Fodor's

NEW ENGLAND

MAY   2015

WELCOME TO NEW ENGLAND

New England's distinctive sights and landscapes make it a classic American destination. Vermont's and New Hampshire's blazing fall foliage, Connecticut's colonial towns, and Maine's rocky coast are just a few regional icons. Massachusetts, home to Boston's stirring Revolutionary-era sites, is one of many places where history comes alive. You can sample the good life too, with visits to Newport's Gilded Age mansions in Rhode Island or a stay in a sleek country inn. Enjoy nature's bounty, whether you're skiing, hiking, or simply taking in a magnificent view.

TOP REASONS TO GO

★ **Fall Foliage:** Scenic drives and walks reveal America's best festival of colors.

★ **History:** The Freedom Trail, Mystic Seaport, and more preserve a fascinating past.

★ **Small Towns:** A perfect day includes strolling a town green and locavore dining.

★ **The Coast:** Towering lighthouses and pristine beaches, plus whale-watching and sailing.

★ **Outdoor Fun:** Top draws are Acadia National Park, Cape Cod, and the Appalachian Trail.

★ **Regional Food:** Maine lobster and blueberries, Vermont maple syrup and cheese.

Fodor's NEW ENGLAND

Publisher: Amanda D'Acierno, *Senior Vice President*

Editorial: Arabella Bowen, *Editor in Chief*; Linda Cabasin, *Editorial Director*

Design: Fabrizio La Rocca, *Vice President, Creative Director*; Tina Malaney, *Associate Art Director*; Chie Ushio, *Senior Designer*; Ann McBride, *Production Designer*

Photography: Melanie Marin, *Associate Director of Photography*; Jessica Parkhill and Jennifer Romains, *Researchers*

Maps: Rebecca Baer, *Senior Map Editor*; Mark Stroud, Moon Street Cartography, and David Lindroth *Cartographers*

Production: Linda Schmidt, *Managing Editor*; Evangelos Vasilakis, *Associate Managing Editor*; Angela L. McLean, *Senior Production Manager*

Sales: Jacqueline Lebow, *Sales Director*

Marketing & Publicity: Heather Dalton, *Marketing Director*; Katherine Punia, *Senior Publicist*

Business & Operations: Susan Livingston, *Vice President, Strategic Business Planning*; Sue Daulton, *Vice President, Operations*

Fodors.com: Megan Bell, *Executive Director, Revenue & Business Development*; Yasmin Marinaro, *Senior Director, Marketing & Partnerships*

Copyright © 2014 by Fodor's Travel, a division of Random House LLC

Writers: Bethany Cassin Beckerlegge, Fred Bouchard, Seth Brown, Mike Dunphy, Frances Folsom, Debbie Hagan, Brian Kevin, Kim Foley MacKinnon, Doug Norris, Victoria Abbott Riccardi, Josh Rogol, Mary Ruoff, Laura V. Scheel

Editors: Salwa Jabado (*lead project editor*), Mark Sullivan, Kristan Schiller (*Boston editor*)

Editorial Contributors: Róisín Cameron, Amanda Sadlowski

Production Editor: Carrie Parker

31st Edition

ISBN 978-0-8041-4217-5

ISSN 0192-3412

All details in this book are based on information supplied to us at press time. Always confirm information when it matters, especially if you're making a detour to visit a specific place. Fodor's expressly disclaims any liability, loss, or risk, personal or otherwise, that is incurred as a consequence of the use of any of the contents of this book.

SPECIAL SALES

This book is available at special discounts for bulk purchases for sales promotions or premiums. For more information, e-mail specialmarkets@randomhouse.com

PRINTED IN THE UNITED STATES OF AMERICA

10 9 8 7 6 5 4 3 2 1

CONTENTS

Fodor's Features

A Celebration of Color. 36
Follow the Redbrick Road 82
A Whale of a Tale. 192
Antiques and Crafts Shopping. 321
The Mansions of Newport 398
Let it Snow 491
Hiking the Appalachian Trail 563
Maine's Lighthouses 698

6 < **Contents**

MAPS

ABOUT THIS GUIDE

Fodor's Recommendations

Everything in this guide is worth doing—we don't cover what isn't—but exceptional sights, hotels, and restaurants are recognized with additional accolades. Fodor'sChoice★ indicates our top recommendations; and **Best Bets** call attention to notable hotels and restaurants in various categories. Care to nominate a new place? Visit Fodors.com/contact-us.

Trip Costs

We list prices wherever possible to help you budget well. Hotel and restaurant price categories from **$** to **$$$$** are noted alongside each recommendation. For hotels, we include the lowest cost of a standard double room in high season. For restaurants, we cite the average price of a main course at dinner or, if dinner isn't served, at lunch. For attractions, we always list adult admission fees; discounts are usually available for children, students, and senior citizens.

Hotels

Our local writers vet every hotel to recommend the best overnights in each price category, from budget to expensive. Unless otherwise specified, you can expect private bath, phone, and TV in your room. For expanded hotel reviews, facilities, and deals, visit Fodors.com.

Restaurants

Unless we state otherwise, restaurants are open for lunch and dinner daily. We mention dress code only when there's a specific requirement and reservations only when they're essential or not accepted. To make restaurant reservations, visit Fodors.com.

Credit Cards

The hotels and restaurants in this guide typically accept credit cards. If not, we'll say so.

Top Picks
★ Fodor'sChoice

Listings
⊠ Address
⊠ Branch address
☎ Telephone
🖷 Fax
⊕ Website
✉ E-mail
🖃 Admission fee
🕙 Open/closed times
Ⓜ Subway
✢ Directions or Map coordinates

Hotels & Restaurants
🏨 Hotel
🛏 Number of rooms
🍽 Meal plans
✕ Restaurant
🍴 Reservations
👔 Dress code
🚫 No credit cards
Ⓢ Price

Other
⇨ See also
☞ Take note
⛳ Golf facilities

EXPERIENCE
NEW ENGLAND

WHAT'S WHERE

The following numbers refer to chapters.

3 Boston. Massachusetts's capital city is also New England's hub. Boston's many universities make it a cosmopolitan town, but there are also blue-collar roots in the distinct neighborhoods. This is the cradle of American democracy, a place where soaring skyscrapers cast shadows on Colonial graveyards.

4 Cape Cod, Nantucket, and Martha's Vineyard. Great beaches, delicious seafood, and artsy shopping districts fill scenic Cape Cod, chic Martha's Vineyard, and cozy Nantucket.

5 The Berkshires and Western Massachusetts. The mountainous Berkshires live up to the storybook image of rural New England; there's also a thriving arts community. Farther east, the Pioneer Valley is home to a string of historic settlements.

6 Connecticut. The densely populated southwest region contrasts with the sparsely populated northeastern Quiet Corner, known for antiquing. Small shoreline villages line the southeastern coast and are near a pair of casinos. The Connecticut River Valley and Litchfield Hills have grand old inns, rolling farmlands, and state parks.

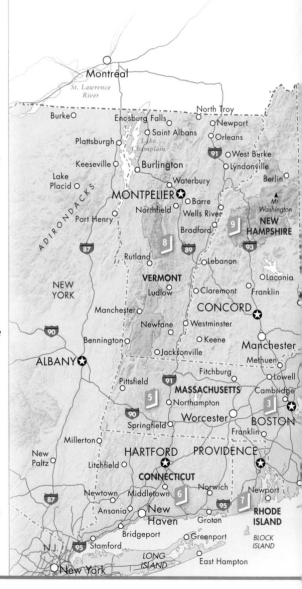

7 Rhode Island. The smallest of the six New England states is home to great sailing and glitzy mansions in Newport. South County has sparsely populated beaches and rolling farmland; scenic Block Island is just a short ferry ride away.

8 Vermont. Vermont has farms, freshly starched New England towns, quiet back roads, and bustling ski resorts.

9 New Hampshire. Portsmouth is the star of the independent state's 18-mile coastline. The Lakes Region is a popular summertime escape; the White Mountains' dramatic vistas attract photographers and adventurous hikers farther north.

10 Inland Maine. The largest New England state's rugged interior, including the Western Lakes and vast North Woods regions, attracts skiers, hikers, campers, anglers, and other outdoors enthusiasts.

11 The Maine Coast. Classic townscapes, rocky shorelines punctuated by sandy beaches, and picturesque downtowns draw vacationers to Maine like a magnet. Acadia National Park is where majestic mountains meet the coast; Bar Harbor is the park's gateway town.

NEW ENGLAND PLANNER

Average Temperatures

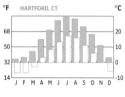

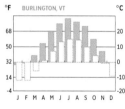

When to Go

All six New England states are year-round destinations. Winter is popular with skiers, summer draws beach lovers, and fall delights those who love the bursts of autumnal color. Spring can also be a great time, with sugar shacks transforming maple sap into all sorts of tasty things. ■TIP→ **You'll probably want to avoid rural areas during mud season (April) and black-fly season (mid-May to mid-June).**

Memorial Day signals migration to the beaches and the mountains, and summer begins in earnest on July 4. Those who want to drive to Cape Cod in July or August, beware: on Friday and Sunday weekenders clog the overburdened U.S. 6. The same applies to the Maine Coast and its feeder roads, Interstate 95 and U.S. 1.

In the fall, a rainbow of reds, oranges, yellows, purples, and other vibrant hues emerges. The first scarlet and gold colors appear in mid-September in northern areas; "peak" color occurs at different times from year to year. Generally, it's best to visit the northern reaches in late September and early October and move south as October progresses.

CLIMATE

In winter, coastal New England is cold and damp; inland temperatures may be lower, but generally drier conditions make them easier to bear. Snowfall is heaviest in the interior mountains and can range up to several hundred inches per year in northern Maine, New Hampshire, and Vermont. Spring is often windy and rainy; in some years winter appears to segue almost immediately into summer. Coastal areas can be quite humid in summer, while inland, particularly at higher elevations, there's a prevalence of cool summer nights. Autumn temperatures can be mild even into October.

Getting Here and Around

⇨ *For more information, see Travel Smart New England.*

Air Travel: The main gateway to New England is Boston's Logan International Airport (BOS). Other New England airports include Bradley International Airport (BDL, 12 miles north of Hartford), T.F. Green Airport (PVD, just outside Providence), Manchester Boston Regional Airport (MHT, in New Hampshire), Portland International Jetport (PWM, in Maine), and Burlington International Airport (BTV, in Vermont).

Car Travel: New England is best explored by car. Areas in the interior are largely without heavy traffic and congestion, and parking is consistently easy to find. Coastal New England is considerably more congested, and parking can be hard to find or expensive in Boston, Providence, and many smaller resort towns along the coast. Still, a car is typically the best way to get around even on the coast (though once you arrive, you may want to explore on foot, on a bike, or by public transportation). In New England's interior, public transportation options are more limited and a car is almost necessary.

Train Travel: Amtrak offers frequent daily service to several New England destinations, including Boston; Portland, Maine; coastal New Hampshire; several points in Vermont; and Pittsfield, Springfield, Worcester, and Framingham, Massachusetts. The Massachusetts Bay Transportation Authority (MBTA) connects Boston with outlying areas.

TRAVEL TIMES FROM BOSTON TO:	BY AIR	BY CAR	BY BUS	BY TRAIN
Acadia National Park (ME)	1 hour	5 hours	not applicable	not applicable
Burlington, VT	no direct flight	3½ hours	4½–5 hours	8¾ hours
Hartford, CT	no direct flight	1¾ hours	2–2¾ hours	4–4½ hours
New York, NY	¾–1 hour	4 hours	4½–7 hours	3½–4¼ hours
Portland, ME	no direct flight	2 hours	2¼ hours	2½ hours
Providence, RI	no direct flight	1 hour	1 hour	½–¾ hour
Provincetown, MA	½ hour	2¼ hours	3–3½ hours	not applicable

Visitor Information

Each New England state provides a helpful free information kit, including a guidebook, map, and listings of attractions and events. All include listings and advertisements for lodging and dining establishments. Each state also has an official website with material on sights and lodgings; most of these sites have a calendar of events and other special features.

Contacts
Greater Boston Convention & Visitors Bureau
☎ 888/733–2678, 617/536–4100 ⊕ www.bostonusa.com.
Connecticut Commission on Culture & Tourism
☎ 888/288–4748
⊕ www.ctvisit.com.
Maine Office of Tourism
☎ 888/624–6345
⊕ www.visitmaine.com.
Massachusetts Office of Travel and Tourism
☎ 800/227–6277, 617/973–8500
⊕ www.massvacation.com.
New Hampshire Division of Travel and Tourism Development ☎ 603/386–4664
⊕ www.visitnh.gov.
Rhode Island Tourism Division ☎ 800/556–2484
⊕ www.visitrhodeisland.com.
Vermont Department of Tourism and Marketing
☎ 802/828–3237, 800/837–6668
⊕ www.vermontvacation.com.

NEW ENGLAND TODAY

The People

The idea of the self-reliant, thrifty, and often stoic New England Yankee has taken on almost mythic proportions in American folklore, but in some parts of New England—especially in rural Maine, New Hampshire, and Vermont—there still is some truth to this image, which shouldn't come as a surprise. You need to be independent if you farm an isolated field, live in the middle of a vast forest, or work a fishing boat miles off the coast. Like any part of the country, there are stark differences between urban New Englanders and those you encounter outside the cities. Both, though, are usually fiercely proud of the region, its rugged beauty, and its contributions to the nation. New Englanders also tend to be well educated.

In terms of ethnicity, Vermont, Maine, and New Hampshire are three of the nation's four whitest states. African American and Asian populations are increasing, especially in Massachusetts and Connecticut. In northern Maine there is a heavy French-Canadian influence from nearby Québec.

The Politics

Though they're often portrayed as liberals, New Englanders are actually more complex when it comes to politics. The region's representation in both the U. S. Senate and the House of Representatives is heavily Democratic. Voters in New Hampshire, which hosts the nation's first primary each presidential election season, tend to lean conservative, but with a distinctly libertarian slant, as do residents in many rural portions of New England.

During the civil rights era in the 1960s, racial tension in Boston was high, with people clashing in the streets over public school segregation. In 2006, however, Massachusetts residents elected Deval Patrick, the second black governor ever to be elected in the United States. In 2004 Massachusetts became the first state to allow same-sex marriage. Today it's legal in all six New England states.

The Economy

Long gone are the days when New England's shoe and textile industries sailed overseas, when many a mill town suffered blows to employment and self-image. In recent years the unemployment rate has fallen below the national average (though Rhode Island has one of the highest in the country at 9.1%).

In Maine the lobster-fishing industry (about 70% of the state's seafood industry) is rebounding steadily after a number of tough years. Lobster prices dropped nearly $2 per pound between 2005 and 2009, bottoming out during the 2008 global economic slide. However, prices have recovered somewhat in the last few years and in 2012 Maine fishermen hauled in a record-setting 126 million pounds of lobster, doubling their catch from a decade ago.

Exports are a major part of the modern New England economy, consisting heavily of computer and other electronics, chemicals, and specialized machinery. The Boston area is home to a thriving biotech industry. The service industries are also strong, especially in the insurance and financial sectors, which have a long history in Hartford. Some towns are known for a particular export: Groton, Connecticut, and Bath, Maine, both have naval shipyards supplying the military with high-technology ships and submarines; Springfield, Massachusetts, is a gun-manufacturing center; and Barre, Vermont, quarries granite. Assorted foods produced include maple syrup, blueberries, cranberries, lobster, and other seafood.

Sports

Fans from all five states follow Massachusetts's sports teams as if they were their own. The state's capital is home to three of the region's four major sports teams—Boston Red Sox baseball, Boston Bruins hockey, and Boston Celtics basketball. The New England Patriots (football) play in the small suburb of Foxboro, about 30 miles southwest of Downtown Boston.

New England is currently enjoying a period of unprecedented sports success, as the region's teams have racked up seven titles since 2002. The most recent squad to claim a championship (the franchise's first since 1972) is the Boston Bruins, after besting the Vancouver Canucks in the 2011 Stanley Cup Finals.

Red Sox fans, often referred to as Red Sox Nation, are some of the most fanatical in the country. The 2004 World Series marked the pinnacle of bliss for many New Englanders after witnessing their beloved BoSox win, ending an 86-year drought. The Sox would do it again three years later, in 2007, and yet again in 2013.

The Patriots charged into the 21st century, winning three out of four Super Bowls, from 2002 to 2005, but the Pats' last two trips to the big game ended in heartbreak after upsets in both 2008 and 2012 to the New York Giants.

Not to be left out, the Celtics advanced their status as one of basketball's marquee franchises, capturing an NBA record 17th title in 2008 (the Los Angeles Lakers have since equaled the Celtics' title bounty, besting Boston in the 2010 Finals).

Held each spring, the Boston Marathon is New England's largest sporting event, attracting more than 500,000 spectators. Started in 1897, the world's oldest annual marathon attracts more than 20,000 competitors.

The Language

As people move around, the local accents have begun to blend, creating more of a general New England accent. (In fact, in some urban areas you may not hear any accent.) Linguistic differences, however, are still evident in some places, especially close to the coast.

Boston's distinct accent is similar in tone to that of New York City's Bronx, and is noted by the dropping of the R in certain places, as in the pronunciation of the famous sports arena "the Gahden." Bostonians also lengthen their vowels, so chowder sounds like "chowdah." Town names in Massachusetts are often spoken very differently than they are spelled; Gloucester, for example, becomes "Glawstuh." Bostonians also rush their speech, so "Hi, how are you?" is "hihawaya?" and "Did you eat?" sounds like "Jeet?"

Connecticut, Maine, and Rhode Island also have a Boston-like accent with nuanced differences. Rhode Islanders drop their R's at the end of words and use an "aw" sound for the O or A in words like "coffee" or "talk" but an "ah" sound for the short O's in words like "Providence" and "mom." In Connecticut and New Hampshire the accent is not nearly as strong, but it comes out in certain words, like how locals pronounce Concord ("Cahn-cuhd").

Meanwhile, true Mainers drop or soften their R's—making their favorite dish "lobstah"; they also often accentuate the vowel, so a one-word syllable can be pronounced like two, meaning "here" may become "hee-yuh."

QUINTESSENTIAL NEW ENGLAND

Fall Foliage

It's impossible to discuss New England without mentioning that time of year when the region's deciduous (leaf-shedding) trees—maples, oaks, birches, and beeches—explode in reds, yellows, oranges, and other rich hues. Autumn is the most colorful season in New England, but it can be finicky, defined as much by the weather as it is by the species of trees; a single rainstorm can strip trees of their grandeur. What happens in one part of the region doesn't necessarily happen in another, and if you have the time you can follow the colors from one area to the next. You'll be competing with thousands of other like-minded leaf peepers, so be sure to book lodging early. Your preparedness will pay off the first time you drive down a winding country road aflame in the bright sun of a New England autumn day.

The Coast

The coast of New England is both workplace and playground. From the 17th century, boatbuilders sprung up in one town after another to support the shipping and fishing trades. Today, the boatyards are far fewer than in historical times, but shipping and especially fishing remain important to the economy on the coast and beyond. It's not all work and no play—some of the classic wooden sailboats now serve cruise goers, and some fishermen have traded in their lobster boats for whale-watching vessels. The coast's lighthouses are another New England staple; more than 60 of these beacons of light line Maine's jagged coast like sentinels along the shore. In Massachusetts, Cape Cod is a beachcombers' paradise, and the relatively chilly waters of the North Atlantic don't scare away swimmers come summertime.

New Englanders are a varied group joined by a shared past and a singular pride in their roots. It's therefore no surprise that New England spans a spectrum of activities and locales, yet offers visitors and residents alike distinct experiences that still can perfectly define the region.

Food, Glorious Food

Maine lobster. Vermont Grade A maple syrup. Portuguese sausage from Cape Cod. Blueberries from Maine. Fine food prepared under the influence of every region of Italy in Boston's North End (there's plenty of Italian to go around on Atwells Avenue in Providence's Federal Hill, too). This is just a sampling to whet your appetite. New England dining is truly a feast for the gastronomist, and it runs the gamut from the simply prepared to the most artistic of presentations: from blueberry pie just as Grandma used to make to molecular gastronomy in some Boston restaurants. Local ingredients and sustainable methods are common in foodie-focused cities and also Vermont. Chefs who grew up here sometimes leave to learn their trade, only to return and enrich the dining scene, but the region is attracting newcomers as well.

Artisans

New England's independent artisans have built a thriving cottage industry. Some of the finest potters spin their wheels on the coast, and one-of-a-kind jewelry is wrought in silver, pewter, and other metals. Modern furniture makers take classic simple New England designs, including those of the Shakers and Quakers, and refine them for buyers eager to pay for expert craftsmanship. The varied landscapes of Vermont and New Hampshire, with their respective Green and White mountains; Massachusetts, with its Berkshire Mountains, Pioneer Valley, and historic coast; Connecticut, with its southern shore; and Rhode Island, with its oceanfront cliffs, have patiently sat for thousands of painters, whose canvases are sold in small shops and local museums.

NEW ENGLAND TOP ATTRACTIONS

Acadia National Park

(A) Hosting more than 2 million visitors annually, this wonder of the Maine Coast was the first national park established east of the Mississippi River. It is regularly one of the most visited in the United States. In the warmer months, take a drive around Mount Desert Island's 27-mile Park Loop Road to acquaint yourself with the area and indulge in spectacular views of the mountains and the sea. Head to the top of Cadillac Mountain for amazing 360-degree views (especially popular at sunrise) or bike the scenic 45-mile carriage-road system, inspecting each of the 17 stone bridges along the way. Go on a park ranger–led boat trip in search of local wildlife such as porpoises, seals, and seabirds or cruise to the fjordlike bay of Somes Sound, where steep rocky cliffs jut out of the sea. Adorable Bar Harbor is the park's gateway town.

Appalachian Trail

(B) The 2,180-mile Appalachian Trail, running from Springer Mountain, Georgia, to Katahdin, Maine, cuts through five New England states: Connecticut, Massachusetts, New Hampshire, Vermont, and Maine. Though the trail is best known as a weeks-long endurance test for expert hikers, many short stretches can be walked in a few hours. "AT" terrain in Maine and New Hampshire can be quite challenging; the trail is a bit more manageable in southern New England. If you're a complete novice, you can also drive to many of the trailheads—if only to say you've set foot on the country's most famous walk.

Baxter State Park

(C) Over the span of 32 years, from 1930 to 1962, former Maine governor Percival Baxter began buying and donating parcels of land, with the goal of creating a natural park in the wilds of northern Maine. The result is Baxter State Park: more than

200,000 acres containing numerous lakes and streams, plus Mt. Katahdin, Maine's tallest peak and the northern terminus of the Appalachian Trail. Offering frequent sightings of moose, white-tailed deer, and black bear, and attracting only 60,000 visitors a year, Baxter State Park provides a wilderness experience not found elsewhere in New England.

Boston

(D) New England's largest and most cosmopolitan city is the region's hub for modern commerce, education, and culture, and the early history of the United States is never far from view. Orient yourself with a 360-degree view from the Prudential Skywalk Observation Deck before you hit the ground exploring. The 50-acre Boston Common is the oldest city park in the nation; across the street is the Public Garden, where a ride on a Swan Boat has been a popular pastime and a harbinger of spring since 1877. Two lanterns hung from the Old North Church kicked off the Revolutionary War and made Paul Revere a legend; the Freedom Trail is a 2.5-mile route that winds past 16 of the city's most historic landmarks. Be sure to include a visit to the Museum of Fine Arts, containing more than 450,000 works of art from almost every corner of the world, including Egyptian mummies and Asian scrolls.

Cape Cod National Seashore

(E) Comprising 40 miles of sandy beaches and nearly 44,000 acres of a landscape that has been the muse of countless painters and photographers, the Cape Cod National Seashore features the best of what New England has to offer. Since its designation in 1961 by President John F. Kennedy, it has become the perfect place for explorers and strollers looking for an untouched stretch of coastline. An exhaustive number of programs—from guided bird walks to surf rescue demonstrations to snorkeling in Wellfleet's kettle ponds—take place year-round; most are free.

Green Mountains

(F) Vermont takes its nickname (the Green Mountain State) and its actual name (*verts monts* is "green mountains" in French) from this 250-mile-long mountain range that forms the spine of the state. Part of the Appalachian Mountains, the Green Mountains are a wild paradise filled with rugged hiking trails (most notably the Long Trail and the Appalachian Trail), unspoiled forests, quaint towns, and some of the East Coast's best ski resorts. About 400,000 acres are protected in Green Mountain National Forest.

Lake Winnipesaukee

(G) As fun to fish as it is to pronounce, the largest (and longest) lake in New Hampshire is home to three species of trout, small- and largemouth bass, bluegill, and more. The 72-square-mile lake and its more than 250 islands also contain beaches, arcades, water parks, and countless other fun family diversions. In summer, Winnipesaukee buzzes with activity as travelers flock to resort towns like Wolfeboro, Weirs Beach, and Meredith.

Maine Coast

(H) Counting all its nooks, crannies, and crags, Maine's coast would stretch for thousands of miles if you could pull it straight. The Southern Coast is the most visited section, stretching north from Kittery to just outside Portland, but don't let that stop you from heading farther "Down East" (Maine-speak for "up the coast"). Despite the cold North Atlantic waters, beachgoers enjoy miles of sandy—or, more frequently, rocky—beaches, with sweeping views of lighthouses, forested islands, and the wide-open sea.

Mt. Washington

(I) New England's highest mountain, this New Hampshire peak has been scaled by many a car (as the bumper stickers will attest). You can also take a cog railway to the top or, if you're an intrepid hiker,

navigate a maze of trails. The weather station here recorded a wind gust of 231 mph in April 1934—the highest wind speed ever recorded at a surface station until it was surpassed in 1996 by a 253 mph gust on Australia's Barrow Island. Bundle up if you make the trek—the average temperature at the summit is below freezing.

Mystic

(J) Home to two great museums—Mystic Seaport (known for its collection of historic ships and re-creation of a 19th-century seaside village) and the Mystic Aquarium and Institute for Exploration—this Connecticut seaside town is one of the state's biggest draws. When you finish touring the town's two impressive institutions, peruse the boutiques and galleries downtown.

Newport

(K) Rhode Island's treasure trove has preserved Colonial buildings and Gilded Age mansions like no other city in the country. Here you'll find more than 200 pre-Revolutionary structures and scores of jaw-dropping, ridiculously over-the-top castles from the late 19th century. Newport is also a picturesque seaside town and one of the world's great sailing capitals.

Portland Head Light

(L) One of the most photographed lighthouses in the nation, the historic white stone Portland Head Light was commissioned by George Washington and completed in 1791 for the whopping sum of $2,250. It welcomes nearly 1 million visitors each year and features an informative museum in the Victorian-style innkeeper's cottage. The lighthouse is in Fort Williams Park, about 2 miles from the town center of Cape Elizabeth, at the southwest entrance of Portland harbor.

TOP EXPERIENCES

Peep a Leaf

Tourist season in most of New England is concentrated in the late spring and summer, but there's a resurgence in September and October, especially in the northern states, when leaf peepers from all corners descend by the car- and busload to see the leaves turn red, yellow, orange, and all shades in between. Foliage season can be fragile and unpredictable—temperature, winds, and rain all influence when the leaves turn and how long they remain on the trees—but that makes the season even more precious. Apple picking at a local orchard and searching for the perfect pumpkin for a jack-o'-lantern among the falling leaves are quintessential New England experiences.

Comb a Beach

Whether sandy or rocky, New England beaches can be filled with flotsam and jetsam. Anything from crab traps unmoored by heavy waves to colored sea glass worn smooth by the water to lost watches, jewelry, and the like can appear at your feet. Also common are shells of sea urchins, clams, and other bivalves. During certain times of the year sand dollars of all sizes and colors are plentiful—you may even find one still whole.

Take Yourself Out to a Ballgame

Fenway Park has been the home of the Boston Red Sox since it opened in 1912, and is the oldest ballpark in the major leagues. Though the cheapest seats and farthest from the field, the bleachers are quite popular with the faithful, who gather to drink beer in plastic cups and watch as batters attempt to clear the 37-foot-tall left-field wall known as the Green Monster. Seat 21 of Section 42, Row 37 in the right-field bleachers is painted red in honor of the longest measurable home run

ever hit at Fenway, Ted Williams's legendary 502-foot blast on June 9, 1946. To get an up-close and inexpensive look at some of the game's next rising stars, visit the Red Sox triple-A farm team, the Paw Sox, located in Pawtucket, Rhode Island. During the summer, the Cape Cod Baseball League features some of the nation's best young collegiate talent.

Hit the Slopes

Though the mountain snow in New England is not as legendary as the powder out west (and, in fact, can be downright unpleasant when packed snow becomes crusty ice), skiing is quite popular here. Vermont has several ski areas, with Killington ranking among the largest resorts in the Northeast: its nearly 200 trails span seven mountains. New Hampshire's White Mountains and Massachusetts's Berkshires also cater to snow-sport lovers, while Sunday River and Sugarloaf in Maine are perennial favorites with advanced-intermediate and expert skiers. Beginners (and lift-ticket bargain hunters) can choose from a number of small but fun hills throughout northern New England.

Eat a Maine Lobster

Maine lobsters are world renowned, and lobstermen and fish markets all along the coast will pack a live lobster in seaweed for overnight shipment to almost anywhere nationwide. These delectable crustaceans are available throughout New England, but without a doubt the best place to eat them is near the waters of origin. Lobster meat is sweet, especially the claws, and most agree that simple preparation is the best way to go: steamed and eaten with drawn butter or pulled into chunks and placed in a toasted hot dog bun—the famous New England lobster

roll. There are two types of lobster rolls to try: traditional Maine style features a cold lobster salad with a leaf of lettuce and the barest amount of mayonnaise, while the Connecticut lobster roll is served warm with drawn butter and no mayo. Don't forget to save room for New England's other culinary treasure: *chowdah*. No two clam chowders taste the same, but they're all delicious.

Rise and Shine at a B&B

New England's distinctive architecture, much of it originating in the 18th and 19th centuries, has resulted in beautiful buildings of all shapes and sizes, many of which have been restored as bed-and-breakfasts. These inns typify the cozy, down-home, and historic feel of New England, and are an ideal lodging choice. This is especially true when the weather is cold, and the warm ambience of many of these inns more than justifies the slightly higher prices you'll pay here versus a hotel or motel.

Watch a Whale

The deep, cold waters of the North Atlantic serve as feeding grounds and migration routes for a variety of whales, including the fin, humpback, the occasional blue, and endangered white whales. Cape Cod and Maine's Southern Coast and Mid-Coast regions are the best places to hop aboard a whale-watching boat, but tours also depart from Boston Harbor. Some boat captains go so far as to guarantee at least a single sighting. The tours head to the whale feeding grounds about 20 miles offshore, where the majestic animals are numerous. The whale-watching season varies by tour skipper, but generally runs from April through October.

Fair Thee Well

New Englanders love their fairs and festivals. Maine-iacs celebrate the moose, clam, lobster, and blueberry. Maple sugar and maple syrup are feted in Vermont, while "live free or die" New Hampshire honors American independence. Newport, Rhode Island, hosts two highly regarded music festivals, one folk and one jazz. Many rural communities throughout New England hold agricultural fairs in late August and September.

Find the Perfect Souvenir

Artists and craftspeople abound in New England, meaning that finding the perfect souvenir of your vacation will be an enjoyable hunt. Whether you choose a watercolor of a picturesque fishing village, a functional and beautiful piece of handmade pottery, or a handcrafted piece of jewelry, you'll be supporting the local economy while taking a little piece of the region home with you.

Get Up Close and Personal with Nature

New England might be known for its flashy foliage in the fall and spectacular slopes in the winter, but the outdoors in the spring and summer delights all the senses as well. You can breathe in the ocean air as you drive along the Maine Coast or amble on Newport's 3½-mile Cliff Walk. Alternatively, enjoy the fragrance of the mountains and forests in the Berkshires, Vermont's Green Mountains, and New Hampshire's White Mountains while hiking along the Appalachian Trail. You may observe such animals as moose and bear. Close to the ocean there are numerous chances to see birds, seals, dolphins, and whales.

Savor Sweet Stuff

Summer vacations in New England go hand in hand with sweet treats; it's difficult to visit without sampling homemade fudge at an old-fashioned candy store, buying an ice cream for your sweetie, or bringing home some saltwater taffy to share with the folks back at the ranch. Be sure to try a Maine specialty—the whoopie pie. Made from two chocolate circles of cake with vanilla cream filling in between, it's a delectable Maine tradition. If you are visiting Maine when the tiny wild blueberry is in season, take every opportunity to savor this flavorful fruit, whether in pie, muffin, or pancake form, and you'll understand its legendary culinary status. In Vermont, go on a factory tour at Ben & Jerry's, and have a delicious cone afterward. The Green Mountain state's favorite sons by no means have the market cornered on ice cream goodness; you'll find excellent frozen treats in every corner of the region (Cape Cod is an especially blessed area). In Boston, head to the Italian North End for legendary cannoli. You can even have dessert for breakfast when you top your pancakes with Vermont's maple syrup.

Check Out Lighthouses

Maine's long and jagged coastline is home to more than 60 lighthouses, perched high on rocky ledges or on the tips of wayward islands. Though modern technology in navigation has made many of the lights obsolete, preservation groups restore and maintain many of them and often make them accessible to the public. Some of the state's more famous lights include Portland Head Light, commissioned by President George Washington in 1787 and immortalized in one of Edward Hopper's paintings; Two Lights, a few miles down the coast in Cape Elizabeth; and West Quoddy Head, on the easternmost tip

of land in the United States. Some lighthouses are privately owned and others accessible only by boat, but plenty are within easy reach and open to the public, some with museums and tours. At the Maine Lighthouse Museum in Rockland, visitors can view a collection of Fresnel lenses and Coast Guard artifacts.

Sail the Coast

The coastline of northern New England is a sailor's paradise, complete with hidden coves, windswept islands, and picture-perfect harbors where you can pick up a mooring for the night. With nearly 3,500 miles of undulating, rocky shoreline, you could spend a lifetime of summers sailing the waters off the Maine Coast and never see it all. If you're not one of the lucky few with a sailboat to call your own, there are many companies that offer sailboat charters, whether for day trips or weeklong excursions. It might sound like an expensive getaway, but as meals and drinks are usually included, an overnight sailing charter might not cost any more than a seaside hotel room, plus you have an experienced captain to provide history and insight along the voyage.

Get the First Sight of First Light

At 1,530 feet, Cadillac Mountain, in Maine's Acadia National Park, is the highest mountain on the New England coast—so what better place to view the sunrise? Drive the winding and narrow 3½-mile road to the summit before dawn (not accessible when the Loop Road is closed in the winter), and you could be the first person in the United States to see the summer sun's rays. (Note that this depends on the time of year; sometimes the first sunrise is at West Quoddy Head Lighthouse in Lubec, Maine).

NEW ENGLAND WITH KIDS

Children's Museum, Boston. Make bubbles, climb through a maze, and while away some hours in "Adventure Zone" at this fun museum just for tykes in Downtown Boston. A special play area for those under three lets them run around in a safe environment. Festivals happen throughout the year. (⇨ *Chapter 3.*)

Hampton Beach, New Hampshire. This seaside diversion draws families to its almost Coney Island–like fun. Along the boardwalk, kids enjoy arcade games, parasailing, live music, and an annual children's festival. They can even learn how saltwater taffy is made. (⇨ *Chapter 9.*)

Magic Wings Butterfly Conservatory & Gardens, Deerfield, Massachusetts. Almost 4,000 free-flying native and tropical butterflies are the star attraction here, contained within an 8,000-square-foot glassed enclosure that keeps the temperature upward of 80°F year-round. Relax around the Japanese koi pond on one of numerous benches and watch the kids chase the colorful creatures as they flit about. Or walk outside to the Iron Butterfly Outdoor Gardens, where flowers attract even more butterflies. (⇨ *Chapter 5.*)

Mystic Aquarium and Institute for Exploration, Mystic, Connecticut. This aquarium and research institute is one of only four North American facilities to feature endangered Steller sea lions, and New England's only beluga whale calls the aquarium home. Kids can touch a cownose ray, and you'll also see African penguins, harbor seals, graceful sea horses, Pacific octopuses, and sand tiger sharks. Nearby Mystic Seaport is another great attraction for kids and families. (⇨ *Chapter 6.*)

Montshire Museum of Science, Norwich, Vermont. This interactive museum uses more than 60 hands-on exhibits to explore nature and technology. The building sits amid 110 acres of woodlands and nature trails. Live animals are on-site as well. (⇨ *Chapter 8.*)

Massachusetts Audubon Wellfleet Bay Wildlife Sanctuary, South Wellfleet, Massachusetts. With its numerous programs and its beautiful salt-marsh surroundings, this is a favorite migration stop for Cape vacationers year-round. Five miles of nature trails weave throughout the sanctuary's 1,100 acres of marsh, beach, and woods. If you're careful and quiet, you might be able to get close to seals basking in the sun or birds such as the great blue heron. Naturalists are on hand for guided walks and lectures. (⇨ *Chapter 4.*)

Plimoth Plantation, Plymouth, Massachusetts. Want to know what life was like in Colonial America? A visit to this living-history museum is like stepping into a time machine and zooming back to the year 1627. Guides are dressed in period costume and act like early-17th-century Pilgrims. (⇨ *Chapter 3.*)

Shelburne Farms, Shelburne, Vermont. This working dairy farm is also an educational and cultural resource center. Visitors can watch artisans make the farm's famous cheddar cheese from the milk of more than 100 purebred and registered Brown Swiss cows. A children's farmyard and walking trails round out the experience. (⇨ *Chapter 8.*)

Southworth Planetarium, Portland, Maine. This University of Southern Maine facility offers classes such as night-sky mythology and introductory astronomy. The 30-foot dome houses a star theater complete with lasers, digital sounds, and a star projector that displays more than 5,000 heavenly bodies. (⇨ *Chapter 11.*)

FLAVORS OF NEW ENGLAND

The locavore movement has officially hit New England. New farms, greenmarkets, and gourmet food shops are sprouting up every day and chefs are exploring more farm-to-table options.

FOOD FESTIVALS

Wilton Blueberry Festival, Wilton, Maine. You can pick your own wild blueberries and sample baked goods from pancakes to pies at the annual Wilton Blueberry Festival (⊕ *www.wiltonbbf.com*), which takes place in early August.

Keene Pumpkin Festival, Keene, New Hampshire. Locals attempt to set the world record for most lighted pumpkins at the annual Keene Pumpkin Festival (⊕ *pumpkinfestival2011.org*), which takes place in mid-to-late October. Enjoy hayrides and contests from pie eating to pumpkin-seed spitting.

Maine Lobster Festival, Rockland, Maine. Stuff your face with lobster tails and claws during this lobstravaganza (⊕ *www.mainelobsterfestival.com*) in late July and early August. With almost 20,000 pounds of delicious crustacean at your finger tips, leaving hungry is unthinkable.

Vermont Cheesemakers Festival, Shelburne, Vermont. Artisanal cheeses and local beer and wine highlight this daylong festival (⊕ *www.vtcheesefest.com*) in late July. Sample more than 200 cheese varieties from 40 local cheese makers in the Coach Barn of Shelburne Farms.

Chowderfest, Boston, Massachusetts. Thousands gather at City Hall Plaza for the annual Chowderfest (⊕ *www.bostonharborfest.com*) in early July. The chowder cook-off is part of Harborfest, Boston's yearly festivities centered around Independence Day.

SPECIALTIES BY STATE

Massachusetts

Concord grapes started growing in the namesake Massachusetts village way back in 1849. **Cranberries** are cultivated on marshy bogs, mostly in Massachusetts. Known as "Little Italy," Boston's North End contains almost 90 Italian restaurants; you'll find everything from hole-in-the-wall pizza joints to elegant eateries serving regional cuisine from every corner of the boot. No trip here is complete without a post-dinner **cannoli** from Mike's Pastry.

For more than 100 years fisherman and whalers of Portuguese and Azorean decent have called the seaside village of Provincetown home. Some say Provincetown Portuguese Bakery's decadent *malassadas* (fried dough dusted with sugar) are worth the trip alone.

Connecticut

The iconic **New Haven–style pizza,** a decidedly thin-crust pie cooked in a brick oven, can be found at several pizzerias in town. The original creator, Frank Pepe Pizzeria Napoletana, has been around since 1925, while two blocks away is Sally's Apizza, established in 1938. If you prefer a newcomer, try BAR, a nightclub-cum-microbrewery popular with the college crowd. At any of the above, ask for fresh *mootz* (mozzarella in East Coast speak). **Connecticut-style lobster rolls,** warm lobster meat served on a bun doused with drawn butter, are another statewide specialty.

Over the past decade the state has also become known for its **wines.** Chardonnay, Riesling, Cabernet Sauvignon, and many other grape varietals are grown to produce local wines throughout New England, but Connecticut's wine production

stands out. The Connecticut Wine Trail is a collection of 25 vineyards, separated into the Western Trail in the Litchfield Hills and the Eastern Trail located near the southeastern shore. Hopkins Vineyard (Western Trail) overlooking Lake Waramaug and Jonathan Edwards Winery (Eastern Trail) are two of the most admired stops along the trail.

Rhode Island

Rhode Islanders are partial to **johnnycakes,** a cornmeal flatbread that was once a staple of Early American gastronomy. They also like to sip **cabinets**—milk shakes, often made with coffee and celery salt (also known as frappés in other parts of New England).

The Ocean State may be a small one, but its capital's food reputation is big, thanks to its status as the home of Johnson & Wales, an upper-echelon culinary academy. Some of its graduates have opened restaurants in Providence, drawing discriminating diners from near and far. Savor Italian food along Providence's Atwells Avenue in the Federal Hill neighborhood or nosh with the posh at upscale river-view establishments in downtown Providence.

Vermont

Vermonters are big on **maple syrup** straight up and in candies, but dairy products take top billing in this state. Milk and cream from the region's dairy farms are used in cheeses, like the famous **cheddars;** and in **ice cream,** like famed Ben & Jerry's. Willow Hill Farm in Milton, Vermont, is famous for its sheep's milk cheeses. Try the savory Vaquero Blue, a blue cheese made from both sheep and cow's milk. For a family-friendly stop, check out Shelburne Farms' children's farmyard. On the shore of Lake Champlain, Shelburne Farms uses only purebred Brown Swiss cows to make its famous farmhouse cheddar. In addition to the Vermont Cheesemakers Festival, Shelburne attracts visitors year-round to taste mouthwatering cheeses and explore walking trails.

New Hampshire

Northern New Hampshire's cuisine carries a heavy French-Canadian influence. One of the most enticing francophone creations is *poutine* (french fries covered with cheese curds and gravy). The local **corn chowder** substitutes corn for clams and bacon, putting a twist on a Northeastern classic. Smuttynose Brewing Company, a craft brewery in Portsmouth, offers tours and tastings.

Maine

Lobster classics include **boiled lobster**—a staple at "in the rough" picnic-bench-and-paper-plate spots along the Maine Coast—and **lobster rolls,** a lobster meat–and-mayo or melted-butter preparation served in a toasted hot dog bun.

Blueberries, strawberries, raspberries, and **blackberries** grow wild (and on farms) all over the Northeast in the summertime. Blueberry pancakes with maple syrup, blueberry muffins, and blueberry pies are very popular, especially in coastal Maine. Mainers also love **whoopie pies,** cakelike cookies sandwiched together with frosting.

Portland's waterfront Commercial Street is bookended by two typical Maine diners, Gilbert's Chowderhouse and Becky's Diner. The former has one of the state's finest lobster rolls and homemade clam cakes; the latter opens for breakfast at 4 am to feed the fishermen before they head out to sea. Order a slice of fresh pie or buy one whole to take with you.

OUTDOOR ADVENTURES

BEACHCOMBING AND SWIMMING

Long, wide beaches edge the New England coast from southern Maine to southern Connecticut, with dozens dotting the shores of Cape Cod, Martha's Vineyard, and Nantucket. Many of the beaches have lifeguards on duty in season; some have picnic facilities, restrooms, changing facilities, and concession stands. Depending on the locale, you may need a parking sticker to use the lot.

When to Go

The waters are at their warmest in August, though they're cold even at the height of summer along much of Maine, New Hampshire, and Massachusetts. Inland, small lake beaches abound, most notably in New Hampshire and Vermont. The best time to beachcomb is after the tide has gone out, when the retreating water has left behind its treasures. Early spring is an especially good time to see sand dollars washed up on beaches.

What to Look For

The best part of beachcombing is that you never quite know what you'll find at your feet. Sea glass—nothing more than man-made glass worn smooth from its seaward journeys—is common and most prized in rare shades of blue. You'll also find shells in abundance: blue mussels, tiny periwinkles, razor (or "jackknife") clams, ridged scallops, and briny oysters, with their rough outside shell and lovely mother-of-pearl interiors.

Best Beaches

Block Island, Rhode Island. Twelve miles off Rhode Island's coast, this 10-square-mile island has 17 miles of shoreline, 365 freshwater ponds, and plenty of hiking trails. Due to its rolling green hills, some liken the island to Ireland. Take the hour-long ferry from Port Judith.

Cape Cod National Seashore, Massachusetts. With more than 150 beaches—roughly 40 miles worth—Cape Cod has enough to keep any beachcomber happy and sandy year-round. They range from the tourist-packed sand in Dennis to the almost untouched stretches of coast protected by the Cape Cod National Seashore. Favorite activities include swimming, bicycling, and even dune-buggy excursions.

Gloucester Beaches, Massachusetts. Along the North Shore, Gloucester is the oldest seaport in the nation. Its trio of beaches—Good Harbor Beach, Long Beach, and Wingaersheek Beach—cool those coming north of Boston for some sun and sand.

Hampton Beach State Park, New Hampshire. The Granite State's ocean shore is short, but this state park along historic Route 1 takes full advantage of the space it has. In addition to swimming and fishing, there are campsites with full hookups for RVs and an amphitheater with a band shell for fair-weather concerts.

Old Orchard Beach, Maine. Think Coney Island on a smaller scale. There's a white-sand beach to be sure (lapped by cold North Atlantic waters), but many come to ride the Pirate Ship at Palace Playland, drop quarters at the arcade, and browse the multitude of trinket-and-T-shirt shops.

Reid State Park, Maine. The water is cold much of the year, but this beach just west of Sheepscot Bay on Georgetown Island is a beautiful and quiet place to look for sand dollars or climb the rocks at low tide, exploring tidal pools. Great views can be had from the park's rocky Griffith Head.

BICYCLING

Biking on a road through New England's countryside is an idyllic way to spend a day. Many ski resorts allow mountain bikes in summer.

Bike Tours

There are a multitude of tour operators and magnificent trails throughout New England, and many bike shops rent and repair bicycles. Urban Adventours in Downtown Boston provides both tours and rentals complete with helmet, lock, and Boston bike map. Bike New England offers cycling routes and maps throughout the Northeast.

Safety

On the road, watch for trucks and stay as close as possible to the side of the road, in single file. On the trail, ride within your limits and keep your eyes peeled for hikers and horses (both of which have the right of way), as well as dogs. Always wear a helmet and carry plenty of water.

Best Rides

Acadia National Park, Maine. At the heart of this popular park is the 45-mile network of historic carriage roads covered in crushed rock that bicyclists share only with equestrians and hikers. Hybrid or mountain bikes are the way to go here, so leave your road bike at home. Fit and experienced riders can ascend the road to the top of Cadillac Mountain, but take caution: heavy traffic in high season can make this a dangerous proposition.

All Along the Coast. U.S. 1, Maine. The major road that travels along the Maine Coast is only a narrow two-lane highway for most of its route, but it is still one of the country's most historic highways. As a result, it's very popular in spring, summer, and fall with serious long-distance bike riders.

Boston, Massachusetts. Commuters and hard-core cyclists alike buzz along the streets and bike paths of New England's largest city. For a scenic ride, the 17-mile-long Dr. Paul Dudley White Bike Path can't be beat. It hugs the Charles River, with great views of practicing crew teams, the spires of Harvard University, and the city skyline. Or, for a bit of history with your ride, hop on the 10-mile-long Minuteman Bikeway, which runs from the Alewife T stop (on the Red Line, in North Cambridge), through Lexington and all the way to Bedford. From here you can cycle to Concord, following the path the minutemen traveled on the first day of the American Revolution.

Cape Cod, Massachusetts. Cape Cod has miles of bike trails, some paralleling the national seashore, most on level terrain. On either side of the Cape Cod Canal is an easy, 7-mile, straight trail with views of the canal traffic. Extending 22 miles from South Dennis to Wellfleet, the Cape Cod Rail Trail is a converted rail bed that is now a paved, mostly flat bike path passing through a handful of the Cape's scenic towns, offering plenty of opportunity to take side trips.

Killington Resort, Vermont. Following the lead of many ski resorts in the western United States, Killington allows fat-tire riders on many of its ski trails after the snow has melted. Stunt riders can enjoy the jumps and bumps of the mountain-bike park.

Portland, Maine. The paved Eastern Prom Trail extends from the edge of the Old Port to East End Beach, then to Back Bay for a 6-mile loop, before returning.

BOATING

Along many of New England's larger lakes, sailboats, rowboats, canoes, kayaks, and outboards are available for rent at local marinas. Sailboats are available for rent at a number of seacoast locations, but you may be required to prove your seaworthiness. Lessons are frequently available.

What to Wear

It can get cold on the water, especially while sailing, so dress in layers and bring along a windbreaker and fleece even if it's warm on land. Don't wear cotton or jeans: once they get wet, they stay wet and will leave you chilled. Sunscreen, sunglasses (with Croakies so they don't fall overboard), and a hat are also musts, as are drinking water and high-energy snacks, especially for canoe and kayak expeditions.

Best Boating

Allagash Wilderness Waterway, Maine. This scenic and remote waterway—92 miles of lakes, ponds, rivers, and streams—is part of the 740-mile Northern Forest Canoe Trail, which also floats through New York, Vermont, and New Hampshire.

Lake Champlain, Vermont. Called by some the sixth Great Lake, 435-square-mile Lake Champlain is bordered by Vermont's Green Mountains to the east and the Adirondacks of New York to the west. Burlington, Vermont, is the largest lakeside city and a good bet for renting a boat—be it canoe, kayak, rowboat, skiff, or motorboat. Attractions include numerous islands and deep-blue water that's often brushed by pleasant New England breezes.

Lakes Region, New Hampshire. Lake Winnipesaukee is the largest lake in New Hampshire, but there are many puddles large and small worth dipping a paddle into. Squam Lake is a tranquil lake made famous by *On Golden Pond*, Lake Wentworth has a state park with a boat launch, bathhouse, and picnic tables.

Mystic, Connecticut. The world's largest maritime museum, Mystic Seaport, is also a good place to get out on the water. A wide variety of sailing programs are available here—including lessons on a 61-foot schooner—as is instruction on powerboating. If you're eager to test your skills against other sailors, there's also a weekly race series.

Newport and Block Island, Rhode Island. Narragansett Bay, Newport Harbor, and Block Island Sound are among the premier sailing areas in the world. Newport hosted the America's Cup, yachting's most prestigious race, from 1930 to 1983. Numerous outfitters provide public and private sailing tours, sailing lessons, and boat rentals.

Rockland, Maine. For a guided trip on the water, consider a windjammer excursion out of Rockland, Camden, or Rockport. From day sails to multiday cruises, trips cost between $50 and $1,000, and include meals. Check The Maine Windjammer Association (⊕ *www.sailmainecoast.com*) or Windjammer Cruises (⊕ *www.mainewindjammercruises.com*) for more information.

GOLF

Golf caught on early in New England. In fact, Newport Country Club hosted the first-ever U.S. Open Championship in 1895. It is one of the five founding members of the U.S. Golf Association and recognized as one of the first 100 golf clubs in America.

The region has an ample supply of public and semiprivate courses, many of which are part of distinctive resorts or even ski areas. One dilemma facing golfers is keeping their eye on the ball instead of the scenery. The views are marvelous at Balsams Wilderness grand resort in Dixville Notch, New Hampshire, and the nearby course at the splendid old Mount Washington Hotel in Bretton Woods. During prime season, make sure you reserve ahead for tee times, particularly near urban areas and at resorts.

Best Tees

The Gleneagles Golf Course at the Equinox, Vermont. One of the stateliest resorts in all of New England, the Equinox opened in 1769 and has hosted the likes of Teddy Roosevelt and Mary Todd Lincoln. The golf course is par-71 and 6,423 yards, and is especially alluring in the fall when the trees that line the fairways explode in color. After golf, go to the 13,000-square-foot spa for some pampering. The resort is ringed by mountain splendor.

Newton Commonwealth Golf Course, Massachusetts. Minutes from Downtown Boston, this municipal golf course is open to the public seven days a week. Even with 18 holes it isn't a long course, but it can't be beat for a quick break from sightseeing in Beantown.

Pinehills Golf Club, Massachusetts. Located in Plymouth, less than an hour from Boston, Pinehills features a pair of five-star golf courses—one designed by Jack Nicklaus and the other by Rees Jones. Shaped by two of the world's premier golf course architects and adorned with top-notch facilities, this public course is widely recognized as one of the best in New England.

Samoset Resort on the Ocean, Maine. Few things match playing 18 holes on a championship course that's bordered by the North Atlantic. In Rockport, Maine, along Penobscot Bay, Samoset Resort's course is open from May through October. Book a room at the luxurious hotel here to make it a complete golf vacation.

HIKING

Probably the most famous trails in the region are the 270-mile Long Trail, which runs north–south through the center of Vermont, and the Maine-to-Georgia Appalachian Trail, which runs through New England on both private and public land. The Appalachian Mountain Club (AMC) maintains a system of staffed huts in New Hampshire's Presidential Range, with bunk space and meals available by reservation. State parks throughout the region afford good hiking.

Safety

There are few real hazards to hiking, but a little preparedness goes a long way. Know your limits, and make sure the terrain you are about to embark on doesn't exceed your abilities. Check the trail map carefully and pay attention to elevation changes, which make a huge difference in the difficulty of a hike (a steep 1-mile-long trail is much tougher to negotiate than a flat 2- or even 3-mile trail). Bring layers of clothing to accommodate changing weather and always carry enough drinking water. Before you go, be sure to tell someone where you're going and how long you expect to be gone.

Best Hikes

Appalachian Trail, Massachusetts, Connecticut, Vermont, New Hampshire, Maine. This path from Georgia to Maine is as great for a short day hike as it is for a challenging six-month endurance test. The popular trail is marked by rectangular white blazes which are kept up and relatively easy to follow.

Mt. Washington, New Hampshire. The cog railroad and the auto road to the summit are popular routes up New England's highest mountain, but for those with stamina and legs of steel it's one heck of a hike. There are a handful of trails to the top, the most popular beginning at Pinkham Notch Visitor Center. Be sure to dress in layers and have some warm clothing for the frequent winds toward the peak.

The Long Trail, Vermont. Following the main ridge of the Green Mountains from one end of Vermont to the other, this is the nation's oldest long-distance trail. In fact, some say it was the inspiration for the Appalachian Trail. Hardy hikers make a go of its 270-mile length, but day hikers can drop in and out at many places along the way.

HISTORY YOU CAN SEE

History lies thick on the ground in New England—from Pilgrims to pirates, witches to whalers, the American Revolution to the Industrial Revolution.

Pilgrim's Progress

The story of the Pilgrims comes alive when you visit New England. From Provincetown (where the *Mayflower* actually first landed) to Plymouth and throughout Cape Cod, these early New England settlers left an indelible mark on the region. Their contemporaries, the Puritans, founded the city of Boston. Both groups, seeking religious freedom, planted the seeds for the founding of the United States.

What to See:

In Plymouth (south of Boston) you can visit **Plimoth Plantation**, *Mayflower II*, the **National Monument to the Forefathers**, and, of course, **Plymouth Rock** itself *(⇨ Side Trips from Boston in Chapter 3)*. On Cape Cod, visit **First Encounter Beach** in Eastham and the **Pilgrim Monument** in Provincetown *(⇨ Cape Cod in Chapter 4)*.

Talkin' 'Bout a Revolution

New England is the cradle of democracy. Home to many of the patriots who launched the American Revolution and the war's first battles, here you can see real evidence of the events you read about in history class. From battlefields to the Boston Tea Party ship, New England (and especially Massachusetts) is filled with touchstones of our national story.

What to See:

In Boston, walk the **Freedom Trail** *(⇨ Boston in Chapter 3)* or just be on the lookout for markers and plaques as you walk around Downtown—you can literally trip over history wherever you step. Outside the city, **Lexington** and **Concord** *(⇨ The North Shore and South of Boston in Chapter 3)* are easy visits for a quick primer on the start of the American Revolution.

Sea to Shining Sea

New England has a proud (and long) maritime history. From the *Mayflower* to boatbuilders in Maine who still produce wooden ships, you'll feel New England's seafaring traditions anywhere on the coast here. Many museums tell the story of the region's contributions to shipbuilding, nautical exploration, and whaling. And although the latter is no longer a pillar of the local economy, today you can go visit Earth's largest mammals on whale-watching expeditions that leave from many points along the New England coast.

What to See:

One of the nation's most famous ships, the USS *Constitution,* is docked in Charlestown, Massachusetts, just outside of Boston *(⇨ Exploring Boston in Chapter 3)*. The **Maine Maritime Museum** in Bath, Maine, is the last remaining intact shipyard in the United States to have built large wooden sailing vessels *(⇨ Portland and Environs in Chapter 11)*. But the granddaddy of New England maritime experiences is undoubtedly **Mystic Seaport,** where almost 500 vessels are preserved *(⇨ New Haven to Mystic in Chapter 6)*.

Frozen in Time

New England preserves its past like no other region of the United States. In addition to countless museums, historic sites, refurbished homes, and historical markers, the area has several wonderfully preserved villages, each trying to capture a specific moment in time.

What to See:

A mile-long stretch of Main Street in Deerfield, Massachusetts, contains a remarkably well-preserved portion of an

18th-century village. **Historic Deerfield** (⇨ *The Pioneer Valley in Chapter 5*) contains more than a dozen homes built between 1730 and 1850, all maintained as interpretive museums. Together, they house more than 25,000 artifacts harking back to a quintessential New England town.

One of the country's finest re-creations of a Colonial-era village, **Old Sturbridge Village** (⇨ *The Pioneer Valley in Chapter 5*) emulates an early-19th-century New England town, with more than 40 historic buildings moved here from other communities. Guides clad in period costumes do the sort of activities that villagers did back in the day: farmers plow, blacksmiths pound, and bakers bake. A slice of quintessential New England life, the village represents a period of transition brought about by the growing significance of commerce and manufacturing, improvements in agriculture and transportation, and various social changes.

Near Lake Champlain, the **Shelburne Museum** (⇨ *Northern Vermont in Chapter 8*) spans 39 exhibition halls—many of which are restored 18th- and 19th-century buildings relocated here from locales throughout New England and New York. The sheer size and breadth of the museum's collections are dizzying. On display are more than 150,000 artifacts and works of art, as well as period structures that include a one-room schoolhouse, a lighthouse, a covered bridge, and even the 220-foot steamboat *Ticonderoga,* which once sailed Lake Champlain and is the last side-wheel steamboat of its kind. Landscaping recalls a classic New England village and features more than 400 lilac trees and various gardens.

Writing the Story of America

The list of New England writers who have shaped American culture is long indeed. Massachusetts alone has produced great poets in every generation: Anne Bradstreet, Phillis Wheatley, Emily Dickinson, Henry Wadsworth Longfellow, William Cullen Bryant, e.e. cummings, Robert Lowell, Elizabeth Bishop, Sylvia Plath, and Anne Sexton. Bay State writers include Louisa May Alcott, author of the enduring classic *Little Women*; Nathaniel Hawthorne, who re-created the Salem of his Puritan ancestors in *The Scarlet Letter*; Herman Melville, who wrote *Moby-Dick* in a house at the foot of Mt. Greylock; Eugene O'Neill, whose early plays were produced at a makeshift theater in Provincetown on Cape Cod; Lowell native Jack Kerouac, author of *On the Road*; and John Cheever, chronicler of suburban angst. Mark Twain, arguably the most famous American author of all time, lived in Connecticut for much of his writing career (in Hartford and later Redding).

What to See:

Many homes of famous New England writers are preserved. An especially rich stop is **Concord, Massachusetts,** where you can see the homes of Alcott, Ralph Waldo Emerson, Henry David Thoreau, and Hawthorne (as well as Thoreau's Walden Pond). You can visit their graves (as well as those of other authors) in the Author's Ridge section of the town's **Sleepy Hollow Cemetery** (⇨ *Side Trips from Boston in Chapter 3*). Another favorite stop is the **Mark Twain House** in Hartford, Connecticut (⇨ *Hartford and the Connecticut River Valley in Chapter 6*).

BEST FALL FOLIAGE
DRIVES & ROAD TRIPS

A CELEBRATION

Picture this: one scarlet maple offset by the stark white spire of a country church, a whole hillside of brilliant foliage foregrounded by a vintage barn or perhaps a covered bridge that straddles a cobalt river. Such iconic scenes have launched a thousand postcards and turned New England into the ultimate fall destination for leaf peepers.

OF COLOR

By Susan MacCallum-Whitcomb

Mother Nature, of course, puts on an annual autumn performance elsewhere, but this one is a showstopper. Like the landscape, the mix of deciduous (leaf-shedding) trees is remarkably varied here and creates a broader than usual palette. New England's abundant evergreens lend contrast, making the display even more vivid. Every September and October, leaf peepers arrive to cruise along country lanes, join outdoor adventures, or simply stroll on town greens.

Did you know the brilliant shades actually lurk in the leaves all year long? Leaves contain three pigments. The green chlorophyll, so dominant in summer that it obscures the red anthocyanins and orangey-yellow carotenoids, decreases in fall and reveals a crayon box of color.

Above, Vermont's Green Mountains are multicolored in the fall (and often white in winter).

PREDICTING THE PEAK

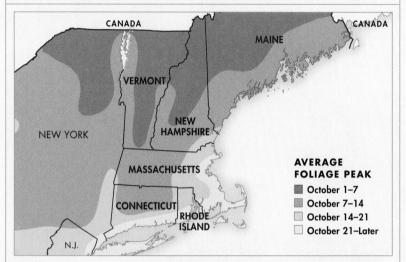

AVERAGE FOLIAGE PEAK
- October 1–7
- October 7–14
- October 14–21
- October 21–Later

LOCATION

Pinning down precisely when colors will appear remains an inexact science, although location plays a major role. Typically, the transformation begins in the highest and northernmost parts of New England in mid-September, then moves steadily into lower altitudes and southern sectors throughout October.

For trip planning, think in terms of regions rather than states. In Maine (a huge state that runs north–south) leaf color can peak anytime from the fourth week of September to the third week of October, depending on the locale.

WEATHER

Early September weather is another deciding factor. From the foliage aficionado's perspective, the ideal scenario is calm, temperate days capped by nights that are cool but still above freezing. If the weather is too warm, it delays the onset of the season. If it's too dry or windy, the leaves shrivel up or blow off.

COLOR CHECK RESOURCES

Curious about current conditions? In season, each state maintains a dedicated Web site reporting on foliage conditions. Weather Channel has peak viewing maps and Foliage Network uses a network of spotters to chart changes.

- **Connecticut:** ☎ 800/282–6863 ⊕ www.ct.gov/dep
- **Foliage Network:** ⊕ www.foliagenetwork.com
- **Maine:** ☎ 888/624–6345 ⊕ www.maine.gov/doc/foliage
- **Massachusetts:** ☎ 617/973–8500 ⊕ www.massvacation.com
- **New Hampshire:** ☎ 800/258–3608 ⊕ www.visitnh.gov
- **Rhode Island:** ☎ 800/556–2484 ⊕ www.visitri.com
- **Vermont:** ☎ 800/837–6668 ⊕ www.foliage-vermont.com
- **Weather Channel:** ⊕ www.weather.com

TOP TREES FOR COLOR

A **AMERICAN BEECH.** This tree's smooth, steel-gray trunk is crowned with gold, copper, and bronze-tinted leaves in autumn, giving it a metallic sheen. Though the elliptical leaves sometimes hang on all winter, its "fruit" goes fast because beechnuts are a popular snack for birds, squirrels, and even bears.

B **NORTHERN RED OAK.** The upside of oaks is that they retain their fall shading until late in the season—the downside is that, for most species, that color is a boring brown. Happily, the northern red isn't like other members of the oak family. Its elongated, flame-shaped leaves turn fiery crimson and incandescent orange.

C **QUAKING ASPEN.** Eyes and ears both prove useful when identifying this aspen. Look for small, ovate leaves that usually become almost flaxen. Or listen for the leaves' quake: a sound, audible in even a gentle breeze, which the U.S. Forest Service likens to that made by "thousands of fluttering butterfly wings."

D **SUGAR MAPLE.** The leaf of the largest North American maple species is so lovely that Canada put it on its national flag. Each generally has five multi-pointed lobes—plus enough anthocyanin to produce a deep red color. The tree itself produces plentiful sap and is the cornerstone of New England's syrup industry.

E **WHITE ASH.** This tall tree typically grows to between 65 to 100 feet. Baseball enthusiasts admire the wood (which is used to craft bats); while foliage fans admire the compound leaves, each consisting of five to nine slightly serrated, tapering leaflets. They range in hue from burgundy and purple to amber.

F **WHITE BIRCH.** A papery, light, bright bark makes this slender hardwood easily recognizable. Centuries ago, Native Americans used birch wood to make everything from canoes to medicinal teas. Today's photographers know the bark also makes great pictures since it provides a sharp contrast to the tree's vibrant yellow leaves.

FANTASTIC FALL ITINERARY

The Berkshires

Fall is the perfect time to visit New England—country roads wind through dense forests exploding into reds, oranges, yellows, and purples. For inspiration, here is an itinerary for the truly ambitious that links the most stunning foliage areas; choose a section to explore more closely. Like autumn itself, this route works its way south from northern Vermont into Connecticut, with one or two days in each area.

VERMONT

NORTHWEST VERMONT

In Burlington, the elms will be turning colors on the University of Vermont campus. You can ride the ferry across Lake Champlain for great views of Vermont's Green Mountains and New York's Adirondacks. After visiting the resort town of Stowe, detour off Route 100 beneath the cliffs of Smugglers' Notch. The north country's palette unfolds in Newport, where the blue waters of Lake Memphremagog reflect the foliage. (⇨ Northern Vermont in Chapter 8.)

NORTHEAST KINGDOM

After a side trip along Lake Willoughby, explore St. Johnsbury, where the Fairbanks Museum and St. Johnsbury Athenaeum reveal Victorian tastes in art and natural-history collecting. In Peacham, stock up for a picnic at the Peacham Store. (⇨ Northern Vermont in Chapter 8.)

NEW HAMPSHIRE

WHITE MOUNTAINS AND LAKES REGION

In New Hampshire, Interstate 93 narrows as it winds through craggy Franconia Notch. Get off the interstate for the sinuous Kancamagus Highway portion of Route 112 that passes through the mountains to Conway. In Center Harbor, in the Lakes Region, you can ride the MS Mount Washington for views of the Lake Winnipesaukee shoreline, or ascend to Moultonborough's Castle in the Clouds for a falcon's-eye look at the colors. (⇨ The White Mountains and Lakes Region in Chapter 9.)

MT. MONADNOCK

In Concord, stop at the Museum of New Hampshire History and the State House. Several trails climb Mt. Monadnock, near Jaffrey Center, and colorful vistas extend as far as Boston. (⇨ The Monadnocks and Merrimack Valley in Chapter 9.)

⇨ For local drives perfect for an afternoon, also see our Fall Foliage Drive Spotlights on Western Massachusetts, Connecticut, Rhode Island, Vermont, New Hampshire, and Inland Maine.

THE MOOSE IS LOOSE!

Take "Moose Crossing" signs seriously because things won't end well if you hit an animal that stands six feet tall and weighs 1,200 pounds. Some 40,000 reside in northern New England. To search out these ungainly creatures in the wild, consider an orgaznized moose safari in northern New Hampshire or Maine.

MASSACHUSETTS

THE MOHAWK TRAIL

In Shelburne Falls, Massachusetts, the Bridge of Flowers displays the last of autumn's blossoms. Follow the Mohawk Trail section of Route 2 as it ascends into the Berkshire Hills—and stop to take in the view at the hairpin turn just east of North Adams (or drive up Mt. Greylock, the tallest peak in New England, for more stunning vistas). In Williamstown, the Sterling and Francine Clark Art Institute houses a collection of impressionist works. (⇨ *The Pioneer Valley and the Berkshires in Chapter 5.*)

THE BERKSHIRES

The scenery around Lenox, Stockbridge, and Great Barrington has long attracted the talented and the wealthy. Near U.S. 7, you can visit the homes of novelist Edith Wharton (the Mount, in Lenox), sculptor Daniel Chester French (Chesterwood, in Stockbridge), and diplomat Joseph Choate (Naumkeag, in Stockbridge). (⇨ *The Berkshires in Chapter 5.*)

CONNECTICUT

THE LITCHFIELD HILLS

This area of Connecticut combines the feel of upcountry New England with exclusive urban polish. The wooded shores of Lake Waramaug are home to country inns and wineries in pretty towns. Litchfield has a perfect village green—an idealized New England town center. (⇨ *The Litchfield Hills in Chapter 6.*)

FOLIAGE PHOTO HINT

Don't just snap the big panoramic views. Look for single, brilliantly colored trees with interesting elements nearby, like a weathered gray stone wall or a freshly painted white church. These images are often more evocative than big blobs of color or panoramic shots.

LEAF PEEPER PLANNER

Hot-air balloons and ski-lift rides give a different perspective on fall's color.

Enjoying fall doesn't necessarily require a multistate road trip. If you are short on time (or energy), a simple autumnal stroll might be just the ticket: many state parks even offer free short ranger-led rambles.

HIKE AND BIKE ON A TOUR

You can sign on for foliage-focused hiking holidays with **Country Walkers** (☎ 800/464–9255 ⊕ www.countrywalkers.com) and **Boundless Journeys** (☎ 800/941–8010 ⊕ www.boundlessjourneys.com); or cycling ones with **Bike Vermont** (☎ 800/257–2226 ⊕ www.bikevt.com) and **VBT Bicycling Vacations** (☎ 800/245–3868, ⊕ www.vbt.com). Individual state tourism boards list similar operators elsewhere.

SOAR ABOVE THE CROWDS

New Hampshire's Cannon Mountain (☎ 603/823–8800 ⊕ www.cannonmt.com) is only one of several New England ski resorts that provides gondola or aerial tram rides during foliage season. Area hot-air balloon operators, like **Balloons of Vermont, LLC** (☎ 802/369–0213 ⊕ www.balloonsofvermont.com), help you take it in from the top.

ROOM AT THE INN?

Accommodations fill quickly in autumn. Vermont's top lodgings sell out months in advance for the first two weeks in October. So book early and expect a two-night minimum stay requirement. If you can't find a quaint inn, try basing yourself at a B&B or off-season ski resort. Also, be prepared for some sticker shock; if you can travel midweek, you'll often save quite a bit.

RIDE THE RAILS OR THE CURRENT

Board the **Essex Steam Train** for a ride through the Connecticut countryside (☎ 800/377–3987 ⊕ www.essexsteamtrain.com) or float through northern Rhode Island on the **Blackstone Valley Explorer** riverboat (☎ 401/724–2200 ⊕ www.rivertourblackstone.com).

MASSACHUSETTS FALL FOLIAGE DRIVE

When fall foliage season arrives, the Berkshires are the place to appreciate the autumnal grandeur. Winding roads lined with dramatic trees ablaze—notably maples, birches, and beeches—pass alongside meadows, pasture, farmland, mountains, rivers, and lakes.

Although this complete scenic loop is only about 35 miles, you could easily spend the day making your way leisurely along the circuit. Begin in North Adams, a city transformed by art, and spend some time at the Massachusetts Museum of Contemporary Art (MASS MoCA). Just west of downtown off Route 2, the Notch Road leads into the **Mt. Greylock State Reservation,** ambling upward to the summit. At 3,491 feet, it's the state's highest point and affords expansive views of the countryside. Hike any of the many trails throughout the park, picnic at the peak, or stay for a meal at the rustic **Bascom Lodge.** Continue your descent on the Notch Road to Rockwell Road to exit the park and join Route 7 South.

BEST TIME TO GO

Peak season for leaf viewing in the Berkshires generally happens in mid-October. Trees growing near waterways—and they are plentiful in the area—tend to have more vibrant colors that peak a bit sooner. The state regularly updates fall foliage information by phone and online (☎ *800/632–8038* ⊕ *www.massvacation.com*).

Follow Route 7 South into the small town center of Lanesborough, where you'll turn left onto Summer Street. Horse farms and wide-open pastures make up the landscape, with distant mountain peaks hovering grandly in the background. If you want to pick your own apples, take a 1½-mile detour off Summer Street and stop at **Lakeview Orchard**.

Summer Street continues to tiny Berkshire Village, where you'll pick up Route 8 heading back toward North Adams. Running parallel to Route 8 from Lanesborough to Adams, is the paved **Ashuwillticook Rail Trail** for biking and walking. Right in the midst of two mountain ranges, the trail abuts wetlands, mixed woodland (including beech, birch, and maple trees), the Hoosac River, and the Cheshire Reservoir. In Cheshire, **Whitney's Farm Market** is busy on fall weekends with pony rides, pumpkin picking, a corn maze, and hayrides; plus it sells baked goods like the pumpkin whoopie pie.

Continuing on Route 8, you'll start to leave farm country as you make your way back to North Adams. Once a part of its much larger neighbor, the town of Adams still has active mills and the **Susan B. Anthony Birthplace Museum**. The 1817 Federal home of her birth has been fully restored.

NEED A BREAK?

Bascom Lodge. Built in the 1930s, this mountain-top lodge retains its rustic charm with no-frills but comfortable lodging and a restaurant in a stunning setting. ⊠ *Mt. Greylock State Reservation, Adams* ☎ *413/743–1591* ⊕ *www.bascomlodge.net* ⊘ *Closed Nov.–May.*

Lakeview Orchard. At Lakeview Orchard you can pick your own bushel of apples (or other fruits) and sample freshly pressed cider. There's a bevy of homemade pies and pastries, but make sure to sample the cider donuts. ⊠ *94 Old Cheshire Rd., Lanesboro* ☎ *413/448–6009* ⊕ *www.lakevieworchard. com* ⊘ *Early July–Oct., Tues.–Sun. 10–4:30.*

Whitney's Farm Market. Whitney's Farm has a large market with baked goods, fresh flowers, and seasonal fruit that you can pick yourself. ⊠ *1775 S. State Rd., Cheshire* ☎ *413/442–4749* ⊕ *www.whitneysfarm.com* ⊘ *Apr.–Dec., Mon.–Sat. 9–7, Sun. 9–6.*

CONNECTICUT FALL FOLIAGE DRIVE

Hidden in the heart of Litchfield County is the crossroads village of New Preston, perched above a 40-foot waterfall on the Aspetuck River. Just north of here you'll find Lake Waramaug, nestled in the rolling foothills and Mt. Tom, both ablaze with rich color every fall.

Start in New Milford and stroll along historic Main Street. Here you'll find New England's longest green and many shops, galleries, and restaurants within a short walk. Hop in the car and drive south on Main Street, then turn left to head north on wooded Route 202. About 4 miles north of the town green is the **Silo at Hunt Hill Farm Trust.** The former property of the late Skitch Henderson, onetime music director of NBC and the New York Pops, consists of a gallery, cooking school, and gift store housed in the buildings of two farms dating to the 1700s. Continue north on Route 202 to the junction of Route 45 and follow signs for Lake Waramaug.

—Bethany Cassin Beckerlegge

BEST TIME TO GO

Peak foliage in Connecticut occurs between early October and mid-November, according to the state's Department of Environmental Protection (⊕ *www.ct.gov/dep*). In season, the website includes daily updates on leaf color. Hope for a wet spring, warmer fall days, and cool (but not too cool) nights for the most dramatic color display.

Route 45 will bring you through the tiny village center of New Preston; stop here for a bit of shopping at **Dawn Hill Antiques.** Take 45 north and follow signs for Lake Waramaug. The 8-mile drive around the lake is stunning in autumn with the fiery foliage of the red maples, rusty brown oaks, and yellow birches reflected in the water. The beach area of **Lake Waramaug State Park** (about halfway around the lake) is a great place for a picnic, or perhaps even a quick dip on a warm fall day. **Hopkins Vineyard** is open daily for wine tasting; head to its Hayloft Wine Bar to enjoy a glass of wine and the spectacular lake views.

After completing a loop of Lake Waramaug, head back to Route 202 North toward Litchfield. Another excellent leaf-peeping locale is **Mt. Tom State Park,** about 3 miles or so from the junction of Routes 45 and 202. Here you can hike the mile-long trail to the summit and climb to the top of a stone tower that provides 360-degree views of the countryside's colors—the vibrant magenta-reds of the sugar maples are always among the most dazzling. After your hike, continue north on Route 202, ending your journey in the quintessential New England town of Litchfield. Peruse the shops and galleries in the town center and end the day with a dinner at the chic **West Street Grill.**

It's only about 30 miles from New Milford to the center of Litchfield, but with stops at the Silo at Hunt Hill, Lake Waramaug, and Mt. Tom you could easily spend half the day enjoying the scenery.

NEED A BREAK?

Dawn Hill Antiques.
This shop is filled with antiques that the owners have discovered on their regular trips to Sweden. ⊠ *11 Main St., New Preston* ☎ *860/868–0066* ⊕ *www.dawnhillantiques. com.*

Hopkins Vineyard.
This vineyard offers wine tastings and produces more than 13 varieties of wine, from sparkling to dessert. A wine bar in the hayloft serves a fine cheese-and-pâté board and has views of the lake. ⊠ *25 Hopkins Rd., off N. Shore Rd., New Preston* ☎ *860/868–7954* ⊕ *www.hopkinsvineyard. com* ⊠ *$6.50 for a tasting, $12 for a tour* ⊙ *Hours vary.*

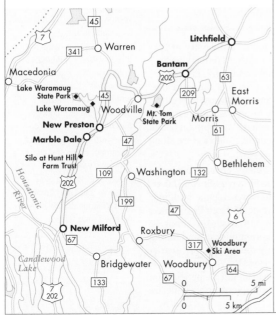

RHODE ISLAND FALL FOLIAGE DRIVE

Rhode Island's state tree is the red maple, which turns shades of gold, purple, and scarlet in fall and is common across the state.

But this small state is also home to a diversity of species like scarlet oak, white oak, northern red oak, yellow birch, gray birch, ash, black cherry and more. Pine forests dominate southern woodlands, reserving the most dramatic leaf peeping for the northern and western regions. You'll find dense forests, rolling meadows with centuries-old stone walls, an occasional orchard or pumpkin patch, and the quintessential New England country store along the way.

This tour through the state's quieter corners begins in Providence, where you can stroll across **Brown University's** handsome campus of dignified academic buildings and towering shade trees. Drive north from Providence, via Route 112 and then Route 114 north for about 12 miles to Cumberland, a rural community of undulating woodland crowned by a canopy of sugar maple, scarlet oak, and birch trees. Stop at **Diamond Hill Vineyards**, whose vineyards and apple orchards yield an intriguing selection of wines—the sparkling cider and spiced-apple wine are perfect on a cool October day.

BEST TIME TO GO

Foliage peaks in most of Rhode Island in the second week of October, especially in the state's northwest corner where the elevation is highest. Color can last a good two weeks in a year with no big storms and lots of cool, crisp fall nights. Autumn splendor can continue into the beginning of November along the coast. Tiverton's Weetamoo Woods and Pardon Gray Preserve and Little Compton's Wilbour Woods have great walking trails.

Drive west about 12 miles on Route 116 through Greenville, turning west on U.S. 44 for 7 miles to the tiny hamlet of Chepachet.

The rest of the tour meanders through some of Rhode Island's most pastoral countryside. In quaint Chepachet, Colonial and Victorian buildings contain antiques shops and quirky stores. Don't miss **Brown & Hopkins**, one of the country's oldest continuously operating general stores (including an old-fashioned candy counter), or the **Tavern on Main**, a rambling 18th-century restaurant that's perfect for a lunch stop.

Follow U.S. 44 west 5 miles through the burst of changing leaves in **Pulaski Memorial State Forest**. Turn left onto Route 94 and follow this for about 13 miles to Route 102, and then continue southeast another 20 miles to Exeter. The most undeveloped route from Chepachet to Exeter is lined with pristine hardwood forests, with an abundance of red maple, white oak, beech, elm, and poplar trees.

From Route 102, detour south in Exeter 1½ miles down Route 2 to **Schartner Farm** for a corn maze or hayride and cider and pumpkin pie. Backtrack to Route 102 and continue east 4 miles to the Colonial seaport of Wickford, whose pretty harbor opens to Narragansett Bay. The town's oak- and beech-shaded lanes are perfect for a late-afternoon stroll among the gift shops, galleries, and boutiques.

The drive is a total of about 80 miles and takes from four to eight hours, depending on stops.

NEED A BREAK?

Brown & Hopkins Country Store. Opened in 1809, Brown & Hopkins Country Store carries candles, reproduction antiques, penny candy, and handmade soaps. ⊠ *1179 Putnam Pike, Chepachet* ☎ *401/568–4830* ⊕ *www.brownandhopkins. com* ⊘ *Mon.–Sat. 10–5, Sun. 11–5.*

Diamond Hill Vineyards. This winery produces wine from pinot noir grapes grown on-site. It also makes a variety of seasonal wines from locally grown fruit. ⊠ *3145 Diamond Hill Rd., Cumberland* ☎ *401/333–2751* ⊕ *www. favorlabel.com* ⊘ *Thurs.– Sat. noon–5, Sun. noon–3.*

Schartner Farm. This farm store is popular during the fall for cider, pumpkin pie, and hayrides. ⊠ *1 Arnold Pl., Exeter* ☎ *401/294–2044* ⊕ *www.schartnerfarms.com* ⊘ *Daily 8–sunset.*

Tavern on Main. For lunch, try the homemade seafood stuffies or the lobster roll. ⊠ *1157 Putnam Pike, Chepachet* ☎ *401/710–9788* ⊕ *www.tavernonmainri.com* ⊘ *Closed Mon. and Tues.*

VERMONT FALL FOLIAGE DRIVE

Nearly 80% of Vermont is forested, with cities few and far between. The interior of Vermont is a rural playground for leaf peepers, and it's widely considered to have the most intense range of foliage colors anywhere on the continent. The few distractions from the dark reds, yellows, oranges, and russets—the tiny towns and hamlets—are as pristine as nature itself.

Begin this drive in Manchester Village, along the old-fashioned, well-to-do homes lining Main Street, and drive south to Arlington, North Bennington, and Old Bennington. Stop first just a mile south along 7A at **Hildene**, the Lincoln family home. The 412 acres of explorable grounds here are ablaze with color, and the views over the Battenkill Valley are as good as any you can find anywhere. Continue south another mile along 7A to **Equinox Nursery**, where you can pick your own pumpkin from a huge patch, try delicious apple cider and cider doughnuts, and take in the stunning countryside. A few more miles south along 7A is the small town of Arlington.

BEST TIME TO GO

Late September and early October are the times to go, with the southern area peaking about a week later than the north. Remember to book hotels in advance. The state has a Fall Foliage Hotline and an online interactive map (☎ 800/828–3239 ⊕ *www. foliage-vermont.com*). The drive from Manchester to Bennington outlined here is just 30 minutes, but a relaxed day is best to take in all the sights.

From 7A in Arlington you can take two adventurous and stunning detours. One is pure foliage: follow 313 west a few miles to the New York State border for more beautiful views. Or head east a mile to East Arlington where delightful stores await you, including a chocolate emporium. (You can continue even farther east from this spot to Kelly Stand Road leading into the Green Mountains; this is a little-known route that can't be beat.) Back on 7A South in Arlington, stop at the **Cheese House**, the delightfully cheesy roadside attraction.

Farther south into Shaftsbury is **Clear Brook Farm**, a brilliant place for cider and fresh produce and pumpkins. Robert Frost spent much of his life in South Shaftsbury, and you can learn about his life at his former home, the **Stone House.** From South Shaftsbury take Route 67 through North Bennington and continue on to Route 67A in Old Bennington. Go up the 306-foot-high **Bennington Battle Monument** to survey the seasonal views across four states. Back down from the clouds, walk a few serene blocks to the cemetery of the **Old First Church**, where Robert Frost is buried, and contemplate his autumnal poem, "Nothing Gold Can Stay."

NEED A BREAK?

Equinox Valley Nursery. This nursery carries fresh produce, seasonal snacks, and is full of family-friendly fall activities—a corn maze, pumpkin golf (mini golf played with small pumpkins), hay rides, and pumpkin carving. ⊠ *1158 Main St., Manchester* ☎ *802/362–2610* ⊕ *www. equinoxvalleynursery.com* ⊡ *Free.*

Clear Brook Farm. Set on more than 25 acres, Clear Brook Farm sells its own organic produce, in addition to baked goods and other seasonal treats. ⊠ *47 Hidden Valley Rd., Manchester* ☎ *802/442–4273* ⊕ *www. clearbrookfarm.com.*

The Cheese House. Get your Vermont cheddar fix at the The Cheese House, which also sells maple syrup and other local products and gifts. ⊠ *5187 Vermont Rte. 7A, Arlington* ☎ *802/375–9033* ⊕ *www. thevermontcheesehouse. com* ⊡ *Free* ⊙ *Closed Tues.*

NEW HAMPSHIRE FALL FOLIAGE DRIVE

With its quaint villages graced with green commons, white town halls, and covered bridges, southwestern New Hampshire is dominated by the imposing rocky summit of Mt. Monadnock and brilliant colors in fall. Kancamagus Highway is another classic foliage route, but for more solitude and less traffic, try this more accessible route that peaks a few weeks later than the state's far north.

The Granite State is the second-most forested state in the nation; by Columbus Day the colors of the leaves of its maple, birch, elm, oak, beech, and ash trees range from green to gold, purple to red, and orange to auburn. Routes 12, 101, 202, and 124 compose a loop around Mt. Monadnock. Start in Keene with a cup of coffee at Prime Roast; for New Hampshire–made products, take a walk on Main Street or detour west on Route 9 to reach **Stonewall Farm** for something more country.

BEST TIME TO GO

Early October is best time to view foliage in southern New Hampshire, but the time can vary by up to four weeks. For daily leaf changes, contact **Visit New Hampshire** (☎ *800/258-3608* ⊕ *www.visitnh.gov*).

PLANNING YOUR TIME

Expect to travel about 55 miles. The journey can take up to a full day if you stop to explore along the way.

From Keene, travel east on Route 101 through Dublin and over Pack Monadnock, a 2,290-foot peak (not to be confused with the 3,165-foot Grand, or Mt. Monadnock). In quaint **Peterborough**, browse the local stores, whose attitude and selection mirror the state's independent spirit.

Then turn south on Route 202 toward Jaffrey Village. Just west on Route 124, in historic Jaffrey Center, be sure to visit the **Meeting House Cemetery,** where author Willa Cather is buried. A side trip, 4 miles south on Route 202, leads to the majestic **Cathedral of the Pines** in Rindge, one of the best places in the region for foliage viewing because the ever-greens offset the brilliant shades of red.

Heading west on Route 124, you can take Dublin Road to the main entrance of **Monadnock State Park** or continue along to the Old Toll Road parking area for one of the most popular routes up the mountain, the **Halfway House Trail**. All the hiking trails have great views, including the area's many lakes. Continuing on Route 124, you come to Fitzwilliam and Route 12; turn north back to Keene.

NEED A BREAK?

Stonewall Farm.
This nonprofit working farm teaches about the importance of agriculture. The farm offers an active schedule of events, including maple sugaring and seasonal horse-drawn hayrides. Walking trails wind throughout the farm—in winter you can borrow snowshoes for free. Young children love the discovery room, and the interactive greenhouse is geared for all ages. ✉ *242 Chesterfield Rd., Keene* ☎ *603/357–7278* ⊕ *www.stonewallfarm.org* ☉ *Weekdays 9–4:30.*

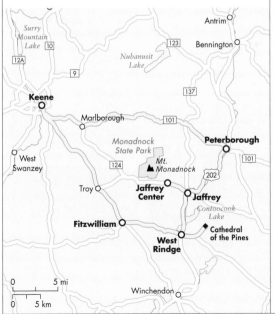

INLAND MAINE FALL FOLIAGE DRIVE

Swaths of pine, spruce, and fir trees offset the red, orange, and yellow of maples and birches along this popular foliage drive through Western Maine's mountains, but hardwoods largely dominate the landscape.

Wending its way to the four-season resort town of Rangeley, near its northern terminus, the route passes by or near stunning overlooks, forest-lined lakes, waterfalls, hiking trails, and a state park.

From Mexico, Route 17 heads north from U.S. 2, flowing past old homesteads and fields along the Swift River Valley before making the winding, mountainous ascent to **Height of Land**, the drive's literal pinnacle. This must-stop overlook has off-road parking, interpretive panels, stone seating, and a path to the nearby **Appalachian Trail**. Mountain vistas are reflected in the many (and often connected) lakes, ponds, rivers, and streams. On a clear day you can see west to New Hampshire and Canada. **Mooselookmeguntic Lake** and **Upper Richardson Lake** seem to float in the sea of forestland below. A few miles north of here is an overlook for Rangeley Lake, also with interpretive panels.

BEST TIME TO GO

Fall color usually peaks in the Rangeley area in the first or second week of October. Get fall foliage updates at ⊕ *www.mainefoliage.com.*

PLANNING YOUR TIME

The Rangeley Lakes National Scenic Byway (⊕ *www.byways.org*) makes up much of this 59-mile drive (1½ hours without stops), but plan for a relaxed full day of exploring.

In tiny, welcoming Oquossoc, where Routes 17 and 4 meet, **The Farmer's Daughter** welcomes passersby with displays of pumpkins and mums during autumn. Inside the seasonal specialty foods store you can pick up apple cider and picnic items. Or stop at the **Gingerbread House Restaurant** for a meal, or just ice cream or baked goods. The hamlet is also home to the **Rangeley Outdoor Sporting Heritage Museum**, where you can learn why visitors have come here to fish, hunt, and enjoy the outdoors since the mid-1800s.

Rangeley, 7 miles east on Route 4, has restaurants, inns, waterfront parks, and outdoorsy shops. The countryside sweeps into view along public hiking trails at both **Saddleback Maine** ski resort and the 175-acre **Wilhelm Reich Museum**.

The road to **Rangeley Lake State Park** is accessible from both Routes 4 and 17, as is the **Appalachian Trail**. Overhanging foliage frames waterfalls at the scenic rest areas at or near each end of the drive: Smalls Falls on Route 4, the byway's eastern terminus, and Coos Canyon on Route 17 en route to Height of Land. Both spots have several falls, swimming holes, and paths with views of the drops. Coos Canyon is along the Swift River, a destination for recreational gold panning. You can rent or buy panning equipment at **Coos Canyon Rock and Gift**, across from its namesake. It also sells sandwiches and snacks.

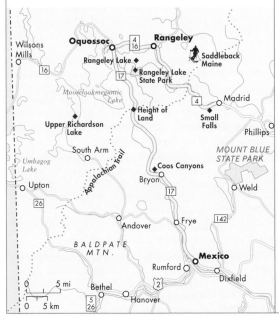

NEED A BREAK?

The Farmer's Daughter. At The Farmer's Daughter, much of the produce—including pumpkins and gourds come fall—is from the family farm. At the bakery counter you can buy a cup of coffee or apple cider in season. ✉ *13 Rumford Rd., Oquossoc* ☎ *207/864–2492.*

Wilhelm Reich Museum. This museum showcases the life and work of controversial physician-scientist Wilhelm Reich (1897–1957). There are magnificent views from the observatory and the many trails on the 175-acre grounds. ✉ *19 Orgonon Circle, off Rte. 4, Rangeley* ☎ *207/864–3443* ⊕ *www.wilhelmreichtrust. org* ✑ *Museum $6, grounds free* ☉ *Museum July and Aug., Wed.– Sun. 1–5; Sept., Sat. 1–5. Grounds daily 9–5.*

Rangeley Lakes Heritage Trust. This trust protects 13,000 acres of area land. It has trail maps and information about outdoor activities in the area. ✉ *52 Carry Rd., Oquossoc* ☎ *207/864–7311* ⊕ *www.rlht.org.*

GREAT ITINERARIES

CAPE COD

Classic Beaches and Bustling Villages, 7 Days

Cape Cod can be all things to all visitors, with quiet villages and lively resorts, gentle bay-side wavelets and crashing surf. A car is the best way to meander along Massachusetts's beach-lined, arm-shaped peninsula and explore the Cape, but in the busier town centers—such as Falmouth, Hyannis, Chatham, and Provincetown—you can get around quite easily on foot. Keep in mind that traffic leading onto the Cape is particularly bad on Friday, and traffic in the other direction is rough on Sunday. Cross as early in the day as possible.

DAY 1: HYANNIS
(30- to 90-minute drive from the bridge to Hyannis, depending on traffic)

The best way to spend a week on the Cape is to pick a central location and use that as a launching point to explore. Begin by crossing the Bourne Bridge and head east on U.S. 6 toward Hyannis—make this centrally located, larger town your headquarters.

The crowded Mid Cape is a center of activity, and its heart is **Hyannis.** Here you can take a cruise around the harbor or go on a deep-sea-fishing trip. There are shops and restaurants along Main Street and plenty of kid-friendly amusements. Fans of John F. Kennedy shouldn't miss the museum in his honor. End the day with a concert at the **Cape Cod Melody Tent.**

DAY 2: FALMOUTH
(30- to 45-minute drive from Hyannis)

For your first excursion, wander along Route 28 until you reach **Falmouth** in the Upper Cape. Here you can stroll around the village green, duck into some of the historic houses, and stop at the **Waquoit**

Bay National Estuarine Research Reserve for a walk along the barrier beach. Take some time to check out the village of **Woods Hole,** the center for international marine research, and the year-round ferry port for Martha's Vineyard. A small aquarium has regional sea-life exhibits. If you have extra time, head north to the lovely old town of **Sandwich,** known for the **Sandwich Glass Museum,** and the beautiful grounds and collection of antique cars at **Heritage Museums and Gardens.**

DAY 3: BARNSTABLE, YARMOUTH PORT, DENNIS
(20-minute drive from Hyannis to Dennis)

Spend your day exploring the northern reaches of the Mid Cape with a drive along scenic Route 6A, which passes through the charming, slow-paced villages of **Barnstable, Yarmouth Port,** and **Dennis.** There are beaches and salt marshes, antiques shops and galleries, and old graveyards along this route. Yarmouth Port's **Bass Hole Boardwalk** makes for a particularly beautiful stroll. In Dennis there are historic houses to tour, and the **Cape Museum of Fine Arts** merits a stop. End the day by climbing 30-foot **Scargo Tower** to watch the sun set. At night you can catch a film at the **Cape Cinema,** on the grounds of the **Cape Playhouse.**

If you're traveling with kids, spend some time in the southern sections of Yarmouth and Dennis, where Route 28 passes by countless amusement centers and miniature-golf courses.

DAY 4: CHATHAM
(30-minute drive from Hyannis)

Chatham, with its handsome Main Street, is a perfect destination for strolling, shopping, and dining. A trip to the nearby **Monomoy Islands** is a must for bird-watchers and nature lovers. Back in town, you

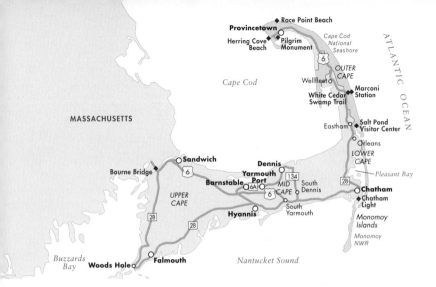

can watch glassblowing at the **Chatham Glass Company,** visit the **Atwood House Museum,** and drive over to take in the view from **Chatham Light.**

DAY 5: CAPE COD NATIONAL SEASHORE

(1½-hour drive from Hyannis to Provincetown)

On Day 5, leave your Hyannis hub and head for the farther reaches of Cape Cod. Take U.S. 6 east, before making a slight detour onto the less commercial end of Route 28. On the way north toward Orleans you'll drive past sailboat-speckled views of Pleasant Bay.

Stop in Eastham at the Cape Cod National Seashore's **Salt Pond Visitor Center.** Take time to stroll along one of the beaches—there are more than 40 miles of pristine sand from which to choose—or bike on the many picturesque trails. Head slightly farther north to historic **Marconi Station,** which was the landing point for the transatlantic telegraph early in the 20th century, or park your car in **Wellfleet**'s historic downtown, where you'll find a bounty of intriguing shops and galleries. It's also worth walking the short but stunning **White Cedar Swamp Trail.** Continue on to Provincetown to spend your first of two nights at the tip of the Cape.

DAYS 6 AND 7: PROVINCETOWN

Bustling **Provincetown** sits at the very end of the Cape, and there's a lot to see and do here. Catch a whale-watching boat and take a trolley tour through town, or bike through the **Cape Cod National Seashore** on its miles of trails. Climb the **Pilgrim Monument** for a spectacular view of the area—on an exceptionally clear day you can see the Boston skyline. Visit the museums, shops, and art galleries, or spend the afternoon swimming and sunning on the beaches at **Herring Cove** or **Race Point.**

NEW HAVEN TO BOSTON

A Culinary Tour, 5 Days

Sample some of the splendid culinary fare the northeast has to offer in this short jaunt between New Haven and Boston. New Haven, Providence, and Boston all make the case for having the finest Italian cuisine in the region, which leaves you to judge whose cuisine reigns supreme. History buffs can also get their fill while exploring New England's Colonial and maritime past.

DAY 1: NEW HAVEN

Start your journey in **New Haven,** Connecticut. The Constitution State's second-largest city is home to **Yale University,** named for British shipping merchant Elihu Yale. Take a one-hour walking tour

with one of the university's guides and feast your eyes on the iconic Gothic-style structures that adorn the campus. After you've worked up an appetite, a stop for New Haven–style pizza is a must. Less than a mile from campus are two staples known for thin-crust pies cooked in brick ovens: **Frank Pepe Pizzeria Napoletana** and **Sally's Apizza**. For the burger enthusiast, there's **Louis' Lunch** on Crown Street. Don't ask for ketchup: it's been taboo here since they opened in 1895. Spend your first night in New Haven.

DAY 2: NEW HAVEN TO PROVIDENCE

(1-hour drive from New Haven to Mystic; 50-minute drive from Mystic to Providence)

On your second day, get an early start, and head east on Interstate 95 to make your way toward Providence, Rhode Island. There are plenty of small towns bursting with New England's maritime history along Connecticut's shoreline. Stop in New London, Niantic, or **Stonington** and explore the region's rich seafaring history. If you're planning on making one stop on the way to Rhode Island, the seaside village of **Mystic** is worth at least a half day to explore the seaport or take a boat out on the water. **Mystic Seaport**, with its almost 500 shipping vessels and more

than 60 preserved historic buildings, will transport you back to 19th-century New England. For those looking to try their luck at a game of chance, take a slight detour north on Interstate 395 to either of Connecticut's two casinos, **Foxwood's Resort Casino** or **Mohegan Sun**. Overnight in Providence or any of the seaside towns along the way.

DAY 3: PROVIDENCE

Rhode Island's capital holds treasures like **Benefit Street**, with its Federal-era homes, and the **Museum of Art** at the **Rhode Island School of Design**. Be sure to savor a knockout Italian meal on Atwells Avenue in the **Federal Hill** neighborhood—**Pane e Vino** is a popular choice. For dessert, it's hard to top the cannoli at **Scialo Bros. Bakery**. If you're visiting in early June, sample authentic eats from all over Italy, while live music fills the streets, during the **Federal Hill Stroll**. On summer nights, catch a Paw Sox baseball game at McCoy Stadium in the neighboring town of **Pawtucket**, the home of the beloved Boston Red Sox Triple-A farm team. Also in the warmer months, typically late May through early November, Providence hosts **WaterFire**, a public celebration of art and performance. The festival's 100 bonfires on the rivers of downtown Providence will attract tens of thousands of viewers for the 20th anniversary in 2014.

DAYS 4 AND 5: BOSTON
(1-hour drive from Providence)

A short drive north on Interstate 95 will bring you to Boston, New England's cultural and commercial hub. To savor Boston's centuries-old ties to the sea, take a half-day stroll by **Faneuil Hall** and **Quincy Market** or a boat tour of the harbor (you can even head out on a whale-watching tour from here). In Boston, famous buildings such as Faneuil Hall are not merely civic landmarks, but national icons. From the **Boston Common**, the 2.5-mile **Freedom Trail** links treasures of American liberty such as the **USS Constitution** (better known as "Old Ironsides") and the **Old North Church** (of "one if by land, two if by sea" fame). Be sure to walk the gas-lighted streets of **Beacon Hill**, too.

Boston's **North End** is the oldest residential neighborhood in the city, and has great dining options like **Antico Forno,** which offers pizza baked in a wood-burning brick oven. The following day, either explore the massive **Museum of Fine Arts** and the grand boulevards and shops of **Back Bay,** or visit colorful **Cambridge,** home of **Harvard University** and the **Massachusetts Institute of Technology.** Lively **Harvard Square** is a perfect place to do some people-watching or catch a street performance. The **All Star Sandwich Bar** is an excellent choice for lunch. For an experience unique to the Boston area, head a few miles south of the city along U.S. 1 to Dorchester's **Boston Bowl** to cap off your trip with candlepin bowling. Here, at all hours of the night, Bay Staters play a smaller version of 10-pin bowling that uses balls weighing less than 3 pounds and allows participants to bowl three balls per frame instead of two.

MASSACHUSETTS, NEW HAMPSHIRE, AND MAINE
The Coast and Mountains, 7 Days

Revel in the coastlines of three New England states—Massachusetts, New Hampshire, and Maine—on the path from the region's largest city, Boston, to the its highest peak, Mt. Washington. An assortment of New England's coastal treasures are at your fingertips as you pilot the ins and outs of the jagged northeastern coastline, before ascending the heights of the White Mountains.

DAY 1: THE NORTH SHORE AND NEW HAMPSHIRE COAST
(1-hour drive from Boston to Portsmouth)

Kick off your trek by leaving city life behind in Boston and head for the North Shore of Massachusetts. In **Salem,** the **Peabody Essex Museum** and the **Salem Maritime National Historic Site** chronicle the country's early shipping fortunes. Spend some time exploring more of the North Shore, including the old fishing port of **Gloucester,** and **Rockport,** one possible place to buy that seascape painted in oils. **Newburyport,** with its Federal-style shipowners' homes, is home to the **Parker River National Wildlife Refuge,** beloved by birders and beach walkers.

New Hampshire fronts the Atlantic for a scant 18 miles, but its coastal landmarks range from honky-tonk **Hampton Beach** to quiet **Odiorne Point State Park** in Rye and pretty Portsmouth, where the cream of pre-Revolutionary society built Georgian- and Federal-style mansions—visit a few at the **Strawbery Banke Museum.** Stay the night in **Portsmouth** at the centrally located **Ale House Inn.**

DAY 2: THE YORKS
(30-minute drive from Portsmouth)

Much of the appeal of the Maine Coast lies in its geographical contrasts, from its long stretches of swimming and walking beaches in the south to the cliff-edged, rugged, rocky coasts in the north. And not unlike the physical differences of the shoreline, each town along the way reveals a slightly different character, starting with **York.**

In **York Village** take a leisurely stroll through the seven buildings of the **Old York Historical Society,** getting a glimpse of 18th-century life in this gentrified town. Spend time wandering amid the shops or walking the nature trails and beaches around York Harbor. There are several grand lodging options here, most with views of the harbor. If you prefer a livelier pace, continue on to **York Beach,** a haven for families with plenty of entertainment venues. Stop at **Fox's Lobster House** after visiting **Nubble Light** for a seaside lunch or dinner.

DAY 3: OGUNQUIT AND THE KENNEBUNKS
(35-minute drive from York)

For well over a century, **Ogunquit** has been a favorite vacation spot for those looking to combine the natural beauty of the ocean with a sophisticated environment. Take a morning walk along the **Marginal Way** to see the waves crashing on the rocks. In **Perkins Cove,** have lunch, stroll the shopping areas, or sign on with a lobster-boat cruise to learn about Maine's most important fishery—the state's lobster industry supplies more than 90% of the world's lobster intake. See the extraordinary collection at the **Ogunquit Museum of American Art,** take in a performance at one of the several theater venues, or just spend time on the beach.

Head north to the Kennebunks, allowing at least two hours to wander through the shops and historic homes of **Dock Square** in **Kennebunkport.** This is an ideal place to rent a bike and amble around the backstreets, head out on Ocean Avenue to view the large mansions, or ride to one of the several beaches to relax a while. Spend your third night in Kennebunkport.

DAYS 4 AND 5: PORTLAND
(45-minute drive from Kennebunkport)

If you have time, you can easily spend several days in **Portland,** Maine's largest city, exploring its historic neighborhoods, shopping and eating in the **Old Port,** or visiting one of several excellent museums. A brief side trip to **Cape Elizabeth** takes you to **Portland Head Light,** Maine's first

2

lighthouse, which was commissioned by George Washington in 1787. The lighthouse is on the grounds of **Fort Williams Park** and is an excellent place to bring a picnic. Be sure to spend some time wandering the ample grounds. There are also excellent walking trails (and views) at nearby **Two Lights State Park.** If you want to take a boat tour while in Portland, get a ticket for Casco Bay Lines and see some of the islands that dot the bay. Spend two nights in Portland.

DAY 6: BRETTON WOODS
(3-hour drive from Portland)

Wake up early and drive to Bretton Woods, where you will spend nights six and seven. The driving time from Portland to Bretton Woods is approximately three hours, due to two-lane, steep mountain roads. ■ TIP→ **Be sure to drive a four-wheel-drive vehicle in winter.** Drive northwest along U.S. 302 toward **Sebago Lake,** a popular water-sports area in the summer, and continue on toward the time-honored New England towns of Naples and Bridgton. Just 15 miles from the border of New Hampshire, and nearing Crawford Notch, U.S. 302 begins to thread through New Hampshire's **White Mountains,** passing beneath brooding **Mt. Washington** before arriving in **Bretton Woods.**

DAY 7: THE WHITE MOUNTAINS

In Bretton Woods, the **Mt. Washington Cog Railway** still chugs to the summit, and the **Mount Washington Hotel** recalls the glory days of White Mountain resorts. Beloved winter activities here include snowshoeing and skiing on the grounds of the Mount Washington Hotel. Afterward, defrost with a cup of steaming hot cider while checking out vintage photos of the International Monetary Conference, held here in 1944.

MAINE'S NORTHERN COAST

Portland to Acadia National Park, 6 Days

Lighthouses, beaches, lobster rolls, and water sports—Maine's northern coast has something for everyone. Quaint seaside villages and towns line the shore as U.S. 1 winds its way toward the easternmost swath of land in the United States at Quoddy Head State Park. Maine's only National Park, Acadia, is a highlight of the tour, drawing more than 2 million visitors per year.

DAY 1: PORTLAND TO BRUNSWICK

Use Maine's maritime capital as your jumping-off point to head farther up the Maine Coast, or, as Mainers call it, "Down East." Plan to spend half of your first day in Portland, then head to Brunswick for the night.

Portland shows off its restored waterfront at the **Old Port.** From there, before you depart, you can grab a bite at either of two classic Maine eateries: **Gilbert's Chowderhouse** or **Becky's Diner.** For a peek at the freshest catch of the day, wander over to the **Harbor Fish Market,** a Portland institution since 1968, and gaze upon Maine lobsters and other delectable seafood. Two lighthouses on nearby **Cape Elizabeth, Two Lights** and **Portland Head,** still stand vigil.

Following U.S. 1, travel northeast along the ragged, island-strewn coast of Down East Maine and make your first stop at the retail outlets of **Freeport,** home of **L.L. Bean.** More than 3 million people visit the massive flagship store every year, where you can find everything from outerwear to camping equipment. Just 10 miles north of Freeport on U.S. 1, **Brunswick,** Maine

is home to the campus of **Bowdoin College** and also features a superb coastline for kayaking. Spend the night in Brunswick at one of the many inns that line U.S. 1.

DAY 2: BATH
(1-hour-and-45-minute drive from Brunswick to Rockland)

From Brunswick, head to **Bath**, Maine's shipbuilding capital, and tour the **Maine Maritime Museum**, stopping for lunch on the waterfront. Check out the boutiques and antiques shops, or take in the plentitude of beautiful homes. From here it's a 30-minute drive down Route 127 to **Reid State Park**, where you will find a quiet beach lining Sheepscot Bay, and maybe even a sand dollar or two to take home if you arrive at low tide. For a stunning vista, make your way to **Griffith Head.**

Drive north on Georgetown Island and reconnect with U.S. 1. Continue through the towns of **Wiscasset** and **Damariscotta**, where you may find yourself pulling over to stop at the outdoor flea markets and intriguing antiques shops that line the road. Another hour from here is **Rockland**, Maine, where you'll spend your second night.

DAY 3: ROCKLAND, CAMDEN, AND CASTINE
(1½-hour drive from Rockland to Castine)

From Rockland, spend the day cruising on one of the majestic schooners that set sail from here or reserve a tee time at **Somerset Resorts'** 18-hole championship course that overlooks the Rockland Harbor. If you're an art lover, save some time for Rockland's **Farnsworth Art Museum** and the **Wyeth Center.**

In **Camden** and Castine, exquisite inns occupy homes built from inland Maine's gold and timber. These are perfect places to stay overnight as you make your way closer to Acadia National Park. Camden is a beautiful seaside town with hundreds of boats bobbing in the harbor, immaculately kept antique homes, streets lined with boutiques and specialty stores, and restaurants serving lobster at every turn. The modest (by Maine standards, anyway) hills of nearby Mt. Battie offer good hiking and a great spot from which to picnic and view the surrounding area. Camden is one of the hubs for the beloved and historic windjammer fleet—there is no better way to see the area than from the deck of one of these graceful beauties.

2

DAYS 4 AND 5: MOUNT DESERT ISLAND AND ACADIA NATIONAL PARK
(1-hour-and-15-minute-drive from Castine to Bar Harbor)

On Day 4, head out early for **Bar Harbor** and plan to spend two nights here, using the bustling village as jumping-off point for the park—Bar Harbor is less than 5 miles from the entrance to **Mount Desert Island**'s 27-mile Park Loop Road. Spend at least a day exploring **Acadia National Park,** Maine's only national park and its most popular tourist destination. Popular ways of enjoying the island's natural beauty include kayaking along the coast, biking the 45-mile, historic, unpaved, carriage-road system, and driving to the summit of **Cadillac Mountain** to enjoy the stunning panorama.

DAY 6: BAR HARBOR TO QUODDY HEAD STATE PARK
(2½-hour drive from Bar Harbor)

About 100 miles farther along U.S. 1 and "Way Down East" is **Quoddy Head State Park** in Lubec, Maine. Here, on the easternmost tip of land in the United States, sits the **West Quoddy Head Lighthouse,** one of 60 lighthouses that dot Maine's rugged coastline. Depending on the time of year, you might be lucky enough to catch the East Coast's first sunrise.

CONNECTICUT AND RHODE ISLAND

Connecticut Wineries and Rhode Island Mansions, 5 Days

Travel through Connecticut's Lower River Valleys as you meander toward the state's Eastern Wine Trail. Besides savoring different wine varietals from the area's best vineyards and wineries, get a taste of New England's literary and maritime history along the way. Finish your tour by gawking at Newport's grand mansions.

DAY 1: HARTFORD

Embark on your journey from **Hartford,** Connecticut. The **Mark Twain House** resembles a Mississippi steamboat beached in a Victorian neighborhood (adjacent to it is the **Harriet Beecher Stowe House** museum). Downtown, you can visit the Nutmeg State's ornate **State Capitol** and the **Wadsworth Atheneum,** which houses fine Impressionist and Hudson River School paintings. Sports buffs: the **Naismith Memorial Basketball Hall of Fame** is only a quick detour up Interstate 91, in **Springfield,** Massachusetts, where Dr. James Naismith invented basketball in 1891. Spend your first night in Hartford.

DAY 2: CONNECTICUT RIVER VALLEY AND SOUTHEASTERN SHORE
(1-hour-and-45-minute-drive from Hartford to Mystic)

Just a half-hour southeast of Hartford along Route 2 is the first wine stop, **Priam Vineyards,** in Colchester. Sample any of the boutique wines before bearing south to explore the centuries-old towns of **Essex, Chester,** and **Haddam** that dot the banks of the Connecticut River. In Essex, take a ride on the **Essex Steam Train**—the 12-mile excursion showcases the area's well-preserved countryside.

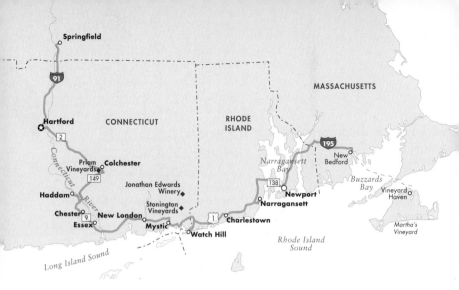

Continue on to **New London**, Connecticut, home of the **U.S. Coast Guard Academy**, and board the **USCGS Eagle** (when in port) or tour the museum, which details more than 200 years of Coast Guard maritime history. In **Mystic** the days of wooden ships and whaling adventures live on at **Mystic Seaport**. Spend your second night in Mystic.

DAY 3: EASTERN WINE TRAIL
(25-minute drive from Mystic to Watch Hill)

A patchwork of six wineries that make up the heart of the **Eastern Wine Trail** sits in this tiny southeastern corner of Connecticut. Taste from each of the picturesque vineyards until you find the perfect bottle to take home. Many of the wineries offer self-guided walks through peaceful vineyards, allowing you to roam on your own. **Stonington Vineyards** has daily guided tours, and **Jonathan Edwards Winery**, perched above the Atlantic, is a serene setting for picnics. Cap off the day by crossing the state line into Rhode Island and spend the night in **Watch Hill**.

DAYS 4 AND 5: RHODE ISLAND'S BEACHES AND NEWPORT'S MANSIONS
(1-hour drive from Watch Hill to Newport)

En route to Newport along U.S. 1 from **Watch Hill**, sandy beaches dot the coast in **Charlestown** and **Narragansett**. If it's summer and the weather is fine, spend the afternoon at the beach before continuing on to Newport. Despite its Colonial downtown and seaside parks, to most people **Newport** means mansions—it is the most opulent enclave of private homes ever built in the United States. Turn-of-the-20th-century "summer cottages" such as the **Breakers** and **Marble House** are must-sees. Embark on the scenic **Cliff Walk** for remarkable views of the mansions on one side and of the Atlantic on the other.

Newport is known to many as the sailing capital of the East Coast, and you might get the best feel for it by cruising its famous harbor on a schooner. Tours generally last around 90 minutes and some come complete with beverages and snacks. Tennis enthusiasts can visit the **International Tennis Hall of Fame**. Along with exhibits focusing on the legends of the game is the unique interior, designed by architect Stanford White. You can easily spend a few days exploring Newport. For a side trip, less than one hour east of Newport is New Bedford, Massachusetts, where you can board year-round ferry service to **Martha's Vineyard**. This Bay State seaside town was once a major whaling center; exhibits at the **New Bedford Whaling Museum** capture this vanished world.

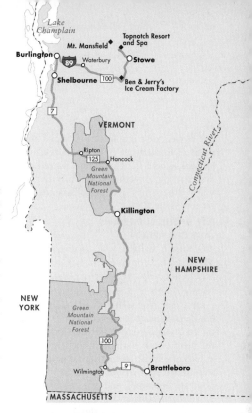

VERMONT

Best of the Green Mountain State, 7 Days

Following roads that weave through the Green Mountains and charming towns, this 200-mile journey is ideal for all seasons. It has Vermont covered from top to bottom.

DAY 1: BRATTLEBORO

Artsy **Brattleboro** is the perfect place to begin a tour of Vermont and is worth a day to do some shopping and exploring. Take in a movie at the art-deco **Latchis Theatre,** browse in a bookstore, or simply grab a cup of joe and people-watch. For dinner, make a reservation well in advance at tiny **T.J. Buckley's,** one of the best restaurants in the state. Spend one night in Brattleboro.

DAY 2: BRATTLEBORO TO KILLINGTON
(2½-hour drive from Brattleboro)

Depart from Brattleboro heading west on Route 9 and link up with Route 100 in Wilmington. As you travel north along the eastern edge of **Green Mountain National Forest,** you'll pass a plethora of panoramic overlooks and delightful ski towns. Stop to snap a photo or take a moment to peruse what's for sale at a funky general store, as you meander toward gigantic Killington Peak. Spend the night in **Killington,** the largest ski resort in Vermont. Skiers: one of the closest places to the slopes to stay is **The Mountain Top Inn & Resort.**

DAYS 3 AND 4: KILLINGTON

Wake up early to carve the mountain's fresh powder in winter. In summer, enjoy trails long after the ground has thawed, when they are opened to mountain bikers and hikers. For a more leisurely activity, try your hand at the 18-hole disc-golf course. Spend two nights here exploring Killington's more than 20 lifts and 140 trails.

DAY 5: KILLINGTON TO BURLINGTON
(2½-hour drive from Killington)

Continue on Route 100 north until you reach Hancock and then head west onto Route 125 as you enter the land of poet Robert Frost. Frost spent almost 40 years living in Vermont, and summered in the nearby tiny mountain town of Ripton, where he wrote numerous poems. Plaques along the 1.2-mile **Robert Frost Interpretive Trail,** a quiet woodland walk that takes about 30 minutes, display commemorative quotes from his poems, including his timeless piece, "The Road Not Taken." After your stroll, head north on U.S. 7 until you hit Burlington.

Burlington, Vermont's largest city and home to the **University of Vermont,** is located on the eastern shore of Lake Champlain. Bustling in the summer and fall, the **Burlington Farmers' Market** is filled with everything from organic meats and cheeses to freshly cut flowers and maple syrup. Spend the night in Burlington. At night, check out **Nectar's,** where the band Phish played its first bar gig, or wander into any of the many other pubs and cafés that attract local musicians.

DAY 6: SHELBURNE AND LAKE CHAMPLAIN

(10-minute drive from Burlington to Magic Hat; 20-minute drive from Burlington to Shelburne Farms)

Basing yourself in Burlington, you can take a day trip south to the **Magic Hat Brewing Company,** in operation since 1994, on your second day in the area. It was at the forefront of Vermont's microbrewery explosion. Take a free half-hour guided or self-guided tour of the Artifactory (even dogs are welcome), and wet your whistle by filling a growler from one of the 48 taps pumping out year-round, seasonal, and experimental brews. With one brewery for about every 24,000 Vermonters, the Green Mountain State is tops in the United States. A stone's throw farther down U.S. 7, in **Shelburne,** is family-friendly **Shelburne Farms.** Watch the process of making cheese from start to finish or wander the gorgeous 1,400-acre estate designed by Frederick Law Olmsted, co-creator of New York's Central Park. The grounds overlook beautiful **Lake Champlain** and are the perfect place to picnic. If you're visiting in late July, don't miss the **Vermont Cheesemakers Festival,** showcasing more than 200 varieties of cheese crafted by 40 local purveyors. If you can't get enough, you can opt to spend the night at Shelburne Farms.

DAY 7: STOWE

(1-hour drive from Burlington to Stowe)

A 30-minute drive down Interstate 89 from Burlington reunites you with Route 100 in the small town of Waterbury. Head north toward Stowe, and, in under 2 miles you can make the obligatory pit stop at **Ben & Jerry's Ice Cream Factory.** The factory tour offers a behind-the-scenes look at how the ice cream is made; you can taste some of the limited-release creations only available at the factory.

Next, set out for the village of **Stowe.** Proximity to Mt. Mansfield, Vermont's highest peak at 4,395 feet, has made Stowe a popular ski destination since the 1930s. If there's snow on the ground, hit the slopes, hitch a ride on a one-horse open sleigh, or simply put your feet up by the fire and enjoy a Heady Topper beer (an unfiltered, hoppy, American Double IPA beloved by Vermonters). In warmer weather, pop into the cute shops and art galleries that line the town's main street and sample some of the finest cheddar cheese and maple syrup that Vermont has to offer. Rejuvenate yourself at **Topnotch Resort and Spa,** which offers more than 100 different treatments. Spend your final night here.

BOSTON AND ENVIRONS

WELCOME TO BOSTON AND ENVIRONS

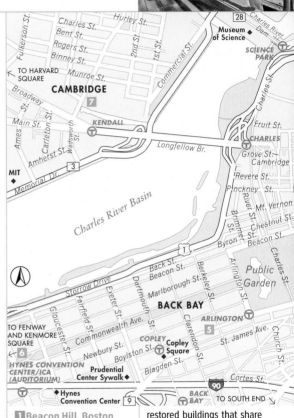

TOP REASONS TO GO

★ **Freedom's Ring:**
Walk through America's early history on the 2½-mile Freedom Trail that snakes through town.

★ **Ivy-Draped Campus:**
Hang in Harvard Square like a collegiate or hit the university's museums: the Sackler (ancient art), the Botanical Museum, the Peabody (archeology), and the Natural History Museum.

★ **Posh Purchases:**
Strap on some stilettos and join the quest for fashionable finds on Newbury Street, Boston's answer to Manhattan's 5th Avenue.

★ **Sacred Ground:**
Root for (or boo) the Red Sox at baseball's most hallowed shrine, Fenway Park.

★ **Tea Time:** Interact with the city's history at the Boston Tea Party Ships & Museum: greet re-enactors and explore replicas of the ships at the actual spot where the tea met the sea.

1 Beacon Hill, Boston Common, and the Old West End. The Brahmins' old stomping ground has many landmarks (Boston Common and the State House among them). The Old West End has the Museum of Science and TD Garden.

2 Government Center and the North End. The sterile Government Center area is home to lovely Faneuil Hall and the trio of restored buildings that share its name. The small North End is full of history and a strong Italian influence.

3 Charlestown. Charlestown's Freedom Trail sights can't be missed—literally. The Bunker Hill Monument is a towering tribute to a pivotal 1775 battle; the USS *Constitution*, a towering tangle of masts and rigging, highlights the neighborhood's naval heritage.

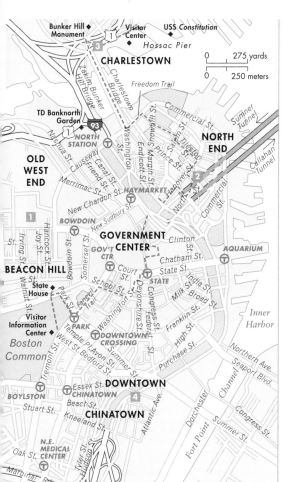

CHARLESTOWN

Bunker Hill Monument · Visitor Center · USS *Constitution* · Hossac Pier

0 — 275 yards
0 — 250 meters

Freedom Trail

TD Banknorth Garden

NORTH STATION

OLD WEST END

NORTH END

HAYMARKET

BOWDOIN

GOVERNMENT CENTER
GOV'T CTR

AQUARIUM

BEACON HILL

State House

STATE

Inner Harbor

Visitor Information Center

PARK

DOWNTOWN CROSSING

Boston Common

DOWNTOWN

BOYLSTON

CHINATOWN

CHINATOWN

N.E. MEDICAL CENTER

GETTING ORIENTED

3

With such a complex identity, it's no surprise that Boston, despite its relatively small size, offers visitors a diverse set of experiences. History buffs—and just about everyone else—will spend a day or more following the thick red line of the Freedom Trail and tracing Revolutionary history through town. Shopaholics can join the quest for fashionable finds on Newbury Street, while sports fiends gravitate toward Fenway Park for a tour (or if very lucky, a game) of the beloved Boston Red Sox's home. The Museum of Fine Art's expansive catalog of French Impressionists and American painters, the Isabella Stewart Gardner Museum's palazzo of painting masters, and the Institute of Contemporary Art's modern works satisfy any artistic taste.

4 Downtown. This maze-like section of central Boston encompasses the Financial District and Downtown Crossing (a retail zone); as well as Chinatown, the revived Theater District, plus portions of the Freedom Trail and HarborWalk.

5 The Back Bay. Back Bay's chichi shops, upscale restaurants, and deluxe lodgings sit alongside attractions like the Public Garden and Public Library.

6 The Fenway. Sox fans, art lovers, and college students all frequent the Fens. Fenway Park, the Museum of Fine Arts, and the Isabella Stewart Gardner Museum are here.

7 Cambridge. A separate city across the Charles River, Cambridge has long been a haven for intellectuals and iconoclasts. Along with Harvard and MIT, you'll find bookstores, cafés, and funky boutiques.

FENWAY PARK

For baseball fans Fenway Park is Mecca: a trip there is a religious pilgrimage to the home of former baseball greats such as Ted Williams and Carl Yastrzemski. The Boston Red Sox have played here since 1912, making Fenway the oldest Major League ballpark. The scoreboard is still operated by hand, and fans still clamor for cramped, uncomfortable seats.

(above) Take yourself out to a ballgame at legendary Fenway Park. (lower right) Iconic sox mark the park walls. (upper right) Flags adorn the epicenter of Red Sox Nation.

For much of the ballpark's history Babe Ruth's specter loomed large. After winning five titles by 1918 (including the first World Series in 1903), the team endured an 86-year title drought after trading away the Sultan of Swat. The team vexed generations of fans with colossal late-season collapses, post-season bungles, and losses to the hated New York Yankees. The Sox snapped the spell in 2004, defeating the Yanks in the American League Championship Series after being down 3–0 and sweeping the St. Louis Cardinals in the World Series. The Red Sox won it all again in 2007, completely exorcising "The Curse" in 2013.

FUN FACT

A lone red seat in the right-field bleachers marks where Ted Williams' 502-foot shot—the longest measurable home run hit inside Fenway Park—landed on June 9, 1946.

TICKET TIPS

Can't get tickets? At Gate E two hours before the game, a handful of tickets are sold. There's a one-ticket limit, so everyone must be in line.

THE NATION
The Red Sox have the most rabid fan base in baseball. They follow the team with an intensity usually seen in religious cults. The Pats and Celtics may be champion-caliber teams, too, but this is first and foremost a Red Sox town.

THE MONSTER
Fenway's most dominant feature is the 37-foot-high "Green Monster," the wall that looms over left field. It's just over 300 feet from home plate and in the field of play, so deep fly balls that would have been outs in other parks sometimes become home runs. The Monster also stops line drives that would have been over the walls of other stadiums.

THE MUSIC
Fans sing "Take Me Out to the Ballgame" during the 7th inning stretch in every ballpark… but at Fenway they also sing Neil Diamond's "Sweet Caroline" in the middle of the 8th. If the Sox win, the Standell's "Dirty Water" blasts over the loudspeakers at the game's end.

THE CURSE
In 1920 the Red Sox traded pitcher Babe Ruth to the Yankees, where he became a home-run-hitting baseball legend. Some fans—most famously *Boston Globe* columnist Dan Shaughnessy, who wrote a book called *The Curse of the Bambino*—blamed this move for the team's 86-year title drought, but others will claim that "The Curse" was just a media-driven storyline used to explain the team's past woes. Still, fans who watched a ground ball roll between Bill Buckner's legs in the 1986 World Series or saw Aaron Boone's winning home run in the 2003 American League Division Series swear the curse was real.

THE SPORTS GUY
For an in-depth view of the psyche of a die-hard Red Sox fan, pick up a copy of Bill Simmons's book *Now I Can Die in Peace*. Simmons, a native New Englander, writes for ESPN.com and is the editor-in-chief of Grantland.com.

VISIT THE NATION
Can't get tickets but still want to experience the excitement of a Red Sox game? Then head down to the park and hang out on Yawkey Way, which borders the stadium. On game days it's closed to cars and filled with vendors, creating a street-fair atmosphere. Duck into a nearby sports bar (there are many) and enjoy the game with other fans who couldn't secure seats. A favorite is the Cask 'n Flagon, at Brookline Avenue and Lansdowne Street, across the street from Fenway. The closet you can get to Fenway without buying a ticket is the **Bleacher Bar** (✉ *82A Lansdowne St.*), which actually has a huge window in the center field wall overlooking the field. If you want to see a game from this unique vantage point, get here early—it starts filling up a few hours before game time.

Updated by
Kim Foley
MacKinnon

There's history and culture around every bend in Boston — skyscrapers nestle next to historic hotels, while modern marketplaces line the antique cobblestone streets. But to Bostonians, living in a city that blends yesterday and today is just another day in their beloved Beantown.

It's difficult to fit Boston into a stereotype because of the city's many layers. The deepest is the historical one, the place where musket-bearing revolutionaries vowed to hang together or hang separately. The next tier, a dense spread of Brahmin fortune and fortitude, might be labeled the Hub. It was this elite caste of Boston society, descended from wealthy English Protestants who first settled the state, that funded and patronized the city's universities and cultural institutions, gaining Boston the label "the Athens of America" and felt only pride in the slogan "Banned in Boston." Over that layer lies Beantown, home to the Red Sox faithful and the raucous Bruins fans who crowded the old Boston "*Gah*-den"; this is the city whose ethnic loyalties account for its many distinct neighborhoods. Crowning these layers are the students who converge on the area's universities and colleges every fall.

PLANNING

WHEN TO GO

Summer brings reliable sunshine, sailboats to Boston Harbor, concerts to the Esplanade, and café tables to assorted sidewalks. If you're dreaming of a classic shore vacation, summer is prime.

Weather-wise, late spring and fall are the optimal times to visit Boston. Aside from mild temperatures, the former offers blooming gardens throughout the city and the latter sees the surrounding countryside ablaze with brilliantly colored foliage. At both times expect crowds.

Autumn attracts hordes of leaf peepers, and more than 250,000 students flood into the area each September, then pull out in May and June. Hotels and restaurants fill up quickly on move-in, move-out, and graduation weekends.

Winters are cold and windy.

PLANNING YOUR TIME

If you have a couple of days, hit Boston's highlights—Beacon Hill, the Freedom Trail, and the Public Garden—the first day, and then check out the Museum of Fine Arts or the Isabella Stewart Gardner Museum the morning of the second day. Reserve day two's afternoon for an excursion to Harvard or shopping on Newbury Street.

GETTING HERE AND AROUND

AIR TRAVEL

Boston's major airport, Logan International (BOS), is across the harbor from Downtown, about 2 miles outside the city center, and can be reached by taxi, water taxi, or bus/subway via MBTA's Silver or Blue line). Logan has four passenger terminals, identified by letters A, B, C, and E. A free airport shuttle runs between the terminals and airport hotels. Some airlines use different terminals for international and domestic flights; most international flights arrive at Terminal E. A visitor center in Terminal C offers tourist information. T. F. Green Airport, in Providence, Rhode Island, and the Manchester Boston Regional Airport in Manchester, New Hampshire, are both about an hour from Boston.

Airport Information Logan International Airport (Boston) ⊠ *I–90 east to Ted Williams Tunnel, Boston* ☎ *800/235–6426* ⊕ *www.massport.com/logan* Ⓜ *Airport.* **Manchester Boston Regional Airport** ⊠ *Off I–293/Rte. 101, Exit 2, Manchester, NH, Manchester, New Hampshire* ☎ *603/624–6556* ⊕ *www.flymanchester.com.* **T.F. Green Airport** ⊠ *Off I–95, Exit 13, Providence, RI, 2000 Post Rd., Warwick, Rhode Island* ☎ *888/268–7222, 401/691–2471* ⊕ *www.pvdairport.com.*

CAR TRAVEL

In a place where roads often evolved from cow paths, driving is no simple task. A surfeit of one-way streets and inconsistent signage add to the confusion. Street parking is hard to come by, as much of it is resident-permit-only. Your own car is helpful if you're taking side trips, but for exploring the city it will only be a burden. Also, Bostonians give terrible directions, since few of them actually drive.

PUBLIC TRANSIT

The "T," as the Massachusetts Bay Transportation Authority's subway system is nicknamed, is the cornerstone of an efficient, far-reaching public transit network that also includes aboveground trains, buses, and ferries. Its five color-coded lines will put you within a block of almost anywhere you want to go. Subways operate from about 5:30 am to 12:30 pm, as do buses, which crisscross the city and reach into suburbia.

A standard adult subway fare is $1.70 with a CharlieCard or $2 with a ticket or cash. For buses it's $1.25 with a CharlieCard or $1.50 with a ticket or cash (more if you are using an Inner or Outer Express bus). Commuter rail and ferry fares vary by route; yet all options charge seniors and students reduced prices, and kids under 12 ride free with a paying adult. Contact the MBTA (☎ *617/222–3200 or 800/392–6100* ⊕ *www.mbta.com*) for schedules, routes, and rates.

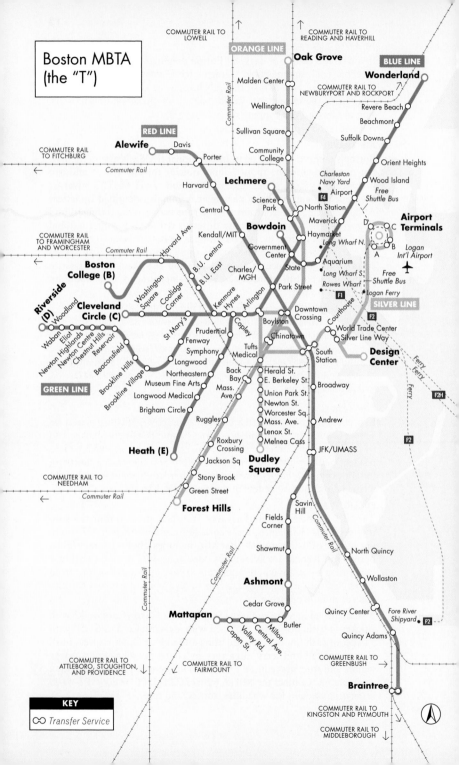

Boston MBTA (the "T")

COMMUTER RAIL TO LOWELL

COMMUTER RAIL TO READING AND HAVERHILL

ORANGE LINE

Oak Grove

BLUE LINE

Wonderland

Malden Center

COMMUTER RAIL TO NEWBURYPORT AND ROCKPORT

Revere Beach

Wellington

Beachmont

Sullivan Square

Suffolk Downs

RED LINE

Community College

Orient Heights

Alewife

Davis

Porter

Wood Island

Charlestown Navy Yard

Free Shuttle Bus

Harvard

Lechmere

Airport

Science Park

Maverick

Bowdoin

North Station

D'

Airport Terminals

Central

Haymarket

C

Kendall/MIT

Long Wharf N.

B

Government Center

Charles/MGH

State

Logan Int'l Airport

A

Boston College (B)

B.U. Central

B.U. East

Long Wharf S.

Free Shuttle Bus

Washington Square

Coolidge Corner

Kenmore

Arlington

Park Street

Rowes Wharf

Logan Ferry

Riverside (D)

Cleveland Circle (C)

Hynes

Aquarium

Woodland

St Mary's

Copley

Boylston

Downtown Crossing

Courthouse

SILVER LINE

Waban
Eliot
Newton Highlands
Newton Centre
Chestnut Hills

Reservoir

Chinatown

World Trade Center

Silver Line Way

Beaconsfield

Prudential

Fenway

Symphony

Longwood

Tufts Medical

South Station

Design Center

Brookline Hills

Brookline Village

Northeastern

Museum Fine Arts

Herald St.
E. Berkeley St.
Union Park St.
Newton St.
Worcester Sq.
Mass. Ave.
Lenox St.
Melnea Cass

Broadway

GREEN LINE

Longwood Medical

Back Bay

Mass. Ave.

Brigham Circle

Andrew

Ruggles

Heath (E)

Roxbury Crossing

JFK/UMASS

COMMUTER RAIL TO NEEDHAM

Jackson Sq

Dudley Square

Stony Brook

Green Street

Savin Hill

Forest Hills

Fields Corner

Shawmut

North Quincy

Wollaston

Ashmont

Cedar Grove

COMMUTER RAIL TO ATTLEBORO, STOUGHTON, AND PROVIDENCE

COMMUTER RAIL TO FAIRMOUNT

Mattapan

Milton

Butler

Quincy Center

Fore River Shipyard

Capen St.
Valley Rd.
Central Ave.

Quincy Adams

COMMUTER RAIL TO GREENBUSH

Braintree

COMMUTER RAIL TO KINGSTON AND PLYMOUTH

COMMUTER RAIL TO MIDDLEBOROUGH

KEY

∞ *Transfer Service*

TAXI TRAVEL

Cabs are available 24/7. Rides within the city cost $2.60 for the first 1/7 mile and 40¢ for each 1/7 mile thereafter (tolls, where applicable, are extra).

VISITOR INFORMATION

Contact the city and state tourism offices for details about seasonal events, discount passes, trip planning, and attraction information. The National Park Service has a Boston office for Boston's historic sites that provides maps and directions. The Welcome Center and Boston Common Visitor Information Center offer general information. The Cambridge Tourism Office's information booth is in Harvard Square, near the main entrance to the Harvard T stop.

Contacts Boston Common Visitor Information Center ⊠ *148 Tremont St., where Freedom Trail begins, Downtown, Boston* ☎ *888/733–2678* ⊕ *www.thefreedomtrail.org/visitor/boston-common.html.* **National Parks Service Visitor Center** ⊠ *Faneuil Hall, Downtown, Boston* ☎ *617/242–5642* ⊕ *www.nps.gov/bost.* **Cambridge Tourism Office** ⊠ *4 Brattle St., Harvard Sq., Cambridge* ☎ *800/862–5678, 617/441–2884* ⊕ *www.cambridge-usa.org.* **Greater Boston Convention and Visitors Bureau** ⊠ *2 Copley Pl., Suite 105, Back Bay, Boston* ☎ *888/733–2678, 617/536–4100* ⊕ *www.bostonusa.com.* **Massachusetts Office of Travel and Tourism** ⊠ *State Transportation Bldg., 10 Park Plaza, Suite 4510, Back Bay, Boston* ☎ *800/227–6277, 617/973–8500* ⊕ *www.massvacation.com.*

ONLINE RESOURCES

Boston.com, home of the *Boston Globe* online, has news and feature articles, ample travel information, and links to towns throughout Massachusetts. The site for Boston's arts and entertainment weekly, the *Boston Phoenix* (⊕ *www.bostonphoenix.com*) has nightlife, movie, restaurant, and arts listings. The Bostonian Society (⊕ *bostonhistory.org*) answers some frequently asked questions about Beantown history on their website. The iBoston (⊕ *www.iboston.org*) page has wonderful photographs of architecturally and historically important buildings. *The Improper Bostonian* (⊕ *www.improper.com*) and *WickedLocal* (⊕ *www.wickedlocal.com*) provide a more relaxed (and irreverent) take on Boston news and information.

Boston.com ⊕ *www.boston.com.* **Bostonian Society** ⊕ *bostonhistory.org.* **iBoston** ⊕ *www.iboston.org.* **The Improper Bostonian** ⊕ *www.improper.com.* **Wicked Local** ⊕ *www.wickedlocal.com.*

Safety Transportation Security Administration (*TSA*). ⊕ *www.tsa.gov.*

EXPLORING BOSTON

BEACON HILL AND BOSTON COMMON

Past and present home of the old-money elite, contender for the "Most Beautiful" award among the city's neighborhoods, and hallowed address for many literary lights, Beacon Hill is Boston at its most Bostonian. The redbrick elegance of its narrow streets sends you back to the 19th century just as surely as if you had stumbled into a time machine. But Beacon Hill residents would never make the social faux pas of being out of date. The neighborhood is home to hip boutiques and trendy restaurants frequented by young, affluent professionals rather than DAR (Daughters of the American Revolution) matrons.

FAMILY

Fodor's Choice

★

Boston Common. Nothing is more central to Boston than the Common, the oldest public park in the United States and undoubtedly the largest and most famous of the town commons around which New England settlements were traditionally arranged. Dating from 1634, Boston Common started as 50 acres where the freemen of Boston could graze their cattle. (Cows were banned in 1830.) Latin names are affixed to many of the Common's trees; it was once expected that proper Boston schoolchildren be able to translate them.

On Tremont Street near Boylston stands the 1888 **Boston Massacre Memorial**; the sculpted hand of one of the victims has a distinct shine from years of sightseers' caresses. The Common's highest ground, near the park's Parkman Bandstand, was once called Flagstaff Hill. It's now surmounted by the **Soldiers and Sailors Monument,** honoring Civil War troops. The Common's only body of water is the **Frog Pond,** a tame and frog-free concrete depression used as a children's wading pool during steamy summer days and for ice-skating in winter. It marks the original site of a natural pond that inspired Edgar Allan Poe to call Bostonians "Frogpondians." In 1848 a gushing fountain of piped-in water was created to inaugurate Boston's municipal water system.

On the Beacon Street side of the Common sits the splendidly restored **Robert Gould Shaw 54th Regiment Memorial,** executed in deep-relief bronze by Augustus Saint-Gaudens in 1897. It commemorates the 54th Massachusetts Regiment, the first Civil War unit made up of free black people, led by the young Brahmin Robert Gould Shaw. He and half of his troops died in an assault on South Carolina's Fort Wagner; their story inspired the 1989 movie *Glory.* The monument—first intended to depict only Shaw until his abolitionist family demanded it honor his regiment as well—figures in works by the poets John Berryman and Robert Lowell, both of whom lived on the north slope of Beacon Hill in the 1940s. This magnificent memorial makes a fitting first stop on the Black Heritage Trail. ✉ *Bounded by Beacon, Charles, Tremont, and Park Sts., Beacon Hill* Ⓜ *Park St., Boylston.*

Central Burying Ground. The Central Burying Ground may seem an odd feature for a public park, but remember that in 1756, when the land was set aside, this was a lonely corner of the Common. It's the final resting place of Tories and Patriots alike, as well as many British

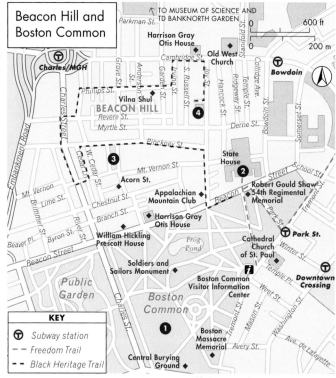

Beacon Hill and Boston Common

TO MUSEUM OF SCIENCE AND
TO BANKNORTH GARDEN

KEY

  Subway station

– – Freedom Trail

– – Black Heritage Trail

casualties of the Battle of Bunker Hill. The most famous person buried here is Gilbert Stuart, the portraitist best known for his likenesses of George and Martha Washington; he died a poor man in 1828. The Burying Ground is open daily 9–5. ✉ *Boylston St. near Tremont, Beacon Hill* ⊕ *www.cityofboston.gov/parks/hbgi/CentralBuryingCentral. asp* Ⓜ *Park St., Boylston.*

Louisburg Square. One of Beacon Hill's most charming corners, Louisburg Square (proper Bostonians always pronounce the "s") was an 1840s model for a townhouse development that was never built on the Hill because of space restrictions. Today, the grassy square, enclosed by a wrought-iron fence, belongs collectively to the owners of the houses facing it. The statue at the north end of the green is of Columbus, the one at the south end of Aristides the Just; both were donated in 1850 by a Greek merchant who lived on the square. The houses, most of which are now divided into apartments and condominiums, have seen their share of famous tenants, including author and critic William Dean Howells at Nos. 4 and 16, and the Alcotts at No. 10 (Louisa May not only lived but also died here, on the day of her father's funeral). In 1852 the singer Jenny Lind was married in the parlor of No. 20. Louisburg Square is also the current home of U.S. Secretary of State John Kerry.

DID YOU KNOW?

For a taste of Boston's watery side, take a walk on the 47-mile HarborWalk between major attractions (like the New England Aquarium), picturesque piers, working wharves, and even urban beaches.

There's a legend that Louisburg Square was the location of the Rev. William Blaxton's spring, although there's no water there today. Blaxton, or Blackstone, was one of the first Bostonians, having come to the Shawmut Peninsula in the mid-1620s. When the Puritans, who had settled in Charlestown, found their water supply inadequate, Blaxton invited them to move across the river, where he assured them they would find an "excellent spring." Just a few years later, he sold them all but 6 acres of the peninsula he had bought from the Native Americans and decamped to Rhode Island, seeking greater seclusion; a plaque at 50 Beacon Street commemorates him. ⊠ *Between Mt. Vernon and Pickney Sts., Beacon Hill* Ⓜ *Park St.*

FAMILY

Fodor's Choice

★

Museum of African American History. Ever since runaway slave Crispus Attucks became one of the famous victims of the Boston Massacre of 1770, the African American community of Boston has played an important part in the city's history. Throughout the 19th century, abolition was the cause célèbre for Boston's intellectual elite, and during that time, blacks came to thrive in neighborhoods throughout the city. The Museum of African American History was established in 1964 to promote this history. The umbrella organization includes a trio of historic sites: the Abiel Smith School, the first public school in the nation built specifically for black children; the African Meeting House, where in 1832 the New England Anti-Slavery Society was formed under the leadership of William Lloyd Garrison; and the African Meeting House on the island of Nantucket, off the coast of Cape Cod. Park Service personnel continue to lead tours of the **Black Heritage Trail,** starting from the Shaw Memorial. The museum is the site of activities, including lectures, children's storytelling, and concerts focusing on black composers. ⊠ *46 Joy St., Beacon Hill* ☎ *617/725–0022* ⊕ *www.afroammuseum.org* ✉ *$5* ☻ *Mon.–Sat. 10–4* Ⓜ *Park St.*

State House. On July 4, 1795, the surviving fathers of the Revolution were on hand to enshrine the ideals of their new Commonwealth in a graceful seat of government designed by Charles Bulfinch. Governor Samuel Adams and Paul Revere laid the cornerstone; Revere would later roll the copper sheathing for the dome.

Bulfinch's neoclassical design is poised between Georgian and Federal; its finest features are the delicate Corinthian columns of the portico, the graceful pediment and window arches, and the vast yet visually weightless golden dome (gilded in 1874 and again in 1997). During World War II the dome was painted gray so that it would not reflect moonlight during blackouts and thereby offer a target to anticipated Axis bombers. It's capped with a pinecone, a symbol of the importance of pinewood, which was integral to the construction of Boston's early houses and churches; it also serves as a reminder of the state's early connection to Maine, once part of Massachusetts.

Inside the building are Doric Hall, with its statuary and portraits; the Hall of Flags, where an exhibit shows the battle flags from all the wars in which Massachusetts regiments have participated; the Great Hall, an open space used for state functions that houses 351 flags from the cities and towns of Massachusetts; the governor's office; and the chambers of the House and Senate. The Great Hall contains a giant, modernistic clock designed by New York artist R. M. Fischer. Its installation in 1986 at a cost of $100,000 was roundly slammed as a symbol of legislative extravagance. There's also a wealth of statuary, including figures of Horace Mann, Daniel Webster, and a youthful-looking President John F. Kennedy in full stride. Just outside Doric Hall is *Hear Us*, a series of six bronze busts honoring the contributions of women to public life in Massachusetts. But perhaps the best-known piece of artwork in the building is the carved wooden *Sacred Cod*, mounted in the Old State House in 1784 as a symbol of the commonwealth's maritime wealth. It was moved, with much fanfare, to Bulfinch's structure in 1798. By 1895, when it was hung in the new House chambers, the representatives had begun to consider the Cod their unofficial mascot—so much so that when *Harvard Lampoon* wags "codnapped" it in 1933, the House refused to meet in session until the fish was returned, three days later. You can take a guided tour or do a self-guided tour. ⊠ *Beacon St. between Hancock and Bowdoin Sts., Beacon Hill* ☎ 617/727–3676 ⊕ *www.sec.state.ma.us/trs/ trsidx.htm* ⊠ *Free* ⊗ *Weekdays 8:45–5. 30-minute guided tours 10–3:30. Advance reservations requested.* Ⓜ *Park St.*

> ### DID YOU KNOW?
>
> Beacon Hill's north slope played a key part in African American history. A community of free blacks lived here in the 1800s; many worshipped at the African Meeting House, established in 1805 and still standing. It came to be known as the "Black Faneuil Hall" for the fervent antislavery activism that started within its walls.

THE OLD WEST END

A few decades ago this district—separated from Beacon Hill by Cambridge Street—resembled a typical medieval city: thoroughfares that twisted and turned, maddening one-way lanes, and streets that were a veritable hive of people. Today little remains of the *old* Old West End except for a few brick tenements and a handful of monuments, including the first house built for Harrison Gray Otis. The biggest surviving structures with any real history are two public institutions, Massachusetts General Hospital and the former Suffolk County Jail, which dates from 1849. The onetime prison is now part of the luxurious, and wryly named, Liberty Hotel. Here you'll also find TD Banknorth Garden, the home away from home for loyal Bruins and Celtics fans. In addition, the innovative Museum of Science is one of the neighborhood's more modern attractions. The newest addition to the skyline here is the Leonard P. Zakim Bunker Hill Bridge, which spans the Charles River just across from the TD Banknorth Garden.

FAMILY

Fodor's Choice

★

Museum of Science. With 15-foot lightning bolts in the Theater of Electricity and a 20-foot-long Tyrannosaurus rex model, this is just the place to ignite any child's scientific curiosity. Located just north of Massachusetts General Hospital, the museum sits astride the Charles River Dam. More than 550 exhibits cover astronomy, astrophysics, anthropology, medical progress, computers, the organic and inorganic earth sciences, and much more. The emphasis is on hands-on education.

Continued on page 89

FOLLOW THE REDBRICK ROAD

BOSTON'S FREEDOM TRAIL

by Mike Nalepa

Paul Revere

Benjamin Franklin

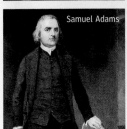

Samuel Adams

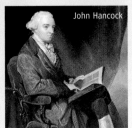

John Hancock

Paul Revere's ride

3

IN FOCUS FOLLOW THE REDBRICK ROAD: BOSTON'S FREEDOM TRAIL

The Freedom Trail is more than a collection of historic sites related to the American Revolution or a suggested itinerary connecting Boston's unique neighborhoods. It's a chance to walk in the footsteps of our forefathers—literally, by following a crimson path on public sidewalks—and pay tribute to the figures all school kids know, like Paul Revere, John Hancock, and Ben Franklin. In history-proud Boston, past and present intersect before your eyes not as a re-creation but as living history accessible to all.

Boston played a key role in the dramatic events leading up to the American Revolution. Many of the founding fathers called the city home, and many of the initial meetings and actions that sparked the fight against the British took place here. In one day, you can visit Faneuil Hall—the "Cradle of Liberty"—where outraged colonial radicals met to oppose British authority; the site of the incendiary Boston Massacre; and the Old North Church, where lanterns hung to signal Paul Revere on his thrilling midnight ride. Colonists may have originally landed in Jamestown and Plymouth, but if you really want to see where America began, come to Boston.

Boston Common, Founder's Statue

🌐 www.nps.gov/bost
🌐 www.thefreedomtrail.org

☎ 617/242–5642

💳 Admission to the Freedom Trail itself is free. Several museum sites charge for admission. However, most attractions are free monuments, parks, and landmarks.

The 1729 Old South Meeting House, where many protesters gathered during the American Revolution.

PLANNING YOUR TRAIL TRIP

THE ROUTE

The 2½-mi Freedom Trail begins at Boston Common, winds through Downtown, Government Center, and the North End, and ends in Charlestown at the USS *Constitution*. The entire Freedom Trail is marked by a red line on the sidewalk; it's made of paint or brick at various points on the Trail. ⇨ *For more information on Freedom Trail sites, see listings in Neighborhood chapters.*

GETTING HERE AND BACK

The route starts near the Park Street T stop. When you've completed the Freedom Trail, head for the nearby Charlestown water shuttle, which goes directly to the downtown area. For schedules and maps, visit ⊕ *www.mbta.com.*

TIMING

If you're stopping at a few (or all) of the 16 sites, it takes a full day to complete the route comfortably. ■TIP➔ If you have children in tow, you may want to split the trail into two or more days.

VISITOR CENTERS

There are Freedom Trail information centers in Boston Common (Tremont Street), at 15 State Street (near the Old State House), and at the Charlestown Navy Yard Visitor Center (in Building 5).

TOURS

The National Park Service's free 90-minute Freedom Trail walking tours begin at the Boston National Historical Park Visitor Center at 15 State Street and cover sites from the Old South Meeting House to the Old North Church. Check online for times; it's a good idea to show up at least 30 minutes early, as the popular tours are limited to 30 people.

Half-hour tours of the USS *Constitution* are offered Tuesday through Sunday. Note that visitors to the ship must go through security screening.

FUEL UP

The trail winds through the heart of Downtown Boston, so finding a quick bite or a nice sit-down meal isn't difficult. Quincy Market, near Faneuil Hall, is packed with cafés and eateries. Another good lunch choice is one of the North End's wonderful Italian restaurants.

WHAT'S NEARBY

For a short break from revolutionary history, be sure to check out the major attractions nearby, including the Boston Public Garden, New England Aquarium, and Union Oyster House.

Above: In front of the Old State House a cobblestone circle marks the site of the Boston Massacre.

TOP SIGHTS

Benjamin Franklin Statue

Boston Common

The Granary Burial Grounds

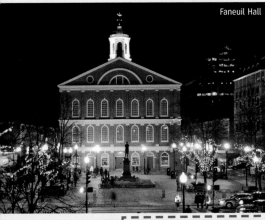
Faneuil Hall

Park Street Church

Old North Church

Bunker Hill Monument

BOSTON COMMON TO FANEUIL HALL

Old State House

GOVERNMENT CENTER

Cambridge St.

0 — 100 yards
0 — 100 meters

Hancock St.
Joy St.
Bowdoin St.
Somerset St.
Court St.
Clinton

Faneuil Hall · **Boston National Historic Park Visitor Center**

Chatham St.

BEACON HILL

State House

Mt. Vernon St.

King's Chapel and Burying Ground

School St.

Old State House

Boston Massacre Site

State St.

India St.
Kilby St.
Milk St.
Broad St.

Walnut St.

Granary Burying Ground

Old Corner Bookstore

Beacon St.

Park St.

Ben Franklin Statue

Congress St.
Devonshire St.
Federal St.
Arch St.
Franklin St.

Boston Common

Park Street Church

PARK ST.

Old South Meeting House

Washington St.

Start: near the Park Street T stop.

Freedom Trail Foundation Center Information

KEY

--- *Freedom Trail*

Many of the Freedom Trail sites between Boston Common and the North End are close together. Walking this 1-mile segment of the trail makes for a pleasant morning.

THE ROUTE

Begin at ★ **Boston Common,** then head for the **State House,** Boston's finest example of Federal architecture. Several blocks away is the **Park Street Church,** whose 217-foot steeple is considered to be the most beautiful in New England. The church was actually founded in 1809, and it played a key role in the movement to abolish slavery.

Reposing in the church's shadows is the ★ **Granary Burying Ground,** final resting place of Samuel Adams, John Hancock, and Paul Revere. A short stroll to Downtown brings you to **King's Chapel,** founded in 1686 by King James II for the Church of England.

Follow the trail past the **Benjamin Franklin statue** to the **Old Corner Bookstore** site, where Hawthorne, Emerson, and Longfellow were published. Nearby is the **Old South Meeting House,** where arguments in 1773 led to the Boston Tea Party. Overlooking the site of the Boston Massacre is the city's oldest public building, the **Old State House,** a Georgian beauty.

In 1770 the Boston Massacre occurred directly in front of here—look for the commemorative stone circle.

Cross the plaza to ★ **Faneuil Hall** and explore where Samuel Adams railed against "taxation without representation." ■TIP→ A good mid-trail break is the shops and eateries of Faneuil Hall Marketplace, which includes Quincy Market.

Old Corner Book Store Site

★ = **Fodor's**Choice ★ = Highly Recommended ☺ = Family Friendly

NORTH END TO CHARLESTOWN

USS Constitution

Freedom Trail sites be-
tween Faneuil Hall and
Charlestown are more
spread out along
1½ miles. The sites here,
though more difficult to
reach, are certainly worth
the walk.

THE ROUTE

When you depart Faneuil Hall,
follow the red stripe to the
North End, Boston's Little Italy.

The ⌁ **Paul Revere House**
takes you back 200 years—
here are the hero's own
saddlebags, a toddy warmer,
and a pine cradle made from
a molasses cask. It's also
air-conditioned in the summer, so try to stop here in
mid-afternoon to escape the
heat. Next to the Paul Revere
House is one of the city's
oldest brick buildings, the
Pierce-Hichborn House.

Next, peek inside a place
guaranteed to trigger a wave
of patriotism: the ★ **Old
North Church** of "One if by
land, two if by sea" fame.
Then head toward **Copp's**

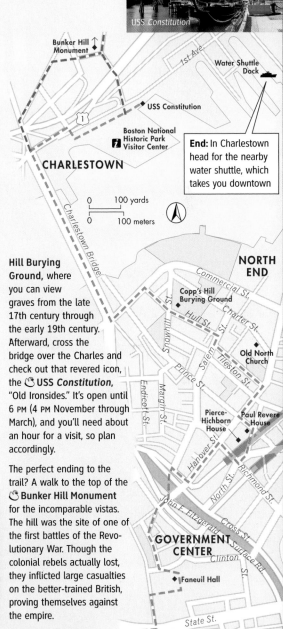

Paul Revere House

**Hill Burying
Ground,** where
you can view
graves from the late
17th century through
the early 19th century.
Afterward, cross the
bridge over the Charles and
check out that revered icon,
the ⌁ **USS Constitution,**
"Old Ironsides." It's open until
6 PM (4 PM November through
March), and you'll need about
an hour for a visit, so plan
accordingly.

The perfect ending to the
trail? A walk to the top of the
⌁ **Bunker Hill Monument**
for the incomparable vistas.
The hill was the site of one of
the first battles of the Revolutionary War. Though the
colonial rebels actually lost,
they inflicted large casualties
on the better-trained British,
proving themselves against
the empire.

End: In Charlestown
head for the nearby
water shuttle, which
takes you downtown

DID YOU KNOW?

If the Freedom Trail leaves you eager to see more Revolutionary War sites, drive about 30 minutes to Lexington and Concord, where the "shot heard 'round the world" launched the first battles in 1775.

The Charles Hayden Planetarium, with its sophisticated multimedia system based on a Zeiss planetarium projector, produces exciting programs on astronomical discoveries. Laser light shows, with laser graphics and computer animation, are scheduled Thursday through Sunday evenings. The museum also includes the Mugar Omni Theater, a five-story dome screen. The theater's state-of-the-art sound system provides extra-sharp acoustics, and the huge projection allows the audience to practically experience the action on-screen. Try to get tickets in advance online or by phone; call or check the museum's website for showtimes: www.mos.org. ✉ *Science Park at Charles River Dam, Old West End* ☎ *617/723–2500* ⊕ *www.mos.org* ✉ *$23* ☉ *July 5–Labor Day, Sat.–Thurs. 9–7, Fri. 9–9; after Labor Day–July 4, Sat.–Thurs. 9–5, Fri. 9–9* Ⓜ *Science Park.*

FAMILY **TD Garden.** Diehards still moan about the loss of the old Boston Garden, a much more intimate venue than this mammoth facility, which opened in 1995. Regardless, the home of the Celtics (basketball) and Bruins (hockey) is still known as the good old "Gah-den," and its air-conditioning, comfier seats, improved food selection, 1,200-vehicle parking garage, and nearly double number of bathrooms, has won grudging acceptance. The Garden also serves as a concert venue, featuring big-name acts like Justin Timberlake and Nine Inch Nails. On occasion there are public-skating events in winter; call ahead for information. ✉ *100 Legends Way, Old West End* ☎ *617/624–1050* ⊕ *www.tdbanknorthgarden.com* Ⓜ *North Station.*

Sports Museum of New England. The fifth and sixth levels of the TD Garden house the Sports Museum of New England, where displays of memorabilia and photographs showcase local sports history and legends. Take a tour of the locker and interview rooms (off-season only), test your sports knowledge with interactive games, and see how you stand up to life-size statues of heroes Carl Yastrzemski and Larry Bird. The museum is generally open daily 10–4, but call ahead to confirm. Admission is $10. ✉ *Use west premium seating entrance* ☎ *617/624–1234* ⊕ *www.sportsmuseum.org* ✉ *$10.*

GOVERNMENT CENTER

This is a section of town Bostonians love to hate. Not only does Government Center house what they can't fight—City Hall—but it also contains some of the bleakest architecture since the advent of poured concrete. But though the stark, treeless plain surrounding City Hall has been roundly jeered, the expanse is enlivened by feisty political rallies, free summer concerts, and the occasional festival.

Faneuil Hall. The single building facing Congress Street is the real Faneuil Hall, though locals often give that name to all five buildings in this shopping complex. Bostonians pronounce it *Fan-*yoo'uhl or *Fan-*yuhl. Like other Boston landmarks, Faneuil Hall has evolved over many years. It was erected in 1742, the gift of wealthy merchant Peter Faneuil, who wanted the hall to serve as both a place for town meetings and a public market. It burned in 1761 and was immediately reconstructed according to the original plan of its designer, the Scottish portrait painter

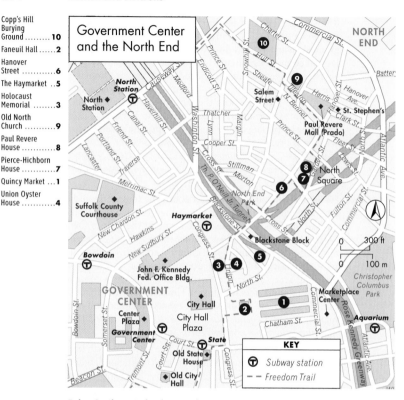

John Smibert (who lies in the Granary Burying Ground). In 1763 the political leader James Otis helped inaugurate the era that culminated in American independence when he dedicated the rebuilt hall to the cause of liberty.

In 1772 Samuel Adams stood here and first suggested that Massachusetts and the other colonies organize a Committee of Correspondence to maintain semiclandestine lines of communication in the face of hardening British repression. In later years the hall again lived up to Otis's dedication when the abolitionists Wendell Phillips and Charles Sumner pleaded for support from its podium. The tradition continues to this day: in presidential-election years the hall is the site of debates between contenders in the Massachusetts primary.

Faneuil Hall was substantially enlarged and remodeled in 1805 according to a Greek Revival design of the noted architect Charles Bulfinch; this is the building you see today. Its purposes remain the same: the balconied Great Hall is available to citizens' groups on presentation of a request signed by a required number of responsible parties; it also plays host to regular concerts.

Inside Faneuil Hall are dozens of paintings of famous Americans, including the mural *Webster's Reply to Hayne* and Gilbert Stuart's portrait of Washington at Dorchester Heights. Park rangers give informational talks about the history and importance of Faneuil Hall every half hour. There are interactive displays about Boston sights and National Park Service rangers at the Visitor Center on the first floor can provide maps and other information.

Faneuil Hall has always sat in the middle of Boston's main marketplace. When such men as Andrew Jackson and Daniel Webster debated the future of the Republic here, the fragrances of bacon and snuff—sold by merchants in **Quincy Market** across the road—greeted their noses. Today the aroma of coffee wafts through the hall from a snack bar. The shops at ground level sell New England bric-a-brac. ⊠ *Faneuil Hall Sq., Government Center* ☎ *617/523–1300* ⊕ *www.cityofboston.gov/ freedomtrail/faneuilhall.asp* ⊡ *Free* ⊙ *Great Hall daily 9–5; informational talks every ½ hr. Shops Mon.–Sat. 10 am–9 pm, Sun. 11 am–6 pm. Visitor center daily 9–5* Ⓜ *Government Center, Aquarium, State.*

Ancient & Honorable Artillery Company of Massachusetts. On the building's top floors are the headquarters and museum of the Ancient & Honorable Artillery Company of Massachusetts. Founded in 1638, it's the oldest militia in the Western Hemisphere, and the third oldest in the world, after the Swiss Guard and the Honorable Artillery Company of London. Its status is now strictly ceremonial, but it's justly proud of the arms, uniforms, and other artifacts on display. Admission is free. The museum is open weekdays 9 to 3. ☎ *617/227–1638* ⊕ *www.ahac.us.com.*

The Haymarket. Loud, self-promoting vendors pack this exuberant maze of a marketplace at Marshall and Blackstone streets on Friday and Saturday from dawn to dusk (most vendors are usually gone by 5). Pushcart vendors hawk fruits and vegetables against a backdrop of fish, meat, and cheese shops. The accumulation of debris left every evening has been celebrated in a whimsical 1976 public-arts project—Mags Harries's *Asaroton*, a Greek word meaning "unswept floors"—consisting of bronze fruit peels and other detritus smashed into pavement. Another Harries piece, a bronze depiction of a gathering of stray gloves, tumbles down between the escalators in the Porter Square T station in Cambridge. At Creek Square, near the Haymarket, is the **Boston Stone.** Set into a brick wall, this was allegedly a marker used as milepost zero in measuring distances from Boston. ⊠ *Marshall and Blackstone Sts., Government Center* ⊙ *Fri. and Sat. 7 am–mid-afternoon* Ⓜ *Government Center.*

Fodor'sChoice
★
Holocaust Memorial. At night its six 50-foot-high glass-and-steel towers glow like ghosts. During the day the monument seems at odds with the 18th-century streetscape of Blackstone Square behind it. Shoehorned into the north end of Union Park, the Holocaust Memorial is the work of Stanley Saitowitz, whose design was selected through an international competition; the finished memorial was dedicated in 1995. Recollections by Holocaust survivors are set into the glass-and-granite walls; the upper levels of the towers are etched with 6 million numbers in random sequence, symbolizing the Jewish victims of the Nazi horror. Manufactured steam from grates in the granite base makes for a particularly haunting scene after dark. ⊠ *Union St. near Hanover St., Government Center* ☎ *617/457–8755* ⊕ *www.nehm.org.*

Quincy Market. Not everyone likes Quincy Market, also known as Faneuil Hall Marketplace; some people prefer grit to polish, and disdain the shiny cafés and boutiques. But there's no denying that this pioneer effort at urban recycling set the tone for many similar projects throughout the country, and that it has brought tremendous vitality to a once-tired corner of Boston. Quincy Market continues to attract huge crowds of tourists and locals throughout the year. In the early '70s, demolition was a distinct possibility for the decrepit buildings. Fortunately, with the participation of the Boston Redevelopment Authority, architect Benjamin Thompson planned a renovation of Quincy Market, and the Rouse Corporation of Baltimore undertook its restoration, which was completed in 1976. Try to look beyond the shop windows to the grand design of the market buildings themselves; they represent a vision of the market as urban centerpiece, an idea whose time has certainly come again.

> **THE STORY BEHIND THE GRASSHOPPER**
>
> Why is the gold-plated weather vane atop Faneuil Hall's cupola in the shape of a grasshopper? One apocryphal story has it that Sir Thomas Gresham—founder of London's Royal Exchange—was discovered in a field in 1519 as a babe by children chasing grasshoppers. He later placed a gilded metal version of the insect over the Exchange to commemorate his salvation. Years later Peter Faneuil admired the critter (a symbol of good luck) and had a model of it mounted over Faneuil Hall. The 8-pound, 52-inch-long grasshopper is the only unmodified part of the original structure.

The market consists of three block-long annexes: **Quincy Market, North Market,** and **South Market,** each 535 feet long and across a plaza from Faneuil Hall. The structures were designed in 1826 by Alexander Parris as part of a public-works project instituted by Boston's second mayor, Josiah Quincy, to alleviate the cramped conditions of Faneuil Hall and clean up the refuse that collected in Town Dock, the pond behind it. The central structure, made of granite, with a Doric colonnade at either end and topped by a classical dome and rotunda, has kept its traditional market-stall layout, but the stalls now purvey international and specialty foods: sushi, frozen yogurt, bagels, calzones, sausage-on-a-stick, Chinese noodles, barbecue, and baklava, plus all the boutique chocolate-chip cookies your heart desires. This is perhaps Boston's best locale for grazing.

Along the arcades on either side of the Central Market are vendors selling sweatshirts, photographs of Boston, and arts and crafts—some schlocky, some not—alongside a couple of patioed bars and restaurants. The North and South markets house a mixture of chain stores and specialty boutiques. Quintessential Boston remains here only in Durgin Park, opened in 1826 and known for its plain interior, brassy waitresses, and large portions of traditional New England fare.

A greenhouse flower market on the north side of Faneuil Hall provides a splash of color; during the winter holidays, trees along the cobblestone walks are strung with thousands of sparkling lights. In summer up to 50,000 people a day descend on the market; the outdoor cafés are an excellent spot to watch the hordes if you can find a seat. Year-round the pedestrian walkways draw street performers, and rings of strollers form around magicians and musicians. ⊠ *Bordered by Clinton, Commercial, and Chatham Sts., Government Center* ☎ *617/523–1300* ⊕ *www.faneuilhallmarketplace.com* ⊙ *Mon.–Sat. 10–9, Sun. 11–6. Restaurants and bars generally open daily 11 am–2 am; food stalls open earlier* Ⓜ *Government Center, Aquarium, State.*

Union Oyster House. Billed as the oldest restaurant in continuous service in the United States, the Union Oyster House first opened its doors as the Atwood & Bacon Oyster House in 1826. Charles Forster of Maine was the first American to use the curious invention of the toothpick on these premises. And John F. Kennedy was also among its patrons; his favorite booth has been dedicated to his memory. The charming facade is constructed of Flemish bond brick and adorned with Victorian-style signage. With its scallop, clam, and lobster dishes—as well as the de rigueur oyster—the menu hasn't changed much since the restaurant's early days (though the prices have). ⊠ *41 Union St., Government Center* ☎ *617/227–2750* ⊕ *www.unionoysterhouse.com* ⊙ *Sun.–Thurs. 11–9:30, Fri. and Sat. 11–10; bar open until midnight* Ⓜ *Haymarket.*

THE NORTH END

The warren of small streets on the northeast side of Government Center is the North End, Boston's Little Italy. In the 17th century the North End *was* Boston, as much of the rest of the peninsula was still under water or had yet to be cleared. Here the town grew rich for a century and a half before the birth of American independence. The quarter's dwindling ethnic character lingers along Salem or Hanover Street, where you can still hear people speaking with Abruzzese accents.

Copp's Hill Burying Ground. An ancient and melancholy air hovers like a fine mist over this Colonial-era burial ground. The North End graveyard incorporates four cemeteries established between 1660 and 1819. Near the Charter Street gate is the tomb of the Mather family, the dynasty of church divines (Cotton and Increase were the most famous sons) who held sway in Boston during the heyday of the old theocracy. Also buried here is Robert Newman, who crept into the steeple of the Old North Church to hang the lanterns warning of the British attack the night of Paul Revere's ride. Look for the tombstone of Captain Daniel Malcolm; it's pockmarked with musket-ball fire from British soldiers, who used the stones for target practice. Across the street at 44 Hull is the **narrowest house in Boston**—it's a mere 10 feet across. ⊠ *Intersection of Hull and Snowhill Sts., North End* ⊕ *www.cityofboston.gov/freedomtrail/coppshill.asp* ⊙ *Daily 9–5* Ⓜ *North Station.*

Hanover Street. This is the North End's main thoroughfare, along with the smaller and narrower Salem Street. It was named for the ruling dynasty of 18th- and 19th-century England; the label was retained after the Revolution, despite a flurry of patriotic renaming (King Street became State Street, for example). Hanover's business center is thick with restaurants, pastry shops, and Italian cafés; on weekends Italian immigrants who have moved to the suburbs return to share an espresso with old friends and maybe catch a soccer game broadcast via satellite. Hanover is one of Boston's oldest public roads, once the site of the residences of the Rev. Cotton Mather and the colonial-era patriot Dr. Joseph Warren, as well as a small dry-goods store run by Eben D. Jordan—who went on to launch the Jordan Marsh department stores. ⊠ *North End.*

Fodor's Choice　**Old North Church.** At one end of the **Paul Revere Mall** is a church famous
★　　not only for being the oldest standing church building in Boston (built in 1723) but for housing the two lanterns that glimmered from its steeple on the night of April 18, 1775. This is Christ, or Old North, Church, where Paul Revere and the young sexton Robert Newman managed that night to signal the departure by water of the British regulars to Lexington and Concord.

Although William Price designed the structure after studying Christopher Wren's London churches, Old North—which still has an active Episcopal congregation (including descendants of the Reveres)—is an impressive building in its own right. Inside, note the gallery and the graceful arrangement of pews; the bust of George Washington, pronounced by the Marquis de Lafayette to be the truest likeness of the general he ever saw; the brass chandeliers, made in Amsterdam in 1700 and installed here in 1724; and the clock, the oldest still running in an American public building. The pews—No. 54 belonged to the Revere family—have the tallest walls in the United States because of the little charcoal-burning foot warmers. Try to visit when changes are rung on the bells, after the 11 am Sunday service; they bear the inscription, "We are the first ring of bells cast for the British Empire in North America." On the Sunday closest to April 18, descendants of the patriots reenact the raising of the lanterns in the church belfry during a special evening service. Visitors are welcome to drop in, but to see the bell-ringing chamber and the crypts, take the 30-minute behind-the-scenes tour offered Monday–Saturday.

Behind the church is the **Washington Memorial Garden,** where volunteers cultivate a plot devoted to plants and flowers favored in the 18th century. The garden is studded with several unusual commemorative plaques, including one for the Rev. George Burrough, who was hanged in the Salem witch trials in 1692; Robert Newman was his great-grandson. In another niche hangs the "Third Lantern," dedicated in 1976 to mark the country's bicentennial celebration. ⊠ *193 Salem St., North End* ☎ *617/523–6676* ⊕ *www.oldnorth.com* ☉ *Jan. and Feb., Tues.–Sun. 10–4; Mar.–May, daily 9–5; June–Oct., daily 9–6; Nov. and Dec., daily 10–5. Sun. services at 9 and 11 am* Ⓜ *Haymarket, North Station.*

FAMILY　**Paul Revere House.** Originally on the site was the parsonage of the Second Church of Boston, home to the Rev. Increase Mather, the Second Church's minister. Mather's house burned in the great fire of 1676, and the house that Revere was to occupy was built on its location about four years later, nearly a hundred years before Revere's 1775 midnight ride through Middlesex County. Revere owned it from 1770 until 1800, although he lived there for only 10 years and rented it out for the next two decades. Pre-1900 photographs show it as a shabby warren of storefronts and apartments. The clapboard sheathing is a replacement, but 90% of the framework is original; note the Elizabethan-style overhang and leaded windowpanes. A few Revere furnishings are on display here, and just gazing at his silverwork—much more of which is displayed at the Museum of Fine Arts—brings the man alive. ■**TIP→ Special events are scheduled throughout the year, many designed with children in mind.**

The immediate neighborhood also has Revere associations. The little park in North Square is named after Rachel Revere, his second wife, and the adjacent brick **Pierce-Hichborn House** once belonged to relatives of Revere. The garden connecting the Revere house and the Pierce-Hichborn House is planted with flowers and medicinal herbs favored in Revere's day. ✉ *19 North Sq., North End* ☎ *617/523–2338* ⊕ *www.paulreverehouse. org* ✇ *$3.50, $5.50 with Pierce-Hichborn House* ☼ *Mid-April–Oct. 9:30–5:15, Nov.–mid-April 9:30–4:15. Closed Mondays Jan.–March.* Ⓜ *Haymarket, Aquarium, Government Center.*

Pierce-Hichborn House. One of the city's oldest brick buildings, this structure, just to the left of the Paul Revere House, was once owned by Nathaniel Hichborn, a boatbuilder and Revere's cousin on his mother's side. Built about 1711 for a window maker named Moses Pierce, the Pierce-Hichborn House is an excellent example of early Georgian architecture. The home's symmetrical style was a radical change from the wood-frame Tudor buildings, such as the Revere House, then common. Its four rooms are furnished with modest 18th-century furniture, providing a peek into typical middle-class life. ✉ *29 North Sq., North End* ☎ *617/523–2338* ✇ *$2, $5.50 with Paul Revere House* ☼ *Guided tours only; call to schedule* Ⓜ *Haymarket, Aquarium, Government Center.*

A STICKY SUBJECT

Boston has had its share of grim historic events, from massacres to stranglers, but on the sheer weirdness scale, nothing beats the Great Molasses Flood. In 1919 a steel container of molasses exploded on the Boston Harbor waterfront, killing 21 people and 20 horses. More than 2.3 million gallons of goo oozed onto unsuspecting citizenry. Some say you can still smell molasses on the waterfront during steamy weather.

CHARLESTOWN

Boston started here. Charlestown was a thriving settlement a year before colonials headed across the Charles River at William Blaxton's invitation to found the city proper. Today the district's attractions include two of the most visible—and vertical—monuments in Boston: the Bunker Hill Monument, which commemorates the grisly battle that became a symbol of patriotic resistance against the British, and the USS *Constitution*, whose masts continue to tower over the waterfront where she was built more than 200 years ago.

Fodor's Choice
★
Bunker Hill Monument. Three misunderstandings surround this famous monument. First, the Battle of Bunker Hill was actually fought on Breed's Hill, which is where the monument sits today. (The real Bunker Hill is about ½ mile to the north of the monument; it's slightly taller than Breed's Hill.) Bunker was the original planned locale for the

battle, and for that reason its name stuck. Second, although the battle is generally considered a colonial success, the Americans lost. It was a Pyrrhic victory for the British Redcoats, who sacrificed nearly half of their 2,200 men; American casualties numbered 400–600. And third: the famous war cry "Don't fire until you see the whites of their eyes" may never have been uttered by American Colonel William Prescott or General Israel Putnam, but if either one did shout it, he was quoting an old Prussian command made necessary by the notorious inaccuracy of the musket. No matter. The Americans did employ a deadly delayed-action strategy on June 17, 1775, and conclusively proved themselves worthy fighters, capable of defeating the forces of the British Empire.

Among the dead were the brilliant young American doctor and political activist Joseph Warren, recently commissioned as a major general but fighting as a private, and the British Major John Pitcairn, who two months before had led the Redcoats into Lexington. Pitcairn is believed to be buried in the crypt of Old North Church.

In 1823 the committee formed to construct a monument on the site of the battle chose the form of an Egyptian obelisk. Architect Solomon Willard designed a 221-foot-tall granite obelisk, a tremendous feat of engineering for its day. The Marquis de Lafayette laid the cornerstone of the monument in 1825, but because of a nagging lack of funds, it wasn't dedicated until 1843. Daniel Webster's stirring words at the ceremony commemorating the laying of its cornerstone have gone down in history: "Let it rise! Let it rise, till it meets the sun in his coming. Let the earliest light of the morning gild it, and parting day linger and play upon its summit."

The monument's zenith is reached by a flight of 294 steps. There's no elevator, but the views from the observatory are worth the effort of the arduous climb. A statue of Colonel Prescott stands guard at the base. In the Bunker Hill Museum across the street, artifacts and exhibits tell the story of the battle, while a detailed diorama shows the action in miniature. ⊠ *Monument Sq., Charlestown* ☎ 617/242-5641 ⊕ *www.nps.gov/bost/historyculture/bhm.htm* ⊠ *Free* ☉ *Museum daily 9–5, monument daily 9–4:30* Ⓜ *Community College.*

FAMILY
Fodor'sChoice
★

USS *Constitution*. Better known as "Old Ironsides," the USS *Constitution* rides proudly at anchor in her berth at the Charlestown Navy Yard. The oldest commissioned ship in the U.S. fleet is a battlewagon of the old school, of the days of "wooden ships and iron men"—when she and her crew of 200 succeeded at the perilous task of asserting the sovereignty of an improbable new nation. Every July 4 and on certain other occasions she's towed out for a turnabout in Boston Harbor, the very place her keel was laid in 1797.

The venerable craft has narrowly escaped the scrap heap several times in her long history. She was launched on October 21, 1797, as part of the nation's fledgling navy. Her hull was made of live oak, the toughest wood grown in North America; her bottom was sheathed in copper, provided by Paul Revere at a nominal cost. Her principal service was during Thomas Jefferson's campaign against the Barbary pirates, off the coast of North Africa, and in the War of 1812. In 42 engagements her record was 42–0.

The nickname "Old Ironsides" was acquired during the War of 1812, when shots from the British warship *Guerrière* appeared to bounce off her hull. Talk of scrapping the ship began as early as 1830, but she was saved by a public campaign sparked by Oliver Wendell Holmes's poem "Old Ironsides." She underwent a major restoration in the early 1990s, and only about 8%–10% of her original wood remains in place, including the keel, the heart of the ship. Today she continues, the oldest commissioned warship afloat in the world, to be a part of the U.S. Navy.

The men and women who look after the *Constitution,* regular navy personnel, maintain a 24-hour watch. Sailors show visitors around the ship, guiding them to her top, or spar, deck, and the gun deck below. Another treat when visiting the ship is the spectacular view of Boston across Boston Harbor. Take a few minutes to explore the excellent Navy Yard Visitor Center for an overview before boarding. ■ TIP→ Instead of taking the T, you can get closer to the ship by taking MBTA Bus 93 to Chelsea Street from Haymarket. Or you can take the Boston Harbor Cruise water shuttle from Long Wharf to Pier 4. ⊠ *Charlestown Navy Yard, 55 Constitution Rd., Charlestown* ☎ *617/242–7511* ⊕ *www. history.navy.mil/ussconstitution* ⊠ *Free* ⊙ *Apr. 1–Sept., Tues.–Sun. 10–6; Oct., Tues.–Sun. 10–4; Nov.–Mar., Thurs.–Sun. 10–4; last tour at 3:30* Ⓜ *North Station.*

DOWNTOWN

Boston's commercial and financial districts—the area commonly called Downtown—are in a maze of streets that seem to have been laid out with little logic; they are village lanes now lined with modern 40-story office towers. Just as the Great Fire of 1872 swept the old Financial District clear, the Downtown construction in more-recent times has obliterated many of the buildings where 19th-century Boston businessmen sat in front of their rolltop desks. Yet historic sites remain tucked among the skyscrapers; a number of them have been linked together to make up a fascinating section of the Freedom Trail.

The area is bordered by State Street on the north and by South Station and Chinatown on the south. Tremont Street and the Common form the west boundary, and the harbor wharves the eastern edge. Locals navigate the tangle of thoroughfares in between, but few of them manage to give intelligible directions, so carry a map.

FAMILY **Boston Tea Party Ships & Museum.** After a lengthy renovation, the museum reopened in the summer of 2012 at the Congress Street Bridge, where Griffin's Wharf was, the actual spot where the Boston Tea Party took place on December 16, 1773. Visitors can check out *The Beaver II,* a historic reproduction of one of the ships forcibly boarded and unloaded the night Boston Harbor became a teapot, along with a reproduction of the *Eleanor,* another of the ships (the third ship, the *Dartmouth,* is slated to be built in 2014). The museum is big on interaction. Actors in period costumes greet patrons, and after assigning them a colonial persona, ask a few people to heave boxes of tea into the water. Inside, there are 3D Holograms, talking portraits, and

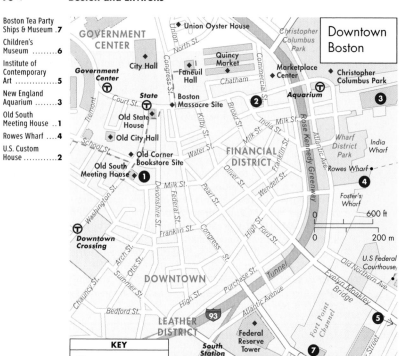

even the Robinson Half Tea Chest, one of two original tea chests known to exist. Outside, you can explore replicas of the ships, meet re-enactors, or drink a cup of tea in Abigail's Tea Room, which has one of the best views around. ⊠ *Fort Point Channel at Congress St. Bridge, Downtown* ⊕ *www.bostonteapartyship.com* ☒ *$25 (check website for discounts)* ⊘ *Daily 10–5* Ⓜ *South Station.*

FAMILY

Fodor'sChoice

★

Children's Museum. Most children have so much fun here that they don't realize they're actually learning something. Creative hands-on exhibits demonstrate scientific laws, cultural diversity, and problem solving. Some of the most popular stops are also the simplest, like the bubble-making machinery and the two-story climbing maze. At the Japanese House you're invited to take off your shoes and step inside a two-story silk merchant's home from Kyoto. The "Boston Black" exhibit stimulates dialogue about ethnicity and community, and children can play at a Cape Verdean restaurant and the African Queen Beauty Salon. In the toddler PlaySpace, children under three can run free in a safe environment. There's also a full schedule of special exhibits, festivals, and performances. ⊠ *308 Congress St., Downtown* ☎ *617/426–6500* ⊕ *www.bostonkids.org* ☒ *$14, Fri. 5–9 $1* ⊘ *Sat.–Thurs. 10–5, Fri. 10–9* Ⓜ *South Station.*

Fodor'sChoice   **Institute of Contemporary Art.** Housed in a breathtaking cantilevered edi-
★   fice that juts out over the Boston waterfront, the ICA moved to this
site in 2006 as part of a massive reinvention that's seeing the museum
grow into one of Boston's most exciting attractions. Since its foundation in 1936, the institute has cultivated its cutting-edge status: it's
played host to works by Edvard Munch, Egon Schiele, and Oskar
Kokoschka. Early in their careers, Andy Warhol, Robert Rauschenberg, and Roy Lichtenstein each mounted pivotal exhibitions here.
Now the ICA is building a major permanent collection for the first
time in its history, while continuing to showcase innovative paintings, videos, installations, and multimedia shows. The performing
arts get their due in the museum's theater, and the Water Café features cuisine from local seasonal ingredients. In nice weather you can
sit outside and enjoy the views. ⊠ *100 Northern Ave., South Boston*
☎ *617/478–3100* ⊕ *www.icaboston.org* ⊠ *$15, free Thurs. 5–9, free
for families last Sat. of every month (except Dec.)* ⊘ *Tues. and Wed.
10–5, Thurs. and Fri. 10–9, weekends 10–5. Tours on select weekends
at 2 and select Thurs. at 6* Ⓜ *Courthouse.*

Old South Meeting House. This is the second-oldest church building in
Boston, and were it not for Longfellow's celebration of the Old North
in "Paul Revere's Ride," it might well be the most famous. Some of the
fiercest of the town meetings that led to the Revolution were held here,
culminating in the gathering of December 16, 1773, which was called by
Samuel Adams to confront the crisis of three ships, laden with dutiable
tea, anchored at Griffin's Wharf. The activists wanted the tea returned
to England, but the governor would not permit it—and the rest is history. To cries of "Boston Harbor a teapot tonight!" and John Hancock's
"Let every man do what is right in his own eyes," the protesters poured
out of the Old South, headed to the wharf with their waiting comrades,
and dumped 18,000 pounds' worth of tea into the water.

One of the earliest members of the congregation was an African slave
named Phillis Wheatley, who had been educated by her owners. In 1773
a book of her poems was printed (by a London publisher), making her
the first published African-American poet. She later traveled to London, where she was received as a celebrity, but was again overtaken by
poverty and died in obscurity at age 31.

The church suffered no small amount of indignity in the Revolution: its
pews were ripped out by occupying British troops, and the interior was
used for riding exercises by General John Burgoyne's light dragoons.
A century later it escaped destruction in the Great Fire of 1872, only
to be threatened with demolition by developers. Interestingly, it was
the first successful preservation effort in New England. The building
opened as an independent, non-profit museum in 1877 and contains
the last remaining example of a two-tiered gallery in a New England
meetinghouse. The pulpit is a combination of two pulpits that were both
original to the meetinghouse during points in the Victorian era. The
white barrel portion of the pulpit dates from 1858 and the mahogany
wine glass portion in the front dates from 1808.

NEW ENGLAND AQUARIUM

✉ *Central Wharf between Central and Milk Sts., 1 Central Wharf, Downtown* ☎ *617/973–5200* ⊕ *www. neaq.org* 🎫 *$24.95, IMAX $9.95* ⊘ *July–early Sept., Sun.–Thurs. 9–6, Fri. and Sat. 9–7; early Sept.–June, weekdays 9–5, weekends 9–6* Ⓜ *Aquarium, State.*

This aquarium challenges you to imagine life under and around the sea. Its glass-and-steel exterior is constructed to mimic fish scales, and seals bark outside. Inside the main facility you'll see penguins, sea otters, sharks, and other exotic sea creatures—more than 30,000 animals, with 800 different species.

Highlights

In the semi-enclosed outdoor space of the New Balance Foundation Marine Mammal Center, visitors can enjoy the antics of northern fur seals and sea lions while gazing out at Boston Harbor.

The real show-stopper, though, is the four-story, 200,000-gallon ocean-reef tank, one of the largest of its kind in the world, which was renovated in 2013. Ramps winding around the tank lead to the top level and allow you to view the inhabitants from many vantage points. Up top, the new Yawkey Coral Reef Center features a seven-tank exhibit gallery that gives a close-up look at animals that might not be easily seen on the reef. Don't miss the five-times-a-day feedings; each lasts nearly an hour and takes divers 24 feet into the tank.

The aquarium has one of the largest exhibits of jellies in the country, with thousands of jellyfish (some grown in the museum's labs.)

Get up close to sharks and rays at the Trust Family Foundation Shark and Ray Touch Tank, the largest of its kind on the East Coast. The Blue Planet Action Center is a hands-on and interactive educational experience where visitors have the chance to see shark and lobster nurseries.

At the Edge of the Sea exhibit children can gingerly pick up starfish and other creatures. Whale-watch cruises leave from the aquarium's dock from April to October, and cost $45. There is also a 6½-story-high IMAX theater.

TIPS

■ If you are planning to see an IMAX show as well as check out the aquarium, buy a combo ticket; you'll save $5 for the adult ticket.

■ Also buy the combo ticket if you'd like to do the whale watch and the Aquarium, you'll save $12 if you purchase them together.

■ Save yourself the torture of waiting in long weekend lines, and purchase your tickets ahead of time online. You can skip ahead of the crowd and pick up your tickets at the will-call window, or print them out at home.

The Voices of Protest exhibit celebrates Old South as a forum for free speech from Revolutionary days to the present. ✉ *310 Washington St., Downtown* ☎ *617/482–6439* ⊕ *www.oldsouthmeetinghouse. org* ✏ *$6* ⊙ *Apr.–Oct., daily 9:30–5; Nov.–Mar., daily 10–4* Ⓜ *State, Downtown Crossing.*

Rowes Wharf. Take a Beacon Hill redbrick town house, blow it up to the *n*th power, and you get this 15-story Skidmore, Owings & Merrill extravaganza from 1987, one of the more welcome additions to the Boston Harbor skyline. From under the complex's gateway six-story arch, you can get great views of Boston Harbor and the yachts docked at the marina. Water shuttles pull up here from Logan Airport—the most intriguing way to enter the city. A windswept stroll along the HarborWalk waterfront promenade at dusk makes for an unforgettable sunset on clear days. ✉ *Atlantic Ave. south of India Wharf* Ⓜ *Aquarium.*

U.S. Custom House. This 1847 structure resembles a Greek Revival temple that appears to have sprouted a tower. It's just that. This is the work of architects Ammi Young and Isaiah Rogers—at least, the bottom part is. The tower was added in 1915, at which time the Custom House became Boston's tallest building. It remains one of the most visible and best loved structures in the city's skyline. To appreciate the grafting job, go inside and look at the domed rotunda. The outer surface of that dome was once the roof of the building, but now the dome is embedded in the base of the tower.

The federal government moved out of the Custom House in 1987 and sold it to the city of Boston, which, in turn, sold it to the Marriott Corporation, which has converted the building into hotel space and luxury time-share units, a move that disturbed some historical purists. You can now sip a cocktail in the hotel's Counting Room Lounge after 6 pm, or visit the 26th-floor observation deck for a fee. The magnificent Rotunda Room sports maritime prints and antique artifacts, courtesy of the Peabody Essex Museum in Salem. ✉ *3 McKinley Sq., Downtown* ☎ *617/310–6300* Ⓜ *State, Aquarium.*

THE BACK BAY

In the folklore of American neighborhoods, the Back Bay stands as a symbol of propriety and high social standing. Before the 1850s it really was a bay, a tidal flat that formed the south bank of a distended Charles River. The filling in of land along the isthmus that joined Boston to the mainland (the Neck) began in 1850, and resulted in the creation of the South End. To the north a narrow causeway called the Mill Dam (later Beacon Street) was built in 1814 to separate the Back Bay from the Charles. By the late 1800s Bostonians had filled in the shallows to as far as the marshland known as the Fenway, and the original 783-acre peninsula had been expanded by about 450 acres. Thus the waters of Back Bay became the neighborhood of Back Bay.

Heavily influenced by the then-recent rebuilding of Paris according to the plans of Baron Georges-Eugène Haussmann, the Back Bay planners created thoroughfares that resemble Parisian boulevards. Almost immediately, fashionable families began to decamp from Beacon Hill

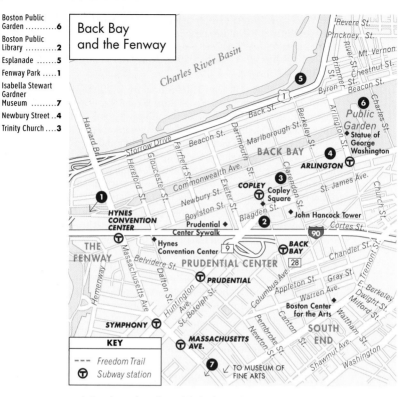

and South End and establish themselves in the Back Bay's brick and brownstone row houses. By 1900 the streets between the Public Garden and Massachusetts Avenue had become the smartest, most desirable neighborhood in all of Boston.

Today the area retains its posh spirit, but mansions are no longer the main draw. Locals and tourists flock to the commercial streets of Boylston and Newbury to shop at boutiques, galleries, and the usual mall stores. Many of the bars and restaurants have patio seating and bay windows. The Boston Public Library, Symphony Hall, and numerous churches ensure that high culture is not lost amid the frenzy of consumerism.

TOP ATTRACTIONS

FAMILY
Fodor'sChoice
★

Boston Public Garden. Although the Boston Public Garden is often lumped together with Boston Common, the two are separate entities with different histories and purposes and a distinct boundary between them at Charles Street. The Common has been public land since Boston was founded in 1630, whereas the Public Garden belongs to a newer Boston, occupying what had been salt marshes on the edge of the Common. By 1837 the tract was covered with an abundance of ornamental plantings donated by a group of private citizens. The area was defined in 1856 by the building of Arlington Street, and in 1860 the architect George Meacham was commissioned to plan the park.

The central feature of the Public Garden is its irregularly shaped pond, intended to appear, from any vantage point along its banks, much larger than its nearly 4 acres. Near the Swan Boat dock is what has been described as the world's smallest suspension bridge, designed in 1867 to cross the pond at its narrowest point.

The Public Garden is America's oldest botanical garden, and has the finest formal plantings in central Boston. The beds along the main walkways are replanted for spring and summer. The tulips during the first two weeks of May are especially colorful, and there's a sampling of native and European tree species.

The dominant work among the park's statuary is Thomas Ball's equestrian **George Washington** (1869), which faces the head of Commonwealth Avenue at the Arlington Street gate. This is Washington in a triumphant pose as liberator, surveying a scene that, from where he stood with his cannons at Dorchester Heights, would have included an immense stretch of blue water. Several dozen yards to the north of Washington (to the right if you're facing Commonwealth Avenue) is the granite-and-red-marble **Ether Monument,** donated in 1866 by Thomas Lee to commemorate the advent of anesthesia 20 years earlier at nearby Massachusetts General Hospital. Other Public Garden monuments include statues of the Unitarian preacher and transcendentalist William Ellery Channing, at the corner opposite his Arlington Street Church; Edward Everett Hale, the author (*The Man Without a Country*) and philanthropist, at the Charles Street Gate; and the abolitionist senator Charles Sumner and the Civil War hero Colonel Thomas Cass, along Boylston Street.

The park contains a special delight for the young at heart; follow the children quack-quacking along the pathway between the pond and the park entrance at Charles and Beacon streets to the *Make Way for Ducklings* bronzes sculpted by Nancy Schön, a tribute to the 1941 classic children's story by Robert McCloskey. ⊠ *Bounded by Arlington, Boylston, Charles, and Beacon Sts., Back Bay* Ⓜ *Arlington.*

Swan Boats. The pond has been famous since 1877 for its foot-pedal-powered (by a captain) Swan Boats, which make leisurely cruises during warm months. The pond is favored by ducks and swans, and for the modest price of a few boat rides you can amuse children here for an hour or more. ☎ *617/522–1966* ⊕ *www.swanboats.com* 🖾 *Swan Boats $3 adults; $1.50 children* ☉ *Swan Boats mid-Apr.–June 20, daily 10–4; June 21–Labor Day, daily 10–5; day after Labor Day–mid-Sept., weekdays noon–4, weekends 10–4.*

Fodor's Choice ★ **Boston Public Library.** This venerable institution is a handsome temple to literature and a valuable research library. The Renaissance Revival building was opened in 1895; a 1972 addition emulates the mass and proportion of the original, though not its extraordinary detail; this skylighted annex houses the library's circulating collections.

You don't need a library card to enjoy the magnificent art. The murals at the head of the staircase, depicting the nine muses, are the work of the French artist Puvis de Chavannes; those in the book-request processing room to the right are Edwin Abbey's interpretations of the Holy Grail legend. Upstairs, in the public areas leading to the fine-arts, music,

Shoppers take a break at a Newbury Street café.

and rare-books collections, is John Singer Sargent's mural series on the *Triumph of Religion*, shining with renewed color after its cleaning and restoration in 2003. The corridor leading from the annex opens onto the Renaissance-style **courtyard**—an exact copy of the one in Rome's Palazzo della Cancelleria—around which the original library is built. A covered arcade furnished with chairs rings a fountain; you can bring books or lunch into the courtyard, which is open all the hours the library is open, and escape the bustle of the city. Beyond the courtyard is the main entrance hall of the 1895 building, with its immense stone lions by Louis St. Gaudens, vaulted ceiling, and marble staircase. The corridor at the top of the stairs leads to **Bates Hall**, one of Boston's most sumptuous interior spaces. This is the main reference reading room, 218 feet long with a barrel-arch ceiling 50 feet high. ⊠ *700 Boylston St., at Copley Sq., Back Bay* ☎ *617/536–5400* ⊕ *www.bpl. org* ⊘ *Mon.–Thurs. 9–9, Fri. and Sat. 9–5, Sun. 1–5 (Oct.–June). Free guided art and architecture tours Mon. at 2:30, Tues. and Thurs. at 6, Wed., Fri., and Sat. at 11* Ⓜ *Copley.*

QUICK BITES

Courtyard. You can take a lunch break at the Courtyard or the MapRoom Café, adjoining restaurants in the Boston Public Library. Breakfast and lunch are served in the 1895 Map Room, and the main restaurant, which overlooks the courtyard, is open for lunch and afternoon tea. The Courtyard is open weekdays 11:30–2:30 for lunch and Wednesday–Friday 2–4 for tea. The MapRoom Café is open Monday–Saturday 9–5. ⊠ *700 Boylston St., at Copley Sq., Back Bay* ☎ *617/859–2251* ⊕ *www.thecateredaffair. com/bpl/courtyard.*

Trinity Church. In his 1877 masterpiece, architect Henry Hobson Richardson brought his Romanesque Revival style to maturity; all the aesthetic elements for which he was famous come together magnificently—bold polychromatic masonry, careful arrangement of masses, sumptuously carved interior woodwork—in this crowning centerpiece of Copley Square. A full appreciation of its architecture requires an understanding of the logistical problems of building it here. The Back Bay is a reclaimed wetland with a high water table. Bedrock, or at least stable glacial till, lies far beneath wet clay. Like all older Back Bay buildings, Trinity Church sits on submerged wooden pilings. But its central tower weighs 9,500 tons, and most of the 4,500 pilings beneath the building are under that tremendous central mass. The pilings are checked regularly for sinkage by means of a hatch in the basement.

> **FRUGAL FUN**
>
> Take a cue from locals and sign up for one of the Boston Park Rangers' programs. Top picks include a visit to the city stables to meet the Mounties and their horses, regularly scheduled readings of Robert McCloskey's *Make Way for Ducklings* in Boston's Public Garden, and city scavenger hunts geared for families. Contact **Boston Parks and Recreation** (☎ 617/635–7487 ⊕ www.cityofboston.gov/parks/parkrangers).

Richardson engaged some of the best artists of his day—John LaFarge, William Morris, and Edward Burne-Jones among them—to execute the paintings and stained glass that make this a monument to everything that was right about the pre-Raphaelite spirit and the nascent aesthetic of Morris's Arts and Crafts movement. LaFarge's intricate paintings and ornamented ceilings received a much-needed overhaul during the extensive renovations completed in 2005. Along the north side of the church, note the Augustus Saint-Gaudens statue of Phillips Brooks—the most charismatic rector in New England, who almost single-handedly got Trinity built and furnished. Shining light of Harvard's religious community and lyricist of "O Little Town of Bethlehem," Brooks is shown here with Christ touching his shoulder in approval. For a nice respite, try to catch one of the Friday organ concerts beginning at 12:15. ■ TIP→ **The 11:15 Sunday service is usually followed by a free guided tour.** ✉ *206 Clarendon St., Back Bay* ☎ *617/536–0944* ⊕ *trinitychurchboston.org* ✉ *Entrance free, guided and self-guided tours $7* ☉ *Sept.–June Mon., Fri., and Sat. 9–5, Tues.–Thurs. 9–6, Sun. 1–6; services Sun. at 7:45, 9, and 11:15 am and 6 pm. Tours take place several times daily; call to confirm times. Last admission 30 min prior to closing. Hrs change slightly in the summer* Ⓜ *Copley.*

WORTH NOTING

Esplanade. Near the corner of Beacon and Arlington streets, the Arthur Fiedler Footbridge crosses Storrow Drive to the 3-mi-long Esplanade and the **Hatch Memorial Shell.** The free concerts here in summer include the Boston Pops' immensely popular televised July 4 performance. For shows like this, Bostonians haul lawn chairs and blankets to the lawn in front of the shell; bring a take-out lunch from a nearby restaurant, find an empty spot—no mean feat, so come early—and you'll feel right at home. An impressive stone bust of the late maestro Arthur Fiedler watches over the walkers, joggers, picnickers, and sunbathers who fill the Esplanade's paths on pleasant days. Here, too, is the turn-of-the-20th-century **Union Boat Club Boathouse,** headquarters for the country's oldest private rowing club. ⊠ *Back Bay* ⊕ *www.esplanadeassociation.org.*

Newbury Street. Eight-block-long Newbury Street has been compared to New York's 5th Avenue, and certainly this is the city's poshest shopping area, with branches of Chanel, Brooks Brothers, Diane von Furstenberg, Burberry, and other top names in fashion. But here the pricey boutiques are more intimate than grand, and people live above the trendy restaurants and ubiquitous hair salons, giving the place a neighborhood feel. Toward the Mass Ave. end, cafés proliferate and the stores get funkier, ending with Newbury Comics and Urban Outfitters. ⊠ *From Arlington St. to Mass Ave., Back Bay* Ⓜ *Hynes, Copley.*

THE FENWAY

The marshland known as the Back Bay Fens gave this section of Boston its name, but two quirky institutions give it its character: Fenway Park, home of Boston's beloved Red Sox, and the Isabella Stewart Gardner Museum, the legacy of a high-living Brahmin who attended a concert at Symphony Hall in 1912 wearing a headband that read, "Oh, You Red Sox." Not far from the Gardner is another major cultural magnet: the Museum of Fine Arts. Kenmore Square, a favorite haunt for Boston University students, adds a bit of funky flavor to the mix.

Fodor's Choice ★ **Fenway Park.** For 86 years, the Boston Red Sox suffered a World Series dry spell, a streak of bad luck that fans attributed to the "Curse of the Bambino," which, stories have it, struck the team in 1920 when they sold Babe Ruth (the "Bambino") to the New York Yankees. All that changed in 2004, when a maverick squad broke the curse in a thrilling seven-game series against the team's nemesis in the series semifinals. This win against the Yankees was followed by a four-game sweep of St. Louis in the finals. Boston, and its citizens' ingrained sense of pessimism, hasn't been the same since. The repeat World Series wins in 2007 and 2013 cemented Bostonians' sense that the universe had finally begun working correctly and made Red Sox caps the residents' semiofficial uniform. ⇨ *See the Fenway Park spotlight in the Sports and the Outdoors chapter for more information.* ⊠ *4 Yawkey Way, between Van Ness and Lansdowne Sts., The Fenway* ☎ *877/733–7699 box office, 617/226–6666 tours* ⊕ *www. redsox.com* ⊠ *Tours $16* ☉ *Tours run daily 9–5, on the hour.* Ⓜ *Kenmore.*

Fodor's Choice ★ **Isabella Stewart Gardner Museum.** A spirited young society woman, Isabella Stewart came in 1860 from New York—where ladies were more commonly seen and heard than in Boston—to marry John Lowell Gardner, one of Boston's leading citizens. "Mrs. Jack" promptly set about becoming the most un-Bostonian of the Proper Bostonians. She decided to build the Venetian palazzo to hold her collected arts in an isolated corner of Boston's newest neighborhood. Her will stipulated that the building remain exactly as she left it—paintings, furniture, and the smallest object in a hall cabinet—and that is as it has remained. Today, it's probably America's most idiosyncratic treasure house.

MUSEUM OF FINE ARTS

✉ *465 Huntington Ave., The Fenway* ☎ *617/267–9300* ⊕ *www.mfa.org* ✉ *$25 (good for two days in a 10-day period)* ⊘ *Sat.–Tues. 10–4:45, Wed.–Fri. 10–9:45. 1-hr tours daily; call for scheduled times* Ⓜ *Museum.*

TIPS

■ The year-round cocktail party "MFA First Fridays," from 6 to 9:30—held monthly—has become quite the social event. Stop by to admire the art in a festive atmosphere.

■ Be aware that the museum will require you to check any bag larger than 11 inches by 15 inches, even if it's your purse. So save that oversize bag for another day and bring along only the essentials.

Count on staying a while if you have any hope of seeing what's here. Eclecticism and thoroughness, often an incompatible pair, have coexisted agreeably at the MFA since its earliest days. From Renaissance and baroque masters to Impressionist marvels, African masks and sublime samples of Native American pottery to contemporary crafts, the collections are happily shorn of both cultural snobbery and shortsighted trendiness.

Highlights

The MFA's collection of approximately 450,000 objects was built from a core of paintings and sculpture from the Boston Athenaeum, historical portraits from the city of Boston, and donations by area universities. The MFA has more than 70 works by John Single-ton Copley; major paintings by Winslow Homer, John Singer Sargent, Fitz Henry Lane, and Edward Hopper; and a wealth of American works ranging from native New England folk art and colonial portraiture to New York abstract expressionism of the 1950s and 1960s. Also of particular note are the John Singer Sargent murals adorning the Rotunda. They were unveiled at the museum in 1921 and make for a dazzling first impression on visitors coming through the Huntington Avenue entrance.

American decorative arts are also liberally represented, particularly those of New England in the years before the Civil War. Native son Paul Revere, much more than a sounder of alarms, is amply represented as well, with superb silver teapots, sauceboats, and other tableware.

More than thirty galleries contain the MFA's European painting and sculpture collection, dating from the 11th century to the 20th. Contemporary art has a dynamic home in the MFA's dramatic I. M. Pei–designed building.

Gardner's palazzo contains a trove of amazing paintings—including such masterpieces as Titian's *Europa,* Giotto's *Presentation of Christ in the Temple,* Piero della Francesca's *Hercules,* and John Singer Sargent's *El Jaleo.* Spanish leather panels, Renaissance hooded fireplaces, and Gothic tapestries accent salons; eight balconies adorn the majestic Venetian courtyard. There's a Raphael Room, Spanish Cloister, Gothic Room, Chinese Loggia, and a magnificent Tapestry Room for concerts, where Gardner entertained Henry James and Edith Wharton. An adjacent gallery houses the works of participants in the museum's artist-in-residence program.

There are some conspicuously bare spots on the walls. On March 18, 1990, the Gardner was the target of a sensational art heist. Thieves disguised as police officers stole 12 works, including Vermeer's *The Concert.* To date, none of the art has been recovered, despite a $5-million reward. Because Mrs. Gardner's will prohibited substituting other works for any stolen art, empty expanses of wall identify spots where the paintings once hung.

A new addition to the museum opened in 2012. The Renzo Piano–designed building houses a music hall, exhibit space, classrooms, and conservation labs, where Gardner's works can be repaired and preserved. ✉ *280 The Fenway, The Fenway* ☎ *617/566–1401, 617/566–1088 café* ⊕ *www. gardnermuseum.org* 💲 *$15* ⊙ *Museum Wed.–Mon. 11–5, Thurs. 11–9, open some holidays; café Tues.–Fri. 11:30–4, weekends 11–4* Ⓜ *Museum.*

EXPLORING CAMBRIDGE

Updated by
Kim Foley
MacKinnon

Across the Charles River is the überliberal academic enclave of Cambridge. The city is punctuated at one end by the funky tech-noids of MIT and at the other by the grand academic fortress that is Harvard University. Civic life connects the two camps into an urban stew of 100,000 residents who represent nearly every nationality in the world, work at every kind of job from tenured professor to taxi driver, and are passionate about living on this side of the river.

The Charles River is the Cantabrigians' backyard, and there's virtually no place in Cambridge more than a 10-minute walk from its banks. Strolling, running, or biking here is one of the great pleasures of Cambridge, and views include graceful bridges, the distant Boston skyline, crew teams rowing through the calm water, and the elegant spires of Harvard soaring into the sky.

No visit to Cambridge is complete without an afternoon in Harvard Square. It's home to every variation of the human condition; Nobel laureates, homeless buskers, trust-fund babies, and working-class Joes mill around the same piece of real estate. Walk down Brattle Street past Henry Wadsworth Longfellow's house. Farther along Massachusetts Avenue is Central Square, an ethnic melting pot of people and restaurants. Ten minutes more brings you to MIT, with its eclectic architecture from postwar pedestrian to Frank Gehry's futuristic fantasyland. In addition to providing a stellar view, the Massachusetts Avenue Bridge, spanning the Charles from Cambridge to Boston, is also notorious in MIT lore for its Smoot measurements.

Harvard Art Museums. In 2014 the combined collections of the Busch-Reisinger and Fogg museums (which closed in 2008) and the Arthur M. Sackler Museum (which closed in 2013) will be represented under one roof with the umbrella name Harvard Art Museums. Barring any possible delays, Harvard Art Museums are slated to open in late 2014, housed in a new facility designed by architect Renzo Piano. Highlights include American and European paintings, sculptures, and decorative arts from the Fogg Museum; works by German expressionists, materials related to the Bauhaus, and postwar contemporary art from German-speaking Europe from the Busch-Reisinger Museum. The collection will also include ancient Greek and Roman sculpture, Chinese jades, and Islamic ceramics from the Sackler Museum. ⊠ *32 Quincy St., Cambridge* ☎ *617/495–9400* ⊕ *www.harvardartmuseums. org* Ⓜ *Harvard.*

FAMILY **Harvard Museum of Natural History.** Many museums promise something
Fodor'sChoice for every member of the family; the vast Harvard Museum complex
★ actually delivers. In 2012 Harvard University created a new consortium, the Harvard Museums of Science & Culture, uniting under one administration several of its most visited public museums. The Harvard Museum of Natural History (which exhibits specimens from the Museum of Comparative Zoology, Harvard University Herbaria, and the Mineralogical and Geological Museum) displays some 12,000 specimens, including dinosaurs, rare minerals, hundreds of mammals and birds, and Harvard's world famous Blaschka Glass Flowers. The museum combines historic exhibits drawn from the university's vast collections with new and changing multimedia exhibitions such as *New England Forests and Mollusks: Shelled Masters of the Marine Realm*, and the renovated Earth & Planetary Sciences gallery. ■TIP➔ **Check the website for children's events and special engagements, which occur throughout the year.** ⊠ *26 Oxford St., Cambridge* ☎ *617/495–3045* ⊕ *www.hmnh.harvard.edu* 🎟 *$12; free for Massachusetts residents year-round, Sun. 9–noon and Sept.–May, Wed. 3–5. Ticket includes admission to the Peabody Museum.* ☉ *Daily 9–5* Ⓜ *Harvard.*

FAMILY **Harvard Square.** Tides of students, tourists, political-cause proponents,
Fodor'sChoice and bizarre street creatures are all part of the nonstop pedestrian flow
★ at this most celebrated of Cambridge crossroads.

Harvard Square is where Mass Ave., coming from Boston, turns and widens into a triangle broad enough to accommodate a brick peninsula (above the T station). The restored 1928 kiosk in the center of the square once served as the entrance to the MBTA station (it's now Out of Town News, a fantastic newsstand). Harvard Yard, with its lecture halls, residential houses, libraries, and museums, is one long border of the square; the other three are composed of clusters of banks and a wide variety of restaurants and shops.

On an average afternoon you'll hear earnest conversations in dozens of foreign languages; see every kind of youthful uniform from Goth to impeccable prep; wander by street musicians playing Andean flutes, singing opera, and doing excellent Stevie Wonder or Edith Piaf imitations; and watch a tense outdoor game of pickup chess between a

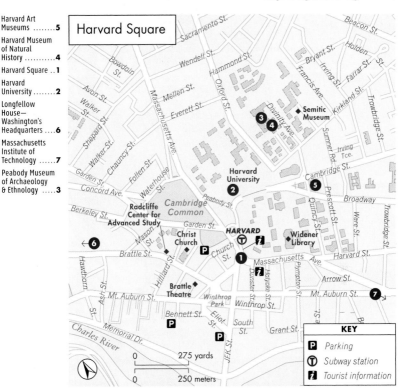

street-tough kid and an older gent wearing a beard and a beret while you slurp a cappuccino or an ice cream cone (the two major food groups here). An afternoon in the square is people-watching raised to a high art; the parade of quirkiness never quits.

As entertaining as the locals are, the historic buildings are worth noting. Even if you're only a visitor (as opposed to a prospective student), it's still a thrill to walk though the big brick-and-wrought-iron gates to Harvard Yard, past the residence halls and statues, on up to Widener Library.

Across Garden Street, through an ornamental arch, is **Cambridge Common,** decreed a public pasture in 1631. It's said that under a large tree that once stood in this meadow George Washington took command of the Continental Army on July 3, 1775. A stone memorial now marks the site of the "Washington Elm." Also on the Common is the Irish Famine Memorial by Derry artist Maurice Herron, unveiled in 1997 to coincide with the 150th anniversary of "Black '47," the deadliest year of the potato famine. It depicts a desperate Irish mother sending her child off to America. At the center of the Common a large memorial commemorates the Union soldiers and sailors who lost their lives in the Civil War. On the far side of the Common (on Waterhouse St. between Garden St. and Massachusetts Ave.) is a fantastic park. ⊕ *www.harvardsquare. com* Ⓜ *Harvard.*

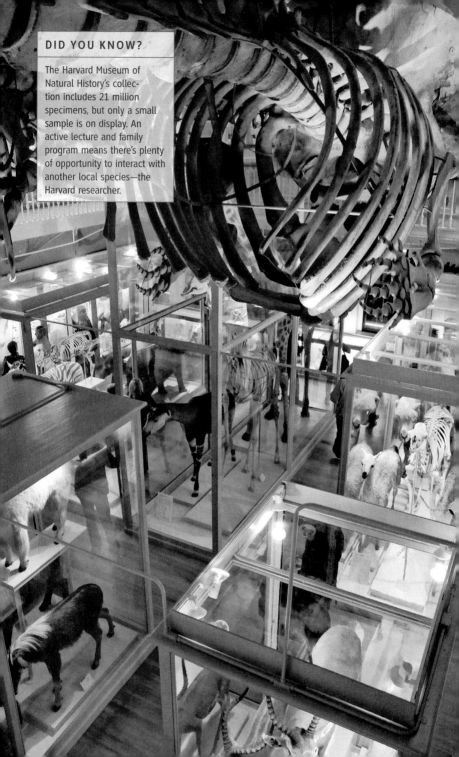

Broadway Marketplace. The Broadway Marketplace is just around the corner from Harvard Yard. Besides the excellent fresh produce, there's a selection of sandwiches and prepared meals; choose one to be heated up and then grab a seat for a quick, delicious (if pricey) bite. Every Thursday (5–7 pm) there's a wine, beer, or liquor tasting, a great way to mingle with locals. ✉ *468 Broadway, Cambridge* ☎ *617/547–2334* ⊕ *www.broadwaymarketplace.com.*

Harvard University. The tree-studded, shady, and redbrick expanse of Harvard Yard—the very center of Harvard University—has weathered the footsteps of Harvard students for hundreds of years. In 1636 the Great and General Court of the Massachusetts Bay Colony voted funds to establish the colony's first college, and a year later chose Cambridge as the site. Named in 1639 for John Harvard, a young Charlestown clergyman who died in 1638 and left the college his entire library and half his estate, Harvard remained the only college in the New World until 1693, by which time it was firmly established as a respected center of learning. Local wags refer to Harvard as WGU—World's Greatest University—and it's certainly the oldest and most famous American university.

Although the college dates from the 17th century, the oldest buildings in Harvard Yard are from the 18th century (though you'll sometimes see archaeologists digging here for evidence of older structures). Together the buildings chronicle American architecture from the colonial era to the present. **Holden Chapel,** completed in 1744, is a Georgian gem. The graceful **University Hall** was designed in 1815 by Charles Bulfinch. An 1884 statue of John Harvard by Daniel Chester French stands outside; ironically for a school with the motto of "Veritas" ("Truth"), the model for the statue was a member of the class of 1882 and not Harvard himself. **Sever Hall,** completed in 1880 and designed by Henry Hobson Richardson, represents the Romanesque revival that was followed by the neoclassical (note the pillared facade of Widener Library) and the neo-Georgian, represented by the sumptuous brick houses along the Charles River, many of which are now undergraduate residences. **Memorial Church,** a graceful steepled edifice of modified Colonial Revival design, was dedicated in 1932. Just north of the Yard is **Memorial Hall,** completed in 1878 as a memorial to Harvard men who died in the Union cause; it's High Victorian both inside and out. It also contains the 1,166-seat Sanders Theatre, which serves as the university's largest lecture hall, site of year-round concerts by students and professionals, and the venue for the festive Christmas Revels.

Many of Harvard's cultural and scholarly facilities are important sights in themselves, including the **Harvard Museum of Natural History,** the **Peabody Museum of Archaeology & Ethnology,** and the **Widener Library.** Be aware that most campus buildings, other than museums and concert halls, are off-limits to the general public. ✉ *Bounded by Massachusetts Ave. and Mt. Auburn, Holyoke, and Dunster Sts., Cambridge* ☎ *617/495–1000* ⊕ *www.harvard.edu* Ⓜ *Harvard.*

Harvard University Events & Information Center. Harvard University Events & Information Center, run by students, includes a small library, a video-viewing area, computer terminals, and an exhibit space. It also distributes maps of the university area and has free student-led tours of Harvard Yard. The tour doesn't include visits to museums, and it doesn't take you into campus buildings, but it provides a fine orientation. The information center is open year-round (except during spring recess and other semester breaks), Monday through Saturday 9 to 5. Tours are offered September through May, every hour between 10 and 4 (except during university breaks). From the end of June through August, guides offer tours every half-hour; however, it's best to call ahead to confirm times. Groups of 20 or more can schedule tours ahead. You can also download a mobile tour if you have a smartphone. ⊠ *Holyoke Center, 1350 Massachusetts Ave., Cambridge* ☎ *617/495–1573* ⊕ *www.harvard.edu/visitors*

Longfellow House-Washington's Headquarters. If there's one historic house to visit in Cambridge, this is it. Henry Wadsworth Longfellow, the poet whose stirring tales of the Village Blacksmith, Evangeline, Hiawatha, and Paul Revere's midnight ride thrilled 19th-century America, once lived in this elegant mansion. One of several original Tory Row homes on Brattle Street, the house was built in 1759 by John Vassall Jr., and George Washington lived here during the Siege of Boston from July 1775 to April 1776. Longfellow first boarded here in 1837, and later received the house as a gift from his father-in-law on his marriage to Frances Appleton, who burned to death here in an accident in 1861. For 45 years Longfellow wrote his famous verses here and filled the house with the exuberant spirit of his own work and that of his literary circle, which included Ralph Waldo Emerson, Nathaniel Hawthorne, and Charles Sumner, an abolitionist senator. Longfellow died in 1882, but his presence in the house lives on—from the Longfellow family furniture to the wallpaper to the books on the shelves (many the poet's own). The home is preserved and run by the National Park Service; free 45-minute guided tours of the house are offered hourly. The formal garden is the perfect place to relax. ■TIP➜ **Longfellow Park, across the street, is the place to stand to take photos of the house.** The park was created to preserve the view immortalized in the poet's "To the River Charles." ⊠ *105 Brattle St., Cambridge* ☎ *617/876–4491* ⊕ *www.nps. gov/long* ▢ *Free* ☉ *Grounds daily dawn to dusk; house May–Oct., Wed.–Sun. 9:30–4:30* Ⓜ *Harvard.*

Massachusetts Institute of Technology. This once-tidy engineering school at right angles to the Charles River is growing like a sprawling adolescent, consuming old industrial buildings and city blocks with every passing year. Once dissed as "the factory," particularly by its Ivy League neighbor, Harvard University, MIT mints graduates that are the sharp blades on the edge of the information revolution. It's perennially in the top five of U.S. News and World Report's college rankings.

Founded in 1861, MIT moved to Cambridge from Copley Square in the Back Bay in 1916. It has long since fulfilled the predictions of its founder, the geologist William Barton Rogers, that it would surpass "the universities of the land in the accuracy and the extent of its teachings in all branches of positive science." Its emphasis shifted in the 1930s from practical engineering and mechanics to the outer limits of scientific fields.

Architecture is important at MIT. Although the original buildings were obviously designed by and for scientists, many represent pioneering designs of their times. The **Kresge Auditorium,** designed by Eero Saarinen, with a curving roof and unusual thrust, rests on three, instead of four, points. The nondenominational **MIT Chapel,** a circular Saarinen design, is lighted primarily by a roof oculus that focuses natural light on the altar and by reflections from the water in a small surrounding moat; it's topped by an aluminum sculpture by Theodore Roszak. The serpentine **Baker House,** now a dormitory, was designed in 1947 by the Finnish architect Alvar Aalto in such a way as to provide every room with a view of the Charles River. Sculptures by Henry Moore and other notable artists dot the campus. The latest addition is the newly minted Green Center, punctuated by the splash of color that is Sol Lewitt's 5,500-square-foot mosaic floor mural.

The East Campus, which has grown around the university's original neoclassical buildings of 1916, also has outstanding modern architecture and sculpture, including the stark high-rise **Green Building** by I. M. Pei, housing the Earth Science Center. Just outside is Alexander Calder's giant stabile (a stationary mobile) *The Big Sail.* Another Pei work on the East Campus is the **Wiesner Building,** designed in 1985, which houses the **List Visual Arts Center.** Architect Frank Gehry made his mark on the campus with the cockeyed, improbable **Ray & Maria Stata Center,** a complex of buildings on Vassar Street. The center houses computer, artificial intelligence, and information systems laboratories, and is reputedly as confusing to navigate on the inside as it is to follow on the outside. East Campus's **Great Dome,** which looms over neoclassical Killian Court, has often been the target of student "hacks" and has at various times supported a telephone booth with a ringing phone, a life-size statue of a cow, and a campus police cruiser. Nearby, the domed **Rogers Building** has earned unusual notoriety as the center of a series of hallways and tunnels dubbed "the infinite corridor." Twice each winter the sun's path lines up perfectly with the corridor's axis, and at dusk students line the third-floor hallway to watch the sun set through the westernmost window. The phenomenon is known as "MIT-henge."

MIT maintains an information center in the Rogers Building, and offers free tours of the campus weekdays at 11 and 3. Check the schedule, as the tours are often suspended during school holidays. General hours for the information center are weekdays 9–5. ⊠ *77 Massachusetts Ave., Cambridge* ☎ *617/253–4795* ⊕ *www.mit.edu* Ⓜ *Kendall/MIT.*

Peabody Museum of Archaeology & Ethnology. With one of the world's outstanding anthropological collections, the Peabody focuses on Native American and Central and South American cultures. The Hall of the North American Indian is particularly outstanding, with art, textiles, and models of traditional dwellings from across the continent. The Mesoamerican room juxtaposes ancient relief carvings and weavings with contemporary works from the Maya and other peoples. ☒ *11 Divinity Ave., Cambridge* 🕾 *617/496–1027* ⊕ *www.peabody.harvard. edu* 🖃 *$12, includes admission to Harvard Museum of Natural History, accessible through the museum; free for Massachusetts residents on Sun. 9–noon year-round and Wed. 3–5 Sept.–May (excluding commercial groups).* ⊙ *Daily 9–5* Ⓜ *Harvard.*

WHERE TO EAT

Updated by
Victoria Abbott
Riccardi

In a city synonymous with tradition, Boston chefs have spent recent years rewriting culinary history. The stuffy, wood-paneled formality is gone; the endless renditions of chowdah, lobster, and cod have retired. A crop of young chefs has ascended, opening small, upscale neighborhood spots that use New England ingredients to delicious effect.

Traditional eats can still be found (Durgin-Park remains as the best place to get baked beans), but many diners now gravitate toward innovative food in understated environs. Whether you're looking for casual French, down-home Southern cooking, some of the best sushi in the country, or Vietnamese *banh mi* sandwiches, Boston restaurants are ready to deliver. The fish and shellfish brought in from nearby shores continue to inform the regional cuisine: expect to see several seafood options on local menus, but don't expect them to be boiled or dumped into the lobster stew that JFK loved. Instead, you might be offered swordfish with salsa verde, cornmeal-crusted scallops, or lobster cassoulet with black truffles.

In many ways, though, Boston remains solidly skeptical of trends. If you close your eyes in the North End, Boston's Little Italy, you can easily imagine you're in Rome circa 1955. And over in the university culture of Cambridge, places like East Coast Grill and Oleana espoused the locovore and slow-food movements before they became buzzwords. *Prices in the reviews are the average cost of a main course at dinner or, if dinner is not served, at lunch.*

Use the coordinate (⊕ B2) at the end of each listing to locate a site on the Where to Eat and Stay in Boston map.

BACK BAY AND SOUTH END

$$$

SEAFOOD

Fodor's Choice

★

✕ **Atlantic Fish Co.** Designed to look like an ocean vessel with gorgeous wood finishes and nautical artwork, this local seafood restaurant delivers first-class seafood, so fresh that the extensive menus are printed daily to reflect the day's catch served broiled, baked, blackened, fried, grilled, or pan-seared. Unsnap your starched napkin and begin with a platter of chilled seafood (lobster, little necks, oysters, crab, and shrimp), followed by the standout seafood bolognese (made with ground seafood instead of meat) or any one of the specialties ranging from simple fried Ipswich clams to pan-seared bass in an unctuous lobster cream sauce. The sea bass chowder with bacon is a delectable alternative to the common clam-based versions around town. Steak and chicken are available for culinary landlubbers. $ *Average main: $31 ⊠ 761 Boylston St., Back Bay ☎ 617/267–4000 ⊕ www.atlanticfishco.com ✛ C5.*

$$ ✕ **The Butcher Shop.** Chef Barbara Lynch has remade the classic meat
AMERICAN market as a polished wine bar–cum–hangout, and it's just the kind of high-quality, low-pretense spot every neighborhood could use. Stop in for a glass of wine and a casual, quick snack of homemade prosciutto and salami or a plate of artisanal cheeses. Or linger longer over dinner specials like tagliatelle bolognese and juicy prime rib-eye. Reservations are accepted for parties of six or more. $ *Average main: $19 ⊠ 552 Tremont St., South End ☎ 617/423–4800 ⊕ www. thebutchershopboston.com Ⓜ Back Bay/South End ✛ E6.*

$$$$ ✕ **Clio.** Years ago, when Ken Oringer opened his snazzy leopard skin–
FRENCH lined hot spot in the tasteful boutique Eliot Hotel, the hordes were
Fodor'sChoice fighting over reservations. A 2012 face-lift doubled the size of the bar
★ and made things considerably less formal, save for the food. Oppulent offerings like foie gras, Maine lobster, and Kobe sirloin enhanced with flavor-rich foams, emulsions, and bubbles still dominate the menu, along with a few fail-safe options, like crispy chicken and Scottish salmon. A magnet for romantics and die-hard foodies, the place continues to serve some of the city's most fanciful, well-crafted meals. Cocktail aficionados will appreciate the creative and sophisticated bar offerings. $ *Average main: $39 ⊠ Eliot Hotel, 370 Commonwealth Ave., Back Bay ☎ 617/536–7200 ⊕ www.cliorestaurant.com ⌖ Reservations essential ☾ No lunch Ⓜ Hynes ✛ B5.*

$$ ✕ **Eastern Standard Kitchen and Drinks.** A vivid red awning beckons
AMERICAN patrons of this spacious brasserie-style restaurant. The bar area and red
Fodor'sChoice banquettes are filled most nights with Boston's power players (members
★ of the Red Sox management are known to stop in), thirtysomethings, and students from the nearby universities all noshing on raw-bar specialties and comfort dishes such as lamb-sausage rigatoni, rib eye, and burgers. It's a Sunday brunch hot spot, especially on game days (the Big Green Monster is a very short walk away). The cocktail list is one of the best in town, filled with old classics and new concoctions, and in addition to a boutique wine list there is a reserve list for rare beers. A covered, heated patio offers alfresco dining year-round. $ *Average main: $24 ⊠ 528 Commonwealth Ave., Kenmore Sq. ☎ 617/532–9100 ⊕ www.easternstandardboston.com Ⓜ Kenmore ✛ A5.*

$ ✕ **Flour Bakery + Café.** When folks in the South End need coffee, a sand-
AMERICAN wich, or a raspberry crumb bar—or just a place to sit and chat—they
FAMILY come here. A communal table in the middle acts as a gathering spot,
Fodor'sChoice around which diners enjoy homemade soups, hearty bean and grain sal-
★ ads, and specialty sandwiches like grilled chicken with Brie and arugula, or a BLT with applewood-smoked bacon. Of course, it's the irresistible sweets, like pecan sticky buns, lemon tarts, and double chocolate cookies that require a trip to Flour, which has proven so popular that owner Joanne Chang has opened three more locations—in the Fort Point

BEST BETS FOR BOSTON DINING

Channel neighborhood, Cambridge (by MIT), and Back Bay. $ Average main: $7 ⊠ 1595 Washington St., South End ☎ 617/267–4300 ⊕ www.flourbakery.com ⌖ Reservations not accepted Ⓜ Mass. Ave. ✢ E6. $ Average main: $7 ⊠ 12 Farnsworth St., Fort Point Channel ☎ 617/338–4333 Ⓜ South Station ✢ E6.

$$ · AMERICAN · × **Franklin Café.** This place has jumped to the head of the class by keeping things simple yet effective. (The litmus test: local chefs gather here to wind down after work.) Try the succulent turkey meatloaf off the regular menu or the tomato-roasted eggplant offered on both the vegetarian and gluten-free menus. The vibe is generally more that of a bar than a restaurant (hence the many bartender awards), so be forewarned that it can get loud. The wait for a table (there are only 7 booths and 2 tables) can be downright impossible on weekend nights, and desserts are not served. On the upside, food is served until 1:30 am and cocktails until 2 am. $ Average main: $18 ⊠ 278 Shawmut Ave., South End ☎ 617/350–0010 ⊕ www.franklincafe.com ⌖ Reservations not accepted ⊘ No lunch Ⓜ South End ✢ E6.

$$$$
STEAKHOUSE

✕ **Grill 23 & Bar.** Pinstripe suits, dark paneling, Persian rugs, and waiters in white jackets give this single-location steak house a posh demeanor. The food is anything but predictable, with dishes such as seasonally dressed tartars (steak and tuna) and weekly cuts of all-natural beef like the 14-ounce dry-aged New York sirloin. Seafood specialties such as spicy scallops with mushroom dumplings and baby artichokes give beef sales a run for their money. Desserts, such as the decadent Valrhona chocolate layer cake, rank far above those of the average steak house. Make sure to leave room. Ⓢ *Average main: $40* ✉ *161 Berkeley St., Back Bay* ☎ *617/542–2255* ⊕ *grill23.com* ⊙ *No lunch* Ⓜ *Back Bay/South End* ✛ *E5.*

$$$
FRENCH
Fodor's Choice
★

✕ **Hamersley's Bistro.** Famous for wearing a Red Sox cap instead of a toque, Gordon Hamersley has earned a national reputation, thanks to signature dishes such as roast chicken, spicy halibut, and souffléed lemon custard. His devotion to locally sourced, market-fresh ingredients makes dining at his restaurant a sheer joy, no matter what the season. Dishes, including several vegetarian options, arrive carefully prepared and lusty yet unpretentious, which explains why he's one of Boston's great chefs. The warm, butter-yellow space has a full bar with two tables for walk-ins, a small dining room, and a larger main room that looks into the open kitchen. Brunch is served Sunday. Ⓢ *Average main: $30* ✉ *553 Tremont St., South End* ☎ *617/423–2700* ⊕ *www.hamersleysbistro.com* ⊙ *No lunch* Ⓜ *Back Bay/South End* ✛ *B6.*

$$$$
FRENCH
Fodor's Choice
★

✕ **L'Espalier.** In 2008 L'Espalier left its longtime home in a Back Bay town house, reopening beside the Mandarin Oriental Hotel. The new locale, with its floor-to-ceiling windows and modern decor, looks decidedly different. But chef-owner Frank McClelland's dishes—from caviar and roasted foie gras to garlicky beef tenderloin with braised short ribs and wild mushrooms—are as elegant as ever. In the evening a three-course prix-fixe, six-course seasonal degustation, and over 10-course chef's journey menu tempt discriminating diners. A budget-minded power lunch as well as à la carte options are available weekday afternoons. Finger sandwiches and sublime sweets are served for weekend tea; the salon menu hits the spot for post-work drinks and nibbles, like a perfectly ripe fromage flight from the city's premier cheese trolley. Ⓢ *Average main: $125* ✉ *774 Boylston St., Back Bay* ☎ *617/262–3023* ⊕ *www.lespalier.com* ⌂ *Reservations essential* Ⓜ *Copley* ✛ *C5.*

$$$$
FRENCH
Fodor's Choice
★

✕ **Mistral.** Polished service and upscale yet unpretentious dishes, like beef-tenderloin pizza topped with mashed potatoes and white-truffle oil, make Mistral a perennial South End hot spot. Grab a table by the arched, floor-to-ceiling windows or a seat at the always-buzzing bar—either way, there'll be plenty to see in this airy white room with a Provençal-theme decor. Boston's fashionable set has been coming here for years, which speaks to chef Jamie Mammano's consistently excellent French-Mediterranean cuisine with fail-safe favorites like tuna tartare, duck with cherries, and French Dover sole. The menu rarely changes—but no one's complaining. Unlike many trendy restaurants, Mistral sticks to what it does best. Brunch is served on Sunday. Ⓢ *Average main: $36* ✉ *223 Columbus Ave., South End* ☎ *617/867–9300* ⊕ *mistralbistro.com* ⊙ *No lunch* ✛ *E5.*

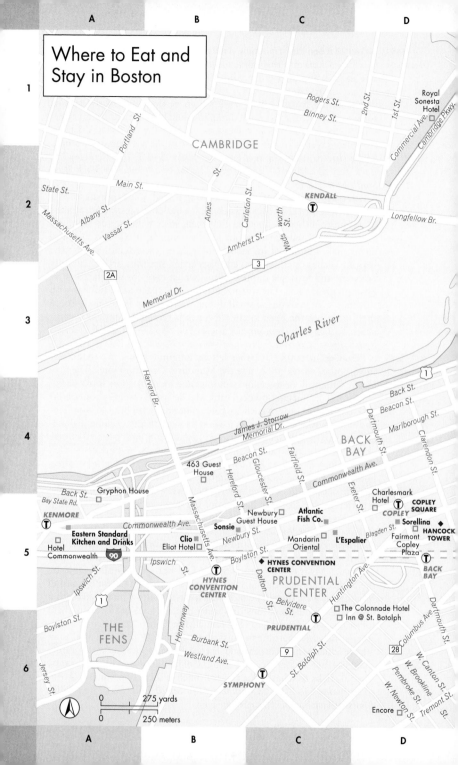

Where to Eat and Stay in Boston

A · **B** · **C** · **D**

1

Rogers St.
Binney St.
2nd St.
1st St.
Commercial Ave.
Royal Sonesta Hotel
Cambridge Pkwy.

CAMBRIDGE

Portland St.
St.

2

State St.
Main St.
Albany St.
Vassar St.
Ames St.
Carleton St.
worth St.
Wads St.
KENDALL
Longfellow Br.
Massachusetts Ave.
Amherst St.
3

2A
Memorial Dr.
Charles River

3

Harvard Br.

4

James J. Storrow Memorial Dr.
Beacon St.
Fairfield St.
Back St.
Beacon St.
Dartmouth St.
Marlborough St.
Clarendon St.
BACK BAY
463 Guest House
Beacon St.
Gloucester St.
Hereford St.
Exeter St.

Back St.
Bay State Rd.
Gryphon House
KENMORE
Commonwealth Ave.
Massachusetts Ave.
Newbury Guest House
Sonsie
Newbury St.
Atlantic Fish Co.
Charlesmark Hotel
COPLEY
COPLEY SQUARE
Hotel Commonwealth
Eastern Standard Kitchen and Drinks
90
Clio
Eliot Hotel
Mandarin Oriental
L'Espalier
Blagden St.
Sorellina
Fairmont Copley Plaza
HANCOCK TOWER
BACK BAY
5

Ipswich St.
Boylston St.
1
Ipswich
Boylston St.
Hemenway
Dalton St.
HYNES CONVENTION CENTER
HYNES CONVENTION CENTER
PRUDENTIAL CENTER
Huntington Ave.
Belvidere St.
PRUDENTIAL
The Colonnade Hotel
Inn @ St. Botolph
Dartmouth St.
Columbus Ave.
28
W. Canton St.
W. Brookline
Pembroke St.
W. Newton St.
Tremont St.

THE FENS
Burbank St.
Westland Ave.
9
St. Botolph St.

6

Jersey St.
SYMPHONY
Encore

0 — 275 yards
0 — 250 meters

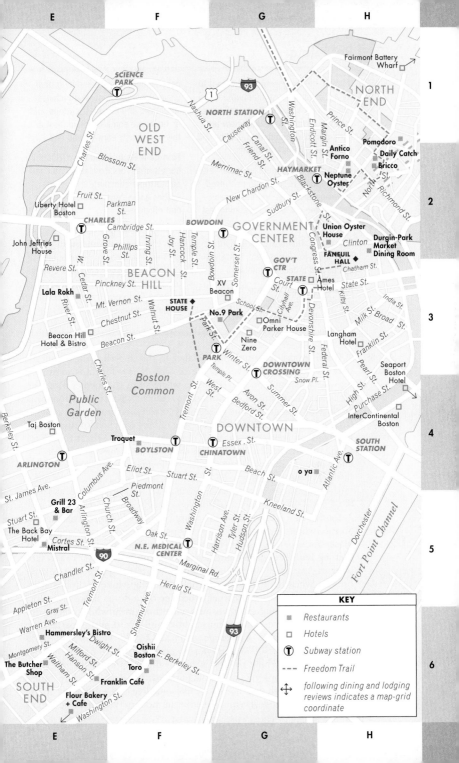

CLOSE UP

Refueling

If you're on the go, you might want to try a local chain restaurant where you can stop for a quick bite or get some takeout. The places listed below are fairly priced, committed to quality, and use decent, fresh ingredients.

B.Good. This chainlet's avocado- and salsa-topped veggie burgers, baked sweet-potato fries, and sesame-ginger chicken salad are redefining fast food in Boston.

Bertucci's. Thin-crust pizzas fly fast from the brick ovens here, along with pastas and a decent tiramisu.

BoLoCo. For quick, cheap, healthful, and high-quality wraps and burritos, this is easily the city's most dependable (and also locally based) chain. BoLoCo's menu also includes smoothies and breakfast options, and its hours are some of the longest in this notoriously early-to-bed city.

Finagle A Bagel. Find fresh, doughy bagels in flavors from jalapeño cheddar to triple chocolate, plus sandwiches and salads. Service is swift and efficient.

UBurger. Better-than-average burgers with toppings that lean toward the gourmet (sautéed mushrooms, blue cheese) and a great chocolate frappe (Boston-ese for milkshake) make this spot the East Coast's answer to California's much-loved In-n-Out.

$$$ JAPANESE

🍴 **Oishii Boston.** Although the entrance to this superb sushi restaurant may elude you, simply follow the crowds of raw fish fans streaming into the sleek, gray industrial space, where sushi chef-owner Ting Yen turns succulent morsels of seafood into edible enchantment. From tuna tartar with sesame oil and golden caviar to crunchy tempura oysters, from lobster salad maki to grilled Wagyu beef with shallot-sake sauce, this larger, tonier incarnation of Yen's über-popular 14-seat restaurant Oishii in Chestnut Hill allows him to spread his wings. The vibe is hip and so are the diners. While the delectable nine-course *omakase* (chef's tasting) is quite a splurge ($150), the set lunch specials (*kaiseki*) offer fabulous value. [$] *Average main: $28* ✉ *1166 Washington St., South End* ☎ *617/482–8868* 🌐 *www.oishiiboston.com* 🕒 *Closed Mon.* ✥ *F6.*

$$ AMERICAN

🍴 **Sonsie.** Café society blossoms along Newbury Street, particularly at Sonsie, where a well-heeled crowd sips coffee up front or angles for places at the bar. Lunch and dinner dishes, such as charcoal duck breast and leg with brown rice and five-spice turnips, are basic bistro fare with an American twist. The restaurant is a terrific place for weekend brunch, when the light pours through the long windows, and is at its most vibrant in warm weather, when the open doors make for colorful people-watching. A downstairs wine room meanwhile offers more intimacy. The late-night menu (nightly until 12:30 am) is perfect for after-hours cravings. [$] *Average main: $23* ✉ *327 Newbury St., Back Bay* ☎ *617/351–2500* 🌐 *sonsieboston.com* [M] *Hynes* ✥ *B5.*

$$$$ ITALIAN

🍴 **Sorellina.** Everything about this upscale Italian spot is oversized, from its space near Copley Square to its portions. The sexy, all-white dining room is filled with well-heeled locals (some live in the gorgeous apartment building above it) who come for the modern twist on basic Italian dishes. Grilled octopus with squid-ink couscous, various versions of carpaccio, and the signature tuna tartare dot the list of starters, while veal saltimbocca with wild mushrooms and truffled whipped potato takes the spotlight. Just save room for dessert: it's always a highlight here. $ *Average main: $41* ⊠ *1 Huntington Ave., Back Bay* ☎ *617/412–4600* ⊕ *www.sorellinaboston.com* ☉ *No lunch* Ⓜ *Copley, Back Bay* ✛ *D5.*

$$$ ✕**Toro.** The opening buzz from chefs Ken Oringer and Jamie Bisson-
SPANISH nette's tapas joint still remains—for good reason. Small plates such
Fodor'sChoice as grilled corn with aioli and cotija cheese are hefty enough to make
★ a meal out of a few, or you can share the regular or vegetarian paella with a group. An all-Spanish wine list complements the plates. Crowds have been known to wait it out for more than an hour for dinner. Aim to go for lunch during the week for a less hetic, but just as satisfying experience. $ *Average main: $30* ⊠ *1704 Washington St., South End* ☎ *617/536–4300* ⊕ *www.toro-restaurant.com* ⌫ *Reservations not accepted* Ⓜ *Mass. Ave.* ✛ *F6.*

$$$$ ✕**Troquet.** Despite boasting what might well be Boston's longest wine
FRENCH FUSION list, with nearly 500 vintages (more than 45 of which are available by
Fodor'sChoice the glass), plus an unobstructed view of the Common, this French fusion
★ spot flies somewhat under the radar. Still, locals know that Troquet offers all the ingredients for a lovely evening: a quietly elegant dining room, decadent dishes like bacon-wrapped veal sirloin and sticky-toffee pudding, and a knowledgeable yet unpretentious staff. The menu includes by-the-glass wine recommendations after each entrée, so you're sure to sip something delicious and appropriate. $ *Average main: $37* ⊠ *140 Boylston St., Back Bay* ☎ *617/695–9463* ⊕ *www.troquetboston. com* ☉ *Closed Sun. and Mon. No lunch* Ⓜ *Boylston* ✛ *F4.*

BEACON HILL

$$ ✕**Lala Rokh.** A rotating gallery of Persian art, ranging from miniatures
MIDDLE EASTERN and medieval maps to modern photographs, adorns the walls of this beautifully detailed fantasy of food and art. The cuisine focuses on the Azerbaijanian corner of what is now northwest Iran, including exotically spiced specialties and dishes such as eggplant puree, *pollo* (rice dishes), kebabs, *fesanjoon* (pomegranate-walnut sauce), and lamb stews. The staff obviously enjoys explaining the menu, and the wine list is well selected for foods that often defy wine matches. $ *Average main: $22* ⊠ *97 Mt. Vernon St., Beacon Hill* ☎ *617/720–5511* ⊕ *www. lalarokh.com* ☉ *No lunch weekends* Ⓜ *Charles/MGH* ✛ *E3.*

$$$$ ✕**No. 9 Park.** The stellar cuisine at Chef Barbara Lynch's first restaurant
EUROPEAN continues to draw plenty of well-deserved attention from its place in
Fodor'sChoice the shadow of the State House's golden dome. Settle into the plush but
★ unpretentious dining room and indulge in pumpkin risotto with rare lamb or the memorably rich prune-stuffed gnocchi drizzled with bits of foie gras, the latter of which is always offered even if you don't see it on the menu. The wine list bobs and weaves into new territory, but is always well chosen, and the savvy bartenders are of the classic ilk, so you'll find plenty of classics and very few cloying, dessertlike sips here. $ *Average main: $39* ⊠ *9 Park St., Beacon Hill* ☎ *617/742–9991* ⊕ *www.no9park.com* Ⓜ *Park St.* ✛ *G3.*

DOWNTOWN

$$$$ JAPANESE Fodor's Choice ★ 🍴 **o ya.** Despite its side-street location and hidden door, o ya isn't exactly a secret: dining critics from the *New York Times*, *Bon Appetit*, and *Food & Wine* have all named this tiny, improvisational sushi spot among the best in the country. Chef Tim Cushman's nigiri menu features squid-ink bubbles, homemade potato chips—even foie gras. Other dishes offer a nod to New England, such as the braised pork with Boston baked beans and grilled lobster with a light shiso tempura. Cushman's wife Nancy oversees an extensive sake list that includes sparkling and aged varieties. [$] *Average main: $36* ✉ *9 East St., Leather District* ☎ *617/654–9900* 🌐 *www.oyarestaurantboston.com* 🕒 *Closed Sun. and Mon. No lunch* [M] *South Station* ✥ *G4.*

GOVERNMENT CENTER/FANEUIL HALL

$$ AMERICAN 🍴 **Durgin-Park Market Dining Room.** You should be hungry enough to cope with enormous portions, yet not so hungry you can't tolerate a long wait (or sharing a table with others). Durgin-Park was serving its same hearty New England fare (Indian pudding, baked beans, corned beef and cabbage, and a prime rib that hangs over the edge of the plate) back when Faneuil Hall was a working market instead of a tourist attraction. The service is as brusque as it was when fishmongers and boat captains dined here, but that's just part of its charm. [$] *Average main: $19* ✉ *340 Faneuil Hall Market Pl., North Market Bldg., Faneuil Hall* ☎ *617/227–2038* 🌐 *www.arkrestaurants.com/durgin_park.html* [M] *Government Center* ✥ *H2.*

$$$ SEAFOOD 🍴 **Union Oyster House.** Established in 1826, this is Boston's oldest continuing restaurant, and almost every tourist considers it a must-see. If you like, you can have what Daniel Webster had—oysters on the half shell at the ground-floor raw bar, which is the oldest part of the restaurant and still the best. The rooms at the top of the narrow staircase are dark and have low ceilings—very Ye Olde New England—and plenty of nonrestaurant history. The small tables and chairs (as well as the endless lines and kitschy nostalgia) are as much a part of the charm as the simple and decent (albeit pricey) food. On weekends, especially in summer, make reservations a few days ahead or risk enduring waits of historic proportions. There is valet parking after 5:30 pm Monday through Saturday. One cautionary note: Locals hardly ever eat here. [$] *Average main: $25* ✉ *41 Union St., Government Center* ☎ *617/227–2750* 🌐 *www.unionoysterhouse.com* [M] *Haymarket* ✥ *H2.*

NORTH END

$ ITALIAN Fodor's Choice ★ 🍴 **Antico Forno.** Many of the menu choices here come from the eponymous wood-burning brick oven, which turns out surprisingly delicate pizzas simply topped with tomato and fresh buffalo mozzarella. Though its pizzas receive top billing, Antico excels at a variety of Italian country dishes. Don't overlook the hearty baked dishes and handmade pastas; the specialty, gnocchi, is rich and creamy but light. The joint is cramped and noisy, but also homey and comfortable—which means that your meal will resemble a raucous dinner with an adopted Italian family. $ *Average main: $17* ⊠ *93 Salem St., North End* ☎ *617/723–6733* ⊕ *www.anticofornoboston.com* Ⓜ *Haymarket* ✛ *H2.*

$$$$

ITALIAN

✕**Bricco.** A sophisticated but unpretentious enclave of nouveau Italian, Bricco has carved out quite a following. And no wonder: the handmade pastas alone are argument for a reservation. Simple but well-balanced main courses such as roast chicken marinated in seven spices and a brimming *brodetto* (fish stew) with half a lobster and a pile of seafood may linger in your memory. You're likely to want to linger in the warm room, too, gazing through the floor-to-ceiling windows while sipping a glass of Sangiovese from the Italian and American wine list. $ *Average main: $40* ⊠ *241 Hanover St., North End* ☎ *617/248–6800* ⊕ *www. bricco.com* ⏿ *Reservations essential* ☽ *No lunch* Ⓜ *Haymarket* ✛ *H2.*

$

SEAFOOD

✕**Daily Catch.** You've just got to love this shoebox-size place—for the noise, the intimacy, the complete absence of pretense, and, above all, the food, which proved so popular, it spawned two other locations (one in Brookline and another in Boston's Seaport area). Compact and brightly lighted, this storefront restaurant has been a local staple for 40 years and for good reason. With garlic and olive oil forming the foundation for almost every dish, this cheerful, bustling spot specializes in big skillets of calamari dishes, black squid-ink pastas, and linguine with clam sauce that would seem less perfect if served on fine white china versus the actual cooking pan that's placed in front of you with an efficient flourish as soon as it leaves the stove. $ *Average main: $15* ⊠ *323 Hanover St., North End* ☎ *617/523–8567* ⊕ *www.dailycatch.com* ⏿ *Reservations not accepted* ▭ *No credit cards* Ⓜ *Haymarket* ✛ *H2.*

$$$

SEAFOOD

Fodor's Choice

★

✕**Neptune Oyster.** This *piccolo* oyster bar, the first of its kind in the neighborhood, has only 22 chairs, but the long marble bar adorned with mirrors has extra seating for 15 more patrons, who can watch the oyster shuckers deftly undo handfuls of bivalves to savor by the dozen or on a *plateau di frutti di mare,* a gleaming tower of oysters and other raw-bar items piled over ice that you can order from the slip of paper they pass out listing each day's crustacean options. Dishes change seasonally, but a couple of year-round favorites include the North End Cioppino (fish stew) and the lobster roll that, hot or cold, overflows with meat. Service is prompt even when it gets busy (as it is most of the time). Go early to avoid a long wait. $ *Average main: $32* ⊠ *63 Salem St., North End* ☎ *617/742–3474* ⊕ *www.neptuneoyster.com* ⏿ *Reservations not accepted* Ⓜ *Haymarket* ✛ *H2.*

$$

ITALIAN

✕**Pomodoro.** This teeny trattoria—just nine tables—is worth the wait, with excellent country Italian favorites such as rigatoni with white beans and arugula, a veal scaloppini with sweet onion balsamic glaze, and a light-but-filling zuppa di pesce. The best choice could well be the classic linguini, accompanied by a bottle of Vernaccia. Pomodoro doesn't serve dessert, but it's easy to find great espresso and pastries in the cafés on Hanover Street. $ *Average main: $24* ⊠ *319 Hanover St., North End* ☎ *617/367–4348* ⏿ *Reservations essential* ▭ *No credit cards* ☽ *No lunch weekdays* Ⓜ *Haymarket* ✛ *H1.*

CAMBRIDGE

Use the coordinate (⊕ B2) at the end of each listing to locate a site on the Where to Eat and Stay in Cambridge map.

$
AMERICAN
Fodor's Choice ★

🍴 **All Star Sandwich Bar.** This brightly colored place with about a dozen tables has a strict definition of what makes a sandwich: no wraps. The owners have put together a list of classics, like crispy, overstuffed Reubens and beef on weck, which are served quickly from an open kitchen. Their famous Atomic Meatloaf Meltdown has been highlighted on a number of foodie networks. Not into sandwiches? Soups, salads, a burger, and chili are available, along with a small selection of beer and wine. If pies are more your thing, sister restaurant All-Star Pizza Bar is just across the street. [$] *Average main: $9* ✉ *1245 Cambridge St.* ☎ *617/868–3065* 🌐 *www.allstarsandwichbar.com* ✍ *Reservations not accepted* [M] *Central/Inman* ⊕ *A4.*

$$
MODERN AMERICAN
Fodor's Choice ★

🍴 **Area Four.** A bona fide hit from day one, everything at this glass-enclosed eatery in the avante-garde Technology Square area is scrumptious–from the morning sticky buns and excellent dark coffee at the cafe to the clam-bacon pizza in the casual dining room. A central wood-fired oven turns out chewy-crusted pies and small skillets of mac & cheese with croissant crumbs and crackly-skinned chicken over wilted greens. You will find only local, seasonal, and sustainable cooking here. [$] *Average main: $18* ✉ *500 Technology Sq.* ☎ *617/758-4444* 🌐 *www.areafour.com* ⊕ *B6.*

$$
AMERICAN

🍴 **East Coast Grill and Raw Bar.** Owner-chef-author Chris Schlesinger built his national reputation on grilled foods and red-hot condiments. The Texas style beef brisket and North Carolina shredded pork are still here, but this restaurant has made an extraordinary play to establish itself in the front ranks of fish restaurants. Spices and condiments are more restrained, and Schlesinger has compiled a wine list bold and flavorful enough to match the highly spiced food. The dining space is completely informal. In addition to Saturday lunch, weekends include a killer Sunday brunch (complete with cornbread-crusted French toast and a do-it-yourself Bloody Mary bar). [$] *Average main: $24* ✉ *1271 Cambridge St.* ☎ *617/491–6568* 🌐 *www.eastcoastgrill.net* [M] *Central* ⊕ *A4.*

$$$
SOUTHERN
Fodor's Choice ★

🍴 **Hungry Mother.** You'll forget you're well above the Mason-Dixon line when you enter this Kendall Square gem, where Virginia-born chef Barry Maiden whips up Southern-inspired comfort food with a hint of French sophistication—and New England ingredients. From fried green tomatoes to cornbread with sorghum butter, from Berkshire pork loin to apple bread pudding, this cozy two-story bistro serves up decidedly soul-warming fare, as well as excellent house-mixed drinks, such as the "#43," a concotion of rye, tawny Port, maple syrup, and bitters. [$] *Average main: $26* ✉ *233 Cardinal Medeiros Ave., Kendall Square* ☎ *617/499–0090* ⏲ *Closed Mon. No lunch Sat.–Thu.* [M] *Kendall/MIT* ⊕ *B6.*

$$$
MEDITERRANEAN
Fodor's Choice ★

🍴 **Oleana.** With three restaurants (including Sofra in Cambridge and Sarma in Somerville), and a cookbook to her name, chef-owner Ana Sortun is one of the city's culinary treasures. So is Oleana, which specializes in zesty Eastern Mediterranean *meze* (small plates) plumped up with fresh-picked produce from her husband's nearby Siena Farms. Although the menu changes often, look for the hot, crispy fried mussels starter

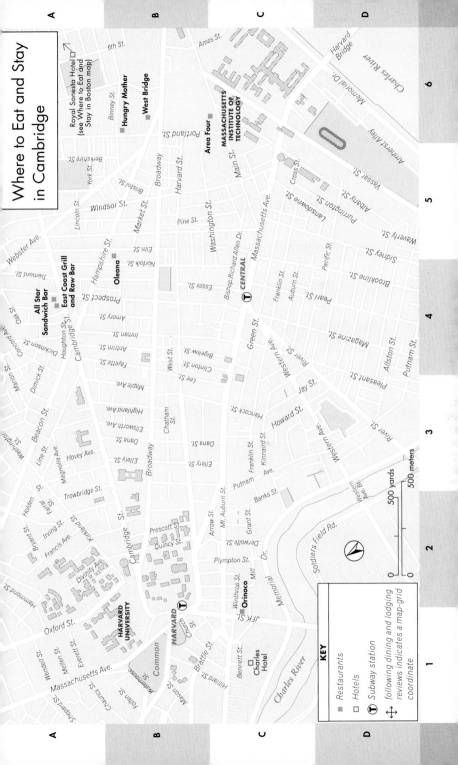

Where to Eat and Stay in Cambridge

Royal Sonesta Hotel (see Where to Eat and Stay in Boston map)

6th St.
Binney St.
Berkshire St.
York St.
Lincoln St.
Webster Ave.
Tremont St.
Oak St.
Concord Ave.
Marion St.
Dickinson St.
Dimick St.
Beacon St.
Line St.
Washington St.
Magnolia Ave.
Hovey Ave.
Trowbridge St.
Holden St.
Farr St.
Irving St.
Francis Ave.
Kirkland St.
Hammond St.
Oxford St.
Wendell St.
Mellen St.
Everett St.
Massachusetts Ave.
Chauncy St.
Shepard St.
Mason St.
Waterhouse St.
Bryant St.
Divinity Ave.
Sacramento St.

Hungry Mother
West Bridge

Binney St.
Broadway
Harvard St.
Windsor St.
Market St.
Pine St.
Hampshire St.
Elm St.
Norfolk St.
Oleana
Prospect St.
Amory St.
Inman St.
Antrim St.
Fayette St.
West St.
Clinton St.
Bigelow St.
Lee St.
Maple Ave.
Highland Ave.
Ellsworth Ave.
Dana St.
Chatham St.
Dana St.
Ellery St.
Broadway
Prescott St.
Quincy St.
Cambridge St.
Houghton St.
Cambridge St.

All Star Sandwich Bar
East Coast Grill and Raw Bar

Ames St.

Area Four

Portland St.
MASSACHUSETTS INSTITUTE OF TECHNOLOGY
Main St.
Cross St.
Landsdowne St.
Purrington St.
Albany St.
Vassar St.
Sidney St.
Pacific St.
Franklin St.
Auburn St.
Brookline St.
Pearl St.
Magazine St.
Allston St.
Putnam St.
Pleasant St.
River St.
Western Ave.
Jay St.
Howard St.
Hancock St.
Franklin St.
Kinnard St.
Putnam Ave.
Banks St.
Mt. Auburn St.
Grant St.
Arrow St.
Dewolfe St.
Plympton St.
Winthrop St.
JFK St.
Mill
Memorial Dr.
Soldiers Field Rd.
Western Ave. Br.
River St.

Washington St.
Essex St.
Bishop Richard Allen Dr.
Green St.
Massachusetts Ave.
Western Ave.

T CENTRAL

Waverly St.
Harvard Bridge
Memorial Dr.
Amherst Alley
Charles River

T HARVARD
Church St.
Orinoco
Brattle St.
Hilliard St.
Bennett St.
Mason St.
Harvard Common
HARVARD UNIVERSITY

□ Charles Hotel

Charles River

N
0   500 yards
0   500 meters

KEY
- ■ Restaurants
- □ Hotels
- **T** Subway station
- ↔ following dining and lodging reviews indicates a map-grid coordinate

A   B   C   D

1   2   3   4   5   6

and the smoky eggplant puree beside tamarind-glazed beef. Lamb gets jacked up with Turkish spices, while duck gets accented with saffron and hazelnuts. In warm weather the back patio garden is a hidden utopia. [$] *Average main: $26* ✉ *134 Hampshire St.* ☎ *617/661–0505* 🌐 *www.oleanarestaurant.com* ✍ *Reservations essential* ⏲ *No lunch* [M] *Central* ✥ *B5.*

$ LATIN AMERICAN Fodor's Choice ★

🍴 **Orinoco.** It's easy to miss this red clapboard, Latin American restaurant located down an alleyway in Harvard Square. Don't. Owner Andres Banger's dream to bring bountiful plates of super-fresh family fare from his home country of Venezuala to Cambridge (as well as Brookline and the South End), will reward you with delectable, palm-sized *arepas*, or crispy, hot cornflour pockets stuffed with beans, cheese, and pork; *pabellon criollo*, moist shredded beef with stewed beans, rice, and plantains; and red chile adobo-marinated, charred *pollo* (chicken). Empanadas, hearty salads, and stuffed French-bread sandwiches at lunch, along with a small selection of wine and beer, round out the very affordable menu at this casual eatery. When weather permits, ask for a seat on the hidden back patio, a quiet flower- and fountain-filled oasis that makes the rest of the world feel very far away. [$] *Average main: $17* ✉ *56 JFK St., Harvard Sq.* ☎ *617/354–6900* 🌐 *www.orinocokitchen.com* ✍ *Reservations not accepted* ⏲ *Closed Mon.* ✥ *C1*

$$$ MODERN AMERICAN Fodor's Choice ★

🍴 **West Bridge.** Prosecco on tap and serious cocktails may draw area techies, MIT folks, and neighborhood hipsters into this happening white, window-filled room with exposed ceiling pipes in Kendall Square, but it's the small and large plates of lusty, flavor-rich food that keeps them lingering. The gooey duck egg in a jar served over potato puree with crisp duck skin is a must; also try the roasted cauliflower with hazelnuts and tawny-skinned roast chicken for two. Many menu offerings can be tweaked for vegetarians and a broad selection of unusual beers and wines by the glass means every bite will have a great sip to match. [$] *Average main: $26* ✉ *1 Kendall Sq., Kendall Sq.* ☎ *617/945–0221* 🌐 *www.westbridgerestaurant.com* ⏲ *No lunch weekends* ✥ *B6.*

WHERE TO STAY

Updated by Frances Folsom

At one time great lodging was scarce in Boston. If you were a persnickety blue blood in town to visit relatives, you checked into the Charles or the old Ritz on Newbury. If you were a parent in town to see your kid graduate from one of the city's many universities, you suffered through a stay at a run-down chain. And if you were a young couple in town for a little romance, well, you could just forget it. A dearth of suitable rooms practically defined Boston. Oh, how things have changed.

In the early 2000s, Boston finally got wise to modernization, and a rush of new construction took the local hotel scene by storm. Sleek, boutique accommodations began inviting guests to Cambridge and Downtown, areas once relegated to alumni and business traveler sets. New, mega-luxury lodgings like the Mandarin Oriental and the Taj (the latter, in that old Ritz spot) infiltrated posh Back Bay, while high-end, hipster-friendly spots like the W Boston and Ames are drawing visitors to

	NEIGHBORHOOD VIBE	PROS	CONS
Beacon Hill and Boston Common	Old brick and stone buildings host luxe boutique hotels and B&Bs on the hill or along busy, preppy Charles Street; some skyscraper lodging right on Boston Common.	Safe, quaint area with lamp-lit streets; chain-free upscale shopping and dining; outdoor fun abounds in the park; good T access.	Street parking is extremely hard to come by; not budget friendly; very close to noisy hospital; hills can be very steep.
Downtown	The city's financial center hums with activity and busy hotels during the week; new boutique lodging is moving in to compete with the big-box chains.	Excellent area for business travelers; frequent low weekend rates; good T and bus access; walking distance to Theater District and some museums.	All but dead at night; expensive garage parking during the day; Downtown Crossing is mobbed at lunchtime and on weekends; poorly marked streets.
The Back Bay	High-priced hotels in the city's poshest neighborhood, home to excellent shops, restaurants, bars, spas, and salons. Commonwealth Avenue is lined with historic mansions.	Easy, central location; safe, beautiful area to walk around at night; ample T access; excellent people-watching.	Rooms, shopping, and eating can be ridiculously expensive; Newbury Street is overcrowded with tourists on weekends.
The South End	Small, funky lodgings in a very hip and happening (and gay-friendly) area packed with awesome independent restaurants and shops.	The city's best dining scene; easy T and bus access; myriad parks; walking distance from the Back Bay and Downtown; safe along the main avenues at night.	Some bordering blocks turn seedy after dusk; difficult street parking (and few garages); only a handful of hotel options.
The Fenway and Kenmore Square	A sampling of large and small hotels and inns, plus two hostels; the area is a mix of students, young professionals, and die-hard Sox fans.	Close to Fenway Park (home of the Red Sox); up-and-coming dining scene; less expensive than most 'hoods; very accessible by T.	Impossible street parking on game days (and pricey garages); expect big crowds for concert and sporting events; some bars are loud and tacky.
Boston Outskirts	Mostly midsize chain hotels in student neighborhoods full of coffee shops, convenience stores, and rowdy college bars.	Serviceable airport lodging near Logan; cheap rates on rooms in Brighton, Allston, and parts of Brookline; easier driving than Downtown.	No overnight street parking in Brookline; far from Boston center and museums, shopping, and the river; some areas get dicey at night; T rides into the city proper can take an hour.
Cambridge	A mix of grand and small hotels pepper the hip, multi-university neighborhood; expect loads of young freethinkers and efficient (if laid-back) service.	Hallowed academia; verdant squares; good low- and high-cost eating and lodging; excellent neighborhood restaurants; very few chain anythings.	Spotty T access; less of a city feel; a few areas can be very quiet and slightly dodgy at night; lots of one-way streets make driving difficult.

3

up-and-coming areas in Downtown. Even mostly residential areas like the South End now draw discerning boarders, thanks to the revamped Chandler and the nearby Inn@St. Botolph.

Speaking of revamped, it seems that nearly every hotel in town just got a face-lift. From spruced up decor (good-bye, grandma's bedspread; hello, puffy white duvets) to hopping restaurant-bars to new spas and fitness centers, Boston's lodgings are feeling the competitive heat and acting accordingly. You don't just get a room anymore—you get an experience.

Many properties have stellar weekend deals, so you may be able to try an upscale Fodor's Choice even if you thought it was out of your budget.

Use the coordinate (✛ B2) at the end of each listing to locate a site on the Where to Eat and Stay in Boston map.

Prices in the reviews are the lowest cost of a standard double room in high season.

BACK BAY

$
B&B/INN

🛏 **463 Beacon Street Guest House.** Though there's no sign on the door of this handsome brownstone, international visitors and college students have discovered the rooming house—and quickly warmed to its slightly quirky, old-auntie charm. **Pros:** Newbury Street is three blocks away; the Charles River and Esplanade are one block in the other direction. **Cons:** some rooms have a two-person occupancy limit, and because of the layout, the house isn't appropriate for children under 7. Ⓢ *Rooms from: $125* ✉ *463 Beacon St., Back Bay* ☎ *617/536–1302* ⊕ *www.463beacon.com* ⇲ *20 rooms, 17 with bath* ⭘ *No meals* Ⓜ *Hynes* ✛ *B4.*

$$
HOTEL
Fodor'sChoice
★

🛏 **Charlesmark Hotel.** Hipsters and romantics who'd rather spend their cash on a great meal than a hotel bill have put this late-19th-century former residential row house on the map. **Pros:** fantastic price for the location; free Wi-Fi. **Cons:** some might feel crowded by compact rooms and hallways. Ⓢ *Rooms from: $239* ✉ *655 Boylston St., Back Bay* ☎ *617/247–1212* ⊕ *www.thecharlesmarkhotel.com* ⇲ *40 rooms* ⭘ *Breakfast* Ⓜ *Copley* ✛ *D5.*

$$$$
HOTEL
FAMILY

🛏 **Colonnade Hotel.** Thanks to a $25-million dollar makeover in 2013 that included a spruced-up facade, new windows, and updated room decor, the Colonnade went from an '80s brass-and-mahogany showcase to a clean, modern environs injected with hues of khaki, chocolate, and chrome. **Pros:** roof-deck pool; across from Prudential Center shopping; good Red Sox packages. **Cons:** Huntington Avenue can get clogged with rush-hour traffic; on summer days the pool is packed by 11 am. Ⓢ *Rooms from: $479* ✉ *120 Huntington Ave., Back Bay* ☎ *617/424–7000, 800/962–3030* ⊕ *www.colonnadehotel.com* ⇲ *276 rooms, 9 suites* ⭘ *No meals* Ⓜ *Back Bay, Prudential Center* ✛ *C6.*

$$$$
HOTEL
Fodor'sChoice
★

🛏 **Eliot Hotel.** One of the city's best small hotels is on posh Commonwealth Avenue, modeled after Paris's epic Champs Élysées, and it expertly merges the old blue-blood Boston aesthetic with modern flair (like zebra-print rugs mingling with crystal chandeliers); everyone from well-heeled Sox fans to traveling CEOs to tony college parents

BEST BETS FOR BOSTON LODGING

Fodor's Choice ★

Charles Hotel, $$$, p. 135
Charlesmark Hotel, $$, p. 130
Eliot Hotel, $$$$, p. 130
Fairmont Copley Plaza, $$$, p. 131
Gryphon House, $$$, p. 134
Hotel Commonwealth, $$$, p. 134
Inn@St. Botolph, $$$, p. 131
Liberty Hotel Boston, $$$$, p. 132
Nine Zero, $$$, p. 133
XV Beacon, $$$$, p. 132

By Price

$

463 Beacon Street Guest House, p. 130
John Jeffries House, p. 132

$$

Charlesmark Hotel, p. 130
Encore, p. 134

$$$

Beacon Hill Hotel & Bistro, p. 132
Charles Hotel, p. 135
Fairmont Copley Plaza, p. 131
Gryphon House, p. 134
Hotel Commonwealth, p. 134
Inn@St. Botolph, p. 131
Langham Hotel, p. 133
Nine Zero, p. 133
Seaport Boston Hotel, p. 134

$$$$

Colonnade Hotel, p. 130
Eliot Hotel, p. 130
Fairmont Battery Wharf, p. 133
InterContinental Boston, p. 133
Liberty Hotel Boston, p. 132
Mandarin Oriental Boston, p. 132
XV Beacon, p. 132

By Experience

BEST LOCATION

Charles Hotel, p. 135
Nine Zero, p. 133

has noticed. **Pros:** super location; top-notch restaurants; pet-friendly; beautiful rooms. **Cons:** very expensive; some complain of elevator noise. [$] *Rooms from: $485* ✉ *370 Commonwealth Ave., Back Bay* ☎ *617/267–1607, 800/443–5468* 🌐 *www.eliothotel.com* 🛏 *16 rooms, 79 suites* 🍴 *No meals* [M] *Hynes* ⊕ *B5.*

$$$ HOTEL FAMILY Fodor's Choice ★ **Fairmont Copley Plaza.** Past guests, including one Judy Garland, felt at home in this decadent, unabashedly romantic hotel that underwent a $20-million renovation in early 2012. **Pros:** very elegant. **Cons:** tiny bathrooms with scratchy towels; charge for Internet access (no charge on Fairmont Presidentt's Club level). [$] *Rooms from: $369* ✉ *138 St. James Ave., Back Bay* ☎ *617/267–5300, 866/540–4417* 🌐 *www.fairmont.com/copley-plaza-boston* 🛏 *366 rooms, 17 suites* 🍴 *No meals* [M] *Copley, Back Bay* ⊕ *D5.*

$$$ B&B/INN FAMILY Fodor's Choice ★ **Inn@St. Botolph.** The posh yet homey 16-room Inn@St. Botolph follows a groundbreaking new hotel model—no front desk, no restaurant, and no valet (there is, however, an office on-site that is staffed 24/7). **Pros:** affordable style; free satellite TV and Wi-Fi; free transit to top area restaurants, where guests also get "preferred" pricing. **Cons:** DIY parking; for those who need hand-holding, there's no front desk. [$] *Rooms from: $379* ✉ *99 St. Botolph St., Back Bay* ☎ *617/236–8099* 🌐 *www.innatstbotolph.com* 🛏 *16 rooms* 🍴 *Breakfast* [M] *Prudential* ⊕ *C6.*

$$$$ HOTEL FAMILY **Mandarin Oriental Boston.** With too many amenities to list, the 148-room hotel has helped redefine luxury in town (pay attention, Ritz and Four Seasons) since opening in 2008, and it offers services many guests are calling "out of this world." **Pros:** amazing service; very quiet; good-size rooms. **Cons:** small fitness center; exorbitantly expensive; average views. [$] *Rooms from: $600* ✉ *776 Boylston St., Back Bay* ☎ *617/535–8888* 🌐 *www.mandarinoriental.com/boston* 🛏 *136 rooms, 12 suites* 🍴 *No meals* [M] *Prudential, Copley* ✥ *C5.*

$$$ HOTEL FAMILY **Taj Boston Hotel.** Standing guard at the corner of fashionable Newbury Street and the Public Garden, the old-school elegant Taj is doing its best to win over the old Ritz fans (it was formerly the landmark Ritz-Carlton Boston), as well as woo new guests, with discounted weekend rates and a soft renovation. **Pros:** white-glove service; great views; proximity to shopping, dining, and the park. **Cons:** occasionally snobby staff; frequently barren restaurant. [$] *Rooms from: $399* ✉ *15 Arlington St., Back Bay* ☎ *617/536–5700* 🌐 *www.tajhotels.com* 🛏 *273 rooms, 45 suites* 🍴 *No meals* [M] *Arlington* ✥ *E4.*

BEACON HILL

$$$ B&B/INN **Beacon Hill Hotel & Bistro.** This home away from home—or, rather, full-service version of home where you hardly have to lift a finger (unless it's to dial room service)—is within walking distance of the Public Garden, Back Bay, Government Center, and the river Esplanade. **Pros:** free Wi-Fi; many nearby shops and restaurants; chef Jason Bonds' decadent Sunday brunch at the ground-floor bistro. **Cons:** neighborhood parking is nonexistent; the rooms are somewhat small. [$] *Rooms from: $325* ✉ *25 Charles St., Beacon Hill* ☎ *617/723–7575* 🌐 *www.beaconhillhotel.com* 🛏 *12 rooms, 1 suite* 🍴 *Breakfast* [M] *Arlington, Charles/MGH* ✥ *E3.*

$ B&B/INN **John Jeffries House.** Right next to the Charles/MGH stop, the John Jeffries isn't only easily accessible, it's affordable—a veritable home run in this city. **Pros:** great Beacon Hill location; free Wi-Fi; good value. **Cons:** there's a busy (and noisy) hospital across the street; no spa or gym facilities. [$] *Rooms from: $125* ✉ *14 David G. Mugar Way, Beacon Hill* ☎ *617/367–1866* 🌐 *www.johnjeffrieshouse.com* 🛏 *23 rooms, 23 suites* 🍴 *Breakfast* [M] *Charles/MGH* ✥ *E2.*

$$$$ HOTEL Fodor's Choice ★ **Liberty Hotel Boston.** Since it opened in late 2007, the buzz surrounding the chic Liberty—formerly Boston's Charles Street Jail—was at first deafening, with bankers, tech geeks, foreign playboys, and fashionistas all scrambling to call it their own; a few years later, the hype has thankfully died down, though it's still part retreat, part nightclub. **Pros:** Scampo's mouthwatering house-made mozzarella bar; bustling nightlife; proximity to the river and Beacon Hill. **Cons:** loud in-house nightlife; long waits at bars and restaurants. [$] *Rooms from: $699* ✉ *215 Charles St., Beacon Hill* ☎ *617/224–4000* 🌐 *www.libertyhotel.com* 🛏 *288 rooms, 10 suites* 🍴 *No meals* [M] *Charles/MGH* ✥ *E2.*

$$$$ HOTEL Fodor's Choice ★ **XV Beacon.** The 1903 beaux arts exterior of one of the city's first small luxury hotels is a study in understated class and elegance. **Pros:** in-room massages; chef Jamie Mammano's steak house, Mooo; free pet stays. **Cons:** some rooms are very small; mattresses are just average; can be expensive on weekends during peak months (May, June,

September, October). $ *Rooms from: $575* ⊠ *15 Beacon St., Beacon Hill* ☎ *617/670–1500, 877/982–3226* ⊕ *www.xvbeacon.com* ⟿ *63 rooms* ❙❍❙ *No meals* Ⓜ *Government Center, Park St.* ✛ *G3.*

DOWNTOWN

$$$

HOTEL

🖼 **Ames Hotel.** One of the newest players on the Boston scene, the 114-room Ames is all New England modernity even though it's run by the hip Morgans Hotel Group (think the Delano and Shore Club in Miami). **Pros:** very cool design; cushy beds; limo service. **Cons:** far from South End and Back Bay shopping. $ *Rooms from: $350* ⊠ *1 Court St., Downtown* ☎ *617/979–8100, 888/697–1791* ⊕ *www.ameshotel.com* ⟿ *114 rooms* ❙❍❙ *No meals* Ⓜ *State, Government Ctr* ✛ *H3.*

$$$$

HOTEL

FAMILY

🖼 **Fairmont Battery Wharf.** One of the growing number of lodgings clustered along Boston's ever-expanding Harborwalk—a pretty pedestrian path that runs from Charlestown to Dorchester—this Fairmont looks more like a gated community than a chain hotel. **Pros:** great water views; access to Harborwalk; close to the North End. **Cons:** far from Newbury Street and South End shopping; 15- to 20-minute walk to nearest T stations. $ *Rooms from: $499* ⊠ *3 Battery Wharf, Downtown* ☎ *617/994–9000, 800/257–7544* ⊕ *www.fairmont.com/ battery-wharf-boston* ⟿ *120 rooms, 30 suites* Ⓜ *Haymarket, North Station* ✛ *H1.*

$$$$

HOTEL

🖼 **InterContinental Boston.** Call it the anti-boutique hotel: The 424-room InterContinental, facing both the waterfront and the Rose Kennedy Greenway, consists of two opulent, 22-story towers wrapped in blue glass. **Pros:** upper-floor rooms have great views; cool bathrooms; close to Financial District and South Station. **Cons:** huge function rooms mean lots of conventioneers; far from Newbury Street and South End shopping; guests say the soundproofing could be better. $ *Rooms from: $429* ⊠ *510 Atlantic Ave., Downtown/Waterfront* ☎ *617/747–1000, 866/493–6495* ⊕ *www.intercontinentalboston.com* ⟿ *424 rooms, 38 suites* ❙❍❙ *No meals* Ⓜ *South Station* ✛ *H4.*

$$$

HOTEL

🖼 **Langham Hotel.** This 1922 Renaissance Revival landmark (the former Federal Reserve Building) strikes an admirable balance between historic, old-world charm and sleek, modern appointments. **Pros:** ideal spot for business travelers; fabulous Sunday brunch and weekend Chocolate Bar at Café Fleuri; the beautiful Post Office Square park adjacent to the Langham is a quiet oasis. **Cons:** downtown location feels remote on weekends; pricey during the week; expensive valet parking. $ *Rooms from: $395* ⊠ *250 Franklin St., Downtown* ☎ *617/451–1900, 800/543–4300* ⊕ *www.boston.langhamhotels.com* ⟿ *318 rooms, 17 suites* ❙❍❙ *No meals* Ⓜ *South Station* ✛ *H3.*

$$$

HOTEL

FAMILY

Fodor's Choice

★

🖼 **Nine Zero.** Hotel rooms can get a little lonely, and that's why this downtown spot instated its "guppy love" program; yes, that's right, you get a pet fish on loan. **Pros:** pet- and kid-friendly; lobby wine-tasting every evening (from 5 to 6); Etro bath products. **Cons:** smallish rooms; high parking fees. $ *Rooms from: $386* ⊠ *90 Tremont St., Downtown* ☎ *617/772–5800, 866/906–9090* ⊕ *www.ninezero.com* ⟿ *185 rooms, 5 suites* ❙❍❙ *No meals* Ⓜ *Park St., Government Center* ✛ *G3.*

$$$ 🖼 **Omni Parker House.** If any hotel says "Boston," it's this one, where JFK
HOTEL proposed to Jackie, and Charles Dickens gave his first reading of "A
FAMILY Christmas Carol"—in fact, you may well see a Dickens impersonator in
the lobby, since history tours always include the Parker House on their
routes. **Pros:** historic property; near Downtown Crossing on the Free-
dom Trail. **Cons:** small rooms, some quite dark; thin-walled rooms can
be noisy. $ *Rooms from: $339* ⊠ *60 School St., Downtown* 🕾 *617/227–*
8600, 800/843–6664 ⊕ *www.omniparkerhouse.com* ⟿ *551 rooms, 21*
suites ⫯⊙⫯ *No meals* Ⓜ *Government Center, Park St.* ✢ *G3*

$$$ 🖼 **Seaport Boston Hotel.** Chances are, if you've ever been to Boston on
HOTEL business, you've already stayed at the Seaport, where guest rooms are
among the biggest in the city. **Pros:** on-site Wave Health & Fitness Club;
close to a newly developed restaurant scene offering 20 dining options;
free Wi-Fi. **Cons:** far from city center. $ *Rooms from: $369* ⊠ *World*
Trade Center, 1 Seaport La., Downtown/Seaport District 🕾 *617/385–*
4000, 800/440–3318 ⊕ *www.seaportboston.com* ⟿ *428 rooms* ⫯⊙⫯ *No*
meals Ⓜ *World Trade Center* ✢ *H4.*

SOUTH END

$ 🖼 **Encore.** Innkeepers Reinhold Mahler and David Miller, an architect
B&B/INN and creative set designer, respectively, have pooled their creative ener-
gies into this South End lodging gem, proving that they know a thing
or two about ambience. **Pros:** trendy South End location; free Wi-Fi;
Bang & Olufson sound systems. **Cons:** small breakfast nook; two-night
minimums on weekends; no elevator. $ *Rooms from: $155* ⊠ *116 W.*
Newton St., South End 🕾 *617/247–3425* ⊕ *www.encorebandb.com*
⟿ *3 rooms* ⫯⊙⫯ *Breakfast* Ⓜ *Back Bay, Mass. Ave.* ✢ *D6*

KENMORE SQUARE

$$$ 🖼 **Gryphon House.** The staff in this value-packed four-story, 19th-century
B&B/INN brownstone is helpful and friendly, and the suites are thematically deco-
Fodor'sChoice rated: one evokes rustic Italy; another is inspired by neo-Gothic art.
★ **Pros:** elegant suites are lush and spacious; gas fireplaces in all rooms;
free Wi-Fi. **Cons:** may be too fussy for some; there's no elevator or
handicapped access. $ *Rooms from: $300* ⊠ *9 Bay State Rd., Kenmore*
Sq. 🕾 *617/375–9003, 877/375–9003* ⊕ *www.innboston.com* ⟿ *8 suites*
⫯⊙⫯ *Breakfast* Ⓜ *Kenmore* ✢ *A5.*

$$$ 🖼 **Hotel Commonwealth.** Luxury and service without pretense makes this
HOTEL hip spot a solid choice—no wonder rumor has it that Bono and the Boss
Fodor'sChoice have walked the hallways of the Hotel Commonwealth, as have a host
★ of local celebs and visitors intent on branching out of the downtown
Boston hospitality scene. **Pros:** down bedding; perfect locale for Red Sox
fans; happening bar scene at Eastern Standard; free Wi-Fi. **Cons:** area
is mobbed during Sox games; small gym. $ *Rooms from: $399* ⊠ *500*
Commonwealth Ave., Kenmore Square 🕾 *617/933–5000, 866/784–*
4000 ⊕ *www.hotelcommonwealth.com* ⟿ *149 rooms, 5 suites* ⫯⊙⫯ *No*
meals Ⓜ *Kenmore* ✢ *A5.*

CAMBRIDGE

Use the coordinate (✛ B2) at the end of each listing to locate a site on the Where to Eat and Stay in Cambridge map.

$$$ **Charles Hotel.** It used to be that the Charles was *the* place to stay in
HOTEL Cambridge, and while other luxury hotels have since arrived to give
FAMILY it a little healthy competition, this Harvard Square staple is standing
Fodor's Choice strong. **Pros:** two blocks from the T Redline to Boston; on-site jazz club
★ and hip Noir bar; outdoor skating rink in winter. **Cons:** luxury comes
at a price. $ *Rooms from: $399* ⊠ *1 Bennett St.* ☎ *617/864–1200,
800/882–1818* ⊕ *www.charleshotel.com* ⤳ *249 rooms, 45 suites* ⦿ *No
meals* Ⓜ *Harvard* ✛ *C1.*

$$$ **Royal Sonesta Hotel.** Right next to the Charles River, the certified-green
HOTEL Sonesta has one of the best city skyline and sunset views in Boston. **Pros:**
FAMILY walk to Museum of Science and T to downtown Boston; complimentary
shuttle to Cambridge area attractions; nice pool. **Cons:** parking is not
free. $ *Rooms from: $379* ⊠ *40 Edwin Land Blvd., off Memorial Dr.*
☎ *617/806–4200, 800/766–3782* ⊕ *www.sonesta.com/boston* ⤳ *379
rooms, 21 suites* ⦿ *No meals* Ⓜ *Lechmere* ✛ *A6.*

NIGHTLIFE AND THE ARTS

NIGHTLIFE

Updated by
Fred Bouchard

BEACON HILL

BARS

Cheers. This pub was dismantled in England, shipped to Boston, reassembled, and named the Bull & Finch Pub. It later became the inspiration for the TV show *Cheers*, although it doesn't look anything like the bar in the now-classic TV series. ■TIP➡ **There's a model of the Hollywood set in the upstairs bar.** ⊠ *Hampshire House, 84 Beacon St., Beacon Hill* ☎ *617/227–9605* ⊕ *www.cheersboston.com* Ⓜ *Park St., Charles/MGH.*

The Sevens Ale House. This vintage bar is an easygoing alternative to Beacon Hill's tony stuffiness, with its dark tones, simple bar setup, dart board, well-poured pints, and decent wines. It's pleasantly un-trendy. ⊠ *77 Charles St., Beacon Hill* ☎ *617/523–9074* Ⓜ *Charles/MGH.*

GOVERNMENT CENTER

BARS

Black Rose. Very much like a Dublin pub, the Black Rose is decorated with family crests, pictures of Ireland, and portraits of the likes of Samuel Beckett, Lady Gregory, and James Joyce. Its Faneuil Hall location draws as many tourists as locals, but nightly shows, beginning at 9:30, by traditional Irish and contemporary musicians, make it worth braving the crowds. ⊠ *160 State St., Faneuil Hall* ☎ *617/742–2286* Ⓜ *Aquarium, State.*

CHARLESTOWN
BARS

Warren Tavern. Massachusetts' oldest watering hole, rebuilt in 1780, was frequented by Paul Revere; even George Washington had a few drinks here. Today its main clientele are tourists and Charlestown professionals. It's an easy stop for a pint en route to the Bunker Hill Monument or historic Navy Yard. Try the house-made potato chips with your ale of choice. There are singers on Wednesdays and Thursdays beginning around 9 pm. ⊠ *2 Pleasant St., Charlestown* ☎ *617/241–8142* ⊕ *www.warrentavern.com* Ⓜ *Community College.*

> ### THE REAL CHEERS
>
> TV's *Cheers* may have ended in 1993, but that doesn't stop die-hard fans from paying their respects at the "real" Cheers bar on Beacon Street (or its second location in Faneuil Hall). Although the inspiration for the TV show doesn't quite look like its fictional double, the same atmosphere of good spirits persists. You can find your own kind of notoriety here by devouring the double-decker "Giant Norm burger" and adding your name to the Hall of Fame.

DOWNTOWN
DANCE CLUBS

Gypsy Bar. With its rich red velvet and crystal chandeliers, Gypsy Bar calls to mind the decadence of a dark European castle. Rows of video screens broadcast the Fashion Network, adding a sexier, more modern touch. Thirtysomething revelers and European students snack on lime-and-ginger-marinated tiger shrimp and sip "See You in Church" martinis (vodka with fresh marmalade) while the trendy dance floor throbs to Top 40 and house music. ⊠ *116 Boylston St., Theater District* ☎ *617/482–7799* ⊕ *www.gypsybarboston.com* Ⓜ *Boylston.*

BACK BAY
MUSIC CLUBS

Red Room @ Cafe 939. By day a Berklee College coffee and snack bar, the Cafe by night opens its tidy, scarlet 150-seat concert space. Run and booked by students, it's an ideal venue for aspiring student bands and indies on the rise. Minimal refreshments are served (no alcohol) in this dedicated concert space, but it shares a foyer with Cactus Club. Cover charges range from zero to $12. ⊠ *939 Boylston St., Back Bay* ☎ *617/747–2261* ⊕ *www.cafe939.com* Ⓜ *Hynes.*

THE SOUTH END
BARS

Franklin Café. This neighborhood institution is known for great martinis, microbrews on tap, and upscale pub food. There's no placard bearing its name; just look for the martini sign (or the crowd waiting for a dinner table) to know you're there. Note that this is a bar for drinking and socializing, but there's no entertainment here. ⊠ *278 Shawmut Ave., South End* ☎ *617/350–0010* ⊕ *www.franklincafe.com* Ⓜ *Back Bay/South End.*

THE FENWAY
BARS
Boston Beer Works. This is a "naked brewery," with all the works exposed—the tanks, pipes, and gleaming stainless-steel and copper kettles used in producing beer. Seasonal brews, in addition to 16 microbrews on tap, draw students, young adults, and tourists alike to the original location (its sibling by the TD Garden is popular, too). The atmosphere is too crowded and noisy for intimate chats, and good luck trying to get in when there's a home game. ⊠ *61 Brookline Ave., The Fenway* ☎ *617/536–2337* ⊕ *www.beerworks.net* Ⓜ *Kenmore.*

ALLSTON
ROCK CLUBS
Fodor's Choice **Paradise Rock Club.** This iconic bandbox near Boston University is famed
★ for bringing up big-name talent (think U2 and Dresden Dolls), hosting Coldplay, and nurturing local rock and hip-hop acts. Two tiers of booths provide good sight lines from all angles, even some intimate, out-of-the-way corners. Four bars quench the crowd's thirst, and food is available. Some shows are for 18-plus only. The newer Paradise Lounge next door is a more intimate space to catch local (often acoustic) songsters, literary readings, poetry slams, and other artsy events. Most tickets run $15–$30. ⊠ *967–969 Commonwealth Ave., Allston* ☎ *617/562–8800* ⊕ *crossroadspresents.com/paradise-rock-club* Ⓜ *Pleasant St.*

Scullers Jazz Club. Since 1989 this intimate and amiable venue has presented the top names in jazz, Latin, and contemporary, as well as blues, soul, cabaret, and world music. Impresario Fred Taylor continues to welcome jazz greats to Boston, like Harry Connick, Jr., Wynton Marsalis, Diana Krall, and Tony Bennett, with performances Wednesday through Saturday nights at 8 and 10; tickets are $20–$50 per show, discounted with dinner in the Green Room. Buying tickets in advance is advised. ⊠ *Doubletree Guest Suites hotel, 400 Soldiers Field Rd., Allston* ☎ *617/562–4111* ⊕ *www.scullersjazz.com* Ⓜ *BU West, Bus 47, or CT2.*

SOMERVILLE
MUSIC CLUBS
Johnny D's Uptown. This is as close as Boston gets to a rural roadhouse: good eats and good music, where every seat is a good seat. The line-up leans into Cajun, country, rockabilly, blues, roots, with a bit of jazz, Latin, and poetry. Come early for Southern and Mediterranean bistro food, or on weekends enjoy the popular jazz brunch both days until 2:30 pm and open blues jam on Sunday afternoons. During Trivia Mondays, hot dogs are a buck-fifty. Those under 21 may visit with a parent or guardian. ⊠ *17 Holland St., Somerville* ☎ *617/776–9667 recorded info, 617/776–2004* ⊕ *johnnyds.com* Ⓜ *Davis.*

CAMBRIDGE
BLUES AND R&B CLUBS
Cantab Lounge/Third Rail. This place hums every night with live bands cranking out rhythm and blues, soul, funk, rock, or bluegrass. The Third Rail bar downstairs hosts major poetry slams, open-mic readings, and Club Bohemia nights. Its diverse under-40 crowd is friendly and informal. ⊠ *738 Massachusetts Ave., Cambridge* ☎ *617/354–2685* ⊕ *www.cantab-lounge.com* ⊟ *No credit cards* Ⓜ *Central.*

JAZZ CLUBS

Regattabar. Once the go-to club for name jazz acts, Regattabar has lately scaled back its music roster to host private events. Regulars still include top guitarists (John Scofield, Mike Stern, Wayne Krantz, Pat Martino) and local favorites (Mike Bono, Matt Savage). Tickets for shows are $20–$35. The dark 250-seat club with jaunty nautical decor offers reasonably priced fare and drinks. ⊠ *Charles Hotel, 1 Bennett St., Cambridge* ☎ *617/661–5000 hotel, 617/395–7757 tickets* ⊕ *www. regattabarjazz.com* Ⓜ *Harvard.*

Ryles Jazz Club. Soft lights, mirrors, and good barbecue set the mood for fine jazz on the ground-floor mainstage, host to a steady showcase since the 1960s of new bands, favored locals, and stars like McCoy Tyner and Maynard Ferguson. But Ryles leads a merry double life, because meanwhile, the upstairs dancehall has earned its spurs as a Latin dancers' destination. There's world music Wednesdays and occasionally open-mic poetry. Ryles' ever-popular Sunday jazz brunch requires reservations. The reasonable cover charge varies and there's free parking for patrons. ⊠ *212 Hampshire St., Cambridge* ☎ *617/876–9330* ⊕ *www. ryles.com* Ⓜ *Bus 69, 83, or 91.*

MUSIC CLUBS

Sinclair. Bringing a long-awaited sophisticated rock music and dining venue to Harvard Square, the Sinclair has factory-chic decor, a serious beverage list, creative mixology, and thoughtful comfort cuisine. Its adventurous, near-nightly calendar boasts indie rock, with enticing flings into world and jazz. Accommodating 500, here's a party made to order for grown-ups, academic and streetwise. ⊠ *52 Church St., Harvard Sq., Cambridge* ☎ *617/547–5200* ⊕ *www.sinclaircambridge. com* Ⓜ *Harvard Square.*

ROCK CLUBS

Middle East Restaurant & Nightclub. This nightclub has balanced its kebab-and-falafel menu with three ever-active performance spaces to carve its niche as one of New England's most eclectic alternative rock venues. National and local acts vie for the large upstairs, tiny corner, and cavernous downstairs rooms. Phenoms like the Mighty Mighty Bosstones got their start here. Music-world celebs drop by when playing town. There's also belly dancing, folk, jazz, country-rock, and dancing at Zu Zu. ⊠ *472–480 Massachusetts Ave., Cambridge* ☎ *617/497–0576, 617/864–3278* ⊕ *www.mideastclub.com* Ⓜ *Central.*

THE ARTS

BEACON HILL

CONCERTS

Fodor'sChoice ★ **Hatch Memorial Shell.** On the bank of the Charles River, this wonderful acoustic shell, 100 feet wide and wood-inlaid, is home to the Boston Pops' famous Fourth of July concert and dozens of other free summer concerts and events. Local radio stations air music shows and festivals here from April through October. Friday Flicks, often animated for children, are screened at sunset. ⊠ *Off Storrow Dr. at embankment, Beacon Hill* ☎ *617/626–4970* ⊕ *www.mass.gov* Ⓜ *Charles/MGH, Arlington.*

DOWNTOWN AND SOUTH BOSTON
CONCERTS
Bank of America Pavilion. Up to 5,000 people gather on the waterfront for breathtaking summertime concerts. National pop, folk, and country headliners play the huge white tent from mid-June to mid-September. In chilly months the scene turns to TD Garden or Comcast Center. ⊠ *290 Northern Ave., South Boston* ☎ *617/728–1600* ⊕ *www.bankofamericapavilion.net* Ⓜ *South Station.*

Boston Opera House. The glittering, regilded Boston Opera House hosts plays, musicals, and traveling Broadway shows (long runs for *Wicked, Once*) and also books performers as diverse as Sarah Brightman, B.B. King, and Pat Metheny. The magnificent building, constructed in 1926, also hosts Boston Ballet's iconic holiday sellout, Tchaikovsky's *Nutcracker.* ⊠ *539 Washington St., Downtown* ☎ *617/259–3400* ⊕ *www.bostonoperahouseonline.com* Ⓜ *Boylston, Chinatown, Downtown Crossing, Park St.*

BACK BAY
CONCERTS
Berklee Performance Center. The main stage for the internationally renowned Berklee College of Music, the "BPC" is best known for its jazz and pop programs, but also hosts folk performers, rock acts, and pop stars such as Andrew Bird, Aimee Mann, and Henry Rollins. Bargain alert: excellent student and faculty shows and showcases and clinics by famous performers are abundant and cost next to nothing. ⊠ *136 Massachusetts Ave., Back Bay* ☎ *617/747–2261 box office* ⊕ *www.berklee.edu/BPC* Ⓜ *Hynes.*

New England Conservatory's Jordan Hall. One of the world's acoustic treasures, New England Conservatory's Jordan Hall is ideal for solo and string quartet recitals yet spacious enough for chamber and full orchestras. The pin-drop intimacy of this all-wood, 1,000-seat hall is in demand year-round for ensembles visiting and local. Boston Philharmonic and Boston Baroque perform here regularly. Dozens of free faculty and student concerts, jazz and classical, are a best-kept secret. ⊠ *30 Gainsborough St., Back Bay* ☎ *617/585–1260 box office* ⊕ *necmusic.edu/calendar_event* Ⓜ *Symphony.*

Symphony Hall. While Boston's Symphony Hall—the home of the Boston Symphony Orchestra and the Boston Pops—is considered among the best in the world for its sublime acoustics, it's also worth visiting to enjoy its other merits. The stage is framed by an enormous organ facade and an intricate golden proscenium. Above the second balcony are 16 replicas of Greek and Roman statues, which, like the rest of the Hall, marry the acoustic and aesthetic by creating niches and uneven surfaces to enhance the acoustics of the space. Although acoustical science was a brand-new field of research when Professor Wallace Sabine planned the interior, not one of the 2,500 seats is a bad one—the secret is the box-within-a-box design. ⊠ *301 Massachusetts Ave., Back Bay* ☎ *888/266–1200 box office, 617/638–9390 tours* ⊕ *www.bso.org* ☉ *Free walk-up tours Oct.–May, Wed. at 4 and some Sat. at 2* Ⓜ *Symphony.*

OPERA

Boston Lyric Opera. At Citi Performing Arts Center's Schubert Theater, the Boston Lyric Opera stages four full productions each season—three classics and a 20th-century work. Recent highlights have included Mozart's *Magic Flute* and Verdi's *Rigoletto*. ⊠ *11 Ave. de Lafayette, Downtown* ☎ *617/542–4912, 617/542–6772 audience services office* ⊕ *blo.org* Ⓜ *Boylston.*

THEATER

Huntington Theatre Company. Boston's largest resident theater company consistently performs a high-quality mix of 20th-century plays, new works, and classics under the artistic direction of Peter DuBois, and commissions artists to produce original dramas. The Huntington performs at two locations: at the Boston University Theatre and at the Calderwood Theatre Pavilion in the South End. ⊠ *Boston University Theatre, 264 Huntington Ave., Back Bay* ☎ *617/266–0800 box office* ⊕ *www. huntingtontheatre.org* Ⓜ *Symphony* ⊠ *Calderwood Theatre Pavilion, Boston Center for the Arts, 527 Tremont St., South End* ☎ *617/426–5000* ⊕ *www.bcaonline.org* Ⓜ *Back Bay/South End, Copley.*

THE SOUTH END

BALLET

Boston Ballet. The city's premier dance company performs at the Boston Opera House. In addition to a world-class repertory of classical and high-spirited modern works, it presents an elaborate signature *Nutcracker* during the holidays. ⊠ *19 Clarendon St., South End* ☎ *617/695–6950* ⊕ *www.bostonballet.org* Ⓜ *Back Bay.*

THEATER

Boston Center for the Arts. Of Boston's multiple arts organizations, this nonprofit arts-and-culture complex is the one that is closest to "the people." Here you can see the work of budding playwrights, check out rotating exhibits from contemporary artists, or stop in for a curator's talk and other special events. The BCA houses six performance spaces, a community music center, the Mills Art Gallery, and studio space for some 40 Boston-based contemporary artists. ⊠ *539 Tremont St., South End* ☎ *617/426–5000* ⊕ *www.bcaonline.org* ☜ *Free* ☉ *Weekdays 9–5; Mills Gallery Wed. and Sun. noon–5, Thurs.–Sat. noon–9* Ⓜ *Back Bay/South End.*

CAMBRIDGE

BALLET

José Mateo's Ballet Theatre. This troupe is building an exciting, contemporary repertory under Cuban-born José Mateo, the resident artistic director-choreographer. Performances, which include an original *Nutcracker,* take place October through April at the **Sanctuary Theatre,** a beautifully converted former church at Massachusetts Avenue and Harvard Street in Harvard Square. ⊠ *400 Harvard St., Cambridge* ☎ *617/354–7467* ⊕ *www.ballettheatre.org* Ⓜ *Harvard.*

FILM

Brattle Theatre. A classic moviegoer's iconic den with 230 seats, Brattle Theatre shows classic movies, new foreign and indie films, theme series, and directors' cuts. Tickets sell out for its annual much-acclaimed Humphrey Bogart festival, scheduled around Harvard's exam period; the

Bugs Bunny Film Festival in February; *Trailer Treats,* an annual fundraiser featuring classic and modern movie previews; and DocYard, a stunning series of documentaries. At Christmastime, expect seasonal movies like *It's a Wonderful Life* and *Holiday Inn.* ✉ *40 Brattle St., Harvard Sq., Cambridge* ☎ *617/876–6837* ⊕ *brattlefilm.org* Ⓜ *Harvard.*

Harvard Film Archive. Screening independent, foreign, classic, and experimental films rarely seen in commercial cinemas, Harvard Film Archive is open to the public Friday through Monday. The 200-seat theater, with pristine film and digital projection, is located in the stunning brick-and-glass Carpenter Visual Arts Center, Le Corbusier's only American building. Tickets are $9. ✉ *Carpenter Center for the Visual Arts, 24 Quincy St., Cambridge* ☎ *617/495–4700* ⊕ *hcl.harvard.edu/hfa* Ⓜ *Harvard.*

THEATER

American Repertory Theater. New director Diane Paulus at the helm is edging the ART into packing sell-out shows and winning Tonys for revivals of *Pippin* and *The Gershwins' Porgy and Bess.* The theater stages experimental, classic, and contemporary plays, often with unusual lighting and stage design, edgy scores, and multimedia effects. It boasts multiple venues. Loeb Drama Center has two theaters; the smaller black-box often stages productions by the irreverent Harvard-Radcliffe Dramatic Club. Oberon, a modern theater space with flexible stage design at 2 Arrow Street, engages young audiences in immersive theater, like the "disco-ball and hustle queen" extravaganza, *The Donkey Show,* on Saturday nights. ✉ *64 Brattle St., Harvard Sq., Cambridge* ☎ *617/547–8300* ⊕ *americanrepertorytheater.org* Ⓜ *Harvard.*

SPORTS AND THE OUTDOORS

Updated by
Kim Foley
MacKinnon

Everything you've heard about the zeal of Boston fans is true; you cheer, and you pray, and you root some more. "Red Sox Nation" witnessed a miracle in 2004, with the reverse of the curse and the team's first World Series victory since 1918.

Then in 2007 and 2013 they proved it wasn't just a fluke with two more Series wins. In 2008 the Celtics ended their 18-year NBA championship drought with a victory over longtime rivals the LA Lakers. And three-time champions the New England Patriots are still a force to be reckoned with.

Bostonians' fervor for sports is equally evident in their leisure-time activities. Harsh winters keep locals wrapped up for months, only to emerge at the earliest sign of oncoming spring. Once the mercury tops freezing and the snows begin to melt, Boston's extensive parks, paths, woods, and waterways teem with sun worshippers and athletes.

NATURAL PARKS AND BEACHES

Arnold Arboretum. The sumptuously landscaped Arnold Arboretum is open all year to joggers and in-line skaters. Volunteer docents give free walking tours in spring, summer, and fall. ✉ *125 Arborway, Jamaica Plain* ☎ *617/524–1718* ⊕ *www.arboretum.harvard.edu* Ⓜ *Forest Hills.*

Candlepin Bowling

Back in 1880 Justin White adjusted the size of his pins at his Worcester, Massachussetts, bowling hall, giving birth to candlepin bowling, a highly popular pint-sized version of ten-pin bowling. Now played almost exclusively in northern New England and in the Canadian Maritime Provinces, candlepin bowling is a game of power and accuracy.

Paradoxically, candlepin bowling is both much easier and far more difficult than regular bowling. The balls are significantly smaller, weighing less than 3 pounds. There are no finger holes, and players of all ages and abilities can whip the ball down the alley. But because both the ball and the pins are lighter, it is far more difficult to bowl strikes and spares. Players are allowed three throws per frame, and bowlers may hit fallen pins (called wood) to knock down other pins. There has never been a perfect "300" score. The top score is 245. Good players score around 100 to 110, and novice players should be content with a score of 90.

A handful of alleys are in and around Boston, and many of them maintain their own quirky charm and history.

Needham Bowlaway. Founded in 1917, this tiny alley's eight cramped lanes are tucked away down a flight of stairs. Fans say Bowlaway is like bowling in your own basement. The charge is $25 per lane per hour ($20 before noon weekdays). ■ TIP → Note that this is a drive-to only destination (no subway station is anywhere nearby). ⊠ *16 Chestnut St., Needham* ☎ *781/449–4060* ⊕ *www.needhambowl.com.*

Boston Bowl. Open 24 hours a day, Boston Bowl attracts a more adult crowd. It has pool tables, a game room, both 10-pin and candlestick bowling, and a restaurant and bar. ⊠ *820 Morrissey Blvd., Dorchester* ☎ *617/825–3800* ⊕ *www.bostonbowl.com.*

Sacco's Bowl Haven. The '50s decor here "makes bowling the way it was, the way it is." Run by the fourth generation of the Sacco family, the alleys include a Flatbread Company pizzeria. Its 10 lanes are open all day until midnight and run $25 per hour. ⊠ *45 Day St., Somerville* ☎ *617/776–0552.*

FAMILY
Fodor'sChoice
★

Boston Harbor Islands National Park Area. Comprising 34 islands and peninsulas, the Boston Harbor Islands National Park Area is somewhat of a hidden gem for nature lovers and history buffs, with miles of lightly traveled trails and shoreline and several little-visited historic sites to explore. The focal point of the national park is 39-acre Georges Island, where you'll find the partially restored pre–Civil War Fort Warren that once held Confederate prisoners. Other islands worth visiting include Peddocks Island, which holds the remains of Fort Andrews, and Spectacle Island, a popular destination for swimming (with lifeguards). Lovells, Peddocks, Grape, and Bumpkin islands all allow camping with a permit from late June through Labor Day. Peddocks also has yurts available. Pets and alcohol are not allowed on the Harbor Islands. ⊠ *Visitor Pavilion, 191 W. Atlantic Ave., Downtown* ☎ *617/223–8666* ⊕ *www.bostonislands.com* Ⓜ *Aquarium.*

National Park Service. The NPS is a good source for information about camping, transportation, and the like. ☎ 617/223–8666 ⊕ *www. nps.gov/bost/index.htm.*

Rose Fitzgerald Kennedy Greenway. After Boston's Central Artery (I–93) was moved underground as part of the Big Dig project, the state transformed the footprint of the former highway into the Rose Fitzgerald Kennedy Greenway, a gorgeous 1½-mile-long ribbon of parks boasting fountains, organically maintained lawns and landscapes, hundreds of trees, and chairs, tables, and umbrellas for the public's use. The Greenway stretches from the North End (New Sudbury and Cross streets) to Chinatown (Kneeland and Hudson streets), curving through the heart of downtown, just a few blocks from the harbor in most places.

The Conservancy, a non-profit foundation, operates, maintains, and progams the park with more than 350 events each year, including concerts, exercise classes, and farmer's and artisan markets. A mobile food program features more than 20 food trucks and carts operating seasonally in several locations on the Greenway, with the heart of the activity at Dewey Square Park. In 2013 a one-of-a-kind carousel was installed, with 36 seats featuring 14 characters native to the Boston area, including a lobster, rabbit, grasshopper, and falcon. ⊠ *Downtown* ☎ *617/292–0020* ⊕ *www.rosekennedygreenway.org* Ⓜ *South Station, North Station, Aquarium, Haymarket.*

FAMILY

Fodor'sChoice

★

Emerald Necklace. The nine large public parks known as Boston's Emerald Necklace stretch 5 miles from the Back Bay Fens to Franklin Park in Dorchester, and include Arnold Arboretum, Jamaica Pond, Olmsted Park, and the Riverway. The linear parks, designed by master landscape architect Frederick Law Olmsted more than 100 years ago, remain a well-groomed urban masterpiece. Locals take pride in and happily make use of its open spaces and its pathways and bridges connecting rivers and ponds. ⊕ *www.emeraldnecklace.org.*

Emerald Necklace Conservancy. This conservancy maintains a regular calendar of nature walks and other events in the parks. ⊠ *125 The Fenway, Fens* ☎ *617/522–2700* ⊕ *www.emeraldnecklace.org* Ⓜ *Museum of Fine Arts, Northeastern.*

Boston Parks & Recreation Department. Rangers with the Boston Parks & Recreation Department lead tours highlighting the area's historic sites and surprising ecological diversity. ⊠ *1010 Massachusetts Ave.* ☎ *617/635–4505* ⊕ *www.cityofboston.gov/parks/parkrangers.*

Harbor Express. Boston Best Cruises offers ferries to the Harbor Islands from Long Wharf (Downtown) or the Hingham Shipyard to Georges Island or Spectacle Island (in summer). High-speed catamarans run daily from May through mid-October and cost $15. Other islands can be reached by the free inter-island water shuttles that depart from Georges Island. ☎ *617/770–0400* ⊕ *bostonsbestcruises.com.*

PARTICIPANT SPORTS

BICYCLING

It's common to see suited-up doctors, lawyers, and businessmen commuting on two wheels through Downtown; unfortunately, bike lanes are few and far between. Boston's dedicated bike paths are well used, as much by joggers and in-line skaters as by bicyclists.

Back Bay Bicycles. Road bikes rent here for $65 per day (weekly rates are also available)—cash only. ⊠ *362 Commonwealth Ave., Back Bay* ☎ *617/247–2336* ⊕ *www.backbaybicycles.com.*

Community Bicycle Supply. This South End place rents cycles from April through October. ⊠ *496 Tremont St., at E. Berkeley St., South End* ☎ *617/542–8623* ⊕ *www.communitybicycle.com* Ⓜ *Back Back.*

Department of Conservation & Recreation (*DCR*). For other path locations, consult the Department of Conservation & Recreation Web site. ⊕ *www.mass.gov/dcr.*

Dr. Paul Dudley White Bike Path. This 17-mile long path follows both banks of the Charles River as it winds from Watertown Square to the Museum of Science. ⊠ *Watertown.*

Massachusetts Bicycle Coalition (*MassBike*). This advocacy group works to improve conditions for area cyclists, has information on organized rides, and sells good bike maps of Boston and the state. Thanks to MassBike's lobbying efforts, the MBTA now allows bicycles on subway and commuter-rail trains during nonpeak hours. ⊠ *171 Milk St., Suite 33, Downtown* ☎ *617/542–2453* ⊕ *www.massbike.org.*

BOATING

Except when frozen over, the waterways coursing through the city serve as a playground for boaters of all stripes. All types of pleasure craft, with the exception of inflatables, are allowed from the Charles River and Inner Harbor to North Washington Street on the waters of Boston Harbor, Dorchester inner and outer bays, and the Neponset River from the Granite Avenue Bridge to Dorchester Bay.

Boat Drop Sites. There are several boat drop sites along the Charles.

Clarendon Street ⊠ *Back Bay* Ⓜ *Copley, Arlington.*

Hatch Shell ⊠ *Embankment Rd., Back Bay* Ⓜ *Arlington, Boylston, Charles/MGH.*

Pinckney Street Landing ⊠ *Back Bay* Ⓜ *Charles/MGH.*

Brooks Street ⊠ *Nonantum Rd., Brighton.*

Richard T. Artesani Playground ⊠ *Off Soldiers Field Rd., Brighton.*

Charles River Dam, Museum of Science ⊠ *Cambridge* Ⓜ *Science Park Station.*

Watertown Square ⊠ *Charles River Rd., Watertown.*

Charles River Watershed Association. This association publishes detailed boating information on its website. ☎ *781/788–0007* ⊕ *www.charlesriver.org.*

Many of the local University teams row on the Charles River.

SPECTATOR SPORTS

BASEBALL

⇨ *See the Fenway Park spotlight.*

BASKETBALL

Boston Celtics. One of the most storied franchises in the National Basketball Association, the Boston Celtics have won the NBA championship 17 times since 1957, more than any other team in the league. The last title came in 2008, after a solid defeat of longtime rivals (the LA Lakers) ended an 18-year championship dry spell. Basketball season runs from late October to April, and playoffs last until mid-June. ⊠ *TD Garden, Old West End* ☎ *866/423–5849, 617/931–2222 Ticketmaster* ⊕ *www.celtics.com.*

FOOTBALL

New England Patriots. Boston has been building a football dynasty over the past decade, starting with the New England Patriots' come-from-behind victory against the favored St. Louis Rams in the 2002 Super Bowl. Coach Bill Belichick and heartthrob quarterback Tom Brady then brought the team two more championship rings in 2004 and 2005, and have made Patriots fans as zealous as their baseball counterparts. Exhibition football games begin in August, and the season runs through the playoffs in January. The state-of-the-art Gillette Stadium is in Foxboro, 30 mi southwest of Boston. ⊠ *Gillette Stadium, Rte. 1, off I–95 Exit 9, Foxboro* ☎ *800/745–3000 Ticketmaster* ⊕ *www.patriots.com* Ⓜ *Gillette Stadium.*

HOCKEY

Beanpot Hockey Tournament. Boston College, Boston University, Harvard, and Northeastern teams face off every February in the Beanpot Hockey Tournament at the TD Garden. The colleges in this fiercely contested tournament traditionally yield some of the finest squads in the country. ⊠ *TD Garden* ⊕ *www.beanpothockey.com* Ⓜ *North Station.*

Boston Bruins. Beantown's hockey team is on the ice from September until April, frequently on Thursday and Saturday evenings. Playoffs last through early June. ⊠ *TD Garden, 100 Legends Way, Old West End* ☎ *617/624–2327* ⊕ *www.bostonbruins.com* Ⓜ *North Station.*

RUNNING

Fodor's Choice
★

Boston Marathon. Every Patriots' Day (the third Monday in April), fans gather along the Hopkinton–to–Boston route of the Boston Marathon to cheer on more than 25,000 runners from all over the world. The race ends near Copley Square in the Back Bay. ⊠ *Copley Square, Back Bay* ⊕ *www.baa.org* Ⓜ *Copley, Arlington.*

Boston Athletic Association. For information, call the Boston Athletic Association. ☎ *617/236–1652* ⊕ *www.bostonmarathon.org.*

SHOPPING

Updated
by Frances
Folsom

Boston's shops are generally open Monday through Saturday from 10 or 11 until 6 or 7 and Sunday noon to 5. Many stay open until 8 pm one night a week, usually Thursday. Malls are open Monday through Saturday from 9 or 10 until 8 or 9 and Sunday noon to 6.

MAJOR SHOPPING DISTRICTS

Boston's shops and department stores are concentrated in the area bounded by Quincy Market, the Back Bay, and Downtown. There are plenty of bargains in the Downtown Crossing area. The South End's gentrification creates its own kind of consumerist milieus, from housewares shops to avant-garde art galleries. In Cambridge you can find lots of shopping around Harvard and Central squares, with independent boutiques migrating west along Massachusetts Avenue (or Mass Ave., as almost everyone else calls it) toward Porter Square and beyond.

BOSTON

Boylston Street. Parallel to Newbury Street is Boylston Street, where a few standout shops such as Pompanoosuc Mills (hand-crafted furnishings) are scattered among the other chains and restaurants.

Charles Street. Pretty Charles Street, running north to south, is crammed beginning to end with top-notch antiques stores such as Judith Dowling Asian Art, Eugene Galleries, and Devonia, as well as a handful of independently owned fashion boutiques whose prices reflect their high Beacon Hill rents. River Street, parallel to Charles Street, is also an excellent source for antiques. Both are easy walks from the Charles Street T stop on the Red Line. Ⓜ *Charles/MGH.*

Copley Place. Two modern structures dominate Copley Square—the **John Hancock Tower** off the southeast corner and the even more assertive Copley Place skyscraper on the southwest. An upscale, glass-and-brass urban mall built between 1980 and 1984, Copley Place includes two major hotels: the high-rise Westin and the Marriott Copley Place. Dozens of shops, restaurants, and offices are attractively grouped on several levels, surrounding bright, open indoor spaces. ⊠ *100 Huntington Ave., Back Bay* ⊕ *www.simon.com/mall/copley-place* ⊙ *Shopping galleries Mon.–Sat. 10–8, Sun. noon–6* Ⓜ *Copley.*

Faneuil Hall Marketplace. This complex is both huge and hugely popular (drawing 22 million people a year), but not necessarily unique—most of its independent shops have given way to Banana Republic, Urban Outfitters, and other chains. The place has plenty of history, one of the area's great à la carte casual dining experiences (Quincy Market), pushcarts sell everything from apparel to jewelry to candy to Boston souvenirs, and buskers perform crowd-pleasing feats such as break dancing. ⊠ *Bounded by Congress St., Atlantic Ave., the Waterfront, and Government Center, Downtown* ☎ *617/523–1300* ⊕ *www. faneuilhallmarketplace.com* Ⓜ *Government Center.*

Newbury Street. Boston's version of LA's Rodeo Drive, all of Newbury Street is a shoppers' paradise, from high-end names such as Brooks Brothers to tiny specialty shops such as the Fish and Bone. Upscale clothing stores, up-to-the-minute art galleries, and dazzling jewelers line the street near the Public Garden. As you head toward Massachusetts Avenue, Newbury gets funkier and the cacophony builds, with skateboarders zipping through traffic and garbage-pail drummers burning licks outside hip boutiques. The big-name stores run from Arlington Street to the Prudential Center. ⊕ *www.newbury-st.com* Ⓜ *Arlington, Copley, Hynes.*

Prudential Center. A skywalk connects Copley Place to the Prudential Center. The Pru, as it's often called, contains moderately priced chain stores such as Ann Taylor and the Body Shop, and is anchored by Saks Fifth Avenue and Lord and Taylor. ⊠ *800 Boylston St., Back Bay* ☎ *800/746–7778* ⊕ *www.prudentialcenter.com* Ⓜ *Prudential.*

South End. Merchants here are benefiting from the ongoing gentrification that has brought high real-estate prices and trendy restaurants to the area. Explore the chic home-furnishings and gift shops that line Tremont Street, starting at Berkeley Street. The MBTA's Silver Line bus runs through the South End. ⊕ *www.south-end-boston.com* Ⓜ *Back Bay.*

CAMBRIDGE

Harvard Square. Harvard Square takes up just a few blocks but holds more than 150 stores selling clothes, books, records, furnishings, and specialty items. ⊠ *Cambridge* Ⓜ *Harvard.*

Brattle Street. A handful of chains and independent boutiques are clustered on Brattle Street. ⊠ *Behind Harvard Sq., Cambridge* Ⓜ *Harvard.*

Porter Square. This spot in north Cambridge has distinctive clothing stores, as well as crafts shops, coffee shops, natural-food stores, restaurants, and bars with live music. ⊠ *West on Mass Ave. from Harvard Sq., Cambridge* Ⓜ *Porter Square.*

SHOPPING BY NEIGHBORHOOD

BEACON HILL

CLOTHING AND SHOES

Crush Boutique. This garden-level shop is perfect for everyday work essentials, weekend casual outfits, and even party-girl attire. You'll also find affordable jewelry and handbags to dress up any ensemble. **TIP→ Crush's Newbury Street shop (between Fairfield and Gloucester streets) has a more LA vibe to it.** ✉ *131 Charles St., Beacon Hill* ☎ *617/720–0010* 🌐 *www.shopcrushboutique.com* Ⓜ *Charles/MGH.*

Moxie. The selection is always fashion-forward and sophisticated at this home to the season's hottest shoes. ✉ *51 Charles St., Beacon Hill* ☎ *617/557–9991* 🌐 *www.moxieboston.com* Ⓜ *Charles/MGH.*

Wish. The contemporary women's boutique is home to beloved brands including Diane von Furstenberg, Theory, and Joie. Be sure to stop by in the cooler months—their cashmere selection is otherworldly. ✉ *49 Charles St., Beacon Hill* ☎ *617/227–4441* 🌐 *thewishboston.wordpress.com* Ⓜ *Charles/MGH.*

Helen's Leather Shop. Choose from half a dozen brands of boots (Lucchese, Nocona, Dan Post, Tony Lama, Justin, and Frye); then browse through the leather sandals, jackets, briefcases, luggage, and accessories. ✉ *110 Charles St., Beacon Hill* ☎ *617/742–2077* 🌐 *www.helensleather.com* ⏲ *Closed Tues. May–Oct.* Ⓜ *Charles/MGH.*

BACK BAY

CLOTHING AND SHOES

Alan Bilzerian. Satisfying the Euro crowd, this store sells luxe men's and women's clothing by such fashion darlings as Yohji Yamamoto and Ann Demeulemeester. ✉ *34 Newbury St., Back Bay* ☎ *617/536–1001* 🌐 *www.alanbilzerian.com* ⏲ *Closed Sun.* Ⓜ *Arlington.*

Anne Fontaine. You can never have too many white shirts—especially if they're designed by this Parisienne. The simple, sophisticated designs are mostly executed in cotton and priced around $160. ✉ *318 Boylston St., Back Bay* ☎ *617/423–0366* 🌐 *www.annefontaine.com* Ⓜ *Arlington, Boylston.*

Jos. A. Bank Clothiers. Like Brooks Brothers, the national chain Joseph Bank is well known to the conservatively well dressed everywhere. ✉ *399 Boylston St., Back Bay* ☎ *617/536–5050* 🌐 *www.josbank.com* Ⓜ *Arlington.*

DEPARTMENT STORES

Barneys New York. The hoopla (not to mention the party) generated by this store's arrival was surprising in a city where everything new is viewed with trepidation. But clearly Boston's denizens have embraced the lofty, two-story space because it's filled with cutting-edge lines like Comme des Garçons and Nina Ricci, as well as a few bargains in the second-level Co-op section. ✉ *100 Huntington Ave., Back Bay* ☎ *617/385–3300* 🌐 *www.barneys.com* Ⓜ *Copley.*

Lord & Taylor. Somewhat overstuffed with merchandise, this Boston branch of the popular national chain is a reliable stop for classic clothing by such designers as Anne Klein and Ralph Lauren, along with accessories, cosmetics, and jewelry. ✉ *760 Boylston St., Back Bay* ☎ *617/262–6000* ⊕ *www.lordandtaylor.com* Ⓜ *Prudential Center.*

Neiman Marcus. At its Back Bay location, the flashy Texas-based retailer jokingly referred to by some as "Needless Markup" has three levels of swank designers and a jaw-dropping shoe section, as well as cosmetics and housewares. ✉ *5 Copley Pl., Back Bay* ☎ *617/536–3660* ⊕ *www. neimanmarcus.com* Ⓜ *Back Bay.*

SPECIALTY STORES
The Fish and Bone. This boutique is dedicated to all things cat and dog. Choose from the enormous selection of collars, toys, and food. ✉ *217 Newbury St., Back Bay* ☎ *857/753–4176* ⊕ *www.thefishandbone.com* Ⓜ *Arlington.*

THRIFT SHOPS
Second Time Around. Okay, so $700 isn't all that cheap for a used suit—but what if it's Chanel? Many of the items here, from jeans to fur coats, are new merchandise; the rest is on consignment. The staff makes periodic markdowns, ranging from 20% to 50% over a 90-day period. ✉ *176 Newbury St., Back Bay* ☎ *617/247–3504* ⊕ *www. secondtimearound.net* Ⓜ *Copley.*

ART GALLERIES
Copley Society of Art. After more than a century, this nonprofit membership organization continues to present the works of well-known and aspiring New England artists. ✉ *158 Newbury St., Back Bay* ☎ *617/536– 5049* ⊕ *www.copleysociety.org* ⊘ *Closed Mon. (by appt. only)* Ⓜ *Copley.*

DOWNTOWN
BOOKS
Brattle Book Shop. The late George Gloss built this into Boston's best used- and rare-book shop. Today his son Kenneth fields queries from passionate book lovers. If the book you want is out of print, Brattle has it or can probably find it. The store has been in operation since 1825. ✉ *9 West St., Downtown* ☎ *617/542–0210, 800/447–9595* ⊕ *www. brattlebookshop.com* ⊘ *Closed Sun.* Ⓜ *Downtown Crossing.*

CLOTHING AND SHOES
Fodor'sChoice ★ **Louis Boston.** Impeccably tailored designs, subtly updated classics, and the latest Italian styles highlight a wide selection of imported clothing and accessories. Visiting celebrities might be trolling the racks along with you as jazz spills out into the street from the adjoining Sam's Restaurant. ✉ *60 Northern Ave., South Boston* ☎ *617/262–6100* ⊕ *www. louisboston.com* Ⓜ *South Station.*

DEPARTMENT STORES
Macy's. Three floors offer men's and women's clothing and shoes, housewares, and cosmetics. Although top designers and a fur salon are part of the mix, Macy's Boston location doesn't feel exclusive; instead, it's a popular source for family basics. ✉ *450 Washington St., Downtown* ☎ *617/357–3000* ⊕ *www.macys.com* Ⓜ *Downtown Crossing.*

The Harvard Coop has peddled books to university students since 1882.

SOUTH END

CRAFTS

Gracie Finn's. This trendy South End shop is well stocked with crafts from local artisans; items for sale include pottery, wooden toys, notecards, and luxurious soaps. It's not open in the evenings. ✉ *10 Union Park St., South End* ☎ *617/357–0321* ⊕ *www.graciefinn.com* Ⓜ *Back Bay.*

TOYS

Tadpole. This is a treasure trove of educational games, dolls, trucks, blocks, and every other necessity for a kid's toy chest. Stock up on baby gear and essentials as well. ✉ *58 Clarendon St., South End* ☎ *617/778–1788* ⊕ *www.shoptadpole.com* Ⓜ *Back Bay.*

CAMBRIDGE

ANTIQUES

Cambridge Antique Market. Off the beaten track, this antiques hot spot has a selection bordering on overwhelming: five floors of goods ranging from 19th-century furniture to vintage clothing, much of it reasonably priced. There are two parking lots next to the building. ✉ *201 Monsignor O'Brien Hwy., Cambridge* ☎ *617/868–9655* ⊕ *www. marketantique.com* ⊙ *Closed Sun.* Ⓜ *Lechmere.*

CLOTHING AND SHOES

Mint Julep. Cute dresses, playful skirts, and form-fitting tops make up the selection here. The Cambridge location is a little larger and easier to navigate, but Brookline houses the original. ✉ *6 Church St., Cambridge* ☎ *617/576–6468* ⊕ *www.shopmintjulep.com* Ⓜ *Harvard.*

BOOKS

Schoenhof's. The friendly staff helps patrons navigate through thousands of foreign books, many in French, German, Italian, and Spanish. ✉ *76 Mount Auburn St., Cambridge* ☎ *617/547–8855* ⊕ *www.schoenhofs. com* ⊗ *Closed Sun.* Ⓜ *Harvard.*

Fodor's Choice ★ **Harvard Book Store.** The intellectual community is well served here, with a slew of new titles upstairs and used and remaindered books downstairs. The collection's diversity has made the store a favored destination for academics. ✉ *1256 Massachusetts Ave., Cambridge* ☎ *617/661–1515* ⊕ *www.harvard.com* Ⓜ *Harvard.*

TOYS

FAMILY **The Curious George Store.** Time can really slip away from you in this jungle of kids books and gifts. Decorated with tropical plants, a fake hut, and tot-size chairs, and equipped with puzzles, toys, activity sets, and books of all kinds for all ages, this store is a wonderland for kids and a parent's salvation on a rainy day. ✉ *1 JFK St., Harvard Sq., Cambridge* ☎ *617/498–0062* ⊕ *thecuriousgeorgestore.com* Ⓜ *Harvard.*

SIDE TRIPS FROM BOSTON

LEXINGTON

16 miles northwest of Boston.

Discontented with the British, American colonials burst into action in Lexington in April 1775. On April 18, patriot leader Paul Revere alerted the town that British soldiers were approaching. The next day, as the British advance troops arrived in Lexington on their march toward Concord, the Minutemen were waiting to confront the Redcoats in what became the first skirmish of the Revolutionary War.

These first military encounters of the American Revolution are very much a part of present-day Lexington, a modern suburban town that sprawls out from the historic sites near its center. Although the downtown area is generally lively, with ice cream and coffee shops, boutiques, and a great little movie theater, the town becomes especially animated each Patriots' Day (April 19, but celebrated on the third Monday in April), when costume-clad groups re-create the Minutemen's battle maneuvers and Paul Revere rides again.

To learn more about the city and the 1775 clash, stop by the **Lexington Visitor Center.**

GETTING HERE AND AROUND

Massachusetts Bay Transportation Authority (MBTA) operates bus service in the greater Boston area and serves Lexington.

ESSENTIALS

Bus Contacts MBTA ☎ *800/392–6100, 617/222–3200, 617/222–5146 TTY* ⊕ *www.mbta.com.*

Visitor Information Lexington Visitors Center ✉ *1875 Massachusetts Ave.* ☎ *781/862–1450* ⊕ *www.lexingtonchamber.org.*

Tours Liberty Ride. April through October, guided trolley tours visit many of the historic sites in Lexington and Concord. Tickets are good for 24 hours and allow on-off privileges. If you don't get off, the tour is about 90 minutes. It begins at the Lexington Visitor Center at 1875 Massachusetts Avenue. ☎ 781/862–0500 ⊕ tourlexington.us/libertyride.html ☜ $25 ♡ Daily June–Oct., weekends Apr.–May ☞ Dial extension 260.

TOUR BY PHONE

Half-hour cell-phone audio tours of various parts of Minute Man National Historical Park are available for $5.99 apiece. They start at the visitor center, Hartwell Tavern, and Concord's North Bridge entrance—just look for the audio tour signs and call ☎ 703/286–2755.

EXPLORING

Battle Green. It was on this 2-acre triangle of land, on April 19, 1775, that the first confrontation between British soldiers, who were marching from Boston toward Concord, and the colonial militia known as the Minutemen took place. The Minutemen—so called because they were able to prepare themselves at a moment's notice—were led by Captain John Parker, whose role in the American Revolution is commemorated in Henry Hudson Kitson's renowned 1900 *Minuteman* statue. Facing downtown Lexington at the tip of Battle Green, the statue's in a traffic island, and therefore makes for a difficult photo op. ⊠ *Junction of Massachusetts Ave. and Bedford St.*

Buckman Tavern. While waiting for the arrival of the British on the morning of April 19, 1775, the Minutemen gathered at this 1690 tavern. A half-hour tour takes in the tavern's seven rooms, which have been restored to the way they looked in the 1770s. Among the items on display is an old front door with a hole made by a British musket ball. ⊠ *1 Bedford St.* ☎ *781/862–1703* ⊕ *www.lexingtonhistory.org* ☜ *$7; $12 combination ticket includes Hancock-Clarke House and Munroe Tavern* ♡ *Apr.–Oct., daily 10–4.*

Hancock-Clarke House. On April 18, 1775, Paul Revere came here to warn patriots John Hancock and Sam Adams (who were staying at the house while attending the Provincial Congress in nearby Concord) of the advance of British troops. Hancock and Adams, on whose heads the British king had put a price, fled to avoid capture. The house, a parsonage built in 1698, is a 10-minute walk from Lexington Common. Inside are the pistols of the British major John Pitcairn, as well as period furnishings and portraits. ⊠ *36 Hancock St.* ☎ *781/862–1703* ⊕ *www.lexingtonhistory.org* ☜ *$7; $12 combination ticket includes Buckman Tavern and Munroe Tavern* ♡ *Apr.–May, Sat.–Sun. 10–4; June–Oct., daily 10–4.*

FAMILY **Minute Man National Historical Park.** West of Lexington's center stretches this 1,000-acre, three-parcel park that also extends into nearby Lincoln and Concord (⇨ *Concord, Exploring*). Begin your park visit at Lexington's **Minute Man Visitor Center** to see its free multimedia presentation, "The Road to Revolution," a captivating introduction to the events of April 1775. Then, continuing along Highway 2A toward Concord, you pass the point where Revere's midnight ride ended with

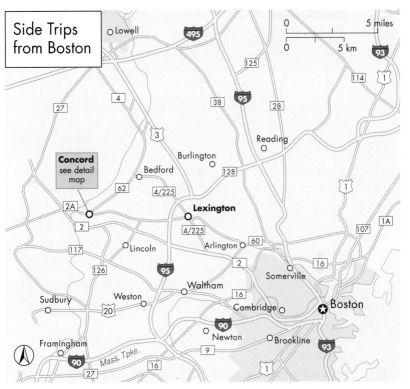

Side Trips
from Boston

his capture by the British; it's marked with a boulder and plaque, as well as an enclosure where rangers sometimes give educational presentations. You can also visit the 1732 **Hartwell Tavern** (open mid-April through late May, weekends 9:30–5:30, and late May through late October, daily 9:30–5:30), a restored drover's (driver's) tavern staffed by park employees in period costume; they frequently demonstrate musket firing or open-hearth cooking, and children are likely to enjoy the reproduction colonial toys. ⊠ *250 North Great Rd.(Hwy. 2A), ¼ mi west of Hwy. 128* ☎ *978/369–6993* ⊕ *www.nps.gov/mima* ⊗ *North Bridge Visitor Center, hrs vary according to season.*

Munroe Tavern. As April 19, 1775, dragged on, British forces met fierce resistance in Concord. Dazed and demoralized after the battle at Concord's Old North Bridge, the British backtracked and regrouped at this 1695 tavern 1 mile east of Lexington Common, while the Munroe family hid in nearby woods. The troops then retreated through what is now the town of Arlington. After a bloody battle there, they returned to Boston. Tours of the tavern last about 30 minutes. ⊠ *1332 Massachusetts Ave.* ☎ *781/862–1703* ⊕ *www.lexingtonhistory.org* ✉ *$7; $12 combination ticket includes Hancock-Clarke House and Buckman Tavern* ⊗ *June–Oct., noon–4.*

National Heritage Museum. View artifacts from all facets of American life, put in social and political context. Specializing in the history of American Freemasonry and Fraternalism, the changing exhibits and lectures also focus on local events leading up to April 1775 and illustrates Revolutionary-era life through everyday objects such as blacksmithing tools, bloodletting paraphernalia, and dental instruments, including a "tooth key" used to extract teeth. ⊠ *33 Marrett Rd., Hwy. 2A at Massachusetts Ave.* ☎ *781/861–6559* ⊕ *www.monh.org* 💵 *Donations accepted* ☉ *Wed.–Sat. 10–4:30.*

CONCORD

About 10 miles west of Lexington, 21 miles northwest of Boston.

The Concord of today is a modern suburb with a busy center filled with arty shops, places to eat, and (recalling the literary history made here) old bookstores. Autumn lovers, take note: Concord is a great place to start a fall foliage tour. From Boston, head west along Route 2 to Concord, and then continue on to find harvest stands and apple picking around Harvard and Stow.

GETTING HERE AND AROUND

The MBTA runs buses to Concord. On the MBTA Commuter Rail, Concord is a 40-minute ride on the Fitchburg Line, which departs from Boston's North Station.

ESSENTIALS

Bus and Train Contact MBTA ☎ *617/222–3200, 800/392–6100* ⊕ *www.mbta.com.*

Visitor Information Concord Visitor Center ⊠ *58 Main St.* ☎ *978/369–3120* ⊕ *www.concordchamberofcommerce.org* ☉ *Daily 10–4 Mar.–Dec.*

EXPLORING

FAMILY **Concord Museum.** The original contents of Emerson's private study, as well as the world's largest collection of Thoreau artifacts, reside in this 1930 Colonial Revival building just east of the town center. The museum provides a good overview of the town's history, from its original American Indian settlement to the present. Highlights include American Indian artifacts, furnishings from Thoreau's Walden Pond cabin (there's a replica of the cabin itself on the museum's lawn), and one of the two lanterns hung at Boston's Old North Church to signal that the British were coming by sea. ■ TIP→ **If you've brought children, ask for a free family activity pack.** ⊠ *200 Lexington Rd., entrance on Cambridge Tpke.* ☎ *978/369–9763* ⊕ *www.concordmuseum.org* 💵 *$10* ☉ *Jan.– Mar., Mon.–Sat. 11–4, Sun. 1–4; Apr., May, and Sept.–Dec., Mon.–Sat. 9–5, Sun. noon–5; June–Aug., daily 9–5.*

FAMILY **Minute Man National Historical Park.** Along Highway 2A is a three-parcel park with 1,000 acres. The park contains many of the sites important to Concord's role in the Revolution, including Old North Bridge, as well as two visitor centers, one each in Concord and Lexington (⇨ *Lexington, Essentials*). Although the initial Revolutionary War sorties were in Lexington, word of the American losses spread rapidly to surrounding towns: when the British marched into Concord,

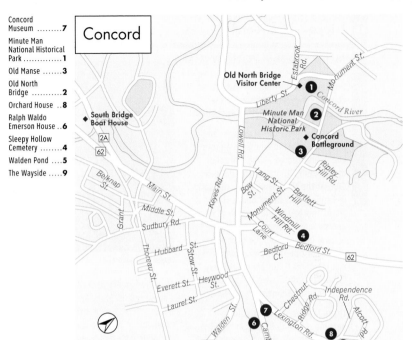

more than 400 Minutemen were waiting. A marker set in the stone wall along Liberty Street, behind the North Bridge Visitor Center, announces, "On this field the minutemen and militia formed before marching down to the fight at the bridge." ⊠ *Bounded by Monument St., Liberty St., and Lowell Rd.* ⊕ *www.nps.gov/mima* ⊗ *Grounds daily dawn–dusk.*

North Bridge Visitor Center ⊠ *174 Liberty St.* ☎ *978/369–6993* ⊗ *Apr.–Oct., daily 9–5; Nov., daily 9–4; call for winter hrs.*

Old Manse. The Reverend William Emerson, grandfather of Ralph Waldo Emerson, watched rebels and redcoats battle from behind his home, which was within sight of the Old North Bridge. The house, built in 1770, was occupied continuously by the Emerson family for almost two centuries, except for a 3½-year period during which Nathaniel Hawthorne rented it. Furnishings date from the late 18th century. Tours run throughout the day and last 45 minutes, with a new tour starting within 15 minutes of when the first person signs up. ⊠ *269 Monument St.* ☎ *978/369–3909* ⊕ *www.thetrustees.org/ places-to-visit/greater-boston/old-manse.html* ⊠ *$8* ⊗ *Mid-Apr.–Oct., Mon.–Sat. 10–5, Sun. noon–5; Nov.–Mar. Tours Thurs. and Fri. 2, 3, and 4 pm and weekends noon–4:30 (weather permitting).*

Literary Concord

The first wholly American literary movement was born in Concord, the tiny town west of Boston that, quite coincidentally, also witnessed the beginning of the American Revolution.

Under the influence of essayist and poet Ralph Waldo Emerson, a group eventually known as the Transcendental Club (but called the Hedges Club at the time) assembled regularly in Emerson's Concord home. Henry David Thoreau, a fellow townsman and famous proponent of self-reliance, was an integral club member, along with such others as pioneering feminist Margaret Fuller and poet Ellery Channing, both drawn to Concord simply because of Emerson's presence.

Louisa May Alcott

These are the names that have become indelible bylines in high school anthologies and college syllabi, but Concord also produced beloved authors outside the Transcendentalist movement. These writers include Louisa May Alcott of *Little Women* fame and children's book author Harriet Lothrop, pseudonymously known as Margaret Sydney. Even Nathaniel Hawthorne, whose various temporary homes around Massachusetts constitute a literary trail all their own, resided in Concord during the early and later portions of his career.

The cumulative inkwells of these authors have bestowed upon Concord a literary legacy unique in the United States, both for its influence on literature in general and for the quantity of related sights packed within such a small radius. From Alcott's Orchard House to Hawthorne's Old Manse, nearly all of their houses remain standing, well-preserved and open for tours.

The Thoreau Institute, within walking distance of a reconstruction of Thoreau's famous cabin in the woods at Walden Pond, is a repository of his papers and original editions. Emerson's study sits in the Concord Museum, across the street from his house. Even their final resting places are here, on Authors Ridge in Sleepy Hollow Cemetery, a few short blocks from the town common. **Concord Bike Tours** (☎ *978/697–1897* ⊕ *www.concordbiketours.com*) will guide you through the sites on two wheels, usually April through November (weather permitting).

Old North Bridge. A half-mile from Concord center, at this bridge, the Concord Minutemen turned the tables on the British on the morning of April 19, 1775. The Americans didn't fire first, but when two of their own fell dead from a Redcoat volley, Major John Buttrick of Concord roared, "Fire, fellow soldiers, for God's sake, fire." The Minutemen released volley after volley, and the Redcoats fled. Daniel Chester

French's famous statue *The Minuteman* (1875) honors the country's first freedom fighters. Inscribed at the foot of the statue are words Ralph Waldo Emerson wrote in 1837 describing the confrontation: "By the rude bridge that arched the flood / Their flag to April's breeze unfurled / Here once the embattled farmers stood / And fired the shot heard round the world." The lovely wooded surroundings give a sense of what the landscape was like in more rural times. ⊠ *Concord Center, Near Minute Man Monument* ⊕ *www.nps.gov/mima.*

Orchard House. The dark brown exterior of Louisa May Alcott's family home sharply contrasts with the light, wit, and energy so much in evidence inside. Named for the apple orchard that once surrounded it, Orchard House was the Alcott family home from 1857 to 1877. Here Louisa wrote *Little Women*, based on her life with her three sisters; and her father, Bronson, founded his school of philosophy—the building remains behind the house. Because Orchard House had just one owner after the Alcotts left, and because it became a museum in 1911, many of the original furnishings remain, including the semicircular shelf-desk where Louisa wrote *Little Women.* ⊠ *399 Lexington Rd.* ☎ *978/369–4118* ⊕ *www.louisamayalcott.org* ⊠ *$9* ⊙ *Apr.–Oct., Mon.–Sat. 10–4:30, Sun. 1–4:30; Nov.–Dec. and Jan. 3–Mar., Sat.–Sun. 11–3, Sat. 10–4:30, Sun. 1–4:30. Half-hour tours begin every 30 mins Apr.–Oct.; call for off-season schedule.*

Ralph Waldo Emerson House. The 19th-century essayist and poet Ralph Waldo Emerson lived briefly in the Old Manse in 1834–35, then moved to this home, where he lived until his death in 1882. Here he wrote the *Essays.* Except for artifacts from Emerson's study, now at the nearby Concord Museum, the Emerson House furnishings have been preserved as the writer left them, down to his hat resting on the newel post. You must join one of the half-hour-long tours to see the interior. ⊠ *28 Cambridge Tpke., at Lexington Rd.* ☎ *978/369–2236* ⊕ *www. nps.gov/nr/travel/massachusetts_conservation/ralph_waldo_emerson_ house.html* ⊠ *$8* ⊙ *Mid-Apr.–mid-Oct., Thurs.–Sat. 10–4:30, Sun. 1–4:30; call for tour schedule.*

Sleepy Hollow Cemetery. In the Author's Ridge section of this cemetery are the graves of American literary greats Louisa May Alcott, Ralph Waldo Emerson, Henry David Thoreau, and Nathaniel Hawthorne. Each Memorial Day Alcott's grave is decorated in commemoration of her death. ⊠ *Bedford St. (Hwy. 62)* ☎ *978/318–3233* ⊙ *Daily dawn–dusk.*

Fodor'sChoice
★ **Walden Pond.** For lovers of early American literature, a trip to Concord isn't complete without a pilgrimage to Henry David Thoreau's most famous residence. Here, in 1845, at age 28, Thoreau moved into a one-room cabin—built for $28.12—on the shore of this 100-foot-deep kettle hole formed by the retreat of an ancient glacier. Living alone for the next two years, Thoreau discovered the benefits of solitude and the beauties of nature. The essays in *Walden,* published in 1854, are a mixture of philosophy, nature writing, and proto-ecology. The site of the first cabin is staked out in stone. A full-size, authentically furnished replica of the cabin stands about ½ mile from the original

Retrace Henry David Thoreau's steps at Walden Pond.

site, near the Walden Pond State Reservation parking lot. Even when it's closed, you can peek through its windows. Now, as in Thoreau's time, the pond is a delightful summertime spot for swimming, fishing, and rowing, and there's hiking in the nearby woods. To get to Walden Pond State Reservation from the center of Concord—a trip of only 1½ miles—take Concord's Main Street a block west from Monument Square, turn left onto Walden Street, and head for the intersection of Highways 2 and 126. Cross over Highway 2 onto Highway 126, heading south for ½ mile. ⊠ *915 Walden St.(Hwy. 126)* ☎ *978/369-3254* ⊕ *www.mass.gov/dcr/parks/walden* ✉ *Free, parking $5* ☉ *Daily 8 am– sunset weather permitting.*

The Wayside. Nathaniel Hawthorne lived at the Old Manse in 1842–45, working on stories and sketches; he then moved to Salem (where he wrote *The Scarlet Letter*) and later to Lenox (*The House of the Seven Gables*). In 1852 he returned to Concord, bought this rambling structure called The Wayside, and lived here until his death in 1864. The home certainly appealed to literary types: the subsequent owner of The Wayside, Margaret Sidney, wrote the children's book *Five Little Peppers and How They Grew* (1881), and before Hawthorne moved in, the Alcotts lived here, from 1845 to 1848. An exhibit center, in the former barn, provides information about the Wayside authors and links them to major events in American history. Hawthorne's tower study, with his stand-up writing desk, is substantially as he left it. ⊠ *455 Lexington Rd.* ☎ *978/318-7863* ⊕ *www.nps.gov* ✉ *$5* ☉ *Open by guided tour only, May–Oct.; call for reservations.*

WHERE TO EAT

$$ ✕ **Main Streets Market & Cafe.** Cyclists, families, and sightseers pack into
AMERICAN this brick building, which was used to store munitions during the Revolutionary War. Wood floors and blackboard menus add a touch of nostalgia, but the extensive menu includes many modern hits. Breakfast offerings include a quiche and breakfast sandwich of the day. At lunch, the grilled panini are excellent; they also serve flatbread pizza and pub fare. At night heartier offerings dominate the menu, including baked lobster mac and cheese, scallop and shrimp risotto, and a Yankee pot roast dinner. There's a full bar, live music five nights a week, and in summer the small alley outside leads to a counter that serves ice cream. It's open late on Friday and Saturday nights. $ *Average main: $18* ✉ *42 Main St.* ☎ *978/369–9948* ⊕ *www.mainstreetsmarketandcafe.com* ⊗ *No dinner Sun.*

THE NORTH SHORE

The slice of Massachusetts's Atlantic Coast known as the North Shore extends past Boston to the Cape Ann region just shy of the New Hampshire border. In addition to miles of woods and beaches, the North Shore's highlights include Marblehead, a classic New England sea town; Salem, which thrives on a history of witches, writers, and maritime trades; Gloucester, the oldest seaport in America; Rockport, rich with crafts shops and artists' studios; and Newburyport, with its redbrick center and clapboard mansions, and a handful of typical New England towns in between. Bustling during the short summer season and breathtaking during the autumn foliage, the North Shore is calmer (and colder) between November and June. Many restaurants, inns, and attractions operate on reduced hours during the off-season.

MARBLEHEAD

17 miles north of Boston.

Marblehead, with its narrow and winding streets, beautifully preserved clapboard homes, sea captains' mansions, and harbor, looks much as it must have when it was founded in 1629 by fishermen from Cornwall and the Channel Islands. One of New England's premier sailing capitals, Marblehead attracts boats from along the Eastern Seaboard each July during Race Week—first held in 1889. Parking in town can be difficult; lots at the end of Front Street or on State Street by the Landing restaurant are the best options.

ESSENTIALS

Visitor Information Marblehead Chamber of Commerce Information Booth ✉ *62 Pleasant St.* ☎ *781/631–2868* ⊕ *www.visitmarblehead.com.*

EXPLORING

Abbott Hall. The town's Victorian-era municipal building, built in 1876, displays Archibald Willard's painting *The Spirit of '76*. Many visitors, familiar since childhood with this image of the three Revolutionary veterans with fife, drum, and flag, are surprised to find the original in an otherwise unassuming town hall. Also on-site is a small naval museum exploring Marblehead's maritime past. ✉ *188 Washington St.* ☎ *781/631–0000* ⊗ *Free* ⊗ *Call for hrs.*

The 1768 Jeremiah Lee Mansion. Marblehead's 18th-century high society is exemplified in this mansion run by the Marblehead Museum and Historical Society. Colonel Lee was the wealthiest merchant and ship owner in Massachusetts in 1768, and although few original furnishings remain, the unique hand-painted wallpaper and fine collection of traditional North Shore furniture provide clues to the life of an American gentleman. Across the street at the main museum (open year round), the J.O.J. Frost Folk Art Gallery pays tribute the town's talented 19th-century native son; there are also exhibits focusing on the Civil War. ✉ *161 Washington St.* ☎ *781/631–1768* 🌐 *www.marbleheadmuseum.org/LeeMansion.htm* 🎟 *$5* 🕒 *Lee Mansion June–Oct., Tues.–Sat. 10–4; Marblehead Museum Tues.–Sat. 10–4.*

Fort Sewall. Magnificent views of Marblehead, of the harbor, the Misery Islands, and the Atlantic are best enjoyed from this fort built in 1644 atop the rocky cliffs of the harbor. Used as a defense against the French in 1742 as well as during the War of 1812, Fort Sewall is today open to the public as community parkland. Barracks and underground quarters can still be seen, and Revolutionary War reenactments by members of the modern-day Glover's Marblehead Regiment are staged at the fort annually. ✉ *End of Front St.* ☎ *781/631–1000* 🌐 *www.marblehead.org/index.aspx?NID=1012* 🎟 *Free* 🕒 *Daily sunrise–sunset.*

WHERE TO EAT AND STAY

$$ SEAFOOD 🍴 **The Landing.** Decorated in nautical blues and whites, this pleasant restaurant sits right on Marblehead harbor, with a deck that's nearly in the water. The restaurant offers classic New England fare like clam chowder and broiled scrod, and serves brunch on Sunday. The pub area has a lighter menu and local feel. [$] *Average main: $12* ✉ *81 Front St.* ☎ *781/639–1266* 🌐 *www.thelandingrestaurant.com.*

$$ B&B/INN Fodor's Choice ★ 🏨 **Harbor Light Inn.** Housed in a pair of adjoining 18th-century mansions in the heart of Old Town Marblehead, this elegant inn features many rooms with canopy beds, brick fireplaces, and Jacuzzis. **Pros:** nice location amid period homes; on-site tavern with pub menu. **Cons:** limited parking; many one-way and narrow streets make this town somewhat confusing to get around in by car and the inn tricky to find. [$] *Rooms from: $149* ✉ *58 Washington St.* ☎ *781/631–2186* 🌐 *www.harborlightinn.com* 🛏 *20 rooms, 3 apartments.*

SALEM

16 miles northeast of Boston, 4 miles west of Marblehead.

Known for years as the Witch City, Salem is redefining itself. Though numerous witch-related attractions and shops still draw tourists, there's much more to the city. But first, a bit on its bewitched past...

The witchcraft hysteria emerged from the trials of 1692, when several Salem-area girls fell ill and accused some of the townspeople of casting spells on them. More than 150 men and women were charged with practicing witchcraft, a crime punishable by death. After the trials later that year, 19 people were hanged and one man was crushed to death.

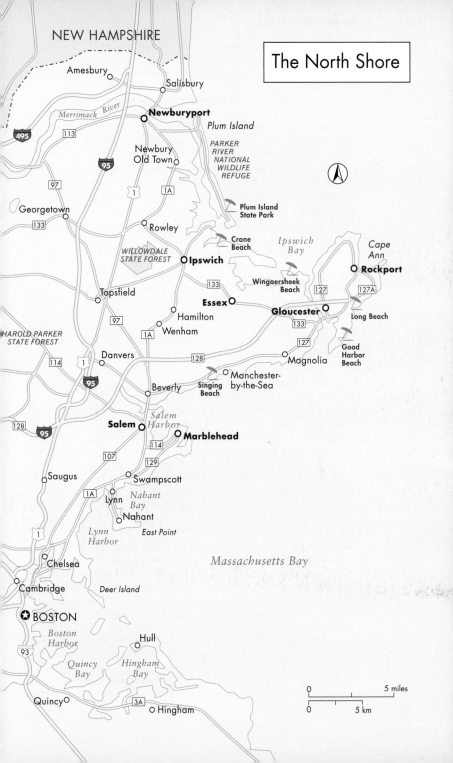

Though the witch trials might have built Salem's infamy, it'd be a mistake to ignore the town's rich maritime and creative traditions, which played integral roles in the country's evolution. Frigates out of Salem opened the Far East trade routes and generated the wealth that created America's first millionaires. Among its native talents are writer Nathaniel Hawthorne, the intellectual Peabody Sisters, navigator Nathaniel Bowditch, and architect Samuel McIntire. This creative spirit is today celebrated in Salem's internationally recognized museums, waterfront shops and restaurants, galleries, and wide common.

To learn more on the area, stop by the **Regional Visitor's Center**. Innovatively designed in the Old Salem Armory, the center has exhibits, a 27-minute film, maps, and a gift shop.

ESSENTIALS

Visitor Information Destination Salem ⊠ *93 Washington St.* ☎ *978/744–3663, 877/725–3662* ⊕ *www.salem.org.* **Regional Visitor's Center** ⊠ *2 New Liberty St.* ☎ *978/740–1650* ⊕ *www.nps.gov/ner/sama* ☺ *Daily 9–5.*

EXPLORING

House of the Seven Gables. Immortalized in Nathaniel Hawthorne's classic novel, this site itself is a literary treasure. Built in 1668 and also known as the Turner-Ingersoll Mansion, the house includes a secret staircase, a garret containing an antique scale model of the house, and some of the finest Georgian interiors in the country. Also on the property is the small house where Hawthorne was born in 1804; built in 1750, it was moved from its original location a few blocks away. ⊠ *115 Derby St.* ☎ *978/744–0991* ⊕ *www.7gables.org* ⊠ *$12.50* ☺ *Nov.–Dec., and mid-Jan.–June, daily 10–5; July–Oct., daily 10–7.*

Fodor'sChoice
★
Peabody Essex Museum. Salem's world-class museum celebrates maritime art, history, and the spoils of the Asian export trade. Its 30 galleries, housed in a contemplative blend of modern design, represent a diverse range of styles; exhibits include pieces ranging from American decorative and seamen's art to idea studios and photography. While there, be sure to tour the Yin Yu Tang house. This fabulous 200-year-old house dates to the Qing Dynasty (1644–1911) of China. The museum brought it over from China in sections and reassembled it here. ⊠ *East India Sq.* ☎ *978/745–9500, 866/745–1876* ⊕ *www.pem. org* ⊠ *$15* ☺ *Tues.–Sun. 10–5; Mon. holidays 10–5.*

Salem Maritime National Historic Site. Near Derby Wharf, this 9¼-acre site focuses on Salem's heritage as a major seaport with a thriving overseas trade. It includes an orientation center with an 18-minute film; the 1762 home of Elias Derby, America's first millionaire; the 1819 Customs House, made famous in Nathaniel Hawthorne's *The Scarlet Letter*; and a replica of the *Friendship*, a 171-foot, three-masted 1797 merchant vessel. There's also an active lighthouse dating from 1871, as well as the nation's last surviving 18th-century wharves. The West India Goods Store, across the street, is still a working 19th-century store, with glass jars of spices, teas, and coffees. New to the site is the 1770 Pedrick Store House, moved from nearby Marblehead and reassembled right on Derby Wharf; the two-story structure once played a vital role in the

CLOSE UP

The First Witch Trial

It was in Danvers, not Salem, that the first witch trial was held, originating with the family of Samuel Parris, a minister who moved to the area in 1680 from Barbados, bringing with him two slaves, including one named Tituba. In 1691 Samuel's daughter, Betty, and niece, Abigail, began having "fits." Tituba, who had told Betty and Abigail stories of magic and witchcraft from her homeland, baked a "witch cake" to identify the witches who were harming the girls. The girls in turn accused Tituba of witchcraft. After three days of "questioning," which included beatings from Samuel and a promise from him to free her if she cooperated, Tituba confessed to meeting the devil (in the form of a black hog or dog). She also claimed there were other witches in the village, confirming the girls' accusations against Sarah Good and Sarah Osborne, but she refused to name any others. Tituba's trial prompted the frenzy that led to the deaths of 20 accused "witches."

3

lucrative merchant seaside trade. ✉ *193 Derby St.* ☎ *978/740–1650* 🌐 *www.nps.gov/sama* 🎟 *Site free, tours $5* 🕑 *Hrs vary.*

Salem Witch Museum. An informative, if somewhat hokey, introduction to the 1692 witchcraft hysteria, this museum has a short walk-through exhibit, "Witches: Evolving Perceptions," that describes witch hunts through the years. ✉ *19 1/2 N. Washington Sq.* ☎ *978/744–1692* 🌐 *www.salemwitchmuseum.com* 🎟 *$9* 🕑 *Daily 10–5; July and Aug., daily 10–7.*

WHERE TO EAT AND STAY

$$ SEAFOOD 🍴 **Finz Seafood & Grill.** This contemporary seafood restaurant on Pickering Wharf treats patrons to prime canal views. Seafood potpie and lobster rolls highlight the lunch menu, while sesame-crusted tuna or steamed lobster are dinner favorites. Nab a seat on the outdoor deck when the weather's fine and eat practically among the boats. There's also live music on Thursday and Friday nights. [$] *Average main: $21* ✉ *76 Wharf St.* ☎ *978/744–8485* 🌐 *www.hipfinz.com.*

$$ B&B/INN 🏨 **Amelia Payson House.** Built in 1845, this Greek Revival house is a comfortable bed-and-breakfast near all the historic attractions. **Pros:** spotless; cozy; decorated in period furniture. **Cons:** no children under 14. [$] *Rooms from: $135* ✉ *16 Winter St.* ☎ *978/744–8304* 🌐 *www.ameliapaysonhouse.com* 🛏 *3 rooms* 🕑 *Closed Dec.–Apr.* 🍽 *Breakfast.*

$$ HOTEL 🏨 **The Hawthorne Hotel.** Elegantly restored, this full-service landmark hotel celebrates the town's most famous writer and is within walking distance of the town common, museums, and waterfront. **Pros:** lovely, historic lobby; parking available behind hotel; easy walking access to all the town's features. **Cons:** many rooms are small. [$] *Rooms from: $144* ✉ *18 Washington Sq. W* ☎ *978/744–4080, 800/729–7829* 🌐 *www.hawthornehotel.com* 🛏 *93 rooms.*

ARTS AND ENTERTAINMENT

THEATER

Cry Innocent: The People versus Bridget Bishop. This show, the longest continuously running play north of Boston, transports audience members to Bridget Bishop's trial of 1692. After hearing historical testimonies, the audience cross-examines the witnesses and must then decide the verdict. Actors respond in character revealing much about the Puritan frame of mind. Each show is different and allows audience members to play their "part" in history. ✉ *Old Town Hall, 32 Derby Sq.* ☎ *978/867–4767* ⊕ *www.cryinnocentsalem.com* 🖃 *$12* ⊙ *July–Oct., showtimes vary.*

GLOUCESTER

37 miles northeast of Boston, 8 miles northeast of Manchester-by-the-Sea.

On Gloucester's fine seaside promenade is a famous statue of a man steering a ship's wheel, his eyes searching the horizon. The statue, which honors those who go down to the sea in ships, was commissioned by the town citizens in celebration of Gloucester's 300th anniversary in 1923. The oldest seaport in the nation (with some of the North Shore's best beaches) is still a major fishing port. Sebastian Junger's 1997 book *A Perfect Storm* was an account of the fate of the *Andrea Gail,* a Gloucester fishing boat caught in the storm of the century in October 1991. In 2000 the book was made into a movie, filmed on location in Gloucester.

ESSENTIALS

Visitor Information Cape Ann Chamber of Commerce ✉ *33 Commercial St.* ☎ *978/283–1601* ⊕ *www.capeannchamber.com.*

EXPLORING

The Cape Ann Historical Association. Downtown in the Captain Elias Davis 1804 house, this is Gloucester's surprising museum and gallery. It reflects the town's commitment to artists, and has the world's largest collection by maritime luminist Fitz Henry (Hugh) Lane. There's also an excellent exhibit on Gloucester's maritime history. ✉ *27 Pleasant St.* ☎ *978/283–0455* ⊕ *www.capeannmuseum.org* 🖃 *$10* ⊙ *Tues.–Sat. 10–5, Sun. 1–4.*

Hammond Castle Museum. Inventor John Hays Hammond Jr. built this structure in 1926 to resemble a "medieval" stone castle. Hammond is credited with more than 500 patents, including inventions associated with the organ that bears his name. The museum contains medieval-style furnishings and paintings, and the Great Hall houses an impressive 8,200-pipe organ. From the castle you can see Norman's Woe Rock, made famous by Longfellow in his poem "The Wreck of the Hesperus." ✉ *80 Hesperus Ave., south side of Gloucester off Rte. 127* ☎ *978/283–2080, 978/283–7673* ⊕ *www.hammondcastle.org* 🖃 *$9* ⊙ *May–early June, weekends and mid-June–Oct., daily; call for hrs.*

Rocky Neck. The town's creative side thrives in this neighborhood, the first-settled artists' colony in the United States. Its alumni include Winslow Homer, Maurice Prendergast, Jane Peter, and Cecilia Beaux. ✉ *53 Rocky Neck Ave.* ☎ *978/282–0917* ⊕ *www.rockyneckartcolony.org* ⊙ *Galleries 10–10, May 15–Oct. 15. Call or check website for winter hrs.*

WHERE TO EAT AND STAY

$ ✕ **The Franklin Cafe.** This contemporary nightspot offers bistro-style
AMERICAN chicken, roast cod, and steak frites, perfect for the late-night crowd
(it's open until midnight). Live jazz is on tap most Tuesday evenings.
Look for the signature martini glass over the door. $ *Average main:
$20* ⊠ *118 Main St.* ☎ *978/283–7888* ⊕ *www.franklincafe.com*
⊗ *No lunch.*

$ ✕ **Passports.** With an eclectic lunch and dinner menu—hence the name—
ECLECTIC Passports is a bright and airy café with French, Spanish, and Thai
dishes, as well as lobster sandwiches. Early risers can opt for breakfast,
which is served only on Sunday mornings. The fried calamari and house
haddock are favorites here, and there's always local art hanging on the
walls for patrons to buy. Occasionally there are wine tastings. $ *Average main: $15* ⊠ *110 Main St.* ☎ *978/281–3680.*

$$ 🛏 **Cape Ann's Marina Resort & Spa.** This year-round hotel less than a mile
RESORT from Gloucester comes alive in summer. **Pros:** guests get a free river
FAMILY cruise during summer; free Wi-Fi. **Cons:** "resort" is a misnomer—the
hotel is surrounded by parking lots; expect motel quality. $ *Rooms
from: $175* ⊠ *75 Essex Ave.* ☎ *978/283–2116, 800/626–7660* ⊕ *www.
capeannmarina.com* ⇗ *31 rooms* ⦿ *No meals.*

$$ 🛏 **Cape Ann Motor Inn.** On the sands of Long Beach, this three-story,
HOTEL shingled motel has no-frills rooms except for the balconies and ocean
views. **Pros:** exceptional view from every room; kids under 5 stay free.
Cons: thin walls; motel quality; summer season can be loud and crowded.
$ *Rooms from: $175* ⊠ *33 Rockport Rd.* ☎ *978/281–2900, 800/464–
8439* ⊕ *www.capeannmotorinn.com* ⇗ *30 rooms, 1 suite* ⦿ *Breakfast.*

SPORTS AND THE OUTDOORS

BEACHES

Gloucester has some of the best beaches on the North Shore. From
Memorial Day through mid-September, parking costs $20 on weekdays
and $25 on weekends, when the lots often fill by 10 am.

Good Harbor Beach. This beach has calm waters and soft sand, and is
surrounded by grassy dunes, making it perfect any time of year. In summer (June, July, and August) it is lifeguard patrolled and there is a snack
bar if you don't feel like packing in food. The restrooms and showers
are clean and wheelchair accessible, and you can pick up beach toys at
the concessions. **Amenities:** restrooms, showers, concessions. **Best for:**
swimming and playing on the shore. ■TIP→ **On weekdays parking is
plentiful, but the lot fills by 10 am on weekends. In June green flies can
be bothersome.** ⊠ *Easily signposted from Rte. 127A* 🅿 *Parking $20
per car; $25 on weekends and holidays.*

Long Beach. Just as its name implies, this soft-sand beach is long, and it's
also broad. It draws crowds from the houses that border it, particularly
on weekends. Cape Ann Motor Inn is nearby. **Amenities:** none. **Best
for:** families. ■TIP→ **Very limited parking. Don't even think of parking
in neighborhood streets if you don't have a town parking sticker—you
will be towed.** ⊠ *Off Rte. 127A on Gloucester-Rockport town line.*

Wingaersheek Beach. With white sand and dunes, Wingaersheek Beach
is a well-protected cove. The white Annisquam lighthouse is in the

bay. The beach is known for its miles of white sand and calm waters. **■ TIP→ On weekends arrive early. The parking lot generally fills up by mid-morning. Amenities: restrooms; food and drink. Best for: families; surf boarding.** ✉ *Exit 13 off Rte. 128* 🌐 *www.gloucester-ma.gov/index.aspx?nid=299* 🚗 *Limited parking, $20 per car; $25 on weekends and holidays.*

BOATING

Thomas E. Lannon. Consider a sail along the harbor and coast aboard the 65-foot schooner *Thomas E. Lannon*, crafted in Essex in 1996 and modeled after the great boats built a century before. From mid-May through mid-October there are several two-hour sails, including trips that let you enjoy the sunset or participate in a lobster bake. Tickets are $40. ✉ *41 Rogers St., next to Gloucester House restaurant* ☎ *978/281–6634* 🌐 *www.schooner.org.*

ROCKPORT

41 miles northeast of Boston, 4 miles northeast of Gloucester on Rte. 127.

Rockport, at the very tip of Cape Ann, derives its name from the local granite formations. Many Boston-area structures are made of stone cut from its long-gone quarries. Today the town is a tourist center with a well-marked, centralized downtown that is easy to navigate and access on foot. Unlike typical tourist-trap landmarks, Rockport's shops sell quality arts, clothing, and gifts, and its restaurants serve seafood or home-baked cookies rather than fast food. Walk past shops and colorful clapboard houses to the end of Bearskin Neck for an impressive view of the Atlantic Ocean and the old, weather-beaten lobster shack known as Motif No. 1 because of its popularity as a subject for amateur painters and photographers.

ESSENTIALS

Visitor Information **Rockport Chamber of Commerce** ✉ *33 Commercial St., Gloucester* ☎ *978/546–6575* 🌐 *www.rockportusa.com.*

WHERE TO EAT AND STAY

$$ SEAFOOD 🍴 **Brackett's Ocean View.** A big bay window in this quiet, homey restaurant provides an excellent view across Sandy Bay. The menu includes chowders, fish cakes, and other seafood dishes. [$] *Average main: $18* ✉ *25 Main St.* ☎ *978/546–2797* 🌐 *www.bracketts.com* 🕒 *Closed Nov.–Mar.*

$$ B&B/INN 🏨 **Addison Choate Inn.** Just a minute's walk from both the center of Rockport and the train station, this 1851 inn sits in a prime location. **Pros:** proximity to the ocean, shopping, and train station. **Cons:** only one bedroom on the first floor. [$] *Rooms from: $159* ✉ *49 Broadway* ☎ *978/546–7543, 800/245–7543* 🌐 *www.addisonchoateinn.com* 🛏 *5 rooms* 🕒 *Closed Nov.–Apr.* 🍽 *Breakfast.*

$$ B&B/INN Fodor's Choice ★ 🏨 **Sally Webster Inn.** This inn with local flavor and within walking range of town activities was named for a member of Hannah Jumper's "Hatchet Gang," teetotalers who smashed up the town's liquor stores in 1856 and turned Rockport into the dry town it remained until as recently as 2007. **Pros:** homey atmosphere in an excellent location with attentive staff. **Cons:** some rooms accessed via stairs. [$] *Rooms from: $140* ✉ *34 Mt. Pleasant St.* ☎ *978/546–9251* 🌐 *www.sallywebster.com* 🛏 *7 rooms* 🍽 *Breakfast.*

Kids enjoy the white sands of Wingaersheek Beach in Gloucester.

ESSEX

35 miles northeast of Boston, 12 miles west of Rockport.

The small seafaring town of Essex, once an important shipbuilding center, is surrounded by salt marshes and is filled with antiques stores and seafood restaurants.

GETTING HERE AND AROUND

Head west out of Cape Ann on Rte. 128, turning north on Rte. 133.

ESSENTIALS

Visitor Information Escape to Essex 🌐 *www.visitessexma.com.*

EXPLORING

FAMILY **Essex Shipbuilding Museum.** At what is still an active shipyard, this museum traces the evolution of the American schooner, which was first created in Essex. The museum sometimes offers shipbuilding demonstrations. One-hour tours take in the museum's many buildings and boats, especially the *Evelina M. Goulart*—one of only seven remaining Essex-built schooners. ✉ *66 Main St.(Rte. 133)* ☎ *978/768–7541* 🌐 *www.essexshipbuildingmuseum.org* 🎫 *$7* 🕒 *Mid-May–mid-Oct. Wed.–Sun. 10–5.*

WHERE TO EAT

$$ SEAFOOD FAMILY Fodor's Choice ★ 🍴 **Woodman's of Essex.** According to local legend, this is where Lawrence "Chubby" Woodman invented the first fried clam back in 1916. Today this sprawling wooden shack with indoor booths and outdoor picnic tables is *the* place for seafood in the rough. Besides fried clams, you can tuck into clam chowder, lobster rolls, or the popular "downriver" lobster combo. [$] *Average main: $16* ✉ *121 Main St.(Rte. 133)* ☎ *978/768–2559, 800/649–1773* 🌐 *www.woodmans.com.*

IPSWICH

30 miles north of Boston, 6 miles northwest of Essex.

Quiet little Ipswich, settled in 1633 and famous for its clams, is said to have more 17th-century houses standing and occupied than any other place in America; more than 40 were built before 1725. Information and a booklet with a suggested walking tour are available at the **Ipswich Visitor Information Center.**

ESSENTIALS

Visitor Information Ipswich Visitor Information Center ⊠ *36 S. Main St. (Rte. 1A)* ☎ *978/356–8540* ⊕ *www.ipswichvisitorcenter.org* ⊗ *Closed Nov.–Apr. Closed May weekdays.*

EXPLORING

Castle Hill on the Crane Estate. This 59-room Stuart-style mansion, built in 1927 for Richard Crane—of the Crane plumbing company—and his family, is part of the Crane Estate, a stretch of more than 2,100 acres along the Essex and Ipswich rivers, encompassing Castle Hill, Crane Beach, and the Crane Wildlife Refuge. Although the original furnishings were sold at auction, the mansion has been elaborately refurnished in period style; photographs in most of the rooms show their original appearance. The Great House is open for one-hour tours and also hosts concerts and other events. Inquire about seasonal programs like fly-fishing or kayaking. If you're looking for an opulent and exquisite overnight stay, book a room at the onsite Inn at Castle Hill. ⊠ *Argilla Rd.* ☎ *978/356–4351* ⊠ *Fees vary* ⊗ *Memorial Day– Columbus Day weekend, Wed.–Sat., call for hrs.*

SPORTS AND THE OUTDOORS

FAMILY **Crane Beach.** Crane Beach, one of New England's most beautiful beaches, is a sandy, 4-mile-long stretch backed by dunes and a nature trail. Public parking is available, but on a nice summer weekend it's usually full before lunch. There are lifeguards, a snack bar, and changing rooms. Check ahead before visiting mid-July to early August, when greenhead flies terrorize sunbathers. ■ TIP→ **The Ipswich Essex Explorer bus runs between the Ipswich train station and Crane Beach weekends and holidays from June to September; the $5 pass includes round-trip bus fare and beach admission. Contact the Ipswich Visitor Information Center for information.** ⊠ *310 Argilla Rd.* ☎ *978/356–4354* ⊠ *Fees vary* ⊗ *Daily 8–sunset.*

HIKING

FAMILY **Ipswich River Wildlife Sanctuary.** The Massachusetts Audubon Society's Ipswich River Wildlife Sanctuary has trails through marshland hills, where there are remains of early colonial settlements as well as abundant wildlife. Make sure to grab some birdseed and get a trail map from the office. Enjoy bridges, man-made rock structures, and other surprises on the Rockery Trail. ⊠ *87 Perkins Row, southwest of Ipswich, 1 mile off Rte. 97, Topsfield* ☎ *978/887–9264* ⊕ *www.massaudubon.org* ⊠ *$4* ⊗ *Hrs vary seasonally.*

WHERE TO EAT

$ SEAFOOD FAMILY Fodor'sChoice ★ 🍴 **Clam Box.** Shaped like a giant fried clam box, this small roadside stand is the best place to sample Ipswich's famous bivalves. Since 1938 locals and tourists have been lining up for clams, oysters, scallops, and onion rings. [$] *Average main: $14* ✉ *246 High St.(Rte. 1A)* ☎ *978/356–9707* 🌐 *www.ipswichma.com/clambox* ✍ *Reservations not accepted* 🕒 *Closed late Nov.–Feb.*

$ SEAFOOD 🍴 **Stone Soup Café.** This cheery café provides consistently good food. Excellent breakfasts include omelets, French toast, and assorted pancakes; lunch features chowders, pot roast, or delicious Cuban sandwiches. Its clam chowder took home the town's annual prize six years in a row. Dinner can include lobster bisque, porcini ravioli, or whatever contemporary fare the chef is inspired to cook from the day's farm-stand finds. [$] *Average main: $8* ✉ *141 High St., off Rte. 1A* ☎ *978/356–4222* 💳 *No credit cards* 🕒 *Closed Mon.–Tues.*

3

NEWBURYPORT

38 miles north of Boston, 12 miles north of Ipswich on Rte. 1A.

Newburyport's High Street is lined with some of the finest examples of Federal-period (roughly, 1790–1810) mansions in New England. The city was once a leading port and shipbuilding center; the houses were built for prosperous sea captains. Although Newburyport's maritime significance ended with the decline of the clipper ships, the town was revived in the 1970s. Today the town has shops, restaurants, galleries, and a waterfront park and boardwalk. Newburyport is walker-friendly, with well-marked restrooms and free parking all day down by the water.

A stroll through the **Waterfront Park and Promenade** offers a view of the harbor as well as the fishing and pleasure boats that moor here.

A causeway leads from Newburyport to a narrow piece of land known as Plum Island, which harbors a summer colony at one end.

EXPLORING

Custom House Maritime Museum. Built in 1835 in Greek Revival style, this museum contains exhibits on maritime history, ship models, tools, and paintings. ✉ *25 Water St.* ☎ *978/462–8681* 🌐 *www.customhousemaritimemuseum.org* 🎟 *$7* 🕒 *Hrs vary seasonally.*

WHERE TO EAT AND STAY

$$ SEAFOOD 🍴 **Glenn's Restaurant & Cool Bar.** A block from the waterfront parking lot, Glenn's offers creative combinations from around the world, with the occasional New England twist. The ever-changing menu might include sesame-crusted yellowfin tuna or house-smoked babyback ribs. There's live jazz or blues on Sunday. [$] *Average main: $23* ✉ *44 Merrimac St.* ☎ *978/465–3811* 🌐 *www.glennsrestaurant.com* 🕒 *Closed Mon. No lunch.*

$$ B&B/INN 🏨 **Clark Currier Inn.** Once the home of the 19th-century sea captain Thomas March Clark, this 1803 Federal mansion has been beautifully restored. **Pros:** easy to find; close to shopping and the oceanfront; good for couples looking for a peaceful and quiet experience. **Cons:** children under 10 not allowed; rooms can get hot in summer. [$] *Rooms from:*

$165 ⊠ 45 Green St. ☎ 978/465–8363 ⊕ www.clarkcurrierinn.com ⮑ 7 rooms, 1 suite ⦾ Breakfast.

SPORTS AND THE OUTDOORS

Parker River National Wildlife Refuge. On Plum Island, this 4,662-acre refuge of salt marsh, freshwater marsh, beaches, and dunes is one of the few natural barrier beach–dune–salt marsh complexes left on the Northeast coast. Here you can bird-watch, fish, swim, and pick plums and cranberries. The refuge is a popular place in summer, especially on weekends; cars begin to line up at the gate before 7 am. There's no restriction on the number of people using the beach, but only a limited number of cars are let in; no pets are allowed in the refuge. ⊠ *6 Plum Island Tpke.* ☎ *978/465–5753* ⊕ *www.fws.gov/refuge/parker_river* ⧉ *$5 per car, bicycles and walk-ins $2* ⊘ *Daily dawn–dusk. Beach usually closed during nesting season in spring and early summer.*

FAMILY
Fodor'sChoice
★

Salisbury Beach State Reservation. Relax at the long sandy beach, launch a boat, or just enjoy the water. From Newburyport center, follow Bridge Road north, take a right on Beach Road, and follow it until you reach State Reservation Road. The park is popular with campers; reservations in summer are made many months ahead to ensure a spot. ⊠ *Rte. 1A, 5 miles northeast of Newburyport, Beach Rd., Rte. 1A, Salisbury* ☎ *978/462–4481* ⊕ *www.mass.gov/dcr* ⧉ *Beach free, parking $9.*

SHOPPING

Todd Farm Flea Market. A New England tradition since 1971, the Todd Farm Flea Market features up to 240 vendors from all over New England and New York. It's open every Sunday from mid-April through late November, though its busiest months are May, September, and October. Merchandise varies from antique furniture, clocks, jewelry, recordings, and tools to fishing rods, golf accessories, honey products, cedar fencing, vintage toys, and seasonal plants and flowers. Antiques hunters often arrive before the sun comes up for the best deals. ⊠ *285 Main St., Rte. 1A, Rowley* ☎ *978/948–3300* ⊕ *www.toddfarm.com* ⊘ *Apr.–Nov., Sun. 5 am–3 pm.*

SOUTH OF BOSTON

People from all over the world travel south of Boston to visit Plymouth for a glimpse into the country's earliest beginnings. The two main stops are the Plimoth Plantation, which re-creates the everyday life of the Pilgrims; and the *Mayflower II*, which gives you an idea of how frightening the journey across the Atlantic must have been. As you may guess, November in Plymouth brings special events focused on Thanksgiving. Farther south, New Bedford recalls the world of whaling.

EN
ROUTE

While driving from Boston to Plymouth, stop at **Quincy** to visit the Adams National Historic Park.

Adams National Historic Park. Receive a guided visit of the birthplaces, homes, and graves of Presidents John Adams and his son John Quincy Adams. You also can see the park as part of a trolley tour of the property and family church. ⊠ *Carriage house, 135 Adams St., visitor* *center and bookstore, 1250 Hancock St., Quincy* ☎ *617/770–1175* ⊕ *www.nps.gov/adam* ⬛ *$5* ⊙ *Tours 9–5 daily; last tour at 3:15, mid-Apr.–mid-Nov.*

PLYMOUTH

40 miles south of Boston.

On December 26, 1620, 102 weary men, women, and children disembarked from the *Mayflower* to found the first permanent European settlement north of Virginia. Today Plymouth is characterized by narrow streets, clapboard mansions, shops, antiques stores, and a scenic waterfront. To mark Thanksgiving, the town holds a parade, historic-house tours, and other activities. Historic statues dot the town, including depictions of William Bradford, Pilgrim leader and governor of Plymouth Colony for more than 30 years, on Water Street; a Pilgrim maiden in Brewster Gardens; and Massasoit, the Wampanoag chief who helped the Pilgrims survive, on Carver Street.

ESSENTIALS

Visitor Information Plymouth Visitor Information Center ⬠ *130 Water St., at Hwy. 44* ☎ *508/747–7533, 800/872–1620* ⊕ *www.visit-plymouth.com* ⊙ *Hrs vary seasonally; check website or call.*

EXPLORING

FAMILY **Mayflower II.** This seaworthy replica of the 1620 *Mayflower* was built in England through research and a bit of guesswork, then sailed across the Atlantic in 1957. As you explore the interior and exterior of the ship, sailors in modern dress answer your questions about both the reproduction and the original ship, while costumed guides provide a 17th-century perspective. Plymouth Rock is nearby. ⬠ *State Pier* ☎ *508/746–1622* ⊕ *www.plimoth.org* ⬛ *$10, $35 with Heritage Pass admission to Plimoth Plantation* ⊙ *Late Mar.–Nov., daily 9–5.*

FAMILY
Fodor's Choice
★
Plimoth Plantation. Over the entrance to this popular attraction is the caution: You are now entering 1627. Believe it. Against the backdrop of the Atlantic Ocean, and 3 miles south of downtown Plymouth, this Pilgrim village has been carefully re-created, from the thatch roofs, cramped quarters, and open fireplaces to the long-horned livestock. Throw away your preconception of white collars and funny hats; through ongoing research, the Plimoth staff has developed a portrait of the Pilgrims that's more complex than the dour folk in school textbooks. Listen to the accents of the "residents," who never break out of character. You might see them plucking ducks, cooking rabbit stew, or tending gardens. Feel free to engage them in conversation about their life, but expect only curious looks if you ask about anything that happened after 1627. "Thanksgiving: Memory, Myth & Meaning," an exhibit in the visitor center, offers a fresh perspective on the 1621 harvest celebration that is now known as "the first Thanksgiving." Note that there's not a lot of shade here in summer. ⬠ *137 Warren Ave.(Hwy. 3A)* ☎ *508/746–1622* ⊕ *www.plimoth.org* ⬛ *Combination passes for three sites start at $28* ⊙ *Hrs vary seasonally.*

DID YOU KNOW?

Plimoth Plantation is about more than Pilgrims. It also honors Native Americans at Wampanoag Site. Visit a traditional house, learn about family life, and chat with Wampanoag people. Note that presenters are not in character as at the plantation site.

FAMILY **Pilgrim Hall Museum.** From the waterfront sights it's a short walk to one of the country's oldest public museums. Established in 1824, Pilgrim Hall Museum transports you back to the time of the Pilgrims' landing with objects carried by those weary travelers to the New World. Included are a carved chest, a remarkably well-preserved wicker cradle, Myles Standish's sword, John Alden's Bible, American Indian artifacts, and the remains of the *Sparrow Hawk,* a sailing ship that was wrecked in 1626. ✉ *75 Court St.(Rte. 3A)* ☎ *508/746–1620* ⊕ *www.pilgrimhall.org* ✉ *$8* ☉ *Feb.–Dec., daily 9:30–4:30 including Thanksgiving Day.*

Sparrow House. Built in 1640, this is Plymouth's oldest structure. It is among several historic houses in town that are open for visits. You can peek into a pair of rooms furnished in the spartan style of the Pilgrims' era. The contemporary crafts gallery also on the premises seems somewhat incongruous, but the works on view are of high quality. ✉ *42 Summer St.* ☎ *508/747–1240* ⊕ *www.sparrowhouse.com* ✉ *House $2, gallery free* ☉ *Daily 10–5.*

WHERE TO EAT AND STAY

$$$ ✕ **Blue-eyed Crab Grille & Raw Bar.** Grab a seat on the outside deck over-
SEAFOOD looking the water at this friendly, somewhat funky (plastic fish dangling from the ceiling) fresh-fish shack. If the local Island Creek raw oysters are on the menu, go for them! Otherwise start with thick crab bisque full of hunks of floating crabmeat or the steamed mussels. Dinner entrées include seafood stew with chorizo and sweet potatoes and the classic fish-and-chips. Locals come for the brunch specials, too, like grilled shrimp and poached eggs over red-pepper grits, the lobster omelet, and banana-ginger pancakes. $ *Average main: $22* ✉ *170 Water St.* ☎ *508/747–6776* ⊕ *www.blueeyedcrab.com.*

$ ⌂ **Best Western Cold Spring.** Walk to the waterfront and downtown Plym-
HOTEL outh from this clean, family-friendly two-story motel. **Pros:** free park-
FAMILY ing; half-mile from Plymouth Rock and *Mayflower II;* some of the best wallet-pleasing rates in the area. **Cons:** basic rooms without much character. $ *Rooms from: $140* ✉ *188 Court St.* ☎ *508/746–2222, 800/678–8667* ⊕ *www.bestwesternmassachusetts.com* ⬐ *56 rooms* ◯| *Breakfast.*

NEW BEDFORD

45 miles southwest of Plymouth, 50 miles south of Boston.

In 1652 colonists from Plymouth settled in the area that now includes the city of New Bedford. The city has a long maritime tradition, beginning as a shipbuilding center and small whaling port in the late 1700s. By the mid-1800s it had developed into a center of North American whaling. Today New Bedford has the largest fishing fleet on the East Coast. Although much of the town is industrial, the restored historic district near the water is a delight. It was here that Herman Melville set his masterpiece, *Moby-Dick,* a novel about whaling.

ESSENTIALS

Visitor Information New Bedford Office of Tourism ✉ *Waterfront Visitor Center, Pier 3, 52 Co op Wharf #3* ☎ *800/508–5353, 508/979–1745* ⊕ *www.newbedford-ma.gov/Tourism/DestinationNB/visitorcenter.html.*

EXPLORING

FAMILY **New Bedford Whaling Museum.** Established in 1903, this is the world's largest museum of its kind. A highlight is the skeleton of a 66-foot blue whale, one of only three on view anywhere. An interactive exhibit lets you listen to the underwater sounds of whales, dolphins, and other sea life—plus the sounds of a thunderstorm and a whale-watching boat—as a whale might hear them. You can also peruse the collection of scrimshaw, visit exhibits on regional history, and climb aboard an 89-foot, half-scale model of the 1826 whaling ship *Lagoda*—the world's largest ship model. A small chapel across the street from the museum is the one described in *Moby-Dick*. ✉ *18 Johnny Cake Hill* ☎ *508/997–0046* 🌐 *www.whalingmuseum.org* 🎟 *$14* 🕒 *May–Sept., daily 9-5, Oct.–Apr. Tues.–Sat. 9–4; Sun. 11–4.*

FAMILY **New Bedford Whaling National Historical Park.** The city's whaling tradition is commemorated at this park that takes up 13 blocks of the waterfront historic district. The park visitor center, housed in an 1853 Greek Revival building that was once a bank, provides maps and information about whaling-related sites. Free walking tours of the park leave from the visitor center at 10:30, 12:30, and 2:30 in July and August. ✉ *33 William St.* ☎ *508/996–4095* 🌐 *www.nps.gov/nebe* 🎟 *Free* 🕒 *Daily 9–5.*

Rotch-Jones-Duff House & Garden Museum. For a glimpse of upper-class life during New Bedford's whaling heyday, head one-half mile south of downtown to this 1834 Greek Revival mansion. Amid a full city block of gardens, the home housed three prominent families in the 1800s and is filled with elegant furnishings from the era, including a mahogany piano, a massive marble-top sideboard, and portraits of the house's occupants. A free self-guided audio tour is available. ✉ *396 County St.* ☎ *508/997–1401* 🌐 *www.rjdmuseum.org* 🎟 *$6* 🕒 *Mon.–Sat. 10–4, Sun. noon–4.*

WHERE TO EAT

$$ PORTUGUESE 🍴 **Antonio's.** Expect the wait to be long and the dining room to be loud, but it's worth the hassle to sample the traditional fare of New Bedford's large Portuguese population at this friendly, unadorned restaurant. Dishes include hearty portions of pork and shellfish stew, *bacalau* (salt cod), and grilled sardines, often on plates piled high with crispy fried potatoes and rice. [$] *Average main: $15* ✉ *267 Coggeshall St., near intersection of I–195 and Hwy. 18* ☎ *508/990–3636* 🌐 *www.antoniosnewbedford.com.*

$$ SEAFOOD FAMILY 🍴 **Davy's Locker.** A huge seafood menu is the main draw at this spot overlooking Buzzards Bay. Choose from more than a dozen shrimp preparations, or a choice of healthful entrées—dishes prepared with olive oil, vegetables, garlic, and herbs. For landlubbers, chicken, steak, ribs, and the like are also available. [$] *Average main: $15* ✉ *1480 E. Rodney French Blvd.* ☎ *508/992–7359* 🌐 *www.davyslockerrestaurant.com.*

CAPE COD, MARTHA'S VINEYARD, AND NANTUCKET

WELCOME TO CAPE COD, MARTHA'S VINEYARD, AND NANTUCKET

TOP REASONS TO GO

★ **Beaches:** Cape Cod's picturesque beaches are the ultimate reason to go. The high sand dunes, gorgeous sunsets, and never-ending sea will get you every time.

★ **Visiting Lighthouses:** Lighthouses rise along Cape Cod's coast like architectural exclamation marks. Highlights include Eastham's beautiful Nauset Light and Chatham and Nobska lights for their spectacular views.

★ **Biking the Trails:** The Cape Cod Rail Trail from South Dennis to South Wellfleet is the definitive bike route, with 25 miles of relatively flat terrain. Martha's Vineyard and Nantucket have dedicated bike paths.

★ **Setting Sail:** Area tour operators offer everything from sunset schooner cruises to charter fishing expeditions. Mid-April through October, whale-watching adventures are popular.

★ **Browsing the Galleries:** The Cape was a prominent art colony in the 19th century and today it has a number of galleries.

1 Cape Cod. Typically divided into regions—the Upper, Mid, Lower, and Outer—Cape Cod is a place of many moods. The Upper Cape (closest to the bridges) has Cape Cod's oldest towns, plus fine beaches and fascinating little museums. The Mid Cape has sophisticated Colonial-era hamlets but also motels and miniature golf courses. In the midst of it all sits Hyannis, the Cape's unofficial capital. The Lower Cape has casual clam shacks, lovely lighthouses, funky art galleries, and stellar natural attractions. The narrow "forearm" of the Outer Cape is famous for sand dunes, crashing surf, and scrubby pines. Frenetic and fun-loving Provincetown is a leading gay getaway.

2 Martha's Vineyard. The Vineyard lies 5 miles off the Cape's southwest tip. The Down-Island towns are the most popular and most populated, but much of what makes this island special is found in its rural Up-Island reaches where dirt roads lead past crystalline ponds, cranberry bogs, and conservation lands.

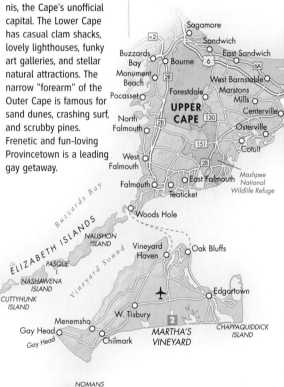

3 Nantucket. Nantucket, or "Far Away Island" in the Wampanoag tongue, is some 25 miles south of Hyannis. Ferries dock in pretty Nantucket Town, where tourism services are concentrated. The rest of the island is mostly residential (trophy houses abound), and nearly all roads terminate in tiny beach communities.

GETTING ORIENTED

Henry David Thoreau, who famously traveled the sparsely populated mid-19th-century Cape Cod, likened the peninsula to "a bare and bended arm." Indeed—looking at a map the outline is obvious, and many people hold their own arm aloft and point to various places from shoulder to fist when asked for directions.

There are three main roads that travel, more or less, the entire Cape: U.S. Highway 6, Route 28, and Route 6A, a designated historic road also called the Old King's Highway. Most visitors stick to these main byways, though the back roads can save time and aggravation in summer.

The Cape is surrounded by water, though it's not a true island. Several bodies of water define the peninsula's land and seascapes: Just off the mainland to the southeast are the gentler, warmer waters of Buzzards Bay, Vineyard Sound, and Nantucket Sound. Cape Cod Bay extends north to the tip of Provincetown, where it meets the Atlantic Ocean.

4

Map labels

OUTER CAPE

Provincetown

Long Point

North Truro

Cape Cod National Seashore

Wellfleet

Cape Cod Bay

Wellfleet Harbor

North Eastham

LOWER CAPE

Eastham

CAPE COD 1

Orleans

East Orleans

Brewster

East Dennis

Dennis

Long Pond

South Orleans

Yarmouth Port

South Dennis

East Harwich

Barnstable

MID CAPE

Dennis Port

Chatham

Harwich Port

West Chatham

Hyannis

S. Yarmouth

Hyannis Port

Monomoy Nat'l Wildlife Refuge

MONOMOY ISLAND

Monomoy Point

0   6 mi
0   6 km

Nantucket Sound

Great Point

NANTUCKET

3

TUCKERNUCK ISLAND

Nantucket

Sankaty Head

Siasconset

CAPE COD NATIONAL SEASHORE

John F. Kennedy certainly knew a good thing when he saw it. During his presidency, Kennedy marked off a magnificent 40-mile swath of the Massachusetts coast, protecting it for future generations. Today the Cape Cod National Seashore remains the Cape's signature site.

Encompassing more than 44,000 acres of coastline from Chatham to Provincetown, the park is truly a national treasure. Without protection, such expansive beauty would surely have been lost to rampant overdevelopment long ago. Within its borders are extraordinary ocean beaches, dramatic dunes, ancient swamps, salt marshes, and wetlands; pitch-pine and scrub-oak forest; much wildlife; and a number of historic structures open for touring.

There's no question that the National Seashore's beaches are the main attractions for sunbathers, swimmers, and surfers. It's not at all uncommon for the parking lots to fill up by 11 am on hot, sunny days. Arrive early to find your spot on the sand, or venture out on some of the less-traveled trails to find solitude in the high season.

BEST TIME TO GO

Swimming is best in summer; the park becomes sublime in the fall with golden salt-marsh grasses and ruby-red cranberry bogs. Winter and early spring nearly guarantee you'll have the place to yourself.

CONTACT INFO

Cape Cod National Seashore ⊠ Doane Rd. off U.S. 6 02642 ☎ 508/255–3421 ⊕ www.nps.gov/caco ☜ Free ☉ Daily 9–4:30.

BEST WAYS TO EXPLORE

TAKE A WALK

Walking the marked trails, beaches, and wooded fire roads is an excellent way to truly experience the diverse natural splendor within the park. There are 11 self-guided trails that begin at various points, leading through shaded swamps, alongside marshes, and through meadows, forest, and dunes. Most of the terrain is flat and sometimes sandy.

RIDE A BIKE

Three well-maintained bicycle trails run through parts of the park. In Eastham the short Nauset Trail heads from the Salt Pond Visitor Center through the woods and out to Coast Guard Beach. Truro's Head, off the Meadow Trail, edges a large salt meadow that's an ideal place for birding. The most physically demanding—and most dramatic—of the park's bike trails is the Province Lands Trail, more than 7 miles of steep hills and hairpin curves through forest and sand dunes. Mountain bikers can make their own trails on the miles of fire roads.

SEE THE SIGHTS

Several historic homes and sites are open for touring; there are also a few notable overlooks easily accessible by car. Climb the steep steps of lighthouses in Eastham and Truro or see rescue reenactments at the Old Harbor Life-Saving Station in Provincetown. Scenic overlooks include Eastham's exquisite Fort Hill area; Wellfleet's Marconi Station Site, where the first transatlantic wireless message was sent in 1903; Truro's Pilgrim Heights; and Provincetown's scenic 2-mile Race Point Road.

TOUR WITH A RANGER

From mid-April through Thanksgiving there is a full schedule of mostly free ranger-guided activities. Combining history, folklore, science, and nature, rangers take visitors right to the source, whether for a full-moon hike in the dunes, a campfire on the beach, a paddling trip, or a photography workshop.

SHIFTING SANDS

Forged by massive moving glaciers more than 20,000 years ago, Cape Cod's landscape is still in perpetual motion, continually shaped by the powerful forces of sand, wind, and water. The Cape's land is slowly giving way to rising ocean levels and erosion, losing an average of nearly 4 feet of outer beach per year. Many a home or structure has succumbed to the unrelenting ocean over the years; some—like Truro's Highland Light and Eastham's Nauset Light—have been moved to safety. Eventually Cape Cod will likely be lost to the sea, though not for thousands of years.

You'll see many signs on beaches and trails asking walkers to keep off the dunes. Take heed, for much of the fragile landscape of the outer Cape is held together by its dune formations and the vegetation that grows within them.

4

CAPE COD, MARTHA'S VINEYARD, AND NANTUCKET BEST BEACHES

Blessed by a great variety of surrounding waters, Cape Cod, Martha's Vineyard, and Nantucket boast some of the world's best beaches. They face the wild, bracing surf of the Atlantic Ocean on one side, while the warmer and gentler waters of Cape Cod Bay or the Nantucket Sound sweep the opposite shores.

Cape Cod alone has more than 150 beaches—enough to keep the most inveterate beachcomber busy all year long. One can still capture that sense of adventure that enchanted Thoreau so long ago while walking the isolated stretches of towering dune-backed beaches from Eastham to Provincetown. Families love the easy access and more placid beaches of the bay and sound, which tend to be more crowded. If saltwater isn't your thing, the Cape has dozens of freshwater kettle holes inland that were carved in the far-distant past by receding glaciers. Aside from warm, salt-free water, some—like Scargo Lake in Dennis—are also blessed with sandy beaches.

HISTORY LESSON

In this centuries-old area even a fun-in-the-sun day can double as a history lesson. In the Lower Cape, Eastham's popular **First Encounter Beach** has a bronze plaque that marks the spot where Myles Standish and his *Mayflower* buddies first encountered Native Americans in 1620.

UPPER CAPE

For Families: Parents love **Old Silver**—a long crescent of soft white sand in North Falmouth—for its comparatively calm, warm water, and kids like poking around the shallow tidal pools full of sea life.

MID CAPE

For Wanderers: Stretching some 6 miles across a peninsula that ends at Sandy Neck Light, **Sandy Neck Beach** in West Barnstable offers a spectacular combination of sand, sea, and dunes perfect for strolling and watching the plentiful birdlife.

For Active Types: Encompassing 1½ miles of soft white sand on Nantucket Sound, busy West Dennis Beach has plenty of space to try windsurfing, play a game of beach volleyball, or just sit back and enjoy the people-watching.

LOWER CAPE

For Traditionalists: Locals contend that Eastham's **Nauset Light Beach and Coast Guard Beach**, both set within the **Cape Cod National Seashore**, are the quintessential beaches. Combining serious surf, sweeping expanses of sand, magnificent dunes, and mesmerizing views, these spots deliver on the wow factor.

For Bird-Watchers: On the barrier beaches of the **Monomoy National Wildlife Refuge,** accessible by boat tours from Chatham, you're bound to see more sandpipers and plovers than people. Summer through early fall, shorebirds and

waterfowl flock here to nest, rest, and feast in tidal flats.

OUTER CAPE

For Surfers: Wave-blasted **White Crest Beach** in Wellfleet is one of the preeminent places on the peninsula to hang 10.

For Views: After the winding drive amid the dunes and scrub in the National Seashore, **Race Point Beach** in Provincetown literally is the end of the road. Cape Cod Bay and the Atlantic meet here in a powerful tumbling of waves; views are vast and include extraordinary sunsets as well whale sightings.

For Night Owls: After-hours it's tough to beat **Cahoon Hollow Beach** in Wellfleet. The water here is chilly but the music at the Beachcomber bar and restaurant is hot.

MARTHA'S VINEYARD

For Photographers: Perhaps no beach in this camera-ready region is more photogenic than that below the **Aquinnah Cliffs**. The multicolored clay cliffs face west, allowing for gorgeous shots at sunset.

NANTUCKET

For Sand Castle Connoisseurs: Jetties Beach has the finest sand castle building material. Hordes gather to prove it during Sandcastle & Sculpture Day, held annually in mid-August.

Updated by Laura V. Scheel

Even if you haven't visited Cape Cod and Islands, you can likely—and accurately—imagine "sand dunes and salty air, quaint little villages here and there." As the 1950s Patti Page song promises, "you're sure to fall in love with old Cape Cod."

Cape Codders are fiercely protective of the environment. Despite some occasionally rampant development, planners have been careful to preserve nature and encourage responsible, eco-conscious building. Nearly 30% of the Cape's 412 square miles is protected from development, and another 35% has not yet been developed (on Nantucket and Martha's Vineyard, the percentages of protected land are far higher). Opportunities for sports and recreation abound, as the region is rife with biking and hiking trails, serene beaches, and waterways for boating and fishing.

The area is also rich in history. Many don't realize that the Pilgrims landed here first: in November 1620 the lost and travel-weary sailors dropped anchor in what is now Provincetown Harbor and spent five weeks here, scouring the area for food and possible settlement. Were it not for the aid of the resident Native Americans, the strangers would have barely survived. Even so, they set sail again for fairer lands, ending up across Cape Cod Bay in Plymouth.

Virtually every period style of residential American architecture is well represented on Cape Cod, including—of course—that seminal form named for the region, the Cape-style house. These low, one-and-a-half-story domiciles with clapboard or shingle (more traditionally the latter in these parts) siding and gable roofs have been a fixture since the late 17th century. You'll also find grand Georgian and Federal mansions from the Colonial era, as well as handsome Greek Revival, Italianate, and Second Empire houses that date to Victorian times. Many of the most prominent residences were built for ship captains and sea merchants. In recent decades the region has seen an influx of angular, glassy, contemporary homes, many with soaring windows and skylights and massive wraparound porches that take advantage of their enviable sea views.

PLANNING

WHEN TO GO

The Cape and Islands teem with activity during high season: roughly late June to Labor Day. If you're dreaming of a classic shore vacation, this is prime time.

However, with the dream come daunting crowds and high costs. Fall has begun to rival summer in popularity, at least on weekends through late October, when the weather is temperate and the scenery remarkable. Many restaurants, shops, and hotels remain open in winter, too, making the area desirable even during the coldest months. The region enjoys fairly moderate weather most of the year, with highs typically in the upper 70s and 80s in summer, and in the upper 30s and lower 40s in winter. Snow and rain are not uncommon during the cooler months, and it can be windy any time.

HYANNIS AVG. TEMPS.

Jan.	Feb.	Mar.	Apr.	May	June
40°F/4°C	41°F/5°C	42°F/6°C	53°F/12°C	62°F/17°C	71°F/22°C

July	Aug.	Sept.	Oct.	Nov.	Dec.
78°F/26°C	76°F/24°C	70°F/21°C	59°F/15°C	49°F/9°C	40°F/4°C

PLANNING YOUR TIME

As the towns are all quite distinct on Cape Cod, it's best to cater your trip based on your interests: an outdoors enthusiast would want to head to the National Seashore region; those who prefer shopping and amusements would do better in the Mid-Cape area. A full-day trip to Nantucket to wander the historic downtown is manageable; several days is best to appreciate Martha's Vineyard's diversity.

GETTING HERE AND AROUND

AIR TRAVEL

The major air gateways are Boston's Logan International Airport and Providence's T. F. Green International Airport. Smaller municipal airports are in Barnstable, Martha's Vineyard, Nantucket, and Provincetown.

CAR TRAVEL

Cape Cod is easily reached from Boston via Route 3 and from Providence via Interstate 195. Once you cross Cape Cod Canal, you can follow U.S. 6. Without any traffic, it takes about 60 to 90 minutes to reach the canal from either Boston or Providence. Allow an extra 30 to 60 minutes in peak periods.

Parking, in general, can be a challenge in summer, especially in congested downtowns and at popular beaches. If you can walk, bike, carpool, or cab it somewhere, do so. But unless you are planning to focus your attention on a single community, you'll probably need a car. Taking a vehicle onto the island ferries is expensive and requires reservations (another option is renting upon arrival).

FERRY TRAVEL

Martha's Vineyard and Nantucket are easily reached by passenger ferries (traditional and high-speed boats) from several Cape towns. Trip times vary from as little as 45 minutes to about two hours and range in price from about $8 one way up to $35. In season, ferries connect Boston and Plymouth with Provincetown.

RESTAURANTS

Cape Cod kitchens have long been closely associated with seafood—the waters off the Cape and Islands yield a bounty of lobsters, clams, oysters, scallops, and myriad fish that make their way onto local menus. In addition to the region's strong Portuguese influence, globally inspired and contemporary fare commonly flavor restaurant offerings. Also gaining in popularity is the use of locally—and often organically—raised produce, meat, and dairy.

Note that ordering an expensive lobster dinner may push your meal into a higher price category than this guide's price range shows for the restaurant.

You can indulge in fresh local seafood and clambakes at seat-yourself shanties for a lower price than at their fine-dining counterparts. Often, the tackier the style (plastic fish on the walls), the better the seafood. These laid-back local haunts usually operate a fish market on the premises and are in every town on the Cape. *Prices in the reviews are the average cost of a main course at dinner or, if dinner is not served, at lunch.*

HOTELS

Dozens of heritage buildings now welcome overnight guests, so you can bed down in a former sea captain's home or a converted church. Scores of rental homes and condominiums are available for long-term stays. Several large resorts encompass numerous amenities—swimming, golf, restaurants, children's programs—all on one property, but often lack the intimate charm and serenity of the smaller establishments. Large chain hotels are frew in the region; the vast majority of lodging properties are locally owned. You'll want to make reservations for inns well in advance during peak summer periods. Smoking is prohibited in all Massachusetts hotels. *Prices in the reviews are the lowest cost of a standard double room in high season.*

CAPE COD

Continually shaped by ocean currents, this windswept land of sandy beaches and dunes has compelling natural beauty. Everyone comes for the seaside, yet the crimson cranberry bogs, forests of birch and beech, freshwater ponds, and marshlands that grace the interior are just as splendid. Local history is fascinating; whale-watching provides an exhilarating experience of the natural world; cycling trails lace the landscape; shops purvey everything from antiques to pure kitsch; and you can dine on simple fresh seafood, creative contemporary cuisine, or most anything in between.

Separated from the Massachusetts mainland by the 18-mile Cape Cod Canal—at 480 feet, the world's widest sea-level canal—and linked to it by two heavily trafficked bridges, the Cape is likened in shape to an outstretched arm bent at the elbow, its Provincetown fist turned back toward the mainland.

Each of the Cape's 15 towns is broken up into villages, which is where things can get complicated. The town of Barnstable, for example, consists of Barnstable, West Barnstable, Cotuit, Marston Mills, Osterville, Centerville, and Hyannis. The terms Upper Cape and Lower Cape can also be confusing. Upper Cape—think upper arm, as in the shape of the Cape—refers to the towns of Bourne, Sandwich, Falmouth, and Mashpee. Mid Cape includes Barnstable, Hyannis, Yarmouth, and Dennis. Brewster, Harwich, Chatham, Orleans, and Eastham make up the Lower Cape. The Outer Cape consists of Wellfleet, Truro, and Provincetown. ⇨ *The towns have been arranged geographically, starting with the Upper Cape and ending with the Outer Cape.*

ESSENTIALS

Visitor Information Cape Cod Chamber of Commerce
✉ *Shoot Flying Hill Rd., off U.S. 6 and Rte. 132, Centerville* ☎ *508/362–3225* ⊕ *www.capecodchamber.org.*

SANDWICH

3 miles east of Sagamore Bridge, 11 miles west of Barnstable.

Fodor's Choice ★ The oldest town on Cape Cod, Sandwich was established in 1637 by some of the Plymouth Pilgrims and incorporated on March 6, 1638. Today it is a well-preserved, quintessential New England village with a white-columned town hall and streets lined with 18th- and 19th-century houses.

ESSENTIALS

Visitor Information Sandwich Chamber of Commerce ✉ *502 Rte. 130, Sandwich Center* ☎ *508/833–9755* ⊕ *www.sandwichchamber.com.*

EXPLORING

FAMILY
Fodor's Choice ★ **Heritage Museums and Gardens.** These 100 beautifully landscaped acres overlooking the upper end of Shawme Pond are one of the region's top draws. Paths crisscross the grounds, which include gardens planted with hostas, heather, herbs, and fruit trees. Rhododendrons are in full glory from mid-May through mid-June, and daylilies reach their peak from mid-July through early August. In 1967 pharmaceuticals magnate Josiah K. Lilly III purchased the estate and turned it into a nonprofit museum. A highlight is the reproduction Shaker Round Barn, which showcases classic and historic cars—including a 1919 Pierce-Arrow, a 1915 Milburn Light Electric, a 1911 Stanley Steamer, and a 1930 yellow-and-green Duesenberg built for movie star Gary Cooper. The art museum has an extraordinary collection of New England folk art, including paintings, weather vanes, Nantucket baskets, and scrimshaw. Both adults and children can enjoy riding on a Coney Island–style carousel dating from the early 20th century. Other features include Hidden Hollow, an outdoor activity center for families with children.

A shuttle bus—equipped with a wheelchair lift and space to stow baby strollers—transports visitors on certain days. In summer, concerts are held in the gardens, often on Wednesday or Saturday evening or Sunday afternoon. The center of the complex is about ¾ mile on foot from the in-town end of Shawme Pond. ✉ *67 Grove St., Sandwich Center* ☎ *508/888–3300* 🌐 *www.heritagemuseumsandgardens.org* 🎟 *$15* 🕒 *Apr.–June and Sept.–Nov., daily 10–5; Jul. and Aug., Thurs.–Tues. 10–5, Wed. 10–8.*

Sandwich Boardwalk. The long sweep of Cape Cod Bay stretches out around the beach at the end of the Sandwich Boardwalk, where a platform provides fine views, especially at sunset. You can look out toward Sandy Neck, Wellfleet, and Provincetown or toward the white cliffs beyond Sagamore. Near this mostly rocky beach are dunes covered with rugosa roses, which have a delicious fragrance; this is a good place for birding. The creeks running through the salt marsh make for great canoeing. From the town center it's about a mile to the boardwalk; cross Route 6A on Jarves Street, and at its end turn left, then right, and continue to the boardwalk parking lot. ✉ *End of Jarves St., Sandwich Center.*

Sandwich Glass Museum. Shimmering glass was manufactured here more than a century ago, and the the Sandwich Glass Museum shows you what the factory looked in its heyday. There's an "ingredient room" showcasing a wide spectrum of glass colors along with the minerals added to the sand to obtain them, and an outstanding collection of blown and pressed glass in many shapes and hues. Large lamps, vases, and pitchers are impressive, as are the hundreds of candlesticks on display. There are daily glassblowing demonstrations between 10 and 3. The extensive gift shop sells some handsome reproductions, including some made by local and national artisans. The museum also hosts historic walking tours on certain days from June through October. ✉ *129 Main St., Sandwich Center* ☎ *508/888–0251* 🌐 *www.sandwichglassmuseum.org* 🎟 *$6* 🕒 *Apr.–Dec., daily 9:30–5; Feb. and Mar., Wed.–Sun. 9:30–4.*

WHERE TO EAT AND STAY

$$$ SEAFOOD

🍴 **Pilot House.** Views of the bustling Cape Cod Canal abound from this casual spot's enviable waterside perch. Seafood is the main catch here, though there are a few alternatives in the form of hefty burgers, steaks, and prime rib. Scallops, clams, oysters, and mussels get top billing, usually served fried among heaps of steaming french fries. For something a bit healthier, opt for broiled or baked. There's a pianist in the dining room every Friday and Saturday, and live music on the patio in warmer months. [$] *Average main: $21* ✉ *14 Gallo Rd., Sandwich Center* ☎ *508/888–8889* 🌐 *www.pilothousecapecod.com.*

$$$ B&B/INN Fodor's Choice ★

🏨 **Belfry Inne & Bistro.** This one-of-a-kind inn includes a 1901 former church, an ornate wood-frame 1882 Victorian, and an 1827 Federal-style house. **Pros:** great in-town location; bright, beautiful, and spacious rooms. **Cons:** some steep stairs. [$] *Rooms from: $189* ✉ *8 Jarves St.* ☎ *508/888–8550, 800/844–4542* 🌐 *www.belfryinn.com* 🛏 *23 rooms* 🕒 *Closed Jan.* 🍽 *Breakfast.*

$$$ B&B/INN

🏨 **1750 Inn at Sandwich Center.** Gracious hosts Jan and Charlie Preus have created a warm and inviting inn that's appealing whether you seek quiet seclusion or the opportunity to mingle with fellow guests. **Pros:** easy access to town center; innkeepers really know the area; appealing package options. **Cons:** some steep, narrow stairs. $ *Rooms from: $179* ⊠ *118 Tupper Rd.* ☏ *508/888–6958, 800/249–6949* ⊕ *www. innatsandwich.com* ⤳ *5 rooms* ⊘ *Closed Jan.–Mar.* ⧍ *Breakfast.*

NIGHTLIFE

British Beer Company. This traditional British "public house" has a great menu that includes fish, ribs, and pizza. Sunday evenings feature karaoke; a variety of bands perform Thursday through Saturday nights. There are two other Cape locations in Falmouth and Hyannis. ⊠ *46 Rte. 6A* ☏ *508/833–9590* ⊕ *www.britishbeer.com.*

SHOPPING

Fodor's Choice **Titcomb's Bookshop.** You'll find used, rare, and new books here, includ-
★   ing a large collection of Americana. There's also an extensive selection of children's books. ⊠ *432 Rte. 6A, East Sandwich* ☏ *508/888–2331* ⊕ *www.titcombsbookshop.com.*

FALMOUTH

15 miles south of Bourne Bridge, 20 miles South of Sandwich.

Falmouth, the Cape's second-largest town, was settled in 1660. Much of Falmouth today is suburban, with a mix of old and new developments and a large year-round population. Many residents commute to other towns on the Cape, to southeastern Massachusetts, and even to Boston. The town has a quaint village center, with a typically old New England village green and a shop-lined Main Street. South of town center, Falmouth faces Nantucket Sound and has several often-crowded beaches popular with families. To the east, the Falmouth Heights neighborhood mixes inns, B&Bs, and private homes, nestled close together on residential streets leading to the sea. Bustling Grand Avenue, the main drag in Falmouth Heights, hugs the shore and the beach.

The village of Woods Hole, part of Falmouth, is home to several major scientific institutions, and is a departure point for ferries to Martha's Vineyard.

GETTING HERE AND AROUND

Heading from the Bourne Bridge toward Falmouth, County Road and Route 28A are prettier alternatives to Route 28, and Sippewisset Road meanders near Buzzards Bay between West Falmouth and Woods Hole.

If you're coming from Falmouth to Woods Hole, either ride your bicycle down the straight and flat Shining Sea Trail or take the Cape Cod Regional Transit Authority's WHOOSH trolley. In summer the basically one-street village overflows with thousands of visiting scientists, students, and tourists heading to the islands. Parking, limited to a relatively small number of metered spots on the street, can be nearly impossible.

ESSENTIALS

Transportation Contacts Cape Cod Regional Transit Authority
☏ *800/352–7155* ⊕ *www.capecodtransit.org.*

Visitor Information Falmouth Chamber of Commerce & Visitor Center
⊠ *20 Academy La.* ☏ *508/548–8500, 800/526–8532*
⊕ *www.falmouthchamber.com.*

EXPLORING

Marine Biological Laboratory–Woods Hole Oceanographic Institution Library. With more than 5,000 scientific journals in 40 languages, this is one of the world's best collections of biological, ecological, and oceanographic literature. The Rare Books Room contains photographs, monographs, and prints, as well as journal collections that date from 1665.

Unless you are a scientific researcher, the only way you can get in to see the library is by taking the hour-long tours. Led by retired scientists, the tours include an introductory slide show as well as stops at the library and the marine resources center. Reservations are required. ⊠ *7 Marine Biological Laboratory St., off Water St., Woods Hole* ☎ *508/289–7423* ⊕ *www.mbl.edu* ⊠ *Free* ☉ *Tours June–Aug., weekdays at 1 and 2.*

Nobska Light. This imposing lighthouse has spectacular views from its base of the nearby Elizabeth Islands and of Martha's Vineyard, across Vineyard Sound. The 42-foot cast-iron tower, lined with brick, was built in 1876 with a stationary light. It shines red to indicate dangerous waters or white for safe passage. Since the light was automated in 1985, the adjacent keeper's quarters have been the headquarters of the Coast Guard group commander—a fitting passing of the torch from one safe-guarder of ships to another. The interior is open to the public through scheduled tours arranged by the U.S. Coast Guard. ⊠ *233 Nobska Rd., Woods Hole* ⊕ *www.lighthouse.cc/nobska* ⊠ *Free* ☉ *Tours by appt.*

FAMILY **Waquoit Bay National Estuarine Research Reserve.** Encompassing 3,000 acres of estuaries, woodlands, salt marshes, and barrier beaches, this research reserve is a good place for walking, kayaking, fishing, and birding. The visitor center's interactive exhibit, outside on the lawn, lets kids trace the path of a raindrop through its journey from cloud to land to river. In July and August there are nature programs for families, including an outdoor lecture series on Tuesday evenings.

South Cape Beach is part of the reserve; you can lie out on the sand or join one of the interpretive walks. **Flat Pond Trail** runs through several different habitats, including fresh- and saltwater marshes. You can reach **Washburn Island** on your own by boat, or by joining a Saturday morning tour. It offers 330 acres of pine barrens and trails, swimming, and 10 wilderness campsites (an advance reservation and permit are required). ⊠ *149 Rte. 28, 3 miles west of Mashpee rotary, Waquoit* ☎ *508/457–0495* ⊕ *www.waquoitbayreserve.org* ⊠ *Free* ☉ *Visitor center Mon.–Sat. 10–4.*

FAMILY
Fodor's Choice
★
Woods Hole Science Aquarium. This impressive facility displays 16 large tanks and many more smaller ones filled with regional fish and shellfish. The rooms are small, but they are crammed with stuff to see. Magnifying glasses and a dissecting scope help you examine marine life. Several hands-on pools hold banded lobsters, crabs, snails, starfish, and other creatures. The stars of the show are two harbor seals, on view in the outdoor pool near the entrance; watch their feedings, most days, at 11 and 4. ⊠ *166 Water St., Woods Hole* ☎ *508/495–2001* ⊕ *aquarium. nefsc.noaa.gov* ⊠ *Free* ☉ *Tues.–Sat. 11–4.*

WHERE TO EAT AND STAY

$$
SEAFOOD

✕ **The Clam Shack.** The fried clams are crisp and fresh at this basic seafood joint right on Falmouth Harbor. The meaty lobster roll and the fish-and-chips platter are good choices, too. Place your order at the counter and then take your tray to the picnic tables on the roof deck for the best views. More tables are on the dock in back, or you can squeeze into the tiny dining room. Just don't plan on a late night here—the Shack closes most evenings around 8. $ *Average main: $16* ✉ *227 Clinton Ave., Falmouth Harbor* ☎ *508/540–7758* ⊘ *Closed early Sept.–mid May.*

$$$
ITALIAN
Fodor'sChoice
★

✕ **La Cucina Sul Mare.** Northern Italian and Mediterranean cooking distinguishes this classy, popular place. The staff is friendly and the setting is both intimate and festive, if a bit crowded. The *zuppa de pesce*, a medley of seafood sautéed in olive oil and garlic and finished in a white-wine, herb-and-tomato broth, is a specialty. Make sure to come hungry—the portions here are huge—and expect a long wait during prime hours in season. ■TIP→ **Use the call-ahead wait list to get a jump on the line.** $ *Average main: $25* ✉ *237 Main St., Falmouth Center* ☎ *508/548–5600* ⊕ *www.lacucinasulmare.com* ⟵ *Reservations not accepted.*

$$$$
B&B/INN

▦ **The Captain's Manor Inn.** With its expansive landscaped grounds ringed by a wrought-iron fence, this elegant 1849 Italianate inn with a wrap-around porch resembles a private estate. **Pros:** walk to town center; elegant setting. **Cons:** not for those with small children; long stairway to second-floor rooms. $ *Rooms from: $255* ✉ *27 W. Main St., Falmouth Center* ☎ *508/388–7336* ⊕ *www.captainsmanorinn.com* ⟵ *8 rooms* ⏅ *Breakfast.*

$$
B&B/INN

▦ **Coonamessett Inn.** At this delightful inn five buildings of one- and two-bedroom suites ring a landscaped lawn that leads to a scenic wooded pond. **Pros:** lush grounds; high marks in romantic-dining setting. **Cons:** weddings are a constant here. $ *Rooms from: $170* ✉ *311 Gifford St., at Jones Rd.* ☎ *508/548–2300* ⊕ *www.capecodrestaurants.org/coonamessett* ⟵ *28 suites, 1 cottage* ⏅ *Breakfast.*

$$$
B&B/INN
Fodor'sChoice
★

▦ **Inn on the Sound.** At this understated but stylish inn, perched on a bluff overlooking Vineyard Sound, the living room and most of the guest rooms face the water. **Pros:** grand water views; elegant setting. **Cons:** not an in-town location; not for those with small children. $ *Rooms from: $245* ✉ *313 Grand Ave., Falmouth Heights* ☎ *508/457–9666, 800/564–9668* ⊕ *www.innonthesound.com* ⟵ *10 rooms* ⏅ *Breakfast.*

SPORTS AND THE OUTDOORS

BEACHES

FAMILY
Old Silver Beach. This long, beautiful crescent of soft white sand is bordered by the Sea Crest Beach Resort at one end. It's especially good for small children because a sandbar keeps it shallow at the southern end and creates tidal pools full of crabs and minnows. Very popular, this beach has its share of crowds on nice, sunny days. **Amenities:** food and drink; lifeguards; parking (fee); showers; toilets. **Best for:** swimming; walking. ✉ *296 Quaker Rd., North Falmouth.*

Continued on page 198

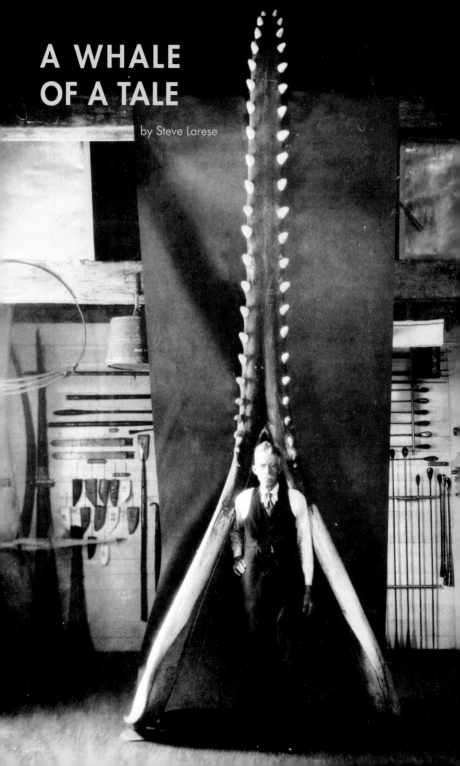

A WHALE OF A TALE

by Steve Larese

WHALING IN NEW ENGLAND TIMELINE

Cameras have replaced harpoons in the waters north of Cape Cod. While you can learn about New England's whaling history and perhaps see whales in the distance from shore, a whale-watching excursion is the best way to connect with these magnificent creatures—who may be just as curious about you as you are about them.

Once relentlessly hunted around the world by New Englanders, whales today are celebrated as intelligent, friendly, and curious creatures. Whales are still important to the region's economy and culture, but now in the form of ecotourism. Easily accessible from several ports in Massachusetts, the 842-square-mi Stellwagen Bank National Marine Sanctuary attracts finback, humpback, minke, and right whales who feed and frolic here twice a year during their migration. The same conditions that made the Stellwagen Bank area of the mouth of Massachusetts Bay a good hunting ground make it a good viewing area. Temperature, currents, and nutrients combine to produce plankton, krill, and fish to feed marine mammals.

(opposite) Whaling museum custodian and a sperm whale jaw in the 1930s. (top) Hunted to near extinction, humpbacks today number about 60,000, and are found in oceans worldwide.

ON LAND: MARINE AND MARITIME MUSEUMS

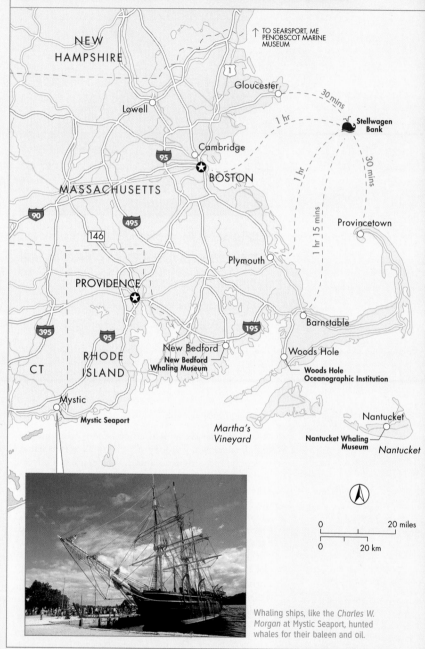

NEW HAMPSHIRE

TO SEARSPORT, ME
PENOBSCOT MARINE
MUSEUM

Gloucester

30 mins

Lowell

1 hr

Stellwagen
Bank

Cambridge

30 mins

BOSTON

MASSACHUSETTS

1 hr

90

495

146

Provincetown

1 hr 15 mins

Plymouth

PROVIDENCE

395

195

Barnstable

95

RHODE
ISLAND

New Bedford
New Bedford
Whaling Museum

Woods Hole

CT

Woods Hole
Oceanographic Institution

Mystic

Mystic Seaport

Martha's
Vineyard

Nantucket

Nantucket Whaling
Museum

Nantucket

0 — 20 miles

0 — 20 km

Whaling ships, like the *Charles W.
Morgan* at Mystic Seaport, hunted
whales for their baleen and oil.

Even landlubbers can learn about whales and whaling at these top New England institutions.

Nantucket Whaling Museum. This former whale-processing center and candle factory was converted into a museum in 1929. See art made by sailors, including masterful scrimshaw—intricate nautical scenes carved into whale bone or teeth and filled in with ink ⊠ *Nantucket, Massachusetts* ☎ *508/228–1894* ⊕ *www.nha.org.*

★ **New Bedford Whaling Museum.** More than 200,000 artifacts are collected here, from ships' logbooks to harpoons. A must-see is the 89-foot, half-scale model of the 1826 whaling ship *Lagoda* ⊠ *New Bedford, Massachusetts* ☎ *508/ 997–0046* ⊕ *www.whalingmuseum.org.*

New Bedford Whaling National Historical Park. The visitor center for this 13-block waterfront park provides maps and information about whaling-related sites, including a sea captain's mansion and restored whaling schooner. ⊠ *New Bedford, Massachusetts,* ☎ *508/996–4095* ⊕ *www.nps.gov/nebe.*

★ **Mystic Seaport.** Actors portray life in a 19th-century seafaring village at this 37-acre living-history museum. Don't miss the 1841 *Charles W. Morgan,* the world's only surviving wooden whaling ship ⊠ *Mystic, Connecticut* ☎ *860/572– 5302* ⊕ *www.mysticseaport.org.*

Penobscot Marine Museum. Maine's seafaring history and mostly shore-whaling industry is detailed inside seven historic buildings ⊠ *Searsport, Maine* ☎ *207/548–2529* ⊕ *www.penobscot marinemuseum.org.*

THE GREAT WHITE WHALE

Herman Melville based his 1851 classic *Moby-Dick: or, The Whale* on the true story of the *Essex*, which was sunk in 1821 by huge whale; an albino sperm whale called Mocha Dick; and his time aboard the whaling ship *Acushnet*.

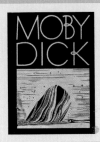

Nantucket Whaling Museum

New Bedford Whaling Museum

Mystic Seaport

★ = **Fodor's** Choice

AT SEA: WHALE-WATCHING TOURS

COMMON NORTH ATLANTIC SPECIES

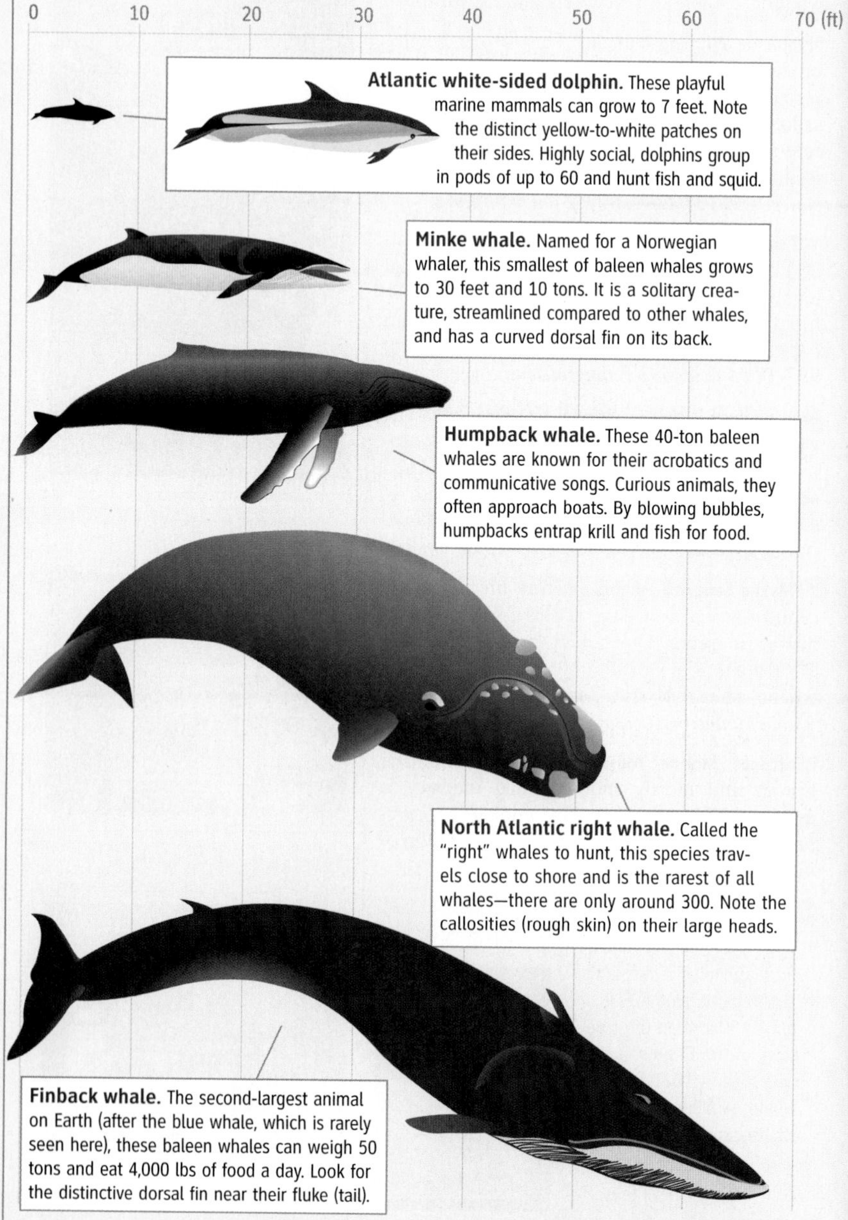

0   10   20   30   40   50   60   70 (ft)

Atlantic white-sided dolphin. These playful marine mammals can grow to 7 feet. Note the distinct yellow-to-white patches on their sides. Highly social, dolphins group in pods of up to 60 and hunt fish and squid.

Minke whale. Named for a Norwegian whaler, this smallest of baleen whales grows to 30 feet and 10 tons. It is a solitary creature, streamlined compared to other whales, and has a curved dorsal fin on its back.

Humpback whale. These 40-ton baleen whales are known for their acrobatics and communicative songs. Curious animals, they often approach boats. By blowing bubbles, humpbacks entrap krill and fish for food.

North Atlantic right whale. Called the "right" whales to hunt, this species travels close to shore and is the rarest of all whales—there are only around 300. Note the callosities (rough skin) on their large heads.

Finback whale. The second-largest animal on Earth (after the blue whale, which is rarely seen here), these baleen whales can weigh 50 tons and eat 4,000 lbs of food a day. Look for the distinctive dorsal fin near their fluke (tail).

4

SEAWORTHY TRIP TIPS

When to Go: Tours operate April through October; May through September are the most active months in the Stellwagen Bank area.

Ports of Departure: Boats leave from Barnstable and Provincetown on Cape Cod, and Plymouth, Boston, and Gloucester, cutting across Cape Cod Bay to the Stellwagen area. Book tours at least a day ahead in the height of the summer season. Hyannis Whale Watcher in Barnstable, the Dolphin Fleet, Portuguese Princess, Captain John's Whale Watch in Plymouth, the New England Aquarium and Boston Harbor Cruises in Boston are just a few of your options. *See Thar She Blows box in this chapter for more information.*

Cost: Around $40. Check company Web sites for coupons.

What to Expect: All companies abide by guidelines so as not to harass whales. Tours last 3 to 4 hours and almost always encounter whales; if not, vouchers are often given for another tour. Passengers are encouraged to watch the horizon for water spouts, which indicate a surfaced whale clearing its blowhole to breathe air. Upon spotting an animal, the boat slows and approaches the whale to a safe distance; often, whales will approach an idling boat and even swim underneath it.

What to Bring: Plastic bags protect binoculars and cameras from damp spray. Most boats have a concession stand, but pack bottled water and snacks.
■ TIP➡ **Kids (and adults) will appreciate games or other items to pass the time in between whale sightings.**

What to Wear: Wear rubber-soled footwear for slick decks. A waterproof outer layer and layers of clothing will help in

Hyannis Whale Watcher Cruises, Cape Cod Bay

varied conditions, as will sunscreen, sunglasses, and a hat that can be secured. Most boats have cabins where you can warm up and get out of the wind.

Comforting Advice: Small seat cushions like those used at sporting events may be appreciated. Consider taking motion-sickness medication before setting out. Ginger candy and acupressure wristbands can also help. If you feel queasy, get some fresh air and focus your eyes on a stable feature on the shore or horizon.

Photo Hints: Use a fast shutter speed, or sport mode, to avoid blurry photographs. Most whales will be a distance from the boat; have a telephoto lens ready. To avoid shutter delay on your point-and-shoot camera, lock the focus at infinity so you don't miss that breaching whale shot.

DID YOU KNOW?

Most boats have a naturalist aboard to discuss the whales and their environment. Many companies contribute to population studies by reporting the individual whales they spot. Whale tails, called flukes, are distinct and used like fingerprints for identification.

BIKING

Fodor's Choice ★ **Shining Sea Bikeway.** The wonderful Shining Sea Bikeway is an 11-mile paved bike path through four of Falmouth's villages, running from Woods Hole to North Falmouth. It follows the shore of Buzzards Bay, providing water views and dips into oak and pine woods; a detour onto Church Street takes you to Nobska Light. A brochure is available at the trailheads. If you're taking your bike to Martha's Vineyard, park in one of Falmouth's Steamship Authority lots and ride to the ferry. Free shuttles from Falmouth to the Woods Hole ferry dock have bike carriers.

FISHING

Eastman's Sport & Tackle. Freshwater ponds are good for perch, pickerel, trout, and more; get the required license (along with rental gear) at Eastman's Sport & Tackle. It's a good resource if you are looking for local guides. ⊠ *783 Main St., Falmouth Center* ☎ *508/548–6900* ⊕ *www.eastmanstackle.com.*

SHOPPING

Bean & Cod. This specialty food shop sells cheeses, breads, great sandwiches, and picnic fixings, along with coffees and teas. The store also packs and ships gift baskets. ⊠ *140 Main St., Falmouth Center* ☎ *508/548–8840.*

HYANNIS

23 miles east of the Bourne Bridge, 21 miles northeast of Falmouth.

Perhaps best known for its association with the Kennedy clan, the Hyannis area was also a vacation site for President Ulysses S. Grant in 1874 and later for President Grover Cleveland. A bustling year-round hub of activity, Hyannis has the Cape's largest concentration of businesses, shops, malls, hotels and motels, restaurants, and entertainment venues.

GETTING HERE AND AROUND

There's plenty of public parking around town, on both sides of Main Street as well as in several public parking lots. The island ferry companies have designated parking lots (daily fee is about $15 in summer season) with free shuttles to the docks. Hyannis is the Cape's transit hub and is served by a number of bus routes.

ESSENTIALS

Transportation Contacts Cape Flyer ⊠ *215 Iyannough Rd.* ☎ *508/775–8504* ⊕ *www.capeflyer.com.* **Hyannis Transportation Center** ⊠ *215 Iyanough Rd., Barnstable* ☎ *800/352–7155* ⊕ *www.capecodtransit.org.*

Visitor Information Hyannis Chamber of Commerce ⊠ *397 Main St.* ☎ *508/775–2201* ⊕ *www.hyannis.com.*

EXPLORING

John F. Kennedy Hyannis Museum. In Main Street's Old Town Hall, this museum explores JFK's Cape years (1934–63) through enlarged and annotated photographs culled from the archives of the JFK Library near Boston, as well as a seven-minute video narrated by Walter Cronkite. Also on-site is the **Cape Cod Baseball League Hall of Fame and Museum,** housed in several rooms in the basement of the JFK museum (which is

CLOSE UP

Clam Shacks

Cape Codders have been clamming for generations, and their iconic mollusks are a celebrated part of the culture here. Classic clam shacks are known for their bountiful baskets of crispy fried clams, which, according to Cape Codders, should always be ordered "whole"—that is, with the bellies. Fried clams are never the only item on the menu. Typical fare also includes clam chowder, lobster rolls, fried fish, scallops, shrimp, coleslaw, fries, potato salad, and other non-seafood items. The quintessential experience usually involves ordering at one window, picking up at another, and eating at a picnic table—hopefully one with a beach or harbor view! A few of our favorites on Cape Cod include The Clam Shack in Falmouth, Mac's Seafood in Wellfleet, and Arnold's Lobster & Clam Bar in Eastham. The Bite in Menemsha on Martha's Vineyard is also worth a try.

appropriately referred to as "The Dugout"). Plaques of Hall of Famers, autographed items from former players who went on to play professional ball, and other Cape League memorabilia are on view; several films about the league and baseball itself are played continuously. ✉ *397 Main St.* ☎ *508/790–3077* 🌐 *www.jfkhyannismuseum.org* 🎟 *$8, includes baseball museum* 🕐 *Late Feb.–Mar., Thurs.–Sat. 10–4, Sun. noon–4; mid-Apr.–Memorial Day, Mon.–Sat. 10–4, Sun. noon–4; Memorial Day–Oct., Mon.–Sat. 9–5, Sun. noon–5; Nov., Fri. and Sat. 10–4, Sun. noon–4.*

WHERE TO EAT

$$$$ BRAZILIAN Fodor's Choice ★

🍴 **Brazilian Grill.** The Cape has a large Brazilian population, and you can find many of these residents, plus plenty of satisfied visitors, at this all-you-can-eat churrascaria. Be prepared for some serious feasting—this experience is not for nibblers or vegetarians. Waiters circulate through the dining room offering more than a dozen grilled meats—beef, pork, chicken, sausage, and even quail—on swordlike skewers. You can help yourself to a buffet of soups, salads, and side dishes, including *farofa* (a couscous-like dish made of manioc), plantains, rice, and beans. The atmosphere is often loud and jovial. For dessert, the homemade flan is the best choice. [$] *Average main: $32* ✉ *680 Main St.* ☎ *508/771–0109* 🌐 *www.braziliangrill-capecod.com* 🕐 *No lunch weekends.*

$$$ ECLECTIC Fodor's Choice ★

🍴 **Naked Oyster.** With its own oyster farm in nearby Barnstable, this restaurant—as well as its clientele—benefits from near-daily deliveries of the succulent bivalves. More than 1,000 oysters are eaten here on an average summer weekend. You'll always find close to two dozen raw and "dressed" oyster dishes (such as barbecue oysters on the half shell with blue cheese, caramelized onions, and bacon). There's also a nice range of non-oyster entrées, salads, and appetizers. The oyster stew is also out of this world. Exposed brick walls inside and a few street-side tables outside add to the pleasurable dining experience. [$] *Average main: $28* ✉ *410 Main St.* ☎ *508/778–6500* 🌐 *www.nakedoyster.com.*

$$$ EUROPEAN

🍴 **The Paddock.** The Paddock is synonymous with tried-and-true formal dining on the Cape, with sumptuous upholstery in the main dining room and old-style wicker on the breezy summer porch. The authentic Victorian style complements a menu that is traditional yet subtly innovative—fresh ingredients are combined in novel ways: Chatham scrod comes with lemon-thyme bread crumbs and a rich lobster sauce. The steak au poivre, with several varieties of crushed peppercorns, is masterful; the fire-roasted salmon is stuffed with lobster, goat cheese, and finished with a beurre blanc. $ *Average main: $28* ⊠ *20 Scudder Ave.* ☎ *508/775–7677* ⊕ *www.paddockcapecod.com* ☯ *Closed mid-Nov.–mid-Apr.*

WHERE TO STAY

$$$
HOTEL
Fodor's Choice
★

🛏 **Anchor-In.** Most rooms at this small-scale motel on the north end of Hyannis Harbor have harbor views and small balconies overlooking the water, and its simple street-side appearance belies its spacious and immaculate accommodations, extensive grounds, and warm, B&B-style personal service from Lisa and Skip Simpson. **Pros:** easy walk to downtown; great harbor views. **Cons:** no elevator—second-floor rooms accessed via stairs. $ *Rooms from: $279* ⊠ *1 South St.* ☎ *508/775–0357* ⊕ *www.anchorin.com* ⮐ *42 rooms* ⏺ *Breakfast.*

NIGHTLIFE AND THE ARTS

FAMILY **Cape Cod Melody Tent.** In 1950 actress Gertrude Lawrence and her husband, producer-manager Richard Aldrich, opened the Cape Cod Melody Tent to showcase Broadway musicals and concerts. Today it's the region's top venue for pop concerts and comedy shows. Performers who have played here in the round include the Indigo Girls, Lyle Lovett, Tony Bennett, Diana Krall, and Crosby, Stills & Nash. The Tent also holds an 11 am Wednesday children's theater series in July and August. ⊠ *21 W. Main St.* ☎ *508/775–5630* ⊕ *www.melodytent.com.*

SPORTS AND THE OUTDOORS

BEACH

FAMILY **Kalmus Park Beach.** This wide, sandy beach has an area set aside for windsurfers and a sheltered area that's good for kids. It's a great spot for watching boats go in and out of the harbor. **Amenities:** food and drink; lifeguards; parking (fee); showers; toilets. **Best for:** swimming; walking; windsurfing. ⊠ *End of Ocean St.*

BARNSTABLE

4 miles north of Hyannis.

With nearly 50,000 year-round residents, Barnstable is the largest town on the Cape. It's also the second oldest (founded in 1639). You can get a feeling for its age in Barnstable Village, on and near Main Street (Route 6A), a lovely area of large old homes.

WHERE TO STAY

$$$
B&B/INN

🛏 **Beechwood Inn.** This lovely yellow-and-pale-green 1853 Queen Anne house, named for its two magnificent and aged beech trees, has gingerbread trim and is wrapped by a wide porch with wicker furniture and a glider swing. **Pros:** afternoon tea; seven beaches within a 5-mile radius. **Cons:** narrow, curved stairs. $ *Rooms from: $185* ⊠ *2839 Rte. 6A* ☎ *508/362–6618, 800/609–6618* ⊕ *www.beechwoodinn.com* ⮐ *6 rooms* ⏺ *Breakfast.*

DID YOU KNOW?

Clams can be eaten raw (on the half shell) or cooked. The hard-shell quahogs (CO-hogs) can be divided into littlenecks, cherry stones, and chowders; steamers are another popular Cape bivalve.

$$$ B&B/INN Fodor's Choice ★ **Honeysuckle Hill.** Innkeepers Rick Kowarek and Nancy Hunter-Young provide plenty of thoughtful touches at this 1810 Queen Anne–style cottage—fresh flowers in every room, refrigerators stocked with beverages, and beach chairs with umbrellas (perfect for nearby Sandy Neck Beach). **Pros:** lush gardens on the grounds; tasteful, large rooms; very short drive to Sandy Neck Beach. **Cons:** most rooms are accessed via steep stairs. [$] *Rooms from: $198* ✉ *591 Rte. 6A, West Barnstable* ☎ *508/362–8418, 866/444–5522* 🌐 *www.honeysucklehill.com* 🛏 *4 rooms, 1 suite* 🍴 *Breakfast.*

SPORTS AND THE OUTDOORS

BEACHES

Sandy Neck Beach. Sandy Neck Beach stretches some 6 miles across a peninsula that ends at **Sandy Neck Light.** The beach is one of the Cape's most beautiful—dunes, sand, and bay spread endlessly east, west, and north. The marsh used to be harvested for salt hay; now it's a haven for birds, which are out and about in the greatest numbers in morning and evening. The lighthouse, standing a few feet from the eroding shoreline at the tip of the neck, has been out of commission since 1952. It was built in 1857 to replace an 1827 light, and it used to run on acetylene gas. As you travel east along Route 6A from Sandwich, Sandy Neck Road is just before the Barnstable line, although the beach itself is in West Barnstable. **Amenities**: food and drink; lifeguards; parking (fee); showers; toilets. **Best for**: sunset; swimming; walking. ✉ *Sandy Neck Rd., West Barnstable* ⏲ *Daily 8 am–9 pm (staffed until 5 pm).*

YARMOUTH

Yarmouth Port is 3 miles east of Barnstable Village; West Yarmouth is 2 miles east of Hyannis.

Once known as Mattacheese, or "the planting lands," Yarmouth was settled in 1639 by farmers from the Plymouth Bay Colony. By then the Cape had begun a thriving maritime industry, and men turned to the sea to make their fortunes. Many impressive sea captains' houses—some now B&Bs and museums—still line enchanting Route 6A and nearby side streets, and Yarmouth Port has some real old-time stores in town. West Yarmouth has a very different atmosphere, stretched on busy commercial Route 28 south of Yarmouth Port.

ESSENTIALS

Visitor Information Yarmouth Chamber of Commerce ✉ *424 Rte. 28, West Yarmouth* ☎ *508/778–1008, 800/732–1008* 🌐 *www.yarmouthcapecod.com.*

EXPLORING

FAMILY **Bass Hole Boardwalk.** Taking in one of Yarmouth Port's most beautiful areas, Bass Hole Boardwalk extends over a marshy creek, crosses salt marshes, and winds around vegetated wetlands and upland woods. Gray's Beach is a little crescent of sand with still water that's good for kids inside the roped-in swimming area. At the end of the boardwalk, benches provide a place to relax and look out over abundant marsh life and, across the creek, the beautiful, sandy shores of Dennis's Chapin

Beach. At low tide you can walk out on the flats for almost a mile. ✉ *Center St., near Gray's Beach parking lot.*

Edward Gorey House Museum. Explore the eccentric doodlings and offbeat humor of the late acclaimed artist and illustrator. The regularly changing exhibitions, arranged in the downstairs rooms of Gorey's former home, include drawings of his oddball characters and reveal the mysterious psyche of the sometimes dark but always playful illustrator. ✉ *8 Strawberry La.* ☎ *508/362–3909* 🌐 *www.edwardgoreyhouse.org* 🎫 *$8* 🕓 *Mid-Apr.–June, Thurs.–Sat. 11–4, Sun. noon–4; July–early Oct., Wed.–Sat. 11–4, Sun. noon–4; mid-Oct.–Dec., Fri. and Sat. 11–4, Sun. noon–4.*

QUICK BITES

Jerry's Seafood and Dairy Freeze. Open year-round, this simple shack serves fried clams and onion rings, along with thick frappés (milk shakes), frozen yogurt, and soft-serve ice cream at good prices. ✉ ***654 Rte. 28, West Yarmouth*** ☎ ***508/775–9752.***

WHERE TO EAT AND STAY

$$$ JAPANESE Fodor's Choice ★

🍴 **Inaho.** Yuji Watanabe, chef-owner of the Cape's best Japanese restaurant, makes early-morning journeys to Boston's fish markets to shop for the freshest local catch. His selection of sushi and sashimi is vast and artful, and vegetable and seafood tempura come out of the kitchen fluffy and light. If you're a teriyaki lover, you can't do any better than the chicken's beautiful blend of sweet and sour. Can't decide what to order? He's happy to design a varied and generous tasting menu. One remarkable element of the restaurant is its artful lighting: small pinpoint lights on the food accentuate the presentation in a dramatic way. The serene and simple Japanese garden out back has a traditional koi pond. [$] *Average main: $28* ✉ *157 Main St.* ☎ *508/362–5522* 🌐 *www.inahocapecod.com* 🕓 *Closed Sun. No lunch.*

$ BRITISH

🍴 **The Optimist Café.** From the outside, this bold Gothic Victorian looks like something out of a Brothers Grimm tale, with its steeply pitched roof, fanciful turrets, frilly gingerbread trim, and deep rose-and-green paint job. There is a great selection for breakfast (served all day) and lunch, featuring traditional English fare like smoked fish dishes, curries, scones, and crumpets. Treat yourself to a ploughman's lunch, consisting of cheeses, chutney, and crusty bread. [$] *Average main: $10* ✉ *134 Rte. 6A* ☎ *508/362–1024* 🌐 *www.optimistcafe.com* 🕓 *No dinner.*

$$$$ HOTEL

🏨 **Bayside Resort.** A bit more upscale than most of the properties along Route 28, the Bayside overlooks pristine salt marshes and Lewis Bay. **Pros:** ideal for families with children; close to attractions of busy Route 28. **Cons:** no beach swimming; not for those seeking intimate surroundings. [$] *Rooms from: $259* ✉ *225 Rte. 28, West Yarmouth* ☎ *508/775–5669, 800/243–1114* 🌐 *www.baysideresort.com* 🛏 *128 rooms* 🍽 *Breakfast.*

$$ B&B/INN Fodor's Choice ★

🏨 **Capt. Farris House.** A short spin away from congested Route 28 sits this imposing 1845 Greek Revival home. **Pros:** beautiful grounds; ideal location for exploring Mid Cape area; close to area restaurants and attractions. **Cons:** no elevator; not close to the beach. [$] *Rooms from: $199* ✉ *308 Old Main St., Bass River Village* ☎ *508/760–2818* 🌐 *www.captainfarris.com* 🛏 *6 rooms, 3 suites* 🕓 *Closed Jan.* 🍽 *Breakfast.*

Learn more about the Cape's marshlands, forests, and ponds at the Cape Cod Museum of Natural History in neighboring Brewster.

$$$ B&B/INN Fodor's Choice ★ **Liberty Hill Inn.** Smartly but traditionally furnished common areas—including the high-ceiling parlor, the formal dining room, and the wrap-around porch—are a major draw to this dignified 1825 Greek Revival house. **Pros:** tasteful surroundings; beautiful grounds. **Cons:** some steep stairs; some bathrooms have only small shower stalls; not a waterfront location. [$] *Rooms from: $195* ✉ *77 Rte. 6A* ☎ *508/362–3976* 🌐 *www.libertyhillinn.com* 🛏 *8 rooms, 1 suite* 🍴 *Breakfast.*

NIGHTLIFE AND THE ARTS

Planck's Tavern. Fish tanks illuminate this friendly bar, which hosts live music in a variety of genres on weekends throughout the year. ✉ *6 Bray Farm Rd., off Rte. 6A* ☎ *508/362–6062* 🌐 *www.oliverscapecod.com.*

SHOPPING

Peach Tree Designs. This shop carries home furnishings and decorative accessories, some from local craftspeople. Everything is beautifully made. ✉ *173 Rte. 6A* ☎ *508/362–8317* 🌐 *www.peachtreedesigns.com.*

DENNIS

Dennis Village is 4 miles east of Yarmouth Port; West Dennis is 1 mile east of South Yarmouth.

The backstreets of Dennis Village still retain the Colonial charm of their seafaring days. The town, which was incorporated in 1793, was named for the Reverend Josiah Dennis. There were 379 sea captains living here when fishing, salt making, and shipbuilding were the main industries, and the elegant houses they constructed—now museums and B&Bs—still line the streets.

ESSENTIALS

Visitor Information Dennis Chamber of Commerce ✉ *238 Swan River Rd., West Dennis* ☎ *508/398–3568, 800/243–9920* 🌐 *www.dennischamber.com.*

EXPLORING

Cape Cod Museum of Art. This museum on the grounds of the Cape Playhouse has a permanent collection of more than 850 works by Cape-associated artists. Important pieces include a portrait of a fisherman's wife by Charles Hawthorne, the father of the Provincetown art colony; a 1924 portrait of a Portuguese fisherman's daughter by William Paxton, one of the first artists to summer in Provincetown; a collection of wood-block prints by Varujan Boghosian, a member of Provincetown's Long Point Gallery cooperative; an oil sketch by Karl Knaths, who painted in Provincetown from 1919 until his death in 1971; and works by abstract expressionist Hans Hoffman. ✉ *60 Hope La., Dennis Village* ☎ *508/385–4477* 🌐 *www.ccmoa.org* 🎟 *$9* 🕒 *Tues.–Sat. 10–5, Sun. noon–5.*

WHERE TO EAT AND STAY

$$ SEAFOOD Fodor's Choice ★

🍴 **Cap'n Frosty's.** A great stop after the beach, this barn-shaped seafood shack is where locals go to get their fried seafood. This modest joint has a regular menu supplemented by specials posted on the board and a counter where you order and take a number written on a french-fries box. The staff is young and hardworking, pumping out fresh fried clams and fish-and-chips on paper plates. All frying is done in heart-healthy canola oil, and rice pilaf is offered as a substitute for fries. There's seating inside as well as outside on a shady brick patio. [$] *Average main: $14* ✉ *219 Rte. 6A, Dennis Village* ☎ *508/385–8548* ✍ *Reservations not accepted* 🕒 *Closed early Sept.–mid-Apr.*

$$$ AMERICAN Fodor's Choice ★

🍴 **Red Pheasant.** This is one of the Cape's best cozy country restaurants, with a consistently good kitchen where creative American food, much of it locally sourced and organic, is prepared with elaborate sauces and herb combinations. The sauteed dayboat scallops, for example, are served with butternut squash risotto, pumpkin seeds, and a ginger syrup. The exquisitely roasted rack of lamb Persillade is local favorite; in fall, look for game dishes like venison and quail. Try to reserve a table in the more intimate Garden Room. The expansive wine list is excellent. [$] *Average main: $28* ✉ *905 Rte. 6A, Dennis Village* ☎ *508/385–2133* 🌐 *www.redpheasantinn.com* ✍ *Reservations essential* 🕒 *No lunch.*

$$ B&B/INN Fodor's Choice ★

🏨 **Isaiah Hall B&B Inn.** Lilacs and pink roses trail along the white-picket fence outside this 1857 Greek Revival farmhouse on a quiet residential road near the bay, where innkeepers Jerry and Judy Neal set the scene for a romantic getaway with guest rooms that have country antiques, floral-print wallpapers, fluffy quilts, and Priscilla curtains. **Pros:** beautiful grounds; near beaches and attractions. **Cons:** not for those with children under seven; some very steep steps; some rooms are on the small side. [$] *Rooms from: $150* ✉ *152 Whig St., Box 1007, Dennis Village* ☎ *508/385–9928* 🌐 *www.isaiahhallinn.com* 🛏 *10 rooms, 2 suites* 🍽 *Breakfast.*

NIGHTLIFE AND THE ARTS

FAMILY

Fodor's Choice

★

Cape Playhouse. For Broadway-style dramas, comedies, and musicals, attend a production at the Cape Playhouse, the country's oldest professional summer theater. In 1927 Raymond Moore, who had been working with a theatrical troupe in Provincetown, bought an 1838 Unitarian meetinghouse and converted it into a theater where the original pews still serve as seats. The opening performance was *The Guardsman,* starring Basil Rathbone. Other stars who performed here in the early days—some in their professional stage debuts—include Bette Davis (who first worked here as an usher), Gregory Peck, Lana Turner, Ginger Rogers, Humphrey Bogart, Tallulah Bankhead, and Henry Fonda, who appeared with his then-unknown 20-year-old daughter, Jane. Behind-the-scenes tours are available. The playhouse offers children's theater on Friday morning during July and August. Also part of the 26-acre property are a restaurant, the Cape Cod Museum of Art, and the Cape Cinema. ⊠ *820 Rte. 6A, Dennis Village* ☎ *508/385–3911, 877/385–3911* ⊕ *www.capeplayhouse.com* ☉ *June–Sept.*

Harvest Gallery Wine Bar. Near the Cape Playhouse, this friendly place has an extensive wine list, a good variety of hors d'oeuvres and other nibbles, eclectic artwork, and live music. ⊠ *776 Main St., Dennis Village* ☎ *508/385–2444* ⊕ *www.harvestgallerywinebar.com* ☉ *Closed mid-Jan.–early Apr.*

SPORTS AND THE OUTDOORS

BEACHES

Parking at all Dennis beaches is $20 a day in season ($25 on weekends) for nonresidents.

Corporation Beach. Once a privately owned packet landing, the beautiful crescent of white sand backed by low dunes now serves a decidedly noncorporate purpose as a public beach. **Amenities:** food and drink; lifeguards; parking (fee); showers; toilets. **Best for:** sunset; swimming; walking. ⊠ *Corporation Rd., Dennis Village.*

BREWSTER

7 miles northeast of Dennis, 20 miles east of Sandwich.

Brewster's location on Cape Cod Bay makes it a perfect place to learn about the region's ecology. The Cape Cod Museum of Natural History is here, and the area is rich in conservation lands, state parks, forests, freshwater ponds, and brackish marshes. When the tide is low in Cape Cod Bay, you can stroll the beaches and explore tidal pools up to 2 miles from the shore on the Brewster flats.

ESSENTIALS

Visitor Information Brewster Chamber of Commerce ⊠ *Town Hall, 2198 Rte. 6A* ☎ *508/896–3500* ⊕ *www.brewster-capecod.org.*

EXPLORING

Brewster Store. Built in 1852 as a church, this local landmark is a typical New England general store with such essentials as daily newspapers, penny candy, groceries, and benches out front for conversation. Out back, the Brewster Scoop serves ice cream from mid-June to early September. Upstairs, memorabilia from antique toys to World War II bond posters is displayed. Downstairs there's a working antique nickelodeon; locals warm themselves by the old coal stove in the colder months. ⊠ *1935 Rte. 6A* ☎ *508/896–3744* ⊕ *www. brewsterstore.com.*

FAMILY **Cape Cod Museum of Natural History.**
Fodor's Choice A short drive west from the heart
★ of Brewster, this spacious museum and its pristine grounds include a shop, a natural-history library, and exhibits such as a working beehive and a pond- and sea-life room with live specimens. Walking trails wind through 80 acres of forest, marshland, and ponds, all rich in birds and other wildlife. The exhibit hall upstairs has a wall display of aerial photographs documenting the process by which the famous Chatham sandbar was split in two. In summer there are guided field walks, nature programs, and art classes for preschoolers through ninth graders. ⊠ *869 Rte. 6A, West Brewster* ☎ *508/896–3867* ⊕ *www.ccmnh.org* ☞ *$10* ☾ *June–Sept., daily 9:30–4; Feb. and Mar., Thurs.–Sun. 11–3; Oct.–Dec., Apr., and May, Wed.–Sun. 11–3. Trails open year-round.*

FAMILY **Nickerson State Park.** These 1,961 acres were once part of a vast estate belonging to Roland C. Nickerson, son of Samuel Nickerson, a Chatham native who founded the First National Bank of Chicago. Roland and his wife, Addie, lavishly entertained such visitors as President Grover Cleveland at their private beach and hunting lodge in English country-house style, with coachmen dressed in tails and top hats and a bugler announcing carriages entering the front gates. In 1934 Addie donated the land for the state park in memory of Roland and their son, who died during the 1918 flu epidemic.

The park consists of acres of oak, pitch-pine, hemlock, and spruce forest speckled with seven freshwater kettle ponds formed by glaciers. Some ponds are stocked with trout for fishing. You can swim, canoe, sail, and kayak in the ponds, and bicycle along 8 miles of paved trails that have access to the Cape Cod Rail Trail. Bird-watchers seek out the thrushes, wrens, warblers, woodpeckers, finches, larks, cormorants, great blue herons, hawks, owls, and ospreys. Red foxes and white-tailed deer are occasionally spotted in the woods. ⊠ *3488 Rte. 6A, East Brewster* ☎ *508/896–3491* ⊕ *www.mass.gov/dcr* ☞ *$5* ☾ *Daily dawn–dusk.*

BIKE THE RAIL TRAIL

The Cape's premier bike path, the **Cape Cod Rail Trail** (⊕ *www.mass.gov/dcr*), follows the paved right-of-way of the old Penn Central Railroad. About 25 miles long, the easy-to-moderate trail passes salt marshes, cranberry bogs, and ponds.

The trail starts at the parking lot off Route 134 south of U.S. 6, near Theophilus Smith Road in South Dennis, and it ends at the post office in South Wellfleet. Access points in Brewster are Long Pond Road, Underpass Road, and Nickerson State Park. There's also a spur off the trail that goes to Chatham.

4

WHERE TO EAT AND STAY

$$$$
ECLECTIC

✕ **Bramble Inn.** Inside an inviting 1860s white house in Brewster's historic village center, this romantic property presents well-crafted, globally inspired contemporary fare in four dining rooms. During the warmer months, dine on a patio amid fragrant flower beds. The menu changes often but always includes the assorted seafood curry—the house favorite—which combines lobster, shrimp, scallops, and cod in a light curry sauce with grilled banana, toasted coconut, sliced almonds, and house chutney. If you'd rather graze, opt for the "Bramble Bites"—choose from risottos, skillet roasted mussels, salmon Niçoise, and the like—served in the bar as well as the garden patios. $ *Average main: $32* ⊠ *2019 Rte. 6A, East Brewster* ☎ *508/896-7644* ⊕ *www. brambleinn.com* ⊘ *Closed Mon. and Tues. No lunch.*

$$$$
FRENCH
Fodor'sChoice
★

✕ **Chillingsworth.** One of the crown jewels of Cape restaurants, Chillingsworth combines formal presentation with an excellent French menu and a diverse wine cellar to create a memorable dining experience. Superrich risotto, roast lobster, and grilled Angus sirloin are favorites. Dinner in the main dining rooms is prix fixe and includes seven courses—appetizer, soup, salad, sorbet, entrée, "amusements," and dessert, plus coffee or tea. Less expensive à la carte options for lunch, dinner, and Sunday brunch are served in the more casual, patio-style Bistro. There are also a few guest rooms here for overnighting. $ *Average main: $70* ⊠ *2449 Rte. 6A, East Brewster* ☎ *508/896-3640* ⊕ *www.chillingsworth.com* ⌨ *Reservations essential* ⊘ *Closed Thanksgiving–mid-May.*

$$$
B&B/INN
Fodor'sChoice
★

🛏 **Captain Freeman Inn.** Named for the sea captain who had the home built in 1866, this gracious inn retains its aged elegance with orginal ornate plaster ceiling medallions, marble fireplaces, and sturdy yet graceful construction. **Pros:** authentic historic lodging with modern amenities; free Wi-Fi; walk to town center. **Cons:** not for those with children. $ *Rooms from: $249* ⊠ *15 Breakwater Rd.* ☎ *508/896-7481* ⊕ *www.captainfreemaninn.com* ⌁ *11 rooms* ⦿*Breakfast.*

$$
B&B/INN
Fodor'sChoice
★

🛏 **Old Sea Pines Inn.** With its white-column portico and wraparound veranda overlooking a broad lawn, Old Sea Pines, which housed a "charm and personality" school in the early 1900s, resembles a vintage summer estate. **Pros:** welcomes families; beautiful grounds; reasonable rates. **Cons:** some rooms have shared baths; steep stairway to upper floors. $ *Rooms from: $145* ⊠ *2553 Rte. 6A* ☎ *508/896-6114* ⊕ *www. oldseapinesinn.com* ⌁ *24 rooms, 19 with bath; 5 suites* ⊘ *Closed Dec.– mid-Apr.* ⦿*Breakfast.*

THE ARTS

FAMILY
Cape Cod Repertory Theatre Co. Several impressive productions, from original works to classics, are staged every year in this indoor Arts and Crafts–style theater set way back in the woods. There are mesmerizing outdoor shows for kids offered on weekday mornings during the summer, as well as hour-long puppet shows. ⊠ *3299 Rte. 6A, west of Nickerson State Park, East Brewster* ☎ *508/896–1888* ⊕ *www.caperep. org* ⊘ *May–Nov.*

SPORTS AND THE OUTDOORS

WATER SPORTS

Jack's Boat Rentals. Choose from among canoes, kayaks, pedal boats, sailboats, and sailboards at the two locations of Jack's Boat Rentals in Nickerson State Park (Flax Pond and Cliff Pond). Sign up for sailing lessons offered at Cliff Pond. ✉ *Nickerson State Park, Rte. 6A, at Cliff Pond, East Brewster* ☎ *508/896–8556* 🌐 *www.jacksboatrental.com.*

WORD OF MOUTH

"Route 6A is known as 'Old Kings Highway,' and traveling along this incredibly scenic two-lane road is like a trip back to Colonial days. Lots of old sea captains' homes (especially in Brewster), antiques shops, taverns and inns, art galleries, museums, and peeks of Cape Cod Bay here and there along the way."

—caper64

SHOPPING

Brewster Book Store. A special place, Brewster Book Store is filled to the rafters with all manner of books by local and international authors and has an extensive fiction selection and kids' section. Author signings and children's story times take place year-round. ✉ *2648 Rte. 6A, East Brewster* ☎ *508/896–6543, 800/823–6543* 🌐 *www.brewsterbookstore.com.*

Satucket Farm Stand. Open Memorial Day to Labor Day, this real old-fashioned farm stand offers plenty of local produce as well as homemade baked goods and other treats. ✉ *76 Harwich Rd.* ☎ *508/896–5540* 🌐 *www.satucketfarm.com.*

4

HARWICH

6 miles south of Brewster, 5 miles east of Dennis.

The Cape's famous cranberry industry took off in Harwich in 1844, when Alvin Cahoon was its principal grower. Today you'll still find working cranberry bogs throughout Harwich. Three naturally sheltered harbors on Nantucket Sound make the town, like its English namesake, popular with boaters. You'll find dozens of elegant sailboats and elaborate yachts in Harwich's harbors, plus plenty of charter fishing boats. Each year in August the town pays celebratory homage to its large boating population with a grand regatta, Sails Around the Cape.

ESSENTIALS

Visitor Information Harwich Chamber of Commerce ✉ *1 Schoolhouse Rd., at Rte. 28, Harwich Port* ☎ *508/432–1600, 800/442–7942* 🌐 *www.harwichcc.com.*

WHERE TO EAT

$$$ ITALIAN Fodor's Choice ★

🍴 **Buca's Tuscan Roadhouse.** This romantic roadhouse near the Chatham border, adorned with tiny white lights, wine bottles, and warm-hued walls, might just transport you to Italy—and if it doesn't, the food will. From the baby arugula, goat cheese, pancetta, and pistachio salad to veal with red wine, balsamic butter, sun-dried cherries, and roasted tomatoes, this is mouthwatering Italian fare taken far beyond traditional home cooking. Save room for the signature three-tiered chocolate cake with a coconut-chocolate sauce. [$] *Average main: $27* ✉ *4 Depot Rd.* ☎ *508/432–6900* 🌐 *www.bucasroadhouse.com* ✍ *Reservations essential* ⏲ *No lunch.*

$$$ AMERICAN Fodor's Choice ★

🍴 **Cape Sea Grille.** Sitting primly inside a dashing Gothic Victorian house on a side street off hectic Route 28, this gem with distant sea views cultivates a refined ambience with fresh flowers, white linens, and a vibrant, welcoming atmosphere. Chef-owner Douglas Ramler relies on the freshest ingredients. Specialties from the seasonally changing menu may include pan-seared lobster with pancetta, potatoes, grilled asparagus, and a Calvados-saffron reduction, or grilled Atlantic halibut with smoked bacon, fennel, and basil tart. There's also a generous wine, martini, and drink list. [$] *Average main: $32* ✉ *31 Sea St., Harwich Port* ☎ *508/432–4745* 🌐 *capeseagrille.com* ✍ *Reservations essential* ⏲ *Closed Mon.–Wed. Columbus Day–early Dec. and mid-Dec.–early Apr. No lunch.*

WHERE TO STAY

$$$$ RESORT FAMILY Fodor's Choice ★

🏨 **Wequassett Inn Resort & Golf Club.** Twenty Cape-style cottages and an attractive hotel make up this traditionally elegant resort by the sea. **Pros:** waterfront setting; activities and programs for all ages; babysitting services. **Cons:** rates are very steep; not an in-town location. [$] *Rooms from: $240* ✉ *2173 Orleans Rd. (Rte. 28)* ☎ *508/432–5400, 800/225–7125* 🌐 *www.wequassett.com* 🛏 *115 rooms, 7 suites* ⏲ *Closed Nov.–Mar.* 🍽 *No meals.*

$$$$ B&B/INN

🏨 **Winstead Village Inn.** With its graceful columns and welcoming front veranda, the regal Winstead Inn sits along a quiet street on the edge of downtown. **Pros:** spacious, elegant rooms; pretty pool area. **Cons:** numerous stairs; not for those on a budget. [$] *Rooms from: $305* ✉ *114 Parallel St.* ☎ *508/432–4444, 800/870–4405* 🌐 *www.winsteadinn.com* 🛏 *6 rooms, 2 suites* ⏲ *Closed Nov.–Easter* 🍽 *Breakfast.*

CHATHAM

5 miles east of Harwich.

At the bent elbow of the Cape, with water nearly surrounding it, Chatham has all the charm of a quietly posh seaside resort, with plenty of shops but none of the crass commercialism that plagues some other towns on the Cape. The town has gray-shingle houses with tidy awnings and cheerful flower gardens, an attractive Main Street with crafts and antiques stores alongside dapper cafés, and a five-and-dime. Although it can get crowded in high season—and even on weekends during shoulder seasons—Chatham remains a true New England village.

ESSENTIALS

Visitor Information Chatham Chamber of Commerce ✉ *2377 Main St.* ☎ *508/945–5199, 800/715–5567* 🌐 *www.chathaminfo.com.*

EXPLORING

Atwood House Museum. Built by sea captain Joseph C. Atwood in 1752, this museum has a gambrel roof, hand-hewn floor planks, an old kitchen with a wide hearth and a beehive oven, and some antique dolls and toys. The New Gallery displays portraits of local sea captains. The Joseph C. Lincoln Room has the manuscripts, first editions, and mementos of the Chatham writer, and antique tools are displayed in a room in the basement. The 1974 Durand Wing has collections of seashells from around the world and threaded Sandwich glass, as well as Parian-ware figures, unglazed porcelain vases, figurines, and busts. In a remodeled freight shed are the stunning and provocative murals (1932–45) by Alice Stallknecht Wight portraying religious scenes in Chatham settings. On the grounds are an herb garden, the old turret and lens from the Chatham Light, and a simple camp house rescued from eroding North Beach. ✉ *347 Stage Harbor Rd., West Chatham* ☎ *508/945–2493* 🌐 *www.chathamhistoricalsociety.org* 🎟 *$6* 🕒 *July and Aug., Tues.–Fri. 10–4, Sat. 1–4; June and Sept.–mid-Oct., Tues.–Sat., 1–4.*

Chatham Light. The view from this lighthouse—of the harbor, the sandbars, and the ocean beyond—justifies the crowds. The lighthouse is especially dramatic on a foggy night, as the beacon's light pierces the mist. Coin-operated telescopes allow a close look at the famous "Chatham Break," the result of a fierce 1987 nor'easter that blasted a channel through a barrier beach just off the coast. The U.S. Coast Guard auxiliary, which supervises the lighthouse, offers free tours April to October on most Wednesdays; otherwise, the interior is off-limits. There is free parking in front of the lighthouse, and the 30-minute time limit is closely monitored. ✉ *Main St., near Bridge St., West Chatham.*

4

Fodor's Choice ★ **Monomoy National Wildlife Refuge.** This 2,500-acre preserve includes the Monomoy Islands, a fragile 9-mile-long barrier-beach area south of Chatham. Monomoy's North and South islands were created when a storm divided the former Monomoy Island in 1978. A haven for bird-watchers, the refuge is an important stop along the North Atlantic Flyway for migratory waterfowl and shorebirds—peak migration times are May and late July. It also provides nesting and resting grounds for 285 species, including gulls—great black-backed, herring, and laughing—and several tern species. White-tailed deer wander the islands, and harbor and gray seals frequent the shores in winter. The only structure on the islands is the **South Monomoy Lighthouse,** built in 1849. ✉ *Wikis Way, Morris Island* ☎ *508/945–0594* 🌐 *www.fws.gov/northeast/monomoy.*

Rip Ryder. In season, the Rip Ryder leads for bird- or seal-watching tours. ☎ *508/945–5450* 🌐 *www.monomoyislandferry.com.*

Monomoy Island Excursions. Monomoy Island Excursions offers seal and seabird tours and boat trips out around Monomoy Island on a 43-foot high-speed catamaran. ☎ *508/430–7772* 🌐 *www.monomoyislandexcursions.com.*

Outermost Adventures. Outermost Adventures provides water-taxi services to Monomoy Island and offers fishing, birding, and seal-watching cruises. ☎ *508/945–5858* 🌐 *www.outermostharbor.com.*

WHERE TO EAT AND STAY

$$$ SEAFOOD 🍴 **Impudent Oyster.** This cozy, festive tavern with an unfailingly cheerful staff and superb but reasonably priced seafood occupies a dapper house just off Main Street. It's a great place for a romantic meal or dinner with the kids, and the menu offers light burgers and sandwiches as well as more substantial fare. The mussels with white-wine sauce is a local favorite. The dining room is split-level, with a bar in back. It's always packed, and there's not a ton of seating, so reserve on weekends. [$] *Average main: $27* ✉ *15 Chatham Bars Ave.* ☎ *508/945–3545.*

$$$ SEAFOOD Fodor's Choice ★ 🍴 **Pisces.** An intimate dining room inside a simple yellow house, Pisces serves coastal-inspired fare. If it swims in local waters, you can probably sample it here. A rich chowder of lobster, white truffle oil, and corn is a terrific way to start your meal. Move on to Mediterranean-style fisherman's stew in saffron-lobster broth, or local cod with lemon-caper aioli. Complement your dinner with a selection from the extensive wine list, which offers more than 20 vintages by the glass. [$] *Average main: $27* ✉ *2653 Main St., South Chatham* ☎ *508/432–4600* 🌐 *www.piscesofchatham.com* ✍ *Reservations essential* 🕓 *Closed mid-Oct.–mid-April. No lunch.*

$$$$ B&B/INN 🏨 **Queen Anne Inn.** Built in 1840 as a wedding present for the daughter of a famous clipper-ship captain, the Queen Anne first opened as an inn in 1874; some of the large guest rooms have hand-painted murals, working fireplaces, balconies, and hot tubs. **Pros:** spacious rooms; historic setting. **Cons:** some steep stairs. [$] *Rooms from: $260* ✉ *70 Queen Anne Rd.* ☎ *508/945–0394, 800/545–4667* 🌐 *www.queenanneinn.com* 🛏 *33 rooms* 🕓 *Closed Dec.–mid-Apr.* 🍽 *Breakfast.*

NIGHTLIFE AND THE ARTS

Chatham Squire. With four bars—including a raw bar—this is a rollicking year-round local hangout, drawing a young crowd to the bar side and a mixed crowd of locals to the restaurant. There's live entertainment on weekends. ✉ *487 Main St.* ☎ *508/945–0945* 🌐 *www.thesquire.com.*

SPORTS AND THE OUTDOORS

BEACHES

Harding's Beach. West of Chatham center and on the calmer and warmer waters of Nantucket Sound, Harding's Beach is very popular with families. It can get crowded, so plan to arrive early or late. **Amenities:** food and drink; lifeguards; parking (fee); showers; toilets. **Best for:** swimming; walking; windsurfing. ✉ *Harding's Beach Rd., off Barn Hill Rd., West Chatham.*

SHOPPING

Chatham Jam and Jelly Shop. This shop sells delicious concoctions like rose-petal jelly, apple-lavender chutney, and wild beach plum jelly, as well as all the old standbys. All preserves are made on-site in small batches, and about 75 of the 120-plus varieties are available for sampling (which is encouraged). ✉ *10 Vineyard Ave., at Rte. 28, West Chatham* ☎ *508/945–3052* 🌐 *www.chathamjamandjellyshop.com.*

Yankee Ingenuity. Here you'll find a varied selection of unique jewelry and lamps and a wide assortment of unusual, beautiful trinkets at reasonable (especially for Chatham) prices. ✉ *525 Main St.* ☎ *508/945–1288* 🌐 *www.yankee-ingenuity.com.*

ORLEANS

8 miles north of Chatham, 35 miles east of Sagamore Bridge.

Orleans has a long heritage in fishing and seafaring, and many beautifully preserved homes remain from the Colonial era in the small village of East Orleans, home of the town's Historical Society and Museum. In other areas of town, such as down by Rock Harbor, more modestly grand homes stand near the water's edge.

GETTING HERE AND AROUND

A bus connecting Hyannis and Orleans serves the Lower Cape region. Year-round transport on the Flex service goes from Harwich to Provincetown, serving the towns of Brewster, Orleans, Eastham, Wellfleet, and Truro along the way. In the summer an additional visitor center is open at 8 Eldredge Parkway.

ESSENTIALS

Visitor Information Orleans Chamber of Commerce ✉ *44 Main St.* ☎ *508/255–1386, 800/856–1386* 🌐 *www.capecod-orleans.com.*

EXPLORING

FAMILY **Rock Harbor.** This harbor was the site of a War of 1812 skirmish in which the Orleans militia kept a British warship from docking. In the 19th century Orleans had an active saltworks, and a flourishing packet service between Rock Harbor and Boston developed. Today it's the base of charter-fishing and party boats in season, as well as of a small commercial fishing fleet. Sunsets over the harbor are spectacular, and it's a great place to watch the boats float past. Parking is free. ✉ *Rock Harbor Rd.*

NEED A BREAK? 🍴 **Cottage St. Bakery. Delicious artisanal breads, pastries, cakes, and sweets are made here, as well as healthful breakfast and lunch fare, from homemade granola to hearty soups and hefty sandwiches.** [$] ***Average main: $260*** ✉ ***5 Cottage St.*** ☎ ***508/255–2821.***

WHERE TO EAT AND STAY

$$$ MEDITERRANEAN Fodor's Choice ★ 🍴 **Abba.** In an elegant and intimate setting, Abba serves inspired pan-Mediterranean cuisine. Chef and co-owner Erez Pinhas skillfully combines Middle Eastern, Asian, and southern European flavors in such dishes as herb-crusted rack of venison with shiitake risotto and asparagus in port sauce, and grilled tuna with vegetable nori roll tempura in a balsamic miso-and-mustard sauce. Cushy pillows on the banquettes and soft candlelight flickering from Moroccan glass votives add a touch of opulence. [$] *Average main: $27* ✉ *89 Old Colony Way* ☎ *508/255–8144* 🌐 *www.abbarestaurant.com* ✍ *Reservations essential* ⏲ *No lunch.*

$$$$ B&B/INN Fodor's Choice ★ 🏨 **A Little Inn on Pleasant Bay.** This gorgeously decorated inn occupies a 1798 building on a bluff beside a cranberry bog, and many of the rooms look clear out to the bay for which it's named (others face the lush gardens). **Pros:** great water views; abundant buffet breakfast; spacious baths. **Cons:** not an in-town location; not for those traveling with small children. [$] *Rooms from: $285* ✉ *654 S. Orleans Rd., South Orleans* ☎ *508/255–0780, 888/332–3351* 🌐 *www.alittleinnonpleasantbay.com* 🛏 *9 rooms* ⏲ *Closed Oct.–mid-May* 🍽 *Breakfast.*

SPORTS AND THE OUTDOORS

BEACHES

There is a daily parking fee of $15 from mid-June to Labor Day for both beaches in Orleans.

Nauset Beach. This town-managed beach—not to be confused with Nauset Light Beach on the National Seashore—is a 10-mile sweep of sandy ocean beach with low dunes and large waves good for bodysurfing or board surfing. Despite its size, the massive parking lot often fills up on sunny days; arrive quite early or in the late afternoon if you want to claim a spot. The beach gets extremely crowded in summer; unless you walk a ways, expect to feel very close to your neighbors on the sand. **Amenities:** food and drink; lifeguards; parking (fee); showers; toilets. **Best for:** sunrise; surfing; swimming; walking. ⊠ *Beach Rd., Nauset Heights* ☎ *508/240–3780.*

FAMILY **Skaket Beach.** On Cape Cod Bay, Skaket Beach is a sandy stretch with calm, warm water good for children. When the tide is out, you can walk seemingly endlessly on the sandy flats. The parking lot fills up fast on hot July and August days; try to arrive before 11 or after 2. The many tide pools make this a favorite spot for families. Sunsets here draw a good crowd. **Amenities:** food and drink; lifeguards; parking (fee); showers; toilets. **Best for:** sunset; swimming; walking. ⊠ *Skaket Beach Rd.* ☎ *508/240–3775.*

BOATING AND FISHING

Arey's Pond Boat Yard. There's a sailing school here offering individual and group lessons. The company also rents sailboats. ⊠ *45 Arey's La., off Rte. 28, South Orleans* ☎ *508/255–0994* ⊕ *www.areyspondboatyard.com.*

Many of Orleans's freshwater ponds offer good fishing for perch, pickerel, trout, and more.

Goose Hummock Shop. Fishing licenses and gear are available at the Goose Hummock Shop, which also rents canoes, paddleboards, and kayaks. Lessons and tours are available. ⊠ *15 Rte. 6A* ☎ *508/255–0455* ⊕ *www.goose.com.*

EASTHAM

3 miles north of Orleans, 6 miles south of Wellfleet.

Often overlooked on the speedy drive up toward Provincetown on U.S. 6, Eastham is a town full of hidden treasures. Unlike other towns on the Cape, it has no official town center or Main Street; the highway bisects it, and the town touches both Cape Cod Bay and the Atlantic. Amid the gas stations, convenience stores, restaurants, and large motel complexes, Eastham's wealth of natural beauty takes a little exploring to find.

ESSENTIALS

Visitor Information Eastham Chamber of Commerce ⊠ *1700 Rte. 6, at Governor Prence Rd.* ☎ *508/240–7211* ⊕ *www.easthamchamber.com.*

EXPLORING

FAMILY **Cape Cod National Seashore.** ⇨ *See the highlighted listing, "Cape Cod*

Fodor'sChoice *National Seashore."*

★

WHERE TO EAT AND STAY

$$ ✕ **Arnold's Lobster & Clam Bar.** You can't miss this hot spot on the side SEAFOOD of Route 6: look for the riot of colorful flowers lining the road and the FAMILY patient folks waiting in long lines in the parking lot. That crowd is testament to the freshness and flavors that come out of this busy kitchen for lunch, dinner, and takeout, putting forth everything from grilled

burgers to 3-pound lobsters. Unusual for a clam shack like this is the full bar, offering beer, wine, mixed drinks, and the house specialty, margaritas. There's ice cream and an artfully designed miniature-golf course to keep the kids happy. [$] *Average main: $18* ✉ *3580 State Hwy.* ☎ *508/255–2575* 🌐 *www.arnoldsrestaurant.com* ✍ *Reservations not accepted* ⏲ *Closed Nov.–Apr.*

$$ ITALIAN FAMILY 🍴 **Fairway Restaurant and Pizzeria.** The friendly family-run Fairway specializes in Italian comfort food—try the eggplant Parmesan, fettucine and meatballs, or a well-stuffed calzone—and is also very popular for breakfast. Attached to the Hole in One Donut Shop (a favorite among locals for early-morning coffee and exceptional donuts and muffins), the Fairway puts a jar of crayons on every paper-covered table and sells its own brand of root beer. The pizzas are hearty and filling, rather than the thin-crust variety. [$] *Average main: $15* ✉ *4295 U.S. Rte. 6, North Eastham* ☎ *508/255–3893* 🌐 *www.fairwaycapecod.com* ⏲ *No lunch.*

$$$ B&B/INN Fodor's Choice ★ 🏨 **Fort Hill Bed and Breakfast.** Gordon and Jean Avery run this enchanting, adults-only B&B in an 1864 Greek Revival farmhouse nestled in the tranquil Fort Hill area (it is the only lodging within the National Seashore). **Pros:** pastoral setting; close to nature trails; private and elegant lodging. **Cons:** not for those traveling with children. [$] *Rooms from: $275* ✉ *75 Fort Hill Rd.* ☎ *508/240–2870* 🌐 *www.forthillbedandbreakfast.com* 🛏 *2 suites, 1 cottage* 💳 *No credit cards* 🍽 *Breakfast.*

$$$$ B&B/INN 🏨 **Penny House Inn & Spa.** Tucked behind a wave of privet hedges, this rambling gray-shingle inn's spacious rooms are filled with antiques, collectibles, and wicker furnishings. **Pros:** private and secluded; ideal for a romantic getaway; full range of spa services. **Cons:** off busy U.S. 6; no water views or beachfront. [$] *Rooms from: $238* ✉ *4885 County Rd.* ☎ *508/255–6632, 800/554–1751* 🌐 *www.pennyhouseinn.com* 🛏 *3 rooms, 9 suites* 🍽 *Breakfast.*

$$$ B&B/INN Fodor's Choice ★ 🏨 **Whalewalk Inn & Spa.** On three landscaped acres, this 1830 whaling master's home has wide-plank pine floors, fireplaces, and 19th-century country antiques to provide historical appeal. **Pros:** beautiful grounds; elegantly appointed rooms; decadent spa treatments. **Cons:** not for those traveling with small children. [$] *Rooms from: $190* ✉ *220 Bridge Rd.* ☎ *508/255–0617, 800/440–1281* 🌐 *www.whalewalkinn.com* 🛏 *11 rooms, 6 suites* ⏲ *Closed Dec.–Mar.* 🍽 *Breakfast.*

SPORTS AND THE OUTDOORS

Fodor's Choice ★ **Nauset Light Beach.** Adjacent to Coast Guard Beach, this long, sandy beach is backed by tall dunes, frilly grasses, and heathland. The trail to the Three Sisters lighthouses takes you through a pitch-pine forest. Parking here fills up very quickly in summer; plan to arrive early or you may have to go elsewhere. Nauset charges $15 per car, but you can buy an annual pass for $45 (valid for all six Cape Cod National Seashore beaches). **Amenities:** lifeguards; parking (fee); showers; toilets. **Best for:** sunrise; surfing; swimming; walking. ✉ *Off Ocean View Dr.* 🌐 *www.nps.gov/caco.*

WELLFLEET AND SOUTH WELLFLEET

6 miles north of Eastham, 13 miles southeast of Provincetown.

Still famous for its world-renowned and succulent namesake oysters, Wellfleet is today a tranquil community; many artists and writers call it home. Less than 2 miles wide, it's one of the most attractively developed Cape resort towns, with a number of fine restaurants, historic houses, art galleries, and a good old Main Street in the village proper.

ESSENTIALS

Visitor Information Wellfleet Chamber of Commerce ⊠ *Rte. 6, near the post office, South Wellfleet* ☎ *508/349–2510* ⊕ *www.wellfleetchamber.com.*

EXPLORING

Marconi Station. On the Atlantic side of the Cape is the site of the first transatlantic wireless station erected on the U.S. mainland. It was from here that Italian radio and wireless-telegraphy pioneer Guglielmo Marconi sent the first American wireless message to Europe—"most cordial greetings and good wishes" from President Theodore Roosevelt to King Edward VII of England—on January 18, 1903. There's a lookout deck that offers a vantage point of both the Atlantic and Cape Cod Bay. Off the parking lot, a 1½-mile trail and boardwalk lead through the **Atlantic White Cedar Swamp,** one of the most beautiful trails on the seashore; free maps and guides are available at the trailhead. **Marconi Beach,** south of the Marconi Station on Marconi Beach Road, is one of the National Seashore's lovely ocean beaches. ⊠ *Marconi Site Rd., South Wellfleet* ☎ *508/349–3785* ⊕ *www.nps. gov/caco* ☟ *Free* ☉ *Daily dawn–dusk.*

FAMILY

Fodor's Choice

★

Massachusetts Audubon Wellfleet Bay Wildlife Sanctuary. Encompassing nearly 1,000-acres, this reserve is home to more than 250 species of birds. The jewel of the Massachusetts Audubon Society, the sanctuary is a superb place for walking, birding, and watching the sun set over the salt marsh and bay. The **Esther Underwood Johnson Nature Center** contains two 700-gallon aquariums that offer an up-close look at marine life common to the region's tidal flats and marshlands. From the center you can hike five short nature trails, including a fascinating boardwalk trail that leads over a salt marsh to a small beach—or you can wander through the butterfly garden. The sanctuary has camps for children in July and August and weeklong field schools for adults. ⊠ *291 U.S. 6, South Wellfleet* ☎ *508/349–2615* ⊕ *www.massaudubon.org/wellfleetbay* ☟ *$5* ☉ *Trails daily 8 am–dusk; nature center late May–mid-Oct., daily 8:30–5; mid-Oct.–late May, Tues.–Sun. 8:30–5.*

WHERE TO EAT

$$$

AMERICAN

✕**Finely JP's.** Chef John Pontius consistently turns out wonderful, affordable food full of the best Mediterranean and local influences and ingredients at his beloved restaurant along U.S. 6. Housed in a handsome Arts and Crafts–inspired structure, this spot has long been a local favorite. Appetizers are especially good, among them oysters baked in a white wine-cream sauce and jerk-spiced duck salad with a raspberry vinaigrette. The Wellfleet paella and the roast duck with cranberry-orange sauce draw rave reviews. Off-season hours vary, so call ahead. $ *Average main: $22* ✉ *554 U.S. Rte. 6, South Wellfleet* ☎ *508/349–7500* ⊕ *www.finelyjps.com* ⌚ *Reservations not accepted* ⊘ *No lunch. No brunch June–Sept.*

$$
SEAFOOD
✕ **Mac's Seafood.** Right at Wellfleet Harbor, this ambitious little spot serves some of the freshest seafood around. You can always sit along the pier and soak up the great water views while you chow down. This place serves a vast variety of local fish dishes, plus globe-trotting fare like sushi, grilled scallop burritos, and linguica sausage sandwiches. There's also a selection of smoked fish, pâtés, lobster, and fish you can take home to grill yourself. At 91 Commercial Street is **Mac's Shack,** a funky sit-down restaurant in a rambling mid-19th-century barn overlooking Duck Creek. Look for the lobster boat on the roof. $ *Average main: $18* ✉ *Wellfleet Town Pier, 265 Commercial St., Wellfleet Harbor* ☎ *508/349–9611* ⊕ *www.macsseafood.com* ⊘ *Closed mid-Sept.–late May.*

$$$
AMERICAN
Fodor's Choice
★
✕ **Wicked Oyster.** In a rambling, gray clapboard house, the Wicked Oyster serves up the most-innovative fare in Wellfleet. It's farmhouse sparse inside, with brightly painted walls accented with paintings by local artists. Try the pan-roasted catch of the day with littleneck clams, leeks, bacon, and fingerling potatoes. Oyster stew and the open-face burger (with blue-cheese aioli and applewood-smoked bacon) are among the top lunch dishes. Breakfast is a favorite here—try the smoked-salmon Benedict. There's also an outstanding wine list. Parking is tight at this popular spot in summer. $ *Average main: $25* ✉ *50 Main St., Downtown Wellfleet* ☎ *508/349–3455* ⊕ *www.thewickedo.com* ⊘ *Closed Wed.*

NIGHTLIFE AND THE ARTS

FAMILY
Fodor's Choice
★
Wellfleet Drive-In Theater. A classic Cape experience is the Wellfleet Drive-In Theater, located near the Eastham town line. Regulars spend the night in style: chairs, blankets, and picnic baskets. Films start at dusk nightly from May to September, and there's also a standard indoor cinema with four screens, a miniature-golf course, and a bar and grill. It's also the home of the beloved Wellfleet Flea Market, held weekends from late spring to mid-October. ✉ *51 U.S. 6, South Wellfleet* ☎ *508/349–7176* ⊕ *www.wellfleetcinemas.com.*

SPORTS AND THE OUTDOORS

BEACHES

Cahoon Hollow Beach. The restaurant and music club on top of the dune are the main attractions at Cahoon Hollow Beach, which tends to draw younger and slightly rowdier crowds. It's a big Sunday-afternoon party place. The Beachcomber restaurant has paid parking, which is reimbursed when you buy something to eat or drink. Erosion has made getting to the beach a steep climb. **Amenities:** food and drink; lifeguards; parking (fee); toilets. **Best for:** partiers; surfing; swimming; walking. ✉ *Ocean View Dr., Greater Wellfleet.*

Fodor's Choice
★
Marconi Beach. Marconi Beach, part of the Cape Cod National Seashore, is accessed via a very long and steep series of stairs leading down to the beach. It's popular with surfcasters looking for striped bass or bluefish. Erosion from fierce storms has comprised beach access. **Amenities:** lifeguards; parking (fee); showers; toilets. **Best for:** sunrise; surfing; swimming; walking. ✉ *Marconi Beach Rd., Off U.S. 6, South Wellfleet* ⊕ *www.nps.gov/caco.*

White Crest Beach. White Crest Beach is a prime surfer hangout, where the dudes often spend more time waiting for waves than actually riding them. If you're up to the challenge, join one of the spontaneous volleyball games. The other challenge will be working your way down (and then up) to the water: Mother Nature and her fury have made this a steep trek. **Amenities:** lifeguards; parking (fee); toilets. **Best for:** sunrise; surfing; swimming; walking. ⊠ *Ocean View Dr., Greater Wellfleet.*

BOATING

Jack's Boat Rental. Sailing lessons and guided kayak tours are offered at Jack's, which rents canoes, kayaks, pedal boats, sailboats, surfboards, boogie boards, and sailboards. ⊠ *Gull Pond, U.S. 6 and Cahoon Hollow Rd., Greater Wellfleet* ☎ *508/349–9808, 508/349–7553* ⊕ *jacksboatrental.com.*

EN ROUTE Edward Hopper summered in **Truro** from 1930 to 1967, finding the Cape light ideal for his austere brand of realism. One of the largest towns on the Cape in terms of land area—almost 43 square miles—it's also the smallest in population, with about 1,400 year-round residents. Truro is also the Cape's narrowest town, and from a high perch you can see the Atlantic Ocean on one side and Cape Cod Bay on the other. Its **Highland Light,** also called Cape Cod Light, is the Cape's oldest lighthouse and truly a breathtaking sight. Tours ($4) of the lighthouse are given daily from mid-May to October.

PROVINCETOWN

9 miles northwest of Wellfleet, 62 miles from Sagamore Bridge.

Fodor's Choice
★
Many people know that the Pilgrims stopped here at the curved tip of Cape Cod before proceeding to Plymouth. Historical records suggest that an earlier visitor was Thorvald, brother of Viking Leif Erikson, who came ashore here in AD 1004 to repair the keel of his boat and consequently named the area Kjalarness, or Cape of the Keel. Bartholomew Gosnold came to Provincetown in 1602 and named the area Cape Cod after the abundant codfish he found in the local waters.

Incorporated as a town in 1727, Provincetown was for many decades a bustling seaport, with fishing and whaling as its major industries. In the late 19th century groups of Portuguese fishermen and whalers began to settle here, lending their expertise and culture to an already cosmopolitan town. Fishing is still an important source of income for many Provincetown locals, but now the town ranks among the world's leading whale-watching—rather than whale-hunting—outposts.

Artists began coming here in the late 1890s to take advantage of the unusual Cape Cod light—in fact, Provincetown is the nation's oldest continuous art colony. By 1916, with five art schools flourishing here, painters' easels were nearly as common as shells on the beach. This bohemian community, along with the availability of inexpensive summer lodgings, attracted young rebels and writers as well, including John Reed (*Ten Days That Shook the World*) and Mary Heaton Vorse (*Footnote to Folly*), who in 1915 began the Cape's first significant theater group, the Provincetown Players. The young, then unknown Eugene O'Neill joined them in 1916, when his *Bound East for Cardiff* premiered in a tiny wharf-side East End fish house.

America's original gay resort, Provincetown today is as appealing to artists as it is to gay and lesbian—as well as straight—tourists. Massachusetts's legalization of same-sex marriage has turned the town into the most visibly gay vacation community in America.

GETTING HERE AND AROUND

AIR TRAVEL   Year-round flight service by Cape Air connects Provincetown with Boston's Logan Airport.

CAR TRAVEL   The busiest travel time is early morning—especially on rainy days—when it seems that everyone on Cape Cod is determined to make it to Provincetown. Traffic is heaviest around Wellfleet, and it can be slow going. Driving the 3 miles of Provincetown's main downtown thoroughfare, Commercial Street, in season could take forever. Parking is not one of Provincetown's better amenities, so bike and foot are the best ways to explore the downtown area.

FERRY TRAVEL   Bay State Cruise Company offers standard and high-speed ferry services between Commonwealth Pier in Boston and MacMillan Wharf in Provincetown. High-speed service runs a few times daily from mid-May through September ($83 round-trip); the ride takes 90 minutes. Standard service runs Saturdays only from early July through early September ($46 round-trip); the ride takes three hours. Boston Harbor Cruises runs a fast ferry from Long Wharf in Boston mid-May to mid-October for $83 round-trip. From the State Pier in Plymouth, the Plymouth to Provincetown Express Ferry operates a 90-minute ferry daily from mid-June to mid-September ($42 round-trip).

SHUTTLE
TRAVEL   The Shuttle, run by the Cape Cod Regional Transit Authority, provides a seasonal (mid-June–mid-September) route from Truro, heading into town, with trips to Herring Cove Beach, Race Point Beach, and the Provincetown Airport. Bikes are accommodated.

ESSENTIALS

Transportation Contacts Bay State Cruise Company ⊠ *Commonwealth Pier, 200 Seaport Blvd, Boston* ☎ *617/748–1428, 877/783–3779* ⊕ *www.baystatecruisecompany.com.* **Boston Harbor Cruises** ☎ *617/227–4321, 877/733–9425* ⊕ *www.bostonharborcruises.com.* **Cape Air** ☎ *866/227–3247, 508/771–6944* ⊕ *www.flycapeair.com.* **Provincetown Express Ferry** ⊠ *State Pier, 77 Water St., Plymouth* ☎ *508/747–2400, 800/225–4000* ⊕ *www.provincetownferry.com.*

Visitor Information Provincetown Business Guild ⊠ *3 Freeman St., Downtown Center* ☎ *508/487–2313, 800/637–8696* ⊕ *www.ptown.org.* **Provincetown Chamber of Commerce** ⊠ *Information booth, 307 Commercial St., Downtown Center* ☎ *508/487–3424* ⊕ *www.ptownchamber.com.*

EXPLORING

Commercial Street. Take a casual stroll by the many architectural styles (Greek Revival, Victorian, Second Empire, and Gothic, to name a few) used in the design of the impressive houses for wealthy sea captains and merchants. The Provincetown Historical Society's walking-tour pamphlet is available for $1 at many shops. The center of town is where you'll find the crowds and the best people-watching. The East End has a number of nationally renowned galleries; the West End has a number

Artists and birders flock to the Wellfleet Bay Wildlife Sanctuary, protected by the Massachusetts Audubon Society.

of small inns with neat lawns and elaborate gardens. Commercial Street runs parallel to the water, so there is always a patch of sand close at hand should you need a break.

QUICK BITES

Spiritus. The local bars close at 1 am, at which point this pizza joint becomes the town's epicenter. It's the ultimate place to see and be seen, slice in hand and witty banter at the ready. The same counter serves delectable ice cream from Emack & Bolios, Häagen-Dazs, and Giffords of Maine. ⊠ *190 Commercial St., Downtown Center* ☎ *508/487–2808* ⊕ *www.spirituspizza.com* ▭ *No credit cards* ⊗ *Closed Nov.–Apr.*

Pilgrim Monument. The first thing you'll see in Provincetown is this grandiose edifice, which seems somewhat out of proportion to the rest of the low-rise town. The monument commemorates the Pilgrims' first landing in the New World and their signing of the Mayflower Compact (the first Colonial-American rules of self-governance) before they set off to explore the mainland. Climb the 116 steps and 60 short ramps of the 252-foot-high tower for a panoramic view—dunes on one side, harbor on the other, and the entire bay side of Cape Cod beyond. At the tower's base is a museum of Lower Cape and Provincetown history, with exhibits on whaling, shipwrecks, and scrimshaw. ⊠ *1 High Pole Hill Rd., Downtown Center* ☎ *508/487–1310* ⊕ *www.pilgrim-monument.org* ⌑ *$12* ⊗ *Apr.–late May, mid–Sept.–early Dec., daily 9–5; late May–mid-Sept., daily 9–7; closed Dec.–Mar.*

Fodor's Choice
★

Provincetown Art Association and Museum. Founded in 1914 to collect and show the works of artists with Provincetown connections, this facility has a 1,650-piece permanent collection, displayed in changing exhibits that mix up-and-comers with established 20th-century figures, including Milton Avery, Philip Evergood, William Gropper, Charles Hawthorne, Robert Motherwell, Claes Oldenburg, Man Ray, John Singer Sargent, Andy Warhol, and Agnes Weinrich. A stunning contemporary wing has greatly expanded the exhibit space. The museum store carries books of local interest, including works by or about area artists and authors, as well as posters, crafts, cards, and gift items. Art classes (one day and longer) offer the opportunity to study under such talents as Hilda Neily, Selina Trieff, and Doug Ritter. ✉ *460 Commercial St., East End* ☎ *508/487–1750* 🌐 *www.paam.org* 🎟 *$7* 🕒 *Late May–Sept., Mon.–Thurs. 11–8, Fri. 11–10, weekends 11–5; Oct.–late May, Thurs.–Sun. noon–5.*

WHERE TO EAT

$$$ AMERICAN Fodor's Choice ★

🍴 **Devon's.** This unassuming tiny white cottage—with a dining room that seats just 37 lucky patrons—serves up some of the best food in town, judging by the continual crowds that wait for seats. Specialties from the oft-changing menu include brown butter and herb-roasted Atlantic halibut or grilled Provincetown day-boat scallops. Save some room for knockout desserts like blackberry mousse over ginger-lemon polenta cake with wild-berry coulis. Devon's is also a good spot for breakfast. [$] *Average main: $30* ✉ *401½ Commercial St., Downtown Center* ☎ *508/487–4773* 🌐 *www.devons.org* ✍ *Reservations essential* 🕒 *Closed Wed. and Nov.–mid-May. No lunch.*

$$$ SEAFOOD

🍴 **Lobster Pot.** Provincetown's Lobster Pot is fit to do battle with all the lobster shanties anywhere (and everywhere) else on the Cape—it's often jammed with tourists, but the crowds reflect the generally high quality. The hardworking kitchen turns out classic New England cooking: lobsters, generous and filling seafood platters, and some of the best chowder around. Eat like a local and try the barbeque pepper shrimp. [$] *Average main: $27* ✉ *321 Commercial St., Downtown Center* ☎ *508/487–0842* 🌐 *www.ptownlobsterpot.com* ✍ *Reservations not accepted* 🕒 *Closed Jan.*

$$$ AMERICAN Fodor's Choice ★

🍴 **The Mews.** This perennial favorite with magnificent harbor views focuses on seafood and grilled meats with a cross-cultural flair—popular entrées include roasted vegetable and polenta lasagna with a tomato-olive sauce and "shaking beef," a Vietnamese-inspired dish of beef tenderloin sautéed with scallions and red onions and a lime-black pepper sauce; there's also a lighter bistro menu for smaller appetites. The view of the bay from the bar is nearly perfect, and the gentle lighting makes this a romantic spot to have a drink. The restaurant claims its vodka bar is New England's largest, with more than 275 varieties. Sunday brunch is served from Mother's Day to Columbus Day; fall and winter Monday nights get lively with the very popular open-mike coffeehouse. [$] *Average main: $27* ✉ *429 Commercial St., East End* ☎ *508/487–1500* 🌐 *www.mews.com* 🕒 *No lunch. Brunch Sun. only.*

$$$$ AMERICAN

🍴 **Red Inn.** Inside the striking red house on P-town's West End that's also an enchanting B&B, the Red Inn is perhaps even better known as one of the Outer Cape's most romantic dining destinations—the views are simply stunning. The remarkable setting aside, the inventive contemporary fare as well as the service can be hit-or-miss, especially given the lofty prices. You might start off with the lobster sliders before moving on to chili-rubbed pork chops with ginger cranberry chutney. $ *Average main: $32 ⊠ 15 Commercial St., West End ☎ 508/487–7334 ⊕ www. theredinn.com ⚲ Reservations essential ⊗ Closed Jan–mid-April.*

WHERE TO STAY

$$$
B&B/INN
Fodor'sChoice
★

Brass Key. One of the Cape's most luxurious small resorts, this meticulously kept year-round getaway comprises a beautifully restored main house—originally a sea captain's home built in 1828—and several other carefully groomed buildings and cottages. **Pros:** ultraposh rooms; beautiful and secluded grounds; pool on-site. **Cons:** among the highest rates in town; not for those with children; significant minimum-stay requirements in summer. $ *Rooms from: $319 ⊠ 67 Bradford St., Downtown Center ☎ 508/487–9005, 800/842–9858 ⊕ www.brasskey.com ⇆ 43 rooms ⦿ Breakfast.*

$$
B&B/INN
Fodor'sChoice
★

Christopher's by the Bay. The rooms in this elegant but reasonably priced art-inspired inn are named after the greats—Rembrandt, Picasso, Monet, Van Gogh—and are warmly appointed with brass beds and rich fabrics. **Pros:** excellent value; steps from shopping and dining; friendly and professional service. **Cons:** some rooms share a bath; third-floor rooms are a climb; not for those with children. $ *Rooms from: $175 ⊠ 8 Johnson St., Downtown Center ☎☎ 508/487–9263 ☎ 877/487–9263 ⊕ www.christophersbythebay.com ⇆ 10 rooms, 5 with bath ⦿ Breakfast.*

$$$
B&B/INN
Fodor'sChoice
★

Crowne Pointe Historic Inn and Spa. Created meticulously from six different buildings, this inn has not left a single detail unattended. **Pros:** great on-site amenities; posh and luxurious room decor; professional and well-trained staff. **Cons:** among the highest rates in town; significant minimum-stay requirements in summer; contemporary vibe. $ *Rooms from: $259 ⊠ 82 Bradford St., Downtown Center ☎ 508/487–6767, 877/276– 9631 ⊕ www.crownepointe.com ⇆ 37 rooms, 3 suites ⦿ Breakfast.*

$$$
B&B/INN
Fodor'sChoice
★

White Porch Inn. This sterling, light-filled B&B offers a soothing respite from the bustle of town. **Pros:** fresh and immaculate; steps from East End shopping and dining; enthusiastic and friendly staff. **Cons:** somewhat long walk to West End shopping and businesses. $ *Rooms from: $279 ⊠ 7 Johnson St., Downtown Center ☎ 508/364–2549, 508/487– 0592 ⊕ www.whiteporchinn.com ⇆ 10 rooms ⦿ Breakfast.*

NIGHTLIFE

Atlantic House. Atlantic House is the grandfather of the gay nightlife scene. With a dance club and 2 other bars, there's something for everyone here. ⊠ 4 Masonic Pl., Downtown Center ☎ 508/487–3821 ⊕ www.ahouse.com.

SPORTS AND THE OUTDOORS

BEACHES

Herring Cove Beach. Herring Cove Beach is relatively calm and warm for a National Seashore beach, but it's not as pretty as some because its parking lot isn't hidden behind dunes. It's close to town, so in warm weather it's always crowded. The lot to the right of the bathhouse is a great place to watch the sunset. **Amenities:** food and drink; lifeguards; parking (fee); toilets; showers. **Best for:** sunset; swimming; walking. ⊕ www.nps.gov/caco.

4

Fodor's Choice   **Race Point Beach.** Race Point Beach, one of the Cape Cod National Sea-
★   shore beaches in Provincetown, has a wide swath of sand stretching
far off into the distance around the point and Coast Guard station.
Because of its position facing north, the beach gets sun all day long.
Keep an eye out for whales off-shore; it's also a popular fishing spot.
Amenities: lifeguards; parking (fee); showers; toilets. **Best for:** sunrise;
sunset; surfing; swimming; walking. ⊠ *Race Point Rd., east of U.S. 6*
☎ *508/487–1256* ⊕ *www.nps.gov/caco/index.htm.*

DUNE TOURS

Fodor's Choice   **Art's Dune Tours.** Art's Dune Tours has been taking eager passengers into the
★   dunes of Province Lands since 1946. Bumpy but controlled rides (about
one hour) transport you through sometimes surreal sandy vistas peppered
with beach grass and along a shoreline patrolled by seagulls and sandpipers. On Sunday there is a special Race Point Lighthouse Tour; or head out
at sunset for a stunning ride, available with or without a clambake feast.
⊠ *4 Standish St., Downtown Center* ☎ *508/487–1950, 800/894–1951*
⊕ *www.artsdunetours.com* ⊠ *Regular tours start at $27.*

WHALE-WATCHING

Dolphin Fleet. Tours are accompanied by scientists from the Center for
Coastal Studies in Provincetown, who provide commentary while collecting data on the whales they've been monitoring for years. They
know many of them by name and will tell you about their habits and
histories. These trips are most often exciting and incredibly thrilling
with close-up encounters. ⊠ *Chamber of Commerce Building, Mac-
Millan Wharf, Downtown Center* ☎ *508/240–3636, 800/826–9300*
⊕ *www.whalewatch.com* ⊠ *$44* ☉ *Tours mid-Apr.–Oct.*

SHOPPING

Fodor's Choice   **Julie Heller Gallery.** Julie Heller Gallery has contemporary artists as well
★   as some Provincetown icons. The gallery has works from the Sol Wilson
and Milton Avery estates, as well as from such greats as Robert Motherwell, Agnes Weinrich, and Blanche Lazzell. ⊠ *2 Gosnold St., Downtown
Center* ☎ *508/487–2169* ⊕ *www.juliehellergallery.com.*

MARTHA'S VINEYARD

Far less developed than Cape Cod—thanks to a few local conservation
organizations—yet more cosmopolitan than neighboring Nantucket,
Martha's Vineyard is an island with a double life. From Memorial Day
through Labor Day the quieter (some might say real) Vineyard quickens
into a vibrant, star-studded place.

The busy main port, Vineyard Haven, welcomes day-trippers fresh off
ferries and private yachts to browse in its array of shops. Oak Bluffs,
where pizza and ice cream emporiums reign supreme, has the air of
a Victorian boardwalk. Edgartown is flooded with seekers of chic
who wander tiny streets that hold boutiques, stately whaling captains'
homes, and charming inns.

Summer regulars have included a host of celebrities over the years,
among them Carly Simon, Ted Danson, Spike Lee, and Diane Sawyer.
If you're planning to stay overnight on a summer weekend, be sure to

make reservations well in advance; spring is not too early. Things stay busy on September and October weekends, a favorite time for weddings, but begin to slow down soon after. In many ways the Vineyard's off-season persona is even more appealing than its summer self, with more time to linger over pastoral and ocean vistas, free from the throngs of cars, bicycles, and mopeds.

Retaining its colonial connection, Chilmark is now the only town on the island that remains exclusively "dry. " There are no alcohol sales in shops, and in restaurants you must bring your own wine if you choose to imbibe (often with a healthy "corkage fee"). The towns of Vineyard Haven, West Tisbury, and Aquinnah now allow beer and wine—but no liquor—in restaurants. Oak Bluffs and Edgartown allow liquor sales in restaurants, and there are several package stores where you can buy your own supply to take home.

ESSENTIALS

Visitor Information Martha's Vineyard Chamber of Commerce ✉ *24 Beach Rd., Vineyard Haven* ☎ *508/693–0085, 800/505–4815* ⊕ *www.mvy.com.*

VINEYARD HAVEN (TISBURY)

7 miles southeast of Woods Hole, 3½ miles west of Oak Bluffs, 8 miles northwest of Edgartown.

Most people call this town Vineyard Haven because of the name of the port where ferries arrive, but its official name is Tisbury. Not as high-toned as Edgartown or as honky-tonk as Oak Bluffs, Vineyard Haven blends the past and the present with a touch of the bohemian. Visitors step off the ferry right into the bustle of the harbor, a block from the shops and restaurants of Main Street.

GETTING HERE AND AROUND

It can be handy to have a car to see all of Martha's Vineyard and travel freely. Instead of bringing one over on the ferry in summer it's sometimes easier and more economical to rent a car once you're on the island for the days you plan on exploring. The Martha's Vineyard Transit Authority (VTA) provides regular service to all six towns on the island. The buses can accommodate a limited number of bicycles, and the island has an excellent network of well-maintained bike trails. The VTA also has free in-town shuttle-bus routes in Edgartown and Vineyard Haven.

AIR TRAVEL   Cape Air has regular, year-round flight service to the island from Hyannis, Boston, and Providence's T. F. Green Airport. From New York's LaGuardia Airport, Philadelphia, and Washington, D.C., US Airways Express provides seasonal service.

FERRY TRAVEL   The Steamship Authority runs the only car ferries to Martha's Vineyard, which make the 45-minute trip from Woods Hole on Cape Cod to Vineyard Haven year-round and to Oak Bluffs from late May through mid-October ($8 for passenger fare; $3 for bicycles; $42.50–$68 for a car). In summer and on autumn weekends you must have a reservation if you want to bring your car; passenger reservations are never necessary.

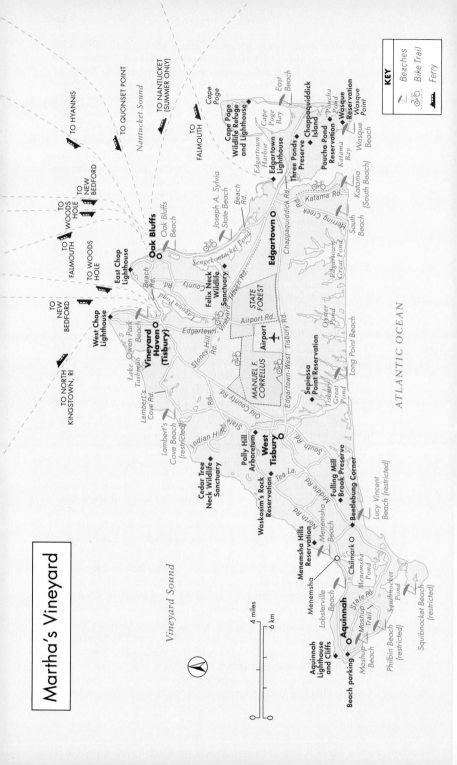

The *Island Queen* makes the 35-minute trip from Falmouth Harbor to Oak Bluffs from late May through early October. Credit cards are not accepted for payment ($20 round-trip). The Vineyard Fast Ferry offers high-speed passenger service to Martha's Vineyard from North Kingstown, Rhode Island—a half-hour south of Providence and a half-hour northwest of Newport. The ride takes 90 minutes, making this a great option for those flying in to T. F. Green Airport, just south of Providence. Service is from late May through early October and costs $49 one way or $74 round-trip.

Hy-Line offers both high-speed and conventional ferry service to Martha's Vineyard from Hyannis. The regular ferries offer a 95-minute run ($22.50) from Hyannis to Oak Bluffs early May to late October. The 55-minute high-speed ferry ($36) runs from late May through late November. Call to reserve a parking space in high season.

Seastreak makes the hour-long trip by high-speed catamaran ($35) from New Bedford to Oak Bluffs and Vineyard Haven from May to the end of October several times daily.

4

ESSENTIALS

Transportation Contacts **Martha's Vineyard Transit Authority** (*VTA*). ☎ *508/693–9940* 🌐 *www.vineyardtransit.com.*

WHERE TO EAT AND STAY

$$$ AMERICAN 🍴 **Black Dog Tavern.** This island landmark—more popular with tourists than locals—lies just steps from the ferry terminal in Vineyard Haven. In July and August the wait for breakfast (with an expansive omelet assortment) can be as much as an hour. Why? Partly because the dining room—roaring fireplace, dark-wood walls, maritime memorabilia, and a grand view of the water—makes everyone feel so at home. The menu is heavy on local fish, chowders, and chops. [$] *Average main: $25* ✉ *20 Beach St. Ext.* ☎ *508/693–9223* 🌐 *www.theblackdog.com* ✍ *Reservations not accepted* 🕒 *October–May, no dinner Sun.–Wed.*

$$$$ B&B/INN 🏨 **Crocker House Inn.** This casual 1890 farmhouse-style inn is tucked into a quiet lane off Main Street, minutes from the ferries and Owen Park Beach. **Pros:** great owners; short walk from town; easygoing vibe. **Cons:** not for those with small children; books up quickly in summer. [$] *Rooms from: $295* ✉ *12 Crocker Ave.* ☎ *508/693–1151, 800/772–0206* 🌐 *www.crockerhouseinn.com* 🛏 *8 rooms* 🍽 *Breakfast.*

$$$ B&B/INN FAMILY 🏨 **Hanover House.** On a half-acre of landscaped lawn within walking distance of the ferry, this children-friendly inn consists of a classic, home-style B&B, a country inn, and a carriage house. **Pros:** good value; 10-minute walk to shops and dining. **Cons:** on busy road; no water or beach views from most units. [$] *Rooms from: $205* ✉ *28 Edgartown Rd.* ☎ *508/693–1066, 800/696–8633* 🌐 *www.hanoverhouseinn.com* 🛏 *13 rooms, 2 suites* 🍽 *Breakfast.*

SPORTS AND THE OUTDOORS

BEACHES

FAMILY **Lake Tashmoo Town Beach.** Swimmers have access to the warm, relatively shallow, brackish Lake Tashmoo from this beach—or cooler, gentler Vineyard Sound. It's a favorite spot for surf casters. **Amenities:** lifeguards; parking (fee); toilets. **Best for:** sunset; swimming. ✉ *End of Herring Creek Rd.*

FAMILY   **Owen Park Beach.** This small, sandy harbor beach is just steps away from the ferry terminal in Vineyard Haven, making it a great spot to catch some last rays before heading home. **Amenities:** lifeguards; toilets. **Best for:** swimming. ⊠ *Off Main St.*

Tisbury Town Beach. This public beach is next to the Vineyard Haven Yacht Club; it is only accessed on foot or by bike: no parking here. But it's a nice place for a picnic. **Amenities:** none. **Best for:** swimming. ⊠ *End of Owen Little Way, off Main St.*

SHOPPING

Fodor'sChoice   **Rainy Day.** As the name suggests, Rainy Day carries gifts and amuse-
★   ments that are perfect for one of the island's gloomy afternoons when you just need a warm, dry diversion. You'll find toys, crafts, cards, soaps, home accessories, gifts, and more. ⊠ *66 Main St.* ☎ *508/693–1830* ⊕ *www.rainydaymv.com.*

OAK BLUFFS

3½ miles east of Vineyard Haven.

Circuit Avenue is the bustling center of the Oak Bluffs action, with most of the town's shops, bars, and restaurants. Colorful gingerbread-trimmed guesthouses and food and souvenir joints enliven Oak Bluffs Harbor, once the setting for several grand hotels (the 1879 Wesley Hotel on Lake Avenue is the last remaining one). This small town is more high-spirited than haute, more fun than refined.

EXPLORING

East Chop Lighthouse. This lighthouse was built out of cast iron in 1876 to replace an 1828 tower (used as part of a semaphore system of visual signaling) that burned down. The 40-foot structure stands high atop a 79-foot bluff with spectacular views of Nantucket Sound. ⊠ *E. Chop Dr.* ☎ *508/627–4441* ⊕ *www.mvmuseum.org* 🎫 *$5* ⊗ *Mid-June–mid-Sept., Sun. 1½ hrs before sunset–½ hr after sunset.*

FAMILY   **Flying Horses Carousel.** A National Historic Landmark, this is the nation's oldest continuously operating merry-go-round. Handcrafted in 1876 (the horses have real horsehair and glass eyes), the ride gives children a taste of entertainment from an era before smartphones. ⊠ *15 Oak Bluffs Ave.* ☎ *508/693–9481* ⊕ *www.mvpreservation.org* 🎫 *$2* ⊗ *Easter–late May, weekends 10–5; late May–early Sept., daily 10–10; early Sept.–mid-Oct., weekdays 11–4:30, weekends 10–5.*

WHERE TO EAT AND STAY

$$ ✕ **Sharky's Cantina.** You may wait awhile to get a table at Sharky's
MEXICAN   Cantina, but once you're in, savor spicy tortilla soup, lobster quesadillas, chicken mole, and gaucho-style skirt steak. There's an extensive margarita list (they're strong here), and for dessert try apple-pie empanadas drizzled with caramel sauce. Limited items from the menu are served until around midnight during the summer season. There's a second location in Edgartown. $ *Average main: $16* ⊠ *31 Circuit Ave.* ☎ *508/693–7501* ⊕ *www.sharkyscantina.com* 🍴 *Reservations not accepted.*

Sacred to the Wampanoag Tribe, the red-hued Aquinnah Cliffs are a popular attraction on Martha's Vineyard.

$$$$
AMERICAN
Fodor's Choice
★

✕ **Sweet Life Café.** Housed in a charming Victorian house, this island favorite's warm hues, low lighting, and handsome antique furniture will make you feel like you've entered someone's home. The cooking is more sophisticated than home-style, however. Dishes are prepared in inventive ways (and change often with the seasons): sautéed halibut is served with sweet-pea risotto, pine nuts, and a marjoram beurre blanc, while the white gazpacho is filled with steamed clams, toasted almonds, sliced red grapes, and paprika oil. The desserts are superb; try the warm chocolate fondant with toasted-almond ice cream. There's outdoor dining by candlelight in a shrub-enclosed garden. $ *Average main: $37* ✉ *63 Upper Circuit Ave.* ☎ *508/696–0200* ⊕ *www.sweetlifemv.com* ⌨ *Reservations essential* ⊘ *Closed Jan.–Mar. No lunch.*

$$$$
B&B/INN

▦ **Pequot Hotel.** In this casual cedar-shingle inn on a tree-lined street, the first floor has a wide porch with rocking chairs—perfect for enjoying coffee or tea with the cookies that are set out in the afternoon. **Pros:** steps from shops and dining; reasonable rates; charmingly offbeat. **Cons:** some rooms are small. $ *Rooms from: $225* ✉ *19 Pequot Ave.* ☎ *508/693–5087, 800/947–8704* ⊕ *www.pequothotel.com* ⤳ *31 rooms, 1 apartment* ⊘ *Closed mid-Oct.–Apr.* ❏ *Breakfast.*

NIGHTLIFE

Offshore Ale. The island's only family brewpub, Offshore Ale, hosts live Latin, folk, and blues year-round and serves its own beer and ales and a terrific pub menu. Cozy up to the fireplace with a pint on cool nights. ✉ *Kennebec Ave.* ☎ *508/693–2626* ⊕ *www.offshoreale.com.*

SPORTS AND THE OUTDOORS

BEACHES

FAMILY **Joseph A. Sylvia State Beach.** This 2-mile-long sandy beach has a view of Cape Cod across Nantucket Sound. Occasional food vendors and calm, warm waters make it a popular spot for families. Arrive early or late in high summer: the parking spots fill up quickly. It's best to bike, walk, or take the shuttle here. **Amenities:** parking (no fee). **Best for:** swimming. ⊠ *Off Beach Rd., between Oak Bluffs and Edgartown.*

FISHING

Dick's Bait & Tackle. You can buy accessories and bait, and check out a current copy of the fishing regulations here. ⊠ *108 New York Ave.* ☏ *508/693–7669.*

GOLF

Farm Neck Golf Club. A semiprivate club on marsh-rimmed Sengekontacket Pond, Farm Neck Golf Club has a driving range and 18 holes in a championship layout. ⊠ *1 Farm Neck Way, off County Rd.* ☏ *508/693–3057* ⊕ *www.farmneck.net* ⛳ *Greens fee: $160 ⅃. 18 holes, 6,807 yds, par 72.*

EDGARTOWN

6 miles southeast of Oak Bluffs.

Once a well-to-do whaling center, Edgartown remains the Vineyard's toniest town and has preserved parts of its elegant past. Sea captains' houses from the 18th and 19th centuries, with well-manicured gardens and lawns, line the streets.

EXPLORING

Chappaquiddick Island. A sparsely populated area with many nature preserves, Chappaquiddick Island, 1 mile southeast of Edgartown, makes for a pleasant day trip or bike ride on a sunny day. The "island" is actually connected to the Vineyard by a long sand spit that begins in South Beach in Katama. It's a spectacular 2¾-mile walk, or you can take the ferry, which departs about every five minutes. On the island's Mytoi preserve, a boardwalk runs through part of the grounds, where you're apt to see box turtles and hear the sounds of songbirds. Elsewhere you can fish, sunbathe, or even dip into the surf—use caution, as the currents are strong. ⊠ *Chappaquiddick Rd.*

FAMILY **Felix Neck Wildlife Sanctuary.** The 350-acre Massachusetts Audubon Society preserve, 3 miles outside Edgartown toward Oak Bluffs and Vineyard Haven, has 4 miles of hiking trails traversing marshland, fields, woods, seashore, and waterfowl and reptile ponds. Naturalist-led events include sunset hikes, stargazing, snake or bird walks, and canoeing. ⊠ *100 Felix Neck Rd., off Edgartown–Vineyard Haven Rd.* ☏ *508/627–4850* ⊕ *www.massaudubon.org* ⛳ *$4* ☉ *June–Aug., Mon.– Sat. 9–4, Sun. 10–3; Sept.–May, weekdays 9–4, Sat. 10–3, Sun. noon–3. Trails daily sunrise–dusk.*

Fodor's Choice **Mytoi.** The Trustees of Reservations' 14-acre preserve is a serene, beau-
★ tifully tended, Japanese-inspired garden with a creek-fed pool spanned by a bridge and rimmed with Japanese maples, azaleas, bamboo, and irises. A boardwalk runs through part of the grounds, where you're

apt to see box turtles and hear the sounds of songbirds. There are few more-enchanting spots on the island. Restrooms are available. ✉ *56 Dike Bridge Rd., 2 miles from the intersection with Chappaquiddick Rd., Chappaquiddick Island* ☎ *508/627–7689* 🌐 *www.thetrustees.org* 🎟 *Free* 🕒 *Daily sunrise–sunset.*

QUICK BITES

Espresso Love. When you need a pick-me-up, pop into Espresso Love for a cappuccino and a homemade raspberry scone or blueberry muffin. If you prefer something cold, the staff also makes fruit smoothies. Light lunch fare is served: bagel sandwiches, soups, and delicious pastries and cookies—all homemade, of course. ✉ ***17 Church St.*** ☎ ***508/627–9211.***

4

WHERE TO EAT AND STAY

$$$$ FRENCH

🍴 **Alchemy Bistro and Bar.** According to the menu, the definition of *alchemy* is "a magic power having as its asserted aim the discovery of a panacea and the preparation of the elixir of longevity"—lofty goals for a French-style bistro. This high-class version has elegant gray wainscoting, classic paper-covered white tablecloths, old wooden floors, and an opening cut into the ceiling to reveal the second-floor tables. The only things missing are the patina of age and experience—and French working folks' prices—but you can expect quality and imagination. The alcohol list, long and complete, includes cognacs, grappas, and beers. On balmy evenings the half-dozen outdoor tables on the candlelit brick patio are highly coveted. [$] *Average main: $36* ✉ *71 Main St.* ☎ *508/627–9999* ✍ *Reservations essential* 🕒 *No lunch.*

$$$$ AMERICAN Fodor's Choice ★

🍴 **Detente.** A dark, intimate wine bar and restaurant with hardwood floors and rich banquette seating, Detente serves more than a dozen wines by the glass as well as numerous half bottles. Even if you're not much of an oenophile, it's worth a trip just for the innovative food, much of it from local farms and seafood purveyors. Start with a foie gras or tuna tartare, followed by such choice entrées as wild boar, local scallops, or grass-fed beef. [$] *Average main: $35* ✉ *Nevin Sq., off Winter St. between N. Summer and N. Water sts.* ☎ *508/627–8810* 🌐 *www.detentemv.com* ✍ *Reservations essential* 🕒 *Closed Tues. Closed Nov.–late Apr. No lunch.*

$$$$ SEAFOOD FAMILY Fodor's Choice ★

🍴 **Lure Grill.** The airy restaurant at Winnetu Oceanside Resort draws plenty of discerning diners to sample some of the island's most exquisite and creatively prepared seafood. It's the only dining room with a south facing water view, and it's a stunning one at that. You won't find a better lobster dish on the island than Lure's tender butter-poached version topped with roasted corn and fava beans and served alongside buttery corn bread. Locally caught fluke with littleneck clams, leeks, smoked bacon, and a rich chowder broth is another star. If you've got children in tow, you'll appreciate the back dining area, complete with separate play area (you can actually have dinner with the little ones along—without the angry glares from your neighbors). There is a free water taxi from Edgartown to the restaurant; call ahead. [$] *Average main: $34* ✉ *Winnetu Oceanside Resort, Katama Rd.* ☎ *508/627–3663* 🌐 *www.winnetu.com* 🕒 *No lunch.*

$ ✕ **Morning Glory Farm.** This farm store is full of incredible goodies, most
AMERICAN   made or grown on the premises, including fresh farm greens in the sal-
Fodor'sChoice   ads and vegetables in the soups, and homemade pies, breads, quiches,
★   cookies, and cakes. A picnic table and grass to sit on while you eat
make this an ideal place for a simple country lunch. $ *Average main:
$6 ⊠ W. Tisbury Rd.* ☎ *508/627–9003* ⊕ *www.morninggloryfarm.com*
☼ *Closed late Dec.–early May.*

$$$$ 🍴 **Charlotte Inn.** From the moment you walk up to the dark-wood
B&B/INN   Scottish barrister's desk to check in at this regal 1864 inn, you'll be
surrounded by the trappings and customs of a bygone era—beautiful
antique furnishings, objets d'art, and paintings fill the property. **Pros:**
over-the-top lavish; quiet yet convenient location; beautifully landscaped. **Cons:** can feel overly formal; intimidating if you don't adore
museum-quality antiques; not for those with children. $ *Rooms from:
$550 ⊠27 S. Summer St.* ☎ *508/627–4751, 800/735–2478* ⊕ *www.
charlotteinn.net* ⌧ *23 rooms, 2 suites* ⎟⊙⎟ *No meals.*

$$$$ 🍴 **HobKnob.** This 19th-century Gothic Revival boutique hotel blends
B&B/INN   the amenities and service of a luxury property with the ambience and
Fodor'sChoice   charm of a small B&B. **Pros:** spacious rooms; on-site spa; removed
★   from crowds. **Cons:** steep rates; not overlooking harbor; not for those
with small children. $ *Rooms from: $465 ⊠ 128 Main St.* ☎ *508/627–
9510, 800/696–2723* ⊕ *www.hobknob.com* ⌧ *16 rooms, 1 suite*
⎟⊙⎟ *Breakfast.*

SHOPPING

Edgartown Books. This long-time island favorite carries a large selection of island-related titles and periodicals, and the staff will be
happy to make a summer reading recommendation. ⊠ *44 Main St.*
☎ *508/627–8463.*

Old Sculpin Gallery. The Martha's Vineyard Art Association has its headquarters at this gallery, which exhibits works by local juried artists.
On summer Sunday evenings it hosts opening receptions beginning at
5 pm. ⊠ *58 Dock St.* ☎ *508/627–4881* ⊕ *www.oldsculpingallery.org*
☼ *June–mid-Oct., daily 9–9.*

WEST TISBURY

8 miles west of Edgartown, 6½ miles south of Vineyard Haven.

West Tisbury retains its rural appeal and maintains its agricultural
tradition at several active horse and produce farms. The town center
looks very much like a small New England village, complete with a
white-steepled church.

EXPLORING

Sepiessa Point Reservation. A paradise for bird-watchers, Sepiessa Point
Reservation consists of 164 acres on splendid Tisbury Great Pond.
There are expansive pond and ocean views, walking trails around
coves and saltwater marshes, horse trails, swimming areas, and a
boat launch. ⊠ *Tiah's Cove Rd.* ☎ *508/627–7141* ⧉ *Free* ☼ *Daily
sunrise–sunset.*

SHOPPING

Alley's General Store. Step back in time with a visit to Alley's General Store, a local landmark since 1858. Alley's sells a truly general variety of goods: everything from hammers to housewares and dill pickles to sweet muffins as well as great things you find only in a country store. There's even a post office inside. ✉ *299 State Rd.* ☎ *508/693–0088.*

AQUINNAH

4

6½ miles west of Menemsha, 10 miles southwest of West Tisbury, 17 miles southwest of Vineyard Haven.

Aquinnah, called Gay Head until the town voted to change its name in 1997, is an official Native American township. The Wampanoag tribe is the guardian of the 420 acres that constitute the Aquinnah Native American Reservation. Aquinnah (pronounced a-*kwih*-nah) is Wampanoag for "land under the hill." You can get a good view of Menemsha and Nashaquitsa ponds, the woods, and the ocean beyond from Quitsa Pond Lookout on State Road. The town is best known for the red-hued Aquinnah Cliffs.

EXPLORING

Fodor's Choice ★ **Aquinnah Cliffs.** A National Historic Landmark, the spectacular Aquinnah Cliffs are part of the Wampanoag Reservation land. These dramatically striated walls of red clay are the island's major attraction, as evidenced by the tour bus–filled parking lot. Native American crafts and food shops line the short approach to the overlook, from which you can see the Elizabeth Islands to the northeast across Vineyard Sound and Noman's Land Island—a wildlife preserve—3 miles off the Vineyard's southern coast. ✉ *State Rd.*

Gay Head Lighthouse. This brick lighthouse (also called Aquinnah Lighthouse) is stationed precariously atop the rapidly eroding cliffs. Bad weather may affect its opening hours. Parking can be limited here. ✉ *9 Aquinnah Circle* ☎ *508/627–4441* 🌐 *www.mvmuseum.org* 🎟 *$5* 🕒 *Mid-May–mid-Oct., Mon.–Sat. 10–5, Sun. noon–5; Mid-Oct.–mid-May, Mon.–Sat. 10–5.*

WHERE TO EAT

$$ SEAFOOD 🍴 **The Bite.** Fried everything—clams, fish-and-chips, you name it—is on the menu at this simple, roadside shack, where two outdoor picnic tables are the only seating choices and small, medium, and large are the three portion sizes: all of them are perfect if you're craving that classic seaside fried lunch. But don't come on a rainy day, unless you want to get wet—the lines here can be long. [$] *Average main: $14* ✉ *29 Basin Rd., Menemsha* ☎ *509/645–9239* 🌐 *www.thebitemenemsha.com* 💳 *No credit cards* 🕒 *Closed Oct.–late May.*

NANTUCKET

At the height of its prosperity in the early 19th century, the little island of Nantucket was the foremost whaling port in the world. Its harbor bustled with whaling ships and merchant vessels; chandleries, cooperages, and other shops crowded the wharves. Burly ship hands loaded barrels of whale oil onto wagons, which they wheeled along cobblestone streets to refineries and candle factories. Sea breezes carried the smoke and smells of booming industry through town as its inhabitants eagerly took care of business. Shipowners and sea captains built elegant mansions, which today remain remarkably unchanged, thanks to a very strict building code initiated in the 1950s. The entire town of Nantucket is now an official National Historic District encompassing more than 800 pre-1850 structures within 1 square mile.

Day-trippers usually take in the architecture and historical sites, dine at one of the many delightful restaurants, and browse in the pricey boutiques, most of which stay open from mid-April through December. Signature items include Nantucket lightship baskets, originally crafted by sailors whiling away a long watch; artisans who continue the tradition now command prices of $700 and up, and the antiques are exponentially more expensive.

NANTUCKET TOWN

30 miles southeast of Hyannis, 107 miles southeast of Boston.

Nantucket Town has one of the country's finest historic districts, with beautiful 18th- and 19th-century architecture and a museum of whaling history.

GETTING HERE AND AROUND

Arriving by ferry puts you in the center of town. There is little need for a car here to explore; ample public transportation and smoothly paved bike paths can take you to the further reaches with ease. The Nantucket Regional Transit Authority (NRTA) runs shuttle buses from in town to most areas of the island. Service is generally available from late May to mid-October.

AIR TRAVEL   Year-round flight service to Nantucket from Boston and Hyannis is provided by Cape Air, Island Airlines, and Nantucket Airlines. US Airways Express offers seasonal service to the island from Washington, D.C., Philadelphia, and New York's LaGuardia; from Newark Airport in New Jersey, United provides a seasonal route to the island.

FERRY TRAVEL   Hy-Line's high-end, high-speed Grey Lady ferries run between Hyannis and Nantucket year-round in an hour ($39). Hy-Line's slower ferry makes the roughly two-hour trip from Hyannis between early May and late October. The MV *Great Point* offers a first-class section ($28) with a private lounge and a bar or a standard fare ($22.50).

The Steamship Authority runs car-and-passenger ferries from Hyannis year-round, a 2¼-hour trip ($17.50 for passenger fare; $140 to $200 for a car). There's also high-speed passenger ferry service, which takes only an hour, from late March through late December ($35).

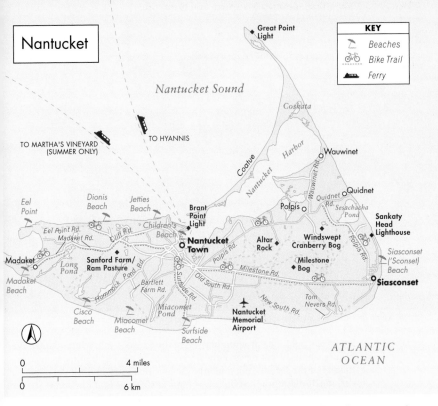

Nantucket

KEY
- Beaches
- Bike Trail
- Ferry

Nantucket Sound

Great Point Light

Coskata

TO MARTHA'S VINEYARD (SUMMER ONLY)

TO HYANNIS

Harbor

Wauwinet

Coatue

Eel Point

Dionis Beach

Jetties Beach

Brant Point Light

Children's Beach

Eel Point Rd.

Madaket Rd.

Cliff Rd.

Madaket

Sanford Farm/ Ram Pasture

Long Pond

Hummock Pond Rd.

Bartlett Farm Rd.

Madaket Beach

Cisco Beach

Miacomet Beach

Miacomet Pond

Surfside Beach

Nantucket Town

Surfside Rd.

Old South Rd.

Polpis Rd.

Altar Rock

Milestone Rd.

Windswept Cranberry Bog

Milestone Bog

Polpis

Quidnet

Quidnet Rd.

Sesachacha Pond

Sankaty Head Lighthouse

Siasconset ('Sconset) Beach

Siasconset

Wauwinet Rd.

Polpis Rd.

New South Rd.

Tom Nevers Rd.

Nantucket Memorial Airport

ATLANTIC OCEAN

0 — 4 miles
0 — 6 km

In season, the passenger-only (some bikes allowed) ferry from Harwich Port to Nantucket is a less hectic alternative to the Hyannis crowd. The Freedom Cruise Line runs express high-speed 75-minute ferries between late May and early October ($39).

ESSENTIALS

Transportation Contacts Nantucket Regional Transit Authority ✉ *3 E. Chestnut St.* ☎ *508/228–7025* ⊕ *www.nrtawave.com.*

Visitor Information Nantucket Chamber of Commerce ✉ *Zero Main St., Nantucket* ☎ *508/228–1700* ⊕ *www.nantucketchamber.org.* **Nantucket Visitor Services and Information Bureau** ✉ *25 Federal St., Nantucket* ☎ *508/228–0925* ⊕ *www.nantucket-ma.gov.*

EXPLORING

African Meeting House. When the island abolished slavery in 1773, Nantucket became a destination for free blacks and escaping slaves. The African Meeting House was built in the 1820s as a schoolhouse, and it functioned as such until 1846, when the island's schools were integrated. A complete restoration has returned the site to its authentic 19th-century appearance. ✉ *29 York St.* ☎ *508/228–9833* ⊕ *www.afroammuseum.org* 🎟 *$5* ☉ *June–Oct., weekdays 11–3, Sat. 11–1, Sun. 1–3.*

Each beach on Nantucket has a unique approach—sometimes getting there is half the fun.

Brant Point Light. The promontory where this 26-foot-tall, white-painted beauty stands offers views of the harbor and town. The point was once the site of the second-oldest lighthouse in the country (1746); the present, much-photographed light was built in 1901. ⊠ *End of Easton St., across the footbridge.*

First Congregational Church. The tower of this church provides the best view of Nantucket—for those willing to climb its 94 steps. Rising 120 feet, the tower is capped by a weather vane depicting a whale catch. Peek in at the church's 1852 trompe l'oeil ceiling. ⊠ *62 Centre St.* ☎ *508/228–0950* ⊕ *www.nantucketfcc.org* ⌸ *Tower tour $5* ⊙ *Mid-June–mid-Oct., Mon.–Sat. 10–4; services Sun. 10 am.*

Nantucket Historical Association (*NHA*). This association maintains an assortment of venerable properties in town. A $20 pass gets you into all the association's sites, including the glorious Whaling Museum. A $6 pass excludes the Whaling Museum but includes the Oldest House, Old Mill, Old Gaol, Greater Light, and the Fire Hose Cart House. Reserve ahead for two very popular walking tours that depart daily from late May to early November: a 60-minute downtown tour and an 80-minute historic house tour. Both cost $10. ☎ *508/228–1894* ⊕ *www.nha.org.*

FAMILY
Fodor's Choice
★

Whaling Museum. With exhibits that include a fully rigged whaleboat and a skeleton of a 46-foot sperm whale, this must-see museum—a complex that includes a restored 1846 spermaceti candle factory—offers a crash course in the island's colorful history. Items on display include harpoons and other whale-hunting implements; portraits of whaling captains and their wives (a few of whom went whaling as well); the South Seas curiosities they brought home; a large collection of sailors' crafts; a full-size tryworks once used to process whale oil; and the original 16-foot-high 1850 lens from Sankaty Head Lighthouse. The Children's Discovery Room provides interactive-learning opportunities. Be sure to climb—or take the elevator—up to the observation deck for a view of the harbor. ✉ *13–15 Broad St.* ☎ *508/228–1894* 🌐 *www.nha.org* 🎫 *$20 (all access pass includes other historic sites)* 🕓 *Mid-Feb.–early Apr., weekends 11–3; mid-Apr.–late May, daily 11–4; late May–Oct., daily 10–5; Nov., weekends 11–4.*

WHERE TO EAT AND STAY

$$$$ MODERN AMERICAN Fodor's Choice ★

🍴 **American Seasons.** Picture a farmhouse gone sexy: That's the mood—wholesome yet seductive—at this candlelit hideaway decorated with Rufus Porter–style murals. Chef Michael LaScola works with a half-dozen island farms to fashion locavore repasts of surpassing artistry. Highlights of his be-here-now menu include seared day-boat scallops with fried green tomatoes and lemon confit, and oven-roasted guinea hen with sweet corn velouté and foie gras jus. The patio bar draws aficionados eager to sample the rich array, piecemeal. [$] *Average main: $35* ✉ *80 Centre St.* ☎ *508/228–7111* 🌐 *www.americanseasons.com* ✍ *Reservations essential* 🕓 *Closed mid-Dec.–mid-Apr. No lunch.*

$$ AMERICAN FAMILY

🍴 **Fog Island Café.** Cherished year-round for its exceptional breakfasts (try the pesto scrambled eggs), Fog Island is just as fine a spot for lunch. The storefront space is cheerily decked out in a fresh country style, and chef-owners Mark and Anne Dawson—both Culinary Institute of America grads—seem determined to provide the best possible service to visitors and local residents alike. [$] *Average main: $14* ✉ *7 S. Water St.* ☎ *508/228–1818* 🌐 *fogisland.com* 🕓 *No dinner. No lunch Sun.*

$$$ ECLECTIC Fodor's Choice ★

🍴 **Lola 41 degrees.** By extending Nantucket's longitude and latitude, you'll not only hit on this hit restaurant's name but touch down on some of the territory that its menu covers. Sushi and sake are specialties, but so are globe-trotting treats like a chili-fired Spanish shrimp salad, grilled wild salmon with tabbouleh and Greek yogurt sauce, or Maine lobster with morel spaghettini and lemon-chive mascarpone. Everywhere this restaurant ventures is good—especially when it ends up heading south for a killer tres leches cake. The place started out as (and remains) a super-popular watering hole for the chic set. [$] *Average main: $26* ✉ *15 S. Beach St.* ☎ *508/325–4001* 🌐 *www.lola41.com* 🕓 *No lunch mid-Apr.–mid-Oct.*

$$$$ MODERN AMERICAN Fodor's Choice ★

🍴 **Straight Wharf.** This loftlike restaurant with a harborside deck has enjoyed legendary status since the mid-1970s, when chef Marion Morash used to get a helping hand from culinary buddy Julia Child. The young couple now in command—Gabriel Frasca and Amanda Lydon—were fast-rising stars on the Boston restaurant scene, but their approach here is the antithesis of flashy; if anything, they have lent this venerable institution a more barefoot air, appropriate to the place and season. Hurricane lamps lend a soft glow to well-spaced tables lined with butcher paper, and dish towels serve as napkins. Intense champions of local crops and catches, the chefs concoct stellar dishes like oysters with Meyer lemon granita, and line-caught halibut with garlic-chive spaetzle. [$] *Average main: $32* ✉ *6 Harbor Sq.* ☎ *508/228–4499* 🌐 *www.straightwharfrestaurant.com* ✍ *Reservations essential* 🕓 *Closed mid-Oct.–mid-May.*

When farmers flood cranberry fields during harvest season, the ripe crimson fruit floats to the surface.

$$$$
RESORT
FAMILY
Fodor's Choice
★

The Nantucket Hotel & Resort. Although this modern, nautically themed beauty opened recently (in 2012), the structure dates back to 1891 and the golden age of grand seaside hotels. **Pros:** Immaculate and large rooms, many with kitchens; ideal for families; full-service restaurant. **Cons:** can be noisy in summer. $ *Rooms from: $475* ⊠ *77 Easton St.* ☎ *508/228–4747, 866/807–6011* ⊕ *www.thenantuckethotel.com* ⇗ *7 rooms, 27 suites, 2 cottages* ¦○¦ *Breakfast.*

$$$$
B&B/INN
Fodor's Choice
★

Union Street Inn. Ken Withrow worked in the hotel business, Deborah Withrow in high-end retail display, and guests get the best of both worlds in this 1770 house, a stone's throw from the bustle of Main Street, that was respectfully yet lavishly restored in 2013. **Pros:** pampering by pros; pervasive good taste. **Cons:** bustle of town; some small rooms; not for those with children. $ *Rooms from: $529* ⊠ *7 Union St.* ☎ *888/517–0707* ⊕ *www.unioninn.com* ⇗ *11 rooms, 1 suite* ⊗ *Closed Nov.–late Apr., except for Christmas stroll* ¦○¦ *Breakfast.*

NIGHTLIFE AND THE ARTS

Chicken Box (*The Box*). Live music—including some big-name bands—plays six nights a week in season, and weekends throughout the year. ⊠ *14 Dave St.* ☎ *508/228–9717* ⊕ *www.thechickenbox.com.*

Muse. This is a year-round venue hosting live bands, including the occasional big-name act. The crowd—the barnlike space can accommodate nearly 400—can get pretty wild. ⊠ *44 Surfside Rd.* ☎ *508/228–6873.*

SPORTS AND THE OUTDOORS

BEACHES

FAMILY **Jetties Beach.** A short bike- or shuttle-bus ride from town, Jetties Beach is popular with families because of its calm surf. It's also a good place to try out kayaks and sailboards. On shore it's a lively scene, with a playground and volleyball nets on the beach and adjacent public tennis courts. There is a boardwalk to the beach (special wheelchairs are available). You'll have a good view of passing ferries—and an even better one if you clamber out on the jetty itself. (Careful, it's slippery.) **Amenities:** food and drink; lifeguards; parking; showers; toilets; water sports. **Best for:** swimming; windsurfing. ⊠ *Bathing Beach Rd., 1½ miles NW of Straight Wharf.*

Fodor's Choice **Surfside Beach.** Surfside Beach, accessible via the Surfside Bike Path (3 ★ miles) or shuttle bus, is the island's most popular surf beach. This wide strand of sand comes fully equipped with conveniences. It draws teens and young adults as well as families and is great for kite flying and, after 5 pm, surf casting. **Amenities:** food and drink; lifeguards; parking; showers; toilets. **Best for:** surfing; swimming; walking. ⊠ *Surfside Rd., South Shore.*

BOATING

Nantucket Community Sailing. Renting sailboats, sailboards, and kayaks at Jetties Beach, NCS also offers youth and adult sailing classes and water-sport clinics for disabled athletes. Its Outrigger Canoe Club— a Polynesian tradition—heads out several evenings a week in season. ⊠ *Jetties Beach, Bathing Beach Rd.* ☎ *508/228–6600* ⊕ *www. nantucketcommunitysailing.org.*

SHOPPING

GALLERIES

Joyce & Seward Johnson Gallery. This gallery is the best place to get an overview of the art scene on the island and pick up a schedule of exhibits and opening receptions. Many members of the Artists' Association of Nantucket also have galleries of their own. ⊠ *19 Washington St.* ☎ *508/228–0294* ⊕ *www.nantucketarts.org.*

Nantucket Looms. Luscious woven-on-the-premises textiles and chunky Susan Lister Locke jewelry are the focus of Nantucket Looms. ⊠ *51 Main St.* ☎ *508/228–1908* ⊕ *www.nantucketlooms.com.*

SIASCONSET

7 miles east of Nantucket Town.

Fodor's Choice First a fishing outpost and then an artist's colony (Broadway actors ★ favored it in the late 19th century), Siasconset—or 'Sconset, in the local vernacular—is a charming cluster of rose-covered cottages linked by driveways of crushed clamshells; at the edges of town the former fishing shacks give way to magnificent sea-view mansions. The small town center consists of a market, post office, café, lunchroom, and a combination liquor store–lending library.

EXPLORING

Altar Rock. A dirt track leads to the island's highest point, Altar Rock, at an elevation of 101 feet, and the view is spectacular. The hill overlooks approximately 4,000 acres of rare coastal heathland laced with paths leading in every direction. ✉ *Altar Rock Rd., 3 miles west of Milestone Rd. Rotary on Polpis Rd.*

WHERE TO EAT AND STAY

$$$$ MODERN AMERICAN

🍴 **Topper's.** The Wauwinet, a lavishly restored 19th-century inn on Nantucket's northeastern shore, is where islanders and visitors alike go to experience utmost luxury, and that includes the food. In the creamy-white dining room, awash with lush linens and glorious flowers, you can choose from a three-course prix fixe or à la carte menu, and more casual fare is on offer out on the deck. Many visitors take advantage of the *Wauwinet Lady* (a complimentary launch docked at the White Elephant, a sister property) to frame the journey with a scenic harbor tour; jitney service is also offered. [$] *Average main: $36* ✉ *The Wauwinet, 120 Wauwinet Rd., Wauwinet* ☎ *508/228–8768* 🌐 *www.wauwinet.com* ✍ *Reservations essential* 🕒 *Closed Nov.–Apr. Brunch Sun. only.*

$$$$ RESORT Fodor's Choice ★

🏨 **The Wauwinet.** This resplendently updated 1850 resort straddles a "haulover" poised between ocean and bay—which means beaches on both sides—and you can head out by complimentary van or launch to partake of utmost pampering (the staff-to-guest ratio exceeds one-on-one). **Pros:** solicitous staff; dual beaches; peaceful setting. **Cons:** not for those with small children; distance from town; overly chichi. [$] *Rooms from: $625* ✉ *120 Wauwinet Rd., Wauwinet* ☎ *508/228–0145* 🌐 *www.wauwinet.com* 🛏 *32 rooms, 4 cottages* 🕒 *Closed Nov.–Apr.* 🍽 *Breakfast.*

SPORTS AND THE OUTDOORS

BIKING

'Sconset Bike Path. This 6.5-mile bike path starts at the rotary east of Nantucket Town and parallels Milestone Road, ending in 'Sconset. It is mostly level, with some gentle hills. Slightly longer (and dippier), the 9-mile Polpis Road Path, veering off to the northeast, is far more scenic and leads to the turnoff to Wauwinet. ✉ *Off Milestone Rd.*

THE BERKSHIRES
AND WESTERN
MASSACHUSETTS

WELCOME TO THE BERKSHIRES AND WESTERN MASSACHUSETTS

TOP REASONS TO GO

★ **The Countryside:**
Rolling hills, dense stands of forest, open pastures, even a few mountains.

★ **Early American History:**
Visit preserved villages, homes, and inns where memories of Colonial history and personalities are kept alive.

★ **Summer Festivals:**
Watch renowned dance companies perform against the Berkshire mountains backdrop at Jacob's Pillow or have the Boston Symphony Orchestra accompany your lawn picnic at Tanglewood in Lenox.

★ **Under-the-Radar Museums:** Western Massachusetts has an eclectic collection of institutions, from the Eric Carle Museum of Picture Book Art to the Basketball Hall of Fame.

★ **College Towns:**
The Pioneer Valley is home to some lovely academic centers: Amherst (University of Massachusetts, Amherst College, and Hampshire College), Northampton (Smith College), and South Hadley (Mount Holyoke College).

1 The Berkshires.
The "hills" you'll see here are actually a continuation of the same range that contains Vermont's Green Mountains. And though it's only a few hours from Boston or New York City, a trip to the Berkshires is a complete escape from all things urban. This is a place of ski resorts and winding forest drives, leaf peeping and gallery browsing. There are extreme sports and extreme spas. If you're looking for a place to recharge your batteries and your soul, you'll be hard-pressed to find a better option in the Northeast—even the Boston Symphony Orchestra comes here for its summer break.

2 Sturbridge and the Pioneer Valley.
Often overshadowed by Boston to the east and the Berkshires to the west, the Pioneer Valley is filled with historic settlements and college towns, natural treasures, and unique museums. Old Sturbridge Village,

a re-created early-19th-century village with restored historic buildings, reenactments, and activities, is the premier attraction here. The main city, Springfield, is home to the Naismith Memorial Basketball Hall of Fame, but most of the area is quite rural—this is where the idyllic New England countryside you've imagined comes to life.

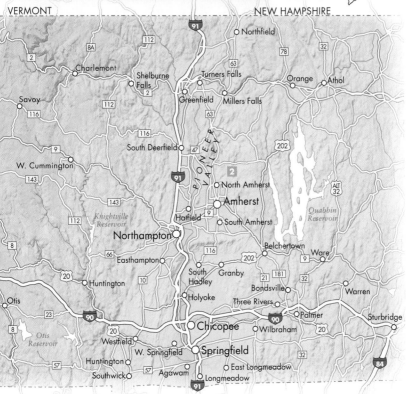

VERMONT   NEW HAMPSHIRE

5

GETTING ORIENTED

Interstate 90, the Massachusetts Turnpike, leads west from Boston to the Berkshires. The main north–south road within the Berkshires is U.S. 7. Highway 2 runs from the northern Berkshires to Greenfield at the head of the Pioneer Valley and continues across Massachusetts into Boston. The scenic section of Highway 2 known as the Mohawk Trail runs from Williamstown to Orange. Interstate 91 runs north–south in the Pioneer Valley in Western Massachusetts.

Updated by
Seth Brown

Rolling terrain defines the landscape of Western Massachusetts. The Pioneer Valley, which runs north to south through the heart of the Bay State, is home to the famed "Five College Consortium," a group of elite institutions including Amherst, Hampshire, Mount Holyoke, UMASS Amherst, and Smith. While they may lack the collegiate density (or bustling metropolis feel) of Boston, areas like Northampton embody the vibrancy that comes from a large population of college students, with various cultural venues and culinary possibilities. In short, it can be a happening sort of place.

While most Bostonians would surely refer to the Pioneer Valley as "Western Massachusetts," the most westerly portion of the state consists of the bucolic Berkshires, a more rural and relaxed region filled with rolling hills and winding mountain roads. Therein sits the "Purple Valley," so named for the encircling mountains—purple hued when seen through an evening haze—as well as for the school colors of the valley's Williams College. Hikers, be they casual trail followers or intrepid mountain climbers, have plenty to see. In autumn, leaf peepers come from all over to drive through the area renowned for its fall foliage, with vibrant oranges, yellows, and reds that exemplify the harvest season in New England.

In addition to its natural advantages, the Berkshires have also become a bastion of arts and culture. A burgeoning arts community has arisen from the ruins of a manufacturing economy, with former mills now serving as artist lofts, and in one case a former electric plant converted into a contemporary art museum. More generally, a number of small museums are sprinkled throughout the region, and myriad craftspeople and artisans live in the Berkshires, many of whom have open studios or display their works in small local galleries.

It would perhaps be presumptuous to proclaim a "renaissance," and yet it cannot be denied that the large concentration of arts and culture in the Berkshires has transformed it to a certain degree. The past few decades have seen not only an influx of artists, but of other revitalizing culture, ranging from boutique shopping to international cuisine, transforming a once-depressed postindustrial area into a hot spot for festivals celebrating everything from ice sculptures to the spoken word.

PLANNING

WHEN TO GO

The dazzling foliage and cool temperatures make fall the best time to visit Western Massachusetts, but the Berkshires and the Pioneer Valley are increasingly a year-round destination. Visit in spring, and witness the burst of color that signals winter's end. Summer is a time of festivals, adventure sports, and outdoor concerts.

Many towns save their best for winter—inns open their doors to carolers and shops serve eggnog. The off-season is the perfect time to try cross-country skiing or spend a night by the fire, tucked under a quilt, catching up on books by Nathaniel Hawthorne or Henry David Thoreau.

GETTING HERE AND AROUND

AIR TRAVEL

Most travelers arrive at Boston's Logan International Airport, the state's major airline hub. From Boston you can reach most parts of the Pioneer Valley in less than two hours by car, and the Berkshires are about three hours' drive from Beantown.

Bradley International Airport in Windsor Locks, Connecticut, 18 miles south of Springfield on Interstate 91, serves the Pioneer Valley and the Berkshires. Other airport alternatives include Manchester Boston Regional Airport in New Hampshire, 50 miles northwest of Boston, and T. F. Green International Airport in Providence, Rhode Island, 59 miles south of Boston.

CAR TRAVEL

Public transportation can be a bit spotty in this region, with buses that don't run on Sunday or during the evening, so you'll almost certainly need a car. But you'll want one anyway so you can take leisurely drives down Routes 2, 7, and 8 to see the fall foliage. Be warned that mountain roads are very winding and not for the fainthearted; if you care less about mountaintop views than you do about settled innards, skip the hairpin turn on Route 2 and approach North Adams from the south instead of the east.

TRAIN TRAVEL

The Northeast Corridor and high-speed Acela services of Amtrak link Boston with the principal cities between it and Washington, D.C. Amtrak's Lake Shore Limited, which stops at Springfield and Pittsfield in the Berkshires, carries passengers from Chicago to Boston. For destinations north and west of Boston, trains depart from Boston's North Station.

Train Information Amtrak ☎ *800/872-7245* ⊕ *www.amtrak.com.*

RESTAURANTS

At country inns in the Southern Berkshires and the Pioneer Valley you can find traditional New England dinners strongly reminiscent of old England: double-cut pork chops, rack of lamb, game, Boston baked beans, Indian pudding, and the dubiously glorified "New England boiled dinner" (slow-boiled meat and vegetables). For those who come to the Berkshires to taste historical tradition, there is plenty of it on the menu.

If you prefer more creative contemporary fare, however, you will not be disappointed. There are various modern cafés and trendy watering holes with inventive menus ranging from fusion cuisine to pizza with inspired toppings.

Perhaps most enticingly, an influx of multiculturalism to the Berkshires has resulted in a number of excellent international food options, especially in the Northern/Central region. In addition to the standard Chinese, Indian, and Thai, visitors can sample Peruvian, Spanish, Columbian, Malaysian, and much more. *Prices in the reviews are the average cost of a main course at dinner or, if dinner is not served, at lunch.*

HOTELS

The signature type of accommodations outside Boston is the country inn; in the Berkshires, where magnificent mansions have been converted into lodgings, the inns reach a very grand scale indeed. Less extravagant and less expensive are bed-and-breakfast establishments, many of them in private homes. Make reservations for inns well in advance during peak periods (summer through winter in the Berkshires). Smoking is banned in all Massachusetts hotels.

Campers can pitch their tents amid acres of pine forest dotted with rivers and lakes or in the shadows of the rolling Berkshire Hills. The camping season in Massachusetts generally runs from Memorial Day to Columbus Day. For more about camping, contact the Massachusetts Department of Conservation and Recreation (☎ *617/626–1250* ⊕ *www. mass.gov/dcr/forparks.htm). Prices in the reviews are the lowest cost of a standard double room in high season.*

VISITOR INFORMATION

The Massachusetts Office of Travel & Tourism's website has plenty of user-friendly information that you can sort by region. For information about fishing, boating, and licenses, call the Massachusetts Department of Fish and Game.

Visitor Information Massachusetts Department of Fish and Game
✉ *251 Causeway St., Suite 400, Boston* ☎ *617/626–1590* ⊕ *www.mass.gov/ dfwele.* **Massachusetts Office of Travel & Tourism** ✉ *10 Park Plaza, Suite 4510, Boston* ☎ *617/973–8500* ⊕ *www.massvacation.com.*

THE BERKSHIRES

Occupying the far western end of the state, the Berkshires are only about 2½ hours by car from Boston and New York City, yet the region lives up to the storybook image of rural New England, with wooded hills, narrow winding roads, and compact historic villages. Summer brings cultural events, including the renowned Tanglewood classical music festival in Lenox. The foliage blazes in fall, skiing is popular in winter, and spring is the time for maple sugaring. The scenic Mohawk Trail runs east to west across the northern section of the Berkshires.

ESSENTIALS

Bus Information Berkshire Regional Transit Authority ☎ *800/499–2782, 413/292–2782* ⊕ *www.berkshirerta.com.*

Visitor Information Berkshires Visitors Bureau ✉ *66 Allen St., Pittsfield* ☎ *413/743–4500, 800/237–5747* ⊕ *www.berkshires.org.*

NORTH ADAMS

130 miles northwest of Boston; 73 miles northwest of Springfield; 20 miles south of Bennington, Vermont.

If you're looking for a Berkshires getaway that combines culture with outdoor fun (and a cool place to stay), put North Adams on your short list. In addition to the Massachusetts Museum of Contemporary Arts (Mass MoCA), North Adams has mills and factory buildings that have been converted into artist studios. The Porches Inn, a row of eye-catching multihued Victorians, has added an additional helping of hip to downtown.

In addition, the 11-mile Ashuwillticook Rail Trail is easily accessible in nearby Adams, as is Mt. Greylock State Reservation, if you explore it on foot via one of the local trailheads.

GETTING HERE AND AROUND

The best way to get to North Adams is either from the south via Pittsfield, or from the west via Williamstown. Either way, once you're in town you can see it all on foot if the weather is good, with almost everything within a few blocks of the town's Main Street—Natural Bridge Park is the exception, but it's still a reasonable walk.

EXPLORING

Down Street Art. This public-arts project includes 31 galleries in downtown North Adams—not surprising, since the city has more contemporary-art spaces than any town in the Berkshires. Catch an "Open Studios" weekend to see the converted artist lofts. ✉ *51 Main St., North Adams, Massachusetts* ☎ *413/663–5253* ⊕ *www.downstreetart.org.*

FAMILY

Fodor's Choice

★

Massachusetts Museum of Contemporary Arts. It's not just the dimensions—13 acres, 27 buildings, more than 250,000 square feet—that are impressive here. The nation's largest center for contemporary visual and performing arts is also one of the finest in the world, drawing equally huge attendances for its exciting gallery exhibits, art shows, concerts, dance, and film presentations. The enormous space in the main gallery allows for massive exhibits that simply wouldn't fit anywhere else, such as Xu Bing's *Phoenix*, two gigantic birds with 90-foot wing spans, or Robert Rauschenberg's monumental *The ¼ Mile or 2 Furlong Piece*. The building, formerly housing the Sprague Electrical Company, is in itself a worthwhile exhibit, and also includes studios, cafés, shops, and the inspiring Kidspace gallery and studio. ⊠ *87 Marshall St.* 🕾 *413/664–4111* ⊕ *www.massmoca.org* 🖅 *$15* ⊗ *July and Aug., daily 10–6; Sept.–June, Wed.–Mon. 11–5.*

Natural Bridge State Park. The city's 48-acre Natural Bridge State Park was named for the 30-foot span that crosses Hudson Brook, and offers numerous appealing views of rocky chasms. The marble arch at the park's center rises in what was a marble quarry from the early 1880s to the mid-1900s. There are picnic sites, hiking trails, and well-maintained restrooms. In winter the park is popular for cross-country skiing. ⊠ *McCauley Rd., Hwy. 8* 🕾 *413/663–6392* ⊕ *www.mass.gov/eea/agencies/dcr/massparks/region-west.*

FAMILY **North Adams Museum of History & Science.** North Adams's best kept secret, this museum has three floors with more than 25 permanent exhibits, including a kid-friendly model of the solar system, a model train, and full-sized reproduction of the Ft. Massachusetts Barracks Room. The building was once part of a railroad yard, and a store sells local historical society publications. ⊠ *Western Gateway Heritage State Park, State St., Bldg. 5A* 🕾 *413/664–4700* ⊕ *www.northadamshistory. org* 🖅 *Free* ⊗ *Nov.–Apr., Sat. 10–4, Sun. 1–4; May–Oct., Thurs.–Sat. 10–4, Sun. 1–4.*

Susan B. Anthony Birthplace Museum. The Susan B. Anthony Birthplace Museum celebrates the extraordinary life and legacy of Susan B. Anthony, who played a pivotal role in winning the right to vote for women. In addition to viewing mementos of the suffrage movement, you can also learn about the abolition and temperance movements. ⊠ *67 East Rd., Adams* 🕾 *413/743–7121* ⊕ *www.susanbanthonybirthplace. com* 🖅 *$6* ⊗ *Late May–mid-Oct., Thurs.–Mon. 10–4; mid-Oct.–late May, Fri. and Sat. 10–4, Sun 11:30–4.*

FAMILY **Western Gateway Heritage State Park.** This park occupies the old Boston & Maine Railroad yard, where the visitor center houses exhibits that trace the impact of train travel on the region. A 30-minute documentary provides a look at the intense labor that went into the construction of the nearby Hoosac Tunnel, and a pedestrian bridge a block from the park offers a good view of tracks going into tunnel. ⊠ *115 State St.* 🕾 *413/663–6312* ⊕ *www.mass.gov/eea/agencies/dcr/massparks/region-west* 🖅 *Free* ⊗ *Visitor center daily 10–5.*

QUICK
BITES

Jack's Hot Dog Stand. A North Adams institution since 1917, Jack's Hot Dog Stand is where locals go for a few hot wieners and hamburgers, with optional cheese and chili. This hole-in-the-wall also serves sweet sausages, onion rings, and fries. It's cash only, closes at 7 pm, and during lunch hour you'll be lucky to find a free stool at the counter. ⊠ *12 Eagle St.* 🕾 *413/664–9006* ⊕ *www.jackshotdogstand.com* ⊗ *Closed Sun.*

Winslow Homer's *West Point, Prout's Neck* is just one of the notable paintings at Williamstown's Clark Art Institute.

WHERE TO EAT

$$ ✕ **España.** In this tasteful eatery, chef Galo Lopez offers an ever-changing array of appealing tapas with a side order of good service. By all means try the roast-vegetable soup, crab cakes, or cheese plate, but the real must-have dish is the *caracoles*, a plate of tender snails and caramelized onions in a rich tomato-based sauce. The paella requires a half-hour wait, but the delicious seafood and rice dish is definitely worth it. For dessert there's the almond flour cake with dulce de leche ice cream. Ⓢ *Average main: $19* ✉ *896 State Rd.* ☎ *413/346–4099* ◷ *Closed Mon. No lunch.*

TAPAS

Fodor's Choice
★

$$$ ✕ **Gramercy Bistro.** Within the Massachusetts Museum of Contemporary Arts complex, the mood and style of this upscale casual eatery makes it easy to forget you are inside a former factory building. The eclectic menu, ranging from chicken-liver mousse to seafood paella, has helped draw a loyal following. Chef-owner Alexander Smith relies on organic meats and locally grown produce when possible, adding serious zip with sauces made from wasabi and fire-roasted poblano peppers. Come by on Sunday for the memorable brunch. Ⓢ *Average main: $24* ✉ *87 Marshall St.* ☎ *413/663–5300* ⊕ *www.gramercybistro.com* ◷ *Closed Tues. No lunch Mon.*

FRENCH FUSION

$$ ✕ **Sushi House.** Right on the main drag, this pan-Asian restaurant offers some of the best dishes in Chinese, Thai, Korean, and Japanese cooking. Start with seaweed salad, then consider a classic noodle dish like pad thai (stir-fried rice noodles) or *pad see ew* (wide, flat noodles with meat and Chinese broccoli). Hot clay pots reveal wonderful dishes like sweet *massaman* curry (a peanut and potato concoction) or spicy *bibim bap* (a bowl of rice and vegetables topped with meat, a fried egg, and hot chili sauce). Ironically, the only thing that isn't uniformly

ASIAN

excellent is the sushi, served at a sushi bar with two big-screen TVs. $ *Average main: $14* ✉ *45 Main St.* ☎ *413/664–9388* ⊗ *Closed Sun.*

WHERE TO STAY

$$$
B&B/INN
Fodor'sChoice
★
🌐 **Porches Inn.** These once-dilapidated mill-workers' houses dating from the 1890s were refurbished and connected with one long porch to become one of New England's quirkiest hotels; they now strike a perfect balance between high-tech and historic—rooms have a mix of retro 1940s and '50s lamps and bungalow-style furnishings, along with stunning bathrooms with slate floors, hot tubs, and mirrors fashioned out of old window frames. **Pros:** outdoor heated pool and hot tub (hot tub is open all year); large guest rooms; walk to town. **Cons:** small breakfast room. $ *Rooms from: $239* ✉ *231 River St.* ☎ *413/664–0400* ⊕ *www.porches.com* ⤴ *47 rooms, 12 suites* ⧖ *Breakfast.*

$$$
B&B/INN
🌐 **Topia Inn.** Just off the Ashuwillticook Rail Trail, this is the greenest inn in the Berkshires: innkeepers Nana Simopoulous and Caryn Heilman transformed a derelict downtown building into an ecofriendly marvel, with solar panels, biofuel heating, and natural clay walls. **Pros:** artsy rooms; organic breakfasts; steam showers and spa tubs. **Cons:** next door to a bar. $ *Rooms from: $210* ✉ *10 Pleasant St., Adams* ☎ *413/743–9600* ⊕ *www.topiainn.com* ⤴ *10 rooms* ⧖ *Breakfast.*

SPORTS AND THE OUTDOORS

KAYAKING

Berkshire Outfitters. If you're itching to explore the Cheshire lakes by kayak, Ashuwillticook Rail Trail by bike, or Mt. Greylock's summit on snowshoes, visit Berkshire Outfitters. Just 300 yards from the Rail Trail, this shop rents bicycles, kayaks, canoes, snowshoes, and cross-country skis, and has a very knowledgeable staff that is happy to dispense trail maps. ✉ *169 Grove St., Adams* ☎ *413/743–5900* ⊕ *www.berkshireoutfitters.com.*

WILLIAMSTOWN

5 miles west of North Adams.

When Colonel Ephraim Williams left money to found a free school in what was then known as West Hoosac, he stipulated that the town's name be changed to Williamstown. Williams College opened in 1793, and even today life in this placid town revolves around it. Graceful campus buildings like the Gothic cathedral, built in 1904, line Main Street. Along Spring Street are a handful of upscale shops and lively eateries.

GETTING HERE AND AROUND

Williamstown includes a lot of farms and rolling hills, but essentially Williamstown proper sits around Route 2, which bisects Williams College. On the college campus you can walk to Spring Street and Water Street, while anything else you want to see is probably just a short drive and brief turn off Route 2 (or a hop onto the BRTA bus).

WORD OF MOUTH

"There are many choices for a stroll, one of the most interesting being the Williams College Campus. This college, established in 1798, has lovely historical buildings, an excellent art museum and a large, modern theater space."

—partypoet1

EXPLORING

Fodor's Choice ★ **Clark Art Institute.** One of the nation's notable small art museums, the Clark Art Institute has a large Renoir collection, as well as canvases by Monet and Pissarro. *The Little Dancer,* an important sculpture by Degas, is another exceptional work on view. Other items include English silver, European and American photography from the 1840s through the 1910s, and 17th- and 18th-century Flemish and Dutch masterworks. ✉ *225 South St.* ☎ *413/458–2303* 🌐 *www.clarkart.edu* 🎟 *June–Nov. $15, Dec.–May free* 🕒 *Sept.–June, Tues.–Sun. 10–5; July and Aug., daily 10–5.*

FAMILY Fodor's Choice ★ **Williams College Museum of Art.** The collection at this fine museum focuses on American and 20th-century art. One of the country's best college art museums, the WCMA's 14,000 objects span a range of eras and cultures. The original octagonal structure facing Main Street was built as a library in 1846, and the rainbow painting above the stairs is a Sol LeWitt, who finished it in 2001. ✉ *15 Lawrence Hall Dr.* ☎ *413/597–2376* 🌐 *wcma.williams.edu* 🎟 *Free* 🕒 *Tues.–Sun. 10–5.*

WHERE TO EAT

$$$ ECLECTIC 🍴 **Mezze Bistro & Bar.** With a beautiful hilltop location and charming grounds, Mezze Bistro & Bar can get crowded in summer, when everyone wants to rub elbows with stars from the Williamstown Theatre Festival. The menu, focused on local and seasonal ingredients, is always in flux, but is bound to contain some fancy options such as roast veal with duck-fat potatoes, or calves' liver with bacon lardons. [$] *Average main: $25* ✉ *777 Cold Spring Rd.* ☎ *413/458–0123* 🌐 *www.mezzerestaurant.com* ✍ *Reservations essential* 🕒 *No lunch.*

$$ AMERICAN Fodor's Choice ★ 🍴 **'6 House Pub.** Set in an old cow barn, this rustic, wood-paneled pub has buckets of character and an interesting array of upholstered furniture at the tables, so you can sit in an old wing chair if you like. Chef Matt Schilling's extensive menu runs the gamut from traditional pub food (burgers and mozzarella sticks) to such upscale vegetarian fare as a grilled plum salad with Granny Smith apples, Gorgonzola, and glazed walnuts, or wild-mushroom-and-cheese ravioli Alfredo. If you love seafood, order the lobster martini appetizer or the lobster roll. Daily specials include prime rib–and-pasta combos, but there's plenty to try on the standard menu. [$] *Average main: $17* ✉ *1896 House Inn, 910 Cold Spring Rd.* ☎ *413/458–1896, 888/999–1896* 🌐 *www.6housepub.com* 🕒 *No lunch Oct.–May.*

WHERE TO STAY

$$$ B&B/INN 🏨 **Guest House at Field Farm.** Built in 1948, this guesthouse contains a fine collection of art on loan from Williams College and the Whitney Museum. **Pros:** great views of the Berkshires; wonderful art collection; luxurious robes and towels. **Cons:** no TV in rooms; not an option for families with young children. [$] *Rooms from: $195* ✉ *554 Sloan Rd.* ☎ *413/458–3135* 🌐 *www.guesthouseatfieldfarm.org* 🛏 *5 rooms* 🕒 *Closed Jan.–Mar.* 🍽 *Breakfast.*

$$$$ HOTEL 🏨 **Orchards Hotel.** Although it's near Route 2 and surrounded by parking lots, this thoroughly proper hostelry compensates with a courtyard filled with fruit trees and a pond stocked with koi. **Pros:** flat-screen

TVs; elegant rooms; good alternative to B&Bs and chain hotels. **Cons:** no coffeemakers in rooms; some guests complain of service lapses; minor signs of wear and tear. $ *Rooms from: $249* ✉ *222 Adams Rd.* ☎ *413/458–9611, 800/225–1517* ⊕ *www.orchardshotel.com* ⤶ *49 rooms* ⦿ *No meals.*

$ ⬚ **River Bend Farm.** Listed on the National Register of Historic Places,
B&B/INN this 1770 Georgian Colonial is not on a river, nor is it a farm, but this rustic inn is a great place to discover simpler times. **Pros:** lovely furnishings; good breakfast; friendly innkeepers. **Cons:** on a busy road; shared bathrooms. $ *Rooms from: $120* ✉ *643 Simonds Rd.* ☎ *413/458–3121* ⊕ *www.riverbendfarmbb.com* ⤶ *4 rooms without bath* ▭ *No credit cards* ☾ *Closed Nov.–Mar.* ⦿ *Breakfast.*

THE ARTS

Fodor's Choice **Williamstown Theatre Festival.** At Williams College, the Williamstown
★ Theatre Festival is summer's hottest ticket. From June through August, the long-running production presents well-known theatrical works with famous performers on the Main Stage and contemporary works on the Nikos Stage. ✉ *'62 Center for Theatre and Dance, 1000 Main St.* ☎ *413/597–3400, 413/597–3399* ⊕ *www.wtfestival.org.*

SPORTS AND THE OUTDOORS

Mt. Greylock State Reservation. The centerpiece of this 10,327-acre reservation south of Williamstown is Mt. Greylock, at 3,491 feet the highest point in Massachusetts. The reservation has facilities for cycling, fishing, horseback riding, camping, and snowmobiling. Many treks—including a portion of the Appalachian Trail—start from the parking lot at the summit, an 8-mile drive from the mountain's base. ✉ *Mt. Greylock State Reservation Visitor Center, 30 Rockwell Rd., Lanesboro* ☎ *413/499–4262* ⊕ *www.mass.gov/eea/agencies/dcr/massparks/region-west.*

SHOPPING

Toonerville Trolley. Some people consider this tiny place to be the best music store in the world. Toonerville Trolley carries hard-to-find jazz, rock, and classical recordings—many on vinyl—curated by a friendly and knowledgeable owner. ✉ *131 Water St.* ☎ *413/458–5229* ⊕ *toonervilletrolleycds.com.*

FAMILY **Where'd You Get That?.** Jam-packed with every imaginable toy and game, as well as some novelty items you'd never have imagined at all, Where'd You Get That? also benefits from the enthusiasm of owners Ken and Michele Gietz. There's also an interesting selection of candies. ✉ *100 Spring St.* ☎ *413/458–2206* ⊕ *www.wygt.com.*

HANCOCK

15 miles south of Williamstown.

Tiny Hancock, the village closest to the Jiminy Peak ski resort, comes into its own in winter. It's also a great base for outdoors enthusiasts year-round, with biking, hiking, and other options in summer.

GETTING HERE AND AROUND

Situated between Williamstown and Lanesborough, Hancock is an oft-overlooked destination for the outdoors person. You can take Route 43 from Williamstown, Route 7 from Pittsfield, or the BRTA bus from Lanesborough, with plenty of mountain views and trees along the way.

EXPLORING

Ioka Valley Farm. Established in the 1930s, this 600-acre farm has pick-your-own pumpkins from mid-September to October, cut-your-own Christmas trees from late November to late December, and a petting farm in June and July. For a real treat between late February and early April, catch a weekend brunch with homemade maple syrup atop pancakes, waffles, and French toast. ⊠ *3475 Rte. 43* ☎ *413/738–5915* ⊕ *www.iokavalleyfarm.com.*

WHERE TO STAY

$$$$
RESORT
🏨 **Country Inn at Jiminy Peak.** Massive stone fireplaces in its lobby and lounge lend this hotel a ski-lodge atmosphere, and the condo-style suites—privately owned but put into a rental pool—accommodate up to four people and have couches and kitchenettes separated from living areas by bars with high stools. **Pros:** on-site restaurant; nice bathrooms; eat-in kitchenettes. **Cons:** hallways are a bit dark; outdoor pool is small. 💲 *Rooms from: $279* ⊠ *37 Corey Rd.* ☎ *413/738–5500, 800/882–8859* ⊕ *www.jiminypeak.com* 🛏 *105 suites* ⍵⊙⍵ *No meals.*

SPORTS AND THE OUTDOORS

Jiminy Peak. The only full-service ski and snowboard resort in the Berkshires, Jiminy Peak is also the largest in southern New England, with a vertical drop of 1,150 feet, 44 trails, and nine lifts. It's mostly a cruising mountain—trails are groomed daily, although some small moguls are left to build up along the side of the slope. The steepest black-diamond runs are on the upper head walls; longer, outer runs make for good intermediate terrain. There's skiing nightly, and snowmaking covers 93% of the skiable terrain. Jiminy also has three terrain parks and a weekends-only mountain coaster, a two-person cart that shoots down the mountain at speeds of up to 25 mph. ⊠ *37 Corey Rd.* ☎ *413/738–5500, 888/454–6469* ⊕ *www.jiminypeak.com.*

PITTSFIELD

21 miles south of Williamstown, 11 miles southeast of Hancock.

Pittsfield is a workaday city without the quaint, rural demeanor of the comparatively small Colonial towns that surround it. There's a positive buzz in Pittsfield these days, though. Symbols of resurgence include the beautifully restored Colonial Theatre, which hosts 250 nights of performances per year, and a spate of new shops and eateries along North Street. City-sponsored art walks and a major renovation of the venerable Berkshire Museum are more evidence of Pittsfield's comeback.

Many of New England's back roads are lined with historic split-rail fences or stone walls.

GETTING HERE AND AROUND

Whether a train or bus drops you at the Intermodal Transportation Station, you'll be just a block from Pittsfield's expansive North Street, along which you can walk to find theatres, museums, interesting stores, and all sorts of restaurants. Bus routes go to the mall and Allendale, elsewhere you'll need to drive.

EXPLORING

FAMILY

Fodor's Choice

★

Berkshire Museum. Opened in 1903, this "universal" museum has a little bit of everything: paintings from the Hudson River School; Alexander Calder's mobiles; natural history, including animals and minerals; and local history. The latter is exemplified by the Hall of Innovation, which showcases Berkshire innovators whose creations range from special effects for *Star Wars* to the paper used for U.S. currency. The 10-foot-high stegosaurus outside the museum advertises the dinosaur gallery, where families can sift through the dig pit for bones, but don't miss the ancient gallery featuring an Egyptian mummy, or the aquarium with a touch tank in the basement. Add to this rotating exhibits such as the Paperworks, and the in-house cinema, and the Berkshire Museum has something for everyone. ⊠ *39 South St.* ☏ *413/443–7171* ⊕ *www. berkshiremuseum.org* ▨ *$13* ⊘ *Mon.–Sat. 10–5, Sun. noon–5.*

Fodor's Choice

★

Hancock Shaker Village. The third Shaker community in America, Hancock was founded in the 1790s. At its peak in the 1840s, the village had almost 300 inhabitants, who made their living farming, selling seeds and herbs, making medicines, and producing crafts. The religious community officially closed in 1960, but visitors today can still see demonstrations of blacksmithing, woodworking, and more. Many examples of

Shaker ingenuity are on display: the Round Stone Barn and the Laundry and Machine Shop are two of the most interesting buildings. There's also a farm (with a wonderful barn), some period gardens, a museum shop with reproduction Shaker furniture, a picnic area, and a café. Visit in April to catch the baby animals at the farm, or in September for the country fair. Traditional Shaker suppers are available only by reservation. ✉ *U.S. 20 and Rte. 41, 6 miles west of Pittsfield* ☎ *413/443–0188, 800/817–1137* 🌐 *www.hancockshakervillage.org* 🎟 *$18* 🕒 *Apr.–June, daily 10–4; July–Oct., daily 10–5.*

WHERE TO EAT

$$$ ITALIAN 🍴 **Elizabeth's.** You'd never guess this little white house was a restaurant, let alone one serving some of the region's best Italian fare. But Elizabeth's, where you feel like you're having dinner at a friend's house, offers a playful menu that emphasizes high-quality ingredients. From the four-cheese lasagna with caramelized onions to the classic pasta puttanesca (olives, garlic, capers, hot pepper), all the richly flavored entrées are accompanied by impressive salads featuring a mix of seasonal greens, vegetables, fruits, and cheeses. Don't pass up the the *bagna coada*, a hot dipping sauce of anchovies, garlic, and olive oil. Cash only. [$] *Average main: $21* ✉ *1264 East St., off Rte. 9* ☎ *413/448–8244* ✍ *Reservations essential* 💳 *No credit cards* 🕒 *Closed Sun.–Tues. No lunch.*

$$ SOUTH AMERICAN 🍴 **La Fogata.** Wondering about the few shelves of South American foods at La Fogata? Owner and chef Miguel Gomez says there was nowhere elsewhere in the area that stocked the ingredients for true Colombian cooking. You may want to buy a jar of mole paste to take home, but it can wait until after you've dined at one of the small tables near the open kitchen. It's hard to go wrong if you order a *plato tipico* (a "typical platter" of grilled steak, fried egg, rice, beans, plantain, avocado, corn patty, and pork rind). Vegetarian options are somewhat uninspiring, but meat and seafood lovers will eat very well. [$] *Average main: $14* ✉ *770 Tyler St.* ☎ *413/443–6969* 🕒 *Closed Mon.*

WHERE TO STAY

$$$ B&B/INN 🏨 **White Horse Inn.** Standing on Pittsfield's busy South Street, this early-20th-century Colonial Revival home provides comfortable rooms appointed with handsome Colonial furnishings. **Pros:** excellent breakfast; knowledgeable innkeepers; very clean. **Cons:** on a busy street. [$] *Rooms from: $220* ✉ *378 South St.* ☎ *413/442–2512* 🌐 *www.whitehorsebb.com* 🛏 *8 rooms* 🍽 *Breakfast.*

THE ARTS

Colonial Theatre. First opened in 1903, this restored theater hosted stars like Helen Hayes and Al Jolson; now guests fill the 780 seats to see artists like Audra McDonald and James Taylor. There are also comedy performances and programs for children. ✉ *111 South St.* ☎ *413/997–4444* 🌐 *www.berkshiretheatregroup.org.*

South Mountain Concerts. For serious music lovers, this is one of the country's most distinguished centers for chamber music events. On the wooded slope of South Mountain, the 500-seat auditorium presents concerts every Sunday in September at 3. ✉ *South St., 2 miles south of Pittsfield center* ☎ *413/442–2106* 🌐 *www.southmountainconcerts.org.*

SPORTS AND THE OUTDOORS

SKIING

Bousquet Ski Area. With a 750-foot vertical drop, Bousquet has 23 trails if you count merging slopes separately. It has some good beginner and intermediate runs, with a few steeper pitches. There are three double chairlifts, two carpet lifts, and a small snowboarding park. Ski instruction is given twice daily on weekdays and thrice on weekends for children ages five and up. In summer, Bousquet offers waterslides, a large activity pool, a miniature golf course, climbing wall, an adventure park, and a zipline. ⊠ *101 Dan Fox Dr., off U.S. 7* ☎ *413/442–8316, 413/442–2436 snow conditions* ⊕ *www.bousquets.com* ☉ *June–Sept. and Dec.–Mar.*

SHOPPING

Whitney's Farm. In addition to offering seasonal pick-your-own blueberries and pumpkins, Whitney's Farm sells fresh produce, herbs, and dairy products. There are also a deli and bakery in the main building. ⊠ *1775 S. State Rd., Cheshire* ☎ *413/442–4749* ⊕ *www.whitneysfarm. com* ☉ *Mon.–Sat. 8–7, Sun. 9–6.*

5

LENOX

10 miles south of Pittsfield, 130 miles west of Boston.

The famed Tanglewood music festival has been a fixture in upscale Lenox for decades, and it's a part of the reason the town remains fiercely popular in summer. Booking a room here or in any of the nearby communities can set you back dearly when music or theatrical events are in town. Many of the town's most impressive homes are downtown; others you can only see by setting off on the curving, tortuous back roads that traverse the region. In the center of the village, a few blocks of shabby-chic Colonial buildings contain shops and eateries.

GETTING HERE AND AROUND

Just off Interstate 90 after passing through Lee, Lenox is a small town a bit south of Pittsfield. Be warned that while the Berkshires are usually blessedly free of traffic, Lenox and environs during the summer Tanglewood season are notable exceptions.

Lenox Chamber of Commerce ⊠ *Lenox Library, 18 Main St.* ☎ *413/637–3646* ⊕ *www.lenox.org.*

EXPLORING

FAMILY **Berkshires Scenic Railway Museum.** In a restored 1903 railroad station in central Lenox, this museum displays antique rail equipment, vintage items, and a large working model railway. ⊠ *10 Willow Creek Rd.* ☎ *413/637–2210* ⊕ *www.berkshirescenicrailroad.org* ☐ *Free* ☉ *Late May–Oct., weekends 9:30–4:30.*

Frelinghuysen Morris House & Studio. This modernist property on a 46-acre site exhibits the works of American abstract artists Suzy Frelinghuysen and George L.K. Morris as well as contemporaries including Pablo Picasso, Georges Braque, and Juan Gris. In addition to the paintings, frescoes, and sculptures, a 57-minute documentary on Frelinghuysen and Morris plays on a continuous loop in the classroom. Tours are offered on the hour—just be aware that it's a long walk to the house. ✉ *92 Hawthorne St.* ☎ *413/637–0166* ⊕ *www.frelinghuysen.org* 🎫 *$12* ⊙ *Late June–early Sept., Thurs.–Sun. 10–3; early Sept.–mid-Oct., Thurs.–Sat. 10–3.*

Fodor'sChoice ★ **The Mount.** This 1902 mansion with myriad classical influences was the summer home of novelist Edith Wharton. The 42-room house and 3 acres of formal gardens were designed by Wharton, who is considered by many to have set the standard for 20th-century interior decoration. In designing The Mount, she followed the principles set forth in her book *The Decoration of Houses* (1897), creating a calm and well-ordered home. Nearly $15 million has been spent to date on an ongoing restoration project that recently restored the third-floor bedroom suite. Summer programs includes free concerts on the terrace. Take one of the guided tours, or schedule a private "ghost tour" after hours. ✉ *2 Plunkett St.* ☎ *413/551–5111, 888/637–1902* ⊕ *www.edithwharton. org* 🎫 *$18* ⊙ *Grounds: dawn to dusk daily. House: May–Oct., daily 10–5; Nov. and Dec., weekends 10–5.*

Ventfort Hall Mansion and Gilded Age Museum. Built in 1893, Ventfort Hall was the summer "cottage" of Sarah Morgan, the sister of financier J.P. Morgan. Lively tours offer a peek into the lifestyles of Lenox's superrich "cottage class." Although the property is being restored, the many rooms that are open reveal the original stained-glass windows and hand-carved woodwork. The museum has rotating exhibits that explore the role of Lenox and the Berkshires as the era's definitive mountain retreat. Victorian high tea is among the highlights. ✉ *104 Walker St.* ☎ *413/637–3206* ⊕ *www.gildedage.org* 🎫 *$15* ⊙ *Weekdays 10–5, weekends 10–3.*

WHERE TO EAT

$$ PERUVIAN Fodor'sChoice ★ ✕ **Alpamayo.** Don't let the hole-in-the-wall vibe fool you; what this place lacks in pretension it more than makes up for in taste. Just order a plate of the much-lauded skewered beef hearts and you'll quickly forget the atmosphere. Ceviche is the specialty of the house, so if you aren't ordering it for your main course, consider a taste as an appetizer. Other options range from typical steaks and seafoods to the delectable mishmash that is *lomo saltado* (Angus beef, onions, tomatoes, and french fries, all sautéed together)—not much to look at, but it has a satisfyingly rich flavor. The caramel custard is a generous serving that two can share, unless one has a sweet tooth. Ⓢ *Average main: $15* ✉ *60 Main St., Lee* ☎ *413/243–6000* ⊕ *www.alpamayorestaurant.com* ⊙ *No lunch Mon.*

$ SOUTHWESTERN ✕ **Baja Charlie's.** If you're looking for a quick bite to break up a full day of sightseeing, grab a seat in the tiny dining area, on the pleasant patio, or order take-out if you're in a hurry. The menu, while small, covers all the standard California-Mexican dishes you'd want, from nachos and tacos to burritos and quesadillas. Best of all, they don't skimp on the meat. Ⓢ *Average main: $11* ✉ *62A W. Center St., Lee* ☎ *413/243–4322.*

$$$ FRENCH ✕ **Bistro Zinc.** Crisp walls, warm tile floors, and tall windows are bright and inviting in this stylishly modern French bistro, which feels like a country house in Provence. The kitchen turns out expertly prepared and refreshingly simple classics like steak frites (with fries), coq au vin, and grilled pork loin with collard greens and baby turnips. The long,

zinc-topped bar, always full and determinedly sophisticated, is the best Lenox can offer for nightlife. $ *Average main: $25* ⊠ *56 Church St.* ☎ *413/637–8800* ⊕ *www.bistrozinc.com.*

$$$ ✕ **Café Lucia.** The menus change with the seasons at this northern Italian
ITALIAN restaurant, so you might find anything from veal piccata with anchovies, lemons, and capers to pan-roasted duck in a fig sauce. The nice porch is one of the best places to take everything in. Weekend reservations are essential, especially when there's a concert at Tanglewood. $ *Average main: $28* ⊠ *80 Church St.* ☎ *413/637–2640* ⊕ *www.cafelucialenox. com* ⌲ *Reservations essential* ⊗ *Closed Mon.; also closed Sun. Nov.– June. No lunch.*

$ ✕ **Chocolate Springs Cafe.** Escape into chocolate bliss here, where even the
BAKERY aromas are intoxicating. This award-winning chocolatier offers wedges
Fodor's Choice of decadent cakes, ice creams and sorbets, and a dazzling array of choco-
★ lates all made on-site from the best cocoa beans. Whether you like your chocolate dark and pure, sugar-free, or even filled with chipotle, you can't go wrong. You can eat at one of a handful of leather couches or wooden chairs and tables, but don't expect so much as a salad or a wrap—it's all chocolate, all the time. $ *Average main: $6* ⊠ *Lenox Commons, 55 Pittsfield/Lenox Rd.* ☎ *413/637–9820* ⊕ *www.chocolatesprings.com.*

$$$ ✕ **Church Street Café.** More laid-back than its nearby competitors, the
CAFÉ rustic Church Street Café offers a minimalist aesthetic, with hardwood floors, recycled metal chairs, and black-and-white photos on the walls. In contrast to the extensive wine list, the menu is a small but intriguing array of globally inspired dishes. From the baked onion-and-Manchego-cheese tart to the cioppino fish stew to the butternut squash lasagna, the dishes served are an international culinary treat that changes seasonally. In warm weather you can dine on a shaded outdoor deck. $ *Average main: $25* ⊠ *65 Church St.* ☎ *413/637–2745* ⊕ *churchstreetlenox.com* ⊗ *Closed Tues. and Wed.*

WHERE TO STAY

$$$ ⌂ **Applegate Inn.** This 1925 Georgian Revival mansion sits at the end of
B&B/INN a regal circular drive, overlooking 6 acres of lush lawns and apple trees. **Pros:** charming dining room; delicious breakfast; heated pool. **Cons:** some traffic noise. $ *Rooms from: $199* ⊠ *279 W. Park St.* ☎ *413/243–4451* ⊕ *applegateinn.com* ⌸ *6 rooms, 5 suites* ⏻ *Breakfast.*

$$$$ ⌂ **Blantyre.** Modeled after a castle in Scotland, this supremely elegant
B&B/INN 1902 manor house sits amid nearly 117 acres of manicured lawns and woodlands. **Pros:** the spa's hot tub is stunning; high-end toiletries in bathrooms; property is exquisitely maintained. **Cons:** some rooms have quirky configurations. $ *Rooms from: $600* ⊠ *16 Blantyre Rd., off U.S. 20* ☎ *413/637–3556* ⊕ *www.blantyre.com* ⌸ *25 rooms, 5 suites, 4 cottages* ⏻ *Breakfast.*

$$$ ⌂ **Brook Farm Inn.** Tucked away in a beautiful wooded glen a short dis-
B&B/INN tance from Tanglewood, this 1880s inn is hosted by innkeepers who are history and music aficionados and often have classical music playing in the fireplace-lighted library. **Pros:** attentive innkeepers; delicious break-fasts; afternoon tea with homemade scones on weekends. **Cons:** books up fast. $ *Rooms from: $189* ⊠ *15 Hawthorne St.* ☎ *413/637–3013, 800/285–7638* ⊕ *brookfarm.com* ⌸ *14 rooms, 1 suite* ⏻ *Breakfast.*

$$$
B&B/INN
Fodor's Choice
★

🏠 **Devonfield Inn.** This grand, yellow-and-cream Federal house sits atop a birch-shaded hillside, dotted with a few quaint outbuildings and 32 acres of rolling meadows. **Pros:** charming innkeepers; good breakfasts; nice pool and lawn. **Cons:** not for families with young kids. $ *Rooms from: $200 ⊠ 85 Stockbridge Rd., Lee* 🕾 *413/243–3298, 800/664–0880* ⊕ *www.devonfield.com* ⇨ *6 rooms, 3 suites, 1 cottage* ¹⁰¹ *Breakfast.*

$$
B&B/INN
Fodor's Choice
★

🏠 **Gateways Inn.** The 1912 summer cottage of Harley Proctor (as in Proctor and Gamble) has had numerous owners during its tenure as a country inn, but current innkeepers Michele and Eiran Gazit have put in thousands of dollars of renovations that make it look better than ever. **Pros:** comfortable rooms; great location in the heart of Lenox; late-night nibbles in the piano bar. **Cons:** lots of stairs; weddings sometimes take over the lobby. $ *Rooms from: $150 ⊠ 51 Walker St.* 🕾 *413/637–2532* ⊕ *www.gatewaysinn.com* ⇨ *11 rooms, 1 suite* ¹⁰¹ *Breakfast.*

THE ARTS

Shakespeare & Company. The works of William Shakespeare and various others writers are performed in three theaters. The Tina Packer Playhouse and Elayne P. Bernstein Theatre are indoors, so you can enjoy productions throughout much of the year. The outdoor Rose Footprint Theatre reflects the dimensions of Shakespeare's first performance space in London, the Rose. ⊠ *70 Kemble St.* 🕾 *413/637–3353* ⊕ *www.shakespeare.org.*

Fodor's Choice
★

Tanglewood. The 200-acre summer home of the Boston Symphony Orchestra, Tanglewood attracts thousands every summer to concerts by world-famous musicians. The 5,000-seat main shed hosts larger concerts; the more intimate Seiji Ozawa Hall (named for the famous conductor) seats around 1,200 and is used for chamber music and solo performances. One of the most rewarding ways to experience Tanglewood is to purchase lawn tickets, arrive early with blankets or lawn chairs, and enjoy a picnic under the stars. Except for the occasional big-name concert, lawn tickets cost less than $20. Inside the shed, tickets vary in price, with most of the good seats costing between $38 and $120. ■ TIP➜ **Consider attending an open rehearsal, offering the same music at a fraction of the price.** ⊠ *297 West St., off Rte. 183* 🕾 *617/266–1492, 888/266–1492* ⊕ *www.tanglewood.org.*

SPORTS AND THE OUTDOORS

HIKING

Pleasant Valley Wildlife Sanctuary. Run by the Massachusetts Audubon Society, this sanctuary abounds with beaver ponds, hardwood forests, and sun-dappled meadows. A whiteboard at the entrance lists recent wildlife sightings, so you know what to watch for on your walk. The various forest trails include loops that range in difficulty from a half-hour stroll around a pond to a three-hour hike up a mountain. Hiking trails are open for cross-country skiing and snowshoeing in winter. ⊠ *472 W. Mountain Rd.* 🕾 *413/637–0320* ⊕ *www.massaudubon.org* 🎫 *$5* ☉ *Nature center Tues.–Fri. 9–4, Sat.–Mon. 10–4.*

Norman Rockwell: Illustrating America

I was showing the America I knew and observed to others who might not have noticed. My fundamental purpose is to interpret the typical American. I am a storyteller.
—Norman Rockwell

If you've ever seen old copies of the *Saturday Evening Post*, no doubt you're familiar with American artist Norman Rockwell. He created 321 covers for the well-regarded magazine, and the *Post* always sold more copies when one of Rockwell's drawings was on the front page. The accomplished artist also illustrated Boy Scouts of America calendars, Christmas cards, children's books, and even a few stamps for the U.S. Postal Service—in 1994 a stamp bearing his image came out in his honor. His illustrations tended to fit the theme of Americana, family, or patriotism.

Born in New York City in 1894, the talented designer had a knack for art early on but strengthened his talent with instruction at the National Academy of Design and the Art Students League. He was only 22 when he sold his first cover to the *Post*. He was married three times and had three sons by his second wife. He died in 1978 in Stockbridge, Massachusetts, where he had lived since 1953.

Norman Rockwell 1920 magazine cover.

Famous works include his *Triple Self-Portrait* and the *Four Freedoms* illustrations done during World War II. They represent freedom of speech, freedom to worship, freedom from want, and freedom from fear. In a poetic twist, in 1977, President Gerald R. Ford bestowed on Rockwell the Presidential Medal of Freedom, the highest civilian honor a U.S. citizen can be given. Ford praised Rockwell for his "vivid and affectionate portraits of our country."

—Debbie Harmsen

HORSEBACK RIDING

Berkshire Horseback Adventures. Travel along the shaded trails of Kennedy Park and Lenox Mountain and enjoy breathtaking views of Berkshire County when you book rides lasting from an hour to a whole day. ✉ *293 Main St.* ☏ *413/637–9090* ⊕ *www.berkshirehorseback.net.*

SPAS

Canyon Ranch. The Berkshires' outpost of Canyon Ranch couldn't be more elegantly old-fashioned; the famous spa is set in Bellefontaine Mansion, an 1897 replica of Le Petit Trianon in Versailles. Looks can be deceiving, though. This holistic spa is home to a state-of-the-art fitness center, with the latest classes and the best equipment—perfect for gym junkies. Choose from more than 40 fitness classes per day, plus lifestyle-management workshops and private consultations with wellness experts in the fields of medicine, nutrition, behavior, and physiology, while trying new fitness techniques, eating great food (even chocolate sauce, craftily made from white grape juice and cocoa), and enjoying the Berkshires countryside on hikes and paddling excursions. ⊠ *165 Kemble St., 9 miles south of Pittsfield* ☎ *800/742–9000, 413/637–4400* ⊕ *www.canyonranch.com.*

OTIS

20 miles southeast of Lenox.

A more rustic alternative to Stockbridge and Lenox, Otis, with a ski area and 20 lakes and ponds, supplies plenty of what made the Berkshires desirable in the first place—the great outdoors. Dining and lodging options are slim; you can stay in Lee or Great Barrington or head southwest to Old Marlborough and stay at the Old Inn on the Green, where you can sample chef Peter Platt's swoon-worthy cuisine. Nearby Becket hosts the outstanding Jacob's Pillow Dance Festival in summer.

GETTING HERE AND AROUND
Interstate 90 to Lee is the fastest way here for many coming from afar; locally Otis lies at the intersection of Routes 8 and 23. With no public transport, Otis is a place you'll be driving to or through.

EXPLORING

Fodor's Choice ★ **Jacob's Pillow Dance Festival.** For 10 weeks every summer, the tiny town of Becket, 8 miles north of Otis, becomes a hub of the dance world. The Jacob's Pillow Dance Festival showcases world-renowned performers of ballet, modern, and international dance. Before the main events, works in progress and even some of the final productions are staged outdoors, often free of charge. ⊠ *358 George Carter Rd., at U.S. 20, Becket* ☎ *413/243–0745* ⊕ *www.jacobspillow.org.*

SPORTS AND THE OUTDOORS
SKI AREA
Otis Ridge. The least expensive ski area in New England, Otis Ridge has long been a haven for beginners and families, but experts will find some challenges here, too. The remote location is quite stunning, the buildings historic. Eleven downhill trails are serviced by four lifts, with 99% snowmaking coverage and night skiing Wednesday through Sunday. ⊠ *159 Monterey Rd., Hwy. 23* ☎ *413/269–4444* ⊕ *www.otisridge.com.*

STOCKBRIDGE

20 miles northwest of Otis, 7 miles south of Lenox.

Stockbridge is the quintessence of small-town New England charm, untainted by large-scale development. It is also the blueprint for small-town America as represented on the covers of the *Saturday Evening Post* by painter Norman Rockwell (the official state artist of Massachusetts). From 1953 until his death in 1978, Rockwell lived in Stockbridge and painted the simple charm of its buildings and residents. James Taylor sang about the town in his hit "Sweet Baby James," as did balladeer Arlo Guthrie in his famous Thanksgiving anthem "Alice's Restaurant," in which he tells what ensued when he tossed some garbage out the back of his Volkswagen bus down a Stockbridge hillside.

Indeed, Stockbridge is the stuff of legend. Travelers have been checking into the Red Lion on Main Street since the 18th century, and Stockbridge is only slightly altered in appearance since that time. In 18th- and 19th-century buildings surrounding the inn are a handful of engaging shops and eateries. The rest of Stockbridge is best appreciated via a country drive or bike ride over its hilly, narrow lanes.

GETTING HERE AND AROUND

Stockbridge is easily accessible from West Stockbridge or Lee, both of which are exits off the Mass Pike. Once here, you can easily walk around the village and drive around the larger area.

ESSENTIALS

Visitor Information Stockbridge Chamber of Commerce ⊠ *50 Main St.* ☎ *413/298–5200, 413/298–5200* ⊕ *www.stockbridgechamber.org.*

EXPLORING

Berkshire Botanical Gardens. This 15-acre garden contains extensive plantings of exotic and native flora—some 2,500 varieties in all—plus greenhouses, ponds, and nature trails. Don't miss annual events like October's Harvest Festival. Tours are available on Friday and Saturday morning. ⊠ *5 W. Stockbridge Rd.* ☎ *413/298–3926* ⊕ *www.berkshirebotanical. org* ⊠ *$15* ⊗ *May–Oct., daily 9–5.*

Fodor'sChoice ★ **Chesterwood.** For 33 years, this was the summer home of the sculptor Daniel Chester French (1850–1931), who created *The Minuteman* in Concord and the Lincoln Memorial's famous seated statue of the president in Washington, D.C. Tours are given of the house, which is maintained in the style of the 1920s, and of the studio, where you can view the casts and models French used to create the Lincoln Memorial. The beautifully landscaped 122-acre grounds also make for an enchanting stroll, bedecked with a contemporary sculpture show during the summer. If you are in the area on Memorial Day weekend, come for the annual classic car show. ⊠ *4 Williamsville Rd., off Hwy. 183* ☎ *413/298–3579* ⊕ *www.chesterwood.org* ⊠ *$16* ⊗ *May–Oct., daily 10–5.*

Naumkeag. This Berkshire cottage once owned by New York lawyer Joseph Choate, ambassador to Great Britain during President William McKinley's administration, provides a glimpse into the gracious living of the Gilded Age. The 44-room gabled mansion, designed by Stanford White in 1886, sits atop Prospect Hill. Its many original furnishings and art span three centuries; the collection of Chinese porcelain is also noteworthy. The meticulously kept 8 acres of formal gardens designed by Fletcher Steele are worth the visit. ⊠ *5 Prospect Hill Rd.* ☎ *413/298–3239* ⊕ *www. thetrustees.org* ⊠ *$15* ⊗ *Memorial Day–Columbus Day, daily 10–5.*

Norman Rockwell Museum. This charming museum traces the career of one of America's most beloved illustrators, beginning with his first *Saturday Evening Post* cover in 1916. The crown jewel of the 570 Rockwell illustrations is the famed "Four Freedoms" gallery, although

Stockbridge's churches are just some of the charming buildings on Main Street.

various works—including self-portraits—are equally charming. The museum also mounts exhibits by other artists. Rockwell's studio was moved to the museum grounds and is complete in every detail. Stroll the 36-acre site, picnic on the grounds, or relax at the outdoor café (open Memorial Day to Columbus Day). There's a child's version of the audio tour with a scavenger-hunt theme, as well as a creativity center with art materials. The museum shop makes it more fun for adults. ✉ *9 Rte. 183* ☎ *413/298–4100* 🌐 *www.nrm.org* 🎟 *$16* ⏲ *May–Oct., daily 10–5; Nov.–Apr., weekdays 10–4, weekends 10–5.*

WHERE TO EAT AND STAY

$$$ ECLECTIC 🍴 **Once Upon a Table.** They picked a cute little name for a cute little restaurant in the mews off Stockbridge's Main Street. The adjective also applies to the upscale eatery's menu, a small but appealing selection of Continental and contemporary American cuisine. After a sourdough rosemary roll, you can try escargot potpie (a puff pastry over a few snails in garlic butter), or entrées like seared crab cakes with capers, rack of lamb with garlic mashed potatoes, or duck in raspberry sauce. [$] *Average main: $25* ✉ *36 Main St.* ☎ *413/298–3870* 🌐 *www.onceuponatablebistro.com* ✍ *Reservations essential* ⏲ *No breakfast weekdays.*

$$$ FRENCH 🍴 **Rouge.** In West Stockbridge, 5 miles northwest of Stockbridge, this French restaurant has been such a success that it's expanded to include a bar and larger dining area. Owner-chef William Merelle is from Provence, where he met his American wife (and co-owner), Maggie, formerly a wine merchant. Try the steak au poivre with arugula, the braised duck with shredded potato cake, or the crispy *pommes frites* (french fries). [$] *Average main: $28* ✉ *3 Center St., West Stockbridge*

📞 *413/232–4111* ⊕ *www.rougerestaurant.com* 🍴 *Reservations essential* ⊙ *Closed Mon. and Tues. No lunch.*

$$
VIETNAMESE ✕ **Truc Orient Express.** Nestled amidst a few shops filled with Vietnamese arts and crafts, this family-owned restaurant has been serving up authentic Vietnamese food for more than 30 years. Trai Duong and Luy Nguyen create a homey atmosphere, as much for the friendly service as the decor that includes a wide staircase just inside the entrance. The menu is a combination of standard favorites like *banh xeo* (Vietnamese rice pancakes) to more adventurous dishes like *ca chien* (whole fried flounder in a pungent fish sauce). $ *Average main: $18* ⊠ *3 Harris St.* 📞 *413/232–4204* ⊙ *Closed Tues. No lunch.*

$$$$
B&B/INN
Fodor'sChoice
★ 🏠 **The Inn at Stockbridge.** Antique furnishings and feather comforters are among the accents in the guest rooms of this 1906 Georgian Revival inn. **Pros:** beautiful grounds; good breakfast; lovely furniture. **Cons:** noise from highway (most noticeable in suites); not within walking distance to town. $ *Rooms from: $310* ⊠ *30 East St.* 📞 *413/298–3337, 888/466–7865* ⊕ *www.stockbridgeinn.com* ⊃ *7 rooms, 8 suites* ⦿*Breakfast.*

$$$$
B&B/INN
Fodor'sChoice
★ 🏠 **The Red Lion Inn.** An inn since 1773, the Red Lion has hosted presidents, senators, and other celebrities, and consists of a large main building and nine annexes. **Pros:** inviting lobby with fireplace; array of rocking chairs on porch; quaintly romantic. **Cons:** pricey dining; puny fitness center; no cell reception. $ *Rooms from: $245* ⊠ *30 Main St.* 📞 *413/298–5545, 413/298–1690* ⊕ *www.redlioninn.com* ⊃ *125 rooms, 25 suites* ⦿*No meals.*

THE ARTS

Berkshire Theatre Festival. Since 1929, this festival has presented plays all summer long. Those on the Main Stage tend to be better-known works with established actors. A smaller theater mounts more experimental works, while the outdoor stage is home to family-friendly shows. You can also catch festival productions at the Colonial Theatre in Pittsfield. ⊠ *6 Main St.* 📞 *413/298–5576* ⊕ *www.berkshiretheatregroup.org.*

SHOPPING AND SPAS

Kripalu Center. You'll see many people sitting peacefully on the grounds as you search for a parking place at this health and yoga retreat in Stockbridge. Kripalu means grace, and there is even a hatha yoga method named after the institution. Meals always include a gluten-free buffet, in addition to more standard fare. ⊠ *57 Interlaken Rd.* 📞 *866/200–5203, 800/741–7353* ⊕ *www.kripalu.org.*

Schantz Galleries. After nearly three decades working with Holsten Galleries, Jim Schantz bought the gallery, and though it's small and tucked away behind a bank, it features some of the finest glasswork in the world. With items from 55 contemporary glass artists—including Dale Chihuly and Lino Tagliapietra—the museum-quality works are truly stunning. ⊠ *3 Elm St.* 📞 *413/298–3044* ⊕ *www.schantzgalleries.com.*

Williams & Sons Country Store. This traditional country store has penny candy, maple goodies, jams and jellies, and an authentic country feel. ⊠ *38 Main St.* 📞 *413/298–3016.*

GREAT BARRINGTON

7 miles southwest of Stockbridge; 13 miles north of Canaan, Connecticut.

The largest town in South County became, in 1781, the first place in the United States to free a slave under due process of law and was also the birthplace, in 1868, of W. E. B. DuBois, the civil rights leader, author, and educator. The many ex–New Yorkers who live in Great Barrington expect great food and service, and the restaurants here deliver complex, delicious fare. The town is also a favorite of antiques hunters, as are the nearby villages of South Egremont and Sheffield.

GETTING HERE AND AROUND
The nearest international airports are Bradley International Airport in Windsor Locks, Connecticut, and Albany International Airport in Albany, New York, but you are better off driving in on Route 7 from either Stockbridge or Canaan, Connecticut. Great Barrington is also on the BRTA bus line from Stockbridge. There's plenty of parking in town, most of which is walkable as well.

ESSENTIALS
Visitor Information Southern Berkshire Chamber of Commerce ⊠ *362 Main St.* ☎ *413/528–1510, 800/269–4825* ⊕ *southernberkshirechamber.com.*

EXPLORING
Vault Gallery. Housed inside a former bank, this small art gallery includes the vault room with the original safe door intact. While the main attraction may be the gallery itself, there are also some lovely paintings and photographs. ⊠ *322 Main St., Great Barrington, Massachusetts* ☎ *413/664–0221* ⊕ *vaultgallery.net/.*

WHERE TO EAT AND STAY

$
PIZZA
✕ **Baba Louie's Sourdough Pizza Co.** Is the pizza here good enough to merit the long lines that sometimes stretch out the door? Possibly. Enjoy the trattoria's rustic interior, and try to ignore the din of the crowd. Baba Louie's offers an interesting array of crusts, with a choice of mild sourdough or organic wheat and spelt-berry. Toppings include roasted sweet potatoes and parsnips, shaved fennel, caramelized onions, and fresh mozzarella with a hint of balsamic vinegar (on the Isabella Pizzarella), or ricotta, red onions, shrimp, pineapple, prosciutto, green chili, and a dusting of coconut (on the Hannah Jo). Weird, but good. $ *Average main: $12* ⊠ *286 Main St.* ☎ *413/528–8100* ⊕ *www.babalouiessourdoughpizzacompany.com* ⌔ *Reservations not accepted.*

$$
JAPANESE
✕ **Bizen.** Although the place can get noisy, this mainstay of Great Barrington's Railroad Street is popular for its Japanese fare. Enlivened by traditional pottery, the dining room has tables that wrap around three sides of a large central sushi bar. If you aren't ordering from the extensive sushi menu, try the *harumaki* (deep-fried lobster and fish in rice paper) or the *una jyu* (grilled river eel in a sweet sauce). Many of the dishes are also organic. $ *Average main: $20* ⊠ *17 Railroad St.* ☎ *413/528–4343.*

CLOSE UP

Massachusetts Farm Stands

Living like a locavore is easy in the Berkshires and Western Massachusetts. The area's many farms, farm stands, and farmers' markets make everything from produce, dairy, and meat to maple syrup, flowers, and Christmas trees. There's spinach, asparagus, maple syrup, and flowers in the spring, an endless array of fruits and veggies at every farm stand in summer, and apples, cranberries, pumpkins, and squash seem to mimic the palette of the fall foliage.

FARM STANDS

A great place to find farm stands is south on Routes 7 and 8. More than 30 run along or just off these routes.

YOU-PICK FARMS

Farms where you pick your own produce are very popular in Massachusetts. It's often berry farms and fruit orchards, but there are also many pick-your-own pumpkin patches, cornfields, and other vegetable farms.

FOR MORE INFORMATION

Berkshire Grown. To learn more about the region's farms, dairies, and farm-to-table restaurants, check out Berkshire Grown. ☎ *413/528–0041* 🌐 *www.berkshiregrown.org.*

Northeast Organic Farming Association. This organization is a great resource for organic produce in Massachusetts. ☎ *978/355–2853* 🌐 *www.nofamass.org.*

—Jen Laskey

$$$ CAFÉ 🍴 **Castle Steet Café.** Chef-owner Michael Ballon wins raves for his simple-but-elegant cuisine and masterful hand with fresh local produce. Local artwork, hardwood floors, and sleek furnishings create an understated interior—a perfect backdrop for oysters on the half shell or duck with black-currant sauce. There's an extensive wine list, and the bread basket has warm offerings from Berkshire Mountain Bakery. The frequent evening jazz may seem ear-splittingly loud if you aren't a fan. [$] *Average main: $23* ✉ *10 Castle St.* ☎ *413/528–5244* 🌐 *www.castlestreetcafe.com* ⏲ *Closed Tues. No lunch.*

$$ B&B/INN 🏨 **Wainright Inn.** Built in 1766 as the Troy Tavern & Inn, this lovely lodging has two wraparound porches leading into an antiques-filled parlor and dining room where the sideboards are filled with fresh flowers and objets d'art. **Pros:** great four-course breakfast; walking distance to downtown; lots of charm. **Cons:** Main Street traffic; no room TVs. [$] *Rooms from: $169* ✉ *518 S. Main St.* ☎ *413/528–2062* 🌐 *www.wainwrightinn.com* 🛏 *10 rooms, 2 suites* 🍽 *Breakfast.*

THE ARTS

Mahaiwe Performing Arts Center. Catch a performance by Arlo Guthrie or Bela Fleck at the Mahaiwe Performing Arts Center. This stunning 1905 theater offers a year-round schedule of music, dance, and film, with performances that range from famed country stars to stand-up comedians. ✉ *14 Castle St.* ☎ *413/528–0100* 🌐 *www.mahaiwe.org.*

SPORTS AND THE OUTDOORS

BICYCLING

The region's terrain is tremendously varied, and it tends to be hilly, but the Berkshires are relatively uncongested and extremely popular for biking, affording cycling enthusiasts of all abilities miles of great riding. The Ashuwillticook (pronounced *Ash*-oo-will-ti-cook) Rail Trail runs from the Pittsfield–Cheshire town line north up through Adams. Partly paved, it traces the old rail line and passes through rugged woodland and alongside Cheshire Lake. This is also a great venue for strolling, jogging, in-line skating, and cross-country skiing. The Berkshires Visitors Bureau distributes a free Berkshire Bike Touring Route, which is a series of relatively short excursions along area roads.

Ashuwillticook Rail Trail. Passing through the Hoosic River Valley, walkers and cyclists enjoy the paved 11-mile Ashuwillticook Rail Trail. ⊠ *Rte. 8, Lanesboro* ☎ *413/442–8928.*

HIKING

A 90-mile swath of the Appalachian Trail cuts through the Berkshires. You'll also find hundreds of miles of trails elsewhere throughout the area's forests and parks.

Appalachian Trail. If you've always dreamed of hiking the Appalachian Trail, consider this moderately strenuous 45-minute hike. At the top of the trail is Ice Gulch, a gorge so deep and cold that there is often ice in it even in summer. Follow the Ice Gulch ridge to the shelter and a large flat rock from which you can see a wide panorama of the valley. ⊠ *Lake Buel Rd.* ⊕ *www.appalachiantrail.org.*

Bartholomew's Cobble. This rock garden beside the Housatonic River (the Native American name means "river beyond the mountains") is a National Natural Landmark with 5 miles of hiking trails passing through fields of wildflowers. The 277-acre site has a visitor center and museum, in addition to the state's largest cottonwood trees. ⊠ *105 Weatogue Rd., Sheffield* ☎ *413/229–8600* ⊠ *$5* ☉ *Daily dawn–dusk.*

Monument Mountain. For great views with minimal effort, hike Monument Mountain, famous as a spot for literary inspiration. Nathaniel Hawthorne and Herman Melville trekked it on August 5, 1850, and sought shelter in a cave when a thunderstorm hit. There they discussed ideas that would become part of a novel called *Moby-Dick*. While poet William Cullen Bryant stayed in the area, he penned a lyrical poem, "Monument Mountain," about a lovesick Mohican maiden who jumped to her death from the cliffs. Feel like hiking? An easy 2.5-mile loop is reachable via a parking lot. ⊠ *U.S. 7, near Rte. 102* ☎ *413/298– 3239* ⊕ *www.thetrustees.org.*

SKI AREAS

Catamount Ski Area. With a 1,000-foot vertical drop, Catamount Ski Area is ideal for family skiing. It has some of the most varied terrain in the Berkshires. There are 34 trails served by six lifts, plus three terrain parks for snowboarders and others. The Sidewinder, an intermediate cruising trail, is more than 1 mile from top to bottom. There's also lighted nighttime boarding and skiing. ⊠ *3290 Rte. 23, South Egremont* ☎ *413/528– 1262, 413/528–1262 snow conditions* ⊕ *www.catamountski.com.*

Ski Butternut. With the longest quad lift in the Berkshires, Ski Butternut is good for skiers of all levels. For snowboarders there are top-to-bottom terrain parks and a beginner park, and eight lanes are available for snow tubing. For downhill skiing, only a steep chute or two interrupt the mellow terrain on 22 trails. Eleven lifts, including four carpet lifts, keep traffic spread out. Ski and snowboard lessons are available. ✉ *380 State Rd.* ☎ *413/528–2000, 413/528–4433 ski school, 800/438–7669 snow conditions* ⊕ *www.skibutternut.com.*

SHOPPING
ANTIQUES
The Great Barrington area, including the small towns of Sheffield and South Egremont, has the Berkshires' greatest concentration of antiques stores. Some shops are open sporadically, and many are closed on Tuesday.

Elise Abrams Antiques. Elise Abrams Antiques sells fine antique china, glassware, and furniture. ✉ *11 Stockbridge Rd.* ☎ *413/528–3201* ⊕ *www.eliseabramsantiques.com.*

Great Barrington Antiques Center. At the Great Barrington Antiques Center, 30 dealers crowd onto one floor selling Oriental rugs, vintage furniture, and smaller decorative pieces. ✉ *964 S. Main St., U.S. 7* ☎ *413/644–8848* ⊕ *www.greatbarringtonantiquescenter.com.*

FOOD
Bizalion. This French specialty food shop carries imported cheeses, cured meats, and olive oils from local producers (who also sell their wares to fancy restaurants in New York City and Martha's Vineyard). Bizalion doubles as an informal eatery where the small menu features appealing sandwiches, including a combination of arugula, pine nuts, prosciutto, goat cheese, and olive oil on toasted bread. ✉ *684 Main St.* ☎ *413/644–9988* ⊕ *www.bizalions.com.*

Blueberry Hill Farm. Blueberries are ripe for the picking in late July and August. Bring your own container and they'll be priced at $2.50 per pound. ✉ *100 East St., Mount Washington* ☎ *413/528–1479* ⊕ *www.austinfarm.com* 🎫 *Free* ☽ *Late July and Aug., weekends 9–5.*

Boardman Farm. This farm offers fresh vegetables, including sweet corn, squash, pumpkins, and more. It's open all day, every day, from mid-July to Thanksgiving. ✉ *64 Hewins St., Sheffield* ☎ *413/229–8554.*

Howden Farm. Pick raspberries from mid-August through mid-October and pumpkins from late September through October. ✉ *303 Rannapo Rd., Sheffield* ☎ *413/229–8481* ⊕ *www.howdenfarm.com* ☽ *Mid-Aug.–mid-Oct., daily 11–5; mid-Oct–end Oct., weekends 11–5.*

Taft Farms. Taft Farms has raspberries from early July through mid-October, and pick-your-own pumpkins from September through October. ✉ *119 Park St. N* ☎ *413/528–1515* ⊕ *www.taftfarms.com* ☽ *Early July–Oct., daily 8–6.*

5

STURBRIDGE AND THE PIONEER VALLEY

A string of historic settlements lines the majestic Connecticut River, the wide and winding waterway that runs through Western Massachusetts. The bustling city of Springfield, known for its family-friendly attractions and museums, along with a cluster of college towns and quaint, rural villages, is part of the Pioneer Valley, which formed the western frontier of New England from the early 1600s until the late 1900s.

Educational pioneers came to this region and created a wealth of major colleges including Mount Holyoke (the first college in the country for women), Amherst, Smith, Hampshire, and the University of Massachusetts. Northampton and Amherst serve as the valley's cultural hubs today; both have become increasingly desirable places to live, drawing former city dwellers who relish the ample natural scenery, sophisticated cultural venues, and lively dining and shopping.

SPRINGFIELD

90 miles west of Boston; 30 miles north of Hartford, Connecticut.

Springfield, easily accessed from Interstates 90 and 91, is the busy hub of the Pioneer Valley. Known as the birthplace of basketball (the game was devised by Canadian gym instructor James Naismith in 1891 as a last-ditch attempt to keep a group of unruly teenagers occupied in winter), the city has a cluster of fine museums and family attractions.

GETTING HERE AND AROUND

Springfield is roughly the center of Massachusetts, which means it's easily accessible by bus, train, or Interstates 90 and 91. Parts of Springfield are walkable, but you're better off with a car, or using the PVTA local bus routes.

ESSENTIALS

Visitor Information Greater Springfield Convention & Visitors Bureau
✉ *1441 Main St.* ☎ *413/787–1548, 800/723–1548* ⊕ *www.valleyvisitor.com.*
Sturbridge Area Tourist Association ✉ *380 Main St., Sturbridge* ☎ *800/628–8379, 508/347–2761* ⊕ *www.sturbridgetownships.com.*

EXPLORING

FAMILY

Fodor'sChoice
★

Naismith Memorial Basketball Hall of Fame. Along the banks of the Connecticut River, this 80,000-square-foot facility is dedicated to Canadian phys-ed instructor Dr. James Naismith, who invented the game here in 1891 during his five years at Springfield's YMCA Training Center. It includes a soaring domed arena where you can practice jumpers, walls of inspirational quotes, dozens of interactive exhibits, and video footage and interviews with former players. The Honors Rings pay tribute to the hall's nearly 300 enshrinees. It's easy to find—just look for the 15-story spire with an illuminated basketball on top. ✉ *1000 W. Columbus Ave.* ☎ *413/781–6500, 877/446–6752* ⊕ *www.hoophall. com* 🎟 *$20* ⊗ *Sun.–Fri. 10–4, Sat. 10–5.*

FAMILY

Six Flags New England. Containing more than 160 rides and shows, this massive attraction is the region's largest theme park and water park. Rides include Batman: The Dark Knight and the Bizarro Superman Ride,

Sturbridge and the Pioneer Valley

VERMONT

Winchendon

Baldwinville

Northfield

Shelburne
Falls

Turners Falls

Orange   Athol

Greenfield

Millers Falls

Deerfield

Montague

Locks Village

New Salem

Barre

South Deerfield

Sunderland

Shutesbury

Wheately

North Hatfield

North Amherst

University
of Massachusetts

Amherst

Quabbin
Reservoir

Hatfield

Amherst College

South Amherst

Northampton

Hampshire
College

Smith College

Belchertown

Easthampton

South Hadley

Lake
Lashaway

Granby

Ware

East Brookfield

Mount Holyoke College

Westover
Air Force Base

Warren

Quaboag
Pond

Southampton

Holyoke

Bondsville

THE PIONEER VALLEY

Three Rivers

Old Sturbridge
Village

Chicopee

Palmer

Fiskdale

Wilbraham

W. Springfield

Sturbridge

Springfield

Holland

Hamilton Reservoir

Agawam

East Longmeadow

Longmeadow

Mashapaug Pond

Congamond
Lakes

Sherwood Manor   CONNECTICUT

0   5 mi

0   5 km

Stafford Springs

which is more than 20 stories tall and has a top speed of 77 mph. ✉ *1623 Main St., Agawam* ☎ *413/786–9300* ⊕ *www.sixflags.com/ newengland* 🎟 *$60* ⊙ *Hrs vary.*

QUICK BITES

La Fiorentina Pastry Shop. Springfield's South End is the home of a lively Little Italy with some excellent restaurants, as well as La Fiorentina Pastry Shop, which has been doling out heavenly pastries and coffees since the 1940s. ✉ *883 Main St.* ☎ *413/732–3151* ⊕ *www.lafiorentinapastry.com* ⊙ *Mon.–Sat. 8–6, Sun. 8–2.*

FAMILY **Springfield Museums.** One of the most ambitious cultural venues in New England, this complex includes four impressive facilities, all for one admission price. The must-see **George Walter Vincent Smith Art Museum** houses a fascinating private art collection that includes 19th-century American paintings by Frederic Church and Albert Bierstadt. A Japanese antiquities room is filled with armor, textiles, and porcelain, as well as carved jade and rock-crystal snuff bottles.

The **Museum of Fine Arts** has paintings by Paul Gauguin, Claude Monet, Pierre-Auguste Renoir, Edgar Degas, Winslow Homer, and J. Alden Weir, as well as 18th-century American paintings and contemporary works by Georgia O'Keeffe, Frank Stella, and George Bellows. Rotating exhibits are open throughout the year. The **Springfield Science Museum** has an Exploration Center of touchable displays, the oldest operating planetarium in the United States, an extensive collection of stuffed and mounted animals, dinosaur exhibits, and the African Hall, through which you can take an interactive tour of that continent's flora and fauna.

The **Museum of Springfield History** tells the story of the town's manufacturing heritage. Springfield was home to the former Indian Motorcycle Company, and the museum has a rich collection of Indian bikes and memorabilia. Also on the grounds is the free **Dr. Seuss National Memorial Sculpture Garden,** an installation of bronze statues depicting scenes from Theodor Geisel's famously whimsical children's books. Born in Springfield in 1904, Geisel was inspired by the animals at Forest Park Zoo, where his father served as director. The statues include a four-foot-tall Lorax, one of his most popular creations. ✉ *220 State St.* ☎ *413/263–6800* ⊕ *www.springfieldmuseums.org* 🎟 *$15* ⊙ *Tues.–Sat. 10–5, Sun. 11–5.*

FAMILY **Zoo in Forest Park and Education Center.** At this leafy, 735-acre retreat, hiking paths wind through the trees, paddleboats navigate Porter Lake, and hungry ducks float on a small pond. The zoo, where Theodore Geisel—better known as Dr. Seuss—found inspiration for his children's books, is home to nearly 200 animals, from black bears and bobcats to lemurs and wallabies. It's manageable in size, and spotting animals in the exhibits is fairly easy, which makes this an especially good stop for families with small children. Another plus: you can purchase small bags of food from the gift shop and feed many of the animals. Leave time to explore the park after you finish the zoo. ✉ *302 Sumner Ave.* ☎ *413/733–2251* ⊕ *www.forestparkzoo.org* 🎟 *$8.50* ⊙ *Weekdays 10–4, Weekends 10–5.*

Costumed historians are part of the 19th-century Old Sturbridge Village.

OFF THE BEATEN PATH

Old Sturbridge Village. Modeled on an early-19th-century New England town, Old Sturbridge Village is a re-creation of a 1790–1840s-era village with more than 40 historic buildings moved here from other towns. Guides wearing period costumes demonstrate home-based crafts like spinning, weaving, and shoemaking. There are several industrial buildings, including a working sawmill. In season, take an informative stagecoach ride, or cruise along the Quinebaug River while you learn about river life in 19th-century New England and catch a glimpse of ducks, geese, turtles, and other local wildlife. ✉ *1 Old Sturbridge Village Rd.* ☎ *508/347–3362, 800/733–1830* 🌐 *www.osv.org* 🎫 *$24* 🕒 *Apr.–late Oct., daily 9:30–5; late Oct.–Mar., Tues.–Sun. 9:30–4.*

WHERE TO EAT

$$ CAJUN

🍴 **Big Mamou.** If you're craving creole food, this casual joint serves up some seriously good Louisiana cuisine. Owner-chef Wayne Booker stands behind the kitchen counter, and his hometown recipes, like sausage and chicken ya-ya (chicken breast wrapped around andouille sausage with creole spices) never fail to satisfy. Other favorites include shrimp-and-sausage jambalaya, barbecue pulled pork, and meat loaf. Added bonus: you can bring your own bottle. [$] *Average main: $15* ✉ *63 Liberty St.* ☎ *413/732–1011* 🌐 *www.chefwaynes-bigmamou.com* ✍ *Reservations not accepted* 🕒 *No dinner Sun.*

$ VIETNAMESE

🍴 **Pho Saigon.** A little out of the way, this tastefully understated eatery serves up some of the area's most authentic Vietnamese cuisine at wallet-pleasing prices. Enjoy the made-from-scratch soups and the shrimp cakes with shredded yams. There are lots of vegetarian options, as well as house specialties like the delectable fried soft-shell crab or the "happy pancake," a rice-batter crepe stuffed with shrimp and chicken. [$] *Average main: $10* ✉ *400 Dickinson St.* ☎ *413/781–4488* 🌐 *www.phosaigonspringfield.com* ⊗ *Closed Wed.*

$$ GERMAN Fodor's Choice ★ 🍴 **Student Prince.** Housed in an old fort, the dark-wood-paneled Student Prince (or the Fort, as the locals call it) is home to one of the largest beer stein and corkscrew collections in the country. Fried Camembert and a few salads notwithstanding, this is a large menu of meats: beef, chicken, seafood, veal, lamb, pork, and sausage. The main attractions here are the German dishes like *hoppel poppel* ("farmer's omelet," with eggs, onion, potato, bacon, and hot dogs), *jaeger schnitzel* (veal steak), sauerbraten served with potato dumplings and cabbage, *eisbein* (pig knuckle), and some especially good sauerkraut. In winter, try the *weisswurst* (sausage made with veal and fresh pork bacon). **■ TIP→ Lunch specials include three courses for under $10.** [$] *Average main: $19* ✉ *8 Fort St.* ☎ *413/788–6628* 🌐 *www.studentprince.com.*

WHERE TO STAY

$$ B&B/INN 🏨 **Naomi's Inn.** This elegantly restored house in a residential neighborhood has three individually decorated suites, all with lush comfort and artistic flair. **Pros:** elegantly designed; deluxe linens and other fabrics; warm and knowledgeable hosts. **Cons:** near the hospital, so you may hear sirens. [$] *Rooms from: $160* ✉ *20 Springfield St.* ☎ *413/433–6019, 888/762–6647* 🌐 *www.naomisinn.net* 🛏 *3 suites* 🍽 *Breakfast.*

$$ B&B/INN Fodor's Choice ★ 🏨 **The Publick House.** Step back in time at this rambling 1771 inn, where the guest rooms have wide plank floors, period antiques and reproductions, and canopy beds. **Pros:** Colonial ambience and architecture; historical significance; log fires and candlelight throughout. **Cons:** rattling pipes; thin walls; small bathrooms. [$] *Rooms from: $139* ✉ *277 Main St., Sturbridge* ☎ *508/347–3313, 800/782–5425* 🌐 *www.publickhouse.com* 🛏 *14 rooms, 3 suites in main inn* 🍽 *No meals.*

SOUTH HADLEY

12 miles north of Springfield.

Nestled in the heart of Pioneer Valley, this small, quiet college town, with a cluster of Main Street cafés and stores, is surrounded by rolling hills and farmlands. It's best known for the Mount Holyoke College Art Museum, one of the finest in the region.

GETTING HERE AND AROUND

With Bradley International Airport and the Springfield Amtrak station to the south, South Hadley is reasonably convenient. You can walk around Mount Holyoke campus, but you'll need to drive to get most anywhere else.

EXPLORING

Mount Holyoke College. Founded in 1837, Mount Holyoke was the first women's college in the United States. Among its alumnae are poet Emily Dickinson and playwright Wendy Wasserstein. The handsome wooded campus, encompassing two lakes and lovely walking or riding trails, was landscaped by Frederick Law Olmsted. ✉ *50 College St.* ☎ *413/538–2000* 🌐 *www.mtholyoke.edu.*

Mount Holyoke College Art Museum. Next to the college greenhouse, this museum contains some 15,000 works, including Asian, European, and American paintings and sculpture, as well as rotating exhibits. ✉ *Lower Lake Rd. and Church Street* ☎ *431/538–2245* 🌐 *www.mtholyoke.edu* 🎫 *Free* 🕑 *Tues.–Fri. 11–5, weekends 1–5.*

WHERE TO EAT AND STAY

$$$ ECLECTIC Fodor's Choice ★ 🍴 **Food 101 Bar & Bistro.** There's nothing basic about this popular, oh-so-calm, candle-lighted eatery across from the Mount Holyoke campus. Dishes are complicated but mostly successful: try the lobster risotto, the upscale *pommes frites* (french fries) with spicy ketchup and wasabi mayonnaise, the pan-seared sea scallops with cauliflower risotto, or the beet, chèvre, and mâche salad in warm curry oil. This spot is a magnet for foodies, yuppies, and college students on their parents' tab. [$] *Average main: $25* ✉ *19 College St.* ☎ *413/535–3101* 🌐 *www.food101bistro.com* 🕑 *Closed Mon. No lunch weekends.*

$$ B&B/INN 🏨 **Daniel Stebbins House Bed & Breakfast.** Within walking distance of downtown and Mount Holyoke, this 1795 Federal-style inn has been elegantly renovated to include four second-floor guest rooms, all with period antiques, fine reproductions, and gas fireplaces. **Pros:** the most elegant choice in town; lush linens and bed coverings; pretty landscaping. **Cons:** thin walls and close quarters. [$] *Rooms from: $135* ✉ *25 Woodbridge St.* ☎ *413/533–2149* 🌐 *www.danielstebbinsbedandbreakfast.com* 🛏 *4 rooms* 🍽 *Breakfast.*

SHOPPING

The Odyssey Bookshop. In addition to stocking 50,000 new and used titles, the Odyssey Bookshop has readings and book signings by locally and nationally known authors. ✉ *9 College St.* ☎ *413/534–7307* 🌐 *www.odysseybks.com.*

NORTHAMPTON

10 miles northeast of South Hadley.

The cultural center of Western Massachusetts is without a doubt the city of Northampton (nicknamed "Noho"), whose vibrant downtown is packed with interesting eateries, lively clubs, and offbeat boutiques. The city attracts artsy types, academics, activists, lesbians and gays, and just about anyone else seeking the culture and sophistication of a big metropolis but the friendliness and easy pace of a small town.

GETTING HERE AND AROUND

Northampton is served by buses from nearby Springfield's train station, although most people will probably arrive by car on Interstate 91. Downtown is crossed by Routes 5, 9, and 10, and walking to most downtown locations is not only possible, but an excellent way to spend an afternoon. Local PVTA buses are also available.

ESSENTIALS

Visitor Information Greater Northampton Chamber of Commerce ✉ *99 Pleasant St.* ☎ *413/584–1900, 800/238–6869* 🌐 *www.explorenorthampton.com.*

5

EXPLORING

Calvin Coolidge Presidential Library and Museum. Opened in 1894, Romanesque-style Forbes Library is one of the city's most distinguished buildings. The Hosmer Gallery on the upper floor has some artwork, but the main draw is the Calvin Coolidge Presidential Library and Museum, within the Forbes Library. Northampton was the 30th president's Massachusetts home, where he practiced law and served as mayor from 1910 to 1911. Some of his papers and memorabilia are collected here, at the only public library in the United States to hold a presidential collection. ✉ *20 West St.* ☎ *413/587–1011* 🌐 *www.forbeslibrary.org* 🕒 *Mon. and Wed. 3–9, Tues. and Thurs. 1–5.*

QUICK BITES

Herrell's Ice Cream. On the lower level of Thorne's Marketplace, Herrell's Ice Cream is famous for its chocolate pudding, vanilla malt, and cinnamon nutmeg flavors, as well as its delicious homemade hot fudge. ✉ ***8 Old South St.*** ☎ ***413/586–9700*** 🌐 **www.herrells.com.**

Smith College. The nation's largest liberal arts college for women opened its doors in 1875 (thanks to heiress Sophia Smith). Renowned for its School of Social Work, Smith has a long list of distinguished alumnae, among them activist Gloria Steinem, chef Julia Child, and writer Margaret Mitchell. One of the most serene campuses in New England, Smith is also a leading center of political and cultural activity. The on-campus Lyman Plant House is worth a visit. The flourishing **Botanic Garden of Smith College** covers the entire 150-acre campus. ✉ *College La.* 🌐 *www.smith.edu.*

Smith College Museum of Art. A floor of skylighted galleries, an enclosed courtyard, and a high-tech library make up this museum, where highlights of the permanent collection include European masterworks by Paul Cézanne, Degas, Auguste Rodin, and Georges Seurat, as well as works by woman artists like Mary Cassatt and Georgia O'Keeffe. ✉ *Brown Fine Arts Center, 22 Elm St., at Bedford Terrace* ☎ *413/585–2760* 🌐 *www.smith.edu/artmuseum* 🎟 *$5* 🕒 *Tues.–Sat. 10–4, Sun. noon–4.*

William Cullen Bryant Homestead. About 20 miles northwest of Northampton, in the scenic hills west of the Pioneer Valley, is the country estate of the 19th-century poet and author William Cullen Bryant. Although the house is closed to visitors, the 195-acre grounds overlooking the Westfield River Valley are a great venue for bird-watching, cross-country skiing, and picnics. ✉ *207 Bryant Rd., Cummington* ☎ *413/634–2244* 🌐 *www.thetrustees.org* 🎟 *Free* 🕒 *Grounds daily sunrise–sunset.*

WHERE TO EAT

$$ ITALIAN

🍴 **Mulino's Restaurant.** In sleek quarters (which also contain the upstairs Bishop's Lounge), this modern trattoria carefully prepares Sicilian-inspired, home-style Italian food. You'll rarely taste a better carbonara sauce this side of the Atlantic, but don't overlook the melt-in-your-mouth veal saltimbocca. Portions are huge, and the wine list is extensive. Parents like to take their college kids here for a special night out. [$] *Average main: $17* ✉ *41 Strong Ave.* ☎ *413/586–8900* 🌐 *mulinos-restaurant.com* 🕒 *No lunch.*

$$ AMERICAN 🍴 **Northampton Brewery.** In a rambling building in Brewster Court, this noisy and often-packed pub has extensive outdoor seating on a deck. The kitchen serves an array of sandwiches and tasty comfort food, including chicken-and-shrimp jambalaya and burgers with blue cheese and caramelized onions. [$] *Average main: $17* ✉ *11 Brewster Ct., near Hampton Ave.* ☎ *413/584–9903* 🌐 *www.northamptonbrewery.com* ✍ *Reservations not accepted.*

$$ ITALIAN Fodor's Choice ★ 🍴 **Spoleto.** A local favorite since the 1980s, Spoleto has moved a block away from its former location in the heart of downtown, but still offers a something-for-everyone menu: beef, chicken, and seafood dishes served with a dash of creative flair and flavor. You'll find pizza and pasta on the menu alongside the more adventurous house-made wild boar sausage or caramelized sea scallops. The Gorgonzola bread is a winner. [$] *Average main: $20* ✉ *1 Bridge St.* ☎ *413/586–6313* 🌐 *www.spoletorestaurants.com* 🕒 *No lunch.*

NIGHTLIFE AND THE ARTS

Diva's Nightclub. This spacious club serves the region's sizable lesbian and gay community with great music that fills the cavernous dance floor. ✉ *492 Pleasant St.* ☎ *413/586–8161* 🌐 *www.divasofnoho.com* 🕒 *Closed Sun. and Mon.*

Fitzwilly's. A reliable choice for a night out, Fitzwilly's draws a friendly mix of locals and tourists for drinks and tasty pub fare. Try the sliders. ✉ *23 Main St.* ☎ *413/584–8666* 🌐 *www.fitzwillys.com.*

Hugo's. A bit of a dive, the dimly lighted Hugo's has cheap beer, affordable pool, a rocking jukebox, and all the local color you'll ever want. ✉ *315 Pleasant St.* ☎ *413/387–6023.*

SPORTS AND THE OUTDOORS

FAMILY **Norwottuck Rail Trail.** Part of the Connecticut River Greenway State Park, this paved 10-mile path links Northampton with Belchertown by way of Amherst. Great for biking, rollerblading, jogging, and cross-country skiing, it runs along the old Boston & Maine Railroad route. Free trail maps are available. ✉ *Hwy. 9, at Damon Rd.* ☎ *413/586–8706.*

SHOPPING

Ten Thousand Villages. A collection of fair-trade crafts from around the world, this shop carries some very stylish jewelry, scarves, and handbags. ✉ *82 Main St.* ☎ *413/582–9338* 🌐 *northampton.tenthousandvillages.com.*

AMHERST

8 miles northeast of Northampton.

Fodor's Choice ★ One of the most visited spots in all of New England, Amherst is known for its scores of world-renowned authors, poets, and artists. The above-average intelligence quotient of its population is no accident, as Amherst is home to a trio of colleges—Amherst, Hampshire, and the University of Massachusetts. The high concentration of college-age humanity bolsters Amherst's downtown area, which includes a wide range of art galleries, music stores, and clothing boutiques.

GETTING HERE AND AROUND

Amherst is a stop on the Amtrak line, and the closest airline is Bradley International in Connecticut. Once you're in town, the PVTA buses are probably your best bet.

ESSENTIALS

Visitor Information Amherst Area Chamber of Commerce ⊠ *28 Amity St.* ☎ *413/253–0700* ⊕ *www.amherstarea.com.*

EXPLORING

Emily Dickinson Museum. The famed Amherst poet lived in this brick Federal-style home. The museum is outfitted with period accoutrements, including original wall hangings and lace curtains. Admission is by guided tour only, and the highlight is getting to see the sunlit bedroom where the poet wrote many of her works. To say that the tour guides are knowledgeable in Dickinson's story would be a massive understatement. Next door is **The Evergreens,** an imposing Italianate Victorian mansion in which Emily's brother Austin and his family resided for more than 50 years. ⊠ *280 Main St.* ☎ *413/542–8161* ⊕ *www.emilydickinsonmuseum.org* ⌲ *$12* ⊗ *Mar.–May and Sept.–mid-Dec., Wed.–Sun. 11–4; June–Aug., Wed.–Mon. 10–5.*

QUICK BITES

The Black Sheep. Newspapers and books are strewn about the tables at this funky downtown café specializing in creative sandwiches, salads, and soups. It's a great place to pick up on the college vibe, enjoy a cup of coffee, or take advantage of free Wi-Fi. ⊠ *79 Main St.* ☎ *413/253–3442* ⊕ *www.blacksheepdeli.com.*

FAMILY

Fodor's Choice ★

Eric Carle Museum of Picture Book Art. If you have kids in tow—or if you just love children's books art—"The Carle" is a must-see. This light-filled museum celebrates and preserves not only the works of renowned children's book author Eric Carle (who penned *The Very Hungry Caterpillar*), but also Maurice Sendak, Lucy Cousins, Petra Mathers, Tomie DePaola, and Leo and Diane Dillon. Puppet shows and storytelling events are part of the museum's ongoing calendar of events. Children are invited to create their own works of art in the museum's studio or read a few classics (or discover new authors) in the library. ⊠ *125 W. Bay Rd.* ☎ *413/658–1100* ⊕ *www.picturebookart.org* ⌲ *$9* ⊗ *Tues.–Fri. 10–4, Sat. 10–5, Sun. noon–5.*

Yiddish Book Center. Founded in 1980 by Aaron Lansky, this nonprofit organization has become a major force in the effort to preserve the Yiddish language and Jewish culture, by rescuing over 1 million Yiddish books that would otherwise have been lost. Built in 1997 on the campus of Hampshire College, the center is housed in a split-roof building that resembles a cluster of houses in a traditional Eastern European shtetl, or village. Inside, a contemporary space contains more than 100,000 books, a kosher dining room, and a visitor center with changing exhibits. ⊠ *1021 West St.* ☎ *413/256–4900* ⊕ *www.yiddishbookcenter.org* ⌲ *$8* ⊗ *Apr.–Oct., Sun.–Fri. 10–4; Nov.–Mar., weekdays 10–4.*

WHERE TO EAT AND STAY

$$ ✕ **Bub's Bar-B-Q.** This rib joint, open for more than three decades, is
BARBECUE one of the best in the state. Maybe it's the tangy, homemade sauce, or
maybe it's side dishes like wilted collard greens, orange-glazed sweet
potatoes, black-eyed corn, and spicy ranch beans. Most likely, it's the
heaping platters of fall-off-the-bone ribs and pulled pork. There's plenty
of outdoor seating when the weather cooperates. $ *Average main: $14*
⊠ *676 Amherst Rd., Sunderland* ☎ *413/548–9630* ⊕ *www.bubsbbq.*
com ☙ *Closed Mon. No lunch Tues.–Fri.*

$$ ✕ **Judie's.** Since 1977, academic types have crowded around small tables
AMERICAN on the glassed-in porch, ordering traditional dishes like grilled chicken
Fodor'sChoice with lobster ravioli, steak and potatoes, seafood gumbo, and probably
★ the best bowl of French onion soup the town has to offer. Your best
bet? Try the more creative popover specials in flavors like gumbo and
shrimp scampi. The atmosphere is hip and artsy; a painting covers each
tabletop. $ *Average main: $17* ⊠ *51 N. Pleasant St.* ☎ *413/253–3491*
⊕ *www.judiesrestaurant.com* ⟡ *Reservations not accepted.*

$ 🛏 **Allen House Inn.** Meticulous attention to detail distinguishes this late-
B&B/INN 19th-century inn owned by a husband-and-wife team. **Pros:** lots of
Fodor'sChoice charm and elegance; great linens; free parking. **Cons:** rooms chock-full
★ of ornate furnishings may be a bit much for some; tiny baths. $ *Rooms*
from: $95 ⊠ *599 Main St.* ☎ *413/253–5000* ⊕ *www.allenhouse.com*
⤵ *14 rooms* ⦿ *Breakfast.*

NIGHTLIFE AND THE ARTS

Amherst Brewing Company. Head to the ABC for its lounge, game room,
and vast selection of beers brewed on the premises. ⊠ *10 University Dr.*
☎ *413/253–4400* ⊕ *www.amherstbrewing.com.*

The Harp. This small but cozy Irish tavern hosts live music on Thursday
afternoon and Friday night. ⊠ *163 Sunderland Rd.* ☎ *413/548–6900*
⊕ *www.theharp.net.*

SHOPPING

Atkins Farms. An institution in the Pioneer Valley, these farms are surrounded by apple orchards and gorgeous views of the Holyoke Ridge.
The market sells produce, baked goods, and specialty foods. Take a
stroll around the outside to find an ice cream shop. ⊠ *1150 West St.*
☎ *413/253–9528* ⊕ *www.atkinsfarms.com.*

DEERFIELD

10 miles northwest of Amherst.

In Deerfield a horse pulling a carriage clip-clops past perfectly maintained
18th-century homes, neighbors tip their hats to strangers, kids play ball in
fields by the river, and the bell of the impossibly beautiful brick church peals
from a white steeple. This is the perfect New England village, though not
without a past darkened by tragedy. Its original Native American inhabitants, the Pocumtucks, were all but wiped out by deadly epidemics and a
war with the Mohawks. English pioneers eagerly settled into this frontier
outpost in the 1660s and 1670s, but two bloody massacres at the hands of
the Native Americans and the French caused the village to be abandoned
until 1707, when construction began on the buildings that remain today.

Historic Deerfield is one of many places in the region to experience America's past through living history.

GETTING HERE AND AROUND

While you can take the train to Springfield, the most direct public transportation to Deerfield is a Peter Pan bus. If you're driving, take Route 10 from the south or Route 2 from the west. Aside from walking around Historic Deerfield, however, you won't get far without a car.

EXPLORING

Fodor's Choice
★

Historic Deerfield. Although it has a turbulent past, this village now basks in a genteel aura. With 52 buildings on 93 acres, Historic Deerfield provides a vivid glimpse into 18th- and 19th-century America. Along the tree-lined main street are 12 museum houses, built between 1720 and 1850; three are open to the public on self-guided tours, and the remainder can be seen by guided tours that begin on the hour. At the **Wells-Thorn House,** various rooms depict life as it changed from 1725 to 1850. The adjacent **Frary House** has arts and crafts from the 1900s on display; the attached Barnard Tavern was the main meeting place for Deerfield's villagers. Also of note is the **Williams House,** the stately home for an affluent early New England couple.

The **Flynt Center of Early New England Life** contains needlework, textiles, and clothing dating back to the 1600s. There's a visitor center at Hall Tavern at 80 Old Main Street. ■ TIP→ Plan at least one full day at Historic Deerfield. ⊠ *Old Main St.* ☎ *413/775–7214* ⊕ *www.historic-deerfield.org* ✉ *$14* ⊙ *Apr.–Dec., daily 9:30–4:30; Jan.–Mar., Flynt Center weekends 9:30–4:30.*

QUICK
BITES

Richardson's Candy Kitchen. The name is no joke—the back half of this store is a kitchen where you can see delectable chocolates being made. A short drive from Historic Deerfield, Richardson's Candy Kitchen makes and sells luscious cream-filled chocolates, truffles, and other handmade confections. Try an almond acorn. ⊠ *500 Greenfield Rd.* ☎ *413/772-0443* ⊕ *www.richardsonscandy.com.*

FAMILY **Magic Wings Butterfly Conservatory & Gardens.** This glass conservatory glitters with more than 4,000 butterflies. Kids love the butterfly nursery, where newborns first take flight. Outside is a three-season garden filled with plants that attract local species. There's also a snack bar, gift shop, and butterfly-themed restaurant. ⊠ *281 Greenfield Rd., South Deerfield* ☎ *413/665-2805* ⊕ *www.magicwings.net* 🖃 *$14* ⊙ *Daily 9–5.*

WHERE TO EAT AND STAY

$$$$
AMERICAN
Fodor's Choice
★

✕ **Chandler's.** One of the area's best restaurants, Chandler's has a candle-lit interior that gives the expansive space an intimate feel. Start out with a pan-seared crab cake with fennel, basil, and lemon juice, then enjoy entrées like grilled salmon with artichoke risotto and duck breast in a blood-orange demi-glace. Even though this is fine dining, Chandler's also has an excellent children's menu. The staff could not be more attentive. 🛈 *Average main: $30* ⊠ *Yankee Candle Village, 25 Deerfield Rd., South Deerfield* ☎ *413/665-1277* ⊕ *chandlers.yankeecandle.com* ⊙ *No dinner Mon. and Tues.*

$$$$
B&B/INN

🛏 **Deerfield Inn.** Period wallpaper and handsome fireplaces add a feeling of authenticity to this historic 1884 inn and tavern. **Pros:** gorgeous architecture; tavern oozes atmosphere; surrounded by museums. **Cons:** bathrooms are basic and tiny; sounds travel through halls (and into rooms). 🛈 *Rooms from: $245* ⊠ *81 Old Main St.* ☎ *413/774-5587, 800/926-3865* ⊕ *www.deerfieldinn.com* 🛌 *23 rooms* 🍴 *Breakfast.*

SHELBURNE FALLS

18 miles northwest of Deerfield.

A tour of New England's fall foliage wouldn't be complete without a trek across the famed Mohawk Trail, a 63-mile section of Highway 2 that runs past picturesque Shelburne Falls. The community, separated from neighboring Buckland by the Deerfield River, is filled with little art galleries and surrounded by orchards, farm stands, and sugar houses.

GETTING HERE AND AROUND

Shelburne Falls lies on Route 2, otherwise known as the Mohawk Trail, useful not only for driving through town, but heading off to the Berkshires as well.

EXPLORING

Bridge of Flowers. From April to October, an arched, 400-foot trolley bridge is transformed into this promenade bursting with color and a wide variety of flowers. ⊠ *Water St.* ☎ *413/625-2544* ⊕ *bridgeofflowersmass.org.*

SPORTS AND THE OUTDOORS

RAFTING

Zoar Outdoor. White-water rafting, canoeing, and kayaking in the Class II–III rapids of the Deerfield River are all popular summer activities. From April to October, Zoar Outdoor conducts kid-friendly rafting trips along 10 miles of challenging rapids, as well as floats along gentler sections of the river. Zipline tours are also offered. ⊠ *7 Main St., off Rte. 2, Charlemont* ☏ *800/532–7483* ⊕ *www.zoaroutdoor.com.*

SHOPPING

Sidehill Farm. This farm sells yogurt and cheese (year-round) and raw milk (April through November) from grass-fed cows. Vegetables and fruits are generally available throughout the year. ⊠ *58 Forget Rd., Hawley* ☏ *413/625–0011* ⊕ *www.sidehillfarm.net.*

6

CONNECTICUT

WELCOME TO CONNECTICUT

TOP REASONS TO GO

★ **Country Driving:** Follow the rolling, twisting roads of Litchfield County, such as U.S. 7, U.S. 44, and Route 63, through the charmed villages of Kent, Salisbury, and Litchfield.

★ **Maritime History:** The village of Mystic is packed with interesting nautical attractions related to Connecticut's rich seafaring history.

★ **Urban Exploring:** Anchored by Yale University, downtown New Haven now (finally) buzzes with hip restaurants, smart boutiques, and acclaimed theaters.

★ **Literary Giants:** In the same historic Hartford neighborhood, you can explore the homes—and legacies—of Mark Twain and Harriett Beecher Stowe.

★ **Antiques Hunting:** You'll find numerous fine shops, galleries, and auction houses specializing in antiques all over the state. Two standout towns: Woodbury and Putnam.

1 Southwestern Connecticut. Enjoy a mix of moneyed bedroom communities and small, dynamic cities, with miles of gorgeous Long Island Sound shoreline. Shop Greenwich Avenue's boutiques, catch a show at the Westport Playhouse, and end with a nightcap in Norwalk's lively SoNo neighborhood.

2 Hartford and the Connecticut River Valley. Get your arts-and-culture fix in Hartford with a visit to the historic Old State House, the Connecticut Science Center, or the Wadsworth Atheneum. Drive south through the Connecticut River Valley for a scenic, small-town New England experience.

GETTING ORIENTED

Connecticut's coastline runs east–west, from the towns of Stonington and Mystic at the Rhode Island border, down to Greenwich in the southwest corner of the state. Head north from the Greenwich vicinity to the hills of Litchfield County in the northwest, bordered by New York and Massachusetts. In the center of the state, you'll find the capital, Hartford: travel south from here to tour the small towns of the Connecticut River Valley. Northeast of Hartford is the less-traveled Quiet Corner, whose rural towns abut Massachusetts and Rhode Island.

6

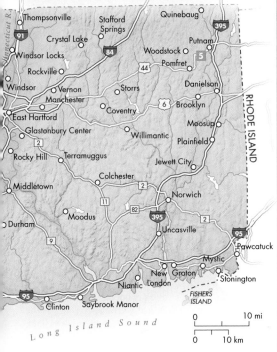

3 The Litchfield Hills. Litchfield County's pastoral countryside is the perfect setting for an autumn weekend: nestle into a romantic country inn, leaf peep around Lake Waramaug, and hunt for undiscovered treasures in the antiques shops of Woodbury.

4 New Haven, Mystic, and the Coast. Wander through Yale's campus or visit the dinosaurs at the Peabody Museum of Natural History before dining at a chic New Haven eatery. Head east along the coastline for unspoiled seaside towns or roll the dice and head inland to the casinos at Foxwoods or Mohegan Sun.

5 The Quiet Corner. The scenic drive along Route 169 through Brooklyn toward Woodstock affords glimpses of authentic Colonial homes, rolling hills, and bucolic views. Try the local wines at Sharpe Hill Vineyard in Pomfret or go antiquing in downtown Putnam.

Updated
by Bethany
Cassin
Beckerlegge

You can travel from just about any point in Connecticut to any other in less than two hours, yet the land you traverse — fewer than 60 miles top to bottom and 100 miles across — is as varied as a drive across the country.

Connecticut's 253 miles of shoreline blows salty sea air over such beach communities as Old Lyme and Stonington. Patchwork hills and peaked mountains fill the state's northwestern corner, and once-upon-a-time mill towns line rivers such as the Housatonic. Connecticut has seemingly endless farmland in the northeast, where cows might outnumber people, as well as chic New York City bedroom communities such as Greenwich and New Canaan, where boutique shopping bags seem to be the dominant species.

Just as diverse as the landscape are the state's residents, who numbered more than 3.5 million at last count. There really is no such thing as the definitive Connecticut Yankee. Yes, families can trace their roots back to the 1600s, when Connecticut was founded as one of the 13 original colonies, but the state motto is "He who transplanted still sustains." And so the face of the Nutmegger is that of the family from Naples now making pizza in New Haven and the farmer in Norfolk whose land dates back five generations, the grandmother in New Britain who makes the state's best pierogi and the ladies who lunch in Westport, the celebrity nestled in the Litchfield Hills and the Bridgeport entrepreneur working to close the gap between Connecticut's struggling cities and its affluent suburbs.

A unifying characteristic of the Connecticut Yankee, however, is inventiveness. Nutmeggers are historically known for both their intellectual abilities and their desire to have a little fun. The nation's first public library was opened in New Haven in 1656 and its first statehouse built in Hartford in 1776; Tapping Reeve opened the first law school in Litchfield in 1784; and West Hartford's Noah Webster published the first dictionary in 1806. On the fun side, note that Lake Compounce in Bristol was the country's first amusement park; Bethel's P. T. Barnum staged the first three-ring circus; and the hamburger, the lollipop, the Frisbee, and the Erector Set were all invented here.

Not surprisingly, Nutmeggers have a healthy respect for their history. For decades, Mystic Seaport, which traces the state's rich maritime past, has been the premier tourist attraction. Today, however, Foxwoods Casino near Ledyard, run by the Mashantucket Pequots, is North America's largest casino, drawing more than 40,000 visitors per day. Thanks in large part to these lures, not to mention rich cultural attractions, cutting-edge restaurants, shopping outlets, first-rate lodgings, and abundant natural beauty (including 92 state parks and 30 state forests), tourism is one of the state's leading industries. Exploring Connecticut reveals a small state that's big in its appeal.

PLANNING

WHEN TO GO

Connecticut is lovely year-round, but fall and spring are particularly appealing times to visit. A fall drive along the state's back roads or the Merritt Parkway (a National Scenic Byway) is a memorable experience. Leaves of yellow, orange, and red color the fall landscape, but the state blooms in springtime, too—town greens are painted with daffodils and tulips, and dogwoods punctuate the rich green countryside. Summer, of course, is prime time for most attractions; travelers have the most options then but also plenty of company, especially along the shore.

PLANNING YOUR TIME

The Nutmeg State is a confluence of different worlds, where farm country meets country homes, and fans of the New York Yankees meet Down-Easter Yankees. To get the best sense of this variety, start in the scenic Litchfield Hills, where you can see historic town greens and trendy cafés. If you have a bit more time, head south to the wealthy southwestern corner of the state and then over to New Haven, with its cultural pleasures. If you have five days or a week, take in the capital city of Hartford and the surrounding towns of the Connecticut River Valley and head down to the southeastern shoreline.

GETTING HERE AND AROUND

AIR TRAVEL

People visiting Connecticut from afar can fly into New York City, Boston, or Providence, or smaller airports in or near Hartford and New Haven.

Airport Contacts Bradley International Airport ⊠ *11 Schoephoester Rd., Windsor Locks* ☎ *860/292–2000* ⊕ *www.bradleyairport.com.*
Tweed New Haven Airport ⊠ *155 Burr St., New Haven* ☎ *203/466–8888* ⊕ *www.flytweed.com.*

CAR TRAVEL

The interstates are the quickest routes between many points in Connecticut, but they can be busy and ugly. From New York City, head north on Interstate 95, which hugs the Connecticut shoreline into Rhode Island, or, to reach the Litchfield Hills and Hartford, head north on Interstate 684, then east on Interstate 84. From central New England, go south on Interstate 91, which bisects Interstate 84 in

Hartford and Interstate 95 in New Haven. From Boston, take Interstate 95 south through Providence or take the Massachusetts Turnpike west to Interstate 84. Interstate 395 runs north–south from southeastern Connecticut to Massachusetts.

Often faster because of less traffic, the historic Merritt Parkway (Route 15) winds between Greenwich and Middletown; U.S. 7 and Route 8, extending between Interstate 95 and the Litchfield Hills; Route 9, which heads south from Hartford through the Connecticut River Valley to Old Saybrook; and scenic Route 169, which meanders through the Quiet Corner.

TRAIN TRAVEL

Amtrak runs from New York to Boston, stopping in Stamford, Bridgeport, and New Haven before heading north through Hartford and several other towns or east to Old Saybrook and Mystic.

Train Contacts Amtrak ☎ *800/872–7245* ⊕ *www.amtrak.com.*
Metro-North Railroad ☎ *877/690–5114* ⊕ *www.mta.info.*

RESTAURANTS

Call it the fennel factor or the arugula influx: southern New England has witnessed a gastronomic revolution. Preparation and ingredients reflect the culinary trends of nearby Manhattan and Boston; indeed, the quality and diversity of Connecticut restaurants now rival those of such sophisticated metropolitan areas. Although traditional favorites remain—such as New England clam chowder, buttery lobster rolls, and fish-and-chips—sliced duck is wrapped in phyllo and served with a ginger-plum sauce (the orange glaze decidedly absent); and everything from lavender to fresh figs is used to season and complement dishes. Dining is increasingly international: you'll find Indian, Vietnamese, Thai, Malaysian, South American, and Japanese restaurants—even Spanish tapas bars—in cities and suburbs. The farm-to-table movement influences what appears on your plate in many establishments, with conscientious chefs partnering up with local farms to provide the best seasonal ingredients. The one drawback of this turn toward sophistication is that finding a dinner entrée for less than $10 is difficult. *Prices in the reviews are the average cost of a main course at dinner or, if dinner is not served, at lunch.*

HOTELS

Connecticut has plenty of business-oriented chain hotels and low-budget motels, along with many of the more unusual and atmospheric inns, resorts, bed-and-breakfasts, and country hotels that are typical of New England. You'll pay dearly for rooms in summer on the coast and in autumn in the hills, where thousands of visitors peek at the changing foliage. Rates are lowest in winter, but so are the temperatures, making spring the best season for bargain seekers. *Prices in the reviews are the lowest cost of a standard double room in high season.*

TOURS

Tour Contacts Connecticut Art Trail. This self-guided tour takes you through 17 museums and historic sites statewide where you can experience European and American art, culture, and history. ✉ *Hartford* ⊕ *www.arttrail.org* ⊠ *$25.* **Connecticut Freedom Trail.** More than 120 historic sights in 50 towns associated with the state's African American heritage can be found on the trail. ☎ *860/256–2800* ⊕ *www.ctfreedomtrail.ct.gov.* **Connecticut Wine Trail.** The wine trail travels among 25 member vineyards. ⊕ *www.ctwine.com.*

VISITOR INFORMATION

Visitor Contacts Connecticut Commission on Culture & Tourism ⊠ *1 Constitution Plaza, 2nd Fl., Hartford* ☎ *888/288–4748* ⊕ *www.ctvisit.com.*

SOUTHWESTERN CONNECTICUT

Southwestern Connecticut is a rich swirl of old New England and new New York. This region consistently reports the highest cost of living and most expensive homes of any area in the country. Its bedroom towns are home primarily to white-collar executives; some still make the hour-plus dash to and from New York, but many drive to Stamford, which is reputed to have more corporate headquarters per square mile than any other U.S. city.

Venture away from the wealthy communities, and you'll discover cities struggling in different stages of urban renewal: Stamford, Norwalk, Bridgeport, and Danbury. These four have some of the region's best cultural and shopping opportunities, but the economic disparity between Connecticut's troubled cities and its upscale towns is perhaps most visible in Fairfield County.

ESSENTIALS

Visitor Information Visit Fairfield County ☎ *860/767–8273* ⊕ *www.visitfairfieldcountyct.com.*

GREENWICH

28 miles northeast of New York City, 64 miles southwest of Hartford.

You'll have no trouble believing that Greenwich is one of the wealthiest towns in the United States when you drive along U.S. 1 (called Route 1 by the locals, as well as West Putnam Avenue, East Putnam Avenue, and the Post Road). The streets here are lined with ritzy car dealers, posh boutiques, oh-so-chic restaurants, and well-heeled, well-to-do residents. Though real estate prices have come down, the median home price in Greenwich hovers around $1.4 million. So bring your platinum card.

GETTING HERE AND AROUND

If you are traveling north from New York City, Greenwich will be the first town in Connecticut once you cross the state border. It's easily accessible from Interstate 95 or the Merritt Parkway if you are coming by car, and is also serviced by Metro-North commuter trains.

EXPLORING

YANKEE DOODLE DANDY

Norwalk is the home of Yankee Doodle Dandies: in 1756, Colonel Thomas Fitch threw together a motley crew of Norwalk soldiers and led them off to fight at Ft. Crailo, near Albany, New York. Supposedly, Norwalk's women gathered feathers for the men to wear as plumes in their caps to give them some appearance of military decorum. Upon the arrival of these foppish warriors, one of the British officers sarcastically dubbed them "macaronis"—slang for dandies. The name caught on, and so did the song.

FAMILY **Audubon Greenwich.** Established in 1942 as the National Audubon Society's first nature-education facility, this center in northern Greenwich is the best location in the area for birdwatching. During the Fall Hawk Watch Festival you can spot more than16 species of hawks, eagles, and vultures. Other annual events include the Spring into Audubon Festival and the bird counts in summer and winter. The center is filled with "real-life" interactive exhibits, galleries, and classrooms, a wildlife observation room, and a deck that offers sweeping views of wildlife activity. Outside are 7 miles of hiking trails passing through 285 acres of woodlands, wetlands, and meadows. ✉ *613 Riversville Rd.* ☎ *203/869–5272* 🌐 *greenwich.audubon.org* 🎟 *$3* 🕒 *Daily 9–5.*

FAMILY Fodor's Choice ★ **Bruce Museum of Arts and Science.** The owner of this 19th-century home, wealthy textile merchant Robert Moffat Bruce, bequeathed it to the town of Greenwich in 1908 with the stipulation that it be used "as a natural history, historical, and art museum." Today this diversity remains, reflected in the museum's collection of some 15,000 objects in fine and decorative arts, natural history, and anthropology, including paintings by Childe Hassam, sculptures by Auguste Rodin, and stained glass by Dale Chihuly. Permanently on display is the spectacular mineral collection. Kids enjoy the touchable meteorite and glow-in-the-dark minerals, as well as the fossilized dinosaur tracks. ✉ *1 Museum Dr., off I–95* ☎ *203/869–0376* 🌐 *www.brucemuseum.org* 🎟 *$7, free Tues.* 🕒 *Tues.–Sat. 10–5, Sun. 1–5.*

WHERE TO EAT AND STAY

$$$$ SEAFOOD 🍴 **Elm Street Oyster House.** Locals come here for outstanding oysters and the freshest fish in town. The colorful artwork gives the slightly cramped dining room a certain cheerfulness; expect a lively crowd on weekends. Menu standouts include the varied selection of fresh oysters from all over the country, classic lobster rolls, and shellfish stew with shrimp, scallops, squid, and clams. [$] *Average main: $34* ✉ *11 W. Elm St.* ☎ *203/629–5795* 🌐 *www.elmstreetoysterhouse.com.*

$$$ ASIAN FUSION 🍴 **Tengda Asian Bistro.** This hopping Asian-fusion hot spot offers consistently good Japanese cuisine with European accents. In a century-old house, the dining room has a rustic yet industrial feel, with exposed brick cozying up next to sculpted steel. Tuck into the crispy firecracker shrimp, sample the spicy mango chicken, or dive into a fresh lobster tempura roll while sipping an exotic cocktail from the diverse drink list. [$] *Average main: $22* ✉ *21 Field Point Rd.* ☎ *203/625–5338.*

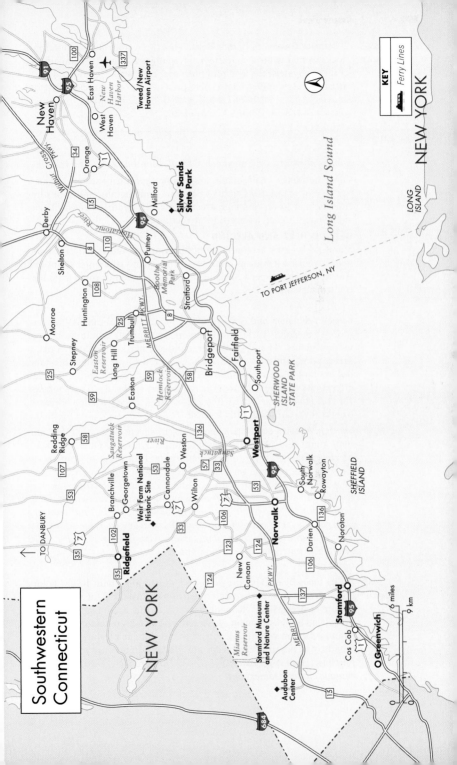

Southwestern Connecticut

NEW YORK

NEW YORK

Long Island Sound

LONG ISLAND

KEY
Ferry Lines

TO PORT JEFFERSON, NY

New Haven Harbor

Tweed/New Haven Airport

East Haven

West Haven

Orange

Milford

Silver Sands State Park

Derby

Shelton

Purney

Stratford

Boothe Memorial Park

Bridgeport

Fairfield

Southport

SHERWOOD ISLAND STATE PARK

Monroe

Huntington

Stepney

Long Hill

Trumbull

Easton

Easton Reservoir

Hemlock Reservoir

Redding Ridge

Saugatuck Reservoir

Westport

Weston

Cannondale

Wilton

South Norwalk

Rowayton

SHEFFIELD ISLAND

Branchville

Georgetown

Weir Farm National Historic Site

Norwalk

Darien

Noroton

Ridgefield

New Canaan

Stamford Museum and Nature Center

Stamford

Cos Cob

Greenwich

Audubon Center

Mianus Reservoir

Saugatuck River

Housatonic River

MERRITT PKWY

MERRITT PKWY

TO DANBURY

TO PORT JEFFERSON, NY

New Haven

Middlesex Pkwy

6 miles

6 km

$$$$ ⓣ **Delamar Greenwich Harbor Hotel.** This three-story luxury hotel just
HOTEL blocks from downtown Greenwich resembles a villa on the Italian Riviera. **Pros:** waterfront location; posh spa; easy walk to downtown restaurants and shopping. **Cons:** super pricey. Ⓢ *Rooms from: $309* ⊠ *500
Steamboat Rd.* ☎ *203/661–9800, 866/335–2627* ⊕ *www.thedelamar.
com* ⤳ *74 rooms, 8 suites* ⏃⃝ *No meals.*

STAMFORD

6 miles northeast of Greenwich, 38 miles southwest of New Haven.

Office buildings, chain hotels, and major department stores dominate
the face of Stamford. Quality restaurants, nightclubs, and shops line
Atlantic and lower Summer streets, however, and have given the city
some much-needed leisure-time attractions.

GETTING HERE AND AROUND

Stamford is easily accessible from Interstate 95 and the Merritt Parkway. It is also a major rail hub for Metro-North commuter trains and
Amtrak; the high-speed Acela makes a stop here on its route from Boston to Washington, D.C.

EXPLORING

Bartlett Arboretum and Gardens. This 91-acre arboretum is home to
more than 2,000 varieties of annuals, perennials, wildflowers, and
woody plants. There's also a greenhouse, marked ecology trails, a
pretty pond, and a boardwalk through a red maple swamp. Brilliant,
bold colors make the wildflower garden stunning in spring. Sunday
afternoons are the time to visit for guided walks. ⊠ *151 Brookdale
Rd., off High Ridge Rd.* ☎ *203/322–6971* ⊕ *www.bartlettarboretum.
org* ⊠ *$6* ☉ *Grounds daily 9–dusk.*

FAMILY **Stamford Museum and Nature Center.** Oxen, sheep, pigs, and other animals roam this 118-acre New England farmstead. Once the estate
of Henri Bendel, the property includes a Tudor-revival stone mansion housing exhibits on natural history, art, and Americana. Also
here are a planetarium with a 22-inch research telescope—perfect
for stargazing—and nature trails winding through the woods. ⊠ *39
Scofieldtown Rd.* ☎ *203/322–1646* ⊕ *www.stamfordmuseum.org*
⊠ *Grounds $10, planetarium and observatory each an additional
$3* ☉ *Grounds daily 9–5; planetarium May–Labor Day, Fri. 8:30
pm–10:30 pm; Sept.–Apr., Fri. 8 pm–10 pm.*

WHERE TO EAT

$$ ✕ **City Limits Diner.** This art deco–style diner, alive with bright colors
AMERICAN and shiny chrome, likes to describe its food as running the gamut from
"haute to homespun." Roughly translated, this is the place for everything from hot pastrami on rye served with an egg cream to pan-roasted
Atlantic salmon with Israeli couscous and shiitake mushrooms. All the
breads, pastries, and ice cream are made in-house and available for
purchase. Ⓢ *Average main: $15* ⊠ *135 Harvard Ave.* ☎ *203/348–7000*
⊕ *www.citylimitsdiner.com.*

NIGHTLIFE AND THE ARTS

NIGHTLIFE

Tigín Pub. Stop in for the perfect pint at this Irish pub with an authentic atmosphere. ⊠ *175 Bedford St.* ☎ *203/353–8444* ⊕ *www. tiginirishpub.com.*

THE ARTS

Stamford Center for the Arts. Plays, comedy shows, musicals, and film festivals are presented in the Palace Theatre. ⊠ *61 Atlantic St.* ☎ *203/325–4466* ⊕ *www.stamfordcenterforthearts.org.*

FAMILY **Stamford Symphony Orchestra.** Performing from October to April, this orchestra offers a popular family concert series. ⊠ *263 Tresser Blvd.* ☎ *203/325–1407* ⊕ *www.stamfordsymphony.org.*

NORWALK

14 miles northeast of Stamford, 47 miles northeast of New York City.

In the 19th century, Norwalk became a major New England port and also manufactured pottery, clocks, watches, shingle nails, and paper. It later fell into neglect, in which it remained for much of the 20th century. In the early 1990s, however, Norwalk's coastal business district was the focus of major redevelopment, which has turned it into a hot spot for trendy shopping, culture, and dining, much of it along the main drag, Washington Street. The stretch is known as SoNo (South Norwalk), and in the evening it is the place to be seen if you're young, single, and living it up in Fairfield County.

GETTING HERE AND AROUND

If you are traveling by car, Norwalk is most easily reached by Interstate 95 and the Merritt Parkway. Metro-North commuter trains also stop here. Exit at the South Norwalk stop to put yourself within walking distance of SoNo shops, restaurants, and bars.

EXPLORING

Lockwood-Mathews Mansion Museum. This ornate tribute to Victorian decorating was built in 1864 as the summer home of LeGrand Lockwood. It remains one the oldest (and finest) surviving Second Empire–style country homes in the United States; it's hard not to be impressed by its octagonal skylighted rotunda and more than 50 rooms of gilt, frescoes, marble, intricate woodwork, and etched glass. ⊠ *295 West Ave.* ☎ *203/838–9799* ⊕ *lockwoodmathewsmansion.com* 🎟 *$10* ☉ *Apr.–Jan., Wed.–Sun. noon–4.*

FAMILY
Fodor's Choice
★

Maritime Aquarium at Norwalk. This 5-acre waterfront center, the cornerstone of the SoNo district, explores the marine life and maritime culture of Long Island Sound. The aquarium's more than 20 habitats include some 1,000 creatures indigenous to the sound, including stately loggerhead sea turtles, happy harbor seals, and the dozens of jellyfish that perform their ghostly ballet in "Jellyfish Encounter." You can see toothy bluefish and sand tiger sharks in the 110,000-gallon Ocean Beyond the Sound aquarium. The center also operates an Environmental Education Center and marine-mammal cruises aboard the *Oceanic,* and has a towering IMAX theater. ⊠ *10 N. Water St.*

Norwalk's Maritime Aquarium is a great way to get eye-to-eye with animals endemic to Long Island Sound, like loggerhead turtles.

☎ *203/852–0700* ⊕ *www.maritimeaquarium.org* ✉ *$19.95* ☉ *Labor Day–June, daily 10–5; July–Labor Day, daily 10–6.*

Sheffield Island and Lighthouse. Adjacent to the Stewart B. McKinney National Wildlife Refuge, this 3-acre park is a prime spot for a picnic. The 1868 lighthouse has four levels, 10 rooms to explore. Clambakes are held Thursday evenings from June through September. To get here, take a ferry from the Hope Dock. ⊠ *Hope Dock, Washington and N. Water Sts.* ☎ *203/838–9444* ✉ *Round-trip ferry service and lighthouse tour $22* ☉ *Ferry Memorial Day–Labor Day, weekdays at 11 and 3, weekends at 11, 2, and 3:30.*

FAMILY **Stepping Stones Museum for Children.** The ColorCoaster, a 27-foot-high mechanical toy in constant motion, is the centerpiece of this hands-on museum. Visit the Energy Lab, where kids can learn about wind, water, and solar power while splashing around the extensive water-play area. For kids three and under there's Tot Town, where they can learn about animals on Old MacDonald's Farm. ⊠ *Mathews Park, 303 West Ave.* ☎ *203/899–0606* ⊕ *www.steppingstonesmuseum.org* ✉ *$15* ☉ *Memorial Day–Labor Day, daily 10–5; Labor Day–Memorial Day, Tues.–Sun. 10–5.*

WHERE TO EAT AND STAY

$$$ ✕ **Match.** In the heart of SoNo, Match uses fresh local ingredients in its
MODERN inventive American dishes. High ceilings, exposed brick, and industrial
AMERICAN fixtures provide a sleek, urban look. Indulge in one of the signature
Fodor'sChoice wood-fired pizzas straight out of the oven, or savor the light-as-air gnoc-
★ chi in a beef, pork, and veal ragu. Complete your meal with a melt-in-your-mouth hot chocolate soufflé topped with raspberries and vanilla

gelato. $ *Average main: $28* ✉ *98 Washington St.* ☎ *203/852–1088* ⊕ *www.matchsono.com* ⊘ *No lunch.*

$$$$ 🛏 **Hotel Zero Degrees Norwalk.** This ultramodern boutique lodging is a
HOTEL great addition in a region where lackluster chain hotels abound. **Pros:** best choice in the area; tasty restaurant; free shuttle service. **Cons:** noise from the nearby train tracks; not walking distance to downtown. $ *Rooms from: $230* ✉ *353 Main Ave.* ☎ *203/750–9800* ⊕ *www. hotelzerodegrees.com/hotels/norwalk* ⏎ *96 rooms* ⏐❍⏐ *Breakfast.*

NIGHTLIFE AND THE ARTS
Barcelona. This wine bar serves exceptional Spanish-style tapas. ✉ *63 N. Main St.* ☎ *203/899–0088* ⊕ *www.barcelonawinebar.com.*

RIDGEFIELD

11 miles north of New Canaan, 43 miles west of New Haven.

In Ridgefield you'll find a rustic Connecticut atmosphere within an hour of Manhattan. The inviting town center is a largely residential sweep of lawns and majestic homes, with a feel more reminiscent of the peaceful Litchfield Hills, even though the town is in the northern reaches of Fairfield County.

GETTING HERE AND AROUND
From Interstate 95 or the Merritt Parkway, head north on Route 7 to Route 33 to reach Ridgefield or take Metro-North to the Branchville station.

EXPLORING
Fodor's Choice   **Aldrich Contemporary Art Museum.** Cutting-edge art is not necessarily
★ what you'd expect to find in a stately 18th-century structure that once served as a general store, a post office, and, for 35 years, a church. Nicknamed "Old Hundred," this historic building is just part of the vast facility, which includes a 25,000-square-foot exhibition space that puts its own twist on traditional New England architecture. The white-clapboard-and-granite structure houses 12 galleries, a screening room, a sound gallery, a 22-foot-high project space for large installations, a 100-seat performance space, and an education center. Outside is a 2-acre sculpture garden. ■ TIP➔ **Stop by on Tuesday, when admission is free.** ✉ *258 Main St.* ☎ *203/438–4519* ⊕ *www.aldrichart.org* 🖘 *$10* ⊘ *Tues.–Sun. noon–5.*

WHERE TO EAT
$$$ ✕ **Luc's Café and Restaurant.** A cozy bistro set inside a stone building with
FRENCH low ceilings and closely spaced tables, Luc's takes full advantage of a handy location in Ridgefield's quaint downtown. The place charms patrons with carefully prepared food and low-key, friendly service. You can opt for a simple salade Niçoise or *croque monsieur* (hot ham and cheese) sandwich or enjoy a classic steak au poivre with a velvety Roquefort sauce and crispy frites. There's an extensive wine list, plus a range of aperitifs and single-malt whiskies. Enjoy live jazz on some evenings. $ *Average main: $22* ✉ *3 Big Shop La.* ☎ *203/894–8522* ⊕ *www.lucscafe.com* ⊘ *Closed Sun.*

6

WESTPORT

15 miles southeast of Ridgefield, 47 miles northeast of New York City.

Westport, an artists' community since the turn of the 20th century, continues to attract creative types. Despite commuters and corporations, the town remains more artsy and cultured than its neighbors.

GETTING HERE AND AROUND

You can reach Westport by car via Interstate 95 (Exit 17 will put you closest to the center of town and main shopping areas) or the Merritt Parkway. Metro-North also has two stops here, Westport (closer to town) and Greens Farms (farther east).

EXPLORING

Sherwood Island State Park. Summer visitors congregate at this state park, which has a 1½-mile sweep of sandy beach, two picnic areas on the water's edge, sports fields, and several food stands that are open seasonally. There's a parking fee Memorial Day to Labor Day. ✉ *Sherwood Island Connector* ☎ *203/226–6983* 🎫 *Free* ⏲ *Daily 8 am–sunset.*

WHERE TO EAT

$$$$ EUROPEAN

🍴 **Da Pietro's Restaurant.** This romantic storefront café serves a savory mix of northern Italian and southern French specialties lovingly prepared by chef-owner Pietro Scotti. Lobster pappardelle; sauteed sea scallops with mushroom risotto; and Paramesan-crusted salmon with linguine and pesto are all delicious choices. Save room for the warm chocolate-lava cake. [$] *Average main: $30* ✉ *36 Riverside Ave.* ☎ *203/454–1213* 🌐 *www.dapietros.com* ⏲ *Closed Sun. No lunch Sat.*

$$$ AMERICAN Fodor's Choice ★

🍴 **Dressing Room.** Beside the Wesport Country Playhouse, this pretheater favorite celebrates regional American, farm-to-table cuisine. Many ingredients are sourced locally; others come from prominent ranches and farms around the country. Highlights include baby back ribs served with an apple-cabbage slaw, and seasonal items like the Connecticut lobster succotash with fresh corn, zucchini, and roasted peppers. A huge fieldstone fireplace warms the rustic-chic dining room, with its sturdy ceiling beams and barn-board walls. [$] *Average main: $25* ✉ *27 Powers Ct.* ☎ *203/226–1114* 🌐 *www.dressingroomrestaurant.com* ⏲ *Closed Mon. No lunch Tues.*

THE ARTS

Levitt Pavilion for the Performing Arts. Enjoy an excellent series of mostly free summer concerts here that range from jazz to classical, folk to blues. ✉ *40 Jesup Rd.* ☎ *203/221–2153* 🌐 *www.levittpavilion.com.*

Westport Country Playhouse. Long associated with benefactors Joanne Woodward and Paul Newman, the venerable and intimate Westport Country Playhouse presents high-quality plays throughout the year. ✉ *25 Powers Ct.* ☎ *203/227–4177* 🌐 *www.westportplayhouse.org.*

Hartford and the Connecticut River Valley

HARTFORD AND THE CONNECTICUT RIVER VALLEY

Westward expansion in the New World began along the meandering Connecticut River. Dutch explorer Adrian Block first explored the area in 1614, and in 1633 a trading post was set up in what is now Hartford. Within five years, throngs of restive Massachusetts Bay colonists had settled in this fertile valley. What followed were more than three centuries of shipbuilding, shad hauling, and river trading with ports as far away as the West Indies and the Mediterranean.

Less touristy than the coast and northwest hills, the Connecticut River Valley is a swath of small villages and uncrowded state parks punctuated by a few small cities and a large one: the capital city of Hartford. South of Hartford, with the exception of industrial Middletown, genuinely quaint hamlets vie for attention with antiques shops, scenic drives, and romantic French restaurants and country inns.

ESSENTIALS

Visitor Information Central Regional Tourism District ✉ *1 Constitution Plaza, 2nd fl., Hartford* ☎ *860/787–9640* ⊕ *www.visitctriver.com.*

ESSEX

29 miles east of New Haven.

Essex, consistently named one of the best small towns in the United States, looks much as it did in the mid-19th century, at the height of its shipbuilding prosperity. So important to the young country was Essex's boat manufacturing that the British burned more than 40 ships here during the War of 1812. Gone are the days of steady trade with the West Indies, when the aroma of imported rum, molasses, and spices hung in the air. Whitewashed houses—many the former roosts of sea captains—line Main Street, which has shops that sell clothing, antiques, paintings and prints, and sweets.

GETTING HERE AND AROUND

The best way to reach Essex is by car; take Interstate 95 to Route 9 north.

EXPLORING

Connecticut River Museum. In an 1878 steamboat warehouse, this museum tells the story of the Connecticut River through maritime artifacts, interactive displays, and ship models. The riverfront museum even has a full-size working reproduction of the world's first submarine, the *American Turtle;* the original was built by David Bushnell in 1775 as a "secret weapon" to win the Revolutionary War. ✉ *67 Main St.* ☎ *860/767–8269* ⊕ *www.ctrivermuseum.org* 🎟 *$8* ⊙ *Tues. 11–5, Wed.–Sun. 10–5.*

SCENIC TRIP

Essex Steam Train and Riverboat. This ride offers some of the best views of the Connecticut River valley from 1920s-era coaches pulled by a vintage steam locomotive and an old-fashioned riverboat. The train, traveling along the Connecticut River through the lower valley, makes a 12-mile

Ride through the Connecticut River Valley on a vintage Essex Steam Train.

round-trip from Essex Station to Deep River Station; from there, if you wish to continue, you board the riverboat for a ride to East Haddam (the open promenade deck on the third level has the best views). ⊠ *Valley Railroad Company, 1 Railroad Ave.* ☎ *860/767–0103* ⊕ *www.essexsteamtrain.com* 🎟 *Train $17, train and boat $26* ⊙ *May–Dec., hrs vary.*

EAST HADDAM

15 miles north of Essex, 28 miles southeast of Hartford.

Fishing, shipping, and musket making were the chief enterprises at East Haddam, the only town in the state that occupies both banks of the Connecticut River. This lovely community retains much of its old-fashioned charm, most of it centered around its historic downtown.

GETTING HERE AND AROUND

The best way to reach East Haddam is by car. From Interstate 95, take Route 9 north to Route 82 east to Route 154 north.

EXPLORING

FAMILY

Fodor's Choice

★

Gillette Castle State Park. The outrageous 24-room oak-and-fieldstone hilltop castle, modeled after medieval castles of the Rhineland and built between 1914 and 1919 by the eccentric actor and dramatist William Gillette, is the park's main attraction. You can tour the castle and hike on trails near the remains of the 3-mile private railroad that chugged about the property until the owner's death in 1937. Gillette, who was born in Hartford, wrote two famous plays about the Civil War and was beloved for his play *Sherlock Holmes* (in which he performed the title role). In his will, he demanded that the castle not fall into the hands of "some blithering saphead who has no conception of where he is or with what surrounded." ⊠ *67 River Rd., off Rte. 82* ☎ *860/526–2336* ⊠ *Park free, castle $6* ۞ *Park daily 8–sunset.*

Fodor'sChoice **Goodspeed Opera House.** This magnificent 1876 Victorian-gingerbread
★ "wedding cake" theater on the Connecticut River—so called for all its turrets, mansard roof, and grand filigree—is widely recognized for its role in the preservation and development of American musical theater. Well over a dozen Goodspeed productions have gone on to Broadway, including *Annie.* Performances take place from April to early December. ⊠ *6 Main St.* ☎ *860/873–8668* ⊕ *goodspeed.org* ⊠ *Tours $5* ۞ *Tours June–Oct., Sat. at 11.*

MIDDLETOWN

15 miles northwest of East Haddam, 24 miles northeast of New Haven.

With its Connecticut River setting, easy access to major highways, and historic architecture, Middletown is a popular destination for recreational boaters and tourists alike. The town's High Street is an architecturally eclectic thoroughfare. Charles Dickens once called it "the loveliest Main Street in America" (Middletown's actual Main Street runs parallel to it a few blocks east).

GETTING HERE AND AROUND
Middletown is best reached by car. From Hartford, follow Interstate 91 south to Route 9 south. From the coast, take Interstate 95 to Route 9 north.

EXPLORING

FAMILY **Dinosaur State Park.** See some 500 tracks left by the dinosaurs that once roamed the area around this park north of Middletown. The tracks are preserved under a giant geodesic dome. You can even make plaster casts of tracks on a special area of the property; call ahead to learn what materials you need to bring. ⊠ *400 West St., east of I–91, Rocky Hill* ☎ *860/529–8423* ⊕ *www.dinosaurstatepark.org* ⊠ *$6* ۞ *Trails daily 9–4, exhibits Tues.–Sun. 9–4:30.*

Wesleyan University. Founded in 1831, Wesleyan University is one of the oldest Methodist institutions of higher education in the country. There are roughly 2,900 undergraduates, which gives Middletown a contemporary, college-town feel. Note the massive, fluted Corinthian columns of the 1828 Greek Revival Russell House at the corner of Washington Street, across from the pink Mediterranean-style Davison Art Center, built 15 years later. Farther on are gingerbreads, towering brownstones, Tudors, and Queen Annes. A few hundred yards up on Church Street, which intersects High Street, is the Olin Library. The 1928 structure was designed by Henry Bacon, the architect of the Lincoln Memorial. ⊠ *High St., 45 Wyllys Ave.* ☎ *860/685–2000* ⊕ *www.wesleyan.edu.*

CLOSE UP

Connecticut's Historic Gardens

These extraordinary Connecticut gardens form Connecticut's Historic Gardens, a "trail" of natural beauties across the state. For more information on each of the gardens, visit ⊕ www.cthistoricgardens.org.

Bellamy-Ferriday House & Garden, Bethlehem. An apple orchard and a circa-1915 formal parterre garden that blossoms with peonies, roses, and lilacs are the highlights of this garden.

Butler-McCook House & Garden, Hartford. Landscape architect Jacob Weidenmann created a Victorian garden that's an amazing respite from downtown city life.

Florence Griswold Museum, Old Lyme. The gardens at the historic Florence Griswold Museum, once the home of a prominent Old Lyme family and then a haven for artists, have been restored to their 1910 appearance and feature hollyhocks and black-eyed Susans.

Glebe House Museum, Woodbury. Legendary British garden writer and designer Gertrude Jekyll designed only three gardens in the United States, and the one at the Glebe House Museum is the only one still in existence. The garden is a classic example of Jekyll's ideas of color harmonies and plant combinations; a hedge of mixed shrubs encloses a mix of perennials.

Harriet Beecher Stowe Center, Hartford. Connecticut's largest magnolia tree, a 100-year-old pink dogwood, an antique rose garden, a wildflower meadow, and a blue cottage garden are the highlights of the grounds.

Griswold Museum in Old Lyme

Hill-Stead Museum, Farmington. The centerpiece of the Hill-Stead Museum is a circa-1920 sunken garden enclosed in a yew hedge and surrounded by a wall of rough stone. At the center of the octagonal design is a summerhouse with 36 flowerbeds and brick walkways radiating outward.

Promisek Beatrix Farrand Garden, Bridgewater. The prolific Beatrix Farrand designed the garden at Promisek Beatrix Farrand Garden, which overflows with beds of annuals and perennials such as hollyhocks, peonies, and always-dashing delphiniums.

Roseland Cottage, Woodstock. At Roseland Cottage, the boxwood parterre garden includes 21 flowerbeds surrounded by boxwood hedges.

Webb-Deane-Stevens Museum, Wethersfield. This Colonial Revival garden is filled with such old-fashioned flowers as peonies, pinks, phlox, hollyhocks, and larkspur, as well as a profusion of roses.

6

Lyman Orchards. Looking for a quintessential New England outing? These orchards just south of Middletown are not to be missed. Get lost in the sunflower maze and then pick your own fruits and vegetables—berries, peaches, pears, apples, and even pumpkins, from June to October. ⊠ *Rtes. 147 and 157, Middlefield* ☎ *860/349–1793* ⊕ *www.lymanorchards.com* ☉ *Nov.–Aug., daily 9–6; Sept. and Oct., daily 9–7.*

WHERE TO EAT

$$
AMERICAN

✕ **O'Rourke's Diner.** Featured on the Food Network's *Diners, Drive-Ins and Dives,* this glass-and-steel classic is the place to go for top-notch diner fare, including creative specialties like the omelet stuffed with roasted portobello mushrooms, Brie, and asparagus. The steamed cheeseburgers are another favorite. Arrive early for lunch, as the lines are often out the door. $ *Average main: $13* ⊠ *728 Main St.* ☎ *860/346–6101* ⊕ *www.orourkesmiddletown.com* ☉ *No dinner.*

WHERE TO STAY

$$$
HOTEL

▣ **Inn at Middletown.** The inn is centrally located in a historic former National Guard Armory in the heart of downtown Middletown. **Pros:** close to Wesleyan campus and steps from downtown shopping; grand old building; large rooms. **Cons:** no real grounds to speak of; rather expensive on weekends when Wesleyan is in session. $ *Rooms from: $195* ⊠ *70 Main St.* ☎ *860/854–6300* ⊕ *www.innatmiddletown.com* ⤺ *88 rooms, 12 suites* ⦿| *No meals.*

NIGHTLIFE AND THE ARTS

THE ARTS

Wesleyan University Center for the Arts. See modern dance or a provocative new play, hear top playwrights and actors discuss their craft, or take in an art exhibit or concert at this college arts center. ⊠ *283 Washington Terr.* ☎ *860/685–3355* ⊕ *www.wesleyan.edu/cfa.*

NIGHTLIFE

Eli Cannon's. At last count, Eli Cannon's had more than 35 beers on draft. This cozy place also has an extensive selection of bottled beers. ⊠ *695 Main St.* ☎ *860/347–3547* ⊕ *www.elicannons.com.*

SHOPPING

Wesleyan Potters. There's more here than just pottery: jewelry, clothing, and weavings are also available from this nonprofit guild. ⊠ *350 S. Main St.* ☎ *860/347–5925* ⊕ *www.wesleyanpotters.com* ☉ *Wed.–Fri. 10–6, Sat. 10–4, Sun. noon–4.*

WETHERSFIELD

7 miles northeast of New Britain, 32 miles northeast of New Haven.

Wethersfield, a vast Hartford suburb, dates from 1634 and has the state's largest—and, some say, most picturesque—historic district, with more than 100 pre-1849 buildings. Old Wethersfield has the oldest firehouse in the state, the oldest historic district in the state, and the oldest continuously operating seed company. Today, this "old" community has new parks and new shops, but history is still its main draw.

GETTING HERE AND AROUND

Wethersfield is only a few miles south of Hartford, and most easily reached by car. From there, take Interstate 91 south to Route 3 south.

EXPLORING

Comstock Ferre & Co. Original tin signs still adorn the inviting post-and-beam buildings of the Comstock Ferre & Co., the country's oldest continuously operating seed company, founded in 1820. The company sells more than 800 varieties of seeds and more than 2,000 varieties of perennials, as well as special seed collections so that you can create your own magical moonlight, Italian herb, or shade garden. ✉ *263 Main St.* ☎ *860/571–6590* ⊕ *www.comstockferre.com* ☾ *Sun.–Fri. 10–4.*

Fodor's Choice **New Britain Museum of American Art.** An important stop for art lovers, ★ this 100-year-old museum's collection of more than 10,000 works from 1740 to the present focuses solely on American art. Among the treasures are paintings by John Singer Sargent, Winslow Homer, and Georgia O'Keeffe, as well as sculpture by Isamu Noguchi. Deserving of special note is the selection of Impressionist artists, including Mary Cassatt, William Merritt Chase, Childe Hassam, and John Henry Twachtman, as well as Thomas Hart Benton's five-panel mural *The Arts of Life in America*. The museum also has a café, a large shop, and a library of art books. ✉ *56 Lexington St., 8 miles west of Wethersfield, New Britain* ☎ *860/229–0257* ⊕ *www.nbmaa.org* 🎟 *$12, free Sat. 10–noon* ☾ *Mon.–Wed. and Fri. 11–5, Thurs. 11–8, Sat. 10–5, Sun. noon–5.*

Webb-Deane-Stevens Museum. For a true sample of Wethersfield's historic past, stop by the Joseph Webb House, the Silas Deane House, and the Isaac Stevens House, next door to each other along Main Street and all built in the mid-to-late 1700s. These well-preserved examples of Georgian architecture reflect their owners' lifestyles as, respectively, a merchant, a diplomat, and a tradesman. The Webb House, a registered National Historic Landmark, was the site of the strategy conference between George Washington and the French general Jean-Baptiste Rochambeau that led to the British defeat at Yorktown. ✉ *211 Main St., off I–91* ☎ *860/529–0612* ⊕ *www.webb-deane-stevens.org* 🎟 *$10* ☾ *May–Oct., Mon. and Wed.–Sat. 10–4, Sun. 1–4; Apr. and Nov., Sat. 10–4, Sun. 1–4; other times by appointment.*

HARTFORD

4 miles north of Wethersfield, 45 miles northwest of New London, 81 miles northeast of Stamford.

Midway between New York City and Boston, Hartford is Connecticut's capital city. Founded in 1635 on the banks of the Connecticut River, Hartford was at various times home to authors Mark Twain and Harriet Beecher Stowe, inventors Samuel and Elizabeth Colt, landscape architect Frederick Law Olmsted, and Ella Grasso, the first woman to be elected a state governor. Today Hartford, where America's insurance industry was born in the early 19th century, is poised for change, with a revitalized downtown core featuring a bustling convention center and top-notch science museum, the Connecticut Science Center. The city is a destination on the verge of discovery.

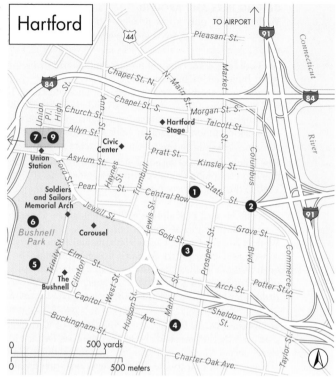

Hartford

GETTING HERE AND AROUND

Hartford is centrally located in the middle of the state. Two main highways meet here; Interstate 91 runs north–south from Western Massachusetts straight through Hartford and on to the Connecticut coastline. Interstate 84 runs generally east to west from Union at the northeast border with Massachusetts to near Danbury at the border of New York. Amtrak also has service to Hartford on its Northeast Regional line. Bradley International Airport in Windsor Locks, 15 minutes north of Hartford, offers flights to more than 30 destinations in the United States, Canada, and the Caribbean.

EXPLORING

TOP ATTRACTIONS

FAMILY **Children's Museum.** A life-size walk-through replica of a 60-foot sperm whale greets patrons at this museum. Located in West Hartford, the museum has a wildlife sanctuary and real-life images beamed in from NASA, plus an exhibit on rocks and fossils that will make a geologist out of your little one. ⊠ *950 Trout Brook Dr., 5 miles west of downtown, West Hartford* ☎ *860/231–2824* ⊕ *www.thechildrensmuseumct. org* ☜ *$14.75* ⊙ *Tues.–Sat. 9–4, Sun. 11–4.*

FAMILY **Connecticut Science Center.** This strikingly modern building, designed by
Fodor's Choice world-renowned architect César Pelli, houses 40,000 square feet of
★ exhibit space under a wavelike roof that appears to float over the structure. Dive into a black hole and examine the moon's craters in the Space
Exploration exhibit, race mini-sailboats and magnetic trains at Forces
in Motion, and discover your hidden athletic talents in the Sports Lab.
Kid Space is perfect for the three- to six-year-old crowd. Complete your
visit by taking in a movie in the 3-D digital theater. The café emphasizes locally sourced cuisine. ✉ *250 Columbus Blvd.* ☎ *860/724–3623*
⊕ *www.ctsciencecenter.org* 🎫 *$19* ⏱ *Tues.–Sun. 10–5.*

Harriet Beecher Stowe Center. Abolitionist and author Harriet Beecher
Stowe (1811–96) spent her final years at this 1871 Victorian Gothic
cottage, now a popular stop on the Connecticut Freedom Trail. The
center was built around the cottage, created as a tribute to the author
of the antislavery novel *Uncle Tom's Cabin.* Stowe's personal writing
table and effects are inside. ✉ *77 Forest St.* ☎ *860/522–9258* ⊕ *www.
harrietbeecherstowecenter.org* 🎫 *$10* ⏱ *Mon.–Sat. 9:30–5:30, Sun.
noon–5.*

Fodor's Choice **Mark Twain House and Museum.** Built in 1874, this building was the home
★ of Samuel Langhorne Clemens, better known as Mark Twain, until
1891. While he and his family lived in this 25-room Victorian mansion,
Twain published seven major novels, including *Tom Sawyer, Huckleberry Finn,* and *The Prince and the Pauper.* The home is one of only two
Louis Comfort Tiffany–designed domestic interiors open to the public.
A contemporary museum on the grounds presents an up-close look at
the author and shows an outstanding Ken Burns documentary on his
life. ✉ *351 Farmington Ave., at Woodland St.* ☎ *860/247–0998* ⊕ *www.
marktwainhouse.org* 🎫 *$16* ⏱ *Apr.–Dec., Mon.–Sat. 9:30–5:30, Sun.
noon–5:30; Jan.–Mar., Mon. and Wed.–Sat. 9:30–5:30, Sun. noon–5:30.*

Fodor's Choice **Wadsworth Atheneum Museum of Art.** With more than 50,000 artworks
★ and artifacts spanning 5,000 years, this is the nation's oldest public art
museum. The first American museum to acquire works by Salvador
Dalí and the Italian artist Caravaggio, it also houses 7,000 items documenting African-American history and culture in partnership with the
Amistad Foundation. Particularly impressive are the museum's baroque,
Impressionist, and Hudson River school collections. ✉ *600 Main St.*
☎ *860/278–2670* ⊕ *www.wadsworthatheneum.org* 🎫 *$10* ⏱ *Wed.–Fri.
11–5, weekends 10–5.*

WORTH NOTING

FAMILY **Bushnell Park.** Fanning out from the State Capitol building, this city park,
created in 1850, was the first public space in the country with natural
landscaping. The original designer, a Swiss-born landscape architect
and botanist named Jacob Weidenmann, planted 157 varieties of trees
and shrubs to create an urban arboretum. Kids love the Bushnell Park
Carousel (open May through September), intricately hand-carved in
1914 by the Artistic Carousel Company of Brooklyn, New York. An
oasis of green, the park has a pond and about 750 trees, including
four state-champion trees. ✉ *Asylum and Trinity Sts.* ☎ *860/232–6710*
⊕ *www.bushnellpark.org.*

Butler-McCook Homestead. Built in 1782, this home housed four generations of Butlers and McCooks until it became a museum in 1971. Inside is Hartford's oldest intact collection of art and antiques, including furnishings, family possessions, and Victorian-era toys that show the evolution of American tastes over nearly 200 years. The beautifully restored Victorian garden was originally designed by Jacob Weidenmann. ⊠ *396 Main St.* ☎ *860/522–1806* ⊕ *www. ctlandmarks.org* ⊡ *$7* ⊙ *Apr., Oct–Dec., Sat.–Sun. 11–4; May–Sept. Thurs.–Sun. 11–4.*

QUICK
BITES

Mozzicato–De Pasquale's Bakery, Pastry Shop & Caffé. Located in Hartford's Little Italy neighborhood along Franklin Avenue, this shop serves delectable Italian pastries in the bakery and espresso, cappuccino, and gelato in the café. ⊠ *329 Franklin Ave.* ☎ *860/296–0426* ⊕ *www.mozzicatobakery.com.*

Old State House. This Federal-style house with an elaborate cupola and roof balustrade was designed in the early 1700s by Charles Bulfinch, architect of the U.S. Capitol. It served as Connecticut's state capitol until a new building opened in 1879, then became Hartford's city hall until 1915. In the 1820 Senate Chamber, where everyone from Abraham Lincoln to George Bush has spoken, you can view a portrait of George Washington by Gilbert Stuart, and in the Courtroom you can find out about the trial of the *Amistad* Africans in the very place where it was first held. In summer, enjoy concerts and a farmers' market; don't forget to stop by the Museum of Natural and Other Curiosities. ⊠ *800 Main St.* ☎ *860/522–6766* ⊕ *www.ctosh.org* ⊡ *$6* ⊙ *Sept.–June weekdays 10–5; July and Aug., Tues.–Sat. 10–5.*

State Capitol. The gold-leaf dome of the State Capitol rises above Bushnell Park. Built in 1878, the building houses the state's executive offices and legislative chamber as well as historical memorabilia. On a tour, you can walk through the Hall of Flags, see a statue of Connecticut state hero Nathan Hale, and observe the proceedings of the General Assembly, when in session, from the public galleries. ⊠ *210 Capitol Ave.* ☎ *860/240–0222* ⊕ *www.cga.ct.gov/capitoltours* ⊡ *Free* ⊙ *Building weekdays 9–3. Tours given hourly, Sept.–June, weekdays 9:15–1:15; July and Aug., weekdays 9:15–2:15.*

OFF THE
BEATEN
PATH

Noah Webster House. This 18th-century farmhouse is the birthplace of the famed author (1758–1843) of the *American Dictionary.* Inside are Webster memorabilia and period furnishings; outside there is a garden planted with herbs, vegetables, and flowers that would have been available to the Websters when they lived here. ⊠ *227 S. Main St., West Hartford* ☎ *860/521–5362* ⊕ *www.noahwebsterhouse.org* ⊡ *$7* ⊙ *Thurs.–Mon. 1–4.*

WHERE TO EAT

$$
PIZZA ✕ **First and Last Tavern.** What looks to be a simple neighborhood joint south of downtown is actually one of the state's most hallowed pizza parlors, serving superb thin-crust pies (locals love the puttanesca) since 1936. The old-fashioned wooden bar in one room is jammed most evenings with suburbia-bound daily-grinders. The main dining

Connecticut's Victorian Gothic state capitol rises from Hartford's Bushnell Park.

room, which is just as noisy, has a brick outer wall covered with celebrity photos. $ *Average main: $18 ⊠ 939 Maple Ave.* ☎ *860/956–6000* ⊕ *www.firstandlasttavern.com* ⌕ *Reservations not accepted.*

$$$$
AMERICAN
Fodor's Choice
★

✕ **Max Downtown.** With its contemporary design, extensive array of martinis, and sophisticated cuisine, Max Downtown is a favorite with the city's well-heeled and a popular after-work spot. Creative entrées include panko-crusted ahi tuna with a pineapple-ginger glaze, jumbo shirmp and sea scallops with a summer vegetable succotash, and a wide range of perfectly prepared steaks with toppings like foie-gras butter and Maytag bleu cheese sauce. Desserts, such as the chocolate-chip ice cream cake or smores crème brûlée, are not to be missed. This restaurant is part of a small empire of excellent Hartford-area restaurants. $ *Average main: $40 ⊠ 185 Asylum St.* ☎ *860/522–2530* ⊕ *www.maxrestaurantgroup.com/downtown* ⌕ *Reservations essential* ⊘ *No lunch weekends.*

$$$
ITALIAN

✕ **Peppercorn's Grill.** This mainstay of Hartford's restaurant scene presents contemporary Italian cuisine in both a lively (colorful murals) and formal (white linens) setting. Enjoy house-made potato gnocchi, ravioli, and top-quality steaks, but save room for the warm chocolate bread pudding and the Valrhona chocolate cake. $ *Average main: $32 ⊠ 357 Main St.* ☎ *860/547–1714* ⊕ *www.peppercornsgrill.com* ⊘ *Closed Sun. No lunch Sat.*

$$$
ECLECTIC

✕ **Trumbull Kitchen.** Upbeat, hip, and casual, Trumbull Kitchen is the place to see and be seen. With leather-clad walls, a loft-style dining area overlooks the action below. The menu has an eclectic and global feel, serving selections such as Thai chicken wings, Québec cheddar-and-bacon fondue, Japanese noodle dishes, and pizzas. Main dishes might include perfectly grilled sirloin steaks, pan-roasted Stonington sea scallops, or perhaps seafood pad thai. $ *Average main: $27* ✉ *150 Trumbull St.* ☎ *860/493–7412* ⊕ *www.maxrestaurantgroup. com* ⊘ *No lunch Sun.*

WHERE TO STAY

$$$$ ⬚ **Hartford Marriott Downtown.** This upscale hotel is connected to the
HOTEL Connecticut Convention Center and conveniently located within walking distance of the Connecticut Science Center, the Wadsworth Atheneum, the Old State House, and other attractions. **Pros:** close to major attractions; in the heart of downtown. **Cons:** convenient location comes at a price. $ *Rooms from: $250* ✉ *200 Columbus Blvd.* ☎ *860/249–8000* ⊕ *www.marriott.com* ⇆ *401 rooms, 8 suites* ⦿*No meals.*

$$$$ ⬚ **Residence Inn Hartford-Downtown.** In the historic Richardson Build-
HOTEL ing, the all-suites Residence Inn is convenient to Pratt Street, Hartford Stage, and the Old State House. **Pros:** spacious rooms; great value; right in middle of downtown. **Cons:** cookie-cutter furnishings. $ *Rooms from: $229* ✉ *942 Main St.* ☎ *860/524–5550, 800/960–5045* ⊕ *www. marriott.com* ⇆ *120 suites* ⦿*Breakfast.*

NIGHTLIFE AND THE ARTS

NIGHTLIFE

Black-Eyed Sally's. For barbecue and blues, head to the laid-back Black-Eyed Sally's. ✉ *350 Asylum St.* ☎ *860/278–7427* ⊕ *www. blackeyedsallys.com.*

THE ARTS

Bushnell. As well as national tours of major musicals, the Bushnell hosts the Hartford Symphony Orchestra. ✉ *166 Capitol Ave.* ☎ *860/987–6000, 888/824–2874* ⊕ *www.bushnell.org.*

Hartford Stage Company. The Tony Award–winning Hartford Stage Company puts on classic and new plays from around the world. ✉ *50 Church St.* ☎ *860/527–5151* ⊕ *www.hartfordstage.org.*

Real Art Ways. Modern and experimental musical compositions are presented here, as well as avant-garde and foreign films. ✉ *56 Arbor St.* ☎ *860/232–1006* ⊕ *www.realartways.org.*

TheatreWorks. This is the Hartford equivalent of off-Broadway, where experimental new dramas are presented. ✉ *233 Pearl St.* ☎ *860/527–7838* ⊕ *www.theaterworkshartford.org.*

FARMINGTON

9 miles southwest of Hartford.

Farmington, incorporated in 1645, is a classic river town with a perfectly preserved main street. This bucolic and affluent suburb of Hartford oozes historical charm. Antiques shops are near the intersection of Routes 4 and 10, along with some excellent house museums.

GETTING HERE AND AROUND

Farmington is most easily reached by car. From Hartford, take Interstate 84 west to Route 4 west.

EXPLORING

Hill-Stead Museum. Converted from a private home into a museum by its talented owner, Theodate Pope, a turn-of-the-20th-century architect, the house has a superb collection of French Impressionist art displayed in situ, including Claude Monet's *Haystacks* and Edouard Manet's *Guitar Player* hanging in the drawing room. Poetry readings take place in the elaborate Beatrix Farrand–designed sunken garden every other week in summer. ✉ *35 Mountain Rd.* ☎ *860/677–4787* 🌐 *www.hillstead.org* 🎟 *$12* 🕐 *Tues.–Sun. 10–4.*

> **WORD OF MOUTH**
>
> "The Hill-Stead Museum is a place where you can find Monets, Manets, Degas, Whistlers, Mary Cassatts, Dürers in a home. I found it very worth a visit. The docent who led our visit was interesting too. I would love to have been able to furnish a home with paintings of such quality, the two Monet Haystacks are wonderful."
>
> —emalloy

WHERE TO EAT AND STAY

$$ ITALIAN — 🍴 **Joey Garlic's.** Come to this Italian eatery for huge portions of classic dishes and a family-friendly atmosphere. Patrons rave about the eggplant fries and the meatball salad. Specialty pizzas and overstuffed grinders are crowd-pleasers as well. [$] *Average main: $16* ✉ *372 Scott Swamp Rd.* ☎ *860/678–7231* 🌐 *www.joeygarlics.com.*

$$ HOTEL — 🏨 **Avon Old Farms Hotel.** A country hotel at the base of Avon Mountain, this 20-acre compound of Colonial-style buildings with manicured grounds sits midway between Farmington and Simsbury. **Pros:** attractive pool area; central location. **Cons:** rooms need a little upgrading. [$] *Rooms from: $139* ✉ *279 Avon Mountain Rd., Avon* ☎ *860/677–1651* 🌐 *www.avonoldfarmshotel.com* 🛏 *160 rooms* 🍽 *Breakfast.*

THE LITCHFIELD HILLS

Fodor's Choice ★ Here in the foothills of the Berkshires is some of the most spectacular and unspoiled scenery in Connecticut. Two highways, Interstate 84 and Route 8, form the southern and eastern boundaries of the region. New York, to the west, and Massachusetts, to the north, complete the rectangle. Grand old inns are plentiful, as are sophisticated eateries. Rolling farmlands abut thick forests, and trails—including a section of the Appalachian Trail—traverse the state parks and forests. Two rivers, the Housatonic and the Farmington, attract anglers and canoeing enthusiasts, and the state's three largest natural lakes, Waramaug, Bantam, and Twin, are here. Sweeping town greens and stately homes anchor Litchfield and New Milford. Kent, New Preston, and Woodbury draw avid antiquers, and Washington and Norfolk provide a glimpse into New England village life as it might have existed two centuries ago.

ESSENTIALS

Visitor Information Litchfield Hills–Northwest Connecticut Convention and Visitors Bureau ☎ *860/567–4506* 🌐 *www.northwestct.com.*

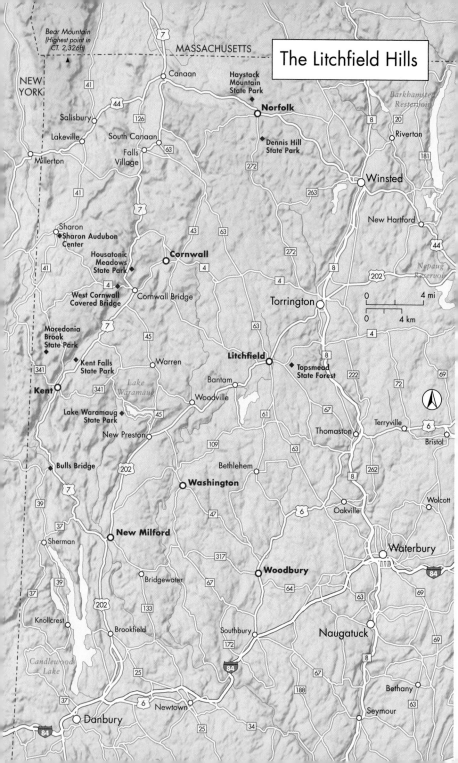

The Litchfield Hills

Bear Mountain
(Highest point in
CT, 2,326ft)

MASSACHUSETTS

NEW YORK

7

Canaan

Haystack
Mountain
State Park

Norfolk

Barkhamsted
Reservoir

41

44

8

20

Salisbury

126

Riverton

Lakeville

South Canaan

63

Dennis Hill
State Park

181

Millerton

Falls
Village

272

Winsted

41

7

263

New Hartford

Sharon
Sharon Audubon
Center

43

63

44

Housatonic
Meadows
State Park

Cornwall

272

8

202

Nepaug
Reservoir

41

4

4

West Cornwall
Covered Bridge

4

Cornwall Bridge

Torrington

4

7

45

63

4

Macedonia
Brook
State Park

Kent Falls
State Park

Warren

Litchfield

8

Topsmead
State Forest

222

72

69

341

Lake
Waramaug

Bantam

67

Terryville

6

Kent

341

Woodville

61

Thomaston

Bristol

Lake Waramaug
State Park

45

New Preston

109

63

8

262

Wolcott

Bulls Bridge

202

Bethlehem

Washington

6

Oakville

39

47

37

New Milford

317

Woodbury

Waterbury

Sherman

67

64

84

39

Bridgewater

63

69

37

Knollcrest

133

8

Brookfield

Southbury

Naugatuck

69

Candlewood
Lake

25

172

84

67

188

37

Danbury

6

Newtown

Bethany

63

84

25

34

Seymour

0   4 mi
0   4 km

NEW MILFORD

28 miles west of Waterbury, 46 miles northeast of Greenwich.

If you're approaching the Litchfield Hills from the south, New Milford is a practical starting point to begin a visit. It was also a starting point for a young cobbler named Roger Sherman, who, in 1743, opened his shop at the corner of Main and Church streets. A Declaration of Independence signatory, Sherman also helped draft the Articles of Confederation and the Constitution. You'll find old shops, galleries, and eateries all within a short stroll of New Milford green.

GETTING HERE AND AROUND

New Milford is best visited by car. From Danbury and points south, take Route 7 to Route 202 to reach the town.

EXPLORING

Silo at Hunt Hill Farm Trust. Once the property of Skitch Henderson, former music director of the New York Pops, this unusual attraction consists of several farm buildings dating back to the 1700s. The Skitch Henderson Living Museum focuses on his collections of musical memorabilia, including rare recordings and scores. Inside a barn is the Silo Store, packed with crafts, cooking supplies, and assorted goodies and sauces. The Silo Gallery presents art shows and literary readings. ✉ *44 Upland Rd., 4 miles north of New Milford* ☎ *860/355–0300* 🌐 *www.thesilo.com* 🎟 *Donation suggested* 🕓 *Wed.–Sat. 10–5, Sun. noon–5.*

6

WHERE TO EAT AND STAY

$$$$ AMERICAN 🍴 **Adrienne.** Set in an 18th-century farmhouse with terraced gardens, Adrienne serves New American cuisine from a seasonal menu. You may be lucky enough to encounter crab-stuffed shrimp wrapped in prosciutto, or grilled lamb chops with mashed blue Peruvian potatoes and French green beans. Sunday brunch (think eggs Florentine, seafood crepes, and vegetable scampi) on the outdoor terrace is always popular. There's live jazz on the first Sunday of every month. [$] *Average main: $30* ✉ *218 Kent Rd.* ☎ *860/354–6001* 🌐 *www.adriennerestaurant.com* 🕓 *Closed Mon. No lunch.*

$$ BARBECUE 🍴 **The Cookhouse.** Stop here for some of the best "slow-smoked" barbecue in Connecticut. The casual, family-friendly spot offers a wide variety of comfort-food staples. Try the chicken-fried steak, cookhouse meat loaf, or the delicious baby back ribs. Come hungry on Thursday night—it's all-you-can-eat barbecue for $21, and it comes with a free pint of beer. [$] *Average main: $20* ✉ *31 Danbury Rd.* ☎ *860/355-4111* 🌐 *thecookhouse.com.*

$$ B&B/INN 🏨 **The Homestead Inn.** High on a hill overlooking New Milford's town green, this place opened as an inn in 1928. **Pros:** reasonably priced; close to shops and restaurants. **Cons:** on a busy street. [$] *Rooms from: $160* ✉ *5 Elm St.* ☎ *860/354–4080* 🌐 *www.homesteadct.com* 🛏 *14 rooms, 1 suite* 🍽 *Breakfast.*

KENT

14 miles northwest of New Milford.

Kent has the area's greatest concentration of art galleries, some nationally renowned. Home to a prep school of the same name, Kent once held many ironworks. The Schaghticoke Indian Reservation is also here. During the Revolutionary War, 100 Schaghticokes helped defend the colonies by transmitting messages of army intelligence from the Litchfield Hills to Long Island Sound along the hilltops by way of shouts and drumbeats.

GETTING HERE AND AROUND

To reach Kent by car, travel north on Route 7 from New Milford.

EXPLORING

Eric Sloane Museum and Kent Iron Furnace. Hardware-store buffs and vintage-tool aficionados will feel right at home at this museum. Artist and author Eric Sloane (1905–85) was fascinated by Early American woodworking tools, and his collection showcases examples of American craftsmanship from the 17th to the 19th centuries. The museum contains a re-creation of Sloane's last studio and also encompasses the ruins of a 19th-century iron furnace. Sloane's books and prints, which celebrate vanishing aspects of Americana such as barns and covered bridges, are on sale here. ✉ *31 Kent-Cornwall Rd.* ☎ *860/927–3849* 🎟 *$8* 🕒 *Late May–late Oct., Thurs.–Sun. 10–4.*

Macedonia Brook State Park. The early-season trout fishing is superb at 2,300-acre Macedonia Brook State Park, where you can also hike and cross-country ski. ✉ *159 Macedonia Brook Rd., off Rte. 341* ☎ *860/927–3238* 🎟 *Free* 🕒 *Daily 8–sunset.*

WHERE TO STAY

$$$$ B&B/INN Fodor'sChoice ★

🏨 **The Inn at Kent Falls.** This 18th-century Colonial carefully preserves the charm of the past while providing every convenience today's travelers expect. **Pros:** stylish rooms; country setting; excellent breakfasts. **Cons:** queen rooms are on the small side. [$] *Rooms from: $320* ✉ *107 Kent Cornwall Rd.* ☎ *860/927–3197* 🌐 *www.theinnatkentfalls.com* 🛏 *6 rooms* 🍴 *Breakfast.*

SPORTS AND THE OUTDOORS

Appalachian Trail. The Appalachian Trail's longest river walk, off Route 341, is this almost-8-mile hike from Kent to Cornwall Bridge along the Housatonic River.

EN ROUTE

Kent Falls State Park. Heading north from Kent toward Cornwall, you'll pass the entrance to 295-acre Kent Falls State Park, where you can hike a short way to one of the most impressive waterfalls in the state and picnic in the green meadows at the base of the falls. There is a $15 fee for parking. ✉ *U.S. 7* ☎ *860/927–3238* 🎟 *Free* 🕒 *Daily 8–7.*

SHOPPING

House of Books. Stop in here for a great selection of books for readers of all ages, along with local maps, cards, and art supplies. ✉ *10 N. Main St.* ☎ *860/927–4104* 🌐 *www.hobooks.com.*

Be patient on back roads: Many covered bridges, like this one in West Cornwall, are one-lane only.

Kent Coffee and Chocolate Company. This shop sells delicious organic chocolates, and many of the homemade varieties are filled with roasted nuts and fruits. It's also a great place to stop for coffee and tea. ⊠ *8 N. Main St.* ☎ *860/927–1445* ⊕ *www.kentcoffee.com.*

Three Monkeys and Me. Here you'll find out-of-the-ordinary children's casual clothes. There's also a toy room with unique gifts for young people. ⊠ *Kent Village Barns, Fulling La.* ☎ *860/927–4549* ⊕ *three-monkeysandme.com.*

CORNWALL

12 miles northeast of Kent.

Connecticut's Cornwalls can get confusing. There's Cornwall, Cornwall Bridge, West Cornwall, Cornwall Hollow, East Cornwall, and North Cornwall. This quiet corner of the Litchfield Hills is known for its fantastic vistas of woods and mountains and its covered bridge, which spans the Housatonic.

GETTING HERE AND AROUND
Head north on Route 7 to reach Cornwall from Kent.

EXPLORING
Housatonic Meadows State Park. The park is marked by its tall pine trees near the Housatonic River and has terrific riverside campsites. Fly-fishers consider this 2-miles stretch of the river among the best places in New England to test their skills against trout and bass. ⊠ *U.S. 7, Cornwall Bridge* ☎ *860/927–3238* ⊕ *www.ct.gov/deep/cwp/view. asp?a=2716&q=325220.*

FAMILY **Sharon Audubon Center.** With 11 miles of hiking trails, this 1,147-acre property—a mixture of forests, meadows, wetlands, ponds, and streams—provides myriad hiking opportunities. It's also home to Princess, an American crow, who shares the visitor center with small hawks, an owl, and other animals in a live-animal display. Also here is a natural-history museum and children's adventure center. An aviary houses a bald eagle, a red-tailed hawk, and two turkey vultures. ✉ *325 Cornwall Bridge Rd., Sharon* ☎ *860/364–0520* 🌐 *www.sharon.audubon.org* 🎟 *$3* 🕐 *Tues.–Sat. 9–5, Sun. 1–5, trails daily dawn–dusk.*

West Cornwall Bridge. A romantic reminder of the past, this one-lane bridge is several miles up U.S. 7 on Route 128 in West Cornwall. The bridge was built in 1841 and incorporates strut techniques that were copied by bridge builders around the country. ✉ *Junction of Rte. 7 and Rte. 128.*

WHERE TO STAY

$$$ B&B/INN 🏨 **Cornwall Inn.** This 19th-century inn combines country charm with contemporary elegance; eight rustic rooms in the adjacent lodge are slightly more private and have cedar-post beds. **Pros:** tranquil setting; lovely grounds; welcoming to kids and pets. **Cons:** a bit far from neighboring towns. [$] *Rooms from: $199* ✉ *270 Kent Rd. S* ☎ *860/672–6884, 800/786–6884* 🌐 *www.cornwallinn.com* 🛏 *12 rooms, 1 suite* 🍴 *Breakfast.*

SPORTS AND THE OUTDOORS

CANOEING AND KAYAKING

Clarke Outdoors. This outfitter rents canoes, kayaks, and rafts and operates 10-mile trips from Falls Village to Housatonic Meadows State Park. ✉ *163 Rte. 7, 1 mile south of covered bridge, West Cornwall* ☎ *860/672–6365* 🌐 *www.clarkeoutdoors.com.*

FISHING

Housatonic Anglers. Enjoy a half- or full-day fishing trip on the Housatonic River and its tributaries with this company. You can also take fly-fishing lessons. ✉ *26 Bolton Hill Rd.* ☎ *860/672–4457* 🌐 *www.housatonicanglers.com.*

Housatonic River Outfitters. This outfitter operates a full-service fly shop, leads guided trips of the region, runs classes in fly-fishing, and stocks a good selection of vintage and modern gear. ✉ *24 Kent Rd., Cornwall Bridge* ☎ *860/672–1010* 🌐 *www.dryflies.com.*

SKIING

Mohawk Mountain. The 25 trails at Mohawk Mountain, ranging down 650 vertical feet, include plenty of intermediate terrain, with a few trails for beginners and a few steeper sections for more advanced skiers toward the top of the mountain. A small section is devoted to snowboarders. Trails are serviced by four triple lifts and one double; 12 trails are lighted for night skiing. The base lodge has munchies and a retail shop, and halfway up the slope the Pine Lodge Restaurant has an outdoor patio. ✉ *46 Great Hollow Rd., off Rte. 4* ☎ *860/672–6100, 800/895–5222* 🌐 *www.mohawkmtn.com.*

NORFOLK

23 miles northeast of Cornwall, 59 miles north of New Haven.

Thanks to its severe climate and terrain, Norfolk is one of the best-preserved villages in the Northeast. Notable industrialists have been summering here for two centuries, and many enormous homesteads still exist. The striking town green, at the junction of Route 272 and U.S. 44, has a fountain designed by Augustus Saint-Gaudens and executed by Stanford White at its southern corner. It stands as a memorial to Joseph Battell, who turned Norfolk into a major trading center.

GETTING HERE AND AROUND

To reach Norfolk by car from points north or south, use Route 272.

EXPLORING

Dennis Hill State Park. Dr. Frederick Shepard Dennis, former owner of the 240 acres now making up the park, lavishly entertained guests, among them President William Howard Taft and several Connecticut governors, in the stone pavilion at the summit of the estate. From its 1,627-foot height, you can see Haystack Mountain, New Hampshire, and, on a clear day, New Haven harbor, all the way across the state. Picnic on the park's grounds or hike one of its many trails. ✉ *Rte. 272* ☎ *860/482–1817* 🌐 *www.ct.gov/deep/cwp/view.asp?a=2716&q=325186* 🎟 *Free* 🕐 *Daily 8 am–dusk.*

Haystack Mountain State Park. One of the most spectacular views in the state can be seen from this park via its challenging trail to the top. If you'd rather drive, a road takes you halfway up. ✉ *Rte. 272* ☎ *860/482–1817* 🌐 *www.ct.gov/deep/cwp/view.asp?a=2716&q=325216.*

WHERE TO STAY

$$$ B&B/INN 🏨 **Manor House Inn.** Among this 1898 Bavarian Tudor's remarkable appointments are its beamed ceilings, graceful arches, and antique beds—not to mention the 20 stained-glass windows designed by Louis Comfort Tiffany. **Pros:** sumptuous decor; lavish breakfasts; peaceful atmosphere. **Cons:** no phone or TV in the rooms (and cell-phone reception is iffy in these parts); no Internet offered. [$] *Rooms from: $215* ✉ *69 Maple Ave.* ☎ *860/542–5690, 866/542–5690* 🌐 *www.manorhouse-norfolk.com* 🛏 *8 rooms, 1 suite* 🍴 *Breakfast.*

$$$$ B&B/INN 🏨 **Mountain View Inn.** Perfectly restored and lovingly maintained, this gracious country retreat welcomes you with expansive lawns and a lovely wraparound porch. **Pros:** meticulously maintained; gracious innkeepers; great location. **Cons:** Victorian decor not everyone's cup of tea. [$] *Rooms from: $225* ✉ *67 Litchfield Rd.* ☎ *860/542–6991, 866/792–7812* 🌐 *www.mvinn.com* 🛏 *7 rooms* 🍴 *Breakfast.*

THE ARTS

Infinity Music Hall. Built in 1883, this newly renovated 300-seat music hall hosts more than 200 shows a year by local performers and nationally known groups. ✉ *20 Greenwoods Rd.* ☎ *866/666–6306* 🌐 *www.infinityhall.com.*

Norfolk Chamber Music Festival. Held at the Music Shed on the 70-acre Ellen Battell Stoeckel Estate, the Norfolk Chamber Music Festival presents world-renowned artists and ensembles on Friday and Saturday evenings in summer. Students from the Yale School of Music perform on Thursday evening and Saturday morning. Stroll the 70-acre grounds or visit the art gallery. ⊠ *Ellen Battell Stoeckel Estate, 20 Litchfield Rd.* ☎ *860/542–3000* ⊕ *www.yale.edu/norfolk.*

SHOPPING

Norfolk Artisans Guild. The shop carries works by more than 60 local artisans—from hand-stitched pillows to one-of-a-kind baskets. ⊠ *10 Station Pl.* ☎ *860/542–5055* ⊗ *Fri. and Sat. 10–5, Sun. noon–4.*

LITCHFIELD

20 miles south of Norfolk, 34 miles west of Hartford.

Everything in Litchfield, the wealthiest and most noteworthy town in the Litchfield Hills, seems to exist on a larger scale than in neighboring burgs, especially the impressive Litchfield Green and the white Colonial and Greek Revival homes that line the broad elm-shaded streets. Harriet Beecher Stowe, author of *Uncle Tom's Cabin,* and her brother, abolitionist preacher Henry Ward Beecher, were born and raised in Litchfield, and many famous Americans earned their law degrees at the Litchfield Law School. Today lovely but expensive boutiques and restaurants line the downtown.

GETTING HERE AND AROUND

To reach Litchfield by car from points north or south, take Route 8 to Route 118 west.

EXPLORING

Litchfield History Museum. In this well-regarded museum, seven well-organized galleries highlight family life and work during the 50 years after the American Revolution. The extensive reference library has information about the town's historic buildings, including the Sheldon Tavern (where George Washington slept on several occasions) and the Litchfield Female Academy, where in the late 1700s Sarah Pierce taught girls not just sewing and deportment but mathematics and history. ⊠ *7 South St., at Rtes. 63 and 118* ☎ *860/567–4501* ⊕ *www.litchfieldhistoricalsociety.org* ⊠ *$5, includes Tapping Reeve House and Litchfield Law School* ⊗ *Mid-Apr.–late Nov., Tues.–Sat. 11–5, Sun. 1–5.*

Tapping Reeve House and Litchfield Law School. In 1773, Judge Tapping Reeve enrolled his first student, Aaron Burr, in what became the first law school in the country. (Before Judge Reeve, students studied the law as apprentices, not in formal classes.) This school is dedicated to Reeve's achievement and to the notable students who passed through its halls, including three U.S. Supreme Court justices. This museum is one of the state's most worthy attractions, with multimedia exhibits, an excellent introductory film, and restored facilities. ⊠ *82 South St.* ☎ *860/567–4501* ⊕ *www.litchfieldhistoricalsociety.org* ⊠ *$5, includes Litchfield History Museum* ⊗ *Mid-Apr.–late Nov., Tues.–Sat. 11–5, Sun. 1–5.*

Explore White Memorial Conservation Center on the boardwalks, nature trails, and bird-watching platforms.

Fodor's Choice ★ **White Memorial Conservation Center.** This 4,000-acre nature preserve houses top-notch natural-history exhibits. There are 30 bird-watching platforms, two self-guided nature trails, several boardwalks, boating facilities, and 35 miles of hiking, cross-country skiing, and horseback-riding trails. ✉ *80 Whitehall Rd., off U.S. 202* ☎ *860/567–0857* 🌐 *www.whitememorialcc.org* 🎟 *Grounds free, conservation center $6* ⏲ *Grounds daily dawn to dusk; conservation center Mon.–Sat. 9–5, Sun. noon–5.*

WHERE TO EAT AND STAY

$$$ AMERICAN 🍴 **The Village.** Beloved by visitors and locals alike, this storefront eatery in a redbrick townhouse serves tasty, unfussy food—inexpensive pub grub in one room, updated contemporary American cuisine in the other. Whether you order a burger or horseradish-and-Parmesan-crusted salmon, you're bound to be pleased. [$] *Average main: $22* ✉ *25 West St.* ☎ *860/567–8307* 🌐 *www.village-litchfield.com.*

$$$$ AMERICAN 🍴 **West Street Grill.** This sophisticated dining room on the town green is *the* place to see and be seen. Dinner selections might include pan-roasted cod with leeks and asparagus, braised short ribs over a Gorgonzola-polenta cake, or organic Irish salmon with fingerling potatoes. The ice creams and sorbets, made by the restaurant, are worth every calorie. [$] *Average main: $32* ✉ *43 West St.* ☎ *860/567–3885* 🌐 *www.weststreetgrill.net.*

$$$$ RESORT Fodor's Choice ★ 🏨 **Winvian.** This 113-acre hideaway consists of 18 of the most imaginatively themed and luxuriously outfitted cottages you'll ever lay eyes on. **Pros:** whimsical and super-plush accommodations; outstanding cuisine; stunning setting. **Cons:** super pricey. [$] *Rooms from: $650* ✉ *155 Alain*

White Rd., Morris ☎ 860/567–9600 🌐 www.winvian.com 🛏 18 cottages, 1 suite 🍴 Multiple meal plans.

SPORTS AND THE OUTDOORS

HORSEBACK RIDING

Lee's Riding Stable. This stable leads trail and pony rides. ✉ *57 E. Litchfield Rd.* ☎ *860/567–0785* 🌐 *www.windfieldmorganfarm.com/lees.html.*

SHOPPING

Jeffrey Tillou Antiques. This antiques store specializes in 18th- and 19th-century American furniture and paintings. ✉ *39 West St.* ☎ *860/567–9693* 🌐 *www.tillouantiques.com.*

WASHINGTON

14 miles southwest of Litchfield.

The beautiful buildings of The Gunnery prep school mingle with stately Colonials and churches in Washington, one of the best-preserved Colonial towns in Connecticut. The Mayflower Inn, south of The Gunnery on Route 47, attracts an exclusive clientele. In 1779 Washington, which was settled in 1734, became the first town in the United States to be named for the first president.

GETTING HERE AND AROUND

Washington is best visited by car. Route 47 runs through town, connecting it with New Preston to the north and Woodbury to the south.

EXPLORING

The Institute for American Indian Studies. The exhibits in this small but excellent and thoughtfully arranged collection detail the history and continuing presence of more than 10,000 years of Native American life in New England. Highlights include nature trails, a simulated archaeological site, and an authentically constructed Algonquian Village with wigwams, a longhouse, a rock shelter, and more. A gift shop presents the work of some of the country's best Native American artists. ✉ *38 Curtis Rd., off Rte. 199* ☎ *860/868–0518* 🌐 *www.iaismuseum.org* 🎟 *$5* 🕒 *Mon.–Sat. 10–5, Sun. noon–5.*

WHERE TO STAY

$$$$ RESORT Fodor's Choice ★

🏨 **Mayflower Inn & Spa.** Though the most expensive suites at this inn cost upwards of $1,000 a night, the elegant Mayflower is often booked months in advance. **Pros:** perfected landscaped grounds; solicitous but relaxed service; outstanding spa. **Cons:** very pricey. [$] *Rooms from: $850* ✉ *118 Woodbury Rd.* ☎ *860/868–9466* 🌐 *www.mayflowerinn.com* 🛏 *19 rooms, 11 suites* 🍴 *No meals.*

Continued on page 328

ANTIQUES AND CRAFTS SHOPPING
SOMETHING OLD, SOMETHING NEW
By Christina Valhouli

Forget the mall. In New England, shoppers can pick up serious antiques or quirky bric-a-brac in old mills and converted barns. Or hit funky galleries or annual craft fairs to meet artisans and buy one-of-a-kind products. Your souvenirs will be as memorable as the shopping experience.

Alongside New England's wealth of early American history is some of the best antique and craft shopping in the country—and often in beautiful settings perfect for browsing. You can explore galleries in converted farmhouses, craft shops clustered around the village green, or a picturesque Main Street (Woodstock, Vermont, or Camden, Maine, are good bets). Drive through historic coastal towns, like Essex, Massachusetts, where finds such as sun-bleached, centuries-old wooden tables or antique compasses evoke the area's maritime heritage.

Picture-perfect towns like Blue Hill, Maine, and Chester, Connecticut, are home to plenty of contemporary artists' galleries and cooperatives, like the Connecticut River Artisans, which showcases handmade quilts, jewelry, and ceramics; or try your luck at the Frog Hollow Craft Center in Burlington, Vermont.

Top Left, Hand-blown glass. Top right, Brimfield Antique Show. Bottom, antique pocket watch.

GREAT FINDS: CRAFTS

When most people think of a typical New England look, the austere lines of a Shaker table or the colorful patterns in a quilt come to mind. Artisans here still make crafts the old-fashioned way, but a new generation of glassblowers, potters, and weavers is creating products that will appeal to modernistas.

QUILTS. Today's quilters continue to produce traditional quilts, but there are plenty of contemporary styles available. Instead of star patterns, go for bold stripes or blocky squares made from funky fabrics. Buy one for your bed or to hang; baby quilts start around $100.

SHAKER-STYLE FURNITURE. The Shakers believed that form must follow function, and a typical Shaker design is clean, straight-lined, and devoid of decoration. Carpenters still make Shaker-inspired furniture, including ladderback chairs, tables, and bookcases. Chairs start around $300.

FELT. Humble felt is simply unspun wool that has been rolled and beaten into a solid form, but it's one of the most versatile (and eco-friendly) products around. Contemporary artists fashion felt into handbags, rugs, and even lightweight sculptures. Handbags start at $60.

CERAMICS. Visit a pottery studio or an art gallery and choose from ceramic plates and mugs or sturdier stoneware products that can survive the dishwasher. Small ceramic pieces start at $25.

WOOD-TURNED BOWLS. Hand- or wood-turned bowls are individually shaped on a lathe from solid blocks of wood. Each piece has a unique size, shape, grain pattern, and color. Look for rare spalted wood bowls—highly valued for their patterns and rich contrasts. Bowls are around $40 and up.

BLOWN GLASS. It's worth a trip to a glass-blowing studio just to see the artisans blow a gob of molten glass into a beautiful object. Best bets include colorful vases, bowls, and sculptures; handblown glass is typically $100 to $500.

GREAT FINDS: ANTIQUES

Antiques can run the gamut from auction-worthy pieces to decorative trinkets and vintage items from the '40s, '50s and '60s. Antique trends come and go, but popular New England buys include "smalls" like old prints and glass bottles. Don't be put off if you don't know a lot about antiques—however, do keep in mind that a true antique must be at least 100 years old.

KITCHEN TOOLS. Although you won't be tempted to cook with an old iron cauldron, items like engraved stove plates, mortar and pestles, and spoon racks look great on display for about $40–$180.

■TIP→
Start a collection easily with two or more of the same item (salt and pepper shakers) or style (speckled graniteware).

PENS. Hardly anyone writes letters anymore, which makes collecting old pens even more special. Parker pens from the 1970s are airplane inspired, while antique fountain pens are sheathed in beautiful wood or mother of pearl (and a joy to use). Prices are $100 up to thousands.

MIRRORS. If your taste runs toward the ornate, browse for 19th-century Federal and Queen Anne–style gilt mirrors. For something smaller and more understated, try a concave or vintage sunburst mirror. Prices range from $200–$2,000.

JEWELRY. Cuff links, earrings, and brooches make great gifts and will take up little room in your luggage. Antique jewelry runs the gamut from fun beaded necklaces to delicate Art Deco pieces. Prices start at $20.

MAPS. Frame an old nautical chart or map of a town you vacationed in for a stylish memento. Reproductions are easier on the wallet but still look good. Prices start at $40 for prints and run up to the thousands for antiques.

AMERICANA. This can be anything from painted signs to photographs of historic villages or kitschy porcelain figurines that evoke what it means to be American. Items inspired by the Stars and Stripes make colorful decorative accents for a country home feel. Postcards and other small items start at $5.

TOP SHOPPING ROUTES & SIGHTS

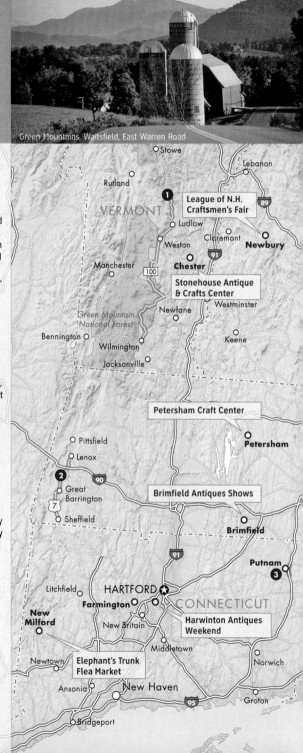

Green Mountains, Waitsfield, East Warren Road

One of the most effective and fun ways to shop is to hop in the car and drive through sleepy, scenic towns. On several key shopping routes in New England, stretches of road are absolutely packed with shops. Charles Street in Boston and downtown Providence and Portland are ideal, compact urban shopping areas for walking. If you do have wheels, try these routes.

❶ Route 100. One of the most picturesque drives in the Green Mountain State, this winding road goes from Wilmington north all the way up to Stowe. You'll pass craft studios, general stores like the Vermont Country Store in Weston, and plenty of red barns and covered bridges.

❷ Route 7, Berkshire County. Practically the entire route is chock-a-block with antiques stores. The Berkshire County Antiques and Art Dealers Association (⊕ www. bcaada.com) publishes a handy guide to the various shops. Key Western Massachusetts shopping towns include Great Barrington, Sheffield, and Lenox.

❸ Main Street, Putnam. Most of the town has a stuck-in-time quality, so it's a great place to spend the day the northeastern part of the state. The majority of antique stores are clustered around Main Street and its offshoots. Start your hunt at the massive Antiques Marketplace.

ANTIQUES

Antique Shop, Shefield, Berkshires

The
WHITE ELEPHANT
SHOP

White Elephant Shop, Essex

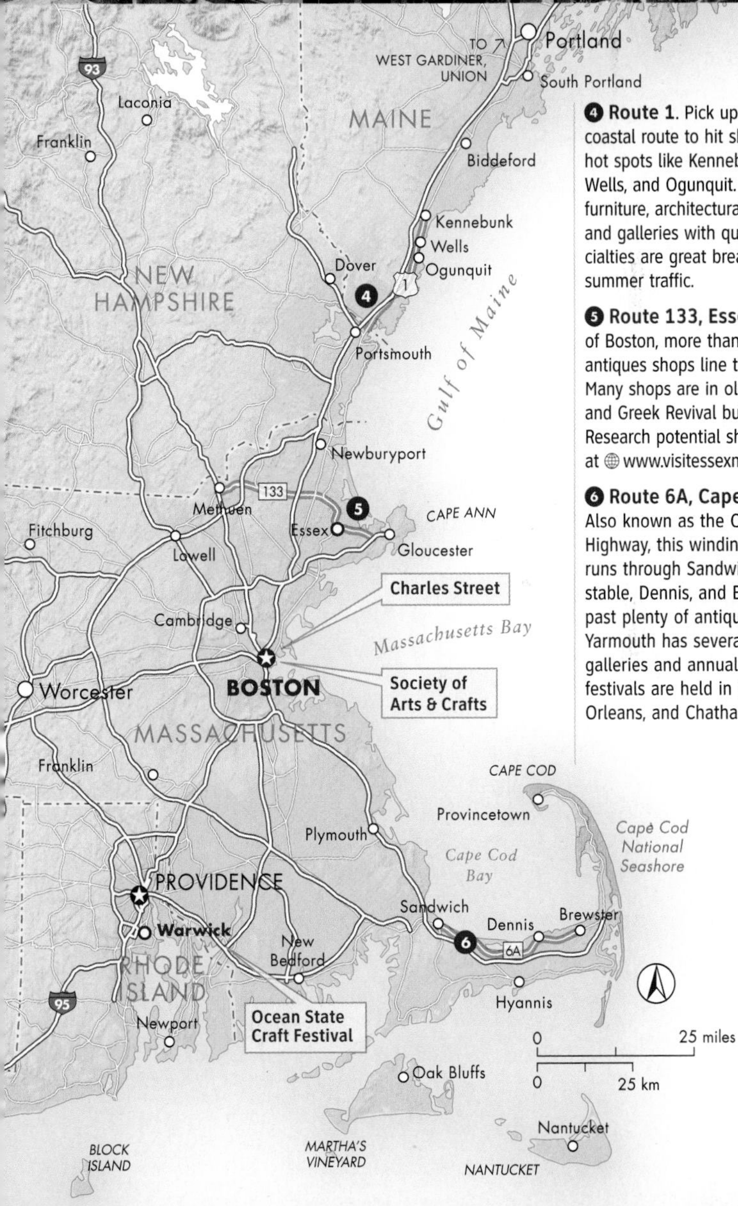
Portland
TO WEST GARDINER, UNION
South Portland
MAINE
93
Laconia
Franklin
Biddeford
Kennebunk
Wells
Ogunquit
Dover
1
NEW HAMPSHIRE
Gulf of Maine
Portsmouth
Newburyport
133
Methuen
Essex
CAPE ANN
Fitchburg
Lowell
Gloucester
Charles Street
Cambridge
Massachusetts Bay
Worcester
BOSTON
Society of Arts & Crafts
MASSACHUSETTS
Franklin
CAPE COD
Provincetown
Cape Cod National Seashore
Plymouth
Cape Cod Bay
PROVIDENCE
Sandwich
Dennis
Brewster
Warwick
New Bedford
6A
RHODE ISLAND
95
Hyannis
Newport
Ocean State Craft Festival
0
25 miles
0
25 km
Oak Bluffs
Nantucket
BLOCK ISLAND
MARTHA'S VINEYARD
NANTUCKET

4 Route 1. Pick up this Maine coastal route to hit shopping hot spots like Kennebunk, Wells, and Ogunquit. Colonial furniture, architectural antiques, and galleries with quirky specialties are great breaks from summer traffic.

5 Route 133, Essex. North of Boston, more than 30 antiques shops line this road. Many shops are in old Colonial and Greek Revival buildings. Research potential shops online at 🌐 www.visitessexma.com).

6 Route 6A, Cape Cod. Also known as the Old King's Highway, this winding route runs through Sandwich, Barnstable, Dennis, and Brewster past plenty of antiques shops. Yarmouth has several art galleries and annual crafts festivals are held in Falmouth, Orleans, and Chatham.

WHERE TO GET THE GOODS

Depending on your budget, there are plenty of places to shop. Take your pick from artisan studios, art galleries, auction houses, and multi-dealer antique centers. Some antiques shops are one step above flea markets, so prices can vary widely. Antiques shows and craft fairs also offer excellent one-stop shopping opportunities.

TOP ANTIQUES SHOWS

★ **Brimfield Antique and Collectible Shows**, Brimfield, Massachusetts. May, July and September (⊕ *www.brimfieldshow.com*).

Elephant's Trunk Country Flea Market, New Milford, Connecticut. Most Sundays except in December and March (⊕ *www.etflea.com*).

Harwinton Antiques Weekend, Connecticut. June and September (⊕ *www.farmingtonantiques weekend.com*).

Maine Antiques Festival, Union, Maine. August (⊕ *www.maineantique fest.com*).

Top, Ceramics sold along Route 100, Vermont.

Right, antique rocking horse.

TOP CRAFT FAIRS AND CENTERS

Center for Maine Crafts West Gardiner, Maine (⊕ *mainecrafts.org*).

★ **League of New Hampshire Craftsmen's Fair**, Newbury, New Hampshire. August (⊕ *www.nhcrafts.org*).

Ocean State Artisans Holiday Craft Festival, Warwick, Rhode Island. November (⊕ *www.oceanstateartisans.com*).

Petersham Craft Center, Petersham, Massachusetts (⊕ *www.petershamcraftcenter.org*).

Society of Arts and Crafts, Boston, Massachusetts (⊕ *www.societyofcrafts.org*).

Stonehouse Antique and Crafts Center, Chester, Vermont (☎ 802/875–4477).

6

IN FOCUS ANTIQUES AND CRAFTS SHOPPING

SHOPPING KNOW-HOW

Many shops are often closed on Sundays and Mondays. Call ahead to confirm. Before you whip out the credit card (or a wad of cash), there are a few other things to remember.

■ Unless you're an expert, it can be difficult to tell if an item is a reproduction or a genuine antique. Buy a price guide or a reference book like Miller's *Antiques & Collectibles* or *Kovel's* to have an idea of a fair value.

■ To ensure you are buying from a legitimate source, make sure the dealer belongs to a professional organization.

■ Think carefully about shipping costs for bulky items. It's also a good idea to carry with you some key measurements from your house.

■ If you find a piece that you love, check it carefully for any flaws. Point out any dings or scratches and use it as a bargaining chip when negotiating a price.

■ Always remember the golden rule: Buy what you love at a price you can afford.

WOODBURY

10 miles southeast of Washington.

More antiques shops may be in the quickly growing town of Woodbury than in all the towns in the rest of the Litchfield Hills combined. Five magnificent churches and the Greek Revival King Solomon's Temple, formerly a Masonic lodge, line U.S. 6; they represent some of the best-preserved examples of Colonial religious architecture in New England.

GETTING HERE AND AROUND

To reach Woodbury by car from Washington, take Route 47 south to Route 6.

EXPLORING

Glebe House Museum and The Gertrude Jekyll Garden. This property consists of the large, antiques-filled, gambrel-roof Colonial in which Dr. Samuel Seabury was elected the first Episcopal bishop in the United States, in 1783, and its historic garden. The latter was designed in the 1920s by renowned British horticulturist Gertrude Jekyll. Though small, it is a classic, old-fashioned English-style garden and the only one of the three gardens Jekyll designed in the United States still in existence. ✉ *49 Hollow Rd.* ☎ *203/263–2855* 🌐 *www.theglebehouse.org* 🎟 *$5* ⏲ *May–Oct., Wed.–Sun. 1–4; Nov., weekends 1–4.*

WHERE TO EAT AND STAY

$$$ AMERICAN Fodor's Choice ★ 🍴 **Good News Café.** Carole Peck is a well-known name throughout New England, and since this café opened in 1992, foodies have been flocking to Woodbury to sample her superb cuisine. The emphasis is on healthy, innovative, and surprisingly well-priced fare: wok-seared Gulf shrimp with new potatoes, grilled green beans, and a garlic aioli or the Nantucket cod with spinach and matchstick potatoes are good choices. In the simpler room next to the bar, you can order from a less expensive café menu. [$] *Average main: $27* ✉ *694 Main St. S* ☎ *203/266–4663* 🌐 *www.good-news-cafe.com* ⏲ *Closed Tues.*

$$$ B&B/INN 🏨 **Cornucopia at Oldfield.** A short drive from Woodbury antiques shops and restaurants, this Federal house has a bounty of pleasing comforts, from high-quality antiques and soft bedding to floral gardens and a pool surrounded by a private hedge. **Pros:** fine antiques; beautifully kept grounds; modern in-room amenities. **Cons:** on somewhat busy road. [$] *Rooms from: $175* ✉ *782 N. Main St., Southbury* ☎ *203/267–6772* 🌐 *www.cornucopiabnb.com* 🛏 *4 rooms, 1 suite* 🍽 *Breakfast.*

SHOPPING

Country Loft Antiques. This antiques shop specializes in 18th- and 19th-century country French antiques. ✉ *557 Main St. S* ☎ *203/266–4500* 🌐 *www.countryloftantiques.com.*

Mill House Antiques. The Mill House carries formal and country English and French furniture and has the state's largest collection of Welsh dressers. ✉ *1068 Main St. N* ☎ *203/263–3446* 🌐 *www.millhouseantiquesandgardens.com.*

Monique Shay Antiques & Designs. The six barns that make up Monique Shay's are lined with French Canadian country antiques. ✉ *920 Main St. S* ☎ *203/263–3186* 🌐 *www.moniqueshay.com.*

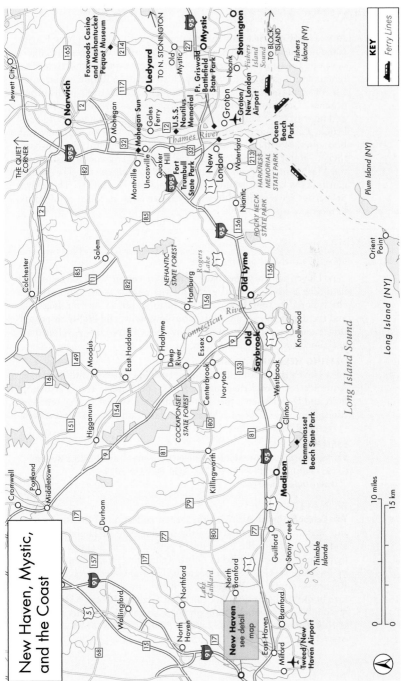

New Haven, Mystic, and the Coast

KEY

Ferry Lines

THE QUIET CORNER

Jewett City

Norwich

Foxwoods Casino and Mashantucket Pequot Museum

Ledyard

TO N. STONINGTON

Mystic

Old Mystic

Stonington

Noank

Fishers Island Sound

Fishers Island (NY)

TO BLOCK ISLAND

Mohegan

Mohegan Sun

Gales Ferry

U.S.S. Nautilus Memorial

Ft. Griswold Battlefield State Park

Groton

Groton/ New London Airport

New London

Thames River

Montville

Uncasville

Quaker Hill

Fort Trumbull State Park

Waterford

Ocean Beach Park

Plum Island (NY)

Salem

Niantic

Rocky Neck State Park

HARKNESS MEMORIAL STATE PARK

Colchester

Nehantic State Forest

Rogers Lake

Hamburg

Old Lyme

Orient Point

Moodus

Hadlyme

Connecticut River

Essex

Old Saybrook

Knollwood

Long Island Sound

East Haddam

Deep River

Centerbrook

Ivoryton

Westbrook

Long Island (NY)

Higganum

Cockaponset State Forest

Clinton

Cromwell

Portland

Middletown

Killingworth

Hammonasset Beach State Park

Madison

Durham

Guilford

Stony Creek

Thimble Islands

Wallingford

Northford

Lake Gaillard

North Branford

New Haven see detail map

East Haven

Milford

Tweed/New Haven Airport

North Haven

Branford

10 miles

15 km

NEW HAVEN, MYSTIC, AND THE COAST

As you drive northeast along Interstate 95, culturally rich New Haven is the final urban obstacle between southwestern Connecticut's over-developed coast and southeastern Connecticut's quieter shoreline. The remainder of the jagged coast, which stretches to Rhode Island, con-sists of small coastal villages, quiet hamlets, and relatively undisturbed beaches. The only interruptions along this seashore are the industry and piers of New London and Groton. Mystic, Stonington, Old Say-brook, Clinton, and Guilford are havens for fans of antiques and boutiques. North of Groton, near the town of Ledyard, the Mashan-tucket Pequot Reservation owns and operates Foxwoods Casino and the Mashantucket Pequot Museum & Research Center. The Mohe-gan Indians run the Mohegan Sun casino in Uncasville. These two properties have added noteworthy hotels and marquee restaurants in recent years.

NEW HAVEN

46 miles northeast of Greenwich.

New Haven's history goes back to the 17th century, when its squares, including a lovely central green for the public, were laid out. The city is home to Yale University. The historic district surrounding Yale and the distinctive shops, prestigious museums, and highly respected theaters downtown are a major draw. New Haven has developed an acclaimed restaurant scene in recent years.

GETTING HERE AND AROUND

New Haven is accessible by car from both Interstate 95 and Route 15. Amtrak's Northeast Regional and high-speed Acela trains also stop here, and New Haven is the end of the line for Metro-North commuter trains from New York City. Shore Line East train service connects New Haven and New London.

ESSENTIALS

Visitor Information Greater New Haven Convention and Visitors Bureau ⊠ *195 Church St., 14th Fl.* ☏ *203/777–8550, 800/332–7829* ⊕ *www.visitnewhaven.com.*

TOP ATTRACTIONS

Fodor'sChoice ★ **Yale Center for British Art.** With the largest collection of British art out-side Britain, the center surveys the development of English art, life, and thought from the Elizabethan period to the present. The sky-lighted galleries of architect Louis I. Kahn's final work contain works by John Constable, William Hogarth, Thomas Gainsborough, Joshua Reynolds, and J. M. W. Turner, to name but a few. You'll also find rare books and paintings documenting English history. ■TIP➜ **There are ongoing renovations through 2015, so call ahead before visiting.** ⊠ *1080 Chapel St.* ☏ *203/432–2800, 877/274–8278* ⊕ *britishart.yale. edu* ☞ *Free* ⊗ *Tues.–Sat. 10–5, Sun. noon–5.*

Connecticut Lobster Rolls

Behold the lobster roll. Sweet, succulent, and sinfully rich, it's the ultimate buttery icon of a Connecticut summer. Other New England states may prefer to chill out with lobster rolls created from a cool mix of lobster meat, mayonnaise, and chopped celery, but Nutmeggers like their one-of-a-kind rolls served hot, hot, hot.

The traditional Connecticut lobster roll, said to have been invented in the early 1930s at Perry's, a now-defunct seafood shack on the Boston Post Road in Milford, consists of nothing more than plump chunks of hot lobster meat and melted butter served on a butter-toasted roll. In other words: heaven on a bun. From seafood shanties along the shore to more gourmet getaways farther inland, Connecticut is fairly swimming with eateries that offer these revered rolls. Three favorites:

Abbott's Lobster in the Rough, Noank. A lobster roll at Abbott's Lobster in the Rough is best enjoyed seated at a picnic table at the edge of Noank Harbor watching the boats bob by.

Lenny and Joe's Fish Tale, Madison. At Lenny and Joe's Fish Tale, kids of all ages love to eat their lobster rolls or fried seafood outdoors by a hand-carved Dentzel carousel with flying horses (and a whale, frog, lion, seal, and more), which the restaurant runs from early May through early October.

Marnick's, Stratford. You can take your lobster roll to go for a picnic on a small beach on the Long Island Sound, or enjoy a leisurely after-dinner stroll along the sea wall here.

6

QUICK
BITES

Sugar Bakery and Sweet Shop. Winning Food Network's Cupcake Wars put this little East Haven bakery on the map. Stop in to try one of the 25 different types of cupcakes rotated daily. With flavors like cannoli, cookie dough, and the Elvis (banana cupcake with peanut butter and jelly buttercream frosting) you're bound to find one (or more) to fuel your perfect sugar high. ⊠ *422 Main St., East Haven* ☎ *203/469–0851* ⊕ *www.thesugarbakery.com.*

Yale University. New Haven as a manufacturing center dates from the 19th century, but the city owes its fame to merchant Elihu Yale. In 1718 Yale's contributions enabled the Collegiate School, founded in 1701 at Saybrook, to settle in New Haven, where it changed its name to Yale University. This is one of the nation's great universities, and its campus holds some handsome neo-Gothic buildings and noteworthy museums. The university's guides conduct one-hour walking tours that include Connecticut Hall in the Old Campus, which has had a number of illustrious past residents. ⊠ *Yale Visitor Center, 149 Elm St.* ☎ *203/432–2300* ⊕ *www.yale.edu/visitor* ☒ *Free* ☉ *Tours weekdays at 10:30 and 2, weekends at 1:30* ☞ *Tours start from 149 Elm St. on north side of New Haven Green.*

WORTH NOTING

Beinecke Rare Book and Manuscript Library. The collections here include a Gutenberg Bible, illuminated manuscripts, and original Audubon bird prints, but the building is almost as much of an attraction—the walls are made of marble cut so thin that the light shines through, making the interior a breathtaking sight on sunny days. ⊠ *121 Wall St.* ☎ *203/432–2977* ⊕ *www.library.yale.edu/beinecke* 🎟 *Free* ☉ *Mon.–Thurs. 9–7, Fri. 9–5, Sat. noon–5.*

New Haven Green. Bordered on the west side by the Yale campus, the green is a fine example of early urban planning. As early as 1638, village elders set aside the 16-acre plot as a town common. Three early-19th-century churches—the Gothic-style **Trinity Episcopal Church,** the Georgian-style **Center Congregational Church,** and the predominantly Federal-style **United Church**—contribute to its present appeal. ⊠ *Between Church and College Sts.*

FAMILY **Peabody Museum of Natural History.** Opened in 1876, the Peabody, with more than 11 million specimens, is one of the largest natural history museums in the nation. In addition to exhibits on Andean, Mesoamerican, and Pacific cultures, the venerable museum has an excellent collection of birds, including a stuffed dodo and passenger pigeon. The main attractions for children and amateur paleontologists alike are some of the world's earliest reconstructions of dinosaur skeletons. ⊠ *170 Whitney Ave.* ☎ *203/432–5050* ⊕ *www.peabody.yale.edu* 🎟 *$9* ☉ *Mon.–Sat. 10–5, Sun. noon–5.*

Yale University Art Gallery. Since its founding in 1832, this art gallery has amassed more than 200,000 works from around the world, dating from ancient Egypt to the present day. Highlights include works by Vincent van Gogh, Edouard Manet, Claude Monet, Pablo Picasso, Winslow Homer, and Thomas Eakins, as well as Etruscan and Greek vases, Chinese ceramics and bronzes, early Italian paintings, and a collection of American decorative arts that is considered one of the world's finest. The gallery's landmark main building is also of note. Opened in 1953, it was Louis I. Kahn's first major commission and the first modernist building on the neo-Gothic Yale campus. ⊠ *1111 Chapel St.* ☎ *203/432–0600* ⊕ *www.yale.edu/artgallery* 🎟 *Free* ☉ *Tues.–Fri. 10–5, weekends 11–5.*

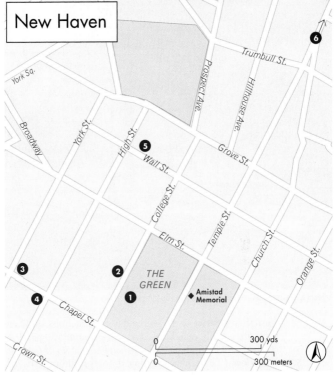

WHERE TO EAT

$$$ ✕ **Barcelona.** There's no need to take a transatlantic flight for authentic
SPANISH Spanish cuisine when you can feast on tapas right here in New Haven.
This place delivers in both dining and decor (think a 2,000-bottle
wine cellar, open kitchen, and massive wall-sized mural of a Spanish
bullfighter). There are entrées on the menu, but the tapas are a bet-
ter bet: the chorizo with sweet-and-sour figs offers an intensely rich
bite, the organic greens with goat-cheese croquettes nicely balances
tastes and textures, and the *gambas al ajillo* (sautéed shrimp with
garlic, sherry, and *guindilla* peppers) are full of flavor. $ *Average
main: $22* ⊠ *Omni New Haven Hotel, 155 Temple St., Downtown*
☎ *203/848–3000* ⊕ *www.barcelonawinebar.com* ⌕ *Reservations
essential* ⊗ *No lunch*.

$$ ✕ **Caseus Fromagerie Bistro.** The aroma of high-quality aged cheese will
AMERICAN hit you as you walk into this two-level bistro and fromagerie. On the
bottom floor you can buy cheeses to go, in addition to other goodies
like artisanal chocolates, jams, and olive oils. Visit the upstairs bistro
to linger over the decadent mac and cheese (made in three different
varieties: chèvre, raclette, and Comté), the grilled cheese made with
the bistro's "best melting cheeses," or the onion soup topped with no
fewer than six cheeses. All the ingredients are all natural and organic,
and dishes that do not include cheese, like the half chicken roasted with

Yale's leafy campus is home to many neo-Gothic buildings.

fresh thyme butter or the seared day-boat scallops with heirloom toma-toes, are equally delightful. $ *Average main: $20* ✉ *93 Whitney Ave.* ☎ *203/624–3373* ⊕ *www.caseusnewhaven.com* ☉ *Closed Sun.*

$$$ ✗ **Heirloom.** This isn't your typical hotel restaurant: occupying half of
AMERICAN the lobby of The Study at Yale, this contemporary American eatery has casually refined decor and a chalkboard menu. Dine during the day if you want to enjoy the sunlight pouring in through the floor-to-ceiling windows. The seasonal menu emphasizes the freshest locally sourced ingredients. Highlights include squash-blossom tempura stuffed with ricotta, or cornmeal-crusted sea bass with crispy okra and blistered tomatoes. The bar is great for a pre- or postdinner cocktail. $ *Average main: $25* ✉ *The Study at Yale, 1157 Chapel St., Downtown* ☎ *203/503–3900* ⊕ *www.studyhotels.com.*

$$$$ ✗ **Ibiza.** Come here for some of the region's most outstanding Spanish
SPANISH cuisine. Tall ceilings, multipaned windows, exposed brick, and vibrant
Fodor's Choice murals create a backdrop for such extraordinary dishes as steamed
★ lobster with sautéed shiitake and oyster mushrooms, endive foam, and fingerling potatoes, or quail cooked two ways with root vegetables and caramelized onions. A tasting menu is a great way to sample it all. $ *Average main: $32* ✉ *39 High St.* ☎ *203/865–1933* ⊕ *www. ibizanewhaven.com* ☉ *Closed Sun. No lunch Mon.–Thurs. and Sat.*

$ ✗ **Louis' Lunch.** This all-American luncheonette on the National Register
AMERICAN of Historic Places claims to be the birthplace of the hamburger. Its first-rate burgers are cooked in an old-fashioned upright broiler and served with either a slice of tomato or cheese on two pieces of toast. As most customers who come from far and wide for these tasty morsels agree, it doesn't get much better than that. Thursday to Saturday, the place is

open until 2 am. $ *Average main: $10* ✉ *263 Crown St., Downtown* ☎ *203/562–5507* ⊕ *www.louislunch.com* ▭ *No credit cards* ⊙ *Closed Sun. and Mon. No dinner Tues. and Wed.*

$$
PIZZA
✕**Modern Apizza.** It's not what Modern Apizza has that sets it apart from the rest, but rather what it doesn't have: toppings. The pizzeria's signature "plain" pie is a thin crust with a layer of tomato sauce and a sprinkling of Parmesan cheese. If you want "mootz" (mozzarella in New Haven–speak), then you have to ask for it. But why mess with a classic? Modern Apizza has been serving its signature pies since 1934, and business is still booming. $ *Average main: $19* ✉ *874 State St., Downtown* ☎ *203/776–5306* ⊕ *www.modernapizza.com.*

$$
PIZZA
✕**Pepe's Pizzeria.** Does this place serve the best pizza in the world, as so many reviewers claim? If it doesn't, it comes close. Pizza is the only thing on the menu—try the justifiably famous white-clam pie (it's especially good topped with bacon). Expect to wait an hour or more for a table—or, on weekend evenings, come after 10. $ *Average main: $16* ✉ *157 Wooster St., Downtown* ☎ *203/865–5762* ⊕ *www.pepespizzeria. com* ⌾ *Reservations not accepted* ▭ *No credit cards.*

$$$
PIZZA
✕**Sally's Apizza.** This place has been a rival of Frank Pepe's since 1938, when Salvatore Consiglio, Pepe's nephew, decided to break away from his relatives and open his own pizzeria. The result of this family feud is two competing pizzerias and a divided city: those who believe Frank Pepe's serves the best pizza and those who are devoted to Sally's. All the pizzas here are hand tossed and baked in a coal-fired oven. Try a slice topped with fresh tomato for a little taste of pizza heaven. $ *Average main: $22* ✉ *237 Wooster St., Downtown* ☎ *203/624–5271* ⊕ *www.sallysapizza.com.*

$$$$
BRASSERIE
✕**Union League Cafe.** In a gorgeous Beaux-Arts dining room, this lively brasserie wins high marks for its updated French cuisine. Diners rave about the mussels with curry, ginger, and coconut milk, and wax poetic when describing the perfectly executed beef tenderloin with watercress and a whole-grain-mustard sauce. The knowledgeable staff is happy to recommend complementary wine pairings for whatever dishes you select. The prices are steep, but most think it's worth the splurge. $ *Average main: $36* ✉ *1032 Chapel St., Downtown* ☎ *203/562–4299* ⊕ *unionleaguecafe.com.*

$$$
ECLECTIC
✕**Zinc.** In a sexy, dimly lighted storefront space looking toward the glorious city green, Zinc turns heads with its artfully prepared, globally inspired cooking. You can't go wrong with starters like the grilled shrimp with polenta grits, shiitake mushrooms, and bacon, or the Saigon beef lettuce wraps with peanuts, chili, and garlic. The pan-seared barramundi in a blue-cornmeal crust with sweet-and-sour kale is a standout among the entrées. $ *Average main: $28* ✉ *964 Chapel St., Downtown* ☎ *203/624–0507* ⊕ *www.zincfood.com* ⊙ *Closed Sun. and Mon. No lunch Sat.*

WHERE TO STAY

$$$
HOTEL
▦**Omni Hotels & Resorts.** This comfortable hotel is near the heart of New Haven and outfitted with all the modern amenities. **Pros:** upscale furnishings; nice gym and spa; walking distance from many shops and restaurants. **Cons:** somewhat steep rates; in busy part of downtown. $ *Rooms from: $200* ✉ *155 Temple St.* ☎ *203/772–6664* ⊕ *www. omnihotels.com* ⤳ *299 rooms, 7 suites* ⦿ *No meals.*

CLOSE UP

New Haven Pizza 101

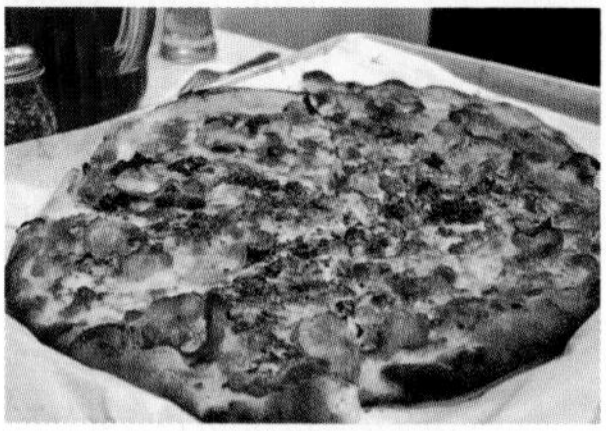

New Haven has been on pizza-lovers' radar for decades. The apizza (pronounced "ah-beetz" by locals) is defined by its thin, chewy crust, which makes for a unique—and, some would argue, superior—pizza experience. From white clam pies to mashed-potato-topped concoctions, here are our picks for the area's best pizzas (⇨ *see Where to Eat for more details).*

It doesn't surprise us that **BAR** (⇨ *see Nightlife*), a nightclub-cum-microbrewery, is in a college town and that its signature pie just happens to be bacon-and-mashed-potato-topped pizza—a college student's comfort-food dream. If you want to taste what this place does best, push aside any creeping thoughts of carbs and calories, and go for the masterpiece, a slightly charred, crispy-crusted pizza, topped with a thin layer of creamy mashed potatoes and bits of bacon.

Pepe's Pizzeria is where it all began: in 1925 Frank Pepe opened this eponymous pizza place and created what would become the iconic New Haven–style pizza. Eager customers line up for hours to get a taste of the famous thin-crust pies, in particular, Frank Pepe's pièce de résistance—the white clam pizza. This masterful creation consists of olive oil, garlic, oregano, grated Parmesan cheese, and littleneck clams atop a thin crust.

It's not what **Modern Apizza** has that sets it apart from the rest, but rather what it doesn't have: toppings. The pizzeria's signature "plain" pie is a thin crust with a layer of tomato sauce and just a sprinkling of Parmesan cheese. If you want mootz (mozzarella in New Haven–speak), then you have to ask for it. But why mess with a classic? Modern Apizza has been serving its signature pies since 1934, and business is still booming.

Just two blocks from Pepe's on Wooster Street (considered to be New Haven's Little Italy) is **Sally's Apizza**, a rival of Frank Pepe's since 1938, when Salvatore Consiglio, Pepe's nephew, decided to break away from his relatives and open his own pizzeria. The result of this family feud is two competing pizzerias and a divided city: those who believe Frank Pepe's serves the best pizza and those who are devoted to Sally's.

—Carolyn Galgano

$$$$ HOTEL 🏨 **The Study at Yale.** With bellhops dressed as newsies, a pair of spectacles emblazoned on all of the hotel's signature items, and overflowing bookshelves in the hotel's lobby and suites, The Study is a chic lodging for the scholarly set. **Pros:** destination restaurant; attentive staff; in the middle of the action. **Cons:** small gym; only one computer in the lobby. [$] *Rooms from: $250* ✉ *1157 Chapel St.* ☎ *203/503–3900* 🌐 *www.studyhotels.com* 🛏 *117 rooms, 7 suites* 🍴 *No meals.*

NIGHTLIFE AND THE ARTS

NIGHTLIFE

Anna Liffey's. This is one of the city's liveliest Irish pubs. ⊠ *17 Whitney Ave.* ☎ *203/773–1776* ⊕ *www.annaliffeys.com.*

BAR. This spot is a cross between a nightclub, a brick-oven pizzeria, and a brewpub. ⊠ *254 Crown St.* ☎ *203/495–1111* ⊕ *www.barnightclub.com.*

Delaney's Tap Room. Simply put, this is a beer-lover's paradise. With nearly 50 ever-rotating beers on tap, and dozens more by the bottle, there's something for everyone. ⊠ *882 Whalley Ave.* ☎ *203/397–5494* ⊕ *www.delaneystaproom.com.*

Toad's Place of New Haven. Alternative and traditional rock bands play at Toad's Place. ⊠ *300 York St.* ☎ *203/624–8623* ⊕ *www.toadsplace.com.*

THE ARTS

Long Wharf Theatre. The well-regarded Long Wharf Theatre presents works by contemporary writers and revivals of neglected classics. ⊠ *222 Sargent Dr.* ☎ *203/787–4282* ⊕ *www.longwharf.org.*

New Haven Symphony Orchestra. The New Haven Symphony Orchestra plays at Yale University's Woolsey Hall. ⊠ *Woolsey Hall, 500 College St., at Grove St.* ☎ *203/865–0831* ⊕ *www.newhavensymphony.org.*

Woolsey Hall. Built in 1901 to commemorate Yale's bicentennial, Woolsey Hall hosts performances by the New Haven Symphony Orchestra and the Philharmonia Orchestra of Yale, as well as recitals on the Newberry Memorial Organ. ⊠ *500 College St., at Grove St.* ⊕ *www.yale.edu/woolsey*

Shubert Performing Arts Center. Broadway musicals, dance performances, and classical music concerts are on the bill at the Shubert Performing Arts Center. ⊠ *247 College St.* ☎ *203/624–1825* ⊕ *www.shubert.com.*

Yale Repertory Theatre. This theater premieres new plays and mounts fresh interpretations of the classics. ⊠ *1120 Chapel St.* ☎ *203/432–1234* ⊕ *www.yalerep.org.*

Yale School of Music. Most events in the impressive roster of performances by the Yale School of Music take place in Sprague Memorial Hall. ⊠ *470 College St.* ☎ *203/432–4158* ⊕ *www.yale.edu/music.*

SHOPPING

Atticus Bookstore & Café. This independent bookseller in the heart of Yale University offers a full cafe menu you can enjoy while devouring the latest bestseller. ⊠ *1082 Chapel St.* ☎ *203/776–4040* ⊕ *atticusbookstorecafe.com.*

MADISON

22 miles east of New Haven, 62 miles northeast of Greenwich.

Coastal Madison has an understated charm. Ice cream parlors, antiques stores, and quirky gift boutiques prosper along U.S. 1, the town's main street. Stately Colonial homes line the town green, site of many a summer antiques fair and arts-and-crafts festival. The Madison shoreline, particularly the white stretch of sand known as Hammonasset Beach and its parallel boardwalk, draws visitors year-round.

GETTING HERE AND AROUND

Madison is accessible by car and train. Drive north on Interstate 95 from New Haven, or take the Shore Line East train to the Madison stop.

WHERE TO STAY AND EAT

$$ ✕ **Lenny and Joe's Fish Tale.** At Lenny and Joe's Fish Tale, kids of all ages
SEAFOOD love to eat their lobster rolls or fried seafood outdoors by a hand-carved Dentzel carousel with flying horses (and a whale, frog, lion, seal, and more), which the restaurant runs from early May through early October. $ *Average main: $18* ⌧ *1301 Boston Post Rd.* ☎ *203/245–7289* ⊕ *www.ljfishtale.com.*

$$$ 🏨 **Scranton Seahorse Inn.** In the heart of Madison, this historic inn run by
B&B/INN pastry chef Michael Hafford offers a restful retreat within walking distance of the beach and shops. **Pros:** central location; gracious innkeeper; meticulous attention to detail. **Cons:** books up quickly. $ *Rooms from: $185* ⌧ *818 Boston Post Rd.* ☎ *203/245–0550* ⊕ *scrantonseahorseinn. com* ↩ *7 rooms* ⑩ *Breakfast.*

SPORTS AND THE OUTDOORS

Hammonasset Beach State Park. The largest of the state's shoreline sanctuaries, Hammonasset Beach State Park has 2 miles of white-sand beaches, a top-notch nature center, excellent birding, and a hugely popular campground with about 55 sites. **Amenities:** food and drink; lifeguards; showers; toilets. **Best for:** swimming; walking. ⌧ *1288 Boston Post Rd., off I–95* ☎ *203/245–2785 park, 203/245–1817 campground* 🆓 *Free.*

OLD SAYBROOK

9 miles east of Madison, 29 miles east of New Haven.

Old Saybrook, once a lively shipbuilding and fishing town, bustles with summer vacationers and antiques shoppers. Its downtown is an especially pleasing place for a window-shopping stroll. At the end of the afternoon, stop at the old-fashioned soda fountain, where you can share a sundae with your sweetie.

GETTING HERE AND AROUND

Drive north on Interstate 95 to Route 154 to reach Old Saybrook. The town is also serviced by Amtrak's Northeast Regional trains, and the Shore Line East commuter trains.

WHERE TO EAT AND STAY

$$$ ✕ **Café Routier.** Grilled hanger steak with cauliflower gratin and seared
FRENCH scallops with pancetta and butternut squash puree are among the favorites at this bistro, which specializes in regional favorites and seasonal dishes. Check out the Mood Lounge for smaller plates meant for sharing and excellent cocktails. $ *Average main: $26* ⌧ *1353 Boston Post Rd., 5 miles west of Old Saybrook, Westbrook* ☎ *860/399–8700* ⊕ *www. caferoutier.com* ⊘ *No lunch.*

$$$$ 🏨 **Saybrook Point Inn & Spa.** Rooms at the cushy Saybrook Point Inn
HOTEL are done up in 18th-century style, with reproductions of British furnishings and Impressionist art. **Pros:** tasteful decor; excellent brunch. **Cons:** pricey; you'll need a car to get downtown. $ *Rooms from: $279*

✉ 2 Bridge St. ☎ 860/395–2000, 800/243–0212 🌐 www.saybrook.com 🛏 82 rooms; some condos also available 🍴 No meals.

SHOPPING

Old Saybrook Antiques Center. More than 125 dealers selling every type of antique imaginable operate out of the Old Saybrook Antiques Center. *✉ 756 Middlesex Tpke. ☎ 860/388–1600 🌐 www.oldsaybrookantiques.com 🕒 Daily 10–4.*

Saybrook Country Barn. You'll find everything you need to outfit a home in country style, from tiger-maple dining-room tables to hand-painted pottery. *✉ 2 Main St. ☎ 860/388–0891 🌐 www.saybrookcountrybarn.com.*

OLD LYME

4 miles east of Old Saybrook, 40 miles south of Hartford.

Old Lyme, on the other side of the Connecticut River from Old Saybrook, is renowned among art lovers for its past as the home of the Lyme Art Colony, the most famous gathering of Impressionist painters in the United States. Artists continue to be attracted to the area for its lovely countryside and shoreline. The town also has handsome old houses, many built for sea captains.

GETTING HERE AND AROUND

Old Lyme is best reached by car. Drive north on Interstate 95 from Old Saybrook.

EXPLORING

Fodor's Choice ★ **Florence Griswold Museum.** Central to Old Lyme's artistic reputation is this grand late-Georgian-style mansion, which served as a boardinghouse for members of the Lyme Art Colony in the first decades of the 20th century. When artists like Willard Metcalf, Clark Voorhees, Childe Hassam, and Henry Ward Ranger flocked to the area to paint its varied landscape, Miss Florence Griswold offered housing as well as artistic encouragement. The house has been restored to its 1910 appearance, when the colony was in full flower (clues to the house's layout and decor were gleaned from members' paintings). The museum's 10,000-square-foot Krieble Gallery, on the riverfront, hosts changing exhibitions of American art. *✉ 96 Lyme St. ☎ 860/434–5542 🌐 www.florencegriswoldmuseum.org 🎫 $9 🕒 Tues.–Sat. 10–5, Sun. 1–5.*

WHERE TO STAY

$$$$ B&B/INN Fodor's Choice ★ 🏨 **Bee and Thistle Inn and Spa.** Behind a weathered stone wall in the historic district sits this three-story 1756 Colonial house with 5½ acres of broad lawns, formal gardens, and herbaceous borders. **Pros:** a short walk from Griswold Museum; lovely old home; fantastic restaurant. **Cons:** can hear noise from Interstate 95; lacks some modern amenities. *[$] Rooms from: $242 ✉ 100 Lyme St. ☎ 860/434–1667 🌐 www.beeandthistleinn.com 🛏 11 rooms 🍴 Breakfast.*

NORWICH

27 miles northeast of Old Saybrook, 37 miles southeast of Hartford.

Outstanding Georgian and Victorian structures surround the triangular town green in Norwich, and more can be found downtown by the Thames River. The former mill town is hard at work at restoration and rehabilitation efforts. So eye-catching are these brightly colored structures that the Paint Quality Institute has designated the town one of the "Prettiest Painted Places in New England."

GETTING HERE AND AROUND

To reach Norwich from the coast by car, take Interstate 95 to Interstate 395 north to Route 82 east.

EXPLORING

Slater Memorial Museum & Converse Art Gallery. On the grounds of the Norwich Free Academy, this museum houses one of the country's largest collections of Greek, Roman, and Renaissance plaster casts of some of the world's greatest sculptures, including the Winged Victory, Venus de Milo, and Michelangelo's *Pietà*. The Converse Art Gallery, adjacent to the museum, hosts six to eight shows a year, many of which focus on Connecticut artists and craftsmen as well as student work. ✉ *108 Crescent St.* ☎ *860/887–2506* 🌐 *www.norwichfreeacademy.com* 🎟 *$3* 🕒 *Tues.–Fri. 9–4, weekends 1–4.*

WHERE TO STAY

$$$$ B&B/INN 🏨 **Spa at Norwich Inn.** On 42 rolling acres right by the Thames River, this Georgian-style inn is best known for its spa, which offers an entire spectrum of skin-care regimens, body treatments, and fitness classes. **Pros:** one of the best spas in the state; beautiful grounds; tasty food. **Cons:** oriented toward spa guests; tired room decor in need of an upgrade. [$] *Rooms from: $339* ✉ *607 W. Thames St.* ☎ *860/425–3500, 800/275–4772* 🌐 *www.thespaatnorwichinn.com* 🛏 *49 rooms, 54 villas* 🍴 *No meals.*

LEDYARD

10 miles south of Norwich, 37 miles southeast of Hartford.

Ledyard, in the woods of southeastern Connecticut between Norwich and the coastline, is known first and foremost for the vast Mashantucket Pequot Tribal Nation's Foxwoods Resort Casino. With the opening of the excellent Mashantucket Pequot Museum & Research Center, however, the tribe has moved beyond gaming to educating the public about its history, as well as that of other Northeast Woodland tribes.

GETTING HERE AND AROUND

Driving is probably the best way to get to Ledyard; take Interstate 95 to Route 2 west. If you are only planning to visit Foxwoods, there are many coach bus companies that run charter trips directly there. See 🌐 *www.foxwoods.com/bybus.aspx* for more information.

EXPLORING

Foxwoods Resort Casino. On the Mashantucket Pequot Indian Reservation near Ledyard, Foxwoods is the largest resort casino in North America. The skylighted compound draws 40,000-plus visitors daily to its more than 6,200 slot machines, 380 gaming tables, and a 3,200-seat bingo parlor. This 4.7-million-square-foot complex includes the Grand Pequot Tower, the Great Cedar Hotel, and the Two Trees Inn, which have more than 1,400 rooms combined, as well as a full-service spa, retail concourse, food court, and numerous restaurants. Also on-site is the MGM Grand at Foxwoods, an ultraluxury branch of the Las Vegas gaming resort that adds another 825 posh rooms and suites, plus several notable restaurants. ✉ *350 Trolley Line Blvd., Mashantucket* ☎ *800/369–9663* 🌐 *www.foxwoods.com* 🕐 *Daily 24 hrs.*

FAMILY Fodor's Choice ★ **Mashantucket Pequot Museum & Research Center.** A large complex a mile from Foxwoods, this museum brings the history and culture of Northeastern Woodland tribes in general and the Pequots in particular to life in exquisite detail. Some highlights include views of an 18,000-year-old glacial crevasse, a caribou hunt from 11,000 years ago, and a 17th-century fort. Perhaps most remarkable is a sprawling "immersion environment"—a 16th-century village with more than 50 life-size figures and real smells and sounds. Audio devices provide detailed information about the sights. A full-service restaurant serves both Native and traditional American cuisine. ✉ *110 Pequot Tr., Mashantucket* ☎ *800/411–9671* 🌐 *www.pequotmuseum.org* 🎟 *$20* 🕐 *Wed.–Sat. 10–4.*

Mohegan Sun. The Mohegan Indians, known as the Wolf People, operate this casino west of Ledyard and just south of Norwich, which has more than 300,000 square feet of gaming space, including 6,000 slot machines and more than 250 gaming tables. Also part of the complex: the Kids Quest family-entertainment center, a 130,000-square-foot shopping mall, more than 40 restaurants and food-and-beverage suppliers, and a 34-story, 1,200-room luxury hotel with a full-service spa. A 10,000-seat arena hosts major national acts and is home to the WNBA's Connecticut Sun, and a swanky 300-seat cabaret hosts intimate shows and comedy acts. Mohegan After Dark is a 22,000-square-foot complex with three nightclubs. ✉ *1 Mohegan Sun Blvd., off I–395, Uncasville* ☎ *888/226–7711* 🌐 *www.mohegansun.com* 🕐 *Daily 24 hrs.*

WHERE TO STAY

$$$ HOTEL 🏨 **Grand Pequot Tower.** Mere steps from the gaming floors, this expansive 17-story showpiece contains deluxe rooms and suites updated with modern decor in pleasantly neutral tones. **Pros:** elegant rooms; easy access to the casino; nice views from upper floors. **Cons:** not much to entice if you're not gambling. [$] *Rooms from: $199* ✉ *Foxwoods Resort Casino, 350 Trolley Line Blvd., Mashantucket* ☎ *860/312–5044, 800/369–9663* 🌐 *www.foxwoods.com* 🛏 *824 rooms* 🍴 *No meals.*

$$$
HOTEL
MGM Grand at Foxwoods. This lavishly appointed hotel offers stylish accommodations just seconds away from the casino's action. **Pros:** elegant rooms; easy access to the casino; nice views from upper floors. **Cons:** if you're not a gambler, this might not be your scene. $ *Rooms from: $199* ⊠ *Foxwoods Resort Casino, 350 Trolley Line Blvd., Mashantucket* ☎ *800/369–9663* ⊕ *www.foxwoods.com* ⇆ *825 rooms* ◉ *No meals.*

$$$
HOTEL
Mohegan Sun. The emphasis of this 34-story hotel is on luxury. **Pros:** numerous fine restaurants are steps from lobby; incredible views from upper floors; excellent spa and fitness center. **Cons:** better like casinos. $ *Rooms from: $199* ⊠ *1 Mohegan Sun Blvd., Uncasville* ☎ *888/777–7922* ⊕ *www.mohegansun.com* ⇆ *1,020 rooms, 180 suites* ◉ *No meals.*

$$$
B&B/INN
Stonecroft. A sunny 1807 Georgian Colonial on 6½ acres of green meadows, woodlands, and rambling stone walls is the center of Stonecroft. **Pros:** scenic and verdant grounds; cheerful service. **Cons:** secluded location requires a car to get around. $ *Rooms from: $205* ⊠ *515 Pumpkin Hill Rd.* ☎ *800/772–0774* ⊕ *www.stonecroft.com* ⇆ *10 rooms* ◉ *Breakfast.*

MYSTIC

8 miles south of Ledyard.

Mystic has devoted itself to recapturing the seafaring spirit of the 18th and 19th centuries. Some of the nation's fastest clipper ships were built here in the mid-19th century; today's Mystic Seaport is the state's most popular museum. Downtown Mystic has an interesting collection of boutiques and galleries.

GETTING HERE AND AROUND
By car, take Interstate 95 to Route 27 south to reach Mystic. Amtrak's Northeast Regional train service also stops here.

ESSENTIALS
Visitor Information Mystic Country–Eastern Regional Tourism District ⊠ *27 Coogan Blvd., Bldg. 3A* ☎ *860/536–8822* ⊕ *mysticcountry.com.*

EXPLORING

FAMILY
Fodor'sChoice
★
Mystic Aquarium. The famous Arctic Coast exhibit—which holds 800,000 gallons of water, measures 165 feet at its longest point by 85 feet at its widest point, and ranges from just inches to 16½ feet deep—is just a small part of this revered establishment. You can also check out world-renowned ocean explorer Dr. Robert Ballard's Institute for Exploration and its Nautilus Live Theater, which features live video from the E/V *Nautilus* ship as it explores wrecks. You can also see African penguins, harbor seals, graceful sea horses, Pacific octopuses, and sand tiger sharks. Don't miss feeding time at the Ray Touch Pool, where rays suction sand eels right out of your hand. The animals here go through 1,000 pounds of herring, capelin, and squid each day. Juno, a male beluga whale, is responsible for consuming 85 pounds of that himself. ■TIP→ **For an up-close-and-personal experience with a beluga whale, take part in the Trainer for Day ($375) or**

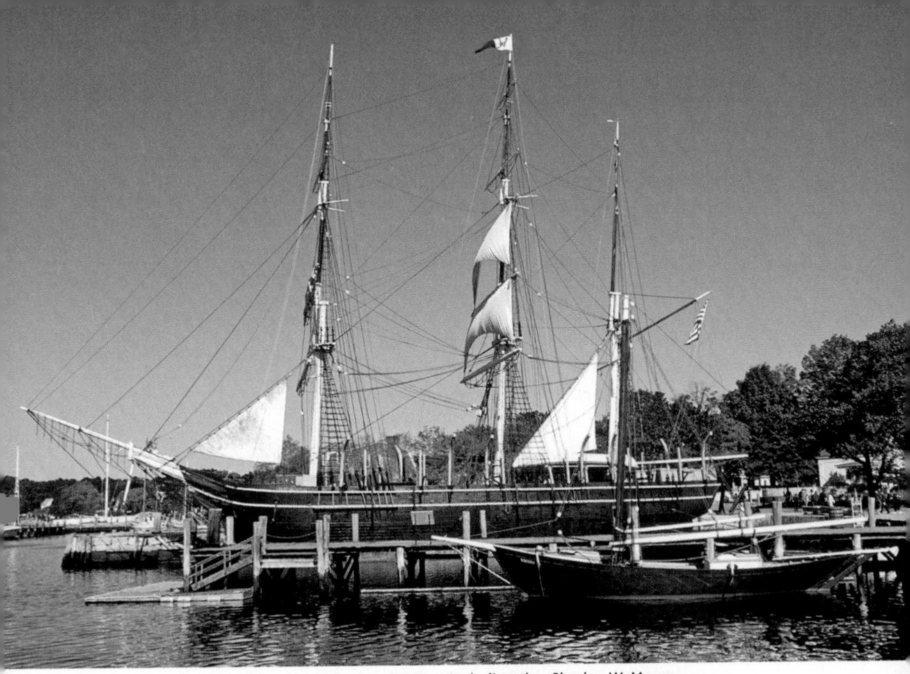

Mystic Seaport includes a number of vessels you can tour, including the *Charles W. Morgan*.

Beluga Encounter ($145) programs. Both allow you to touch and interact with these magnificent animals. ✉ *55 Coogan Blvd.* ☎ *860/572–5955* 🌐 *www.mysticaquarium.org* 🎟 *$29.95* 🕒 *Mar. and Sept.–Nov., daily 9–4; Apr.–Aug., daily 9–5; Dec.–Feb., daily 10–4.*

FAMILY
Fodor's Choice ★
Mystic Seaport. The world's largest maritime museum, Mystic Seaport encompasses 37 acres of indoor and outdoor exhibits with more than 1 million artifacts that provide a fascinating look at the area's rich shipbuilding and seafaring heritage. In the narrow streets and historic homes and buildings (some moved here from other sites), craftspeople give demonstrations of open-hearth cooking, weaving, and other skills of yesteryear. The museum's more than 500 vessels include the *Charles W. Morgan*, the last remaining wooden whaling ship afloat, and the 1882 training ship *Joseph Conrad*. You can climb aboard for a look or for sail-setting demonstrations and reenactments of whale hunts. **■ TIP→ Children under five are admitted free.** ✉ *75 Greenmanville Ave., 1 mile south of I–95* ☎ *860/572–0711* 🌐 *www.mysticseaport.org* 🎟 *$24* 🕒 *Apr.–Oct., daily 9–5; Nov. and Dec., daily 10–4; Jan.–Mar., call for hrs.*

WHERE TO EAT

$$
SEAFOOD
Fodor's Choice ★
🍴 **Abbott's Lobster in the Rough.** If you want some of the state's best lobsters, mussels, crabs, or clams on the half shell, head down to this unassuming seaside lobster shack in sleepy Noank, a few miles southwest of Mystic. Most seating is outdoors or on the dock, where the views of Noank Harbor are magnificent. [$] *Average main: $18* ✉ *117 Pearl St., Noank* ☎ *860/536–7719* 🌐 *www.abbotts-lobster.com.*

$$$
SEAFOOD
✕ **Go Fish.** This sophisticated restaurant captures all the tastes—and colors—of the ocean. There's a raw bar, wine bar, coffee bar, and a black-granite sushi bar, which, with its myriad tiny, briny morsels, is worth the trip in itself. The menu lists options for vegetarians and carnivores and offers many of its main dishes in smaller portions that are perfect for passing around. The lobster ravioli in a light cream sauce is a must-try. $ *Average main: $25* ⊠ *Olde Mistick Village, 27 Coogan Blvd.* ☎ *860/536–2662* ⊕ *www.gofishct.com.*

WHERE TO STAY

$$$
B&B/INN
🛏 **Old Mystic Inn.** This 1784 inn was once a well-regarded bookstore, so it's no surprise that rooms in the cozy main house and carriage house are named after New England authors. **Pros:** beautifully kept historic house; quiet neighborhood; friendly host. **Cons:** need a car to get into downtown. $ *Rooms from: $205* ⊠ *52 Main St.* ☎ *860/572–9422* ⊕ *www.oldmysticinn.com* ⤴ *8 rooms* ⦿ *Breakfast.*

$$$
HOTEL
🛏 **Whaler's Inn.** A perfect compromise between a chain motel and a country inn, this complex with public rooms furnished with lovely antiques is one block from the Mystic River and downtown. **Pros:** within walking distance of downtown shopping; excellent restaurant. **Cons:** rooms in motel-style building have less character; on a busy street. $ *Rooms from: $200* ⊠ *20 E. Main St.* ☎ *860/536–1506* ⊕ *www. whalersinnmystic.com* ⤴ *49 rooms* ⦿ *Breakfast.*

SHOPPING

Finer Line Gallery. This gallery exhibits prints with nautical themes, including some local scenes. ⊠ *48 W. Main St.* ☎ *860/536–8339* ⊕ *www.finerlinegallery.com.*

Olde Mistick Village. Resembling an early-1700s American village, Olde Mistick Village has more than 50 shops selling everything from crafts and clothing to souvenirs and munchies. ⊠ *27 Coogan Blvd.* ☎ *860/536–4941* ⊕ *www.oldemistickvillage.com.*

Whyevernot. This is a colorful spot for clothing, jewelry, pottery, linens, handmade papers, and much more. ⊠ *17 W. Main St.* ☎ *860/536–6209* ⊕ *www.whyevernot.com.*

SETTING SAIL AT MYSTIC SEAPORT

Kids can learn the ropes—literally—of what it takes to be a sailor during Mystic Seaport's many sailing classes and camps. Younger children and those who wish to stay on shore can sign up for courses on building boats (including how to varnish them), blacksmithing, carving, and roping (from knotting to splicing). The Seaport's planetarium also offers instruction on navigating a ship by the stars. Prices for classes vary. Call Mystic Seaport (☎ *860/572–5322*) or see its website (⊕ *www.mysticseaport.org*) for details.

STONINGTON

7 miles southeast of Mystic, 57 miles east of New Haven.

The pretty village of Stonington pokes into Fishers Island Sound. A quiet fishing community clustered around white-spired churches, Stonington is far less commercial than Mystic. In the 19th century, though, it was a bustling whaling, sealing, and transportation center. Historic buildings line the town green and border both sides of Water Street up to the imposing Old Lighthouse Museum.

GETTING HERE AND AROUND

From Mystic by car, take Route 1 north (you'll actually be heading due east so don't be concerned) to Route 1A.

EXPLORING

Old Lighthouse Museum. This museum occupies a lighthouse that was built in 1823 and moved to higher ground 17 years later. Climb to the top of the tower for a spectacular view of Long Island Sound and three states. Six rooms of exhibits depict the varied history of the small coastal town. ✉ *7 Water St.* ☎ *860/535–1440* 🌐 *www.stoningtonhistory.org* 🎟 *$9* 🕑 *May–Oct., Thurs.–Tues 10–5.*

Stonington Vineyards. At this small coastal winery you can browse through the works of local artists in the gallery or enjoy a picnic lunch on the grounds. The vineyard's Seaport White, a vidal-chardonnay blend, is a nice accompaniment. ✉ *523 Taugwonk Rd.* ☎ *860/535–1222* 🌐 *www.stoningtonvineyards.com* 🎟 *$12 tasting, free tour* 🕑 *May–Nov., daily 11–5, tours at 2; Jan.–Apr. weekdays 12–4, weekends 11–5.*

WHERE TO STAY

$$$ B&B/INN Fodor's Choice ★

🏨 **Inn at Stonington.** The views of Stonington Harbor and Fishers Island Sound are spectacular from this waterfront inn in the heart of Stonington Village. **Pros:** smartly furnished rooms; walking distance from village shops and dining; great water views. **Cons:** no restaurant. [$] *Rooms from: $220* ✉ *60 Water St.* ☎ *860/535–2000* 🌐 *www.innatstonington.com* 🛏 *18 rooms* 🍴 *Breakfast.*

THE QUIET CORNER

Few visitors to Connecticut experience the old-fashioned ways of the state's "Quiet Corner," a vast patch of sparsely populated towns that seem a world away from the rest of the state. The Quiet Corner has a reclusive allure: people used to leave New York City for the Litchfield Hills; now many leave for northeastern Connecticut, where the stretch of Route 169 from Brooklyn past Woodstock has been named a National Scenic Byway.

The cultural capital of the Quiet Corner is Putnam, a small mill city on the Quinebaug River whose formerly industrial town center has been transformed into a year-round antiques mart. Smaller jewels are Pomfret and Woodstock—two towns where authentic Colonial homesteads still seem to outnumber the contemporary, charmless clones that are springing up all too rapidly across the state.

POMFRET

51 miles north of Stonington; 6 miles north of Brooklyn.

Pomfret, one of the grandest towns in the region, was once known as the inland Newport because it attracted the wealthy, who summered here in large "cottages." Today it is a quiet stopping-off point along Route 169, designated one of the most scenic byways in the country by the National Scenic Byway Program.

GETTING HERE AND AROUND

Pomfret is best visited by car; Route 169 runs right through the center of town. From Interstate 395, take Route 44 west to Route 169 south.

EXPLORING

Connecticut Audubon Society Center at Pomfret. Adjacent to more than 700 acres of rolling meadows, grasslands, and forests, this nature center offers natural-history exhibits and seasonal lectures and workshops. Miles of trails provide excellent birding: look for the ruby-crowned kinglet, yellow-rumped warbler, and blue-headed vireo. ✉ *218 Day Rd.* ☎ *860/928–4948* 🌐 *www.ctaudubon.org/center-at-pomfret* 🎟 *Free* ⏲ *Sanctuary daily dawn–dusk; center weekdays 9–4, weekends, noon–4.*

Sharpe Hill Vineyard. Centered on an 18th-century-style barn in the hills of Pomfret, this vineyard offers tastings of its excellent wines and serves lunch and dinner in a European-style wine garden and relaxed restaurant (reservations are essential). Try Ballet of Angels, a heavenly semidry white, one of the more popular wines from New England. ✉ *108 Wade Rd.* ☎ *860/974–3549* 🌐 *www.sharpehill.com* 🎟 *Tastings $7–$12* ⏲ *Fri.–Sun. 11–5.*

WHERE TO EAT

$$$$ EUROPEAN Fodor's Choice ★
🍴 **Golden Lamb Buttery.** Connecticut's most unusual dining experience has achieved almost legendary status. Eating here, in a converted barn on a 1,000-acre farm, is far more than a chance to enjoy good Continental food: it's a social and gastronomical event. There is one seating each for lunch and dinner; choose from one of four entrées, which might include roast duck or chateaubriand. The dinner prix fixe is $75, but lunch has an à la carte menu. There is a hay wagon that you can ride before dinner (a musician accompanies you). [$] *Average main: $75* ✉ *499 Wolf Den Rd., off Rte. 169, Brooklyn* ☎ *860/774–4423* 🌐 *www.thegoldenlamb.com* ✍ *Reservations essential* 👔 *Jacket and tie* ⏲ *Closed Sun. and Mon. No dinner Tues.–Thurs.*

$$ AMERICAN
🍴 **Vanilla Bean Café.** Homemade soups, sandwiches, and baked goods have long been a tradition at this café inside a restored 19th-century barn. Dinner specials might include pan-seared blackfish with local squash or wild mushroom mac and cheese. Belgian waffles and blueberry pancakes are breakfast highlights. There are also an art gallery and folk entertainment. [$] *Average main: $16* ✉ *450 Deerfield Rd.* ☎ *860/928–1562* 🌐 *www.thevanillabeancafe.com* ⏲ *No dinner Mon. and Tues.*

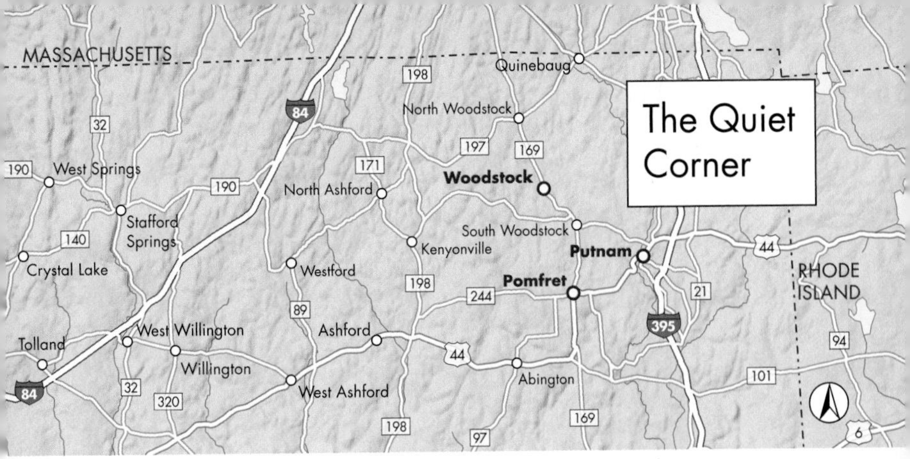

PUTNAM

5 miles northeast of Pomfret.

Ambitious antiques dealers have reinvented Putnam, a mill town 30 miles west of Providence, Rhode Island, that was neglected after the Depression. Putnam's downtown, with more than 400 antiques dealers, is the heart of the Quiet Corner's antiques trade.

6

GETTING HERE AND AROUND

By car, take Route 44 east from Pomfret to reach Putnam.

WHERE TO EAT

$$$ AMERICAN 🍴 **85 Main.** This stylish bistro is *the* place to go for a break from antiquing. Typical lunchtime offerings include roasted corn and clam chowder, pesto chicken salad, and burgers with fries; dinner could be maple-glazed sea scallops or veal Bolognese. There's also a raw bar and a full sushi bar. [$] *Average main: $27* ✉ *85 Main St.* ☎ *860/928–1660* 🌐 *www.85main.com.*

SHOPPING

Antiques Marketplace. This four-level emporium features more than 350 dealers selling everything from fine furniture to tchotchkes. ✉ *109 Main St.* ☎ *860/928–0442* 🌐 *www.antiquesmarketplace.com.*

Arts & Framing. Head here for antique art and art restoration and framing services. ✉ *112 Main St.* ☎ *860/963–0105* 🌐 *www.artsandframingputnam.com.*

WOODSTOCK

5 miles northwest of Putnam.

The landscape of this enchanting town is splendid in every season—the rolling hills seem to stretch for miles. Scenic roads lead past antiques shops, a country inn in the grand tradition, orchards, grassy fields and grazing livestock, and the fairgrounds of one of the state's oldest agricultural fairs, held each Labor Day weekend.

GETTING HERE AND AROUND

To reach Woodstock by car from Putnam, follow Route 171 west to Route 169 north.

EXPLORING

Roseland Cottage. This pink board-and-batten Gothic-Revival house was built in 1846 as a summer home for New York silk merchant, publisher, and abolitionist Henry C. Bowen. The house and outbuildings (including a carriage house with a private bowling alley) hold a prominent place in history, having hosted four U.S. presidents (Ulysses S. Grant, Rutherford B. Hayes, William Henry Harrison, and William McKinley). The parterre garden includes 21 flower beds surrounded by 600 yards of boxwood hedge. ✉ *556 Rte. 169* ☎ *860/928–4074* 🌐 *www.historicnewengland.org/historic-properties/homes/roseland-cottage* 🎟 *$8* 🕒 *June–mid-Oct., Wed.–Sun. 11–4.*

WHERE TO STAY

$$$ B&B/INN 🏨 **The Inn at Woodstock Hill.** Filled with antiques, this inn overlooking the countryside has rooms with four-poster beds, handsome fireplaces, pitched ceilings, and timber beams. **Pros:** beautiful grounds; pretty rooms. **Cons:** traditional decor is very old-fashioned; somewhat remote; expensive restaurant. [$] *Rooms from: $200* ✉ *94 Plaine Hill Rd., South Woodstock* ☎ *860/928–0528* 🌐 *www.woodstockhill.com* 🛏 *21 rooms* 🍴 *Breakfast.*

SHOPPING

Christmas Barn. This country store has 12 rooms of holiday decorations. ✉ *835 Rte. 169* ☎ *860/928–7652* 🌐 *www.thechristmasbarnonline.com.*

Scranton's Shops. This store sells the wares of 60 regional artisans. ✉ *300 Rte. 169* ☎ *860/928–3738* 🌐 *www.scrantonsshops.com.*

Whispering Hill Farm. Supplies for rug hooking and braiding, quilting, and needlework, plus an assortment of antiques are all on sale here. ✉ *18 Castle Rock Rd.* ☎ *860/928–0162* 🌐 *whispering-hill.com.*

RHODE ISLAND

WELCOME TO RHODE ISLAND

TOP REASONS TO GO

★ **Mansions:** See how the one-percenters lived during Newport's Gilded Age with a tour of Cornelius Vanderbilt's opulent 70-room "summer cottage" known as The Breakers.

★ **Historic Street:** Follow along Benefit Street on Providence's East Side for a mile of history and see ornate homes built by leading Colonial merchants.

★ **Nature:** Block Island is one of the most serene spots on the Eastern Seaboard, especially at Rodman's Hollow, a glacial outwash basin, where winding paths lead to the sea.

★ **Sand:** Take your pick from South County's numerous sugary-white beaches, including Scarborough State Beach in Narragansett.

★ **Food Enclave:** From food trucks to upscale dining, Providence has an exciting culinary scene fueled in large part by young Johnson & Wales University–trained chefs.

1 Providence. Visit Rhode Island's capital city on an empty stomach so you can fill up on its exciting culinary scene, anchored by one of New England's most treasured Little Italy neighborhoods, Federal Hill. Prestigious colleges give Providence intellectual and cultural vitality while restored Colonial houses on the East Side preserve its history.

2 The Blackstone Valley. The Blackstone River powered the factories that led America's industrial revolution in the 19th century. Now it's the focal point of renewed interest in northern Rhode Island as a destination where several fascinating museums document the rise of industry over the past 200 years.

3 South County. Visit some of southern New England's most accessible and scenic stretches of beach and you'll be happy to discover the ocean warm and welcoming in the summer. Explore nature preserves or take a fishing charter trip out of Galilee, Snug Harbor, or Jerusalem. Get off the beaten path on Route 1A and stop in antiques shops and galleries along the way.

4 Newport County and East Bay. No socks required in this longtime yachting enclave where boat crews unwind after a day on the water with a dark and stormy. Take in the beaches, Colonial architecture, professional tennis, and the dramatic views of the Newport Pell Bridge. Go fly a kite in Brenton Point State Park.

5 Block Island. This laid-back island with 17 miles of beaches—including Crescent Beach, one of New England's best beaches—offers an idyllic seaside escape in summer. Best of all, it's less crowded than Martha's Vineyard and Nantucket. Relax at one of its rambling Victorian inns and B&Bs (most lacking in-room TVs and phones) and take in busy shops and restaurants.

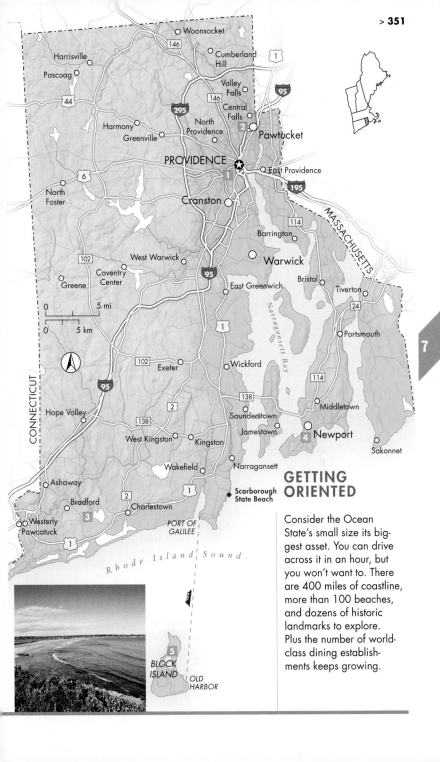

Woonsocket

146

Cumberland Hill

1

Harrisville

Pascoag

Valley Falls

146

295

44

Central Falls

95

Harmony

North Providence

2

Greenville

PROVIDENCE

Pawtucket

East Providence

6

195

North Foster

Cranston

MASSACHUSETTS

114

Barrington

102

West Warwick

Warwick

Coventry Center

95

Bristol

Greene

East Greenwich

Tiverton

0   5 mi

24

0   5 km

1

Portsmouth

7

102

Exeter

Wickford

138

Middletown

Hope Valley

2

138

Saunderstown

114

West Kingston

Jamestown

4

Newport

Kingston

CONNECTICUT

95

Wakefield

Narragansett

Sakonnet

Ashaway

Scarborough State Beach

GETTING ORIENTED

Bradford

2

Charlestown

3

Westerly
Pawcatuck

1

PORT OF GALILEE

R h o d e   I s l a n d   S o u n d

5

BLOCK ISLAND

OLD HARBOR

Consider the Ocean State's small size its biggest asset. You can drive across it in an hour, but you won't want to. There are 400 miles of coastline, more than 100 beaches, and dozens of historic landmarks to explore. Plus the number of world-class dining establishments keeps growing.

Narragansett Bay

Updated by
Doug Norris

"Rhode Island: 3% Bigger at Low Tide," reads a best-selling T-shirt by designer Hilary Treadwell. It's a bit of an exaggeration: the state geologist actually calculates .5%. But the smallest state's size is a big source of pride given all there is to do and see within its 1,500 square miles (one-third of those are water). The visitor may find it hard to choose from so many experiences: historic tours, fine dining, and WaterFire in Providence; apple picking and canal-boat rides in the Blackstone Valley; fishing trips and hitting the beach in South County or Block Island; pedaling along Bristol's bike path; and taking sunset sails and touring Gilded Age mansions in Newport.

Rhode Island and Providence Plantations, the state's official name, has a long history of forward thinking and a spirit of determination and innovation symbolized by the 11-foot-tall bronze Independent Man atop its marble-domed State House. The first of the 13 colonies to declare independence from Britain can also claim the first successful textile mill in Pawtucket, America's oldest synagogue in Newport, and the first lunch wagon in Providence. A state founded on the principle of religious liberty drew Baptists, Jews, Quakers, and others throughout the 17th and 18th centuries, then flourished with factories, silver foundries, and jewelry companies that drew workers from French Canada, Italy, Ireland, England, Portugal, and Eastern Europe.

The state's leaders keep working to make Rhode Island a dynamic place to live and work in and to visit for the 21st century. They moved a highway to carry on the revitalization of Downtown Providence, made infrastructure improvements at Fort Adams State Park in Newport to host international yacht-racing events, extended commuter rail service linking Providence to T. F. Green Airport and Wickford, and planned bike-path expansions in South County and Blackstone Valley. Rhode Island's 39 cities and towns—none more than 50 miles apart—offer natural attractions, inspired culinary artistry, and many opportunities to relax and take in its scenic vistas.

PLANNING

WHEN TO GO

Summer, with its renowned arts and music festivals and gorgeous beach days, is a great time to visit Rhode Island. But visitors will find fun and exciting things to do here all year-round. The shoulder seasons of April–May and September–October offer pleasant weather and more affordable accommodations. Late fall, winter, and early spring have their own charms, such as restaurant weeks in Providence, Newport, and Narragansett, when popular eateries join together to promote special three-course prix-fixe menus.

Newport has the Newport Jazz and Newport Folk festivals in late July and early August as well as the Newport Music Festival for classical-music fans in July. Take the ferry to Block Island for a fun day trip or relaxing overnight stay and experience its low-key, less crowded beaches.

Late October is a good time to catch fall foliage in the Blackstone Valley, around the University of Rhode Island or in picturesque Tiverton and Little Compton. The return of students to the several colleges of Providence gives the capital city energy and a youthful vibe.

PLANNING YOUR TIME

By car it's an hour or less from any one place in Rhode Island to another. Though the distances are short, the state is densely populated, so allow extra time for traffic congestion.

Most of the sights in Providence can be seen in one day. The Blackstone Valley can also occupy a day (potentially as an afternoon side trip from Providence). Newport, though not even 12 square miles, offers enough to see in two days. The same can be said for South County, with its superb beaches. With a week, you can visit all four regions of the state as well as Block Island.

GETTING HERE AND AROUND

AIR TRAVEL

Rhode Island's main airport is T. F. Green in Warwick, which is served by most domestic air carriers. Boston's Logan Airport is only an hour away. The major car-rental agencies have branches at both airports.

Air Contacts T. F. Green Airport ✉ *2000 Post Rd., off I–95, Warwick* ☎ *401/691–2471, 888/268–7222* ⊕ *www.pvdairport.com.*

CAR TRAVEL

New England's main highway, Interstate 95, cuts diagonally through Rhode Island, spanning 43 miles from the Connecticut border to the Massachusetts line.

Interstate 195 southeast from Providence leads to New Bedford, Massachusetts, and Cape Cod. Route 146 northwest from Providence leads to Worcester, Massachusetts, and Interstate 90, passing through the Blackstone Valley. U.S. 1 follows much of the Rhode Island coast east from Connecticut before turning north to Providence. Route 138 heads east from Route 1 to Jamestown, Newport, and Portsmouth, in easternmost Rhode Island. Route 114 leads south from East Providence down through the East Bay community of Bristol and then to Newport.

Once you're here, a car is your best way to get around the state, although it's quite practical to explore Providence and Newport on foot and using public transportation. Parking is easy to find outside of cities, though challenging and sometimes expensive in Downtown Providence and Newport.

RESTAURANTS

Rhode Island's restaurant scene has flourished over the past decade, fueled by the creative passion of award-winning chefs, many in their twenties and early thirties, who have elevated fine dining to an art form. Abundant fresh seafood also makes for outstanding fish-and-chips, clam chowder, and stuffed quahogs (the hard clam that is the official state shell), which are all best enjoyed at one of the state's many clam shacks. Then there is regional fare such as the thin corn pancake cooked on a griddle known as the johnnycake, as well as coffee milk, Del's frozen lemonade, and Gray's Ice Cream. Authentic Italian restaurants can be found in Providence's Federal Hill neighborhood. *Prices in the reviews are the average cost of a main course at dinner or, if dinner is not served, at lunch.*

HOTELS

The major chain hotels are represented in Rhode Island, but the state's many smaller B&Bs and other inns provide a more intimate experience. Rates are very seasonal; in Newport, for example, winter rates are often half those of summer. Many inns in coastal towns are closed in winter. *Prices in the reviews are the lowest cost of a standard double room in high season.*

VISITOR INFORMATION

Rhode Island Department of Economic Development, Tourism Division
☎ *800/556–2484* ⊕ *www.visitrhodeisland.com.*

PROVIDENCE

Big-city sophistication with small-city charm: Providence has the best of both worlds. The capital city's thriving arts community, prestigious academic institutions Brown University and the Rhode Island School of Design, renowned restaurant scene, and revitalized Downtown make it an exciting place to be. And Providence's convenient location, close to Boston without being too close, warrants a stop on any New England tour.

The city underwent a renaissance in the 1990s when the two rivers that merge to form the Providence River were uncovered and moved to create Waterplace Park, now the setting for the popular summer evening series of bonfires on the river known as WaterFire. The

OUTDOOR ACTIVITIES

FISHING

Department of Environmental Management's Division of Licensing. For information on where to buy licenses for freshwater fishing, contact the Department of Environmental Management's Division of Licensing. ☎ *401/222-3576* ⊕ *www.dem.ri.gov.*

A saltwater fishing license costs $10 and is good for a year.

Appalachian Mountain Club (*AMC*). One of the best trail guides for the region is the *AMC Massachusetts and Rhode Island Trail Guide*, available at local outdoors shops or from the Appalachian Mountain Club. Rhode Island's affiliate, the Narragansett Chapter, was founded in 1921 and has around 2,500 members. ⊠ *5 Joy St., Boston, Massachusetts* ☎ *800/372-1758* ⊕ *www.amcnarragansett.org.*

HIKING

Audubon Society of Rhode Island. The Audubon Society of Rhode Island leads interesting hikes and field expeditions around the state. ⊠ *12 Sanderson Rd., Smithfield* ☎ *401/949-5454* ⊕ *www.asri.org.*

relocation of Interstate 195 has again changed the city's landscape, leading to the impressive new Providence River Bridge, reconnecting Downtown and the Jewelry District, and allowing improvements to India Point Park.

GETTING ORIENTED

The narrow Providence River cuts through the city's Downtown from north to south. West of the river lies the compact business district. A largely Italian neighborhood, Federal Hill, pushes west from here along Atwells Avenue. On the north side of Downtown is the white-marble State House. South Main and Benefit streets run parallel to the river, on the East Side. College Hill constitutes the western half of the East Side. At the top of College Hill, Thayer Street runs north to south. Don't confuse the city of East Providence with Providence's East Side.

GETTING HERE AND AROUND

AIR TRAVEL T. F. Green Airport, 10 miles south of Providence, has scheduled daily flights by most major airlines, including Cape Air, Delta, JetBlue, Southwest, United , and US Airways. By cab, the ride from T. F. Green Airport to Downtown Providence takes about 15 minutes and costs about $28 to $32. The Airport Taxi & Limousine Service shuttle, running from the airport to Downtown hotels, Rhode Island School of Design, and Brown University, costs $11 per person each way.

BUS TRAVEL At Kennedy Plaza in Downtown Providence you can board the local Rhode Island Public Transit Authority (RIPTA) buses or trolleys. The Route 92 trolley links Federal Hill to the East Side and the Route 6 trolley links Downtown to the Roger Williams Park and Zoo. RIPTA fares are $2 per ride; an all-day pass is $6. Exact-cash fare is needed when boarding buses or change is distributed back in a fare card. RIPTA buses also service T. F. Green Airport; Route 14 links the airport to Kennedy Plaza.

TRAIN TRAVEL When traveling between New York City and Boston, Amtrak makes stops at Westerly, Kingston, and Providence. The Massachusetts Bay Transportation Authority (MBTA) commuter rail service connects Boston and Providence to T. F. Green Airport and Wickford Junction during weekday morning and evening rush hours for a little more than half the cost of an Amtrak ride. MBTA provides weekday service year-round with runs scheduled from early morning to noon and late afternoon to approximately 10:15 pm. The fare from the airport to Providence is $2.25 per person or $10 between T. F. Green and Boston's South Station.

> ### TASTE OF ITALY TOUR
>
> **Savoring Federal Hill.** For an insider's tour of Providence's own "Little Italy," sign up for a Cindy Salvato's three-hour walking and tasting tour ($50) that takes you into a half dozen of Federal Hill's long standing establishments (including a bakery, an Italian specialty store, and wine shop). ☎ 401/934–2149 ⊕ savoringrhodeisland.com.

PARKING Overnight parking is not generally allowed on Providence streets. During the day it can be difficult to find curbside parking, especially Downtown and on Federal and College hills. There is a large parking garage at Providence Place mall.

TOURS **Providence Preservation Society.** The Providence Preservation Society publishes five booklets describing self-guided walking tours of the city available for $3 each at its headquarters. The tours include Benefit Street, the city's waterfront, Downtown, the Elmwood section, and the Armory District. ⊠ *21 Meeting St., at Benefit St.* ☎ *401/831–7440* ⊕ *www.ppsri. org* ⊗ *Weekdays 9–5.*

ESSENTIALS

Transportation Contacts Airport Taxi & Limousine Service ☎ *401/737–2868* ⊕ *www.airporttaxiri.com.* **Amtrak** ☎ *800/872–7245* ⊕ *www.amtrak.com.* **Massachusetts Bay Transportation Authority** (*MBTA*). ☎ *617/722–3200, 617/222–3538* ⊕ *www.mbta.com.* **Rhode Island Public Transit Authority** (*RIPTA*). ⊠ *Kennedy Plaza Passenger Terminal, 1 Kennedy Plaza, Downtown* ☎ *401/781–9400* ⊕ *www.ripta.com.*

Visitor Information Providence Warwick Convention & Visitors Bureau ⊠ *144 Westminster St.* ☎ *401/456–0200, 800/233–1636* ⊕ *www.goprovidence.com.*

DOWNTOWN

TOP ATTRACTIONS

Federal Hill. You're as likely to hear Italian as English in this neighborhood. The stripe down Atwells Avenue is painted in red, white, and green, and a huge *pignoli* (pinenut), an Italian symbol of abundance and quality, hangs on an arch soaring over the street. Grocers sell pastas, pastries, and usually hard-to-find Italian groceries. During the Federal Hill Stroll (usually held in early June) festivalgoers enjoy music and sample signature cuisine at numerous eateries within a ¾-mile stretch of Atwells Avenue. ⊠ *379 Atwells Ave., Federal Hill* ⊕ *www.federalhillprov.com.*

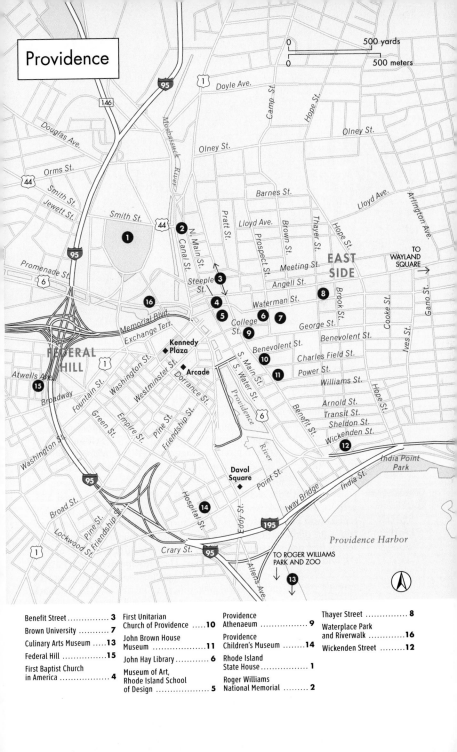

Providence

0 — 500 yards
0 — 500 meters

Doyle Ave.
Camp St.
Hope St.
Olney St.
Douglas Ave.
Orms St.
Smith St.
Jewett St.
Smith St.
Moshassuck River
Barnes St.
Lloyd Ave.
Arlington Ave.
Olney St.
N. Main St.
Pratt St.
Lloyd Ave.
Brown St.
Thayer St.
Hope St.
Canal St.
Prospect St.
Meeting St.
EAST SIDE
TO WAYLAND SQUARE
Promenade St.
Steeple St.
Angell St.
Brook St.
Cooke St.
Ives St.
Gano St.
Memorial Blvd.
Waterman St.
College St.
George St.
Exchange Terr.
Kennedy Plaza
Benevolent St.
Benevolent St.
FEDERAL HILL
Washington St.
S. Main St.
S. Water St.
Charles Field St.
Atwells Ave.
Arcade
Westminster St.
Dorrance St.
Power St.
Williams St.
Broadway
Fountain St.
Green St.
Empire St.
Pine St.
Friendship St.
Providence River
Benefit St.
Arnold St.
Transit St.
Sheldon St.
Wickenden St.
Hope St.
Washington St.
Davol Square
Point St.
India Point Park
Broad St.
Pine St.
Hospital St.
Providence River
Iway Bridge
India St.
Lockwood St.
Friendship St.
Crary St.
Allens Ave.
Providence Harbor
TO ROGER WILLIAMS PARK AND ZOO

Benefit Street 3
Brown University 7
Culinary Arts Museum 13
Federal Hill 15
First Baptist Church in America 4

First Unitarian Church of Providence 10
John Brown House Museum 11
John Hay Library 6
Museum of Art, Rhode Island School of Design 5

Providence Athenaeum 9
Providence Children's Museum 14
Rhode Island State House 1
Roger Williams National Memorial 2

Thayer Street 8
Waterplace Park and Riverwalk 16
Wickenden Street 12

In the last 20 years, the Providence riverfront has been beautified, highlighting the river that divides the city.

First Baptist Church in America. This historic house of worship was built in 1775 for a congregation established in 1638 by Roger Williams and his fellow Puritan dissenters. One of the finest examples of Georgian architecture in Colonial America, the church was built to seat 1,200 people and to this day is used for Brown University's baccalaureate ceremony. The 185-foot steeple was put up in 3½ days. The auditorium's large crystal chandelier from Ireland was installed in 1792. Self-guided tour booklets are available in multiple languages. ⊠ *75 N. Main St., Downtown* ☎ *401/454–3418* ⊕ *www.fbcia.org* ✉ *$2* ☉ *Weekdays 10–noon and 1–3. Guided tours Memorial Day–Labor Day.*

OFF THE BEATEN PATH

Roger Williams Park and Zoo. Plan a full day to take in this regal 435-acre Victorian park where you can picnic, feed the ducks in the lakes, rent a swan paddleboat, or ride a Victorian-style carousel. The 40-acre zoo—one of the nation's oldest— has African elephants, Masai giraffes, zebras, red pandas, snow leopards, moon bears, gibbons, giant anteaters, and river otters in natural settings. The **Museum of Natural History** has a collection of more than 250,000 specimens, including preserved animals, plants, rocks, fossils, and ethnographic objects. The **Cormack Planetarium** has a 2 pm show on weekends year-round and daily in the summer months. The **Botanical Center** has two greenhouses and 12,000 square feet of indoor gardens. ⊠ *1000 Elmwood Ave., South Providence* ☎ *401/785–9450 museum, 401/785–3510 zoo* ⊕ *www.rogerwilliamsparkzoo.org and providenceri.gov/museum* ✉ Zoo: *$14.95; planetarium and museum $3; botanical center $3* ☉ Zoo: *daily 9–4; museum: daily 10-5; botanical center: Tues.–Sun. 11–4.*

WORTH NOTING

FAMILY **Providence Children's Museum.** At Rhode Island's only hands-on children's museum, kids and their families play and learn in vibrant interactive environments including "Water Ways," a playground of pumps and fountains; "Coming to Rhode Island," a time-traveling adventure through state history; and "Littlewoods," with a cave and a climbing tree for toddlers. Kids can also investigate the awesome power of air, explore a two-story-high climbing maze, and enjoy a picnic in the Children's Garden. ✉ *100 South St., Downtown* ☎ *401/273–5437* ⊕ *www.childrenmuseum.org* ✆ *$8.50* ☉ *Sept.–Mar., Tues.–Sun. 9–6; Apr.–Labor Day., daily 9–6.*

Rhode Island State House. Designed by the noted firm of McKim, Mead & White, Rhode Island's 1904 capitol building has one of the world's largest self-supporting marble domes. The gilded Independent Man statue that tops the dome was struck by lightning 27 times before lightning rods were installed in 1975. The State Library on the north side of the second floor has the military accoutrements of Nathaniel Greene, Washington's second-in-command during the Revolutionary War, plus the state flag on board Apollo 11's first lunar landing mission in 1969. In the State Room is a full-length portrait of George Washington by Rhode Islander Gilbert Stuart. The original 1663 parchment charter granted by King Charles II to the colony of Rhode Island is the centerpiece of the museum, opened on the charter's 350th anniversary. Guided tours lasting 50 minutes are offered weekday mornings. ✉ *82 Smith St., Downtown* ☎ *401/222–3983* ⊕ *www. sos.ri.gov/publicinfo/tours* ☉ *Weekdays 8:30–4:30; tours weekdays 9, 10, and 11.*

Roger Williams National Memorial. This 4½-acre park dedicated to Rhode Island's founder has a symbolic well to mark the site of the spring around which Roger Williams built Providence's original settlement in 1636. A visitor center has a five-minute film about the park's namesake. A demonstration garden shows how Native Americans cultivated corn, beans, and squash and English colonists grew herbs. The park has several picnic tables and 20 free parking spaces, though a two-hour limit is strictly enforced. ✉ *282 N. Main St., Downtown* ☎ *401/521–7266* ⊕ *www.nps.gov/rowi* ✆ *Free* ☉ *June–early Oct., daily 9–5; mid-Oct.– May, daily 9–4:30.*

Waterplace Park and Riverwalk. Venetian-style footbridges, cobblestone walkways, and an amphitheater encircling a tidal pond set the tone at this 4-acre tract. Near the junction of three rivers—the Woonasquatucket, Providence, and Moshassuck—the park is a gathering place for free concerts and open-air ballroom dancing in the summer. It's also the site of the popular **WaterFire**, a multimedia installation featuring music and nearly 100 burning braziers that rise from the water between dusk and midnight. WaterFire attracts nearly 1 million visitors annually. ✉ *Memorial Blvd., Steeple St., and Exchange St., Downtown* ☎ *401/273–1155* ⊕ *www.waterfire.org.*

Culinary Arts Museum. This offbeat museum on the campus of Johnson & Wales University celebrates the joy of cooking and eating throughout human history. There's an authentic 1920s diner, ancient Chinese culinary vessels, displays of mayonnaise makers, marshmallow beaters, other kitchen gadgets, and vintage menus. Unique exhibitions and collections include ephemera on Rhode Island food novelties and contributions by immigrant cultures to the state's rich culinary tradition. ⊠ *315 Harborside Blvd., South Providence* ☎ *401/598–2805* ⊕ *www.culinary. org* ⊠ *$7* ⊙ *Tues.–Sun. 10–5.*

EAST SIDE

TOP ATTRACTIONS

Fodor'sChoice
★

Benefit Street. The centerpiece of any visit to Providence is this "mile of history" where the city's wealthiest families lived in the 18th and early 19th centuries. Benefit Street is home to the one of the highest concentrations of Colonial architecture and passes through the campuses of Brown University and the Rhode Island School of Design. The Rhode Island Historical Society conducts 90-minute tours that cost $14 and depart from the John Brown House Museum at 11 am Tuesday to Saturday between mid-June and mid-October. ⊠ *Benefit St., Downtown* ☎ *401/273–7507* ⊕ *www.rihs.org.*

Brown University. Founded in 1764, this Ivy League institution is the nation's seventh-oldest college and has more than 40 academic departments, including the Warren Alpert Medical School. On a stroll through the College Hill campus you'll encounter Gothic and Beaux-Arts structures as well as the imposing Prospect Street gates, which open twice a year—in fall to welcome the students and spring to bid them farewell. Free one-hour university tours conducted by current students depart from the Stephen Robert '62 Campus Center on the Main Green. Public events include outdoor Shakespeare performances and a summer open-air movie series hosted by the Granoff Center for the Creative Arts. The Haffenreffer Museum of Anthropology on the ground floor of Manning Hall has exhibits showcasing artifacts from around the world. The David Winton Bell Gallery in the List Art Center hosts several major art exhibitions a year. ⊠ *Stephen Robert '62 Campus Center, 75 Waterman St., East Side* ☎ *401/863–2378* ⊕ *www.brown.edu.*

Thayer Street. Bustling Thayer Street bears a proud old New England name and is very much a part of life at Brown University. You'll find restaurants from Greek to Korean, fashion boutiques, shops selling vintage clothing and funky gifts, and the Avon Cinema in the blocks between Waterman and Bowen streets. ⊠ *Thayer St., between Waterman and Bowen Sts., East Side.*

John Brown House Museum. Rhode Island's most famous 18th-century home was the stately residence of John Brown, a wealthy businessman, slave trader, politician, and China Trade merchant. Finished in 1788, John Brown's three-story brick mansion was designed by his brother Joseph Brown, who also designed the First Baptist Meeting House. The stately house is a perfect example of late-Georgian-early-Federal design and made quite the impression on John Quincy Adams, who

Roger Williams

It was an unthinkable idea: a complete separation of church and state. Break the tie between church and state and where would the government get its authority? The answer threatened the Puritan way of life. And that's why in the winter of 1636 the Massachusetts Bay Colony banished a certain preacher with radical opinions named Roger Williams. He fled south into the wilderness with the goal of establishing a new colony of religious tolerance and arranged to buy land from the Narragansett sachems Cononicus and Miantonomo at the confluence of the Woonasquatucket and Moshassuck rivers. Word spread that this new settlement Williams named Providence was a place where civil power rested in the hands of the people. Those persecuted for their beliefs flocked to Providence, which grew into a prosperous Colonial shipping port. What started out as a radical experiment became the basis of American democracy.

called it "the most magnificent and elegant private mansion that I have ever seen on this continent." An ardent patriot, John Brown was a famous participant in the burning of the British customs ship *Gaspee* in 1772. Guided tours are given every 90 minutes. ⊠ *52 Power St., East Side* ☎ *401/273–7507* ⊕ *www.rihs.org/museums/john-brown-house* ⊠ *$10* ⊙ *Apr.–Nov., Tues.–Fri. 1:30–4, Sat. 10–4; Dec.–Mar., Fri. and Sat. 10–4.*

FAMILY

Fodor's Choice
★

Museum of Art, Rhode Island School of Design. This museum houses more than 86,000 objects ranging from ancient art to work by contemporary artists from across the globe. Highlights include Impressionist paintings, Gorham silver, Newport furniture, an ancient Egyptian mummy, and a 12th-century Buddha—the largest historic Japanese wooden sculpture in the United States. Artists represented include major figures in the history of visual art and culture, including Cézanne, Chanel, Copley, Degas, Hirst, Homer, LeWitt, Matisse, Manet, Picasso, Rothko, Sargent, Turner, Twombly, van Gogh, and Warhol—to name a few. ⊠ *224 Benefit St., East Side* ☎ *401/454–6500* ⊕ *www.risdmuseum.org* ⊠ *$12* ⊙ *Tues., Wed., and Fri.–Sun. 10–5, Thurs. 10–9.*

Providence Athenaeum. Philadelphia architect William Strickland designed this 1838 Greek Revival building. Here Edgar Allan Poe courted poet Sarah Helen Whitman and signed a periodical in the collection containing a piece he published anonymously. An 1870s Manet print that illustrated Poe's "The Raven" hangs in the rare book room, which also contains two medieval illuminated manuscripts. Raven signs are posted at eight points of interest on a self-guided library tour. Among them is a special cabinet modeled after an Egyptian temple to house the library's multivolume imperial edition of *Description de l'Egypte* (1809–22), commissioned by Napoléon. ■ TIP→ **If you need to log on, the library has Wi-Fi.** ⊠ *251 Benefit St., East Side* ☎ *401/421–6970* ⊕ *www.providenceathenaeum.org* ⊠ *Free* ⊙ *Sept.–May, Mon.–Thurs. 9–7, Fri. and Sat. 9–5, Sun. 1–5; June–Labor Day, Mon.–Thurs. 9–7, Fri. 9–5, Sat. 9–1.*

WORTH NOTING

First Unitarian Church of Providence. This Romanesque house of worship made of Rhode Island granite was built in 1816. Its steeple houses a 2,500-pound bell, the largest ever cast in Paul Revere's foundry. ⊠ *1 Benevolent St., at Benefit St., East Side* ☎ *401/421–7970* ⊕ *www. firstunitarianprov.org* ⊠ *Free* ⊘ *Aug.–mid-July, weekdays 9–4.*

John Hay Library. Built in 1910 and named for Abraham Lincoln's secretary, the "Hay" houses Brown University Library's collections of rare books and manuscripts. World-class collections of Lincoln-related items, H.P. Lovecraft letters, and toy soldiers are of particular interest. The library is open to the public, but you need a photo ID to enter. ⊠ *20 Prospect St., East Side* ☎ *401/863–2146* ⊕ *library.brown.edu/about/ hay* ⊠ *Free* ⊘ *Sept.–mid-Dec. and Feb.–May, Mon.–Thurs., 10–6, Fri. 10–5; mid-Dec.–Jan. and June–Aug., weekdays 10–5.*

QUICK BITES

✕ **Seven Stars Bakery.** For first-rate coffee and espresso drinks with artful foam, venture up Hope Street to the bustling Seven Stars Bakery, located in a converted garage. You'll also find pecan sticky buns, brownies, cookies, and sandwiches on fresh baguettes. ⊠ *820 Hope St., East Side* ☎ *401/521–2200* ⊕ *www.sevenstarsbakery.com* ⊘ *Weekdays 6 am–6:30 pm; weekends 7–6.*

Wickenden Street. Named for a Baptist minister who was one of Providence's first settlers, this main artery in the Fox Point district is home to antiques stores, art galleries, and trendy cafés. It also hosts the Coffee Exchange, one of the area's most popular gathering spots. Once a working-class Portuguese neighborhood, the Wickenden Street area has seen steady gentrification over the years. But Our Lady of the Rosary Church on Traverse Street still conducts two Sunday morning Masses in Portuguese. ⊠ *Wickenden St.*

WHERE TO EAT

The hard part is deciding which one of Providence's many superb dining spots to visit. If you're in the mood for Italian, you'll enjoy a stroll through Federal Hill on Atwells Avenue. Downtown is home to excellent fine-dining establishments, while the East Side has great neighborhood and upscale casual restaurants as well as an assortment of spots with hip ambience and international cuisine.

DOWNTOWN

$$$
ITALIAN
Fodor'sChoice
★

✕ **Bacaro.** The two levels at this lively Italian restaurant founded by chef Brian Kingsford and partner Jennifer Matta offer unique dining experiences. The informal first floor has a deli case stocked with cured salami, cheeses, olives, and traditional Italian-style tapas. Upstairs is a more traditional dining room with impressive views of the Providence River. Every table receives a separate *salumeria cicchetteria* menu checklist and selections come on a beautifully presented board. Rely on the very knowledgeable servers to guide you around the frequently changing menu, which emphasizes seasonal, local ingredients. The pan-seared duck breast with creamy red-wine risotto inspires as much awe as the

The Independent Man atop Rhode Island's marble-domed capitol building symbolizes the smallest state's spirit of free thinking.

high ceilings and exposed wood beams. The hard part is saving room for dessert—the pear and walnut crisp tart for two can actually feed four. [$] *Average main: $27* ✉ *262 S. Water St., Downtown* ☎ *401/751–3700* 🌐 *www.bacarorestaurant.net* 🕓 *Closed Sun. and Mon. No lunch.*

$$ MODERN AMERICAN 🍴 **The Dorrance.** The opulent first floor of what was once the Union Trust Building is home to one of Providence's best-known purveyors of farm-to-table food. Siena marble, ornate plaster detailing, and stained-glass windows lend a Newport-mansion vibe, but the long bar is populated by young professionals enjoying handcrafted creative cocktails. The Up N' Cumber cocktail with cucumber vodka, St-Germain, lime juice, and ginger beer is divine. A one-page menu of small and large plates offers creative dishes made from local, fresh ingredients. [$] *Average main: $20* ✉ *60 Dorrance St., Downtown* ☎ *401/521–6000* 🌐 *www.thedorrance.com* 🕓 *Closed Sun. and Mon. No lunch.*

$$$ MODERN AMERICAN 🍴 **Gracie's.** The city's best spot for a romantic meal is Table 21 in a cozy, private alcove at Ellen Gracyalny's stellar downtown restaurant. Located across the street from Trinity Rep, Gracie's mixes sophistication with whimsy in the main dining room with star-themed decor. Executive chef Matthew Varga is known for wowing guests with pleasant little surprises. The amazing triple-cooked potato medallion accompanying mouthwatering Chatham cod loin might make you reevaluate your low-carb diet. The service here is excellent. A three-course prix-fixe menu for $40 is available nightly, but for true excitement, opt for Varga's five- or seven-course tasting and see what delights come your way. [$] *Average main: $28* ✉ *194 Washington St., Downtown* ☎ *401/272–7811* 🌐 *www.graciesprov.com* 🕓 *Closed Sun. and Mon. No lunch.*

$$$ SEAFOOD 🍴 **Hemenway's Seafood Grill & Oyster Bar.** In a city where culinary newcomers tend to garner all the attention, Hemenway's continues to be one of the great seafood restaurants. The menu includes New England staples like a perfectly cracked baked stuffed lobster with lump crab and scallop stuffing, fried whole belly clams, and baked, fried, or grilled George's Bank sea scallops. Inspired chef's specialties include a prosciutto-wrapped rainbow trout and a Portuguese-style grilled littleneck clam appetizer with *chouriço* (spicy Portugese sausage), savory broth, and grilled bread. The wine list is extensive, and martini lovers will have a hard time making a decision here. High ceilings and huge windows grace the dining room, which looks out on the city's World War II Memorial. In warm weather, dine outside on the front patio. [$] *Average main: $28* ✉ *121 S. Main St., Downtown* ☎ *401/351–8570* 🌐 *www.hemenwaysrestaurant.com.*

$$ AMERICAN 🍴 **Local 121.** What was once the lobby of the Dreyfus Hotel has been transformed into an elegant restaurant where the focus is on locally raised foods from area farms, fishermen, and food artisans. Local 121's posh dining room has a dark-brown-and-white color scheme, stylish light fixtures, and comfortable round booths; the more casual Tap Room has a long wood bar and stained-glass windows. The varied menu changes seasonally and features a fresh pasta and local catch of the day. [$] *Average main: $20* ✉ *121 Washington St., Downtown* ☎ *401/274–2121* 🌐 *www.local121.com* 🕒 *No lunch Mon.*

$$$$ MODERN AMERICAN 🍴 **Mill's Tavern.** The lasagna-inspired Cobb salad—served as a square of perfectly chopped eggs, vegetables, and bacon on a bed of Bibb lettuce—is just one of many examples of culinary artistry you'll find here. This upscale tavern has handsome brick walls and vaulted casement ceilings. The menu, which includes a raw bar and selections from the wood-burning oven and rotisserie, consists of contemporary French-influenced American fare that changes quarterly to emphasize local and seasonal ingredients. If you decide not to go for the Angus rib eye with house-made steak sauce, the pan-roasted Scottish salmon over French lentils with citrus tomato jam is noteworthy. Take advantage of the $29.95 three-course fixed-price menu on weeknights. [$] *Average main: $30* ✉ *101 N. Main St., Downtown* ☎ *401/272–3331* 🌐 *www.millstavernrestaurant.com* 🕒 *No lunch.*

$$ AMERICAN 🍴 **The ROI.** Housed in a downstairs space in the old Jewelry District, the ROI generates a hip, urban vibe. Jazz plays as you descend into the restaurant to a sleek, dark interior of tables, booths, and a curved bar, entering what feels like a modern throwback to the city's speakeasy past. The music is as much of a draw as the food; bands play nightly on a large stage. The menu aims to please with an emphasis on seasonal ingredients and cozy dishes like polenta fries, grilled pizza, and half-pound burgers made with antibiotic-free beef. [$] *Average main: $13* ✉ *150 Chestnut St., Downtown* ☎ *401/272–2161* 🌐 *theroiprov.com* 🕒 *Closed Mon.*

$ CAFÉ 🍴 **Tazza.** Skip the bland buffet at your hotel and head to this great, light-filled space where the real coffee drinkers congregate. They come for Tazza's robust house blend brewed mad-scientist-style with siphon pots that boil water heated by halogen lamps. The result is a cup of joe without bitterness or acidity. You can also opt to get your brew hand poured over coffee grounds directly into your cup. The unique brunch menu combines lunch fare like grilled pizza and Angus bacon burgers with a variety of sweet and savory breakfast options like beignets and shrimp-and-cheddar grits. Plan to return for weeknight raw bar specials, great cocktails, and the adventurous dinner menu featuring local lamb loin and Rhode Island striped bass. ■ **TIP→ Tazza sponsors free outdoor movies in the lot next door on Thursday, June through October.** [$] *Average main: $9* ✉ *250 Westminster St., Downtown* ☎ *401/421–3300* 🌐 *www.tazzacaffe.com.*

EAST SIDE

$$$ ITALIAN 🍴 **Al Forno.** When it opened in 1980, Al Forno, which means "from the oven" in Italian, put Providence on the national dining map, and it continues to garner ebullient praise from critics and patrons. The oven produces a number of stellar dishes, among them thin-crust pizzas, roasted duck with prune-stuffed gnocchi, spicy roasted clams, and bacon-wrapped wild boar loin. Also consider the extraordinary pastas, such as house-made cavatelli with prosciutto and butternut squash. For dessert, look to the pear-and-walnut tart. [$] *Average main: $24* ✉ *577 S. Main St., East Side* ☎ *401/273–9760* 🌐 *www.alforno.com* ✍ *Reservations not accepted* ⏲ *Closed Sun. and Mon. No lunch.*

$$$ BISTRO 🍴 **Chez Pascal.** You know this French bistro will be welcoming and unpretentious from its logo, a trio of pigs in striped shirts and berets. Located in a peaceful residential neighborhood, Chez Pascal seats 80, yet a dividing wall makes it feel intimate and romantic. The menu always offers escargots baked in butter, garlic, and parsley and a house-butchered pork of the day, but also reflects locally available seasonal produce. Lunch is served in an open kitchen inside the main dining room called the Wurst Kitchen. ■ **TIP→ A take-out window serving sausages and sandwiches is open during lunch Tuesday to Saturday.** [$] *Average main: $26* ✉ *960 Hope St., East Side* ☎ *401/421–4422* 🌐 *www.chez-pascal.com* ⏲ *Closed Sun. No lunch Mon.*

$$ FRENCH 🍴 **Red Stripe.** A giant fork hangs on the outside of this lively neighborhood brasserie in Wayland Square. They do things big here, from the popular 10-ounce Angus burger to the everything-but-the-kitchen-sink chopped salad. The Prince Edward Island mussels come with a choice of savory broth and hand-cut frites and are uncovered tableside with a flouish, releasing aromatic steam. Menu highlights include lavender-scented brick chicken and cider beer–brined pork tenderloin. [$] *Average main: $16* ✉ *465 Angell St., East Side* ☎ *401/437–6950* 🌐 *redstriperestaurants.com.*

FEDERAL HILL

$ ITALIAN 🍴 **Angelo's Civita Farnese.** Since 1924, boisterous Angelo's has been serving up reliably good home-style red-sauce fare with old-world charm. The third-generation, family-owned restaurant in the heart of Federal Hill has a little bar and affordable prices. Locals come for the chicken Parmesan, veal and peppers, and broiled or fried hand-cut pork chops. [$] *Average main: $12* ✉ *141 Atwells Ave., Federal Hill* ☎ *401/621–8171* 🌐 *www.angelosonthehill.com.*

7

$$$
MODERN
AMERICAN
Fodor's Choice
★

✕ **Nick's on Broadway.** What might pass as a no-frills luncheonette from the street is actually a trendy West End restaurant with some of the best breakfast food in Rhode Island, plus extraordinary lunches and dinners. Young chef Derek Wagner delights morning patrons with vanilla-battered French toast with warm fruit compote; later in the day he prepares a knockout pulled-pork sandwich with cheddar and caramelized onion. Foodies will appreciate Wagner's passionate embrace of the farm-to-table movement, not to mention his attention to detail—his outstanding homemade mustard may occupy a small place on the charcuterie plate but it speaks volumes. Ask for a seat at the polished wood counter for a front-row view of the well-choreographed show in the open kitchen, and try the chocolate-bacon bread pudding for dessert. $ *Average main: $24* ⊠ *500 Broadway, Federal Hill* ☎ *401/421–0286* ⊕ *www.nicksonbroadway.com* ☏ *Closed Mon. and Tues. No dinner Sun.*

$$$
ITALIAN

✕ **Pane e Vino.** This popular Federal Hill spot, whose name means "bread and wine" in Italian, offers fresh ingredients presented in a straightforward way. Portions are big in the Rhode Island comfort food tradition: appetizers like the braised escarole, house-made sausage, and cannellini beans over grilled artisanal bread are more like a lunch portion. Share a starch course if you dare, but keep in mind that the veal chop may rival the one that tipped over Fred Flintstone's car. A $22.95 per person prix-fixe menu is available weekdays from 5 to 7 and all day Sunday. The dining room staff provides excellent service, and tables in front near the window are especially suited for a romantic dinner. ■TIP→ **A gluten-free menu is also available.** $ *Average main: $25* ⊠ *365 Atwells Ave., Federal Hill* ☎ *401/223–2230* ⊕ *www.panevino.net* ☏ *No lunch.*

$$
ITALIAN

✕ **Siena.** Among Federal Hill's 30 or so restaurants, Siena generates the most buzz, and for good reason: the *branzino* (Chilean sea bass) with scallops in a creamy scallion sauce and the pasta with a rich Bolognese are legendary. It's best to split an appetizer, as portions here are huge, though you might want to keep the delicious *involtini di melanzane*, eggplant rolled with prosciutto and ricotta and baked in tangy marinara sauce, all to yourself. The silky-white *pasta e fagioli* under the menu's antipasti section is a meal in itself. The excellent wine list is usually augmented by special additions available by bottle or glass, and the well-trained waitstaff can help you make the perfect pairing. ■TIP→ **Ask for a table by the large windows, as the stylish back dining room can get noisy.** $ *Average main: $20* ⊠ *238 Atwells Ave., Federal Hill* ☎ *401/521–3311* ⊕ *www.sienari.com* ☏ *No lunch.*

WHERE TO STAY

DOWNTOWN

$$
B&B/INN

▦ **Christopher Dodge House.** Rooms on the east side of this three-story 1858 Italianate brick town house have direct views of the State House, though Interstate 95 lies between the two. **Pros:** huge windows in rooms; free passes to a nearby health club. **Cons:** Interstate 95 may be too close for light sleepers. $ *Rooms from: $149* ⊠ *11 W. Park St., Downtown* ☎ *401/351–6111* ⊕ *www.providence-hotel.com* ➫ *14 rooms* ◉❙ *Breakfast.*

$$ **Hotel Providence.** In the heart of the city's Arts and Entertainment
HOTEL District, this intimate boutique hotel sets the standard for elegant decor and attentive service. **Pros:** attentive staff; plush rooms; "doggie lounge" has treats for pets. **Cons:** late risers may not appreciate the 8 am pealing of Grace Church's 16 bells. *$ Rooms from: $159 ⌧ 139 Mathewson St., Downtown* ☎ *401/861–8000, 800/861–8990* ⊕ *www. hotelprovidence.com ↻ 64 rooms, 16 suites* ⍟ *No meals.*

$$ **Providence Biltmore.** The city's beloved landmark since 1922, the
HOTEL Providence Biltmore has been treated to a multimillion-dollar renovation that has brought the rooms up to the 21st century. **Pros:** spacious suites; great location. **Cons:** ongoing renovations. *$ Rooms from: $164 ⌧ Kennedy Plaza, 11 Dorrance St., Downtown* ☎ *401/421– 0700, 800/294–7709* ⊕ *www.providencebiltmore.com ↻ 292 rooms, 185 suites* ⍟ *No meals.*

$$$ **Renaissance Providence Downtown Hotel.** This luxury hotel occupies
HOTEL one of Providence's most mysterious buildings, a stately nine-story
Fodor's Choice neoclassical building constructed as a Masonic temple but never
★ occupied. **Pros:** terrific location next door to Providence Place Mall; super-comfortable linens and bedding. **Cons:** some rooms have small windows. *$ Rooms from: $209 ⌧ 5 Ave. of the Arts, Downtown* ☎ *401/919–5000, 800/468–3571* ⊕ *www.renaissanceprovidence.com ↻ 272 rooms, 7 suites* ⍟ *No meals.*

EAST SIDE

$$ **The Old Court Bed & Breakfast.** Parents of Brown and Rhode Island
B&B/INN School of Design students book their stays in this three-story Italianate inn on historic Benefit Street a few years before graduation. **Pros:** on a regal residential street; elegant furnishings; friendly service. **Cons:** small bathrooms; closets sized for 19th-century wardrobes. *$ Rooms from: $145 ⌧ 144 Benefit St., East Side* ☎ *401/751–2002* ⊕ *www.oldcourt. com ↻ 10 rooms* ⍟ *Breakfast.*

FEDERAL HILL

$$ **Hotel Dolce Villa.** This small, well-managed inn is the only accom-
HOTEL modation actually in Federal Hill—it overlooks DePasquale Square and its vibrant cafés, gelato stands, and gourmet markets. **Pros:** great value; fun location with sister restaurant Caffe Dolce Vita next door; huge suites. **Cons:** modern white decor and carpets starting to show wear; no gym. *$ Rooms from: $159 ⌧ 63 DePasquale Sq., Federal Hill* ☎ *401/383–7031* ⊕ *www.dolcevillari.com ↻ 14 suites* ⍟ *No meals.*

NIGHTLIFE AND THE ARTS

For events listings, consult the daily *Providence Journal* or the website ⊕ *golocalprov.com.* The weekly *Providence Phoenix* or *Providence Monthly* are both free in restaurants and shops.

NIGHTLIFE

DOWNTOWN

BARS **Mirabar.** Long-running Mirabar is one of the most popular gay clubs in Providence. ⌧ *15 Elbow St., Downtown* ☎ *401/331–6761* ⊕ *www.mirabar.com.*

AS220. Hear original music from techno-pop and hip-hop to folk and jazz at this gallery and performance space. Spoken word and poetry slams, comedy nights, and open mikes are also scheduled. The bar always has a dozen rotating beers on tap. ⊠ *115 Empire St., Downtown* ☎ *401/861–9190* ⊕ *www.as220.org.*

Lupo's Heartbreak Hotel. Housed in a five-story theater, this legendary music venue hosts nationally known alternative, rock, blues, and punk bands. ⊠ *79 Washington St., Downtown* ☎ *401/331–5876* ⊕ *www.lupos.com.*

Point Street Dueling Pianos. Two pianists play whatever the audience wants to hear, from "Happy Birthday" to "Piano Man" to an assortment of rock and roll, heavy metal, and pop. If you're in the mood to sing, they may invite you on stage. Reservations are taken for table seating on Friday and Saturday nights. ⊠ *3 Davol Sq., Downtown* ☎ *401/270–7828* ⊕ *www.pointstreetpianos.com.*

Rí Rá Irish Pub. Corned beef and cabbage is on the menu year-round at this atmospheric pub. Inside the vintage Union Station building, the interior was shipped here, piece by piece, from County Mayo, Ireland. Pop and rock cover bands play Wednesday to Sunday night. ⊠ *50 Exchange Terr., Downtown* ☎ *401/272–1953* ⊕ *www.rira.com.*

EAST SIDE

BARS **Hot Club.** This place is fashionable with young professionals, university professors, and politicians. Summer nights find a crowd on the outdoor deck overlooking the Providence River. For cheap eats, try local favorites like the saugy dog or the stuffed quahog. ⊠ *575 S. Water St., East Side* ☎ *401/861–9007.*

FEDERAL HILL

BARS **Lili Marlene's.** An easygoing bar and with cozy booths, Lili Marlene's cultivates a loyal following among in-the-know locals who like martinis and beer, good burgers, and free pool. ⊠ *422 Atwells Ave., Federal Hill* ☎ *401/751–4996.*

THE ARTS

FILM

Cable Car Cinema & Cafe. This espresso bar and neighborhood art house showcases a fine slate of foreign and independent flicks. Seating is on couches and old-school theater chairs. Get beer and wine at the concession stand. ⊠ *204 S. Main St., Downtown* ☎ *401/272–3970* ⊕ *www.cablecarcinema.com.*

GALLERY TOURS

Gallery Night Providence. During Gallery Night, held the third Thursday evening of every month March through November, 25 galleries and museums hold open houses and mount special exhibitions. ⊠ *1 Citizens Plaza, Downtown* ☎ *401/490–2042* ⊕ *www.gallerynight.info.*

MUSIC

Providence Performing Arts Center. Having arrowly escaped the wrecking ball in the 1970s, the 3,200-seat Providence Performing Arts Center is listed on the National Register of Historic Places. Major renovations restored the stage, lobby, and arcade to their original splendor when it opened in 1928 as a Loew's Movie Palace. It hosts Broadway shows, concerts, and other large-scale events. Its mighty Wurlitzer pipe organ is a source of pride. ⊠ *220 Weybosset St., Downtown* ☎ *401/421–2787* ⊕ *www.ppacri.org.*

Veterans Memorial Auditorium. The 1,900-seat Veterans Memorial Auditorium (known locally as "the Vets") has a proscenium stage and exquisite interior and hosts concerts, opera, and dance performances. From September to May, this is the home of the Rhode Island Philharmonic. ⊠ *1 Ave. of the Arts, Downtown* ☎ *401/421–2787* ⊕ *www.vmari.com.*

THEATER

Brown University Theater. Every winter, Brown University's renowned graduate playwriting program presents the Writing is Live festival of new plays. A lively summer theater program through the university's partnership with Trinity Rep offers professional productions for the cost of a movie ticket. Dance performances take place in the Ashamu Dance studio and in the Stuart Theatre. ⊠ *Catherine Bryan Dill Center for the Performing Arts, 77 Waterman St., East Side* ☎ *401/863–2838* ⊕ *www.brown.edu/tickets.*

Trinity Repertory Company. This troupe present classic plays, intimate musicals, and new works by young playwrights, as well as an annual version of *A Christmas Carol,* in the renovated Lederer Theater, which opened as the Emery Majestic vaudeville house in 1917. ⊠ *201 Washington St., Downtown* ☎ *401/351–4242* ⊕ *www.trinityrep.com* ☯ *Box office Tues.–Sun. noon–8.*

SPORTS AND THE OUTDOORS

BIKING

East Bay Bicycle Path. The 14½-mile East Bay Bicycle Path connects Providence's India Point Park to Independence Park in Bristol. Along the way, you pass eight parks and deck bridges with views of coves and saltwater marshes. The route is extremely popular on weekends, and is typically congested when the weather's fine. ■ TIP→ Save a few quarters for the homemade lemonade stands, operated by neighborhood children along the route. ⊠ *India Point Park, India St.* ☎ *401/253–7482* ⊕ *www.dot.ri.gov/bikeri/east_bay_bike_path.asp.*

BOATING

Prime boating areas include the Providence River, the Seekonk River, and Narragansett Bay.

Narragansett Boat Club. Experienced scullers can join a group for afternoon rowing on the Seekonk and Providence rivers with the Narragansett Boat Club. The club offers classes in sculling and rowing for beginners. ⊠ *2 River Rd., East Side* ☎ *401/272–1838* ⊕ *www.rownbc.org.*

ICE-SKATING

Bank of America City Center. The 14,000-square-foot outdoor ice rink is twice the size of the one at New York City's Rockefeller Plaza. The facility is open daily from late November to mid-March. In the summer, it hosts concerts, festivals, and other events. ⊠ *2 Kennedy Plaza, Downtown* ☎ *401/331–5544* ⊕ *www.providenceskating.com* 🎟 *Skating $7 adults; $4 seniors, military, children age 12 and younger; rentals $5* ☯ *Late Nov.–mid-Mar., weekdays 10–10, weekends 11–10.*

SHOPPING

Providence has a handful of small but engaging shopping areas. In Fox Point, Wickenden Street contains many antiques stores and several art galleries. Near Brown University, Thayer Street has a number of boutiques, though there has been an influx of chain stores. With its eclectic collection of specialty stores, always-trendy Hope Street has branded itself as the East Side's Main Street. Downtown's Westminster Street has morphed into a strip of independently owned fashion boutiques, galleries, and design stores.

DOWNTOWN

ANTIQUES AND HOME FURNISHINGS

Craftland. Artsy fans will rejoice in the array of arts and crafts to be found at Craftland. Jewelry, notecards, prints, silk-screened T-shirts, fashion accessories, bags, and other sparkly handmade objects by local artists are for sale at this colorful shop and gallery. ⊠ *235 Westminster St., Downtown* ☎ *401/272–4285* ⊕ *www.craftlandshop.com* ☺ *Mon.– Sat., 10–6, Sun. 11–5.*

HomeStyle. Along increasingly gentrified Westminster Street, drop by HomeStyle for eye-catching objets d'art, stylish housewares, and other decorative items. ⊠ *229 Westminster St., Downtown* ☎ *401/277–1159* ⊕ *www.homestyleri.com.*

Tilden-Thurber Gallery. A Providence landmark since 1895, the building houses the country's largest collection of classical and Colonial furniture and antiques. ⊠ *292 Westminster St., at Mathewson St., Downtown* ☎ *401/272–3200* ⊕ *www.tildenthurber.com* ☺ *Sat. 11–5.*

ART GALLERIES

risd|works. This shop has a selection of quirky kitchen gadgets, hand-blown glass, jewelry, and prints by Rhode Island School of Design faculty and alumni, including *Family Guy* creator Seth MacFarlane's custom RISD T-shirt. ⊠ *20 N. Main St., Downtown* ☎ *401/277–4949* ⊕ *www.risdworks.com* ☺ *Tues., Wed., and Fri.–Sun. 10–5, Thurs. 10–9.*

FOOD

Tony's Colonial Food store. This superb grocery and deli stocks freshly prepared foods to eat on the premises or take with you. Tony's offers a family-friendly atmosphere and the finest Italian meats and cheeses; imported vinegars and olive oils; and candies and confections, all at reasonable prices. Try the Italian grinder, a Rhode Island lunch staple. ⊠ *311 Atwells Ave., Downtown* ☎ *401/621–8675* ⊕ *tonyscolonial. mybigcommerce.com.*

Fodor'sChoice ★ **Venda Ravioli.** One of the best gourmet shops in New England, Venda Ravioli surrounds you with the sights, scents, and flavors of Italy as you choose from an amazing selection of imported foods. The lively banter between customers and employees adds to the convivial atmosphere. Stop here for lunch, or grab an espresso or gelato at the bar. ⊠ *275 Atwells Ave., Downtown* ☎ *401/421–9105* ⊕ *www. vendaravioli.com.*

JEWELRY
Copacetic Rudely Elegant Jewelry. Expect the unusual at this shop, which sells handmade jewelry, gadgets, and clocks created by more than 100 artists. ⊠ *17 Peck St., Downtown* ☎ *401/273–0470* ⊕ *www. copaceticjewelry.com* ⊗ *Weekdays 10–6, Sat. 10–4.*

MALLS
Arcade. Built in 1828, the Arcade is filled with contemporary shops and restaurants on the first floor. A National Historic Landmark, the Greek Revival building has entrances on Westminster and Weybosset streets. ⊠ *65 Weybosset St., Downtown* ☎ *401/454–4568* ⊕ *www. arcadeprovidence.com.*

EAST SIDE

ANTIQUES AND HOME FURNISHINGS
Butterfield. Owner Mindy Matouk has an eye for edgy but elegant home decor like cowhide rugs, contemporary crystal chandeliers, and all kinds of artsy pillows. ⊠ *187 Wayland Ave., East Side* ☎ *401/273–3331.*

Frog + Toad. Browse the eclectic selection of home decor, jewelry, and fashions from local designers at this small curiosity shop and gift boutique. ⊠ *795 Hope St., East Side* ☎ *401/831–3434* ⊕ *hopestreetprov. com/frog-toad* ⊗ *Mon.–Sat. 10–6, Sun. noon–6.*

ART GALLERIES
Bert Gallery. This gallery displays late-19th- and early-20th-century paintings by regional artists. ⊠ *540 S. Water St., East Side* ☎ *401/751– 2628* ⊕ *www.bertgallery.com.*

The Peaceable Kingdom. This gallery stocks folk art from around the world, including weavings and rugs, clothing and jewelry, masks and musical instruments. In October, hundreds of colorful skeletons are on display in anticipation of the Mexican Day of the Dead. ⊠ *116 Ives St., East Side* ☎ *401/351–3472* ⊕ *www.pkgifts.com.*

FEDERAL HILL

FOOD
Scialo Bros. Bakery. Get your cannoli fix at this family-owned bakery that has been around since 1916. ⊠ *257 Atwells Ave.* ☎ *401/421–0986, 877/421–0986* ⊕ *www.scialobakery.com.*

THE BLACKSTONE VALLEY

In 1790, young British engineer Samuel Slater arrived in Providence with the knowledge he gained from apprenticing in English cotton mills. It was a crime to export machinery designs for cotton-cloth making, but Slater had memorized much of what he saw. He found backers, and partners and three years later a mill opened at Pawtucket Falls in the Blackstone River. Eventually hundreds of mills were operating up and down the river from Worcester to Providence, transforming a young nation's agriculture-dominated economy and launching an industrial revolution. The Blackstone Valley helped make America the world's industrial powerhouse for a century and a half, luring immigrants to the region to work in its factories to make textiles as well as barbed wire, space suits, and even Mr. Potato Head. Much of that industry is now gone, and many old mills have been renovated and converted to condominiums, offices, and gallery spaces. But the scenic river, the focus of ongoing environmental remediation efforts, remains a main attraction to the region, which includes the Rhode Island communities of Woonsocket, Pawtucket, Central Falls, Cumberland, Lincoln, North Smithfield, Smithfield, Glocester, and Burrillville. The Blackstone River Valley National Heritage Corridor designation aims to preserve and interpret the area's landscape and history.

EXPLORING

Blackstone Valley Explorer. Running from Central Falls (June through mid-August) and Woonsocket (late August through late October), the 40-passenger riverboat *Blackstone Valley Explorer* offers tours on Sunday afternoons on the Blackstone River. The 45-minute narrated tour describes the area's ecology and industrial history. ⊠ *Central Falls Landing, 45 Madeira Ave., Central Falls* ☎ *800/454–2882, 401/724–2200* ⊕ *www.rivertourblackstone.com* ✆ *$10.*

PAWTUCKET

5 miles north of Providence.

Northeast of Providence, Pawtucket is Rhode Island's fourth-largest city with a population of more than 71,000 living in its 8.7 square miles. In Algonquian, "petuket" means "at the falls in the river." In 1671, ironworker Joseph Jenks built a forge and gristmill on the west bank of the Seekonk River at the falls where the Blackstone River reaches sea level, establishing a village that would grow on both sides of the fast-running river. The city shaped the Industrial Revolution, reaching its manufacturing peak in the late 19th century. Many industries moved south or died out in the 20th century, leaving numerous vacant mills for which city officials continue to pursue adaptive reuse projects. Pawtucket is still home to the headquarters of toy manufacturer Hasbro. Its thriving arts and cultural scene includes the Sandra Feinstein-Gamm Theatre, originally founded in Providence and now occupying the annex of the historic Pawtucket Armory, and the Hope Artiste Village, a mix of art studios, lofts, retail shops, light-industrial workshops, and the Met music venue.

ESSENTIALS

Visitor Information Blackstone Valley Visitor Center ⊠ *175 Main St.* ☎ *401/724–2200, 800/454–2882* ⊕ *www.tourblackstone.com* ✆ *Free* ⊙ *Mon.-Sat. 10–5, Sun. 1–5.*

EXPLORING

FAMILY **Slater Memorial Park.** Within the stately grounds of this park along Ten Mile River are picnic tables, tennis courts, playground, a dog park, and a river walk. The park's **Looff Carousel,** built by Charles I.D. Looff in 1894, has 39 horses, three dogs, a lion, a camel, a giraffe, and two chariots that are the earliest examples of the Danish immigrant's work. Rides are only 25¢. The Pawtucket chapter of the Daughters of the American Revolution gives tours by appointment of the park's **Daggett House,** which dates to 1685. ⊠ *825 Armistice Blvd.*

☎ 401/728–0500 park information 🌐 www.experiencepawtucket.org 🎟 Free 🕒 Park daily dawn–dusk. Carousel Apr.–June, Sept., and Oct., weekends 11–5; July and Aug., daily 11–5.

FAMILY Fodor's Choice ★ **Slater Mill Museum.** Concord and Lexington may lay legitimate claim to what Ralph Waldo Emerson called "the shot heard round the world" in 1776, but Pawtucket's Slater Mill would provide the necessary economic shot in the arm through its own industrial revolution and secure America's sovereign independence in the decades that followed. Built in 1793, this National Historic Landmark was the first successful water-powered spinning mill in America, and spawned the textile manufacturing industry. The museum complex explores America's second revolution, with expert interpretive guides dressed in period clothing who demonstrate the fiber to yarn, and the yarn to fabric processes, and discuss how industrialization forever changed this nation. On-site are collections of hand-operated and -powered machinery, a 120-seat theater, two gift shops, a gallery, and a recreational park. *✉ 67 Roosevelt Ave. ☎ 401/725–8638 🌐 www.slatermill.org 🎟 $12 🕒 Mar. and Apr., weekends 11–3; May and June, Tues.–Sun. 10–4; July–Oct., daily 10-4; Nov., weekends 10–4.*

WHERE TO EAT

$ DINER 🍴 **Modern Diner.** The line is often out the door on weekends for a seat in this 1941 Sterling Streamliner eatery. Breakfast—try the hash Benedict, lobster cheese grits, or cranberry pecan pancakes—is served all day, meaning until this family-run diner closes at 2. The burgundy-and-tan railway car simulation was the first diner to be listed on the National Register of Historic Places. There's a modern addition with retro counter seating. *[$] Average main: $8 ✉ 364 East Ave. ☎ 401/726–8390 💳 No credit cards 🕒 No dinner.*

$$ INDIAN 🍴 **Rasoi.** Taking its name from the Hindi word for kitchen, Rasoi has an affordable menu featuring cuisine from 27 regions of India. Just over the Providence line into Pawtucket, young professionals flock here for the grilled lamb kebabs, seafood stew, chicken cooked in a clay oven, and numerous vegetarian options. The menu indicates spicy, gluten-free, and vegan selections. The stylish dining room has a rectangular bar and warm orange walls, gold-specked blue floors, and red decorative panels. *[$] Average main: $15 ✉ 727 East Ave. ☎ 401/728–5500 🌐 www.indianrestaurantsri.com/rasoi.*

NIGHTLIFE AND THE ARTS

Sandra Feinstein–Gamm Theatre. Known for its Shakespearean performances, the theatre also produces edgy productions of classic and contemporary works in an intimate 137-seat setting. Its season runs from fall through spring. *✉ 172 Exchange St. ☎ 401/723–4266 🌐 www.gammtheatre.org.*

SPORTS AND THE OUTDOORS

Pawtucket Red Sox. From April to early September, the Pawtucket Red Sox, the Triple-A international league affiliate of the Boston Red Sox, play approximately 70 home games at the 10,000-seat McCoy Stadium. *✉ 1 Ben Mondor Way ☎ 401/724–7300 🌐 www.pawsox.com 🎟 Tickets $8–$12.*

Slater Mill in Pawtucket is regarded as the first factory in the country; it produced cotton, using water power.

WOONSOCKET

10 miles north of Pawtucket, 15 miles north of Providence.

There are two theories regarding the origin and meaning of the city's name, both attributed to the language of the Native Americans who lived here before white settlers. One definition joins "woone" meaning thunder and "socket" meaning mist, given the city's location at the largest falls of the Blackstone River. Historians also suggest that the name refers to the Woonsocket Hill in present day North Smithfield, some 3 miles southwest of the city, which was mentioned by Roger Williams in a 1660 letter. Woonsocket is home to one of the best museums about immigrant factory life and textile milling in the country. It is also home to the headquarters of Fortune 500 company CVS Corporation.

EXPLORING

FAMILY
Fodor's Choice
★
Museum of Work and Culture. In a former textile mill, this interactive museum examines the lives of American factory workers and owners during the Industrial Revolution. Focusing on French Canadian immigrants to Woonsocket's mills, the museum's cleverly laid-out walk-through exhibits begin with a 19th-century Québécois farmhouse, then continue with displays of life in a 20th-century tenement, Catholic school, church, and on the shop floor. The genesis of the textile workers' union is described, as are the events that led to the National Textile Strike of 1934. There is also an engaging presentation about child labor. ✉ *42 S. Main St.* ☎ *401/769–9675* ⊕ *www.rihs.org* ✉ *$8* ⊘ *Tues.–Fri., 9:30–4, Sat. 10–4, Sun. 1–4.*

WHERE TO EAT AND STAY

$ SEAFOOD 🍴 **Ye Olde English Fish & Chips.** Folks come from all over to savor the affordable, fresh fried fish and hand-cut potatoes at this local institution in Market Square. The family-owned Ye Olde English Fish & Chips, which celebrated its 90th anniversary in 2012, has a wood-paneled dining room for a casual and relaxed feast. The clam chowder and clam cakes are very good. [$] *Average main: $10* ✉ *25 S. Main St.* ☎ *401/762–3637* ⏲ *Closed Sun. and Mon.*

$ B&B/INN 🏨 **The Pillsbury House Bed & Breakfast.** Tucked away on historic Prospect Street, a half mile from the Blackstone River, is this lovely 1875 Victorian. **Pros:** stunning architecture; great rates. **Cons:** old-fashioned decor isn't for everyone. [$] *Rooms from: $95* ✉ *341 Prospect St.* ☎ *401/766–7983, 800/205–4112* 🌐 *www.pillsburyhouse.com* 🛏 *3 rooms, 1 suite* 🍽 *Breakfast.*

NIGHTLIFE AND THE ARTS

Chan's. Hear renowned blues and jazz performers along with folk, cabaret, and comedy acts, and enjoy fine Chinese cuisine at Chan's. Reservations are advisable, and tickets average $10 to $25. ✉ *267 Main St.* ☎ *401/765–1900* 🌐 *www.chanseggrollsandjazz.com.*

7

SOUTH COUNTY

Although officially called Washington County, the southwestern region of Rhode Island is home to beautiful seaside villages, unspoiled beaches, and parks and management areas that offer great hiking, kayaking, and running opportunities. More laid-back than Newport and Providence, the area has always been a summertime destination, but South County's 11 towns have grown into a region of year-round residents. With a student body of more than 13,000 undergraduate and 3,000 graduate students, the University of Rhode Island occupies a 1,200-acre campus in Kingston as well as a 153-acre waterfront campus in Narragansett where its Graduate School of Oceanography is located.

ESSENTIALS

Visitor Information **South County Tourism Council** ✉ *4808 Tower Hill Rd., Suite 101, Wakefield* ☎ *401/789–4422, 800/548–4662* 🌐 *www.southcountyri.com.*

WESTERLY

50 miles southwest of Providence, 100 miles southwest of Boston, 140 miles northeast of New York City.

The picturesque downtown business district in this town of 18,000 people bordering Pawcatuck, Connecticut, has more than 55 structures on the National Register of Historic Places, galleries and artist studios, and a 14.5-acre Victorian strolling park. Once a busy little railroad town in the late 19th century, Westerly is now a stop on the New York–Boston Amtrak corridor. The town was once known for its red granite used in monuments around the country. It has since sprawled out along U.S. 1 and grown to include seven villages—Westerly itself, or downtown

Westerly, Watch Hill, Dunn's Corners, Misquamicut, Bradford, Shelter Harbor, and Weekapaug—encompassing a 33-square-mile area.

GETTING HERE AND AROUND

When traveling between New York City and Boston, Amtrak makes stops at Westerly, Kingston, and Providence.

WHERE TO EAT AND STAY

$$
AMERICAN

✕ **Bridge.** Named for a nearby bridge spanning the Pawcatuck River, this restaurant offers affordable American regional cuisine with an emphasis on local seafood and comfort food. The menu includes a flavorful meat loaf, lobster mac and cheese, and chicken potpie, along with the popular grilled fish tacos. The riverside bar and outdoor patio are great for taking in summer concerts in the park right across the narrow river or watching the annual Westerly-Pawcatuck Duck Race, when 20,000 rubber duckies are cast into the river to raise money for local schools. $ *Average main: $18* ⊠ *37 Main St.* ☎ *401/348–9700.*

$$$
B&B/INN

🏠 **Shelter Harbor.** Set back off Route 1, this early-19th-century farmhouse inn and restaurant in the village of Shelter Harbor is a quiet retreat 5 miles from downtown Westerly. **Pros:** quiet location; beautiful grounds; great water views. **Cons:** bathrooms could use updating. $ *Rooms from: $192* ⊠ *10 Wagner Rd., off U.S. 1, Shelter Harbor* ☎ *401/322–8883, 800/468–8883* ⊕ *www.shelterharborinn.com* ⇆ *24 rooms* ◎❘ *Breakfast.*

NIGHTLIFE

Knickerbocker Cafe. The band Roomful of Blues was born at "The Knick" and still gigs at this music club near the Westerly train station. The venue hosts R&B, jazz, blues, and alt-country touring acts and dance parties. ⊠ *35 Railroad Ave.* ☎ *401/315–5070* ⊕ *www.theknickerbockercafe.com.*

SPORTS AND THE OUTDOORS

Westerly Public Library and Wilcox Park. Designed and created in 1898 by Warren Manning (an associate of Frederick Law Olmsted), this 14½-acre Victorian strolling park in the heart of downtown Westerly boasts a pond, meadow, arboretum, perennial garden, sculptures, fountains, and monuments. A garden market, arts festivals, and Shakespeare in the park productions are held periodically. The library's Hoxie Gallery holds monthly art exhibitions. ⊠ *44 Broad St.* ☎ *401/596–2877* ⊕ *www.westerlylibrary.org.*

WATCH HILL

6 miles south of downtown Westerly.

The quintessential New England seaside village has quite the inventory of well-kept summerhouses owned by wealthy families for generations. Parking can be difficult on Bay Street, the tiny business district with boutiques, cafés, and the historic carousel. Watch Hill has almost 2 miles of gorgeous beaches, including Napatree Point Conservation Area, a great spot to see shorebirds and raptors and take in the sunset.

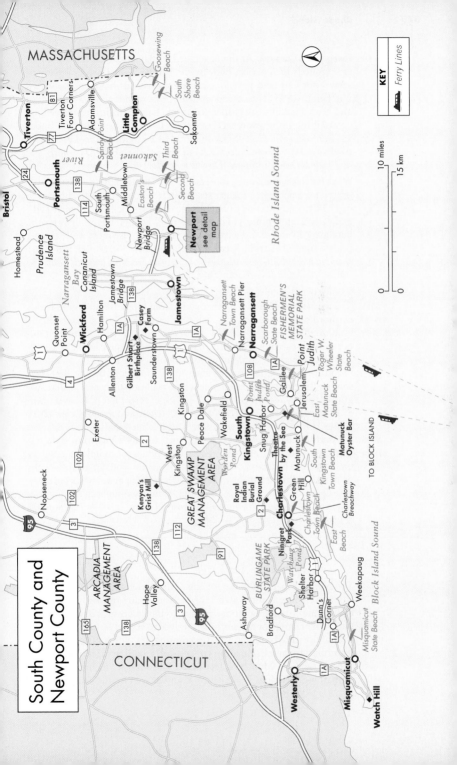

EXPLORING

FAMILY   **Flying Horse Carousel.** At the beach end of Bay Street is one of the oldest carousels in America, built by the Charles W.F. Dare Company of New York City and part of a traveling carnival that came to Watch Hill before 1883. The carved woden horses with real horsehair manes and leather saddles are suspended from chains attached to the ceiling, creating the impression the horses are flying. Riders must be under 12. ⊠ *151 Bay St.* ☎ *401/348–6007* ✍ *$1.50* ☉ *Mid-June–Labor Day, weekdays 10–9, weekends and holidays 9–9; Memorial Day–mid-June and Labor Day–Columbus Day, weekends 9–9.*

Watch Hill Lighthouse. A tiny museum at this 1808 lighthouse contains the original Fresnel light, mariner sea chests, photographs of the hurricane of 1938, documentation of famous local shipwrecks, and shots of 19th- and early-20th-century sailing vessels off Watch Hill. Parking is for the handicapped and senior citizens only; everyone else must walk along a private road off Larkin Road. ⊠ *14 Lighthouse Rd.* ☎ *401/596–7761* ⊕ *www.watchhilllighthousekeepers.org* ✍ *Free* ☉ *Grounds daily 8–sunset. Museum July–Labor Day, Tues. and Thurs. 1–3.*

WHERE TO STAY

$$$$ **Ocean House.** High on bluffs overlooking Block Island Sound is this
RESORT   extraordinary replica of the Victorian grand hotel of the same name
Fodor'sChoice   built on the same spot in 1868. **Pros:** exceptional service; private sand
★   beach with cabanas; full-size championship croquet lawn; spa with 25-meter lap pool; complimentary cooking classes led by a resident "food forager." **Cons:** rooms start at $715 a night during high season; two-night minimum on weekends; traditionalists may dislike no-gratuity policy resulting from $32-per-night resort fee. $ *Rooms from: $715* ⊠ *1 Bluff Ave.* ☎ *401/584–7000* ⊕ *www.oceanhouseri.com* ⇆ *49 rooms, 23 residences, 13 signature suites* ℟ *No meals.*

$$$$ **Watch Hill Inn Residences.** Comprising an 1845 Victorian-style inn
RENTAL   and a modern addition, this upscale condominium complex has sunny one- and two-bedroom condos and apartments rented nightly, weekly, or monthly. **Pros:** steps from beaches and shops; many units have private decks; Wi-Fi and other amenities. **Cons:** two-night minimum stay required. $ *Rooms from: $350* ⊠ *38-44 Bay St.* ☎ *401/348–6300* ⊕ *www.watchhillinn.com* ⇆ *24 apartments* ℟ *No meals.*

MISQUAMICUT

2½ miles northeast of Watch Hill.

The Native American name for this 7-mile-long strip of sandy beachfront stretching from Watch Hill to Weekapaug means "Red Fish," referencing Atlantic salmon, common to the Pawcatuck River and also the original name for the entire Westerly area settled in 1661. Today it's a family-oriented summer vacation destination with amusement parks featuring a carousel, miniature golf, go-carts, batting cages, waterslides, and kiddie rides. Hop on a Jet Ski, paddle a kayak, or find a spot for sunbathing. Evenings bring concerts and movies on the beach.

EXPLORING

FAMILY **Atlantic Beach Park.** The largest and most popular of the several kid-oriented amusements along Misquamicut Beach, this festive facility has lots to keep families busy, including a carousel, bumper cars, a minigolf course, waterslides, batting cages, a roller coaster, a hurricane simulator, and a large arcade with more than 75 video and other games. ⊠ *323 Atlantic Ave.* ☎ *401/322–0504* ⊕ *www.atlanticbeachpark.com* 🎫 *Free; $2 per ride* ☉ *Mid-June–Labor Day, daily; mid-May–mid-June and Labor Day–mid-Oct., weekends; hrs vary.*

WHERE TO STAY

$$$ 🖼 **Breezeway Resort.** A great choice for families, this well-maintained
HOTEL boutique motel is only two-tenths of a mile away from the ocean. **Pros:** nice range of room configurations; beach towels provided; laundry on-site. **Cons:** a bit noisy with so many kids; most rooms don't have Wi-Fi. $ *Rooms from: $189* ⊠ *70 Winnapaug Rd.* ☎ *401/348–8953, 800/462–8872* ⊕ *www.breezewayresort.com* 🛏 *30 rooms, 25 suites* ☉ *Closed late Oct. through early May* ◯ *Breakfast.*

SPORTS AND THE OUTDOORS

Misquamicut State Beach. Half-mile-long Misquamicut State Beach is the state's longest beach, part of the several-mile-long stretch that makes up Misquamicut. Expect the 2,100-space parking lot to fill up on sunny summer holiday weekends. **Amenities:** food and drink; lifeguards; parking (fee); showers; toilets. **Best for:** sunset; swimming; walking. ⊠ *257 Atlantic Ave.* ☎ *401/596–9097* ⊕ *www.riparks.com/locations/locationmisquamicut.html* ☉ *May–Memorial Day, weekends 9–6; Memorial Day–Labor Day, daily 9–6.*

CHARLESTOWN

12 miles northeast of Misquamicut.

Named after King Charles II, Charlestown had previously been a part of Westerly until it was incorporated in 1738. The 37-square-mile town of about 7,800 people is centrally located between New London, Connecticut, and Providence, both a 40-minute drive. Approximately 20% of Charlestown is conservation and recreation land, including Burlingame State Park, Ninigret Wildlife Refuge, Ninigret Park, and East Beach. Its secluded coastline makes the town a great spot for swimming, sailing, surfing, beachcombing, and boating. Charlestown is also home to the Narragansett Indian Tribe Reservation, which holds the oldest recorded annual powwow in North America every August.

EXPLORING

Ninigret National Wildlife Refuge. Spring brings great opportunites to view the male American woodcock's mating ritual at this 400-acre sanctuary. But bird-watchers flock here year-round to commune with nature among 9 miles of trails and diverse upland and wetland habitats, including grasslands, shrublands, wooded swamps, and freshwater ponds. There's an abandoned naval air station on Ninigret Pond, the state's largest coastal salt pond and a great place to watch the sunset. Explore an impressive collection of wildlife and natural history displays at the

Kettle Pond Visitor Center on the other side of Route 1. ⊠ *50 Bend Rd., off Rte. 1* ☎ *401/364–9124* ⊕ *www.fws.gov/ninigret/complex* ⊠ *Free* ⊙ *Daily dawn–dusk; visitor center daily 10–4.*

Ninigret Park. This 227-acre park off Old Post Road on the site of a World War II–era naval air training base features picnic grounds, ball fields, playground, a bike path, tennis and basketball courts, a criterium bicycle course, nature trails, a disc-golf course, and a 3-acre spring-fed swimming pond. A nature center and observatory are located across from one another within the park. The Charlestown Seafood Festival is held here every August. ⊠ *5 Park La., off Rte. 1* ☎ *401/364–1222* ⊠ *Free* ⊙ *Daily 8–sunset.*

> ### RHODE ISLAND TREATS
>
> **Coffee Milk.** The official state drink, coffee milk is like chocolate milk but made instead with coffee-flavored syrup; the preferred coffee syrup is Autocrat Coffee Syrup.
>
> **Del's Frozen Lemonade.** A finalist for official state drink, you can get one of these refreshingly cold drinks from one of many Del's trucks making the rounds in the summer or a Del's storefront.
>
> **NY System Wieners.** Try a hot dog "done all the way"—topped with meat sauce, mustard, onions, and celery salt; they are said to be a great hangover cure.

SPORTS AND THE OUTDOORS

PARKS

Burlingame State Park. This 2,100-acre park has nature trails, picnic and swimming areas, and boating and fishing on crystal clear Watchaug Pond. ⊠ *1 Burlingame Rd.* ☎ *401/322–8910* ⊕ *www.riparks.com/locations/locationburlingame.html* ⊠ *Free* ⊙ *Mid-Apr.–mid-Oct.*

BEACHES

Blue Shutters Beach. Located just west of the Ninigret Conservation Area, Blue Shutters offers wonderful views of Block Island Sound and is a popular escape for families. Beachgoers can see Block Island and Long Island from the shaded deck of the pavilion. **Amenities:** lifeguards; outdoor showers; toilets; changing rooms; on-site parking (fee); food and drink; picnic tables; beach-accessible wheelchairs available at no cost. **Best for:** beachcombing; sunsets; sandcastle building. ⊠ *East Beach Road, Charlestown* ☎ *401/364-1206.*

Charlestown Town Beach. The Town of Charlestown owns 450 feet of oceanfront and has concessions and sparkling bathroom facilities with outdoor rinsing stations. **Amenities:** parking (fee); lifeguards; showers; toilets. **Best for:** solitude; surfing; swimming; windsurfing. ⊠ *557 Charlestown Beach Rd.* ☎ *401/364–1208* ⊠ *Parking $20 weekends, $15 weekdays.*

East Beach. This unspoiled narrow barrier beach is the place for tranquility. Spanning 3 miles of shoreline that fronts and separates Ninigret Pond from the ocean, it's quite a contrast to Narragansett's bustling Scarborough Beach. Parking is limited and fills up quickly. Be careful when swimming, as the ocean side is known for riptides. **Amenities:** lifeguards; parking (fee); toilets. **Best for:** swimming; walking. ⊠ *E. Beach Rd., off Rte. 1* ☎ *401/322–0450* ⊠ *Parking $14 weeends, $20 weekdays.*

BOATING

Ocean House Marina. This full-service marina on scenic Ninigret Pond offers fuel, fishing supplies, and boat rentals. ✉ *60 Town Dock Rd., off U.S. 1* ☎ *401/364–6040* 🌐 *www.oceanhousemarina.com.*

SHOPPING

FAMILY **Fantastic Umbrella Factory.** With a hippie vibe, the kid-friendly Fantastic Umbrella Factory has five rustic shops built around a wild garden. For sale are hardy, unusual daylilies and other plants, interesting jewelry, vintage eyewear, soy candles, creative pottery, blown glass, penny candy, and incense. In the South County Artisans Loft you can meet local artists and view their wares in a renovated second-floor barn space. For 50¢ you can scoop a cone full of seeds to feed the fenced-in emus, guinea hens, and ducks. There is also the BYOB Small Axe Cafe serving organic foods. ✉ *4820 Old Post Rd., off U.S. 1* ☎ *401/364–1060* 🌐 *www.fantasticumbrellafactory.com* 🕓 *Memorial Day–Labor Day, daily 10–6; Labor Day–Memorial Day, daily 10–5.*

SOUTH KINGSTOWN

10 miles northeast of Charlestown.

Originally incorporated in 1674 as Kings Town, this rural community was the site of the Great Swamp Fight in 1675, the battle in which Colonial soldiers gave King Philip his greatest defeat. Almost a third of South Kingstown's 57 square miles is protected open space. There are two beaches, three rivers, and several salt ponds, making it a great place for fishing and boating. The town of about 30,000 people claims a total of 14 distinct villages, including Wakefield, Snug Harbor, Matunuck, and Kingston, home of the University of Rhode Island.

7

EXPLORING

Kenyon's Grist Mill. On the bank of the Queen's River, Kenyon's Grist Mill still grinds cornmeal for johnnycakes the old-fashioned way, with enormous granite millstones quarried from Westerly. Private tours of approximately 1 to 1½ hours can be arranged. The mill hosts an annual johnnycake festival every October. Production continues through the winter, although the shop isn't open. ✉ *21 Glen Rock Rd., West Kingston* ☎ *401/783–4054, 800/753–6966* 🌐 *www.kenyonsgristmill.com* 🎟 *Tour $6* 🕓 *Mid-Apr.–Dec. weekdays 9–4, weekends 11–4.*

WHERE TO EAT

$$ SEAFOOD Fodor's Choice ★ 🍴 **Matunuck Oyster Bar.** Shuckers are hard at work at the raw bar in this awesome waterside restaurant, an offshoot of the nearby Matunuck Oyster Farm. This year-round business committed to mixing fresh local produce with farm-raised and wild-caught seafood draws a crowd. Thankfully, a valet ensures you're able to park your vehicle. Sunset is the best time to take in the view with a glass of wine while enjoying Point Judith calamari with cherry peppers and arugula, whole-belly fried clams, and different varieties of crisp, briny Rhode Island oysters, cherrystones, and littleneck clams. **■ TIP→ Lines are long, especially in summer. Snag a table outside if you can.** [$] *Average main: $20* ✉ *629 Succotash Rd., East Matunuck* ☎ *401/783–4202* 🌐 *www.rhodyoysters.com* ✍ *Reservations not accepted.*

NIGHTLIFE AND THE ARTS

Ocean Mist. The Ocean Mist has a beachfront deck where you can watch surfers on the point and catch some rays. Live bands, including rock and reggae acts, perform nightly in summer and on weekends the rest of the year. Considered one of Rhode Island's best hangouts, the "Mist," as it's called by locals, is that cozy, worn sweatshirt of a beach bar that every coastal state wishes it had. ⊠ *895 Matunuck Beach Rd., Matunuck* ☎ *401/782–3740* ⊕ *www.oceanmist.net.*

Fodor's Choice ★ **Theatre by the Sea.** Enjoy summer stock as it was meant to be performed at this old 500-seat barn-theater a quarter mile from the ocean. Broadway musicals get the royal treatment here with directors, choreographers, and performers coming from New York City. The season of four summer musicals extends from late May to early September. Dramatic sunsets, flickering fireflies, and shimmering fog are among the natural attractions that often accompany evening performances. ⊠ *364 Cards Pond Rd., Matunuck* ☎ *401/782–8587* ⊕ *www.theatrebythesea.com.*

SPORTS AND THE OUTDOORS

BEACHES

East Matunuck State Beach. East Matunuck State Beach is popular with the college crowd for its vigorous waves, white sands, and picnic areas. Crabs, mussels, and starfish populate the rock reef that extends to the right of Matunuck Beach. ⚠ **Currents can be strong, so keep an eye on kids. Amenities:** food and drink; lifeguards; parking (fee); showers; toilets. **Best for:** surfing; swimming; walking; windsurfing. ⊠ *950 Succotash Rd.* ☎ *401/789–8585* ⊕ *www.riparks.com/locations/ locationeastmatunuck.html* 🅿 *Parking $20 weekdays, $14 weekends.*

South Kingstown Town Beach. The 1/3-mile-long South Kingstown Town Beach, with a playground, boardwalk, volleyball court, and picnic tables, cannot be seen from the road and doesn't fill as quickly as the nearby state beaches. The beach has moderate surf. **Amenities:** lifeguards; parking (fee); toilets. **Best for:** sunset; swimming; walking. ⊠ *719 Matunuck Beach Rd.* ☎ *401/789–9301* 🅿 *Parking $20.*

BOATING AND FISHING

Snug Harbor Marina. On the docks at Snug Harbor, an annual shark tournament the weekend after July 4th means you'll see mako, blue, and the occasional tiger shark being weighed in. The harbor is a fine spot for kayaking. Snug Harbor Marina sells bait, arranges fishing charters, and rents sea kayaks. ⊠ *410 Gooseberry Rd., Wakefield* ☎ *401/783–7766* ⊕ *www.snugharbormarina.com.*

NARRAGANSETT

5 miles east of Wakefield.

A popular summer resort destination during the Victorian era, Narragansett still has as its main landmark The Towers, the last remaining section of the famous 1886 Narragansett Pier Casino designed by McKim, Mead, and White. The town is home to a large commercial fishing fleet and four beaches. Take a scenic drive down Route 1A to

Point Judith Lighthouse is just one of 21 such beacons in the Ocean State.

see the ocean and grand old shingle-style homes. You'll eventually wind up at Point Judith Lighthouse, which has been in operation since the 19th century.

EXPLORING

Point Judith Lighthouse. From the port of Galilee it's a short drive to this 1857 lighthouse with a beautiful ocean view. The lighthouse is on an active Coast Guard Station. ⊠ *1470 Ocean Rd.* ☎ *401/789–0444* ⊕ *www.newenglandlighthouses.net/point-judith.html* ⊠ *Free* ☉ *Daily dawn–dusk.*

FAMILY **Port of Galilee.** This little corner of Narragansett is a working fishing village where you can watch fishermen unload their catch, eat at a fish shack, or go for a swim at either of two state beaches. The port is the major hub for year-round ferry service to Block Island. ⊠ *301 Great Island Rd.* ☎ *401/783–5551* ⊕ *www.dem.ri.gov/programs/bnatres/ coastal/index.htm.*

Block Island Ferry. If you're headed to Block Island, the Interstate Navigation Company offers two types of ferry service from Point Judith. Year-round there's regular service, which takes 55 minutes and costs $25 round-trip. From Memorial Day to Columbus Day a high-speed ferry takes 30 minutes and costs $36 round-trip. Cars are allowed only on the regular service. ■TIP➔ **A Block Island Ferry Bloody Mary is a favorite beverage for some riders, but it's not recommended for the easily seasick.** ⊠ *Galilee State Pier, 304 Great Island Rd.* ☎ *401/783–7996, 866/783–7996* ⊕ *www.blockislandferry.com.*

FAMILY **South County Museum.** Set on part of early-19th-century Rhode Island governor William Sprague's former estate (now a town park), the museum founded in 1933 holds 25,000 artifacts dating from pre-European settlement to the mid-20th century. Six exhibit buildings include a printshop, blacksmith and carpentry shops, and a textile arts center. A living-history farm has Romney sheep, Nubian goats, and a flock of Rhode Island Red Heritage chickens, the state bird. **TIP→ The annual chick hatching has become a popular Independence Day tradition for local families.** ✉ *Strathmore St., off Rte. 1A, 115 Strathmore St.* ☎ *401/783–5400* 🌐 *www.southcountymuseum.org* 🎟 *$6* 🕒 *May, June, and Sept., Fri. and Sat. 10–4; July and Aug., Wed.–Sat. 10–4.*

WHERE TO EAT

$$ SEAFOOD FAMILY Fodor's Choice ★ 🍴 **Aunt Carrie's.** Family owned for four generations, this iconic Point Judith dining hall has been a must for Rhode Islanders every summer since it opened in 1920. Its peerless location and unpretentious atmosphere are the main draws, along with comfortable favorites like clam cakes, steamers, and fish-and-chips. For a true native experience, try the Rhode Island Shore Dinner, an orgy of seafood served in several courses. The clam chowder comes three ways: red, white, and clear. Lobster is used many dishes, including a tasty BLT. Many of the recipes for namesake Carrie Cooper's pies are still in use, and some folks have been known to drive more than an hour just for the Indian pudding, a traditional dessert made with cornmeal, molasses, and spices. Eat in the 125-seat dining hall or order at the take-out window and head to the picnic tables across the street, although the lines for both can get pretty long in the thick of summer. The restaurant is BYOB. [$] *Average main: $19* ✉ *1240 Ocean Rd., Point Judith* ☎ *401/783–7930* 🌐 *www.auntcarriesri.com* ✍ *Reservations not accepted* 🕒 *Closed weekdays Oct.–Mar.*

$$$ SEAFOOD 🍴 **Coast Guard House.** A plaque on the dining room wall commemorates how this Ocean Road landmark can't be any closer to the sea: the dining room was under water when Hurricane Bob hit in 1991. While the two open decks draw a crowd in the nice weather, enjoy a table by the huge bank of windows inside when the sea is stormy. Originally built in 1888 as a U.S. Life Saving Service Station, many of the property's architectural details have been preserved, and historic photos line the walls in the spacious and sleek bar area. Seafood often comes from the nearby Port of Galilee. [$] *Average main: $21* ✉ *40 Ocean Rd.* ☎ *401/789–0700* 🌐 *www.thecoastguardhouse.com.*

$ ECLECTIC 🍴 **Crazy Burger Cafe & Juice Bar.** Vegetarians, vegans, and omnivores flock to this funky BYOB café not far from Narragansett Town Beach for smoothies, creative juice blends like pear-ginger-apple, eclectic burgers, and sweet-potato fries. Breakfast, served until 4 pm every day, features popular Mexican-style eggs and spinach crepes. White Christmas lights and colorful cloth napkins are part of the decor, as is a red phone booth behind the counter housing condiments (the place makes its own ketchup). The waitstaff is friendly but usually very busy. Expect a bit of a wait until you can settle into a comfy booth and contemplate the extensive menu. [$] *Average main: $10* ✉ *144 Boon St.* ☎ *401/783–1810* 🌐 *www.crazyburger.com* ✍ *Reservations not accepted.*

$$ ⅹ **George's of Galilee.** Owned by the same family since 1948, this local
SEAFOOD landmark near Salty Brine State Beach serves traditional Rhode Island
favorites, including clambakes and "stuffies" (stuffed quahogs). Get
your fried and broiled seafood here at reasonable prices; George's buys
its ingredients directly from the boats in Galilee. The real draw is the
large second-floor bar, an open-air space where you can enjoy a fruity
rum punch in a fish bowl you can take home as a souvenir. There's
a sleek black-granite bar, an outdoor patio, and a fire pit. $ *Average main: $17 ⊠ 250 Sand Hill Cove Rd.* ☎ *401/783–2306* ⊕ *www.
georgesofgalilee.com* ⌕ *Reservations not accepted* ☉ *Closed Jan.–mid-
Feb. No dinner mid-Feb.–Mar., Mon.–Thurs.*

$$ ⅹ **Trio.** Close to Narragansett's best beaches, this welcoming place
SEAFOOD emphasizes seafood as well as classic comfort food favorites. The menu
includes fluke, snapper, striped bass, and local oysters while elevating
Atlantic salmon to new culinary heights with a sexy barbecue glaze.
Grilled meats, baked oysters, house-made pasta dishes, and an artisanal
pizza of the moment are other highlights. The global wine list includes
some two dozen great by-the-glass options. The patio is open for dining
in summer months. Vintage photos of turn-of-the-20th-century beachgoers decorate the walls of the cool-hued dining room and expansive
bar area. $ *Average main: $18 ⊠ 15 Kingstown Rd.* ☎ *401/792–4333*
⊕ *www.trio-ri.com* ☉ *No lunch weekdays.*

WHERE TO STAY

$$ 🛏 **Blueberry Cove Inn.** On an attractive, tree-lined, residential street, this
B&B/INN historic inn dating from the 1870s has warmly furnished rooms that
balance well-chosen antiques and tasteful, modern color schemes. **Pros:**
four-tenths of a mile from Narragansett Town Beach; beach towels and
chairs available; outstanding breakfasts. **Cons:** two-night stay required
July, August, and most weekends May–November; three-night stays
required for summer holidays. $ *Rooms from: $150 ⊠ 75 Kingstown
Rd.* ☎ *401/792–9865, 800/478–1426* ⊕ *www.blueberrycoveinn.com*
◿ *7 rooms, 2 suites* ⦿| *Breakfast.*

$$ 🛏 **The Richards Bed & Breakfast.** The white rope hammock behind this
B&B/INN secluded circa-1884 English-style stone mansion is where you want to
be. **Pros:** lots of quiet; remarkable architecture; great breakfast. **Cons:**
a bit of a walk from the beach; no TV in rooms. $ *Rooms from: $160
⊠ 144 Gibson Ave.* ☎ *401/789–7746* ⊕ *www.therichardsbnb.com* ◿ *3
rooms, 1 suite* ⊟ *No credit cards* ⦿| *Breakfast.*

SPORTS AND THE OUTDOORS

Appalachian Mountain Club. The Narragansett Chapter of the Appalachian Mountain Club was founded in 1921 and has around 2,500 members. The Rhode Island affiliate meets regularly for hiking, kayaking,
climbing, and cross-country skiing excursions. ⊠ *5 Joy Street, Boston,
Massachusetts* ☎ *603/523-0636* ⊕ *www.amcnarragansett.org.*

BEACHES

Narragansett Town Beach. This crowded and lively beach is perfect for
bodysurfing, sunbathing, people-watching, sandcastle-making, crab-hunt-
ing, and strolling its half-mile length. A sea wall (with free parking for
early arrivals) stretches along Ocean Road and attracts an eclectic crowd,

including guitarists and motorcyclists. Covering approximately 19 acres, Narragansett Town Beach has a beautiful sandy beachfront. **Amenities:** food and drink; lifeguards; parking (fee); showers; toilets. **Best for:** surfing; swimming; walking. ⊠ *39 Boston Neck Rd.* ☎ *401/783–6430* ⊕ *www. narragansettri.gov* ✉ *$6; parking $10 weekdays, $15 weekends.*

Roger W. Wheeler State Beach. This beach, still known to some locals as Sand Hill Cove, has fine white sand, calm water, and a slight drop-off. It's a perennial favorite for parents with young children. **Amenities:** food and drink; lifeguards; parking (fee); showers; toilets. **Best for:** sunrise; sunset; swimming; walking. ⊠ *100 Sand Hill Cove Rd.* ☎ *401/789– 3563* ⊕ *www.riparks.com/locations/locationrogerwheeler.html.*

Salty Brine State Beach. Formerly known as Galilee State Beach, the beach was renamed for a Rhode Island radio legend in 1990. It's a small but popular destination, especially for families with young children. Located at the state's largest commercial fishing port of Galilee, Salty Brine is permeated with the sights, sounds, and scents of Rhode Island's daily fishing culture. The beach is near a cluster of lively seafood restaurants and offers the best seat in the state for viewing the steady parade of ferries, fishing boats, and charters moving in and out of the channel. **Amenities:** food and drink; lifeguards; parking (fee); showers; toilets. **Best for:** sunrise; sunset; swimming; walking. ⊠ *254 Great Rd., Narragansett.*

Fodor'sChoice ★ **Scarborough State Beach.** With generally moderate surf, the 42-acre Scarborough State Beach has stunning views of where Narragansett Bay empties into the ocean. There's a concrete boardwalk with gazebos and an observation tower. A grassy section on the south end of the beach is popular for kite flying and picnicking. **Amenities:** food and drink; lifeguards; parking (fee); showers; toilets. **Best for:** surfing; swimming; walking; windsurfing. ⊠ *870 Ocean Rd.* ☎ *401/789–2324* ✉ *Parking $28 weekends, $20 weekdays.*

FISHING

Prowler. International Game Fishing World Fishing Hall of Famer Captain Al Anderson—credited with tagging more fish for science than anyone worldwide—can take you fishing for tuna, bluefish, and striped bass on the 42-foot *Prowler.* ⊠ *State Charter Boat Dock, State St.* ☎ *401/783–8487* ⊕ *www.prowlerchartersri.com.*

Seven B's V. The 80-foot *Seven B's V* holds up to 120 passengers and offers daily fishing trips. ⊠ *Port of Galilee Dock RR, 30 State St.* ☎ *401/789–9250* ⊕ *www.sevenbs.com.*

SURFING

Narragansett Surf & Skate Shop. Narragansett Surf and Skate rents surfboards, body boards, and wetsuits and offers surfing and stand-up paddle lessons for individuals and groups. ⊠ *74 Narragansett Ave.* ☎ *401/789–7890* ⊕ *narragansettsurfandskate.com.*

WHALE-WATCHING

Lady Frances. During July and August, whale-watching excursions aboard *Lady Frances* take you through warm waters where you'll get a chance to spot finback whales and other species. The company also offers a range of fishing trips. ■**TIP→ The family specials on Tuesday and Friday are a good deal.** ⊠ *33 State St., Point Judith* ☎ *401/783–4988* ⊕ *www. francesfleet.com* ✉ *$45* ⊗ *July and Aug., Tues. and Thurs.–Sat. at 1 pm.*

WICKFORD

12 miles north of Narragansett Pier, 15 miles south of Providence.

A quaint village on a small harbor, Wickford has dozens of 18th- and 19th-century homes, historical churches, antiques shops, and boutiques selling jewelry, home accents and gifts, and clothing. Wickford hosts Daffodil Days in the spring, an annual arts festival in July, and the Festival of Lights in December.

EXPLORING

Casey Farm. In the 19th century this 1751 farmstead overlooking Narragansett Bay was the summer residence of the Casey family, who leased the land to tenant farmers. Today this community-supported farm is operated by resident managers who raise organic vegetables. Nearly 30 miles of stone walls surround the 300-acre farmstead. ■TIP→ A weekly farmers' market takes place Saturday from May to October. ✉ *2325 Boston Neck Rd., Saunderstown* ☎ *401/295–1030* ⊕ *www.historicnewengland.org* ✑ *$4* ☉ *June–mid-Oct., Tues.–Thurs. 1–5, Sat. 9–2.*

Old Narragansett Church. Built in 1707, making it one of the oldest Episcopal churches in America, the Old Narragansett Church has no heat or electricity. But St. Paul's Parish continues to hold weekend services here, and offers free 30-minute guided tours during summer months. One of the four Colonial parishes, the church has pew boxes, a wineglass pulpit, and an upstairs gallery where enslaved people were once welcomed to worship. The organ dates to 1680. ✉ *62 Church La.* ☎ *401/294–4357* ⊕ *www.stpaulswickford.org* ☉ *July and Aug., Thurs.–Mon. 11–4.*

Smith's Castle. Built in 1678 by Richard Smith Jr., this beautifully preserved saltbox plantation house replaced an earlier fortified house built by Smith's father. The former house had been burned during hostilities in King Philip's War. Originally the site of a trading post established by Roger Williams, it also includes a marked mass grave where 40 colonists killed in the Great Swamp battle of 1676 are buried. The land was part of a great plantation during the 18th century, spanning more than 3,000 acres worked by slaves and indentured laborers, and was later a large dairy farm. Saved from the wrecking ball by preservationists in 1949, the castle today appears much like it was in 1740. Smith's Castle hosts an annual Strawberry Festival each June and other special events. ✉ *55 Richard Smith Dr., 1 mile north of Wickford* ☎ *401/294–3521* ⊕ *www.smithscastle.org* ✑ *$6* ☉ *May and Sept.–mid-Oct., noon–4; Fri.–Sun., noon–4; June–Aug. Thurs.–Sun., noon–4; tours given on the hour.*

Gilbert Stuart Birthplace and Museum. Built in 1751, the childhood home of America's foremost portrait artist is set on 23 acres in the woods on a pristine millpond and stream with Colonial herb gardens, nature trails, and a fish ladder. Gilbert Stuart was born in 1755 in the gambrel-roofed house above his father's snuff mill. There is also a fully restored gristmill with the original granite millstones used to grind local whitecap flint corn into cornmeal. Stuart would paint more than 1,000 portraits, including presidents George Washington, John Adams, Thomas Jefferson, James Madison, James Monroe, and John Quincy

EN ROUTE

Adams. You might see visiting artists painting and photographing the picturesque grounds. Guided tours are given on the hour. ■ TIP→ **The grounds are open throughout April for the annual herring run, a spring tradition.** ✉ *815 Gilbert Stuart Rd., Saunderstown* ☎ *401/294–3001* ⊕ *www.gilbertstuartmuseum.com* 🖃 *$7* ⊙ *May–Oct., Mon., Tues., Fri., and Sat. 11–4, Sun. noon–4.*

SPORTS AND THE OUTDOORS
BOATING
Kayak Centre. In Wickford Harbor, the Kayak Centre rents kayaks and stand-up paddleboards and offers lessons. ✉ *9 Phillips St.* ☎ *401/295–4400* ⊕ *www.kayakcentre.com* ⊙ *Tuesday.*

SHOPPING
ANTIQUES
Wickford Art Association. This gallery hosts juried arts shows and sponsors July's Wickford Art Festival. ✉ *36 Beach St.* ☎ *401/294–6840* ⊕ *www.wickfordart.org* ⊙ *Tues.–Sat. 11–3, Sun. noon–3.*

CRAFTS
Five Main. This small fine-art gallery represents local and nationally known artists, photographers, and jewelry designers. You'll find inspired landscapes and seascapes as well as a collection of vintage pottery. ✉ *5 Main St.* ☎ *401/294–6280* ⊕ *www.fivemain.com.*

The Mermaid's Purl. This welcoming yarn shop has a great selection of organic cotton, bamboo, alpaca, merino wool, and cashmere yarns, felting supplies, beads and buttons, books and patterns, and knitting and crochet needles. Wednesday "knit-ins" invite you to bring in a work in progress. ✉ *1 West St.* ☎ *401/268–3899* ⊕ *www.themermaidspurl.com* ⊙ *Mon.–Sat. 10–5, Sun. noon–5.*

NEWPORT COUNTY AND EAST BAY

Newport is one of the great sailing cities of the world and the host to world-class jazz, blues, folk, classical music, and film festivals. Colonial houses and Gilded Age mansions grace the city. Besides Newport itself, Newport County also encompasses the two other communities of Aquidneck Island—Middletown and Portsmouth—plus Conanicut Island, also known as Jamestown, to the west, and Tiverton and Little Compton, abutting Massachusetts to the east. Little Compton is a remote, idyllic town that presents a strong contrast to Newport's quick pace. Narrow and scenic Mount Hope Bridge carries traffic north from Aquidneck Island to Bristol, the most charming of the three towns that make up the East Bay region, which is encompassed entirely within Bristol County, one of the nation's smallest geographically.

GETTING HERE AND AROUND
You'll need to cross at least one of four major bridges to reach Newport County. The largest is the Newport Pell Bridge, spanning Narragansett Bay's East Passage via Route 138 and linking the island community of Jamestown and Newport. Motorists without a Rhode Island-issued EZ-Pass transponder have to pay $4 to cross it. Newport anchors Aquidneck Island, also home to the towns of Middletown and

Portsmouth. From the north end of Portsmouth, Route 24 takes you across the Sakonnet River Bridge (for a 10¢ toll) to Tiverton. Follow Route 77 south through Tiverton to reach quiet Little Compton. From the northwest end of Portsmouth, you cross the Mount Hope Bridge to reach the charming town of Bristol in Bristol County, home to the oldest continuous 4th of July parade in the country. The Jamestown–Verrazano Bridge connects Jamestown to North Kingstown over Narragansett Bay's West Passage.

FERRY TRAVEL Visitors headed to Newport from the west can save themselves the hassle of parking in Newport and the Newport Pell Bridge toll by parking their cars for free in Jamestown and boarding the Jamestown Newport Ferry. Conanicut Marine operates the 40-foot passenger ferry from One East Ferry Wharf in Jamestown and offers free van shuttle service to a large parking area at nearby Taylor Point. The ferry runs daily mid-June through Labor Day and on weekends Memorial Day weekend through mid-June and late September through Columbus Day. The ferry links the village of Jamestown to Rose Island, Fort Adams State Park, Perrotti Park, Bowen's Wharf, and Waites Wharf. An $18 round-trip rate is good for all day but one-way passage rates and bicycle rates are available. Ferry service starts at 9:15 am in Jamestown, and the last run leaves Newport around 7:20 (or around 11 pm on weekends.)

Oldport Marine Services operates a harbor shuttle service Monday through Thursday from noon to 6 pm and Friday, Saturday, and Sunday from 11 am to 7 pm ($10 all day, $6 round-trip, $3 one way). The shuttle lands at Perrotti Park, Bowen's Wharf, Ann Street Pier, International Yacht Restoration School, the Sail Newport dock, Fort Adams, and Goat Island.

TAXI TRAVEL Cozy Cab runs a daily shuttle service ($25 each way) between T. F. Green Airport (in Warwick) and the Newport Visitors' Information Center, as well as major hotels.

PARKING In Newport a number of lots around town offer pay parking (the largest and most economical is the garage behind the Newport Visitors' Information Center); street parking can be difficult to find in summer.

ESSENTIALS

Transportation Contacts Cozy Cab ☎ *401/846–1500, 800/846–1502* ⊕ *www.cozytrans.com.* **Jamestown Newport Ferry** ✉ *1 East Ferry Wharf, Jamestown* ☎ *401/423–9900* ⊕ *www.jamestownnewportferry.com* 🎫 *$18.50 round-trip* ⊙ *Memorial Day–Columbus Day.* **Oldport Marine Services** ✉ *1 Sayer's Wharf, Newport* ☎ *401/847–9109* ⊕ *www.oldportmarine.com.*

Visitor Information Discover Newport ✉ *23 America's Cup Ave., Newport* ☎ *401/845–9123, 800/976–5122* ⊕ *www.gonewport.com* ⊙ *Daily 9–4* ⊙ *Thanksgiving Day, Christmas Eve and Christmas Day.*

JAMESTOWN

25 miles south of Providence, 3 miles west of Newport.

Surrounded by Narragansett Bay's East and West passages, Conanicut Island comprises the town of Jamestown. About 9 miles long and 1 mile wide, the island is home to beautiful state parks, historic Beavertail Lighthouse, farmland, and a downtown village with a quaint mix of shops and restaurants.

EXPLORING

Jamestown Windmill. Once common in Rhode Island, this English-designed smock windmill built in 1787 ground corn for more than 100 years—and it still works. You can enter the three-story, octagonal structure and see the 18th-century technology. ✉ *378 N. Main Rd.* ☎ *401/423–0784* 🌐 *www.jamestownhistoricalsociety.org* 🎟 *Free* 🕐 *Mid-June–Columbus Day, weekends 1–4.*

Watson Farm. In 1789, Job Watson purchased this piece of rich farmland on Conanicut Island, and five generations of his family cultivated the land for next two centuries. Thomas Carr Watson bequeathed the 265 acres to Historic New England when he died in 1979. Still a working farm using sustainable practices, the farm produces grass-fed beef and lamb as well as wool blankets for local markets. The annual Sheep Shearing Day takes place on the second Saturday in May, when you can visit the baby lambs, see the flock being shorn by local shearers, and watch spinning and weaving demonstrations. You can also stroll 2 miles of trails and view seasonal farm activities. ✉ *455 North Rd.* ☎ *401/423–0005* 🌐 *www.historicnewengland.com/historic-properties/homes//* 🎟 *$4* 🕐 *June–mid-Oct., Tues., Thurs., and Sun. 1–5.*

WHERE TO EAT AND STAY

$$$ SEAFOOD 🍴 **Jamestown FiSH.** This upscale Jamestown restaurant showcases the ocean's underappreciated species like sable, char, and cuttlefish. The adventurous menu changes often to reflect available fresh seafood and produce. Try the spicy fish tomato bisque that's a refreshing alternative to New England clam chowder, though you can get that here, too. The downstairs has a cool blue dining room with white table linens, Italian water glasses, and a gas fireplace. The upstairs bar area has a patio offering great views of Newport Bridge lit up at night. Patio seating is first-come, first-served, though you can make reservations for the indoor dining room. [$] *Average main: $28* ✉ *14 Narragansett Ave.* ☎ *401/423–3474* 🌐 *www.jamestownfishri.com* 🕐 *No lunch.*

$$ B&B/INN 🏨 **East Bay B&B.** This 1893 Victorian is peaceful day and night, even though it's only a block from Jamestown's two main streets and wharf. **Pros:** great value compared to Newport accommodations; large rooms; fireplace in common area. **Cons:** small showers; only three parking spaces; no kids under 12. [$] *Rooms from: $149* ✉ *14 Union St.* ☎ *401/423–0330, 800/243–1107* 🌐 *www.eastbaybnb.com* 🛏 *4 rooms* 🍽 *Breakfast.*

SPORTS AND THE OUTDOORS

PARKS

Beavertail State Park. Water conditions range from tranquil to harrowing at this park straddling the southern tip of Conanicut Island. However, on a clear, calm day the park's craggy shoreline seems intended for sunning, hiking, and climbing. There are restrooms with composting toilets open daily year-round. On several dates between May and October the Beavertail Lighthouse Museum Association opens the 1856 **Beavertail Lighthouse,** letting you climb 49 steps to enjoy the magnificent panorama from the observation deck. A museum is in what was the lighthouse keeper's quarters, and the old steam-engine room has a saltwater aquarium with local species. ⊠ *800 Beavertail Rd.* ☎ *401/423–3270* ⊕ *www.beavertaillight.org* ✉ *Free* ☉ *Museum mid-June–Labor Day, daily 10–4; Memorial Day–mid-June and Labor Day–Columbus Day, weekends noon–3.*

Fort Wetherill State Park. An outcropping of stone cliffs at the tip of the southeastern peninsula, this green space has 26 picnic tables and walking paths with scenic overlooks. There's also a boat ramp. The park is a favorite of scuba divers, and is a popular site for viewing Tall Ship parades and America's Cup races. Public restrooms are open daily April to October. ⊠ *3 Fort Wetherill Rd.* ☎ *401/423–1771* ⊕ *www. riparks.com/locations/locationfortwetherill.html* ✉ *Free* ☉ *Daily dawn–dusk.*

BEACHES

FAMILY **Mackerel Cove Beach.** Sandy Mackerel Cove, also known as Jamestown Town Beach, is sheltered from the currents of Narragansett Bay, making it a great spot for families. **Amenities:** food and drink; lifeguards; parking (fee); toilets. **Best for:** sunrise; sunset; swimming; walking. ⊠ *Beavertail Rd.* ✉ *Free, parking $15.*

GOLF

Jamestown Golf Course. From the 5th hole of Jamestown Golf Course you can see three bridges: Jamestown, Newport, and Mt. Hope. A limited pro shop and full bar and grill are on-site. ⊠ *245 Conanicus Ave.* ☎ *401/423–9930* ⊕ *www.jamestowngolf.com* ✉ *Greens fee: $18* ⚐ *9 holes, 6096 yards, par 72.*

NEWPORT

30 miles south of Providence, 80 miles south of Boston.

Established in 1639 by a small band of religious dissenters led by William Coddington and Nicholas Easton, the city by the sea became a haven for those who believed in religious freedom. Newport's deepwater harbor at the mouth of Narragansett Bay ensured its success as a leading Colonial port, and a building boom produced hundreds of houses and many landmarks that still survive today. These include the Wanton-Lyman-Hazard House and the White Horse Tavern, both built during the 17th century, plus Trinity Church, Touro Synagogue, the Colony House, and the Redwood Library, all built in the 18th century.

British troops occupied Newport from 1776–1779, causing half the city's population to flee and ending a golden age of prosperity. The economic downturn that followed may not have been so great for its citizens but it certainly was for preserving Newport's architectural heritage, as few had the capital to raze buildings and replace them with bigger and better ones. By the mid-19th century the city had gained a reputation as the summer playground for the very wealthy, who built enormous mansions overlooking the Atlantic. These so-called "summer cottages," occupied for only six to eight weeks a year by the Vanderbilts, Berwinds, Astors, and Belmonts, helped establish the best young American architects. The presence of these wealthy families also brought the New York Yacht Club, which made Newport the venue for the America's Cup races beginning in 1930 until the 1983 loss to the Australians.

The Gilded Age mansions of Bellevue Avenue are what many people associate most with Newport. These late-19th-century homes are almost obscenely grand, laden with ornate rococo detail and designed with a determined one-upmanship.

Pedestrian-friendly Newport has so much else to offer in a relatively small geographical area— beaches, seafood restaurants, galleries, shopping, and cultural life. Summer can be crowded, but fall and spring are increasingly popular times of the year to visit.

TOURS

BOAT TOURS   More than a dozen yacht companies operate tours of Newport Harbor and Narragansett Bay. Outings usually run two hours and cost about $25 to $35 per person.

Classic Cruises of Newport. You have your choice of three different vessels at Classic Cruises of Newport. The 19th-century *Madeleine* is 72-foot schooner that cruises around the harbor. Built for two New Jersey mobsters to carry "hooch," the 1929 yacht *RumRunner II* evokes the days of smuggling along the coast. The *Arabella,* a three-masted staysail schooner, sails into secluded coves and harbors. Choose from a variety of tours, including gorgeous sunset sails. ⊠ *24 Bannister's Wharf* ☎ *401/847–0298* ⊕ *www.cruisenewport.com.*

Newport Majestic Cruises. The 92-foot double-decker luxury yacht *Majestic* takes passengers out on Narragansett Bay to see lighthouses, the Newport Pell Bridge, and other landmarks. Brunch, lunch, and dinner cruises are available. Seal-watching tours are offered in winter. ⊠ *2 Bowen's Ferry Landing* ☎ *401/849–3575* ⊕ *www.newportmajestic.com.*

Sightsailing of Newport. The 80-foot schooner *Aquidneck* and two sailboats depart from Bowen's Wharf for up to two-hour tours of Newport Harbor and Narragansett Bay. ⊠ *Bowen's Wharf, America's Cup Ave.* ☎ *401/849–3333* ⊕ *www.sightsailing.com.*

TROLLEY   **Viking Tours of Newport.** Take a trolley tour of Newport daily from April
TOURS   through October and on Tuesday and Saturday November through March. ⊠ *44 Long Wharf Mall* ☎ *401/847–6921* ⊕ *www.vikingtours newport.com.*

WALKING
TOURS **Newport Historical Society.** Various walking tours are available from late March through early January. ✉ *127 Thames St.* ☎ *401/841–8770* ⊕ *www.newporthistorytours.org.*

EXPLORING

DOWNTOWN NEWPORT

More than 200 pre-Revolutionary buildings (mostly private residences) remain in Newport. But you'll also find other noteworthy landmarks such as St. Mary's Church at the corner of Spring Street and Memorial Boulevard West where John Fitzgerald Kennedy and Jacqueline Bouvier were married on September 12, 1953. In summer traffic is thick, and the narrow one-way streets can be frustrating. Consider parking in a pay lot and leaving your car behind to walk the downtown area. The Ocean Drive and Bellevue Avenue are nice to see from a bicycle.

Colony House. Completed in 1741, this National Historic Landmark on Washington Square was the center of political activity in Colonial Newport. The Declaration of Independence was read from its steps on July 20, 1776, and later British troops used this structure as a barracks during their occupation of Newport. In 1781 George Washington met here with French commander Count Rochambeau, cementing the alliance that led to the American victory at Yorktown. The Newport Historical Society manages the Colony House and offers guided tours. ✉ *Washington Sq.* ☎ *401/841–8770* ⊕ *www.newporthistory.org* 🎟 *$12 walking tour; $8 site tour* ☉ *Daily 11–3.*

Common Burial Ground. Among those buried in this graveyard, which dates back to the 17th century, are several governors, a Declaration of Independence signer, famous lighthouse keeper Ida Lewis, and Desire Tripp, whose unusual February 1786 gravestone commemorates the amputation of her arm. Many tombstones were made in the stone carving shop of John Stevens, which opened in 1705 and is still in operation. ✉ *Farewell St.* ☎ *401/841–8770* ⊕ *www.newporthistory. org* 🎟 *Free.*

Great Friends Meeting House. The oldest house of worship in Rhode Island reflects the quiet reserve and steadfast faith of Colonial Quakers, who gathered here to discuss theology, peaceful alternatives to war, and the abolition of slavery. Built in 1699, the two-story shingle structure has wide-plank floors, simple benches, a balcony, and a beamed ceiling. ✉ *29 Farewell St.* ☎ *401/841–8770* ⊕ *www. newporthistory.org* 🎟 *$8 tour* ☉ *Daily 11–3.*

Hunter House. The oldest house owned and maintained by the Preservation Society of Newport, the 1748 Hunter House served as the Revolutionary War headquarters of French admiral Charles Louis d'Arsac de Ternay after its Loyalist owner fled the city. Characterized by a balustraded gambrel roof and heavy stud construction, it is an excellent example of an early Georgian frame residence. The carved pineapple over the doorway was a symbol of welcome throughout Colonial America. A collection of Colonial furniture includes pieces crafted by Newport's famed 18th-century Townsend-Goddard family of cabinetmakers and paintings by Cosmo Alexander, Gilbert Stuart, and Samuel

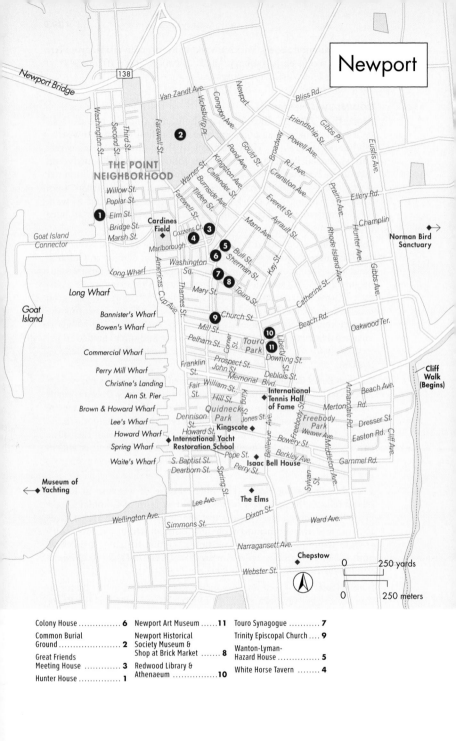

Newport

138

Newport Bridge

Washington St.
Second St.
Third St.
Farewell St.

Van Zandt Ave.
Vicksburg Pl.
Congdon Ave.

Newport
Bliss Rd.
Friendship St.
Gibbs Pl.

Powell Ave.
Broadway
R.I. Ave.
Cranston Ave.

Eustis Ave.

THE POINT NEIGHBORHOOD

Willow St.
Poplar St.
Elm St.
Bridge St.
Marsh St.

Warner St.
Kingston Ave.
Pond Ave.
Gould St.

Everett St.
Ayrault St.

Ellery Rd.
Champlin

Norman Bird Sanctuary

Goat Island Connector

Cardines Field
Cozzens Ct.
Marlborough
Callender St.
Burnside St.
Tilden St.
Farewell St.

Bull St.
Sherman St.
Mann Ave.

Prairie Ave.
Rhode Island Ave.
Hunter Ave.

Washington Sq.
Mary St.
Touro St.

Key St.
Catherine St.

Gibbs Ave.

Long Wharf

Americas Cup Ave.
Thames St.

Church St.

Beach Rd.
Oakwood Ter.

Goat Island

Bannister's Wharf
Bowen's Wharf

Mill St.
Pelham St.

Corner St.

Touro Park
Downing St.
Liberty St.

Cliff Walk (Begins)

Commercial Wharf
Perry Mill Wharf
Christine's Landing
Ann St. Pier
Brown & Howard Wharf
Lee's Wharf
Howard Wharf
Spring Wharf
Waite's Wharf

Franklin St.
Prospect St.
John St.
Memorial Blvd.
Deblois St.

Fair St.
William St.
Hill St.
King St.

International Tennis Hall of Fame

Annandale Rd.
Beach Ave.
Mertonde Rd.
Dresser St.
Easton Rd.

Quidnick Park

Dennison St.
Howard St.
Jones St.

Kingscote

Freebody Park
Weaver Ave.
Bowery St.
Middleton Ave.

Cliff Ave.

International Yacht Restoration School

S. Baptist St.
Dearborn St.
Pope St.
Perry St.
Spring St.
Berkley Ave.
Gammel Rd.

Isaac Bell House

Sylvan St.

Museum of Yachting

Lee Ave.
The Elms
Dixon St.
Ward Ave.

Wellington Ave.
Simmons St.

Narragansett Ave.

Chepstow

Webster St.

| 0 | 250 yards |
| 0 | 250 meters |

King. The house is named after ambassador William Hunter, President Andrew Jackson's charge d'affaires to Brazil. ⊠ *54 Washington St.* ☏ *401/847–1000* ⊕ *www.newportmansions.org* ✎ *$28* ☉ *Late June–mid–Oct., daily 10–6; tours at 10:30, 11:30, 12:30, 2, 3, 4, 5.*

Newport Art Museum. More than a century old, the Newport Art Museum and Art Association has three buildings: the 1864 Griswold House designed by Richard Morris Hunt (a National Historic Landmark), the Cushing Gallery, and the Coleman Center for Creative Studies. The galleries exhibit works from the museum's impressive holdings and the local and regional contemporary art scene. In the museum's permanent collection are works by Fitz Henry Lane, George Inness, William Trost Richards, John La Farge, Nancy Elizabeth Prophet, Gilbert Stuart, and Helena Sturtevant, as well as contemporary artists like Dale Chihuly, Howard Ben Tre, and Joseph Norman. ⊠ *76 Bellevue Ave.* ☏ *401/848–8200* ⊕ *www.newportartmuseum.org* ✎ *$10* ☉ *Nov.–Apr., Tues.–Sat. 10–4, Sun. noon–4; May–Oct., Tues.–Sat. 10–5, Sun. noon–5.*

Newport Historical Society Museum & Shop at Brick Market. Take guided walking and site tours departing from the Newport Historical Society's information center and museum in the 1762 Brick Market on Washington Square. Designed by Peter Harrison, the building houses a gift shop and a Newport history exhibit. ⊠ *127 Thames St.* ☏ *401/841–8770* ⊕ *www.newporthistory.org* ✎ *$4* ☉ *Daily 10–5.*

Redwood Library & Athenaeum. In 1747, Abraham Redwood gave 500 pounds sterling to purchase a library of arts and sciences; three years later, this Georgian-Palladian-style building opened with 751 titles. More than half the original collection vanished during the British occupation of Newport, but almost all of it has been recovered or replaced. Paintings on display include five portraits by Gilbert Stuart. Look for the portrait of the colonial governor's wife whose low neckline was later masked with a bouquet by Stuart's daughter Jane at the patron's behest. A guided 35-minute tour is offered daily at 2 pm. ⊠ *50 Bellevue Ave.* ☏ *401/847–0292* ⊕ *www.redwoodlibrary. org* ✎ *Free, tour $5* ☉ *Mon.–Wed., Fri., and Sat. 9:30–5:30, Thurs. 9:30–8, Sun. 1–5.*

Fodor'sChoice **Touro Synagogue.** In 1658 more than a dozen Jewish families whose
★ ancestors had fled Spain and Portugal during the Inquisition founded a congregation in Newport. A century later, Peter Harrison designed a two-story Palladian house of worship for the congregation. George Washington wrote a famous letter to the congregation in which he pledged the new American nation "would give to bigotry no sanction, to persecution no assistance." The oldest surviving synagogue in the country, it was dedicated in 1763 and its simple exterior and elegant interior remain virtually unchanged. A small trapdoor in the platform upon which the Torah is read symbolizes the days of persecution when Jews were forced to worship in secret. The John L. Loeb Visitors Center has two floors of state-of-the-art exhibits on early American Jewish life and Newport's Colonial history. ■TIP→ **The last synagogue tour is generally an hour before the visitor center closes.** ⊠ *85 Touro St.*

7

☎ *401/847–4794* ⊕ *www.tourosynagogue.org* ✉ *$12* ⊙ *May and June, Sun.–Fri. 11:30–2:30; July and Aug., Sun.–Fri. 9:30–4:30; Sept. and Oct., Sun–Fri. 9:30–2:30; Nov.–Apr., Sun. 11:30–2:30.*

QUICK BITES

la maison de COCO. Enjoy your tea-infused *chocolat chaud* in a bowl at this little French café across from the Hotel Viking. Owner and pastry chef Michele De Luca-Verley makes truffles daily with fresh cream from a Tiverton dairy farm. ✉ *28 Bellevue Ave.* ☎ *401/845–2626* ⊕ *www.lamaisondecoco.com.*

Rosemary & Thyme. The Brie, pear, and prosciutto on a grilled baguette (known affectionately to locals as the "BPP") has earned a cult following at this little boulangerie and café. But you may have a hard time deciding between several outstanding European street-food-inspired sandwiches. ✉ *382 Spring St.* ☎ *401/619–3338* ⊕ *www.rosemaryandthymecafe.com.*

Trinity Episcopal Church. George Washington once sat in the distinguished visitor pew close to the distinctive three-tier wineglass pulpit. Completed in 1726, the church is similar to Boston's Old North Church, both inspired by the designs of Sir Christopher Wren. Trinity's 1733 London-made organ is believed to be the first big pipe organ in the 13 colonies. Among those buried in the churchyard's historic cemetery is French Admiral D'Arsac de Ternay, commander of the allied French Navy in Newport who was buried with special permission in 1780 as there were then no Roman Catholic cemeteries in New England. ✉ *Queen Anne Sq., 145 Spring St.* ☎ *401/846–0660* ⊕ *www. trinitynewport.org* ✉ *$5* ⊙ *May and June, weekdays 11–2; July and Aug., Sat. 10–3; Sept.–mid-Oct., weekdays 10–3; mid-Oct.–Dec., Sat. 1–3, Sun. 11:30–3.*

Wanton-Lyman-Hazard House. As Newport's oldest house museum, this late-17th-century residence presents a window on the city's Colonial and Revolutionary history. The dark-red building was the site of the city's Stamp Act riot of 1765. After the British Parliament levied a tax on most printed material, the Sons of Liberty stormed the house, which was occupied by a prominent Loyalist. ✉ *17 Broadway* ☎ *401/846–0813* ⊕ *www.newporthistory.org* ✉ *$8 site tour* ⊙ *Daily 11–3.*

White Horse Tavern. America's oldest tavern was originally built in 1652 as a two-room, two-story residence, but was converted to a tavern in 1673 by William Mayes, Sr., father of a notorious pirate. It served as a meeting place of the Colony's General Assembly, Criminal Court, and City Council. Now a fine-dining restaurant, the White Horse's gambrel roof, low dark-beam ceilings, cavernous fireplace, and uneven plank floors convey Newport's Colonial charm. ✉ *26 Marlborough St.* ☎ *401/849–3600* ⊕ *whitehorsetavern.us.*

GREATER NEWPORT

Just outside of downtown you can begin discovering elaborate, stunning mansions. Along the waterfront, these "summer cottages" were built by wealthy families in the late 1800s and early 1900s as seasonal residences.

Fodor's Choice **The Breakers.** The 70-room summer estate of Cornelius Vanderbilt
★ II, president of the New York Central Railroad, was built in 1895.
Architect Richard Morris Hunt modeled the four-story residence after
the 16th-century Italian Renaissance palaces. This mansion is not
only big but grand—be sure to look for the sculpted figures tucked
above the pillars. The interior includes rare marble, alabaster and
gilded rooms, with open-air terraces revealing magnificent ocean
views. Noteworthy are a blue marble fireplace, rose alabaster pillars in the dining room, and a porch with a mosaic ceiling that took
Italian artisans six months, lying on their backs, to install. ⊠ *44
Ochre Point Ave.* ☎ *401/847–1000* ⊕ *www.newportmansions.org*
🎫 *$19.50* ◷ *Jan.–mid-Mar., daily 10–5; mid-March–June, daily 9–6;
July–Labor Day, daily 9–7; Sept.–mid-Nov. daily 9–6; mid-Nov.–
early Jan., daily 9–5.*

Chateau-sur-Mer. Built in 1852 as an Italianate-style villa for China
trade merchant William Shepard Wetmore, Chateau-sur-Mer was
Newport's first grand residence until the construction of the Vanderbilt houses 40 years later. In 1857 Wetmore threw an extravagant,
unprecedented gala for 2,500 people, ushering in the Gilded Age in
Newport. The house is a treasure trove of Victorian architecture, furniture, wallpapers, ceramics, and stenciling. See hand-carved Italian
woodwork, Chinese porcelains, and Japanese and Egyptian Revival
stenciled wallpapers. The grounds have some rare trees from Mongo-
lia. ⊠ *474 Bellevue Ave.* ☎ *401/847–1000* ⊕ *www.newportmansions.
org* 🎫 *$14.50* ◷ *Mid-March–mid-Nov., daily 10–6.*

Chepstow. Though not as grand as other Newport mansions, this Ital-
ianate-style villa with a mansard roof houses a remarkable collection
of art and furniture gathered by the Morris family of New York City.
Its collection of important 19th-century American paintings includes
Hudson River landscapes. Built in 1861, the home was designed by
Newport architect George Champlin Mason. ⊠ *120 Narragansett Ave.*
☎ *401/847–1000* ⊕ *www.newportmansions.org* 🎫 *$14.50* ◷ *Late
June–mid-Oct., daily 10–6.*

Fodor's Choice **The Elms.** Architect Horace Trumbauer modeled this graceful 48-room
★ French neoclassical mansion and its grounds after the Château
d'Asnières near Paris. The Elms was built for Edward Julius Ber-
wind, a bituminous-coal baron, in 1901 and was one of the first in
Newport to be fully electrified. At the foot of the 10-acre estate is
a spectacular sunken garden. The Behind the Scenes tours, which
offer a glimpse into the life of staff and the operations (such as the
boiler room and kitchen) of the mansion, is one of the best of any of
these mansion tours. ⊠ *367 Bellevue Ave.* ☎ *401/847–1000* ⊕ *www.
newportmansions.org* 🎫 *$14.50* ◷ *Jan.–mid-Feb., weekends 10–4;
mid-Feb.–mid-March, daily 10–5; mid-March–late Nov., daily 10–6;
late Nov.–early Jan., daily 10–5.*

7

Continued on page 404

Above left, stair hall of Château-sur-Mer, the first of the Bellevue Avenue mansions.

Opposite, Romantic Rosecliff's terracotta tiles look magical at dusk.

Below left, Statues of cherubs watch over the exterior of the Elms.

Right, Go behind the entrance gate on a tour of the Breakers.

The Mansions of Newport

GILDED AGE GEMS

By Andrew Collins, Debbie Harmsen, and Janine Weisman

Would you call a home with 70 rooms a cottage? If not, you're obviously not Cornelius Vanderbilt II. The Breakers, the "summer cottage" of the 19th-century multimillionaire, is one of a dozen mansions in Newport that are now by far the city's top attractions. Many of the homes are open to the public for tours, giving you a peek into the lives of the privileged.

THE SOCIAL SCENE

The Breakers dining room, just one of the opulent mansion's 70 rooms.

To truly appreciate a visit to Newport's mansions, you need to understand the times and the players—those who built these opulent homes and summered here for six weeks a year.

Newport at the turn of the 20th century was where the socialites of Boston, New York, and Philadelphia came for the summer. They were among the richest people in America at the time—from railroad tycoons and coal barons to plantation owners.

The era during which they lived here, the late 1800s up through the 1920s, is often referred to as the Gilded Age, a term coined by Mark Twain and co-author Charles Dudley Warner in a book by the same name. It was a time when who you knew was everything. Caroline Schermerhorn Astor was the queen of New York and

Newport society; her list of the "Four Hundred" was the first social register. Three übersocialites were Alva Vanderbilt Belmont, Mary Ann (Mamie) Fish, and Tessie Oelrichs. These ladies who seriously lunched threw most of *the* parties in Newport.

While the women gossiped, planned soirees, and dressed and redressed thoughout the summer days, the men were usually off yachting.

In terms of the deepest pockets, the two heavyweight families during Newport's Gilded Age were the Vanderbilts and the Astors.

Madeleine Force was only 19 when she married John Jacob Astor IV at the Beechwood mansion in 1911; he was 47.

LEADING FAMILIES

Beechwood will soon be reinvented as an art museum.

Alva Vanderbilt Belmont

Cornelius Vanderbilt

John Jacob Astor IV

John Jacob Astor

THE VANDERBILTS Cornelius Vanderbilt I, called Commodore Cornelius Vanderbilt, built his empire on steamships and railroads. Cornelius had amassed almost $100 million before he died in 1877. He gave most of it to his son William Henry, who, also shrewd in the railroading business, nearly doubled the family fortune over the next decade. William Henry Vanderbilt willed $70 million to his son Cornelius Vanderbilt II, who became the chairman and president of New York Central Railroad; and $55 million to son William K. Vanderbilt, who also managed railroads for a while and saw his yacht, *The Defender*, win the America's Cup in 1895. One of Cornelius Vanderbilt II's sons, Alfred Gwynne Vanderbilt, died on the *Lusitania*, which sank three years after the *Titanic*. **Visit:** The Breakers, Marble House.

THE ASTORS Meanwhile, in the Astor camp, John Jacob Astor IV, who perished on the *Titanic*, had the riches his great-granddad had made in the fur trade as well as his own millions earned from successful real estate ventures, including New York City hotels such as the St. Regis and the Astoria (later the Waldorf–Astoria). His mother was Caroline Astor. Her mansion, Beechwood, is now owned by Oracle CEO Larry Ellison.

7

IN FOCUS THE MANSIONS OF NEWPORT

WHICH MANSION SHOULD I VISIT?

Even though the Newport "summer cottages" were inhabited for only six weeks each year, it would take you almost that long to explore all the grand rooms and manicured grounds. Each mansion has its own style and unique features. Here are the characteristics of each to help you choose those you'd like to visit:

★ **The Breakers:** The most opulent; enormous Italian Renaissance mansion built by Cornelius Vanderbilt II; tours are often big and very crowded; open most of the year.

Château-sur-Mer: The prettiest gardens and grounds; High Victorian–style mansion built in 1852; enlarged and modified in 1870s by Richard Morris Hunt.

Chepstow: Italianate villa with a fine collection of art; a bit less wow factor; summer hours only.

★ **The Elms:** A French chatea-style home with 10 acres of stunningly restored grounds; new guided servant quarters tour takes you into a hidden dormitory, roof, and basement; open most of the year.

Hunter House: Fantastic collection of Colonial furniture; downtown location, not on Bellevue Avenue; pricey admission; summer hours only.

Isaac Bell House: Currently undergoing restoration; less dramatic shingled Victorian displays an unusual mix of influences; less visited; summer hours only.

Kingscote: Gothic Revival–style home includes early Tiffany glass; one of the first summer cottages built in 1841; summer hours only.

★ **Marble House:** Outrageously opulent and sometimes crowded; former Vanderbilt home modeled on Petit Trianon in Versailles; tour at your own pace with digital audio tour; open most of the year.

Rosecliff: Romantic 1902 mansion; modeled after Grand Trianon in Versailles; somewhat crowded tours.

Rough Point: More contemporary perspective in 20th-century furniture; 1889 English manor–style home; tours are expensive and have limited availability.

Portrait of Mrs. Cornelius Vanderbilt II circa 1880, The Breakers.

Consider viewing mansions from the Cliff Walk for a different perspective.

Marble House at night.

TOP EXPERIENCE

★ **Cliff Walk.** See the backyards of Newport's famous oceanfront Gilded Age mansions while strolling along this 3½-mile public access walkway. The designated National Recreation Trail stretches from Memorial Boulevard at the west end of Easton's Beach (also called First Beach) southerly to the east end of Bailey's Beach. Along the way you'll pass the Breakers, Rosecliff, and Marble House and its Chinese Tea House. The north half of the walk is paved but the trail turns to large flat boulders south of Ruggles Avenue. Be prepared for increasingly rough terrain not suitable for small children, strollers, or people with mobility problems. Park on either Memorial Boulevard or Narragansett Avenue.

FAMILY **Fort Adams State Park.** The largest coastal fortification in the United States is at Fort Adams State Park, home to the Newport Folk and Jazz festivals. From mid-May through Columbus Day the nonprofit Fort Adams Trust offers tours of the fort where soldiers lived from 1824 to 1950. You can explore the fort's overlooks and tunnels or walk along its impressive walls. The views of Newport Harbor and Narragansett Bay are exquisite. The fort is reputed to be haunted, and is often open for ghost hunting tours in the days leading up to Halloween. ⊠ *90 Fort Adams Dr.* ☎ *401/841–0707* ⊕ *www.fortadams.org* ✑ *Park free; fort guided tours $12; self-guided tours $6* ⊙ *Daily 7:30–dusk.*

> **SCENIC DRIVE**
>
> **Ocean Drive.** There really isn't a street called Ocean Drive, but the name has come to indicate the roughly 10-mile scenic route from Bellevue Avenue at the intersection of Memorial Boulevard, heading south to Ocean Avenue and out to Castle Hill Avenue, Ridge Road, and Harrison Avenue. About halfway, you'll come to the 89-acre Brenton Point State Park, a premiere destination for kite enthusiasts and picnickers with free parking. ⊠ *Bellevue Ave.*

International Tennis Hall of Fame & Museum. Tennis fans and lovers of history, art, and architecture will enjoy a visiting the birthplace of American tournament tennis. Its museum contains clothing worn by the sport's biggest stars, video highlights of great matches, and the 1874 patent from Queen Victoria for the game of lawn tennis, among other memorabilia. The 6-acre site is home to the shingle-style Newport Casino, which opened in 1880 and was designed by architects McKim, Mead & White, a grandstand, and the recently restored Casino Theatre. The 13 grass tennis courts, one clay court, and an indoor tennis facility are open to the public for play. In early July the Hall of Fame hosts the prestigious Hall of Fame Tennis Championships. ⊠ *194 Bellevue Ave.* ☎ *401/849–3990* ⊕ *www.tennisfame.com* ✑ *$12, $3 grounds pass only* ⊙ *Daily 9:30–5.*

International Yacht Restoration School. You can watch work being done on historically significant sailboats and powerboats from an elevated catwalk inside the 1903 Restoration Hall—a large brick building that was once an electric power plant. The 2½-acre campus on lower Thames Street is also home to the 1831 Aquidneck Mill, which has a maritime reference library with more than 4,000 nautical titles, including some 100 rare books, logbooks, yacht registers, and yacht club directories. Also see ongoing restoration of the 1885 racing schooner *Coronet.* ⊠ *449 Thames St.* ☎ *401/848–5777* ⊕ *www.iyrs.org* ⊙ *Weekdays 9–5; library Tues.–Thurs. noon–6, Fri. and Sat. noon–5.*

Isaac Bell House. Revolutionary in its design when it was completed in 1883, the shingle-style Isaac Bell House combines Old English and European architecture with Colonial American and exotic details, such as a sweeping open floor plan and bamboo-style porch columns. It was designed by McKim, Mead & White for wealthy cotton broker Isaac Bell. ⊠ *70 Perry St., at Bellevue Ave.* ☎ *401/847–1000* ⊕ *www.newportmansions.org* ✑ *$14.50* ⊙ *Late June–mid-Oct., daily 10–6.*

Kingscote. This Gothic Revival mansion completed in 1841 for Georgia plantation owner Geoge Noble Jones was one of Newport's first summer cottages. Richard Upjohn designed Kingscote, which was rebuilt in 1881 for the King family. The dining room contains one of the first installations of Tiffany glass windows and a cork ceiling. Furnishings reflect the King family's involvement in the China Trade. ⊠ *253 Bellevue Ave.* ☎ *401/847–1000* ⊕ *www.newportmansions.org* ⊑ *$14.50* ⊘ *Mid-May–mid-Oct., daily 10–6.*

Fodor'sChoice
★

Marble House. One of the most opulent of the Newport mansions, Marble House contains 500,000 cubic feet of marble. The house was built from 1888 to 1892 by William Vanderbilt, who gave it as a gift to his wife, Alva, for her 39th birthday. The house was designed by the architect Richard Morris Hunt, who took inspiration from the Petit Trianon at Versailles. The Vanderbilts divorced in 1895 and Alva married Oliver H.P. Belmont, moving down the street to Belcourt Castle. After his death, she reopened Marble House, and had the Chinese Tea House built on the back lawn where she hosted "Votes for Women" rallies. ⊠ *596 Bellevue Ave.* ☎ *401/847–1000* ⊕ *www.newportmansions.org* ⊑ *$14.50* ⊘ *Early Jan.–mid-Feb., weekends 10–5; mid-Feb.–mid-Mar., daily 10–4; mid-Mar.–late Nov., daily 10–6; late Nov.–early Jan., daily 10–5.*

National Museum of American Illustration. This museum exhibits original work by Norman Rockwell, J.C. Leyendecker, Maxfield Parrish, N.C. Wyeth, and many others spanning the "Golden Age of American Illustration" (1895–1945). All 323 printed *Saturday Evening Post* covers are on display. The 1898 Beaux-Arts adaptation of an 18th-century French chateau was designed by the same architects responsible for the New York Public Library and other landmarks. Frederick Law Olmsted designed the adjacent grounds. ⊠ *492 Bellevue Ave.* ☎ *401/851–8949* ⊕ *www. americanillustration.org* ⊑ *$18* ⊘ *Memorial Day–Labor Day, hrs vary.*

FAMILY **Norman Bird Sanctuary.** Stroll through the woods or hike to the top of Hanging Rock for a spectacular view at this 325-acre sanctuary for more than 300 species of birds, plus deer, fox, mink, turtles, and rabbits. The sanctuary has about 7 miles of trails. The visitor center in a 19th-century barn highlights Rhode Island's natural history with a variety of wildlife and ecosystem exhibits spanning from the time of Native Americans before white settlers arrived to the present. ■TIP➔ **The raucous dawn chorus of birdsong in the spring is one of the great wildlife experiences in Rhode Island.** ⊠ *583 Third Beach Rd., Middletown* ☎ *401/846–2577* ⊕ *www.normanbirdsanctuary.org* ⊑ *$6* ⊘ *Daily 9–5.*

Rosecliff. Built in 1902, Newport's most romantic mansion was commissioned by Tessie Hermann Oelrichs, who inherited a Nevada silver fortune from her father. Stanford White modeled the palace after the Grand Trianon at Versailles. Rosecliff has a heart-shaped staircase and Newport's largest private ballroom. Rosecliff stayed in the Oelrichs family until 1941, went through several ownership changes and then was purchased by Mr. and Mrs. J. Edgar Monroe of New Orleans in 1947. The Monroes were known for throwing big parties. Some scenes from *The Great Gatsby* and *True Lies* were filmed here. ⊠ *548 Bellevue Ave.* ☎ *401/847–1000* ⊕ *www.newportmansions.org* ⊑ *$14.50* ⊘ *Mid-March–late Nov., daily 10-6.*

Fodor's Choice ★ **Rough Point.** Tobacco heiress and preservationist Doris Duke furnished her 39,000-square-foot English manorial-style house at the southern end of Bellevue Avenue with family treasures and fine art and antiques she purchased on her world travels. Highlights include paintings by Renoir, van Dyck and Gainsborough, numerous Chinese porcelains, Turkish carpets and Belgian tapestries, and a suite of Louis XVI chairs. Duke's two camels Baby and Princess (which came with an airplane she had purchased from a Middle Eastern businessman) once summered here on the expansive grounds designed by landscape architect Frederick Law Olmsted. Duke bequeathed the oceanfront house with all its contents to the Newport Restoration Foundation to operate as a museum after her death. Each year, the foundation assembles an exhibit devoted to Duke's lifestyle and interests that is included in guided tours. ✉ *680 Bellevue Ave.* ☎ *401/847–8344* 🌐 *www.newportrestoration.org* 🎟 *$25* 🕒 *Mid-Apr.–mid-May, Thurs.–Sat. 10–2; mid-May–early Nov., Tues.–Sat. 9:45–3:45.*

WORD OF MOUTH

"Mansion time! I love cool houses, particularly old and/or fancy mansions. Our first stop was The Elms. This place had the best gardens, reminiscent of what you'd see in Europe.

Next stop, Rosecliff. Then, we headed to Marble House. The marble was amazing. Both Rosecliff and Marble House are wonderfully situated facing the water."

—aggiegirl

WHERE TO EAT

$$$$ AMERICAN Fodor's Choice ★ 🍴 **Castle Hill Inn.** No other place can compete with the spectacular water views from the Sunset Room, one of four dining rooms inside the historic main inn. A perfect spot for a romantic dinner, Castle Hill also offers a great value two-course lunch menu that allows you to watch the clouds drift past while savoring ethereal cuisine. The three-course prix-fixe menu displays a passion for simple New England food done well, re-creating a clambake with littlenecks and plump *chouriço*-filled Georges Bank scallops. Produce comes from local growers listed right on the menu. The popular Sunday brunch offers lobster hash and a Rhody omelet of the day made from fresh farm vegetables and artisanal cheeses. [$] *Average main: $75* ✉ *590 Ocean Dr.* ☎ *888/466–1355, 401/849–3800* 🌐 *www.castlehillinn.com* ✍ *Reservations essential.*

$$$ WINE BAR 🍴 **Fluke Wine, Bar & Kitchen.** Cocktails made with freshly pressed juices are the best way to start your meal at this modern hot spot. The ever-changing menu has a well-conceived mix of snacks, cheeses, and charcuterie plus rotating small- and large-plate offerings. Seafood options like pan-seared scallops are compelling choices for freshness and imaginative side pairings like celery root, unsmoked Italian bacon, and pumpkin-seed pesto. [$] *Average main: $28* ✉ *41 Bowen's Wharf* ☎ *401/849–7778* 🌐 *www.flukewinebar.com* 🕒 *No lunch.*

$ DINER 🍴 **Franklin Spa.** A local landmark where the line can be out the door on summer weekend mornings, Franklin Spa's satisfying breakfasts are worth the wait. The Portuguese Sailor (grilled *chouriço* and egg with melted cheese on Portuguese sweet bread) is a house specialty. Healthy options include egg-white omelets, fresh-squeezed orange juice, and fruit smoothies made with fat-free yogurt. Owner and avid fisherman Rocky Botelho is at the grill most days. The service is extremely friendly. $ *Average main: $8* ⊠ *229 Spring St.* ☎ *401/847–3540* ⌂ *Reservations not accepted* ⊟ *No credit cards.*

$$$$ ✕ **Restaurant Bouchard.** Regional takes on French cuisine fill the menu
FRENCH at this upscale yet homey establishment inside a stately gambrel-roof 1785 Colonial on Thames Street. Nightly specials are based on the fresh catch from Rhode Island waters, which might include scallops, swordfish, and clams, as well as classics like sautéed duck breast with a ground-coffee crust, finished with a brandy-balsamic sauce. The wine list offers a nice range of New and Old World varietals. ■TIP➤ **Kids must be older than seven to enter the dining room.** $ *Average main: $29* ⊠ *505 Thames St.* ☎ *401/846–0123* ⊕ *www.bouchardnewport. com* ⊘ *No lunch. Closed Tues.*

$$$$ ✕ **Spiced Pear.** For atmosphere, service, and exceptional food, the Spiced
MODERN Pear is the ultimate fine-dining triple threat. Overlooking Easton's Beach
AMERICAN and the north end of the Cliff Walk, this refined open-kitchen restaurant
Fodor'sChoice has attentive tuxedoed waiters, an extensive wine list, and a creative
★ New England dinner menu. Selections include a butter-poached Maine lobster and wild Burgundy escargot. Lunch has the absurdly delicious Kobe beef GQ burger. The Bar, which has lighter fare and a signature martini, hosts a popular Friday-night jazz series. $ *Average main: $38* ⊠ *The Chanler at Cliff Walk, 117 Memorial Blvd.* ☎ *401/847–2244* ⊕ *www.thechanler.com/dining.*

$$$$ ✕ **Tallulah on Thames.** The menu here changes a few times a week in
MODERN order to use the freshest, locally sourced seafood and produce. You
AMERICAN can always count on an imaginative take on traditional New England fare and artful presentation. Deconstructed chowder and other soups are poured right at your table. Wednesdays from November through April draw a cult following for specialty burgers made from grass-fed black Angus sourced from Black Bird Farm in Smithfield. An attentive and knowledgeable staff offers expertise on wine selections from boutique vineyards and prix-fixe selections. Artisanal chocolates make an exquisite end to every meal. $ *Average main: $34* ⊠ *464 Thames St.* ☎ *401/849–2433* ⊕ *www.tallulahonthames.com* ⊘ *Closed Mon. and Tues. No lunch.*

$$$$ ✕ **22 Bowen's Wine Bar & Grille.** Excellent service, world-class steaks, and
STEAKHOUSE an extensive, award-winning wine list make dinner here a memorable
Fodor'sChoice experience. Floor-to-ceiling windows allow you to watch the world go
★ by on the wharf outside. The USDA Prime beef and premium Hereford center-cut fillets are handpicked and aged a minimum of 14 and 21 days, respectively, for premium flavor and texture. Sushi-grade tuna, Rhode Island–style calamari (with hot peppers), and Maine lobster are on the menu, too. A three-course prix-fixe dinner menu is a good deal at $30. Gluten-free options are available. $ *Average main: $36* ⊠ *22 Bowen's Wharf* ☎ *401/841–8884* ⊕ *www.22bowens.com.*

WHERE TO STAY

$$
B&B/INN
[icon] **Architect's Inn.** Built in 1873 by noted Newport architect George Champlin Mason, this distinctive Swiss chalet–inspired house has good-sized rooms done up in classic Victorian style. **Pros:** friendly hosts cater to your dietary needs, and can make kosher dishes; central but quiet location. **Cons:** you're asked to go shoeless to protect wood floors; some may find the decor too knickknacky. [$] *Rooms from: $150* ✉ *2 Sunnyside Pl., off Bellevue Ave.* ☎ *401/845–2547, 877/466–2547* ⊕ *www.architectsinn.com* ⤳ *5 suites* ⦿❙ *Breakfast.*

$$$$
HOTEL
Fodor's Choice
★
[icon] **Castle Hill Inn and Resort.** Built as a summer house in 1874 for scientist and explorer Alexander Agassiz, this luxurious and romantic getaway on a 40-acre peninsula has its own private beach and trails to the Castle Hill Lighthouse. **Pros:** stunning views; superb restaurant; variety of rooms. **Cons:** 3 miles from downtown Newport; expensive rates. [$] *Rooms from: $682* ✉ *590 Ocean Dr.* ☎ *401/849–3800, 888/466–1355* ⊕ *www.castlehillinn.com* ⤳ *35 rooms, 3 suites* ⦿❙ *Breakfast.*

$$$$
HOTEL
Fodor's Choice
★
[icon] **The Chanler at Cliff Walk.** The custom-designed rooms at this landmark boutique hotel on the Cliff Walk represent the most unusual and luxurious accommodations in Newport. **Pros:** panoramic water views from many rooms; two or three flat-screen TVs per room; great on-site restaurant. **Cons:** no elevator; some rooms have steps to access bathroom; traffic can be noisy. [$] *Rooms from: $599* ✉ *117 Memorial Blvd.* ☎ *401/847–1300, 401/847–1300* ⊕ *www.thechanler.com* ⤳ *7 rooms, 13 suites* ⦿❙ *Breakfast.*

$$$$
B&B/INN
[icon] **Francis Malbone House.** The design of this stately painted-brick house is attributed to Peter Harrison, the same architect behind Touro Synagogue and the Redwood Library. **Pros:** steps from many restaurants and shops; highly professional service; fireplaces in each room. **Cons:** Thames Street abounds with tourists in summer. [$] *Rooms from: $275* ✉ *392 Thames St.* ☎ *401/846–0392, 800/846–0392* ⊕ *www.malbone.com* ⤳ *17 rooms, 3 suites* ⦿❙ *Breakfast.*

$$$$
HOTEL
[icon] **Hydrangea House Inn.** Rosie, the house Bichon, keeps watch at this mid-19th-century inn with decadent suites and rooms that exude romance. **Pros:** central location; huge rooms; highly personal service. **Cons:** slightly over-the-top decor. [$] *Rooms from: $295* ✉ *16 Bellevue Ave.* ☎ *401/846–4435, 800/945–4667* ⊕ *www.hydrangeahouse.com* ⤳ *3 rooms, 7 suites* ⦿❙ *Breakfast.*

$$
B&B/INN
[icon] **Spring Street Inn.** This romantic B&B in a well-maintained 1858 Victorian is the real deal, offering some of the most attractive rates in downtown Newport. **Pros:** on a quiet but centrally located street; breakfast is terrific. **Cons:** small showers. [$] *Rooms from: $159* ✉ *353 Spring St.* ☎ *401/847–4767* ⊕ *www.springstreetinn.com* ⤳ *6 rooms, 1 suite* ⊘ *Closed late Nov.–mid-May* ⦿❙ *Breakfast.*

$$$$
HOTEL
Fodor's Choice
★
[icon] **Vanderbilt Grace.** Built in 1909 by Alfred Gwynne Vanderbilt for his mistress, Agnes O'Brien Ruiz, this Grace Hotel property aims to impress, and does. **Pros:** highly personalized service; full-service spa and indoor and outdoor pools; stylish snooker room. **Cons:** on a narrow street that's busy in summer; municipal parking lot next door. [$] *Rooms from: $495* ✉ *41 Mary St.* ☎ *401/846–6200* ⊕ *www.gracehotels.com/vanderbilt* ⤳ *33 rooms, 29 suites* ⦿❙ *No meals.*

NIGHTLIFE AND THE ARTS

To sample Newport's lively nightlife, you need only stroll down Thames Street or the southern end of Broadway after dark. Pick up the free *Newport Mercury* or *Newport This Week* or visit ⊕ *www.newportri. com* for entertainment listings and news on featured events.

BARS

Candy Store. This is the best place to sip a dark and stormy and rub elbows with yacht crews. The walls are covered with photos from the halcyon days of Newport's America's Cup supremacy. If you're up for dancing, head downstairs to the Boom Boom Room. ⊠ *Clarke Cooke House, Bannister's Wharf* ☎ *401/849–2900* ⊕ *www.bannistersnewport. com/clarke_candy_grill.html.*

Fastnet Pub. Named for the Fastnet Lighthouse off the coast of Cork, Ireland, the Fastnet Pub hosts Irish sessions every Sunday evening when guest musicians, singers, and dancers familiar with traditional repertoire are invited to participate. ⊠ *3 Broadway* ☎ *401/845–9311* ⊕ *thefast-netpub.com.*

FESTIVALS

Newport Folk Festival. Bob Dylan made his premiere national performance at the 1963 Newport Folk Festival. Two years later some fans booed when he went electric, marking a shift in his own musical trajectory and the start of a larger cultural shift from folk to rock. Held the last weekend in July, the folk fest continues stretching boundaries and keeping things fresh with multiple stages and acts spanning folk, blues, country, bluegrass, folk rock, alt-country, indie folk, and folk punk. Lineups mix veteran performers like Jackson Browne, Patty Griffin, and Arlo Guthrie with younger stars like Conor Oberst, Brandi Carlile, and Deer Tick. The festival is held rain or shine, and seating is general admission on a large uncovered lawn. ⊠ *Fort Adams State Park, Harrison Ave.* ☎ *401/848–5055* ⊕ *www.newportfolkfest.net* ▭ *$84 per day.*

Newport Jazz Festival. The grandfather of all jazz festivals, founded by George Wein in 1954, takes place the first weekend in August aand features both jazz veterans and up-and-coming artists. Performers in recent years have included Esperanza Spalding, Wynton Marsalis, Dianne Reeves, The Bad Plus with Bill Frisell, Dr. John, and Maria Schneider Orchestra. The festival is held rain or shine with open-air lawn seating. ⊠ *Fort Adams State Park, Harrison Ave.* ☎ *401/848–5055, 800/745–3000* ⊕ *newportjazzfest.net* ▭ *$84 per day.*

Fodor's Choice ★ **Newport Music Festival.** A great way to experience a Newport mansion is to take in one of the 60 or so classical music concerts presented every July during the Newport Music Festival. Morning, afternoon, evening, and even midnight performances by world-class artists are scheduled at The Elms, The Breakers, and other venues. Selected works are chosen from 19th-century chamber music, vocal repertoire, and Romantic-era piano literature. Every year features at least one American debut and a tribute to a composer. ☎ *401/849–0700, 401/846–1133* ⊕ *www. newportmusic.org* ▭ *Tickets $20–$75.*

FILM

FAMILY **newportFILM.** Enjoy sneak peeks of films before they open elsewhere thanks to this nonprofit group that hosts outdoor screenings and mini-festivals with programming for adults and kids throughout the year. Founded in 2010, the group promotes documentary filmmaking to encourage community dialogue. ✉ *174 Bellevue Ave., Suite 314* ☎ *401/649–2784* ⊕ *www.newportfilm.com.*

SPORTS AND THE OUTDOORS

BASEBALL

FAMILY **Cardines Field.** One of America's oldest ballparks with a circa-1908 original backdrop is home to the Newport Gulls of the New England Collegiate Baseball League. Home games from June through early August draw a family-friendly crowd to watch some of tomorrow's major leaguers play ball. The field hosted barnstorming all-stars in the early 20th century, including Negro League clubs such as the Baltimore Elite Giants, the New York Black Yankees, and the Boston Royal Giants. ✉ *20 America's Cup Ave., Downtown* ⊕ *www.newportgulls.com* 💲 *$4.*

BEACHES

Easton's Beach. Also known as First Beach, Easton's Beach is a ¾-mile-long surf beach with a boardwalk, vintage carousel, aquarium, and playground. Public facilities include restrooms, indoor and outdoor showers, a skate park, an elevator and beach wheelchairs for persons with disabilities. The snack bar's twin lobster rolls are very popular and a great deal. **Amenities:** food and drink; lifeguards; parking (fee); showers; toilets. **Best for:** sunrise; sunset; swimming; walking. ✉ *175 Memorial Blvd.* ☎ *401/845–5810* ⊕ *www.cityofnewport.com/ departments/enterprise-fund/beach/home.cfm* ⊙ *Memorial Day– Labor Day, daily 9–6.*

Sachuest Beach. This 1¼-mile-long sandy beach has a popular surfing spot on its west end. Surfboard and stand-up paddleboard rentals are available. **Amenities:** food and drink; lifeguards; parking (fee); showers; toilets. **Best for:** surfing; swimming; walking; windsurfing. ✉ *305 Sachuest Point Rd., Middletown* ☎ *401/849–2822* ⊕ *www. middletownri.com/government/6/43/sachuest-beaches-campground* 💲 *Parking $10–$20* ⊙ *Memorial Day–Labor Day, daily 8–6.*

Third Beach. On the Sakonnet River, Third Beach is more peaceful than the nearby ocean beaches and is a great spot for families. It has a boat ramp and is a favorite of windsurfers. You'll find a mobile concession stand on weekends. **Amenities:** parking (fee); lifeguards. **Best for:** swimming; walking; windsurfing. ✉ *Third Beach Rd., Middletown* ☎ *401/849–2822* ⊕ *www.middletownri.com/government/6/43/ sachuest-beaches-campground.*

BIKING

The 12-mile swing down Bellevue Avenue to Ocean Drive and back offers amazing coastal views.

Ten Speed Spokes. This shop rents hybrid bikes for $35 per day. Road bikes are $45. ✉ *18 Elm St.* ☎ *401/847–5609* ⊕ *www.tenspeedspokes.com.*

Newport's naturally well-protected harbor has made the city a sailing capital.

BOATING AND DIVING

The Dive Shop. This shop rents, sells, and services dive equipment, refills air tanks, and offers PADI instruction and certification. It also conducts group "fun dives" close to shore. ✉ *550 Thames St.* ☎ *401/847–9293* ⊕ *www.thediveshopnewport.com.*

Sail Newport. Take a private two-hour sailing lesson or rent 19- or 22-foot sailboats or kayaks at Sail Newport, New England's largest public sailing center. ✉ *Ft. Adams State Park, 60 Ft. Adams Dr.* ☎ *401/846–1983* ⊕ *www.sailnewport.org.*

FISHING

Fishin' Off. This outfitter runs charter-fishing trips in Narragansett Bay and coastal Rhode Island waters mid-May through October on a 36-foot Trojan cabin cruiser. ☎ *401/683–8080.*

The Saltwater Edge. This company conducts guided trips, gives lessons, and sells tackle for both fly-fishing and surf casting. ✉ *47 Valley Rd., Middletown* ☎ *401/842–0062, 866/793–6733* ⊕ *www.saltwateredge.com.*

POLO

Newport International Polo Series. Teams from around the U.S. and the world compete in Saturday evening matches at Glen Farm in Portsmouth. Spectators are invited to stomp divots at the half and then mingle with players and pet the horses after the match. Arrive early with a picnic for a choice tailgating spot. The concession stand has a bar and grilled fare. Matches take place Saturday, June through August, starting at 5 pm, and in September beginning at 4 pm. ✉ *715 E. Main Rd., Portsmouth* ☎ *401/846–0200* ⊕ *www.nptpolo.com* 🎟 *$12–$20* 🕒 *June–Sept., Sat., match times vary.*

SHOPPING

Many of Newport's shops and art and crafts galleries are on Thames Street, Spring Street, and at Bowen's and Bannister's wharves. The Brick Market area—between Thames Street and America's Cup Avenue—has more than 40 shops. Bellevue Avenue just south of Memorial Boulevard (near the International Tennis Hall of Fame) contains a strip of high-end fashion and home decor boutiques and gift shops.

ANTIQUES

Aardvark Antiques. This shop specializes in distinctive architectural salvage such as mantels, doors, stained glass, fountains, and garden statuary. ⊠ *9 Connell Hwy.* ☎ *401/849–7233, 800/446–1052* ⊕ *www. aardvarkantiques.com.*

The Drawing Room of Newport. Inside The Drawing Room of Newport you'll find an extraordinary collection of Art Nouveau Zsolnay pottery from Hungary as well as museum-quality lighting fixtures, antique glass, fine porcelain, and vintage Newport postcards from the 1890s through World War II. ⊠ *152 Spring St.* ☎ *401/841–5060* ⊕ *www. drawrm.com* ☉ *Daily 11–5.*

ART AND CRAFTS GALLERIES

Arnold Art. This gallery exhibits original paintings and prints of landscapes and seascapes by Rhode Island artists. ⊠ *210 Thames St.* ☎ *401/847–2273* ⊕ *www.arnoldart.com.*

DeBlois Gallery. This gallery exhibits work by southern New England artists. Artworks on display include paintings, photography, sculpture, and ceramics. ⊠ *134 Aquidneck Ave., Middletown* ☎ *401/847–9977* ⊕ *www.debloisgallery.com* ☉ *Mar.–Dec., Tues.–Sun. noon–5.*

Harbor Fine Art. A gallery and studio space for several notable artists around the region, Harbor Fine Arts features landscapes and seascapes in oil. ⊠ *33 Bannister's Wharf* ☎ *401/338–4462* ⊕ *www.harborfineart. com* ☉ *Daily 10–6.*

Thames Glass. Watch Matthew Buechner and his team of glassblowers at work making blown-glass gifts through a window in the gallery at Thames Glass. Sign up for a lesson to make an ornament, paperweight, or vase out of molten glass. ⊠ *688 Thames St.* ☎ *401/846–0576* ⊕ *www.thamesglass.com* ☉ *Jan.–June, Mon.–Sat. 10–5, Sun. noon–5; July–Dec., Mon.–Sat. 10–6, Sun. noon–5.*

BEACH GEAR

Water Brothers. This is the place to go for surf supplies, including bathing suits, wet suits, sunscreen, sunglasses, surfboards, and all styles of skateboards. Owner Sid Abruzzi, a legend in the East Coast surf community, records a new surf report daily to keep sufers apprised of local waves. ⊠ *23 Memorial Blvd.* ☎ *401/846–7873* ⊕ *originalwaterbrothers.com.*

CLOTHING

Angela Moore. Look to Angela Moore for stylish resort threads and signature hand-painted beaded jewelry. ⊠ *190 Bellevue Ave.* ☎ *401/619– 1900* ⊕ *www.angelamoore.com.*

FOOD

Newport Wine Cellar. This specialty wine and craft-beer merchant offers lively Wednesday night wine classes, pairings of wine and cheese on Friday, and complimentary tastings on Saturday. ✉ *24 Bellevue Ave.* ☎ *401/619–3966* ⊕ *www.newportwinecellar.com.*

JEWELRY

Alloy. At this shop Tamar Kern displays her signature stackable cone rings plus unique designs by two dozen other leading contemporary artists. ✉ *125 Bellevue Ave.* ☎ *401/619–2265* ⊕ *alloygallery.com.*

PORTSMOUTH

11 miles north of Newport.

Founded by religious dissident Anne Hutchinson, who led a group of settlers to the area in 1638 after being banished from the Massachusetts Bay Colony, Portsmouth is Rhode Island's second-oldest community. The town was the site of the Battle of Rhode Island on August 29, 1778, when American troops, who included a locally recruited African American regiment, withdrew to Bristol and Tiverton, leaving Aquidneck Island under British control. Covering a 23.3-mile area, Portsmouth has a population of more than 17,000. The town is also home to many yacht builders and boat dealers.

EXPLORING

FAMILY **Green Animals Topiary Garden.** Fanciful animals, a sailing ship, and geometric shapes populate this large topiary garden on a Victorian estate that served as a Fall River, Massachusetts, textile mill owner's summer residence. Also here are flower gardens, winding pathways, and the 1872 white clapboard house that displays original family furnishings and an antique toy collection. ✉ *380 Cory's La., off Rte. 114* ☎ *401/683–1267* ⊕ *www.newportmansions.org* 🎫 *$14.50* 🕐 *Mid-May–Oct., daily 10–6.*

SPORTS AND THE OUTDOORS

BEACHES

Sandy Point Beach. Sandy Point Beach is a choice spot for families and beginning windsurfers because of the calm surf along the Sakonnet River. Lifeguards are on duty Memorial Day through Labor Day. **Amenities:** food and drink; lifeguards; parking (fee); showers; toilets. **Best for:** solitude; swimming; walking; windsurfing. ✉ *Sandy Point Ave.* ☎ *401/297–1263* 🎫 *$7 weekdays, $12 weekends.*

BRISTOL

5 miles north of Portsmouth, 20 miles southeast of Providence.

Midway between Newport and Providence—each a 30-minute drive—patriotic Bristol sits on a 10-square-mile peninsula between Narragansett Bay on its west and Mount Hope Bay on its east. The main thoroughfare through the town's charming business district, Hope Street, is painted with a red-white-and-blue center stripe in honor of the town's annual 4th of July Celebration dating back to 1785, making it the oldest continuous celebration of its kind in the United States.

A horse, an elephant, and a bunny are just some of the creatures at Green Animals Topiary Garden in Portsmouth.

Bristol was once a boatbuilding center; the Herreshoff Manufacturing Company built five consecutive America's Cup Defenders between 1893 and 1920. The southern end of the East Bay Bike Path lies at Independence Park. The bike path crosses the access road for Colt State Park, a great spot for picnics and kite flying.

EXPLORING

Blithewold Mansion, Gardens, and Arboretum. Starting with a sea of daffodils in April, this 33-acre estate on Bristol Harbor blooms all the way until fall. Highlights include fragant pink chestnut roses and one of largest giant sequoia trees on the East Coast. The 45-room English-style manor house is filled with original antiques and artwork. ✉ *101 Ferry Rd.* ☎ *401/253–2707* ⊕ *www.blithewold.org* ✉ *$11* ⊗ *Grounds daily 10–5; mansion mid-Apr.–Columbus Day, Tues.–Sun. 10–4.*

Herreshoff Marine Museum / America's Cup Hall Of Fame. This maritime museum honors the maker of yachts for eight consecutive America's Cup defenses as well as the sport of yachting. Its collection includes more than 60 boats, ranging from the 8½-foot dinghy *Nathanael* to 75-foot successful America's Cup defender *Defiant.* The **Hall of Fame** was founded in 1992 as an arm of the museum by Halsey Herreshoff, a four-time America's Cup defender and grandson of yacht designer Nathanael Herreshoff. The museum hosts talks on yacht design and restoration and operates a sailing school for kids and adults. ✉ *1 Burnside St.* ☎ *401/253–5000* ⊕ *www.herreshoff.org* ✉ *$10* ⊗ *Late Apr.–Aug., daily 10–5; Sept., Tues.–Sun. 10–5; Oct., Wed.–Sun. 10–5; Nov. and Dec., Fri.–Sun. 10–5.*

OFF THE BEATEN PATH

Warren. North of Bristol, Warren has the distinction of being the smallest town in the smallest county in the smallest state in the United States. Home to a thriving arts scene, the town is one of the state's nine "Tax-Free Arts Districts" allowing sales-tax free purchases at its galleries. The East Bay Bike Path travels through its commercial district, so stop to get a Del's frozen lemonade. Warren also claims the stellar 2nd Story Theatre, which stages cutting-edge comedies and dramas. ✉ *Warren* 🌐 *discoverwarren.com.*

WHERE TO EAT AND STAY

$ CAFÉ

🍴 **Beehive Cafe.** This aptly named two-story café is abuzz with college students and foodies who appreciate fresh-baked bread and the famous butternut squash sandwich, made with roasted butternut squash, tangy-sweet pesto, carmelized onions, and Vermont cheddar. The breakfast menu, served every day until 3:30, includes gingerbread pancakes, sweet potato biscuits, and homemade granola. Order at the register and you'll receive a plastic animal to mark your table for the waitress. [$] *Average main: $9* ✉ *10 Franklin St.* ☎ *401/396–9994* 🌐 *www.thebeehivecafe.com* 🕒 *No dinner Sun.–Wed.*

$$$ ECLECTIC Fodor's Choice ★

🍴 **DeWolf Tavern.** A notorious 1818 rum distillery is now one of the state's most distinctive restaurants—look for the timber ceilings, African granite from slave ship ballasts in the walls, and framed sections of early-19th-century graffiti-covered plaster. Chef Sai Viswanath reinvents traditional New England fare with lobster roasted in a 900-degree tandoor oven, seared local sea scallops with chestnut spaetzle and a thyme-garam masala sauce, and seafood stew simmered in a coconut, coriander, star anise, and mustard-seed broth. Save room for the homemade cardamom ice cream. Alfresco dining on the second-story back deck at sunset is one of summer's great pleasures. In winter, ask to reserve Table 36 near the fireplace in the upstairs dining room. [$] *Average main: $28* ✉ *259 Thames St.* ☎ *401/254–2005* 🌐 *www.dewolftavern.com* ✍ *Reservations essential.*

$$$ MODERN AMERICAN

🍴 **Persimmon.** This intimate neighborhood bistro just off the main street has seating for only 38 patrons, so reservations are essential on summer weekends. Neutral walls, white table linens, and simple but elegant china focus your attention on the artfully composed dishes of chef Champe Speidel, who owns the restaurant with his wife Lisa. The kitchen staff uses tweezers to arrange the petite greens on each plate. The meats, bacon, and sausage on the seasonal menu come from the owner's own butcher shop. Appetizers include an excellent pan-seared foie gras. [$] *Average main: $27* ✉ *31 State St.* ☎ *401/254–7474* 🌐 *www.persimmonbristol.com* 🕒 *Closed Mon. Closed Sun. Jan.–Apr. No lunch.*

$$$ ITALIAN

🍴 **Roberto's.** The East Bay's best Italian restaurant can compete with any establishment on Federal Hill with its delicious braciole, 10 classic veal and chicken preparations, and owner Robert Vanderhoof's thoughtful wine list covering Italy, France, Australia, and California. One wall of the elegant dining room has a lovely mural of Tuscany painted by renowned local artist Kendra Ferreira, the mother of Roberto's Johnson & Wales University–trained chef Christian Ferreira. Be prepared to wait; this place is bustling every night of the week. Reservations are essential on busy summer weekends. *[$] Average main: $22 ✉ 450 Hope St. ☎ 401/254–9732 🌐 www.robertosofbristol.com ⏲ No lunch.*

$$ HOTEL 🏨 **Bristol Harbor Inn.** Part of Thames Street Landing, this waterfront hotel was constructed with timber and architectural detailing from an 1818 rum distillery and warehouse that once stood on the site. **Pros:** reasonably priced for a waterfront hotel; stellar restaurant; convenient location. **Cons:** other than shops and marina, there are no exterior grounds. *[$] Rooms from: $135 ✉ 259 Thames St. ☎ 401/254–1444, 866/254–1444 🌐 www.bristolharborinn.com 🛏 40 rooms, 8 suites 🍴 Breakfast.*

SPORTS AND THE OUTDOORS

BIKING

East Bay Bike Path. Flat and affording majestic views of Narragansett Bay, the 14½-mile East Bay Bike Path connects Providence to Bristol's charming downtown. *✉ Colt State Park, Hope St. ☎ 401/253–7482 🌐 www.riparks.com.*

TIVERTON/LITTLE COMPTON

10 miles south of Bristol to Tiverton Four Corners.

The southeastern corner of Rhode Island was originally inhabited by the Sakonnet tribe, led by Awashonks, a cousin of Metacomet (known as King Philip). The name means "the black goose comes." Tiverton and Little Compton were part of Massachusetts until 1747.

From Route 24 at the Sakonnet River Bridge, take Route 77 south for about 5¾ miles to reach historic Tiverton Four Corners, where you'll find the 1730 Chase-Cory House. Continuing south to Little Compton you'll pass rolling estates, lovely homes, farmlands, woods, and a gentle western shoreline. Consider a hike in Tiverton's Weetamoo Woods or Little Compton's Wilbour Woods. Options for dining and accommodations are rather limited in the area, though you will find it a pleasant afternoon drive from Newport or Bristol.

EXPLORING

Gray's Ice Cream. More than 40 flavors of ice cream, all of them made on the premises, are available at Gray's Ice Cream. A Tiverton Four Corners landmark since 1923, it's a summertime pilgrimage destination for people from every corner of the state. Coffee is the go-to flavor for most Rhode Islanders, but specialties such as Indian pudding and apple caramel spice also delight. *✉ 16 East Rd., Tiverton ☎ 401/624–4500 🌐 graysicecream.com ⏲ Nov.–April, daily 6:30 am–7 pm; May–Oct., Mon.–Thurs. 6:30 am–9 pm, Fri., Sat. and Sun. 6:30 am–10 pm.*

Little Compton Commons. This quintessential rural New England town square is actually more of a long triangle anchored by the Georgian-style United Congregational Church. Among the headstones in the nearby cemetery you'll find one for Elizabeth Padobie, said to be the first white girl born in New England. Surrounding the green are a rock wall and all the elements of a small community: town hall, community center, police station, school, library, general store, and restaurant. *✉ 40 Commons 🌐 www.little-compton.com.*

Rhode Island isn't just about regattas; working boats are common on the water, too.

Sakonnet Point. A scenic drive down Route 77 ends at this quiet, southeastern corner of Rhode Island and an Army Corp of Engineers breakwater people like to fish off or walk along to view the harbor. The 1884 Sakonnet Lighthouse on Little Cormorant Rock is not open to the public. Parking is limited in the area. ⊠ *Sakonnet Point, 19 Bluff Head Ave.*

Carolyn's Sakonnet Vineyard. The 50 acres at this vineyard produce about 30,000 cases a year, including an award-winning peach-lemon flavored Vidal Blanc and a dark, fruity blend of Cabernet Franc and Chancellor named Rhode Island Red. The vineyard extends tasting-room hours during the summer, when it hosts a concert series on Thursday evening. For $10, you can enjoy a tasting of six different wines and keep the glass. ⊠ *162 W. Main Rd.* ☎ *401/635–8486* ⊕ *www.sakonnetwine.com* ▭ *Free* ☉ *Memorial Day–Columbus Day, daily 10–6; Nov.–Memorial Day, daily 11–5.*

Tiverton Four Corners. From Route 24, head south on Route 77 to historic Tiverton Four Corners. At the Four Corners Arts Center, in the historic Soule-Seabury House, there's an annual antiques show, art festivals and exhibits, concerts and dances, and other special events. ⊠ *Tiverton* ⊕ *www.tivertonfourcorners.com.*

SPORTS AND THE OUTDOORS

HIKING

Weetamoo Woods. There are more than 10 miles of walking trails in this 850-acre nature preserve that's home to a coastal oak-holly forest, an Atlantic white cedar swamp, two grassland meadows, Early American cellar holes, and the remains of a mid-19th-century village sawmill. The main entrance to Weetamoo Woods, a quarter-mile east of Tiverton

Four Corners, has a parking area and a kiosk with maps. Weetamoo Woods takes its name from the last sachem of the Pocasset Tribe of Wampanoag Indians. ⊠ *Rte. 179, Tiverton* ☎ *401/625–1300* ⊕ *www. tivertonlandtrust.org.*

Wilbour Woods. This 30-acre hollow with picnic tables and a waterfall is a good place for a casual hike along a mile-long marked loop that winds along and over Dundery Brook. The trail includes a boulder dedicated to Queen Awashonks, who ruled the local Saugkonnates tribe during the early Colonial period. ⊠ *111 Swamp Rd.*

BLOCK ISLAND

About 12 miles off Rhode Island's southern coast, Block Island is the smallest state's answer to nearby bigger and ritzier Martha's Vineyard and Nantucket. With 17 miles of beaches that—unlike many of those on its Massachusetts sister islands—are open to everyone, it has been a vacation destination since the 19th century. Despite the number of summer visitors and thanks to the efforts of local conservationists, the island's beauty remains intact (more than 43% of the land is preserved); its 365 freshwater ponds support thousands of species of birds that migrate seasonally along the Atlantic Flyway.

The original inhabitants of the island were Native Americans who called it Manisses, or "isle of the little god." Following a 1614 visit by Dutch explorer Adrian Block, the island was given the name Adrian's Eyelant, and later Block Island. In 1661 it was settled by farmers and fishermen from Massachusetts Bay Colony, who established its second official name, the Town of New Shoreham, when it became part of Rhode Island in 1672.

Block Island, with 950 year-round residents, is a laid-back community. You can dine at any of the island's establishments in shorts and a T-shirt. The busiest season, when the population explodes to about 15,000, is between May and Columbus Day—at other times most restaurants, inns, stores, and visitor services close down. If you plan to stay overnight in summer, make reservations well in advance; for weekends in July and August, March is not too early.

GETTING HERE AND AROUND

AIR TRAVEL New England Airlines operates scheduled flights from Westerly to Block Island State Airport.

FERRY TRAVEL There's year-round car-and-passenger ferry service to Block Island from the Port of Galilee, in the town of Narragansett in South County. Seasonal passenger-only ferry service is available from Newport; New London, Connecticut; and Montauk, New York. All the ferry companies permit bicycles, with the fares for these ranging from $3 to $10 each way.

The most heavily trafficked route is Block Island Ferry's traditional car-passenger service and high-speed passenger service between Block Island's Old Harbor and Galilee. By conventional ferry, the one-hour trip is about $14 one way for passengers (rates fluctuate with oil prices) and $50 for automobiles, and runs from one or two times a day in winter to 10 times a day in peak season. Make car reservations well

Block Island

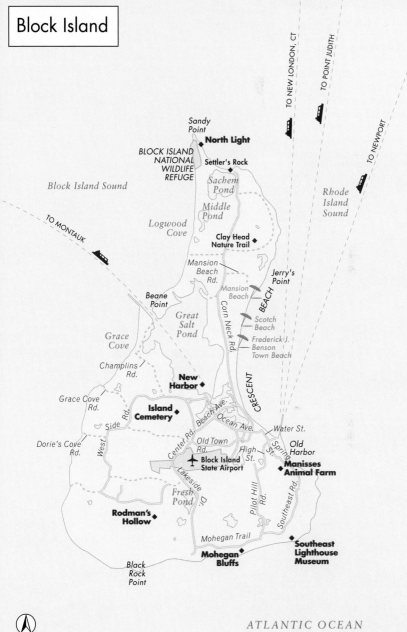

TO NEW LONDON, CT

TO POINT JUDITH

TO NEWPORT

Block Island Sound

Sandy Point

North Light

BLOCK ISLAND NATIONAL WILDLIFE REFUGE

Settler's Rock

Sachem Pond

Middle Pond

Logwood Cove

Clay Head Nature Trail

Rhode Island Sound

Mansion Beach Rd.

Jerry's Point

Mansion Beach

Beane Point

Great Salt Pond

BEACH

Scotch Beach

Grace Cove

Frederick J. Benson Town Beach

Champlins Rd.

Corn Neck Rd.

TO MONTAUK

New Harbor

CRESCENT

Grace Cove Rd.

Island Cemetery

Beach Ave.

Ocean Ave.

Water St.

Dorie's Cove Rd.

Side Rd.

West Rd.

Center Rd.

Old Town Rd.

High St.

Spring St.

Old Harbor

Block Island State Airport

Manisses Animal Farm

Lakeside Dr.

Fresh Pond

Pilot Hill Rd.

Southeast Rd.

Rodman's Hollow

Mohegan Trail

Mohegan Bluffs

Southeast Lighthouse Museum

Black Rock Point

ATLANTIC OCEAN

0	1/2 mile
0	1 km

ahead by telephone. Arrive 45 minutes ahead in high season to allow time to find parking in the pay lots that surround the docks ($10 to $15 a day). From early June to mid-October the high-speed service makes four to six daily 30-minute trips ($19 one way) along the same route. There is no auto service on the high-speed; passenger reservations are recommended.

Block Island Ferry also operates a seasonal service from Newport's Fort Adams State Park to Old Harbor. The passengers-only ferry leaves Newport for Block Island once a day from July through Labor Day at 9:15 am and leaves Block Island at 4:45 pm. One-way rates are about $25.50 (no reservations or credit cards are accepted in Newport). Approximate sailing time is 70 minutes.

From late May to mid-October a high-speed passenger-only ferry operated by Block Island Express runs between New London, Connecticut, and Old Harbor. The ferry departs from New London every three hours, three or four times a day, and takes a little more than an hour. Tickets are $25 one way. Reservations are recommended.

Viking Fleet runs high-speed passenger service from Montauk, Long Island, to Block Island from late May to mid-October. The boat departs from Montauk at 10 am and leaves Block Island at 5 pm, plus an additional trip on Sundays in July and August that departs from Block Island at 11:30 am and Montauk at 3:30 pm. Fare is $50 one way. Travel time is one hour; the ferry docks at New Harbor.

GETTING AROUND Block Island has two harbors, Old Harbor and New Harbor. Approaching the island by sea from New London, Newport, or Point Judith, you'll see Old Harbor, the island's only village, and its group of Victorian hotels, the largest left intact on the New England coast. Most of the smaller inns, shops, and restaurants are also here, and it's a short walk from the ferry landing to most of the interesting sights as well as many accommodations.

A car isn't necessary but can be helpful if you're staying far from Old Harbor or visiting for long. You can rent one at Block Island Car Rental.

ESSENTIALS

Transportation Contacts Block Island State Airport ⊠ *Center Rd.* ☎ *401/466–5511.* **Block Island Bike and Car Rental** ⊠ *Ocean Ave., New Harbor* ☎ *401/466–2297* ⊕ *www.blockislandinfo.com.* **Block Island Express** ⊠ *2 Ferry St., New London, Connecticut* ☎ *401/466–2212, 860/444–4624* ⊕ *www.goblockisland.com.* **Block Island Ferry** ⊠ *304 Great Island Rd., Narragansett* ☎ *401/783–7996, 866/783–7996* ⊕ *www.blockislandferry.com.* **New England Airlines** ☎ *800/243–2460* ⊕ *www.block-island.com/nea.* **Viking Fleet** ⊠ *462 West Lake Dr., Montauk, New York* ☎ *631/668–5700* ⊕ *www.vikingfleet.com.*

Visitor Information Block Island Chamber of Commerce ⊠ *1 Water St.* ☎ *401/466–2982, 800/383–2474* ⊕ *www.blockislandchamber.com.*

EXPLORING

TOP ATTRACTIONS

Mohegan Bluffs. The 200-foot cliffs along Mohegan Trail, the island's southernmost road, are named for an Indian battle in which the local Manisses defeated an attacking band of Mohegans. From Payne Overlook, west of the Southeast Lighthouse, you can see to Montauk Point on Long Island. An intimidating set of stairs leads down almost to the bottom; erosion means there's then a short but treacherous rocky scramble before you reach the beach. It is pebbly at the base of the stairs but sandy in the cove to the west, with lively surf that attracts surfers. ■TIP➔ **Wear walking shoes and don't attempt the descent unless you're in reasonably good shape.** ✉ *Mohegan Trail.*

North Light. This 1867 granite lighthouse on the northernmost tip of the Block Island National Wildlife Refuge serves as a maritime museum. The refuge is home to American oystercatchers, piping plovers, and other rare migrating birds. From a parking lot at the end of Corn Neck Road it's a ¾-mile hike over sand to the lighthouse. Seals sun themselves on nearby Sandy Point during winter months. ✉ *Block Island National Wildlife Refuge, Corn Neck Rd.* ☎ *401/466–3200* ⊕ *www.blockislandchamber.com* 🎫 *Donation suggested* ⊗ *July 5–Labor Day, Thurs.–Mon. 10–4.*

Fodor's Choice **Rodman's Hollow.** This easy-to-find nature preserve is many people's first
★ point of contact with the island's Greenway Trail system. The main trail runs south about 1 mile to clay bluffs with great ocean views, from which a winding path descends to the rocky beach below. Side trails cross the 50-acre hollow, offering longer hikes and the allure of getting mildly lost. The striking, if muted, natural beauty makes it easy to understand why, 40 years ago, this was the property that first awoke the local land conservation movement, now close to achieving its goal of preserving half the island. Geology buffs will delight in this fine example of a glacial outwash basin; nature lovers may enjoy looking for the Block Island meadow vole, the state-threatened northern harrier, and endangered American burying beetle. A small parking lot sits just south of Cooneymus Road near a stone marker. ✉ *Cooneymus Rd.*

Southeast Lighthouse Museum. The small repository is inside a "rescued" 1873 redbrick beacon with gingerbread detail that was moved back 360 feet from the eroded clay cliffs. The lighthouse is a National Historic Landmark; tours are offered during the summer. ✉ *122 Mohegan Tr.* ☎ *401/466–5009* 🎫 *Tours $10* ⊗ *Memorial Day–Labor Day, daily 10–4.*

WORTH NOTING

FAMILY **Manisses Animal Farm.** Animals you never knew existed—like the zedonk, a cross between a zebra and a donkey—are on display at this farm. Fainting goats (goats whose legs stiffen when excited, causing them to fall over), camels, llamas, emus, and kangaroos will gladly take handouts of the pellets provided. Black swans stroll about, and lemurs leap around their own enclosure. A herd of gentle alpacas helps provide fibers for the adjacent North Light Fibers textile mill. ✉ *Off Spring St.* ☎ *401/466–2421* 🎫 *Free* ⊗ *Daily dawn–dusk.*

Rodman's Hollow boasts cliffside trails that may be enjoyed on foot or horseback.

New Harbor. The Great Salt Pond has a culture all its own, centered on the three marinas, two hotels, and five restaurants clustered along its southern shore that make up this commercial area about a 20-minute walk from Old Harbor. Up to 2,000 boats create a forest of masts on summer weekends, drawn by sail races and fishing tournaments, while on the quiet north and east shores, clammers and windsurfers claim the tidal flats. Two landmark buildings preserved in the island's historic red-and-white idiom overlook the waters: the decommissioned Coast Guard Building at the cut where oceangoing boats enter and leave; and the Narragansett Inn, the only Victorian hotel still run by the family that built it. The Montauk ferry docks at Champlin's, the largest of the marinas. ✉ *Great Salt Pond.*

WHERE TO EAT

$$ AMERICAN 🍴 **The Beachead.** The food—especially the Rhode Island clam chowder—is consistently great, the price is right, and you won't feel like a tourist at this local favorite. Catch ocean breezes on the patio, or in stormy weather sit at the bar and watch breakers roll in 30 feet away. The menu and service are unpretentious; stop in for a grilled tuna or chicken sandwich at lunch, or try more ambitious fare at dinner like Portuguese mussels linguica or steak au poivre. The kitchen brings its talent for reliability and quality to Payne's Dock, where it runs the Burger Bar at lunch and dinner during boating season. [$] *Average main: $18* ✉ *Corn Neck Rd.* ☎ *401/466–2249* 🌐 *thebeachead.com* ✍ *Reservations not accepted* 🕒 *Closed Dec.–Apr.*

$$$ AMERICAN 🍴 **Eli's.** This intimate bistro is the source of some of Block Island's most creative cuisine, built around the theme of Asian comfort food. Menu items change seasonally, but might include appetizers of tuna poke, wakame salad, sriracha aioli, and homemade wonton chips. Eclectic main dishes range from spring lamb osso bucco with ceci beans and a citrus-herb gremolata to seared red snapper with baby bok choy to grilled Chinese-style pork belly. The pastry chef enjoys local fame for her bread pudding. Wait times can be long, and the tiny bar, a favorite of locals, is prime real estate. [$] *Average main: $25* ✉ *456 Chapel St.* ☎ *401/466–5230* 🌐 *www.elisblockisland.com* ✍ *Reservations not accepted* 🕒 *Closed Nov.–Mar. No lunch.*

$$$ SEAFOOD 🍴 **Finn's.** A Block Island institution, Finn's serves fresh, reliable fried and broiled seafood and a wonderful smoked bluefish pâté. The island's best bet for simple steamed lobster, this is also the spot for an unfussy lunch such as the Workman's Special—a burger, coleslaw, and fries. Eat inside or out on the deck, or get food to go from the takeout window and raw bar. Finn's Fish Market is in the same building and its lobster tanks and ice tables are the best source for local seafood to cook at home or over a beach fire. [$] *Average main: $26* ✉ *Ferry Landing, 212 Water St., Old Harbor* ☎ *401/466–2473* 🌐 *finnsseafood.com* ✍ *Reservations not accepted* 🕒 *Closed mid-Oct.–May.*

$ VEGETARIAN 🍴 **Froozies.** What began as a smoothie bar on the back porch of the National Hotel has evolved into a standout sandwich joint, with hearty but healthy options, a varied vegetarian menu, and good people-watching. Active types stop by early for a black bean–and-avocado breakfast burrito and fair-trade coffee. Night owls roll in late morning for hangover-cure smoothies and the Grilled Pondsider, one of the best takes on a grilled cheese ever invented, with pesto, mozzarella, sun-dried tomatoes, sunflower seeds, and spinach. [$] *Average main: $8* ✉ *26 Dodge St.* ☎ *401/466–2230* 🌐 *www.frooziesblockisland.com* ✍ *Reservations not accepted* 🕒 *Closed Oct.–May.*

$$$ MODERN AMERICAN Fodor's Choice ★ 🍴 **Manisses Restaurant.** The chef at the island's premier restaurant for American cuisine uses herbs and vegetables from the hotel's garden and locally caught seafood to prepare such superb dishes as lobster johnnycakes with sweet corn salsa and fennel pollen butter or grilled swordfish with lobster mashed potatoes and a lemon beurre blanc. Fans of red meat appreciate the tandoori beef tenderloin skewers with chickpea salad and grilled naan, or the braised short ribs with house-made kimchi, garlicky spinach, and sushi rice. A wide selection of small plates make this a place to splurge without breaking the bank, and the garden seating around a fountain is tranquil. [$] *Average main: $26* ✉ *Hotel Manisses, 1 Spring St.* ☎ *401/466–2421, 800/626–4773* 🌐 *www.blockislandresorts.com* 🕒 *Closed late Oct.–Apr.*

WHERE TO STAY

It's advisable to book lodgings well in advance, especially for weekends in July and August, when many hotels ask for a two-night minimum; the Chamber of Commerce runs a room reservation service that's handy for last-minute trips. Many visitors rent homes for stays of a week or more.

$$$ HOTEL **The Atlantic Inn.** Perched on a hill of floral gardens and undulating lawns, away from the hubbub of the Old Harbor area, this long, white, classic 1879 Victorian resort has big windows, high ceilings, a sweeping staircase, and lovely views. **Pros:** spectacular hilltop location; beautiful veranda for whiling away the afternoon; grand decor. **Cons:** no TVs or high-speed Internet in rooms. [$] *Rooms from: $200* ✉ *359 High St.* ☎ *401/466–5883, 800/224–7422* 🌐 *www.atlanticinn.com* *20 rooms, 1 suite* ⏲ *Closed late Oct.–mid-Apr.* 🍴 *Breakfast.*

$$ B&B/INN **Blue Dory Inn.** This Old Harbor district inn, with a main building and three small shingle-and-clapboard outbuildings, has been a guesthouse since its construction in 1898. **Pros:** great in-town location; relatively affordable. **Cons:** some units are small. [$] *Rooms from: $165* ✉ *61 Dodge St.* ☎ *401/466–5891, 800/992–7290* 🌐 *www.blockislandinns.com* *11 rooms, 4 cottages, 3 suites* 🍴 *Breakfast.*

$$$$ B&B/INN Fodor's Choice ★ **Payne's Harbor View Inn.** This 2002 inn, designed to blend with the island's historic architecture, occupies a breezy hillside overlooking the Great Salt Pond and is just minutes from Crescent Beach. **Pros:** relatively inexpensive for luxurious feel; kayak rentals; Wi-Fi and TVs. **Cons:** books up fast. [$] *Rooms from: $235* ✉ *Ocean Ave. and Beach Ave.* ☎ *401/466–5758* 🌐 *www.paynesharborviewinn.com* *10 rooms* 🍴 *Breakfast.*

$$$$ B&B/INN **The Rose Farm Inn.** With simple accommodations in a late-19th-century farmhouse and more luxurious units across a country lane inside a more modern structure, this property is set on a 20-acre pastoral farmstead. **Pros:** great spot for weddings; choice of accommodations; quiet setting yet easy walk to Old Harbor. **Cons:** bathrooms in Farm House a bit rustic; few in-room amenities. [$] *Rooms from: $234* ✉ *Roslyn Rd., off High St.* ☎ *401/466–2034* 🌐 *www.rosefarminn.com* *19 rooms, 17 with bath* ⏲ *Closed mid-Oct.–early May* 🍴 *Breakfast.*

NIGHTLIFE

Nightlife, at least in season, is one of Block Island's highlights, and you have approximately two dozen places to grab a drink. Check the *Block Island Times* for band listings.

Atlantic Inn. Of the island's many gracious Victorian hotel porches, the Atlantic Inn's is still the best one to begin your summer evening. Locals and visitors alike enjoy inventive cocktails, an award-winning wine list, well-prepared tapas, and an unparalleled view of Old Harbor in the setting sun. Croquet mallets are available at the front desk. ✉ *359 High St.* ☎ *401/466–5883* 🌐 *www.atlanticinn.com.*

Captain Nick's. This place sets itself apart from the others by hosting June's Block Island Music Festival, a free roundup of soon-to-be-discovered bands from around the country. It has a two-level bar, live music inside and out, and a suntanned crowd to ogle. Disco Mondays have been an island tradition for more than two decades. The owner, a gifted pianist and singer, performs Tuesday and Wednesday. Sushi is served Thursday to Sunday. ✉ *34 Ocean Ave.* ☎ *401/466–5670* 🌐 *www.captainnicks.com.*

7

Mahogany Shoals. A tiny shack built over the water at Payne's Dock, Mahogany Shoals is where Irish sea chanteys are the evening entertainment of choice. It has expanded, gracefully, with an outdoor bar and an upper-level deck. It remains the best place on the island to enjoy a quiet drink, peer at beautiful yachts, and catch a breeze on even the hottest of nights. ⊠ *Payne's Dock, 133 Ocean Ave.*

SPORTS AND THE OUTDOORS

BEACHES

The east side of the island has a number of beaches, which, like the rest of Rhode Island's coastline, offer temperate, warm waters that are ideal for swimming from June through around September.

Fodor's Choice ★ **Crescent Beach.** This 3-mile-long beach runs north from Old Harbor, and its white sands become wider and crowds thinner the farther away from town you go. It is divided into three smaller beaches, each with its own access point from Corn Neck Road. Farthest north is Mansion Beach: look for the sign, then follow the dirt road to the right. From the parking area, it's a short hike to reach what is easily one of New England's most beautiful beaches. In the morning you may spot deer on the dunes, while surfers dot Jerry's Point to the north. Closer to Old Harbor, Scotch Beach, with its small parking lot directly off Corn Neck Road, is a mecca for young adults. **Amenities:** food and drink; lifeguards; parking (no fee); showers; toilets. **Best for:** sunrise; sunset; walking. ⊠ *Corn Neck Rd.*

BIKING

The best way to explore Block Island is by bicycle (about $20 to $30 a day to rent) or moped (about $45 for an hour; $85 to $115 for the day). Most rental places are open spring through fall and have child seats for bikes, and all rent bicycles in a variety of styles and sizes, including mountain bikes, hybrids, tandems, and children's bikes.

Island Moped and Bike Rentals. This shop has bikes of all kinds for daily and weekly rentals and mopeds for hourly to half-day rentals. ⊠ *41 Water St.* ☎ *401/741–2329* ⊕ *www.bimopeds.com.*

Old Harbor Bike Shop. Descend from the Block Island Ferry and get right on a bike at Old Harbor Bike Shop, which also has a location at the Boat Basin marina in New Harbor. ⊠ *Water St., south of ferry dock* ☎ *401/466–2029* ⊕ *www.blockislandtransportation.com/about.htm.*

BOATING

FAMILY **Aldo's Boat Rentals.** At Champlin's Marina, Aldo's Boat Rentals offers all sorts of fun on the quiet waters of the Great Salt Pond, from no-skill-required pontoon boats to zippy sailboats. Bumper boats and paddleboats are fun for kids. ⊠ *Champlin's Marina, West Side Rd., Block Island, New Harbor* ☎ *401/466–2700.*

FAMILY **Pond & Beyond.** Guided wildlife kayak trips around the Great Salt Pond are a specialty at Pond & Beyond. Children 12 and older can join custom tours designed to their skill level, while younger kids will be happy to hang out at the sea-life touch tanks run nearby by the Block Island Maritime Institute. Tours take place from Memorial Day to Columbus Day. ⊠ *Ocean Ave., New Harbor* ☎ *401/578–2773.*

Digging for clams is a fun pastime on Block Island's beaches.

FISHING

Most of Rhode Island's record fish have been caught on Block Island. In fact, it's held the striped bass record (currently a 77.4-pound whopper caught in 2011) since 1984. From almost any beach skilled anglers can land tautog and bass. The New Harbor channel is a good spot to hook bonito and fluke. Shellfishing licenses ($20 a week) may be obtained at the harbormaster's building at the Boat Basin in New Harbor.

Block Island Fishworks. Tiny Block Island Fishworks in New Harbor sells a wide range of tackle, including hand-tied fly-fishing leaders. It also offers charter fishing trips—inshore for bass and blues, offshore for tuna and shark—guide services, and spearfishing lessons. ⊠ *Ocean Ave.* ☎ *401/742–3992* ⊕ *www.bifishworks.com.*

Twin Maples. This shop has been selling bait and handmade lures, sophisticated fishing tackle, and coveted "Eat Fish" T-shirts from its rustic salt-pond setting for more than 60 years. ⊠ *Twin Maples, Beach Ave.* ☎ *401/466–5547* ⊕ *www.twinmaplesblockisland.com.*

HIKING

Fodor'sChoice
★
Clay Head Nature Trail. The outstanding Clay Head Nature Trail meanders past Clay Head Swamp and along 150-foot clay bluffs. Songbirds chirp and flowers bloom along the paths; stick close to the ocean for a stunning hike that ends at Sachem Pond, or venture into the interior's intertwining paths for hours of wandering and blackberrying in an area called the Maze. The trailhead is recognizable by a simple white post marker that lies on the east side of Corn Neck Road about 2 miles north of Old Harbor. ⊠ *Clay Head Trail Rd.*

Greenway. This well-maintained trail system meanders for 28 miles across the island, crossing stone walls and allowing access to places you can't reach any other way. The beaches that ring the island also offer great hikes, from sandy strolls to cliffside bouldering. Trail maps for the Greenway are available at the Block Island Chamber of Commerce. ⊠ *Greenway.*

WATER SPORTS

Block Island Parasail and Watersports. This outfitter will take you parasailing and also rents five-person jet boats and 10-person banana boats. ⊠ *Old Harbor Basin, Water St.* ☎ *401/864–2474* ⊕ *www. blockislandparasail.com* ☽ *June–Oct., daily 9 am–sunset.*

Diamondblue Surf Shop. This shop stocks a full range of surf gear and offers kiteboarding lessons and stand-up paddleboard rentals. ⊠ *Bridgegate Square, Intersection of Dodge St. and Corn Neck Rd.* ☎ *401/466–3145* ⊕ *www.diamondbluebi.com.*

Island Outfitters. This shop sells wet suits, spearguns, and scuba gear, as well as beach wear and bathing suits. ⊠ *227 Weldon's Way* ☎ *401/466–5502.*

SHOPPING

Golddiggers. This jewelry story carries handmade pendants, rings, charms, and bracelets with maritime themes. ⊠ *90 Chapel St.* ☎ *401/466–2611* ⊕ *www.blockislandgolddiggers.com.*

Island Bound Bookstore. This shop has a good selection of fiction and nonfiction titles, including excellent histories of the island. There are art supplies and crafts for kids. ⊠ *New Post Office Bldg., Water St.* ☎ *401/466–8878* ⊕ *www.islandboundbookstore.com.*

Jessie Edwards Studios. This gallery showcases photographs, sculptures, and contemporary American paintings, often with nautical themes. Owner Jessie Edwards does home portraits by commission, and operates the island's only framing shop. ⊠ *New Post Office Bldg., 30 Water St., 2nd fl.* ☎ *401/466–5314* ⊕ *www.jessieedwardsgallery.com.*

Lazy Fish. This eclectic collection of home accessories is curated by a careful eye. The owner is an interior designer who blends old with new to colorful but harmonious effect. ⊠ *235 Dodge St.* ☎ *401/466–2990.*

North Light Fibers. Manisses Animal Farm uses wool from its alpacas, llamas, yaks, and sheep to make beautiful yarns, clothing, and blankets. Classes are offered in knitting, weaving, and felting. ⊠ *Manisses Animal Farm, 10 Spring St.* ☎ *401/466–2050* ⊕ *www.northlightfibers.com.*

VERMONT

WELCOME TO VERMONT

TOP REASONS TO GO

★ **Small-Town Charm:** Vermont rolls out a seemingly never-ending supply of tiny, charming towns made of steeples, general stores, village squares, red barns, and B&Bs.

★ **Ski Resorts:** The East's best skiing takes place in uncrowded, modern facilities, with great views and lots and lots of fresh snow.

★ **Fall Foliage:** Perhaps the most vivid colors in North America wave from the trees in September and October, when the whole state is ablaze.

★ **Gorgeous Landscapes:** This sparsely populated, heavily forested state is an ideal place to find peace and quiet amid the mountains, valleys, and lakes.

★ **Tasty and Healthy Eats:** The state's rich soil and focus on local farming and ingredients yields great cheeses, dairies, orchards, vineyards, local food resources, and restaurants.

1 Southern Vermont. Most people's introduction to the state is southern Vermont, accessible by car from New York and Boston. As elsewhere across the state, you'll find unspoiled towns, romantic B&Bs, rural farms, and pristine forests. There are two notable exceptions: sophisticated Manchester has upscale shopping, and independent Brattleboro remains a hippie outpost and environmentally conscious town.

2 Central Vermont. Similar to southern Vermont in character and geography, central Vermont's star is Stowe, the quintessential ski town east of the Mississippi. Woodstock, Waitsfield, and Middlebury are among its charming small towns.

3 Northern Vermont. The northernmost part of the state is a place of contrasts. Burlington, with dramatic views of Lake Champlain and the Adirondacks, is the state's most populous city at around 60,000 residents; it's an arts-loving, laid-back college town with a sophisticated local food scene. To the east, the landscape becomes increasingly rural, with stupendous natural beauty and almost no significant population, making the Northeast Kingdom a refuge for nature lovers and aficionados of getting away from it all.

GETTING ORIENTED

Vermont can be divided into three regions. The southern part of the state, flanked by Bennington on the west and Brattleboro on the east, played an important role in Vermont's Revolutionary War–era drive to independence (yes, there was once a Republic of Vermont) and its eventual statehood. The central part is characterized by rugged mountains and the gently rolling dairy lands near Lake Champlain. Northern Vermont is home to the state's capital, Montpelier, and its largest city, Burlington, as well as its most rural area, the Northeast Kingdom. The Green Mountains run north to south in the center of the state and are covered in protected national forest.

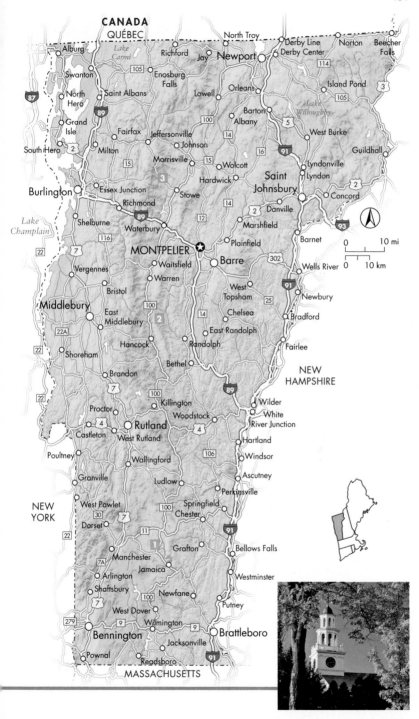

CANADA
QUÉBEC

North Troy

Alburg
Lake
Carmi
Richford
Jay
Newport
Derby Line
Derby Center
Norton
Beecher
Falls

Swanton
Enosburg
Falls
105
Lowell
Orleans
Island Pond
3

North
Hero
Saint Albans
105

Grand
Isle
Fairfax
Albany
Barton
Lake
Willoughby
West Burke
114

South Hero
2
Milton
Jeffersonville
Johnson
100
14
16
91
Lyndonville
Guildhall

Burlington
Essex Junction
Morrisville
15
Wolcott
Hardwick
Saint
Johnsbury
Lyndon
2

Richmond
89
Stowe
Danville
Concord
93

Lake
Champlain
Shelburne
Waterbury
12
Marshfield
2
Barnet

116
MONTPELIER
Plainfield
Wells River
0   10 mi
0   10 km

22
7
Waitsfield
Barre
302
91
Newbury

Vergennes
Warren
West
Topsham
25
Bradford
NEW
HAMPSHIRE

Bristol
100
14
Chelsea
Fairlee
8

Middlebury
East
Middlebury
2
East Randolph

22A
Hancock
Randolph
Wilder

22
Shoreham
Bethel
White
River Junction

Brandon
89
Hartland

22
7
100
Killington
Woodstock
Windsor

Proctor
4
Rutland
Woodstock
4
106
Ascutney

Castleton
West Rutland
Wallingford
Perkinsville

Poultney
Ludlow
Springfield
Chester

NEW
YORK
Granville
West Pawlet
30
7
100
Bellows Falls

22
Dorset
11
Grafton
91

1
Manchester
Jamaica
Westminster

7A
Arlington
Newfane

Shaftsbury
100
Putney

7
West Dover
Wilmington
9

279
Bennington
Jacksonville
Brattleboro

Pownal
Readsboro
91

MASSACHUSETTS

Updated by
Mike Dunphy

Vermont is an entire state of hidden treasures and unspoiled scenery. Wander anywhere in the state—nearly 80% is forest—and you'll travel a pristine countryside dotted with farms and framed by mountains. Tiny towns with picturesque church steeples, village greens, and clapboard Colonial-era houses are perfect for exploring.

Sprawl has no place here. Highways are devoid of billboards by law, and on some roads cows still stop traffic twice a day en route to and from the pasture. In spring, sap boils in sugarhouses, some built generations ago, and up the road a chef trained at the New England Culinary Institute in Montpelier might use the resulting maple syrup to glaze a pork tenderloin.

It's the landscape, for the most part, that attracts people to Vermont. The rolling hills belie the rugged terrain underneath the green canopy of forest growth. In summer, clear lakes and streams provide ample opportunities for swimming, boating, and fishing; the hills attract hikers and mountain bikers. The more than 14,000 miles of roads, many of them only intermittently traveled by cars, are great for biking. In fall the leaves have their last hurrah, painting the mountainsides a stunning show of yellow, gold, red, and orange. Vermont has the best ski resorts in the eastern United States, centered along the spine of the Green Mountains running north to south. The traditional heart of skiing is the town of Stowe. Almost anywhere you go, any time of year, it will make you reach for your camera.

Vermont may seem locked in time, but technological sophistication appears where you least expect it: wireless Internet access in a 19th-century farmhouse-turned-inn and cell phone coverage from the state's highest peaks. Like an old farmhouse under renovation, Vermont's historic exterior is still the main attraction.

PLANNING

WHEN TO GO

In summer the state is lush and green, although in winter the hills and towns are blanketed with snow and skiers travel from around the world to challenge Vermont's peaks. Fall, however, is always the most amazing time to come. If you have never seen the kaleidoscope of Vermont's autumn colors, it's well worth braving the slow-moving traffic and paying the extra money for fall lodging. The only time things really slow down is during "mud" season—otherwise known as late spring. Even innkeepers have told guests to come another time. Activities in the Champlain Islands essentially come to a halt in the winter, except for ice fishing and snowmobiling. Two of the state's biggest attractions, Shelburne Farms and the Shelburne Museum, are closed mid-October through April. Otherwise, Vermont is open for business all year.

PLANNING YOUR TIME

There are many ways to take advantage of Vermont's beauty: skiing or hiking its mountains, biking or driving its back roads, fishing or sailing its waters, shopping for local products, visiting its museums and sights, or simply finding the perfect inn and never leaving the front porch.

Distances are relatively short, yet the mountains and back roads will slow a traveler's pace. You can see a representative north–south section of Vermont in a few days; if you have up to a week, you can hit the highlights. Note that many inns have two-night-minimum stays on weekends and holidays.

GETTING HERE AND AROUND

AIR TRAVEL

Delta, JetBlue, United, Porter Airlines, and US Airways fly into Burlington International Airport. Rutland State Airport has daily service to and from Boston on Cape Air.

BOAT TRAVEL

Lake Champlain Ferries. This company operates three ferry routes between the Vermont and New York shores: Grand Isle–Plattsburgh, NY; Burlington–Port Kent, NY; and Charlotte–Essex, NY. ☎ *802/864–9804* ⊕ *www.ferries.com.*

CAR TRAVEL

Vermont is divided by a mountainous north–south middle, with a main highway on either side: scenic Route 7 on the western side and Interstate 91 (which begins in New Haven and runs through Hartford, central Massachusetts, and along the Connecticut River in Vermont to the Canadian border) on the east. Interstate 89 runs from New Hampshire across central Vermont from White River Junction to Burlington and up to the Canadian border. For current road conditions, call ☎ *800/429–7623.*

TRAIN TRAVEL

Amtrak. Amtrak has daytime service linking Washington, D.C., with Brattleboro, Bellows Falls, White River Junction, Montpelier, Waterbury, Essex Junction, and St. Albans via the *Vermonter.* Amtrak's *Ethan*

Allen Express connects New York City with Castleton and Rutland. ☎ *800/872-7245* ⊕ *www.amtrak.com.*

RESTAURANTS

Everything that makes Vermont good and wholesome is distilled in its eateries, making the regional cuisine much more defined than that in neighboring states. With an almost political intensity, farmers and chefs have banded together to insist on utilizing Vermont's wonderful bounty. Especially in summer, the produce and meats are impeccable. Many of the state's restaurants belong to the **Vermont Fresh Network** (⊕ *www. vermontfresh.net*), a partnership that encourages chefs to create menus from local produce.

Great chefs are coming to Vermont for the quality of life, and the New England Culinary Institute is a recruiting ground for new talent. Seasonal menus use local fresh herbs and vegetables along with native game. Look for imaginative approaches to native New England foods such as maple syrup (Vermont is the largest U.S. producer), dairy products (especially cheese), native fruits and berries, "new Vermont" products such as salsa and salad dressings, and venison, quail, pheasant, and other game.

Your chances of finding a table for dinner vary with the season: lengthy waits are common in tourist centers at peak times (a reservation is always advisable); the slow months are April and November. Some of the best dining is at country inns. *Prices in the reviews are the average cost of a main course at dinner or, if dinner is not served, at lunch.*

HOTELS

Vermont's only large chain hotels are in Burlington and Rutland. Elsewhere it's just quaint inns, bed-and-breakfasts, and small motels. The many lovely and sometimes quite luxurious inns and B&Bs provide what many people consider the quintessential Vermont lodging experience. Most areas have traditional base ski condos; at these you sacrifice charm for ski-and-stay deals and proximity to the lifts. Rates are highest during foliage season, from late September to mid-October, and lowest in late spring and November, although many properties close during these times. Winter is high season at Vermont's ski resorts. *Prices in the reviews are the lowest cost of a standard double room in high season.*

TOURS

Country Inns Along the Trail. This company arranges guided and self-guided hiking, skiing, and biking trips from inn to inn in Vermont. ✉ *52 Park St., Brandon* ☎ *802/247-3300, 800/838-3301* ⊕ *www.inntoinn. com.*

P.O.M.G. Bike Tours of Vermont. This outfitter, whose name is short for "Peace Of Mind Guaranteed," leads weekend and multiday bike tours around the state. ☎ *802/434-2270, 888/635-2453* ⊕ *www.pomgbike. com.*

Ski Vermont/Vermont Ski Areas Association. For skiing information, contact Ski Vermont/Vermont Ski Areas Association. ✉ *26 State St., Montpelier* ☎ *802/223-2439* ⊕ *www.skivermont.com.*

Vermont Bicycle Touring. This guide company leads bike tours across the state. ☎ *802/453–4811, 800/245–3868* ⊕ *www.vbt.com.*

VISITOR INFORMATION

Vermont Seasonal Hotline. This useful hotline has tips on peak foliage viewing locations and times, up-to-date snow conditions, and seasonal events. ☎ *802/828–3239.*

Vermont Department of Tourism and Marketing ⊠ *6 Baldwin St., Drawer 33, Montpelier* ☎ *802/828–3237, 800/837–6668* ⊕ *www.vermontvacation. com.*

Regional Contacts Northeast Kingdom Travel and Tourism Association ☎ *802/626–8511, 800/884–8001* ⊕ *www.travelthekingdom.com.*

SOUTHERN VERMONT

Cross into the Green Mountain State from Massachusetts on Interstate 91, and you might feel as if you've entered a new country. There isn't a town in sight. What you see are forested hills punctuated by rolling pastures. When you reach Brattleboro, no fast-food joints or strip malls line the exits to signal your arrival at southeastern Vermont's gateway city. En route to downtown, you pass by Victorian-era homes on tree-lined streets. From Brattleboro you can cross over the spine of the Green Mountains toward Bennington and Manchester.

The state's southwest corner is the southern terminus of the Green Mountain National Forest, dotted with lakes, threaded with trails and old forest roads, and home to four big ski resorts: Bromley, Stratton, Mount Snow, and Haystack Mountain.

8

BRATTLEBORO

60 miles south of White River Junction.

Brattleboro has drawn political activists and earnest counter-culturists since the 1960s. Today the arty town of 12,000 is still politically and culturally active, making it Vermont's most offbeat outside of Burlington.

GETTING HERE AND AROUND

Brattleboro is near the intersection of Route 9, the principal east–west highway also known as the Molly Stark Trail, and Interstate 91. For downtown, use Exit 2 from Interstate 91.

ESSENTIALS

Visitor Information Brattleboro Area Chamber of Commerce ⊠ *180 Main St.* ☎ *802/254–4565, 877/254–4565* ⊕ *www.brattleborochamber.org.*

EXPLORING

Brattleboro Museum and Art Center. Downtown is the hub of Brattleboro's art scene, with this museum in historic Union Station at the forefront. It presents changing exhibits created by locally, nationally, and internationally renowned artists. ⊠ *10 Vernon St.* ☎ *802/257–0124* ⊕ *www. brattleboromuseum.org* 🖾 *$8* ⊘ *Sun., Mon., Wed., Thurs., 11–5; Fri., 11–7; Sat., 10–5.*

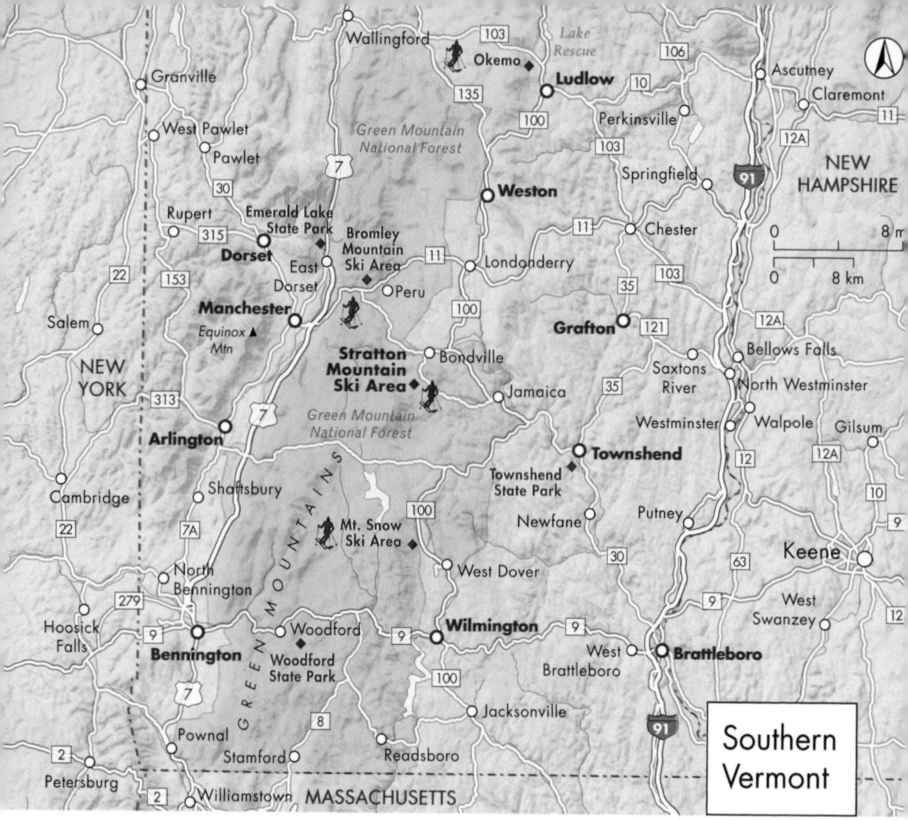

OFF THE BEATEN PATH

Putney. Nine miles upriver, this small town, with a population just short of 3,000, is the country cousin of bustling Brattleboro and is a haven for writers, artists, and craftspeople. There are dozens of pottery studios to visit and a few orchards. Each November dozens of artisans and craftsmen open their studios and homes for a live demonstrations and plenty of fun during the Putney Craft Tour. ✉ *Putney.*

WHERE TO EAT

$ AMERICAN

🍴 **Brattleboro Food Co-op.** This foodie hot spot has many charms, including different grades of self-serve maple syrup and reusable containers to store your bounty. Pick up a plate of curry chicken at the deli counter, then eat it in the glassy café area or out on the river-view patio. Local and organic is the focus in dishes like beef *satay* (skewered grilled meat). The newly expanded deli serves fabulous sandwiches. [$] *Average main: $8* ✉ *2 Main St.* ☎ *802/257–0236* 🌐 *www.brattleborofoodcoop.com.*

$$ ITALIAN

🍴 **Fireworks.** Stop by this trendy, airy, and colorful trattoria-style restaurant for flatbread pizzas, pastas, and salads any night of the week. In nice weather, check out the back patio. Try the daily specials and well-mixed cocktails. [$] *Average main: $16* ✉ *69-73 Main St.* ☎ *802/254-2073* 🌐 *www.fireworksrestaurant.net/brattleboro* 🕑 *No lunch.*

OUTDOOR ACTIVITIES

Biking: Vermont, especially the often-deserted roads of the Northeast Kingdom, is great bicycle-touring country. Many companies lead weekend tours and weeklong trips throughout the state. If you'd like to go it on your own, most chambers of commerce have brochures highlighting good cycling routes in their area.

Canoeing and Kayaking: Getting on Vermont's many rivers and lakes is a great way to experience nature. Outfitters can be found almost anywhere there's water.

Fishing: Central Vermont is the heart of the state's warm-water lake and pond fishing area. Lake Champlain, stocked annually with salmon and lake trout, has become the state's ice-fishing capital.

Hiking: Vermont is an ideal state for hiking—nearly 80% of the state is forest, and trails are everywhere. The Long Trail runs the length of the state. It was the first portion of the Appalachian Tral to be completed and inspired the rest of the trail. Many bookstores in the state have numerous volumes dedicated to local hiking.

Skiing: The Green Mountains run through the middle of Vermont like a bumpy spine, visible from almost every point in the state; generous accumulations of snow make them an ideal site for skiing. Route 100 is also known as Skier's Highway, passing by 13 of the state's ski areas.

$$$$
AMERICAN
Fodor'sChoice
★

✕ **Peter Havens.** Since coming under the ownership of chef Zachary Corbin, Peter Havens has added a new layer of polish to its already sterling reputation. This chic little bistro seems to know just how to perfectly prepare and present everything on the menu, drawing heavily on local sources. One room is painted a warm red, another in sage; both are punctuated by a rotating exhibitions of paintings, creating a look that is one of the most sophisticated in the state. Whatever your main dish, start off with the fabulous tuna tartare and a seasonal cocktail or glass from the superb wine list. $ *Average main: $30* ⊠ *32 Elliot St.* ☎ *802/257-3333* ⊕ *www.peterhavens.com* ☾ *Closed Mon. and Tues. No lunch.*

$$$$
AMERICAN
Fodor'sChoice
★

✕ **T.J. Buckley's.** It's easy to miss this tiny restaurant, but it's worth seeking out as one of the most romantic eateries in Vermont. Open the doors to the sleek black 1920s diner and enter what amounts to a very intimate theater, with a mere 18 seats for the show. The stage is an open kitchen, the flames a few feet away, and working under the whisper of jazz and candlelight is the star of the show: Michael Fuller, the dashing owner and sole chef, who has been at the helm for 30 years. The contemporary menu is conveyed verbally each day and is based on locally available ingredients. $ *Average main: $40* ⊠ *132 Elliot St.* ☎ *802/257-4922* ⊕ *www.tjbuckleys.com* ⚑ *Reservations essential* ☾ *Closed Mon.–Wed.*

$$
BARBECUE

✕ **Top of the Hill Grill.** Don't let the diminutive size of this roadside smokehouse deceive you. It houses some big flavors that locals line up for: hickory-smoked ribs, apple-smoked turkey, beef brisket, and pulled pork, to name a few. Homemade pecan pie is the dessert of choice.

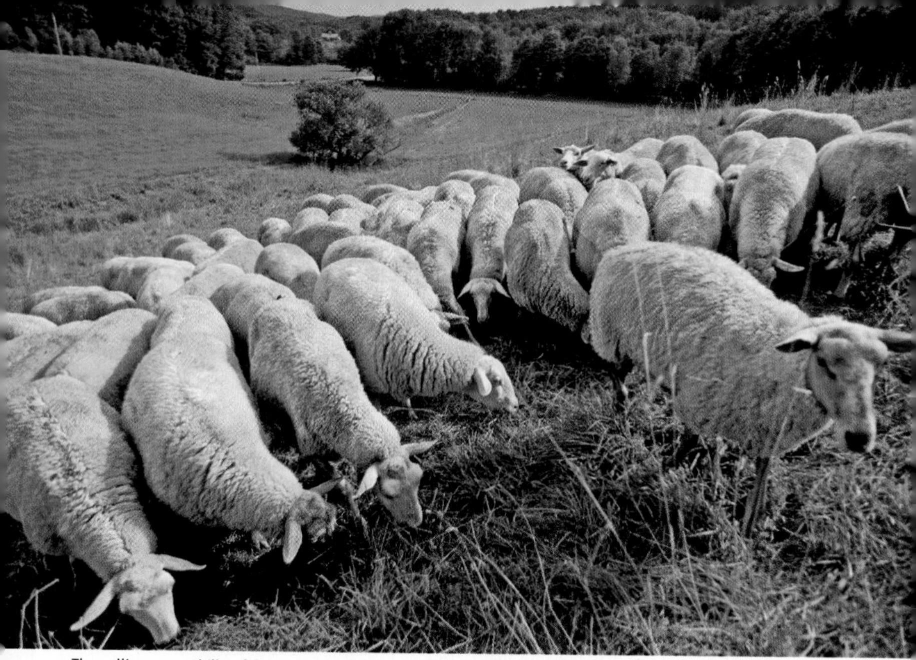

The rolling green hills of Putney are home to many organic farm operations.

The restaurant probably has the best view in town, with outdoor picnic tables and a cozy enclosed area overlooking the West River. [$] *Average main: $15* ✉ *632 Putney Rd.* ☎ *802/258–9178* 🌐 *www.topofthehillgrill.com* 💳 *No credit cards* 🕒 *Closed Nov.–Mar.*

WHERE TO STAY

$$$$ B&B/INN Fodor's Choice ★ 🏨 **Forty Putney Road.** Realizing her dream to run an inn, Rhonda Calhoun took over this French-style manse and has added her own colorful touch to the original features. **Pros:** caring host makes you feel like a guest, not a customer **Cons:** tight parking. [$] *Rooms from: $239* ✉ *192 Putney Rd.* ☎ *802/254–6268, 800/941–2413* 🌐 *www.fortyputneyroad.com* 🛏 *5 rooms, 1 suite* 🍴 *Breakfast.*

$$$ B&B/INN Fodor's Choice ★ 🏨 **Hickory Ridge House.** If you're looking for a relaxing country getaway, this 1808 Federal-style mansion, a former sheep farm set on a wide meadow, is a sure bet. **Pros:** peaceful, property; great breakfast; quintessential B&B experience. **Cons:** not walking distance from town. [$] *Rooms from: $175* ✉ *53 Hickory Ridge Rd., 11 miles north of Brattleboro, Putney* ☎ *802/387–5709, 800/380–9218* 🌐 *www.hickoryridgehouse.com* 🛏 *6 rooms, 1 cottage* 🍴 *Breakfast.*

$ HOTEL 🏨 **Latchis Hotel.** To stay in the heart of town, you won't find a more economical option than the three-story Latchis. **Pros:** heart-of-town location; lots of personality; reasonable rates. **Cons:** limited breakfast. [$] *Rooms from: $110* ✉ *50 Main St.* ☎ *802/254–6300, 800/798–6301* 🌐 *www.latchis.com* 🛏 *30 rooms, 3 suites* 🍴 *Breakfast.*

NIGHTLIFE AND THE ARTS

THE ARTS

Latchis Theater. This art-deco movie theater, complete with statues and frescoes, shows four films at a time and hosts art exhibits. ✉ *50 Main St.* ☎ *802/254–6300* ⊕ *www. latchis.com.*

NIGHTLIFE

Metropolis Wine Bar & Cocktail Lounge. This popular lounge serves up signature infused cocktails, wine, and local beer, as well as finger food and live music. It has a hip, festive atmosphere. ✉ *55 Elliot St.* ☎ *802/254–8500* ⊕ *www. metropoliswinebar.com.*

BILLBOARDS AND VERMONT

Did you know that there are no billboards in Vermont? The state banned them in 1967 (similar laws exist in Maine, Alaska, and Hawaii), and the last one came down in 1975, so when you look out your window, you see trees and other scenic sights, not advertisements. (It may make playing the alphabet game with your child a bit difficult.)

NEED A BREAK?

Mocha Joe's Cafe. This gathering spot for coffee and conversation takes great care in sourcing beans from places like Kenya, Ethiopia, and Guatemala. This is ground zero for Brattleboro's contemporary bohemian spirit. ✉ *82 Main St., at Elliot St.* ☎ *802/257–5637* ⊕ *www.mochajoes.com.*

SPORTS AND THE OUTDOORS

BIKING

Brattleboro Bicycle Shop. This shop rents hybrid bikes and does repair work. Maps and equipment are available. ✉ *165 Main St.* ☎ *802/254–8644* ⊕ *www.bratbike.com.*

CANOEING

Vermont Canoe Touring Center. Canoes and kayaks are available for rent here. ✉ *451 Putney Rd.* ☎ *802/257–5008* ⊕ *www. vermontcanoetouringcenter.com.*

SHOPPING

ART

Gallery in the Woods. This funky three-floor store sells art, jewelry, and light fixtures from around the world. Rotating shows take place in the upstairs and downstairs galleries. ✉ *145 Main St.* ☎ *802/257–4777* ⊕ *www.galleryinthewoods.com.*

Vermont Artisan Designs. Ceramics, glass, wood, clothing, jewelry, and furniture from more than 300 artists are on display here. Rotating shows are in the small gallery upstairs. ✉ *106 Main St.* ☎ *802/257–7044* ⊕ *www.vtart.com.*

BOOKS

Brattleboro Books. With more than 25,000 used books, this is a great spot to browse. ✉ *36 Elliot St.* ☎ *802/257–7777* ⊕ *brattleborobooks. com* ⊗ *Mon.–Sat. 10–6, Sun. 11–5.*

8

FOOD

Serenity Herbs and Teas. Even if you're not an avid tea drinker, it's hard not to admire the passion and expertise of the proprietors of this elegant shop. Ask what makes a true Earl Grey and you'll learn more than you ever thought possible. All teas are hand-blended in the back. ✉ *60 Elliot St.* 🌐 *www.serenityherbsandteas.com* 🕒 *Wed.–Sat. 11–5.*

WILMINGTON

18 miles west of Brattleboro.

The village of Wilmington, with its classic Main Street lined with 18th- and 19th-century buildings, anchors the Mount Snow Valley. Most of the valley's lodging and dining establishments, however, line Route 100, which travels 5 miles north to West Dover and Mount Snow, where skiers flock on winter weekends. The area abounds with cultural activity year-round, from concerts to art exhibits.

GETTING HERE AND AROUND

Wilmington is at the junction of Routes 9 and 100. West Dover and Mount Snow are a few miles to the north along Route 100.

ESSENTIALS

Visitor Information Mount Snow Valley Chamber of Commerce ✉ *21 W. Main St.* ☎ *802/464–8092, 877/887–6884* 🌐 *www.visitvermont.com.*

EXPLORING

FAMILY **Adams Farm.** At this working farm you can collect fresh eggs from the chicken coop, feed a rabbit, milk a goat, ride a tractor or a pony, or take sleigh rides in winter. A livestock barn is open November to mid-June; the animals roam free the rest of the year. ✉ *15 Higley Hill Rd., off Rte. 100* ☎ *802/464–3762* 🌐 *www.adamsfamilyfarm.com* 🎟 *$6.95* 🕒 *Mid-June–Oct., daily 10–4; Nov.–mid-June, Wed.–Sun. 10–4.*

FAMILY **Southern Vermont Natural History Museum.** This museum, 5 miles east of Wilmington, houses one of New England's largest collections of mounted birds, including three extinct species and a complete collection of mammals native to the Northeast. The museum also has live hawk and owl exhibits. There's also an adjacent 600-acre nature preserve. ✉ *7599 Rte. 9* ☎ *802/464–0048* 🌐 *www.vermontmuseum.org* 🎟 *$5* 🕒 *Weekdays 10–4, weekends 10–5.*

WHERE TO EAT

$$$ EUROPEAN 🍴 **Inn at Sawmill Farm.** No other restaurant in Vermont aims as high with its haute Continental food, wine, and service as the restaurant at Sawmill. Order a beer and the bottle is served chilled in a small ice bucket, as if it were champagne. This reverent service and deference to potables come from the top: chef-owner Brill Williams passionately cares for his 17,000-bottle cellar, the biggest restaurant collection in the state. Try the potato-crusted fish of the day served in beurre blanc or grilled loin of venison. Gourmands of Mount Snow, this is your place. [$] *Average main: $23* ✉ *7 Crosstown Rd., at Rte. 100, West Dover* ☎ *802/464–8131, 800/493–1133* 🌐 *www.theinnatsawmillfarm.com* 🕒 *Closed early Apr.–late May. No lunch.*

CLOSE UP

Vermont Maple Syrup

Vermont is one of the country's smallest states, but it's the largest producer of maple syrup. A visit to a maple farm is a great way to learn all about sugaring, the process of taking maple tree sap and making syrup. Sap is stored in a sugar maple tree's roots in the winter, and in the spring when conditions are just right, the sap runs up and is capable of being tapped. Tapping season takes place in March and April, which is when all maple in the state is produced.

Maple sap is collected in buckets.

One of the best parts of visiting a maple farm is getting to taste the four grades of syrup. As the sugaring season goes on and days get warmer, the sap becomes progressively darker and stronger flavored. Color, clarity, and flavor define the four grades of syrup. Is one grade better than another? Nope. It's just a question of taste. Sap drawn early in the season produces the lightest color, and has the most delicate flavor: this is called Vermont Fancy. Vermont Grade A Medium Amber has a mellow flavor. Vermont Grade A Dark Amber is much more robust, and Vermont Grade B is the most flavorful, making it often the favorite of first-time tasters.

Is one syrup better than another? Can you actually tell the difference? You'd need an exceptionally nuanced palate to discern between one Vermont syrup and another, but aesthetics can alter taste, and authenticity counts. So when visiting a maple farm, make sure that this is a place that actually makes its own syrup, as opposed to just bottling or selling someone else's.

Morse Farm Maple Sugarworks. There's no better introduction to Vermont mapling than a visit to Morse Farm Maple Sugarworks in Montpelier,

Vermont. Burr Morse's family has been mapling for more than 200 years, longer than anyone else in the state. Attractions here include a free tour of a sugar house, tastings, and an outdoor museum and woodshed theater. ⊠ *1168 County Rd., Montpelier* ☎ *800/242–2740* ⊕ *www.morse farm.com.*

Vermont Maple Syrup. There are approximately 50 maple farms that are free and open all year to the public. The official industry Web site for Vermont Maple Syrup is a great resource that has a map of maple farms that host tours, a directory of producers open year-round, and a list of places you can order maple by mail. In addition, you can learn about the Annual Maple Open House weekend, which is when sugarhouses throughout the state open their doors to the public. ⊕ *www.vermont maple.org.*

—Michael de Zayas

8

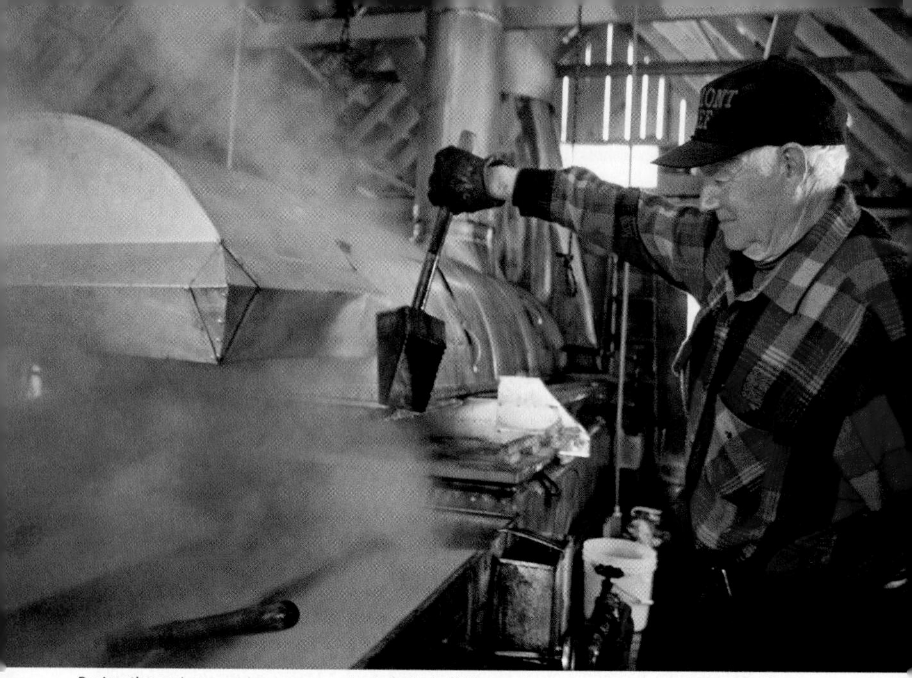

During the spring sugaring season water is boiled off the maple sap to concentrate the syrup's flavor.

WHERE TO STAY

$$$ B&B/INN **Deerhill Inn.** The picture of a quintessential New England inn, this is a truly charming spot. **Pros:** great restaurant; nicely renovated rooms. **Cons:** must drive to town and resort. [$] *Rooms from: $185* ✉ *14 Valley View Rd., West Dover* ☎ *802/464–3100, 800/993–3379* 🌐 *www.deerhill.com* 🛏 *10 rooms, 3 suites* 🍴 *Breakfast.*

$$$$ RESORT FAMILY **Grand Summit Hotel.** The hotel at Mount Snow is an easy choice for skiers who don't care about anything but getting on the slopes as quickly as possible. **Pros:** easy ski access; modern property. **Cons:** somewhat bland decor. [$] *Rooms from: $328* ✉ *89 Grand Summit Way, West Dover* ☎ *800/245-7669* 🌐 *www.mountsnow.com* 🛏 *104 rooms, 93 suites* 🍴 *No meals.*

$$$ B&B/INN **The Inn at Sawmill Farm.** Full of character and charm, this inn in a converted barn has common rooms elegantly accented with English chintzes, antiques, and Oriental rugs. **Pros:** spacious grounds; attentive service. **Cons:** overload of floral prints in some rooms; room size varies. [$] *Rooms from: $175* ✉ *7 Crosstown Rd., at Rte. 100, West Dover* ☎ *802/464–8131, 800/493–1133* 🌐 *www.theinnatsawmillfarm.com* 🛏 *21 rooms* ⏲ *Closed early-Apr.–late May* 🍴 *Multiple meal plans.*

$$$ B&B/INN **White House of Wilmington.** It's hard to miss this 1915 Federal-style mansion standing imposingly atop a high hill east of Wilmington. **Pros:** intriguing property; intimate dining. **Cons:** not in town, so you have to drive to everything; no children under eight. [$] *Rooms from: $220* ✉ *178 Rte. 9* ☎ *802/464–2135, 800/541–2135* 🌐 *www.whitehouseinn.com* 🛏 *15 rooms, 1 suite* 🍴 *Breakfast.*

SPORTS AND THE OUTDOORS

BOATING

Green Mountain Flagship Company. Canoes and kayaks are available for rent from May through Columbus Day on Lake Whitingham. ⊠ *389 Rte. 9, 2 miles west of Wilmington* ☎ *802/464–2975.*

Molly Stark State Park. Molly Stark State Park is home to some of the state's most popular snowshoe trails. Mount Olga Trail is a relatively easy 1.7-mile hike climaxing with a 360-degree view of southern Vermont and northern Massachusetts. ⊠ *705 Rte. 9 East* ☎ *802/464–5460* ⊕ *www.vtstate parks.com/htm/mollystark.htm.*

SKI AREAS

Mount Snow. The closest major ski area to all of the Northeast's big cities, Mount Snow has a full roster of year-round activities. It prides itself on its 253 snowmaking fan guns, more than any other resort in North America. There are four major downhill areas. The main mountain is mostly intermediate terrain, while the north face includes the majority of the expert terrain. The south face, Sunbrook, has wide, sunny trails. The trails are served by 20 lifts, including three high-speed quads and a six-passeger bubble lift called the Bluebird Express. The ski school's instruction program is designed to help skiers of all abilities, including kids. In summer, the 800-acre resort has an 18-hole golf course, 45 miles of mountain-biking trails, and an extensive network of hiking trails. ⊠ *39 Mount Snow Rd., West Dover* ☎ *802/464–3333, 802/464–2151 snow conditions* ⊕ *www.mountsnow.com.*

Timber Creek. North of Snow Mountian, this appealingly small cross-country skiing and snowshoeing center has 4½ miles of groomed loops, equipment rentals, and ski lessons. ⊠ *R1 Tomber Creek Rd., at Rte. 100, West Dover* ☎ *802/464–0999* ⊕ *www.timbercreekxc.com.*

SHOPPING

Quaigh Design Centre. For half a century, this store has been seling great pottery and artwork from Britain and New England, including works by Vermont woodcut artist Mary Azarian. Scottish woolens are also on offer. ⊠ *11 W. Main St.* ☎ *802/464–2780.*

BENNINGTON

21 miles west of Wilmington.

Bennington is the commercial focus of Vermont's southwest corner and home to the renowned Bennington College. It's really three towns in one: Downtown Bennington, Old Bennington, and North Bennington.

The poet Robert Frost is buried in Bennington at the Old First Church, "Vermont's Colonial Shrine."

Downtown Bennington has retained much of the industrial character it developed in the 19th century, when paper mills, gristmills, and potteries formed the city's economic base. The outskirts of town are commercial and not worth a stop, so make your way right into Downtown and Old Bennington to appreciate the true charm of the area.

GETTING HERE AND AROUND

The heart of modern Bennington is at the intersection of U.S. 7 and Route 9. Old Bennington is a couple of miles west on Route 9, at Monument Avenue. North Bennington is a few miles north on Route 67A.

ESSENTIALS

Visitor Information Bennington Area Chamber of Commerce ⊠ *100 Veterans Memorial Dr.* ☎ *802/447–3311, 800/229–0252* ⊕ *www.bennington.com.*

EXPLORING

TOP ATTRACTIONS

FAMILY **Bennington Battle Monument.** This 306-foot stone obelisk—with an elevator to the top—commemorates General John Stark's victory over the British, who attempted to capture Bennington's stockpile of supplies. Inside the monument you can learn all about the battle, which took place near Walloomsac Heights in New York state on August 16, 1777, and helped bring about the surrender of the British commander "Gentleman Johnny" Burgoyne two months later. The summit provides commanding views of the Massachusetts Berkshires, the New York Adirondacks, and the Vermont Green Mountains. ⊠ *15 Monument Circle, Old Bennington* ☎ *802/447–0550* ⊕ *www.historicsites.vermont. gov* ⊑ *$3* ⊙ *Mid-Apr.–Oct., daily 9–5.*

Bennington Museum. The rich collections at this museum include military artifacts, early tools, dolls, and the Bennington Flag, one of the oldest of the Stars and Stripes in existence. One room is devoted to early Bennington pottery, and another examines life here during the Gilded Age. There's glass and metalwork by Tiffany, but the museum's highlight may still remain the largest public collection of the work of Grandma Moses (1860–1961), the popular self-taught artist who lived and painted in the area. ✉ *75 Main St., Old Bennington* ☎ *802/447–1571* 🌐 *www.benningtonmuseum.com* 🎟 *$10* 🕒 *July–Oct. daily 10–5; Nov., Dec., and Feb.–June, Thurs.–Tues. 10–5.*

Robert Frost Stone House Museum. It was to the town of Shaftsbury that poet Robert Frost came in 1920 "to plant a new Garden of Eden with a thousand apple trees of some unforbidden variety." The museum tells the story of the nine years (1920–29) Frost spent living in the house with his wife and four children. (He passed the 1930s in a house up the road in Shaftsbury, now owned by a producer Norman Lear.) It was here that he penned "Stopping by Woods on a Snowy Evening" and published two books of poems. Seven of the Frost family's original 80 acres can be wandered. Among the apple boughs you just might find inspiration of your own. ✉ *121 Historic Rte. 7A, Shaftsbury* ☎ *802/447–6200* 🌐 *www.frostfriends.org* 🎟 *$5* 🕒 *May–Nov., daily 10–5.*

WORTH NOTING

Old Bennington. West of downtown, this National Register Historic District is well endowed with stately Colonial and Victorian mansions. The famous Catamount Tavern, where Ethan Allen organized the Green Mountain Boys to capture Fort Ticonderoga in 1775, now contains a bronze statue of Vermont's now-extinct indigenous mountain lion. ✉ *Monument Ave., Old Bennington.*

The Old First Church. In the graveyard of this church, the tombstone of the poet Robert Frost proclaims, "I had a lover's quarrel with the world." ✉ *1 Monument Cir, at Monument Ave., Old Bennington* ☎ *802/447–1223* 🌐 *www.oldfirstchurchbenn.org* 🎟 *Free.*

WHERE TO EAT

$ DINER 🍴 **Blue Benn Diner.** Breakfast is served all day in this authentic diner, where the eats include turkey hash and breakfast burritos with scrambled eggs, sausage, and chilies, plus pancakes of all imaginable varieties. The menu lists many vegetarian selections. Lines may be long, especially on weekends: locals and tourists alike can't stay away. [$] *Average main: $10* ✉ *314 North St.* ☎ *802/442–5140* ✍ *Reservations not accepted* 💳 *No credit cards.*

WHERE TO STAY

$$ B&B/INN 🏨 **The Eddington House Inn.** You can thank Patti Eddington for maintaining this three-bedroom house, the best value in all of Vermont. **Pros:** budget prices for great B&B; privacy and gentle service. **Cons:** slightly off usual tourist track; only three rooms so it fills up fast. [$] *Rooms from: $139* ✉ *21 Main St., North Bennington* ☎ *802/442–1511* 🌐 *www.eddingtonhouseinn.com* 🛏 *3 suites* 🍽 *Breakfast.*

8

$$
B&B/INN
Fodor's Choice
★

Four Chimneys Inn. One of the best inns in Vermont, this three-story 1915 neo-Georgian looks out over a substantial lawn and a wonderful old stone wall. **Pros:** stately mansion that's extremely well kept; formal dining; nicely renovated rooms. **Cons:** common room/bar closes early. $ *Rooms from: $149* ⊠ *21 West Rd., Old Bennington* ☎ *802/447–3500* ⊕ *www.fourchimneys.com* ⇴ *9 rooms, 2 suites* ⏌⋓*Breakfast.*

THE ARTS

Vermont Arts Exchange. The fun and funky "basement music series" is presented in a lower-level cabaret space in an old factory building. Buy tickets in advance for the best contemporary music performances in town. ⊠ *29 Sage St., North Bennington* ☎ *802/442–5549* ⊕ *www.vtartxchange.org/bms.php.*

Bennington Center for the Arts. Cultural events, including exhibitions by local and national artists, take place here. It's home to the Oldcastle Theatre Company, whose season runs April to November. ⊠ *44 Gypsy La.* ☎ *802/442–7158* ⊕ *www.thebennington.org.*

SPORTS AND THE OUTDOORS

Lake Shaftsbury State Park. You'll find a swimming beach, nature trails, boat and canoe rentals, and a snack bar at this pretty park. ⊠ *262 Shaftsbury State Park Rd., 10½ miles north of Bennington* ☎ *802/375–9978* ⊕ *www.vtstateparks.com/htm/shaftsbury.htm.*

Woodford State Park. This park has an activities center on Adams Reservoir, a playground, boat and canoe rentals, and nature trails. ⊠ *142 State Park Rd., 10 miles east of Bennington* ☎ *802/447–7169* ⊕ *www.vtstateparks.com/htm/woodford.htm.*

SHOPPING

The Apple Barn & Country Bake Shop. This shop sells home-baked goodies, fresh cider, Vermont cheeses, maple syrup, and 30 varieties of apples. You can pick berries here too, making it a fun family stop. You can watch them making cider donuts at the bakery and café on weekends. ⊠ *604 Rte. 7S, 1½ miles south of downtown Bennington* ☎ *802/447–7780* ⊕ *theapplebarn.com.*

The Bennington Bookshop. The state's oldest independent bookstore sells the latest releases an offers free Wi-Fi. ⊠ *467 Main St.* ☎ *802/442–5059.*

Bennington Potters Yard. The showroom at the Bennington Potters Yard stocks goods from the famed Bennington Potters. Take a self-guided tour to see the potters working in the yard. ⊠ *324 County St.* ☎ *802/447–7531, 800/205–8033* ⊕ *www.benningtonpotters.com* ⏱ *Weekdays 9–6.*

Now & Then Books. This great used bookstore, located in an upstairs shop, has nearly 45,000 volumes in stock. ⊠ *439 Main St.* ☎ *802/442–5566* ⊕ *www.nowandthenbooksvt.com.*

ARLINGTON

15 miles north of Bennington.

Smaller than Bennington and more down-to-earth than upper-crust Manchester to the north, Arlington exudes a certain Rockwellian folksiness, and it should. Illustrator Norman Rockwell lived here from 1939 to 1953, and many of his neighbors served as models for his portraits of small-town life.

GETTING HERE AND AROUND

Arlington is at the intersection of Routes 313 and 7A. Take 313 West to reach West Arlington.

EXPLORING

West Arlington. A covered bridge leads to the quaint town green of West Arlington, where Norman Rockwell once lived. River Road runs along the south side of the Battenkill River, a scenic drive. If you continue west along Route 313, you'll come to the Wayside Country Store, a real charmer, where you can pick up sandwiches and chat with locals. The store is frequently mentioned in the Vermont columns written by Christopher Kimball, editor of *Cooks Illustrated.* ✉ *Rte. 313 W.*

WHERE TO STAY

$$$ B&B/INN 🏨 **The Arlington Inn.** Greek Revival columns at this 1847 home lend it an imposing presence in the middle of town, but the atmosphere is friendly and old-fashioned. **Pros:** heart-of-town location; friendly atmosphere. **Cons:** expensive dining. [$] *Rooms from: $199* ✉ *3904 Historic Rte. 7A* ☎ *802/375–6532* 🌐 *www.arlingtoninn.com* 🛏 *13 rooms, 5 suites* 🍴 *Multiple meal plans.*

$$$ B&B/INN FAMILY 🏨 **West Mountain Inn.** This 1810 farmhouse sits on 150 acres on the side of a mountain, offering hiking trails and easy access to the Battenkill River, where you can canoe or go tubing. **Pros:** mountainside location; lots of activities; great if you have kids. **Cons:** outdated bathrooms. [$] *Rooms from: $195* ✉ *144 West Mountain Inn Rd., at Rte. 313* ☎ *802/375–6516* 🌐 *www.westmountaininn.com* 🛏 *14 rooms, 6 suites* 🍴 *Multiple meal plans.*

SPORTS AND THE OUTDOORS

BattenKill Canoe. This outfitter rents canoes for trips along the Battenkill River, which runs directly behind the shop. If you're hooked, they also run bigger white-water trips as well as inn-to-inn tours. ✉ *6328 Historic Rte. 7A* ☎ *802/362–2800, 800/421–5268* 🌐 *www.battenkill.com.*

SHOPPING

ANTIQUES

East Arlington Antiques Center. More than 70 dealers display their wares at East Arlington Antiques Center, which is in a converted 1930s movie theater. Among the finds is one of the country's best stoneware collections. ✉ *1152 East Arlington Rd., East Arlington* ☎ *802/375–6144* 🕒 *Daily 10–5.*

GIFTS

FAMILY **Village Peddler.** This shop has a "chocolatorium" where you can learn all about cocoa. It sells fudge and other candies and stocks a large collection of teddy bears. ✉ *261 Old Mill Rd., East Arlington* ☎ *802/375–6037* 🌐 *www.villagepeddlervt.com.*

The formal gardens and mansion at Robert Todd Lincoln's Hildene are a far cry from his father's log cabin.

MANCHESTER

9 miles northeast of Arlington.

Well-to-do Manchester has been a popular summer retreat since the mid-19th century, when city dwellers traveled north to take in the cool clean air at the foot of 3,816-foot Mt. Equinox. Manchester Village's tree-shaded marble sidewalks and stately old homes—Main Street here could hardly be more picture perfect—reflect the luxurious resort lifestyle of more than a century ago. A mile north on 7A, Manchester Center is the commercial twin to Colonial Manchester Village, as well as where you'll find the town's famed upscale factory outlets doing business in attractive faux-Colonial shops.

Manchester Village also houses the world headquarters of Orvis, the outdoor goods brand that began here in the 19th century and has greatly influenced the town ever since. Its complex includes a fly-fishing school with lessons in its casting ponds and the Battenkill River.

GETTING HERE AND AROUND

Manchester is the main town for the ski resorts of Stratton and Bromley and is roughly 15 minutes from either on Routes 11 and 30. It's 15 minutes north of Arlington, 30 minutes north of Bennington and south of Rutland on Routes 7 and 7A. Take 7A for a more scenic drive.

ESSENTIALS

Visitor Information Green Mountain National Forest Visitor Center ⊠ *2538 Depot St.* ☎ *802/362-2307* ⊕ *www.fs.fed.us/r9/gmfl* ☽ *Weekdays 8-4:30.* **Manchester and the Mountains Regional Chamber of Commerce** ⊠ *39 Bonnet St.* ☎ *802/362-6313, 800/362-4144* ⊕ *www.visitmanchestervt.com.*

EXPLORING

American Museum of Fly Fishing. This museum houses the world's largest collection of angling art and angling-related objects. Rotating exhibitions draw from a permanent collection of more than 1,500 rods, 800 reels, 30,000 flies, and the tackle of notables like Winslow Homer, Bing Crosby, and Jimmy Carter. Every August, a fly-fishing festival has vendors selling antique equipment. You can also practice your casting out back. ✉ *4104 Main St.* ☎ *802/362–3300* ⊕ *www.amff.com* 💲 *$5* ⊙ *Tues.–Sat 10–4.*

FAMILY
Fodor's Choice
★

Hildene. The Lincoln Family Home is a twofold treat, providing historical insight into the life of the Lincolns while escorting you through the lavish Manchester life of the 1900s. Abraham had only one son who survived to adulthood, Robert Todd Lincoln, who served as secretary of war and head of the Pullman Company. Robert bought the beautifully preserved 412-acre estate and built a 24-room mansion where he and his descendants lived from 1905 to 1975. The sturdy Georgian Revival house holds many of the family's prized possessions, including one of three surviving stovepipe hats owned by Abraham and a Lincoln Bible. When the 1,000-pipe aeolian organ is played, the music reverberates as though from the mansion's very bones.

Rising from a 10-acre meadow, the new Hildene Farm, which opened in 2008, is magnificent. The agriculture center is built in a traditional style—post-and-beam construction of timber felled and milled on the estate—and has informative farming displays that recall the family's use of this land. Best of all, you can meet the resident goats and watch goat cheese being made.

The highlight, though, may be the elaborate formal gardens: in June a thousand peonies bloom. When conditions permit, you can cross-country ski and snowshoe on the property. Robert's carriage house now houses a gorgeous museum store and welcome center that showcase, among other things, a live bee exhibit. In good weather Jessie Lincoln's 1928 vintage Franklin car is parked out front. Allow half a day for exploring Hildene. ✉ *1005 Hildene Rd., at Rte. 7A* ☎ *802/362–1788* ⊕ *www.hildene.org* 💲 *Tour $16* ⊙ *Daily 9:30–4:30.*

Fodor's Choice
★

Southern Vermont Arts Center. At the end of a long, winding driveway, this complex houses rotating exhibits and a permanent collection of more than 800 19th- and 20th-century American artworks. The original building, a graceful Georgian mansion set on 100 acres, now is home to 10 galleries with pieces by more than 600 artists, many of them from Vermont. The building also hosts concerts, performances, and film screenings. In summer and fall, lunch at the pleasant restaurant with magnificent views. ✉ *930 SVAC Dr., West Rd.* ☎ *802/362–1405* ⊕ *www.svac.org* 💲 *$6* ⊙ *Tues.–Sat. 10–5, Sun. noon–5.*

WHERE TO EAT

$$$$
FRENCH

✕ **Bistro Henry.** The presence of chef-owner Henry Bronson accounts for the continual popularity of this friendly place, as does the fact that dishes are about $5 cheaper than at the town's other upscale restaurants. The bistro menu includes classics like a peppery steak au poivre and a medium-rare duck breast served with a crispy leg, then mixes things up with eclectic dishes like tuna with wasabi and soy, crab cakes in a Cajun rémoulade, and delicious seared scallops with lemon-ginger risotto. The wine list is extensive, and Dina Bronson's desserts are memorable—indulge in the "gooey chocolate cake," a great molten treat paired with a homemade malt ice cream. [$] *Average main: $29* ✉ *1942 Depot St., 3 miles east of Manchester Center* ☎ *802/362–4982* 🌐 *www.bistrohenry.com* 🕒 *Closed Mon. No lunch.*

$$$$ EUROPEAN 🍴 **Chantecleer.** There is something wonderful about eating by candlelight in an old barn. Chantecleer's dining rooms (in winter ask to sit by the great fieldstone fireplace) are wonderfully romantic, especially with the collection of roosters atop the wooden beams. The menu leans toward the Continental with starters like a fine escargots glazed with Pernod in a hazelnut and parsley butter. Crowd pleasers include Colorado rack of lamb and whole Dover sole filleted table-side. A recipe from the chef's Swiss hometown makes a winning winter dessert: Basel Rathaus Torte, a delicious hazelnut layer cake. [$] *Average main: $38* ✉ *8 Reed Farm La., 3½ miles north of Manchester, East Dorset* ☎ *802/362–1616* 🌐 *www.chantecleerrestaurant.com* ✍ *Reservations essential* 🕒 *Closed Nov., Apr., and Sun.–Tues. No lunch.*

$$$$ STEAKHOUSE 🍴 **Chop House.** Walk to the very back room of the Equinox's Marsh Tavern, past a velvet curtain, and you'll have entered a different eatery—a wonderful, very expensive steak house called the Chop House. The dining room has a bit of history—the marble above the fireplace is chiseled L. L. ORVIS 1832 (and way before he claimed the spot, the Green Mountain Boys gathered here to plan their resistance). Today, you'll yield to aged corn- or grass-fed beef broiled at 1,700 degrees and finished with herb butter. The New York strip, rib eye, filet mignon, milk-fed veal chops, and seafood are delicious, a must for deep-pocketed carnivores. [$] *Average main: $44* ✉ *3567 Main St.* ☎ *802/362–4700* 🌐 *www.equinoxresort.com* 🕒 *No lunch.*

$$ PIZZA 🍴 **Depot 62 Bistro.** The best pizzas in town are topped with terrific fresh ingredients and served in the middle of a high-end antiques showroom, making this Turkish-Mediterranean restaurant a local secret worth knowing about. The wood-fired oven yields masterful results—like the arugula pizza, a beehive of fresh greens atop a thin crust. This a great place for lunch or an inexpensive but satisfying dinner. Sit on your own or at the long communal table. [$] *Average main: $18* ✉ *515 Depot St.* ☎ *802/366–8181* 🌐 *www.depot62.us.*

$$$ FRENCH 🍴 **Mistral's at Toll Gate.** This classic French restaurant is tucked in a grotto on the climb to Bromley Mountain. The two dining rooms are perched over the Bromley Brook, and at night lights magically illuminate a small waterfall. Ask for a window table. Specialties include Chateaubriand béarnaise and rack of lamb with rosemary for two. Chef Dana Markey's crispy sweetbreads with Dijonnaise sauce are a favorite. [$] *Average main: $25* ✉ *10 Toll Gate Rd., off Rte. 11/30* ☎ *802/362–1779* 🌐 *www.mistralsattollgate.com* 🕒 *Closed Wed. Closed Tues. Nov.–June. No lunch.*

$$$ ECLECTIC Fodor's Choice ★ 🍴 **Perfect Wife.** Owner-chef Amy Chamberlain, a Manchester native, creates a fun, freestyle atmosphere with dishes like Peking duck rolled in Mandarin pancakes and sesame-crusted yellowfin tuna topped with crispy rice sticks. There are two entrances: one to the charming

restaurant on the lower level and another to the Other Woman Tavern above. The tavern is one of the livelier local spots in town, with live music on weekends and a pub menu with burgers, potpies in winter, and Vermont microbrews on tap. $ *Average main: $27* ✉ *2594 Depot St., 2½ miles east of Manchester Center* ☎ *802/362–2817* ⊕ *www. perfectwife.com* ⊙ *Closed Sun. No lunch.*

$$$$
AMERICAN
✕ **The Reluctant Panther Inn & Restaurant.** The dining room at this luxurious inn is a large, modern space where rich woods and high ceilings meld into a kind of nouveau Vermont aesthetic. The contemporary American cuisine emphasizes farm-to-table ingredients and has earned the restaurant "Gold Barn" honors from the Vermont Fresh Network. The dinner menu includes grilled Hollandeer Farm venison and pan-roasted pheasant breast. You can pair your choice with a bottle from the award-winning wine list. In the warmer months, sit outside on the lovely landscaped patio, which has a raw bar on Thursday to Saturday evenings. $ *Average main: $36* ✉ *39 West Rd.* ☎ *800/822–2331, 802/362–2568* ⊕ *www.reluctantpanther.com* ⊙ *No lunch.*

$$$$
ECLECTIC
Fodor'sChoice
★
✕ **The Silver Fork.** This popular, intimate bistro with Caribbean flair is owned by husband-and-wife team Mark and Melody French. The owners spent years living in Puerto Rico, and the flavors of the island are reflected in their menu. Start with savory olive tapenade and warm rosemary flatbread, then sample the salmon seared on mango with greens, or dig into crispy crab cakes. There are also more Continental offerings on the sophisticated international menu like veal ragu and warm apple-cinnamon beignets. Be sure to reserve one of the six tables ahead of time, or sit at the wine bar for a casual and romantic dinner with a bottle from the impressive wine list or a maple martini. $ *Average main: $29* ✉ *4201 Main St., across from Orvis Flagship Store* ☎ *802/768–8444* ⊕ *www.thesilverforkvt.com* ⌃ *Reservations essential* ⊙ *Closed Sun. No lunch.*

$$
AMERICAN
✕ **Ye Olde Tavern.** This circa-1790 Colonial inn serves up Yankee favorites like pot roast and cheddar-and-ale onion soup along with plenty of local New England charm. A favorite of regulars and visitors alike, the tavern serves excellent food in a casual, colorful setting with fireplaces. The cozy tap room is a nice spot to stop for a drink and a taste of Vermont. $ *Average main: $20* ✉ *5183 Main St.* ☎ *802/362–0611* ⊕ *www.yeoldetavern.net.*

WHERE TO STAY

$$$$
RESORT
🛏 **The Equinox.** The Equinox defines the geographic center and historic heart of Manchester Village, and has been *the* fancy hotel in town—and in the state—since the 18th century. **Pros:** heart-of-town location; full-service hotel; great golf and spa. **Cons:** corporate feel; spotty service; overrun by New Yorkers on weekends. $ *Rooms from: $294* ✉ *3567 Main St.* ☎ *802/362–4700, 888/367–7625* ⊕ *www.equinoxresort.com* ⇱ *164 rooms, 29 suites* ⦿ *No meals.*

$$$
B&B/INN
Fodor'sChoice
★
🛏 **Wilburton Inn.** Stepping into this hilltop 1902 Tudor style mansion, you might think you've walked into a lavish film set. **Pros:** beautiful setting with easy access to Manchester; fine dining. **Cons:** limited indoor facilities; popular wedding site. $ *Rooms from: $190* ✉ *257 River Rd.*

8

☎ *802/362–2500, 800/648–4944* ⊕ *www.wilburton.com* ⋍ *30 rooms, 4 suites* ⦿ *Breakfast.*

NIGHTLIFE AND THE ARTS

Falcon Bar. This sophisticated bar at the Equinox Resort has live music on weekends. Don't miss the wonderful outdoor deck—in winter, the place to be is around the giant Vermont slate fire pit. ⊠ *Equinox Resort, 3567 Main St.* ☎ *800/362–4747* ⊕ *www.equinoxresort.com.*

SPORTS AND THE OUTDOORS

BIKING

Battenkill Sports Bicycle Shop. This shop rents, sells, and repairs bikes and provides maps and route suggestions. ⊠ *1240 Depot St., off Rte. 7* ☎ *802/362–2734, 800/340–2734* ⊕ *www.battenkillsports.com.*

FISHING

Battenkill Anglers. Teaching the art and science of fly-fishing, Battenkill Anglers offers both private and group lessons. ⊠ *6204 Main St.* ☎ *802/379–1444* ⊕ *www.battenkillangler.com.*

Orvis Fly-Fishing School. This nationally renowned school offers courses mid-April to mid-October, ranging from two-hour pond trips with casting lessons and fishing with private instructors to two-day advanced classes on the Battenkill. ⊠ *6204 Rte. 7A, Manchester Center* ☎ *802/362–4604* ⊕ *www.orvis.com/schools.*

HIKING

There are bountiful hiking trails in the Green Mountain National Forest. Shorter hikes begin at the Equinox Resort, which owns about 1,000 acres of forest and has a great trail system open to the public.

Long Trail. One of the most popular segments of Vermont's Long Trail leads to the top of Bromley Mountain. The strenuous 5.4-mile round-trip takes about four hours. ⊠ *Rte. 11/30* ⊕ *www.greenmountainclub.org.*

Lye Brook Falls. This 4.6-mile hike starts off Glen Road and ends at Vermont's most impressive cataract, Lye Brook Falls. The moderate hike takes four hours. ⊠ *Manchester East Rd.*

Mountain Goat. Stop here for hiking, cross-country-skiing, and snow-shoeing equipment, as well as lots of warm clothing. ⊠ *4886 Main St.* ☎ *802/362–5159* ⊕ *mountaingoat.com.*

ICE-SKATING

Riley Rink at Hunter Park. This Olympic-size indoor ice rink has skate rentals and a concession stand. ⊠ *410 Hunter Park Rd.* ☎ *802/362–0150, 866/866–2086* ⊕ *www.rileyrink.com.*

SHOPPING AND SPAS

ART AND ANTIQUES

Long Ago & Far Away. This store specializes in fine indigenous artwork, including Inuit stone sculpture. ⊠ *Green Mountain Village Shops, 4963 Main St.* ☎ *802/362–3435* ⊕ *www.longagoandfaraway.com.*

Tilting at Windmills Gallery. This large gallery displays the paintings and sculpture of nationally known artists. ⊠ *24 Highland Ave.* ☎ *802/362–3022* ⊕ *www.tilting.com.*

Manchester Designer Outlets' Colonial-style architecture helps blend upscale discount shopping with the surrounding town.

BOOKS

FAMILY **Northshire Bookstore.** The heart of Manchester Center, this bookstore is adored by visitors and residents for its ambience, selection, and service. Up the iron staircase is a second floor dedicated to children's books, toys, and clothes. Connected to the bookstore is the Spiral Press Café, where you can sit for a grilled pesto-chicken sandwich or a latte and scone. ✉ *4869 Main St.* ☎ *802/362–2200, 800/437–3700* ⊕ *www. northshire.com.*

CLOTHING

Manchester Designer Outlets. This is the most upscale collection of stores in northern New England—and every store is a discount outlet. The architecture reflects the surrounding homes, so the place looks a bit like a Colonial village. The long list of upscale clothiers here includes Kate Spade, Yves DeLorme, Michael Kors, Ann Taylor, Tumi, BCBG, Armani, Coach, Polo Ralph Lauren, Brooks Brothers, and Theory. ✉ *97 Depot St.* ☎ *802/362–3736, 800/955–7467* ⊕ *www. manchesterdesigneroutlets.com.*

Orvis Flagship Store. The lodge-like Orvis Flagship Store has a trout pond as well as the company's latest clothing, fly-fishing gear, and pet supplies. It's a required shopping destination for many visitors—the Orvis name is pure Manchester. There are demonstrations of how fly rods are constructed and tested. ✉ *4200 Rte. 7A* ☎ *802/362–3750* ⊕ *www. orvis.com.*

SPAS

Spa at Equinox. With mahogany doors and beadboard wainscoting, this spa feels like a country estate. At one end is an indoor pool and outdoor hot tub; at the other end are the treatment rooms. The signature 80-minute Spirit of Vermont combines Reiki, reflexology, and massage. In the co-ed relaxation room, you can nestle into overstuffed chairs next to a two-sided fireplace made of Vermont gneiss. The locker rooms, with marble accents and pottery-bowl wash basins, have steam rooms and saunas. ⊠ *Equinox Resort, 3567 Rte. 7A, Manchester* ☎ *802/362–4700* ⊕ *www.equinoxresort.com.*

DORSET

7 miles north of Manchester.

Lying at the foot of many mountains and with a village green surrounded by white clapboard homes and inns, Dorset has a solid claim to the title of Vermont's most picture-perfect town. The town has just 2,000 residents, but two of the state's best and oldest general stores.

The country's first commercial marble quarry opened here in 1785. Dozens followed suit, providing the marble for the main research branch of the New York City Public Library and many Fifth Avenue mansions, among other notable landmarks, as well as the sidewalks here and in Manchester. A remarkable private home made entirely of marble can be seen on Dorset West Road, a beautiful residential road west of the town green. The marble Dorset Church on the green features two Tiffany stained-glass windows.

EXPLORING

FAMILY
Fodor's Choice
★

Dorset Quarry. On hot summer days the sight of dozens of families jumping, swimming, and basking in the sun around this massive 60-foot-deep swimming hole makes it one of the most wholesome and picturesque recreational spots in the region. First mined in 1785, the stone from the country's oldest commercial marble quarry went to build the main branch of the New York Public Library and Montreal Museum of Fine Arts. ⊠ *Rte. 30* ▨ *Free.*

FAMILY **Merck Forest & Farmland Center.** This 3,100-acre educational center has 30 miles of nature trails for hiking, cross-country skiing, snowshoeing, and horseback riding. You can visit the 60-acre farm, which grows organic fruit and vegetables (and purchase them at the farm stand), and check out the horses, cows, sheep, pigs, and chickens. You're even welcome to help out with the chores. ⊠ *3270 Rte. 315, Rupert* ☎ *802/394–7836* ⊕ *www.merckforest.org* ▨ *Free* ☺ *Visitor center daily 9–4.*

WHERE TO EAT

$$$
AMERICAN

✕ **The Dorset Inn.** Built in 1796, this inn has been continuously operating ever since. The comfortable tavern, which serves the same menu as the more formal dining room, is popular with locals, and Patrick, the amiable veteran bartender, will make you feel at home. Popular choices include the Taylor Farm Gouda fondue and the maple-glazed duck breast. A member of the Vermont Fresh Network, the restaurant benefits greatly from its strong connections with local farmers and chefs.

$ *Average main: $22* ✉ *Dorset Green, 8 Church St.* ☎ *802/867–5500* 🌐 *www.dorsetinn.com.*

$$$$ ECLECTIC 🍴 **Inn at West View Farm.** Chef-owner Raymond Chen was the lead line cook at New York City's Mercer Kitchen under Jean-Georges Vongerichten before opening this local-ingredient-friendly restaurant. You'll find traditional floral wallpaper and soft classical music, but that's where the similarities to Dorset's other eateries end. Chen's dishes are skillful and practiced, starting with an amuse-bouche such as salt cod over pesto. French influences are evident in the sautéed mushrooms and mascarpone ravioli in white truffle oil. Asian notes are evident, too, as in the lemongrass ginger soup with shiitake mushrooms that's ladled over grilled shrimp. A tavern serves enticing, inexpensive small dishes. $ *Average main: $31* ✉ *2928 Rte. 30* ☎ *802/867–5715, 800/769–4903* 🌐 *www.westviewfarm.com* 🕒 *Closed Tues. and Wed.*

WHERE TO STAY

$$$$ HOTEL 🏨 **Barrows House.** If you've had enough of the ubiquitous floral fabrics found in many New England inns, this renovated 19th-century manse, once the residence of the town's pastor, is a pleasant alternative. **Pros:** perhaps the best bar and restaurant in town; chintz-free decor. **Cons:** rooms can become drafty in cold weather. $ *Rooms from: $245* ✉ *3156 Rte. 30* ☎ *802/867–4455* 🌐 *www.barrowshouse.com* 🛏 *18 rooms, 9 suites, 3 cottages* 🍽 *Breakfast.*

$$$ B&B/INN 🏨 **Squire House Bed & Breakfast.** On a wonderfully quiet road, this inn has three rooms that combine modern comforts and antique fixtures. **Pros:** big estate feels like your own; well-maintained rooms. **Cons:** bathrooms less exciting than rooms; no credit cards. $ *Rooms from: $210* ✉ *3395 Dorset West Rd.* ☎ *802/867–0281* 🌐 *www.squirehouse.com* 🛏 *2 rooms, 1 suite* 💳 *No credit cards* 🍽 *Breakfast.*

THE ARTS

Dorset Playhouse. Dorset is home to a prestigious summer theater troupe that presents the annual Dorset Theater Festival. Plays are presented in a wonderful converted pre-Revolutionary War barn. ✉ *Dorset Playhouse, 104 Cheney Rd.* ☎ *802/867–5777* 🌐 *www.dorsetplayers.org.*

SPORTS AND THE OUTDOORS

Emerald Lake State Park. This park has a marked nature trail, a small beach, boat rentals, and a snack bar. ✉ *65 Emerald Lake La., East Dorset* ☎ *802/362–1655* 🌐 *www.vtstateparks.com/htm/emerald.htm* 🎟 *$3.*

SHOPPING

Dorset Union Store. Dating from 1816, this general store makes good prepared dinners, has a big wine selection, and sells interesting gifts. ✉ *Dorset Green, Church St.* ☎ *802/867–4400* 🌐 *www.dorsetunionstore.com* 🕒 *Mon.–Sat. 7–6, Sun. 8–5.*

H. N. Williams General Store. Started in 1840 by William Williams, this authentic country store has been run by the same family for six generations. This is one of those unique places where you can buy both maple syrup and ammo and catch up on posted town announcements. A farmers' market is held outside on Sundays in summer. ✉ *2732 Rte. 30* ☎ *802/867–5353* 🌐 *www.hnwilliams.com.*

STRATTON

26 miles southeast of Dorset.

Stratton is really Stratton Mountain Resort—a mountaintop ski resort with a self-contained "town center" of shops, restaurants, and lodgings clustered at the base of the slopes. When the snow melts, golf, tennis, and a host of other summer activities are big attractions, but the ski village remains quiet. For those arriving from the north along Route 30, Bondville is the town at the base of the mountain. At the junction of Routes 30 and 100 is the tiny Vermont village of Jamaica, with its own cluster of inns and restaurants on the east side of the mountain.

GETTING HERE AND AROUND

From Manchester or Route 7, follow Route 11/30 east until they split. Route 11 continues past Bromley ski mountain while Route 30 turns south 10 minutes toward Bondville, the town closest to Stratton Mountain.

WHERE TO EAT

$$$$ AMERICAN 🍴 **The Red Fox Inn.** This two-level converted barn has the best nightlife in southern Vermont and a fun dining room to boot. The upper level is the restaurant—the big A-frame has wagon wheels and a carriage suspended from the ceiling. Settle in near the huge fireplace for beef tenderloin, roasted half duckling, or penne alla vodka. The apple pie was served at the 2009 and 2013 presidental inaugurations. Downstairs in the tavern, open year-round, there's Irish music, half-price Guinness, and fish-and-chips on Wednesday. On the premises are some relaxed, no-frills accommodations. [$] *Average main: $30* ✉ *103 Winhall Hollow Rd., Bondville* ☎ *802/297–2488* 🌐 *www.redfoxinn.com* 🕒 *No lunch. Closed Mon.–Wed. June–Oct.*

WHERE TO STAY

$$ RENTAL 🏨 **Long Trail House.** Directly across the street from the ski village, this condo complex is one of the closest to the slopes. **Pros:** across from skiing; reasonable rates available; outdoor heated pool. **Cons:** room decor varies; two-night stay required on weekends. [$] *Rooms from: $165* ✉ *5 Village Lodge Rd.* ☎ *802/297–4000, 800/787–2886* 🌐 *www.stratton.com* 🛏 *100 units* 🍽 *No meals.*

$$$$ B&B/INN Fodor's Choice ★ 🏨 **Three Mountain Inn.** A 1780s tavern, the romantic Three Mountain Inn in downtown Jamaica feels authentically Colonial, from the wide-plank paneling to the low ceilings. **Pros:** charming B&B; well-kept rooms; great dinners. **Cons:** can be expensive. [$] *Rooms from: $234* ✉ *30 Depot St., 10 miles northeast of Stratton, Jamaica* ☎ *802/874–4140* 🌐 *www.threemountaininn.com* 🛏 *14 rooms, 1 suite* 🍽 *Breakfast.*

NIGHTLIFE AND THE ARTS

Fodor's Choice ★ **Johnny Seesaw's.** Near Bromley Mountain, Johnny Seesaw's is a classic rustic ski lodge with two huge fireplaces and a relaxed attitude. There's live acoustical music on weekends, a separate games room, and an excellent comfort-food menu. ✉ *3574 Rte. 11, Peru* ☎ *802/824–5533, 800/424–2729* 🌐 *www.jseesaw.com.*

Mulligan's. Popular Mulligan's hosts bands or DJs in the downstairs Green Door Pub on weekends. ⊠ *Stratton Village Sq. 11B, Mountain Rd., Bondville* ☎ *802/297–9293.*

SPORTS AND THE OUTDOORS

SKI AREAS

Bromley. About 20 minutes from Stratton, Bromley is a favorite with families. The 46 trails are evenly divided between beginner, intermediate, and expert. The resort runs a child-care center for kids ages 6 weeks to 6 years and hosts children's programs for ages 3 to 17. Beginning skiers and snowboarders have expanded access to terrain-based training in the dedicated Learning Zone, while everyone can unwind in the newly renovated base lodge. An added bonus: the trails face south, making for glorious skiing in spring and on warm winter days. ⊠ *3984 Vermont Rte. 11, Peru* ☎ *802/824–5522, 800/865–4786* ⊕ *www.bromley.com.*

Stratton Mountain. About 30 minutes from Manchester, sophisticated Stratton Mountain draws affluent families and young professionals. An entire village, with a covered parking structure for 700 cars, sits at the base of the mountain. In summer Stratton has 15 outdoor clay tennis courts, 27 holes of golf, and hiking trails accessed by a gondola. The sports center, open year-round, has a 25-meter indoor pool, a hot tub, a steam room, and a fitness facility.

In terms of downhill skiing, Stratton prides itself on its immaculate grooming, making it excellent for cruising. The lower part of the mountain is beginner to low-intermediate, served by several chairlifts, including one high-speed six passenger. The upper mountain is served by several chairlifts, including a six passenger and a 12-passenger gondola. Down the face are the expert trails, and on either side are intermediate cruising runs with a smattering of wide beginner slopes. The third sector, the Sun Bowl, is off to one side with two six-passenger lifts serving two expert trails and plenty of intermediate terrain. Snowmaking covers 95% of the slopes. In all, Stratton has 12 lifts that service 94 trails and more than 115 acres of glades. There's also 11 miles of cross-country skiing. An on-site day-care center takes children from six weeks to five years old for indoor activities and outdoor excursions. Children also love careening down one of four groomed lift-serviced lanes at the resort's Coca Cola Tube Park. ⊠ *5 Village Rd., Bondville* ☎ *802/297–4211 snow conditions, 800/787–2886* ⊕ *www.stratton.com.*

WESTON

17 miles north of Stratton.

Best known for the Vermont Country Store, Weston was one of the first Vermont towns to discover its own intrinsic loveliness—and marketability. With its summer theater, classic town green with a Victorian bandstand, and an assortment of shops, the little village really lives up to its vaunted image.

WHERE TO STAY

$$$$ B&B/INN **The Inn at Weston.** Highlighting the country elegance of this 1848 inn, a short walk from the town green and a stone's throw from four ski mountains, is innkeeper Bob Aldrich's collection of 500 orchid species—rare and beautiful specimens surround the dining table in the gazebo. **Pros:** great rooms; terrific town location. **Cons:** top-end rooms are expensive. [$] *Rooms from: $235* ✉ *630 Main St.* ☎ *802/824–6789* 🌐 *www.innweston.com* 🛏 *13 rooms* 🍴 *Breakfast.*

THE ARTS

Weston Playhouse. The oldest professional theater in Vermont produces plays, musicals, and other works. The season runs from late June to early September. ✉ *703 Main St., off Rte. 100* ☎ *802/824–5288* 🌐 *www.westonplayhouse.org.*

SHOPPING

The Vermont Country Store. This store opened in 1946 and is still run by the Orton family, though it has become something of an empire, with a large catalog and online business. One room is set aside for Vermont Common Crackers and bins of fudge and other candy. In others you'll find nearly forgotten items such as Lilac Vegetol aftershave, as well as practical items such as sturdy outdoor clothing. Nostalgia-evoking implements dangle from the rafters. There's a second location on Route 103 in Rockingham. ✉ *657 Main St.* ☎ *802/824–3184* 🌐 *www.vermontcountrystore.com.*

LUDLOW

9 miles northeast of Weston.

Ludlow is a largely nondescript industrial town whose major draw is Okemo, one of Vermont's largest and most popular ski resorts.

WHERE TO EAT

$$ AMERICAN 🍴 **Coleman Brook Tavern.** Slopeside at the Jackson Gore Inn, Coleman Brook is the fanciest and most expensive of Okemo's 19 places to eat, but it's not formal—you'll find ski-boot-wearing diners crowding the tables at lunch. Big wing chairs and large banquettes line window bays. Ask to sit in the Wine Room, a separate section where tables are surrounded by the noteworthy collection of wines. Start with a pound of mussels steamed in butter, garlic, white wine, and fresh herbs. Then move on to the sesame seed–crusted ahi tuna served over green-tea soba noodles in a ginger-miso broth. The s'mores dessert is cooked with a tabletop "campfire." [$] *Average main: $20* ✉ *111 Jackson Gore Rd., Okemo* ☎ *802/228–1435.*

$ PIZZA FAMILY 🍴 **Goodman's American Pie.** This pizzeria has the best wood-fired oven pizza in town. It also has character to spare—sit in chairs from old ski lifts and order from a counter that was once a purple VW bus. Though it's on Main Street, it's set back and kind of hidden—you may consider it your Ludlow secret. Locals and Okemo regulars already in the know stop by to design their own pizza from 25 ingredients; there is also a section of six specials. The Rip Curl has mozzarella, Asiago, ricotta, chicken, fresh garlic, and fresh tomatoes. Slices are available.

You never know what you'll find at a rambling general store like Weston's Vermont Country Store.

Arcade games are in the back. $ *Average main: $8* ⊠ *106 Main St.* ☎ *802/228–4271* ▭ *No credit cards* ◷ *Closed Wed.*

$$
ECLECTIC

✕**Harry's.** The local favorite when you want to eat a little out of town, this casual roadside restaurant 5 miles northwest of Ludlow has a number of international influences. Traditional contemporary entrées such as pork tenderloin are at one end of the menu and Mexican dishes at the other. The large and tasty burrito, made with fresh cilantro and black beans, is one of the best bargains around. Chef-owner Trip Pearce also owns the equally popular Little Harry's in Rutland. $ *Average main: $19* ⊠ *3621 Rte. 103, Mount Holly* ☎ *802/259–2996* ⊕ *www. harryscafe.com* ◷ *Closed Mon. and Tues. No lunch.*

$$
ECLECTIC
Fodor'sChoice
★

✕**The Inn at Weathersfield.** One of Vermont's best restaurants, this is a culinary gem inside an 18th-century countryside inn. A chalkboard in the foyer lists the farms that grow the food you'll eat here on any given night. Executive chef Jean-Luc Matecap, who has extensive experience cooking for top restaurants in France, Nantucket, and his native Vermont, is passionate about local ingredients. The inn's farm-to-table cuisine is showcased in an à la carte tavern menu, chalkboard specials, and two nightly prix-fixe menus in the formal dining room. The first ($59) includes meats such as roasted Cavendish game birds and dry-aged Black Watch Farm sirloin; the second ($45) offers vegetarian and gluten-free dishes. Service is excellent, and the wine list is large and reasonably priced. If it's summer, enjoy your meal on the patio. $ *Average main: $20* ⊠ *1342 Rte. 106, 15 miles east of Ludlow, Perkinsville* ☎ *802/263–9217* ⊕ *www.innatweathersfield.com* ◷ *No lunch. Closed Mon., Tues., and Apr. and beginning of Nov.*

8

CLOSE UP

Vermont Artisanal Cheese

Vermont is the artisanal cheese capital of the country, with more than 40 creameries (and growing fast) that are open to the public—carefully churning out hundreds of different cheeses. Many creameries are "farmstead" operations, meaning that the animals that provide the milk are on-site where their milk is made into cheese. If you eat enough cheese during your time in the state, you may be able to differentiate between the many types of milk (cow, goat, sheep, or even water buffalo), as well as make associations between the geography and climate of where you are and the taste of the cheese you eat.

This is one of the reasons why taking a walk around a dairy is a great idea: you can see the process in action, from grazing to aging to eating. Almost all dairies welcome visitors, though it's universally recommended that you call ahead to plan your visit.

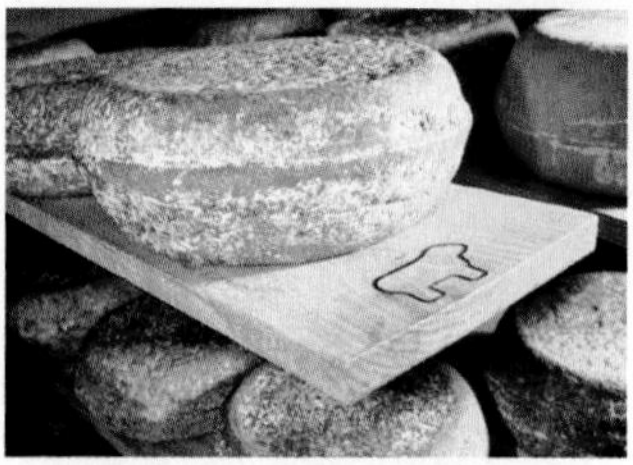

Vermont sheep's milk cheese.

Vermont Cheese Council. This group has developed the Vermont Cheese Trail, a map of 44 creameries with contact information for each. ☎ *866/261–8595* 🌐 *www.vtcheese.com.*

Vermont Cheesemakers Festival. If you're a real cheese lover, definitely plan your trip to Vermont around the state's world-class food event, the annual Vermont Cheesemakers Festival—each July over 40 cheesemakers gather in Shelburne to sell and sample their various cheeses. 🌐 *www.vtcheesefest.com.*

—Michael de Zayas

WHERE TO STAY

$$$ B&B/INN 🏨 **Inn at Water's Edge.** Former Long Islanders Bruce and Tina Verdrager converted their old ski house and barns into this comfortably refined haven, perfect for those who want to ski but don't want to stay in town. **Pros:** bucolic setting on a lakefront; interesting house. **Cons:** ordinary B&B rooms. [$] *Rooms from: $175* ✉ *45 Kingdom Rd., 5 miles north of town* ☎ *802/228–8143, 888/706–9736* 🌐 *www.innatwatersedge.com* 🛏 *9 rooms, 2 suites* 🍴 *Multiple meal plans.*

$$$ B&B/INN 🏨 **Inn at Weathersfield.** This is the kind of place where relaxation rules—unless you want to take advantage of year-round seasonal sports like hiking, cross-country skiing, and even apple picking. **Pros:** dynamite restaurant and tavern; laid-back inn; quiet setting. **Cons:** 15-mile drive from the Okemo slopes. [$] *Rooms from: $179* ✉ *1342 Rte. 106, Perkinsville* ☎ *802/263–9217* 🌐 *www.innatweathersfield.com* 🛏 *12 rooms* ⏲ *Closed first two weeks in Nov.* 🍴 *Breakfast.*

$$ HOTEL FAMILY 🏨 **Jackson Gore Village.** This slope-side base lodge is the place to stay if your aim is convenience to Okemo's slopes. **Pros:** ski-in ski-out at base of mountain; good for families. **Cons:** chaotic and noisy on weekends;

expensive. $ *Rooms from: $162* ✉ *77 Okemo Ridge Rd., off Rte. 103* ☎ *802/228–1400, 800/786–5366* ⊕ *www.okemo.com* ⮡ *263 rooms.*

SPORTS AND THE OUTDOORS

SKI AREAS

Okemo Mountain Resort. Family-owned since 1982 and still run by Tim and Diane Mueller, Okemo Mountain Resort has evolved into a major year-round resort, now with two base areas. At 2,200 feet, Okemo has the highest vertical drop of any resort in southern Vermont. Beginner trails extend above both base areas, with more challenging terrain higher on the mountains. Intermediate trails are the theme here, but experts will find steep trails and glades at Jackson Gore and on the South Face. The total 120 trails are served by an efficient system of 24 lifts, including nine quads, three triple chairlifts, and seven surface lifts; 96% of the trails are covered by snowmaking. Okemo has six terrain parks for skiers and snowboarders, including one for beginners, a progression park, and 500-foot-long superpipe. For cross-country skiing, the Okemo Valley Nordic Center has 14 miles of groomed cross-country trails and 8 miles dedicated to snowshoeing. For ice-skating, the resort's roofed Ice House rink near the Jackson Gore base area is open mid-December to April, with rentals and entry costing $4 each. A tubing facility can also be found there, with four groomed lanes serviced by a conveyor-style lift Friday and Saturday 3-6 pm.

If you're looking for non-snow-related activities, you can play basketball and tennis at the Ice House next to Jackson Gore Inn or perfect your swing at the 18-hole course at the Okemo Valley Golf Club. The Spring House, next to the entrance of Jackson Gore Inn, has a great kids' pool with slides, a racquetball court, fitness center, and sauna. ✉ *77 Okemo Ridge Rd.* ☎ *802/228–4041, 802/228–5222 snow conditions* ⊕ *www.okemo.com.*

GRAFTON

20 miles south of Ludlow.

Out-of-the-way Grafton is as much a historical museum as a town. During its heyday, citizens grazed some 10,000 sheep and spun their wool into sturdy yarn for locally woven fabric. When the market for wool declined, so did Grafton. Then in 1963 the Windham Foundation—Vermont's second-largest private foundation—commenced the town's rehabilitation. Not only was the Old Tavern preserved (now called The Grafton Inn), but so were many other commercial and residential structures in the village center.

EXPLORING

Historical Society Museum. The Historical Society Museum documents the town's history with exhibits that change yearly. ✉ *147 Main St.* ☎ *802/843–2584* ⊕ *www.graftonhistory.info* 🏷 *$3* ☉ *Memorial Day–Columbus Day, Thurs.–Mon. 10–4. Closed Tues. and Wed.*

WHERE TO STAY

$$$$ B&B/INN [icon] **The Grafton Inn.** One of the country's oldest operating inns, this 1801 classic encourages you to linger on the wraparound porches, in the authentically Colonial common rooms, or with a book by the fire in the old-fashioned library. **Pros:** classic Vermont inn and tavern; professionally run; appealing common areas. **Cons:** rooms are attractive but not stellar. [$] *Rooms from: $225* ✉ *92 Main St.* ☎ *802/843–2231, 800/843–1801* 🌐 *www.graftoninnvermont.com* 🛏 *38 rooms, 7 suites* 🍴 *Breakfast.*

SHOPPING

Gallery North Star. Inside this restored 1877 home original oil paintings, watercolors, lithographs, and sculptures by more than 30 New England artists are on display. ✉ *151 Townshend Rd.* ☎ *802/843–2465* 🌐 *www.gnsgrafton.com* 🕑 *Daily 10–5.*

Grafton Village Cheese Company. Sample the best of Vermont cheddar at the Grafton Village Cheese Company's downtown wine and cheese shop. ✉ *56 Townshend Rd.* ☎ *800/472–3866, 802/843–2221* 🌐 *www.graftonvillagecheese.com.*

TOWNSHEND

9 miles south of Grafton.

One of a string of attractive villages along the banks of the West River, Townshend embodies the Vermont ideal of a lovely town green presided over by a gracefully proportioned church spire. The spire belongs to the 1790 Congregational Meeting House, one of the state's oldest houses of worship. North on Route 30 is the Scott Bridge, the state's longest single-span covered bridge. It makes for a pretty photo although it is closed to foot and vehicle traffic.

OFF THE BEATEN PATH

Newfane. With a village green surrounded by pristine white buildings, Newfane, 6 miles southeast of Townshend, is sometimes described as the quintessential New England small town. The 1839 First Congregational Church and the Windham County Court House, with 17 green-shuttered windows and a rounded cupola, are often open. The building with the four-pointed spire is Union Hall, built in 1832. ✉ *Newfane* 🌐 *www.newfanevt.com.*

WHERE TO EAT

$ DINER ✕ **Townshend Dam Diner.** Folks come from miles around to enjoy traditional fare such as meat loaf, roast beef, chili, and croquettes, as well as Townshend-raised bison burgers and creative daily specials. Breakfast, served all day, includes such tasty treats as raspberry-chocolate-chip walnut pancakes and homemade French toast. You can sit at any of the collection of 1930s enamel-top tables or in the big swivel chairs at the U-shaped counter. The diner is a few miles northwest of the village on Route 30. [$] *Average main: $8* ✉ *5929 Rte. 30, West Townshend* ☎ *802/874–4107* 💳 *No credit cards* 🕑 *Closed Tues.*

WHERE TO STAY

$ B&B/INN **Boardman House.** This handsome Greek Revival home on the town green combines modern comfort with the relaxed charm of a 19th-century farmhouse. **Pros:** inexpensive; perfect village green location. **Cons:** no phone, and cell-phone reception is bad. [$] *Rooms from: $80* ✉ *Grafton Rd.* ☎ *802/365–4086* *4 rooms, 1 suite* *No credit cards* 🍴 *Breakfast.*

$$$$ B&B/INN **Windham Hill Inn.** As there's not too much to do nearby, you might find yourself sitting by a fire or swimming in the outdoor pool at this inn, part of the Relais & Chateau collection. **Pros:** lovely views; exceedingly cozy spa. **Cons:** extremely expensive; staff not always helpful. [$] *Rooms from: $305* ✉ *311 Lawrence Dr., West Townshend* ☎ *802/874–4080, 800/944–4080* 🌐 *www.windhamhill.com* *11 rooms, 10 suites, 1 cottage* 🍴 *Breakfast.*

SPORTS AND THE OUTDOORS

Townshend State Park. At Townshend State Park you'll find a sandy beach on the West River and a trail that parallels the river for almost 2 miles, topping out on Bald Mountain Dam. Up the dam, the trail follows switchbacks literally carved into the stone apron. ✉ *2755 State Forest Rd.* ☎ *802/365–7500* 🌐 *www.vtstateparks.com/htm/townshend.htm.*

SHOPPING

Newfane Country Store. You'll find delicious homemade fudge, locally made jams and jellies, and colorful quilts—which can also be custom ordered—at this pleasant shop. ✉ *598 Rte. 30, Newfane* ☎ *802/365–7916* 🌐 *www.newfanecountrystore.com.*

CENTRAL VERMONT

Central Vermont's economy once centered on marble quarrying and mills. But today, as in much of the rest of the state, tourism drives the economic engine. The center of the dynamo is Killington, the East's largest downhill resort, but there's more to discover in central Vermont than high-speed chairlifts and slope-side condos. The old mills of Quechee and Middlebury are now home to restaurants and shops, giving wonderful views of the waterfalls that once powered the mill turbines. Woodstock has upscale shops and a national historic park. Away from these settlements, the protected (except for occasional logging) lands of the Green Mountain National Forest are laced with hiking trails.

Our coverage of towns begins with Norwich, on U.S. 5 near Interstate 91 at the state's eastern edge, winds west toward U.S. 7, then continues north to Middlebury before heading over the spine of the Green Mountains to Waitsfield.

NORWICH

6 miles north of White River Junction.

On the bank of the Connecticut River, Norwich boasts beautifully maintained 18th- and 19th-century homes set about a handsome green. Nor-

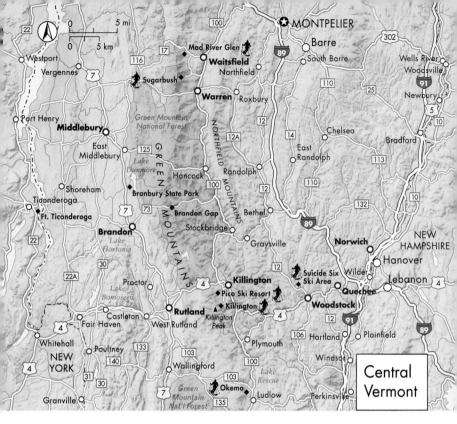

wich is the Vermont sister to sophisticated Hanover, New Hampshire (home of Dartmouth College), over the river.

GETTING HERE AND AROUND

Most attractions are off Interstate 91; the town sits a mile to the west.

EXPLORING

FAMILY
Fodor'sChoice
★

Montshire Museum of Science. Numerous hands-on exhibits at this science museum explore nature and technology. Kids can make giant bubbles, see images from NASA space telescopes, watch marine life swim in aquariums, and explore a maze of outdoor trails by the river. Adults will happily join the fun. An ideal destination for a rainy day, this is one of the finest museums in New England. ⊠ *1 Montshire Rd.* ☎ *802/649–2200* ⊕ *www.montshire.org* 🖃 *$14* ⊙ *Daily 10–5.*

SPORTS AND THE OUTDOORS

Lake Morey Ice Skating Trail. For the most fun you can have on skates, head to American's longest ice-skating trail. From January to March the lake freezes over and is groomed for ice-skating, providing a magical 4½-mile route amid forested hillsides. Bring your own skates or rent them at the Lake Morey Resort, which maintains the trail. ⊠ *1 Clubhouse Rd., Fairlee* ☎ *800/423–1211* ⊕ *www.lakemoreyresort.com.*

SHOPPING

King Arthur Flour Baker's Store. This shop is a must-see for those who love bread. The shelves are stocked with all the ingredients and tools in the company's *Baker's Catalogue,* including flours, mixes, and local jams and syrups. The bakery has a viewing area where you can watch products being made, and you can buy baked goods or sandwiches. ⊠ *135 U.S. 5 S* ☎ *802/649–3881, 800/827–6836* ⊕ *www.kingarthurflour.com* ⊗ *Weekdays 8 am–9 pm, weekends 9–5.*

QUECHEE

11 miles southwest of Norwich, 6 miles west of White River Junction.

A historic mill town, Quechee sits just upriver from its namesake gorge, an impressive 165-foot-deep canyon cut by the Ottauquechee River. Most people view the gorge from U.S. 4. To escape the crowds, hike along the gorge or scramble down one of several trails to the river.

EXPLORING

FAMILY
Fodor's Choice
★

Simon Pearce. The main attraction in the village is this glassblowing factory, store, and restaurant, set in a restored woolen mill by a waterfall. Water power still drives the factory's furnace. Take a free self-guided tour of the downstairs factory floor and see the amazing glassblowers at work (great for kids, too!). The store sells beautifully crafted contemporary glass and ceramic tableware. Seconds and discontinued items are available on a first-come, first-served basis. An excellent, sophisticated restaurant with outstanding views of the falls uses the Simon Pearce glassware and is justly popular. ⊠ *The Mill, 1760 Quechee Main St.* ☎ *802/295–1470* ⊕ *www.simonpearce.com* ⊗ *Daily 10–9.*

FAMILY

Vermont Institute of Natural Science Nature Center. Next to Quechee Gorge, this science center has 17 raptor exhibits, including bald eagles, peregrine falcons, and owls. All the caged birds have been found injured and are unable to survive in the wild. "Raptors up Close," a 30-minute live bird program, starts daily at 1:30. ⊠ *6565 Woodstock Rd.* ☎ *802/359–5000* ⊕ *www.vinsweb.org* ✉ *$13* ⊗ *Late June–Oct., daily 10–5:30; Nov.–early Apr., daily 10–4; mid-Apr.–mid-June, daily 10–5.*

WHERE TO EAT AND STAY

$$$
AMERICAN
Fodor's Choice
★

✕ **Simon Pearce.** Sparkling glassware from the studio downstairs, exposed brick, flickering candles, and large windows overlooking the falls of the roaring Ottauquechee River create an ideal setting for contemporary American cuisine. The food is widely considered to be worthy of a pilgrimage. Horseradish-crusted blue cod with crispy leeks, herb mashed potatoes, and balsamic shallot reduction as well as roast duck with mango chutney sauce are house specialties; the wine cellar holds several hundred vintages. Ⓢ *Average main: $28* ⊠ *The Mill, 1760 Main St.* ☎ *802/295–1470* ⊕ *www.simonpearce.com.*

$$$$
B&B/INN

The Parker House Inn. This beautiful 1857 house on the National Historic Register was once home to Senator Joseph Parker, who also owned the textile mill next door. **Pros:** riverfront location; spacious rooms. **Cons:** no yard. Ⓢ *Rooms from: $245* ⊠ *1792 Main St.* ☎ *802/295–6077* ⊕ *www.theparkerhouseinn.com* ⇦ *7 rooms, 1 suite* ⍟ *Breakfast.*

8

$$$ B&B/INN [icon] **Quechee Inn at Marshland Farm.** Each room in this handsomely restored 1793 country home has Queen Anne–style furnishings and period antiques. **Pros:** historic house; spacious grounds. **Cons:** some bathrooms are dated. [$] *Rooms from: $175* ✉ *1119 Main St.* ☎ *802/295–3133, 800/235–3133* 🌐 *www.quecheeinn.com* 🛏 *22 rooms, 3 suites* 🍴 *Breakfast.*

SPORTS AND THE OUTDOORS

Wilderness Trails and the Vermont Fly Fishing School. This school leads fly-fishing workshops, rents mountain bikes, and arranges canoe and kayak trips. In winter the company conducts cross-country and snowshoe treks. ✉ *1119 Quechee Main St.* ☎ *802/295–7620* 🌐 *www.scenesofvermont.com/wildernesstrails.*

SHOPPING

ANTIQUES AND CRAFTS

Quechee Gorge Village. Hundreds of dealers sell their wares at the Quechee Gorge Village, an antiques and crafts mall in a reconstructed barn that also houses a country store and a classic diner. A merry-go-round and a small-scale working railroad operate when weather permits. ✉ *573 Woodstock Rd., U.S. 4* ☎ *802/295–1550, 802/295–1550* 🌐 *www.quecheegorge.com.*

CLOTHING AND MORE

Scotland by the Yard. This store sells all things Celtic, from kilts to Argyle jackets and tartan ties. ✉ *8828 Woodstock Rd.* ☎ *802/295–5351, 800/295–5351* 🌐 *www.scotlandbytheyard.com.*

WOODSTOCK

4 miles west of Quechee.

Woodstock is a Currier & Ives print come to life. Well-maintained Federal-style houses surround the tree-lined village green, which is not far from a covered bridge. The town owes much of its pristine appearance to the Rockefeller family's interest in historic preservation and land conservation and to native George Perkins Marsh, a congressman, diplomat, and conservationist who wrote the pioneering book *Man and Nature* (1864) about humanity's use and abuse of the land. Only busy U.S. 4 detracts from the town's quaintness.

ESSENTIALS

Visitor Information Woodstock Vermont Area Chamber of Commerce ✉ *59 Central St.* ☎ *802/457–3555, 888/496–6378* 🌐 *www.woodstockvt.com.*

EXPLORING

FAMILY **Billings Farm and Museum.** Founded by Frederick Billings in 1871, this is one of the oldest operating dairy farms in the country. In addition to watching the herds of Jersey cows, horses, and other farm animals at work and play, you can tour the restored 1890 farm house and learn about 19th-century farming and domestic life in the adjacent barns. The biggest takeaway, however, is a renewed belief in sustainable agriculture and stewardship of the land. ✉ *69 Old River Rd., ½ mile*

Simon Pearce is a glassblowing factory, store, and restaurant; the factory's furnace is still powered by hydroelectricity from Quechee Falls.

north of Woodstock ☎ *802/457–2355* ⊕ *www.billingsfarm.org* 🎫 *$12* ⊗ *May–late Oct., daily 10–5; Nov.–Feb., weekends 10–3:30.*

Marsh-Billings-Rockefeller National Historical Park. This 555-acre park is Vermont's only national park and the nation's first to focus on conserving natural resources. The pristine and stunning park includes Frederick Billings's mansion, gardens, and carriage roads. The entire property was the gift of Laurance S. Rockefeller, who lived here with his late wife Mary, Billings's granddaughter. You can learn more at the visitor center, tour the residential complex with a guide every hour on the hour, and explore the 20 miles of trails and old carriage roads that climb Mt. Tom. ✉ *54 Elm St.* ☎ *802/457–3368* ⊕ *www.nps.gov/mabi* 🎫 *Tour $8* ⊗ *May–Oct., mansion and garden tours 10–5; grounds daily dawn–dusk.*

WHERE TO EAT

$$$$
AMERICAN

✗ **Barnard Inn Restaurant and Max's Tavern.** The dining room in this 1796 brick farmhouse exudes 18th-century charm, but the food is decidedly from the 21st century. Former San Francisco restaurant chef-owners Will Dodson and Ruth Schimmelpfennig create inventive three- and four-course prix-fixe menus ($65 to $75) with such delicacies as venison medallions and chili and house-made chive-and-nutmeg potato gnocchi. In the back is a local favorite, Max's Tavern, which serves upscale pub fare such as beer-battered oysters and dry-rubbed pulled pork. $ *Average main: $65* ✉ *5518 Rte. 12, 8 miles north of Woodstock, Barnard* ☎ *802/234–9961* ⊕ *barnardinn.com* 🍴 *Reservations essential* ⊗ *Closed Sun. and Mon. No lunch.*

$$$$ AMERICAN 🍴 **Cloudland Farm.** Representative of the wildly popular local food scene in Vermont, Cloudland Farm offers thrice-weekly prix-fixe dinners—Thursday, Friday, and Saturday—with all the seasonal ingredients fresh from the farm or other growers. Cloudland's own pork and beef feature in such main dishes as maple-glazed ham roast with an apple-and-onion compote or beef shank osso bucco with sauteed kale and beef bacon. Desserts, such as homemade carrot cake with red wine caramel and carrot jam, are delicious. With the table literally on the farm, this is a unique farm-to-table experience and worth the short drive from Woodstock. [$] *Average main: $30* ✉ *1101 Cloudland Rd., North Pomfret* ☎ *802/457–2599* 🌐 *www.cloudlandfarm.com* ✍ *Reservations essential* ⏲ *Closed Mar. and Sun.–Wed. No lunch.*

$$$ CAFÉ 🍴 **Keeper's Café.** Creatively prepared, moderately priced fare draws customers from all over the region to this cozy café. Chef Chris Loucka's menus include such organic dishes as the char-grilled kielbasa and the arugula-and-beet salad. Blackboard specials change daily. Housed inside a former general store, the three dining rooms feel relaxed, with locals table-hopping to chat with friends. [$] *Average main: $22* ✉ *3685 Rte. 106, 12 miles south of Woodstock, Reading* ☎ *802/484–9090* 🌐 *www.keeperscafe.com* ⏲ *Closed Sun. and Mon. No lunch.*

$$$ ITALIAN Fodor's Choice ★ 🍴 **Pane e Saluto.** Don't let the size fool you—meals at this little upstairs restaurant are exciting and memorable, thanks to young couple Deirdre and Caleb Barber. Reserve well in advance, as the small space fills up fast. Hip decor, an intimately small space, and Heekin's discreetly passionate front-of-house direction all come together to complement the Barbers' slow-food-inspired passion for flavorful, local and farm-raised dishes. Try *ragu d'agnello e maiale* (spaghetti with an *abruzzese* ragu from roasted pork and lamb) followed by *cotechino e lenticche* (garlic sausage with lentils). You might expect such an *osteria* in Berkeley or Brooklyn, but this tiny spot pumps life into the blood of old Woodstock. [$] *Average main: $21* ✉ *61 Central St.* ☎ *802/457–4882* 🌐 *www.osteriapaneesalute.com* ✍ *Reservations essential* ⏲ *Closed Mon., Tues., and Wed. and Apr. and Nov. No lunch.*

$$$ FRENCH 🍴 **The Prince & The Pauper.** Modern French and American fare with a Vermont accent is the focus of this candlelit Colonial restaurant off the town green. The grilled duck breast might have an Asian five-spice sauce, and the boneless rack of lamb is wrapped in puff pastry and splashed with Bordelaise sauce. A three-course prix-fixe menu is available for $49; a less expensive bistro menu is available in the lounge. If you like the artwork hanging above your table, feel free to buy it. [$] *Average main: $21* ✉ *24 Elm St.* ☎ *802/457–1818* 🌐 *www.princeandpauper.com* ⏲ *No lunch.*

WHERE TO STAY

$$$ B&B/INN 🏨 **The Fan House.** If you're searching for an authentic inn in the heart of a small, quaint Vermont town, consider this Colonial-style house dating from 1840. **Pros:** center of old town; plenty of creature comforts; good library. **Cons:** upstairs rooms can be cool in winter. [$] *Rooms from: $200* ✉ *6297 Rt. 12 N* ☎ *802/234–6704* 🌐 *www.thefanhouse.com* 🛏 *3 rooms* 💳 *No credit cards* ⏲ *Closed Apr.* 🍽 *Breakfast.*

The upscale Woodstock area is known as Vermont's horse country.

$$$$
B&B/INN
🏨 **Kedron Valley Inn.** You're likely to fall in love at the first sight of this 1828 three-story brick building, which forms the centerpiece of a 15-acre retreat. **Pros:** good food; quiet setting. **Cons:** 5 miles south of Woodstock. $ *Rooms from: $259* ✉ *4778 South Rd., South Woodstock* ☎ *802/457–1473, 800/836–1193* ⊕ *www.kedronvalleyinn.com* ⏎ *24 rooms, 1 suites* ☉ *Closed Apr.* ⧉ *Breakfast.*

$$
HOTEL
🏨 **The Shire Riverview Motel.** Many rooms in this immaculate motel have decks, and almost all have fabulous views of Ottauquechee River, which runs right along the building. **Pros:** inexpensive access to the heart of Woodstock; views. **Cons:** basic rooms; unexciting exterior. $ *Rooms from: $158* ✉ *46 Pleasant St.* ☎ *802/457–2211* ⊕ *www.shiremotel.com* ⏎ *42 rooms, 1 suite* ⧉ *No meals.*

$$$$
ALL-INCLUSIVE
Fodor's Choice
★
🏨 **Twin Farms.** Let's just get it out: Twin Farms is the best lodging in Vermont. And if you can afford it—stays begin at well over $1,000 a night—you'll want to experience it. Each incredible accommodation is furnished with a blend of high art (Jasper Johns, Milton Avery, Cy Twombly), gorgeous folk art, and furniture that goes beyond comfortable sophistication. **Pros:** impeccable service; stunning rooms; sensational meals. **Cons:** incredibly steep prices $ *Rooms from: $1600* ✉ *452 Royalton Tpke., Barnard* ☎ *802/234–9999* ⊕ *www.twinfarms. com* ⏎ *10 rooms, 10 cottages* ☉ *Closed Apr.* ⧉ *All-inclusive.*

$$$$
RESORT
Fodor's Choice
★
🏨 **The Woodstock Inn & Resort.** This resort sits in the middle of it all. **Pros:** attractive and historic property; excellent food; soothing spa. **Cons:** can lack intimacy. $ *Rooms from: $300* ✉ *14 The Green* ☎ *802/457–1100, 800/448–7900* ⊕ *www.woodstockinn.com* ⏎ *135 rooms, 7 suites* ⧉ *No meals.*

8

SPORTS AND THE OUTDOORS

GOLF

Woodstock Inn & Resort Golf Club. Robert Trent Jones Sr. designed this challenging course at the Woodstock Inn & Resort. ⊠ *Woodstock Inn & Resort, 14 The Green* ☎ *802/457–1100* ⊕ *www.woodstockinn.com* ▧ *Greens fee: $89 weekdays, $109 weekends* ⅃ *18 holes, 6000 yards, par 70.*

SHOPPING AND SPAS

CRAFTS

Collective. This funky and attractive shop sells local jewelry, glass, pottery, and clothing. ⊠ *47 Central St.* ☎ *802/457–1298* ⊕ *www.collective-theartofcraft.com* ☉ *Mon.–Sat.10–5, Sun. 11–4.*

FOOD

Sugarbush Farm. Take the Taftsville Covered Bridge to Sugarbush Farm, where you'll learn how maple sugar is made and get to sample as much maple syrup as you'd like. The farm also makes excellent cheeses. ⊠ *591 Sugarbush Farm Rd., off Rte. 4* ☎ *802/457–1757, 800/281–1757* ⊕ *www.sugarbushfarm.com* ☉ *Daily 10–5.*

Taftsville Country Store. East of town, the Taftsville Country Store sells a wide selection of Vermont cheeses, moderately priced wines, and Vermont specialty foods. ⊠ *404 Woodstock Rd., Taftsville* ☎ *802/457–1135, 800/854–0013* ⊕ *www.taftsville.com.*

Village Butcher. This emporium of Vermont edibles has great sandwiches, cheeses, local beers, and delicious baked goods—perfect for a picnic or lunch-on-the-go. ⊠ *18 Elm St.* ☎ *802/457–2756.*

Woodstock Farmers' Market. The market is a year-round buffet of local produce, fresh fish, and excellent sandwiches and pastries. The maple-walnut scones go fast, so get there early. ⊠ *468 Woodstock Rd. (U.S. 4)* ☎ *802/457–3658* ⊕ *www.woodstockfarmersmarket.com* ☉ *Tues.–Sat. 7:30–7, Sun. 9–6.*

GALLERIES

Gallery on the Green. This corner gallery in one of Woodstock's oldest buildings showcases paintings depicting regional landscapes by more than 26 New England artists. ⊠ *One the Green* ☎ *802/457–4956* ⊕ *www.galleryonthegreen.com.*

SPAS

Out of the Woods Spa at Twin Farms. A visit to Twin Farms is a trip to another world, and a treatment at the on-site spa completes the journey. Set in the woods of the charming estate of Nobel Prize–winning writer Sinclair Lewis, the spa expounds a philosophy of wellness that goes well beyond the realm of massages and skin treatments. Employing an organic product line by Vermont-based Tata Harper and Lunaroma, the spa offers a range of facials, polishes, aromatherapy, and mud wraps, but the star remains the 120-minute Ultimate Body Treatment, which administers a heavenly reboot to your skin and muscles. ⊠ *Twin Farms, 452 Royalton Tpke., Barnard* ☎ *802/234–9999* ⊕ *www. twinfarms.com/experience/spa.*

Spa at the Woodstock Inn and Resort. The spa features a stunning 10,000-square-foot nature-inspired facility with 10 treatment rooms, a full-service salon, and sophisticated shop dedicated to wellness and relaxation. The elegant, minimalist design accentuates its beautiful setting: natural light pours into the sparking dressing rooms and the comfortable firelit Great Room. An outdoor meditation courtyard has a soaking pool and a Scandinavian-style sauna that face the sky. The mood is peaceful, quiet and serene; choose from a wide array of treatments and organic products. Each season has its own 100-minute signature treatment. ✉ *Woodstock Inn and Resort, 14 The Green, Woodstock* ☎ *802/457–6697* 🌐 *www.woodstockinn.com/Activities/Spa.*

KILLINGTON

15 miles east of Rutland.

With only a gas station, post office, motel, and a few shops at the intersection of Routes 4 and 100, it's difficult to tell that the East's largest ski resort is nearby. The village of Killington is characterized by unfortunate strip development along the access road to the ski resort. But the 360-degree views atop Killington Peak, accessible by the resort's gondola, make it worth the drive.

WHERE TO STAY

$$ B&B/INN 🏨 **Birch Ridge Inn.** A slate-covered carriageway about a mile from the Killington ski resort leads to one of the area's most popular off-mountain stays, a former executive retreat in two renovated A-frames. **Pros:** quirky design; well-maintained property; tasty cuisine. **Cons:** oddly furnished; outdated style. [$] *Rooms from: $150* ✉ *37 Butler Rd.* ☎ *802/422–4293, 800/435–8566* 🌐 *www.birchridge.com* 🛏 *10 rooms* 🕒 *Closed May* 🍴 *Breakfast.*

$$$$ RESORT FAMILY 🏨 **The Mountain Top Inn & Resort.** This cross-country skiing and horseback riding haven has stunning views and laid-back yet luxurious accommodations. **Pros:** family-friendly vibe; a great spot for outdoor activities. **Cons:** expensive for what it is. [$] *Rooms from: $275* ✉ *195 Mountain Top Rd., Chittenden* ☎ *802/483–2311* 🌐 *www.mountaintopinn.com* 🛏 *32 rooms, 4 cabins, 3 cottages, 18 homes* 🍴 *Breakfast.*

$$$$ RESORT 🏨 **The Woods Resort & Spa.** These upscale two- and three-bedroom town houses stand in wooded lots along a winding road leading to the spa. **Pros:** contemporary facility; spacious rooms; lots of layout choices. **Cons:** lacks traditional Vermont feel. [$] *Rooms from: $250* ✉ *53 Woods La.* ☎ *802/422–3139, 866/785–8904* 🌐 *www.woodsresortandspa.com* 🛏 *107 units* 🍴 *No meals.*

NIGHTLIFE

Inn at Long Trail. On weekends, listen to live Irish music and sip draft Guinness at the Inn at Long Trail. ✉ *709 Rte. 4* ☎ *800/325–2540* 🌐 *www.innatlongtrail.com.*

Pickle Barrel Night Club. During ski season the Pickle Barrel Night Club has live music on Friday and Saturday. After 8 the crowd moves downstairs for dancing, sometimes to big-name bands. ✉ *1741 Killington Rd.* ☎ *802/422–3035* 🌐 *www.picklebarrelnightclub.com.*

Outback. This friendly place serves an all-you-can-eat pizza buffet on Monday nights. With a focus on live music, it's open year-round. ⊠ *2841 Killington Rd.* ☏ *802/422–9885.*

Wobbly Barn. Twentysomethings dance at the Wobbly Barn, open during ski season. ⊠ *2229 Killington Rd.* ☏ *802/422–6171* ⊕ *www.wobblybarn.com.*

SPORTS AND THE OUTDOORS

BIKING

True Wheels Bike Shop. This shop rents bicycles and has information on local routes. ⊠ *2886 Killington Rd.* ☏ *802/422–3234, 877/487–9972* ⊕ *www.truewheels.com.*

CROSS-COUNTRY SKIING

The Mountain Top Inn & Resort. This resort has 37 miles of hilly trails groomed for cross-country skiing, 24 miles of which can be used for skate skiing. You can also enjoy snowshoeing, ice skating, and snowmobile and sleigh rides. In the summer there's horseback riding, clay-bird shooting, fishing, hiking, sand volleyball, and water sports. ⊠ *195 Mountaintop Rd., Chittenden* ☏ *802/483–6089, 802/483–2311* ⊕ *www.mountaintopinn.com.*

FISHING

Gifford Woods State Park. Kent Pond in Gifford Woods State Park is a terrific fishing spot. ⊠ *34 Gifford Woods Rd., ½ mile north of U.S. 4* ☏ *802/775–5354* ⊕ *www.vtstateparks.com/htm/gifford.cfm.*

GOLF

Killington Golf Course. At its namesake resort, the Killington Golf Course has a challenging layout. ⊠ *4763 Killington Rd.* ☏ *802/422–6200* ⊕ *www.killington.com/summer/golf_course* ⊠ *Greens fee: $50 weekdays, $60 weekends* ⌘ *18 holes, 6,186 yards, par 72.*

HIKING

Deer Leap Trail. This 3-mile round-trip hike leads to a great view overlooking Sherburne Gap and Pico Peak. ⊠ *Rte. 4, near Inn at Long Trail, Rutland* ⊕ *www.greenmountainhikingtrails.com/deerleap.html.*

SKI AREAS

Fodor's Choice ★ **Killington.** "Megamountain" aptly describes Killington. Thanks to its extensive snowmaking system, the resort typically opens in early November, and the lifts often run into late April or early May. Après-ski activities are plentiful and have been rated the best in the region by national ski magazines. Killington ticket holders can also ski at Pico Mountain: a shuttle connects the two areas.

In terms of downhill skiing, it would probably take weeks to test all 212 trails on the seven mountains of the Killington complex. There are 29 lifts, including 2 gondolas, 11 quads (including 7 high-speed express quads), 5 triples, and a Magic Carpet. The K-1 Express Gondola goes to the area's highest elevation, 4,241-foot Killington Peak. The Skyeship Gondola starts on U.S. 4, far below Killington's main base lodge. ■TIP→ Savvy skiers park at the base of the Skyeship Gondola to avoid the more crowded access road.

Although Killington has a vertical drop of 3,050 feet, only gentle trails like the Juggernaut go from top to bottom. The skiing includes everything from Outer Limits, the East's steepest and longest mogul trail, to 6½-mile Great Eastern. In the glades, underbrush and low branches have been cleared to provide tree skiing. Killington's 22-foot Superpipe is one of the best rated in the East. Instruction programs are available for youngsters ages 3 to 8; those 6 to12 can join an all-day program. The Killington–Pico complex also has a host of summer activities, including mountain biking, hiking, and golf. ⊠ 4763 Killington Rd. ☎ 802/422–6200, 802/422–6200 snow conditions ⊕ www.killington.com.

Pico. When weekend hordes hit Killington, the locals head to Pico. One of Killington's "seven peaks," Pico is physically separated from its parent resort. The 57 trails range from elevator-shaft steep to challenging intermediate trails near the summit, with easier terrain near the bottom of the mountain's 2,000-foot vertical. The learning slope is separated from the upper mountain, so hotshots won't bomb through it. The lower express quad can get crowded, but the upper one rarely has a line. ⊠ 73 Alpine Dr., Mendon ☎ 802/422–6200, 866/667–7426 ⊕ www.picomountain.com.

SNOWMOBILE TOURS

Snowmobile Vermont. Blazing down forest trails on a snowmobile is one way Vermonters embrace the winter landscapes. Rentals are available through Snowmobile Vermont at several locations including Killington and Okemo. Both have hour-long guided tours across groomed ski trails ($99). If you're feeling more adventurous, take the two-hour backcountry tour through 25 miles of Calvin Coolidge State Forest ($149). ⊠ 170 Rte. 100, Bridgewater Corners ☎ 802/422–2121 ⊕ www.snowmobilevermont.com.

RUTLAND

15 miles southwest of Killington, 32 miles south of Middlebury.

On and around U.S. 7 in Rutland are strips of shopping centers and a seemingly endless row of traffic lights—very un-Vermont. Two blocks west, however, stand the mansions of the marble magnates. The county farmers' market is held in Depot Park Saturdays 9–2. Note: while Rutland is a good central base to grab a bite and see some interesting marble, it's not a place to spend too much time sightseeing.

ESSENTIALS

Visitor Information Rutland Region Chamber of Commerce ⊠ 50 Merchants Row ☎ 802/773-2747, 800/756-8880 ⊕ www.rutlandvermont.com.

EXPLORING

Chaffee Art Center. Housed in a beautiful mansion, this arts center exhibits the work of more than 200 Vermont artists. A second location is open downtown on Merchants Row. ⊠ 16 S. Main St. ☎ 802/775–0356 ⊕ www.chaffeeartcenter.org ☑ Free ⊗ Thurs.–Sat. 10–6.

New England Maple Museum. Maple syrup is Vermont's signature product, and this museum north of Rutland explains the history and process of turning sap into syrup. If you don't get a chance to visit a sugarhouse,

8

this is a fine place to sample the different grades and pick up some souvenirs. ✉ *4578 U.S. 7, 9 miles south of Brandon, Pittsford* ☎ *802/483–9414* 🌐 *www.maplemuseum.com* 🎟 *Museum $5* 🕐 *Late May–Oct., daily 9:30–5:30; Nov., Dec., and mid-Mar.–late May, daily 10–4.*

Paramount Theatre. The highlight of downtown is this 838-seat gilded playhouse, an architectural gem dating from 1913. The gorgeous theater is home to music, theater, and films, as well as stand-up comedy. ✉ *30 Center St.* ☎ *802/775–0570* 🌐 *www.paramountvt.org.*

Vermont Marble Museum. This monument to marble highlights one of the main industries in this region. The hall of presidents has a carved bust of each U.S. president, and in the marble chapel is a replica of Leonardo da Vinci's *Last Supper.* Elsewhere you can watch a sculptor-in-residence at work, compare marble from around the world, and check out the Vermont Marble Company's original "stone library." A short walk away is the original quarry, which helped finish the U.S. Supreme Court. ✉ *52 Main St., off Rte. 3, Proctor* ☎ *802/459–2300, 800/427–1396* 🌐 *www.vermont-marble.com* 🎟 *$7* 🕐 *Mid-May–Oct., daily 9–5:30.*

Wilson Castle. Completed in 1867, this 32-room mansion was built over the course of eight years by a Vermonter who married a British aristocrat. Within the opulent setting are 84 stained-glass windows (one inset with 32 Australian opals), hand-painted Italian frescoes, and 13 fireplaces. It's magnificently furnished with European and Asian objets d'art. ✉ *2708 West St., Proctor* ☎ *802/773–3284* 🌐 *www.wilsoncastle.com* 🎟 *$10* 🕐 *Daily 9–5; last tour at 5.*

WHERE TO EAT

$$ ECLECTIC 🍴 **Little Harry's.** Locals have packed this restaurant ever since chef-owners Trip Pearce and Jack Mangan brought Vermont cheddar ravioli and lamb lo mein to downtown Rutland in 1997. This place is "Little" compared to the bigger Harry's, near Ludlow. The 17 tabletops are adorned with laminated photos of the regulars. If you have a big appetite but a small budget, try the vegetarian red curry—it's under $12. [$] *Average main: $18* ✉ *121 West St.* ☎ *802/747–4848* 🌐 *littleharrys.com* 🕐 *No lunch.*

SPORTS AND THE OUTDOORS

BOATING

Lake Bomoseen Marina. Rent pontoon boats, speedboats, paddleboards, and kayaks at Lake Bomoseen Marina. ✉ *145 Creek Rd., off Rte. 4A* ☎ *802/265–4611* 🌐 *www.woodardmarine.com.*

HIKING

Mountain Travelers. This place sells hiking, sporting, and boating equipment; gives advice on local hikes; and rents skis. ✉ *147 Rte. 4 E* ☎ *802/775–0814.*

BRANDON

15 miles northwest of Rutland.

Thanks to an active artists' guild, tiny Brandon is making a name for itself. In 2003 the Brandon Artists Guild, led by American folk artist Warren Kimble, auctioned 40 life-size fiberglass pigs painted by local artists. The "Really Really Pig Show" raised money for the guild and has brought small-town fame ever since to this community through its yearly shows. Brandon is also home to the Basin Bluegrass Festival, held in July.

ESSENTIALS

Visitor Information Brandon Visitor Center ⊠ *4 Grove St.* ☎ *802/247–6401* ⊕ *brandon.org.*

EXPLORING

Brandon Museum at the Stephen A. Douglas Birthplace. The famous Early American statesman was born in this house in 1813. He left 20 years later to establish himself as a lawyer, becoming a three-time U.S. senator and arguing more cases before the U.S. Supreme Court than anyone else. This museum recounts the early Douglas years, early Brandon history, and the antislavery movement in Vermont—the first state to abolish it. ⊠ *4 Grove St., at U.S. 7* ☎ *802/247–6401* ⊕ *www.brandon.org* ⊠ *Free* ☉ *Mid-May–mid-Oct., daily 11–4.*

WHERE TO EAT AND STAY

$$
CAFÉ
✕ **Café Provence.** Robert Barral, former director of the New England Culinary Institute, graces Brandon with this informal eatery named after his birthplace. One story above the main street, the café with hints of Provence—flowered seat cushions and dried-flower window valences—specializes in eclectic farm-fresh dishes. Goat-cheese cake with mesclun greens, braised veal cheeks and caramelized endive, and a portobello pizza from the restaurant's hearth oven are just a few of the choices. Breakfast offerings include buttery pastries, eggs Benedict, and breakfast pizza. Outdoor seating can be had under large umbrellas. $ *Average main: $20* ⊠ *11 Center St.* ☎ *802/247–9997* ⊕ *www.cafeprovencevt.com.*

$$$$
B&B/INN
Fodor'sChoice
★
Blueberry Hill Inn. In Green Mountain National Forest, 5½ miles off a mountain pass on a dirt road, you'll find this secluded inn with lush gardens and a pond with a wood-fired sauna on its bank. **Pros:** peaceful setting within the national forest; lots of activities; great food. **Cons:** fills up with wedding parties. $ *Rooms from: $269* ⊠ *1307 Goshen–Ripton Rd., Goshen* ☎ *802/247–6735, 800/448–0707* ⊕ *www.blueberryhillinn.com* ⇖ *12 rooms* ⍩⏐ *Some meals.*

$$$
B&B/INN
The Lilac Inn. The best B&B in town has spacious, cheery, and comfortable rooms in a central setting half a block from the heart of Brandon. **Pros:** big manor house; walking distance to town; charming rooms. **Cons:** busy in summer with weddings. $ *Rooms from: $220* ⊠ *53 Park St.* ☎ *802/247–5463, 800/221–0720* ⊕ *www.lilacinn.com* ⇖ *8 rooms, 1 suite* ⍩⏐ *Breakfast.*

SPORTS AND THE OUTDOORS

PARKS

Moosalamoo National Recreation Area. Covering more than 20,000 acres of the Green Mountain National Forest, this recreation area northeast of Brandon delights the hikers, mountain bikers, and cross-country skiers who enjoy the 60-plus miles of trails through gorgeous terrain. If there is anywhere to stop and smell the flowers in Vermont, this is it. ☎ *800/448–0707* ⊕ *www.moosalamoo.org.*

GOLF

Neshobe Golf Club. This bent-grass course has terrific views of the Green Mountains. Several local inns offer golf packages. ⊠ *224 Town Farm Rd.* ☎ *802/247–3611* ⊕ *www.neshobe.com* 🖃 *Greens fee: $49–$60* 🏌 *18 holes, 6,500 yards, par 72.*

HIKING

Branbury State Park. On the shores of Lake Dunmore, Branbury State Park sits near Moosalamoo National Recreation Area. A large turnout on Route 53 marks a moderate trail to the Falls of Lana. ⊠ *Rte. 53.*

Mt. Horrid. For great views from a vertigo-inducing cliff, hike up the Long Trail to Mt. Horrid. The steep, hour-long hike starts at the top of Brandon Gap, about 8 miles east of Brandon. ⊠ *Rte. 73.*

Mt. Independence State Historic Site. West of Brandon, four trails—two short ones of less than 1 mile each and two longer ones—lead to the abandoned Revolutionary War fortifications at Mt. Independence State Historic Site. To reach them, take the first left turn off Route 73 west of Orwell and go right at the fork. The parking lot is on the left at the top of the hill. ⊠ *28 Shoales Dr., Orwell* ⊕ *www.historicsites.vermont. gov/directory/mount_independence.*

SHOPPING

The Inside Scoop and Antiques by the Falls. A husband-and-wife team runs these two separate and equally fun-loving businesses under one roof: a colorful ice cream stand and penny candy store and an antiques store filled floor to ceiling with Americana. ⊠ *22 Park St., East Brandon* ☎ *802/247–6600.*

MIDDLEBURY

17 miles north of Brandon, 34 miles south of Burlington.

In the late 1800s Middlebury was the largest Vermont community west of the Green Mountains, an industrial center of river-powered wool and grain mills. This is Robert Frost country: Vermont's late poet laureate spent 23 summers at a farm east of Middlebury. Still a cultural and economic hub amid the Champlain Valley's serene pastoral patchwork and the home of top-notch Middlebury College, the picturesque town and rolling countryside invite a day of exploration.

EXPLORING

Middlebury College. Founded in 1800, Middlebury College was conceived as a more godly alternative to the worldly University of Vermont, but has no religious affiliation today. In the middle of town, the early-19th-century stone buildings contrast provocatively with the postmodern architecture of the **Mahaney Center for the Arts,** which offers music, theater, and dance performances throughout the year. ⊠ *131 College St.* ☎ *802/443–5000* ⊕ *www.middlebury.edu.*

Robert Frost Interpretive Trail. About a mile west of Middlebury College's Bread Loaf campus, this easy 1.2-mile trail winds through quiet woodlands. Plaques along the way bear quotations from Frost's poems. A picnic area is across the road from the trailhead. ⊠ *Rte. 125, 10 miles east of downtown.*

FAMILY **University of Vermont Morgan Horse Farm.** The Morgan horse—Vermont's official state animal—has an even temper, stamina, and slightly truncated legs in proportion to its body. This farm, about 2½ miles west of Middlebury, is a breeding and training center where in summer you can tour the stables and paddocks. ✉ *74 Battell Dr., off Morgan Horse Farm Rd., Weybridge* ☎ *802/388–2011* ⊕ *www.uvm.edu/morgan* 🖥 *$5* ⊗ *May–Oct., daily 9–4.*

Vermont Folklife Center. In the Masonic Hall, exhibits include photography, antiques, folk paintings, manuscripts, and other artifacts and contemporary works that examine facets of Vermont life. ✉ *88 Main St.* ☎ *802/388–4964* ⊕ *www.vermontfolklifecenter.org* 🖥 *Donations accepted* ⊗ *Tues.–Sat. 10–5.*

OFF THE BEATEN PATH

Fort Ticonderoga Ferry. Established in 1759, the Fort Ti cable ferry crosses Lake Champlain between Shoreham and Fort Ticonderoga, New York, at one of the oldest ferry crossings in North America. The trip takes seven minutes. ✉ *4831 Rte. 74W, Shoreham* ☎ *802/897–7999* ⊕ *www. forttiferry.com* 🖥 *Cars $9; bicycles $2; pedestrians $1* ⊗ *May, June, Sept., and Oct:, daily 7–6; July–Sept., 7–7.*

WHERE TO EAT

$$
PIZZA

✕ **American Flatbread Middlebury Hearth.** On weekends this is the most happening spot in town, and no wonder: the pizza is extraordinary, and the attitude is pure Vermont. Wood-fired clay domes create masterful thin crusts from organically grown wheat. Besides the innovative, delicious pizzas, try an organic mesclun salad tossed in the house gingertamari vinaigrette. If you love pizza, you're in for a treat. There are also locations in Waitsfield and Burlington. 💲 *Average main: $20* ✉ *137 Maple St.* ☎ *802/388–3300* ⊕ *www.americanflatbread.com* ⚓ *Reservations not accepted* ⊗ *No lunch. No dinner Sun. and Mon.*

$$
AMERICAN

✕ **The Bobcat Cafe & Brewery.** Worth the drive from Middlebury to the small, quaint town of Bristol, The Bobcat is the place to be in the area. Fun, funky, and hip, this charming eatery is nice enough for a date but casual enough for the whole family. Choose from a wide range of great offerings from burgers to cornmeal-crusted haddock and wash it down with excellent house-brewed beer. For something special, try the maple-brined pork loin or the peach upside-down cake for dessert. 💲 *Average main: $18* ✉ *5 Main St., Bristol* ☎ *802/453–3311* ⊕ *www. bobcatcafe.com* ⊗ *No lunch.*

$$$
AMERICAN
Fodor's Choice
★

✕ **Mary's at Baldwin Creek.** People drive from the far reaches of Vermont to dine at this restaurant just beyond the charming, little-known town of Bristol, 13 miles northeast of Middlebury. Plan time to visit the sprawling gardens that surround this beautiful property—they represent the slow approach to cooking that earned this restaurant its stellar reputation. Seasonal fare bursts to life here with hearty fare like the summer lasagna packed with vegetables and the near-legendary garlic soup, a creamy year-round staple that seems genetically engineered to please. Desserts, however, are hit or miss. 💲 *Average main: $25* ✉ *1868 North Rte. 116, Bristol* ☎ *802/453–2432* ⊕ *www.innatbaldwincreek. com* ⊗ *Closed Mon. and Tues.*

8

$$ MODERN AMERICAN 🍴 **The Storm Cafe.** There's no setting in town quite like this restaurant's deck, overlooking Otter Creek Falls at one end of a long footbridge. Even if you're not here in summer, the eclectic, ever-changing menu at this small restaurant in the old Frog Hollow Mill makes it worth a visit any time of year. Spicy calamari and vegetable curry are favorites, as are the large salads. [$] *Average main: $20* ✉ *3 Mill St.* ☎ *802/388–1063* 🌐 *www.thestormcafe.com* 🕒 *No dinner Sun. and Mon.*

WHERE TO STAY

$$ B&B/INN 🏨 **Inn on the Green.** On the National Register of Historic Places, this 1803 inn and carriage house sit in the center of bucolic Middlebury near the stunning campus of Middlebury College. **Pros:** ideal location; great breakfast. **Cons:** rooms can be small and close together. [$] *Rooms from: $170* ✉ *71 S. Pleasant St.* ☎ *802/388–7512* 🌐 *www.innonthegreen.com* 🛏 *9 rooms, 2 suites* 🍽 *Breakfast.*

$$ B&B/INN 🏨 **Swift House Inn.** The 1814 Georgian home of a 19th-century governor showcases white-panel wainscoting, mahogany furnishings, and marble fireplaces. **Pros:** attractive, spacious, well-kept rooms; professionally run. **Cons:** near to but not quite in the heart of town. [$] *Rooms from: $169* ✉ *25 Stewart La.* ☎ *866/388–9925* 🌐 *www.swifthouseinn.com* 🛏 *20 rooms* 🍽 *Breakfast.*

SHOPPING

Edgewater Gallery. This gallery alongside Otter Creek is about as picturesque as you can get. However, there are plenty of impressive paintings, jewelry, ceramics, and pieces of furniture inside the bright, airy space to steal your attention as well. Exhibitions rotate regularly, demonstrating the owner's ambition to be more gallery than shop (although all pieces are for sale). ✉ *1 Mill St.* ☎ *802/458–0098* 🌐 *www.edgewatergallery-vt.com.*

Historic Marble Works. This renovated marble manufacturing facility has a collection of shops and eateries set amid quarrying equipment and factory buildings. ✉ *2 Maple St.* ☎ *802/388–3701.*

Danforth Pewter. In addition to the lovely handcrafted pewter vases, lamps, and jewelry, this store offers you a front-row seat to the art of pewter spinning in the back workshop. There's also a small museum. ✉ *52 Seymour St.* ☎ *800/222–3142* 🌐 *www.danforthpewter.com*

WAITSFIELD AND WARREN

32 miles northeast (Waitsfield) and 25 miles east (Warren) of Middlebury.

Skiers discovered the high peaks overlooking the pastoral Mad River Valley in the 1940s. Now the valley and its two towns, Waitsfield and Warren, attract the hip, the adventurous, and the low-key. Warren is tiny and adorable, with a general store that attracts tour buses. The gently carved ridges cradling the valley and the swell of pastures and fields lining the river seem to keep notions of ski-resort sprawl at bay. With a map from the Sugarbush Chamber of Commerce you can investigate back roads off Route 100 that have exhilarating valley views.

Sheep's cheese is just one of the many food products that contribute to great fresh local meals in Vermont.

8

ESSENTIALS

Visitor Information Mad River Valley Chamber of Commerce ✉ *4061 Main St.* ☎ *802/496–3409, 800/828–4748* 🌐 *www.madrivervalley.com.*

WHERE TO EAT

$$ PIZZA Fodor's Choice ★ 🍴 **American Flatbread Waitsfield.** Is this the best pizza experience in the world? It just may be. In summer you can dine outside around fire pits in the beautiful valley. The organically grown flour and vegetables and the wood-fired clay ovens transform the pizza into something magical. One of our favorites is the maple-fennel sausage pie topped with sun-dried tomatoes, caramelized onions, cheese, and herbs; it's a dream, as are the more traditional flavors. This is the original American Flatbread location—plan your trip around it. Seats can be hard to come by, but if you stay at the adjoining inn, they're reserved. [$] *Average main: $18* ✉ *46 Lareau Rd., off Rte. 100* ☎ *802/496–8856* 🌐 *www.americanflatbread.com* ✍ *Reservations not accepted* ⏲ *Closed Mon.–Wed. No lunch.*

$$$ MODERN AMERICAN 🍴 **Common Man.** This restaurant is in a big 1800s barn with hand-hewn rafters and crystal chandeliers hanging from the beams. That's the Common Man for you: fancy and après-ski all at once. Bottles of Moët & Chandon signed by the customers who ordered them sit atop the beams. The eclectic, sophisticated New American cuisine highlights locally grown produce and meats. The menu might include a roasted beet salad with goat cheese and fennel in an orange vinaigrette, duck breast with butternut squash puree, or seared black bass with sticky rice and bok choy. Dinner is served by candlelight. Couples sit by the big fireplace. [$] *Average main: $25* ✉ *3209 German Flats Rd., Warren*

☎ 802/583–2800 🌐 *www.commonmanrestaurant.com* ⏲ *Closed Sun. and Mon. No lunch.*

WHERE TO STAY

$$$ B&B/INN **The Inn at Round Barn Farm.** A Shaker-style round barn (one of only five in Vermont) is the centerpiece of this B&B, but what you'll remember when you leave is how comfortable a stay here is. **Pros:** great trails, gardens, and rooms; tasty breakfasts; unique architecture. **Cons:** no restaurant; fills up for wedding parties. [$] *Rooms from: $205* ✉ *1661 E. Warren Rd.* ☎ *802/496–2276* 🌐 *www.theroundbarn.com* *11 rooms, 1 suite* 🍴 *Breakfast.*

$$$$ B&B/INN Fodor's Choice ★ **The Pitcher Inn.** Sublime is a word which comes to mind when thinking about a night at the elegant Pitcher Inn, one of Vermont's trio of Relais & Châteaux properties. **Pros:** exceptional service; fabulous restaurant; beautiful location. **Cons:** at some point, you have to go home. [$] *Rooms from: $425* ✉ *275 Main St., Warren* ☎ *802/496–6350, 888/867–4824* 🌐 *www.pitcherinn.com* *9 rooms, 2 suites* 🍴 *Breakfast.*

NIGHTLIFE AND THE ARTS

THE ARTS

Green Mountain Cultural Center. The Green Mountain Cultural Center hosts concerts, art exhibits, and educational workshops. ✉ *Inn at Round Barn Farm, 1661 E. Warren Rd.* ☎ *802/496-4759* 🌐 *www.theroundbarn.com.*

NIGHTLIFE

Purple Moon Pub. Live bands play most weekends at Purple Moon Pub. ✉ *6163 Main St.(Rte. 100)* ☎ *802/496–3422* 🌐 *www.purplemoonpub.com.*

Fodor's Choice ★ **Tracks.** Downstairs at the Pitcher Inn, this comfortable tavern has a tasteful lodge-style setting complete with a crackling fireplace. It has a terrific bar menu—try the seared scallops over sweet potatoes and bacon or the local pork chops. There's also an excellent wine selection, billiard tables, dart boards, and a fun shuffleboard game played on a long table. ✉ *Pitcher Inn, 275 Main St, ., Warren* ☎ *802/493–6350* 🌐 *www.pitcherinn.com.*

SPORTS AND THE OUTDOORS

GOLF

Sugarbush Resort Golf Club. Great views and challenging play are the trademarks of the Robert Trent Jones Sr.–designed mountain course. ✉ *Sugarbush, 1840 Sugarbush Access Rd., Warren* ☎ *802/583–6300* 🌐 *www.sugarbush.com* *Greens fee: $40–$100* ⛳ *18 holes, 6,464 yards, par 72.*

MULTI-SPORT OUTFITTER

Clearwater Sports. This outfitter rents canoes and kayaks and leads guided river trips in the warmer months. When the weather turns cold it offers snowshoe and backcountry ski tours. ✉ *4147 Main St.* ☎ *802/496–2708* 🌐 *clearwatersports.com.*

SKI AREAS

Blueberry Lake Cross Country and Snowshoeing Center. This ski area has 18 miles of trails through thickly wooded glades. ⊠ *424 Plunkton Rd., East Warren* ☎ *802/496–6687* ⊕ *www.blueberrylakeskivt.com.*

Mad River Glen. A pristine alpine experience, Mad River attracts rugged individualists looking for less polished terrain. The area was developed in the late 1940s, and has changed relatively little since then. It remains one of only three resorts in the country that ban snowboarding. Mad River is steep, with natural slopes that follow the mountain's fall lines. The terrain changes constantly on the 45 interconnected trails, of which 33% are beginner, 27% are intermediate, and 41% are expert. Five lifts—including one of two surviving single chairlifts in the country—service the mountain's 2,037-foot vertical drop. Most of Mad River's trails are covered only by natural snow. The kids' ski school runs classes for little ones ages 4 to 12.

Known as the capital of free-heel skiing, Mad River Glen sponsors Telemark programs throughout the season. Every March the North America Telemark Organization Festival attracts up to 1,400 visitors. Snowshoeing is also an option. There is a $5 fee to use the snowshoe trails, and rentals are available. ⊠ *Rte. 17* ☎ *802/496–3551, 802/496–2001 snow conditions* ⊕ *www.madriverglen.com.*

Sugarbush. Sugarbush has remade itself as a true skier's mountain, with steep, natural snow glades and fall-line drops. Not as rough around the edges as Mad River Glen, Sugarbush also has well-groomed intermediate and beginner terrain. A computer-controlled system for snowmaking has increased coverage to 70%. At the base of the mountain are condominiums, restaurants, shops, bars, and a sports center.

Sugarbush is two distinct, connected mountain complexes connected by the Slide Brook Express quad. Lincoln Peak, with a vertical drop of 2,400 feet, is known for formidable steeps, especially on Castlerock. Mount Ellen has more beginner runs near the bottom, with steep fall-line pitches on the upper half of the 2,650 vertical feet. There are 111 trails in all: 22% beginner, 46% intermediate, 32% expert. The resort has 18 lifts: seven quads (including four high-speed versions), three triples, four doubles, and four surface lifts. There's half- and full-day instruction available for children ages 4 to 12 and supervised ski-and-ride programs for teens. Sugarbear Forest, a terrain garden, has fun bumps and jumps. ⊠ *1840 Sugarbush Access Rd., accessible from Rte. 100 or 17, Warren* ☎ *802/583–6300, 802/583–7669 snow conditions* ⊕ *www.sugarbush.com.*

SHOPPING

All Things Bright and Beautiful. This eccentric Victorian house is jammed to the rafters with stuffed animals of all shapes, sizes, and colors, as well as folk art, European glass, and Christmas ornaments. ⊠ *27 Bridge St.* ☎ *802/496–3997* ⊕ *www.allthingsbright.com.*

The Warren Store. This general store has everything you'd hope to find in tiny but sophisticated Vermont: a nice selection of local beer and wine, cheeses, baked goods, strong coffee, and delicious sandwiches and prepared foods. In summer, grab a quick lunch on the small deck by the water; in winter, warm up at the woodstove. ■TIP→ **Don't forget to head upstairs for an eclectic selection of warm, wooly clothing and accessories.** ⊠ *284 Main St., Warren* ☎ *802/496–3864* ⊕ *www. warrenstore.com* ⊗ *Mon.–Sat. 8–7, Sun. 8–6.*

NORTHERN VERMONT

Vermont's northernmost region presents the state's greatest contrasts. To the west, Burlington and its suburbs have grown so rapidly that rural wags now say that Burlington's greatest advantage is that it's "close to Vermont." The north country also harbors Vermont's tiny but charming capital, Montpelier, and its highest mountain, Mt. Mansfield, site of the famous Stowe and Smugglers' Notch ski resorts. To the northeast of Montpelier is a sparsely populated and heavily wooded territory that former Senator George Aiken dubbed the "Northeast Kingdom." It's the domain of loggers, farmers, and avid outdoors enthusiasts.

MONTPELIER

38 miles southeast of Burlington, 115 miles north of Brattleboro.

With only about 8,000 residents, little Montpelier is the country's smallest capital city. But it has a youthful energy—and certainly an independent spirit—that makes it seem almost as large as Burlington. The well-preserved downtown bustles with state and city workers walking to meetings and restaurants, or students heading to one of the funky coffee shops.

EXPLORING

Hope Cemetery. The "Granite Capital of the World," Barre lies just 7 miles east of Montpelier. On a hilltop north of town you'll find one of the world's most gorgeous cemeteries. Many of the superbly crafted tombstones were carved by the stonecutters themselves to demonstrate their skill. A few embrace the avant-garde, while others take defined shapes lake a racecar, biplane, and soccer ball. ⊠ *201 Maple Ave, Barre.*

FAMILY
Fodor'sChoice
★
Morse Farm Maple Sugarworks. With eight generations of sugaring, the Morses may be the oldest maple family in existence, so you're sure to find an authentic maple farm experience here. Burr Morse heads up the operation now, along with his son Tom, but you can still see Burr's father hamming it up in a hilarious video playing in the Woodshed Theater. More than 3,000 trees produce the syrup (sample all the grades), candy, cream, and and sugar in their gift shop. Surrounding trails offer pleasant strolls in summer and prime cross-country skiing in winter. ⊠ *1168 County Rd.* ☎ *800/242–2740* ⊕ *www.morsefarm.com* ⊠ *Free.*

Vermont History Museum. The collection here was begun in 1838 and features all things Vermont, from a catamount (the now-extinct local cougar) to Ethan Allen's shoe buckles. The museum store has a great collection of books, prints, and gifts. ⊠ *109 State St.* ☎ *802/828–2291* ⊕ *www.vermonthistory.org* ⊠ *$5* ⊗ *Tues.–Sat. 10–4.*

QUICK
BITES
✕**La Brioche Bakery. This is a great downtown stop for breakfast and lunch. New England Culinary Institute students are up at 4 am preparing breads for thankful locals. There's a nice selection of soups, salads, and**

8

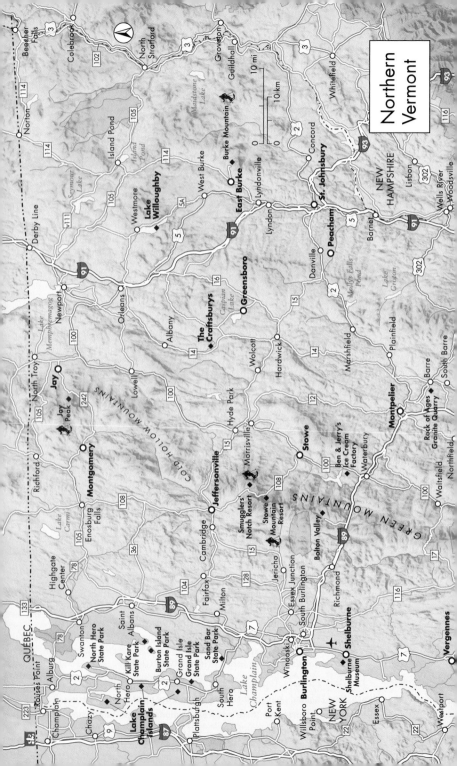

Northern Vermont

sandwiches, but it's the pastries that are the most tempting. [$] *Average main: $425* ✉ *89 Main St.* ☎ *802/229-0443* 🌐 *www.neci.edu/labrioche.*

Vermont State House. The regal capitol building surrounded by forest is emblematic of this proudly rural state. With the gleaming dome topped by the goddess of agriculture and columns of Barre granite measuring 6 feet in diameter, the statehouse is home to the country's oldest legislative chambers still in their original condition. Half-hour tours take you through the governor's office and the house and senate chambers. Interior paintings and exhibits make much of Vermont's sterling Civil War record. ✉ *115 State St.* ☎ *802/828-2228* 🎟 *Donations accepted* ⏲ *Weekdays 8–4; tours July–mid-Oct., weekdays every ½ hr 10–3:30, Sat. 11–3.*

OFF THE BEATEN PATH

Rock of Ages Granite Quarry. The attractions here range from the awe-inspiring (the quarry resembles the Grand Canyon in miniature) to the mildly ghoulish (you can consult a directory of tombstone dealers throughout the country) to the whimsical (an outdoor granite bowling alley). You might recognize the sheer walls of the quarry from *Batman and Robin,* the film starring George Clooney and Arnold Schwarzenegger. At the crafts center, skilled artisans sculpt monuments and blast stone, while at the quarries themselves 25-ton blocks of stone are cut from sheer 475-foot walls by workers who clearly earn their pay. ✉ *560 Graniteville Rd., off I–89, Graniteville* ☎ *802/476-3119* 🌐 *www.rockofages.com* 🎟 *Tours $5* ⏲ *Visitor center May–Oct., Mon.–Sat. 9–5.*

WHERE TO EAT

$$$ ECLECTIC

🍴 **Ariel's.** Well off the beaten path, this small restaurant overlooking a lake is worth the drive down a dirt road. The chef prepares small, medium, and large plates of New England–inspired cuisine based on local sources. Favorites include herb-crusted lamb loin and line-caught swordfish. Don't leave without ordering a board of Vermont cheeses, which pair especially well with the excellent wine selection. [$] *Average main: $26* ✉ *29 Stone Rd., 18 miles south of Montpelier, Brookfield* ☎ *802/276-3939* 🌐 *www.arielsrestaurant.com* ⏲ *Closed Nov. and Apr.; Mon. and Tues. May–Oct.; Sun.–Thurs. Dec.–Mar. No lunch.*

$$ AMERICAN

🍴 **NECI on Main.** Nearly everyone working here is a student at the New England Culinary Institute, but the quality and inventiveness of the food is anything but beginner's luck. The menu changes seasonally, but soups and Misty Knoll Farm free-range chicken are reliable winners. The lounge downstairs offers the same menu, but in a more casual atmosphere. Sunday brunch is very popular, and reservations are strongly recommended. [$] *Average main: $20* ✉ *118 Main St.* ☎ *802/223-3188* 🌐 *www.neci.edu* ⏲ *Closed Mon. No dinner Sun.*

$$ ITALIAN

🍴 **Sarducci's.** Legislative lunches have been a lot more leisurely since Sarducci's came along to fill the trattoria void in Vermont's capital. These bright, cheerful rooms alongside the Winooski River are a local favorite for pizza fresh from wood-fired ovens, wonderfully textured homemade Italian breads, and imaginative dishes like pasta *pugliese,* which marries penne with basil, black olives, roasted eggplant, portobello mushrooms, and sun-dried tomatoes. [$] *Average main: $17* ✉ *3 Main St.* ☎ *802/223-0229* 🌐 *www.sarducci s.com* ⏲ *No lunch Sun.*

$ ✕ **The Skinny Pancake.** This dine-in creperie makes a great stop for break-
CAFÉ   fast, lunch, or an easy dinner. The Breakfast Monster, made with eggs
and local Cabot cheddar, is a winner. For lunch, try the spinach and feta
crepes, the Veggie Monster, or the Lamb Fetatastic, made with local lamb
sausage, baby spinach, Vermont feta, and kalamata olives. If you're in
the mood for dessert, sample the Nutella crepe or the Pooh Bear served
with warm local honey and cinnamon. ⓈＡverage main: $9 ⊠ 89 Main
St., Monpelier ☎ 802/262–2253 ⊕ www.skinnypancake.com.

$$ ✕ **That's Life Soup.** As the name indicates, soup is the focus of this tiny,
INTERNATIONAL   bright restaurant. The selections here are delicious and warming, per-
haps the best in the state. The ever-changing menu incorporates a truly
global influence and a lot of quirkiness, with flavors like South Ameri-
can chipotle pork stew and Tuscan ribollita. There are few tables, so
it's best to aim for off-peak hours. Ⓢ Average main: $18 ⊠ 41 Elm St.,
Montpelier ☎ 802/223–5333.

$$ ✕ **Three Penny Taproom.** This hip, lively taproom is quickly becoming one
ECLECTIC   of the best in Vermont. The Three Penny serves a wide array of craft
Fodor'sChoice   beers, including the coveted and hard-to-get Hill Farmstead. Now with
★   a full menu and expanded seating, the pub is a dining destination as
well, sharing an award for the state's best burger. The vibe feels straight
out of an artsy neighborhood in Brussels but with the earthiness of Vermont. Ⓢ Average main: $15 ⊠ 108 Main St ☎ 802/223–8277 ⊕ www.
threepennytaproom.com.

WHERE TO STAY

$$ ▦ **Inn at Montpelier.** The town's most charming lodging option, this lov-
B&B/INN   ingly tended inn dating from 1830 has rooms filled with antique four-
poster beds and Windsor chairs. **Pros:** beautiful home; relaxed central
setting; amazing porch. **Cons:** some rooms are small. Ⓢ Rooms from:
$150 ⊠ 147 Main St. ☎ 802/223–2727 ⊕ www.innatmontpelier.com
⤏ 19 rooms ⦿ Breakfast.

SHOPPING

Artisans Hand Craft Gallery. For more than 30 years, Maggie Neale has
been celebrating and supporting Vermont's craft community. Her store
houses jewelry, textiles, sculpture, and paintings by many local artists.
⊠ 89 Main St. ☎ 802/229-9492 ⊕ www.artisanshand.com.

Vermont Butter & Cheese Creamery. One of the leaders of the artisanal
cheese movement, Vermont Butter & Cheese invites curious cheese afi-
cionados to visit its 4,000-square-foot creamery where gem-like goat
cheeses such as Bonne Bouche—a perfectly balanced, cloud-like cheese—
are made weekdays. It's in Websterville, southwest of the city. ⊠ 40 Pit-
man Rd., Websterville ☎ 800/884–6287 ⊕ www.vermontcreamery.com.

Zutano. For hip newborn, baby, and toddler clothing designed in Vermont,
head to Zutano. ⊠ 79 Main St. ☎ 802/223–2229 ⊕ www.zutano.com.

EN
ROUTE   **Ben & Jerry's Ice Cream Factory.** On your way to Stowe, be sure to stop
at Ben & Jerry's Ice Cream Factory. Ben Cohen and Jerry Greenfield
began selling ice cream from a renovated gas station in Burlington in
the 1970s. The tour only skims the surface of the behind-the-scenes
goings-on at the plant—a flaw forgiven when the free samples are dished
out. ⊠ 1281 Waterbury-Stowe Rd., 1 mile north of I–89, Waterbury

☎ *802/846–1500* ⊕ *www.benjerry.com* ▨ *Tour $4* ☉ *Late Oct.–June, daily 10–6; July–mid-Aug., daily 9–9; mid-Aug.–late Oct., daily 9–7. Tours run every half hour.*

Cabot Creamery. The state's biggest cheese producer, Cabot Creamery has a visitor center where you can learn about the dairy industry. ⊠ *2878 Main St., 5 miles north of U.S. 2, Cabot* ☎ *800/837–4261* ⊕ *www. cabotcheese.coop* ▨ *$2* ☉ *June–Oct., daily 9–5; Nov., Dec., and Feb.– May, Mon.–Sat. 9–4; Jan., Mon.–Sat. 10–4.*

STOWE

22 miles northwest of Montpelier, 36 miles east of Burlington.

Fodor's Choice ★ Long before skiing came to Stowe in the 1930s, the rolling hills and valleys beneath Vermont's highest peak, 4,395-foot Mt. Mansfield, attracted summer tourists looking for a reprieve from city heat. Most stayed at one of two inns in the village of Stowe. When skiing made the town a winter destination, the arriving skiers outnumbered the hotel beds, so locals took them in. This spirit of hospitality continues, and many of these homes are now lovely country inns. The village itself is tiny, just a few blocks of shops and restaurants clustered around a picture-perfect white church with a lofty steeple, but it serves as the anchor for Mountain Road, which leads north past restaurants, lodges, and shops on its way to Stowe's fabled slopes.

ESSENTIALS

Visitor Information Stowe Area Association ☎ *802/253–7321, 877/467–8693* ⊕ *www.gostowe.com.*

EXPLORING

Trapp Family Lodge. Built by the von Trapp family of *The Sound of Music* fame, this Tyrolean lodge and its grounds are the site of a popular outdoor music series in the summer. You can hike along the trails in warm weather, or go cross-country skiing in winter. The lodge's café, overlooking a breathtaking mountain vista, serves tasty food and local beers; a ski-in cabin offers homemade soups, sandwiches, and hot chocolate. There's also a fine-dining restaurant on the premises. ⊠ *700 Trapp Hill Rd.* ☎ *802/253–8511, 800/826–7000* ⊕ *www.trappfamily.com.*

Vermont Ski and Snowboard Museum. The state's skiing and snowboarding history is documented here with myriad exhibits. ⊠ *1 S. Main St.* ☎ *802/253–9911* ⊕ *www.vtssm.com* ▨ *$5* ☉ *Wed.–Mon. noon–5.*

WHERE TO EAT

$$
AMERICAN
✕ **Harrison's Restaurant.** For an excellent dinner at a warm and unpretentious American bistro, go no further than Harrison's in downtown Stowe. A lively local scene, cozy booths by the fireplace, and a creative menu paired with a variety of fine wines and local beers make this a perfect stop for couples and families alike. Stop in for braised short ribs in blackberry-chipotle barbecue sauce, sirloin bistro steak, or lobster mac 'n' cheese made with Cabot cheddar. The bar is also inviting—it's a nice place to dine alone or chat over a drink with a local. $ *Average main: $20* ⊠ *25 Main St., behind TD Bank* ☎ *802/253–7773* ⊕ *www. harrisonsstowe.com* ⌕ *Reservations essential* ☉ *No lunch.*

$$$
ECLECTIC
Fodor'sChoice
★

✕ Hen of the Wood. Ask Vermont's great chefs where they go for a tremendous meal, and Hen of the Wood inevitably tops the list. The setting is riveting: a converted 1835 grist mill beside a waterfall. Inside the underground level of the mill, a sunken pit formerly housing the grindstone is now filled with tables, thick wood beams, and uneven stone walls dotted with tiny candles that make the ambience decidedly romantic. Sophisticated dishes showcase the abundance of local produce, meat, and cheese. A typical plate on the daily changing menu may feature goat's milk dumplings, a local farm pork loin, grass-fed rib eye, and a wild Alaskan halibut. This is very nearly the perfect Vermont dining experience. In the warmer months, beg for a coveted patio table overlooking a dramatic series of falls. A second branch of the restaurant is in Burlington. $ *Average main: $25* ⊠ *92 Stowe St., Waterbury* ☎ *802/244–7300* ⊕ *www.henofthewood.com* ⌂ *Reservations essential* ⊘ *Closed Sun. No lunch.*

$$$$
EUROPEAN

✕ Michael's on the Hill. Swiss-born chef Michael Kloeti trained in Europe and New York before opening this dining establishment in a 19th-century farmhouse outside Stowe. In addition to à la carte options, Michael's two four-course prix-fixe menus ($47 and $67) highlight European cuisine with farm-to-table earthiness, perhaps best seen in dishes like spice-roasted duck breast and venison navarin. The menu changes seasonally. $ *Average main: $32* ⊠ *4182 Stowe-Waterbury Rd., 6 miles south of Stowe, Waterbury Center* ☎ *802/244–7476* ⊕ *www. michaelsonthehill.com* ⊘ *Closed Tues. No lunch.*

$
AMERICAN

✕ Prohibition Pig. The Alchemist, a very popular downtown restaurant, closed a few years back, but new owners have brought the place roaring back to life. Prohibition Pig is just as good, with more or less the same hip look and layout of the previous incarnation. It also still serves the same fabulous local brews and barbecue-friendly bistro cuisine like duck-fat fries, roasted brisket, and pit-smoked chicken. A young, energetic crowed creates a fun vibe. $ *Average main: $12* ⊠ *23 S. Main St., Waterbury* ☎ *802/244–4120* ⊕ *prohibitionpig.com* ⊘ *No lunch Mon.–Thurs.*

$
CAFÉ

✕ Red Hen Baking Co. If you're a devotee of artisanal bakeries, it'd be a mistake not to trek the 15 miles away from Stowe to have lunch, pick up fresh baked bread, or sample a sweet treat here. Try the ham-and-cheese croissants, sticky buns, homemade soups, and savory sandwiches. Red Hen supplies bread to some of the state's best restaurants, including Hen of the Wood, and is open daily. $ *Average main: $8* ⊠ *961 Rte. 2, Middlesex* ☎ *802/223–5200* ⊕ *www.redhenbaking.com* ⌂ *Reservations not accepted* ⊘ *No dinner.*

WHERE TO STAY

$$$
B&B/INN

⬚ Green Mountain Inn. Welcoming guests since 1833, this classic redbrick inn gives you access to the buzz of downtown. **Pros:** fun location; lively tavern; and lots of character. **Cons:** farther from skiing than other area hotels. $ *Rooms from: $189* ⊠ *18 Main St.* ☎ *802/253–7301, 800/253–7302* ⊕ *www.greenmountaininn.com* ⇆ *103 rooms* ⦿ *No meals.*

$$$$
B&B/INN

⬚ Stone Hill Inn. A contemporary B&B where classical music plays in the hallways, the Stone Hill Inn has rooms with two-sink vanities and two-person whirlpools in front of double-sided fireplaces. **Pros:**

Continued on page 498

LET IT SNOW

WINTER ACTIVITIES IN VERMONT

by Elise Coroneos

SKIING AND SNOWBOARDING IN VERMONT

Less than 5 mi from the Canadian border, Jay Peak is Vermont's northernmost ski resort.

Ever since America's first ski tow opened in a farmer's pasture near Woodstock in January 1934, skiers have headed en masse to Vermont in winter. Today, 19 alpine and 30 nordic ski areas range in size and are spread across the state, from Mount Snow in the south to Jay Peak near the Canadian border. The snowmaking equipment has also become more comprehensive over the years, with more than 75% of the trails in the state using man-made snow. Here are some of the best ski areas by various categories:

GREAT FOR KIDS **Smugglers' Notch, Okemo,** and **Bromley Mountain** all offer terrific kids' programs, with classes organized by age categories and by skill level. Kids as young as 3 (4 at some ski areas) can start learning. Child care, with activities like stories, singing, and arts and crafts, are available for those too young to ski; some ski areas, like Smuggler's Notch, offer babysitting with no minimum age daytime and evening.

BEST FOR BEGINNERS Beginner terrain makes up nearly half of the mountain at **Stratton,** where options include private and group lessons for first-timers. Also good are small but family-friendly **Bolton Valley** and **Bromley Mountains,** which both designate a third of their slopes for beginners.

EXPERT TERRAIN The slopes at **Jay Peak** and massive **Killington** are most notable for their steepness and pockets of glades. About 40% of the runs at these two resorts are advanced or expert. Due to its far north location, Jay Peak tends to get the most snow, making it ideal for those skilled in plowing through fresh powder. Another favorite with advanced skiers is Central Vermont's **Mad River Glen,** where many slopes are ungroomed (natural) and the motto is "Ski it if you can." In addition, **Sugarbush, Stowe,** and **Smugglers' Notch** are all revered for their challenging untamed side country.

Mount Mansfield is better known as Stowe.   Stratton Mountain clocktower

NIGHT SKIING Come late afternoon, **Bolton Valley** is hopping. That's because it's the only location in Vermont for night skiing. Ski and ride under the lights from 4 until 8 Wednesday through Saturday, followed by a later après-ski scene.

APRÈS-SKI The social scenes at **Killington, Sugarbush,** and **Stowe** are the most noteworthy (and crowded). Warm up after a day in the snow in Killington with all-you-can-eat pizza on Monday nights and daily happy hour specials at the Outback, or stop by the always popular Wobbly Barn. For live music, try Castlerock Pub in Sugarbush or the Matterhorn Bar in Stowe.

SNOWBOARDING Boarders (and some skiers) will love the latest features for freestyle tricks in Vermont. **Stratton** has a half pipe, rail garden, and four other parks. **Mount Snow's** Carinthia Peak is an all-terrain park–dedicated mountain, the only of its kind in New England. Head to **Killington** for Burton Stash, another beautiful all-natural features terrain park. **Okemo** has a superpipe and eight terrain parks and a gladed park with all-natural features. Note that snowboarding is not allowed at skiing cooperative **Mad River Glen.**

CROSS-COUNTRY To experience the best of cross-country skiing in the state, simply follow the Catamount Trail, a 300-mile nordic route from southern Vermont to Canada. **The Trapp Family Lodge** in Stowe has 37 miles of groomed cross-country trails and 62 miles of back-country trails. Another top option is **The Mountain Top Inn & Resort,** just outside of Killington. Its Nordic Ski and Snowshoe Center provides instruction for newcomers, along with hot drinks and lunches when it is time to take a break and warm up.

TELEMARK Ungroomed snow and tree skiing are a natural fit with free-heel skiing at **Mad River Glen. Bromley** and **Jay Peak** also have telemark rentals and instruction.

MOUNTAIN-RESORT TRIP PLANNER

TIMING

■ **Snow Season.** Winter sports time is typically from Thanksgiving through April, weather permitting. Holidays are the most crowded.

■ **March Madness.** Most of the season's snow tends to come in March, so that's the time to go if you want to ski on fresh, nature-made powder. To increase your odds, choose a ski area in the northern part of the state.

■ **Summer Scene.** During summertime, many ski resorts reinvent themselves as prime destinations for golfers, zipline and canopy tours, mountain bikers, and weddings. Other summer visitors come to the mountains to enjoy hiking trails, climbing walls, aquatic centers, chairlift and horseback rides, or a variety of festivals.

■ **Avoid Long Lift Lines.** Try to hit the slopes early—many lifts start at 8 or 9 am, with ticket windows opening a half-hour earlier. Then take a mid-morning break as lines start to get longer and head out again when others come in for lunch.

SAVINGS TIPS

■ **Choose a Condo.** Especially if you're planning to stay for a week, save money on food by opting for a condominum unit with a kitchen. You can shop at the supermarket and cook breakfast and dinner.

■ **Rent Smart.** Consider ski rental options in the villages rather than those at the mountain. Renting right at the ski area may be more convenient, but it may also cost more.

■ **Discount Lift Tickets.** Online tickets are often the least expensive; multi-day discounts and and ski-and-stay packages will also lower your costs. Good for those who can plan ahead, early-bird tickets often go on sale before the ski season even starts.

■ **Hit the Peaks Off-peak.** In order to secure the best deals at the most competitive rates, avoid booking during school holidays. President's Week in February is the busiest, because that's when Northeastern schools have their spring break.

Top left, Killington's six mountains make up the largest ski area in Vermont. Top right, Stratton has a Snowboard-cross course.

THINK WARM THOUGHTS

It can get cold on the slopes, so be prepared. Consider proper face warmth and smart layering, plus ski-specific socks, or purchase a pair each of inexpensive hand and feet warmers that fit easily in your gloves and boots. Helmets, which can also be rented, provide not only added safety but warmth.

VERMONT SKI AREAS BY THE NUMBERS

Okemo's wide slopes attract snowbirds to Ludlow in Central Vermont.

Numbers are a helpful way to compare mountains, but remember that each resort has a distinct personality. This list is composed of ski areas in Vermont with at least 100 skiable acres. For more information, see individual resort listings.

SKI AREA	Vertical Drop	Skiable Acres	# of Trails & Lifts	Terrain Type ●	■	◆◆◆	Snowboarding Options
Bolton Valley	1,704	300	70/6	36%	37%	27%	Terrain park
Bromley	1,334	178	46/10	32%	37%	31%	Terrain park
Burke Mountain	2,011	270	50/6	10%	44%	46%	Terrain park
Jay Peak	2,153	385	78/22	22%	39%	41%	Terrain park
Killington	3,050	752	155/22	28%	33%	39%	Terrain park, Half-pipe
Mad River Glen	2,037	115	45/9	30%	30%	40%	Snowboarding not allowed
Mount Snow	1,700	588	80/20	14%	73%	13%	Terrain park, Half-pipe
Okemo	2,200	655	120/19	31%	38%	31%	Terrain park, Superpipe, RossCross terrain cross park
Pico Mountain	1,967	468	57/7	18%	46%	36%	Triple Slope, terrain park
Smugglers' Notch	2,610	311	78/8	19%	50%	31%	Terrain park
Stowe	2,160	485	116/13	16%	59%	25%	Terrain park, Half-pipe
Stratton	2,003	625	97/11	42%	31%	27%	Terrain park, Half-pipe, Snowboardcross course
Sugarbush	2,600	578	111/16	20%	45%	35%	Terrain park

CONTACT THE EXPERTS

Ski Vermont (☏ *802/223-2439* ⊕ *www. skivermont.com*), a non-profit association in Montpelier, Vermont, and **Vermont Department of Tourism** (⊕ *www.vermontvacation. com*) are great resources for travelers planning a wintertime trip to Vermont.

KNOW YOUR SIGNS

On trail maps and the mountains, trails are rated and marked:

● Beginner   ◆ Advanced

■ Intermediate   ◆◆ Expert

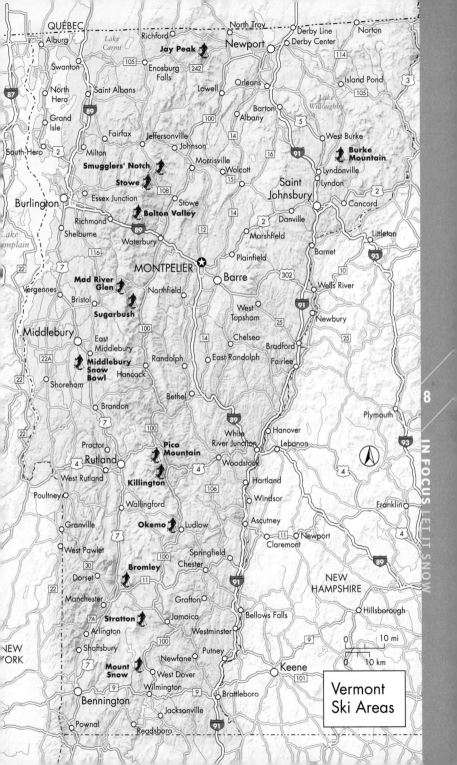

QUÉBEC

Alburg

Lake Carmi

Richford
North Troy
Newport
Derby Line
Derby Center
Norton

Jay Peak

Swanton

Enosburg Falls

105

242

Orleans

Island Pond

114

105

3

North Hero

Saint Albans

Lowell

Barton

Albany

5

West Burke

Lyndonville

Burke Mountain

16

91

Grand Isle

Fairfax

Jeffersonville

Johnson

100

14

Saint Johnsbury

Lyndon

2

South Hero

87

89

2

Milton

Morrisville

Wolcott

Concord

Smugglers' Notch

15

Essex Junction

Stowe

108

Stowe

Burlington

Bolton Valley

Danville

Littleton

Richmond

Shelburne

Waterbury

12

14

Marshfield

2

Barnet

93

Lake Champlain

116

Plainfield

Wells River

10

22

7

MONTPELIER

Barre

302

91

Newbury

Vergennes

Mad River Glen

Northfield

West Topsham

25

Bristol

Sugarbush

Chelsea

Bradford

25

Middlebury

East Middlebury

100

14

East Randolph

Fairlee

22A

Randolph

Hancock

Middlebury Snow Bowl

Shoreham

Bethel

Brandon

22

7

100

White River Junction

Hanover

Plymouth

93

Proctor

Pico Mountain

Woodstock

Lebanon

Rutland

4

Killington

Hartland

4

Franklin

4

West Rutland

106

Windsor

Poultney

Wallingford

Ascutney

11

Newport

89

Granville

7

Okemo

Ludlow

Claremont

West Pawlet

100

Springfield

Chester

30

Bromley

NEW HAMPSHIRE

Dorset

11

Manchester

Grafton

Hillsborough

7A

Stratton

Jamaica

Bellows Falls

Arlington

Westminster

Shaftsbury

100

Newfane

Putney

9

NEW YORK

7

Mount Snow

West Dover

Keene

Bennington

9

Wilmington

9

Brattleboro

101

Jacksonville

Pownal

Readsboro

91

8

IN FOCUS LET IT SNOW

0   10 mi
0   10 km

Vermont Ski Areas

very comfortable rooms; convenient location. **Cons:** grounds could use a bit of grooming. $ *Rooms from: $380* ⊠ *89 Houston Farm Rd.* ☎ *802/253–6282* ⊕ *www.stonehillinn.com* ⤴ *9 rooms* ⊚ *Breakfast.*

$$$$ ⊞ **Stoweflake Mountain Resort and Spa.** With one of the largest spas in the
RESORT area, Stowflake lets you enjoy a hydrotherapy waterfall that cascades into a hot tub, an herb and flower labyrinth, and a fitness center reached via a covered bridge. **Pros:** nice spa; wide range of rooms. **Cons:** maze-like layout can make rooms a bit hard to find. $ *Rooms from: $279* ⊠ *1746 Mountain Rd.* ☎ *802/253–7355* ⊕ *www.stoweflake.com* ⤴ *120 rooms, 60 town houses* ⊚ *No meals.*

$ ⊞ **Stowe Motel & Snowdrift.** This family-owned motel sits on 16 acres
HOTEL across the river from one of the area's favorite hiking trails. **Pros:**
FAMILY inexpensive rates; complimentary bikes; friendly game room. **Cons:** motel-style accommodations. $ *Rooms from: $120* ⊠ *2043 Mountain Rd.* ☎ *802/253–7629, 800/829–7629* ⊕ *www.stowemotel.com* ⤴ *52 rooms, 4 suites, 4 houses* ⊚ *Breakfast.*

$$$$ ⊞ **Stowe Mountain Lodge.** At the base of the ski slopes, Stowe Mountain
RESORT Lodge would be king of the hill for location alone, but a stay here
Fodor'sChoice also treats to you many perks. **Pros:** perfect setting; great concierge;
★ activities galore. **Cons:** somewhat sterile feel; no separate kids' pool. $ *Rooms from: $350* ⊠ *7412 Mountain Rd.* ☎ *802/253–3560* ⊕ *www. stowemountainlodge.com* ⤴ *312 rooms* ⊚ *No meals.*

$$$$ ⊞ **Topnotch Resort.** On 120 acres overlooking Mt. Mansfield, this posh
RESORT property has a contemporary look and an outstanding spa. **Pros:**
Fodor'sChoice outdoor heated pool facing the mountains; impeccable service; fam-
★ ily-friendly atmosphere. **Cons:** boutique style may not be for every-one. $ *Rooms from: $250* ⊠ *4000 Mountain Rd.* ☎ *802/253–8585, 800/451–8686* ⊕ *www.topnotchresort.com* ⤴ *71 rooms, 9 suites, 14 town houses* ⊚ *Multiple meal plans.*

NIGHTLIFE AND THE ARTS

THE ARTS

Spruce Peak Performing Arts Center. This center hosts a wide variety of visual and performing arts, including theater, music, and dance. ⊠ *122 Hourglass Dr.* ☎ *802/760–4634* ⊕ *www.sprucepeakarts.org.*

NIGHTLIFE

Matterhorn. This nightspot hosts live music and dancing on week-ends during the ski season. If you'd rather just watch, there's a sep-arate martini bar. ⊠ *4969 Mountain Rd.* ☎ *802/253–8198* ⊕ *www. matterhornbar.com.*

SPORTS AND THE OUTDOORS

CANOEING AND KAYAKING

Umiak Outdoor Outfitters. This full-service outfitter rents canoes and kay-aks. It has outposts on the Winooski River in Waterbury, at North Beach in Burlington, and on the Lamoille River in Jeffersonville. ⊠ *849 S. Main St.* ☎ *802/253–2317* ⊕ *www.umiak.com.*

FISHING

The Fly Rod Shop. This shop provides a guide service, offers fly-tying and casting classes, and rents tackle and other equipment. ⊠ *2703 Waterbury Rd., 1½ miles south of Stowe* ☎ *802/253–7346* ⊕ *www. flyrodshop.com.*

GOLF

Stowe Country Club. A scenic 18-hole golf course, a driving range, and a putting green are available at Stowe Country Club. ⊠ *744 Cape Cod Rd.* ☎ *802/253–4893* ⛳ *Greens fee: $65–$115* ⊙ *18 holes, 6,185 yards, par 72.*

HIKING

Mt. Mansfield. Ascending Mt. Mansfield makes for a challenging day hike. Trails lead from Mountain Road to the summit, where they meet the north-to-south Long Trail. Views take in New Hampshire's White Mountains, New York's Adirondacks, and southern Québec. The Green Mountain Club publishes a trail guide. ⊠ *Mountain Rd.* ☎ *802/244– 7037* ⊕ *www.greenmountainclub.org.*

SLEDDING

FAMILY **Peacepups Dog Sledding.** This company offers two-hour day tours and one-hour night tours using a team of eight Siberian huskies. You can ride inside a padded toboggan or join in the driving using a two-person tandem sled. The cost is $275 per day or $175 at night. If you prefer to walk the trails yourself, snowshoe rentals are also available. ⊠ *239 Cross Rd., Lake Elmore* ☎ *802/888–7733* ⊕ *www.peacepupsdogsledding.com* ⊙ *Mid-Dec.–Mar., Wed. and Fri.–Sun. at 10, noon, and 2.*

SKI AREA

Stowe Mountain Resort. The name of the village is Stowe and the name of the mountain is Mt. Mansfield, but to generations of skiers, the area, it's all just plain Stowe. The area's mystique attracts as many serious skiers as social ones. Improved snowmaking, new lifts, and free shuttle buses that gather skiers from lodges, inns, and motels along Mountain Road have made Stowe much more convenient. Yet the traditions remain: the Winter Carnival in January and the Sugar Slalom in April, to name two. Three base lodges provide the essentials, including two on-mountain restaurants.

The resort has 27 miles of groomed cross-country trails and 18 miles of backcountry trails. Four interconnecting cross-country ski areas have more than 90 miles of groomed trails within the town of Stowe. Mt. Mansfield, with an elevation of 4,395 feet and a vertical drop of 2,360 feet, is one of the giants among Eastern ski mountains. Its symmetrical shape allows skiers of all abilities long, satisfying runs from the summit. The famous Front Four (National, Liftline, Starr, and Goat) are the intimidating expert runs, yet there is plenty of intermediate skiing and one long beginner trail. Mansfield's satellite sector is a network of intermediate trails and one expert trail off a basin served by a gondola. Spruce Peak, separate from the main mountain, is a teaching hill and offers a pleasant experience for intermediates and beginners.

In addition to the high-speed, eight-passenger gondola, Stowe has 13 lifts, including two quads, two triples, and four double chairlifts, a carpet lift, plus one handle tow, to service its 116 trails. Night-skiing trails are accessed by the gondola. The resort has 80% snowmaking coverage. Snowboard facilities include a half pipe and two terrain parks—one for beginners, at Spruce Peak, and one for experts, on the Mt. Mansfield side. Children's programs are headquartered at Spruce Peak, with ski-school programs for ages 3 to 12. ⊠ *5781 Mountain Rd.* ☎ *802/253–3000, 802/253–3600 snow conditions* ⊕ *www.stowe.com.*

SHOPPING AND SPAS

In Stowe, Mountain Road is lined with shops from town up toward the ski area. North of Stowe, shops line Route 100 from Interstate 89.

FOOD

Cabot Cheese Annex Store. In addition to the shelves of Vermont-made jams, mustards, crackers, and maple products, the store features a long central table with samples of a dozen Cabot cheeses. ⊠ *2657 Waterbury-Stowe Rd., 2½ miles north of I–89* ☎ *802/244–6334* ⊕ *www.cabotcheese.coop.*

FAMILY
Fodor's Choice
★

Cold Hollow Cider Mill. Watch apples pressed into fabulous cider at the Cold Hollow Cider Mill. The on-site store also sells apple butter, jams and jellies, and Vermont-made handicrafts. Kids get free cider popsicles. ⊠ *3600 Waterbury-Stowe Rd., 3 miles north of I–89, Waterbury Center* ☎ *800/327–7537* ⊕ *www.coldhollow.com.*

SPAS

Spa at Stoweflake. One of the largest spas in New England, the Spa at Stoweflake features a massaging hydrotherapeutic waterfall, a Hungarian mineral pool, 30 treatment rooms, and 120 services like the Bingham Falls Renewal, named after a local waterfall. This treatment begins with a body scrub and a Vichy shower, followed by an aromatherapy oil massage. The spacious men's and women's sanctuaries have saunas, steam rooms, and whirlpool tubs. ⊠ *Stoweflake Mountain resort and Spa, 1746 Mountain Rd.* ☎ *802/760–1083* ⊕ *www.stoweflake.com.*

Spa at Topnotch. An aura of calm pervades the Spa at Topnotch, with its birchwood doors and accents, natural light, and cool colors. Signature services include the Mount Mansfield Saucha, a three-stage herbal body treatment, and the Little River Stone Massage, which uses's the resort's own wood-spice oil. Locker areas are spacious and spotless, with saunas, steam rooms, and whirlpool tubs. Classes in tai chi, yoga, and Pilates are offered throughout the day in the nearby fitness center. ⊠ *Topnotch Resort and Spa, 4000 Mountain Rd.* ☎ *802/253–6463* ⊕ *www.topnotchresort.com.*

Spa and Wellness Center at Stowe Mountain Lodge. This 21,000-square-foot facility has 19 treatment rooms, a fitness center, and an outdoor pool and hot tub. In addition to the expected array of facials, scrubs, and massages for adults, the spa offers a separate program for kids. ⊠ *Stowe Mountain Lodge, 7412 Mountain Rd.* ☎ *802/253–3560* ⊕ *www.stowemountainlodge.com.*

JEFFERSONVILLE

30 miles west of Craftsbury, 18 miles north of Stowe.

Jeffersonville is just over Smugglers' Notch from Stowe but miles away in feel and attitude. In summer you can drive over the notch road as it curves precipitously around boulders that have fallen from the cliffs above, then pass open meadows and old farmhouses and sugar shacks on the way down to town. Below the notch, Smugglers' Notch Ski Resort is the hub of activity year-round. Downtown Jeffersonville, once home to an artists' colony, is quiet but has excellent dining and nice art galleries.

EXPLORING

Boyden Valley Winery. West of Jeffersonville, this winery conducts tours and tastings and showcases an excellent selection of Vermont specialty products and local handicrafts. The winery's Big Barn Red is satisfyingly full-bodied, but the real fun may be in the ice wines, maple creme liqueur, and hard cider. ⊠ *Junction of Rtes. 15 and 104, Cambridge* ☎ *802/644–8151* ⊕ *www.boydenvalley.com* ☼ *Daily 10–5.*

WHERE TO EAT AND STAY

$$
AMERICAN

✕ **158 Main Restaurant & Bakery.** The best and most popular restaurant in Jeffersonville, 158 Main easily earns its accolades. For breakfast, locals love the "Two Eggs Basic," which comes with two eggs any style, homemade toast, and home fries for $4. Portions are big; prices are not. Menu selections for dinner range from sesame-seared yellowfin tuna with wok-seared vegetables to hanger steak with a maple-chipotle sauce. Sunday brunch is very popular. Ⓢ *Average main: $16* ⊠ *158 Main St.* ☎ *802/644–8100* ⊕ *www.158Main.com* ⚑ *Reservations not accepted* ☼ *Closed Mon. No dinner Sun.*

$$$$
RESORT
FAMILY
Fodor'sChoice
★

🏨 **Smugglers' Notch Resort.** With four giant water parks for summer fun and just about every winter activity imaginable, this family resort has amenities other places can only dream about. **Pros:** great place for families to learn to ski. **Cons:** not a romantic getaway for couples. Ⓢ *Rooms from: $388* ⊠ *4323 Rte. 108 S* ☎ *802/644–8851, 800/419–4615* ⊕ *www.smuggs.com* ⇆ *600 condominiums* ⦿ *No meals.*

SPORTS AND THE OUTDOORS

KAYAKING

Vermont Canoe and Kayak. This outfitter rents canoes and kayaks for use on the Lamoille River and leads guided canoe trips to Boyden Valley Winery. ⊠ *4807 Rte. 15* ☎ *802/644–8336* ⊕ *www.vermontcanoeandkayak. com.*

LLAMA RIDES

Applecheek Farm. Applecheek Farm runs daytime and evening hay and sleigh rides, llama treks, and farm tours. ⊠ *567 McFarlane Rd., Hyde Park* ☎ *802/888–4482* ⊕ *www.applecheekfarm.com.*

Northern Vermont Llama Co. These llamas carry everything, including snacks and lunches for half-day treks along the trails of Smugglers' Notch. Advance reservations are essential for the trips, offered from late May to Labor Day. ⊠ *766 Lapland Rd., Waterville* ☎ *802/644–2257* ⊕ *www.northernvermontllamaco.com.*

SKI AREA

FAMILY   **Smugglers' Notch.** The "granddaddy of all family resorts," Smuggler's Notch consistently wins accolades for its family programs. Its children's ski school is one of the best in the country—possibly *the* best—but there are challenges for skiers of all levels. This was the first ski area in the East to designate a triple-black-diamond run, the Black Hole.

The self-contained village has outdoor ice-skating and snow tubing. For Nordic skiing, the area has 18 miles of groomed and tracked trails and 12 miles of snowshoe trails. For downhill skiing, the resort has three mountains. The highest, Madonna, with a vertical drop of 2,610 feet, has trails connecting it to 1,500-foot Sterling. The third mountain, 1,150-foot Morse, can be reached via trails and a shuttle bus.

The tops of each of the mountains have expert terrain—a couple of double-black diamonds and a triple-black-diamond make Madonna memorable. Intermediate trails fill the lower sections, and Morse has many beginner trails. The 78 trails are served by eight lifts, including six chairs and two surface lifts. Top-to-bottom snowmaking allows for 62% coverage. There are five terrain parks, including one for beginners. A snowboarding park is for kids three to six. There's a full roster of summertime amenities, including waterslides, hiking programs, a treetop obstacle course, a zipline canopy tour, and crafts workshops. ✉ *4323 Rte. 108 S* ☎ *802/644–8851, 800/419–4615* ⊕ *www.smuggs.com.*

SHOPPING

ANTIQUES

Route 15 between Jeffersonville and Johnson is dubbed the "antiques highway."

Smugglers' Notch Antiques. In a rambling barn, this shop sells antiques, collectibles, and custom-made furniture from 60 dealers. ✉ *906 Rte. 108 S* ☎ *802/644–2100* ⊕ *smugglersnotchantiques.com.*

CLOTHING

Fodor'sChoice   **Johnson Woolen Mills.** This factory store has great deals on woolen blan-
★   kets, household goods, and the famous Johnson outerwear. ✉ *51 Lower Main St. E, 9 miles east of Jeffersonville, Johnson* ☎ *802/635–2271* ⊕ *www.johnsonwoolenmills.com.*

BURLINGTON

31 miles southwest of Jeffersonville, 76 miles south of Montreal, 349 miles north of New York City, 223 miles northwest of Boston.

Fodor'sChoice   As you drive along Main Street toward downtown Burlington, it's easy
★   to see why this four-college city is so often called one of the most livable small cities in the United States. Downtown is filled with hip restaurants and bars, art galleries, and the Church Street Marketplace—a bustling pedestrian mall with trendy shops, crafts vendors, street performers, and sidewalk cafés. Just beyond, Lake Champlain shimmers beneath the towering Adirondacks on the New York shore. On the shores of the lake, Burlington's revitalized waterfront teems with outdoors enthusiasts who bike or stroll along its recreation path, picnic on the grass, and ply the waters in sailboats and motor craft in summer.

BURLINGTON'S LOCAL FOOD MOVEMENT

Burlington is exploding on the national food scene as one of the hubs of the local food movement. Known for its excellent soil and abundance of local organic farms—as showcased in its huge weekly farmers' market (Saturday, May through October) and popular outdoor summertime farm suppers—this health-conscious and liberal city is home to restaurants and markets with a foodie's focus on fresh, high-quality ingredients rivaling those of a much larger city. Burlington residents are likely to be seen biking to pick up their weekly CSA share at the Intervale (the city's huge web of community gardens), doing some weeding in their own urban garden plots, or stopping by one of the farms to pick berries or flowers on their way to a dinner party.

EXPLORING

FAMILY **ECHO Lake Aquarium and Science Center.** This center gives kids and adults a chance to learn about the Lake Champlain region through more than 100 interactive exhibits. You can also get an up-close look at 70 species of indigenous animals. ⊠ *1 College St.* ☎ *802/864–1848* ⊕ *www. echovermont.org* ☒ *$13.50* ⊗ *Daily 10–5.*

Ethan Allen Homestead Museum. When Vermont hero Ethan Allen retired from his revolutionary activities, he purchased 350 acres along the Winooski River and built this modest cabin in 1787. The original structure is a real slice of 18th-century life, including such frontier hallmarks as saw-cut boards and an open hearth for cooking. A kitchen garden resembles the one the Allens would have had. There's also a visitor center and miles of biking and hiking trails. In warmer months, climb Ethan Allen Tower at the west end of the property for stupendous views of Lake Champlain and the Green Mountains. Don't forget mosquito repellent. ⊠ *1 Ethan Allen Homestead, off Rte. 127* ☎ *802/865–4556* ⊕ *www.ethanallenhomestead.org* ☒ *$7* ⊗ *May–Oct., Thurs.–Mon. 10–4.*

Magic Hat Brewing Company. You can tour the Magic Hat brewery, which puts out 400 bottles a minute. The free tour includes free beer samples and the Growler Bar has 48 beers on tap. ⊠ *5 Bartlett Bay Rd., South Burlington* ☎ *802/658–2739* ⊕ *magichat.net* ☒ *Free* ⊗ *Mon.–Sat. 10–6, Sun. noon–5.*

University of Vermont. Crowning the hilltop above Burlington is the University of Vermont, known as UVM for the abbreviation of its Latin name, Universitas Viridis Montis, meaning the University of the Green Mountains. With more than 10,000 students, this is the state's principal institution of higher learning. The most architecturally impressive buildings face the green and have gorgeous lake views, as does the statue of founder Ira Allen, Ethan's brother. ⊠ *85 South Prospect St.* ☎ *802/656–3131* ⊕ *www.uvm.edu.*

WHERE TO EAT

$$ ✕ **American Flatbread Burlington.** It might be worth going to college in
PIZZA   Burlington just to be able to gather with friends at this wildly popular
Fodor's Choice   organic pizza place. Seating is first-come, first-served, and the scene is
★   bustling with locals and visitors sipping house-made brews. The wood-
fired clay dome is where the cooks create delicious pies like the Punc-
tuated Equilibrium, which has kalamata olives, roasted red peppers,
goat cheese, fresh rosemary, red onions, mozzarella, and garlic. Fresh
salads topped with locally made cheese are also popular. Here's to the
college life! $ *Average main: $17* ⊠ *115 St. Paul St.* ☎ *802/861–2999*
⊕ *americanflatbread.com* ⚐ *Reservations not accepted.*

$$$ ✕ **Bluebird Tavern.** Hidden away off the main downtown drag, this trendy
MODERN   bistro is a foodie favorite, with a chic French-bistro setting, open-air
AMERICAN   kitchen, and a fabulous bar serving some of the best cocktails in town.
It's also one of the few places in town to serve the coveted Hill Farm-
stead beer. Try the Sunday night suppers for local comfort food, or come
any night for mussels, oysters, burgers, and homemade pasta. If you
prefer a more intimate feel, dine at the bar. $ *Average main: $25* ⊠ *86
St Paul St.* ☎ *802/540–1786* ⊕ *www.bluebirdvermont.com.*

$ ✕ **Bove's.** Since 1941, this petite old-school eatery has been feeding Bur-
ITALIAN   lingtonians tasty and affordable Italian cuisine. Now in the third generation, the family and its fabulous lasagna and spaghetti are held deep
in the hearts of locals. The dishes have remained mostly unchanged,
making them the city's most time-tested fare. $ *Average main: $8* ⊠ *68
Pearl St.* ☎ *802/864–6651* ⊕ *www.boves.com* ☉ *Closed Sun. and Mon.
No lunch Tues.–Thurs.*

$$ ✕ **Farmhouse Tap & Grill.** This is one of the most popular restaurants
AMERICAN   in town, so don't be put off by the line on a typical weekend night.
Fodor's Choice   Known for using only local beef, cheese, and produce, this farm-to-table
★   experience is laid-back in style but one of the finest meals in the area.
Specialities include excellent burgers, chicken and biscuits, wonderful
local cheese and charcuterie plates, and a great wine and craft-beer
selection. ■TIP→ **Put your name on the list and have a drink at the cozy
downstairs Tap Room or the outdoor beer garden while you wait.** If the
wait feels too long, try El Cortijo, its small taqueria down the street, for
locally raised beef or chicken tacos and terrific margaritas. $ *Average
main: $18* ⊠ *160 Bank St.* ☎ *802/859–0888* ⊕ *www.farmhousetg.com.*

$$$$ ✕ **Guild and Company Steakhouse.** Vermont's best steak can be found
STEAKHOUSE   roasting over hardwood coals in the open kitchens of Guild and Com-
pany. All the meat is sourced from local farms, dry-aged a minimum of
21 days, and cooked to absolute perfection. The space itself is also a
treat, with antique chicken feeders serving as light fixtures and a soap-
stone-topped bar in the center. Lighter fare is available, but make sure
at least one person in your party orders the rib eye. $ *Average main:
$48* ⊠ *1633 Williston Rd.* ☎ *802/497–1207* ⊕ *www.guildandcompany.
com* ☉ *No lunch.*

$$$ ✕ **Hen of the Wood Burlington.** Arguably Vermont's best restaurant, Hen of
MODERN   the Wood has yielded to the desires of its ravenous fans with a branch in
AMERICAN   Burlington. With a more urban feel than that of the original location in
Fodor's Choice   Waterbury, the restaurant serves the same inventive yet down-to-earth
★   cuisine that sets diners' hearts aflutter and tongues wagging. Drop your

Vermont by Bike

Road biking in the Green Mountains.

Vermont has more than 16,000 miles of roads, and almost 80% of them are town roads that see little high-speed traffic, making them ideal for scenic bike rides. More than half are dirt roads, making them especially suitable for mountain biking. Although mountain-bike trails and old farm and logging roads wind through the Green Mountain State, most are on private property and are, therefore, not mapped. Several mountain-biking centers around the state have extensive trail networks (and maps) that will keep avid fat-tire fans happy for a few hours or a few days. To road bike in Vermont, you'll want a map and preferably a bicycle with at least 10 gears. The only roads that prohibit cycling are the four-lane highways and Routes 7 and 4 in Rutland.

TOP ROAD BIKING ROUTES:
To make a relatively easy 16-mile loop, begin at the blinker on U.S. 7 in **Shelburne** and follow Mt. Philo Road south to Hinesburg Road, then west

to Charlotte. Lake Road, Orchard Road, and Mouth of River Road go past orchards and berry fields. Bostwick Road returns to U.S. 7.

In the heart of the central Green Mountains is a moderate 18-mile loop on Routes 4, 100, and 100A that passes Calvin Coolidge's home in **Plymouth Notch.**

West of **Rutland** is a beautiful 27-mile ride on Routes 140, 30, and 133 that passes swimming holes, then hugs the shore of Lake St. Catherine. Start in Middletown Springs.

A scenic 43-mile ride in the **Northeast Kingdom** passes through pleasant Peacham and the birches and maples of Groton State Forest. Start in Danville and follow Peacham Road, then Routes 302 and 232 and U.S. 2.

For a real test, try the 48-mile ride over **Middlebury and Brandon Gaps** on Routes 125 and 73, which connect via Routes 153 and 100.

8

finger anywhere on the menu and you can't go wrong, especially with dishes like brown butter crepes stuffed with chanterelles and smoked bluefish toast in buttermilk. If you ever need to say "I love you," this is the place. [$] *Average main: $27* ✉ *55 Cherry St.* ☎ *802/540–0534* 🌐 *www.henofthewood.com* 🕓 *No lunch.*

$$$$ AMERICAN 🍴 **Juniper.** The Hotel Vermont has generated excitement not just for its new-school accommodations, but also for its ground-floor restaurant and bar. Its delightful design—a perfect blend of boutique chic and real Vermont, with reclaimed, antique, red-oak floors; black granite walls; and a free-flowing layout—is only part of the fun. The rest is in the inventive menu, which includes juniper-roasted quail and apple-wood-smoked pickled eggs, and possibly the best cocktail list in town. Weather permitting, you can stay toasty on the outdoor patio with its central fire pit. [$] *Average main: $29* ✉ *41 Cherry St.* ☎ *802/651–5027* 🌐 *www.hotelvt.com/dining-drinking/juniper* 🕓 *No lunch.*

$$$ CAFÉ 🍴 **Leunig's Bistro & Cafe.** This popular café delivers alfresco bistro cuisine, a friendly European-style bar, and live jazz. Favorite entrées include salade Niçoise, *soupe au pistou,* and beef bourguignon. Fans of crème brûlée: this place makes the best in town. A prix-fixe dinner for two goes for $30, and it's one of the city's best bargains. An expanded upstairs lounge offers cocktails, a nice wine selection, and local cheese plates and other light fare. This is a great spot for weekend brunch. [$] *Average main: $28* ✉ *115 Church St.* ☎ *802/863–3759* 🌐 *www.leunigsbistro.com.*

$ AMERICAN FAMILY 🍴 **Penny Cluse Cafe.** This popular breakfast and brunch spot is often busy and buzzing with activity. Weekend lines can be long, but locals think it's worth the wait for the famous gingerbread-blueberry pancakes, warm buscuits with herb gravy, huevos rancheros, and homemade banana bread. [$] *Average main: $10* ✉ *169 Cherry St.* ☎ *802/651–8834* 🌐 *www.pennycluse.com* 🕓 *No dinner.*

$$ CHINESE 🍴 **A Single Pebble.** The creative, authentic Chinese fare served on the first floor of this charming residential row house includes traditional clay-pot dishes as well as wok specialties like beef with fresh baby bok choy and chicken with peanuts and chili peppers. The dry-fried green beans (sautéed with flecks of pork, black beans, preserved vegetables, and garlic) are a house specialty, as is "mock eel," braised shiitake mushrooms served in a crispy ginger sauce. All dishes can be made without meat. ■ **TIP→ Try the dim sum on Sunday from 11:30–1:45.** [$] *Average main: $20* ✉ *133 Bank St.* ☎ *802/865–5200* 🌐 *www.asinglepebble.com* ✍ *Reservations essential.*

$$$ ITALIAN 🍴 **Trattoria Delia.** If you didn't manage a trip to Umbria this year, the next best thing is this charming Italian country eatery around the corner from City Hall Park. Game and fresh produce are the stars; try the wild boar braised in red wine, tomatoes, rosemary, and sage served on soft polenta. Wood-grilled items are also a specialty. In winter, try to reserve a table near the fire. [$] *Average main: $25* ✉ *152 St. Paul St.* ☎ *802/864–5253* 🌐 *www.trattoriadelia.com* ✍ *Reservations essential* 🕓 *No lunch.*

$ AMERICAN 🍴 **Zabby and Elf's Stone Soup.** A perfect place to stop for a delicious and healthful lunch or early dinner, Stone Soup offers all-local produce and organic ingredients showcased in fresh salads, wonderful soups, homemade breads, and a wide array of baked goods. There are many veggie and vegan options. $ *Average main: $12* ✉ *211 College St.* ☎ *802/862–7616* ⊕ *www.stonesoupvt.com* ��� *Closed Sun.*

WHERE TO STAY

$$$$
HOTEL
Fodor'sChoice
★

🏨 **Hotel Vermont.** Ever since the Hotel Vermont opened its doors in 2013, guests have been stepping inside with acute curiosity and walking out with copious praise. **Pros:** destination restaurant; gorgeous rooms; unbelievable service. **Cons:** luxury doesn't come cheap. $ *Rooms from: $299* ✉ *41 Cherry St.* ☎ *802/651–0080* ⊕ *www.hotelvt.com* 💤 *120 rooms, 5 suites* ⎟◎⎟ *No meals.*

$$
B&B/INN

🏨 **The Lang House on Main Street.** Within walking distance of downtown but in the historic hill section of town, this grand 1881 Victorian home charms completely with its period furnishings, fine woodwork, plaster detailing, and stained-glass windows. **Pros:** family-friendly vibe; interesting location; well run. **Cons:** no elevator. $ *Rooms from: $165* ✉ *360 Main St.* ☎ *802/652–2500, 877/919–9799* ⊕ *www.langhouse. com* 💤 *11 rooms* ⎟◎⎟ *Breakfast.*

$$
B&B/INN

🏨 **Willard Street Inn.** High in the historic hill section of Burlington, this ivy-covered house with an exterior marble staircase and English gardens incorporates elements of Queen Anne and Georgian Revival styles. **Pros:** innkeepers passionate about their job; lots of friendly attention. **Cons:** a tad old-fashioned; walk to downtown can be a drag in winter. $ *Rooms from: $170* ✉ *349 S. Willard St.* ☎ *802/651–8710, 800/577– 8712* ⊕ *www.willardstreetinn.com* 💤 *14 rooms* ⎟◎⎟ *Breakfast.*

NIGHTLIFE AND THE ARTS

THE ARTS

Fodor'sChoice
★

Flynn Center for the Performing Arts. A grandiose art-deco gem, the Flynn Theatre is the cultural heart of Burlington. In addition to being home to Vermont's largest musical theater company, it also hosts the Vermont Symphony Orchestra as well as big-name acts like Neko Case, Elvis Costello, and the like. The adjacent Flynn Space is a coveted spot for more off-beat, experimental performances. ✉ *153 Main St.* ☎ *802/863– 5966* ⊕ *www.flynncenter.org.*

NIGHTLIFE

The Farmhouse Tap & Grill. The Tap Room, downstairs from the hugely popular Farmhouse Tap & Grill, serves a wide range of local artisan beers, wines, and small plates in a cozy and buzzing fireside setting reminiscent of a Colorado lodge tavern. Featuring local foods—try the great cheese plates—and a seasonal outdoor beer garden in summertime, this is the place to see and be seen in downtown Burlington. It's also one of just four places in town to get the coveted Hill Farmstead beer on tap. ✉ *160 Bank St.* ☎ *802/859–0888* ⊕ *www. farmhousetg.com.*

Higher Ground. When you feel like shaking it up to live music, come to Higher Ground—it gets the lion's share of local and national musicians. ✉ *1214 Williston Rd., South Burlington* ☎ *802/652–0777* ⊕ *www. highergroundmusic.com.*

Nectar's. The band Phish got its start at Nectar's, which is always jumping to the sounds of local bands and never charges a cover. Don't leave

8

Burlington's pedestrian-only Church Street Marketplace and the nearby shores of Lake Champlain are great for exploring.

without a helping of the bar's famous fries and gravy. ✉ *188 Main St.* ☎ *802/658–4771* ⊕ *www.liveatnectars.com.*

Vermont Pub & Brewery. Vermont's first brewpub still makes its own beer and remains a popular spot, especially in warm weather when locals head to the outdoor patio. Folk musicians play here regularly. ✉ *144 College St.* ☎ *802/865–0500* ⊕ *www.vermontbrewery.com.*

SPORTS AND THE OUTDOORS

BEACHES

FAMILY **North Beach.** Along Burlington's "new" North End, a long line of beaches stretches to the Winooski River delta, beginning with North Beach, which has a grassy picnic area, snack bar, and boat rentals. Neighboring Leddy Park offers a more secluded beach. **Amenities:** food and drink; lifeguards; parking (fee); showers; toilets. **Best for:** partiers; swimming; walking; windsurfing. ✉ *North Beach Park, 52 Institute Rd., off North Ave.* ☎ *802/864–0123* ⊕ *www.enjoyburlington.com/ northbeach.cfm.*

BIKING

FAMILY **Burlington Bike Path.** Anyone who's put the rubber to the pedal on the 7.5-
Fodor's Choice mile Burlington Bike Path and its almost equally long northern exten-
★ sion on the Island Line Trail sings its praises. Along the way there are endless postcard views of Lake Champlain and the Adirondack Mountains. The northern end of the trail is slightly more rugged and windswept, so dress accordingly. ☎ *802/864–0123* ⊕ *www.enjoyburlington. com/parks/bikepath1.cfm.*

North Star Sports. In addition to stocking an extensive supply of sports apparel and accessories, this family-owned shop rents bikes and provides maps of cycling routes. ⊠ *100 Main St.* ☎ *802/863–3832* ⊕ *northstarsportsvt.com.*

Ski Rack. Burlington's one-stop shop for winter sports equipment, the Ski Rack also rents bikes and sells running gear throughout the year. ⊠ *85 Main St.* ☎ *802/658–3313, 800/882–4530* ⊕ *www.skirack.com.*

True North Kayak Tours. This company conducts two- and five-hour guided kayak tours of Lake Champlain that include talks about the region's natural history. It also offers customized lessons and runs a kayak camp for kids. ⊠ *25 Nash Pl.* ☎ *802/238–7695* ⊕ *www.vermontkayak.com.*

BOATING

Burlington Community Boathouse. This boathouse houses the city's marina and a summertime watering hole called Splash, one of the best places to watch the sun set over the lake. ⊠ *Burlington Harbor, College St.* ☎ *802/865–3377* ⊕ *www.enjoyburlington.com/waterfront.cfm.*

Lake Champlain Shoreline Cruises. The three-level *Spirit of Ethan Allen III,* a 363-passenger vessel, offers narrated cruises, themed dinners, and sunset sails with stunning views of the Adirondacks and the Green Mountains. ⊠ *Burlington Boat House, 1 College St.* ☎ *802/862–8300* ⊕ *www.soea.com* ⌑ *$16* ☾ *Late May–mid-Oct., daily 10–9.*

FAMILY **Community Sailing Center.** In addition to renting dinghies, keelboats, and kayaks, the Community Sailing Center offers classes geared to all levels. ⊠ *1 Lake St.* ☎ *802/864–2499* ⊕ *www.communitysailingcenter.org.*

SKI AREA

Bolton Valley Resort. About 25 miles from Burlington, Bolton Valley Resort is a family favorite. In addition to 71 downhill ski trails (more than half rated for intermediates and beginners), Bolton has 62 miles of cross-country and snowshoe trails, night skiing, and a sports center. ⊠ *4302 Bolton Valley Access Rd., Bolton* ☎ *802/434–3444, 877/926–5866* ⊕ *www.boltonvalley.com.*

SHOPPING

With each passing year, Burlington's industrial South End attracts ever greater numbers of artists and craftspeople, who set up studios, shops, and galleries in the former factories and warehouses along Pine Street. The district's annual "Art Hop" is the city's largest art celebration, and a roaring good time.

CRAFTS

Bennington Potters North. In addition to its popular pottery, Bennington Potters North stocks interesting kitchen items. ⊠ *127 College St.* ☎ *802/863–2221* ⊕ *www.benningtonpotters.com.*

Frog Hollow. This nonprofit collective sells contemporary and traditional crafts by more than 200 Vermont artisans. ⊠ *85 Church St.* ☎ *802/863–6458* ⊕ *www.froghollow.org.*

FOOD

Lake Champlain Chocolates. This chocolatier makes sensational truffles, caramels, candies, fudge, and even hot chocolate. The chocolates are all natural, made in Vermont, and make a great edible souvenir. ⊠ *750 Pine St.* ☎ *800/465–5909* ⊕ *www.lakechamplainchocolates.com.*

MARKETS

Fodor's Choice ★ **Burlington Farmers' Market.** Burlington's lively farmers' market is an absolute must-see when visiting in summer or fall. Located in the center of town, the Saturday market is jam-packed with local farmers selling a colorful array of organic produce, flowers, baked goods, maple syrup, meats, cheeses, prepared foods, and crafts. There's live music on the green, fresh cider and doughnuts in the fall, and the best people-watching in the state. From November to March it's held every other Saturday at Memorial Auditorium. ⊠ *City Hall Park, corner of College St. and St. Paul St.* ☎ *802/310–5172* ⊕ *www.burlingtonfarmersmarket. org* ☉ *Late May–Oct., Sat. 8:30–2.*

FAMILY
Fodor's Choice ★ **Church Street Marketplace.** For more than 30 years, this pedestrian-only thoroughfare has served as the heartbeat of Burlington, with lots of boutiques, cafés, restaurants, and street vendors during the day and a lively bar and live-music scene at night. On sunny days there are few better places to be in Burlington. ⊠ *2 Church St.* ☎ *802/863–1648* ⊕ *www. churchstmarketplace.com.*

OFF THE
BEATEN
PATH
Green Mountain Audubon Nature Center. This is a wonderful place to discover Vermont's outdoor wonders. The center's 255 acres of diverse habitats are a sanctuary for all things wild, and the 5 miles of trails provide an opportunity to explore the workings of differing natural communities. Events include dusk walks, wildflower and birding rambles, nature workshops, and educational activities for children and adults. The center is 18 miles southeast of Burlington. ⊠ *255 Sherman Hollow Rd., Huntington* ☎ *802/434–3068* ⊕ *vt.audubon.org* ✉ *Donations accepted* ☉ *Mon.–Sat. 8:30–5.*

SHELBURNE

5 miles south of Burlington.

A few miles south of Burlington, the Champlain Valley gives way to fertile farmland, affording stunning views of the rugged Adirondacks across the lake. In the middle of this farmland is the village of Shelburne (and just farther south, beautiful and more rural Charlotte), chartered in the mid-18th century and partly a bedroom community for Burlington. Stunning Shelburne Farms is worth at least a few hours of exploring, as are Shelburne Orchards in fall when you can pick your own apples and drink fresh cider while admiring breathtaking views of the lake and mountains beyond.

GETTING HERE AND AROUND

Shelburne is south of Burlington after the town of South Burlington, notable for its very un-Vermont traffic and commercial and fast food–franchised stretch of U.S. 7. It's easy to confuse Shelburne Farms—2 miles west of town on the lake, with Shelburne Museum, which is just south of town directly on Route 7, but you'll want to make time for both.

EXPLORING

FAMILY Fodor's Choice ★ **Shelburne Farms.** Founded in the 1880s as a private estate for two very rich New Yorkers, this 1,400-acre farm is much more than an exquisite landscape: it's an educational and cultural resource center with a working dairy farm, an award-winning cheese producer, an organic market garden, and a bakery whose aroma of fresh bread and pastries is an olfactory treat. It's a brilliant place for parents to expose their kids to the dignity of farm work and the joys of compassionate animal husbandry—indeed, children and adults alike will get a kick out of hunting for eggs in the oversize coop and milking a cow. Frederick Law Olmsted, co-creator of New York's Central Park, designed the magnificent grounds overlooking Lake Champlain. If you fall in love with the scenery, arrange a romantic dinner at the lakefront mansion or spend the night. ✉ *1611 Harbor Rd., west of U.S. 7* ☎ *802/985–8498* 🌐 *www.shelburnefarms.org* 🎫 *$8* 🕑 *Visitor center mid-May–mid-Oct., daily 9–5:30; mid-Oct.–mid-May, daily 10–5.*

FAMILY Fodor's Choice ★ **Shelburne Museum.** You can trace much of New England's history simply by wandering through the 45 acres and 38 buildings of this museum. The outstanding 150,000-object collection of art, design, and Americana consists of antique furniture, farm tools, fine and folk art, quilts, trade signs, and weather vanes. There are also more than 200 carriages and sleighs. In total, 25 buildings were moved to the museum, including an old-fashioned jail, an 1871 lighthouse, and even a 220-foot steamboat, the *Ticonderoga*. The Pizzagalli Center for Art and Education is open year-round with changing exhibitions and programs for kids and adults. ✉ *6000 Shelburne Rd.* ☎ *802/985–3346* 🌐 *www.shelburnemuseum.org* 🎫 *$22* 🕑 *May–Oct., daily 10–5; Nov.–Apr., Tues.–Sun. 10–5.*

Shelburne Vineyard. On Route 7 you'll see rows and rows of organically grown vines. Visit the attractive tasting room and learn how wine is made. ✉ *6308 Shelburne Rd.* ☎ *802/985–8222* 🌐 *www.shelburnevineyard.com* 🎫 *$5.*

FAMILY **Vermont Teddy Bear Company.** On the 30-minute tour of this fun-filled factory you'll hear more puns than you ever thought possible and learn how a few homemade bears, sold from a cart on Church Street, have turned into a multimillion-dollar business. Patrons and children can relax, eat, and play under a large canvas tent in summer or wander the beautiful 57-acre property. ✉ *6655 Shelburne Rd.* ☎ *802/985–3001* 🌐 *www.vermontteddybear.com* 🎫 *Tour $4* 🕑 *July–Oct., daily 9:30–5; Nov.–June, daily 10–4.*

WHERE TO EAT

$$ ECLECTIC 🍴 **The Bearded Frog.** This is the top restaurant in the Shelburne area, perfect for a casual dinner in its cozy bar or for a more upscale ambience in the attractive, sophisticated dining room. In the bar, try the soups, burgers, and terrific cocktails, or take them to the somewhat more formal dining room and add the fresh salads topped with local blue cheese, seared scallops, excellent grilled fish, steaks, and decadent desserts. [$] *Average main: $20* ✉ *5247 Shelburne Rd.* ☎ *802/985–9877* 🌐 *www.thebeardedfrog.com* 🕑 *No lunch.*

$$$ AMERICAN Fodor's Choice ★ 🍴 **The Dining Room at the Inn at Shelburne Farms.** Dinner here will make you dream of F. Scott Fitzgerald. Piano music wafts from the library, and you can carry a drink through the rooms of this 1880s mansion, gazing across a long lawn and formal gardens on the shore of dark Lake Champlain—you'll swear Jay Gatsby is about to come down the stairs. Count on just-grown ingredients that come from the market gardens as well as flavorful locally grown venison, beef, pork, and chicken. On weekends a spectacular spread of produce is set up next to a cocktail bar with fresh specialties. The dining room overlooks the lake, and the Sunday brunch is the area's best. Breakfast is served as well. [$] *Average main: $27* ✉ *Inn at Shelburne Farms, 1611 Harbor Rd.* ☎ *802/985–8498* 🌐 *www.shelburnefarms.org* 🕒 *Closed mid-May–mid-Oct.*

WHERE TO STAY

$$ B&B/INN 🏨 **Heart of the Village Inn.** Each of the elegantly furnished rooms at this B&B in a restored 1886 Queen Anne Victorian provides coziness and comfort. **Pros:** adorable village B&B; friendly owners; well run. **Cons:** near to but not within Shelburne Farms. [$] *Rooms from: $170* ✉ *5347 Shelburne Rd.* ☎ *802/985–9060, 866/985–9060* 🌐 *www.heartofthevillage.com* 🛏 *9 rooms* 🍽 *Breakfast.*

$$$ B&B/INN Fodor's Choice ★ 🏨 **The Inn at Shelburne Farms.** It's hard not to feel a little bit like an aristocrat at this exquisite turn-of-the-20th-century Tudor-style inn, one of the most memorable properties in the country. **Pros:** stately lakefront setting in a fantastic historic mansion; great service; wonderful value; great restaurant. **Cons:** some may miss having a TV in the room; closed in winter; must book far in advance. [$] *Rooms from: $165* ✉ *1611 Harbor Rd.* ☎ *802/985–8498* 🌐 *www.shelburnefarms.org* 🛏 *24 rooms, 17 with bath; 2 cottages; 1 house* 🕒 *Closed mid-Oct.–mid-May* 🍽 *No meals.*

$$$$ B&B/INN Fodor's Choice ★ 🏨 **Mt. Philo Inn.** If you've grown tired of the ubiquitous floral wallpaper of so many traditional New England inns, Jane and Dave Garbose's charming Mt. Philo Inn is a good place to check out. **Pros:** space, and lots of it; elegant rooms; great art collection. **Cons:** a bit remote. [$] *Rooms from: $240* ✉ *27 Inn Rd., Charlotte* ☎ *802/425–3335* 🌐 *www.mtphiloinn.com* 🛏 *4 suites* 🍽 *No meals.*

SHOPPING

The Shelburne Country Store. When you enter the The Shelburne Country Store, you'll step back in time. Walk past the potbellied stove and take in the aroma emanating from the fudge neatly piled behind huge antique glass cases. The store specializes in candles, weather vanes, glassware, and local foods. ✉ *29 Falls Rd., off U.S. 7* ☎ *800/660–3657* 🌐 *www.shelburnecountrystore.com.*

VERGENNES

12 miles south of Shelburne.

Vermont's oldest city, founded in 1788, is also the third oldest in New England. The downtown area is a compact district of restored Victorian homes and public buildings with a few good eateries sprinkled throughout. Main Street slopes down to Otter Creek Falls, where cannonballs

Shelburne Museum's many attractions include the *Ticonderoga* steamship and other pieces from New England's past.

were made during the War of 1812. The statue of Thomas MacDonough on the green immortalizes the victor of the Battle of Plattsburgh in 1814.

ESSENTIALS

Visitor Information Addison County Chamber of Commerce ⊠ *93 Court St., Middlebury* 🕾 *802/388–7951* ⊕ *www.addisoncounty.com.*

OFF THE BEATEN PATH

Lake Champlain Maritime Museum. This museum documents centuries of activity on the historically significant lake. Climb aboard a replica of Benedict Arnold's Revolutionary War gunboat moored in the lake, learn about shipwrecks, and watch craftsmen work at traditional boatbuilding and blacksmithing. ⊠ *4472 Basin Harbor Rd., 7 miles west of Vergennes, Basin Harbor* 🕾 *802/475–2022* ⊕ *www.lcmm.org* 🖃 *$10* ⊗ *May–mid-Oct., daily 10–5.*

WHERE TO EAT AND STAY

$$$
ECLECTIC

✕ **Starry Night Café.** This chic restaurant is one of the hottest spots around. The proprietors combine artisanal tableware and furniture with a seasonal, farm-to-table cuisine like grilled pork belly and almond-encrusted salmon. The walls also host rotating shows by local artists. Ⓢ *Average main: $24* ⊠ *5371 Rte. 7, 5 miles north of Vergennes, Ferrisburg* 🕾 *802/877–6316* ⊕ *www.starrynightcafe.com* ⚞ *Reservations essential* ⊗ *Closed Mon. and Tues. No lunch.*

$$$$
RESORT
FAMILY
Fodor's Choice
★

Basin Harbor Club. On 700 acres overlooking Lake Champlain, this ultimate family resort provides luxurious accommodations and a full roster of amenities, including an 18-hole golf course, a 48-foot tour boat, and morning and evening children's programs. **Pros:** gorgeous lakeside property; activities galore. **Cons:** open only half the year; pricey. Ⓢ *Rooms from: $240* ⊠ *4800 Basin Harbor Rd.* 🕾 *802/475–2311,*

800/622–4000 🌐 www.basinharbor.com 🛏 32 rooms, 14 suites in 3 guesthouses, 73 cottages ⏲ Closed mid-Oct.–mid-May 🍴 Breakfast.

SHOPPING

Dakin Farm. Cob-smoked ham, aged cheddar cheese, maple syrup made on-site, and other specialty foods can be found here. You can also visit the ham smokehouse and watch the waxing and sealing of the cheeses. *✉ 5797 Rte. 7, 5 miles north of Vergennes ☎ 800/993–2546 🌐 www.dakinfarm.com.*

LAKE CHAMPLAIN ISLANDS

Lake Champlain stretches more than 100 miles south from the Canadian border and forms the northern part of the boundary between New York and Vermont. Within it is an elongated archipelago composed of several islands—Isle La Motte, North Hero, Grand Isle, South Hero—and the Alburg Peninsula. With a temperate climate, the islands hold several apple orchards and are a center of water recreation in summer and ice fishing in winter. A scenic drive through the islands on U.S. 2 begins at Interstate 89 and travels north to Alburg Center; Route 78 takes you back to the mainland.

ESSENTIALS

Visitor Information **Lake Champlain Regional Chamber of Commerce** *✉ 60 Main St., Suite 100, Burlington ☎ 802/863–3489, 877/686–5253 🌐 www.vermont.org.* **Lake Champlain Islands Chamber of Commerce** *✉ 3501 US Rte. 2, Suite 100, North Hero ☎ 802/372–8400, 800/262–5226 🌐 www.champlainislands.com.*

EXPLORING

Snow Farm Vineyard and Winery. Vermont's first vineyard was started here in 1996; today the winery specializes in nontraditional botanical hybrid grapes to withstand the local climate. Take a self-guided tour, sip some samples in the tasting room, and picnic and listen to music at the free concerts on the lawn Thursday evenings mid-June through Labor Day. *✉ 190 W. Shore Rd., South Hero ☎ 802/372–9463 🌐 www.snowfarm.com 🎟 Free ⏲ May–Dec., daily 11–5.*

St. Anne's Shrine. This spot marks the site where French soldiers and Jesuits put ashore in 1665 and built a fort, creating Vermont's first European settlement. The state's first Roman Catholic Mass was celebrated here on July 26, 1666. *✉ 92 St. Anne's Rd., Isle La Motte ☎ 802/928–3362 🌐 www.saintannesshrine.org 🎟 Free ⏲ Mid-May–mid-Oct., daily 9–4; Nov–Apr., hrs vary.*

WHERE TO STAY

$$ B&B/INN FAMILY 🏨 **North Hero House Inn and Restaurant.** This inn has four buildings right on Lake Champlain, including the 1891 Colonial Revival main house with nine guest rooms, a restaurant, a pub room, library, and sitting room. **Pros:** relaxed complex; superb lakefront setting. **Cons:** closed in winter. *[$] Rooms from: $170 ✉ 3643 U.S. Rural Rte. 2, North Hero ☎ 802/372–4732, 888/525–3644 🌐 www.northherohouse.com 🛏 23 rooms, 3 suites ⏲ Closed Nov.–Mar. 🍴 Breakfast.*

$$ HOTEL **Ruthcliffe Lodge & Restaurant.** Good food and splendid scenery make this off-the-beaten-path motel directly on Lake Champlain a great value. **Pros:** inexpensive rates; serene setting; laid-back vibe. **Cons:** rooms simple, not luxurious. [$] *Rooms from: $149* ✉ *1002 Quarry Rd., Isle La Motte* ☎ *802/928–3200* 🌐 *www.ruthcliffe.com* *7 rooms* 🕒 *Closed Columbus Day–mid-May* 🍴 *Breakfast.*

SPORTS AND THE OUTDOORS

Apple Island Resort. Apple Island Resort rents pontoon boats, rowboats, canoes, kayaks, and motorboats. ✉ *71 US Rte. 2, South Hero* ☎ *802/372–3922* 🌐 *appleislandresort.com.*

Hero's Welcome. This shop rents bikes, canoes, kayaks, and paddleboats. In winter, there are skates, cross-country skis, and snowshoes. ✉ *3643 U.S. 2, North Hero* ☎ *802/372–4161, 800/372–4376* 🌐 *heroswelcome.com.*

Missisquoi National Wildlife Refuge. On the mainland east of the Alburg Peninsula, the Missisquoi National Wildlife Refuge consists of 6,729 acres of federally protected wetlands, meadows, and woods. It's a beautiful area for bird-watching, canoeing, or walking nature trails. ✉ *29 Tabor Rd., 36 miles north of Burlington, Swanton* ☎ *802/868–4781* 🌐 *www.fws.gov/refuge/missisquoi.*

Sand Bar State Park. One of Vermont's best swimming beaches is at Sand Bar State Park, along with a snack bar, changing room, and boat rentals. ✉ *1215 U.S. 2, South Hero* ☎ *802/893–2825* 🌐 *www.vtstateparks.com/htm/sandbar.htm* 🎟 *$3.50* 🕒 *Memorial Day weekend–Labor Day weekend, daily dawn–dusk.*

SHOPPING

Allenholm Farm. Open May to December, this farm store sells exemplary local produce, has a pick-your-own apple orchard, and features an animal-petting paddock. ✉ *150 South St., South Hero* ☎ *802/372–5566* 🌐 *www.allenholm.com.*

MONTGOMERY AND JAY

51 miles northeast of Burlington.

Montgomery is a small village near the Canadian border and Jay Peak ski resort. Amid the surrounding countryside are seven covered bridges.

OFF THE BEATEN PATH **Lake Memphremagog.** Vermont's second-largest body of water, Lake Memphremagog extends from Newport 33 miles north into Canada. Prouty Beach in Newport has tennis courts, boat rentals, and a 9-hole disc golf course. Watch the sun set from the deck of the East Side Restaurant, which serves excellent burgers and prime rib. ✉ *242 Prouty Beach Rd., Newport* ☎ *802/334–6345.*

SPORTS AND THE OUTDOORS

ICE-SKATING

FAMILY **Ice Haus Arena.** The sprawling Ice Haus Arena has a professional-size hockey rink and seating for 400 spectators. You can practice your stick and puck skills, and public skating is available several times a week. If you just want to watch, check out the several tournaments that take

place throughout most of the year. ✉ *830 Jay Peak Rd., Jay* ☎ *802/988–2611* ⊕ *www.jaypeakresort.com.*

SKI AREAS

Hazen's Notch Cross Country Ski Center and B&B. Delightfully remote at any time of the year, this center has 40 miles of marked and groomed trails and rents equipment and snowshoes. ✉ *1419 Hazen's Notch Rd.* ☎ *802/326–4799* ⊕ *www.hazensnotch.org.*

Jay Peak. Sticking up out of the flat farmland, Jay Peak averages 380 inches of snow a year—more than any other Vermont ski area. It's renowned for its glade skiing and powder. Jay Peak has two interconnected mountains for downhill skiing, the highest reaching nearly 4,000 feet with a vertical drop of 2,153 feet. The smaller mountain has straight-fall-line, expert terrain that eases mid-mountain into an intermediate pitch. Beginners should stick near the bottom on trails off the Metro quad lift. The area's 78 trails, including 21 glades and two chutes, are served by eight lifts, including Vermont's only tramway and a long detachable quad. The area also has three quads, a triple, and a double chairlift; and two moving carpets. Jay has 80% snowmaking coverage. The area also has four terrain parks, each rated for different abilities, and a state-of-the art ice arena for hockey, figure skating, and curling. There are ski-school programs for children ages 3 to 18.

Jay Peak runs tram rides to the summit from mid-June through Labor Day and mid-September through Columbus Day. In the winter snowshoes can be rented, and guided walks are led by a naturalist. Telemark rentals and instruction are available. ✉ *830 Jay Peak Rd., Jay* ☎ *802/988–2611* ⊕ *www.jaypeakresort.com.*

WHERE TO STAY

$$$
HOTEL
FAMILY
🏨 **Hotel Jay & Jay Peak Condominiums.** Centrally located in the ski resort's base area, the hotel and its simply furnished rooms are a favorite for families. **Pros:** great for skiers; wide range of accommodations; kids 14 and under stay and eat free. **Cons:** can get noisy; not very intimate; service isn't always helpful. 💲*Rooms from: $201* ✉ *4850 Rte. 242* ☎ *802/988–2611* ⊕ *www.jaypeakresort.com* ⮑ *172 suites, 94 condominiums* ❑*Some meals.*

$$
B&B/INN
🏨 **The INN.** Innkeepers Nick Barletta and Scott Pasfield have transformed this older property into a smart chalet-style lodging with tons of character. **Pros:** walking distance from shops and supplies. **Cons:** noise from bar can seep into nearby rooms. 💲*Rooms from: $159* ✉ *241 Main St.* ☎ *802/326-4391* ⊕ *www.theinn.us* ⮑ *11 rooms* ❑*No meals.*

$$$$
B&B/INN
🏨 **Phineas Swann Bed & Breakfast Inn.** The top-hatted bulldog on the sign of this 1880 farmhouse isn't just a mascot: it reveals the hotel's welcoming attitude to pet owners. **Pros:** walking distance from shops and supplies. **Cons:** decor is a tad old-fashioned. 💲*Rooms from: $449* ✉ *195 Main St.* ☎ *802/326-4306* ⊕ *phineasswann.com* ⮑ *3 rooms, 6 suites* ❑*Breakfast.*

EN
ROUTE
Northeast Kingdom. Routes 14, 5, 58, and 100 make a scenic drive around the Northeast Kingdom, named for the remoteness and stalwart independence that have helped preserve its rural nature. You can extend the loop and head east on Route 105 to the city of Newport on

Lake Memphremagog. Some of the most unspoiled areas in all Vermont are on the drive south from Newport on either U.S. 5 or Interstate 91 (the latter is faster, but the former is prettier).

LAKE WILLOUGHBY

30 miles southeast of Montgomery (summer route; 50 miles by winter route), 28 miles north of St. Johnsbury.

EXPLORING

FAMILY   **Bread and Puppet Museum.** This ramshackle barn houses a surrealistic collection of props used by the world-renowned Bread and Puppet Theater. The troupe has been performing social and political commentary with the towering (they're supported by people on stilts), eerily expressive puppets for 50 years. In July and August, there are performances on Sunday at 2:30. ⊠ *753 Heights Rd., 1 mile east of Rte. 16, Glover* ☎ *802/525–3031* ⊕ *www.breadandpuppet.org* ✉ *Donations accepted* ☉ *June–Oct., daily 10–6.*

Lake Willoughby. The cliffs of Mt. Pisgah and Mt. Hor drop to the edge of Lake Willoughby on opposite shores, giving this beautiful, deep, glacially carved lake a striking resemblance to a Norwegian fjord. The trails to the top of Mt. Pisgah reward hikers with glorious views. ⊠ *Westmore.*

EAST BURKE

17 miles south of Lake Willoughby.

Once a sleepy village, East Burke is now the Northeast Kingdom's outdoor-activity hub. The Kingdom Trails attract thousands of mountain bikers in summer and fall. In winter, many trails are groomed for cross-country skiing.

ESSENTIALS

Kingdom Trails Association ☎ *802/626–0737* ⊕ *www.kingdomtrails.org.*

WHERE TO STAY

$$$ 🛏 **The Wildflower Inn.** The hilltop views are breathtaking at this rambling, family-oriented complex of old farm buildings on 570 acres. **Pros:** kid-friendly resort; relaxed atmosphere; lots of activities. **Cons:** most rooms have basic furnishings. $ *Rooms from: $200* ⊠ *2059 Darling Hill Rd., 5 miles west of East Burke, Lyndonville* ☎ *802/626–8310, 800/627–8310* ⊕ *www.wildflowerinn.com* 🛏 *10 rooms, 13 suites, 1 cottage* ☉ *Closed Apr. and Nov.* ⦿| *Breakfast.*

RESORT
FAMILY

SPORTS AND THE OUTDOORS

BIKING

East Burke Sports. This shop rents and repairs mountain bikes, kayaks, skis, snowboards, and snowshoes. ⊠ *439 Rte. 114* ☎ *802/626–3215* ⊕ *www.eastburkesports.com.*

Kingdom Trails. Locals maintain this 110-mile network of trails for mountain biking and hiking in the summer, and 37 miles for snowshoeing and cross-country skiing in the winter. ⊠ *478 Rte. 114* ☎ *802/626–0737* ⊕ *www.kingdomtrails.com.*

Catch a show and some social commentary at the Bread and Puppet Theater in summer, or visit the museum year-round.

Village Sport Shop. This shop rents bikes, canoes, kayaks, paddleboats, skis, and snowshoes. ✉ *511 Broad St., Lyndonville* ☎ *802/626–8448* ⊕ *www.villagesportshop.com.*

SKI AREA

Burke Mountain. About an hour's drive from Montpelier is Burke Mountain ski resort. Racers stick to the Training Slope, served by its own lift. The other 55 trails and glades are a quiet playground. ✉ *1 Mountain Rd.* ☎ *802/626–7300* ⊕ *www.skiburke.com.*

8

ST. JOHNSBURY

16 miles south of East Burke, 39 miles northeast of Montpelier.

St. Johnsbury, the southern gateway to the Northeast Kingdom, was chartered in 1786. But its identity was established after 1830, when Thaddeus Fairbanks invented the platform scale, a device that revolutionized weighing methods. The Fairbanks family's philanthropic efforts gave the city a strong cultural and architectural imprint. Today St. J, as the locals call it, is the friendly, adventure-sports-happy hub of the Northeast Kingdom.

EXPLORING

FAMILY **Dog Mountain.** Artist Stephen Huneck was famous for his colorful folk art sculptures and paintings of dogs. Much more than an art gallery–gift shop, this deeply moving place is complete with a chapel where animal lovers can reflect on their beloved pets. Above all, this is a place to bring your dog: there is a swimming pond and hiking trails. ✉ *143 Parks*

Rd., off Spaulding Rd. ☎ *800/449–2580* 🌐 *www.dogmt.com* 🎟 *Free* 🕒 *May–August: Daily 10–5; October–May, Thurs.–Mon. 11–4.*

FAMILY Fodor's Choice ★ **Fairbanks Museum and Planetarium.** This odd and deeply thrilling little museum displays the eccentric collection of Franklin Fairbanks, who surely had one of the most inquisitive minds in American history. He built this magnificent barrel-vaulted gallery in 1889 to house the specimens of plants, animals, birds, reptiles, and collections of folk art and dolls—and a seemingly unending variety of beautifully mounted curios—he had picked up around the world. The museum showcases over 175,000 items, but it's surprisingly easy to feast your eyes on everything here without getting a museum headache. There's also a popular 45-seat planetarium, the state's only public planetarium; as well the Eye on the Sky Weather Gallery, home to live NPR weather broadcasts. ✉ *1302 Main St.* ☎ *802/748–2372* 🌐 *www.fairbanksmuseum.org* 🎟 *Museum $8; planetarium $5* 🕒 *Apr.–Oct., Mon.–Sat. 9–5, Sun. 1–5; Nov.–Mar., Tues.–Sat. 9–5, Sun. 1–5.*

Fodor's Choice ★ **St. Johnsbury Athenaeum.** With its polished Victorian woodwork, dramatic paneling, and ornate circular staircases, this building is both the town library (one of the nicest you're likely to ever come across) and one of the oldest art galleries in the country, housing more than 100 original works mainly of the Hudson River school. Albert Bierstadt's enormous *Domes of Yosemite* dominates the beautiful painting gallery. ✉ *1171 Main St.* ☎ *802/748–8291* 🌐 *www.stjathenaeum.org* 🎟 *Free* 🕒 *Weekdays 10–5:30, Sat. 10–3.*

OFF THE BEATEN PATH **Peacham.** Tiny Peacham, 10 miles southwest of St. Johnsbury, is on almost every tour group's list of "must-sees." With views extending to the White Mountains of New Hampshire and a white-steeple church, Peacham is perhaps the most photographed town in New England. The movie adaptation of *Ethan Frome,* starring Liam Neeson, was filmed here. Next door, the **Peacham Corner Guild** sells local handcrafts. The **Peacham Store** offers tasty soups and stews. ✉ *Peacham* 🌐 *www.peacham.net.*

WHERE TO STAY

$$$ B&B/INN 🏨 **Rabbit Hill Inn.** Few inns in New England have the word-of-mouth buzz that Rabbit Hill seems to earn from satisfied guests. **Pros:** attractive, spacious rooms; romantic; lovely grounds; good food. **Cons:** might be too quiet a setting for some. [$] *Rooms from: $210* ✉ *48 Lower Waterford Rd., 11 miles south of St. Johnsbury, Lower Waterford* 🌐 *www.rabbithillinn.com* 🛏 *19 rooms* 🕒 *Closed 1st 3 wks in Apr., 1st 2 wks in Nov.* 🍴 *Breakfast.*

NEW HAMPSHIRE

WELCOME TO NEW HAMPSHIRE

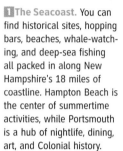

TOP REASONS TO GO

★ **The White Mountains:** Great for hiking and skiing, these rugged, dramatic peaks and notches are unforgettable.

★ **Lake Winnipesaukee:** Water parks, arcades, boat cruises, and classic summer camps make for a family fun summer.

★ **Fall Foliage:** Head to the Kancamagus Highway in the fall for one of America's best drives or seek out a lesser-known route that's just as stunning.

★ **Portsmouth:** Less than an hour from Boston, this great American city has coastline allure, colorful Colonial architecture, romantic dining, and fine arts and crafts.

★ **Pristine Towns:** Jaffrey Center, Walpole, Tamworth, Center Sandwich, and Jackson are among the most charming tiny villages in New England.

1 **The Seacoast.** You can find historical sites, hopping bars, beaches, whale-watching, and deep-sea fishing all packed in along New Hampshire's 18 miles of coastline. Hampton Beach is the center of summertime activities, while Portsmouth is a hub of nightlife, dining, art, and Colonial history.

2 **Lakes Region.** Throughout central New Hampshire are lakes and more lakes. The largest, Lake Winnipesaukee, has 240 miles of coastline and attracts all sorts of water sports enthusiasts, but there are many more secluded and quiet lakes with enchanting bed-and-breakfasts where relaxation is the main activity.

3 **The White Mountains.** Skiing, snowshoeing, and snowboarding in the winter; hiking, biking, and riding scenic railways in the summer—the Whites, as locals call their mountains, have plenty of natural wonders within a stone's throw from the roads, but other spots call for lung-busting hikes. Mt. Washington, the tallest mountain in the Northeast, can be conquered by trail, train, or car.

4 **Dartmouth–Lake Sunapee.** Quiet villages can be found throughout the region. Many of them are barely removed from Colonial times, but some thrive as centers of arts and education and are filled with quaint shops. Hanover, the home of 240-year-old Dartmouth College, retains that true New England college-town feel, with ivy-draped buildings and cobblestone walkways. Lake Sunapee is a wonderful place to swim, fish, or enjoy a cruise.

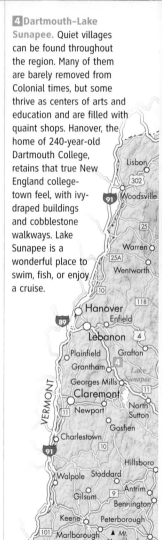

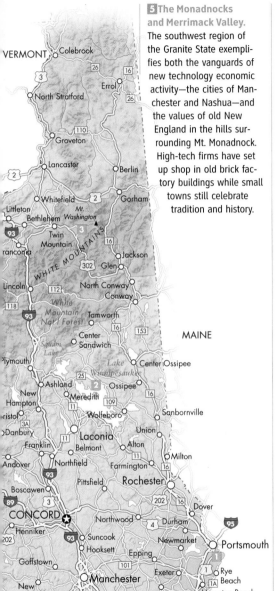

5 The Monadnocks and Merrimack Valley.
The southwest region of the Granite State exemplifies both the vanguards of new technology economic activity—the cities of Manchester and Nashua—and the values of old New England in the hills surrounding Mt. Monadnock. High-tech firms have set up shop in old brick factory buildings while small towns still celebrate tradition and history.

GETTING ORIENTED

Although New Hampshire has three interstates running through it (I–95, I–93, and I–89), most of its regions are accessible only on smaller roads. From Boston or Portland, Maine, Interstate 95 provides the best access to Portsmouth and the beaches along the coast, though many people like to drive along Route 1A, which parallels the coast. North of Portsmouth, Route 16 leads to the White Mountains, whose precipitous peaks seem to rise out of nowhere, and the lakes region, home to Lake Winnipesaukee. From there, Interstate 93 cuts north toward Franconia and Littleton and south into Concord, Manchester, and Nashua. State roads east and north of Interstate 93 lead to Dixville Notch, which casts the first vote in presidential elections, and the Connecticut Lakes. Following the Connecticut River takes you to Hanover, home of Dartmouth College, Claremont, Charleston, Walpole, and Keene. From Concord, travelers head west to reach the Monadnock Region.

9

Updated by
Debbie Hagan

New Hampshire residents have often been called cantanker-ous, but beneath that crusty exterior is often hospitality and friendliness. The state's motto was coined by New Hamp-shire native General John Stark, who led the Colonial Army in its hard-fought battle of Bennington, Vermont, in 1777. "Live free or die; death is not the worst of evils," he said, in a letter written 20 years after the battle. The residents of the Granite State have taken "Live Free or Die" to heart, defin-ing themselves by that principle for more than 200 years.

The state is often identified more by what it is not than by what it is. It lacks Vermont's folksy charm. Maine's coast is grander. But New Hampshire's independent spirit, mountain peaks, clear air, and spar-kling lakes have attracted trailblazers and artists for centuries. Ralph Waldo Emerson, Henry David Thoreau, Nathaniel Hawthorne, and Louisa May Alcott all visited and wrote about the state, sparking a strong literary tradition that continues today. It also has a strong politi-cal history: it was the first colony to declare independence from Great Britain, the first to adopt a state constitution, and the first to require that constitution be referred to the people for approval.

The state's diverse terrain makes it popular with everyone from avid adventurers to young families looking for easy access to nature. You can hike, climb, ski, snowboard, snowshoe, and fish as well as explore on snowmobiles, sailboats, and mountain bikes. Natives have no objection to others enjoying the state's beauty as long as they leave some money behind. New Hampshire has long resisted both sales and income taxes, so tourism brings in much-needed revenue.

With a number of its cities consistently rated among the most livable in the nation, New Hampshire has seen considerable growth over the past decade. Longtime residents worry that the state will soon take on two personalities: one of rapidly growing cities to the southeast and the other of quiet villages to the west and north. Although newcomers have brought change, the independent nature of the people and the state's natural beauty remain constant.

PLANNING

WHEN TO GO

Summer and fall are the best times to visit most of New Hampshire. Winter is a great time to travel to the White Mountains, but most other tourist sites in the state, including the Portsmouth museums and many attractions in the Lakes Region, are closed due to snow and cold weather. In summer people flock to beaches, mountain trails, and lake boat ramps. In the cities, festivals showcase music, theater, and crafts. Fall brings leaf peepers, especially to the White Mountains and along the Kancamagus Highway (Route 112). Skiers and snowboarders take to the slopes in winter, when Christmas lights and carnivals brighten the long, dark nights. Spring's unpredictable weather—along with April's mud and late May's black flies—tends to deter visitors. Still, the season has its joys, not the least of which is the appearance of the state flower, the purple lilac, from mid-May to early June as well as colorful rhododendrons.

PLANNING YOUR TIME

Some people come to New Hampshire to hike or ski the mountains, fish and sail the lakes, or cycle along the back roads. Others prefer to drive through scenic towns, visiting museums and shops. Although New Hampshire is a small state, roads curve around lakes and mountains, making distances longer than they appear. You can get a taste of the coast, lake, and mountain areas in three to five days; eight days gives you time to make a more complete loop.

GETTING HERE AND AROUND

AIR TRAVEL

Manchester Boston Regional Airport is the state's largest and has non-stop service to more than 20 cities. Boston's Logan Airport is within one to three hours of most places in New Hampshire, as is Bradley International in Hartford, Connecticut.

CAR TRAVEL

New Hampshire is an easy drive north from Boston and serves as a good base for exploring northern New England. Many destinations are near major highways, so getting around by car is a great way to travel. Interstate 93 stretches from Boston to Littleton and on into neighboring Vermont. Interstate 89 will get you from Concord to Hanover and eventually to Burlington, Vermont. To the east, Interstate 95, which is a toll road, passes through southern New Hampshire's coastal area on its way from Massachusetts to Maine. Throughout the state are quiet backcountry lanes and winding roads that might take a little longer but can make for some of the best parts of the journey.

Speed limits on interstate and limited-access highways are usually 65 mph, except in heavily settled areas, where 55 mph is the norm. On state and U.S. routes, speed limits vary considerably. On any given stretch, the limit may be anywhere from 25 mph to 55 mph, so watch the signs carefully. Right turns on red lights are permitted unless otherwise indicated.

TRAIN TRAVEL

Amtrak. Amtrak runs its *Downeaster* service from Boston to Portland, Maine, with stops in Exeter, Durham, and Dover. ☎ *800/872–7245* ⊕ *www.amtrak.com.*

RESTAURANTS

New Hampshire prides itself on seafood—not just lobster but also salmon pie, steamed mussels, fried clams, and seared tuna. Across the state you'll find country taverns with upscale Continental and American menus, many of them embracing regional ingredients. Alongside a growing number of contemporary eateries are such state traditions as greasy-spoon diners, pizzerias, and pubs that serve hearty comfort fare. Reservations are almost never required, and dress is casual in nearly every eatery.

Prices in the reviews are the average cost of a main course at dinner or, if dinner is not served, at lunch.

HOTELS

In the mid-19th century wealthy Bostonians retreated to imposing New Hampshire country homes in summer months. Grand hotels were built across the state, especially in the White Mountains, when the area competed with Saratoga Springs, Newport, and Bar Harbor to draw the nation's elite vacationers. Today a handful of these hotel-resorts survive, with their large cooking staffs and tradition of top-notch service. Many of the vacation houses have been converted into inns and B&Bs. The smallest have only a couple of rooms and are typically done in period style. The largest contain 30 or more rooms and suites and have in-room fireplaces and even hot tubs. You'll also find a great many well-kept, often family-owned motor lodges—particularly in the White Mountains and Lakes regions. In the ski areas expect the usual ski condos and lodges. In the Merrimack River valley, as well as along major highways, chain hotels and motels prevail. There are numerous campgrounds across the state, which accommodate RVs as well. The White Mountains provide an excellent base for camping and hiking.

Prices in the reviews are the lowest cost of a standard double room in high season.

THE SEACOAST

New Hampshire's 18-mile stretch of coastline packs in a wealth of scenery and diversions. The honky-tonk of Hampton Beach gets plenty of attention, good and bad, but first-timers are often surprised by the significant chunk of shoreline that remains pristine—especially through the town of Rye. This section begins in the regional hub, Portsmouth, cuts down the coast to the beaches, branches inland to the prep-school town of Exeter, and runs back up north through Dover, Durham (home of the University of New Hampshire), and Rochester. From here it's a short drive to the Lakes Region.

OUTDOOR ACTIVITIES

Hitting the trails by boot and ski, fishing, kayaking and canoeing, biking, or just plain old walking will undoubtedly be a part of your visit.

Biking: Many ski resorts in the White Mountains offer mountain-biking opportunities, providing chairlift rides to the top and trails for all skill levels at the bottom. Some of the state's best road biking is along the Kancamagus Highway and around Lake Sunapee.

Hiking: For the more adventurous, hiking the trails in the White Mountains or along the Appalachian Trail is their reason for visiting. For those more interested in less arduous treks, there are plenty of day hikes in the White Mountain National Forest and state parks such as Pisgah, the state's largest, in Cheshire County, the Crawford Notch and Franconia Notch state parks in the Whites, and Mt. Monadnock.

Skiing: Ski areas abound in New Hampshire—try Bretton Woods, Mt. Sunapee, Waterville Valley, or Canon Mountain. For cross-country skiing, nothing beats Gunstock Mountain Resort, with 32 miles of trails, also open for snowshoeing. Or visit Franconia Village, which has 37 miles of cross-country trails.

ESSENTIALS

Visitor Information Seacoast New Hampshire & South Coast Maine
☎ 603/427–2020 ⊕ www.seacoastnh.com.

PORTSMOUTH

47 miles southeast of Concord; 50 miles southwest of Portland, Maine; 56 miles north of Boston.

Fodor's Choice ★

Settled in 1623 as Strawbery Banke, Portsmouth became a prosperous port before the Revolutionary War, and, like similarly wealthy Newport, Rhode Island, it harbored many Tory sympathizers throughout the campaign. Filled with grand residential architecture spanning the 18th through early 20th centuries, this city of 23,000 has many historic homes, including the collection of 40-plus buildings that make up the Strawbery Banke Museum. With hip eateries, quirky shops, swank cocktail bars, respected theaters, and jumping live-music venues, this sheltered harbor city is a hot destination. Downtown, especially around elegant Market Square, buzzes with conviviality.

GETTING HERE AND AROUND

Interstate 95 and Route 1 run through Portsmouth. From the west, take Route 101 and from the north take Route 16. Amtrak runs through Durham, which is a short drive from the coast. Once in Portsmouth, you can walk about the downtown, though you'll want a car for farther attractions.

ESSENTIALS

Bus and Trolley COAST Bus ☎ 603/743–5777 ⊕ www.coastbus.org.

Taxi Anchor Taxi ☎ 603/436–1888. **Portsmouth Taxi** ☎ 603/431–6811.

Visitor Information **Greater Portsmouth Chamber of Commerce** ⊠ *500 Market St.* ☎ *603/610–5510* ⊕ *www.portsmouthchamber.org.*

TOURS

Prescott Park Arts Festival. This outdoor festival presents theater, dance, and musical events from June through August. ⊠ *105 Marcy St.* ☎ *603/436–2848* ⊕ *www.prescottpark.org.*

Discover Portsmouth. Part welcome center and part museum, Discover Portsmouth, operated by the Portsmouth Historical Society, is where you'll not only learn about daily events, history tours, and walking trails, but also see art and historical exhibits. Sign up here for a guided walking tour, stock up on city maps, and learn about the Portsmouth Harbour Trail, a route that passes more than 70 points of scenic and historical significance. ⊠ *10 Middle St.* ☎ *603/436–8433* ⊕ *www.portsmouthhistory.org* ⊠ *Free* ☉ *Apr.–late-Dec., daily 10–5.*

Portsmouth Black Heritage Trail. Important sites of African-American history are along the self-guided walk on the Portsmouth Black Heritage Trail. Included are the New Hampshire Gazette Printing Office, where skilled slave Primus Fowle operated the paper's printing press for some 50 years beginning in 1756, and the city's 1866 Election Hall, outside of which the city's black citizens held annual celebrations of the Emancipation Proclamation. Call about guided tours. ⊠ *Discover Portsmouth, 10 Middle St.* ☎ *603/380–1231* ⊕ *www.portsmouthhistory.org* ⊠ *Donations welcome.*

EXPLORING

TOP ATTRACTIONS

Albacore Park. Built here in 1953, the USS *Albacore* is docked at this visitor center in Albacore Park. You can board the prototype submarine, which was a floating laboratory designed to test an innovative hull design, dive brakes, and sonar systems for the Navy. The nearby Memorial Garden and its reflecting pool are dedicated to those who have lost their lives in submarine service. ⊠ *600 Market St.* ☎ *603/436–3680* ⊕ *www.ussalbacore.org* ⊠ *$6* ☉ *Memorial Day–Columbus Day, daily 9:30–5; Columbus Day–Memorial Day, Thurs.–Mon. 9:30–4.*

Great Bay Estuarine National Research Reserve. Just inland from Portsmouth is one of southeastern New Hampshire's most precious assets. Amid its 10,235 acres of open and tidal waters and mudflats you can spot blue herons, ospreys, and snowy egrets, particularly during spring and fall migrations. The Great Bay Discovery Center has indoor and outdoor exhibits, a library and bookshop, and a 1,700-foot boardwalk, as well as other trails through mudflats and upland forest. ⊠ *89 Depot Rd., Greenland* ☎ *603/778–0015* ⊕ *www.greatbay.org* ⊠ *Free* ☉ *Visitor Center May–Sept., Wed.–Sun. 10–4; Oct., weekends 10–4.*

John Paul Jones House. This was a boardinghouse when the Revolutionary War hero lived here while supervising shipbuilding for the Continental Navy. The 1758 hip-roofed structure displays furniture, costumes, glass, guns, portraits, and documents from the late 18th century. The collection specializes in textiles, particularly some extraordinary embroidery samplers from the early 19th century. ⊠ *43 Middle St.* ☎ *603/436–8420* ⊕ *www.portsmouthhistory.org* ⊠ *$6* ☉ *May–Oct., daily 11–5.*

New Hampshire
Coast

Redhook Ale Brewery. Tours here end with a beer tasting, but you can also stop in the Cataqua Public House for a mug of ale and a bite to eat. The grounds are home to many events during the summer, including August's Redhookfest. ⊠ *Pease International Tradeport, 1 Redhook Way* ☎ *603/430–8600* ⊕ *www.redhook.com* ⊠ *$5* ☉ *Sun.–Thurs. 1–5, Fri. and Sat. noon–6.*

FAMILY

Fodor's Choice
★

Strawbery Banke Museum. The first English settlers named the area around today's Portsmouth for the wild strawberries along the shores of the Piscataqua River. The name survives in this 10-acre outdoor history museum, one of the largest in New England. The compound has 46 buildings dating from 1695 to 1820—some restored and furnished to a particular period, others used for historical exhibits. Half the interior of the Drisco House, built in 1795, depicts its use as a dry-goods store in Colonial times, whereas the living room and kitchen are decorated as they were in the 1950s, showing how buildings were adapted over time. The Shapiro House has been restored to reflect the life of the Russian Jewish immigrant family who lived in the home in the early 1900s. Perhaps the most opulent house, done in decadent Victorian style, is the 1860 Goodwin Mansion, former home of Governor Ichabod Goodwin. ⊠ *14 Hancock St.* ☎ *603/433–1100* ⊕ *www.strawberybanke.org* ⊠ *$18* ☉ *May–Oct., daily 10–5.*

WORTH NOTING

FAMILY **Fort Constitution Historic Site.** On the nearby island of New Castle, Fort Constitution was built in 1631 and then rebuilt in 1666 as Fort William and Mary, a British stronghold overlooking Portsmouth Harbor. The fort earned its fame in 1774, when patriots raided it in one of Revolutionary America's first overtly defiant acts against King George III. The rebels later used the captured munitions against the British at the Battle of Bunker Hill. Great view of Portsmouth Lighthouse, next door. Park at the Battery Farnsworth and walk into the Coast Guard installation to the fort. ⊠ *25 Wentworth Rd., next to the Coast Guard Station* ☎ *603/436–1552* ⊕ *www.nhstateparks.org* ⌲ *Free* ◷ *Daily 8–4.*

Moffatt-Ladd House and Garden. The period interior of this 1763 home tells the story of Portsmouth's merchant class through portraits, letters, and furnishings. The Colonial Revival garden includes a horse chestnut tree planted by General William Whipple when he returned home after signing the Declaration of Independence in 1776. ⊠ *154 Market St.* ☎ *603/436–8221* ⊕ *www.moffattladd.org* ⌲ *Garden and house $6, garden only $2* ◷ *Early June–mid-Oct., Mon.–Sat. 11–5, Sun. 1–5.*

QUICK
BITES

Annabelle's Natural Ice Cream. Drop by Annabelle's Natural Ice Cream for a dish of New Hampshire Pure maple walnut or rich vanilla ice cream made with golden egg yolks. ⊠ 49 Ceres St. ☎ 603/436–3400 ⊕ www. annabellesicecream.com.

Breaking New Grounds. If you're going out to dinner, skip the coffee and dessert and head here instead. The only problem is choosing from among the many types of sweets, from pastries to gelati. In nice weather, sit outside and soak up the street entertainment. ⊠ 14 Market Sq. ☎ 603/436–9555 ⊕ www.bngcoffee.com.

Warner House. The main features of this quiet 1716 gem are the curious folk-art murals lining the hall staircase, which may be the oldest-known murals in the United States still gracing their original structure. This house, a noted example of Georgian architecture, contains original art, furnishings, and extraordinary examples of area craftsmanship. The west-wall lightning rod is believed to have been installed in 1762 under the supervision of Benjamin Franklin. ⊠ *150 Daniel St.* ☎ *603/436–5909* ⊕ *www.warnerhouse.org* ⌲ *$5* ◷ *June–Oct., Wed.–Mon. 11–4.*

Wentworth-Coolidge Mansion Historic Site. A National Historic Landmark now part of Little Harbor State Park, this was originally the residence of Benning Wentworth, New Hampshire's first royal governor (1753–70). Notable among its period furnishings is the carved pine mantelpiece in the council chamber. Wentworth's imported lilac trees bloom each May. Call ahead for house tours, offered on the hour. ⊠ *375 Little Harbor Rd., near South Street Cemetery* ☎ *603/436–6607* ⊕ *www. nhstateparks.org* ⌲ *$5* ◷ *Late May–mid-June and Sept.–mid-Oct., weekends 10–4; mid-June–Aug., Wed.–Sun. 10–4.*

Strawbery Banke Museum includes period gardens and 46 historic buildings.

Isles of Shoals. Many of these nine small, rocky islands (eight at high tide) retain earthy names—Hog and Smuttynose to cite but two—given them by 17th-century fishermen. A history of piracy, murder, and ghosts surrounds the archipelago, long populated by an independent lot who, according to one writer, hadn't the sense to winter on the mainland. Celia Thaxter, a native islander, romanticized these islands with her poetry in *Among the Isles of Shoals* (1873). In the late 19th century **Appledore Island** became an offshore retreat for Thaxter's coterie of writers, musicians, and artists. **Star Island** contains a small museum, the Rutledge Marine Lab, with interactive family exhibits. From May to late October you can take a narrated history cruise of the Isles of Shoals, a day trip to Star Island, or a walking tour of Star Island with Isles of Shoals Steamship Company. ⊠ *315 Market St.* ☎ *800/441–4620* ⊕ *www.islesofshoals.com.*

Prescott Park. Picnicking is popular at this waterfront park. A large formal garden with fountains is perfect for whiling away an afternoon. The park contains Point of Graves, Portsmouth's oldest burial ground, and two 17th-century warehouses. The Prescott Park Arts Festival, a summer-long event, includes a multitude of concerts, outdoor movies, and food festivals. ⊠ *Marcy St.* ☎ *603/436–2848* ⊕ *www.prescottpark.org.*

Water Country. New Hampshire's largest water park has an tube ride, a wave pool, and 15 waterslides. ⊠ *2300 Lafayette Rd.* ☎ *603/427–1111* ⊕ *www.watercountry.com* ⊠ *$39* ☉ *Mid-June–Labor Day, hours vary.*

A boat tour of Portsmouth Harbor is popular in warm weather, and a great introduction to the city's maritime heritage.

WHERE TO EAT

$$$
INTERNATIONAL
Fodor's Choice
★

✕ **Black Trumpet Bistro.** Award-winning chef Evan Mallett combines bold flavors from Latin America, North Africa, Turkey, and Mexico in the fare he serves in this romantic little restaurant with views of the water. The menu is constantly changing, offering such surprises as roasted allium soup, rabbit-and-mushroom enchiladas, and potato-and-cheese pierogies with smoked corn bisque and a sautéed kale–and-blueberry salad. Mallett belongs to the Heirloom Harvest Project, and brings unusual vegetables, sometimes in surprising colors, to the table. Vegetarians will always find out-of-the-ordinary entrées. The atmosphere is quiet, and walk-ins may find a table in the upstairs wine bar. $ *Average main: $25* ✉ *29 Ceres St.* ☎ *603/431–0887* ⊕ *www.blacktrumpetbistro. com* ◷ *No lunch.*

$$
CARIBBEAN

✕ **Blue Mermaid Island Grill.** This fun, colorful place is good for seafood, sandwiches, and quesadillas, as well as house-cut yucca chips. Specialties include plantain-encrusted cod topped with grilled mango vinaigrette and served with grilled banana–sweet potato hash, a chipotle-and-honey-marinated sirloin, and braised short ribs with an island rub. In summer you can eat on a deck that overlooks some adorable Colonial homes. There's live music most nights. $ *Average main: $20* ✉ *409 The Hill* ☎ *603/427–2583* ⊕ *www.bluemermaid.com.*

$$
AMERICAN
FAMILY

✕ **Friendly Toast.** The biggest and best breakfast in town is served at this funky, wildly colorful diner loaded with bric-a-brac. Coconut Cakes (buttermilk pancakes, chocolate chips, coconut, and cashews), Drunkard French toast (with a Grand Marnier–and-raspberry sauce), and hefty omelets are favorites. Also enjoy the homemade breads and muffins. The place serves lunch and dinner, and a late-night crowd gathers after the bars close. $ *Average main: $13* ✉ *113 Congress St.* ☎ *603/430–2154* ⊕ *www.thefriendlytoast.net.*

$$$ ✕ **Jumpin' Jay's Fish Cafe.** A wildly popular downtown spot, this offbeat,
SEAFOOD dimly lighted eatery has a changing menu of fresh seafood from as far away as Iceland and Costa Rica. Try the steamed Prince Edward Island mussels with jalapeños, spicy ginger, and saffron sauce, or the haddock with lemon, white wine, and capers. You can't go wrong with one of the fresh catches topped with one of seven different sauces. Singles like to gather at the central bar for dinner and furtive glances. $ *Average main: $25* ✉ *150 Congress St.* ☎ *603/766–3474* ⊕ *www.jumpinjays.com.*

$$$$ ✕ **Library Restaurant.** In this bibliophile's dream, the 12-foot hand-carved
STEAKHOUSE ceiling and the Spanish mahogany walls were constructed by the Pullman Car Woodworkers in 1889. Although the kitchen creates lighter dishes such as jumbo crab cakes and crispy fried shrimp in sweet chili sauce, the mainstays are thick-cut, juicy steaks and chops. The crushed-peppercorn steak is meat heaven. Choose from six different rich, creamy sauces, including hollandaise and Gorgonzola, plus an array of fresh vegetables. The English-style pub serves nearly 100 martinis made from over 250 brands of international vodkas. Sunday brunch is also popular. $ *Average main: $30* ✉ *401 State St.* ☎ *603/431–5202* ⊕ *www.libraryrestaurant.com.*

$$ ✕ **Poco's Bow Street Cantina.** This casual but contemporary eatery turns
LATIN AMERICAN out exceptional Southwestern and Latin American cuisine. Cajun red snapper tacos, fried calamari, and lobster quesadillas are among the best choices. Most tables have great views of the Piscataqua River. The downstairs bar and spacious outdoor deck are local hangouts. Try one of the craft cocktails, such as the cucumber martini. $ *Average main: $14* ✉ *37 Bow St.* ☎ *603/431–5967* ⊕ *www.pocosbowstreetcantina.com* ⟷ *Reservations not accepted.*

WHERE TO STAY

$$$ 🛏 **Ale House Inn.** Talk about prime location: this urban-style hotel is
HOTEL steps from the city's historic houses, boutiques, and restaurants. **Pros:** great location; complimentary tickets to local theater; bicycles for local jaunts. **Cons:** no breakfast. $ *Rooms from: $199* ✉ *121 Bow St.* ☎ *603/431–7760* ⊕ *www.alehouseinn.com* ⟷ *10 rooms* ⎮⚌⎮ *No meals.*

$$$ 🛏 **Martin Hill Inn.** You may fall in love with this adorable yellow 1815
B&B/INN house surrounded by flower-filled gardens. **Pros:** lovely building; central location; furnished with real antiques. **Cons:** not in historic district. $ *Rooms from: $185* ✉ *404 Islington St.* ☎ *603/436–2287* ⊕ *www.martinhillinn.com* ⟷ *7 rooms* ⎮⚌⎮ *Breakfast.*

$$$$ 🛏 **Wentworth by the Sea.** What's not to love about this white colossus
RESORT overlooking the sea on New Castle Island? **Pros:** great spa; spectacu-
Fodor's Choice lar Sunday brunch; lovely oceanfront perch. **Cons:** not in downtown
★ Portsmouth. $ *Rooms from: $429* ✉ *588 Wentworth Rd., New Castle* ☎ *603/422–7322, 866/240–6313* ⊕ *www.wentworth.com* ⟷ *161 rooms, 31 suites* ⎮⚌⎮ *No meals.*

9

Four of the nine rocky Isles of Shoals belong to New Hampshire; the other five belong to Maine.

NIGHTLIFE AND THE ARTS
THE ARTS
Music Hall. Beloved for its acoustics, the 1878 Music Hall brings the best touring events to the seacoast—from classical and pop concerts to dance and theater. The hall also screens art films. ⊠ *28 Chestnut St.* ☎ *603/436–2400* ⊕ *www.themusichall.org.*

NIGHTLIFE
BARS **Two Ceres Street.** This lively bar serves such original martinis as the Lumberjack, with Maker's Mark and maple syrup, and the Hammer and Sickle, with Grey Goose vodka, peperoncini, and olive juice. ⊠ *2 Ceres St.* ☎ *603/433–2373* ⊕ *www.twocerestreet.com.*

MUSIC **Portsmouth Gas Light Co.** This brick-oven pizzeria hosts local rock bands in its lounge, courtyard, and slick upstairs space. ⊠ *64 Market St.* ☎ *603/430–9122* ⊕ *www.portsmouthgaslight.com.*

The Press Room. People come from Boston and Portland just to hang out at the Press Room, which showcases folk, jazz, blues, and blue-grass performers nightly. ⊠ *77 Daniel St.* ☎ *603/431–5186* ⊕ *www. pressroomnh.com.*

The Red Door Lounge. Discover the local music scene at the Red Door Lounge, open every night except Tuesday. Indie music fans shouldn't miss Monday night's Hush Hush Sweet Harlot live music series. ⊠ *107 State St.* ⊕ *www.reddoorportsmouth.com.*

SPORTS AND THE OUTDOORS
BOAT TOURS

Gundalow Company. Sail the Piscataqua River in a flat-bottom gundalow built at Strawbery Banke. Help the crew haul up lobster traps and trawl for plankton, or buy a picnic lunch from the White Apron Café (next door to the office) and sit back and enjoy the spectacular views. Learn all about the region's history from an onboard educator. Cruises run Memorial Day to Columbus Day. ✉ *60 Marcy St.* ☎ *603/433–9505* ⊕ *www.gundalow.org.*

Isles of Shoals Steamship Company. This company runs cruises aboard the *Thomas Laighton*, a replica of a Victorian steamship, May through October. Cruises take you to the Isles of Shoals, Portsmouth Harbor, or the nearby lighthouses. Lunches and light snacks are available on board, or you can bring your own. ✉ *Barker Wharf, 315 Market St.* ☎ *603/431–5500, 800/441–4620* ⊕ *www.islesofshoals.com.*

Portsmouth Harbor Cruises. From May to October, Portsmouth Harbor Cruises operates tours of Portsmouth Harbor, foliage trips on the Cocheco River, and sunset cruises aboard the MV *Heritage.* ✉ *64 Ceres Str.* ☎ *603/436–8084, 800/776–0915* ⊕ *www.portsmouthharbor.com.*

Portsmouth Kayak Adventures. Explore the Piscataqua River Basin and the New Hampshire coastline on a guided kayak tour with Portsmouth Kayak Adventures. Beginners are welcome (instruction included). Tours are run daily from June through mid-October, at 10, 2, and 6. ✉ *185 Wentworth Rd.* ☎ *603/559–1000* ⊕ *www.portsmouthkayak.com.*

SHOPPING

Market Square, in the center of town, has gift and clothing boutiques, book and gourmet food shops, and exquisite crafts stores.

Byrne & Carlson. Watch elegant chocolates being made in the European tradition in this small shop. ✉ *121 State St.* ☎ *888/559–9778* ⊕ *www.byrneandcarlson.com.*

Nahcotta. Stylish ceramics, jewelry, glassware, and art fill this contemporary design boutique. ✉ *110 Congress St.* ☎ *603/433–1705* ⊕ *www.nahcotta.com.*

N.W. Barrett Gallery. Handmade jewelry, pottery, and glass are featured in this fine gallery. You'll also find one-of-a-kind lamps and rocking chairs. ✉ *53 Market St.* ☎ *603/431–4262* ⊕ *www.nwbarrett.com.*

Piscataqua Fine Arts. This gallery mainly shows works of master woodcutter Don Gorvett, who creates spellbinding scenes of New England's coast, particularly the Portsmouth area. There are also works by some of New England's finest printmakers, including Sidney Hurwitz, Alex deConstant, Peter Vincent, and Sean Hurley. ✉ *123 Market St.* ☎ *603/436–7278* ⊕ *www.dongorvettgallery.com.*

Three Graces Gallery. The gallery showcases an unusual mix of paintings, sculpture, jewelry and other art; watch for monthly changing exhibitions. ✉ *105 Market St.* ☎ *603/436–1988* ⊕ *www.threegracesgallery.com.*

RYE

8 miles south of Portsmouth.

On Route 1A as it winds south through Rye you'll pass a group of late-19th- and early-20th-century mansions known as **Millionaires' Row.** Because of the way the road curves, the drive south along this route is breathtaking. In 1623 the first Europeans established a settlement at Odiorne Point in what is now the largely undeveloped and picturesque town of Rye, making it the birthplace of New Hampshire. Today the area's main draws are a lovely state park, oceanfront beaches, and the views from Route 1A. Strict town laws have prohibited commercial development in Rye, creating a dramatic contrast with its frenetic neighbor Hampton Beach.

EXPLORING

FAMILY Fodor's Choice ★ **Odiorne Point State Park.** These 330 acres of protected land are where David Thompson established the first permanent European settlement in what is now New Hampshire. Several nature trails with informative panels describe the park's military history, and you can enjoy vistas of the nearby Isles of Shoals. The rocky shore's tidal pools shelter crabs, periwinkles, and sea anemones. Throughout the year the **Seacoast Science Center** hosts exhibits on the area's natural history. The tidal-pool touch tank and 1,000-gallon Gulf of Maine deepwater aquarium are popular with kids. There are also guided nature walks. ✉ *570 Ocean Blvd.* ☎ *603/436–8043* 🌐 *www.seacoastsciencecenter.org* 🎟 *$7* 🕒 *Science center Mar.–Oct., daily 10–5; Nov.–Feb., Sat.–Mon. 10–5.*

WHERE TO EAT

$$$ AMERICAN 🍴 **The Carriage House.** Across from Jenness Beach, this elegant cottage serves innovative dishes with a Continental flair. Standouts include penne teeming with fresh seafood, creative curries, and steak with peppercorns. Savor a hot-fudge ice-cream croissant for dessert. Upstairs is a wood-paneled tavern with ocean views. [$] *Average main: $26* ✉ *2263 Ocean Blvd.* ☎ *603/964–8251* 🌐 *www.carriagehouserye.com* 🕒 *No lunch.*

SPORTS AND THE OUTDOORS

BEACHES

Jenness State Beach. Good for swimming and sunning, this long sand beach is a favorite among locals who enjoy fewer people and nice waves for bodysurfing. Wide and shallow, Jenness Beach is a great place for kids to run and build sand castles. **Amenities:** lifeguards; parking (fee); showers; toilets. **Best for:** swimming; walking; surfing. ✉ *2280 Ocean Blvd.* ☎ *603/436–1552* 🌐 *www.nhstateparks.org* 🎟 *Parking $2 per hour May–Sept.*

Wallis Sands State Beach. This family-friendly swimmers' beach has bright white sands, a picnic area, a store, and beautiful views of the Isles of Shoals. **Amenities:** food and drink; lifeguards; parking (no fee); showers; toilets. **Best for:** swimming; walking. ✉ *1050 Ocean Blvd.* 🌐 *www.nhstateparks.org* 🎟 *$15 per car* 🕒 *June–Labor Day, weekdays 8–4, weekends 8–6.*

FISHING AND WHALE-WATCHING

Atlantic Fleet. For a full- or half-day deep-sea angling charter, try Atlantic Fleet. Whale-watching trips are also available. ✉ *1870 Ocean Blvd.* ☎ *603/964–5220, 800/942–5364* 🌐 *www.atlanticwhalewatch.com.*

Granite State Whale Watch. This outfit conducts naturalist-led whale-watching tours aboard the 100-passenger MV *Granite State* from May to mid-October. ✉ *Rye Harbor State Marina, 1860 Ocean Blvd.* ☎ *603/964–5545, 800/964–5545* 🌐 *www.granitestatewhalewatch.com* 🎟 *$36.*

HAMPTON BEACH

8 miles south of Rye.

FAMILY This is an authentic seaside amusement center—the domain of fried-dough stands, loud music, arcade games, palm readers, parasailing, and bronzed bodies. The 3-mile-long boardwalk, where kids play games and see how saltwater taffy is made, looks like a leftover from the 1940s; in fact, the whole community remains remarkably free of modern franchises. Free outdoor concerts are held on many a summer evening, and once a week there's a fireworks display. An estimated 150,000 people visit the town and its free public beach on the 4th of July, and it draws plenty of people until late September, when things close up.

GETTING HERE AND AROUND

Interstate 95 is the fastest way to get to Hampton, but the town is best seen by driving on Route 1A, which follows the coast and offers access to a number of beaches. Route 1 is the quickest way to get around, but be prepared for strip malls and stoplights.

ESSENTIALS

Visitor Information **Hampton Area Chamber of Commerce** ✉ *160 Ocean Blvd.* ☎ *603/926–8718* 🌐 *www.hamptonchamber.com.*

EXPLORING

Fuller Gardens. Away from the beach crowds is this small late-1920s estate garden designed in the Colonial Revival style by landscape architect Arthur Shurtleff. It encompasses 1,700 rosebushes, a hosta garden, a Japanese garden, and a tropical conservatory. ✉ *10 Willow Ave., North Hampton* ☎ *603/964–5414* 🌐 *www.fullergardens.org* 🎟 *$9* 🕐 *Mid-May–mid-Oct., daily 10–5:30.*

WHERE TO EAT AND STAY

$$$ AMERICAN 🍴 **Ron's Landing.** Among the motels lining Ocean Boulevard is this casually elegant restaurant. The seared ahi tuna with a citrus, chili, and soy glaze is one of the tastiest starters. Outstanding entrées include the oven-roasted salmon with a cream sauce, slivered almonds, and sliced apples, or the baked haddock stuffed with scallops and lobster and served with lemon-dill butter. From many tables you can enjoy sweeping ocean views. Brunch is popular. [$] *Average main: $28* ✉ *379 Ocean Blvd.* ☎ *603/929–2122* 🌐 *www.ronslanding.com* 🕐 *Closed Mon. Closed Tues., Sept.–June. No lunch.*

$$$$
HOTEL

☺ **Ashworth by the Sea.** You'll be surprised how contemporary this across-from-the-beach hotel feels, even though it's been around for a century. **Pros:** center-of-town location; comfortable rooftop bar; open all year. **Cons:** breakfast not included; very busy. $ *Rooms from: $349* ✉ *295 Ocean Blvd.* ☎ *603/926–6762, 800/345–6736* ⊕ *www. ashworthhotel.com* ⤳ *98 rooms, 7 suites* ❍| *No meals.*

NIGHTLIFE

Hampton Beach Casino Ballroom. Despite its name, the Hampton Beach Casino Ballroom isn't a gambling establishment but a late-19th-century auditorium that has hosted everyone from Janis Joplin to Jerry Seinfeld, George Carlin, and B.B. King. Performances in the 1,800-seat space run from April to October. ✉ *169 Ocean Blvd.* ☎ *603/929–4100* ⊕ *www. casinoballroom.com.*

SPORTS AND THE OUTDOORS

BEACHES

Hampton Beach State Park. At the mouth of the Hampton River stretches this long sand beach with a boardwalk that runs along restaurants, attractions, and hotels. There's a visitor center (open year-round), multiple picnic areas, and a seasonal store. **Amenities:** food and drink; lifeguards; parking (fee); showers; toilets. **Best for:** swimming. ✉ *160 Ocean Blvd.* ☎ *603/926–3784* ⊕ *www.nhstateparks.org* ⤳ *Parking $15.*

FISHING AND WHALE-WATCHING

Several companies conduct whale-watching excursions as well as half-day, full-day, and nighttime cruises. Most leave from the Hampton State Pier on Route 1A.

Al Gauron Deep Sea Fishing. This company maintains a fleet of three boats for whale-watching cruises and fishing charters. ✉ *State Pier, 1 Ocean Blvd.* ☎ *603/926–2469, 800/905–7820* ⊕ *www.algauron.com.*

Eastman's Docks. This company offers whale-watching and fishing cruises. ✉ *River St., Seabrook* ☎ *603/474–3461* ⊕ *www.eastmansdocks.com.*

Smith & Gilmore. Enjoy half-day and full-day deep-sea fishing expeditions with Smith & Gilmore. ✉ *State Pier, Ocean Blvd.* ☎ *603/926–3503, 877/272–4005* ⊕ *www.smithandgilmore.com.*

EN
ROUTE

Applecrest Farm Orchards. At the 400-acre Applecrest Farm Orchards you can pick your own apples and berries or buy fresh fruit pies and cookies, homemade ice cream, and many other tasty treats. Fall brings cider pressing, hayrides, pumpkins, and music on weekends. Author John Irving worked here as a teenager, and his experiences inspired the book *The Cider House Rules.* ✉ *133 Exeter Rd., Hampton Falls* ☎ *603/926–3721* ⊕ *www.applecrest.com* ☾ *May–Dec., daily 8–6.*

EXETER

9 miles northwest of Hampton, 52 miles north of Boston, 47 miles southeast of Concord.

Fodor'sChoice
★

During the Revolutionary War, Exeter was the state capital, and it was here amid intense patriotic fervor that the first state constitution and the first Declaration of Independence from Great Britain were put to paper. These days Exeter shares more in appearance and personality with Boston's blue-blooded satellite communities than the rest of New Hampshire—indeed, plenty of locals commute to Beantown. Cheerful cafés, coffeehouses, and shops with artisan-made wares make up this bustling town center.

GETTING HERE AND AROUND

Amtrak's *Downeaster* service stops here between Boston and Portland, Maine. On the road, it's 9 miles northwest of Hampton on Route 111. Route 101 is also a good way to get to Exeter from the east or west. The town itself is easy to walk around.

ESSENTIALS

Visitor Information Exeter Area Chamber of Commerce ✉ *24 Front St., #101* ☎ *603/772–2411* 🌐 *www.exeterarea.org.*

EXPLORING

American Independence Museum. This museum celebrates the birth of the nation. The story unfolds during the course of a guided tour focusing on the Gilman family, who lived in the house during the Revolutionary era. See drafts of the U.S. Constitution and the first Purple Heart as well as letters and documents written by George Washington and the household furnishings of John Taylor Gilman, one of New Hampshire's early governors. In July the museum hosts the American Independence Festival. ✉ *Ladd-Gilman House, 1 Governor's La.* ☎ *603/772–2622* 🌐 *www.independencemuseum.org* 🎫 *$6* 🕒 *Mid-May–Dec., Thurs.–Sat. 10–4.*

Phillips Exeter Academy. The 1,000 high school students at Phillips Exeter Academy lend energy to the town. The grounds, open to the public, resemble an elite Ivy League university campus. The Louis Kahn–designed library is the largest secondary-school library in the world. The Lamont Gallery, in the Frederick R. Mayer Art Center, offers free contemporary art exhibits. ✉ *20 Main St.* ☎ *603/772–4311* 🌐 *www.exeter.edu.*

9

WHERE TO EAT

$ AMERICAN 🍴 **The Green Bean.** This serve-yourself retaurant makes it easy when you can't decide between the delicious homemade soups, sandwiches, and salads. All the soups are made daily, including curried butternut squash, spicy corn chowder, and tarragon potato with peas. Perfect for dunking are sandwiches like turkey with cranberry and stuffing or veggie and walnut pesto. The early-morning menu includes breakfast burritos, French toast, and ham and eggs. It's a popular spot for those on the go, but if you have the time, sit in the delightful little courtyard for a quiet view of the town. [$] *Average main: $6* ✉ *33 Water St.* ☎ *603/778–7585* 🌐 *www.nhgreenbean.com* 🕒 *No dinner.*

$ AMERICAN 🍴 **Loaf and Ladle.** There are three components to this down-to-earth place's success: quality, price, and location. The name refers to homemade bread (more than 30 kinds) and soup (100 varieties are offered on a rotating basis). Choose a chunk of anadama bread, made with cornmeal and molasses, to go with your soup, and take your meal to one of the two decks that hover over the Exeter River. It's simple and homey. $ *Average main: $6* ✉ *9 Water St.* ☎ *603/778–8955* ⚓ *Reservations not accepted* ⊘ *Closed Tues. and Wed. No dinner.*

$$
AMERICAN

✕ **The Tavern At River's Edge.** A convivial downtown gathering spot on the Exeter River, this downstairs tavern pulls in parents of prep-school kids, college students, and suburbanites. It may be informal, but the kitchen turns out surprisingly sophisticated meals. Start with sautéed ragout of mushrooms stewed in a Marsala cream sauce with sun-dried tomatoes, roasted shallots, garlic, and Asiago cheese, then move on to a lobster risotto with wild mushrooms and asparagus. In the bar, lighter fare is on offer. $ *Average main: $16* ✉ *163 Water St.* ☎ *603/772–7393* ⊕ *www.tavernatriversedge.com.*

WHERE TO STAY

$$
B&B/INN

🏨 **The Exeter Inn.** This elegant, brick, Georgian-style inn on the Phillips Exeter Academy campus has been the choice of visiting parents since it opened in the 1930s. **Pros:** well-designed rooms; elegant feel; near the center of town. **Cons:** a walk to the shops. $ *Rooms from: $139* ✉ *90 Front St.* ☎ *603/772–5901, 800/782–8444* ⊕ *www.theexeterinn.com* ⮑ *46 rooms, 5 suites* ⦿ *No meals.*

$$$
B&B/INN
Fodor'sChoice
★

🏨 **Inn by the Bandstand.** New owners have spruced up this charming B&B, located in the heart of town. **Pros:** perfect in-town location; bikes available; friendly staff. **Cons:** some ongoing renovations. $ *Rooms from: $179* ✉ *6 Front St.* ☎ *603/772–6352, 877/239–3837* ⊕ *www.innbythebandstand.com* ⮑ *9 rooms, 4 suites* ⦿ *Breakfast.*

SHOPPING

Exeter Fine Crafts. Prestigious Exeter Fine Crafts shows an impressive selection of juried pottery, paintings, jewelry, textiles, glassware, and other fine creations by more than 300 of northern New England's top artisans. ✉ *61 Water St.* ☎ *603/778–8282* ⊕ *www.exeterfinecrafts.com.*

A Picture's Worth a Thousand Words. A destination for bibliophiles, this shop offers rare books, town histories, old maps, and antique and contemporary prints. ✉ *65 Water St.* ☎ *603/778–1991* ⊕ *www.apwatw.com.*

Willow. You'll never know what you'll find at this creative shop, which stocks interesting antiques, finely stitched linens, handcrafted jewelry, woven throws, organic teas, gardening accessories, and gorgeous bags. ✉ *183 Water St.* ☎ *603/773–9666.*

DURHAM

12 miles north of Exeter, 11 miles northwest of Portsmouth.

Settled in 1635 and the home of General John Sullivan, a Revolutionary War hero and three-time New Hampshire governor, Durham was where Sullivan and his band of rebel patriots stored the gunpowder they captured from Ft. William and Mary in New Castle. Easy access to Great Bay via the Oyster River made Durham a maritime hub in the 19th century. Among the lures today are the water, farms that welcome visitors, and the University of New Hampshire, which occupies much of the town's center.

GETTING HERE AND AROUND

By car, Durham can be reached on Route 108 from the north or south and Route 4 from Portsmouth from the east or Concord from the west. The *Downeaster* Amtrak train stops here between Boston and Portland, Maine.

ESSENTIALS

Visitor Information University of New Hampshire ☎ *603/862–1234* 🌐 *www.unh.edu.*

EXPLORING

Museum of Art. Noted items in this gallery's collection include 19th-century Japanese wood-block prints, Boston expressionist works, and art of New England. It's on the campus of the University of New Hampshire. ✉ *Paul Creative Arts Center, 30 College Rd.* ☎ *603/862–3712* 🌐 *www.unh.edu/moa* 🎟 *Free* 🕒 *Sept.–May, Mon.–Wed. 10–4, Thurs. 10–8, weekends 1–5.*

WHERE TO EAT AND STAY

$$$ AMERICAN 🍴 **ffrost Sawyer Tavern.** That's not a typo, but an attempt to duplicate a quirky, obsolete spelling of the name of a former owner of this hilltop house. The eccentric stone basement tavern has its original beams, from which hang collections of mugs, hats, and—no way around it—bedpans. There's a terrific old bar. Choose from fine dinner fare, such as grilled porterhouse steak or potato-encrusted haddock. Lunch standards include burgers, pizza, and fish-and-chips. [$] *Average main: $25* ✉ *17 Newmarket Rd.* ☎ *603/868–7800* 🌐 *www.threechimneysinn.com.*

$$$ B&B/INN 🏨 **Three Chimneys Inn.** This stately yellow structure has graced a hill overlooking the Oyster River since 1649. **Pros:** intimate inn experience; afternoon social hour. **Cons:** have to walk or drive into town. [$] *Rooms from: $189* ✉ *17 Newmarket Rd.* ☎ *603/868–7800, 888/399–9777* 🌐 *www.threechimneysinn.com* 🛏 *23 rooms, 1 suite* 🍽 *Breakfast.*

NIGHTLIFE

Stone Church. Music aficionados head to the Stone Church—in an authentic 1835 former Methodist church—for its craft beers, pub grub, and live rock, jazz, blues, reggae, soul, and folk music. ✉ *5 Granite St., Newmarket* ☎ *603/659–7700* 🌐 *www.stonechurchrocks.com.*

SPORTS AND THE OUTDOORS

Wagon Hill Farm. You can hike several trails or picnic at 130-acre Wagon Hill Farm, overlooking the Oyster River. The old farm wagon on the top of a hill is one of the most photographed sights in New England. Park next to the farmhouse and follow walking trails to the wagon and through the woods to the picnic area by the water. Sledding and cross-country skiing are winter activities. ✉ *U.S. 4, across from Emery Farm.*

SHOPPING

Emery Farm. In the same family for 11 generations, Emery Farm sells fruits and vegetables in summer (including pick-your-own blueberries), pumpkins in fall, and Christmas trees in winter. The farm shop carries breads, pies, and local crafts. Children can pet the resident goats and donkey and ride on a hay wagon on some weekends in September and

New Hampshire Farmers' Markets

Winter squash is in season in New Hampshire from September to October.

Bedford Farmers' Market. Just outside Manchester, the Bedford Farmers' Market has a particularly rich mix of local growers and food purveyors, selling seasonal jams, pasture-raised lamb and chicken, homemade treats for dogs and cats, goats' milk soaps and balms, and even New Hampshire wines. There's usually live music and activities for children at hand. ⊠ *St. Elizabeth Seton Parish, 190 Meetinghouse Road, Bedford ⊕ bedfordfarmersmarket.org ⊙ June–Oct., Tues. 3–6 pm.*

Derry Farmers' Market. A mix of farmers, artisans, and entertainers show you what they're got at this year-round market. The summer and fall markets are held on Wednesday in the municipal parking lot. The winter market is held on Saturday mornings from early December to mid-March inside the Upper Village Hall, 53 East Derry Road. ⊠ *14 Manning St., Derry ☎ 603/434–8974 ⊙ Mid-July–Sept., Wed. 3–7.*

Lebanon Farmers' Market. Lebanon Farmers' Market not only draws more than 50 vendors from throughout the northern Connecticut River valley, but offers live music and concerts following the market. ⊠ *Colburn Park, 51 North Park St., Lebanon ☎ 603/448–5121 ⊕ www.lebanonfarmersmarket. org ⊙ Late May–late Sept., Thurs. 4–7 pm. Winter market, mid-Nov.-April, every third Sat., 10–1, 75 Bank St.*

Portsmouth Farmers' Market. One of the best and longest-running farmers' markets is the Portsmouth Farmers' Market, which features live music and regional treats, such as maple syrup and artisanal cheeses, in addition to seasonal produce. ⊠ *1 Junkins Ave., Portsmouth ⊙ May–early Nov., Sat. 8 am–1 pm.*

Seacoast Growers Association. The market is part of the Seacoast Growers Association, which also has weekly markets in Dover, Durham, Exeter, Newington, and Portsmouth. ⊕ *www.seacoastgrowers.org*

—Andrew Collins

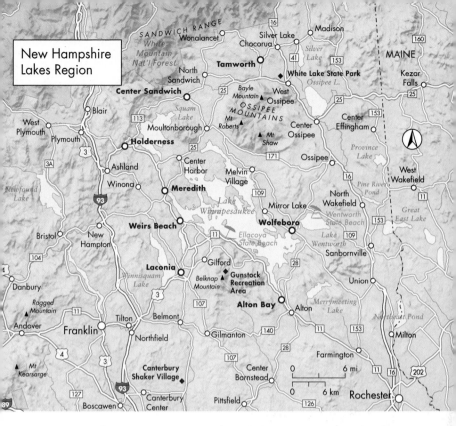

October. ✉ 135 Piscataqua Rd. ☎ 603/742–8495 ⊕ www.emeryfarm.
com ⏱ May–Dec., daily 9–6.

LAKES REGION

Lake Winnipesaukee, a Native American name for "smile of the great
spirit," is the largest of the dozens of lakes scattered across the eastern
half of central New Hampshire. With about 240 miles of shoreline of
inlets and coves, it's the largest in the state. Some claim Winnipesaukee
has an island for each day of the year—the total, though impressive,
falls short: 274.

In contrast to Winnipesaukee, which bustles all summer long, is the
more secluded Squam Lake. Its tranquillity is no doubt what attracted
the producers of *On Golden Pond*; several scenes of the Academy
Award–winning film were shot here. Nearby Lake Wentworth is named
for the state's first royal governor, who, in building his country manor
here, established North America's first summer resort.

Well-preserved Colonial and 19th-century villages are among the
region's many landmarks, and you'll find hiking trails, good antiques
shops, and myriad water-oriented activities. This section begins at

With 240 miles of shoreline, Lake Winnipesaukee is so much more than just the town of Wolfeboro.

Wolfeboro and more or less circles Lake Winnipesaukee clockwise, with several side trips.

ESSENTIALS

Visitor Information Lakes Region Association ☎ *603/286–8008, 800/605–2537* ⊕ *www.lakesregion.org.*

WOLFEBORO

40 miles northeast of Concord, 49 miles northwest of Portsmouth.

Quietly upscale and decidedly preppy Wolfeboro has been a resort since Royal Governor John Wentworth built his summer home on the shore of the lake in 1768. The town bills itself as the oldest summer resort in the country, and its center, bursting with tony boutiques, fringes Lake Winnipesaukee and sees about a tenfold population increase each summer. The century-old, white clapboard buildings of the Brewster Academy prep school bracket the town's southern end. Wolfeboro marches to a steady, relaxed beat, comfortable for all ages.

GETTING HERE AND AROUND

Enter on the west side of Lake Winnipesaukee on Route 28. Be prepared for lots of traffic in the summertime.

ESSENTIALS

Visitor Information Wolfeboro Area Chamber of Commerce ⊠ *32 Central Ave.* ☎ *603/569–2200* ⊕ *www.wolfeborochamber.com.*

EXPLORING

New Hampshire Boat Museum. Two miles northeast of downtown, this museum celebrates New Hampshire's maritime legacy with displays of vintage wooden boats, model boats, antique engines, racing photography, trophies, and vintage marina signs. You can also take a 45-minute narrated ride on the lake in a reproduction triple-cockpit HackerCraft. ✉ *399 Center St.* ☎ *603/569–4554* 🌐 *www.nhbm.org* 🎟 *$7* 🕐 *Memorial Day–Columbus Day, Mon.–Sat. 10–4, Sun. noon–4.*

Wright Museum. Uniforms, vehicles, and other artifacts at this museum illustrate the contributions of those on the home front to the U.S. World War II effort. ✉ *77 Center St.* ☎ *603/569–1212* 🌐 *www.wrightmuseum.org* 🎟 *$10* 🕐 *May–Oct., Mon.–Sat. 10–4, Sun. noon–4.*

QUICK BITES

Kelly's Yum Yum Shop. Picking up freshly baked breads, pastries, cookies, and other sweets in Kelly's Yum Yum Shop has been a tradition since 1948. The butter-crunch cookies are highly addictive. ✉ *16 N. Main St.* ☎ *603/569–1919* 🌐 *www.yumyumshop.net* 🕐 *Closed Nov.–Apr.*

Lydia's Cafe. Brewster Academy students and summer folk converge upon groovy little Lydia's Cafe for espresso, sandwiches, homemade soups, bagels, and desserts. [$] *Average main: $6* ✉ *33 N. Main St.* ☎ *603/569–3991.*

SPORTS AND THE OUTDOORS

BEACH

Wentworth State Beach. Away from the hustle and bustle of Wolfeboro, this no-frills park offers a quiet beach with good fishing, picnic tables and grills, and fields for playing ball. **Amenities:** parking (no fee); showers; toilets. **Best for:** swimming; walking. ✉ *297 Governor Wentworth Hwy.* ☎ *603/569–3699* 🌐 *www.nhstateparks.org* 🎟 *$4.*

HIKING

Abenaki Tower. A quarter-mile hike to the 100-foot post-and-beam Abenaki Tower, followed by a more rigorous climb to the top, rewards you with a view of Lake Winnipesaukee and the Ossipee mountain range. The trailhead is on Route 109 in Tuftonboro. ✉ *Rte. 109, Tuftonboro.*

WATER SPORTS

Scuba divers can explore *The Lady*, the 125-foot-long cruise ship that sank in 30 feet of water off Glendale in 1895.

Dive Winnipesaukee Corp. This corporation runs charters out to wrecks and offers rentals, repairs, scuba sales, boat rentals, and lessons in waterskiing. ✉ *Wolfeboro Bay, 4 N. Main St.* ☎ *603/569–8080* 🌐 *www.divewinnipesaukee.com.*

SHOPPING

The Country Bookseller. You'll find an excellent regional-history section and plenty of children's titles in this independent bookseller, where you can also do a little reading in its small café. ✉ *23A N. Main St.* ☎ *603/569–6030* 🌐 *www.thecountrybookseller.com.*

OUTDOOR OUTFITTERS AND RESOURCES

BIKING

Bike New England. This is an excellent resource for maps, tours, and routes for cyclists all over New England 🌐 *www.bikenewengland.com.*

Bike the Whites. From May to October, Bike the Whites organizes New Hampshire inn-to-inn bike tours. ☎ *800/421–1785* 🌐 *www.bikethewhites.com.*

HIKING

Appalachian Mountain Club. A range of hiking, biking, paddling, and climbing trips are offered at the Appalachian Mountain Club. ☎ *800/372–1758* 🌐 *amc-nh.org/index.php.*

New England Hiking Holidays. Hike across the state with New England Hiking Holidays. ☎ *603/356–9696, 800/869–0949* 🌐 *www.nehikingholidays.com.*

New Hampshire State Parks. Special hikes throughout the year are sponsored by New Hampshire State Parks. ✉ *172 Pembroke Rd., Box 1856, Concord* ☎ *603/271–3556* 🌐 *www.nhstateparks.org.*

U.S. Forest Service. If you want to hike in the White Mountains, the U.S. Forest Service has all the details. ☎ *603/536–6100* 🌐 *www.fs.usda.gov/whitemountain.*

SKIING

Ski New Hampshire. Learn where the best powder is at Ski New Hampshire. ☎ *603/745–9396* 🌐 *www.skinh.com.*

Hampshire Pewter. The artisans at Hampshire Pewter use 16th-century techniques to make pewter tableware, accessories, and gifts. ✉ *9 Railroad Ave.* ☎ *603/569–4944, 800/639–7704* 🌐 *www.hampshirepewter.com.*

WHERE TO EAT

$$ ASIAN 🍴 **East of Suez.** In a countrified lodge on the south side of town, this friendly restaurant serves creative Asian cuisine, with an emphasis on Philippine fare, such as *lumpia* (pork-and-shrimp spring rolls with a sweet-and-sour fruit sauce) and *pancit canton* (panfried egg noodles with sautéed shrimp and pork and Asian vegetables with a sweet oyster sauce). You can also sample Thai red curries, Japanese tempura, and Korean-style flank steak. Gluten-free and vegan options are available. [$] *Average main: $19* ✉ *775 S. Main St.* ☎ *603/569–1648* 🌐 *www.eastofsuez.com* ⏲ *Closed Oct.–mid-May.*

WHERE TO STAY

$$$ B&B/INN 🏨 **Topsides B & B.** At this stylish retreat, refined rooms convey the allure of a particular region, from Martha's Vineyard to coastal France to British fox-hunting country. **Pros:** close to downtown; appealing rooms; great service. **Cons:** some rooms are upstairs. [$] *Rooms from: $195* ✉ *209 S. Main St.* ☎ *603/569–3834* 🌐 *www.topsidesbb.com* 🛏 *5 rooms* 🍽 *Breakfast.*

$$$$ B&B/INN 🏨 **The Wolfeboro Inn.** This 1812 inn has a commanding lakefront location and is a perennial favorite for those visiting Lake Winnipesaukee. **Pros:** lakefront setting; interesting pub. **Cons:** no breakfast. [$] *Rooms*

from: $279 ✉ 90 N. Main St. ☎ 603/569–3016, 800/451–2389 🌐 www.wolfeboroinn.com 🛏 41 rooms, 3 suites.

ALTON BAY

10 miles southwest of Wolfeboro.

Lake Winnipesaukee's southern shore is alive with visitors from the moment the first flower blooms until the last maple sheds its leaves. Two mountain ridges hold 7 miles of the lake in Alton Bay, which is the name of both the inlet and the town at its tip. Cruise boats dock here, and small planes land year-round on the water and the ice. There's a dance pavilion, along with miniature golf, a public beach, and a Victorian-style bandstand.

EXPLORING

Mt. Major. About 5 miles north of Alton Bay, Mt. Major has a 3-mile trail up a series of challenging cliffs. At the top is a four-sided stone shelter built in 1925, but the reward is the spectacular view of Lake Winnipesaukee. ✉ *Rte. 11.*

WHERE TO EAT

$$$$ AMERICAN Fodor's Choice ★

🍴 **The Crystal Quail.** With just four tables tucked inside an 18th-century farmhouse, this restaurant is worth the drive for the sumptuous meals prepared by longtime proprietors Harold and Cynthia Huckaby, who use free-range meats and mostly organic produce and herbs in their cooking. The prix-fixe menu changes daily but might include saffron-garlic soup, a house pâté, mushroom and herb quail, or goose confit with apples and onions. No credit cards are accepted. [$] *Average main: $75* ✉ *202 Pitman Rd., 12 miles south of Alton Bay, Center Barnstead* ☎ *603/269–4151* 🌐 *www.crystalquail.com* ✍ *Reservations essential* 💳 *No credit cards* 🕓 *Closed Mon. and Tues. No lunch* ☞ *BYOB.*

9

WEIRS BEACH

17 miles northwest of Alton Bay.

FAMILY

Weirs Beach is Lake Winnipesaukee's center for arcade activity. Anyone who loves souvenir shops, fireworks, waterslides, hordes of children, and even a drive-in theater will feel right at home. Cruise boats also depart from here.

GETTING HERE AND AROUND

Weirs Beach is just north of Laconia and south of Meredith on Route 3.

EXPLORING

FAMILY

Funspot. The mothership of Lake Winnipesaukee's family-oriented amusement parks, Funspot claims that its more than 500 video games make it the world's largest arcade. You can also work your way through a miniature golf course, a driving range, an indoor golf simulator, and 20 lanes of bowling. Some outdoor attractions are closed in winter months. ✉ *579 Endicott St. N* ☎ *603/366–4377* 🌐 *www.funspotnh.com* 🕓 *Mid-June–Labor Day, daily 9 am–11 pm; Labor Day–mid-June, Sun.–Thurs. 10–10, Fri. and Sat. 10 am–11 pm.*

FAMILY **MS _Mount Washington._** The 230-foot MS _Mount Washington_ offers
Fodor's Choice 2½-hour scenic cruises of Lake Winnipesaukee, departing from Weirs
★ Beach and stopping in Wolfeboro, Alton Bay, Center Harbor, and Meredith (you can board at any of these stops). Evening cruises include live music and a buffet dinner, and the Sunday Champagne brunch cruise includes plenty of bubbly. The same company operates the MV _Sophie C._ ($26), which has been the area's floating post office for more than a century. The boat departs from Weirs Beach with mail and passengers and passes through parts of the lake not accessible by larger ships. The MV _Doris E._ ($18) has one- and two-hour scenic cruises of Meredith Bay throughout the summer. ⊠ _211 Lakeside Ave._ ☎ _603/366–5531, 888/843–6686_ ⊕ _www.cruisenh.com_ ✉ _$29_ ☉ _Mid-May–late Oct., departure times vary._

Winnipesaukee Scenic Railroad. You can board at Weirs Beach or Meredith, and the restored cars of this scenic railroad will carry you along the lakeshore on one- or two-hour rides. Special dinner trips include fall foliage and a harvest meal. ⊠ _154 Main St., Meredith_ ☎ _603/745–2135_ ⊕ _www.hoborr.com_ ✉ _$17_ ☉ _July and Aug., daily; Memorial Day–late June and Labor Day–late Oct., weekends._

NIGHTLIFE AND THE ARTS
New Hampshire Music Festival. Attend award-winning chamber music on Tuesday, classical orchestra on Thursday, and pops concerts on alternate Saturdays from early July to mid-August. The New Hampshire Music Festival's concerts are held in the Silver Arts Center on Main Street in Plymouth. ⊠ _85 Main St., Plymouth_ ☎ _603/535–2787 box office_ ⊕ _www.nhmf.org._

SPORTS AND THE OUTDOORS
BEACH
FAMILY **Ellacoya State Beach.** Families enjoy this secluded park that spans 600 feet along the southwestern shore of Lake Winnipesaukee, offering views of the Sandwich and Ossipee mountains. It's never crowded, and its shallow beach is safe for small children. The park has sheltered picnic tables and a small campground. **Amenities:** parking (no fee); toilets. **Best for:** solitude; swimming. ⊠ _266 Scenic Rd., Gilford_ ☎ _603/293–7821_ ⊕ _www.nhstateparks.org_ ✉ _$5_ ☉ _Late May–mid-June, weekends 9–6; mid-June–mid-Oct., daily 9–6._

BOATING
Thurston's Marina. This marina rents a wide variety of boats as well as ski equipment. ⊠ _18 Endicott St. N_ ☎ _603/366–4811_ ⊕ _www.thurstons marina.com._

GOLF
Pheasant Ridge. In a bucolic setting, this 18-hole course offers great farm and mountain views. ⊠ _140 Country Club Rd., Gilford_ ☎ _603/524–7808_ ⊕ _www.playgolfne.com_ ✉ _Greens fee: $20–$26_ ⚐ _18 holes, 6,044 yards, par 70._

SKI AREA

Gunstock Mountain Resort. High above Lake Winnipesaukee, this ski resort has invested millions to increase snowmaking capabilities, introduce more options for beginners, and add slope-side dining. Thrill Hill, a snow-tubing park, has five runs, a lift service, and 21 acres of terrain parks. The ski area has 55 trails (24 of them open for night skiing) and 32 miles of cross-country and snowshoeing trails. In summer the Mountain Adventure Park offers an adrenaline rush with ziplines, an aerial obstacle course, and scenic chairlift rides. There are also trails for mountain bikes, a skateboarding park, and paddleboats. ⊠ *719 Cherry Valley Rd., Gilford* ☎ *603/293–4341* ⊕ *www.gunstock.com.*

SHOPPING

Pepi Herrmann Crystal. Watch artists at work crafting hand-cut crystal glasses, as well as contemporary tableware, ornaments, and jewelry. ⊠ *3 Waterford Pl., Gilford* ☎ *603/528–1020* ⊕ *www.handcut.com* ⊗ *Closed Sun. and Mon.*

LACONIA

4 miles west of Gilford, 27 miles north of Concord.

The arrival in Laconia—then called Meredith Bridge—of the railroad in 1848 turned the once-sleepy hamlet into the Lakes Region's chief manufacturing hub. It acts today as the area's supply depot, a perfect role given its accessibility to both Winnisquam and Winnipesaukee lakes as well as Interstate 93. It also draws bikers from around the world for Laconia Motorcycle Week in June.

GETTING HERE AND AROUND

The best way to Laconia is on Route 3 or Route 11. Scenic rides from the south include Route 106 and Route 107.

EXPLORING

Belknap Mill. Inside this 1823 textile mill you can see how cloth and clothing were made almost two centuries ago. Belknap Mill contains operating knitting machines, a 1918 hydroelectric power system, and changing exhibits. ⊠ *Mill Plaza, 25 Beacon St. E* ☎ *603/524–8813* ⊕ *www.belknapmill.org* 🎟 *Free* ⊗ *Weekdays 9–5.*

OFF THE BEATEN PATH

Canterbury Shaker Village. Established in 1792, this village flourished in the 1800s and practiced equality of the sexes and races, common ownership, celibacy, and pacifism. The last member of the religious community passed away in 1992. Shakers invented such household items as the clothespin and the flat broom and were known for the simplicity and integrity of their designs. Engaging 60- and 90-minute tours pass through some of the 694-acre property's more than 25 restored buildings, many of them with original furnishings. Crafts demonstrations take place daily. Ask the admissions desk for a map of the many nature trails. The Shaker Box Lunch and Farm Stand offers salads, soups, and baked goods, and sells seasonal vegetables and locally produced maple syrup. A shop sells handcrafted items. ⊠ *288 Shaker Rd., 15 miles south of Laconia via Rte. 106, Canterbury* ☎ *603/783–9511, 866/783–9511*

🌐 *www.shakers.org* 🎟 *$17* 🕒 *Mid-May–Oct., daily 10–5; Nov. and Dec., weekends 10–5.*

WHERE TO STAY

$$$ B&B/INN 🏨 **The Lake House at Ferry Point.** Four miles southwest of Laconia, this home across the street from Lake Winnisquam is a quiet retreat with a dock and small beach. Built in the 1800s as a summer retreat for the Pillsbury family of baking fame, this red Victorian farmhouse has superb views of the lake. White wicker furniture and hanging baskets of flowers grace the 60-foot-long veranda, and the gazebo by the water's edge is a pleasant place to lounge and listen for loons. **Pros:** affordable rates; lovely setting. **Cons:** away from main attractions. [$] *Rooms from: $179* ✉ *100 Lower Bay Rd., Sanbornton* ☎ *603/524–0087* 🌐 *www.lakehouseatferrypoint.com* 🛏 *8 rooms, 1 suite* 🍴 *Breakfast.*

SPORTS AND THE OUTDOORS

FAMILY **Bartlett Beach.** On Lake Winnisquam, this small but pleasant city-run park has a 600-foot-long sand beach. Here you'll find picnic tables and a playground, making it ideal for families, particularly those with small children. **Amenities:** lifeguards; parking (no fee); toilets. **Best for:** swimming. ✉ *99 Winnisquam Ave.* 🎟 *Free.*

FAMILY **Opechee Park.** Nestled in a quiet cove is this medium-sized family-friendly beach with a playground, baseball field, tennis courts, and picnic areas. **Amenities:** parking (no fee); toilets. **Best for:** swimming. ✉ *N. Main St.* 🌐 *www.city.laconia.nh.us* 🎟 *Free.*

SHOPPING

Tanger Outlets Tilton. The more than 56 stores at the Tanger Outlets Tilton include Brooks Brothers, Nike, Eddie Bauer, and Coach. ✉ *120 Laconia Rd., off I–93, Tilton* ☎ *603/286–7880* 🌐 *www.tangeroutlet.com.*

MEREDITH

11 miles north of Laconia.

Meredith is a favored spot for water sports enthusiasts and anglers. For a true taste of Meredith, take a walk down Main Street, just one block from busy Route 3, which is dotted with intimate coffee shops, salons and barber shops, family restaurants, redbrick buildings, antiques stores, and a gun shop. You can pick up area information at a kiosk across from the town docks. One caveat: on busy weekends getting into town from the west can mean sitting in traffic for 30 minutes or more.

ESSENTIALS

Visitor Information Meredith Area Chamber of Commerce ☎ *877/279–6121* 🌐 *www.meredithareachamber.com.*

WHERE TO EAT AND STAY

$$ AMERICAN 🍴 **Lakehouse Grille.** With perhaps the best lake views of any restaurant in the region, this restaurant might be forgiven for ambitious dishes that fall a bit short. Come to this upscale lodge to be near the lake, especially in the convivial bar area, and you'll leave quite happy. The best dishes are old reliables like steak, ribs, and pizza. Breakfast is offered daily,

What's your vessel of choice for exploring New Hampshire's Lakes Region: kayak, canoe, powerboat, or sailboat?

and there's brunch on Sunday. [$] *Average main: $20* ✉ *Church Landing, 281 Daniel Webster Hwy.* ☎ *603/279–5221* 🌐 *www.thecman.com.*

$$$ AMERICAN 🍴 **Mame's.** This 1820s tavern, once the home of the village doctor, now contains a warren of dining rooms with exposed-brick walls, wooden beams, and wide-plank floors. Expect a wide variety of beef, seafood, and chicken plates, but don't be afraid to order the "Luncheon Nightmare," which is pumpernickel topped with turkey, ham, broccoli, and bacon and baked in a cheese sauce. You can also find vegetarian dishes, burgers, sandwiches, and wonderful soups and salads on the menu. Save room for the bread pudding with apples and rum sauce. A cozy tavern upstairs features pub food. [$] *Average main: $23* ✉ *8 Plymouth St.* ☎ *603/279–4631* 🌐 *www.mamesrestaurant.com.*

$$ B&B/INN Fodor's Choice ★ 🏨 **Mill Falls at the Lake.** You have your choice of lodgings here: relaxing Church Landing and Bay Point are on the shore of Lake Winnipesaukee, and convivial Mill Falls is across the street, with a swimming pool and a 19th-century mill that's now a lively shopping area with more than a dozen unique shops. **Pros:** many lodging choices and prices; lakefront rooms; fun environment. **Cons:** expensive; two buildings do not sit on the lake. [$] *Rooms from: $150* ✉ *312 Daniel Webster Hwy., at Rte. 25* ☎ *603/279–7006, 800/622–6455* 🌐 *www.millfalls.com* 🛏 *172 rooms, 15 suites* 🍽 *Breakfast.*

Interlakes Summer Theatre. Broadway musicals are presented at the Interlakes Summer Theatre during its 10-week season of summer stock. ☒ *Interlakes Auditorium, One Laker La., off Rte. 25* ☏ *888/245–6374* ⊕ *www.interlakestheatre.com.*

SPORTS AND THE OUTDOORS

BOATING

Meredith is near the quaint village of Center Harbor, another boating hub that's in the middle of three bays at the northern end of Lake Winnipesaukee.

Meredith Marina. Between May and October, you can rent powerboats and other vessels at this marina. ☒ *2 Bayshore Dr.* ☏ *603/279–7921* ⊕ *www.meredithmarina.com.*

Wild Meadow Canoes & Kayaks. Canoes and kayaks are available at Wild Meadow Canoes & Kayaks. ☒ *6 Whittier Hwy., Center Harbor Village* ☏ *603/253–7536, 800/427–7536* ⊕ *www.wildmeadowcanoes.com.*

HIKING

Red Hill. Off Route 25, Red Hill really does turn red in autumn. The reward at the end of this hiking trail is a view of Squam Lake and the mountains. ☒ *Bean Rd., 7 miles northeast of Meredith.*

SHOPPING

Home Comfort. The owners of Lavinia's Relaxed Dining next door also operate this three-floor showroom of designer furnishings, antiques, and accessories. ☒ *Senters Market, Rte. 25B, Center Harbor Village* ☏ *603/253–6660* ⊕ *www.homecomfortnh.com.*

Keepsake Quilting. Reputedly America's largest quilting shop, this store contains 5,000 bolts of fabric, hundreds of quilting books, and plenty of supplies. There are also gorgeous handmade quilts. ☒ *Senters Market, 12 Main St., Center Harbor* ☏ *603/253–4026, 800/525–8086* ⊕ *www.keepsakequilting.com.*

League of New Hampshire Craftsmen. Here you'll find works by more than 250 area artisans who regularly demonstrate their skills. There are other branches in Littleton, Hanover, North Conway, and Concord. ☒ *279 U.S. 3, next to the Inn at Church Landing* ☏ *603/279–7920* ⊕ *www.nhcrafts.org/meredith.*

Old Print Barn. This shop carries rare prints—Currier & Ives, antique botanicals, and more—from around the world. ☒ *343 Winona Rd., New Hampton* ☏ *603/279–6479* ⊕ *www.theoldprintbarn.com.*

HOLDERNESS

8 miles northwest of Meredith.

Routes 25B and 25 lead to the prim small town of Holderness, between Squam and Little Squam lakes. *On Golden Pond,* starring Katharine Hepburn and Henry Fonda, was filmed on Squam, whose quiet beauty attracts nature lovers.

View simple yet functional furniture, architecture, and crafts at Canterbury Shaker Village.

EXPLORING

FAMILY Fodor's Choice ★ **Squam Lakes Natural Science Center.** A pontoon boat cruise is one of the main attractions at Squam Lakes Natural Science Center, and is the best way to tour the waterfront. Naturalists talk about the animals that make their home here, and give fascinating facts about the loon. This 230-acre property includes a ¾-mile nature trail that passes by trailside exhibits of black bears, bobcats, otters, mountain lions, red and gray foxes, and other native wildlife. The "Up Close to Animals" series in July and August lets you get a good look at these creatures. Children's activities include learning about bugs and wilderness survival skills. ✉ *23 Science Center Rd.* ☎ *603/968–7194* 🌐 *www.nhnature.org* 🎟 *$15* 🕘 *May–Oct., daily 9:30–4:30.*

WHERE TO EAT

$$$$ AMERICAN 🍴 **Manor on Golden Pond Restaurant.** Leaded-glass panes and wood paneling set a decidedly romantic tone at this wonderful inn overlooking Squam Lake. The main dining room is in the manor's original billiard room and features woodwork from 1904. Two others have very different looks: one features white linens, fresh flowers, and candlelight; the other is in the style of a Parisian bistro. The menu changes weekly, but might include lobster risotto, filet mignon, quail, or monkfish. Ask about the fabulous seven-course tasting menu. Breakfast is also served. [$] *Average main: $35* ✉ *31 Manor Dr., corner of U.S. 3 and Shepard Dr.* ☎ *603/968–3348* 🌐 *www.manorongoldenpond.com* ✍ *Reservations essential.*

$$ AMERICAN 🍴 **Walter's Basin.** A former bowling alley in the heart of Holderness makes an unlikely but charming setting for meals overlooking Little

Squam Lake—local boaters dock right beneath the dining room. Among the specialties on this seafood-intensive menu are crostini with pan-fried rainbow trout. Burgers and sandwiches are served in the adjoining tavern. $ *Average main: $20* ⊠ *859 U.S. 3, Little Squam Lake* ☎ *603/968–4412* ⊕ *www.waltersbasin.com.*

WHERE TO STAY

$$$
B&B/INN
Glynn House. Pam, Ingrid, and Glenn Heidenreich operate this beautifully restored 1890s Queen Anne–style Victorian with a turret and wraparound porch and, next door, a handsome 1920s carriage house. **Pros:** luxurious rooms; well-run property; social atmosphere. **Cons:** not much to do in town. $ *Rooms from: $171* ⊠ *59 Highland St., Ashland* ☎ *603/968–3775, 866/686–4362* ⊕ *www.glynnhouse.com* ⊅ *6 rooms, 8 suites* �‖ *Breakfast.*

$$$
B&B/INN
Inn on Golden Pond. Sweet-as-pie Bill and Bonnie Webb run this comfortable and informal B&B a short distance from the lake, to which they provide hiking trail maps. **Pros:** friendly innkeepers; comfortable rooms and common spaces. **Cons:** not directly on the lake; not luxurious. $ *Rooms from: $185* ⊠ *1080 U.S. 3* ☎ *603/968–7269* ⊕ *www. innongoldenpond.com* ⊅ *6 rooms, 2 suites* �‖ *Breakfast.*

$$$$
B&B/INN
Fodor's Choice
★
The Manor on Golden Pond. A name like this is a lot to live up to—and luckily, the Manor on Golden Pond is the most charming inn in the Lakes Region. **Pros:** wood fireplaces; comfy sitting rooms; great food; welcoming hosts. **Cons:** expensive rates. $ *Rooms from: $285* ⊠ *U.S. 3 and Shepard Hill Rd.* ☎ *603/968–3348, 800/545–2141* ⊕ *www. manorongoldenpond.com* ⊅ *21 rooms, 2 suites, 1 cottage.*

$$$
B&B/INN
Squam Lake Inn. Graceful Victorian furnishings fill the nine stylish rooms at this peaceful farmhouse inn just a short stroll from Squam Lake. **Pros:** quiet setting; comfortable beds; big breakfasts. **Cons:** short walk to lake. $ *Rooms from: $185* ⊠ *Shepard Hill Rd.* ☎ *603/968–4417, 800/839–6205* ⊕ *www.squamlakeinn.com* ⊅ *9 rooms* ☾ *Closed mid-Oct.–May* �‖ *Breakfast.*

CENTER SANDWICH

12 miles northeast of Holderness on Route 103.

With Squam Lake to the west and the Sandwich Mountains to the north, Center Sandwich claims one of the prettiest settings of any Lakes Region community. So appealing are the town and its views that John Greenleaf Whittier used the Bearcamp River as the inspiration for his poem "Sunset on the Bearcamp." The town attracts artisans—crafts shops abound among its clutch of charming 18th- and 19th-century buildings.

ESSENTIALS

Visitor Information Squam Lakes Area Chamber of Commerce ☎ *603/968–4494* ⊕ *www.visitsquam.com.* **Sandwich HIstorical Society** ☎ *603/284-6269* ⊕ *www.sandwichhistorical.org.*

EXPLORING

Castle in the Clouds. Looking for all the world like a fairy-tale castle, this wonderful mountaintop estate was finished in 1914. The elaborate mansion has 16 rooms, eight bathrooms, and doors made of lead. Owner Thomas Gustave Plant spent $7 million, the bulk of his fortune, on this project and died penniless in 1941. A tour includes the mansion and the Castle Springs water facility on this high Ossippee Mountain Range property overlooking Lake Winnipesaukee; there's also hiking and pony and horseback rides. ✉ *455 Old Mountain Rd., Moultonborough* ☎ *603/476–5900* 🌐 *www.castleintheclouds.org* 🎫 *$16* 🕑 *Mid-May–early June weekends 10–4; early June–late Oct., daily 10–4.*

Loon Center. Recognizable for its eerie calls and striking black-and-white coloring, the loon resides on many New Hampshire lakes but is threatened by the gradual loss of its habitat. Two trails wind through the 200-acre Loon Center; vantage points on the Loon Nest Trail overlook the spot resident loons sometimes occupy in late spring and summer. ✉ *183 Lee's Mills Rd.* ☎ *603/476–5666* 🌐 *www.loon.org* 🎫 *Free* 🕑 *Columbus Day–Nov. and mid-May–June, Mon.–Sat. 9–5; Dec.–mid-May, Thurs.–Sat. 9–5; July–Columbus Day, daily 9–5.*

WHERE TO EAT

$$ AMERICAN 🍴 **Corner House Inn.** In a converted barn adorned with paintings by local artists, this eatery serves classic American fare. Salads with local greens are a house specialty, but also try the chef's lobster-and-mushroom bisque or the shellfish sauté. Lunch and Sunday brunch are served, and on Thursday evenings there's often storytelling with dinner. [$] *Average main: $18* ✉ *22 Main St.* ☎ *603/284–6219* 🌐 *www.cornerhouseinn.com* 🕑 *No lunch mid-Oct.–mid-June.*

$$$ AMERICAN 🍴 **Lavinia's Relaxed Dining.** Talk about relaxing: that's exactly what you'll want to do in this splendidly restored mansion, built in 1820 by John Coe for his bride Ravinia. Enjoy a glass of wine on the veranda, then sink into a plush chairs in the dining room, where the original French wallpaper, depicting the Seven Wonders of the World, still fills viewers with awe. Start with pumpkin-and-mascarpone ravioli or Gorgonzola-stuffed artichoke hearts, then try the grilled red snapper with pineapple pico de gallo or a lobster potpie. Lighter fare can be ordered in the upstairs lounge. For an unforgettable, romantic evening, reserve the cupola—it seats only two. [$] *Average main: $26* ✉ *Plymouth St. and Lake St., Center Harbor Village* ☎ *603/253–8617* 🌐 *www.laviniasdining.com* 🕑 *No lunch.*

$$$ AMERICAN 🍴 **The Woodshed.** Farm implements and antiques hang on the walls of this enchanting 1860 barn. The fare is mostly traditional New England—prime rib, rack of lamb, marinated chicken—but with some surprises, such as Cajun-blackened pork tenderloin. Either way, the exceptionally fresh ingredients are sure to please. [$] *Average main: $26* ✉ *128 Lee Rd., Moultonborough* ☎ *603/476–2311* 🌐 *www.thewoodshednh.com* 🕑 *Closed Mon.–Wed. mid-Oct.–June.*

9

SHOPPING

Old Country Store and Museum. The store has been selling maple syrup, aged cheeses, penny candy, and other items since 1781. Much of the equipment used in the store is antique, and the free museum displays old farming and forging tools. ✉ *1011 Whittier Hwy.* ☎ *603/476–5750* 🌐 *www.nhcountrystore.com.*

TAMWORTH

13 miles east of Center Sandwich, 20 miles southwest of North Conway.

President Grover Cleveland summered in what remains a village of almost unreal quaintness—it's equally photogenic in verdant summer, during the fall foliage season, or under a blanket of winter snow. Cleveland's son, Francis, returned and founded the acclaimed Barnstormers Theatre in 1931, one of America's first summer theaters and one that continues to this day. Tamworth has a clutch of villages within its borders. At one of them—Chocorua—the view through the birches of Chocorua Lake has been so often photographed that you may experience déjà vu. Rising above the lake is Mt. Chocorua (3,490 feet), which has many good hiking trails.

GETTING HERE AND AROUND

The five villages of Tamworth boast six churches, which are worth a half-day's casual drive to admire their white clapboard elegance. Downtown Tamworth is tiny and can be strolled in a few minutes, but you might linger in the hope to meet one of the town's many resident poets and artists.

EXPLORING

FAMILY **Remick Country Doctor Museum and Farm.** For 99 years (1894–1993) Dr. Edwin Crafts Remick and his father provided medical services to the Tamworth area and operated a family farm. After the younger Remick died, these two houses were turned into the Remick Country Doctor Museum and Farm. The second floor of the house has been kept as it was when Remick passed away; it's a great way to see the life of a country doctor. Each season the still-working farm features a special activity such as maple-syrup making. The farm also has hiking trails and picnicking areas. ✉ *58 Cleveland Hill Rd.* ☎ *603/323–7591, 800/686–6117* 🌐 *www.remickmuseum.org* 🎟 *$5* 🕒 *Labor Day–mid-June, weekdays 10–4; mid-June–Labor Day, weekdays 10–4, Sat. 10–3.*

WHERE TO EAT AND STAY

$$ SEAFOOD FAMILY 🍴 **Jake's Seafood and Grill.** Oars and nautical trappings adorn the wood-paneled walls at this stop between West and Center Ossipee, about 8 miles southeast of Tamworth. The kitchen serves some of eastern New Hampshire's freshest and tastiest seafood, notably lobster pie, fried clams, and seafood casserole. Other choices include steak, ribs, and chicken dishes. [$] *Average main: $17* ✉ *2055 Rte. 16, West Ossipee* ☎ *603/539–2805* 🌐 *www.jakesseafoodco.com* 🕒 *Closed Apr. and Nov.*

$$ SOUTHERN FAMILY 🍴 **Yankee Smokehouse.** This down-home barbecue joint's logo depicting a happy pig foreshadows the gleeful enthusiasm with which patrons dive into the hefty sandwiches of sliced pork and smoked chicken and

immense platters of baby back ribs and smoked sliced beef. Ample sides of slaw, beans, fries, and garlic toast complement the hearty fare. It serves gluten-free items, too. Even Southerners have been known to come away impressed. $ *Average main: $17* ⊠ *Rtes. 16 and 25, about 5 miles southeast of Tamworth* ☎ *603/539–7427* ⊕ *www. yankeesmokehouse.com.*

$$
B&B/INN

Lazy Dog Inn. If you travel with your dog, you've just found your new favorite B&B. **Pros:** mega–dog friendly; super clean; full breakfast. **Cons:** three rooms share baths. $ *Rooms from: $120* ⊠ *201 Rte. 16, Chocorua* ☎ *603/323–8350, 888/323–8350* ⊕ *www.lazydoginn.com* ⌁ *7 rooms, 4 with bath* ⎢○⎢ *Breakfast.*

THE ARTS

Arts Council of Tamworth. The Arts Council of Tamworth produces concerts—soloists, string quartets, revues, children's programs—from September through June and an arts show in late July. ⊠ *77 Main St., Tamworth* ☎ *603/323–8104* ⊕ *www.artstamworth.org/.*

Barnstormers Theatre. This theater puts on eight dramatic and comedic productions during July and August. ⊠ *104 Main St.* ☎ *603/323–8500* ⊕ *www.barnstormerstheatre.org.*

SPORTS AND THE OUTDOORS

White Lake State Park. The 72-acre stand of native pitch pine here is a National Natural Landmark. The park has hiking trails, a sandy beach, trout fishing, canoe rentals, and a picnic area. ⊠ *98 State Park Rd.* ☎ *603/323–7350* ⊕ *www.nhstateparks.org* ⛁ *$5* ☉ *Memorial Day– Labor Day, daily dawn–dusk; Labor Day–mid-Oct., weekends dawn to dusk.*

THE WHITE MOUNTAINS

9

Sailors approaching East Coast harbors frequently mistake the pale peaks of the White Mountains—the highest range in the northeastern United States—for clouds. It was 1642 when explorer Darby Field could no longer contain his curiosity about one mountain in particular. He set off from his Exeter homestead and became the first European to climb what would later be called Mt. Washington. The 6,288-foot peak must have presented Field with formidable obstacles—its summit claims the highest wind velocity in the world ever recorded (231 mph in 1934) and can see snow every month of the year.

Today an auto road and a cog railway lead to the top of Mt. Washington, and people come by the tens of thousands to hike and climb, photograph the vistas, and ski. The peak is part of the Presidential Range, whose peaks are named after early presidents, and part of the White Mountain National Forest, which has roughly 770,000 acres that extend from northern New Hampshire into southwestern Maine. Among the forest's scenic notches (deep mountain passes) are Pinkham, Kinsman, Franconia, and Crawford. From the notches lead trailheads for short hikes and multiday adventures, which are also excellent spots for photographing the majestic White Mountains

This section of the guide begins in Waterville Valley, off Interstate 93, and continues to North Woodstock. It then follows portions of the White Mountains Trail, a 100-mile loop designated as a National Scenic and Cultural Byway.

ESSENTIALS

Visitor Information **White Mountains Visitors Bureau** ✉ *200 Kancamagus Hwy., off I–93, North Woodstock* ☎ *800/346–3687* 🌐 *www.visitwhitemountains.com.* **White Mountain National Forest** ☎ *603/536–6100* 🌐 *www.fs.fed.us/r9/forests/white_mountain.*

WATERVILLE VALLEY

60 miles north of Concord.

The first visitors began arriving in Waterville Valley in 1835. A 10-mile cul-de-sac follows the Mad River and is surrounded by mountains. The valley was first a summer resort and then more of a ski area. Although it's now a year-round getaway, it still has a small-town charm. There are inns, condos, restaurants, shops, conference facilities, a grocery store, and a post office.

GETTING HERE AND AROUND

Depot Camp is a great starting point for hiking, snowshoeing, and cross-country skiing. In town, the Schuss bus has regular stops at the shops in Village Square, the lodges and condos, the Waterville Valley Conference Center, and the ski area. There's enough to do in this small village to keep outdoors enthusiasts busy for several days.

WHERE TO STAY

$$$$ HOTEL 🏨 **Black Bear Lodge.** This family-friendly property has one-bedroom suites that sleep up to six people. **Pros:** affordable rates; perfect for families. **Cons:** basic in its decor and services. [$] *Rooms from: $250* ✉ *3 Village Rd.* ☎ *603/236–4501, 800/349–2327* 🌐 *www.blackbearlodgenh.com* 🛏 *107 suites.*

$$$$ HOTEL 🏨 **Golden Eagle Lodge.** Waterville's premier condominium property—with its steep roof punctuated by dozens of gabled dormers—recalls the grand hotels of an earlier era. **Pros:** most reliable accommodation in town; plenty of elbow room. **Cons:** somewhat bland architecture and decor. [$] *Rooms from: $230* ✉ *28 Packard's Rd.* ☎ *888/703–2453* 🌐 *www.goldeneaglelodge.com* 🛏 *139 condominiums.*

$ HOTEL 🏨 **Snowy Owl Inn & Resort.** You're treated to afternoon wine and cheese in this hotel's atrium lobby, which has a three-story fieldstone fireplace and wonderful watercolors of its namesake. **Pros:** affordable rates; includes Continental breakfast. **Cons:** guests have access to the White Mountain Athletic Club, but pay to use. [$] *Rooms from: $99* ✉ *41 Village Rd.* ☎ *603/236–8383, 800/766–9969* 🌐 *www.snowyowlinn.com* 🛏 *85 rooms* 🍴 *Breakfast.*

SPORTS AND THE OUTDOORS

Waterville Valley Resort. Former U.S. ski-team star Tom Corcoran designed this family-oriented resort. The lodgings and various amenities are about a mile from the slopes, but a shuttle renders a car unnecessary.

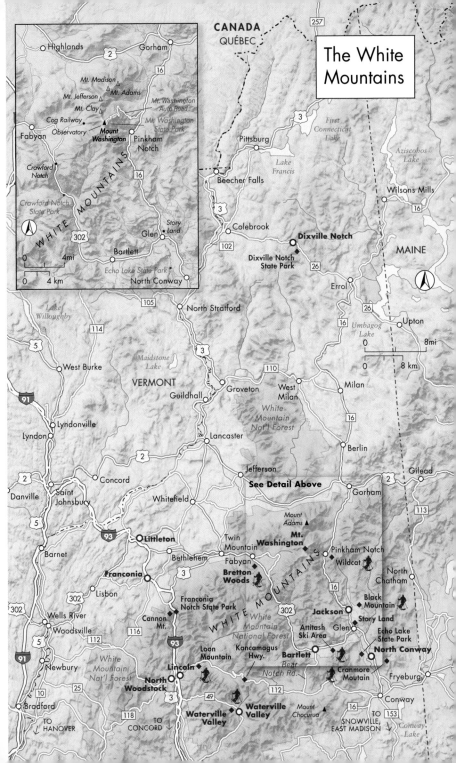

The White Mountains

CANADA
QUÉBEC

Detail (inset map)

Highlands
Gorham
Mt. Madison
Mt. Jefferson
Mt. Adams
Mt. Clay
Mt. Washington Auto Road
Cog Railway
Observatory
Mt. Washington State Park
Mount Washington
Pinkham Notch
Fabyan
Crawford Notch
Crawford Notch State Park
WHITE MOUNTAINS
Glen
Story Land
Bartlett
Echo Lake State Park
North Conway

0   4mi
0   4 km

Main map

Pittsburg
First Connecticut Lake
Lake Francis
Aziscohos Lake
Beecher Falls
Wilsons Mills
Colebrook
Dixville Notch
MAINE
Dixville Notch State Park
Errol
Upton
North Stratford
Umbagog Lake
0   8mi
0   8 km
Lake Willoughby
West Burke
Maidstone Lake
VERMONT
Groveton
White Mountain Nat'l Forest
West Milan
Milan
Guildhall
Lyndonville
Lancaster
Berlin
Lyndon
Jefferson
Gilead
Concord
See Detail Above
Gorham
Danville
Saint Johnsbury
Whitefield
Mount Adams
Mt. Washington
Pinkham Notch
Wildcat
Barnet
Twin Mountain
Littleton
Bethlehem
Fabyan
Bretton Woods
North Chatham
Franconia
Black Mountain
Lisbon
Jackson
Story Land
Wells River
Franconia Notch State Park
Cannon Mt.
White Mountain National Forest
Glen
Echo Lake State Park
Woodsville
WHITE MOUNTAINS
Attitash Ski Area
North Conway
Loon Mountain
Kancamagus Hwy.
Bartlett
Newbury
Lincoln
Bear Notch Rd.
Cranmore Mountain
Fryeburg
North Woodstock
Conway
Bradford
White Mountain Nat'l Forest
Waterville Valley
Waterville Valley
Mount Chocorua
TO SNOWVILLE, EAST MADISON
Conway Lake
TO HANOVER
TO CONCORD

This ski area has hosted more World Cup races than any other in the East, so most advanced skiers will be challenged. Most of the 50 trails are intermediate: straight down the fall line, wide, and agreeably long. About 20 acres of tree-skiing add heart-pounding stimulus. Complete snowmaking coverage ensures good skiing even when nature doesn't cooperate. The Waterville Valley cross-country network, with the ski center in the town square, provides over 43 miles of groomed trails. ⊠ *1 Ski Area Rd.* ☎ *603/236–8311, 800/468–2553 snow conditions, 800/468–2553 lodging* ⊕ *www.waterville.com.*

LINCOLN AND NORTH WOODSTOCK

64 miles north of Concord.

These neighboring towns at the southwestern end of the White Mountains National Forest and one end of the Kancamagus Highway (Route 112) form a lively resort area, especially for Bostonian families who can make an easy day trip straight up Interstate 93 to Exit 32. Festivals, such as the New Hampshire Scottish Highland Games in mid-September, keep Lincoln swarming with people year-round. The town itself is not much of an attraction. Tiny North Woodstock maintains more of a village feel.

GETTING HERE AND AROUND

Lincoln and North Woodstock are places to spend a day shopping in their quaint shops, which are within easy walking distance of each other. It's a pleasant 1-mile stroll between the two towns. On Route 112, which connects the two villages, there is a state visitor center.

ESSENTIALS

Visitor Information Lincoln–Woodstock Chamber of Commerce ☎ *603/745–6621* ⊕ *www.lincolnwoodstock.com.*

EXPLORING

FAMILY **Clark's Trading Post.** Chock-full of hokum, this old-time amusement park is a favorite with families. There are half-hour train rides over a 1904 covered bridge, a museum of Americana inside an 1880s firehouse, a restored gas station filled with antique cars, circus performers, and an Old Man of the Mountain rock-climbing tower. In additition, there's a mining sluice where you can pan for gems. Tour guides tell tall tales and vendors sell popcorn, ice cream, and pizza. There's also a mammoth gift shop and a penny-candy store. ⊠ *110 Daniel Webster Hwy., off I–93, North Lincoln* ☎ *603/745–8913* ⊕ *www.clarkstradingpost. com* ⊆ *$20* ☉ *Mid-June–Aug. and and mid-Sept–mid-Oct., daily 9–5; mid-May–mid-June and early Sept., weekends 9–5.*

FUN TOUR **Hobo Railroad.** Newly restored vintage train cars take you along the scenic shores of the Pemigewassett River. The tours take 80 minutes. Santa Express trains run from late November to late December. ⊠ *64 Railroad St., off Kancamagus Hwy.* ☎ *603/745–2135* ⊕ *www.hoborr.com* ⊆ *$16* ☉ *July–mid-Oct., daily; May, June, and mid-Oct.–late Oct., weekends.*

Continued on page 572

HIKING THE APPALACHIAN TRAIL

Tucked inside the nation's most densely populated corridor, a simple footpath in the wilderness stretches more than 2,100 miles, from Georgia to Maine. The Appalachian Trail passes through some of New England's most spectacular regions, and daytrippers can experience the area's beauty on a multitude of accessible, rewarding hikes.   *By Melissa Kim*

Running along the spine of the Appalachian Mountains, the trail was fully blazed in 1937 and designed to connect anyone and everyone with nature. Within a day's drive of two-thirds of the U.S. population, it draws an estimated two to three million people every year. Through-hikers complete the whole trail in one daunting six-month season, but all ages and abilities can find renewal and perspective here in just a few hours. One-third of the AT passes through New England, and it's safe to say that the farther north you go, the harder the trail gets. New Hampshire and Maine challenge experienced hikers with windy, cold, and isolated peaks.

Top, hiking in New Hampshire's White Mountains. Above, autumn view of Profile Lake, Pemigewasset, NH.

ON THE TRAIL

New England's prime hiking season is in late summer and early fall, when the blaze of foliage viewed from a high peak is unparalleled. Popular trails see high crowds; if you seek solitude, try hiking at sunrise, a peaceful time that's good for wildlife viewing. You'll have to curb your enthusiasm in spring and early summer to avoid mud season in late April and black flies in May and June.

With the right gear, attitude, and preparation, winter can also offer fine opportunities for hiking, snowshoeing, and cross-country skiing.

FOLLOW THE TRAIL

Most hiking trails are marked with blazes, blocks of colored paint on a tree or rock. The AT, and only the AT, is marked by vertical, rectangular 2- by 6-inch white blazes. Two blazes mark route changes; turn in the direction of the top blaze. At higher elevations, you might also see cairns, small piles of rocks carefully placed by trail rangers to show the way when a blaze might be obscured by snow or fog.

Scenic U.S. 302—and the AT—pass through Crawford Notch, a spectacular valley in New Hampshire's White Mountains.

Hikers gather outside Lakes of the Clouds Hut, near the peak of Mount Washington.

TRIP TIPS

WHAT TO WEAR: For clothes, layer with a breathable fabric like polypropylene, starting with a shirt, a fleece, and a wind- or water-resistant shell. Bring gloves, a hat, and a change of socks.

WHAT TO BRING: Carry plenty of water and lightweight high-energy food. Don't forget sunscreen and insect repellent. Bring a map and compass. Just in case: a basic first-aid kit, a flashlight or headlamp, whistle, multi-tool, and matches.

PLAN AHEAD: In your car, leave a change of clothing, especially dry socks and shoes, as well as extra water and food.

PLAY IT SAFE: Tell someone your hiking plan and take a hiking partner. Carry a rescue card with emergency contact information and allergy details.

BE PREPARED: Plan your route and check the weather forecast in advance.

REMEMBER YOUR BEGINNINGS: Look back at the trail especially at the trailhead and at tricky junctions. If you've got a digital camera, photograph trail maps posted at the trailhead or natural landmarks to help you find your way.

WHERE TO STAY

Day hikers looking to extend the adventure can also make the experience as hard or as soft as they choose. Through-hikers combine camping with overnight stays in primitive shelters, mountain huts, comfortable lodges, and resorts just off the trail.

Rustic cabins and lean-tos provide basic shelter in Maine's Baxter State Park. In Maine and New Hampshire, the Appalachian Mountain Club runs four-season lodges as well as a network of mountain huts for backcountry hikers. A hiker code of camaraderie and conviviality prevails in these huts. Experience a night and you might just find yourself dreaming of a through-hike.

FOR MORE INFORMATION

Appalachian Trail Conservancy
(🌐 www.appalachiantrail.org)

Appalachian National Scenic Trail
(🌐 www.nps.gov/appa)

Appalachian Mountain Club
(🌐 www.outdoors.org)

ANIMALS ALONG THE TRAIL

❶ Black bear

Black bears are the most common—and smallest—bear in North America. Clever and adaptable, these adroit mammals will eat whatever they can (though they are primarily vegetarian, favoring berries, grasses, roots, blossoms, and nuts). Not naturally aggressive, black bears usually make themselves scarce when they hear hikers. The largest New England populations are in New Hampshire and Maine.

❷ Moose

Spotting a moose in the wild is unforgettable: their massive size and serene gaze are truly humbling. Treasure the moment, then slowly back away. At more than six feet tall, weighing 750 to 1,000 pounds, a moose is not to be trifled with, particularly during rutting and calving seasons (fall and spring, respectively). Dusk and dawn are the best times to spot the iconic animal; you're most likely to see one in Maine, especially in and around ponds.

⚠ Black flies

Especially fierce in May and June, these pesky flies can upset the tranquility of a hike in the woods as they swarm your face and bite your neck. To ward them off, cover any exposed skin and wear light colors. You'll get some relief on a mountain peak; cold weather and high winds also keep them at bay.

❸ Bald eagles

Countless bird species can be seen and heard along the AT, but what could be more exciting than to catch a glimpse of our national bird as it bounces back from near extinction? Now it's not uncommon to see the majestic bald eagle with its tremendous wing span, white head feathers, and curved yellow beak. The white head and tail distinguish the bald from the golden eagle, a bit less rare but just as thrilling to see. Most of New England's bald eagles are in Maine, but they are now present—albeit in small numbers—in all six states.

WILDFLOWERS ALONG THE TRAIL

❹ Mountain laurel

The clusters of pink and white blooms of the mountain laurel look like bursts of fireworks. Up close, each one has the delicate detail of a lady's parasol. Blooms vary in color, from pure white to darker pink, and have different amounts of red markings. Connecticut's state flower, mountain laurel flourishes in rocky woods, blooming in May and June. Look for the shrub in southern New England; it's rare along the Appalachian trail in Vermont and Maine.

❺ Mountain avens

A member of the rose family, these showy yellow flowers abound in New Hampshire's White Mountains. You can't miss the large buttercup-like blooms on long green stems when they are in bloom from June through August. So common here, yet extremely rare: the only other place in the whole world where you can find mountain avens is on an island off the coast of Nova Scotia.

❻ Painted trillium

You might smell a trillium before you see it; these flowers have an unpleasant odor that may attract the flies that pollinate it. To identify this impressive flower, look for sets of three: three large pointed blue-green leaves, three sepals (small leaves beneath the petals), and three white petals with a brilliant magenta center. It can take four or five years for a trillium to produce one flower, which blooms in May and June in wet woodlands.

❼ Pink lady slippers

These delicate orchids can grow from 6 to 15 inches high and favor specific wet wooded areas in dappled sunlight. The slender stalk rises from a pair of green leaves, then bends a graceful neck to suspend the paper-thin pale pink closed flower. The slow-growing plant needs help from fungus and bees to survive and can live to be 20 years old. New Hampshire's state wildflower, the pink lady slipper blooms in June throughout New England.

● = Somewhat Common ● = Rare

CHOOSE YOUR DAY HIKE

MAINE

GULF HAGAS, Greenville
Difficult, 8-plus mi round-trip, 6–7 hours

This National Natural Landmark in the North Maine Woods is a spectacular sight for the adventurous day hiker. It involves a long drive on logging roads east from Greenville (*see Inland Maine section*) to a remote spot and a slippery, sometimes treacherous 8-mile hike around the rim of what's been dubbed Maine's Grand Canyon. Swimming in one of the sparkling pools under a 30-foot-high waterfall and admiring the views of cliffs, cascades, gorges, and chasms in this slate canyon, otherwise unthinkable in New England, will take your breath away.

TABLE ROCK, Bethel
Medium, 2.4 mi round-trip, 2 hours

Maine's Mahoosuc Range is thought to be one of the most difficult stretches of the entire AT, but north of Bethel at Grafton Notch State Park, day hikes range from easy walks in to cascading water-falls to strenuous climbs up Old Speck's craggy peak. The Table Rock trail offers interesting sights—great views of the notch from the immense slab of granite that gives this trail its name, as well as one of the state's largest system of slab caves—narrow with tall openings unlike underground caves.

NEW HAMPSHIRE

ZEALAND TRAIL, Berlin
Easy, 5.6 mi round-trip, 3.5–4 hours

New Hampshire's Presidential range gets so much attention and traffic that sometimes the equally spectacular Pemigewasset Wilderness, just to its west, gets overlooked. Follow State Route 302 to the trailhead on Zealand Rd. near Bretton Woods. For an easy day hike to one of the Appalachian Mountain Club's excellent overnight huts, take the mostly flat Zealand Trail over bridges and past a beaver swamp to Zealand Pond. The last tenth of a mile is a steep ascent to the mountain retreat, where you might spot an AT through-hiker taking a well-deserved rest. (Most north-bound through-hikers reach this section around July or August.) In winter, you can get here by a lovely cross-country ski trip.

TRAIL NAMES

For through-hikers, doing the AT can be a life-altering experience. One of trail's most respected traditions is the taking of an alter ego: a trail name. Lightning Bolt: fast hiker. Pine Knot: tough as one. Bluebearee: because a bear got all her food on her very first night on the trail.

VERMONT

HARMON HILL, Bennington

Medium to difficult, 3.6 mi round-trip, 3–4 hours

This rugged hike in the Green Mountains goes south along the AT where it coincides with the Long Trail, Vermont's century-old "footpath in the wilderness." From the trail-head on Route 9 just east of Bennington, the first half mile or so is strenuous, with some rock and log staircases and hairpins. The payback is the sweeping view from the top; you'll see Mount Anthony, Bennington and its iconic war monument, and the rolling green hills of the Taconics to the west.

STRATTON MOUNTAIN, Stratton

Difficult, 6.6 mi round-trip, 5–6 hours

A steep and steady climb from the trailhead on Kelly Stand Rd. (between West Wards-boro and Arlington) up the 3,936-foot-high Stratton Moun-tain follows the AT and Long Trail through mixed forests. It's said that this peak is where Benton MacKaye conceived of the idea for the Appalachian Trail in 1921. An observation tower at the summit gives you a great 360-degree view of the Green Mountains. From July to October, you can park at Stratton resort and ride the gondola up (or down) and fol-low the .75-mi Fire Tower Trail to the southern true peak.

MASSACHUSETTS

MOUNT GREYLOCK, North Adams

Easy to difficult, 2 mi round-trip, less than 1 hour

There are many ways to experience Massachusetts's highest peak. From North Adams, follow Route 2 to the Notch Rd. trailheads. For a warm-up, try the Rounds Rock trail (Easy, 0.7 mi) for some spectacular views. Or drive up the 8-mi-long summit road and hike down the Robinson's Point trail (Difficult, 0.8 mi) for the best view of the Hop-per, a glacial cirque that's home to an old-growth red spruce forest. At the sum-mit, the impressive **Bascom Lodge**, built in the 1930s by the Civilian Conservation Corps, provides delicious meals and overnight stays (🌐 www.bascomlodge.net).

CONNECTICUT

LION'S HEAD, Salisbury

Medium, 4.6 mi round-trip, 3.5–4 hours

The AT's 52 miles in Con-necticut take hikers up some modest mountains, including Lion's Head in Salisbury. From the trailhead on State Route 41, follow the white blazes of the AT for two easy miles, then take the blue-blazed Lion's Head Trail for a short, steep push over open ledges to the 1,738-foot summit with its commanding views of pastoral southern New Eng-land. Try this in summer when the mountain laurels—Con-necticut's state flower—are in bloom.

EXPERIENCE MOUNT WASHINGTON

Looking at Mt. Washington from Mt. Bond in the Pemigewasset Wilderness Area, New Hampshire.

Mount Washington is the Northeast's peak of superlatives: worst weather in the world, highest spot in the northeast, windiest place on Earth. It snows in the summer, there are avalanches in winter, and it's foggy 60 percent of the time. Strong 35-mile-per-hour winds are the average, and extreme winds of 100 miles per hour with higher gusts blow year-round. Here, you can literally get blown away.

Explorers, scientists, artists, and botanists have been coming to the mountain for hundreds of years, drawn by its unique geologic features, unusual plants, and exceptional climate.

WHY SO WINDY? The 6,288-foot-high treeless peak is the highest point for miles around, so nothing dampens the force of the wind. Also, the sharp vertical rise causes wind to accelerate. Dramatic changes in air pressure also cause strong, high winds. Add to that the fact that three major storm tracks converge here, and you've got a mountain that has claimed more than 135 lives in the past 150 years.

GOING UP THE MOUNTAIN

An ascent up Mount Washington is for experienced hikers who are prepared for severe, unpredictable weather. Even in summer, cold, wet, foggy, windy conditions prevail. The most popular route to the top is on the eastern face up the Tuckerman Ravine Trail. But countless trails offer plenty of moderate day hikes, like the Alpine Garden Trail, as an alternative to a summit attempt. Start at the Pinkham Notch Visitor Center on Route 16 to review your options.

BACKPACKING ON THE MOUNTAIN

Lakes of the Clouds Hut perches 5,050 feet up the southern shoulder, providing bunkrooms and meals in summer; reservations are required. On the eastern face, the **Hermit Lake Shelter Area** has shelters and tent platforms; to camp here you'll need a first-come, first-served permit from the Visitors Center. Both are operated by the **AMC** (☎ 603/466-2727; 🌐 www.outdoors.org).

NON-HIKING ALTERNATIVES

In the summer, the **Auto Road** (☎ 603/466-3988 ⊕ www.mountwashington autoroad.com) and the **Cog Railway** (☎ 800/922-8825 ⊕ www.thecog.com) present alternate ways up the mountain; both give you a real sense of the mountain's grandeur. In winter, a **SnowCoach** (☎ 603/466-2333 ⊕ www.greatglentrails. com) hauls visitors 4.5 miles up the Auto Road with an option to cross-country ski, telemark, snowshoe, or ride the coach back down.

Lost River Gorge in Kinsman Notch. Parents can enjoy the looks of wonder on their children's faces as they negotiate wooden boardwalks and stairs leading through a granite gorge formed by the roaring waters of the Lost River. One of the 10 caves they can explore is called the Lemon Squeezer (and it's a tight fit). Kids can also pan for gems and search for fossils, while grown-ups might prefer the attractions in the snack bar, gift shop, and nature garden. The park offers weekend lantern tours. ✉ *1712 Lost River Rd., 6 miles west of North Woodstock, N. Woodstock* ☎ *603/745-8720, 800/346-3687* 🌐 *May, June, Sept., and Oct., daily 9–5; July and Aug., daily 9–6* 🎟 *$17* 🕓 *Check Web site for hours.*

Whale's Tale Waterpark. You can float on an inner tube along a gentle river, careen down one of five waterslides, or body-surf in the large wave pool at Whale's Tale Waterpark. There's plenty here for toddlers and small children. ✉ *491 Daniel Webster Hwy., off I–93, North Lincoln* ☎ *603/745-8810* 🌐 *www.whalestalewaterpark.net* 🎟 *$34* 🕓 *Mid-June–late Aug., daily 10–6.*

WHERE TO EAT AND STAY

$$$ AMERICAN FAMILY 🍴 **Woodstock Inn, Station & Brewery.** If you like eateries loaded with character, don't miss this one inside the town's late-1800s train station. The walls are decorated with old maps, historic photographs, and local memorabilia. Then there are fun, curious objects, such as an old phone booth. The menu offers gluten-free items as well as the standard pub fare: pizza, burgers, steaks, and seafood. Gourmet breakfasts are served daily. A brewery on-site makes 17 different varieties; ask your server which ones are on tap. Kids will find a small game room. [$] *Average main: $24* ✉ *135 Main St., off I–93, North Woodstock* ☎ *603/745-3951* 🌐 *www.woodstockinnbrewery.com.*

$$ RESORT FAMILY 🏨 **Indian Head Resort.** The inexpensive and spacious rooms make this the place for families on a budget. **Pros:** great prices; fun for the whole family; near kid-friendly attractions. **Cons:** can be crowded; sometimes hard to get a reservation. [$] *Rooms from: $169* ✉ *664 U.S. 3, 5 miles north of North Woodstock* ☎ *603/745-8000, 800/343-8000* 🌐 *www.indianheadresort.com* 🛏 *98 rooms, 40 cottages.*

$$$$ RESORT 🏨 **Mountain Club on Loon.** If you want a ski-in, ski-out stay on Loon Mountain, this is your best and only option. **Pros:** within walking distance of the lifts; on-site spa; close to the national forest. **Cons:** very busy place in winter. [$] *Rooms from: $225* ✉ *90 Loon Mountain, off Kancamagus Hwy.* ☎ *603/745-2244, 800/229-7829* 🌐 *www.mtnclub.com* 🛏 *117 rooms, 117 suites.*

NIGHTLIFE AND THE ARTS

THE ARTS

FAMILY **Jean's Playhouse.** A popular performing-arts venue, Jean's Playhouse is the area's year-round stage for theater and music. From July to October there's plenty here for kids. ✉ *10 Papermill Dr.* ☎ *603/745-2141* 🌐 *www.papermilltheatre.org.*

NIGHTLIFE

Black Diamond Lounge. For après-ski socializing, skiers head to the Black Diamond Lounge in the Mountain Club at the Loon Mountain ski resort. ⊠ *Loon Mountain, 90 Loon Mountain Rd.* ☎ *603/745–2244* ⊕ *www.mtnclub.com.*

Thunderbird Lounge. Live music, a large dance floor, and great lake views make this a year-round hot spot. ⊠ *Indian Head Resort, 664 U.S. 3, North Lincoln* ☎ *603/745–8000* ⊕ *www.indianheadresort.com.*

SPORTS AND THE OUTDOORS

Loon Mountain. Wide, straight, and consistent intermediate ski trails prevail at Loon, a modern resort on the western edge of the Pemigewasset River. The most advanced among the 61 runs are grouped on the North Peak section, with 2,100 feet of vertical skiing. Beginner trails are set apart. There's snow tubing on the lower slopes, and six terrain parks suitable for all ages and ability levels. In the base lodge are the usual dining and lounging facilities. There are 13 miles of cross-country trails, ice-skating on an outdoor rink, snowshoeing and snowshoeing tours, and a rock-climbing wall in the Loon Mountain Adventure Center. ⊠ *60 Loon Mountain Rd., off the Kancamagus Hwy.* ☎ *603/745–8111, 603/745–8100 snow conditions* ⊕ *www.loonmtn.com.*

Pemi Valley Moose Tours. Eager to see a mighty moose? Embark on a moose-watching bus tour into the northernmost White Mountains. The nearly three-hour trips depart in the early evening for the best wildlife sighting opportunities. The bus is air-conditioned and screens education films about moose. Tours run late April to mid-October. ⊠ *33 Main St., off I–93* ☎ *603/745–2744* ⊕ *www.moosetoursnh.com.*

FRANCONIA

16 miles northwest of Lincoln/North Woodstock on I–93.

Travelers have long passed through the White Mountains via Franconia Notch, and in the late 18th century a town evolved just to the north. It and the region's jagged rock formations and heavy coat of evergreens have stirred the imaginations of Washington Irving, Henry Wadsworth Longfellow, and Nathaniel Hawthorne, who penned a short story about the craggy cliff known as the Old Man of the Mountain. There is almost no town proper to speak of here, just a handful of stores, touched though it is by Interstate 93 (the Franconia Notch Parkway).

Four miles west of Franconia, Sugar Hill is a town of about 500 people. It's famous for its spectacular sunsets and views of the Franconia Mountains, best seen from Sunset Hill, where a row of grand hotels and mansions once stood.

GETTING HERE AND AROUND

Franconia is a small town with not much to offer tourists, but it is an access point for many ski areas and the villages of Sugar Hill, Easton, Bethlehem, Bretton Woods, Littleton, Lincoln, and North Woodstock, towns replete with white church steeples, general stores, country inns, and picturesque farms.

ESSENTIALS

Visitor Information Franconia Notch Chamber of Commerce ☎ *603/823–5661* 🌐 *www.franconianotch.org.*

EXPLORING

Flume Gorge. This 800-foot-long chasm has narrow walls that cause an eerie echo from the gorge's running water. A visit begins at the visitor's center, followed by a stroll along a wooden boardwalk and a series of stairways winding their way to the top of the falls that thunder down the gorge. The 2-mile loop takes a little over an hour. There are also a gift shop, cafeteria, and small museum. ✉ *853 Daniel Webster Hwy.* ☎ *603/745–8391* 🌐 *www.nhstateparks.org* 🎟 *$15* 🕑 *Early May–late Oct., daily 9–5.*

The Frost Place Museum. Robert Frost's year-round home from 1915 to 1920, this is where the poet soaked up the New England life. The place is imbued with the spirit of his work, down to the rusted mailbox in front that's painted "R. Frost" in simple lettering. Two rooms contain memorabilia and signed editions of his books. Out back you can follow short trails marked with lines from his poetry. This place will slow you down and remind you of the intense beauty of the surrounding countryside. Poetry readings are scheduled during many evenings in summer. ✉ *158 Ridge Rd.* ☎ *603/823–5510* 🌐 *www.frostplace.org* 🎟 *$5* 🕑 *June, daily 1–5; July–early Sept., Wed.–Mon. 1–5; mid-Sept.–Oct., Wed.–Mon. 10–5.*

FAMILY **New England Ski Museum.** This small museum lets you travel back in time to see how skiing began as a sport, particularly here in New England. Here you can examine artifacts, clothing, and equipment, as well as Bode Miller's five Olympic medals. For ski enthusiasts, the museum will evoke smiles and a trip down memory lane. ✉ *Franconia Notch State Park, 135 Tramway Dr., next to Cannon Mountain Tramway* 🌐 *www.skimuseum.org* 🎟 *Free* 🕑 *Memorial Day–Apr., daily 10–5.*

Old Man of the Mountain. This somber face in the rock high above Franconia Notch crumbled somewhat unexpectedly in 2003. The iconic image had defined New Hampshire, and the Old Man's "death" stunned and saddened residents. You can see photographs and learn about the history of the Old Man at the visitor center at Flume Gorge. Better yet, follow signs to a small Old Man of the Mountain Park. There you can view the iconic mountain face through newly installed steel rods that seem to literally put the beloved face back on the mountain. ✉ *Rte. 3* 🌐 *www.oldmannh.org* 🎟 *Free* 🕑 *Daily 9–5.*

WHERE TO EAT AND STAY

$ AMERICAN 🍴 **Polly's Pancake Parlor.** In the Dexter family for three generations, Polly's has been serving up pancakes and waffles (from its own original recipe) since the 1930s. Since then, smoked bacon and ham, sandwiches on homemade bread, delicious baked beans, and even gluten-free items have been added to the menu. There are even desserts such as raspberry pie. Much of the food is made from grains ground on-site. The gift shop sells maple products. [$] *Average main: $11* ✉ *672 Rte. 117*

☎ *603/823–5575* 🌐 *www.pollyspancakeparlor.com* ⏲ *Closed weekdays mid-Mar–mid May. No dinner.*

$$$$ AMERICAN Fodor's Choice ★ 🍴 **Sugar Hill Inn.** Inside this romantic 1789 farmhouse you'll find a very elegant dining room where memorable dinners are prepared by chef Val Fortin. Start with a trio of the chef's favorite soups or a butternut squash risotto, followed by a beet-and-anise garden salad. Main courses might include peppercorn-crusted sirloin steak with grilled mushrooms and truffle oil, or a free-range duck served three ways: breast with a bittersweet chocolate sauce, braised leg, and foie-gras ravioli. The creative desserts, such as apple dumpling with pumpkin ice cream or goat cheese crème brûlée with fruit, are all homemade. Because each meal feels individually crafted, the $63 prix-fixe menu is an excellent value. If you like it so much you don't want to leave, the inn has rooms with cozy seating areas next to woodburning fireplaces and wicker chairs on the wraparound porch. [$] *Average main: $63* ✉ *116 Rte. 117* ☎ *603/823–5621* 🌐 *www.sugarhillinn.com* ✍ *Reservations essential* ⏲ *Closed Tues. and Wed. No lunch.*

$$ RESORT 🏨 **Franconia Inn.** At this 120-acre family-friendly resort, you can play tennis on four clay courts, soak in the outdoor heated pool or hot tub, hop aboard a mountain bike, or even soar on a glider. **Pros:** good for kids; amazing views; outdoor heated pool. **Cons:** may be too remote for some. [$] *Rooms from: $169* ✉ *1172 Easton Rd.* ☎ *603/823–5542, 800/473–5299* 🌐 *www.franconiainn.com* 🛏 *34 rooms, 3 suites, 2 2-bedroom cottages* ⏲ *Restaurant closed Apr.–mid-May.*

SPORTS AND THE OUTDOORS

SKI AREAS

Cannon Mountain. This place is rich in New England history. Here you'll find the first aerial tramway in North America, built in 1938, and the view from the top of the 4,080-foot summit (on a clear day) is spectacular. The ride is free with a ski lift ticket; otherwise it's $15. In winter you'll find classic New England ski terrain that runs the gamut from steep pitches off the peak to gentle blue cruisers. In all, Cannon has 73 trails, but beginners may want to head over to the separate Tuckerbrook family area, which offers 13 trails and four lifts. Adventurous types will want to try out the Mittersill area, which has 86 acres of lift-accessed "side country" trails and glades where the snow is au naturel. ✉ *9 Franconia Notch State Park, off Rte. 3* ☎ *603/823–8800* 🌐 *www.cannonmt.com.*

Franconia Village Cross-Country Ski Center. The cross-country ski center at the Franconia Inn has more than 40 miles of groomed and backcountry trails. One popular route leads to Bridal Veil Falls, a great spot for a picnic lunch. You can also enjoy horse-drawn sleigh rides, snowshoeing, snow tubing, and ice-skating on a lighted rink. ✉ *Franconia Inn, 1172 Easton Rd.* ☎ *603/823–5542, 800/473–5299* 🌐 *www.franconiainn.com/cross_country_ski_center.php.*

SHOPPING

Sugar Hill Sampler. In this 1815 barn set high on a hill, you'll find an old-fashioned general store filled with crafts like quilts, lamps, candles, and ornaments, along with a row of gourmet jams, sauces, and condiments. In the back, owner Barbara Serafini has set up a folksy museum with local photos, newspaper clippings, and curiosities (Bette Davis's will is among them). ⊠ *71 Sunset Rd., Sugar Hill* ☎ *603/823–8478* ⊕ *www.sugarhillsampler.com.*

LITTLETON

7 miles north of Franconia and 86 miles north of Concord, on I–93.

One of northern New Hampshire's largest towns (this isn't saying much, mind you) is on a granite shelf along the Ammonoosuc River, whose swift current and drop of 235 feet enabled the community to flourish as a mill center in its early days. Later the railroad came through, and Littleton grew into the region's commerce hub. In the minds of many, it's more a place to stock up on supplies than a bona fide destination, but few communities have worked harder at revitalization. Today intriguing shops and eateries line the adorable Main Street, with its tidy 19th- and early-20th-century buildings that suggest a set in a Jimmy Stewart movie.

EXPLORING

The Rocks Estate. The rambling rock walls and beautifully restored historic buildings of The Rocks Estate, built by John Jacob Glessner of International Harvester, now serves as the 1,400-acre North Country Conservation and Education Center for the Forest Society. The property is open year-round with a variety of natural-history programs, self-guided tours, and hiking trails with excellent views of the Presidential Range. In winter you'll find cross-country ski trails and a select-your-own Christmas tree farm. In spring, watch syrup being made in the New Hampshire Maple Experience Museum. ⊠ *4 Christmas Tree La., Bethlehem* ☎ *603/444–6248* ⊕ *www.therocks.org.*

QUICK BITES **Miller's Cafe & Bakery.** Next to the Riverwalk Covered Bridge, this eatery is a great breakfast or lunch stop, serving fresh salads, award-winning sandwiches, and fabulous baked goods like chocolate-pecan pie. ⊠ **16 Mill St.** ☎ **603/444–2146** ⊕ **www.millerscafeandbakery.com** ⊗ **Closed Mon.**

Thayers Inn. In heart of Littleton sits this former grande dame. While it still welcomes overnight guests, it functions largely as an informal museum. In the lobby and down the hall you'll find photos and memorabilia from movie star Bette Davis's huge birthday bash and artifacts from other illustrious guests, including Ulysses S. Grant, Henry Ford, P. T. Barnum, and Richard Nixon. Request a key to climb up to the cupola for 360-degree view of the town. Two rooms are open to the public: one set up as a guest room from the 1840s and one a scene from *Pollyanna*, written by Littleton native Eleanor Hodgman Porter, born in 1868. ⊠ *111 Main St.* ☎ *603/444–6469* ⊕ *www.thayersinn.com.*

Whitefield. About 11 miles northeast of Littleton, Whitefield became a prominent summer resort in the late 19th century, when wealthy industrialists flocked to this small village in a rolling valley to play golf, ski the slopes, and hobnob with each other. The yellow clapboard Mountain View Grand Hotel, which first opened in 1865, is once again one of New England's grandest resorts. It's worth driving through the courtly Colonial-style center of town—Whitefield was settled in the early 1800s—and up Route 116 just beyond to see this magnificent structure atop a bluff overlooking the Presidentials. ⊠ *Whitefield.*

WHERE TO EAT AND STAY

$$$

AMERICAN

✕ **Tim-bir Alley.** This is a rare find in New Hampshire: an independent restaurant in a contemporary setting that's been serving customers for decades and yet still takes its food seriously. If you're in town, don't miss it. Tim Carr's menu changes weekly and uses regional American ingredients in creative ways. Main dishes might include an eggplant pâté with feta cheese, red pepper, and a tomato-herb marmalade or a basil-and-olive-oil-flavored salmon with a spinach-Brie-pecan pesto. Save room for such desserts as white chocolate–coconut cheesecake. Ⓢ *Average main: $23* ⊠ *7 Main St.* ☎ *603/444–6142* ▭ *No credit cards* ⊘ *Closed Jan.–Apr. and Mon. and Tues. No lunch.*

$$$$

B&B/INN

Fodor's Choice

★

🏨 **Adair Country Inn and Restaurant.** An air of yesteryear refinement infuses Adair, a three-story Georgian Revival home that attorney Frank Hogan built as a wedding present for his daughter in 1927. **Pros:** refined, book-filled spaces; gourmet dinners; gracious service. **Cons:** removed from town. Ⓢ *Rooms from: $245* ⊠ *80 Guider La., off I–93, Bethlehem* ☎ *603/444–2600, 888/444–2600* ⊕ *www.adairinn.com* ⇆ *9 rooms, 1 cottage* ⊘ *Closed Nov. and Apr.* ⦿ *Breakfast.*

SHOPPING

Potato Barn Antiques Center. You'll find 10 dealers under one roof at Potato Barn Antiques Center. Specialties include antique lamps, vintage clothing, costume jewelry, and old tools. ⊠ *960 Lancaster Rd., 6 miles north of Lancaster, Northumberland* ☎ *603/636–2611* ⊕ *www. potatobarnantiques.com.*

Village Book Store. If you're looking for hiking maps or good books about the history of the area, you'll find them here, as well as unusual children's toys and a wide range of adult fiction and nonfiction titles. On the lower level is the League of New Hampshire Craftsmen's shop, featuring glass, prints, ceramics, fiber, and more. ⊠ *81 Main St.* ☎ *603/444–5263* ⊕ *www.booksmusictoys.com.*

BRETTON WOODS

14 miles southeast of Bethlehem; 28 miles northeast of Lincoln/ Woodstock.

In the early 1900s private railcars brought the elite from New York and Philadelphia to the Omni Mount Washington Hotel, the jewel of the White Mountains. A visit to the hotel, which was the site of the 1944 United Nations conference that created the International Monetary Fund and the International Bank for Reconstruction and Development

Bretton Woods is a year-round destination, and especially popular with families.

(and the birth of many conspiracy theories), is not to be missed. The area is also known for its cog railway and Bretton Woods ski resort.

GETTING HERE AND AROUND

Bretton Woods is in the heart of the White Mountains on Route 302. A free shuttle makes it easy to get around the resort's various facilities. Helpful advice on how to enjoy your stay can be found at the concierge and activities desk in the main lobby of the Omni Mount Washington Hotel.

EXPLORING

FAMILY

Fodor's Choice

★

Mount Washington Cog Railway. In 1858, Sylvester Marsh petitioned the state legislature for permission to build a steam railway up Mt. Washington. A politico retorted that he'd have better luck building a railroad to the moon. But 11 years later, the Mount Washington Cog Railway chugged its way up to the summit along a 3-mile track on the west side of the mountain. Today it's one of the state's most beloved attractions—a thrill in either direction. You'll find a small museum about the cog rail at the base. The train runs from May until early December, with varying departure times. A full trip ($64) is three hours, including one hour at the summit. ✉ *3168 Base Station Rd., 6 miles northeast of Bretton Woods* ☎ *603/278–5404, 800/922–8825* ⊕ *www.thecog.com* ✉ *$64.*

WHERE TO EAT

$$$$

AMERICAN

✕ **Bretton Arms Dining Room.** You're likely to have the best meal in the area at this intimate setting. Though the same chef oversees the Omni Mount Washington Hotel's Main Dining Room, the latter is immense, and the Bretton Arms is cozier. Three small interconnected rooms are separated by fireplaces. The menu is seasonal and might include Georges Bank scallops with pureed celery root, baby bok choy, and cipollini onions. Locally sourced food features prominently in all the dishes. [$] *Average main: $30* ✉ *U.S. 302* ☎ *603/278–1000* 🌐 *www.mtwashingtonresort.com* 🕐 *No lunch.*

$$$$ AMERICAN 🍴 **Main Dining Room.** You'd be hard-pressed to find a larger or grander space in New Hampshire than the Omni Mount Washington Hotel's enormous octagonal Main Dining Room, which has massive windows that open onto spectacular views of the Presidential Range. Built in 1902, subtle renovations have brought it into the 21st century. Seasonal dishes are sourced from local New Hampshire farms and suppliers; thus, the menu is constantly changing. On it you might find wild salmon wrapped in buttery pastry served over lobster succotash or a rosemary-scented rack of lamb with candied beets. **TIP→ Appropriate evening wear is expected, meaning no shorts or sneakers.** [$] *Average main: $36* ✉ *Omni Mount Washington Hotel, U.S. 302* ☎ *603/278–1000* 🌐 *www.mtwashingtonresort.com* 🕐 *No lunch.*

$$ AMERICAN FAMILY 🍴 **Fabyan's Station.** A model train circles the dining room at this former railroad station—a nod to the late 19th century, when 60 trains a day stopped here. If you're looking for an easygoing meal, Fabyan's cooks up delicious clam chowder in a bread bowl and a 16-ounce T-bone grilled to perfection. Half the restaurant is a tavern with a long bar, and the other half serves soups, sandwiches, fish, and house-smoked items. There's a kids' menu, too. [$] *Average main: $17* ✉ *Rte. 302, 1 mile north of ski area* ☎ *603/278–2222* 🌐 *www.brettonwoods.com/dining/bretton_woods_dining/overview* ✍ *Reservations not accepted.*

WHERE TO STAY

$$ HOTEL 🏨 **The Lodge.** Freshly renovated throughout, this inexpensive roadside motel gives you free access to all of the resort facilities at Omni Mount Washington Hotel, including the pools, gym, and arcade, which makes it a great deal. **Pros:** inexpensive rates; access to many amenities; free ski shuttle. **Cons:** across street from resort amenities; Continental breakfast only. [$] *Rooms from: $139* ✉ *U.S. 302* ☎ *603/278–1000, 800/680–6600* 🌐 *www.mtwashington.com* 🛏 *50 rooms* 🍴 *Breakfast.*

$$$$ RESORT FAMILY Fodor's Choice ★ 🏨 **Omni Mount Washington Hotel.** The two most memorable sights in the White Mountains would have to be Mt. Washington and the Omni Mount Washington Hotel. **Pros:** beautiful resort; loads of activities; free shuttle to skiing and activities. **Cons:** kids love to run around the hotel. [$] *Rooms from: $229* ✉ *U.S. 302* ☎ *603/278–1000* 🌐 *brettonwoods.com* 🛏 *175 rooms, 25 suites* 🍴 *Multiple meal plans.*

$$$$ B&B/INN Fodor's Choice ★ 🏨 **The Notchland Inn.** Built in 1862 by Sam Bemis, America's grandfather of landscape photography, the house conveys mountain charm on a scale unmatched in New England. **Pros:** middle-of-the-forest setting; marvelous house and common rooms; good dinners. **Cons:** may seem too isolated for some. [$] *Rooms from: $265* ✉ *2 Morey Rd., Harts Location* ☎ *603/374–6131* 🌐 *www.notchland.com* 🛏 *8 rooms, 5 suites, 2 cottages* 🍴 *Breakfast.*

9

SPORTS AND THE OUTDOORS

SKI AREA

FAMILY
Fodor's Choice
★

Bretton Woods. New Hampshire's largest ski area is also one of the country's best family ski resorts. The views of Mt. Washington alone are worth the visit to Bretton Woods; the scenery is especially beautiful from the Latitude 44 restaurant, open during ski season.

This is a great place to learn to ski. Trails appeal mostly to novice and intermediate skiers, including two magic carpet lifts for beginners. There are some steeper pitches near the top of the 1,500-foot vertical and glade skiing to occupy the experts, as well as night skiing and snowboarding on weekends and holidays. Snowboarders enjoy the three terrain parks. The Nordic trail system has 62 miles of cross-country ski trails.

The Hobbit Ski and Snowplay program, for ages 3 to 5, is an introduction to skiing, and the Hobbit Ski and Snowboard School, for ages 4 to 12, has full- and half-day lessons. The complimentary Kinderwoods Winter Playground has a sled carousel, igloos, and a zip line. A snowmobile park at the base area is fun for kids ages 4 to 13. Parents can purchase interchangeable family tickets that allow them to take turns skiing while the other watches the kids—both passes come for the price of one. The ski area also offers an adaptive program for anyone with disabilities.

A recent addition is the year-round Canopy Tour, which has 9 ziplines, two sky bridges, and three rappel stations. Small groups are led by experienced guides. The tour, costing $110, is an exhilarating introduction to flora and fauna of the White Mountains. As with many activities here, kids are welcome. ⊠ *U.S. 302* ☎ *603/278–3320, 603/278–1000 weather conditions* ⊕ *www.brettonwoods.com.*

EN
ROUTE

Crawford Notch State Park. Scenic U.S. 302 winds through the steep, wooded mountains on either side of spectacular Crawford Notch, southeast of Bretton Woods, and passes through Crawford Notch State Park, where you can picnic and take a short hike to Arethusa Falls or the Silver and Flume cascades. The park has a number of roadside photo opportunities. The Willey House Visitor Center has a gift shop, snack bar, and picnic area. ⊠ *1464 U.S. 302, Harts Location* ⊕ *www. nhstateparks.org* ⊠ *$4.*

BARTLETT

18 miles southeast of Bretton Woods.

With Bear Mountain to its south, Mt. Parker to its north, Mt. Cardigan to its west, and the Saco River to its east, Bartlett, incorporated in 1790, has an unforgettable setting. Lovely Bear Notch Road (closed in winter) has the only midpoint access to the Kancamagus Highway. There isn't much town here (dining options are in Glen). It's best known for the Attitash Ski Resort, within walking distance.

WHERE TO EAT

$$ SOUTHWESTERN 🍴 **Margarita Grill.** Après-ski types like to congregate on the enclosed, heated patio and unwind with a margarita. Here you'll find a wide assortment of Tex-Mex and Southwestern specialties, including homemade salsas, wood-fired steaks, ribs, chicken, and burgers. All ingredients are local and fresh, this being a New Hampshire farm-to-table certified restaurant. [$] *Average main: $17* ✉ *78 U.S. 302, Glen* ☎ *603/383–6556* 🌐 *www.margaritagrillnh.com* 🕒 *No lunch weekdays.*

$$ AMERICAN 🍴 **Red Parka Steakhouse & Pub.** This downtown pub has been an institution for nearly 40 years. A family-oriented menu features an all-you-can-eat locally sourced salad bar, hand-cut steaks, and barbecue ribs. The barbecue sauce is made on-site, and beer is served in mason jars. Plan to spend some time reading the dozens and dozens of license plates that adorn the walls of the downstairs pub. You'll also find open mike nights on Monday and live entertainment on Friday and Saturday. [$] *Average main: $18* ✉ *3 Station St., Glen* ☎ *603/383–4344* 🌐 *www.redparkapub.com* ✍ *Reservations not accepted* 🕒 *No lunch.*

WHERE TO STAY

$$$$ HOTEL 🏨 **Attitash Grand Summit Hotel & Conference Center.** If ski-in ski-out convenience is a must, then this is the hotel where you'll want to stay. **Pros:** great location; nice outdoor pool and hot tubs; better price with ski package. **Cons:** generally bland accommodations. [$] *Rooms from: $259* ✉ *U.S. 302* ☎ *603/374–1900, 800/223–7669* 🌐 *www.attitash.com* 🛏 *143 rooms.*

$$$ HOTEL 🏨 **Attitash Mountain Village Resort.** Hidden in a cluster of pine trees across from the ski area is a resort with guest rooms (a few are actually slopeside) that crest the top of this mountain. **Pros:** simple family place; fitness room; nice pools. **Cons:** more functional than posh. [$] *Rooms from: $199* ✉ *784 U.S. 302* ☎ *603/374-6501, 800/862–1600* 🌐 *www.mtwashingtonvalleyaccommodations.com* 🛏 *350 units.*

SPORTS AND THE OUTDOORS

SKI AREA

Attitash Ski Resort. With a vertical drop of 1,760 feet, the Attitash Ski Resort offers a total of 67 trails to explore. Not enough? The adjacent Attitash Bear Peak adds another 1,450 feet of vertical. Here you'll find traditional New England ski runs and challenging terrain, alongside wide-open cruisers that suit all skill levels. There are acres of glades, plus a progressive freestyle terrain park. The Attitash Adventure Center has a rental shop, lessons, and children's programs. ✉ *U.S. 302* ☎ *800/223–7669* 🌐 *www.attitash.com.*

JACKSON

5 miles north of Glen.

Fodor's Choice ★ Just off Route 16 via a red covered bridge, Jackson has retained its storybook New England character. Art and antiques shopping, tennis, golf, fishing, and hiking to waterfalls are among the draws. When the snow falls, Jackson becomes the state's cross-country skiing capital.

9

Four downhill ski areas are nearby. Hotels and B&Bs offer a ski shuttle. Visit Jackson Falls for a wonderful photo opportunity.

ESSENTIALS

Visitor Information **Jackson Area Chamber of Commerce** ☎ *603/383–9356* 🌐 *www.jacksonnh.com.*

EXPLORING

FAMILY **Story Land.** This cluster of fluorescent buildings is a theme park with life-size storybook and nursery-rhyme characters. The 22 rides include a flume ride, a river-raft ride, and a roller coaster. There's also a variety of shows when you need a break. ✉ *850 Rte. 16, Glen* ☎ *603/383–4186* 🌐 *www.storylandnh.com* 🎟 *$32* 🕒 *Memorial Day–early Oct., hrs vary.*

SPORTS AND THE OUTDOORS

SKI AREAS

Black Mountain. Friendly, informal Black Mountain has a warming southern exposure. The Family Passport allows two adults and two kids to ski at highly discounted rates both during the week ($109) and on weekends ($139). That's a great deal, as the regular rates are considered among the lowest in the Mt. Washington Valley. The 40 trails and glades on the 1,100-foot mountain are evenly divided among beginner, intermediate, and expert. There's a nursery for kids over six months old. Enjoy guided horseback riding spring through fall. ✉ *373 Black Mountain Rd.* ☎ *603/383–4490, 800/475–4669 snow conditions* 🌐 *www.blackmt.com.*

Fodor's Choice ★ **Jackson Ski Touring Foundation.** Experts rate this the best-run cross-country ski operation in the country. That's due to the great advice you get from the attentive staff, and also to its 60 miles of groomed trails for skiing, skate skiing, and snowshoeing. The varied terrain offers something for all abilities. Jackson Ski Touring's trails wind through covered bridges and into the picturesque village of Jackson, where you can warm up in cozy, trailside restaurants. Lessons and rentals are available. ✉ *153 Main St.* ☎ *603/383–9355* 🌐 *www.jacksonxc.org.*

WHERE TO EAT

$$ AMERICAN FAMILY 🍴 **Red Fox Bar & Grille.** Some say this big family restaurant overlooking Wentworth Golf Club gets its name from a wily fox with a penchant for stealing golf balls off the fairway. The wide-ranging menu has burgers, barbecued ribs, and wood-fired pizzas, as well as more refined dishes such as seared sea scallops and bourbon steak tips. The Sunday breakfast buffet is very popular. Younger kids will enjoy the playroom, especially if there's a wait for a table. [$] *Average main: $16* ✉ *49 Rte. 16* ☎ *603/383–4949* 🌐 *www.redfoxbarandgrille.com* 🕒 *No lunch Sat.*

$$$ AMERICAN Fodor's Choice ★ 🍴 **Thorn Hill.** This famous inn serves up some of New England's most memorable meals in a romantic atmosphere with low lights and piano music trickling in from the lounge. Many people enjoy dining on the heated porch, which overlooks the Presidential Range. You'll find subtle and flavorful dishes such as pan-seared trout, Peking duck on a scallion pancake with sesame bok choy, and New York sirloin in a blue cheese demi-glace. [$] *Average main: $26* ✉ *42 Thorn Hill Rd.* ☎ *603/383–4242, 800/289–8990* 🌐 *www.innatthornhill.com* 🕒 *No lunch.*

WHERE TO STAY

$$$ B&B/INN **Christmas Farm Inn and Spa.** Despite its wintery name, this 1778 inn is an all-season retreat. **Pros:** kids are welcome; nice indoor and outdoor pools; very close to ski area. **Cons:** can be very busy with kids. [$] *Rooms from: $189* ✉ *3 Blitzen Way, off Rte. 16B* ☎ *603/383–4313, 800/443–5837* 🌐 *www.christmasfarminn.com* 🛏 *22 rooms, 12 suites, 7 cottages* 🍴 *Breakfast.*

$$$ B&B/INN Fodor's Choice ★ **Inn at Jackson.** This bright B&B is impeccably maintained and charmingly furnished. **Pros:** exceptional rooms; peaceful setting; wonderful breakfasts. **Cons:** top-floor rooms lack fireplaces. [$] *Rooms from: $189* ✉ *Corner of Main St. and Thorn Hill Rd.* ☎ *603/383–4321, 800/289–8600* 🌐 *www.innatjackson.com* 🛏 *14 rooms* 🍴 *Breakfast.*

$$$ B&B/INN Fodor's Choice ★ **The Inn at Thorn Hill & Spa.** With a large reception room and sweeping staircase, this inn modeled after an 1891 Stanford White Victorian is breathtaking from the minute you step inside. **Pros:** romantic setting; soothing spa. **Cons:** Wi-Fi works on main floor, but not in the rooms. [$] *Rooms from: $215* ✉ *42 Thorn Hill Rd.* ☎ *800/289–8990, 800/289–8990* 🌐 *www.innatthornhill.com* 🛏 *18 rooms, 5 suites, 3 cottages* 🍴 *Some meals.*

MT. WASHINGTON

20 miles northwest of Jackson.

Mt. Washington. Mt. Washington is the highest peak (6,288 feet) in the northeastern United States and the site of a weather station that recorded the world's highest winds, 231 mph, back in 1934. You can drive to the top, which climbs 4,600 feet in just over 7 miles, in the summer. A number of trailheads circle the mountain and the other peaks in the Presidential Range, but all of them are strenuous. On the summit is Extreme Mount Washington, an interactive museum dedicated to science and weather. A guided bus tour is available, or you can reach the top along several rough hiking trails. Remember that the temperatures atop Mt. Washington will be much colder than those down below—the average year-round is below freezing, and the average wind velocity is 35 mph. ☎ *603/356–2137* 🌐 *www.mountwashington.org.*

SPORTS AND THE OUTDOORS

Great Glen Trails Outdoor Center. This outdoor center at the foot of Mt. Washington is the base for year-around outdoor activities. Renowned for its dramatic 27-mile cross-country trail system, this center gives access to more than 1,100 acres of backcountry. Trees shelter most of the trails, so Mt. Washington's infamous weather isn't such a concern. You can travel to the mountain's upper reaches in nine-passenger vans that are refitted with snowmobile-like treads. You have the option of skiing or snowshoeing down or just enjoying the magnificent winter view. The center has a huge ski and sports shop, food court, climbing wall, and observation deck. In summer it's the base for hiking and biking and has programs in canoeing, kayaking, and fly-fishing. ✉ *1 Mt. Washington Auto Rd.* ☎ *603/466–2333* 🌐 *www.greatglentrails.com.*

Reward your vehicle for tackling the auto road with the obligatory bumper sticker: "This Car Climbed Mt. Washington."

Pinkham Notch. Although not a town per se, scenic Pinkham Notch covers Mt. Washington's eastern side and has several ravines, including famous Tuckerman Ravine. The Appalachian Mountain Club runs a visitor center that provides year-around trail information to hikers, as well as guided hikes, outdoor skills workshops, an outdoors shop, and cafeteria. ✉ *Appalachian Mountain Club Pinkham Notch Visitor Center, 361 Rte. 16* ☎ *603/466–2721* ⊕ *www.outdoors.org* ⊗ *Daily 6:30 am–9 pm.*

Wildcat Mountain. Glade skiers favor Wildcat, with 28 acres of official tree skiing. The 49 runs include some stunning double-black-diamond trails. Experts can zip down the Lynx. Skiers who can hold a wedge should check out the 2½-mile-long Polecat, which offers excellent views of the Presidential Range. The trails are classic New England—narrow and winding—and the views are stunning. Beginners will find gentle terrain and a broad teaching slope. For an adrenaline rush, there's a terrain park. In summer you can zip to the top on the four-passenger gondola, hike the many well-kept trails, and fish in the crystal-clear streams. ✉ *Rte. 16, Jackson* ☎ *603/466–3326, 888/754–9453 snow conditions* ⊕ *www.skiwildcat.com.*

DIXVILLE NOTCH

63 miles north of Mt. Washington, 66 miles northeast of Littleton, 149 miles north of Concord.

Just 12 miles from the Canadian border, this tiny community is known for two things: the Balsams, one of New Hampshire's oldest and most celebrated resorts, and the fact that Dixville Notch and another New Hampshire community, Hart's Location, are the first election districts in the nation to vote in presidential general elections. When the 30 or so Dixville Notch voters file into the little Balsams meeting room on the eve of Election Day and cast their ballots at the stroke of midnight, they invariably make national news.

TOURS

Gorham Moose Tours. One of the favorite pastimes in this area is spotting moose, those large, ungainly, yet elusive members of the deer family. These bus tours lasting up to three hours claim to have a 97% success rate in spotting moose. ✉ *69 Main St., Gorham* ☎ *603/466–2101, 877/986–6673* 🌐 *www.gorhamnh.org* 🎟 *$25* 🕒 *Memorial Day–Sept., departure times vary.*

EXPLORING

FAMILY **Poore Farm Historic Homestead.** Maybe you've visited farm museums before, but certainly not one like this. Originally built in 1825, this farm has survived almost perfectly intact because the Poore family never installed electricity or other modern conveniences. They lived here for a century and a half, and apparently saved everything. The house, barn, outbuildings, and gardens provide a rare opportunity to see how rural New Englanders actually lived, dressed, ate, farmed, and socialized. It's the perfect backdrop for farming demonstrations, music festivals, and discussions about farm life. ✉ *629 Hollow Rd., 7 miles north of Colebrook, Stewartstown* 🌐 *www.poorefarm.org* 🎟 *$5* 🕒 *June–Sept., weekdays 11–1, weekends 11–3.*

OFF THE BEATEN PATH **Pittsburg.** In the Great North Woods, Pittsburg contains the springs that form the Connecticut River. The state's northern tip—a chunk of about 250 square miles—lies within the town's borders. Remote though it is, this frontier town teems with hunters, boaters, fishermen, hikers, and photographers from early summer through winter. Especially in the colder months, moose sightings are common. The town has more than a dozen lodges and several informal eateries. It's about a 90-minute drive from Littleton and 40 minutes from Dixville Notch.

WHERE TO EAT AND STAY

$ FRENCH Fodor's Choice ★ 🍴 **Le Rendez Vous.** You might not expect to find an authentic French pastry shop in the workaday village of Colebrook, 10 miles west of Dixville Notch, but Le Rendez Vous serves fabulous tarts and treats. Understandable, as the owners came from Paris. Drop in to this quaint café—furnished with several tables and armchairs—for hand-dipped Belgian chocolates, buttery croissants, and a tremendous variety of fresh-baked breads, as well as gourmet foods ranging from dried fruits and nuts to lentils, olive oils, and balsamic vinegar. [$] *Average main: $5* ✉ *121 Main St., Colebrook* ☎ *603/237–5150* 🌐 *www.lerendezvousbakerynh.com.*

$$$ AMERICAN 🍴 **Rainbow Grille.** Everyone loves the Rainbow Grille, whether it's for the moose antlers hanging on the pine paneling, views of the sun setting over Black Lake, or the lumberjack-sized meals. Nestled in the Tall Timber Lodge, built in 1946, this restaurant is known for its trout and salmon dishes, as well as for its mesquite-grilled prime rib. The perfect finish to any meal is a slice of bread pudding. Even though this seems

like an out-of-the-way place, don't miss out on a table. Visitors reserve months in advance. $ *Average main: $24* ✉ *609 Beach Rd., Pittsburgh* ☎ *603/538–9556* ⊕ *www.rainbowgrille.com* ⌧ *Reservations essential* ⊙ *Closed Thanksgiving–Mother's Day.*

$ ▦ **Cabins at Lopstick.** In business since 1929, the Cabins at Lopstick
HOTEL have long appealed to outdoors enthusiasts. **Pros:** great views of First Connecticut Lake; full kitchens; great for summer and winter sports. **Cons:** no on-site eatery; no Wi-Fi in most cabins. $ *Rooms from: $99* ✉ *45 Stewart Young Rd., Pittsburgh* ☎ *800/538–6659* ⊕ *www. cabinsatlopstick.com* ⇆ *43 cabins* ⏍ *No meals.*

SPORTS AND THE OUTDOORS

Dixville Notch State Park. In the northernmost notch of the White Mountains, Dixville Notch State Park has a waterfall, two mountain brooks, hiking trails, picnic areas, and restrooms. ✉ *1212 W. Rte. 26* ☎ *603/538–6707* ⊕ *www.nhstateparks.org.*

NORTH CONWAY

76 miles south of Dixville Notch; 7 miles south of Glen; 41 miles east of Lincoln/North Woodstock.

Before the arrival of the outlet stores, the town drew visitors for its inspiring scenery, ski resorts, and access to White Mountain National Forest. Today, however, the feeling of natural splendor is gone. Shopping is the big sport, and businesses line Route 16 for several miles. You'll get a close look at them because traffic slows to a crawl here. You can take scenic West Side Road from Conway to Intervale to circumvent the traffic and take in splendid views.

GETTING HERE AND AROUND

Park near the fire station on Main Street and spend half a day visiting the unique shops and restaurants in this part of town. Taxis can get you around between Conway, North Conway, and Jackson.

ESSENTIALS

Taxi Village Taxi ☎ *603/356–3602.*

Visitor Information North Country Chamber of Commerce ☎ *603/237–8939, 800/698–8939* ⊕ *www.northcountrychamber.org.*

EXPLORING

FAMILY **Conway Scenic Railroad.** Departing from historic North Conway Station, the Conway Scenic Railroad operates trips aboard vintage trains. The Notch Train to Crawford Depot (a 5-hour round-trip) or Fabyan Station (5½ hours) offers wonderful views from a domed observation coach. The Valley Train overlooks Mt. Washington during a 55-minute round-trip journey to Conway or a 1¾-hour excursion to Bartlett. Lunch is served daily from mid-June to late October, and dinner is served four evenings a week. The 1874 station displays lanterns, old tickets and timetables, and other artifacts. Reserve your spot early during foliage season. ✉ *38 Norcross Circle* ☎ *603/356–5251, 800/232–5251* ⊕ *www.conwayscenic.com* ⌦ *$16–$83* ⊙ *Mid-Apr.–mid Dec; departure times vary.*

FAMILY **Hartmann Model Railroad Museum.** All aboard! You can ride a miniature outdoor train at the Hartmann Model Railroad Museum, which also has 10 operating train layouts in scales ranging from G to Z. There's also a hobby shop on the premises. ✉ *15 Town Hall Rd., at Rte. 16, Intervale* ☎ *603/356–9922* 🌐 *www.hartmannrr.com* 🎫 *$6* 🕒 *July and Aug., daily 10–5; Sept.–June, Fri.-Mon. 10–5.*

Weather Discovery Center. Ever wonder what it's like to be in a cabin at the summit of Mt. Washington while 200 mph winds shake the rafters? This fun, interactive museum allows you to experience different weather conditions and learn about how weather affects our lives. There's a twice-daily video link with the scientists hard at work at Mt. Washington Observatory. ✉ *2779 Main St.* ☎ *603/356–2137* 🌐 *www.mountwashington.org/education/center* 🎫 *Free* 🕒 *Daily 10–5.*

WHERE TO EAT

$$ AMERICAN 🍴 **Delaney's Hole in the Wall.** This casual tavern has a real fondness for ski history, displaying early photos of local ski areas, old signs and placards, and odd bits of lift equipment. Entrées range from fajitas that come sizzling out of the kitchen to mussels and scallops sautéed with spiced sausage and Louisiana seasonings. There's an entire menu devoted to sushi. [$] *Average main: $18* ✉ *2966 White Mountain Hwy., ¼ mile north of North Conway Village* ☎ *603/356–7776* 🌐 *www.delaneys.com.*

$$ AMERICAN FAMILY 🍴 **Muddy Moose Restaurant & Pub.** This family restaurant buzzes with the sound of happy kids. The mac and cheese, blueberry-glazed ribs, and hearty burgers are a hit with the small fry, although grown-ups might prefer the pasta and seafood dishes. A unique side dish of carrots with a hint of maple syrup is a pleasant surprise. The Muddy Moose Pie, made of ice cream, fudge, and crumbled Oreos, can feed a family of four. [$] *Average main: $16* ✉ *2344 White Mountain Hwy.* ☎ *603/356–7696* 🌐 *www.muddymoose.com* ✍ *Reservations not accepted.*

$$$ AMERICAN Fodor's Choice ★ 🍴 **The 1785 Inn.** Visitors keep coming back to this special place, not only for its outstanding food, but for its quaint New England charm and spectacular mountain views. The main dining room is in the original 1785 building with a cooking fireplace, Early American antiques, and exposed hand-hewn beams. The restaurant is known for its gracious service (Caesar salads are prepared table-side), extravagant desserts, and drinks that shoot up in flames. Beyond the theatrics, the food by chef Peter Willis is beautifully prepared and flavorful, including the tender seared Maine scallops with a ginger, chili, coconut, and lemongrass sauce, and ruby trout with sweet rice and a seaweed salad. The inn has 17 guest rooms that range from cozy to luxurious. [$] *Average main: $25* ✉ *3582 White Mountain Hwy.* ☎ *603/356–9025* 🌐 *www.the1785inn.com* 🕒 *No lunch.*

WHERE TO STAY

$$ B&B/INN 🏨 **The Buttonwood Inn.** A tranquil oasis in this busy resort area, the Buttonwood Inn sits on Mt. Surprise, 2 miles northeast of North Conway Village. **Pros:** good bedding and amenities; tranquil setting; 6 acres of grounds. **Cons:** unexciting for those not wanting a remote getaway. [$] *Rooms from: $159* ✉ *64 Mt. Surprise Rd.* ☎ *603/356–2625,*

9

Sit back and enjoy the view on the Conway Scenic Railroad.

800/258–2625 🌐 www.buttonwoodinn.com 🛏 10 rooms, 1 suite 🍴 Breakfast.

$$ B&B/INN 🏠 **Darby Field Inn.** After a day in the White Mountains, warm up by the fieldstone fireplace in this inn's common area. **Pros:** romantic setting; an away-from-it-all feel. **Cons:** better for couples than families. [$] *Rooms from: $170 ✉ 185 Chase Hill, Albany ☎ 603/447–2181, 800/426–4147 🌐 www.darbyfield.com 🛏 13 rooms 🕒 Closed Apr. 🍴 Breakfast.*

$$ B&B/INN 🏠 **Snowville Inn.** Journalist Frank Simonds built this gambrel-roofed main house in 1916, and its nicest room has 12 windows that look out over the Presidential Range. **Pros:** spectacular views; fine dining; full breakfast. **Cons:** off the beaten path; Wi-Fi connection unpredictable. [$] *Rooms from: $139 ✉ 136 Stewart Rd., 6 miles southeast of Conway, Snowville ☎ 603/447–2818, 800/447–4345 🌐 snowvillageinn.com 🛏 16 rooms, 1 suite 🍴 Breakfast.*

$$$ RESORT 🏠 **White Mountain Hotel and Resort.** Rooms in this hotel at the base of Whitehorse Ledge have splendid mountain views, and the proximity to White Mountain National Forest and Echo Lake State Park makes you feel farther away from the outlet malls than you actually are. **Pros:** scenic setting that's close to shopping; lots of activities; kids 18 and under stay free. **Cons:** two-night-minimum summer weekends. [$] *Rooms from: $189 ✉ 2560 West Side Rd. ☎ 800/533–6301 🌐 www.whitemountainhotel.com 🛏 69 rooms, 11 suites 🍴 Multiple meal plans.*

SPORTS AND THE OUTDOORS

PARK

Echo Lake State Park. You don't have to be a rock climber to catch views from the 700-foot White Horse and Cathedral ledges. From the top you'll see the entire valley, including Echo Lake, which offers fishing, swimming, boating, and, on quiet days, an excellent opportunity to shout for echoes. ⊠ *68 Echo Lake Rd., off U.S 302, Conway* ☎ *603/356–2672* ⊕ *www.nhstateparks.org* ⊠ *$4* ☉ *Memorial Day–mid-Oct., daily 9–sunset.*

CANOEING AND KAYAKING

Outdoors Saco Bound. This outfitter rents stand-up paddleboards, canoes, and kayaks. It'll even provide transportation for you and your inner tubes for gentle floats down the Saco River. ⊠ *2561 E. Main St., Center Conway* ☎ *603/447–2177* ⊕ *www.sacobound.com.*

FISHING

North Country Angler. One of the best tackle shops in the state, North Country Angler offers casting clinics and guided fly-fishing trips throughout the region. ⊠ *2888 White Mountain Hwy.* ☎ *603/356–6000* ⊕ *www.northcountryangler.com.*

SKI AREAS

Cranmore Mountain Adventure Park. This downhill ski area has been a favorite with families since it opened in 1938. The 57 trails are fun to ski, and five glades have increased the skiable terrain. Most runs are naturally formed intermediates that weave in and out of glades. Beginners have several slopes and routes from the summit; experts must be content with a few short, steep pitches. In addition to the trails, there's snow tubing, a mountain coaster, a giant swing, and a zipline. Snowboarders have five terrain parks. Twilight skiing is offered Saturday and holidays. ⊠ *1 Skimobile Rd.* ☎ *603/356–5543, 603/356–5544 snow conditions* ⊕ *www.cranmore.com.*

King Pine Ski Area at Purity Spring Resort. About 9 miles south of Conway, this family-run ski area has been going strong since 1962. King Pine's 17 gentle trails are ideal for beginner and intermediate skiers; experts won't be challenged except for a brief section of the Pitch Pine trail. There are 9 miles of cross-country ski trails. Indoors, you can enjoy a pool and fitness complex and go ice-skating. In summer the resort has every outdoor activity imaginable, including archery, waterskiing, kayaking, loon-watching, tennis, hiking, mountain biking, and fishing. ⊠ *1251 Eaton Rd., East Madison* ☎ *603/367–8896, 800/373–3754* ⊕ *www.kingpine.com.*

Mt. Washington Valley Ski Touring and Snowshoe Foundation. Nearly 30 miles of groomed cross-country trails weave through the North Conway countryside, maintained by this foundation. Membership to the Mt. Washington Valley Ski Touring Club is required, and can be purchased by the day or year. Equipment rentals are available. ⊠ *279 Rte. 16-302, Intervale* ☎ *603/356–9920* ⊕ *www.mwvskitouring.org.*

9

New Hampshire's Diners

Friendly Toast. In the historic coastal city of Portsmouth, the Friendly Toast might be the most vaunted breakfast spot in the state. Creative fare like Coconut Cakes (pancakes with coconut, chocolate chips, and cashews) and the Hansel and Gretel Waffle (gingerbread waffle topped with pomegranate molasses) keep hungry bellies coming back again and again. ✉ *113 Congress St., Portsmouth* ☎ *603/430–2154* ⊕ *www.thefriendlytoast.net.*

Lou's Restaurant. Dartmouth students and professors hobnob over stellar pancakes, omelets, and breakfast tacos at Lou's Restaurant, a cheap-and-cheerful storefront diner. It serves up prodigious portions of corned-beef hash and eggs Benedict, as well as artfully decorated cupcakes and house-made cider donuts. Just beware of the long lines on weekend mornings. ✉ *30 S. Main St., Hanover* ☎ *603/643–3321* ⊕ *www.lousrestaurant.net.*

Red Arrow Diner. Once declared one of the country's "top 10 diners," the bustling Red Arrow Diner is open around the clock and caters to politicians, students, artists, and regular Janes and Joes in the heart of the Granite State's largest city. The 1922 diner's daily blue plate specials are served on actual blue plates, and you'll find such regular items as kielbasa and beans and house-brewed root beer and cream soda. There's a second location at 63 Union Square in Milford. ✉ *61 Lowell St., Manchester* ☎ *603/626–1118* ⊕ *www.redarrowdiner.com.*

Sunny Day Diner. Up in the skiing and hiking haven of Lincoln, outdoorsy souls fuel up on hearty fare like banana-bread French toast and cherry

Red Arrow Diner in Manchester.

pie à la mode at the cozy Sunny Day Diner, a handsomely restored building from the late 1950s. ✉ *U.S. 3, off I–93, Lincoln* ☎ *603/745–4833.*

Tilt'n Diner. Travelers to the state's Lakes Region have long been familiar with the flashy pink exterior and neon signage of the Tilt'n Diner, a convivial 1950s-style restaurant that's known for its omlets (served every possible way), reuben sandwiches, baked shepherd's pie, and Southern breakfasts—sausage gravy, biscuits, and baked beans with two eggs. Breakfast is served all day. ✉ *61 Laconia Rd., Tilton* ☎ *603/286–2204* ⊕ *www.thecman.com.*

—Andrew Collins

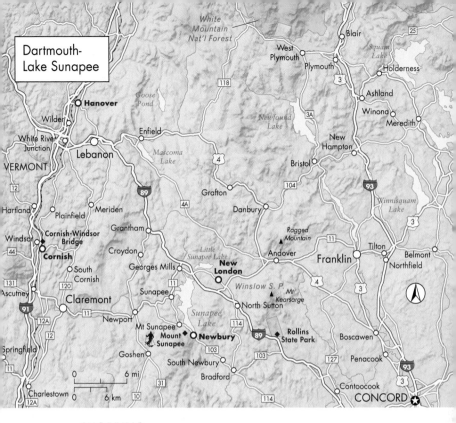

Dartmouth-
Lake Sunapee

SHOPPING

ANTIQUES

Richard Plusch Antiques. This shop deals in period furniture and accessories, including glass, sterling silver, Oriental porcelains, rugs, paintings, and more. ⊠ 2584 *White Mountain Hwy.* ☎ 603/356–3333.

CLOTHING

More than 150 factory outlets—including L. L. Bean, New Balance, Orvis, Columbia, Lenox, Polo, Nike, Anne Klein, and Woolrich—line Route 16.

Joe Jones' Sun & Ski Sports. You'll find outdoor clothing and gear here, as well as the bathing suit you forgot to pack for the hot tub. Joe Jones' also offers rentals of gear and clothing. ⊠ 2709 *White Mountain Hwy.* ☎ 603/356–9411 ⊕ *www.joejonessports.com.*

CRAFTS

Handcrafters Barn. This place stocks the work of 250 area artists and artisans. ⊠ 2473 *White Mountain Hwy.* ☎ 603/356–8996 ⊕ *www.handcraftersbarn.com.*

Zeb's General Store. This old-fashioned country store sells specialty foods, crafts, clothing, and a range of products made in New England. ⊠ 2675 *Main St.* ☎ 603/356–9294, 800/676–9294 ⊕ *www.zebs.com.*

EN
ROUTE
A great place to settle in to the White Mountains, take in one of the greatest panoramas of the mountains, and get visitor info is at the **Intervale Scenic Vista.** The stop, off Route 16 a few miles north of North Conway, is run by the DOT, has a helpful volunteer staff, features a wonderful large topographical map, and has terrific bathrooms.

KANCAMAGUS HIGHWAY

36 miles between Conway and Lincoln/North Woodstock.

Fodor's Choice ★ **Kancamagus Highway.** Interstate 93 is the fastest way to the White Mountains, but it's hardly the most appealing. The section of Route 112 known as the Kancamagus Highway passes through some of the state's most unspoiled mountain scenery—it was one of the first roads in the nation to be designated a National Scenic Byway. The Kanc, as it's called by locals, is punctuated by overlooks and picnic areas, and erupts into fiery color each fall, when photo-snapping drivers really slow things down. In bad weather, check with the White Mountains Visitors Bureau for road conditions. ⊕ *www.kancamagushighway.com.*

SPORTS AND THE OUTDOORS

Lincoln Woods Trail. A couple of short hiking trails off the Kancamagus Highway yield great rewards with relatively little effort. The Lincoln Woods Trail starts from the large parking lot of the Lincoln Woods Visitor Center, 5 miles east of Lincoln. Here you can purchase the $3 pass needed to park in any of the White Mountain National Forest lots or overlooks; stopping briefly to take photos or to use the restrooms at the visitor center is permitted without a pass. The trail crosses a suspension bridge over the Pemigewasset River and follows an old railroad bed for 3 miles along the river. ⊕ *www.fs.usda.gov/whitemountain.*

Sabbaday Falls. The parking and picnic area for Sabbaday Falls, about 15 miles west of Conway, is the trailhead for an easy ½-mile route to a multilevel cascade that plunges through two potholes and a flume. Swimming is not allowed. ⊠ *Kancamagus Hwy.* ⊕ *www.kancamagus highway.com.*

DARTMOUTH–LAKE SUNAPEE

In the west-central part of the state, the towns around prestigious Dartmouth College and rippling Lake Sunapee vary from sleepy, old-fashioned outposts that haven't changed much in decades to bustling, sophisticated towns rife with cafés, art galleries, and boutiques. Among the latter, Hanover and New London are the area's main hubs, both of them increasingly popular as vacation destinations. Although distinct from the Lakes Region, greater Lake Sunapee looks like a miniature Lake Winnipesaukee, albeit with far less commercial development.

For a great drive, follow the Lake Sunapee Scenic and Cultural Byway, which runs for about 25 miles from Georges Mills (a bit northwest of New London) down into Warner, tracing much of the Lake Sunapee shoreline. When you've tired of climbing and swimming and visiting the past, look for small studios of area artists. This part of the state, along with the even quieter Monadnock area to the south, has long been an informal artists' colony where people come to write, paint, and weave in solitude.

ESSENTIALS

Visitor Information Lake Sunapee Region Chamber of Commerce ☎ *603/526–6575, 877/526–6575* 🌐 *www.sunapeevacations.com.*

NEW LONDON

16 miles northwest of Warner, 25 miles west of Tilton.

New London, the home of Colby-Sawyer College (1837), is a good base for exploring the Lake Sunapee region. A campus of stately Colonial-style buildings fronts the vibrant commercial district, where you'll find several cafés and boutiques.

GETTING HERE AND AROUND

From the south, take Exit 11 on Interstate 93 to Crockett Corner and then north on Route 114. From the north, take Exit 12 and travel south on Route 114. Mount Sunapee Ski Area offers a ski shuttle to and from many of the area hotels and B&Bs.

WHERE TO EAT AND STAY

$$ AMERICAN 🍴 **Flying Goose Brew Pub & Grille.** With 12 handcrafted beers and additional seasonal varieties made with hops grown on-site, this inviting restaurant, pub, and solar-powered brewery is a hit with beer connoisseurs. Standouts include juicy ribs, paper-thin onion rings, fresh-cut steaks, and the Memphis burger with pulled pork and coleslaw piled on top. The menu changes twice a year, in the summer and fall. Enjoy live music on Thursday evening. [$] *Average main: $18* ✉ *40 Andover Rd., at the intersection of Rtes. 11 and 114* ☎ *603/526–6899* 🌐 *www.flyinggoose.com.*

$$ B&B/INN 🏨 **Follansbee Inn.** Built in 1840, this quintessential country inn on the shore of Kezar Lake is the kind of place that almost automatically turns strangers into friends. **Pros:** relaxed lakefront setting; clean rooms; nice breakfast. **Cons:** not all rooms have lake views; some Wi-Fi dead zones. [$] *Rooms from: $159* ✉ *2 Keyser St., North Sutton* ☎ *603/927–4221, 800/626–4221* 🌐 *www.follansbeeinn.com* 🛏 *17 rooms* 🍽 *Breakfast.*

$$ B&B/INN 🏨 **The Inn at Pleasant Lake.** Across Pleasant Lake from majestic Mt. Kearsarge, this 1790s inn has spacious rooms filled with country antiques. **Pros:** lakefront with a small beach; kayaks and stand-up paddleboards available. **Cons:** away from town; no cell phone coverage. [$] *Rooms from: $165* ✉ *853 Pleasant St.* ☎ *603/526–6271, 800/626–4907* 🌐 *www.innatpleasantlake.com* 🛏 *10 rooms* 🍽 *Breakfast.*

THE ARTS

New London Barn Playhouse. Broadway-style and children's plays are presented here every summer in New Hampshire's oldest continuously operating theater. ✉ *84 Main St.* ☎ *603/526–6710* 🌐 *www.nlbarn.org.*

9

SPORTS AND THE OUTDOORS

Rollins State Park. A 3½-mile scenic route through Rollins State Park snakes up the southern slope of Mt. Kearsarge, where you can hike a ½-mile trail to the summit. The road often closes in winter due to hazardous conditions. ☒ *1066 Kearsarge Rd., off Rte. 103, Warner* ☏ *603/456–3808* ⊕ *www.nhstateparks.org* 🎫 *$4.*

SHOPPING

Artisan's. This shop carries jewelry, beads, gourmet foods, clothing, and other local crafts. ☒ *11 Pleasant St.* ☏ *603/526–4227* ⊕ *www. artisansnewlondon.com.*

NEWBURY

8 miles southwest of New London.

Newbury is on the edge of Mt. Sunapee State Park. The mountain, which rises to an elevation of nearly 3,000 feet, and the sparkling lake are the region's outdoor recreation centers. The popular League of New Hampshire Craftsmen's Fair, the nation's oldest crafts fair, is held at the base of Mt. Sunapee each August.

GETTING HERE AND AROUND

From New London, take 114 West to 103A South, which follows the eastern coast of Lake Sunapee to Newbury.

EXPLORING

The Fells Historic Estate & Gardens. John M. Hay, who served as private secretary to Abraham Lincoln, built the Fells on Lake Sunapee as a summer home in 1890. House tours offer a glimpse of early-20th-century life on a New Hampshire estate. The grounds are a gardener's delight and include a 100-foot-long perennial garden and a rock garden with a brook flowing through it. Miles of hiking trails can also be accessed from the estate. The 40-minute guided house and garden tours cost an additional $6. ☒ *456 Rte. 103A* ☏ *603/763–4789* ⊕ *www.thefells.org* 🎫 *$10* ☉ *Late June–Labor Day, Wed.–Sun. daily 10–4; late May–late June and Labor Day–Columbus Day, weekends 10–4.*

Sunapee Harbor. On the west side of Lake Sunapee, this an old-fashioned summer resort community with a large marina, a handful of restaurants and shops on the water, a tidy village green with a gazebo, and a small museum. A plaque outside Wild Goose Country Store details some of Lake Sunapee's attributes: for exmaple, it's one of the highest lakes in New Hampshire, and one of the least polluted. Lake Sunapee has brook and lake trout, salmon, smallmouth bass, perch, and pickerel. ☒ *Sunapee* ⊕ *www.sunapeevacations.com.*

WHERE TO EAT

$$

AMERICAN

✕ **Anchorage at Sunapee Harbor.** Fans of this long gray restaurant with a sprawling deck overlooking Sunapee Harbor's marina come as much for the great views as for the dependable—and occasionally creative—American chow. It's as likely a place for a burger or fried seafood platter as for homemade lobster spring rolls. There's also live entertainment some nights—in fact, this is where the founders of the rock band Aerosmith first met back in the early 1970s. $ *Average main: $18* ✉ *71 Main St., Sunapee Harbor* ☎ *603/763–3334* 🌐 *www.theanchorageatsunapeeharbor.com* 🕓 *Closed Oct.–mid-May and Mon.*

WHERE TO STAY

$$$$ RENTAL 🏠 **Sunapee Harbor Cottages.** This charming collection of six private cottages is within a stone's throw of Sunapee Harbor. **Pros:** spacious units; no minimum stays. **Cons:** no maid service; little clothes storage. $ *Rooms from: $225* ✉ *4 Lake Ave., Sunapee Harbor* ☎ *603/763–5052, 866/763–5052* 🌐 *www.sunapeeharborcottages.com* 🛏 *6 cottages* 🍴 *No meals.*

SPORTS AND THE OUTDOORS

BEACHES

Mt. Sunapee State Park Beach. A great family spot, Sunapee State Beach has picnic areas, fishing, and a bathhouse. You can also rent canoes and kayaks, and there's a campground on-site. **Amenities:** lifeguards; parking (no fee); showers; toilets. **Best for:** swimming; walking. ✉ *86 Beach Access Rd.* ☎ *603/763–5561* 🌐 *www.nhstateparks.org* 🎟 *$5* 🕓 *Memorial Day–Labor Day, daily 9–5.*

BOAT TOURS

Lake Sunapee Cruises. Narrated cruises provide a closer look at Lake Sunapee's history and mountain scenery. They run from late May through mid-October, daily in summer and on weekends in spring and fall. ✉ *Town Dock, 81 Main St., Sunapee Harbor* ☎ *603/938–6465* 🌐 *www.sunapeecruises.com* 🎟 *$20.*

MV *Kearsarge*. Two-hour narrated sunset cruises around the lake are offered aboard the MV *Kearsarge*. With departures June to mid-October, the cruises cost $40 and include a buffet dinner. ✉ *Town Dock, 81 Main St., Sunapee Harbor* ☎ *603/938–6465* 🌐 *www.sunapeecruises.com.*

SKI AREA

Mount Sunapee. This family-friendly resort is one of New England's best-kept secrets. The owners have spent millions upgrading snowmaking and grooming equipment and turning this into a four-seasons resort. Mount Sunapee offers over 1,500 vertical feet of downhill excitement, 11 lifts (including three quads), and 66 trails and slopes for all abilities. There are four terrain parks and nine glade trails. In summer the adventure park features a canopy zipline tour, aerial challenge course, an 18-hole disc-golf course, miniature golf, and numerous hiking trails. ✉ *1398 Rte. 103* ☎ *603/763–3500, 603/763–4020 snow conditions* 🌐 *www.mtsunapee.com.*

SHOPPING

Wild Goose Country Store. On the harbor in Sunapee, the Wild Goose Country Store carries teddy bears, penny candy, pottery, and other engaging odds and ends. ✉ *77 Main St., Sunapee* ☎ *603/763–5516.*

HANOVER

12 miles northwest of Enfield; 62 miles northwest of Concord.

Eleazer Wheelock founded Hanover's Dartmouth College in 1769 to educate the Abenaki "and other youth." When he arrived, the town consisted of about 20 families. The college and the town grew symbiotically, with Dartmouth becoming the northernmost Ivy League school. Hanover is still synonymous with Dartmouth, but it's also a respected medical and cultural center for the upper Connecticut River Valley.

GETTING HERE AND AROUND

Lebanon Municipal Airport, near Dartmouth College, is served by Cape Air (in conjunction with JetBlue) from New York. By car, Interstate 91 North or Interstate 89 are the best ways to get to Lebanon, Hanover, and the surrounding area. Plan on spending a day visiting Hanover and to see all the sights on the Dartmouth campus.

Shops, mostly of the independent variety but with a few upscale chains sprinkled in, line Hanover's main street. The commercial district blends almost imperceptibly with the Dartmouth campus. West Lebanon, south of Hanover on the Vermont border, has many more shops.

ESSENTIALS

Airport Lebanon Municipal Airport ⊠ *5 Airport Rd., West Lebanon* 🕾 *603/298–8878* ⊕ *www.flyleb.com.*

Taxi Big Yellow Taxi 🕾 *603/643–8294* ⊕ *www.bigyellowtaxis.com.*

Visitor Information Hanover Area Chamber of Commerce ⊠ *Nugget Arcade Bldg., 53 S. Main St., Suite 216* 🕾 *603/643–3115* ⊕ *www.hanoverchamber.org.*

EXPLORING

Dartmouth College. Robert Frost spent part of a brooding freshman semester at this Ivy League school before giving up college altogether. The buildings that cluster around the green include the **Baker Memorial Library,** which houses such literary treasures as 17th-century editions of William Shakespeare's works. The library is also well known for Mexican artist José Clemente Orozco's 3,000-square-foot murals that depict the story of civilization in the Americas. ⊠ *N. Main and Wentworth Sts.* 🕾 *603/646–1110* ⊕ *www.dartmouth.edu.*

9

QUICK BITES

Dirt Cowboy Cafe. Take a respite from museum-hopping with a cup of espresso, a ham-and-cheese scone, or a freshly baked brownie at the Dirt Cowboy, a café across from the green and beside a used-book store. ⊠ *7 S. Main St.* 🕾 *603/643–1323* ⊕ *www.dirtcowboycafe.com.*

Enfield Shaker Museum. In 1782, two Shaker brothers from Mount Lebanon, New York, arrived on Lake Mascoma's northeastern side, about 12 miles southeast of Hanover. Eventually, they formed Enfield, the ninth of 18 Shaker communities in the United States, and moved it to the lake's southern shore, where they erected more than 200 buildings. The Enfield Shaker Museum preserves the legacy of the Shakers, who numbered 330 members at the village's peak. By 1923 interest in the society had dwindled, and the last 10 members joined the Canterbury community, south of Laconia. A self-guided walking tour takes you through 13 of the remaining buildings, among them an 1849 stone mill. Demonstrations of Shaker crafts techniques and numerous special events take place year-round. ✉ *447 Rte. 4A, Enfield* ☎ *603/632–4346* 🌐 *www.shakermuseum.org* 🎫 *$12* 🕒 *Mon.–Sat. 10–4, Sun. noon–4.*

Hopkins Center for the Arts. If the towering arcade at the entrance to the Hopkins Center for the Arts appears familiar, it's probably because it resembles the project that architect Wallace K. Harrison completed just after designing it: New York City's Metropolitan Opera House at Lincoln Center. The complex includes a 900-seat theater for film showings and concerts, a 480-seat theater for plays, and a black-box theater for new plays. The Dartmouth Symphony Orchestra performs here. ✉ *Dartmout College, 2 East Wheelock St.* ☎ *603/646–2422* 🌐 *hop.dartmouth.edu.*

Hood Museum of Art. In addition to African, Peruvian, Oceanic, Asian, European, and American art, the Hood Museum of Art owns the Pablo Picasso painting *Guitar on a Table*, silver by Paul Revere, and a set of Assyrian reliefs from the 9th century BC. The range of contemporary works, including pieces by John Sloan, William Glackens, Mark Rothko, Fernand Léger, and Joan Miró, is particularly notable. Rivaling the collection is the museum's architecture: a series of austere, copper-roofed, redbrick buildings arranged around a courtyard. Free campus tours are available on request. ✉ *Dartmouth College, Wheelock St.* ☎ *603/646–2808* 🌐 *www.hoodmuseum.dartmouth.edu* 🎫 *Free* 🕒 *Tues. and Thurs.–Sat. 10–5, Wed. 10–9, Sun. noon–5.*

OFF THE BEATEN PATH

Upper Valley. From Hanover you can make a 60-mile drive up Route 10 all the way to Littleton for a highly scenic tour of the upper Connecticut River valley. You'll have views of the river and Vermont's Green Mountains from many points. The road passes through groves of evergreens, over leafy ridges, and through delightful hamlets. Grab gourmet picnic provisions at the general store on Lyme's village common—probably the most pristine of any in the state—and stop at the bluff-top village green in historical Haverhill (28 miles north of Hanover) for a picnic amid the panorama of classic Georgian- and Federal-style mansions and faraway farmsteads.

WHERE TO EAT

$$ AMERICAN

🍴 **Canoe Club.** Bedecked with canoes, paddles, and classic Dartmouth paraphernalia, this festive spot presents live jazz and folk music most nights. The mood may be casual, but the kitchen presents rather imaginative food, including memorable starters like a roasted beet medley with a spiced chocolate sauce and an orange glaze, or steamed mussels in a delectable garlic-and-herb sauce. Among the main courses, the seafood cioppino, with shrimp, scallops, onion, and sweet pepper, is a favorite. There's also a lighter, late-night menu. [$] *Average main: $19* ✉ *27 S. Main St.* ☎ *603/643–9660* 🌐 *www.canoeclub.us.*

$ AMERICAN

🍴 **Lou's Restaurant.** One of the few places in town where students and locals really mix, this place is hard to resist. A Hanover tradition since 1948, this diner-cum-café-cum-bakery serves possibly the best breakfast in the valley—a plate of *migas* (eggs, cheddar, salsa, and guacamole mixed with tortilla chips) can fill you up for the better part of the day;

The Cornish–Windsor Bridge is the second-longest covered bridge in the United States, at 460 feet.

blueberry-cranberry buttermilk pancakes also satisfy. Or grab a seat at the old-fashioned soda fountain and order an ice cream sundae. Lou's can accommodate gluten-free diets, too. $ *Average main: $9* ⊠ *30 S. Main St.* ☏ *603/643–3321* ⊕ *lousrestaurant.net* ☾ *No dinner.*

$$
ITALIAN ✗ **Lui Lui.** The creatively topped thin-crust pizzas and huge portions of pasta are only part of the draw at this chatter-filled eatery; the other is its dramatic setting inside a former power station on the Mascoma River. Pizza picks include the Tuscan (mozzarella topped with tomato and roasted garlic) and the grilled chicken with barbecue sauce. Pasta fans should dive into a bowl of linguine with homemade clam sauce. $ *Average main: $17* ⊠ *8 Glen Rd., West Lebanon* ☏ *603/298–7070* ⊕ *www.luilui.com.*

$$
ECLECTIC ✗ **Murphy's On the Green.** Students, visiting alums, and locals regularly descend upon this popular pub, which has walls lined with shelves of old books. The varied menu features burgers and salads as well as meat loaf, crusted lamb sirloin, and vegetarian dishes like eggplant stuffed with tofu. Check out the extensive beer list. $ *Average main: $19* ⊠ *11 S. Main St.* ☏ *603/643–4075* ⊕ *www.murphysonthegreen.com.*

WHERE TO STAY

$$$$
HOTEL ⌂ **The Hanover Inn.** If you're in town for a Dartmouth event, you'll want to stay on the college's—and the town's—main square. **Pros:** center of campus and town; great service; handy fitness center. **Cons:** breakfast not included; pricey rates. $ *Rooms from: $349* ⊠ *The Green, 2 S. Main St.* ☏ *603/643–4300, 800/443–7024* ⊕ *www.hanoverinn.com* ⇗ *108 rooms, 15 suites* ⦿❘ *No meals.*

$$
B&B/INN
⚏ **Trumbull House.** The nicely decorated guest rooms of this white Colonial-style house—on 16 acres on Hanover's outskirts—have king- or queen-size beds, feather pillows, writing desks, and other comfortable touches, as well as Wi-Fi access. **Pros:** quiet setting; lovely home; big breakfast. **Cons:** 3 miles east of town. $ *Rooms from: $169* ⊠ *40 Etna Rd.* ☎ *603/643–2370, 800/651–5141* ⊕ *www.trumbullhouse.com* ⇨ *4 rooms, 1 suite, 1 cottage* ⓧ *Breakfast.*

SPORTS AND THE OUTDOORS

Ledyard Canoe Club. On the bank of the Connecticut River, the Ledyard Canoe Club of Dartmouth rents canoes, kayaks, and stand-up paddleboats by the hour. ⊠ *Cliffside Trail, near the Ledyard Bridge* ☎ *603/643–6709* ⊕ *www.dartmouth.edu/~lcc.*

CORNISH

22 miles south of Hanover.

Today Cornish is best known for its covered bridges and for being the home of reclusive late author J. D. Salinger, but at the turn of the 20th century the village was known primarily as the home of the country's then most popular novelist, Winston Churchill (no relation to the British prime minister). His novel *Richard Carvell* sold more than a million copies. Churchill was such a celebrity that he hosted Teddy Roosevelt during the president's 1902 visit. At that time Cornish was an enclave of artistic talent. Painter Maxfield Parrish lived and worked here, and sculptor Augustus Saint-Gaudens set up his studio and created the heroic bronzes for which he is known.

GETTING HERE AND AROUND

About 5 miles west of town on Route 44, the Cornish–Windsor Bridge crosses the Connecticut River between New Hampshire and Vermont. The Blacksmith Shop covered bridge is 2 miles east of Route 12A on Town House Road, and the Dingleton Hill covered bridge is 1 mile east of Route 12A on Root Hill Road. Cornish itself is small enough to see in one morning.

EXPLORING

Cornish-Windsor Bridge. This 460-foot bridge, 1½ miles south of the Saint-Gaudens National Historic Site, connects New Hampshire to Vermont across the Connecticut River. It dates from 1866 and is the longest covered wooden bridge in the United States. The notice on the bridge reads: "Walk your horses or pay two dollar fine." ⊠ *Bridge St.*

Fodor'sChoice
★
Saint-Gaudens National Historic Site. Just south of Plainfield, a small lane leads to this historic site, where you can tour sculptor Augustus Saint-Gaudens's house (with his original furnishings), studio, gallery, and 150 acres of grounds and gardens. Scattered throughout are casts of his

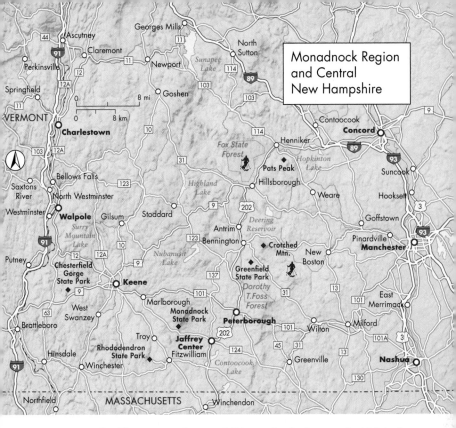

Monadnock Region and Central New Hampshire

works. The property has two hiking trails, the longer of which is the Blow-Me-Down Trail. Concerts are held every Sunday afternoon in July and August. ⊠ *139 Saint-Gaudens Rd., off Rte. 12A* ☎ *603/675–2175* ⊕ *www.nps.gov/saga* ⊠ *$5* ⊙ *Memorial Day–Oct., daily 9–4:30.*

SPORTS AND THE OUTDOORS

North Star Canoe Rentals. Rent a canoe, kayak, or inner tube and enjoy a lazy float down the Connecticut River, with stops en route for swimming and sunbathing. North Star Canoe will bring you back to your car. For a bigger adventure, join in one of the half- or full-day or overnight trips. ⊠ *1356A Rte. 12A* ☎ *603/542–6929* ⊕ *www.kayak-canoe.com.*

THE MONADNOCKS AND MERRIMACK VALLEY

Southwestern and south-central New Hampshire mix village charm with city hustle and bustle across two distinct regions. The Merrimack River Valley has the state's largest and fastest-growing cities: Nashua, Manchester, and Concord. To the west, in the state's sleepy southwestern corner, is the Monadnock region, one of New Hampshire's least developed and most naturally stunning parts. Here you'll find plenty of hiking trails as well as peaceful hilltop hamlets that appear barely changed in the past two centuries. Mt. Monadnock, southern New

Hampshire's largest peak, stands guard over the Monadnock region, which has more than 200 lakes and ponds. Rainbow trout, smallmouth and largemouth bass, and some northern pike swim in Chesterfield's Spofford Lake. Goose Pond, just north of Keene, holds smallmouth bass and white perch.

NASHUA

98 miles south of Lincoln/North Woodstock; 48 miles northwest of Boston; 36 miles south of Concord; 50 miles southeast of Keene.

Once a prosperous manufacturing town that drew thousands of immigrant workers in the late 1800s and early 1900s, Nashua declined following World War II, as many factories shut down or moved to where labor was cheaper. Since the 1970s, however, the metro area has jumped in population, developing into a charming community. Its low-key downtown has classic redbrick buildings along the Nashua River, a tributary of the Merrimack River. Though not visited by tourists as much as other communities in the region, Nashua (population 90,000) has some good restaurants and major shopping centers.

GETTING HERE AND AROUND

A good place to start exploring Nashua is at Main and High streets, where a number of fine restaurants and shops are located. Downtown Nashua has free Wi-Fi.

ESSENTIALS

Taxi D & E Taxi ☎ *603/889–3999.* **SK Taxi** ☎ *603/882–5155.*

EXPLORING

Florence Hyde Speare Memorial Museum. The city's impressive industrial history is retold at this museum that houses the Nashua Historical Society. In this two-story museum you'll find artifacts, early furnishings, photos, a vintage printing press, and a research library. Adjacent to the museum is the Federal-style **Abbot-Spalding House,** furnished with 18th- and 19th-century antiques, art, and household items. ✉ *5 Abbott St.* ☎ *603/883–0015* 🌐 *www.nashuahistoricalsociety.org/spearemuseum* 🎟 *Free* ⏲ *Mar.–late-Nov.,Tues.–Thurs. 10–4.*

WHERE TO EAT

$$$ BISTRO Fodor's Choice ★ 🍴 **MT's Local Kitchen and Wine Bar.** Part hip bistro, part jazzy wine bar, MT's is so popular that even foodies from across the state line drive here. The regularly changing menu highlights local products and might include pork scaloppine with a cognac-soaked raisin pan sauce or wood-grilled Vermont chicken with marinated mushrooms. The pesto fries are legendary. Wood-fired pizzas are also a specialty—try the one topped with soppressata, stewed dates, caramelized onions, ricotta, and pecans. [$] *Average main: $26* ✉ *212 Main St.* ☎ *603/595–9334* 🌐 *www.mtslocal.com.*

$$$ ITALIAN 🍴 **Villa Banca.** On the ground floor of a dramatic, turreted building, this spot with high ceilings and tall windows specializes in traditional and contemporary Italian cooking. Start with Gorgonzola artichokes and move on to pasta Alfredo. The butternut squash ravioli is a sweet delight, and the macadamia nut–encrusted tilapia will satisfy the fish

At the Currier Museum of Art, you can enjoy European and American classics, or visit a nearby Frank Lloyd Wright house.

lover at your table. Note the exotic-martini menu, a big draw at happy hour. $ *Average main: $22* ✉ *194 Main St.* ☎ *603/598–0500* 🌐 *www. villabanca.com* 🕒 *No lunch weekends.*

MANCHESTER

18 miles north of Nashua, 53 miles north of Boston.

Manchester, with 108,000-plus residents, is New Hampshire's largest city. The town grew up around the Amoskeag Falls on the Merrimack River, which fueled small textile mills through the 1700s. By 1828 Boston investors had bought the rights to the Merrimack's water power and built the Amoskeag Mills, which became a testament to New England's manufacturing capabilities. In 1906 the mills employed 17,000 people and weekly churned out more than 4 million yards of cloth. This vast enterprise served as Manchester's entire economic base; when it closed in 1936 the town was devastated.

Today Manchester is mainly a banking and business center. The old mill buildings have been converted into warehouses, classrooms, restaurants, museums, and office space. The city has the state's major airport, as well as the Verizon Wireless Arena, which hosts minor-league hockey matches, concerts, and conventions.

GETTING HERE AND AROUND

Manchester Airport, the state's largest airport, has rapidly become a cost-effective, hassle-free alternative to Boston's Logan Airport, with nonstop service to more than 20 cities. Manchester can be hard to get around, but it offers a number of taxi services.

ESSENTIALS

Airport Manchester-Boston Regional Airport ✉ *1 Airport Rd.* ☎ *603/624–6556* ⊕ *www.flymanchester.com.*

Taxi Manchester Taxi ☎ *603/623-2222.* **Queen City Taxi** ☎ *603/622-0008.*

Visitor Information Greater Manchester Chamber of Commerce ✉ *54 Hanover St.* ☎ *603/666-6600* ⊕ *www.manchester-chamber.org.*

EXPLORING

Amoskeag Fishways. From May to mid-June, salmon, shad, and river herring "climb" the fish ladder at this spot near the Amoskeag Dam. The visitor center has an underwater viewing window and interactive exhibits and programs about the Merrimack River. ✉ *6 Fletcher St.* ☎ *603/626-3474* ⊕ *www.amoskeagfishways.org* ☉ *May and June, daily 9–5; July–Apr., Mon.–Sat. 9–5.*

Fodor's Choice
★

Currier Museum of Art. This renowned art museum not only offers an astounding permanent collection of works by European and American masters, such as Claude Monet, Edward Hopper, Winslow Homer, John Marin, Andrew Wyeth, and Childe Hassam, but presents changing exhibits of contemporary works. Also run by the Currier is the nearby Frank Lloyd Wright–designed Zimmerman House, built in 1950. Wright called this sparse, utterly functional living space "Usonian," an invented term used to describe 50 such smaller homes based on his vision to create distinctly American architecture. It's New England's only Frank Lloyd Wright–designed residence open to the public. ✉ *150 Ash St.* ☎ *603/669–6144, 603/626–4158 house tours* ⊕ *www.currier. org* 🎫 *$12; $20 with Zimmerman House* ☉ *Sun., Mon., and Wed.–Fri. 11–5, Sat. 10–5.*

NIGHTLIFE AND THE ARTS

THE ARTS

The Palace Theatre. Musicals and plays are presented throughout the year at the Palace Theatre. It also hosts comedy acts, the state's philharmonic and symphony orchestras, and the Opera League of New Hampshire. ✉ *80 Hanover St.* ☎ *603/668–5588 box office* ⊕ *www. palacetheatre.org.*

NIGHTLIFE

Club 313. This popular disco's huge dance floor attracts a diverse crowd, especially gays and lesbians. It also features karaoke, a game room, and drag shows. ✉ *93 S. Maple St.* ☎ *603/628–6813* ⊕ *club313nh.com.*

The Yard. Revelers come from all over to drink at the The Yard. Saturday nights are for country line dancing featuring live music and a midnight rodeo. ✉ *1211 S. Mammoth Rd.* ☎ *603/623–3545* ⊕ *www. theyardrestaurant.com.*

WHERE TO EAT

$$
AMERICAN

✕ **Cotton.** Inside one of the old Amoskeag Mills buildings, this eatery has mod lighting and furnishings that give it a swanky atmosphere. For warm weather there's also a patio set in an arbor. Chef Jeffrey Paige, a leader in the farm-to-table movement, specializes in putting a new spin on comfort food. Start with pan-seared crab cakes or the lemongrass chicken salad. The menu changes four times a year but might include an all-natural Delmonico steak or wood-grilled scallops with superb sweet-potato hash. The martinis here are so good they've won awards. $ *Average main: $19* ⊠ *75 Arms St.* ☎ *603/622–5488* ⊕ *www.cottonfood. com* ⊘ *No lunch weekends.*

$ ✕ **Red Arrow Diner.** This tiny diner is ground zero for presidential hope-
AMERICAN fuls in New Hampshire come primary season. The rest of the time, a
Fodor'sChoice mix of hipsters and oldsters, including comedian and Manchester native
★ Adam Sandler, favor this neon-streaked, 24-hour greasy spoon, which has been going strong since 1922. Filling fare—platters of kielbasa, French toast, liver and onions, chicken Parmesan with spaghetti, and the diner's famous panfries—keeps patrons happy. Homemade sodas and éclairs round out the menu. $ *Average main: $10* ⊠ *61 Lowell St.* ☎ *603/626–1118* ⊕ *redarrowdiner.com.*

WHERE TO STAY

$$ ⌂ **Ash Street Inn.** Because it's in an attractive residential neighborhood
B&B/INN of striking Victorian homes, staying in this five-room B&B will give you the best face of Manchester. **Pros:** nicely decorated rooms; walking distance to Currier Museum. **Cons:** not a full-service hotel. $ *Rooms from: $169* ⊠ *118 Ash St.* ☎ *603/668–9908* ⊕ *www.ashstreetinn.com* ⇗ *5 rooms* ⎮○⎮ *Breakfast.*

$$$$ ⌂ **Bedford Village Inn.** If you've decided to sacrifice downtown conve-
B&B/INN niences to venture out to this lovely manor outside of town, its com-forts and beauty will reward you. **Pros:** relaxing setting; exceptional grounds; great restaurant. **Cons:** outside of town. $ *Rooms from: $249* ⊠ *2 Olde Bedford Way, Bedford* ☎ *603/472–2001, 800/852–1166* ⊕ *www.bedfordvillageinn.com* ⇗ *12 suites, 2 apartments, 1 cottage* ⎮○⎮ *No meals.*

$$ ⌂ **Radisson Hotel Manchester Downtown.** Of Manchester's many chain
HOTEL properties, the 12-story Radisson has the most central location—a short walk from Amoskeag Mills and the great dining along Elm Street. **Pros:** downtown location; free airport shuttles; pets are welcome. **Cons:** fee for parking; unexciting decor. $ *Rooms from: $159* ⊠ *700 Elm St.* ☎ *603/625–1000, 800/967–9033* ⊕ *www.radisson.com/manchester-hotel-nh-03101/nhmanch* ⇗ *244 rooms, 6 suites.*

CONCORD

20 miles northwest of Manchester, 67 miles northwest of Boston, 46 miles northwest of Portsmouth.

New Hampshire's capital (population 42,000) is a quiet town that tends to the state's business but little else—the sidewalks roll up promptly at 6. Stop in town to get a glimpse of New Hampshire's State House, which is crowned by a gleaming gold, eagle-topped dome.

GETTING HERE AND AROUND
The Concord on Foot walking trail winds through the historic district, past 50 sites. Pick up a $2 map at the Greater Concord Chamber of Commerce or at stores along the way. Taxis can help get you around town, though Main Street is easy to walk about.

ESSENTIALS

Taxi **Concord Cab** ☎ *603/225–4222.*

Visitor Information Greater Concord Chamber of Commerce ⊠ *49 S. Main St.* ☎ *603/224–2508* ⊕ *www.concordnhchamber.com.*

TOURS

Concord on Foot. The Concord on Foot walking trail winds through the historic district. Pick up a map at the Greater Concord Chamber of Commerce (49 S. Main St.) or stores along the trail.

The Greater Concord Chamber of Commerce. Maps for the walk can be picked up at the Greater Concord The Greater Concord Chamber of Commerce or stores along the trail. ⊠ *49 S. Main St., Concord* ☎ *603/224-2508* ⊕ *www.concordnhchamber.com.*

EXPLORING

FAMILY **McAuliffe-Shepard Discovery Center.** New England's only air-and-space center offers a full day of activities that are mostly focused on the heavens. See yourself in infrared light, learn about lunar spacecraft, examine a replica of the Mercury-Redstone rocket, or experience what it's like to travel in space. You can even try your hand at being a television weather announcer. There's more, including a café and gift shop. ⊠ *New Hampshire Technical Institute, 2 Institute Dr.* ☎ *603/271–7827* ⊕ *www.starhop.com* ⊠ *$9* ⊙ *Mid-June–Labor Day, Mon.–Sat. 10–5, Sun. 11:30–5; Labor Day–mid-June, Thurs.–Sat. 10–5, Sun. 11:30–5.*

New Hampshire Historical Society. Steps from the state capitol, this museum is a great place to learn about the Concord coach, a popular mode of transportation before railroads. Rotating exhibitions may include locally made quilts or historical protraits of residents. ⊠ *6 Eagle Sq.* ☎ *603/228-6688* ⊕ *www.nhhistory.org* ⊠ *$5.50* ⊙ *July–mid. Oct., Tue.–Sat. 9:30–5, Sun. noon–5; Mon. 9:30–5.*

Pierce Manse. Franklin Pierce lived in this Greek-Revival home before he moved to Washington to become the 14th U.S. president. He's buried nearby. ⊠ *14 Horseshoe Pond La.* ☎ *603/225–4555* ⊕ *www.piercemanse.org* ⊠ *$7* ⊙ *Mid-June–early Sept., Tues.–Sat., 11–3; mid-Sept.–mid-Oct., Fri. and Sat, 12–3; otherwise by appt.*

Fodor's Choice ★ **State House.** Take a self-guided tour of this gilt-domed statehouse, a neoclssical treasure built in 1819. This is the oldest capitol building in the nation in which the legislature uses its original chambers. In January through June you can watch the assemblies in action once a week: the 24 senators of the New Hampshire Senate (the fourth-smallest American lawmaking body) meet once a week. In a wild inversion, the state's representatives number 400—one representative per 3,500 residents, a ratio that is a world record. Pick up tour information at the visitors center. While you're there, check out the paraphernalia from decades of presidential primaries. ⊠ *104 N. Main St.* ☎ *603/271–2154* ⊕ *www.gencourt.state.nh.us/NH_Visitorcenter/default.htm* ⊠ *Free* ⊙ *Weekdays 8–4.*

WHERE TO EAT AND STAY

$ AMERICAN 🍴 **Arnie's Place.** If you need a reason to make the 1½-mile detour from Interstate 93, then more than 50 kinds of homemade ice cream should do the trick. Try the toasted-coconut, raspberry, or vanilla flavors. The chocolate shakes are a real treat for chocoholics. The lemon freeze will give you an ice cream headache in no time, but it's worth it. A small dining room is available for dishes such as a barbecue platter (smoked on the premises), hamburgers, and hot dogs, but the five walk-up windows and picnic benches are the way to go. [$] *Average main: $11* ✉ *164 Loudon Rd., off I–93, Concord Heights* ☎ *603/228–3225* 🌐 *www.arniesplace.com* 🕓 *Closed mid-Oct.–late Feb.*

$$ ECLECTIC 🍴 **Barley House.** A lively, old-fashioned tavern practically across from the capitol building and usually buzzing with a mix of politicos, business folks, and tourists, the Barley House serves dependable chow: chorizo-sausage pizzas, burgers smothered with a peppercorn-whiskey sauce, chicken potpies, beer-braised bratwurst, and Mediterranean chicken salad—it's an impressive melting pot of a menu. The bar turns out dozens of interesting beers, on tap and by the bottle, and there's also a decent wine list. It's open until 1 am. [$] *Average main: $20* ✉ *132 N. Main St.* ☎ *603/228–6363* 🌐 *www.thebarleyhouse.com* ✍ *Reservations not accepted* 🕓 *Closed Sun.*

$$ THAI 🍴 **Siam Orchid.** This dark, attractive Thai restaurant with a colorful rickshaw gracing its dining room serves spicy and reasonably authentic dishes with flair. It draws a crowd from the capitol each day for lunch. Try the fiery broiled swordfish with shrimp curry sauce or the pine-nut chicken in an aromatic ginger sauce. [$] *Average main: $18* ✉ *158 N. Main St.* ☎ *603/228–3633* 🌐 *www.siamorchid.net* 🕓 *No lunch weekends.*

$$$ HOTEL 🏨 **The Centennial.** This is the most modern hotel in New Hampshire, and it's home to Granite, the state's most contemporary restaurant and bar, making it a draw for the state's politicians and those doing business here. **Pros:** super-sleek hotel; very comfortable and clean rooms; great bar and restaurant. **Cons:** busy. [$] *Rooms from: $189* ✉ *96 Pleasant St.* ☎ *603/227–9000, 800/360–4839* 🌐 *www.thecentennialhotel.com* 🛏 *27 rooms, 5 suites* 🍽 *No meals.*

NIGHTLIFE AND THE ARTS

Capitol Center for the Arts. The Egyptian-motif artwork, part of the original 1927 decor, has been restored in the Capitol Center for the Arts. The center hosts touring Broadway shows, dance companies, and musical acts. ✉ *44 S. Main St.* ☎ *603/225–1111* 🌐 *www.ccanh.com.*

Hermanos Cocina Mexicana. The lounge at Hermanos Cocina Mexicana stages live jazz Sunday through Thursday nights, and other bands on Saturday nights. ✉ *11 Hills Ave.* ☎ *603/224–5669* 🌐 *www.hermanosmexican.com.*

SHOPPING

Capitol Craftsman Jewelers. Fine jewelry and crafts are sold at Capitol Craftsman Jewelers. ✉ *16 N. Main St.* ☎ *603/224–6166* 🌐 *www.capitolcraftsman.com.*

Mark Knipe Goldsmiths. Near the State House, jewelry designers here create original rings, pendants, earrings, bracelets, and more. ⊠ *2 Capitol Plaza, Main St.* ☎ *603/224–2920* ⊕ *www.knipegold.com.*

CHARLESTOWN

70 miles northwest of Concord.

Charlestown has the state's largest historic district. About 60 homes, handsome examples of Federal, Greek Revival, and Gothic Revival architecture, are clustered about the town center; 10 of them were built before 1800. Several merchants on the main street distribute brochures that describe an interesting walking tour of the district.

GETTING HERE AND AROUND

You can reach Charlestown from Interstate 91, but it's best to follow Route 12 North from Keene for a gorgeous scenic route. Walking about downtown Charlestown should take only 15 minutes of your day, but it's worth admiring the buildings in the town center. The Fort at No. 4 is less than 2 miles from downtown, north on Route 11.

EXPLORING

FAMILY **Fort at No. 4.** In 1747 this fort was an outpost on the periphery of Colonial civilization. That year fewer than 50 militiamen at the fort withstood an attack by 400 French soldiers, ensuring that northern New England remained under British rule. Today costumed interpreters at this living-history museum cook dinner over an open hearth and demonstrate weaving, gardening, and candle making. Each year the museum holds reenactments of militia musters and battles of the French and Indian War. ⊠ *267 Springfield Rd., ½ mile north of Charlestown* ☎ *603/826–5700* ⊕ *www.fortat4.com* ⊡ *$10* ⊗ *May–Aug., Mon.–Sat. 10–4:30, Sun. 10–4; Sept. and Oct., Wed.–Fri. 10–2:30, weekends 10–4.*

SPORTS AND THE OUTDOORS

Morningside Flight Park. Here's a place for the adrenaline junkie: laser tag, ziplines, paragliding, hang gliding, and more. There are lessons too. This place is considered among the best flying areas in the country. Even if you have a fear of flying, stop and watch the bright colors of the gliders as they take off from the 450-foot peak. ⊠ *357 Morningside La., off Rte. 12/11* ☎ *603/542–4416* ⊕ *flymorningside.kittyhawk.com.*

WALPOLE

13 miles south of Charlestown.

Walpole possesses one of the state's most perfect town greens. Bordered by Elm and Washington streets, it's surrounded by homes built about 1790, when the townsfolk constructed a canal around the Great Falls of the Connecticut River and brought commerce and wealth to the area. The town now has 3,200 inhabitants, more than a dozen of whom are millionaires. Walpole is home to Florentine Films, Ken Burns's production company.

GETTING HERE AND AROUND

It's a short jaunt off Route 12, north of Keene. The small downtown is especially photogenic.

WHERE TO EAT

$$ ✕ **The Restaurant at L. A. Burdick Chocolate.** Famous candy maker Larry
FRENCH Burdick, who sells his artful hand-filled and hand-cut chocolates to top
Fodor's Choice restaurants around the Northeast, is a Walpole resident. This restau-
★ rant has the easygoing sophistication of a Parisian café and may tempt
you to linger over an incredibly rich hot chocolate. The Mediterra-
nean-inspired menu utilizes fresh, often local ingredients and changes
daily. Of course, dessert is a big treat here, featuring Burdick's tempting
chocolates and pastries. For dinner, you might start with a selection
of grilled octopus or reduction trio of pâtés, followed by a house beef
stew or honey-roasted duck breast. $ *Average main: $17* ✉ *47 Main
St.* ☎ *603/756–2882* ⊕ *www.burdickchocolate.com.*

SHOPPING

Boggy Meadow Farm. At Boggy Meadow Farm you can watch the
cheese process unfold, from the 200 cows being milked to the finer
process of cheese-making. The farmstead's raw-milk cheeses can be
sampled and purchased in the store, as well as cider donuts and root
vegetables. It's worth a trip just to see the beautiful 400-acre farm.
✉ *13 Boggy Meadow Lane* ☎ *603/756–3300, 877/541–3953* ⊕ *www.
boggymeadowfarm.com.*

KEENE

*17 miles southeast of Walpole; 20 miles northeast of Brattleboro, Ver-
mont; 56 miles southwest of Manchester.*

Keene is the largest city in the state's southwest corner. Its rapidly gen-
trifying main street, with several engaging boutiques and cafés, is Amer-
ica's widest (132 feet). Each year, on the Saturday before Halloween,
locals use the street to hold a Pumpkin Festival, where the small town
competes with big cities such as Boston for the most jack-o'-lanterns
in one place at one time.

ESSENTIALS

Visitor Information Greater Keene Chamber of Commerce ✉ *48 Central
Sq.* ☎ *603/352–1303* ⊕ *www.keenechamber.com.* **Monadnock Travel Council**
☎ *800/432–7864* ⊕ *www.monadnocktravel.com.*

EXPLORING

Keene State College. The hub of the local arts community is this bustling
college. The Thorne-Sagendorph Art Gallery contains a permanent
collection, including works by Richard Meryman, Abbott Handerson
Thayer, and Robert Mapplethorpe. ✉ *229 Main St.* ☎ *603/358–2263*
⊕ *www.keene.edu.*

QUICK
BITES

Prime Roast. Serving up fine coffee, pastries, and art (covering the walls
and tables), Prime Roast is a sensory experience. The beans are roasted
and ground on-site, so they're absolutely fresh. It's two blocks from Keene

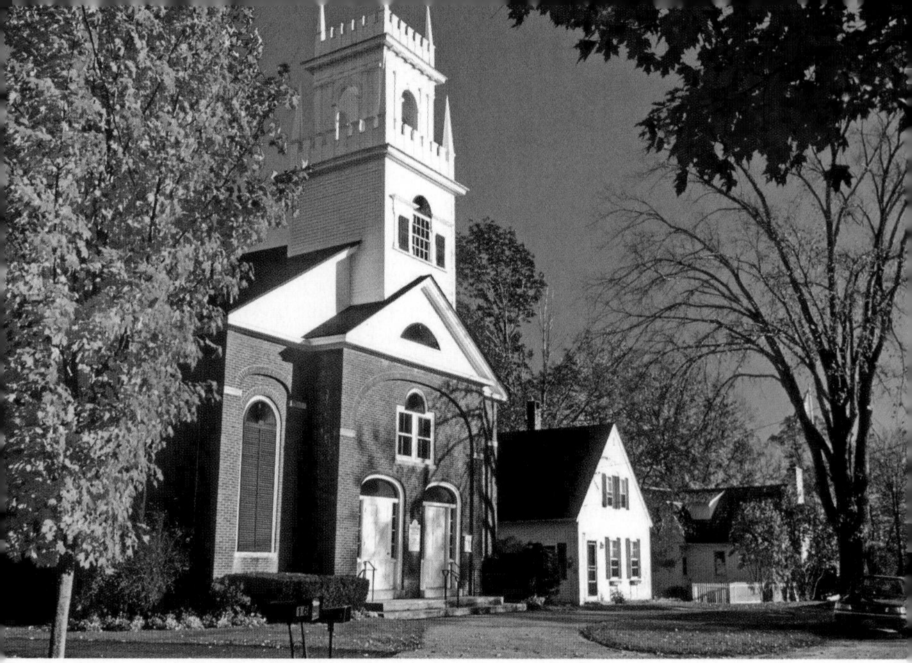

Jaffrey Center is known for its historic buildings and its proximity to Mt. Monadnock.

State College. ✉ *16 Main St.* ☎ *603/352–7874* 🌐 *www.primeroastcoffee.com.*

OFF THE BEATEN PATH

Chesterfield's Route 63. If you're in the mood for a country drive, head west from Keene along Route 9 to Route 63 (about 11 miles) and turn left toward the hilltop town of Chesterfield. This is an especially rewarding journey at sunset, as from many points along the road you can see west out over the Connecticut River valley and into Vermont. The village center consists of little more than a handful of dignified granite buildings and a small general store.

WHERE TO EAT AND STAY

$$ MEDITERRANEAN Fodor's Choice ★

🍴 **Luca's.** A deceptively simple storefront bistro overlooking Keene's graceful town square, Luca's dazzles with epicurean creations influenced by Italy, France, Greece, Spain, and North Africa. Enjoy sautéed shrimp with cilantro pesto and plum tomatoes, three-cheese ravioli with artichoke hearts, or grilled salmon marinated in cumin and coriander. Don't forget to order the locally made gelato or sorbet for dessert. Luca's Market, next door, offers many of the same flavors in wraps, salads, and paninis. [$] *Average main: $20* ✉ *10-11 Central Sq.* ☎ *603/358–3335* 🌐 *www.lucascafe.com.*

$$ B&B/INN

🏨 **Chesterfield Inn.** With views of the hill in the distance, the Chesterfield Inn is nestled on a 10-acre farm. **Pros:** attractive gardens; close to the Connecticut River; includes full breakfast. **Cons:** no dinner on Sunday. [$] *Rooms from: $149* ✉ *20 Cross Rd., West Chesterfield* ☎ *603/256–3211, 800/365–5515* 🌐 *www.chesterfieldinn.com* 🛏 *13 rooms, 2 suites* 🍽 *Breakfast.*

9

$$ 🖼 **The Inn at East Hill Farm.** If you have kids who like animals, meet bliss:
RESORT   a family resort with daylong children's programs on a 160-acre farm
FAMILY   overlooking Mt. Monadnock. **Pros:** rare agritourism and family resort;
activities galore; beautiful setting; no TVs. **Cons:** remote location; noisy
mess-hall dining. $ *Rooms from: $128* ⊠ *460 Monadnock St., 10 miles
southeast of Keene, Troy* 🕾 *603/242–6495, 800/242–6495* ⊕ *www.
east-hill-farm.com* ⇌ *65 rooms* ⦿ *All meals.*

$ 🖼 **The Lane Hotel.** You get a rare urban touch in the sleepy Monadnocks
HOTEL   in this upscale boutique hotel in the middle of Main Street. **Pros:** spa-
cious and comfortable rooms; center of town. **Cons:** no pool. $ *Rooms
from: $99* ⊠ *30 Main St.* 🕾 *603/354–7900, 603/347–7070* ⊕ *www.
thelanehotel.com* ⇌ *33 rooms, 7 suites* ⦿ *Breakfast.*

NIGHTLIFE AND THE ARTS

Colonial Theatre. This renovated 1924 vaudeville theater is now an art
movie house (with the largest movie screen in town) and a stage for
comedy, music, and dance. ⊠ *95 Main St.* 🕾 *603/352–2033* ⊕ *www.
thecolonial.org.*

Elm City Restaurant & Brewery. Located in the Colony Mill, this micro-
brewery is an affordable hangout for everyone from college students to
families. Its menu runs the gamut: burgers, steaks, and seafood. ⊠ *222
West St.* 🕾 *603/355–3335* ⊕ *www.elmcitybrewing.com.*

Redfern Art Center on Brickyard Pond. At Keene State College, the Redfern
Art Center on Brickyard Pond has year-round music, theater, and dance
performances in two theaters and a recital hall. ⊠ *Keene State College,
229 Main St.* 🕾 *603/358–2168* ⊕ *www.keene.edu/racbp.*

SHOPPING

Fairgrounds Antiques. Operating for 40 years, Fairgrounds Antiques is
where vintage shops get their merchandise. There are more than 70
dealers here, and if you're not afraid of a little dust, there's no telling
what kind of treasure you'll find. ⊠ *249 Monadnock Hwy., East Swan-
zey* 🕾 *603/352–4420* ⊙ *Daily 9–5.*

Hannah Grimes Marketplace. Shop here for locally made pottery, kitch-
enware, soaps, greeting cards, toys, and specialty foods. ⊠ *42 Main St.*
🕾 *603/352–6862* ⊕ *hannahgrimesmarketplace.com.*

JAFFREY CENTER

16 miles southeast of Keene.

Novelist Willa Cather came to Jaffrey Center in 1919 and stayed in the
Shattuck Inn, which now stands empty on Dublin Road. Not far from
here, she pitched the tent in which she wrote several chapters of *My
Ántonia.* She returned nearly every summer thereafter until her death
and was buried in the Old Burying Ground, which also contains the
remains of Amos Fortune, a former slave who bought his freedom in
1863 and moved to town when he was 71. Fortune, who was a tanner,
also bought the freedom of his two wives. He died at the age of 91.

GETTING HERE AND AROUND

Jaffrey Center's historic district is on Route 124 and is home to a number of brick buildings. It should take less than an hour to view it in its entirety. Two miles east of town on Route 124 can be found the Old Burying Ground, which is behind the Old Meeting House.

ESSENTIALS

Visitor Information **Jaffrey Chamber of Commerce** ☎ *603/532–4549* 🌐 *www.jaffreychamber.com.*

EXPLORING

Cathedral of the Pines. This outdoor memorial pays tribute to Americans who have sacrificed their lives in service to their country. There's an inspiring view of Mt. Monadnock and Mt. Kearsarge from the Altar of the Nation, which is composed of rock from every U.S. state and territory. All faiths are welcome; organ music for meditation is played at midday from Tuesday through Thursday in July and August. The Memorial Bell Tower, with a carillon of bells from around the world, is built of native stone. Norman Rockwell designed the bronze tablets over the four arches. Flower gardens, an indoor chapel, and a museum of military memorabilia share the hilltop. It's 8 miles southeast of Jaffrey Center. ✉ *10 Hale Hill Rd., off Rte. 119, Rindge* ☎ *603/899–3300* 🌐 *www.cathedralofthepines.org* 🎟 *Free* 🕒 *May–Oct., daily 9–5.*

SPORTS AND THE OUTDOORS

Monadnock State Park. The oft-quoted statistic about Mt. Monadnock is that it's America's most-climbed mountain—third in the world after Japan's Mt. Fuji and China's Mt. Tai. Whether this is true or not, locals agree that it's never lonely at the top. Some days more than 400 people crowd its bald peak. However, when the parking lot fills up, rangers close the park. Thus, an early morning start, especially during fall foliage, is recommended. Monadnock rises to 3,165 feet, and on a clear day the hazy Boston skyline is visible. Five trailheads branch into more than two dozen trails of varying difficulty (though all rigorous) that wend their way to the top. Allow between three and four hours for any round-trip hike. A visitor center has free trail maps as well as exhibits documenting the mountain's history. In winter you can cross-country ski along roughly 12 miles of groomed trails on the lower elevations of the mountain. ✉ *116 Poole Rd., off Rte. 124* ☎ *603/532–8862* 🌐 *www.nhstateparks.org* 🎟 *$5* 🕒 *Daily dawn–dusk* ☞ *No pets.*

WHERE TO EAT AND STAY

$$ AMERICAN 🍴 **J.P. Stephens Restaurant and Tavern.** An appealing choice for lunch or dinner, this rustic-timbered dining room overlooks a small mill pond in Rindge, about 8 miles south of Jaffrey Center. The 1790 building used to house a sawmill, a gristmill, a forge, and a blacksmith. Now it's an all-around good restaurant with live music on weekends. The Cajun-style sirloin is flavorful, and the apple brandy–and-walnut chicken is sweet and brazen. [$] *Average main: $16* ✉ *377 U.S. 202, Rindge* ☎ *603/899–3322* 🌐 *www.jpstephensrestaurant.com* 🕒 *Closed Mon.*

$$ B&B/INN 🏨 **Benjamin Prescott Inn.** Thanks to the dairy farm surrounding this 1853 Colonial house—with its stenciling and wide pine floors—you feel as though you're miles out in the country rather than just minutes from

Jaffrey Center. **Pros:** inexpensive rates; homey and comfortable. **Cons:** some linens a little dated. $ *Rooms from: $129* ✉ *433 Turnpike Rd.* ☎ *603/532–6637* ⊕ *www.benjaminprescottinn.com* ⤶ *7 rooms, 3 suites* ⎮○⎮ *Breakfast.*

$$ ⊡ **The Fitzwilliam Inn.** Once a stagecoach stop, the Fitzwilliam Inn has
B&B/INN graced this picturesque town green since 1786. **Pros:** affordable rates; friendly staff; full country breakfast. **Cons:** modest furnishings for such a grand setting. $ *Rooms from: $125* ✉ *Town Common, 62 Rte. 119 W, Fitzwilliam* ☎ *603/585–9000* ⊕ *www.fitzwilliaminn.com* ⤶ *6 rooms* ⎮○⎮ *Breakfast.*

$ ⊡ **The Monadnock Inn.** Rooms in this 1830s home are painted in lively
B&B/INN lavenders, yellows, or peaches, a cheery presence in the heart of pristine Jaffrey Center, and a perfect place to get away from it all. **Pros:** well-lit rooms with lacy curtains; feels cozy, like grandma's house. **Cons:** limited amenities. $ *Rooms from: $110* ✉ *379 Main St.* ☎ *603/532–7800, 877/510–7019* ⊕ *www.monadnockinn.com* ⤶ *11 rooms, 2 suites* ⎮○⎮ *Breakfast.*

$$ ⊡ **Woodbound Inn.** A favorite with families and outdoors enthusiasts,
B&B/INN this 1819 farmhouse became an inn in 1892. **Pros:** scenic lakefront location; focus on food. **Cons:** older property; simple furnishings; no Wi-Fi service in cabins. $ *Rooms from: $159* ✉ *247 Woodbound Rd., Rindge* ☎ *603/532–8341, 800/688–7770* ⊕ *www.woodboundinn.com* ⤶ *44 rooms, 11 cabins* ⎮○⎮ *Breakfast.*

SHOPPING

Bloomin' Antiques. Fine art and unusual antiques abound in this quaint shop overlooking the town green. ✉ *Village Green, Fitzwilliam Center* ☎ *603/585–6688.*

PETERBOROUGH

9 miles northeast of Jaffrey Center, 30 miles northwest of Nashua, on Route 101.

Thornton Wilder's play *Our Town* was based on Peterborough. The nation's first free public library opened here in 1833. The town, which was the first in the region to be incorporated (1760), is still a commercial and cultural hub.

GETTING HERE AND AROUND

Parking is just off Main Street, with shopping, coffee, and food all close by. Stand on the bridge and watch the roiling waters of the Nubanusit River on the north end of Main Street.

ESSENTIALS

Visitor Information Greater Peterborough Chamber of Commerce ☎ *603/924-7234* ⊕ *www.peterboroughchamber.com.*

EXPLORING

FAMILY **Mariposa Museum.** You can play instruments or try on costumes from around the world and indulge your cultural curiosity at this nonprofit museum dedicated to hands-on exploration of international folk art. The three-floor museum is inside a historic Baptist church, across from the Universalist church in the heart of town. The museum hosts a number of workshops and presentations on dance and arts and crafts. There's also a children's reading nook and a library. ✉ *26 Main St.* ☎ *603/924–4555* 🌐 *www.mariposamuseum.org* 🎫 *$6* 🕒 *July and Aug., daily 11–5; Sept.–June, Wed.–Sun. 11–5.*

WHERE TO STAY

$ B&B/INN 🏨 **Birchwood Inn.** Henry David Thoreau slept here, probably on his way to climb Monadnock or to visit Jaffrey or Peterborough. **Pros:** nice tavern; pleasant rooms. **Cons:** remote small town great for some, not for others. [$] *Rooms from: $109* ✉ *340 Rte. 45, Temple* ☎ *603/878–3285* 🌐 *www.thebirchwoodinn.com* 🛏 *2 rooms, 2 suites* 🍴 *Breakfast.*

$$ B&B/INN 🏨 **The Hancock Inn.** This Federal-style 1789 inn is the real Colonial deal—the oldest in the state and the pride of this idyllic town 8 miles north of Peterborough. **Pros:** quintessential Colonial inn in a perfect New England town; cozy rooms. **Cons:** remote location. [$] *Rooms from: $165* ✉ *33 Main St., Hancock* ☎ *603/525–3318, 800/525–1789* 🌐 *www.hancockinn.com* 🛏 *13 rooms* 🍴 *Breakfast.*

THE ARTS

Monadnock Music. From early July to late August, Monadnock Music sponsors a series of solo recitals, chamber music concerts, and orchestra and opera performances by renowned musicians. Events take place throughout the area on Wednesday through Saturday evenings at 8 and on Sunday at 4. Many of the offerings are free. ✉ *2A Concord St.* ☎ *603/924–7610, 800/868–9613* 🌐 *www.monadnockmusic.org.*

Peterborough Folk Music Society. The society presents folk music concerts by artists such as John Gorka, Greg Brown, and Cheryl Wheeler. Concerts are held monthly October through April in the Peterborough Players Theater, a fantastic repurposed old barn. ✉ *Hadley Rd., off Middle Hancock Rd.* ☎ *603/827–2905* 🌐 *pfmsconcerts.org.*

Peterborough Players. The Peterborough Players have performed since 1933 and stage their productions in a converted barn from late June through mid-September. ✉ *55 Hadley Rd.* ☎ *603/924–7585 box office* 🌐 *www.peterboroughplayers.org.*

SPORTS AND THE OUTDOORS

GOLF

Crotched Mountain Golf Club. At the Donald Ross–designed Crotched Mountain Golf Club you'll find a hilly, rolling 18-hole layout with nice view of the Monadnocks. ✉ *740 Francestown Rd., Francestown* ☎ *603/588–2923* 🌐 *www.crotchedmountaingolfclub.com* 🎫 *Greens fee: $49* ⛳ *18 holes, 6,111 yards, par 71.*

SKI AREA

Crotched Mountain. New Hampshire's southernmost skiing and snowboarding facility has 17 trails, half of them intermediate, and the rest divided pretty evenly between beginner and expert. There's an 875-foot vertical drop. The slopes have ample snowmaking capacity, ensuring good skiing all winter long. Crotched Mountain is famous for its night skiing—if you can stay up you will save on a lift ticket and maybe hear a few good bands. Other facilities include a 40,000-square-foot lodge with a couple of restaurants, a ski school, and a snow camp for youngsters. ⊠ *615 Francestown Rd., Bennington* ☎ *603/588–3668* ⊕ *www.crotchedmountain.com.*

SHOPPING

Depot Square. Whether you're looking for a regional book, gourmet wine and cheese, handmade gifts and crafts, or unusual gardening accessories, these 14 unique shops in the heart of town turn shoppers into treasure hunters. ⊠ *18 Depot St.* ☎ *603/924–6893* ⊕ *www. shoppeterboroughnh.com.*

Dodge Farm Antiques. Sports-related antiques, vintage kitchenware, and vintage children's toys can be found in this small but classy shop. ⊠ *7 School St.* ☎ *917/922–3910* ⊕ *www.dodgefarmantiques.com.*

Eastern Mountain Sports. The retail outlet of Eastern Mountain Sports sells everything from tents to skis to hiking boots, offers hiking and camping classes, and conducts kayaking and canoeing demonstrations. ⊠ *1 Vose Farm Rd.* ☎ *603/924–7231* ⊕ *www.ems.com.*

Sharon Arts Center. This nonprofit art center exhibits thought-provoking, yet completely accessible, edgy contemporary art. It sells the works of 180 regional artists working in media from pottery to fiber. ⊠ *20-40 Depot St.* ☎ *603/924–2787* ⊕ *www.sharonarts.org.*

INLAND MAINE

WELCOME TO INLAND MAINE

TOP REASONS TO GO

★ **Baxter State Park:** Mt. Katahdin, the state's highest peak, stands as a sentry over Baxter's forestland in its "natural wild state."

★ **Moosehead Lake:** Surrounded by mountains, Maine's largest lake—dotted with islands and chiseled with inlets and coves—retains the rugged beauty that so captivated author Henry David Thoreau in the mid-1800s.

★ **Water Sports:** It's easy to get out on the water with scheduled cruises on large inland lakes; marinas and outfitters rent boats, canoes, and kayaks throughout the region and run white-water-rafting trips on several rivers.

★ **Winter Pastimes:** Downhill skiing, snowmobiling, snowshoeing, cross-country skiing, and dogsledding are all popular winter sports.

★ **Foliage Drives:** Maine's best fall foliage is inland, where hardwoods outnumber spruce, fir, and pine trees in many areas.

1 Western Lakes and Mountains. Lakes both quiet and busy, classic New England villages, and ski resorts fit perfectly in the forested landscape. In winter this is ski country; snowmobiling and snowshoeing are also popular. In summer the woods and water draw vacationers for a cool escape. In fall, foliage drives invite exploration of the region's national forest and state parks. In spring there are no crowds, but fishermen, white-water rafters, and canoeists make their way here.

2 The North Woods. Much of the North Woods' private forestland is open for public recreation and best experienced by paddling a canoe or raft, hiking, snowshoeing, snowmobiling, or fishing. Some great destinations are mostly undeveloped: Moosehead Lake, Baxter State Park, and Allagash Wilderness Waterway. Greenville, a laid-back and woodsy resort town, is a good base for day trips—take a drive (go slow!) down a "moose alley."

GETTING ORIENTED

Though Maine is well known for its miles of craggy coastline, the inland part of the state is surprisingly vast and much less populated. Less than an hour's drive from the bays and ocean, huge swaths of forestland are dotted with lakes (sometimes called "ponds" despite their size). Summer camps, ski areas, and small villages populate the mountainous western part of the state, which stretches north along the New Hampshire border to Québec. Quiet waters are easy to find inland, but busier Sebago Lake is just north of coastal Portland, Maine's largest city. In the remote north-central part of the state, wilderness areas beckon outdoors lovers to the North Woods, which extend north and west to Canada.

10

By Mary Ruoff · Unlike Maine's more famous, more populated, and more visited coast, inland Maine is a four-season destination. With strings of lakes and rivers framed by mountainous terrain, hilly pastoral stretches, classic New England villages with restaurants and shops that entice but don't overwhelm, and the region's most extensive wilderness areas, Maine's interior lures visitors in summer, fall, winter, and spring (yes, the slow season, but canoeists, fishermen, and white-water rafters venture inland).

The most visited areas are the Western Lakes and Mountains—stretching east and north from the New Hampshire border—and the North Woods—extending north from central Maine. While much of inland Maine is remote and rugged, opportunities for outdoor recreation are plentiful and renowned, and crowds do form here, though thankfully they're scattered and don't set the tone.

Sebago and Long lakes, north of Portland and the gateway to the Western Lakes and Mountains region, hum with boaters and watercraft in the summer. Sidewalks fill and traffic slows along the causeway in the tourist hub of Naples. Baxter State Park, a 210,000-acre wilderness park in the North Woods, has Mt. Katahdin (an Abenaki Indian word for "Great Mountain"), Maine's highest peak and the terminus of the Appalachian Trail. But while you can hike in much of the park and see few other visitors even during peak season, the treeless, rocky summit of Katahdin and the trails to it are often packed with hikers in July and August and on nice weekends in September and early October.

Come winter, ski resorts wait for big snows and make snow in between. Maine often gets snow when the rest of New England doesn't, or vice versa, so track the weather here if you're coming to partake in winter sports or simply to enjoy the season's serenity. Maine's largest ski resorts, Sugarloaf and Sunday River, are in the Western Lakes and Mountains region. So are up-and-coming Saddleback Mountain in

Rangeley and Shawnee Peak in Bridgton, both family-friendly resorts. But not to worry, the lift lines don't get too long.

"Rusticators" began flocking to Maine to vacation in the mid-1800s, arriving at inland destinations by train or steamship, just as they did on Maine's coast. Escaping the summer heat and city pollution, these wealthy urbanites headed to the mountains to hike, swim, canoe, fish, hunt, and relax, staying at rustic sporting camps or at the grand hotels that cropped up in some of the most scenic spots. Moosehead Lake's Mt. Kineo—a walled outcropping north of Greenville where Indian tribes from throughout the Northeast came for flint-like stone—gave rise to one of the nation's largest and fanciest hotels in the late 1800s. Rangeley was discovered for its sport fishing in the mid-1800s and is still a haven for anglers, who come to fish for "world-class" brook trout and landlocked salmon. Modern streamer fly-fishing was born in the Rangeley region, and many of the local waters are restricted to fly-fishing.

The legacy of the rusticators and the locals who catered to them lives on at the sporting camps still found on inland Maine's remote lakes and rivers, albeit in fewer numbers. It also survives through Maine's unique system of licensed outdoor guides, known as Registered Maine Guides. These days they may lead kayak trips, hiking expeditions, white-water rafting excursions, and moose safaris as well as fishing, hunting, and canoe trips. Guides are happy to show you their license—it's the law that they have one, and some also opt to wear a badge.

PLANNING

WHEN TO GO

Inland's Maine's most popular hiking trails and lakeside beaches may get busy in warm weather, but if splendid isolation is what you crave, you can easily find it. In summer, traffic picks up but rarely creates jams, except in a few spots. Peak lodging rates apply, but moderate weather makes this a great time to visit. Inland Maine gets hotter than the coast, though less so along lakes and at higher elevations. July and August are warmest; September is less busy.

Western Maine is the state's premier destination for leaf peepers—hardwoods are more abundant here than on the coast. Late September through mid-October is peak foliage season.

Maine's largest ski areas can make their own snow; at least one of them opens its doors in mid-November and remains open until May. Inland Maine typically has snow cover by Christmas, so cross-country skiing, snowshoeing, and snowmobiling are in full swing by the end of the year. In ski towns many lodgings charge peak rates in the winter.

Snowmelt ushers in mud season in early spring. Mid-May to mid-June is black fly season; they're especially pesky in the woods but less bothersome in town. Spring is a prime time for canoeing and fishing.

10

PLANNING YOUR TIME

Inland Maine locales are often destinations where visitors stay their entire trip. That's certainly true of those who come to ski at a resort, fish at a remote sporting camp, or just relax at a lakeside cabin. After a day hike on a mountain trail reached by driving gravel logging roads, visitors are unlikely to hurry on to another town. Vacation rental homes and cottages often require a week's stay, as do lakeside cottage resorts. Generally speaking, the farther inland you go, the farther it is between destinations.

GETTING HERE AND AROUND

AIR TRAVEL

Two primary airports serve Maine: Portland International (PWM) and Bangor International (BGR). Portland is closer to the Western Lakes and Mountains area; Bangor is more convenient to the North Woods. Regional flying services, operating from regional and municipal airports, provide access to remote lakes and wilderness areas and offer scenic flights.

CAR TRAVEL

Because Maine is large and rural, a car is essential. U.S. 2 is the major east–west thoroughfare in Western Maine, winding from Bangor to New Hampshire. Interstate 95 is a departure point for many visitors to inland Maine, especially the North Woods. The highway heads inland at Brunswick and is a toll road, the Maine Turnpike, from the New Hampshire border to Augusta. Because of the hilly terrain and abundant lakes and rivers, inland Maine roads are often curvy. Traffic rarely gets heavy, though highways often pass right through instead of around the larger towns, which can slow your trip a bit.

There are few public roads in Maine's North Woods, though private logging roads there are often open to the public (sometimes by permit and fee). When driving these roads, always give lumber-company trucks the right-of-way; loggers must drive in the middle of the road and often can't move over or slow down for cars. Be sure to have a full tank of gas before heading onto the many private roads in the region.

RESTAURANTS

Fear not, lobster lovers: this succulent, emblematic Maine food is on the menu at many inland restaurants, from fancier establishments to roadside places. Lobster dishes are more common than boiled lobster dinners, but look for daily specials. Shrimp, scallops, and other seafood are also menu mainstays, and you may find surprises like bison burgers or steaks from a nearby farm. Organic growers and natural foods producers are planted throughout the state and often sell their food to finer restaurants nearby. Seasonal foods like pumpkins, blackberries, and strawberries make their way into homemade desserts, as do Maine's famed blueberries. Many lakeside resorts and sporting camps have a reputation for good food; some of the latter will cook the fish you catch. *Prices in the reviews are the average cost of a main course at dinner or, if dinner is not served, at lunch.*

HOTELS

Although there is a higher concentration of upscale inns on the coast than inland, you'll find well-run inns, B&Bs, and motels throughout the region, including some sophisticated lodgings. At those located near ski resorts, peak-season rates may apply in winter and summer. The two largest ski resorts, Sunday River and Sugarloaf, offer a choice of hotels and condos. Greenville has the largest selection of lodgings in the North Woods region, with both fine and homey inns. Lakeside sporting camps, from the primitive to the upscale, are popular around Rangeley and the North Woods. Many have cozy cabins heated with woodstoves and serve three hearty meals a day. Conservation organizations also operate wilderness retreats. In Maine's mountains, as on its coast, many small inns and B&Bs don't have air-conditioning. *Prices in the reviews are the lowest cost of a standard double room in high season.*

VISITOR INFORMATION

Maine Office of Tourism ☎ *888/624–6345* ⊕ *www.visitmaine.com.*

Maine Tourism Association ☎ *207/623–0363, 800/767–8709* ⊕ *www. mainetourism.com.*

WESTERN LAKES AND MOUNTAINS

From Sebago Lake, less than 20 miles northwest of Portland, the sparsely populated Western Lakes and Mountains region stretches north and west, bordered by New Hampshire and Québec. Each season offers different outdoor highlights: you can choose from snow sports, hiking, mountain biking, leaf peeping, fishing, swimming, and paddling. The Sebago Lake area bustles with activity in summer. Bridgton is a classic New England town, as is Bethel, in the valley of the Androscoggin River. Sunday River, a major ski resort, is nearby. The more rural Rangeley Lake area brings long stretches of pine, beech, spruce, and sky and more classic inns. Just north of Kingfield is Sugarloaf Mountain Resort, Maine's other big ski resort. Like Sunday River, it offers a host of summer activities.

10

SEBAGO LAKE AREA

20 miles northwest of Portland.

The shores of sprawling Sebago Lake and finger-like Long Lake are popular with water sports enthusiasts, as are Brandy Pond and many other bodies of water in the area. The Songo River links several of these lakes, forming one continuous waterway. Naples, on the causeway separating Long Lake from Brandy Pond, pulses with activity in the summer, when the area swells with seasonal residents and weekend visitors. Open-air cafés overflow with patrons, boats buzz along the water, and families parade along the sidewalk edging Long Lake. On clear days the view includes snowcapped Mt. Washington.

GETTING HERE AND AROUND

Sebago Lake, gateway to Maine's Western Lakes and Mountains, is less than 20 miles from Portland on U.S. 302.

CLOSE UP

Outdoor Activities

People visit inland Maine year-round for hiking, biking (mountain biking is big at ski resorts off-season), camping, fishing, downhill and cross-country skiing, snowshoeing, and snowmobiling.

The Kennebec and Dead rivers, which converge at The Forks in Western Maine, and the West Branch of the Penobscot River, near Millinocket in the North Woods, provide thrilling white-water rafting. Boating, canoeing, and kayaking are also possibilities.

BICYCLING
Bicycle Coalition of Maine. For information on bicycling in Maine, contact the Bicycle Coalition of Maine. ☎ 207/623–4511 ⊕ www.bike maine.org.

FISHING
Maine Department of Inland Fisheries and Wildlife. For information about fishing licenses, contact the Maine Department of Inland Fisheries and Wildlife. ☎ 207/287–8000 ⊕ www.mefishwildlife.com.

HIKING
Maine Appalachian Trail Club. The Maine Appalachian Trail Club publishes seven Appalachian Trail maps

($8) and a Maine trail guide ($30). ⊕ www.matc.org.

Maine Trail Finder. Visitors can find Maine trails to hike, mountain bike, snowshoe, and ski on this website, which includes trail descriptions, photos, user comments, directions, links to maps, weather conditions, and more. ☎ 207/778–0900 ⊕ www. mainetrailfinder.com.

RAFTING
Maine Professional Guides Association. This association helps you find state-licensed guides to lead kayaking, canoeing, and white-water rafting trips. There are also other trips available, ranging from fishing trips to wildlife-watching excursions. ⊕ www. maineguides.org.

SKIING
Ski Maine. For alpine and cross-country skiing information, contact Ski Maine. ☎ 207/773–7669 ⊕ ski maine.com.

SNOWMOBILING
Maine Snowmobile Association. This association's excellent statewide map of about 3,500 miles of interconnected trails is available online. ☎ 207/622–6983 ⊕ www.mesnow. com.

ESSENTIALS

Vacation Rentals Krainin Real Estate ✉ 1539 Roosevelt Tr., Raymond ☎ 207/655–3811 ⊕ www.krainin.com.

Visitor Information Sebago Lakes Region Chamber of Commerce ✉ 747 Roosevelt Tr., Windham ☎ 207/892–8265 ⊕ www.sebagolakeschamber.com.

EXPLORING

Sebago Lake. This is Maine's second-largest lake, and provides Greater Portland's drinking water. Year-round and seasonal dwellings (from simple camps to sprawling showplaces) line the shores of the lake. ✉ Windham ☎ 207/892–8265 ⊕ www.sebagolakeschamber.com.

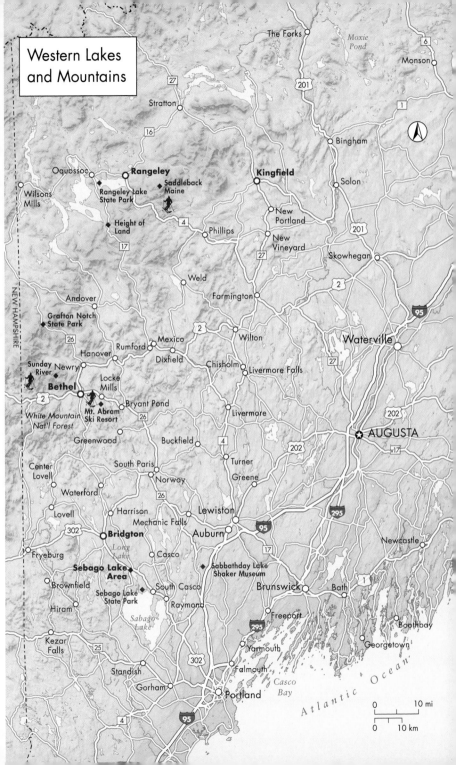

Western Lakes and Mountains

The Forks

Moxie Pond

Monson

6

201

27

Stratton

Bingham

16

Oquossoc

Rangeley

♦ Rangeley Lake State Park

Height of Land

17

Saddleback Maine

Kingfield

Solon

New Portland

201

Phillips

New Vineyard

27

Skowhegan

Wilsons Mills

4

Weld

Farmington

2

Waterville

Andover

26

♦ Grafton Notch State Park

Hanover

Rumford

Mexico

Dixfield

Chisholm

Livermore Falls

Wilton

27

95

Sunday River

Newry

Bethel

2

Locke Mills

Bryant Pond

Mt. Abram Ski Resort

26

Livermore

202

AUGUSTA

White Mountain Nat'l Forest

Greenwood

Buckfield

4

Turner

v17

Center Lovell

South Paris

Norway

Greene

Waterford

26

Lewiston

295

Lovell

Harrison

Mechanic Falls

Auburn

95

Newcastle

302

Bridgton

Long Lake

Casco

17

Fryeburg

Sebago Lake Area

♦ Sabbathday Lake Shaker Museum

Brunswick

Bath

1

Brownfield

Sebago Lake State Park

South Casco

Raymond

Boothbay

Hiram

Sebago Lake

295

Freeport

Georgetown

Kezar Falls

25

Yarmouth

Standish

Falmouth

Casco Bay

Gorham

Portland

Atlantic Ocean

95

4

NEW HAMPSHIRE

0   10 mi

0   10 km

Sebago Lake State Park. This 1,400-acre park on the north shore of Sebago Lake is a great spot for swimming, boating, and fishing for both salmon and togue. A pleasant picnic area is Songo Lock State Historic Site, an operational lock along the twisty, narrow Songo River. Bicycling along the park's roads is a popular pastime in warm weather. Come winter, the park's 6 miles of hiking trails are groomed for cross-country skiing. ✉ *11 Park Access Rd., Casco* ☎ *207/693–6231* 🌐 *www.parksandlands.com* 🎟 *$6.50* 🕒 *9–sunset.*

OFF THE BEATEN PATH

Sabbathday Lake Shaker Village. Established in the late 18th century, this is the last active Shaker community in the world, with only three members. Open for guided one-hour tours are several buildings with Shaker furniture, folk art, tools, farm implements, and crafts from the 18th to the early 20th century. Besides the 1794 Meetinghouse, there's also the 1839 Ministry's Shop, where the elders and eldresses lived until the early 1900s, and the 1821 Sisters' Shop, where household goods and candies were made. The 1850 Boys' Shop has an exhibit on Shaker childhood. You can tour the herb garden on Tuesday and Thursday afternoon in July and August. If you're here in late August, don't miss the popular Maine Native American Summer Market and Demonstration. The shop sells Shaker-produced foods as well as handcrafts by area artisans. ✉ *707 Shaker Rd., near Rte. 26, New Gloucester* ☎ *207/926–4597* 🌐 *www.shaker.lib.me.us* 🎟 *Tour $10* 🕒 *Late May–Columbus Day, Mon.–Sat. 10–4:30.*

WHERE TO STAY

$$$$ RESORT FAMILY

🏨 **Migis Lodge.** Scattered under a canopy of trees along Sebago Lake, the classy pine-paneled cottages at this 125-acre resort have fieldstone fireplaces and are handsomely furnished with colorful rugs and handmade quilts. **Pros:** away-from-it-all feel; woodsy setting; evening cocktail hour. **Cons:** pricey rates; credit cards not accepted. [$] *Rooms from: $670* ✉ *30 Migis Lodge Rd., off U.S. 302, South Casco* ☎ *207/655–4524* 🌐 *www.migis.com* 🛏 *35 cottages, 6 rooms* 💳 *No credit cards* 🕒 *Closed mid-Oct.–mid-June* 🍴 *All meals.*

SPORTS AND THE OUTDOORS

U.S. 302 cuts through Naples, and in the center, at the Naples causeway, you'll find rental craft for fishing or cruising. Sebago and Long lakes are popular areas for sailing, fishing, and motorboating.

FAMILY

Songo River Queen II. Departing from the Naples causeway, *Songo River Queen II,* a 93-foot stern-wheeler, takes passengers on one- and two-hour cruises on Long Lake. ✉ *841 Roosevelt Trail, Naples* ☎ *207/693–6861* 🌐 *www.songoriverqueen.net* 🎟 *$15–$25* 🕒 *July–early Sept., daily; early May–June and early Sept.–mid-Oct., weekends; hrs vary.*

BRIDGTON

8 miles north of Naples, 30 miles south of Bethel.

Bridgton's winding Main Street (U.S. 302) passes picturesque New England townscapes at every curve. On hot summer days kids dive off the dock at the town beach tucked at the end of Highland Lake, just past storefronts with restaurants, galleries, and shops. Just steps from downtown a covered pedestrian bridge leads to 66-acre Pondicherry Park, a nature preserve with wooded trails and two streams. The town has 10 lakes that are popular for boating and fishing. Come winter, people arrive to ski at Shawnee Peak.

The surrounding countryside is a good choice for leaf peepers and outdoors lovers. A few miles north, Harrison anchors the northern end of Long Lake. Come fall, Fryeburg is home to the famed Fryeburg Fair (🌐 *www.fryeburgfair.com*), the region's largest agricultural fair.

GETTING HERE AND AROUND

U.S. 302 runs from Portland up the west side of Long Lake to Bridgton. From here it continues west to Fryeburg, where you can take Route 5 north to Center Lovell.

ESSENTIALS

Vacation Rentals Maine Lakeside Getaways ☎ *207/647–4000, 866/647–8557* 🌐 *www.mainelakesidegetaways.com.*

Visitor Information Greater Bridgton Lakes Region Chamber of Commerce ✉ *101 Portland Rd.* ☎ *207/647–3472* 🌐 *www.mainelakeschamber.com.*

EXPLORING

Rufus Porter Museum and Cultural Heritage Center. Local youth Rufus Porter became a leading folk artist, painting landscape and harbor murals on the walls of New England homes in the early 1800s, including those in the museum's red Cape Cod–style house. Also an inventor, Porter founded *Scientific American* magazine. Early issues are showcased, as are some of his inventions and miniature portraits. Changing exhibits feature 19th-century folk and decorative arts. By 2014 the museum will also include an 1840s house at 121 Main Street. ✉ *67 N. High St.* ☎ *207/647–2828* 🌐 *www.rufusportermuseum.org* 🎟 *$8* 🕒 *Mid-June–mid-Oct., Wed.–Sat. noon–4.*

WHERE TO EAT AND STAY

$$$ CONTEMPORARY 🍴 **Center Lovell Inn & Restaurant.** In summer the best tables for dining at this eye-catching cupola-topped 1805 property—about 15 miles northeast of Bridgton in quiet Center Lovell—are on the wraparound porch, which has sunset views of the White Mountains. Inside, one dining room has mountain views and the other an original iron fireplace that warms diners on cold nights. Herb-crusted rack of lamb, pan-seared filet mignon, and fresh swordfish are menu mainstays; fillet of bison is a welcome occasional special. Eight homey guest rooms and one two-bedroom suite (lodging is year-round) are upstairs and in the adjacent Harmon House. [$] *Average main: $28* ✉ *1107 Main St., Center Lovell* ☎ *207/925–1575, 800/777–2698* 🌐 *www.centerlovellinn.com* 🕒 *No dinner mid-Oct.–late Dec. and Mar.–mid-May.*

$$$$ B&B/INN 🏨 **Noble House Inn.** On a quiet road, this 1903 estate above Highland Lake offers a convenient location, plenty of creature comforts, and a relaxing atmosphere. **Pros:** bottomless cookie jar; ski packages available; canoeing and kayaking in summer. **Cons:** limited lake views; only suites have TVs. [$] *Rooms from: $235* ✉ *81 Highland Rd.* ☎ *207/647–3733, 888/237–4880* 🌐 *www.noblehouseinn.com* 🛏 *4 rooms, 4 suites* 🍽 *Breakfast.*

SPORTS AND THE OUTDOORS

FAMILY **Shawnee Peak.** Just a few miles from Bridgton, Shawnee Peak appeals to families and those who enjoy nighttime skiing—beginner, intermediate, and expert trails are lit most evenings. Five lifts serve 40 trails, six glades, and two terrain parks. The two base lodges have cafeterias; the main lodge also has a restaurant with an expansive deck, a ski school, and a ski shop. Summer visitors can pick blueberries or paddle a canoe on Moose Pond. ✉ *119 Mountain Rd., off U.S. 302* ☎ *207/647–8444* ⊕ *www.shawneepeak.com.*

BETHEL

27 miles north of Bridgton; 65 miles north of Portland.

Bethel is pure New England, a town with white clapboard houses, white-steeple churches, and a mountain vista at the end of every street. The campus of Gould Academy, a college prep school founded in 1836, anchors the east side of downtown. In winter this is ski country: Sunday River, one Maine's big ski resorts, is only a few miles north in Newry. Bethel WinterFest is usually held in February. On the third weekend in July, Mollyockett Days, which includes a parade, fireworks, and frog-jumping contest, honor a Pequawket Indian renowned for her medicinal cures in the early days of white settlement.

GETTING HERE AND AROUND

From the south, both Routes 35 and 5 lead to Bethel, overlapping en route, then splitting from each other several miles south of town. Route 5 is slightly shorter from this point, and especially pretty come fall, with lots of overhanging trees. If you're coming from the west on U.S. 2, you'll pass through the White Mountain National Forest.

ESSENTIALS

Vacation Rentals Four Seasons Realty & Rentals ✉ *32 Parkway Plaza, Suite 1* ☎ *207/824–3776* ⊕ *fourseasonsrealtymaine.com.*

Visitor Information Bethel Area Chamber of Commerce ✉ *8 Station Pl., off Cross St.* ☎ *207/824–2282, 800/442–5826* ⊕ *www.bethelmaine.com.*

EXPLORING

Bethel Historical Society Museum of Regional History. Start your stroll in Bethel here, across from the Village Common. The center's campus comprises two buildings: the 1821 Robinson House and the 1813 Dr. Moses Mason House, both of which are listed on the National Register of Historic Places. The Robinson House has changing and permanent exhibits pertaining to the region's history. One parlor room is a gift shop with a nice book selection. The Moses Mason House has nine period rooms; the front hall and stairway are decorated with Rufus Porter School folk art murals. ✉ *10 Broad St.* ☎ *207/824–2908, 800/824–2910* ⊕ *www.bethelhistorical.org* ✉ *Robinson House free; Mason House $3* ☉ *Robinson House: late Nov.–June, Sept., and Oct., Tues.–Fri. 10–4; July and Aug., Tues.–Fri. 10–4, Sat. 1–4. Mason House: July and Aug., Tues.–Sat. 1–4; Sept.–June, by appointment.*

Grafton Notch State Park. Route 26 runs through this park, which stretches along the Bear River Valley 14 miles north of Bethel and is a favorite foliage drive. It's an easy walk from roadside parking areas to Mother Walker Falls, Moose Cave, and the spectacular Screw Auger Falls. Or pick up the Appalachian Trail for a challenging 8-mile round-trip trek to the viewing platform atop Old Speck Mountain, the state's third-highest peak. Sandwiching the park are the two tracts that make up the state's 9,993-acre Mahoosuc Public Reserved Land. Trails wind through the reserve, offering stunning, if strenuous, backcountry hiking. In winter a popular snowmobile trail runs along the river through the park. ✉ *1941 Bear River Rd., Newry* ☎ *207/624–6080* 🌐 *www.parksandlands.com* 🎟 *$3* 🕒 *Daily, 9–sunset.*

White Mountain National Forest. This forest straddles New Hampshire and Maine, with the highest peaks on the New Hampshire side. The Maine section, though smaller, has magnificent rugged terrain. As for hiking, there's everything from hour-long nature loops to a day hike up Speckled Mountain. The mountain is part of the 11,000-acre Caribou-Speckled Mountain Wilderness Area, one of several in the forest, but the only one entirely within Maine. The most popular Maine access to the national forest is Route 113, which runs south from its terminus at U.S. 2 in Gilead, 10 miles from downtown Bethel. Most of the highway is the Pequawket Trail Maine Scenic Byway, and the section through the forest is spectacular come fall. This stretch is closed in winter, but is used by snowmobilers and cross-country skiers. ✉ *Route 113, off U.S. 2, Gilead* ☎ *603/466–2713* 🌐 *www.fs.fed.us/r9/white* 🎟 *Day pass $3 per car.*

WHERE TO STAY

$ B&B/INN 🏨 **Austin's Holidae House.** At this affordable downtown B&B it's the welcoming hospitality that keeps guests returning—everyone seems to love innkeeper Laurence Austin's British manners. **Pros:** courtesy cordials in parlor; tasty breakfasts; innkeepers help you plan day. **Cons:** some rooms have a dated feel. [$] *Rooms from: $120* ✉ *85 Main St.* ☎ *207/824–3400, 877/224–3400* 🌐 *www.holidaehouse.com* 🛏 *7 rooms* 🍴 *Breakfast.*

EN ROUTE

Artist's Bridge. In the town of Newry, make a short detour to the Artist's Bridge, located about 4 miles northwest of U.S. 2. It's the most painted and photographed of Maine's nine covered bridges. ✉ *Sunday River Rd., Newry.*

Height of Land. A direct but still stunningly scenic route from Bethel to Rangeley is U.S. 2 east to the twin towns of Rumford and Mexico. From the latter, Route 17 heads north to Oquossoc, about an hour's drive. The high point of this route is Height of Land, with its unforgettable views of mountains and the island-studded blue mass of Mooselookmeguntic Lake. In Oquossoc, continue on Route 4 to Rangeley. ✉ *Rte. 17, Rangeley.*

SPORTS AND THE OUTDOORS

MULTI-SPORT OUTFITTERS

Northwoods Outfitters. Northwoods Outfitters outfits for moose-watching, biking, skiing, snowmobiling, snowboarding, canoeing, kayaking, camping, and fishing. They lead trips for many of these activities as well as rent canoes, kayaks, bikes, snowmobiles, snowshoes, ATVs, and more. Shop, get trail advice, and kick back in the Internet café at

One of the Rangeley Lakes, Mooselookmeguntic is said to mean "portage to the moose feeding place" in the Abenaki language.

its downtown outfitters store. They also run an inn and lake rentals as well as shuttle service. ⊠ *5 Lilly Bay Rd., Bethel* ☎ *207/695–3288, 866/223–1380* ⊕ *www.maineoutfitter.com.*

Sun Valley Sports. Take guided fly-fishing excursions, moose and wildlife safaris, and rent canoes and kayaks with Sun Valley Sports. ⊠ *129 Sunday River Rd.* ☎ *207/824–7533* ⊕ *www.sunvalleysports.com.*

CANOEING AND KAYAKING

Bethel Outdoor Adventure. On the Androscoggin River, this outfitter rents canoes and kayaks and leads guided fishing and boating expeditions. Maine Mineralogy Expeditions is based here, offering mine tours and an open-air facility where you can sluice for precious gems. ⊠ *121 Mayville Rd.* ☎ *207/824–4224, 800/533–3607* ⊕ *www.betheloutdoor adventure.com.*

DOGSLEDDING

Mahoosuc Guide Service. This guide company leads day and multiday dogsledding expeditions in the Umbagog National Wildlife Refuge on the Maine–New Hampshire border. In the summer it guides canoe trips here and on rivers in northern Maine. The company runs its own lodging in nearby Newry. ⊠ *1513 Bear River Rd., Newry* ☎ *207/824–2073* ⊕ *www.mahoosuc.com.*

SKI AREAS

FAMILY **Carter's Cross-Country Ski Center.** This cross-country ski center offers about 30 miles of trails for all levels of skiers. Snowshoes, skis, and sleds to pull children are available for rental. The place also rents lodge rooms and ski-in cabins. ⊠ *786 Intervale Rd.* ☎ *207/824–3880, 207/539–4848* ⊕ *www.cartersxcski.com.*

CLOSE UP

Whoopie Pies

When a bill aiming to make the whoopie pie Maine's official dessert was debated in the state legislature, some lawmakers countered that blueberry pie (made with Maine wild blueberries, of course) should have the honor. In the end it did, but what could have been a civil war ended civilly, with whoopie pies designated the "official state treat." Spend a few days anywhere in Maine and you'll notice just how popular the treat is.

The name is misleading: it's a pie only in the sense of a having a filling between two "crusts"—namely, a thick layer of sugary frosting sandwiched between two saucers of rich cake,

usually chocolate. It's said to have Pennsylvania Dutch roots, and may have acquired its distinctive moniker from the jubilant yelp farmers emitted after discovering it in their lunchboxes. Many Mainers dispute this, claiming that the whoopie pie originated here. Typically, the filling is made with butter or shortening; some recipes add Marshmallow Fluff. Many bakers have indulged the temptation to experiment with flavors and ingredients, particularly in the filling but also in the cake, offering pumpkin, raspberry, oatmeal cream, red velvet, peanut butter, and more.

—Michael de Zayas

Mt. Abram. Family-friendly and very affordable, Mt. Abram has 54 trails and glade areas, five lifts, a tubing area, two base lodges, and ski lessons. It's open Thursday through Sunday during the ski season. ⊠ *308 Howe Hill Rd., off Rte. 26, Greenwood* ☎ *207/875–5000* ⊕ *www. skimtabram.com.*

FAMILY

Fodor's Choice

★

Sunday River. What was once a sleepy ski area has evolved into a sprawling resort that attracts skiers from around the world. Stretching for 3 miles, there are 16 lifts service, 135 trails, five terrain parks, and a superpipe. Sunday River has three base areas and several lodging choices, including two slope-side hotels: the family-friendly Grand Summit, located at one of the mountain bases, and the more upscale Jordan Grand, near a summit at the resort's western end. (It's really up there, several miles by vehicle from the base lodges, but during ski season there's a shuttle.) The less costly Snow Cap Inn is a short walk to the slopes. Sunday River is home to Maine Adaptive Sports & Recreation, which provides services for skiers with disabilities. The main South Ridge Base Lodge is the hub for summer activities. ⊠ *15 S. Ridge Rd., off U.S. 2, Newry* ☎ *207/824–3000, 207/824–3000 snow conditions, 800/543–2754 reservations* ⊕ *www.sundayriver.com.*

10

RANGELEY

66 miles north of Bethel.

Rangeley, on the north side of Rangeley Lake on Route 4, has long lured anglers and winter sports enthusiasts to its more than 40 lakes and ponds and 450 square miles of woodlands. Right behind Main Street, Lakeside Park ("Town Park" to locals) has a large swimming area and boat launch. Equally popular in summer or winter, Rangeley has a rough, wilderness feel to it. In late January the Rangeley Lakes Snowmobile Club's Snodeo offers thrilling snowmobile acrobatics, fireworks, and a chili cook-off.

GETTING HERE AND AROUND

To reach Rangeley on a scenic drive through Western Maine, take Route 17 north from U.S. 2 in Mexico to Route 4 in Oquossoc, then head east into town. Route 16 soon joins the highway and from Rangeley continues east to Sugarloaf ski resort and Kingfield.

ESSENTIALS

Vacation Rentals Morton and Furbish Vacation Rentals ⊠ *2478 Main St.* ☏ *207/864–9065, 888/218–4882* ⊕ *www.rangeleyrentals.com.*

Visitor Information Rangeley Lakes Chamber of Commerce ⊠ *6 Park Rd., off Main St.* ☏ *207/864–5364, 800/685–2537* ⊕ *www.rangeleymaine.com.*

EXPLORING

Rangeley Lake State Park. On the south shore of Rangeley Lake, this 869-acre park has superb lakeside scenery, swimming, picnic tables, and a boat ramp. ⊠ *S. Shore Dr., off Rte. 17 or Rte. 4* ☏ *207/624–6080* ⊕ *www.parksandlands.com* 🎫 *$4.50* ⊗ *Daily 9–sunset.*

Rangeley Outdoor Sporting Heritage Museum. Spruce railings and siding on the Rangeley Outdoor Sporting Heritage Museum's facade replicate a local taxidermy shop from about 1900. Inside, the welcome center is an authentic log sporting camp from the same period, when grand hotels and full-service sporting lodges drew well-to-do "rusticators" on long stays. One of the big lures is the exhibit on local fly-tier Carrie Stevens, whose famed streamer flies increased the region's fly-fishing fame in the 1920s. ⊠ *8 Rumford Rd., Oquossoc* ☏ *207/864–3091* ⊕ *www. rangeleyoutdoormuseum.org* 🎫 *$5* ⊗ *Late May–June and Sept.–mid-Oct., Fri. and Sat. 10–2; July and Aug., Wed.–Sun. 10–2.*

Wilhelm Reich Museum. The Wilhelm Reich Museum showcases the life and work of controversial physician-scientist Wilhelm Reich (1897–1957), who believed that a force called orgone energy is in all living matter and the atmosphere. The Orgone Energy Observatory exhibits biographical materials, inventions, and the equipment used in his experiments. The observatory deck has magnificent views of the countryside. In July and August, the museum offers nature programs for all ages. Trails lace the 175-acre grounds. ⊠ *19 Orgonon Cir., off Rte. 4* ☏ *207/864–3443* ⊕ *www.wilhelmreichtrust.org* 🎫 *Museum $6, grounds free* ⊗ *Museum July and Aug., Wed.–Sun. 1–5; Sept., Sat. 1–5. Grounds daily 9–5.*

WHERE TO EAT AND STAY

$$$

AMERICAN

✕ **Gingerbread House Restaurant.** With a fieldstone fireplace in the main dining room, tables scattered around the deck, and an antique marble soda fountain, there are lots of reasons to stop at what really looks like a giant gingerbread house at the edge of the woods. Sandwiches and burgers at lunch give way to crab cakes as appetizers (big enough for a meal) and such interesting entrées as lobster macaroni and cheese and barbecued ribs with a blueberry-chipotle sauce. Locals also come for baked goods or ice cream. $ *Average main: $23* ⊠ *55 Carry Rd.,*

Oquossoc ☎ *207/864–3602* 🌐 *www.gingerbreadhouserestaurant.net* ⏲ *Closed late Oct.–Nov. and Apr.; and Mon.–Thurs. Dec.–Mar., Mon. and Tues. May–late June, and Mon. early Sept.–late Oct.*

$$ B&B/INN FAMILY 🏨 **Country Club Inn.** Built in 1920 as the country club for the adjacent Mingo Springs Golf Course, this hilltop retreat has sweeping mountain and lake views and plenty of charm. **Pros:** loads of board games in living room; superhelpful staff; choice of meal plans. **Cons:** rooms in main building are smaller; no TV in rooms. [$] *Rooms from: $129* ✉ *56 Country Club Rd., off Rte. 4* ☎ *207/864–3831* 🌐 *www.countryclubinnrangeley.com* 🛏 *19 rooms* ⏲ *Closed Nov. and Apr.* 🍴 *Multiple meal plans.*

$$ HOTEL 🏨 **Rangeley Inn.** Painted eggshell blue, this three-story hotel was built around 1900 for wealthy urbanites on vacation. **Pros:** historic hotel; impressive baths (some with claw-foot tubs); canoeing and kayaking on Hayley Pond. **Cons:** no elevator; restaurant open only for dinner. [$] *Rooms from: $130* ✉ *2443 Main St.* ☎ *207/864–3341* 🌐 *www.therangeleyinn.com* 🛏 *40 rooms, 4 suites* ⏲ *Closed Apr.* 🍴 *Breakfast.*

SPORTS AND THE OUTDOORS

BOATING AND FISHING

Rangeley and Mooselookmeguntic lakes are good for canoeing, sailing, fishing, and motorboating. Several outfits rent equipment and provide guide service if needed. Lake fishing for brook trout and landlocked salmon is at its best in May, June, and September. The Rangeley area's rivers and streams are especially popular with fly-fishers, who enjoy the sport from May through October.

GOLF

Mingo Springs Golf Course. This popular course is known for its mountain and water views. You can also take in the views and spot wildlife on the Mingo Springs Trail & Bird Walk, an easy 3-mile loop trail through woods along the course. ✉ *43 Country Club Rd., follow signs from Rte. 4, Rangeley* ☎ *207/864–5021* 🌐 *www.mingosprings.com* 🎫 *Greens fee: $43.*

SEAPLANES

Fodor's Choice ★ **Acadian Seaplanes.** In addition to 15- to 90-minute scenic flights high above the mountains, this seaplane operator offers enticing "fly-in" excursions. You can travel by air to wilderness locales to dine at a sporting camp, spot moose in their natural habitat, or go white-water rafting on the remote Rapid River. The company also provides charter service year-round, including shuttles between Rangeley and airports in Portland, Boston, and New York. ✉ *2640 Main St.* ☎ *207/864–5307* 🌐 *www.acadianseaplanes.com.*

SKI AREAS

Rangeley Lakes Trails Center. About 35 miles of groomed cross-country and snowshoe trails stretch along the side of Saddleback Mountain. The trail network is largely wooded and leads to Saddleback Lake. In warmer weather the trails are popular with mountain bikers, hikers, and runners. A snack bar, known for its tasty soups, is open in winter. ✉ *524 Saddleback Mountain Rd., off Rte. 4, Dallas* ☎ *207/864–4309* 🌐 *www.xcskirangeley.com.*

FAMILY **Saddleback Maine.** A family atmosphere prevails at Saddleback Maine, where the lack of crowds, affordable prices, and spectacular valley views draw return visitors. The 66 trails and glades, accessed by five lifts, are divided about evenly between novice, intermediate, and advanced. A fieldstone fireplace is nestled in the post-and-beam base lodge, which has a second-story pub with views of Saddleback Lake. The resort has a ski school, rental shop, and trailside lodging. Summer guests have access to canoes on Saddleback Lake. ⊠ *976 Saddleback Mountain Rd., off Rte. 4, Dallas* ☎ *207/864–5671, 866/918–2225* ⊕ *www.saddlebackmaine.com.*

KINGFIELD

38 miles east of Rangeley.

In the shadows of Mt. Abram and Sugarloaf Mountain, home to its namesake ski resort, Kingfield has everything a "real" New England town should have: a general store, historic inns, and white clapboard churches.

ESSENTIALS

Visitor Information Franklin County Chamber of Commerce ⊠ *615 Wilton Rd., Farmington* ☎ *207/778–4215* ⊕ *www.franklincountymaine.org.*

EXPLORING

Stanley Museum. Housing a collection of original Stanley Steamer cars built by the Stanley twins—Kingfield's most famous natives—this museum also features exhibits on the glass negative business this inventive pair sold to Eastman Kodak. Also on display are their sister's wonderful photos of everyday country life at the turn of the 20th century. The museum occupies a 1903 Georgian-style former school the Stanleys built for the town. ⊠ *40 School St.* ☎ *207/265–2729* ⊕ *www.stanleymuseum.org* 🖃 *$4* ⊗ *June–Oct., Tues.–Sun. 1–4; Nov.–May., Tues.–Fri. 1–4.*

SPORTS AND THE OUTDOORS

SKI AREAS

FAMILY **Sugarloaf Mountain Resort.** An eye-catching setting, abundant natural snow, and the only above-tree-line lift-service skiing in the East have made Sugarloaf Mountain Resort one of Maine's best-known ski areas. There are 15 lifts, 153 trails and glades, a ski school, and a rental shop. There are two slope-side hotels, and hundreds of slope-side condos with ski-in ski-out access. Sugarloaf Mountain Hotel is in the ski village, while the smaller, more affordable Sugarloaf Inn is just a bit down the mountain. The Outdoor Center has more than 90 miles of cross-country ski trails, as well as snowshoeing and ice-skating. Sugarloaf has plenty for the kids, from tubing to skateboarding. Once you are here, a car is unnecessary—a shuttle connects all mountain operations. Summer is much quieter, but you can mountain bike, go hiking, or play a round on the Robert Trent Jones Jr.–designed golf course. ⊠ *5092 Access Rd., Carrabassett Valley* ☎ *207/237–2000, 800/843–5623 reservations* ⊕ *www.sugarloaf.com.*

Rafting in the North Woods

Virtually all of Maine's white-water rafting takes place on the dam-controlled Kennebec and Dead rivers, which meet at The Forks in Western Maine, and on the West Branch of the Penobscot River, near Millinocket in the North Woods. Guided excursions lasting from a day to several days run rain or shine daily from spring (mid-April on the Kennebec, May on the Dead and the Penobscot) to mid-October.

Maine is New England's premier destination for the sport, which is why thousands of people come here every year to ride the waves. The Kennebec is known for abundant big waves and splashes; the Dead has New England's longest stretch of continuous white water, some 16 miles. The most challenging rapids are on the West Branch of the Penobscot River, a Class V river on the southern border of Baxter State Park outside Millinocket.

Many rafting outfitters operate resort facilities in their base towns. It's not uncommon for outfitters to run trips in both the Millinocket region and The Forks. In recent years operators have added family-friendly rafting trips that take you along some of the gentler stretches of these mighty rivers. North Country Rivers and New England Outdoor Center in Millinocket have many outfitters.

THE NORTH WOODS

Moosehead Lake, the four-season resort town of Greenville, Baxter State Park, and the Allagash Wilderness Waterway are dispersed within Maine's remote North Woods. This vast area in the north-central section of the state is best experienced by canoe or raft; via hiking, snowshoe, cross-country skiing, or snowmobile; or on a fishing trip. Maine's largest lake, Moosehead supplies more in the way of rustic camps, guides, and outfitters than any other northern locale. Its 400-plus miles of shorefront, three-quarters of which is owned by lumber companies or the state, are virtually uninhabited.

10

GREENVILLE

155 miles northeast of Portland; 70 miles northwest of Bangor.

Greenville, tucked at the southern end of island-dotted, mostly forest-lined Moosehead Lake, is an outdoors-lover's paradise. Boating, fishing, and hiking are popular in summer, while snowmobiling and ice fishing reign in winter. The town also has the greatest selection of shops, restaurants, and inns in the North Woods region. Restaurants and lodgings are also clustered 20 miles north in Rockwood, where the Moose River flows through the village and—across from Mt. Kineo's majestic cliffs—into the lake.

GETTING HERE AND AROUND

To reach Greenville from Interstate 95, get off at Exit 157 in Newport and head north, successively, on Routes 7, 23, and 15.

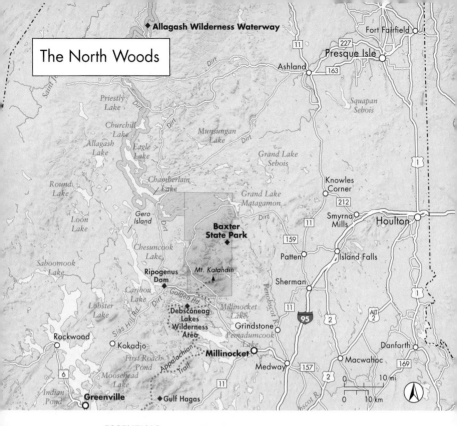

The North Woods

Allagash Wilderness Waterway

Fort Fairfield

Presque Isle

Ashland

Priestly Lake

Churchill Lake

Munsungan Lake

Allagash Lake

Eagle Lake

Grand Lake Sebois

Round Lake

Chamberlain Lake

Grand Lake Matagamon

Knowles Corner

Loon Lake

Gero Island

Baxter State Park

Smyrna Mills

Houlton

Chesuncook Lake

Saboomook Lake

Ripogenus Dam

Mt. Katahdin

Patten

Island Falls

Caribou Lake

Golden Rd.

Sherman

Lobster Lake

Debsconeag Lakes Wilderness Area

Millinocket Lake

Grindstone

Rockwood

Kokadjo

Pemadumcook Lake

Danforth

First Roach Pond

Appalachian Trail

Millinocket

Medway

Macwahoc

Moosehead Lake

Indian Pond

Greenville

Gulf Hagas

ESSENTIALS

Vacation Rentals Northwoods Camp Rentals ✉ *14 Lakeview St.* ☎ *800/251–8042, 207/695–4300* ⊕ *mooseheadrentals.com.*

Visitor Information Moosehead Lake Region Chamber of Commerce ✉ *480 Moosehead Lake Rd.* ☎ *207/695–2702, 888/876–2778* ⊕ *www.moose headlake.org.*

EXPLORING

Lily Bay State Park. Nine miles northeast of Greenville on Moosehead Lake, this park has good lakefront swimming, a 1.6-mi walking trail with water views, two boat-launching ramps, a playground, and two campgrounds with a total of 90 sites. In winter the entrance road is plowed to access the groomed cross-country ski trails and the lake for ice fishing and snowmobiling. ✉ *State Park Rd., turn off Lily Bay Rd., Beaver Cove* ☎ *207/695–2700 mid-May–mid-Oct. only, 207/941–4014* ⊕ *www.parksandlands.com* 🎫 *$4.50, Maine residents $3* ☉ *Daily 9–sunset (mid-Oct.–mid-May no staff, roads not open except on a limited basis during snow season).*

FAMILY

Fodor's Choice

★

Moosehead Historical Society & Museums. Guides in period costume lead tours of the Eveleth-Crafts-Sheridan House, a late-19th-century Victorian mansion filled with period antiques, most original to the home.

> **WORD OF MOUTH**
>
> "Moosehead Lake and Mt. Kineo (in the Greenville area) are beautiful and in my opinion not to be missed."
>
> —clarkgriswold

The Lumberman's Museum, about the region's logging history, is in the carriage house, while the barn next door houses a re-creation of a one-room schoolhouse and a general-store exhibit. You can savor lunch and the architecture of these meticulously maintained buildings from the art-accented Sunken Garden. A mile away in downtown Greenville, the former Universalist Church houses the Center for Moosehead History and Moosehead Lake Aviation Museum. The former has a fine exhibit of Native American artifacts from the Moosehead Lake region, dating from 9,000 BC to the 1700s, while the latter highlights the impact of aviation on the area, from early bush pilots to Greenville's annual International Seaplane Fly-in. ✉ *444 Pritham Ave., Greenville Junction* ☎ *207/695–2909* 🌐 *www.mooseheadhistory.org* 🎟 *Eveleth-Crafts-Sheridan House $5, other museums free* 🕒 *Eveleth-Crafts-Sheridan House: mid-June–mid-Oct., Wed.–Fri. 1–4; Lumberman's Museum: Tues.–Fri. 9–4; Center for Moosehead History and Moosehead Lake Aviation Museum: mid-June–mid-Oct., Thurs.–Sun. 10–4.*

OFF THE BEATEN PATH

Mt. Kineo. Accessed primarily by steamship, Mt. Kineo House was a thriving summer resort for the wealthy set below its namesake's 800-foot cliff on an island-like peninsula north of Greenville. The last of three successive hotels with this name was built in 1884 and became America's largest inland waterfront hotel. It was torn down in 1938, but Kineo remains a pleasant day trip. There's no road access: take a 15-minute boat trip from Rockwood on the seasonal shuttle. Mt. Kineo State Park occupies most of the 1,200-acre peninsula, and you can also play a round on the Mt. Kineo Golf Course, one of the oldest in New England. ✉ *Kineo Dock, Village Rd., Rockwood* ☎ *207/534–9012* 🌐 *www.parksandlands.com* 🎟 *$3* 🕒 *Daily 9–sunset.*

WHERE TO STAY

$$$$ | B&B/INN | Fodor's Choice ★

🏨 **Blair Hill Inn.** Beautiful gardens and a hilltop location with marvelous views over the lake distinguish this 1891 country estate, considered one of New England's top inns. **Pros:** gorgeous rooms; amazing restaurant; 15-acre property has stone paths, wooded picnic area, and trout pond. **Cons:** pricey; no direct lake access. [$] *Rooms from: $398* ✉ *351 Lily Bay Rd.* ☎ *207/695–0224* 🌐 *www.blairhill.com* 🛏 *7 rooms, 1 suite* 🕒 *Closed Nov.–Apr.* 🍴 *Breakfast.*

$$$$ | RESORT | FAMILY | Fodor's Choice ★

🏨 **Appalachian Mountain Club Maine Wilderness Lodges.** When you want to get away from it all, head to the Appalachian Mountain Club's 66,000 acres in Maine's 100-Mile Wilderness—you have a choice of two historic sporting camp retreats, Gorman Chairback and Little Lyford. **Pros:** great for outdoors lovers; far-from-the-crowds feel; laid-back vibe. **Cons:** winter access only by cross-country skis or snowmobile. [$] *Rooms from: $144* ✉ *Off Katahdin Iron Works Rd.* ☎ *603/466–2727* 🌐 *www.outdoors.org/lodging/mainelodges* 🛏 *Gorman Chairback: 12 cabins; Little Lyford: 9 cabins* 🕒 *Closed mid-Mar.–mid-May and late Oct.–late Dec.* 🍴 *All meals.*

SCENIC DRIVE

Golden Road. For a scenic North Woods drive, travel the approximately 20-mile stretch of this private east-west logging road (named for what it cost a paper company to build it) near Baxter State Park northwest of Millinocket. Have patience with ruts and bumps and yield to logging trucks—keep right! At the western end of the drive, the West Branch of the Penobscot River drops 70-plus feet per mile through Ripogenus Gorge, giving white-water rafters a thrilling ride during scheduled releases from Ripogenous Dam. To drive across the dam on Ripogenus Lake and view the gorge, turn on Rip Dam Road (it veers right if you're traveling west). The Crib Works Rapid (Class V) overlook is on Telos Road, about a mile east of Rip Dam Road (parking is on the right after the bridge). Take photos of Baxter's Mt. Katahdin from the footbridge alongside the Golden Road's one-lane Abol Bridge—this view is famed. Park east of the bridge at Abol Bridge Campground or at the parking area west of the bridge. Also just west of the bridge is an access road for Debsconeag Lakes Wilderness Area. At North Woods Trading Post, about nine miles east of the bridge and across from Ambajejus Lake, you can cross between the Golden Road and Millinocket Lake Road (becomes Baxter State Park Road). Turn left for Baxter, right for Millinocket. West of "Rip" Dam the dirt Sias Hill Road heads south from the Golden Road on a backwoods route to Greenville through tiny Kokadjo. ⊠ *Golden Rd., Millinocket.*

SPORTS AND THE OUTDOORS

Togue (lake trout), landlocked salmon, smallmouth bass, and brook trout lure thousands of anglers to the region from ice-out in mid-May until September; the hardiest return in winter to ice fish.

MULTI-SPORT OUTFITTERS

Moose Country Safaris & Eco Tours. In the Greenville area, Moose Country Safaris & Eco Tours leads moose-spotting and bird-watching excursions. There are also snowshoe, hiking, and canoe trips, as well as late-summer meteor shower tours. Spring through fall, the itinerary includes tours of an ice cave near Baxter State Park. ⊠ *191 N. Dexter Rd., Sangerville* ☎ *207/876–4907* ⊕ *www.moosecountrysafaris.com.*

Northwoods Outfitters. This company provides all the gear you'll need for moose-watching, biking, skiing, snowmobiling, snowboarding, canoeing, kayaking, and fishing, among other activities. It also leads day and overnight trips around the region. At its base in downtown Greenville you can pick up sporting goods, get trail advice, or kick back in the Internet café. The company also has its own 16-room motel and lakeside cabin rental. ⊠ *5 Lily Bay Rd.* ☎ *207/695–3288, 866/223–1380* ⊕ *www.maineoutfitter.com.*

BOATING

Allagash Canoe Trips. Run by a husband and wife, both championship paddlers and Registered Maine Guides, this operator offers day, overnight and weeklong canoe trips on the Allagash Wilderness Waterway, the Moose and St. John rivers, and the East and West branches of the

Penobscot River. White-water canoe and kayak trips are run on the Kennebec and Dead rivers. The couple also operates clinics on white-water paddling and kayaking and canoe poling. ✉ *156 Scammon Rd.* ☎ *207/280-1551, 207/280-0191* ⊕ *www.allagashcanoetrips.com.*

SEAPLANES

Currier's Flying Service. You can take sightseeing flights over the Moosehead Lake region with Currier's Flying Service from ice-out until the end of October. ✉ *447 Pritham Ave., Greenville Junction* ☎ *207/695–2778* ⊕ *www.curriersflyingservice.com.*

TOURS

Katahdin Cruises. The Moosehead Marine Museum runs three- and four-and-a-half-hour afternoon trips on Moosehead Lake aboard the *Katahdin,* a 115-foot 1914 steamship converted to diesel. The longer scheduled trips skirt Mt. Kineo's cliffs. Also called *The Kate,* the ship carried resort guests to Mt. Kineo until 1938 and then was used in the logging industry until 1975. The boat and the free shoreside museum have displays about the steamships that transported people and cargo on the lake during a period of about 100 years starting in the 1830s. ✉ *12 Lily Bay Rd.* ☎ *207/695–2716* ⊕ *www.katahdincruises. com* 🖼 *$33–$38* ☉ *Cruises: late June–mid-Oct., Tues.–Sat. at 12:30. Museum: Mon.–Sat. 10–4.*

OFF THE BEATEN PATH

Gulf Hagas. Called the "Grand Canyon of the East," this National Natural Landmark has chasms, cliffs, six large waterfalls, pools, exotic flora, and rock formations. Part of the Appalachian Trail Corridor, the slate-walled gorge east of Greenville is within a remote commercial forest and accessed by gravel logging roads (always yield to trucks). An access fee is usually charged at forest checkpoints, where you can get trail maps and hiking information. From the two parking areas it's a 3- or 3½-mile round-trip hike to Stair Falls on the gorge's western end and the spectacular Screw Auger Falls on the eastern end. These are good choices for families with young children and anyone looking for a moderately difficult hike. Slippery rocks and rugged terrain make for challenging hiking along the rim; a loop route that includes the rim trail is an 8- to 9-mile trek. From the Gulf Hagas Parking Area—the one near the gorge's east end—you must ford the Pleasant River (easily done in summer, but don't attempt it in high water). From Greenville, travel 11 miles east via Pleasant Street (which eventually becomes Katahdin Iron Works Road) to the Hedgehog checkpoint. From here, follow signs to the parking areas at Head of Gulf (2½ miles) or Gulf Hagas (6½ miles). ✉ *Accessed from Katahdin Iron Works Rd.* ⊕ *www. northmainewoods.org.*

10

MILLINOCKET

67 miles north of Bangor, 88 miles northwest of Greenville via Rtes. 6 and 11.

Millinocket, a paper-mill town with a population of about 4,000, is a gateway to Baxter State Park and Maine's North Woods. Although it has a smattering of motels and restaurants, Millinocket is the place to stock up on supplies, fill your gas tank, or grab a hot meal or shower before heading into the wilderness. Numerous rafting and canoeing outfitters and guides are based in the region.

GETTING HERE AND AROUND

From Interstate 95, take Route 157 (Exit 244) west to Millinocket. From here follow signs to Baxter State Park (Millinocket Lake Road becomes Baxter Park State Road), 18 miles from town.

ESSENTIALS

Visitor Information **Katahdin Area Chamber of Commerce** ⊠ *1029 Central St.* ☎ *207/723–4443* ⊕ *www.katahdinmaine.com.*

EXPLORING

Allagash Wilderness Waterway. A spectacular 92-mile corridor of lakes, streams, and rivers, the waterway cuts through northern Maine's vast commercial forests, beginning northwest of Baxter State Park and running north to the town of Allagash, 10 miles from the Canadian border. The Maine Bureau of Parks and Lands has campsites along the waterway, most not accessible by vehicle. From May to mid-October the Allagash is prime canoeing and camping country. It's part of the 740-mile Northern Forest Canoe Trail, which runs from New York to Maine. The complete 92-mile course requires 7 to 10 days. Novices may want to consider going with a guide, as there are many areas with strong rapids. A good outfitter can help plan your route and provide equipment and and transportation. ☎ *207/941–4014* ⊕ *www.maine. gov/allagashwildernesswaterway.*

Fodor's Choice ★ **Baxter State Park.** A gift from Governor Percival Baxter, this is the jewel in the crown of northern Maine, a 210,000-acre wilderness area that surrounds **Mt. Katahdin,** Maine's highest mountain and the terminus of the Appalachian Trail. The 5,267-foot Katahdin draws thousands of hikers every year for the daylong climb to the summit and the stunning views of woods, mountains, and lakes. Three parking lot trailheads lead to its peak; some routes include the hair-raising Knife Edge Ridge. ■ TIP→ Reserve a day-use parking space at the trailheads between May 15 and October 15. The crowds climbing Katahdin can be formidable on clear summer days and fall weekends, so if you crave solitude, tackle one of the 47 other mountains in the park, 20 of which exceed an elevation of 3,000 feet and all of which are accessible from an extensive network of trails. South Turner can be climbed in a morning, and its summit has a great view across the valley. The Owl, the Brothers, and Doubletop Mountain are good day hikes (four to five hours). A trek around Daicey Pond, or from the pond to Big and Little Niagara Falls, are good options for families with young kids. Another option if you only have a couple of hours is renting a canoe at Daicey or Togue ponds. The roads here are unpaved, narrow, and winding; there are no pay phones, gas stations, or stores. The camping is primitive at the park's 10 campgrounds; reserve. The Togue Pond Gate, the park's southern entrance, is 18 miles northwest of Millinocket. Follow signs from Route 157. ⊠ *Baxter State Park Rd.* ☎ *207/723–5140, 207/723–4636 hiking hotline* ⊕ *www.baxterstateparkauthority.com* ✉ *$14 per vehicle* ☉ *Mid-May–mid-Oct., 6 am–10 pm; mid-Oct.–mid-May, sunrise–sunset.*

Debsconeag Lakes Wilderness Area. Bordering the south side of the Golden Road below Baxter State Park, the Nature Conservancy's 46,271-acre Debsconeag Lakes Wilderness Area is renowned for its rare ice cave, old forests, and abundant pristine ponds—more than anywhere else in New England. The access road for the Ice Cave Trail (2-mile round-trip) and Hurd Pond is 17 miles northwest of Millinocket, just west of the Golden Road's Abol Bridge. Near here the Appalachian Trail exits the conservancy land, crossing the bridge en route to Baxter. Before hiking, paddling, fishing, or camping (no fee or reservations needed) in the remote preserve, visit the conservancy's website for directions and other information. Access roads are unmarked, but there are trail kiosks and marked trailheads within the preserve. ⊠ *Golden Road, private logging road, no fee for this section* ⊕ *www.nature.org/maine.*

SPORTS AND THE OUTDOORS

MULTI-SPORT OUTFITTERS

Katahdin Outfitters. Take canoe and kayak expeditions on the Allagash Wilderness Waterway, West Branch of the Penobscot River, and St. John River with Katahdin Outfitters. ⊠ *Millinocket Lake Rd.* ☎ *207/723–5700* ⊕ *www.katahdinoutfitters.com.*

FAMILY

Fodor's Choice
★

New England Outdoor Center. With Baxter State Park's Mt. Katahdin rising beyond the opposite shore at both its locations, this business helps visitors enjoy Maine's pristine North Woods—whether you're relaxing with drink in hand or on a wilderness adventure. Its year-round home base, Twin Pine Camps on Millinocket Lake, 9 miles from the park's southern entrance, has rental cabins and a restaurant and offers a host of guided trips, some within the park. Older log cabins (and a few newer ones) sit beneath tall pines on a grassy nub of land that juts into Millinocket Lake, while spacious upscale "green" units are tucked among trees on a cove. Amenities include kayaks and canoes for use on the lake and a recreation center with a sauna. At the popular River Driver's Restaurant, wood for the trim, wainscoting, bar, and floors was milled from old logs salvaged from local waters. Diners enjoy views of Katahdin beyond rows of windows or the patio, and your dish may have farm-to-table fare from the center's own farm. In addition to running guided snowmobiling, fishing, canoe, kayak, hiking, and moose-watching trips, NEOC rents canoes and kayaks, gives paddling lessons, and rents snowmobiles—it's along Maine's Interconnected Trail System. Trails for hiking, cross-country skiing (11 miles groomed), and mountain biking (to open 2014) are right on the 1,400-acre property. About 2 miles from Baxter, the seasonal Penobscot Outdoor Center is the base for white-water rafting trips on the West Branch of the Penobscot River and has a wooded campground on Pockwockamus Pond. There are tent sites as well as canvas tents and simple wood-frame cabins with cots or bunks and a dim solar light. A circular fireplace anchors the open-plan base lodge, which has a snack bar, pub area, hot tub, and communal outdoor fire pit. A towering window wall provides glimpses of water through trees, and there are waterside camp sites with Katahdin views. ■ TIP→ **Nonguests can use the showers for $2 after hiking or camping at Baxter.** ⊠ *30 Twin Pines Rd.* ✛ *From Millinocket Lake Rd. turn on*

10

Black Cat Rd., go 1 mile to NEOC (stay left on Twin Pines Rd. shortly before NEOC) ☎ *207/723–5438, 800/634–7238* ⊕ *www.neoc.com.*

North Country Rivers. From spring to fall, North Country Rivers runs white-water rafting trips on the Dead and Kennebec rivers in The Forks in western Maine, and on the West Branch of Penobscot River outside Millinocket in the North Woods. North Country's 55-acre resort south of The Forks in Bingham has cabin and cottage rentals, a restaurant, pub, and store. Its Millinocket base is at Big Moose Inn. The outfitter also offers moose and wildlife safaris and rents snowmobiles, mountain and trail bikes, and kayaks. ⊠ *46 Main St., Bingham* ☎ *207/672–4814, 800/348–8871* ⊕ *www.northcountryrivers.com.*

MAINE COAST

WELCOME TO MAINE COAST

TOP REASONS TO GO

★ **Lobster:** It's not a Maine vacation without donning a bib and digging into a steamed lobster with drawn butter for dipping.

★ **Boating:** The coastline of Maine was made for boaters. Whether it's your own boat, a friend's, or a charter, make sure you get out on the water.

★ **Wild Maine Blueberries:** They may be tiny, but the wild blueberries pack a flavorful punch in season (late July to early September).

★ **Cadillac Mountain:** Drive the winding 3½-mile road to the 1,530-foot summit in Acadia National Park for the sunrise.

★ **Perfect Souvenir:** Buy a watercolor, hand-painted pottery, or handcrafted jewelry—artists and craftspeople abound.

1 The Southern Coast. Stretching north from Kittery to just outside Portland, this is Maine's most visited region. The towns along the shore and miles of sandy expanses cater to summer visitors. Old Orchard Beach features Coney Island–like amusements, while Kittery, the Yorks, Wells, and the Kennebunks are more low-key getaways.

2 Portland. Maine's largest and most cosmopolitan city, Portland balances its historic role as a working harbor with its newer identity as a center of sophisticated arts and shopping and innovative restaurants.

3 The Mid-Coast Region. North of Portland, from Brunswick to Monhegan Island, the craggy coastline winds its way around pastoral peninsulas. Its villages boast maritime museums, antiques shops, and beautiful architecture.

Waterville

Augusta

Lewiston

Waldoboro

Auburn

Newcastle

Brunswick

Damariscott[a]

Freeport

Bath

Phippsburg

Boothbay

Yarmouth

Georgetown

Falmouth

Portland

Casco Bay

Saco

Old Orchard Beach

Sanford

Biddeford

0   20 mi

0   20 km

Kennebunk

Kennebunkport

Wells

Ogunquit

York

Kittery

Portsmouth

NEW HAMPSHIRE

Old Town

Newport

Bangor

9

179

9

193

Columbia
Falls

182

Cherryfield

Hancock

Ellsworth

West Gouldsboro

Belfast

Searsport

Bar Harbor

Islesboro

Blue Hill
Peninsula

Mt.
Desert
Island

◆Cadillac Mtn.

Frenchman
Bay

Deer Isle
Village

ACADIA NAT'L
PARK

Camden

Stonington

17

Rockland

Thomaston

Isle
au Haut

Penobscot
Bay

Monhegan
Island

191

Lubec

7

1

Machias

Jonesport

Beals Island

Atlantic Ocean

4 Penobscot Bay.
This region combines lively coastal towns with dramatic natural scenery. Camden is one of Maine's most picture-perfect towns, with its pointed church steeples, antique homes, cozy harbor, and historic windjammer fleet.

5 Blue Hill Peninsula.
Art galleries are plentiful here, and the entire region is ideal for biking, hiking, kayaking, and boating. For many, the peninsula defines the silent beauty of the Maine Coast.

6 Acadia National Park and Mount Desert Island.
Millions come to enjoy Acadia National Park's stunning peaks and vistas of the island's mountains. Bar Harbor is more of a visitor's haven, while Southwest Harbor and Bass Harbor offer quieter retreats.

7 Way Down East. This is the "real" Maine, some say, and it unfurls in thousands of acres of wild blueberry barrens, congestion-free coastlines, and a tangible sense of rugged endurance.

GETTING ORIENTED

Much of the appeal of the Maine Coast lies in its geographical contrasts, from its long stretches of swimming and walking beaches in the south to the cliff-edged, rugged, rocky coasts in the north. And not unlike the physical differences of the coast, each town along the way reveals a slightly different character.

Updated by
Brian Kevin

As you drive across the border into Maine, a sign announces: "The way life should be." Romantics luxuriate in the feeling of a down comforter on a yellow-pine bed or in the sensation of the wind and salt spray on their faces while cruising in a historic windjammer. Families love the unspoiled beaches and safe inlets dotting the shoreline. Hikers are revived while roaming the trails of Acadia National Park, and adventure-seekers kayak along the coast.

The Maine Coast is several places in one. Portland may be Maine's largest metropolitan area, but its attitude is decidedly more big town than small city. South of Portland, Ogunquit, Kennebunkport, Old Orchard Beach, and other resort towns predominate along a reasonably smooth shoreline. North of Portland and Casco Bay, secondary roads turn south off U.S. 1 onto so many oddly chiseled peninsulas that it's possible to drive for days without retracing your route. Slow down to explore the museums, galleries, and shops in the larger towns and the antiques and curio shops and harborside lobster shacks in the smaller fishing villages. Freeport is an entity unto itself, a place where numerous name-brand outlets and specialty stores have sprung up around the retail outpost of famous outfitter L. L. Bean. And no description of the coast would be complete without mention of popular Acadia National Park, with its majestic mountains that are often shrouded in mist.

If you come to Maine seeking an untouched fishing village with locals gathered around a potbellied stove in the general store, you'll likely come away disappointed; that innocent age has passed in all but the most remote spots like Way Down East. Tourism has supplanted fishing, logging, and potato farming as Maine's number one industry, and most areas are well equipped to receive the annual onslaught of visitors. But whether you are stepping outside a cabin for a walk in the woods or watching a boat rock at its anchor, you can sense the wilderness nearby, even on the edges of the most urbanized spots.

PLANNING

WHEN TO GO

Maine's dramatic coastline and pure natural beauty welcome visitors year-round, but note that many smaller museums and attractions are open only for high season—from Memorial Day to mid-October—as are many of the waterside attractions and eateries.

Summer begins in earnest on July 4th, and many smaller inns, B&Bs, and hotels from Kittery on up to the Bar Harbor region are booked a month or two ahead on weekends through August. That's also the case come fall, when the fiery foliage draws leaf peepers. After Halloween, hotel rates drop significantly until ski season begins around Thanksgiving. Along the coast, bed-and-breakfasts that remain open will often rent rooms at far lower prices than in summer.

In spring the fourth Sunday in March is designated as Maine Maple Sunday, and farms throughout the state open their doors to visitors not only to watch sap turn into golden syrup but to sample the sweet results.

PLANNING YOUR TIME

You could easily spend a lifetime's worth of vacations along the Maine Coast and never truly see it all. But if you are determined to travel the coast from end to end, allot at least two weeks to travel comfortably.

Driving in Coastal Maine		
	Miles	Time
Boston–Portland	112	2 hours
Kittery–Portland	50	50 minutes
Portland–Freeport	18	20 minutes
Portland–Camden	80	2 hours
Portland–Bar Harbor	175	3 hours, 20 minutes

GETTING HERE AND AROUND

AIR TRAVEL

Maine has two major international airports, Portland International Jetport and Bangor International Airport, to get you to or close to your coastal destination. Manchester–Boston Regional Airport in New Hampshire is about 45 minutes away from the southern end of the Maine coastline. Boston's Logan Airport is the only truly international airport in the region; it's about 90 minutes south of the Maine border.

CAR TRAVEL

Once you are here the best way to experience the winding back roads of the craggy Maine Coast is in a car. There are miles and miles of roads far from the larger towns that have no bus services, and you won't want to miss discovering your own favorite ocean vista while on a scenic drive.

BUS TRAVEL

The Shoreline Explorer links seasonal trolleys in southern Maine beach towns from the Yorks to the Kennebunks, allowing you to travel between towns without a car.

Shoreline Explorer ☎ *207/459–2932* ⊕ *www.shorelineexplorer.com.*

TRAIN TRAVEL

Amtrak offers regional service from Boston to Portland via its Downeaster line that originates at Boston's North Station and makes six stops in Maine: Wells, Saco, Old Orchard Beach (seasonal), Portland, Freeport, and Brunswick. Greyhound and Concord Coach Lines also offer bus service from Boston to many towns along the Maine Coast. Concord has express service between Portland and Boston's Logan Airport and South Station. Both Concord and Amtrak operate out of the Portland Transportation Center at ✉ *100 Thompson's Point Road.*

RESTAURANTS

Many breakfast spots along the coast open as early as 6 am to serve the going-to-work crowd (in fishing areas as early as 4 am). Lunch generally runs 11–2:30; dinner is usually served 5–9. Only in the larger cities will you find full dinners being offered much later than 9, although in larger towns you can usually find a bar or bistro serving a limited menu late into the evening.

Many restaurants in Maine are closed Monday, though this isn't true in resort areas in high season. However, resort-town eateries often shut down completely in the off-season. *Unless otherwise noted in reviews, restaurants are open daily for lunch and dinner.*

Credit cards are accepted for meals throughout Maine, even in some of the most modest establishments.

The one signature dinner on the Maine Coast is, of course, the lobster dinner. It generally includes boiled lobster, a clam or seafood chowder, corn on the cob, and coleslaw or perhaps a salad. Lobster prices vary from day to day, but generally a full lobster dinner should cost around $25; without all the add-ons, about $18. *Prices in the reviews are the average cost of a main course at dinner or, if dinner is not served, at lunch.*

HOTELS

Beachfront and roadside motels and historic-home B&Bs and inns make up the majority of accommodation options along the Maine Coast. There are a few large luxury resorts, such as the Samoset Resort in Rockport or the Bar Harbor Inn in Bar Harbor, but most accommodations are simple and relatively inexpensive. You will find hotel chains in larger cities and towns, including major tourist destinations like Freeport and Bar Harbor. Many properties close during the off-season— mid-October until mid-May; some that stay open drop their rates dramatically. There is an 8% state hospitality tax on all room rates. *Prices in the reviews are the lowest cost of a standard double room in high season.*

TOURS

No visit to the Maine Coast is complete without some outdoor activity—be it generated by two wheels, two feet, two paddles, or pulling a bag full of clubs.

BICYCLING

The Bicycle Coalition of Main and Explore Maine by Bike are excellent sources for trail maps and other riding information.

Bicycle Coalition of Maine. The well-regarded Bicycle Coalition of Maine's website includes where to rent bikes. ☎ *207/623–4511* ⊕ *www.bikemaine.org.*

Explore Maine by Bike. Run by the Maine Department of Transportation, this helpful website includes an exhaustive list of the state's most popular bike routes. ⊕ *www.exploremaine.org/bike.*

HIKING

Exploring the Maine Coast on foot is a quick way to acclimate to the relaxed pace of life here.

Healthy Maine Walks. Healthy Maine Walks has comprehensive listings for walks that can be done in an hour or less, from park paths to routes that follow roads and streets. ⊕ *www.healthymainewalks.com.*

KAYAKING

Nothing gets you literally off the beaten path like plying the salt waters in a graceful sea kayak.

Maine Association of Sea Kayaking Guides and Instructors. This association lists state-licensed guides and offers information about instructional classes, guided tours, and trip planning. ⊕ *www.maskgi.org.*

Maine Island Trail Association. Seasoned paddlers can join the Maine Island Trail Association ($45) for a map of and full access to Maine's famous sea trail: more than 200 islands and mainland sites, most privately owned but open to members, on a 375-mile path from the southernmost coast to the Canadian Maritimes. Member benefits also include discounts at outfitters and retailers. ☎ *207/761–8225* ⊕ *www.mita.org.*

THE SOUTHERN COAST

Maine's southernmost coastal towns—Kittery, the Yorks, Ogunquit, the Kennebunks, and the Old Orchard Beach area—present a few of the stunning faces of the state's coast, from the miles and miles of inviting sandy beaches to the beautifully kept historic towns and carnival-like attractions. There is something for every taste, whether you seek solitude in a kayak or prefer being caught up in the infectious spirit of fellow vacationers.

North of Kittery, long stretches of hard-packed white-sand beach are closely crowded by nearly unbroken ranks of beach cottages, motels, and oceanfront restaurants. The summer colonies of York Beach and Wells brim with family crowds, T-shirt and gift shops, and shorefront development; nearby wildlife refuges and land reserves promise an easy quiet escape. York Village evokes yesteryear sentiment with its acclaimed historic district, while upscale Ogunquit tantalizes visitors with its array of shops and a cliffside walk.

More than any other region south of Portland, the Kennebunks—and especially Kennebunkport—provide the complete Maine Coast experience: classic townscapes where white-clapboard houses rise from manicured lawns and gardens; rocky shorelines punctuated by sandy beaches; quaint downtown districts packed with gift shops, ice cream stands, and visitors; harbors with lobster boats bobbing alongside yachts; rustic, picnic-tabled restaurants serving lobster and fried seafood; and well-appointed dining rooms. As you continue north, the scents of fried dough and cotton candy mean you've arrived at Maine's version of Coney Island: Old Orchard Beach.

KITTERY

65 miles north of Boston; 3 miles north of Portsmouth, New Hampshire.

One of the earliest settlements in the state of Maine, Kittery suffered its share of British, French, and Native American attacks throughout the 17th and 18th centuries, yet rose to prominence as a vital shipbuilding center. The tradition continues: despite its New Hampshire name, the Portsmouth Naval Shipyard is part of Maine and has been building U.S. submarines since World War I. It was founded in 1800 and built its first warship in 1815. It's not open to the public, but those on boats can pass by and get a glimpse.

Known as the "Gateway to Maine," Kittery has become a major shopping destination thanks to its complex of factory outlets. Flanking both sides of U.S. 1 are more than 120 stores, which attract hordes of shoppers year-round. For something a little less commercial, head east on Route 103 to the hidden Kittery most people miss: the lands around **Kittery Point.** Here you can find hiking and biking trails and great views of the water. With Portsmouth, New Hampshire, across the water, Whaleback Ledge Lighthouse, and the nearby Isles of Shoals, Kittery is a picturesque place to pass some time. The isles and the light, as well as two others, can be seen from two forts along or near this winding stretch of Route 103: Fort McClary State Historic Site and Fort Foster, a town park (both closed to vehicles off-season).

GETTING HERE AND AROUND

Three bridges—on U.S. 1, U.S. 1 Bypass, and Interstate 95—cross the Piscataqua River from Portsmouth, New Hampshire to Kittery. Interstate 95 has three Kittery exits. Route 103 is a scenic coastal drive through Kittery Point to York.

ESSENTIALS

Visitor Information Greater York Region Chamber of Commerce ⊠ *1 Stonewall La., off U.S. 1, York* ☎ *207/363–4422* ⊕ *www.gatewaytomaine. org.* **Kittery Visitor Information Center** ⊠ *U.S. 1 and I–95* ☎ *800/767–8709* ⊕ *www.mainetourism.com.*

WHERE TO EAT

$$$ ✕ **Chauncey Creek Lobster Pound.** From the road you can barely see the
SEAFOOD red roof hovering below the trees, but chances are you can see the cars
FAMILY parked at this popular outdoor restaurant along the high banks of the tidal river, beside a working pier. Brightly colored picnic tables fill the deck and an enclosed eating area. The menu has lots of fresh lobster choices and a raw bar with offerings like clams and oysters. Bring your own beer or wine if you desire alcohol. You can also bring sides and

DID YOU KNOW?

Maine may not have many sandy beaches or warm water, but the rocky shoreline, powerful ocean, and contrasting evergreens have inspired photographers and artists for years.

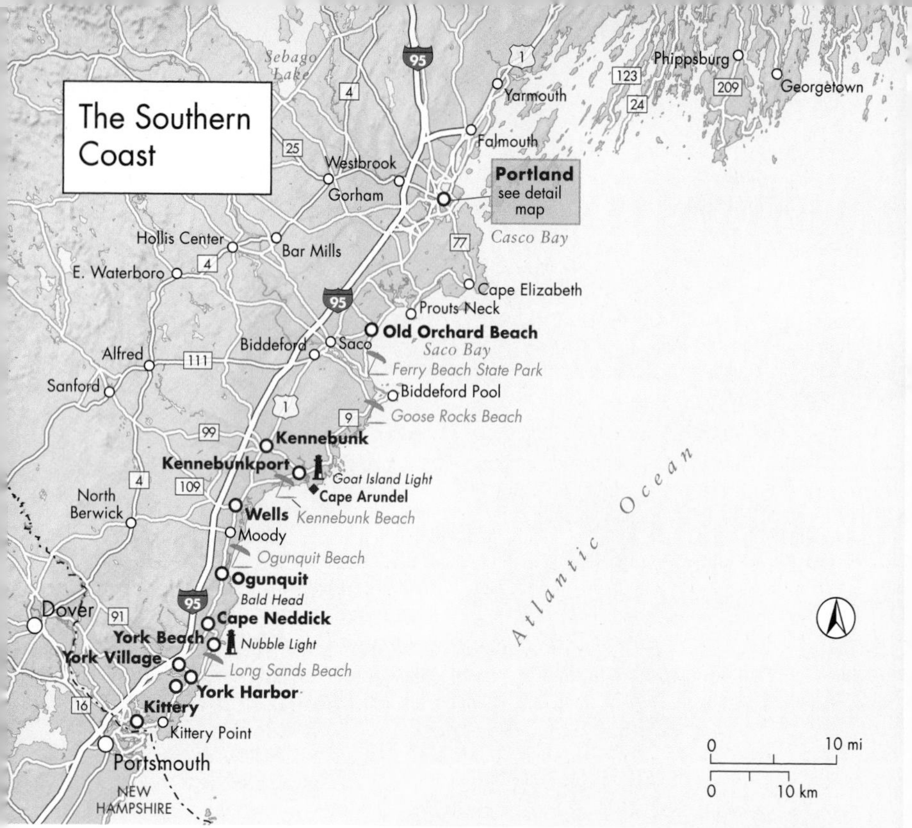

desserts that aren't on the menu. $ *Average main: $22* ✉ *16 Chauncey Creek Rd., Kittery Point* ☎ *207/439–1030* 🌐 *www.chaunceycreek.com* 🕓 *Closed Columbus Day–mid-May. Closed Mon. Labor Day–Columbus Day.*

SPORTS AND THE OUTDOORS

HIKING AND WALKING

Cutts Island Trail. For a peek into the Rachel Carson National Wildlife Refuge, this 2-mile trail leads into the 800-acre Brave Boat Harbor Division. It's one of only a handful of trails in its 11 divisions. It's a prime bird-watching area. There's a kiosk at the trailhead. ✉ *Seapoint Rd.* 🌐 *www.fws.gov/refuge/rachel_carson.*

YORK VILLAGE

8 miles north of Kittery via I–95, U.S. 1, and U.S. 1A.

The actual village of York is quite small, housing the town's basic components of post office, town hall, several shops and galleries, and a stretch of antique homes. As subdued as the town may feel today, the history of York Village reveals a far different character. One of the first permanently settled areas in the state of Maine, it was once witness to great destruction and fierce fighting during the French, Indian, and

British wars; towns and fortunes were sacked, yet the potential for prosperity encouraged the area's citizens continually to rebuild and start anew. Colonial York citizens enjoyed great wealth and success from fishing and lumber as well as a penchant for politics. Angered by the British-imposed taxes, York held its own little-known tea party in 1775 in protest.

GETTING HERE AND AROUND

York is Exit 7 off Interstate 95; follow signs to U.S. 1, the modern commercial strip. From here U.S. 1A winds to the village center and on to York Harbor and York Beach before looping back up to U.S. 1 in Cape Neddick.

EXPLORING

George Marshall Store Gallery. Storefront windows and bead-board trim at the George Marshall Store Gallery, built in 1867, pay homage to its past as a general store, but the focus here is on the present. Changing exhibits focus on prominent and up-and-coming regional artists. ✉ *140 Lindsay Rd.* ☎ *207/351–1083* ⊕ *www.georgemarshallstoregallery. com* ☉ *Mid-May–early Oct., Tues.–Sat. 10–5, Sun. 1–5; Apr.–mid-May and early Oct.–mid-Nov., Wed.–Sat. 10–4, Sun. 1–4; mid-Nov.–Mar., by appt.*

Museums of Old York. Nine historic 18th- and 19th-century buildings, clustered on York Street and along Lindsay Road and the York River, highlight York's rich history starting in early Colonial times. The Old York Gaol (1719) was once the King's Prison for the Province of Maine; inside are dungeons, cells, and the jailer's quarters. The many period rooms in the Emerson-Wilcox House—the main part was built in 1742—display items from daily life here in centuries past, including furniture from as early as the 1600s and an impressive ceramic dishware collection. The 1731 Elizabeth Perkins House reflects the Victorian style of its last occupants, the prominent Perkins family. Buy tickets at the Parsons Education Center, which has changing exhibits, or at the Old York Gaol. ■TIP➔ **Tickets are good for the season.** ✉ *Parsons Education Center, 3 Lindsay Rd.* ☎ *207/363–4974* ⊕ *www.oldyork. org* ☞ *$6 for one museum, $12 for all* ☉ *Memorial Day–mid-Oct., Tues.–Sat. 10–5, Sun. 1–5.*

Stonewall Kitchen. You've probably seen the kitchen's smartly labeled jars of gourmet chutneys, jams, jellies, salsas, and sauces in specialty stores back home. This complex houses the expansive flagship company store, which has a viewing area of the bottling process and stunning gardens. Sample all the mustards, salsas, and dressings you can stand, or have lunch at the café and take-out restaurant. The campus also houses a cooking school where you can join in evening or daytime courses. Reservations are required; most classes are shorter than two hours and cost $45 to $80. ✉ *2 Stonewall La., off U.S. 1* ☎ *877/899–8363* ⊕ *www. stonewallkitchen.com* ☉ *Mon.–Sat. 8–7, Sun. 9–6.*

SHOPPING

Bradley's Custom Framing & Gallery. Watercolors, oils, pastels, and pottery are among the artworks that can be had at Bradley's Custom Framing & Gallery, where many local artists are represented, including the photographer-owner. ✉ *244 York St.* ☎ *207/351–3110.*

Gateway Farmers' Market. Bring a basket for morning shopping at the Gateway Farmers' Market, held in the back lot at the Greater York Region Chamber of Commerce. You'll find fresh local produce, lots of baked goods and artisanal breads, local seafood and meat, fresh flowers, and handcrafted items like soaps and candles. It's a good place to gather the makings for a beach picnic. ✉ *1 Stonewall La., off U.S. 1* ⊕ *www.gatewayfarmersmarket.com* ⊗ *June and Sept.–Columbus Day, Sat. 9–1; July and Aug., Thurs. and Sat. 9–1.*

YORK HARBOR

1 mile from York Village via U.S. 1A.

A short trip from the village proper, York Harbor opens up to the water and offers many places to linger and explore. The harbor is busy with boats of all kinds, while the harbor beach is a good stretch of sand for swimming. Much more formal than the northward York Beach and much quieter, the area retains a somewhat more exclusive air. Perched along the cliffs on the north side of the harbor are huge "cottages" built by wealthy summer residents in the late 1800s, when the area became a premier seaside resort destination with several grand hotels.

GETTING HERE AND AROUND

After passing through York Village to York Harbor, originally called Lower Town, U.S. 1A winds around and heads north to York Beach's village center, a 4-mile trip.

EXPLORING

Sayward-Wheeler House. Built in 1718, the waterfront home was remodeled in the 1760s by Jonathan Sayward, a local merchant who had prospered in the West Indies trade. By 1860 his descendants had opened the house to the public to share the story of their Colonial ancestors. The house, accessible only by guided tour, preserves the decor of a prosperous New England family at the outset of the Revolutionary War. The parlor—considered one of the country's best-preserved Colonial interiors, with a tall clock and mahogany Chippendale-style chairs—looks pretty much as it did when Sayward lived here. ✉ *9 Barrell La. Extension* ☎ *207/384–2454* ⊕ *www.historicnewengland.org* ✉ *$5* ⊗ *June–mid-Oct., 2nd and 4th Sat. of month 11–5.*

WHERE TO EAT

$$$
SEAFOOD
✕ **Dockside Restaurant.** On an island-like peninsula overlooking York Harbor, this restaurant has plenty of seafood on the menu, including popular dishes like haddock stuffed with Maine shrimp and "drunken" lobster—sautéed lobster, scallops, shallots, and herbs in an Irish whiskey cream. There are also treats like beef tenderloin, slow-roasted duckling, seafood chowder, or cakes of native crab and wild mushrooms. Floor-to-ceiling windows in the stair-stepped modern dinning space transport

diners to the water beyond; every seat has a water view. Lighter fare is served in the cozy mahogany bar. Dockside is part of a 7-acre property with lodging rooms and suites in several buildings, from a grand 1895 summer home to condo-style quarters. [$] *Average main: $25* ✉ *22 Harris Island Rd., off Rte. 103, York* ☎ *207/363–2722* 🌐 *www.docksiderestaurant.com* 🕒 *Closed late Oct.–late May and Tues. in June and Sept.*

$$$ SEAFOOD 🍴 **Foster's Downeast Clambake.** Save your appetite for this one. Specializing in the traditional Maine clambake—a feast consisting of rich clam chowder, a pile of mussels and steamers, Maine lobster, corn on the cob, roasted potatoes and onions, and Maine blueberry crumb cake (phew!)—this massive complex provides musical entertainment as well as belly-busting meals. There are also several barbecue offerings. [$] *Average main: $28* ✉ *5 Axholme Rd., at U.S. 1A, York* ☎ *207/363–3255, 800/552–0242* 🌐 *www.fostersclambake.com* 🕒 *Closed early Sept.–late May and weekdays late May–mid-June.*

WHERE TO STAY

$$$ B&B/INN 🏨 **Inn at Tanglewood Hall.** The inn's artfully painted floors, lush wallpapers, and meticulous attention to detail are the fruits of a former designation as a designers' showcase home. **Pros:** authentic historic lodging; serene setting amid gardens; short walk to beaches. **Cons:** no water views. [$] *Rooms from: $195* ✉ *611 York St., York* ☎ *207/351–1075* 🌐 *www.tanglewoodhall.com* 🛏 *4 rooms, 2 suites* 🍽 *Breakfast.*

$$$$ B&B/INN 🏨 **Stage Neck Inn.** Since the 1870s, successive hotels have perched on this tiny rock-clad peninsula beside at York Harbor's entrance. **Pros:** elaborate full-breakfast buffet with scrumptious baked goods; poolside service and snack bar in season; rooms have balconies or deck areas. **Cons:** no suites. [$] *Rooms from: $283* ✉ *8 Stage Neck Rd., off U.S. 1A, York* ☎ *207/363–3850* 🌐 *www.stageneck.com* 🛏 *58 rooms* 🕒 *Closed for 2 wks after Jan. 1* 🍽 *Breakfast.*

$$$ B&B/INN 🏨 **York Harbor Inn.** A mid-17th-century fishing cabin with dark timbers and a fieldstone fireplace forms the heart of this historic inn, which now includes several neighboring buildings that have been added over the years. **Pros:** many rooms have harbor views; close to beaches, scenic walking trails. **Cons:** rooms vary greatly in style, size, and appeal. [$] *Rooms from: $179* ✉ *480 York St., York* ☎ *207/363–5119* 🌐 *www.yorkharborinn.com* 🛏 *60 rooms, 2 suites* 🍽 *Breakfast.*

SPORTS AND THE OUTDOORS

BIKING

Berger's Bike Shop. This former auto garage rents hybrid bikes for local excursions. ✉ *241 York St., York Village* ☎ *207/363–4070* 🌐 *www.bergersbikeshop.com.*

FISHING

Fish Tale Charters. Fish Tale Charters takes anglers on fly-fishing or light tackle charters in search of stripers or juvenile bluefin tuna; trips depart from Town Dock No. 2 in York Harbor. ✉ *Town Dock No. 2, 20 Harris Island Rd., York* ☎ *207/363–3874* 🌐 *www.maineflyfishing.net.*

Rip Tide Charters. Rip Tide Charters goes where the fish are—departure points vary, from Ogunquit to York and Portsmouth, New Hampshire.

It specializes in fly-fishing and light tackle for stripers, mackerel, and bluefish. ☎ *207/337–3608* ⊕ *www.mainestriperfishing.com.*

Shearwater Charters. Shearwater Charters offers light tackle and fly-fishing charters in the York River and along the shoreline from Kittery to Ogunquit. Bait-fishing trips are also available. Departures are from Town Dock #2 in York Harbor. ⊠ *Town Dock #2, 20 Harris Island Rd., York* ☎ *207/363–5324* ⊕ *www.mainestripers.net.*

HIKING AND WALKING

Cliff Walk and Fisherman's Walk. Two walking trails traverse the shore from near Harbor Beach. Just beside it in a small park, the Cliff Walk ascends its granite namesake, running past the summer "cottage" mansions at the harbor entrance. There are some steps, but as signs caution, tread carefully because of erosion. Fisherman's Walk, on the other hand, is an easy stroll. Starting across Stage Neck Road from the beach, it passes waterfront businesses, historic homes, and rocky harbor beaches on the way to York's beloved Wiggly Bridge. This pedestrian suspension bridge alongside Route 103 (there is minimal parking here) leads to Steedman Woods, a public preserve with a shaded loop trail along the York River estuary's ambling waters. You can also enter the preserve near the George Marshall Store in York Village ⊠ *Stage Neck Rd., off U.S. 1A.*

YORK BEACH

6 miles north of York Harbor via U.S. 1A.

Like many shorefront towns in Maine, York Beach has a long history of entertaining summer visitors. Take away today's bikinis and smartphones and it's easy to imagine squealing tourists adorned in the full-length bathing garb of the late 19th century. Just as they did back then, visitors today come here to eat ice cream, enjoy carnival-like novelties, and indulge in the sun and sea air.

York Beach is a real family destination, devoid of all things staid and stuffy—children are meant to be seen and heard here. Just beyond the sands of Short Sand Beach are a host of amusements, from bowling to indoor minigolf and the Fun-O-Rama arcade. Nubble Light is at the tip of the peninsula separating Long Sands and Short Sands beaches. The latter is mostly lined with unpretentious seasonal homes, though motels and restaurants are mixed in.

GETTING HERE AND AROUND

It's a scenic 6 miles to York Beach via the loop road U.S. 1A from its southern intersection with U.S. 1. Although 2 miles longer, it's generally faster to continue north on U.S. 1A to Cape Neddick and take U.S 1A south to the village center, home to Short Sands Beach. Here U.S. 1A is known as Ocean Avenue as it heads north from York Harbor along Long Sands Beach en route to York Beach village and Short Sands Beach. A trolley along U.S. 1 links the beaches in summer. You can also get from beach to beach on a series of residential streets that wind around Nubble Point between these beaches.

York Trolley Co. From late June through Labor Day, York Trolley Co.'s bright red trolleys link Short Sands Beach in York Beach village and nearby Long Sands Beach, running along U.S. 1A with a number of stops. Route maps can be picked up throughout York; fares are $1.50 one way, $3 round-trip. You can also connect with a shuttle service to Ogunquit. ☎ *207/363–9600* 🌐 *www.yorktrolley.com.*

EXPLORING

Nubble Light. On a small island just off the tip of the cape jutting dramatically into the Atlantic Ocean between Long Sands Beach and Short Sands Beach, Nubble Light is one of the most photographed lighthouses on the globe. Direct access is prohibited, but the small Sohier Park right across from the light has parking, historical placards, benches, and a seasonal information center that shares the 1879 light's history. ✉ *End of Nubble Rd., off U.S. 1A, York* ☎ *207/363–3569 Memorial Day weekend–Labor Day* 🌐 *www.nubblelight.org* 🕒 *Park, daily; information center, mid-Apr.–mid-May, daily 9–4; mid-May–late Oct. 9–4.*

FAMILY **York's Wild Kingdom.** Ringed by woods, this popular zoo has an impressive variety of exotic animals and is home to the state's only white Bengal tiger. There's a nostalgic charm to the amusement park, which offers discounts for kids under 13—the target market, since there are no large thrill rides. Many York Beach visitors come just to enjoy the ocean views from the Ferris wheel and share what's advertised as the "seaboard's largest fried dough." ✉ *23 Railroad Ave., off U.S. 1* ☎ *207/363–4911, 800/456–4911* 🌐 *www.yorkzoo.com* 🎟 *$14.75 for zoo; $21.25 for zoo and rides* 🕒 *Zoo late May–late Sept. daily 10–5; amusement park hrs vary.*

WHERE TO EAT AND STAY

$ AMERICAN 🍴 **The Goldenrod.** If you wanted to, you could eat nothing but the famous taffy here, made the same way today as it was back in 1896. The famous Goldenrod Kisses, some 50 tons of which are made per year, are a great attraction, and people line the windows to watch the taffy being made. Aside from the famous candy (there's penny candy, too), this eating place is family oriented, very reasonably priced, and a great place to get ice cream from the old-fashioned soda fountain. Breakfast is served all day, while the simple lunch menu of sandwiches and burgers doubles as dinner, along with a handful of entrées like baked haddock and meat loaf. [$] *Average main: $10* ✉ *2 Railroad Ave.* ☎ *207/363–2621* 🌐 *www.thegoldenrod.com* 🕒 *Closed mid-Oct.–mid-May.*

$$$$ HOTEL 🏨 **Union Bluff Hotel.** This massive, turreted structure still looks much the same as it did when it opened in the mid-19th century. **Pros:** many spectacular ocean views; in the middle of the action. **Cons:** rooms lack any charm or character befitting the inn's origins; not for those looking for a quiet getaway. [$] *Rooms from: $229* ✉ *8 Beach St.* ☎ *207/363–1333, 800/833–0721* 🌐 *www.unionbluff.com* 🛏 *65 rooms, 6 suites* 🍽 *No meals.*

NIGHTLIFE

Inn on the Blues. This hopping music club attracts national bands playing funk, jazz, and reggae, as well as blues. It's open April through December and weekends only in the shoulder seasons. ✉ *7 Ocean Ave., York* ☎ *207/351–3221* 🌐 *www.innontheblues.com.*

CAPE NEDDICK

1 mile north of York Beach via U.S. 1A.

Cape Neddick is one of the less developed of York's areas, but there's not much public access to the water. It has many modest homes, with a sprinkling of businesses catering to locals and visitors. There are a few restaurants and inns but no distinct village hub. Cape Neddick Harbor is at its southern end, beyond York Beach village.

GETTING HERE AND AROUND

U.S. 1A returns to U.S. 1 in Cape Neddick after its 7-mile loop down to the coast starting in southern York near Exit 7 off Interstate 95. U.S. 1 continues north to Ogunquit.

EXPLORING

Mount Agamenticus Park. A park sits atop this humble summit of 692 feet, one of the highest points along the Atlantic seaboard. That may not seem like much, but if you choose to hike to the top, you will be rewarded with incredible views all the way to the White Mountains in New Hampshire. If you don't want to hoof it (though it's not very steep), there is parking at the top. ✉ *Mountain Road, off U.S. 1* ☎ *207/361–1102* 🌐 *www.agamenticus.org* 🕒 *Daily dawn–dusk.*

WHERE TO EAT

$ AMERICAN 🍴 **Flo's Steamed Hot Dogs.** Yes, it seems crazy to highlight a hot-dog stand, but this is no ordinary place. Who would guess that a hot dog could make it into *Saveur* and *Gourmet* magazines? There is something grand about this shabby, red-shingle shack that has been dealing dogs since 1959. The line is out the door most days, but this place is so efficient that the wait isn't long. Flo has passed on, but her son and daughter-in-law keep the business going, satisfying thousands of customers each year. The classic here has mayo and the special sauce—consisting of, among other things, onions and molasses (you can buy a bottle to take home, and you'll want to). [$] *Average main: $3* ✉ *1359 U.S. 1* 🌐 *www.floshotdogs.com* 💳 *No credit cards* 🕒 *Closed Wed. No dinner.*

$$$ ECLECTIC 🍴 **Frankie & Johnny's Restaurant.** If you've had about all the fried seafood you can stand, try this hip spot that focuses on creative cuisine served with flair. There are lots of seafood, poultry, and meat options, homemade pasta choices, and always a few vegetarian dishes (special requests like gluten-free are happily accommodated). The toasted peppercorn-seared sushi-grade tuna, served with coconut risotto on gingered vegetables, is excellent. Pork served with a sweet pear-cream sauce is also a signature dish. Even the breads and most desserts are made by the chef. Entrées include really large dinner salads with fruit and nuts as well as veggies atop the greens. You're welcome to bring your own libations; only cash and checks are accepted. [$] *Average main: $28*

Ogunquit's Perkins Cove is a pleasant place to admire the boats—and wonder at the origin of their names.

✉ *1594 U.S. 1* ☎ *207/363–1909* ⊕ *www.frankie-johnnys.com* ▭ *No credit cards* ◷ *Closed Mon., Tues., and mid-Dec.–early Feb. Closed Wed. mid-Feb.–June and Sept.–early Dec. No lunch.*

SPORTS AND THE OUTDOORS

FISHING

Eldredge Bros. Fly Shop. This shop offers various guided fishing trips, private casting lessons, and, come June, striper and trout "schools." There are fly-tying and rod-building seminars in the off-season. Kayak rentals and rod-and-reel rentals are also available. ✉ *1480 U.S. 1* ☎ *207/363–9269, 877/427–9345* ⊕ *www.eldredgeflyshop.com.*

KAYAKING

Excursions Coastal Maine Outfitting Co. Hop on one of the regularly scheduled guided kayak trips with Excursions Coastal Maine Outfitting Co. You can cruise along the shoreline or sign up for an overnight paddle. Reservations are recommended; trips start at $60. Classes are also offered. ✉ *1740 U.S. 1* ☎ *207/363–0181* ⊕ *www.excursionsinmaine. com.*

SHOPPING

Jeremiah Campbell & Co. Reproductions of 18th- and 19th-century home furnishings are the specialty of Jeremiah Campbell & Co. Everything here is handcrafted, from rugs, decoys, furniture, and lighting to glassware. ✉ *1537 U.S. 1* ☎ *207/363–8499* ⊕ *www.jeremiahcampbell.com* ◷ *Closed Wed.*

OGUNQUIT

8 miles north of the Yorks via U.S. 1.

A resort village since the late 19th century, stylish Ogunquit gained fame as an artists' colony. Today it has become a mini Provincetown, with a gay population that swells in summer. Many inns and small clubs cater to a primarily gay and lesbian clientele. The nightlife in Ogunquit revolves around the precincts of Ogunquit Square and Perkins Cove, where people stroll, often enjoying an after-dinner ice cream cone or espresso. For a scenic drive, take Shore Road from downtown to the 175-foot Bald Head Cliff; you'll be treated to views up and down the coast. On a stormy day the surf can be quite wild here.

GETTING HERE AND AROUND

Parking in the village and at the beach is costly and limited, so leave your car at the hotel and hop the trolley. It costs $1.50 a trip and runs Memorial Day weekend until Columbus Day, with weekend-only service for the first few weeks. From Perkins Cove the trolley runs through town along Shore Road and then down to Ogunquit Beach; it also stops along U.S. 1.

ESSENTIALS

Transportation Information Ogunquit Trolley ☎ *207/646–1411* 🌐 *www.ogunquittrolley.com* 🎫 *$1.50.*

Visitor Information Ogunquit Chamber of Commerce ✉ *36 Main St.* ☎ *207/646–2939* 🌐 *www.ogunquit.org.*

EXPLORING

Perkins Cove. This neck of land off Shore Road in the lower part of Oqunquit village has a jumble of sea-beaten fish houses and buildings that were part of an art school. These have largely been transformed by the tide of tourism into shops and restaurants. When you've had your fill of browsing, stroll out along **Marginal Way,** a mile-long footpath that hugs the shore of a rocky promontory known as Israel's Head. Benches allow you to appreciate the open sea vistas. ✉ *Perkins Cove Rd., off Shore Rd.*

WHERE TO EAT AND STAY

$ AMERICAN 🍴 **Amore Breakfast.** You could hardly find a more satisfying, full-bodied breakfast than at this smart and busy joint just shy of the entrance to Perkins Cove. A lighthearted mix of retro advertising signs adorns the walls of this bright, open, and very bustling dining room. You won't find tired standards here—the only pancakes are German potato. The Oscar Madison omelet combines crabmeat with asparagus and Swiss, topped with a béarnaise sauce. For a really decadent start, opt for the Banana Foster: pecan-coated, cream cheese–stuffed French toast with a side of sautéed bananas in rum syrup. Next door, at the Cafe Amore, you can pick up sandwiches and other light fare. [$] *Average main: $10* ✉ *309 Shore Rd.* ☎ *207/646–6661* 🌐 *www.amorebreakfast.com* 🕒 *Closed mid-Dec.–early Apr. No dinner.*

$$$ HOTEL 🏨 **Ogunquit Resort Motel.** Right along U.S. 1 just a mile north of Ogunquit village, this affordable place is a great choice for families. **Pros:** Continental breakfast is included; good-size rooms; fitness center. **Cons:**

close to highway; no lawns or grounds. [$] *Rooms from: $199* ✉ *719 Main St.* ☎ *877/646–8336* 🌐 *www.ogunquitresort.com* 🛏 *77 rooms, 10 suites* 🍴 *Breakfast.*

WELLS

5 miles north of Ogunquit via U.S. 1.

Lacking any kind of noticeable village center, Wells could be easily overlooked as nothing more than a commercial stretch on U.S. 1 between Ogunquit and the Kennebunks. But look more closely—this is a place where people come to enjoy some of the best beaches on the coast. The town included Ogunquit until 1980. Today this family-oriented beach community has 7 miles of densely populated shoreline, along with nature preserves where you can explore salt marshes and tidal pools.

GETTING HERE AND AROUND

Just $1 per trip, the seasonal Shoreline Trolley serves Wells Beach and Crescent Beach and has many stops along U.S. 1 at motels, campgrounds, restaurants, and so on. You can also catch it at the Wells Transportation Center when the Downeaster (the Amtrak train from Boston to Maine) pulls in.

ESSENTIALS

Transportation Information Shoreline Trolley ☎ *207/324–5762* 🌐 *www.shorelineexplorer.com* 🎟 *$1.*

Visitor Information Wells Chamber of Commerce ✉ *136 Post Rd.* ☎ *207/646–2451* 🌐 *www.wellschamber.org.*

EXPLORING

Rachel Carson National Wildlife Refuge. At the headquarters of the Rachel Carson National Wildlife Refuge, which has 11 divisions from Kittery to Cape Elizabeth, is the Carson Trail, a one-mile loop. The trail traverses a salt marsh and a white-pine forest where migrating birds and waterfowl of many varieties are regularly spotted, and it borders Branch Brook and the Merriland River. ✉ *321 Port Rd.* ☎ *207/646–9226* 🌐 *www.fws.gov/northeast/rachelcarson* 🕒 *Daily sunrise to sunset.*

QUICK BITES

Congdon's Doughnuts. How would you like a really superior doughnut that the same family has been making since 1945? Congdon's Doughnuts bakes about 40 different varieties, though the plain one really gives you an idea of just how good these doughnuts are. Plain, honey-dipped, and black raspberry jelly are the biggest sellers. There are drive-through and takeout windows, or you can sit inside and have breakfast or lunch. Waits can be long for breakfast in summer. ✉ ***1090 Post Rd.*** ☎ ***207/646–4219*** 🌐 ***www.congdons.com.***

WHERE TO EAT AND STAY

$$ SEAFOOD

🍴 **Billy's Chowder House.** Locals and vacationers head to this classic roadside seafood restaurant in the midst of a salt marsh en route to Wells Beach. They come for the generous lobster rolls, haddock sandwiches, and chowders, but there are plenty of non-seafood choices, too. Big windows in the bright dining rooms overlook the marsh, part of the Rachel Carson National Wildlife Refuge. $ *Average main: $15* ✉ *216 Mile Rd.* ☎ *207/646–7558* ⊕ *www.billyschowderhouse.com* ☉ *Closed mid-Dec.–mid-Jan.*

$$
DINER

× **Maine Diner.** One look at the 1953 exterior and you start craving good diner food. You'll get a little more than you're expecting—how many greasy spoons make an award-winning lobster pie? That's the house favorite, as well as a heavenly seafood chowder. There's plenty of fried seafood in addition to the usual diner fare, and breakfast is served all day. Check out the adjacent gift shop, Remember the Maine. $ *Average main: $15* ✉ *2265 Post Rd.* ☎ *207/646–4441* ⊕ *www.mainediner.com* ☉ *Closed at least 1 wk in Jan.*

$$$$
B&B/INN
Fodor's Choice
★

▦ **Haven by the Sea.** Once the summer mission of St. Martha's Church in Kennebunkport, this exquisite inn has retained many of the original details from its former life as a seaside church, including cathedral ceilings and stained-glass windows. **Pros:** unusual structure with elegant appointments; tucked-away massage room. **Cons:** not an in-town location. $ *Rooms from: $239* ✉ *59 Church St.* ☎ *207/646–4194* ⊕ *www. havenbythesea.com* ⤳ *7 rooms, 2 suites, 1 apartment* ⦿❘ *Breakfast.*

SPORTS AND THE OUTDOORS

BEACHES

With its thousands of acres of marsh and preserved land, Wells is a great place to spend a lot of time outdoors. Nearly 7 miles of sand stretch along the boundaries of Wells, making beachgoing a prime occupation. Tidal pools sheltered by rocks are filled with all manner of creatures awaiting discovery. During the summer season a pay-and-display (no quarters, receipt goes on dashboard) parking system is in place at the public beaches.

A summer trolley serves **Crescent Beach,** along Webhannet Drive, and **Wells Beach,** at the end of Mile Road off U.S. 1. There is another parking lot, but no trolley stop, at the north end of Atlantic Avenue, which runs north along the shore from the end of Mile Road. Stretching north from the jetty at Wells Harbor is **Drakes Island Beach** (end of Drakes Island Road off U.S. 1). Lifeguards are on hand at all the beaches, and all have public restrooms.

Crescent Beach. Lined with summer homes, this sandy beach is busy in the summer. The beach and the water are surprisingly clean, considering all the traffic. The swimming's good, and beachgoers can also explore tidal pools and look for seals on the rocks nearby. **Amenities:** food and drink; lifeguards; parking (fee); toilets. **Best for:** swimming. ✉ *Webhannet Dr., south of Mile Rd.* ☎ *207/646–5113.*

Drakes Island Beach. Smaller and quieter than the other two beaches in Wells, Drake's Island Beach is also a little wilder, with rolling sand dunes and access to salt-marsh walking trails at an adjacent estuary. The ice cream truck swings by regularly in the summer. **Amenities:** lifeguards; parking (fee); toilets. **Best for:** walking. ✉ *Island Beach Rd., 1 mile southwest of U.S. 1* ☎ *207/646–5113.*

Wells Beach. The northern end of a two-mile stretch of golden sand, Wells Beach is popular with families and surfers, who line up in the swells and preen on the boardwalk near the arcade and snack shop. The beach's northern tip is a bit quieter, with a long rock jetty perfect for strolling. **Amenities:** food and drink; lifeguards; parking (fee); toilets. **Best for:** surfing; walking. ⊠ *Atlantic Ave., north of Mile Rd.* ☎ *207/646–5113.*

Wheels and Waves. Rent bikes, surfboards, wet suits, boogie boards, kayaks, and all sorts of outdoor gear at Wheels and Waves. ⊠ *365 Post Rd.* ☎ *207/646–5774* ⊕ *www.wheelsnwaves.com.*

KENNEBUNK AND KENNEBUNKPORT

5 miles north of Wells via U.S. 1.

The town centers of Kennebunk and Kennebunkport are separated by 5 miles and two rivers, but united by a common history and a vibe of seaside affluence. Kennebunkport has been a resort area since the 19th century, but its most famous residents have made it even more popular—the presidential Bush family is often in residence in its immense home, which sits dramatically out on Walker's Point on Cape Arundel. The wealth here is as tangible as the sharp sea breezes and the sounds of seagulls overhead. Newer mansions have sprung up alongside the old; a great way to see them is to take a slow drive out along the cape on Ocean Avenue.

Sometimes bypassed on the way to its sister town, Kennebunk has its own appeal. In the 19th century the town was a major shipbuilding center; docks lined the river with hundreds of workers busily crafting the vessels that would bring immense fortune to some of the area's residents. Although the trade is long gone, the evidence that remains of this great wealth exists in Kennebunk's mansions. Kennebunk is a classic small New England town, with an inviting shopping district, steepled churches, and fine examples of 18th- and 19th-century brick and clapboard homes. There are also plenty of natural spaces for walking, swimming, birding, and biking—the Kennebunks' major beaches are here.

Kennebunk's main village sits along U.S. 1, extending west from the Mousam River. The Lower Village is along Routes 9 and 35, 4 miles down Route 35 from the main village, and the drive between the two keeps visitors agog with the splendor of the area's mansions, spread out on both sides of Route 35. To get to the grand and gentle beaches of Kennebunk, continue straight (the road becomes Beach Avenue) at the intersection with Route 9. If you turn left instead, Route 9 will take you across the Kennebunk River, into Kennebunkport's touristy downtown, called Dock Square (or sometimes just "the Port"), a commercial area with restaurants, shops, boat cruises, and galleries. Here you'll find the most activity (and crowds) in the Kennebunks.

GETTING HERE AND AROUND

Take the Intown Trolley for narrated 45-minute jaunts that run daily from Memorial Day weekend through Columbus Day. The $16 fare is valid for the day, so you can hop on and off—or start your journey—at any of the stops. The route includes Kennebunk's beaches and Lower Village and as well as neighboring Kennebunkport's scenery and sights.

The main stop is at 21 Ocean Avenue in Kennebunkport, around the corner from Dock Square.

ESSENTIALS

Visitor Information Intown Trolley ☎ *207/967–3686* ⊕ *www.intowntrolley. com* 🖃 *$16.* **Kennebunk-Kennebunkport Chamber of Commerce** ⊠ *16 Water St.* ☎ *207/967–0857* ⊕ *www.visitthekennebunks.com.*

TOURS

To take a little walking tour of Kennebunk's most notable structures, begin at the Federal-style Brick Store Museum at 117 Main Street. Head south on Main Street (turn left out of the museum) to see several extraordinary 18th- and early-19th-century homes, including the **Lexington Elms** at No. 99 (1799), the **Horace Porter House** at No. 92 (1848), and the **Benjamin Brown House** at No. 85 (1788).

When you've had your fill of historic homes, head back up toward the museum, pass the 1773 **First Parish Unitarian Church** (its Asher Benjamin–style steeple contains an original Paul Revere bell), and turn right onto **Summer Street**. This street is an architectural showcase, revealing an array of styles from Colonial to Federal. Walking past these grand beauties will give you a real sense of the economic prowess and glamour of the long-gone shipbuilding industry.

For a guided 90-minute architectural walking tour of Summer Street, contact the museum at ☎ *207/985–4802.* You can also purchase a $4.95 map that marks historic buildings or a $15.95 guidebook, *Windows on the Past.*

For a dramatic walk along Kennebunkport's rocky coastline and beneath the views of Ocean Avenue's grand mansions, head out on the **Parson's Way Shore Walk**, a paved 4.8-mile round-trip. Begin at Dock Square and follow Ocean Avenue along the river, passing the Colony Hotel and St. Ann's Church, all the way to Walker's Point. Simply turn back from here.

EXPLORING

Brick Store Museum. The cornerstone of this block-long preservation of early-19th-century commercial and residential buildings is William Lord's Brick Store. Built as a dry-goods store in 1825 in the Federal style, the building has an openwork balustrade across the roof line, granite lintels over the windows, and paired chimneys. Exhibits chronicle the Kennebunk area's history and early American decorative and fine arts. The museum leads architectural walking tours of Kennebunk's National Historic District by appointment from late May through September. For $4.95 you can also purchase a map that marks historic buildings. ⊠ *117 Main St.* ☎ *207/985–4802* ⊕ *www.brickstoremuseum. org* 🖃 *$7.50* ⊙ *Tues.–Fri. 10–4:30, Sat. 10–1.*

Dock Square. Clothing boutiques, T-shirt shops, art galleries, and restaurants line this bustling square and spread out along the nearby streets and alleys. Walk onto the drawbridge to admire the tidal Kennebunk River. Cross to the other side and you are in the Lower Village of neighboring Kennebunk. ⊠ *Dock Sq., Kennebunkport.*

First Families Kennebunkport Museum. Also known as White Columns, the imposing Greek Revival mansion with Doric columns is furnished with the belongings of four generations of the Perkins-Nott family. From mid-July through mid-October, the 1853 house is open for guided tours and also serves as a gathering place for village walking tours. It is owned by the Kennebunkport Historical Society, which has several other historic buildings a mile away at 125–135 North Street, including an old jail and schoolhouse. ✉ *8 Maine St., Kennebunkport* ☎ *207/967–2751* ⊕ *www.kporthistory.org* 🏷 *$10* ⊘ *Mid-July–mid-Oct., Mon.–Sat. 11–5.*

First Parish of Kennebunk Unitarian Universalist Church. Built in 1773, just before the American Revolution, this stunning church is a marvel. The 1804 Asher Benjamin–style steeple stands proudly atop the village, and the sounds of the original Paul Revere bell can be heard for miles. The church holds Sunday services at 9:30 am in the summer (10:30 the rest of the year). ✉ *114 Main St.* ☎ *207/985–3700* ⊕ *www. uukennebunk.org.*

Goose Rocks. Three-mile-long Goose Rocks, a 10-minute drive north of town, has plenty of shallow pools for exploring and a good long stretch of smooth sand. It's a favorite of families with small children. Pick up a $15 daily permit at Kennebunkport Town Hall. **Amenities:** parking (fee). **Best for:** walking. ✉ *Dyke Rd., off Rte. 9, Kennebunkport.*

Kennebunk Plains. For an unusual experience, visit this 135-acre grasslands habitat that is home to several rare and endangered species. Locals call it Blueberry Plains, and a good portion of the area is abloom with the hues of ripening wild blueberries in late July. After August 1 you are welcome to pick and eat all the berries you can find. The area is maintained by the Nature Conservancy. ✉ *Webber Hill Rd., 4½ miles northwest of town* ☎ *207/729–5181* ⊕ *www.nature.org* ⊘ *Daily sunrise–sunset.*

FAMILY **Seashore Trolley Museum.** Streetcars were built here from 1872 to 1972, including trolleys for major metropolitan areas: Boston to Budapest, New York to Nagasaki, San Francisco to Sydney. Many of them are beautifully restored and displayed. Best of all, you can take a trolley ride for nearly 4 miles on the tracks of the former Atlantic Shoreline trolley line, with a stop along the way at the museum restoration shop, where trolleys are transformed from junk into gems. The outdoor museum is self-guided. ✉ *195 Log Cabin Rd., Kennebunkport* ☎ *207/967–2712* ⊕ *www.trolleymuseum.org* 🏷 *$10* ⊘ *Memorial Day–Columbus Day, daily 10–5.*

WHERE TO EAT

$$ ✕ **Duffy's Tavern & Grill.** Every small town needs its own lively and
AMERICAN friendly spot, and this bustling spot is Kennebunk's favorite, housed in a former shoe factory with exposed brick, soaring ceilings, and hardwood floors. Right outside are the tumbling waters of the Mousam River as it flows from the dam. There's a large bar with overhead televisions and plenty of seating in the main room, plus a less captivating back section. You'll find lots of comfortable standards like burgers, pizza, and the popular fish-and-chips. The tasty onion rings are hand

dipped. [$] *Average main: $16* ✉ *4 Main St.* ☎ *207/985–0050* 🌐 *www.duffyskennebunk.com.*

$$ AMERICAN 🍴 **Federal Jack's.** Run by the Kennebunkport Brewing Company, this two-story complex is near the bridge from Lower Village into Kennebunkport. All the beers are handcrafted on-site, including Blue Fin Stout and Goat Island Light—try the sampler if you can't decide. In the upstairs restaurant the American pub-style menu includes plenty of seafood; the clam chowder is rich and satisfying. There's also Sunday brunch buffet. The restaurant has two dining rooms and a huge deck that packs in the crowds in the summer. There's live entertainment Thursday through Saturday (Sunday in summer). [$] *Average main: $14* ✉ *8 Western Ave.* ☎ *207/967–4322* 🌐 *www.federaljacks.com.*

$$$ SEAFOOD 🍴 **Mabel's Lobster Claw.** Since the 1950s, Mabel's has been serving lobsters, homemade pies, and lots of seafood for lunch and dinner in this tiny dwelling out on Ocean Avenue. The decor includes paneled walls, wooden booths, autographed photos of various TV stars (plus members of the Bush family). There's outside seating, and paper place mats that illustrate how to eat a Maine lobster. The house favorite is the Lobster Savannah—split and filled with scallops, shrimp, and mushrooms and baked in a Newburg sauce. Save room for the peanut-butter ice cream pie. There's also a take-out window where you can order ice cream and food. [$] *Average main: $25* ✉ *124 Ocean Ave., Kennebunkport* ☎ *207/967–2562* 🌐 *www.mabelslobster.com* ⏲ *Closed Nov.–early Apr.*

$$$ MODERN AMERICAN 🍴 **Pier 77 Restaurant.** The view takes center stage at this establishment. On the ground level Pier 77 is the fine-dining portion with large windows overlooking the harbor. Every seat has a nice view at the restaurant, which serves up sophisticated fare, focusing on meats and seafood. The place is vibrant with live music in summer and a great place for cocktails on the water. Tucked down below, the tiny, tiny but oh-so-funky-and-fun Ramp Bar & Grill pays homage to a really good burger, fried seafood, and other pub-style choices. [$] *Average main: $25* ✉ *77 Pier Rd., Cape Porpoise* ☎ *207/967–8500* 🌐 *www.pier77restaurant.com.*

WHERE TO STAY

$$$$ B&B/INN 🏨 **Bufflehead Cove Inn.** On the Kennebunk River, this gray-shingle B&B sits at the end of a winding dirt road amid fields and apple trees. **Pros:** pastoral setting; riverfront location; perfect for a serene getaway. **Cons:** two-night minimum stay on weekends. [$] *Rooms from: $235* ✉ *18 Bufflehead Cove Rd.* ☎ *207/967–3879* 🌐 *www.buffleheadcove.com* 🛏 *4 rooms, 1 suite, 1 cottage* ⏲ *Closed mid-Nov.–Apr.* 🍽 *Breakfast.*

$$$$ B&B/INN 🏨 **Cape Arundel Inn.** This shingle-style 19th-century mansion, originally one of the area's many summer "cottages," commands a magnificent ocean view that takes in the Bush estate at Walker's Point. **Pros:** extraordinary views from most rooms; across the road from rockbound coast. **Cons:** not for the budget minded. [$] *Rooms from: $410* ✉ *208 Ocean Ave., Kennebunkport* ☎ *207/967–2125* 🌐 *www.capearundelinn.com* 🛏 *14 rooms, 1 suite* ⏲ *Closed late Dec.–late Feb.* 🍽 *Breakfast.*

$$$$ B&B/INN Fodor's Choice ★ 🏨 **The Captain Lord Mansion.** Of all the mansions in Kennebunkport's historic district that have been converted to inns, the 1814 Captain Lord Mansion is the stateliest and most sumptuously appointed. **Pros:** beautiful landscaped grounds; bikes for guests; putting green. **Cons:**

Kennebunk is a classic New England town, while Kennebunkport (pictured) has more upscale inns and shopping.

not a beachfront location. $ *Rooms from: $329* ⊠ *6 Pleasant St., Kennebunkport* ☎ *207/967–3141, 800/522–3141* ⊕ *www.captainlord.com* ⇆ *18 rooms, 2 suites* ❍❘ *Breakfast.*

$$$
RESORT
FAMILY
Fodor's Choice
★

The Colony Hotel. You can't miss this place—it's grand, white, and incredibly large, set majestically atop a rise overlooking the ocean. **Pros:** private beach; heated saltwater swimming pool; activities and entertainment for all ages. **Cons:** not intimate. $ *Rooms from: $199* ⊠ *140 Ocean Ave., Kennebunkport* ☎ *207/967–3331, 800/552–2363* ⊕ *www.colonymaine.com* ⇆ *112 rooms, 11 suites, 2 cottages* ❍ *Closed Nov.–mid-May* ❍❘ *Breakfast.*

$$$$
HOTEL
FAMILY

The Seaside. This handsome seaside property has been in the hands of the Severance family since 1667. **Pros:** great ocean views from upper-floor rooms; tasty breakfast; rates drop significantly in winter. **Cons:** motel-style rooms; not an in-town location. $ *Rooms from: $249* ⊠ *80 Beach Ave.* ☎ *207/967–4461, 800/967–4461* ⊕ *www. kennebunkbeachmaine.com* ⇆ *22 rooms* ❍❘ *Breakfast.*

$$$
B&B/INN

Waldo Emerson Inn. The home itself is a historical gold mine, made grand with unusual maritime architectural touches by a shipbuilder in 1784. **Pros:** good base for exploring Kennebunk and Kennebunkport; authentic historic lodging; complimentary afternoon tea. **Cons:** some steep stairs; no water views or beachfront; not in town. $ *Rooms from: $170* ⊠ *108 Summer St.* ☎ *207/985–4250, 877/521–8776* ⊕ *www. waldoemersoninn.com* ⇆ *4 rooms* ❍❘ *Breakfast.*

$$$$
B&B/INN

White Barn Inn. For a romantic overnight stay, look no further than the exclusive White Barn Inn, known for its attentive, pampering service. **Pros:** about 10 minutes' walk to the beach; elegant spa offers it all; helpful concierge service. **Cons:** prices are steep. $ *Rooms from: $465*

⊠ *37 Beach Ave.* ☎ *207/967–2321* ⊕ *www.whitebarninn.com* ⇆ *13 rooms, 9 suites, 5 cottages* ⚹❘ *Breakfast.*

SPORTS AND THE OUTDOORS

BEACHES

Gooch's Beach. Kennebunk has three beaches, one following the other along Beach Avenue, which is lined with cottages and old Victorians. The most northerly, and closest to downtown Kennebunkport, is Gooch's Beach, the main swimming beach. Next is stony Kennebunk Beach, followed by Mother's Beach, which is popular with families. There's a small playground and tidal puddles for splashing, and rock outcroppings lessen the waves. **Amenities:** lifeguards; parking (fee); toilets. **Best for:** walking; swimming. ⊠ *Beach Ave., south of Hwy. 9.*

FISHING

Cast-Away Fishing Charters. Find and catch fish with Cast-Away Fishing Charters. The captain also offers a lobstering trip that's fun for kids, who can help haul in the traps. ⊠ *Performance Marine, 4-A Western Ave.* ☎ *207/284–1740* ⊕ *www.castawayfishingcharters.com.*

FAMILY **Rugosa.** Lobster-trap hauling trips in the scenic waters off The Kennebunks run daily aboard the *Rugosa* from Memorial Day weekend through early October. ⊠ *Nonantum Resort, 95 Ocean Ave., Kennebunkport* ☎ *207/468–4095* ⊕ *www.rugosalobstertours.com.*

WHALE-WACHING

First Chance. This company leads whale-watching cruises on 85-foot *Nick's Chance.* If you don't see a whale, you get a ticket for a free trip. Scenic lobster cruises are also offered aboard 65-foot *Kylie's Chance.* Trips run daily in summer and on weekends in the shoulder season. ⊠ *Performance Marine, 4-A Western Ave.* ☎ *207/967–5507* ⊕ *www.firstchancewhalewatch.com.*

SHOPPING

Abacus. This shop sells eclectic crafts, jewelry, and furniture. ⊠ *2 Ocean Ave., at Dock Sq., Kennebunkport* ☎ *207/967–0111* ⊕ *www.abacusgallery.com.*

Maine Art. Showcasing works by artists from Maine and New England, Maine Art has a two-story gallery with a sculpture garden. There's also a gallery space on Western Avenue. ⊠ *10 Chase Hill Rd.* ☎ *207/967–0049* ⊕ *www.maine-art.com.*

Mast Cove Galleries. Since 1979, Mast Cove Galleries has been selling paintings and sculpture by artists from New England and beyond. It occupies the barn and first floor of the owner's 1851 village home, which has a sculpture garden. The gallery hosts indoor jazz and blues concerts year-round. ⊠ *2 Mast Cove Ln., Kennebunkport* ☎ *207/967–3453* ⊕ *www.mastcove.com.*

EN ROUTE For a rewarding drive that goes into the reaches of the coastline on the way to Old Orchard Beach, head out of Kennebunkport on Route 9. You'll soon come to the fishing village of Cape Porpoise, where the pier has wondrous views. Continuing on Route 9, plan to do some beach walking at Goose Rocks Beach or Fortunes Rocks Beach, both ideal for stretching your legs or just looking for shells or critters in the tide pools. (Pick up a parking permit first.) Route 9 winds through wooded areas, then heads past the charming resort villages of Camp Ellis and Ocean Park. You could pack a picnic and spend some time at Ferry Beach State Park. The varied landscapes here include forested sections, swamp, beach, a rare stand of tupelo (black gum) trees, and lots of dunes. There are a few miles of marked trails to hike.

OLD ORCHARD BEACH

15 miles north of Kennebunkport; 18 miles south of Portland.

Back in the late 19th century, Old Orchard Beach was a classic, upscale, place-to-be-seen resort area. The railroad brought wealthy families looking for entertainment and the benefits of the fresh sea air. Although a good bit of this aristocratic hue has dulled in more recent times—admittedly, the place is more than a little pleasantly tacky these days—Old Orchard Beach remains a good place for those looking for entertainment by the sea. Many visitors are French Canadian.

The center of the action is a 7-mile strip of sand beach and its accompanying amusement park. Despite the summertime crowds and fried-food odors, the atmosphere can be captivating. During the 1940s and '50s the pier had a dance hall where stars of the time performed. Fire claimed the end of the pier—at one time it jutted out nearly 1,800 feet into the sea—but booths with games and candy concessions still line both sides. In summer the town sponsors fireworks (on Thursday night). Places to stay run the gamut from cheap motels to cottage colonies to full-service seasonal hotels. You won't find free parking in town, but there are ample lots. Amtrak has a seasonal stop here.

GETTING HERE AND AROUND

From Interstate 95, get off at Exit 32 and follow signs. Traveling from the south on U.S. 1, Route 5 heads into town.

ESSENTIALS

Visitor Information Old Orchard Beach Chamber of Commerce ✉ *11 First St.* ☎ *207/934–2500, 800/365–9386* ⊕ *www.oldorchardbeachmaine.com.*

EXPLORING

Ocean Park. A world away from the beach scene lies Ocean Park, on the southwestern edge of town. Locals and visitors like to keep the separation distinct, touting their area as a more peaceful and wholesome family-style village (to that end, there are no alcohol or tobacco sales in this little haven). This vacation community was founded in 1881 by Free Will Baptist leaders as a summer assembly with both religious and educational purposes, following the example of Chautauqua, New York. The 1881 Temple, in an unusual octagon shape, is on the National Register of Historic Places. Today the community hosts an impressive variety of cultural events, from concerts to sand sculpture contests. There's even a public shuffleboard area for vacationers not interested in the neon carnival attractions about a mile up the road. Get an old-fashioned raspberry-lime rickey at the Ocean Park Soda Fountain, at Furber Park. ✉ *14 Temple Ave., Ocean Park* ☎ *207/934–9068* ⊕ *www.oceanpark.org.*

WHERE TO EAT

$$
ECLECTIC

✕ **The Landmark.** In a 1910 Victorian home, this elegant eatery's tables are set either on the glassed-in porch or within high, tin-ceiling rooms. Candles and a collection of fringed Art Nouveau lamps provide a gentle light. The menu has a good selection of seafood and meats, many treated with flavors from various parts of the globe. It's the kind of menu that encourages you to try new things, and you definitely won't be disappointed. From July through Labor Day you can eat outside on the stone patio, sheltered by umbrellas, and order from an "in the rough" dinner menu, with everything cooked on the adjacent grill. Choose from clambake-style meals, charbroiled and marinated skewers, and barbecue ribs. $ *Average main: $20* ⊠ *28 E. Grand Ave.* ☎ *207/934–0156* ⊕ *www.landmarkfinedining.com* ☾ *No lunch.*

$$$
SEAFOOD

✕ **Yellowfin's Restaurant.** Inside this diminutive restaurant housed in an impeccably kept yellow Victorian, the atmosphere is fresh, bright, and appropriately beachy. A giant tank bubbles quietly in the background while its resident colorful fish survey the landscape of white-linen-covered tables adorned with sand and shell centerpieces. Not surprisingly, the house specialty is ahi yellowfin tuna, pan seared and treated with a wasabi glaze; other choices include seared scallops, roasted lamb, and a savory seafood *fra diavolo* (in a spicy tomato sauce). Brunch is offered Sunday year-round. It's strictly BYOB—stock up in nearby Old Orchard Beach. $ *Average main: $23* ⊠ *5 Temple Ave.* ☎ *207/934–1100* ⊕ *yellowfinsrestaurantme.com* ☾ *No lunch.*

PORTLAND

28 miles from Kennebunk via I–95 and I–295.

Maine's largest city is considered small by national standards—its population is just 64,000—but its character, spirit, and appeal make it feel much larger. In fact, it is a cultural and economic center for a metropolitan area of 230,000 residents—almost one-quarter of Maine's entire population. It's well worth at least a day or two of exploration.

A city of many names throughout its history, including Casco and Falmouth, Portland has survived many dramatic transformations. Sheltered by the nearby Casco Bay Islands and blessed with a deep port, Portland was a significant settlement right from its start in the early 17th century. Settlers thrived on fishing and lumbering, repeatedly building up the area while the British, French, and Native Americans continually sacked it. Many considered the region a somewhat dangerous frontier, but its potential for prosperity was so apparent that settlers came anyway to tap its rich natural resources.

In 1632 Portland's first home was built on the Portland Peninsula in the area now known as Munjoy Hill. The British burned the city in 1775, when residents refused to surrender arms, but it was rebuilt and became a major trading center. Much of Portland was destroyed again in the Great Fire on July 4, 1866, when a flicked ash or perhaps a celebratory firecracker started a fire in a boatyard that grew into conflagration; 1,500 buildings burned to the ground.

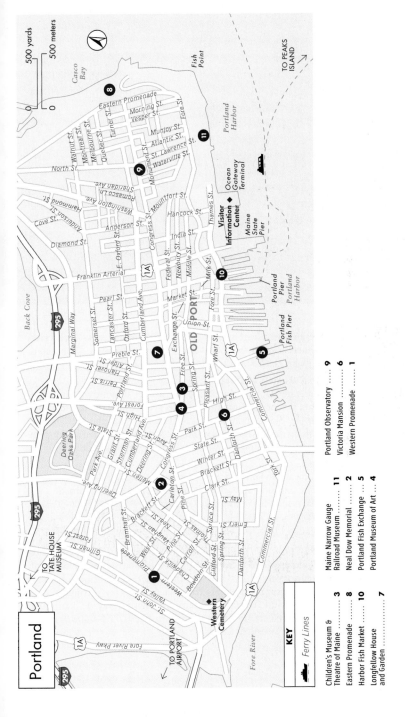

Portland

500 yards
500 meters

Casco Bay

Fish Point

TO PEAKS ISLAND

Eastern Promenade
Morning St.
Vesper St.
Muhjoy St.
Atlantic St.
St. Lawrence St.
Waterville St.

Portland Harbor

North St.

Walnut St.
Montreal St.
Melbourne St.
Quebec St.
Turner St.
Fore St.

Monument St.
Congress St.
Sheridan St.
Romasco Ln.
Washington Ave.

Ocean Gateway Terminal

Hammond St.
Cove St.
Anderson St.
Hammond St.
Mountfort St.

Hancock St.

Diamond St.

Thames St.

Visitor Information Center ◆

Maine State Pier

Franklin Arterial

India St.
Federal St.
Newbury St.
Middle St.
Milk St.

Back Cove

295

Marginal Way

Pearl St.

Market St.

Fore St.

Portland Pier
Portland Harbor

Somerset St.
Lancaster St.
Oxford St.
Cumberland Ave.

Union St.

Portland Fish Pier

Preble St.
Alder St.
Hanover St.
Parris St.
Portland St.

Exchange St.
Free St.

OLD PORT

Spring St.

Wharf St.

Commercial St.

Forest Ave.
Cumberland Ave.
High St.

Pleasant St.

High St.

State St.
Grant St.
Sherman St.
Cumberland Ave.
Deering Ave.
Mellen St.
Carleton St.
Pine St.
Neal St.

Park St.

State St.

Winter St.

Brackett St.

Danforth St.

York St.

Deering Oaks Park

Clark St.

May St.

Park Ave.

Deering Ave.

295

TO TATE HOUSE MUSEUM

Gilman St.
Forest St.

Brackett St.
Bramhall St.
Vaughan St.
Pine St.
Neal St.
Thomas St.
Spruce St.
Carroll St.
Clifford St.

Emery St.

Spring St.

Danforth St.

Commercial St.

Western Promenade

St. John St.
Valley St.
Chadwick St.
Bowdoin St.

Western Cemetery

Fore River Pkwy.

TO PORTLAND AIRPORT

Fore River

KEY
⛴ Ferry Lines

Children's Museum & Theatre of Maine **3**
Eastern Promenade **8**
Harbor Fish Market **10**
Longfellow House and Garden **7**

Maine Narrow Gauge Railroad Museum **11**
Neal Dow Memorial **2**
Portland Fish Exchange ... **5**
Portland Museum of Art ... **4**

Portland Observatory **9**
Victoria Mansion **6**
Western Promenade **1**

Portland's busy harbor is full of working boats, pleasure craft, and ferries headed to the Casco Bay Islands.

Today, there are excellent microbrew and restaurant scenes—many visitors come here just for the food—and a great art museum. The waterfront is a lively place to walk around well into the evening.

GETTING HERE AND AROUND
From Interstate 95, take Interstate 295 to get downtown and onto the Portland Peninsula. Commercial Street runs along the harbor, Fore Street is in one block up in heart of the Old Port, and the Arts District stretches along diagonal Congress Street. Munjoy Hill is on the eastern end of the peninsula and the West End on the opposite side.

ESSENTIALS
Contacts Downtown Portland ⊠ 549 Congress St. ☎ 207/772–6828 ⊕ www. portlandmaine.com. **Greater Portland Convention and Visitors Bureau** ⊠ Visitor Information Center, 14 Ocean Gateway Pier ☎ 207/772–5800 ⊕ www. visitportland.com.

TOURS
BUS TOURS
Portland Discovery Land & Sea Tours. The informative trolley tours of Portland Discovery Land & Sea Tours detail Portland's historical and architectural highlights from Memorial Day through October. Options include combining a city tour with a bay or lighthouse cruise. ⊠ Long Wharf, 170 Commercial St. ☎ 207/774–0808 ⊕ www. portlanddiscovery.com ⊠ $22.

WALKING TOURS

Greater Portland Landmarks. Take 1½-hour walking tours of Portland's historic West End on Friday from July through September with Greater Portland Landmarks. Tours past the neighborhood's Greek Revival mansions and grand Federal-style homes begin at the group's headquarters and cost $10. You can also pick up maps for self-guided tours of the Old Port or the Western Promenade. ✉ *93 High St.* ☎ *207/774–5561* 🌐 *www.portlandlandmarks.org* 🕙 *Tours at 11.*

Maine Foodie Tours. Learn about Portland's culinary history and sample local delights like lobster hors d'oeuvres, organic cheese, and the famous Maine whoopie pie with Maine Foodie Tours. The culinary foot tours include stops at fish mongers, bakeries, and cheese shops that supply Portland's famed restaurants. From summer into early fall you can also take a chocolate tour, a bike-and-brewery tour, or a trolley tour with a stop at a microbrewery. Tours begin at various locales in the Old Port. ☎ *207/233–7485* 🌐 *www.mainefoodietours.com* 🎟 *$39.*

Portland Freedom Trail. The Portland Freedom Trail offers a self-guided tour of sites associated with the Underground Railroad and the anti-slavery movement. ☎ *207/591–9980* 🌐 *www.portlandfreedomtrail.org.*

THE OLD PORT

Fodor's Choice ★ A major international port and a working harbor since the early 17th century, the Old Port bridges the gap between the city's historical commercial activities and those of today. It is home to fishing boats docked alongside whale-watching charters, luxury yachts, cruise ships, and oil tankers from around the globe. Commercial Street parallels the water and is lined with brick buildings and warehouses that were built following the Great Fire of 1866. In the 19th century, candle makers and sail stitchers plied their trades here; today specialty shops, art galleries, and restaurants have taken up residence.

As with much of the city, it's best to park your car and explore the Old Port on foot. You can park at the city garage on Fore Street (between Exchange and Union streets) or opposite the U.S. Custom House at the corner of Fore and Pearl streets. A helpful hint: look for the "Park & Shop" sign on garages and parking lots and get one hour of free parking for each stamp collected at participating shops. Allow a couple of hours to wander at leisure on Market, Exchange, Middle, and Fore streets. The city is very pedestrian-friendly. Maine state law requires vehicles to stop for walkers in crosswalks.

Harbor Fish Market. A Portland favorite since 1968, this freshest-of-the-fresh seafood market ships lobsters and other Maine delectables almost anywhere in the country. A bright-red facade on a working wharf opens into a bustling space with bubbling lobster pens and fish, clams, and other shellfish on ice; employees are as skilled with a fillet knife as sushi chefs. There is also a small retail store. ✉ *9 Custom House Wharf* ☎ *207/775–0251* 🌐 *www.harborfish.com* 🎟 *Free.*

FAMILY **Maine Narrow Gauge Railroad Museum.** Whether you're crazy about old trains or just want to see the sights from a different perspective, the railroad museum has an extensive collection of locomotives and rail coaches and offers scenic tours on narrow-gauge railcars. The 3-mile jaunts run on the hour and take you along Casco Bay, at the foot of the Eastern Promenade. The operating season caps off with a fall harvest ride (complete with cider). During the Christmas season there are Polar Express rides, based on the popular children's book. ⊠ *58 Fore St.* ☎ *207/828–0814* ⊕ *www.mainenarrowgauge.org* ⊡ *Museum $3, train rides $10* ⊗ *May–Oct., daily 10–4.*

NEED A BREAK?

Two Fat Cats Bakery. This bakery's whoopie pies are delicately proportioned, with a smooth and light marshmallow cream filling, and conservative with flavors—no mint-chocolate-chip pies to be found here. ⊠ *47 India St., Portland* ☎ *207/347-5144* ⊕ *www.twofatcatsbakery.com.*

Portland Fish Exchange. You may want to hold your nose for this glimpse into the Old Port's active fish business when you drop by the 20,000-square-foot Portland Fish Exchange. Peek inside coolers teeming with cod, flounder, and monkfish and watch fishermen repairing nets outside. ⊠ *6 Portland Fish Pier* ☎ *207/773–0017* ⊕ *www.pfex. org* ⊡ *Free* ⊗ *Daily 7–3.*

THE ARTS DISTRICT

This district starts at the top of Exchange Street, near the upper end of the Old Port, and extends west past the Portland Museum of Art. Congress Street is the district's central artery. Art galleries, specialty stores, and a score of restaurants line Congress Street. Parking is tricky; two-hour meters dot the sidewalks, but there are several nearby parking garages.

TOP ATTRACTIONS

FAMILY **Children's Museum & Theatre of Maine.** Touching is okay at Portland's small but fun Children's Museum, where kids can pretend they are lobstermen, veterinarians, shopkeepers, or actors in a play. Most exhibits, many of which have a Maine theme, are best for kids 10 and younger. An outside pirate-ship play area is a great place to have a picnic lunch, and don't miss the life-size inflatable humpback whale rising to the ceiling at the whale exhibit. Have a Ball! teaches about the science of motion, letting kids build ramps that make balls speed up, slow down, and leap across tracks. Camera Obscura, an exhibit about optics, provides fascinating panoramic views of the city. It's aimed at adults and older children, so you can purchase a separate admission. ⊠ *142 Free St.* ☎ *207/828–1234* ⊕ *www.kitetails.org* ⊡ *Museum $9; Camera Obscura $4* ⊗ *Memorial Day–Labor Day, daily 10–5; Labor Day–Memorial Day, Mon.–Sat. 10–5.*

Longfellow House and Garden. The boyhood home of the famous American poet is the first brick house in Portland and the oldest building on the peninsula. It's particularly interesting because most of the furnishings, including the young Longfellow's writing desk, are original. Wallpaper, window coverings, and a vibrant painted carpet are period reproductions. Built in 1785, the large dwelling (a third floor was added in 1815) sits back from the street and has a small portico over its entrance and four chimneys surmounting the roof. It's part of the Maine Historical

Society, which includes an adjacent museum with exhibits about Maine life and a research library. After your guided tour, stay for a picnic in the Longfellow Garden; it's open to the public during museum hours. ✉ *489 Congress St.* ☎ *207/774–1822* ⊕ *www.mainehistory.org* ✉ *House and museum $8, gardens free* ☉ *House: May–Oct., Mon.–Sat. 10–5, Sun. noon–5. Museum: May–Oct., Mon.–Sat. 10–5, Sun. noon–5, Nov.– Apr., Mon.–Sat. 10–5.*

Fodor'sChoice **Portland Museum of Art.** Maine's largest public art institution's collec-
★ tion includes fine seascapes and landscapes by Winslow Homer, John Marin, Andrew Wyeth, Edward Hopper, Marsden Hartley, and other American painters. Homer's *Weatherbeaten,* a quintessential Maine Coast image, is here, and the museum owns and displays, on a rotating basis, 16 more of his paintings, plus more than 400 of his illustrations. The museum has works by Monet and Picasso, as well as Degas, Renoir, and Chagall. I. M. Pei designed the strikingly modern Charles Shipman Payson building, which fittingly displays modern art. The nearby L. D. M. Sweat Galleries showcase the collection of 19th-century American art. Special events are held in the gorgeous Federal-style 1801 McLellan House. ✉ *7 Congress Sq.* ☎ *207/775–6148* ⊕ *www.portlandmuseum. org* ✉ *$12, free Fri. 5–9* ☉ *Late May–mid-Oct., Mon.–Thurs. and weekends 10–5, Fri. 10–9; mid-Oct.–late May, Tues.–Thurs. and week- ends 10–5, Fri. 10–9.*

Victoria Mansion. Built between 1858 and 1860, this Italianate mansion is widely regarded as the most sumptuously ornamented dwelling of its period remaining in the country. Architect Henry Austin designed the house for hotelier Ruggles Morse and his wife Olive. The interior design—everything from the plasterwork to the furniture (much of it original)—is the only surviving commission of New York designer Gus- tave Herter. Behind the elegant brownstone exterior of this National Historic Landmark are colorful frescoed walls and ceilings, ornate marble mantelpieces, gilded gas chandeliers, a magnificent 6-foot- by-25-foot stained-glass ceiling window, and a freestanding mahog- any staircase. Guided tours run about 45 minutes and cover all the architectural highlights. Victorian era–themed gifts and art are sold in the museum shop. ✉ *109 Danforth St.* ☎ *207/772–4841* ⊕ *www. victoriamansion.org* ✉ *$15* ☉ *May–Oct., Mon.–Sat. 10–4, Sun. 1–5; Christmas tours day after Thanksgiving–Jan. 3, daily 11–5.*

WORTH NOTING

Eastern Promenade. Of the city's two promenades, this one, often over- looked by tourists, has by far the best view. Gracious Victorian homes, many now converted to condos and apartments, border one side of the street. On the other are 68 acres of hillside parkland that includes Fort Allen Park and, at the base of the hill, the Eastern Prom Trail and tiny East End Beach and Boat Launch. On a sunny day the Eastern Prom is a lovely spot for picnicking and people-watching. ✉ *Extends from Washington Ave. to Fore St.*

Neal Dow Memorial. The mansion, once a stop on the Underground Rail- road, was the home of Civil War general Neal Dow, who became known as the "Father of Prohibition." He was responsible for Maine's adoption of the anti-alcohol bill in 1851, which spurred a national movement. Now a museum, this majestic 1829 Federal-style home is open for guided tours that start on the hour. ☒ *714 Congress St.* ☎ *207/773–7773* ▣ *$5* ⊗ *May–Dec., Mon.–Sat. 11–4; Jan.–Apr., by appt.*

FAMILY   **Portland Observatory.** This octagonal observatory on Munjoy Hill was built in 1807 by Captain Lemuel Moody, a retired sea captain, as a maritime signal tower. Moody used a telescope to identify incoming ships and flags to signal to merchants where to unload their cargo. Held in place by 122 tons of ballast, it's the last remaining historic maritime signal station in the country. The guided tour leads all the way to the dome, where you can step out on the deck and take in views of Portland, the islands, and inland toward the White Mountains. ☒ *138 Congress St.* ☎ *207/774–5561* ⊕ *www.portlandlandmarks.org* ▣ *$9* ⊗ *Memorial Day weekend–Columbus Day, daily 10–5; Thurs. evening sunset tours mid-July–early Sept.*

■ OFF THE
BEATEN
PATH

Tate House Museum. Built astride rose granite steps and a period herb garden overlooking the Stroudwater River on the outskirts of Portland, this magnificent 1755 house was built by Captain George Tate. Tate had been commissioned by the English Crown to organize "the King's Broad Arrow"—the marking and cutting down of gigantic forest trees, which were shipped to England to be fashioned as masts for the British Royal Navy. The house has several period rooms, including a sitting room with some fine English Restoration chairs. With its clapboard still gloriously unpainted, its impressive Palladian doorway, dogleg stairway, unusual clerestory, and gambrel roof, this house will delight all lovers of Early American decorative arts. ☒ *1267 Westbrook St.* ☎ *207/774–6177* ⊕ *www.tatehouse.org* ▣ *$10* ⊗ *Early June–mid-Oct., Wed.–Sat. 10–4, Sun. 1–4.*

THE WEST END

A leisurely walk through Portland's West End, beginning at the top of the Arts District, offers a real treat to historic architecture buffs. The neighborhood, on the National Register of Historic Places, presents an extraordinary display of architectural splendor, from High Victorian Gothic to lush Italianate, Queen Anne, and Colonial Revival.

Western Promenade. A good place to start is at the head of the Western Promenade, which has benches and a nice view. From the Old Port, take Danforth Street all the way up to Vaughn Street; take a right on Vaughn and then an immediate left onto Western Promenade. Pass by the Western Cemetery, Portland's second official burial ground, laid out in 1829 (inside is the ancestral plot of poet Henry Wadsworth Longfellow), and look for street parking. ☒ *Extends from Danforth St. to Bramhall St.*

WHERE TO EAT

America's "Foodiest Small Town" is how one magazine described Portland, which is blessed with exceptional restaurants rivaling those of a far larger city. Fresh seafood, including the famous Maine lobster, is still popular and prevalent, but there are plenty more cuisines to be enjoyed.

Exchange Street, in the Old Port, is a popular place to explore for restaurants, shopping, and summer treats.

More and more restaurants are using local meats, seafood, and organic and local produce as much as possible; changing menus reflect what is available in the region at the moment. As sophisticated as many of these establishments have become, the atmosphere is generally casual; with a few exceptions, you can leave your jacket and tie at home.

Smoking is banned in all restaurants, taverns, and bars in Maine.

$$ DINER 🍴 **Becky's Diner.** You won't find a more local or unfussy place—or one that is more abuzz with conversation at 4 am—than this waterfront institution, way down on the end of Commercial Street. Sitting next to you at the counter or in a neighboring booth could be rubber-booted fishermen back from the sea, college students soothing a hangover, or suited business folks with BlackBerrys. From the upstairs deck you can watch the working waterfront in action. The food is cheap, generous in proportion, and has that satisfying, old-time-diner quality. [$] *Average main: $14* ✉ *390 Commercial St.* ☎ *207/773–7070* 🌐 *www.beckysdiner.com.*

$ MODERN AMERICAN 🍴 **Duckfat.** Even in midafternoon, this small, hip sandwich shop in the Old Port is packed. It concentrates on serving everyday farm-to-table fare: the signature Belgian fries are made with Maine potatoes cooked, yes, in duck fat, and served in paper cones. Sandwiches are made with focaccia bread; choices like tuna melt with Thai chili mayo change seasonally, but the meat loaf and B.G.T. (bacon, tomato, goat cheese) are standards. Drink choices include gelato milk shakes, French-press coffee, lime-mint fountain sodas, beer, and wine. [$] *Average main: $12* ✉ *43 Middle St.* ☎ *207/774–8080* 🌐 *www.duckfat.com* ✍ *Reservations not accepted.*

CLOSE UP

Lobster Shacks

If it's your first time to the Maine Coast, it won't be long before you stumble upon the famous and quintessential seaside eatery, the lobster shack. Also known as a lobster "pound," especially in other parts of New England, this humble establishment serves only two kinds of fresh seafood—lobster and clams. Lobster shacks are essentially wooden huts with picnic tables set around the waterfront. The menu is simplicity itself: steamed lobster or clams by the pound, or a lobster roll. Sides may include potato chips, coleslaw, or corn on the cob. Some pounds are even BYOB—no, not bring your own bib; those are usually provided—but bring your own beer or refreshments.

A signature item at a lobster shack is the lobster dinner. Although this can vary from pound to pound, it generally means the works: a whole steamed lobster, steamed clams, corn on the cob, and potato chips. If the lobster dinner sounds like a bit much, then go for the classic lobster roll, a buttered New England–style hot-dog roll filled with chunks of lobster meat and a bit of mayo. Some pounds will serve it with lemon, some will serve it with butter, and some with even a touch of lettuce or herbs. Purists will serve no toppings at all (and why bother when the unadulterated taste of fresh, sweet lobster meat can't be beat). Most shacks will even have a tank with live lobsters; few will let you pick your own.

We can say this much: the best place to get a lobster dinner or lobster roll is at a shack, and the only authentic ones are right next to the water. There's a general sense that the "purest" pounds are the ones that are the simplest: a wooden shack, right on

A lobster roll: perfection on a bun.

the water with wooden picnic tables, and perhaps most important of all, a beautiful unobstructed view of working lobster boats in a scenic Maine harbor.

Maine Lobster Council. You can find out more about Maine lobster from the Maine Lobster Council. ☎ 207/541–9310 ⊕ www.lobsterfrommaine.com.

—Michael de Zayas

$$$$ MODERN AMERICAN Fodor's Choice ★ 🍴 **Five Fifty-Five.** Classic dishes are cleverly updated at this classy Congress Street spot. The menu changes seasonally to reflect ingredients available from local waters, organic farms, and food purveyors, but seared local diver scallops, served in a buttery carrot-vanilla emulsion, are an exquisite mainstay. So is the mac and cheese, which boasts artisanal cheeses and shaved black truffles. You may also find dishes such as milk-braised rabbit with Himalayan red rice and lemon-dressed local greens. You can try the $65 tasting menu, or come for Sunday brunch. The space, with exposed brick and copper accents, is a former 19th-century firehouse. A sister restaurant, Petite Jacqueline bistro in Longfellow Square, has also earned accolades and fans. [$] *Average main: $29* ✉ *555 Congress St.* ☎ *207/761–0555* 🌐 *www.fivefifty-five.com* 🕑 *No lunch.*

$$ PIZZA FAMILY 🍴 **Flatbread.** Families, students, and bohemian types gather at this popular New England chain pizza place. Two giant wood-fire ovens, where the pies are cooked, are the heart of the soaring, warehouse-like space; in summer you can escape the heat by dining on the deck overlooking the harbor. The simple menu has eight signature pizzas plus weekly veggie and meat specials; everything is homemade, organic, and nitrate-free. Be sure to order the delicious house salad with toasted sesame seeds, seaweed, blue or goat cheese, and ginger-tamarind vinaigrette. **■ TIP→ Waits can be long on weekends and in summer, but you can call a half-hour ahead to get on the waiting list.** [$] *Average main: $13* ✉ *72 Commercial St.* ☎ *207/772–8777* 🌐 *www.flatbreadcompany.com.*

$$$$ MODERN AMERICAN 🍴 **Fore Street.** One of Maine's best chefs, Sam Hayward, opened this restaurant in a renovated warehouse on the edge of the Old Port in 1996. The menu changes daily to reflect the freshest ingredients from Maine's farms and waters. Every copper-top table in the main dining room has a view of the enormous brick oven and soapstone hearth that anchor the open kitchen, where sous-chefs seem to dance as they create such dishes as turnspit-roasted dry-rubbed pork loin, wood-grilled Maine island lamb chop with sun-root puree, and Maine mussels oven roasted in garlic and almond butter. Desserts include artisanal cheeses. In July or August, book two months in advance; otherwise, a week is usually fine. **■ TIP→ Last-minute planners take heart: a third of the tables are reserved for walk-ins.** [$] *Average main: $30* ✉ *288 Fore St.* ☎ *207/775–2717* 🌐 *www.forestreet.biz* 🕑 *No lunch.*

$$ SEAFOOD 🍴 **Gilbert's Chowder House.** This is the real deal, as quintessential as Maine dining can be. Clam rakes and nautical charts hang from the walls of this unpretentious waterfront diner. The flavors are from the depths of the North Atlantic, prepared and presented simply: fish, clam, and seafood chowders (corn, too); fried shrimp; haddock; clam strips; and extraordinary clam cakes. A chalkboard of daily specials often features fish-and-chips. Don't miss out on the lobster roll—a toasted hot-dog bun bursting with claw and tail meat lightly dressed with mayo but otherwise unadulterated. It's classic Maine, fuss free, and presented on a paper plate. [$] *Average main: $19* ✉ *92 Commercial St.* ☎ *207/871–5636* 🌐 *www.gilbertschowderhouse.com.*

$$$$ ECLECTIC 🍴 **Hugo's.** Serving the freshest local organic foods is a high priority at Hugo's, and your server is sure to know everything about various purveyors. Updated daily, the menu at this stylish eatery is made up of

smartly prepared, seasonally inspired dishes like crispy-skin pork belly and crepe-wrapped arctic char. You can choose five courses for $90, or go light with two courses for $45. A 2013 renovation added an open kitchen, a handsome curved bar, and an airy, open-concept dining room. Next door is a sister business, Eventide Oyster Company, with a more casual setting. $ *Average main: $45* ⊠ *88 Middle St.* ☎ *207/774–8538* ⊕ *www.hugos.net* ⊘ *Closed Sun. No lunch.*

$$$
MEDITERRANEAN
Fodor's Choice
★

✕ **Local 188.** There's an infectious vibe at this eclectic Arts District eatery, a foodie hot spot as well as a longtime local favorite. The 2,000-square-foot space has lofty tin ceilings and worn maple floors. Mismatched chandeliers dangle over the dining area, and a pair of antlers crown the open kitchen. Regulars chat with servers about what just-caught seafood will decorate the paella and which organic veggies are starring in the tortillas, one of several tapas choices. You'll find entrées like Casco Bay hake with herb salsa verde, poached purple potatoes, smoked aioli, and beets. Many of the 10 or so draft brews are Maine crafted; there are some 150 mostly European wines. Reservations aren't taken for the large bar side. $ *Average main: $22* ⊠ *685 Congress St.* ☎ *207/761–7909* ⊕ *www.local188.com* ⊘ *No lunch.*

$$$
ECLECTIC

✕ **Walter's.** A fixture in the Old Port since the late 1980s, this relaxed, busy place with a chic modern interior is popular with suits and tourists alike. The seasonally changing menu nicely balances local seafood and meats with Asian and other international flavors. You'll find appetizers like calamari dressed with lemon-and-cherry-pepper aioli and such entrées as crispy duck breast served with spaetzle, baby bok choy, and plum sauce. An inviting bar has a lighter menu; try the mussels or the Greek lamb sliders. $ *Average main: $28* ⊠ *2 Portland Sq.* ☎ *207/871–9258* ⊕ *www.waltersportland.com* ⊘ *Closed Sun. No lunch Sat.*

WHERE TO STAY

As Portland's popularity as a vacation destination has increased, so have its options for overnight visitors. Though several large hotels—geared toward high-tech, amenity-obsessed guests—have been built in the Old Port, they have in no way diminished the success of smaller, more intimate lodgings. Inns and B&Bs have taken up residence throughout the West End, often giving new life to the grand mansions of Portland's wealthy 19th-century businessmen. For the least expensive accommodations, investigate the chain hotels near the Interstate and the airport.

Expect to pay from about $150 a night for a pleasant room (often with complimentary breakfast) within walking distance of the Old Port during high season, and more than $400 for the most luxurious of suites. In the height of the summer season many places are booked; make reservations well in advance, and ask about off-season specials.

$$$$
B&B/INN

The Danforth. A stunning showpiece, this stylish inn was one of Portland's grandest Federal-style dwellings when it was built in 1823. **Pros:** gorgeous rooms; basement billiards room; city views from cupola. **Cons:** small windows in some third-floor rooms. $ *Rooms from: $299* ⊠ *163 Danforth St.* ☎ *207/879–8755, 800/991–6557* ⊕ *www.danforthmaine.com* ⮑ *9 rooms* ⦿| *Breakfast.*

$$$ B&B/INN **Inn on Carleton.** This 1869 Victorian has a curved mahogany staircase to the third floor, a bay window overlooking the street from the front parlor, and gleaming pumpkin pine floors. **Pros:** most rooms have electric fireplaces; English garden with fountain; attentive resident innkeeper. **Cons:** not an easy walk to the Old Port. [$] *Rooms from: $185* ✉ *46 Carleton St.* ☎ *207/775–1910, 800/639–1770* 🌐 *www.innoncarleton.com* 🛏 *6 rooms.*

$$$ B&B/INN **Morrill Mansion.** This 19th-century townhouse has tastefully appointed rooms with well-executed color schemes: blue is a favorite hue here. **Pros:** close to arts district; parlors on each floor for relaxing. **Cons:** not on a grand block. [$] *Rooms from: $200* ✉ *249 Vaughan St.* ☎ *207/774–6900, 888/566–7745* 🌐 *www.morrillmansion.com* 🛏 *6 rooms, 1 suite* 🍴 *Breakfast.*

$$$$ B&B/INN Fodor's Choice ★ **Pomegranate Inn.** The classic facade of this handsome 1884 Italianate in the architecturally rich Western Promenade area gives no hint of the splashy, modern surprises within. **Pros:** surprising decor; many rooms have gas fireplaces; close to Western Promenade. **Cons:** not an easy walk from Old Port. [$] *Rooms from: $259* ✉ *49 Neal St.* ☎ *207/772–1006, 800/356–0408* 🌐 *www.pomegranateinn.com* 🛏 *7 rooms, 1 suite* 🍴 *Breakfast.*

$$$$ HOTEL **Portland Harbor Hotel.** Making luxury its primary focus, the Harbor Hotel has become a favorite with business travelers seeking meetings on a more intimate scale and vacationing guests who want high-quality service and amenities, like the free shuttle to local restaurants and sites. **Pros:** elegant extras; amid the action of the Old Port. **Cons:** smallish lobby. [$] *Rooms from: $299* ✉ *468 Fore St.* ☎ *207/775–9090, 888/798–9090* 🌐 *www.portlandharborhotel.com* 🛏 *87 rooms, 14 suites.*

$$$$ HOTEL **The Portland Regency Hotel & Spa.** Not part of a chain despite the "Regency" name, this brick building in the center of the Old Port served as Portland's armory in the late 19th century. **Pros:** easy walk to sights; lots of room variety for a hotel. **Cons:** lower-than-standard ceilings in many rooms. [$] *Rooms from: $279* ✉ *20 Milk St.* ☎ *207/774–4200, 800/727–3436* 🌐 *www.theregency.com* 🛏 *85 rooms, 10 suites.*

NIGHTLIFE AND THE ARTS

THE ARTS

Art galleries and studios have spread throughout the city, infusing with new life many abandoned yet beautiful old buildings and shops. Many are concentrated along the Congress Street downtown corridor; others are hidden amid the boutiques and restaurants of the Old Port and the East End. A great way to get acquainted with the city's artists is to participate in the First Friday Art Walk, a self-guided, free tour of galleries, museums, and alternative-art venues that happens—you guessed it—on the first Friday of each month.

Merrill Auditorium. This soaring concert hall hosts numerous theatrical and musical events, including performances by the Portland Symphony Orchestra and Portland Opera Repertory Theatre. Ask about organ recitals on the the auditorium's huge 1912 Kotzschmar Memorial Organ. ✉ *20 Myrtle St.* ☎ *207/842–0800* 🌐 *www.porttix.com.*

WHAT'S ON TAP: MICROBREWERIES

One of the nation's microbrew hotbeds, Maine is home to around 40 breweries, and several of the larger ones—Allagash, Geary's, and Shipyard—are in and around Portland. These breweries are open for tours and tastings, but beer lovers may prefer the smaller brewpubs that make their own beer and serve it fresh from their own taps in neighborhood taverns. In the Old Port you'll find Gritty McDuff's, Sebago Brewing Company, and In'finiti Fermentation & Distillation. In Bayside there's Rising Tide and Bunker Brewing Company. If you're in town in November, check out the Maine Brewer's Festival (⊕ www.mainebrewersfestival.com). Pick up a Maine Beer Trail map from the Maine Brewers' Guild (⊕ www.mainebrewersguild.org).

Portland Stage. This company mounts theatrical productions on its two stages from September to May. ⊠ 25-A Forest Ave. ☎ 207/774–0465 ⊕ www.portlandstage.com.

Space Gallery. Space Gallery sparkles as a contemporary art gallery and alternative arts venue, opening its doors to everything from poetry readings to live music to documentary films. The gallery is open daily Wednesday to Saturday. ⊠ 538 Congress St. ☎ 207/828–5600 ⊕ www.space538.org.

NIGHTLIFE

Portland's nightlife scene is largely centered around the bustling Old Port and a few smaller, artsy spots on Congress Street. There's a great emphasis on local, live music and pubs serving award-winning local microbrews. Several hip wine bars have cropped up, serving appetizers along with a full array of specialty wines and whimsical cocktails. It's a fairly youthful scene in Portland, in some spots even rowdy and rough around the edges, but there are plenty of places where you don't have to shout over the din to be heard.

The Big Easy. To catch live local and national acts most any night of the week, try the Big Easy. Everything from blues, jazz, and soul to Grateful Dead covers are played here. ⊠ 55 Market St. ☎ 207/775–2266 ⊕ www.bigeasyportland.com.

Bull Feeney's. For nightly specials, plenty of Guinness, and live entertainment, head to Bull Feeney's, a lively two-story Irish pub and restaurant. ⊠ 375 Fore St. ☎ 207/773–7210.

Gritty McDuff's Portland Brew Pub. Maine's original brewpub serves fine ales, British pub fare, and seafood dishes. There are between six and eight ales on tap, and there's always a seasonal offering. Come on Tuesday and Saturday nights for live music. ⊠ 396 Fore St. ☎ 207/772–2739 ⊕ www.grittys.com.

Fodor's Choice ★ **Novare Res Bier Café.** At tucked-away Novare Res Bier Café, choose from some three dozen rotating drafts and more than 300 bottled brews. Relax on an expansive deck, munch on antipasti, or share a meat and cheese plate. Craft beers from Maine occupy at least eight of the taps at any given time, and the rest span the globe, with an emphasis on Belgian and Trappist brews. ⊠ *4 Canal Plaza, off Exchange St.* ☎ *207/761–2437* ⊕ *www.novaresbiercafe.com.*

Rí Rá. Ths happening Irish pub has live music Thursday through Saturday nights. For a mellower experience, settle into a couch at the upstairs bar. ⊠ *72 Commercial St.* ☎ *207/761–4446* ⊕ *www.rira.com.*

Sonny's. In a Victorian-era bank building with arched windows overlooking an Old Port square, this stylish bar and lounge packs in the late-night crowd. It has quite a list of cocktails, many using house-infused liquors—try the chili tequila. Bluegrass and funk bands play on Thursday; there's a DJ on Saturday. The Latin American cuisine is a winner, too. At night you can order lighter fare like a poblano cheeseburger with yam fries, as well as such entrées as the braised brisket enchilada. Food is served until 10:30 on weekends. ⊠ *83 Exchange St.* ☎ *207/772–7774* ⊕ *www.sonnysportland.com.*

SPORTS AND THE OUTDOORS

When the weather's good, everyone in Portland heads outside. There are also many green spaces nearby Portland, including Fort Williams Park, home to Portland Head Light; Crescent Beach State Park; and Two Lights State Park. All are on the coast south of the city in suburban Cape Elizabeth and offer walking trails, picnic facilities, and water access. Bradbury Mountain State Park, in Pownal, has incredible vistas from its easily climbed peak. In Freeport is Wolfe's Neck Woods State Park, where you can take a guided nature walk and see nesting ospreys. Both are north of Portland.

BICYCLING

Bicycle Coalition of Maine. For state bike trail maps, club and tour listings, or hints on safety, contact the Bicycle Coalition of Maine. Maps are available at the group's headquarters in the Arts District. ⊠ *34 Preble St.* ☎ *207/623–4511* ⊕ *www.bikemaine.org.*

Cycle Mania. Rent bikes downtown at Cycle Mania. The $25 rate includes a helmet and lock. ⊠ *59 Federal St.* ☎ *207/774–2933* ⊕ *www.cyclemania1.com.*

Gorham Bike and Ski. You can rent several types of bikes, including hybrid and tandem models, starting at $25 per day. ⊠ *693 Congress St.* ☎ *207/773–1700* ⊕ *www.gorhambike.com.*

Portland Trails. For local biking information, contact Portland Trails. The staff can tell you about designated paved routes that wind along the water, through parks, and beyond. ⊠ *305 Commercial St.* ☎ *207/775–2411* ⊕ *www.trails.org.*

BOATING

Various Portland-based skippers offer whale-, dolphin-, and seal-watching cruises; excursions to lighthouses and islands; and fishing and lobstering trips. Board the ferry to see the nearby islands. Self-navigators can rent kayaks or canoes.

The Eastern Prom Trail

To experience the city's busy shoreline and grand views of Casco Bay, walkers, runners, and cyclists head out on the 2.1-mile Eastern Prom Trail.

Beginning at the intersection of Commercial and India streets, this paved trail runs along the water at the bottom of the Eastern Promenade, following an old rail bed and running alongside the still-used railroad tracks of the Maine Narrow Gauge Railroad Co. & Museum. There are plenty of places with benches and tables for a picnic break along the way. From the trailhead, it's about 1 mile to the small East End Beach.

Continuing along the trail, you'll pass underneath busy Interstate 295, and emerge at the Back Cove Trail, a popular 3½-mile loop you can connect with for a long trek. To return to the Old Port, backtrack along the trail or head up the steep path to the top of the promenade. Here you can continue along the promenade sidewalk or take the trails through this 68-acre stretch of parkland to the lovely picnic area and playground.

Continuing along the sidewalk toward the Old Port, a gazebo and several old cannons to your left indicate you're at the small Fort Allen Park. Use one of the coin-operated viewing scopes to view Civil War–era Fort Gorges, which never saw action.

Where the Eastern Prom becomes Fore Street, continue on for a few blocks to India Street and take a left, which will bring you back to where you started. Or, continue into the Old Port.

Plan at least an hour to walk the trail with brief stops, or two if you continue along the Back Cove Trail. But if can, make time for the Prom—it's truly an urban jewel.

Casco Bay Lines. Casco Bay Lines operates the ferry service to the seven bay islands with year-round populations. Summer offerings include music cruises, lighthouse excursions, and a trip to Bailey Island with a stopover for lunch. ⊠ *Maine State Pier, 56 Commercial St.* ☎ *207/774–7871* ⊕ *www.cascobaylines.com.*

Lucky Catch Cruises. You'll set sail in a real lobster boat: this company gives you the genuine experience, which includes hauling traps and the chance to purchase the catch. ⊠ *Long Wharf, 170 Commercial St.* ☎ *207/761–0941* ⊕ *www.luckycatch.com.*

Odyssey Whale Watch. From mid-May to mid-October, Odyssey Whale Watch leads whale-watching and deep-sea-fishing excursions. ⊠ *Long Wharf, 170 Commercial St.* ☎ *207/775–0727* ⊕ *www. odysseywhalewatch.com.*

Portland Discovery Land & Sea Tours. For tours of the harbor and Casco Bay, including an up-close look at several lighthouses, try Portland Discovery Land & Sea Tours. ⊠ *Long Wharf, 170 Commercial St.* ☎ *207/774–0808* ⊕ *www.portlanddiscovery.com.*

Portland Paddle. Run by a young pair of Registered Maine Guides, Portland Paddle leads introductory sea kayaking clinics along with guided trips between the Casco Bay islands. Two-hour sunset paddles

($35) are a fave, but the most unusual offering involves a four-hour paddle to the abandoned island military installation of Fort Gorges ($55), where you'll enjoy a short acoustic concert before heading back. Kayak and paddleboard rentals are available. ⊠ *Eastern Promenade, East End Beach, off Cutter St., Portland* ☎ *207/370–9730* ⊕ *www. portlandpaddle.net* ☉ *Closed Nov.–May., appointment only in Oct.*

Portland Schooner Co. This company offers daily windjammer cruises aboard the vintage schooners *Bagheera* and *Wendameen*. You can also arrange overnight trips. Tours are offered May to October. ⊠ *Maine State Pier, 56 Commercial St.* ☎ *207/766–2500* ⊕ *www. portlandschooner.com.*

HOT-AIR BALLOON RIDES

Hot Fun First Class Balloon Flights. Hot Fun First Class Balloon Flights flies mainly sunrise trips and can accommodate up to three people. The price of $300 per person includes a post-flight champagne toast, snacks, and shuttle to the lift-off site. ☎ *207/799–0193* ⊕ *www.hotfun balloons.com.*

SHOPPING

Exchange Street is great for arts and crafts and boutique browsing, while Commercial Street caters to the souvenir hound—gift shops are packed with nautical items, and lobster and moose emblems are emblazoned on everything from T-shirts to shot glasses.

ART AND ANTIQUES

Abacus. This appealing crafts gallery has gift items in glass, wood, and textiles, as well as fine modern jewelry. ⊠ *44 Exchange St.* ☎ *207/772–7188* ⊕ *www.abacusgallery.com.*

Gleason Fine Art. This gallery exhibits sculpture and paintings by Maine and New England artists from the 19th to 21st centuries. ⊠ *545 Congress St.* ☎ *207/699–5599* ⊕ *www.gleasonfineart.com.*

Greenhut Galleries. The contemporary art at this gallery changes with the seasons. Artists represented include David Driskell, an artist and leading art scholar. ⊠ *146 Middle St.* ☎ *207/772–2693, 888/772–2693* ⊕ *www.greenhutgalleries.com.*

Portland Architectural Salvage. A fixer-upper's dream, Portland Architectural Salvage has four floors of unusual reclaimed finds from old buildings, including fixtures, hardware, and stained-glass windows, and also assorted antiques. ⊠ *131 Preble St.* ☎ *207/780–0634* ⊕ *www. portlandsalvage.com.*

BOOKS

Longfellow Books. This shop is known for its good service, author readings, and thoughtful collection of new and used books. There's a little of everything here. ⊠ *1 Monument Way* ☎ *207/772–4045* ⊕ *www. longfellowbooks.com.*

CLOTHING

Bliss. Hip boutique Bliss stocks clothing and accessories by cutting-edge designers, plus jeans by big names like J Brand and Mother. There's also a great selection of Frye boots. ⊠ *58 Exchange St.* ☎ *207/879–7129* ⊕ *www.blissboutiques.com.*

Hélène M. Photos of style icon Audrey Hepburn grace the walls of Hélène M., where you'll find classic, fashionable pieces by designers like Michael Stars, Diane von Furstenberg, and Rebecca Taylor. ⊠ *425 Fore St.* ☎ *207/772–2564* ⊕ *www.helenem.com.*

Material Objects. With an eclectic combination of good-quality consignment and new jewelry and clothing for both men and women, Material Objects makes for an affordable and unusual shopping spree. ⊠ *500 Congress St.* ☎ *207/774–1241.*

Sea Bags. At Sea Bags, totes made from recycled sailcloth and decorated with bright, graphic patterns are sewn right in the store. ⊠ *25 Custom House Wharf* ☎ *888/210–4244* ⊕ *www.seabags.com.*

HOUSEHOLD ITEMS/FURNITURE

Angela Adams. Maine islander Angela Adams specializes in simple but bold geometric motifs parlayed into dramatic rugs (custom, too), canvas totes, bedding, and other home accessories. The shop also carries sleek wood furniture from her husband's woodshop. ⊠ *273 Congress St.* ⊕ *www.angelaadams.com.*

Asia West. For reproduction and antique furnishings with a Far East feel, head to this stylish showroom on the waterfront. ⊠ *219 Commercial St.* ☎ *888/775–0066* ⊕ *www.asiawest.net.*

SIDE TRIPS FROM PORTLAND

CASCO BAY ISLANDS

The islands of Casco Bay are also known as the Calendar Islands because an early explorer mistakenly thought there was one for each day of the year (in reality there are only some 140). These islands range from ledges visible only at low tide to populous Peaks Island, a suburb of Portland. Some are uninhabited; others support year-round communities as well as stores and restaurants. Fort Gorges commands Hog Island Ledge, and Eagle Island is the site of Arctic explorer Admiral Robert Peary's home. The brightly painted ferries of Casco Bay Lines are the islands' lifeline. There is frequent service to the most populated ones, including Peaks, Long, Little Diamond, and Great Diamond.

There is little in the way of overnight lodging on the islands; the population swells during the warmer months due to summer residents. There are few restaurants or organized attractions other than the natural beauty of the islands themselves. Meandering about by bike or on foot is a good way to explore on a day trip.

GETTING HERE AND AROUND

Casco Bay Lines provides ferry service from Portland to the islands of Casco Bay. The *Nova Star,* a passenger ferry service between Portland and Yarmouth, Nova Scotia, is expected to launch in 2014.

ESSENTIALS

Transportation Information Casco Bay Lines ☎ 207/774–7871 ⊕ *www. cascobaylines.com.*

CAPE ELIZABETH

Winslow Homer painted many of his famous oceanscapes from a tiny studio on the rocky peninsula known as Prout's Neck, 12 miles south of Portland. Visitors today navigate a neighborhood of summer homes and a sprawling country-club property for a glimpse of the same dramatic coastline. Follow Highway 77 through South Portland (sometimes called "SoPo"), stopping off for bagels and coffee in its hipper residential neighborhoods. In the affluent bedroom community of Cape Elizabeth, a detour along the two-lane Shore Road shows off the famed Portland Head Light lighthouse and quite a few stunning oceanfront homes.

EXPLORING

Cape Elizabeth Light. This was the first twin lighthouse erected on the Maine coast, in 1828, and the locals still call it Two Lights, but half of the Cape Elizabeth Light was dismantled in 1924 and converted into a private residence The other half still operates, and you can get a great photo of it from the end of Two Lights Road in the surrounding state park of the same name. The lighthouse itself is closed to the public, but you can explore the tidal pools at its base for small snails known as "periwinkles." ⊠ *7 Tower Dr., Cape Elizabeth* ☎ *207/799–5871* ⊕ *www.maine.gov/twolights* ⊠ *$4.50* ⊗ *Daily 9–sunset.*

Fodor's Choice ★ **Portland Head Light.** Familiar to many from photographs and the Edward Hopper's painting *Portland Head-Light* (1927), this lighthouse was commissioned by George Washington in 1787. The towering white stone structure stands over the keeper's quarters, a white home with a blazing red roof, now the Museum at Portland Head Light. The lighthouse is in 90-acre Fort Williams Park, a sprawling green space with walking paths, picnic facilities, a beach and—you guessed it—a cool old fort. ⊠ *Museum, 1000 Shore Rd., Cape Elizabeth* ☎ *207/799–2661* ⊕ *www.portlandheadlight.com* ⊠ *$2* ⊗ *Memorial Day–mid-Oct., daily 10–4; Apr., May, Nov., and Dec., weekends 10–4.*

Scarborough Marsh Audubon Center. You can explore this Maine Audubon Society–run nature center on foot or by canoe on your own, or by signing up for a guided walk or paddle. The salt marsh is Maine's largest and is an excellent place for bird-watching and peaceful paddling along its winding ways. The center has a discovery room for kids, programs for all ages ranging from basket-making to astronomy, and a good gift shop. Tours include birding walks. ⊠ *Pine Point Rd., Scarborough* ☎ *207/883–5100* ⊕ *www.maineaudubon.org* ⊠ *Free; guided tours* *begin at $5* ☉ *Visitor center mid-June–Labor Day, daily 9:30–5:30; Memorial Day–mid-June and Labor Day–Sept., weekends 9:30–5:30.*

Winslow Homer Studio. The great American landscape painter created many of his best-known works in this seaside home between 1883 until his death in 1910. It's easy to see how this rocky, jagged peninsula might have been inspiring. The only way to get a look is on a tour with the Portland Museum of Art, which leads 2½-hour strolls through the historic property. ⊠ *Winslow Homer Rd., Scarborough* ☎ *207/775–6148* ⊕ *www.portlandmuseum.org* ✉ *$55* ☉ *Apr.–Nov., hrs vary.*

WHERE TO EAT AND STAY

$$

SEAFOOD

✕ **The Lobster Shack at Two Lights.** You can't beat the location—right on the water, below the lighthouse pair that gives Two Lights State Park its name—and the food's not bad, either. Enjoy fresh lobster whole or piled into a hot-dog bun with a dollop of mayo. Other menu must-haves include chowder, fried clams, and fish-and-chips. It's been a classic spot since the 1920s. Eat inside or out. $ *Average main: $18* ⊠ *225 Two Lights Rd., Cape Elizabeth* ☎ *207/799–1677* ⊕ *www. lobstershacktwolights.com* ☉ *Closed late Oct.–late Mar.*

$$$$

RESORT

⌗ **Black Point Inn.** Toward the tip of the peninsula that juts into the ocean at Prouts Neck stands this stylish, tastefully updated 1878 resort inn with spectacular views up and down the coast. **Pros:** dramatic setting; geothermally heated pool; discounts in shoulder seasons. **Cons:** "guest service charge" is tacked onto room rate. $ *Rooms from: $500* ⊠ *510 Black Point Rd., Scarborough* ☎ *207/883–2500* ⊕ *www.blackpointinn. com* ⇆ *20 rooms, 5 suites* ☉ *Closed late Oct.–early May* ⍾⊙⍾ *Some meals.*

FREEPORT

17 miles north of Portland via I–295.

Those who flock straight to L.L. Bean and see nothing else of Freeport are missing out. The city's charming backstreets are lined with historic buildings and old clapboard houses, and there's a pretty little harbor on the south side of the Harraseeket River. It's true, many who come to the area do so simply to shop—L.L. Bean is the store that put Freeport on the map, and plenty of outlets and some specialty stores have settled here. Still, if you choose, you can stay a while and experience more than fabulous bargains; beyond the shops are bucolic nature preserves with miles of walking trails and plenty of places for leisurely ambling that don't require the overuse of your credit cards.

GETTING HERE AND AROUND

Interstate 295 has three Freeport exits and passes by on the edge of the downtown area. U.S. 1 is Main Street here.

EXPLORING

Freeport Historical Society. Pick up a village walking map and check out the historical exhibits at the Freeport Historical Society, located in Harrington House, a hybrid Federal- and Greek Revival–style home built in the 1830s. ⊠ *45 Main St.* ☎ *207/865–3170* ⊕ *www.free porthistoricalsociety.org* ☉ *Memorial Day–Labor Day, weekdays 10–5, Sat. 10–2.*

Side trips from Portland and the Mid-Coast Region

Pettengill Farm. The grounds of the Freeport Historical Society's salt-water Pettengill Farm—140 beautifully tended acres along an estuary of the Harraseeket River—are open to the public. It's about a 15-minute walk from the parking area down a farm road to the circa 1800 saltbox farmhouse, which is open by appointment. Little has changed since it was built, it has rare etchings (called sgraffitti) of ships and sea monsters on three bedroom walls. ✉ *Pettengill Rd.* ☎ *207/865–3170* ⊕ *www.freeporthistoricalsociety.org* ☉ *Daily dawn–dusk.*

NEED A BREAK?

Cranberry Island Kitchen. This place ships nationwide, but about half of its "gourmet" whoopie pies (free-range eggs, locally churned butter) are sold at its bakery on Lower Main Street in Freeport, where the offerings include seashell-shaped whoopie pies and filling flavors like espresso chocolate chip and Chambord. ✉ *174 Lower Main St., Freeport* ☎ *207/829–5200* ⊕ *www.cranberryislandkitchen.com.*

WHERE TO EAT AND STAY

$$
SEAFOOD

✕ **Harraseeket Lunch & Lobster Co.** Seafood baskets and lobster dinners are the focus at this popular, bare-bones place beside the town landing in South Freeport. Order at the counter, find a seat inside or out, and expect long lines in summer. $ *Average main: $18* ✉ *36 S. Main St., South Freeport* ☎ *207/865–4888* ⊕ *www.harraseeketlunchandlobster.*

com ✍ *Reservations not accepted* ▭ *No credit cards* ⏲ *Closed mid-Oct.–Apr.*

$$$$ HOTEL Fodor's Choice ★ 🏨 **Harraseeket Inn.** Despite some modern appointments, this large hotel has a country-inn ambience throughout. **Pros:** full breakfast and afternoon tea; elevators and other modern touches; walk to shopping district. **Cons:** additions have diminished some authenticity. [$] *Rooms from: $235* ✉ *162 Main St.* ☎ *207/865–9377, 800/342–6423* 🌐 *www.harraseeketinn.com* 🛏 *82 rooms, 2 suites, 9 town houses* 🍴 *Breakfast.*

NIGHTLIFE AND THE ARTS

L.L. Bean Summer Concert Series. Throughout the summer, L.L.Bean hosts free activities, including concerts, at L.L. Bean Discovery Park. It's set back from Main Street, along a side street the runs between the company's flagship and home furnishings stores. ✉ *L.L. Bean Discovery Park, 95 Main St.* ☎ *877/755–2326* 🌐 *www.llbean.com/events.*

SPORTS AND THE OUTDOORS

CLASSES **L.L. Bean Outdoor Discovery Schools.** It shouldn't come as a surprise that one of the world's largest outdoor outfitters also provides its customers with instructional adventures to go with its products. L.L. Bean's year-round Outdoor Discovery Schools offer courses in canoeing, biking, kayaking, fly-fishing, snowshoeing, cross-country skiing, and other outdoor sports. ✉ *95 Main St.* ☎ *888/552–3261* 🌐 *www.llbean.com/ods.*

SHOPPING

The *Freeport Visitors Guide* lists the more than 200 stores on Main Street, Bow Street, and elsewhere, including Coach, Brooks Brothers, Banana Republic, J. Crew, and Cole Haan. You can pick it up around town.

Edgecomb Potters. Nationally known Edgecomb Potters produces vibrantly colored, hand-thrown porcelain tableware finished with an unusual crystalline glaze. It also sells jewelry, glassware, glass sculptures, and gifts for the home, almost all made by American artisans. ✉ *8 School St.* ☎ *207/865–1705* 🌐 *www.edgecombpotters.com.*

Fodor's Choice ★ **L.L. Bean.** Founded in 1912 as a mail-order merchandiser after its namesake invented a hunting boot, L.L. Bean's giant flagship store attracts more than 3 million shoppers annually and is open 365 days a year in the heart of Freeport's outlet shopping district. You can still find the original hunting boots, along with cotton and wool sweaters; outerwear of all kinds; casual clothing, boots, and shoes for men, women, and kids; and camping equipment. Nearby are the company's home furnishings store, bike, boat, and ski store, and outlet. ✉ *95 Main St.* ☎ *877/755–2326* 🌐 *www.llbean.com.*

R. D. Allen Freeport Jewelers. This shop specializes in brightly colored tourmaline and other gemstones mined in Maine. Most of the pieces are the work of Maine artisans. Watermelon tourmaline is a specialty. ✉ *13 Middle St.* ☎ *207/865–1818, 877/837–3835* 🌐 *www.rdallen.com.*

Thos. Moser Cabinetmakers. Famed local furniture company Thos. Moser Cabinetmakers sells artful, handmade wood pieces with clean, classic lines. The store has information on tours at the workshop a half an hour away in Auburn. ✉ *149 Main St.* ☎ *207/865–4519* 🌐 *www.thosmoser.com.*

THE MID-COAST REGION

11

Lighthouses dot the headlands of Maine's Mid-Coast region, where thousands of miles of coastline wait to be explored. Defined by chiseled peninsulas stretching south from U.S. 1, this area has everything from the sandy beaches and sandbars of Popham Beach to the jutting cliffs of Monhegan Island. If you are intent on hooking a trophy-size fish or catching a glimpse of a whale, there are plenty of cruises available. If you want to explore deserted beaches and secluded coves, kayaks are your best bet. Put in at the Harpswells, or on the Cushing and Saint George peninsulas, or simply paddle among the lobster boats and other vessels that ply the waters here.

Tall ships often visit Maine, sometimes sailing up the Kennebec River for a stopover at Bath's Maine Maritime Museum, on the site of the old Percy & Small Shipyard. Next door to the museum, the Bath Iron Works still builds the U.S. Navy's Aegis-class destroyers.

Along U.S. 1, charming towns, each unique, have an array of attractions. Brunswick, while a bigger, commercial city, has rows of historic brick and clapboard homes and is home to Bowdoin College. Bath is known for its maritime heritage. Wiscasset has arguably the best antiques shopping in the state. On its waterfront you can choose from a variety of seafood shacks competing for the best lobster rolls. Damariscotta, too, is worth a stop for its good seafood restaurants.

South along the peninsulas the scenery opens to glorious vistas of working lobster harbors and marinas. It's here you find the authentic lobster pounds where you can watch your catch come in off the traps. Boothbay Harbor is the quaintest town in the Mid-Coast and a busy tourist destination come summer, with lots of little stores that are perfect for window-shopping. It's one of three towns where you can take a ferry to Monhegan Island, which seems to be inhabited exclusively by painters at their easels, depicting the cliffs and weathered homes with colorful gardens.

ESSENTIALS

Visitor Information Southern Midcoast Maine Chamber ⊠ *Border Trust Business Center, 2 Main St., Topsham* ☎ *877/725–8797* ⊕ *www.midcoastmaine.com.* **State of Maine Visitor Information Center** ⊠ *1100 U.S. 1, off I–95, Yarmouth* ☎ *207/846–0833, 888/624–6345* ⊕ *www.mainetourism.com.*

BRUNSWICK

10 miles north of Freeport via U.S. 1.

Lovely brick and clapboard buildings are the highlight of Brunswick's Federal Street Historic District, which includes Federal Street and Park Row and the stately campus of Bowdoin College. From the intersection of Pleasant and Maine streets, in the center of town, you can walk in any direction and discover an impressive array of restaurants. Seafood? German cuisine? A Chinese buffet that beats out all the competition? It's all here. So are bookstores, gift shops, boutiques, and jewelers.

Below Brunswick are Harpswell Neck and the more than 40 islands that make up the town of Harpswell, known collectively as the Harpswells. Route 123 runs down Harpswell Neck, where small coves shelter lobster boats, and summer cottages are tucked away among birch and spruce trees. On your way down from Cook's Corner to Land's End at the end of Route 24, you cross Sebascodegan Island. Heading east here leads to East Harpswell and Cundy's Harbor. Continuing straight south down Route 24 leads to Orr's Island. Stop at Mackerel Cove to see a real fishing harbor; there are a few parking spaces where you can stop to picnic and look for beach glass or put in your kayaks. Inhale the salt breeze as you cross the world's only cribstone bridge (designed so that water flows freely through gaps between the granite blocks) on your way to Bailey Island, home to a lobster pound made famous thanks in part to a Visa commercial.

GETTING HERE AND AROUND

From Interstate 295 take the Coastal Connector to U.S. 1 in Brunswick. From here Route 24 runs to Bailey Island and Route 123 down Harpswell Neck.

WHERE TO EAT

$$$ ✕ **Cook's Lobster House.** What began as a lobster shack on Bailey's Island
SEAFOOD in 1955 has grown into a huge, internationally famous family-style
FAMILY restaurant with a small gift shop. The restaurant still catches its own
Fodor'sChoice seafood, so you can count on the lobster casserole and the haddock
★ sandwich to be delectable. A shore dinner will still set you back close to $40, but you won't leave hungry after a 1¼-pound lobster with coleslaw, potato, chowder, and mussels or clams. Whether you choose inside or deck seating, you can watch the activity on the water as men check lobster pots and kayakers fan across the bay. $ *Average main: $24 ⊠ 68 Garrison Cove Rd., Bailey Island ☎ 207/833–2818 ⊕ www.cookslobster.com ⌲ Reservations not accepted ⊗ Closed early Jan.–mid-Feb.*

SPORTS AND THE OUTDOORS

H2Outfitters. The coast near Brunswick is full of hidden nooks and crannies waiting to be explored by kayak. H2Outfitters, at the southern end of Orr's Island just before the Cribstone Bridge, is the place in Harpswell to get on the water. It provides top-notch kayaking instruction and also offers half-day, full-day, bed-and-breakfast, and camping trips in the waters off its home base and elsewhere in Maine. ⊠ *1894 Harpswell Island Rd., Orr's Island ☎ 207/833–5257, 800/205–2925 ⊕ www.h2outfitters.com.*

BATH

11 miles north of Brunswick via U.S. 1.

Bath has been a shipbuilding center since 1607. The result of its prosperity can be seen in its handsome mix of Federal, Greek Revival, and Italianate homes along Front, Centre, and Washington streets. In the heart of Bath's historic district are some charming 19th-century homes, including the 1820 Federal-style home at 360 Front Street, the 1810

At the Maine Maritime Museum, a boatbuilder works on a yacht tender, used to ferry people to shore.

Greek Revival mansion at 969 Washington Street, covered with gleaming white clapboards, and the Victorian gem at 1009 Washington Street, painted a distinctive shade of raspberry. All three operate as inns. An easily overlooked site is the town's City Hall. The bell in its tower was cast by Paul Revere in 1805.

The venerable Bath Iron Works completed its first passenger ship in 1890. During World War II, BIW—as it's locally known—launched a new ship every 17 days. It is still building today, turning out destroyers for the U.S. Navy. BIW is one of the state's largest employers, with about 5,600 workers. It's a good idea to avoid U.S. 1 on weekdays from 3:15 pm to 4:30 pm, when a major shift change takes place. You can tour BIW through the Maine Maritime Museum.

GETTING HERE AND AROUND
U.S. 1 passes through downtown and across the Kennebec River at Bath. Downtown is on the north side of the highway along the river.

EXPLORING

Fodor's Choice ★ **Maine Maritime Museum.** No trip to Bath is complete without a visit to this cluster of buildings that once made up the historic Percy & Small Shipyard. Plan on at least half a day—tickets are good for two days because there's so much to see at this museum, which examines the world of shipbuilding and is the only way to tour Bath Iron Works (May to mid-Oct.). From mid-June through Columbus Day, five nature and lighthouse boat tours cruise the scenic Kennebec River—one takes in 10 lights. The 142-foot Grand Banks fishing schooner *Sherman Zwicker* docks here during the same period. Inside the main museum building, exhibits use ship models, paintings, photographs, and historical artifacts

Low tide is the perfect time to explore tidal flats, tide pools, or fish from the shore at Popham Beach State Park.

to tell the maritime history of the region. Hour-long tours of the ship-yard show how these massive wooden ships were built. In the boat shop you can watch boatbuilders wield their tools. A separate historic build-ing houses a fascinating lobstering exhibit. It's worth coming here just to watch the 18-minute video on lobstering written and narrated by E. B. White. A gift shop and bookstore are on the premises, and you can grab a bite to eat in the café or bring a picnic to eat on the grounds. ■TIP→ **Kids ages five and younger get in free.** ⊠ *243 Washington St.* ☎ *207/443–1316* ⊕ *www.mainemaritimemuseum.org* ✉ *$15 (good for 2 days within 7-day period)* ⊙ *Daily 9:30–5.*

OFF THE BEATEN PATH

Popham Beach State Park. The park has bathhouses and picnic tables. At low tide you can walk several miles of tidal flats and also out to a nearby island, where you can explore tide pools or fish off the ledges. It's on a peninsula facing the open Atlantic, between the mouths of the Kennebec and Morse rivers. About a mile from Popham Beach State Park, the road ends at the Civil War–era Fort Popham State Historic Site, an unfinished semicircular granite fort on the sea. Enjoy the beach views at nearby Spinney's Restaurant, or grab a quick bite next door at Percy's Store, which has picnic tables and a path to the beach. **Amenities:** lifeguards; parking (no fee); showers; toilets. **Best for:** swimming; walking. ⊠ *10 Perkins Farm La., off Rte. 209, Phippsburg* ☎ *207/389–1335* ⊕ *www. parksandlands.com* ✉ *$6* ⊙ *Daily 9–sunset.*

WHERE TO EAT AND STAY

$$

BARBECUE

✕ **Beale Street Barbecue.** Ribs are the thing at Maine's oldest (and most authentic) barbecue joint, opened in 1996. Hearty eaters should ask for one of the platters piled high with pulled pork, pulled chicken, or shredded beef. Fried calamari with habanero mayo served with corn bread is a popular appetizer. Enjoy a Maine microbrew at the bar while waiting for your table. $ *Average main: $15* ✉ *215 Water St.* ☎ *207/442–9514* ⊕ *www.mainebbq.com.*

$$$$
RESORT
Fodor's Choice
★

🖼 **Sebasco Harbor Resort.** A family-friendly resort spread across 575 acres on the water near the foot of the Phippsburg Peninsula, this place has a golf course, tennis courts, and a host of other amenities. **Pros:** good choice for families; perfect location; children's activities. **Cons:** no sand beach. $ *Rooms from: $229* ✉ *29 Kenyon Rd., off Rte. 217, Phippsburg* ☎ *207/389–1161, 877/389–1161* ⊕ *www.sebasco. com* ⤳ *107 rooms, 8 suites, 23 cottages* ☉ *Closed late Oct.–mid-May* ⦿ *Some meals.*

WISCASSET

10 miles north of Bath via U.S. 1.

Settled in 1663, Wiscasset sits on the banks of the Sheepscot River. It bills itself "Maine's Prettiest Village," and it's easy to see why: it has graceful churches, old cemeteries, and elegant sea captains' homes (many converted into antiques shops or galleries), and a good wine and specialty foods shop called Treats (stock up here if you're heading north).

Pack a picnic and take it down to the dock on Water Street, where you can watch the fishing boats or grab a lobster roll from Red's Eats or the lobster shack nearby. Wiscasset has expanded its wharf, and this is a great place to catch a breeze on a hot day.

GETTING HERE AND AROUND

U.S. 1 becomes Main Street, and traffic often slows to a crawl come summer. You'll likely have success parking on Water Street rather than Main.

WHERE TO EAT

$
FAST FOOD

✗ **Red's Eats.** You've probably driven right past this little red shack on the Wiscasset side of the bridge if you've visited this area and seen the long line of hungry customers. Red's is a local landmark famous for its hamburgers, hot dogs, lobster and crab rolls, and crispy onion rings and clams fried in their own house-made batters. Maine-made Round Top ice cream is also sold (try blueberry or black raspberry). Enjoy views of the tidal Sheepscot River from picnic tables on the two-level deck or down on the grass by the water. $ *Average main: $12* ✉ *41 Water St.* ☎ *207/882–6128* ⌁ *Reservations not accepted* ⊟ *No credit cards* ☉ *Closed mid-Oct.–mid-Apr.*

SHOPPING

Edgecomb Potters. Not to be missed is Edgecomb Potters, which makes vibrantly colored, exquisitely glazed porcelain that is known around the country. Its store also carries jewelry, glassware, and glass sculptures. ✉ *727 Boothbay Rd., Edgecomb* ☎ *207/882–9493* ⊕ *www. edgecombpotters.com.*

Sheepscot River Pottery. This shop boasts beautifully glazed kitchen tiles as well as kitchenware and home accessories, including sinks. Jewelry

Continued on page 705

MAINE'S LIGHTHOUSES
GUARDIANS OF THE COAST   By John Blodgett

Perched high on rocky ledges, on the tips of wayward islands, and sometimes seemingly on the ocean itself are the more than five dozen lighthouses standing watch along Maine's craggy and ship-busting coastline.

Marshall Point Light

LIGHTING THE WAY: A BIT OF HISTORY

Portland Head Light

Most lighthouses were built in the first half of the 19th century to protect the vessels from running aground at night or when the shoreline was shrouded in fog. Along with the mournful siren of the foghorn and maritime lore, these practical structures have come to symbolize Maine throughout the world.

SHIPWRECKS AND SAFETY

These alluring sentinels of the eastern seaboard today have more form than function, but that certainly was not always the case. Safety was a strong motivating factor in the erection of the lighthouses. Commerce also played a critical role. For example, in 1791 Portland Head light was completed, partially as a response to local merchants' concerns about the rocky entrance to Portland Harbor and the varying depths of the shipping channel, but approval wasn't given until a terrible accident in 1787 in which a 90-ton sloop wrecked. In 1789, the federal government created the U.S. Lighthouse Establishment (later the U.S. Lighthouse Service) to manage them. In 1939 the U.S. Coast Guard took on the job.

Some lighthouses in Maine were built in a much-needed venue, but the points and islands upon which they sat were prone to storm damage. Along with poor construction, this meant that over the years many lighthouses had to be rebuilt or replaced.

LIGHTHOUSES TODAY

In modern times, many of the structures still serve a purpose. Technological advances, such as GPS and radar, are mainly used to navigate through the choppy waters, but a lighthouse or its foghorns are helpful secondary aids, and sometimes the only ones used by recreational boaters. The numerous channel-marking buoys still in existence also are testament to the old tried-and-true methods.

Of the 66 lighthouses along this far northeastern state, 55 are still working, alerting ships (and even small aircraft) of the shoreline's rocky edge. Government agencies, historic preservation organizations, and mostly private individuals own the decommissioned lights.

KEEPERS OF THE LIGHT

Some keepers also used bells and sirens, like this Fog Signal Station on Manana Island in 1898.

Pemaquid Point's fourth-order Fresnel lens

LIFE OF A LIGHTKEEPER

One thing that has changed with the modern era is the disappearance of the lighthouse keeper. In the early 20th century, lighthouses began the conversion from oil-based lighting to electricity. A few decades later, the U.S. Coast Guard switched to automation, phasing out the need for an on-site keeper.

While the keepers of tradition were no longer needed, the traditions of these stalwart, 24/7 employees live on through museum exhibits and retellings of Maine's maritime history, legends, and lore. The tales of a lighthouse keeper's life are the stuff romance novels are made of: adventure, rugged but lonely men, and a beautiful setting along an unpredictable coastline.

The lighthouse keepers of yesterday probably didn't see their own lives so romantically. Their daily narrative was one of hard work and, in some cases, exceptional solitude. A keeper's primary job was to ensure that the lamp was illuminated all day, every day. This meant that oil (whale or coal oil and later kerosene) had to be carried about and wicks trimmed on a regular basis. When fog shrouded the coast, they sounded the solemn horn to pierce through the damp darkness that hid their light. Their quarters were generally small and often attached to the light tower itself. The remote locations of the lights added to the isolation a keeper felt, especially before the advent of radio and telephone, let alone the Internet. Though some brought families with them, the keepers tended to be men who lived alone.

THE LIGHTS 101

Over the years, Fresnel (fray-NELL) lenses were developed in different shapes and sizes so that ship captains could distinguish one lighthouse from another. Invented by Frenchman Augustin Fresnel in the early 19th century, the lens design allows for a greater transmission of light perfectly suited for lighthouse use. Knowing which lighthouse they were near helped captains know which danger was present, such as a submerged ledge or shallow channel. Some lights, such as those at Seguin Island Light, are fixed and don't flash. Other lights are colored red.

DID YOU KNOW?

A lighthouse's personality shines through its flash pattern. For example, Bass Harbor Light (pictured) blinks red every four seconds. Some lights, such as Seguin Island Light, are fixed and don't flash.

LIGHTHOUSE FINDER

Lubec
West Quoddy Head
Old Town
Newport
Farmington
Bangor
Machias
95
179
193
1
Jonesport
Little River Lighthouse
Fort Point
Ellsworth
Searsport
Dyces Head
Narraguagus
Belfast
Castine
Bar Harbor
Prospect Harbor
Winter Harbor
AUGUSTA
26
Grindle Point
Camden
Goose Rocks Light
Mt. Desert Is.
Auburn Lewiston
Rockland Breakwater
Bass Harbor Head
Harrison
Rockland
Burnt Coat Harbor
495
Brunswick
Pemaquid Point
Owls Head
Browns Head
Isle au Haut
Freeport
Bath
Boothbay
Marshall Point
Matinicus Rock
Portland Head
The Cuckolds
Pond Island
Seguin
Portland
Cape Elizabeth (Two Lights)
Monhegan Is.
95
Goat Island
Kennebunk
Kennebunkport
Ogunquit
York
Cape Neddick (Nubble Light)
Whaleback
Kittery
Portsmouth

KEY

🗼 Top Picks

West Quoddy Head

VISITING MAINE'S LIGHTHOUSES

As you travel along the Maine Coast, you won't see lighthouses by watching your odometer—there were no rules about the spacing of lighthouses. The decision as to where to place a lighthouse was a balance between a region's geography and its commercial prosperity and maritime traffic.

Lighthouses dot the shore from as far south as York to the country's eastern-most tip at Lubec. Accessibility varies according to location and other factors. A handful are so remote as to be out-right impossible to reach (except per-haps by kayaking and rock climbing). Some don't allow visitors according to Coast Guard policies, though you can enjoy them through the zoom lens of a camera. Others you can walk right up to and, occasionally, even climb to the top. Lighthouse enthusiasts and preservation groups restore and maintain many of them. All told, approximately 30 light-houses allow some sort of public access.

MUSEUMS, TOURS, AND MORE

Most keeper's quarters are closed to the public, but some of the homes have

SEEK OUT STATE PARKS

■ TIP→ To get the full lighthouse experi-ence your best bet is to visit one that is part of a state or local park. These are gen-erally well kept and tend to allow up-close approach, though typically only outside. While you're at the parks you can picnic or stroll on the trails. Wildlife is often abundant in and near the water; you might spot sea birds and even whales in certain locations (try West Quoddy Head, Portland Head, or Two Lights).

been converted to museums, full of intriguing exhibits on lighthouses, the famous Fresnel lenses used in them, and artifacts of Maine maritime life in general. Talk to the librarians at the **Maine Maritime Museum** in Bath (⊕ *www.mainemaritimemuseum.org*) or sign up for one of the museum's daily light-house cruises to pass by no fewer than ten on the Lighthouse Lovers Cruise. In Rockland, the **Maine Lighthouse Museum** (⊕ *www.mainelighthousemuseum.org*) has the country's largest display of Fresnel lenses. The museum also dis-plays keepers' memorabilia, foghorns, brassware, and more. Maine Open Lighthouse Day is the second Saturday after Labor Day; you can tour and even climb lights usually closed to the public.

For more information, check out the lighthouse page at Maine's official tourism site: ⊕ *www.visitmaine.com/attractions/sightseeing_tours/lighthouse*.

SLEEPING LIGHT: STAYING OVERNIGHT

Goose Rocks, where you can play lighthouse keeper for a week.

Want to stay overnight in a lighthouse? There are several options to do so.

■ TIP → Book lighthouse lodgings as far in advance as possible, up to one year ahead.

Our top pick is **Pemaquid Point Light** (*Newcastle Square Vacation Rentals* ☎ *207/563–6500* ⊕ *www.mainecoast-cottages.com*) because it has one of the most dramatic settings on the Maine coast. Two miles south of **New Harbor**, the second floor of the lighthouse keeper's house is rented out on a weekly basis early May through mid-November to support upkeep of the grounds. When you aren't enjoying the interior, head outdoors: the covered front porch has a rocking-chair view of the ocean. The one-bedroom, one-bath rental sleeps up to a family of four.

Situated smack dab in the middle of a major maritime thoroughfare between two Penobscot Bay islands, **Goose Rocks Light** (☎ *203/400–9565* ⊕ *www.beacon-preservation.org*) offers lodging for the adventuresome—the 51-foot "spark plug" lighthouse is completely surrounded by water. Getting there requires

a ferry ride from Rockland to nearby **North Haven**, a 5- to 10-minute ride by motorboat, and then a climb up an iron-rung ladder from the pitching boat—all based on high tide and winds, of course. There's room for up to eight people. It's a bit more cushy experience than it was for the original keepers: there's a flat-screen TV with DVD player and a selection of music and videos for entertainment. In addition, a hammock hangs on the small deck that encircles the operational light; it's a great place from which to watch the majestic windjammers and the fishing fleet pass by.

Little River Lighthouse (☎ *207/259–3833* ⊕ *www.littleriverlight.org*), along the far northeastern reaches of the coast in **Cutler**, has three rooms available for rent in July and August. You're responsible for food and beverages, linens, towels, and other personal items (don't forget the bug spray), but kitchen and other basics are provided. The lighthouse operators will provide a boat ride to the island upon which the lighthouse sits.

TOP LIGHTHOUSES TO VISIT

BASS HARBOR LIGHT

Familiar to many as the subject of countless photographs is Bass Harbor Light, at the southern end of **Mount Desert Island.** It is within Acadia National Park and 17 miles from the town of Bar Harbor. The station grounds are open year-round.

CAPE ELIZABETH LIGHT

Two Lights State Park is so-named because it's next to two lighthouses. Both of these **Cape Elizabeth** structures were built in 1828. The western light was converted into a private residence in 1924; the eastern light, Cape Elizabeth Light, still projects its automated cylinder of light. The grounds surrounding the building and the lighthouse itself are closed to the public, but the structure is easily viewed and photographed from nearby at the end of Two Lights Road.

CAPE NEDDICK LIGHT

More commonly known as Nubble Light for the smallish offshore expanse of rock it rests upon, Cape Neddick Light sits a few hundred feet off a rock point in **York Beach**. With such a precarious location, its grounds are inaccessible to visitors, but close enough to be exceptionally photogenic, especially during the Christmas season.

MONHEGAN ISLAND LIGHT

Only the adventuresome and the artistic see this light, because **Monhegan Island** is accessible by an approximately one-hour ferry ride. To reach the lighthouse, you have an additional half-mile walk uphill from the ferry dock. The former keeper's quarters is home to the Monhegan Museum, which has exhibits about the island. The tower itself is closed to the public.

PORTLAND HEAD LIGHT

One of Maine's most photographed lighthouses (and its oldest), the famous Portland Head Light was completed in January 1791. At the edge of Fort Williams Park, in **Cape Elizabeth**, the towering white stone lighthouse stands 101 feet above the sea. The Coast Guard operates it and it is not open for tours. However the adjacent keeper's dwelling is now a museum.

WEST QUODDY HEAD LIGHT

Originally built in 1808 by mandate of President Thomas Jefferson, West Quoddy Head Light sits in **Lubec** on the easternmost tip of land in the mainland United States. The 49-foot-high lighthouse with distinctive red and white stripes, is part of Quoddy Head State Park.

Cape Neddick

Portland Head

West Quoddy Head

and other items by local artisans are also on sale. ✉ *34 U.S. 1, Edgecomb* ☎ *207/882–9410* 🌐 *www.sheepscot.com.*

BOOTHBAY

10 miles south of Wiscasset via Rte. 27.

The town of Boothbay includes the village center, Boothbay Harbor, as well as East Boothbay. The shoreline of the Boothbay Peninsula is a craggy stretch of inlets where pleasure craft anchor alongside trawlers and lobster boats. Boothbay Harbor is like a smaller version of Bar Harbor—touristy but friendly and fun—with pretty, winding streets and lots to explore. Commercial Street, Wharf Street, Townsend Avenue, and the By-Way are lined with shops and ice cream parlors.

GETTING HERE AND AROUND

In season, boat trips to Monhegan Island leave from the piers off Commercial Street. Drive out to Ocean Point in East Boothbay for some incredible scenery. Boothbay is 13 miles south of Wiscasset via U.S. 1 and Route 27.

EXPLORING

Coastal Maine Botanical Garden. Set aside a couple of hours to stroll among the roses, lupines, and rhododendrons at the 248-acre Coastal Maine Botanical Garden. In the summer free docent-led tours leave from the visitor center at 11 and 1 on Thursdays and Saturdays. The "children's garden" is a wonderland of stone sculptures, rope bridges, and even a hedge maze. ✉ *132 Botanical Gardens Dr., off Rte. 27, Boothbay* ☎ *207/633–4333* 🌐 *www.mainegardens.org* 🎟 *$14 Apr.–Oct., free Nov.–March.* 🕒 *9–5.*

WHERE TO EAT AND STAY

$$$ SEAFOOD 🍴 **Boat House Bistro.** The multitiered rooftop terrace (complete with an outdoor bar) stays crowded all summer at the Boat House Bistro. Austrian-born chef Karin Guerin dishes up tapas-style small plates ranging from mango empanadas to sweet-potato latkes. For those seeking the full-on Maine experience, there are plenty of seafood options, too, including a different paella each day. The waitstaff is young, friendly, and just as diverse as the menu. [$] *Average main: $21* ✉ *12 By-Way, Boothbay Harbor* ☎ *207/633–0400* 🌐 *www.theboathousebistro.com* 🕒 *Closed mid-Oct.–mid-Apr.*

$$$$ B&B/INN 🏨 **Topside Inn.** The Adirondack chairs on the immense lawn of this historic, hilltop B&B have what is probably the best bay view in town. **Pros:** knockout views; plenty of green space for croquet; easy walk downtown. **Cons:** more guests coming and going than at your average B&B; walls are a bit thin in the annexes. [$] *Rooms from: $330* ✉ *60 McKown St., Boothbay Harbor* ☎ *207/633–5404* 🌐 *www.topsideinn.com* 🛏 *25 rooms* 🕒 *Closed mid-Oct.–mid-May* 🍽 *Breakfast.*

DAMARISCOTTA

8 miles north of Wiscasset via U.S. 1.

The Damariscotta region comprises several communities along the rocky coast. The town itself sits on the water and is a lively place filled with attractive shops and restaurants.

Just across the bridge over the Damariscotta River is the town of Newcastle, between the Sheepscot and Damariscotta rivers. Newcastle was settled in the early 1600s. The earliest inhabitants planted apple trees, but the town later became an industrial center, home to several shipyards and a couple of mills. The oldest Catholic church in New England, St. Patrick's, is here, and it still rings its original Paul Revere bell.

Bremen, which encompasses more than a dozen islands and countless rocky outcrops, has many seasonal homes along the water, and the main industries in the small community are fishing and clamming. Nobleboro, a bit north of here on U.S. 1, was settled in the 1720s by Colonel David Dunbar, sent by the British to rebuild the fort at Pemaquid. Neighboring Waldoboro is situated on the Medomak River and was settled largely by Germans in the mid-1700s. You can still visit the old German Meeting House, built in 1772. The Pemaquid Peninsula stretches south from Damariscotta to include Bristol, South Bristol, Round Pond, New Harbor, and Pemaquid.

GETTING HERE AND AROUND

In Newcastle, U.S. 1B runs from U.S. 1 across the Damariscotta River to Damariscotta. From this road take Route 129 south to South Bristol and Route 130 south to Bristol and New Harbor. From here you can return to U.S. 1 heading north on Route 32 through Round Pond and Bremen. In Waldoboro, turn off U.S. 1 on Jefferson Street to see the historic village center.

ESSENTIALS

Visitor Information Damariscotta Region Chamber of Commerce ☎ *207/563–8340* 🌐 *www.damariscottaregion.com.*

NEED A BREAK?

Moody's Diner. This diner makes whoopie pies of considerable size, prized for their filling above all. ✉ ***1885 Atlantic Hwy., Waldoboro*** ☎ ***207/832–7785*** 🌐 ***www.moodysdiner.com.***

WHERE TO EAT AND STAY

$$ AMERICAN

🍴 **King Eider's Pub & Restaurant.** The classic pub right downtown bills itself as having the finest crab cakes in New England. Start with the fresh local oysters that the Damariscotta region is known for, then move on to entrées like steak-and-ale pie, sea scallop florentine, or sautéed haddock with chips. With exposed-brick walls and low wooden beams, it's a cozy place to enjoy your favorite ale. Stop by on Thursday nights for live music. [$] *Average main: $18* ✉ *2 Elm St.* ☎ *207/563–6008* 🌐 *www.kingeiderspub.com.*

$$$ B&B/INN

🏨 **Newcastle Inn.** A riverside location, tasteful decor, and lots of common areas (inside and out) make this a relaxing country inn. **Pros:** guests can order beer or wine; one suite-like room and two suites with sitting areas. **Cons:** not an in-town location. [$] *Rooms from: $190* ✉ *60 River Rd.,*

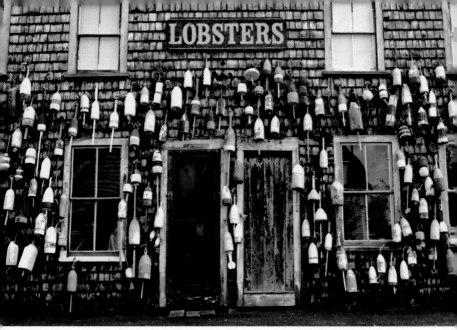

Lobster trap buoys are popular decorations in Maine; the markings represent a particular lobsterman's claim.

Newcastle ☎ 207/563–5685 ⊕ *www.newcastleinn.com* ⇗ *12 rooms, 2 suites* ⏐⊙⏐ *Breakfast.*

PEMAQUID POINT

10 miles south of Damariscotta via U.S. 1, U.S. 1B, and Rte. 130.

Pemaquid Point is the tip of the Pemaquid Peninsula, bordered by Muscongus and Johns bays. It's home to the famous lighthouse of the same name and its attendant fog bell and tiny museum. Also at the bottom of the peninsula, along the Muscongus Bay, is the Nature Conservancy's Rachel Carson Salt Pond Preserve.

GETTING HERE AND AROUND

From U.S. 1, take U.S. 1B into Damariscotta and head south on Route 130 to Pemaquid Point.

EXPLORING

FAMILY **Pemaquid Point Light.** At the end of Route 130, this lighthouse at the tip of the Pemaquid Peninsula looks as though it sprouted from the ragged, tilted chunk of granite that it commands. Most days in the summer you can climb the tower to the light. The former keeper's cottage is now the Fishermen's Museum, which displays historic photographs, scale models, and artifacts that explore commercial fishing in Maine. Also here are the original fog bell and bell house. Pemaquid Art Gallery, on-site, mounts exhibitions by area artists in the summer. There are restrooms and picnic tables. ✉ *3115 Bristol Rd., Pemaquid* ☎ *207/677–2492* ⊕ *www.bristolparks.org* 🎫 *$2* ⊙ *Museum: early May–Oct., daily 9–5.*

WHERE TO EAT AND STAY

$$ SEAFOOD 🍴 **Moscungus Bay Lobster Co.** The food here is practcially guaranteed to be fresh: the lobsters come in off the boat at one of the pier, and the restaurant is at the other. Grab a picnic table and be careful not to hit your head on the colorful, dangling wooden buoys. It's fun to watch the lobstermen unload their catch over lunch. [$] *Average main: $18* ✉ *28 Town Landing Rd., Round Pond* ☎ *207/529–2251* 🌐 *www.mainefreshlobster.com* 🕒 *Closed mid-May–mid-Oct.*

$$ SEAFOOD 🍴 **Round Pond Fisherman's Coop.** Sheltered Moscungus Bay is where you'll find this down-home lobster shack, on the pier so you have pleasant views of the water. Competition with the neighboring Moscungus Bay Lobster Co. keeps the prices low for fresh-off-the-boat lobster and steamers. [$] *Average main: $18* ✉ *25 Town Landing Rd., Round Pond* ☎ *207/529–5725* 🕒 *Closed Labor Day–mid-May.*

$$ B&B/INN 🏨 **Christmas Cove Inn.** If you're traveling with a dog, you'll find few more accommodating spots in Maine than this out-of-the-way place on Rutherford Island. **Pros:** great if you're traveling with dogs; great views from lookout. **Cons:** dogs on premises. [$] *Rooms from: $150* ✉ *53 Coveside Rd., South Bristol* ☎ *207/644–1502, 866/644–1502* 🌐 *www.christmascoveinn.com* 🛏 *7 rooms* 🍽 *No meals.*

SPORTS AND THE OUTDOORS

Hardy Boat Cruises. Mid-May through mid-October, you can take a cruise to Monhegan with Hardy Boat Cruises. The company also offers seal- and puffin-watching trips and lighthouse and fall coastal cruises. ✉ *Shaw's Wharf, 132 State Rte. 32, New Harbor* ☎ *207/677–2026, 800/278–3346* 🌐 *www.hardyboat.com.*

THOMASTON

10 miles northeast of Waldoboro, 72 miles northeast of Portland.

Thomaston is a delightful town, full of beautiful sea captains' homes and dotted with antiques and specialty shops. A National Historic District encompasses parts of High, Main, and Knox streets. The town is the gateway to the two peninsulas; you will see water on both sides as you arrive.

GETTING HERE AND AROUND

U.S. 1 is Main Street through Thomaston. Route 131 runs down the St. George Peninsula from here and Route 97 leads down the Cushing Peninsula and to Friendship.

WHERE TO EAT

$$ AMERICAN 🍴 **Thomaston Cafe.** This is a great place to stop on the long, slow drive up U.S. 1. Works by local artists adorn the walls of this small downtown café, which uses local ingredients as much as possible. It serves an excellent breakfast, including homemade corned beef hash. For lunch there's scrumptious haddock chowder and delicious sandwiches. Try the panfried haddock sandwich lightly breaded with panko bread crumbs, or a salad and crab cakes (sold at breakfast, too). Entrées include lobster ravioli and filet mignon with béarnaise sauce. Sunday brunch is popu-

lar. Ⓢ *Average main: $20* ✉ *154 Main St.* ☎ *207/354–8589* ⊕ *www. thomastoncafe.com* ☉ *Closed Mon. No dinner Sun.–Wed.*

$$
SEAFOOD

✕ **Waterman's Beach Lobster.** This place in South Thomaston is authentic, inexpensive, and scenic, overlooking islands in the Atlantic. You can eat lunch or dinner under the pavilions right next to the beach and pier, or get even closer to the water at picnic tables. In addition to the seafood favorites, Waterman's also sells freshly baked pies and locally made ice cream. It's strictly BYOB. Ⓢ *Average main: $18* ✉ *343 Waterman's Beach Rd., South Thomaston* ☎ *207/596–7819, 207/594–7518* ⊕ *www.watermansbeachlobster.com* ☉ *Closed Oct.–mid-June.*

PORT CLYDE

5 miles south of Tenants Harbor via Rte. 131.

The fishing village of Port Clyde sits at the end of the St. George Peninsula. The road leading here meanders along the St. George River, passing meadows and farmhouses and winding away from the river to the east side of the peninsula, which faces the Atlantic Ocean. Shipbuilding and granite quarrying were big industries here in the 1800s. Later, seafood canneries opened here; you can still buy Port Clyde sardines. Lobster fishing is an economic anchor today, and the quiet village is a haven for artists, with a number of galleries. Marshall Point Lighthouse, right in the harbor, has a small museum.

EXPLORING

Monhegan Island Light. Getting a look at this squat stone lighthouse— from land, anyway—requires a slightly steep, half-mile walk uphill from the island's ferry dock. The lighthouse was automated in 1959, and the former keeper's quarters became the Monhegan Museum shortly thereafter. The tower is open sporadically throughout the summer for short tours. Exhibits at the museum have as much to do with life on the island as they do with the lighthouse itself. ✉ *Lighthouse Hill Rd., ½ mile east of dock, Monhegan* ☎ *207/596–7003* ☉ *Museum July and Aug., daily 11:30–3:30; June and Sept., daily 1:30–3:30.*

PENOBSCOT BAY

Few could deny that Penobscot Bay is one of Maine's most dramatically beautiful regions. Its more than 1,000 miles of coastline is made up of rocky granite boulders, often undeveloped shores, a sprinkling of colorful towns, and views of the sea and islands that are a photographer's dream.

Penobscot Bay stretches 37 miles from Port Clyde in the south to Stonington, the little fishing village at the tip of Deer Isle, in the north. The bay begins where the Penobscot River, New England's second-largest river system, ends, near Stockton Springs, and terminates in the Gulf of Maine, where it is 47 miles wide. It covers an estimated 1,070 square miles and is home to more than 1,800 islands.

Initially, shipbuilding was the primary moneymaker here. In the 1800s, during the days of the great tall ships (or Down Easters, as they were often called), more wooden ships were built in Maine than any other state in the country, and many were constructed along Penobscot Bay. This golden age of billowing sails and wooden sailing ships came to an end with the development of the steam engine. By 1900, sailing ships were no longer a viable commercial venture in Maine. However, as you will see when traveling the coast, the tall ships have not entirely disappeared—some, albeit tiny in number compared to the 1800s heyday, have been revived as recreational boats known as windjammers. Today, once again, there are more tall ships along Penobscot Bay than anywhere else in the country.

ROCKLAND

3 miles north of Thomaston via U.S. 1.

The town is considered the gateway to Penobscot Bay and is the first stop on U.S. 1 offering a glimpse of the often sparkling and island-dotted blue bay. Though once merely a place to pass through on the way to tonier ports like Camden, Rockland now gets attention on its own, thanks to a trio of attractions: the renowned Farnsworth Museum, the increasingly popular summer Lobster Festival, and the lively North Atlantic Blues Festival. Specialty shops and galleries line the main street, and one of the restaurants, Primo (between Camden and the little village of Owls Head), has become nationally famous. The town is still a large fishing port and the commercial hub of this coastal area.

Rockland Harbor bests Camden by one as home to the largest fleet of Maine windjammers. The best place in Rockland to view these beautiful vessels as they sail in and out of the harbor is the mile-long granite breakwater, which bisects the outer portion of Rockland Harbor. To get there, from U.S. 1, head east on Waldo Avenue and then right on Samoset Road; follow this short road to its end.

GETTING HERE AND AROUND

U.S. 1 runs along Main Street here, while U.S. 1A curves through the residential neighborhood west of the business district, offering a faster route if you are passing through.

Visitor Information Penobscot Bay Regional Chamber of Commerce ⊠ *Visitor Center, 1 Park Dr.* ☎ *207/596–0376, 800/223–5459* ⊕ *www.therealmaine.com.*

EXPLORING

Fodor'sChoice **Farnsworth Art Museum.** One of the most important small museums in the
★ country, much of its collection is devoted to Maine-related works of the famous Wyeth family: N. C. Wyeth, an accomplished illustrator whose works were featured in many turn-of-the-20th-century books; his late son Andrew, one of the country's best-known painters; and Andrew's son James, also an accomplished painter, who like his elders before him summers nearby. Galleries in the main building always display some of Andrew Wyeth's works, such as *The Patriot, Witchcraft,* and *Turkey Pond.* The **Wyeth Center,** a former church, shows art by his father and son. The museum's collection also includes works by Fitz Henry Lane, George Bellows, Frank W. Benson, Edward Hopper (as watercolors, they may be "resting"), Louise Nevelson, and Fairfield Porter. Changing

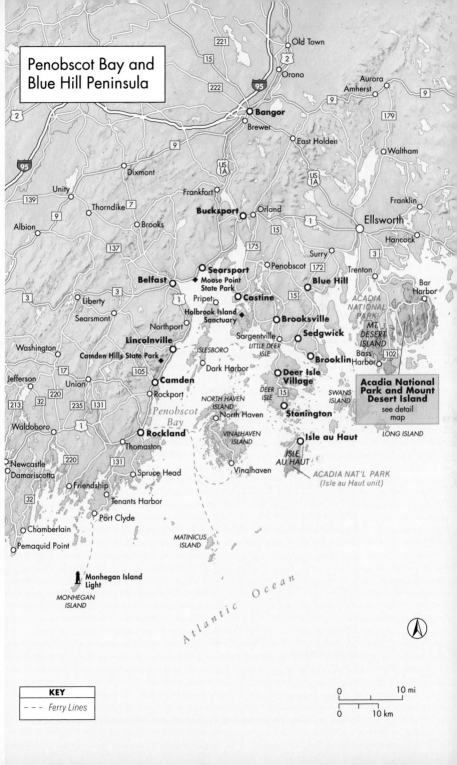

Penobscot Bay and Blue Hill Peninsula

Old Town
Orono
221
15
2
222
95
Bangor
Brewer
2
East Holden
Dixmont
Waltham
Frankfort
9
US 1A
Unity
139
Thorndike
7
Bucksport
Orland
Brooks
Ellsworth
Albion
9
137
175
Hancock
Franklin
Liberty
3
Searsport
Penobscot
172
Surry
3
Trenton
Moose Point State Park
Belfast
Castine
Blue Hill
Searsmont
1
Pripet
15
ACADIA NATIONAL PARK
Washington
Northport
Holbrook Island Sanctuary
Brooksville
Bar Harbor
Lincolnville
Sargentville
Sedgwick
MT. DESERT ISLAND
Jefferson
Camden Hills State Park
ISLESBORO
LITTLE DEER ISLE
Brooklin
Bass Harbor
102
Union
17
105
Camden
Dark Harbor
DEER ISLE
Deer Isle Village
SWANS ISLAND
Acadia National Park and Mount Desert Island
see detail map
213
32
220
235
131
Rockport
NORTH HAVEN ISLAND
North Haven
15
Stonington
LONG ISLAND
Waldoboro
1
Penobscot Bay
Rockland
VINALHAVEN ISLAND
Isle au Haut
Newcastle
220
131
Thomaston
ISLE AU HAUT
Damariscotta
Spruce Head
ACADIA NAT'L PARK (Isle au Haut unit)
32
Friendship
Vinalhaven
Tenants Harbor
Port Clyde
Chamberlain
MATINICUS ISLAND
Pemaquid Point
Monhegan Island Light
MONHEGAN ISLAND
Atlantic Ocean

KEY
- - - Ferry Lines

0   10 mi
0   10 km

CLOSE UP

Windjammer Excursions

A windjammer cruise gives you a chance to admire Maine's dramatic coast from the water.

Nothing defines the Maine coastal experience more than a sailing trip on a windjammer. Windjammers were built all along the East Coast in the 19th and early 20th centuries. Designed primarily to carry cargo, these beauties (most are wood hulled) have a rich past—the *Nathaniel Bowditch* served in World War II, while others plied the waters in the lumbering, granite, fishing, and oystering trades or served as pilot boats. They vary in size but can be as small as 46 feet and hold six passengers (plus a couple of crew members) or more than 130 feet and hold 40 passengers and 10 crew members. During a windjammer excursion passengers are usually able to participate in the navigation, be it hoisting a sail or playing captain at the wheel.

During the Camden Windjammer Festival, held Labor Day weekend, crowds gather to watch the region's fleet sail into the harbor, and most boats are open for tours. The schooner-crew talent show later in the weekend is a bit more irreverent than the majestic arrival ceremony.

Cruises can be anywhere from one to eight days, and day trips usually involve a tour of the harbor and some lighthouse sightseeing. The price, ranging from $230 to $1,100, depending on length of trip, includes all meals. Trips leave from Camden, Rockland, and Rockport. You can get information on the fleets by contacting one of two windjammer organizations:

Maine Windjammer Association ☎ *800/807–9463* ⊕ *www.sailmainecoast.com.* **Maine Windjammer Cruises** ☎ *207/236–2938, 800/736–7981* ⊕ *www.mainewindjammercruises.com.*

exhibits are shown in the **Jamien Morehouse Wing.** The **Farnsworth Homestead,** a handsome circa-1850 Greek Revival dwelling that's part of the museum, retains its original lavish Victorian furnishings and is open late June through mid-October.

In Cushing, a tiny town about 10 miles south of Thomaston on the St. George River, the museum operates the **Olson House,** which is depicted in Andrew Wyeth's famous painting *Christina's World,* as well as in other works by the artist. It's accessible by guided tour only. ✉ *16 Museum St.* ☎ *207/596–6457* 🌐 *www.farnsworthmuseum.org* 🎟 *$12* ⏲ *Jan.–Mar., Wed.–Sun. 10–5; Apr., May, Nov., and Dec., Tues.–Sun. 10–5; June–Oct., Sat.–Tues. and Thurs., 10–5, Wed. and Fri. 10–8.*

FAMILY **Maine Lighthouse Museum.** The lighthouse museum has more than 25 Fresnel lighthouse lenses, as well as a collection of lighthouse artifacts and Coast Guard memorabilia. Permanent exhibits spotlight topics like lighthouse heroines—women who manned the lights when the keepers couldn't—and lightships. ✉ *1 Park Dr.* ☎ *207/594–3301* 🌐 *www.mainelighthousemuseum.org* 🎟 *$5* ⏲ *June–Oct., weekdays 9–5, weekends 10–4; Nov., Dec., and Mar.–May, Thurs. and Fri. 9–5, Sat. 10–4.*

WHERE TO EAT

$$$$ MEDITERRANEAN Fodor's Choice ★

🍴 **Primo.** Award-winning chef Melissa Kelly and her world-class restaurant have been written up in *Gourmet, Bon Appétit,* and *O Magazine.* The upstairs in this restored Victorian home has a funky vibe; downstairs is fancier. Wherever you eat it's farm-to-table here: the eatery raises chickens and pigs, cures meats, produces eggs, and grows produce. Combining fresh Maine ingredients with Mediterranean influences, the daily-changing menu includes dishes like kale salad with creamy garlic dressing, house-made pasta with local squid, and duck with sweet-and-sour rhubarb chutney. Pastry chef Price Kushner creates delectable desserts like cannoli featuring crushed pistachios and amarena cherries. [$] *Average main: $35* ✉ *2 S. Main St.* ☎ *207/596–0770* 🌐 *www.primorestaurant.com* ⏲ *No lunch.*

$$ DINER

🍴 **Rockland Cafe.** It may not look like much from the outside, but Rockland Cafe is one of the most popular eateries in town. It's famous for the size of its breakfasts—don't pass up the fish cakes, also available for lunch and dinner. If you're a late riser, don't worry: breakfast is served until noon (until 4 November to April). At dinner, the seafood combo of shrimp, scallops, clams, and haddock is excellent, or there's also classic liver and onions. [$] *Average main: $15* ✉ *441 Main St.* ☎ *207/596–7556* 🌐 *www.rocklandcafe.com.*

WHERE TO STAY

$$$ B&B/INN

🏨 **Berry Manor Inn.** Originally the residence of Rockland merchant Charles H. Berry, this 1898 shingle-style B&B sits in Rockland's National Historic District. **Pros:** quiet neighborhood; within walking distance of downtown and the harbor; rooms have TVs. **Cons:** not much of a view. [$] *Rooms from: $195* ✉ *81 Talbot Ave.* ☎ *207/596–7696, 800/774–5692* 🌐 *www.berrymanorinn.com* 🛏 *12 rooms* 🍽 *Breakfast.*

$$ B&B/INN

🏨 **LimeRock Inn.** In the center of town in Rockland's National Historic District, the LimeRock Inn puts you within easy walking distance of the Farnsworth Museum and many restaurants. **Pros:** all rooms have

TVs and DVD players; large in-town lot with gazebo. **Cons:** not on the water. $ *Rooms from: $159* ✉ *96 Limerock St.* ☎ *207/594–2257, 800/546–3762* ⊕ *www.limerockinn.com* ⇆ *8 rooms* ⍥ *Breakfast.*

$$$$
RESORT
Fodor's Choice
★

☐ **Samoset Resort.** Occupying 230 waterfront acres on the Rockland–Rockport town line, this all-encompassing resort offers luxurious rooms and suites with private balconies overlooking the water or the grounds. **Pros:** full-service spa; children's programs; activities from basketball to croquet. **Cons:** no beach. $ *Rooms from: $359* ✉ *220 Warrenton St., Rockport* ☎ *207/594–2511, 800/341–1650* ⊕ *www.samoset.com* ⇆ *160 rooms, 18 suites, 4 cottages, 72 condos* ⍥ *Breakfast.*

NIGHTLIFE AND THE ARTS

Maine Lobster Festival. Rockland's annual Maine Lobster Festival, held in early August, is the region's largest annual event. About 10 tons of lobsters are steamed in a huge lobster cooker—you have to see it to believe it. The festival, held in Harbor Park, includes a parade, live entertainment, food booths—and, of course, the crowning of the Maine Sea Goddess. ✉ *Harbor Park, Main St., south of Rte. 1* ☎ *207/596–0376* ⊕ *www.mainelobsterfestival.com.*

FAMILY **North Atlantic Blues Festival.** About a dozen well-known musicians gather for the North Atlantic Blues Festival, a two-day affair held the first full weekend after July 4th. The show officially takes place at the public landing on Rockland Harbor Park, but it also includes a "club crawl" through downtown Rockland on Saturday night. Admission to the festival is $25 in advance, $35 at the gate. ✉ *Harbor Park, Main St.* ☎ *207/691–2248* ⊕ *www.northatlanticbluesfestival.com.*

SPORTS AND THE OUTDOORS

Nathaniel Bowditch. A racing yacht built in 1922 and rebuilt in 1971, the *Nathaniel Bowditch* leads chartered trips lasting from a single afternoon up to four days. ☎ *800/288–4098* ⊕ *www.windjammervacation.com.*

Schooner Heritage. The newest windjammer in Maine's fleet offers three- to six-day cruises, and Captain Doug Lee is a storyteller and author of nautical histories. ✉ *North End Shipyard, 11 Front St., Rockland* ☎ *207/594–8007, 800/648–4544* ⊕ *www.schoonerheritage.com.*

Schooner Summertime. Built with a pointed stern in a pre-Revolutionary War style known as a "pinky" schooner, the *Summertime* heads out on three- to six-day cruises from Rockland (with day sails limited to its home port on Blue Hill Bay, farther up the coast). ✉ *Rockland* ☎ *800/562–8290* ⊕ *www.schoonersummertime.com.*

CAMDEN

8 miles north of Rockland.

Fodor's Choice
★

More than any other town along Penobscot Bay, Camden is the perfect picture-postcard of a Maine coastal village. It is one of the most popular destinations on the Maine Coast, so June through September the town is crowded with visitors, but don't let that scare you away; Camden is worth it. Just come prepared for busy traffic on the town's Main Street (U.S. 1) and make reservations for lodging and restaurants well in advance.

THE PRETTIEST WALK IN THE WORLD

A few years ago *Yankee*, the quintessential magazine of New England, did a cover story on what it called "The Prettiest Walk in the World." The two-lane paved road, which winds up and down, with occasional views of the ocean and the village of Rockport, connects this town with Camden. To judge the merits of the journey of a few miles or so for yourself, you can travel on foot or by car. Begin at the intersection of U.S. 1 and Pascal Avenue. Take a right off U.S. 1 toward Rockport Harbor, then cross the bridge and go up the hill to Central Street. One block later, bear right on Russell Avenue, which becomes Chestnut Street at the Camden town line. Take this all the way to downtown Camden. Lining the way are some of the most beautiful homes in Maine, surrounded by an abundance of flora and fauna. Keep an eye out for Aldermere Farm and its Belted Galloway cows, as well as views of the sparkling ocean. For those who may not know, these rare cows get their name from the foot-wide white "belt" around their middles. The walk or drive is beautiful at any time of the year, but in fall it's breathtaking. Like the rest of New England, the coast of Maine gets a large number of fall-foliage "leaf peepers," and the reds and golds of the chestnut, birch, and elm trees along this winding route are especially beautiful.

Camden is famous not only for its geography, but also for its large fleet of windjammers—relics and replicas from the age of sailing—with their romantic histories and great billowing sails. At just about any hour during the warm months you're likely to see at least one windjammer tied up in the harbor. The excursions, whether for an afternoon or a week, are best from June through September.

The town's compact size makes it perfect for exploring on foot: shops, restaurants, and galleries line Main Street, as well as side streets and alleys around the harbor. Especially worth inclusion on your walking tour is Camden's residential area. It is quite charming and filled with many fascinating old period houses from the time when Federal, Greek Revival, and Victorian architectural styles were the rage among the wealthy. Many of them are now B&Bs. The Chamber of Commerce, at the Public Landing, can provide you with a walking map. Humped on the north side of town are the Camden Hills. Drive or hike to the summit at Camden Hills State Park to enjoy mesmerizing views of the town, harbor, and island-dotted bay.

GETTING HERE AND AROUND

U.S. 1 runs right through Camden. Take Route 90 west from U.S. 1 and rejoin it in Warren to bypass Rockland—this is the quickest route south.

ESSENTIALS

Visitor Information Penobscot Bay Regional Chamber of Commerce
⊠ *Visitor Center, 2 Public Landing* ☎ *207/236–4404, 800/223–5459* ⊕ *www. mainedreamvacation.com.*

WHERE TO EAT

$$$
SEAFOOD

✕ Atlantica. Right on the water's edge, the Atlantica is in a classic weathered shingled building. Its lower deck is cantilevered over the water, offering a romantic setting with great views, and the interior decor is a mix of red walls and contemporary paintings. Fresh seafood with international accents is the specialty here. Favorites include pan-roasted split lobster tails with lemon butter, lobster stuffed with scallops, and pan-roasted king salmon. Everything is made from scratch, including the breads and desserts. There are small plates and lighter offerings like fish tacos. $ *Average main: $27* ⊠ *9 Bayview Landing* ☎ *207/236–6011, 888/507–8514* ⊕ *www.atlanticarestaurant. com* ⌂ *Reservations essential* ⊘ *Closed Nov.–Apr. No lunch.*

$$
SEAFOOD

✕ Cappy's Chowder House. As you would expect from the name, Cappy's clam "chowdah" is the thing to order here—it's been written up in the *New York Times* and *Bon Appétit*—but there are plenty of other seafood specials at this restaurant. Don't be afraid to bring the kids—they'll love the "Crow's Nest" upper level. $ *Average main: $13* ⊠ *1 Main St.* ☎ *207/236–2254* ⊕ *www.cappyschowder.com* ⌂ *Reservations not accepted.*

$$$$
MODERN
AMERICAN

✕ Natalie's Restaurant. One of the most sought-after dining spots in Camden, Natalie's is the creation of Dutch owners Raymond Brunyanszki and Oscar Verest, who brought in executive chef Jon Gaboric in 2013. Located in the Camden Harbour Inn, the restaurant is fine dining with a distinctly Maine flair. Seasonal ingredients set the tone. Choose from two prix-fixe menus (a three-course à la carte for $68 or a seven-course chef's choice for $97), which might feature cabbage-wrapped Maine monkfish or local lamb with root veggies. There's also a five-course lobster tasting menu that may include lobster with peaches and wasabi cream and grilled lobster with carrot puree. In the lounge, you can order small tapas-style dishes or enjoy a predinner cocktail in front of the big fireplace. $ *Average main: $72* ⊠ *Camden Harbour Inn, 83 Bay View St.* ☎ *207/236–7008* ⊕ *www.nataliesrestaurant.com* ⌂ *Reservations essential* ⊘ *Closed Mon. Nov.–May. No lunch.*

WHERE TO STAY

$$$
B&B/INN

☵ Camden Hartstone Inn. This 1835 mansard-roofed Victorian home has been turned into a plush and sophisticated retreat and a fine culinary destination. **Pros:** luxury in the heart of town; extravagant breakfasts; some private entrances. **Cons:** not on water. $ *Rooms from: $199* ⊠ *41 Elm St.* ☎ *207/236–4259, 800/788–4823* ⊕ *www.hartstoneinn.com* ⇱ *12 rooms, 9 suites* ⊚ *Breakfast.*

$$$$
HOTEL

☵ Lord Camden Inn. If you want to be in the center of town and near the harbor, look for this handsome brick building with the bright blue-and-white awnings. **Pros:** large Continental breakfast; suite-like "premier" rooms have balconies and sitting areas. **Cons:** traffic noise in

The view from Camden Hills is a great way to see Penobscot Bay and the town of Camden.

front rooms. $ *Rooms from: $239* ⊠ *24 Main St.* ☎ *207/236–4325, 800/336–4325* ⊕ *www.lordcamdeninn.com* ⤴ *34 rooms, 2 suites* ⭕ *Breakfast.*

$$$$
B&B/INN
Fodor's Choice
★

⬚ **Norumbega Inn.** This welcoming B&B is the one of the most photographed pieces of real estate in Maine, and once you get a look at its castle-like facade, you'll understand why. **Pros:** eye-popping architecture; beautiful views; close to town. **Cons:** stairs to climb. $ *Rooms from: $239* ⊠ *63 High St.* ☎ *207/236–4646, 877/363–4646* ⊕ *www. norumbegainn.com* ⤴ *9 rooms, 2 suites* ⭕ *Breakfast.*

$$$
B&B/INN

⬚ **Whitehall Inn.** The oldest part of the Whitehall is an 1834 white-clapboard sea captain's home, and much of the rest of this historic lodging was built in the early 1900s. **Pros:** short walk to downtown and harbor; breakfast entrée choices. **Cons:** no good water views. $ *Rooms from: $175* ⊠ *52 High St.* ☎ *207/236–3391, 800/789–6565* ⊕ *www. whitehall-inn.com* ⤴ *37 rooms, 4 suites* ☾ *Closed mid-Oct.–mid-May* ⭕ *Breakfast.*

NIGHTLIFE AND THE ARTS

FAMILY **Windjammer Weekend.** One of the biggest and most colorful events of the year is the Camden Windjammer Festival, which takes place over Labor Day weekend. The harbor is packed with historic vessels, and there are lots of good eats. Visitors can tour the ships. ☎ *207/236–4404* ⊕ *www.camdenwindjammerfestival.com.*

SPORTS AND THE OUTDOORS

Angelique. Captain Mike and Lynne McHenry have more than three decades of experience on the high seas. Three- to six-day cruise options aboard the *Angelique* include photography workshops and meteor-watching trips. ⊠ *Camden Harbor* ☎ *800/282–9899* ⊕ *www. sailangelique.com.*

Heron. This schooner, which had a cameo in the movie *The Rum Diary*, offers lunchtime sails, wildlife-watching trips, and sunset cruises. ⊠ *Rockport Marine Park, Pascal Ave., Rockport* ☎ *207/236–8605, 800/599–8605* ⊕ *www.sailheron.com.*

Mary Day. Sailing for more than 50 years, the *Mary Day* is the first schooner in Maine built specifically for vacation excursions. Meals are cooked on an antique wood-fired stove. ⊠ *Camden Harbor, Atlantic Ave.* ☎ *800/992–2218* ⊕ *www.schoonermaryday.com.*

Olad. Captain Aaron Lincoln runs two-hour trips on both the *Olad* and a smaller sailing vessel, spotting lighthouses, coastal mansions, the occasional seal, and the red-footed puffin cousins known as guillemots. Either boat can also be chartered for longer trips. ⊠ *Camden Harbor, Bay View St.* ☎ *207/236–2323* ⊕ *www.maineschooners.com.*

SHOPPING

Camden's downtown area is a shopper's paradise, with lots of interesting places to spend money. Most of the shops and galleries are along Camden's main drag. From the harbor, turn right on Bay View, and walk to Main/High Street. U.S. 1 has lots of names as it runs through Maine. Three are within Camden's town limits—it starts as Elm Street, changes to Main Street, then becomes High Street.

Lily, Lupine & Fern. This full-service florist offers a wonderful array of gourmet foods, chocolates, wines, imported beers, and cheeses. It stocks cigars, too. There's a small deck where you can enjoy harbor views and a cup of coffee. ⊠ *11 Main St.* ☎ *207/236–9600* ⊕ *www.lilylupine.com.*

Planet. In this storefront shop you'll find unique clothing, lots of books, and quality toys, many of them made in Maine. ⊠ *10 Main St.* ☎ *207/236–4410.*

LINCOLNVILLE

6 miles north of Camden via U.S. 1.

Lincolnville's area of most interest—where there are a few restaurants, the ferry to Islesboro, and a swimming beach that attracts folks from neighboring Camden and Belfast—is Lincolnville Beach. The village is tiny; you could go through it in less than a minute. Still, it has a history going back to the Revolution, and you can see a small cannon on the beach here (never used) that was intended to repel the British in the War of 1812.

GETTING HERE AND AROUND

Lincolnville Beach is on U.S. 1, and the town of Lincolnville Center is inland on Route 173.

WHERE TO EAT

$$$

SEAFOOD

FAMILY

✕ **Lobster Pound Restaurant.** If you're looking for an authentic place to enjoy your Maine lobster dinner, this is it. This large restaurant has rustic wooden picnic tables outside, an enclosed patio, and two dining rooms with a gift shop in between. Hundreds of live lobsters are in swimming tanks out back, so feel free to pick your own. There's a full bar, and the wine list includes some local vintages. The classic "shore dinner deluxe" consists of lobster stew or fish chowder, steamed clams or mussels, fried clams, and a 1½-pound lobster, along with side dishes and dessert. Because this is such a big place, you won't have to wait long, even if it's busy. Right on U.S. 1, next to a small beach, the restaurant has beautiful views. [$] *Average main: $22* ✉ *2521 Atlantic Hwy.* ☎ *207/789–5550* 🌐 *www.lobsterpoundmaine.com* 🕘 *Closed mid-Oct.–mid-Apr.*

BELFAST

13 miles north of Lincolnville via U.S. 1.

A number of Maine coastal towns, such as Wiscasset and Damariscotta, like to think of themselves as the prettiest little town in Maine, but Belfast (originally to be named Londonderry) may be the true winner of this title. It has a full variety of charms: a beautiful waterfront; an old and interesting main street climbing up from the harbor; a delightful array of B&Bs, restaurants, and shops; and a friendly population. The downtown even has old-fashioned streetlamps, which set the streets aglow at night.

GETTING HERE AND AROUND

U.S. 1 runs through Belfast as it travels up the coast. From Interstate 95, take U.S. 3 in Augusta to get here. The highways join in Belfast heading north. The information center has a large array of magazines, guidebooks, maps, and brochures that cover the entire Mid-Coast. It also can provide you with a free walking-tour brochure that describes the various historic buildings.

ESSENTIALS

Visitor Information Belfast Area Chamber of Commerce ✉ *14 Main St.* ☎ *207/338–5900* 🌐 *www.belfastmaine.org.*

EXPLORING

In the mid-1800s Belfast was home to a number of wealthy business magnates, ship builders, ship captains, and so on. Their mansions still stand along High Street and in the residential area above it, offering excellent examples of Greek Revival and Federal-style architecture. In fact, the town has one of the best showcases of Greek Revival homes in the state. Don't miss the "White House" where High and Church streets merge several blocks south of downtown.

WHERE TO EAT

$$$ AMERICAN 🍴 **Darby's Restaurant and Pub.** This charming, old-fashioned restaurant and bar is very popular with locals. With pressed-tin ceilings, it has been a bar or a restaurant since it was built in the 1890s. On the walls are works for sale by local artists and old murals of Belfast scenes. Pad thai and chicken with chili and cashews are signature dishes. The menu also has hearty homemade soups and sandwiches and classic fish-and-chips. [$] *Average main: $23* ✉ *155 High St.* ☎ *207/338–2339* 🌐 *www.darbysrestaurant.com.*

$$$
SEAFOOD
Fodor'sChoice
★

✕ **Young's Lobster Pound.** The corrugated-steel building looks more like a fish cannery than a restaurant, but it's one of the best places for an authentic Maine lobster dinner. It sits right on the water's edge, across the harbor from downtown Belfast. When you first walk in, you'll see tanks and tanks of live lobsters of varying size. The traditional meal here is the "shore dinner," consisting of clam chowder or lobster stew, steamed clams or mussels, a 1½-pound boiled lobster, corn on the cob, and chips. Order your dinner at the counter, then find a table inside or on the deck. Surf-and-turf dinners and hot dogs are popular, too. It's BYOB. ■TIP➔ **Don't leave your outdoor table unattended— seagulls love lobster.** ⓢ *Average main: $25* ⊠ *2 Mitchell St., off U.S. 1* ☏ *207/338–1160* ⊕ *youngslobsterpound.webs.com* ⊘ *Takeout only Jan.–Mar.*

NIGHTLIFE AND THE ARTS

Rollie's Bar & Grill. Up a bit from the harbor, Rollie's Bar & Grill has been in business since 1972. The vintage bar is from a 19th-century sailing ship. Rollie's is the town's most popular watering hole, especially with the TVs for watching the big game. It just may serve the best hamburgers in the state, which is why you'll see families here through the dinner hour. Food is served until midnight on Friday and Saturday. ⊠ *37 Main St.* ☏ *207/338–4502* ⊕ *www.rollies.me.*

SEARSPORT

6 miles north of Belfast via U.S. 1.

Searsport is well known as the antiques and flea-market capital of Maine, and with good reason: the Antique Mall alone, on U.S. 1 just north of town, contains the offerings of 70 dealers, and flea markets during the visitor season line both sides of U.S. 1.

Searsport also has a rich history of shipbuilding and seafaring. In the early to mid-1800s there were 10 shipbuilding facilities in Searsport, and the population of the town was about 1,000 people more than it is today because of the ready availability of jobs. By the mid-1800s Searsport was home to more than 200 sailing-ship captains.

GETTING HERE AND AROUND

Downtown Searsport is right along U.S. 1, as is much of the town, which doesn't have lots of side streets. Just north of here in Stockton Springs U.S. 1A leads to Bangor.

EXPLORING

FAMILY
Fodor'sChoice
★

Penobscot Marine Museum. Just off Main Street, this downtown museum explores the maritime culture of the Penobscot Bay region. Exhibits, artifacts, and paintings are in six nearby buildings, most from the first half of the 19th century. One of the former sea captain's homes has period rooms. Outstanding marine art includes a notable collection of works by Thomas and James Buttersworth. There are photos of local sea captains, model ships, lots of scrimshaw, navigational instruments, and tools from the area's history of logging, granite mining, and ice cutting. There are also exhibits just for the kids. ⊠ *5 Church St.*

Learn about Maine's seafaring heritage at the Penobscot Marine Museum.

☎ 207/548–2529 ⊕ *www.penobscotmarinemuseum.org* ✉ *$12* ◷ *Late May–third weekend in Oct., Mon.–Sat. 10–5, Sun. noon–5.*

SHOPPING

Searsport Antique Mall. The area's biggest collection of antiques is in the Searsport Antique Mall, which has more than 70 dealers. ✉ *149 E. Main St.* ☎ *207/548–2640* ⊕ *www.searsportantiquemall.com.*

BUCKSPORT

9 miles north of Searsport via U.S. 1.

The new Penobscot Narrows Bridge, spanning the Penobscot River, welcomes visitors to Bucksport, a town founded in 1763 by Jonathan Buck. Bucksport was the site of the second-worst naval defeat in American history (the first was Pearl Harbor), in 1779, when a British Armada defeated the fledgling American Navy. It became known as "the disaster on the Penobscot." You can learn more about it at the museum in Bucksport or at the Penobscot Marine Museum in Searsport. Fort Knox, Maine's largest historic fort, overlooks the town from across the river. There are magnificent views of the imposing granite structure from the pleasant riverfront walkway downtown.

GETTING HERE AND AROUND

U.S. 1 crosses a bridge into Bucksport; turn left for downtown and right to continue on the highway. Route 15 heads north to Bangor from here.

EXPLORING

FAMILY
Fodor's Choice
★
Penobscot Narrows Bridge & Observatory Tower/Fort Knox Historic Site. An "an engineering marvel" is how experts describe the 2,120-foot-long Penobscot Narrows Bridge, which opened in 2006. It's certainly beautiful to look at—from the surrounding countryside it pops up on the horizon like the towers of a fairy-tale castle. Spanning the Penobscot River across from Bucksport, the bridge's 437-foot observation tower is the highest in the world. An elevator shoots you to the top. Don't miss it—the panoramic views, which take in the hilly countryside and the river as it widens into Penobscot Bay, are breathtaking.

Also here is Fort Knox, the largest historic fort in Maine. It was built between 1844 and 1869, when despite a treaty with Britain settling boundary disputes, invasion was feared—the Brits controlled this region during the Revolutionary War and again during the War of 1812. The fort never saw any actual fighting, but it was used for troop training and as a garrison during the Civil War and the Spanish-American War. Visitors are welcome to explore the passageways and many rooms. Guided tours are given daily during the summer and several days a week in the shoulder seasons. ⊠ *711 Ft. Knox Rd., off U.S. 1, Prospect* ☎ *207/469–6553* ⊕ *www.fortknox.maineguide.com* ✉ *$7 observatory and fort, $4.50 fort only* ☉ *Observatory May, June, Sept., and Oct., daily 9–5; July and Aug., daily 9–6. Fort May–Oct., daily 9–5.*

BANGOR

122 miles north of Portland via I–95, 19 miles north of Bucksport via Rte. 15.

The state's second-largest metropolitan area (Portland is the largest), Bangor is about 20 miles from the coast and is the unofficial capital of northern Maine. Back in the 19th century the most important product and export of the "Queen City" was lumber from the state's vast North Woods. Now, because of its airport, Bangor has become a gateway to Mount Desert Island, Bar Harbor, and Acadia National Park. Along the revitalized waterfront, the American Folk Festival draws big crowds on the last full weekend in August, and an outdoor stage attracts top bands and musicians throughout the summer.

GETTING HERE AND AROUND

Interstate 95 has five Bangor exits, 45 to 49. U.S. 1A loops up to Bangor from Stockton Springs and Ellsworth, near Bar Harbor, and connects with Interstate 395 on the western side of the Bangor area.

ESSENTIALS

Visitor Information Greater Bangor Convention & Visitors Bureau ⊠ *33 Harlow St.* ☎ *207/947–5205, 800/916–6673* ⊕ *www.bangorcvb.org.*

EXPLORING

FAMILY
Maine Discovery Museum. Three floors with more than 60 interactive exhibits let kids explore the state's ecosystem in Nature Trails, learn about other cultures in TradeWinds, step into classic children's books like *Charlotte's Web*—all written by Maine authors—in Booktown, and unearth dinosaur "bones" in DINO Dig. There are also a drop-in

art studio and daily programs on art and other topics. ■ **TIP→ Visitors to Acadia National Park often head here on a rainy day.** ✉ *74 Main St.* ☎ *207/262-7200* 🌐 *www.mainediscoverymuseum.org* 🎟 *$7.50* 🕒 *June–Sept., Mon.–Sat. 10–5, Sun. noon–5; Oct.–May, Tues.–Sat. 10–5, Sun. noon–5.*

NEED A BREAK?

Friars' Bakehouse. Locals say this place has the best whoopie pies in the Bangor area. The bakery and restaurant is run by three Franciscan friars, one of whom spent time in highly regarded culinary programs. ✉ ***21 Central St., Bangor*** ☎ ***207/947-3770.***

Governor's Restaurant & Bakery. The old family-friendly standby Governor's Restaurant and Bakery, with six locations, including Bangor, is famed for its peanut butter whoopie pies as well as the old reliable standard, and can accommodate special flavor combinations by request with 24-hour notice. ✉ ***643 Broadway, Bangor*** ☎ ***207/827-7630*** 🌐 ***www.governorsrestaurant.com.***

WHERE TO STAY

$$ HOTEL 🏨 **Lucerne Inn.** Nestled in the mountains, the Lucerne Inn overlooks beautiful Phillips Lake. **Pros:** golf course across the road. **Cons:** some dated rooms. [$] *Rooms from: $149* ✉ *2517 Main Rd., Dedham* ☎ *207/843-5123, 800/325-5123* 🌐 *www.lucerneinn.com* 🛏 *21 rooms, 10 suites* 🍴 *Breakfast.*

THE BLUE HILL PENINSULA

If you want to see unspoiled Down East Maine landscapes, explore art galleries, savor exquisite meals, or simply enjoy life at an unhurried pace, you should be quite content on the Blue Hill Peninsula.

The large peninsula juts south into Penobscot Bay. Not far from the mainland are the islands of Little Deer Isle, Deer Isle, and, at the latter's tip, the picturesque fishing town of Stonington. A twisting labyrinth of roads winds through blueberry barrens and around picturesque coves, linking the towns of Blue Hill, Brooksville, Sedgwick, and Brooklin. Blue Hill and Castine are the area's primary business hubs. Painters, photographers, sculptors, and other artists are drawn to the area. You can find more than 20 galleries on Deer Isle and in Stonington and at least half as many on the mainland. With its small inns, charming B&Bs, and outstanding restaurants scattered across the area, the Blue Hill Peninsula may just persuade you to leave the rest of the coastline to the tourists.

VISITOR INFORMATION

Contacts Blue Hill Peninsula Chamber of Commerce ✉ *16 South St., Blue Hill* ☎ *207/374-3242* 🌐 *www.bluehillpeninsula.org.* **Deer Isle–Stonington Chamber of Commerce** ✉ *Main St., at Church St., Deer Isle* ☎ *207/348-6124* 🌐 *www.deerisle.com.*

CASTINE

18 miles north of Bucksport via U.S. 1 and Rtes. 175 and 166.

A summer destination for more than 100 years, Castine is a well-preserved seaside village rich in history. The French established a trading post here in 1613, naming the area Pentagoet. A year later Captain John Smith claimed the area for the British. The French regained control of the peninsula with the 1667 Breda Treaty, and Jean Vincent d'Abbadie de St. Castin obtained a land grant in the Pentagoet area, which would later bear his name. Castine's strategic position on Penobscot Bay and its importance as a trading post meant there were many battles for control until 1815. In the 19th century Castine was an important port for trading ships and fishing vessels. Larger ships, the Civil War, and the advent of train travel brought its prominence as a port to an end, but by the late 1800s some of the nation's wealthier citizens had discovered Castine as a pleasant summer retreat.

GETTING HERE AND AROUND

From U.S. 1 in Orland, near Bucksport, Route 175 heads south along the Penobscot River toward Castine. Continue on Route 166 at the crossroads of West Penobscot and after a bit you have the option of taking Route 166A into the village. The roads form a loop; the latter is especially scenic, passing expansive Wadsworth Cove at the mouth of the river as it enters its namesake bay.

EXPLORING

Federal- and Greek Revival–style architecture, rich history, and spectacular views of Penobscot Bay make Castine an ideal spot to spend a day or two. Explore its lively harbor front, two small museums (the Wilson Museum and the Castine Historical Society), and the ruins of a British fort. You can't miss the oversized historical signs throughout the village. An excellent self-guided walking tour is available at local businesses and the historical society. For a nice stroll, park your car at the landing and walk up Main Street toward the white Trinitarian Federated Church. Turn right on Court Street and go one block to the town common. Among the white-clapboard buildings ringing this green space are the Ives House (once the summer home of poet Robert Lowell), the Adams School, the former Abbott School (home to the historical society), and the Unitarian Church, capped by a whimsical belfry. From lower Main Street, head out Perkins Street on foot or by bike or car. You'll pass summer "cottage" mansions and the Wilson Museum on the way to Dyces Head Lighthouse (private), where a path leads to cliffs (careful here) fronting Penobscot Bay, site of a major Revolutionary War battle. You can return on Battle Avenue to make a loop.

WHERE TO EAT

$$ ✕ **Dennett's Wharf.** Originally built as a sail-rigging loft in the early
AMERICAN 1800s, this longtime favorite is a good place for oysters and fresh seafood of all kinds. The waterfront restaurant also serves burgers, sandwiches, and light fare. There are 23 microbrews on tap, including the tasty Dennett's Wharf Rat Ale. Eat in the dining room or outside on the deck—there are covered and open sections, another bar, and

Adirondack chairs if you just stop by for a brew. $ *Average main: $18* ⊠ *15 Sea St.* ☎ *207/326–9045* ⊕ *www.dennettswharf.net* ⊙ *Closed Nov.–mid-Apr.*

SPORTS AND THE OUTDOORS

Castine Kayak International Adventures. At Eaton's Wharf, Castine Kayak Adventures operates tours run by owner Karen Francoeur, a Registered Maine Guide. Sign up for a half day of kayaking along the shore, a full day of kayaking in Penobscot Bay, or nighttime bioluminescent trips— paddling stirs up a type of phytoplankton, causing them to light up like fireflies as they shoot through the water. The company also offers over- night kayak camping trips and rents mountain bikes and kayaks. ⊠ *Eaton's Wharf, 17 Sea St.* ☎ *207/866–3506* ⊕ *www.castinekayak.com.*

BLUE HILL

20 miles east of Castine via Rtes. 166, 175, and 176.

Snuggled between 943-foot Blue Hill Mountain and Blue Hill Bay, the village of Blue Hill sits cozily beside its harbor. Originally known for its granite quarries, copper mines, and shipbuilding, today the town is known for its pottery and galleries, bookstores, antiques shops, and studios that line its streets. The Blue Hill Fair (⊕ *www.bluehillfair.com*), held Labor Day weekend, is a tradition in these parts, with agricultural exhibits, food, rides, and entertainment. A charming little park with a great playground is tucked away on the harbor downtown.

GETTING HERE AND AROUND

From U.S. 1 in Orland, Route 15 heads south to Blue Hill. To continue north on the highway, take Route 172 north to Ellsworth.

WHERE TO EAT AND STAY

$$$$
MODERN
AMERICAN
Fodor's Choice
★

✕ **Arborvine.** Glowing gas fireplaces, period antiques, exposed beams, and hardwood floors covered with Oriental rugs adorn the four can- dlelit dining areas in this renovated Cape Cod–style house. Begin with a salad of mixed greens, sliced beets, and pears with blue cheese crumbled on top. For your entrée, choose from seasonal dishes such as crispy duck with rhubarb and lime glaze or roasted rack of lamb with a basil-and- pine-nut crust. The fresh fish dishes are also superb. Save room for des- serts; the ice cream (chocolate chili!) is homemade. Return when you're in a more casual mood: like the restaurant, the adjacent nautical-theme DeepWater Brew Pub serves dishes made with organic ingredients, as well as its own beer. It's housed in an inviting, historic barn that opens to lawn seating come summer. $ *Average main: $31* ⊠ *33 Tenney Hill* ☎ *207/374–2119* ⊕ *www.arborvine.com* ⊙ *No lunch.*

$$$$
B&B/INN

🛏 **Blue Hill Inn.** One side of this 1830 Federal-style inn was built as a home, but it soon became an inn, adding a wing with a matching facade in the 1850s. **Pros:** plenty of charm; modern suites with kitchens in separate building. **Cons:** some small rooms. $ *Rooms from: $225* ⊠ *40 Union St.* ☎ *207/374–2844, 800/826–7415* ⊕ *www.bluehillinn. com* ⇆ *10 rooms, 3 suites* ⊙ *Closed Nov.–mid-May* �‖ *Breakfast.*

SHOPPING

ART GALLERIES

Blue Hill Bay Gallery. This gallery sells oil and watercolor landscapes and seascapes of Maine and New England from the 19th through the 21st centuries. It also carries the owner's photography. ⊠ *11 Tenny Hill* ☎ *207/374–5773* ⊕ *www.bluehillbaygallery.com.*

POTTERY

North Country Textiles. Huge windows fill this colorful corner store with light, adding to the delight of browsing the handcrafted rag rugs, ornate cotton jackets, felt puppets, knitted items, and dyed artisanal yarns. Almost everything sold at this shop in downtown's Levy Building is handcrafted in Maine. ⊠ *36 Main St.* ☎ *207/374–2715* ⊕ *www.northcountrytextiles.com.*

Rackliffe Pottery. In business since 1969, this shop sells colorful pottery made with lead-free glazes. You can choose between water pitchers, serving platters, tea-and-coffee sets, and sets of canisters, among other lovely items. ⊠ *126 Ellsworth Rd.* ☎ *207/374–2297* ⊕ *www.rackliffepottery.com.*

WINE

Blue Hill Wine Shop. In a restored barn at the rear of one of Blue Hill's earliest houses, the Blue Hill Wine Shop carries more than 1,200 carefully selected wines. Coffee, tea, cheeses, and prewrapped sandwiches are also available. ⊠ *123 Main St.* ☎ *207/374–2161* ⊕ *www.bluehillwineshop.com.*

SEDGWICK, BROOKLIN, AND BROOKSVILLE

Winding through the hills, the roads leading to the villages of Sedgwick, Brooklin, and Brooksville take you past rambling farmhouses, beautiful coves, and blueberry barrens studded with occasional masses of granite.

GETTING HERE AND AROUND

From Blue Hill, Route 175 runs along the bottom of the Blue Hill Peninsula, heading first to Brooklin, then through Sedgwick and Brooksville on its way to U.S. 1 in Orland. Route 176 traverses Sedgwick and Brooksville as it heads west from Blue Hill across the middle of the peninsula. Because this wide peninsula has lots of capes, points, and necks, take care when driving to make sure you're continuing on the right road and not unintentionally looping around. Use a map (don't rely on GPS)—there's a good one in the Blue Hill Peninsula Chamber of Commerce's visitors guide.

Brooklin. The village of Brooklin, originally part of Sedgwick, established itself as an independent town in 1849. Today it's home to the world-famous Wooden Boat School, a 60-acre oceanfront campus offering courses in woodworking, boatbuilding, and seamanship. A small park-like area on the waterfront has a long pier and affords spectacular views of the area's chiseled coast. The school is off the road to Naskeag Point, a sleepy, serenely beautiful spot at the end of the peninsula road with a small rock beach, teeny park, and a home peeking through the trees on the island across the harbor.

Brooksville. The town of Brooksville, incorporated in 1817, is almost completely surrounded by water, with Eggemoggin Reach, Walker Pond, and the Bagaduce River marking its boundaries. Cape Rosier, remote and cove-lined even for this off-the-beaten-path peninsula, is home to Holbrook Island Sanctuary, a state park with hiking trails and a gravel beach.

Sedgwick. Incorporated in 1789, Sedgwick runs along much of Eggemoggin Reach, the body of water separating the mainland from Deer Isle, Little Deer Isle, and Stonington.

WHERE TO EAT

$
SEAFOOD
FAMILY
Fodor's Choice
★

✕ **Bagaduce Lunch.** This tidy fried-fish specialist sits next to the reversing falls on the Bagaduce River. About 10 miles west of Blue Hill, it's the perfect place for an outdoor lunch (no indoor seating). Picnic tables dot this nub of land with water on three sides, and there's a pier to tie up your kayak or boat, or to walk out on to enjoy the lovely view. Clam, shrimp, haddock, or scallop baskets come with onion rings or chips; there are also hot dogs, burgers, and fried chicken fingers. Seals, bald eagles, and ospreys provide natural entertainment in this rich tidal estuary. At low tide kids explore along the shore. $ *Average main: $12* ✉ *145 Franks Flat Rd., Penobscot* ☎ *207/326–4197* ▭ *No credit cards* ☾ *Closed mid-Sept.–late Apr. No dinner Wed.*

$$$
CONTEMPORARY

✕ **Brooklin Inn.** At this small B&B restaurant, in a 1920s bungalow-style building that was the dining room for a long-gone resort, the ambience is pleasantly yesteryear. In summer it expands to include seating on the classic glass-enclosed wraparound porch. The changing menu embraces traditional New England fare without clinging to the past, and all the produce, meats, poultry, and fish are local and often organic. You'll find dishes like crispy duckling with a rhubarb and lime glaze and Frenchman Bay mussels in a Dijon herb cream reduction. There's also an Irish pub downstairs with a menu of oysters, pizza, and sandwiches. The inn has five homey guest rooms. $ *Average main: $22* ✉ *22 Reach Rd., Brooklin* ☎ *207/359–2777* ⊕ *www.brooklininn.com* ⬟ *5 rooms, 3 with bath* ☾ *Closed Mon. and Tues. mid-Oct.–late May. No lunch.*

DEER ISLE VILLAGE

16 miles south of Blue Hill via Rtes. 176 and 15.

Around Deer Isle Village, thick woods give way to tidal coves. Stacks of lobster traps populate the backyards of shingled houses, and dirt roads lead to secluded summer cottages. This region is prized by artists, and studios and galleries are plentiful.

GETTING HERE AND AROUND

From Sedgwick, Route 15 crosses a 1930s suspension bridge onto Little Deer Isle and continues on to the larger Deer Isle.

EXPLORING

Edgar M. Tennis Preserve. Enjoy several miles of woodland and shore trails at the Edgar M. Tennis Preserve. Look for hawks, eagles, and ospreys and wander among old apple trees, fields of wildflowers, and ocean-polished rocks. ✉ *Tennis Rd., Deer Isle* ☎ *207/348–2455* ⊕ *www.islandheritagetrust.org* ✉ *Free* ⊗ *Daily dawn–dusk.*

Haystack Mountain School of Crafts. Want to learn a new craft? This school 6 miles from Deer Isle Village offers one- and two-week courses for people of all skill levels in crafts such as blacksmithing, basketry, printmaking, and weaving. Artisans from around the world present free evening lectures throughout summer. ✉ *89 Haystack School Dr., off Rte. 15* ☎ *207/348–2306* ⊕ *www.haystack-mtn.org* ✉ *$5 for tours* ⊗ *Tours June–Aug., Wed. at 1.*

SHOPPING

Nervous Nellie's Jams and Jellies. Jams and jellies are made right on the property at Nervous Nellie's. There is a tearoom with homemade goodies and also a fanciful sculpture garden with everything from knights to witches to a lobster and a flamingo. They are the works of sculptor Peter Beerits, who operates Nervous Nellie's with his wife. ✉ *598 Sunshine Rd., off Rte. 15, Deer Isle* ☎ *207/348–6182, 800/777–6845* ⊕ *www.nervousnellies.com.*

STONINGTON

6 miles south of Deer Isle.

Stonington is at the southern end of Route 15, which has helped it retain its unspoiled small-town flavor. The boutiques and galleries lining Main Street cater mostly to out-of-towners, though the town remains a fishing and lobstering community at heart. The principal activity is at the waterfront, where boats arrive with the day's catch. The sloped island that rises to the south is Isle au Haut, which contains a remote section of Acadia National Park.

GETTING HERE AND AROUND

From Deer Isle village, Route 15 runs all the way to Stonington at the tip of the island. There is a ferry from here to Isle au Haut.

EXPLORING

Deer Isle Granite Museum. This tiny museum documents Stonington's quarrying tradition. The museum's centerpiece is a working model of quarrying operations on Crotch Island and the town of Stonington at the turn of the last century. Granite was quarried here for Rockefeller Plaza in New York City and the John F. Kennedy Memorial in Arlington National Cemetery, among other well-known structures. ✉ *51 Main St.* ☎ *207/367–6331* ⊕ *www.deerislegranitemuseum.wordpress.com* ✉ *Free* ⊗ *July and Aug., Thurs.–Tues. 9–5.*

SPORTS AND THE OUTDOORS

Old Quarry Ocean Adventures. Departing from Webb Cove and passing Stonington Harbor en route to the outer islands, Captain Bill Baker's refurbished lobster boat takes visitors on puffin-watching, whale-watching, sunset, and lighthouse trips. There's also a three-hour Sightseeing and Natural History Eco-Cruise that goes by Crotch Island, which has one of the area's two active stone quarries, and stops at Green Island, where you can take a dip in a water-filled quarry. There are all-day day trips to bike or kayak on nearby islands, including Isle au Haut. ✉ *130 Settlement Rd.* ☎ *207/367–8977* ⊕ *www.oldquarry.com.*

ISLE AU HAUT

6 miles south of Stonington via ferry.

Isle au Haut thrusts its steeply ridged back out of the sea south of Stonington. French explorer Samuel D. Champlain discovered Isle au Haut—or "High Island"—in 1604, but heaps of shells suggest that native populations lived on or visited the island prior to his arrival. The island is accessible only by mail boat, but the 45-minute journey is well worth the effort. A section of Acadia National Park is here, with miles of trails, and the boat will drop visitors off there in peak season. The island has some seasonal rentals but no inns. With only three stores, you wouldn't think folks would come here to shop. But some do, as the island is home to Black Dinah Chocolatiers (☎ *207/335–5010* ⊕ *www. blackdinahchocolatiers.com*), which makes artful high-end chocolates and has a small café.

GETTING HERE AND AROUND

There's one main road here: it circles the island and goes through the Acadia National Park section. Locals give sections of the road a name. Isle au Haut Boat Services (☎ *207/367–5193* ⊕ *www.isleauhaut.com*) operates daily ferry service between Stonington and Isle au Haut. During the summer season trips increase from two to five Monday through Saturday and one to two on Sunday. From mid-June until late September the boat also stops at Duck Harbor, in the island section of Acadia National Park (it will not unload bicycles, kayaks, or canoes). Ferry service is scaled back in the fall, then returns to the regular or "winter" schedule.

QUICK
BITES

Maine Lobster Lady. Come summer, this former island innkeeper sells yummy quick-eats, many of them made with fish from the local waters and her own organic garden produce. Her "food truck" (actually a tow trailer) is parked near the ranger's station at the Acadia National Park section on Isle au Haut. There are lobster rolls of course, or try a shrimp-salad sandwich with paprika-dill mayo on a homemade roll, or shrimp puffs served in a paper cone. ✉ *Off Main Rd., Isle au Haut* ☎ *207/335–5141* ⊕ *www. mainelobsterlady.com.*

ACADIA NATIONAL PARK AND MOUNT DESERT ISLAND

With some of the most dramatic and varied scenery on the Maine Coast and home to Maine's only national park, Mount Desert Island (pronounced "Mount Dessert" by locals) is Maine's most popular tourist destination, attracting well over 2 million visitors a year. Much of the approximately 12-by-15-mile island belongs to Acadia National Park. The rocky coastline rises starkly from the ocean, appreciable along the

scenic drives. Trails for hikers of all skill levels lead to the rounded tops of the mountains, providing views of Frenchman and Blue Hill bays and beyond. Ponds and lakes beckon you to swim, fish, or boat. Ferries and charter boats provide a different perspective on the island and a chance to explore the outer islands, all of which are part of Maine but not necessarily of Mount Desert. A network of old carriage roads lets you explore Acadia's wooded interior, filled with birds and other wildlife.

Mount Desert Island has four different towns, each with its own personality. The town of Bar Harbor is on the northeastern corner of the island and includes the little villages of Hulls Cove, Salisbury Cove, and Town Hill. The park aside, Bar Harbor is the major tourist destination, with plenty of accommodations, restaurants, and shops. The town of Mount Desert, in the middle of the island, has four main villages: Somesville, Seal Harbor, Otter Creek, and Northeast Harbor, a summer haven for the very wealthy. Southwest Harbor includes the smaller village of Manset south of the village center. Tremont is at the southernmost tip of the island and stretches up the western shore. It includes the villages of Bass Harbor, Bernard, and Seal Cove. Yes, Mount Desert Island is a place with three personalities: the hustling, bustling tourist mecca of Bar Harbor; the "quiet side" on the western half; and the vast natural expanse that is Acadia National Park. But though less congested and smaller, Northeast Harbor and Southwest Harbor are home to inns, campgrounds, restaurants, ferries, galleries, and small museums.

Sponsored by several Mount Desert Island communities as well as Acadia National Park, the Mt. Desert Island Information Center is along Route 3 just before it crosses to Mount Desert Island. The center is loaded with pamphlets about island tours, restaurants, inns, and attractions, including Acadia National Park. You can buy park passes here, and the staff includes a park ranger.

ESSENTIALS

Visitor Information Bar Harbor Chamber of Commerce ⊠ *1201 Bar Harbor Rd., Trenton* ☎ *800/345-4617* ⊕ *www.barharborinfo.com.* **Bar Harbor Information Center** ⊠ *2 Cottage St., Bar Harbor* ☉ *Early May–late Oct.* **Mount Desert Chamber of Commerce** ⊠ *18 Harbor Dr., Northeast Harbor* ☎ *207/276–5040* ⊕ *www.mountdesertchamber.org.* **Mt. Desert Island Information Center at Thompson Island** ⊠ *1319 Bar Harbor Rd., Trenton* ☎ *207/288–3411* ☉ *Mid-May–mid-June, daily 8–5; late June–Aug., daily 8–6; Sept.–mid-Oct., daily 8–5:30.*

BAR HARBOR

34 miles from Blue Hill via Rte. 172 and U.S. 1.

A resort town since the 19th century, Bar Harbor is the artistic, culinary, and social center of Mount Desert Island. It also serves visitors to Acadia National Park with inns, motels, and restaurants. Around the turn of the last century the island was known as the summer haven of the very rich because of its cool breezes. The wealthy built lavish mansions throughout the island, many of which were destroyed in a huge fire that devastated the island in 1947, but many of those that survived have been converted into businesses. Shops are clustered along Main, Mount Desert, and Cottage streets. Take a stroll down West Street, a National Historic District, where you can see some fine old houses.

The island and the surrounding Gulf of Maine are home to a great variety of wildlife: whales, seals, eagles, falcons, ospreys, and puffins (though not right offshore here), and forest dwellers such as deer, foxes, coyotes, and beavers.

THE EARLY BIRD GETS THE SUN

During your visit to Mount Desert, pick a day when you are willing to get up very early, such as 4:30 or 5 am. Drive with a friend to the top of Cadillac Mountain in Acadia National Park. Stand on the highest rock you can find and wait for the sun to come up. When it does, have your friend take a photo of you looking at it and label the photo something like "The first person in the country to see the sun come up on June 1, 2014."

GETTING HERE AND AROUND

In Ellsworth, Route 3 leaves U.S. 1 and heads to Bar Harbor. In season, free Island Explorer buses (🌐 *www.exploreacadia.com* ☎ *207/667–5796*) take visitors to Acadia National Park and other island towns. There is also a passenger ferry to Winter Harbor across Frenchman Bay.

EXPLORING

Abbe Museum. This small museum dedicated to Maine's indigenous tribes—collectively known as the Wabanaki—is the state's only Smithsonian-affiliated facility. The year-round archaeology exhibit displays spear points, bone tools, and other artifacts found around Mount Desert Island. Rotating exhibits often feature contemporary Native American art, and there are frequent demonstrations of everything from boatbuilding to basket weaving. Call on rainy days for impromptu children's activities. A second location, inside the park at Sieur de Monts Spring, features artifacts from the earliest digs around the island. ✉ *26 Mount Desert St.* ☎ *207/288–3519* 🌐 *www.abbemuseum.org* 🎟 *$6* 🕓 *Late May–early Dec., daily 10–5.*

WHERE TO EAT AND STAY

$$$ SEAFOOD Fodor's Choice ★ 🍴 **Burning Tree.** One of the top restaurants in Maine, this easy-to-miss gem with a festive dining room is on Route 3 between Bar Harbor and Otter Creek. The seasonal menu emphasizes freshly caught seafood, and seven species of fish are offered virtually every day, all from the Gulf of Maine. There is always monkfish; you may find it pan-sautéed, glazed with sweet chili sauce, and served with Thai-flavored eggplant and coconut rice. Oven-poached cod and stuffed gray sole are signature dishes. There are always two or three vegetarian options using organic produce, much of it from the owners' garden. [$] *Average main: $22* ✉ *69 Otter Creek Dr., Otter Creek* ☎ *207/288–9331* 🕓 *Closed mid-Oct.–mid-June. No lunch.*

$$$$ HOTEL Fodor's Choice ★ 🏨 **Bar Harbor Inn & Spa.** Originally established in the late 1800s as a men's social club, this waterfront inn has rooms spread among three buildings on well-landscaped grounds. **Pros:** at the harbor; some two-level suites. **Cons:** not right near Acadia National Park. [$] *Rooms from: $209* ✉ *Newport Dr., 1 Newport Dr.* ☎ *207/288–3351, 800/248–3351*

Long ramps on Maine's many docks make it easier to access boats at either high tide or low tide.

⊕ *www.barharborinn.com* ⤫ *138 rooms, 15 suites* ⊘ *Closed late Nov.–mid-Mar.* †◯❙ *Breakfast.*

SPORTS AND THE OUTDOORS

AIR TOURS

Acadia Air Tours. This outfit provides sightseeing flights over Bar Harbor and Acadia National Park. Most tours run from 15 minutes to an hour and range from $150 to $450 for two people. The sunset tour is $50 extra. ⊠ *968 Bar Harbor Rd., Trenton* ☎ *207/667–7627* ⊕ *www.acadiaairtours.com.*

BICYCLING

Acadia Bike. With mountain bikes and hybrids, Acadia Bike rents models that are good for negotiating the carriage roads in Acadia National Park. ⊠ *48 Cottage St.* ☎ *207/288–9605, 800/526–8615* ⊕ *www.acadiabike.com.*

Bar Harbor Bicycle Shop. Rent bikes by the half or full day at the Bar Harbor Bicycle Shop. ⊠ *141 Cottage St.* ☎ *207/288–3886, 800/824–2453* ⊕ *www.barharborbike.com.*

Coastal Kayaking Tours. This outfitter has been leading trips in the scenic waters off Mount Desert Island since 1982. Rentals are provided through its sister business, Acadia Outfitters, on the same downtown street. Trips are limited to no more than 12 people. The season is May through October. ⊠ *48 Cottage St.* ☎ *207/288–9605, 800/526–8615* ⊕ *www.acadiafun.com.*

Downeast Sailing Adventures. Take two-hour and sunset cruises for $35 with six passengers or $50 with fewer. Departures are from Upper Town

Dock in Southwest Harbor and several other locations. ⊠ *Upper Town Dock, Clark Point Rd., Southwest Harbor* ☎ *207/288–2216* ⊕ *www. downeastsail.com.*

FAMILY **Margaret Todd.** The 151-foot four-masted schooner *Margaret Todd* operates 1½- to 2-hour trips three times a day among the islands of Frenchman's Bay The sunset sail has live music, and the 2 pm trip is narrated by an Acadia National Park ranger. Trips are $37.50 and depart from from mid-May to October. ⊠ *Bar Harbor Inn pier, Newport Dr.* ☎ *207/288–4585* ⊕ *www.downeastwindjammer.com.*

WHALE-WATCHING

FAMILY **Bar Harbor Whale Watch Co.** This company has four boats, one of them a 140-foot jet-propelled double-hulled catamaran with spacious decks. It's one of two large catamarans used for whale-watching trips, some of which go at sunset or include a side trip to see puffins. The company also offers lighthouse, lobstering, and seal-watching cruises, and a trip to Acadia National Park's Baker Island. ⊠ *1 West St.* ☎ *207/288–2386, 800/942–5374* ⊕ *www.barharborwhales.com.*

SHOPPING

ART

Alone Moose Fine Crafts. The oldest made-in-Maine gallery in Bar Harbor, Alone Moose Fine Crafts offers bronze wildlife sculptures, jewelry, pottery, and watercolors. ⊠ *78 West St.* ☎ *207/288–4229* ⊕ *www. finemainecrafts.com.*

Eclipse Gallery. The Eclipse Gallery carries handblown glass, ceramics, wood and metal furniture, and home decor items like mirrors and lamps. The gallery is open from mid-May through October. ⊠ *12 Mount Desert St.* ☎ *207/288–9088* ⊕ *www.eclipsegallery.us.*

Island Artisans. this shop sells basketry, pottery, fiber work, and jewelry created by about 150 Maine artisans. ⊠ *99 Main St.* ☎ *207/288–4214* ⊕ *www.islandartisans.com.*

Native Arts Gallery. Silver and gold jewelry is a specialty at Native Arts Gallery, open from May through October. ⊠ *99 Main St.* ☎ *207/288–4474* ⊕ *www.nativeartsgallery.com.*

SPORTING GOODS

Cadillac Mountain Sports. One of the best sporting-goods stores in the state, Cadillac Mountain Sports has developed a following of locals and visitors alike. You can find top-quality climbing, hiking, boating, paddling, and camping equipment. In winter you can rent cross-country skis, ice skates, and snowshoes. ⊠ *26 Cottage St.* ☎ *207/288–4532* ⊕ *www.cadillacmountainsports.com.*

ACADIA NATIONAL PARK

3 miles from Bar Harbor via U.S. 3.

Fodor'sChoice
★
With about 49,000 acres of protected forests, beaches, mountains, and rocky coastline, Acadia National Park is the second-most-visited national park in America (after the Great Smoky Mountains National Park). According to the National Park Service, 2 million people visit

Acadia each year. The park holds some of the most spectacular scenery on the Eastern Seaboard: a rugged coastline of surf-pounded granite and an interior graced by sculpted mountains, quiet ponds, and lush deciduous forests. Cadillac Mountain (named after a Frenchman who explored here in the late 1600s and later founded Detroit) the highest point of land on the East Coast, dominates the

> ### BOOK A CARRIAGE RIDE
>
> If you would like to take a horse-drawn carriage ride down one of the park's roads, you can do so from mid-June to mid-October by making a reservation with Wildwood Stables (☎ 877/276–3622). One of the carriages can accommodate wheelchairs.

park. Although it's rugged, the park also has graceful stone bridges, miles of carriage roads (popular with walkers, runners, and bikers as well as horse-drawn carriages), and the Jordan Pond House restaurant (famous for its popovers).

The 27-mile Park Loop Road provides an excellent introduction, but to truly appreciate the park you must get off the main road and experience it by walking, hiking, biking, sea kayaking, or taking a carriage ride. If you get off the beaten path, you can find places you'll have practically to yourself. Mount Desert Island was once a preserve of summer homes for the very rich (and still is for some), and, because of this, Acadia is the first national park in the United States that was largely created by donations of private land. There are two smaller parts of the park: on Isle au Haut, 15 miles away out in the ocean, and on the Schoodic Peninsula, on the mainland across Frenchman Bay from Mt. Desert.

PARK ESSENTIALS

ADMISSION FEE
A user fee is required May through October—unless arriving on the Island Explorer buses that serve the park and island villages from June 23 through Columbus Day. They are free to ride and also offer free admittance to the park. The per-vehicle fee is $20 for a seven-consecutive-day pass from May through October. You can walk or ride in (bike or motorcycle) on a $5 individual pass, also good for seven days. Or you can use your National Park America the Beautiful Pass, which allows entrance to any national park in the United States. Check ⊕ *www.nps.gov* for details.

ADMISSION HOURS
The park is open 24 hours a day, year-round, but roads are closed from December to mid-April except for the Ocean Drive section of Park Loop Road and a small part of the road that provides access to Jordan Pond.

PARK CONTACT INFORMATION
Acadia National Park ☎ *207/288–3338* ⊕ *www.nps.gov/acad*.

GETTING HERE AND AROUND
Route 3 leads to the island and Bar Harbor from Ellsworth and circles the eastern part of the island. Route 102 is the major road on the west side. Free Island Explorer buses serve the main villages and the park from June 23 through Columbus Day. There are scheduled stops; they

also pick up and drop off passengers anywhere along the park it is safe to stop.

EXPLORING
SCENIC DRIVES AND STOPS

Fodor's Choice ★ **Cadillac Mountain.** At 1,530 feet, this is one of the first places in the United States to see the sun's rays at break of day. It is the highest mountain on the eastern seaboard north of Brazil. Dozens of visitors make the trek to see the sunrise or, for those less inclined to get up so early, sunset. From the smooth summit you have an awesome 360-degree view of the jagged coastline that runs around the island. A small gift shop and some restrooms are the only structures at the top. The road up the mountain is closed from December through mid-May. ⊠ *Cadillac Summit Rd.*

FAMILY
Fodor's Choice ★ **Park Loop Road.** This 27-mile road provides a perfect introduction to the park. You can drive it in an hour, but allow at least half a day so that you can explore the many sites along the way. The route is served by the free Island Explorer buses, which will also pick and drop off anywhere along the route. Traveling south on Park Loop Road toward Sand Beach, you'll reach a small ticket booth, where, if you haven't already, you will need to pay the park entrance fee between May and October. Traffic is one way from the Route 233 entrance to the Stanley Brook Road entrance south of the Jordan Pond House. The section known as Ocean Drive is open year-round, as is a small section that provides access to Jordan Pond from Seal Harbor.

VISITOR CENTER

FAMILY **Hulls Cove Visitor Center.** This is a great spot to get your bearings. A large relief map of Mount Desert Island gives you the lay of the land, and you can watch a free 15-minute video about everything the park has to offer. Pick up guidebooks, maps of hiking trails and carriage roads, schedules for ranger-led tours, and recordings for drive-it-yourself tours. Don't forget to grab a schedule of ranger-led programs, which include guided hikes and other interpretive events. Junior-ranger programs for kids, nature hikes, photography walks, tide-pool explorations, and evening talks are all popular. The Acadia National Park Headquarters, off Route 233 near the north end of Eagle Lake, serves as the park's visitor center during the off-season. ⊠ *Rte. 3, Hulls Cove* ☎ *207/288–3338* ⊕ *www.nps.gov/acad* ☉ *Mid-May–Sept., daily 9–5; Oct., daily 8–4:30.*

SPORTS AND THE OUTDOORS

The best way to see Acadia National Park is to get out of your vehicle and explore on foot or by bicycle or boat. There are more than 45 miles of carriage roads that are perfect for walking and biking in the warmer months and for cross-country skiing and snowshoeing in winter. There are 125 miles of trails for hiking, numerous ponds and

---

ACADIA LEAF PEEPING

The fall foliage in Maine can be spectacular. Because of the moisture, it comes later along the coast, around the middle of October, than it does in the interior of the state. The best way to catch the colors along the coast is travel on the Acadia National Park Loop Road. For up-to-date information, go to ⊕ *www.mainefoliage.com.*

lakes for canoeing or kayaking, two beaches for swimming, and steep cliffs for rock climbing.

HIKING

Acadia National Park maintains more than 125 miles of hiking trails, from easy strolls around lakes and ponds to rigorous treks with climbs up rock faces and scrambles along cliffs. Although

> **CAUTION**
>
> Every few years someone falls off one of the park's trails or cliffs and is swept out to sea. There is a lot of loose, rocky gravel along the shoreline, and sea rocks can often be slippery—so watch your step.

most hiking trails are on the east side of the island, the west side also has some scenic trails. For those wishing for a long climb, try the trails leading up Cadillac Mountain or Dorr Mountain. Another option is to climb Parkman, Sargeant, and Penobscot mountains. Most hiking is done from mid-May to mid-November. Snow falls early in Maine, so from as early as late November to the end of March cross-country skiing and snowshoeing replace hiking. Volunteers groom most of the carriage roads if there's been 4 inches of snow or more. ■TIP→ **You can park at one end of any trail and use the free shuttle bus to get back to your starting point.**

Distances for trails are given for the round-trip hike.

Fodor'sChoice
★
Acadia Mountain Trail. If you're up for a challenge, this is one of the area's best trails. The 2½-mile round-trip climb up Acadia Mountain is steep and strenuous, but the payoff is grand: views of Somes Sound. If you want a guided trip, look into the ranger-led hikes for this trail. ⊠ *Rte. 102* ☎ *207/288–3338* ⊕ *www.nps.gov/acadia.*

Fodor'sChoice
★
Ocean Path Trail. This easily accessible 4.4-mile round-trip trail runs parallel to the Ocean Drive section of the Park Loop Road from Sand Beach to Otter Point. It has some of the best scenery in Maine: cliffs and boulders of pink granite at the ocean's edge, twisted branches of dwarf jack pines, and ocean views that stretch to the horizon. Be sure to save time to stop at **Thunder Hole**, named for the sound the waves make as they thrash through a narrow opening in the granite cliffs, into a sea cave, and whoosh up and out. Steps lead down to the water, where you can watch the wave action close up, but use caution here (access may be limited due to storms), and if venturing onto the outer cliffs along this walk. ⊠ *Ocean Dr. section of Park Loop Rd.*

SWIMMING

The park has two swimming beaches, Sand Beach and Echo Lake Beach. Sand Beach, along Park Loop Road, has changing rooms, restrooms, and a lifeguard on duty from the first full week of June to Labor Day. Echo Lake Beach, on the western side of the island just north of Southwest Harbor, has much warmer water, as well as changing rooms, restrooms, and a lifeguard on duty throughout the summer.

Echo Lake Beach. A quiet lake surrounded by woods in the shadow of Beech Mountain, Echo Lake draws swimmers to its sandy southern shore. The lake bottom is bit muckier than the ocean beaches nearby, but the water is considerably warmer. The surrounding trail network skirts the lake and ascends the mountain. The beach is 2 miles north of

Southwest Harbor. **Amenities:** lifeguards; toilets. **Best for:** swimming. ⊠ *Echo Lake Beach Rd., off Hwy. 102.*

Sand Beach. This pocket beach is hugged by two picturesque rocky outcroppings, and the combination of the crashing waves and the chilly water (peaking at around 55°F) keeps most people on the beach. You'll find some swimmers at the height of summer, but the rest of the year this is a place for strolling and snapping photos. In the shoulder season you'll have the place to yourself. **Amenities:** lifeguards; parking; toilets. **Best for:** sunrise; solitude; walking. ⊠ *Ocean Dr. section of Park Loop Rd., 3 miles south of Hwy. 3.*

NORTHEAST HARBOR

12 miles south of Bar Harbor via Rtes. 3 and 198.

The summer community for some of the nation's wealthiest families, Northeast Harbor has one of the best harbors on the coast, which fills with yachts and powerboats during peak season. Some summer residents rebuilt here after Bar Harbor's Great Fire of 1947 destroyed mansions there.

It's a great place to sign up for a cruise around Somes Sound or to the Cranberry Isles. Other than that, this quiet village has a handful of restaurants, inns, boutiques, and art galleries.

SOMESVILLE

7 miles north of Northeast Harbor via Rte. 198.

Most visitors pass through Somesville on their way to Southwest Harbor, but this well-preserved village, the oldest on the island, is more than a stop along the way. Originally settled by Abraham Somes in 1761, this was once a bustling commercial center with shingle, lumber, and wool mills; a tannery; a varnish factory; and a dye shop. Today Route 102, which passes through the center of town, takes you past a row of white-clapboard houses with black shutters and well-manicured lawns.

SOUTHWEST HARBOR

6 miles south of Somesville via Rte. 102.

Across from Northeast Harbor, Southwest Harbor sits on the south side of the entrance to Somes Sound, which cuts up the center of the island. The town makes for a mellower Acadia base camp than Bar Harbor, with handsome yachts and towering sailboats along the waterfront throughout the summer. Just north of town, trailheads at Echo Lake Beach and Fernald Point access some of the park's less-traveled trails.

BASS HARBOR

10 miles south of Somesville via Rtes. 102 and 102A.

Bass Harbor is a tiny lobstering village with a relaxed atmosphere and a few accommodations and restaurants. If you're looking to get away from the crowds, consider using this hardworking community as your base. Although Bass Harbor does not draw as many tourists as other villages, the Bass Harbor Head Light in Acadia National Park is one of the region's most popular attractions and is undoubtedly one of the most photographed lighthouses in Maine. From Bass Harbor you can hike on the Ship Harbor Nature Trail or take a ferry to Frenchboro or Swans Island.

GETTING HERE AND AROUND

From Bass Harbor the Maine State Ferry Service operates a ferry, the *Captain Henry Lee*, carrying both passengers and vehicles to Swans Island (40 minutes, round-trip $17.50 per person and $49.50 per car with driver) and Frenchboro (50 minutes, round-trip $11.25 per person and $32.25 per car with driver). The Frenchboro ferry doesn't run daily; there's also a passenger-only trip on a smaller boat (same price) from April through November. Round-trip excursions (you don't get off the boat) are $10.

ESSENTIALS

Transportation Information Maine State Ferry Service ✉ *114 Granville Rd.* ☎ *207/244–3254* 🌐 *www.maine.gov/mdot/msfs.*

EXPLORING

Fodor's Choice ★ **Bass Harbor Head Light.** Built in 1858, this lighthouse is one of the most photographed lights in Maine. Now automated, it marks the entrance to Blue Hill Bay. The grounds and residence are Coast Guard property, but two trails around the facility provide excellent views. It's within Acadia National Park, and there is parking. **TIP→ The best place to take a picture is from the rocks below—but watch your step, as they can be slippery.** ✉ *Lighthouse Rd., off Rte. 102A* 🎟 *Free* 🕒 *Daily 9–sunset.*

WHERE TO EAT

$$ SEAFOOD 🍴 **Thurston's Lobster Pound.** Right on Bass Harbor, looking across to the village, Thurston's is easy to spot because of its bright yellow awning. You can buy fresh lobsters to go or sit at covered outdoor tables. Order everything from a grilled-cheese sandwich, soup, or hamburger to a boiled lobster served with clams or mussels. [$] *Average main: $20* ✉ *Steamboat Wharf, 9 Thurston Rd., Bernard* ☎ *207/244–7600* 🌐 *www.thurstonslobster.com* 🕒 *Closed mid-Oct.–mid-May.*

WAY DOWN EAST

Slogans such as "The Real Maine" ring truer Way Down East. The raw, mostly undeveloped coast in this remote region is more accessible than it is farther south. Even in summer here you're likely to have rocky beaches and shady hiking trails to yourself. The slower pace is as calming as a sea breeze.

One innkeeper relates that visitors who plan to stay a few days often opt for a week after learning more about the region's offerings, which include historic sites; museums on local history, culture, and art; national wildlife refuges; state parks and preserves; and increasingly, conservancy-owned public land. Cutler's Bold Coast, with its dramatic granite headlands, is protected from development. Waters near Eastport

have some of the world's highest tides. Lakes perfect for canoeing and kayaking are sprinkled inland, and rivers snake through marshland as they near the many bays. Boulders are strewn on blueberry barrens. Rare plants thrive in coastal bogs and heaths, and dark-purple and pink lupines line the roads in late June.

VISITOR INFORMATION

Many chambers of commerce in the region distribute free copies of the pamphlet "Maine's Washington County: Just Off the Beaten Path," which is several cuts above the usual tourist promotion booklet.

Contacts DownEast and Acadia Regional Tourism ⊠ *87 Milbridge Rd., Cherryfield* ☏ *207/546–3600, 888/665–3278* ⊕ *www.downeastacadia.com.*

SCHOODIC PENINSULA

25 miles east of Ellsworth via U.S. Rte. 1 and Rte. 186.

The landscape of Schoodic Peninsula's craggy coastline, towering evergreens, and views over Frenchman Bay are breathtaking year-round. A drive through the well-to-do summer community of Grindstone Neck shows what Bar Harbor might have been like before so many of its mansions were destroyed in the Great Fire of 1947. Artists and artisans have opened galleries in and around Winter Harbor. Anchored at the foot of the peninsula, Winter Harbor was once part of Gouldsboro, which wraps around it. The southern tip of the peninsula is home to the Schoodic section of Acadia National Park.

GETTING HERE AND AROUND

From U.S. 1, Route 186 loops around the peninsula. Route 195 runs from U.S. 1 to Prospect Harbor and on to its end in Corea.

ESSENTIALS

Visitor Information Schoodic Chamber of Commerce ⊕ *www.acadia-schoodic.org.*

EXPLORING

Within Gouldsboro on the Schoodic Peninsula are several small coastal villages. You drive through Wonsqueak and Birch Harbor after leaving the Schoodic section of Acadia National Park. Near Birch Harbor you can find Prospect Harbor, a small fishing village nearly untouched by tourism. In Corea, there's little to do besides watch the fishermen at work, wander along stone beaches, or gaze out to sea.

Fodor'sChoice
★
Acadia National Park. The only section of Maine's national park that sits on the mainland is at the southern end of the Schoodic Peninsula in the town of Winter Harbor. The park has a scenic 6-mile loop that edges along the coast and yields views of Grindstone Neck, Winter Harbor, Winter Harbor Lighthouse, and, across the water, Cadillac Mountain. At the tip of the point, huge slabs of pink granite lie jumbled along the shore, thrashed unmercifully by the crashing surf, and jack pines cling to life amid the rocks. Fraser Point, at the beginning of the loop, is an ideal place for a picnic. Work off lunch with a hike up Schoodic Head for the panoramic views up and down the coast. During the summer season you can take a passenger ferry to Winter Harbor from Bar

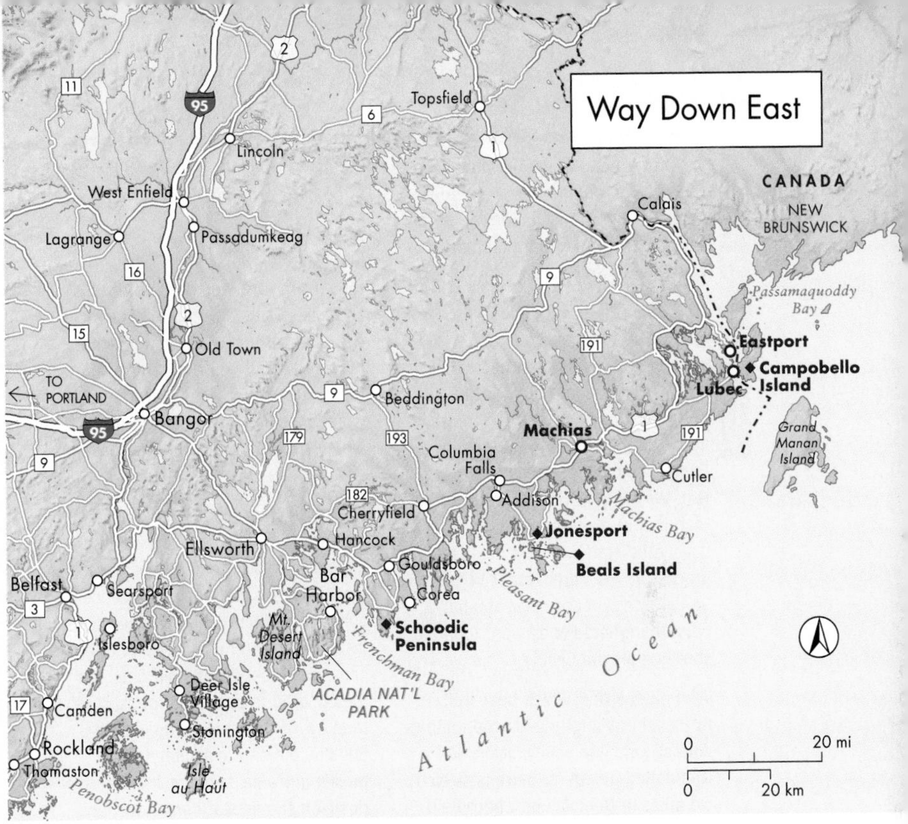

Harbor, then catch the free Island Explorer bus, which stops throughout the park. ✉ *End of Moore Rd., off Rte. 186* ☎ *207/288–3338* 🌐 *www.nps.gov/acad* ⏲ *Daily 24 hrs.*

Schoodic Education and Research Center. In the Schoodic Peninsula section of Acadia National Park, this center offers lectures, workshops, and kid-friendly events about nature. It's worth a drive by just to see the Rockefeller Building, a massive 1935 French Eclectic and Renaissance-style structure with a stone and half-timber facade that housed naval offices and housing. In 2013 the building reopened as a visitor center after an extensive renovation. ✉ *64 Acadia Dr., off Park Loop Rd., 3 miles south of park entrance* ☎ *207/288–1310* 🌐 *www.sercinstitute.org*

WHERE TO EAT AND STAY

$ SEAFOOD 🍴 **Chase's Restaurant.** The orange booths may remind you of a fast-food joint, but this family restaurant has a reputation for serving good, basic fare—in this region that means a lot of fish. There are large and small fried seafood dinners and several more expensive seafood platters. Try the sweet-potato fries as a side. Lunch fare, sold all day, includes wraps and burgers. It's also open for breakfast. [$] *Average main: $10* ✉ *193 Main St.* ☎ *207/963–7171.*

Wild for Blueberries

There's no need to inquire about the cheesecake topping if you dine out in August when the wild blueberry crop comes in. Anything but blueberries would be unthinkable.

Way Down East, wild blueberries have long been a favorite food and a key ingredient in cultural and economic life. Maine produces about a third of the commercial harvest, which totals about 80 million pounds annually, Canada supplying virtually all the rest. Washington County yields more than half of Maine's total crop, which is why the state's largest blueberry processors are here: Jasper Wyman & Son and the predecessor of what is now Cherryfield Foods were founded shortly after the Civil War.

Wild blueberries, which bear fruit every other year, thrive in the region's cold climate and sandy, acidic soil. Undulating blueberry barrens stretch for miles in Deblois and Cherryfield ("the Blueberry Capital of the World") and are scattered throughout Washington County. Look for tufts among low-lying plants along the roadways. In spring the fields shimmer as the small-leaf plants turn myriad shades of mauve, honey orange, and lemon yellow. White flowers appear in June. Fall transforms the barrens into a sea of red.

Amid Cherryfield's barrens, a plaque on a boulder lauds the late J. Burleigh Crane for helping advance an industry that's not as wild as it used to be. Honeybees have been brought in to supplement native pollinators, fields are irrigated, and barrens are burned and mowed to rid plants of disease and insects, reducing the need for pesticides. Most of the barrens in and around Cherryfield are owned by the large blueberry processors.

About 80% of Maine's crop is now harvested with machinery. That requires moving boulders, so the rest continues to be harvested by hand with blueberry rakes, which resemble large forks and pull the berries off their stems. Years ago, year-round residents did the work. Today migrant workers make up 90% of this seasonal labor force.

Blueberries get their dark color from anthocyanins, believed to provide antioxidants. Wild blueberries have more of these anti-aging, anticancer compounds than their cultivated cousins. Smaller and more flavorful than cultivated blueberries, wild ones are mostly used in packaged foods. Less than 1% of the state's crop—about 500,000 pints—is consumed fresh, mostly in Maine. Look for fresh berries (sometimes starting in late July and lasting until early September) at roadside stands, farmers' markets, and supermarkets.

Wild Blueberry Land in Columbia Falls sells everything blueberry, from muffins and candy to socks and books. Find farm stores, stands, and markets statewide, many selling blueberries and blueberry jams and syrups, at ⊕ *www.getrealmaine.com*, a Maine Department of Agriculture site that promotes Maine foods.

—Mary Ruoff

$ B&B/INN FAMILY **Bluff House Inn.** This homey, modern inn is on a secluded hillside with expansive views of Frenchman Bay. **Pros:** good value; largest room has a sitting area with pullout couch. **Cons:** only two rooms have good water views. [$] *Rooms from: $95* ✉ *57 Bluff House Rd., turn off Rte. 186, Gouldsboro* ☎ *207/963–7805* 🌐 *www.bluffinn.com* 🛏 *8 rooms, 1 suite* 🍴 *Breakfast.*

$$ B&B/INN FAMILY Fodor's Choice ★ **Oceanside Meadows Inn.** A must for nature lovers, this lodging sits on a 200-acre preserve dotted with woods, streams, salt marshes, and ponds. **Pros:** one of region's few sand beaches; staff share info about the area over tea. **Cons:** need to cross road to beach. [$] *Rooms from: $149* ✉ *202 Corea Rd., Prospect Harbor* ☎ *207/963–5557* 🌐 *www.oceaninn.com* 🛏 *13 rooms, 2 suites* 🕓 *Closed mid-Oct.–late-May* 🍴 *Breakfast.*

SPORTS AND THE OUTDOORS

KAYAKING

SeaScape Kayaking. Led by a Registered Maine Guide, SeaScape's morning and afternoon kayak tours include an island stop and a blueberry snack. The company also rents canoes, kayaks, and bikes from its location in Birch Harbor. ✉ *Birch Harbor, 18 E. Schoodic Dr.* ☎ *207/963–5806* 🌐 *www.seascapekayaking.com.*

SHOPPING

ANTIQUES AND MORE

U.S. Bells. Hand-cast bronze doorbells and wind chimes are among the items sold at U.S. Bells. You can also buy finely crafted quilts and wood-fired pottery made by the owner's family. Ask for a tour of the foundry. ✉ *56 W. Bay Rd., Prospect Harbor* ☎ *207/963–7184* 🌐 *www.usbells.com.*

ART GALLERIES

Lee Fusion Art Glass. Window glass is fused in a kiln at Lee Fusion Art Glass to create unusual glass dishware. Colorful enamel accents depict birds, lighthouses, flowers, and designs made from doilies. The store is open Memorial Day weekend through Columbus Day. ✉ *679 S. Gouldsboro Rd., Gouldsboro* ☎ *207/963–7280* 🌐 *www.leefusionartglass.com.*

JONESPORT AND BEALS ISLAND

48 miles northeast of Winter Harbor via Rte. 186, U.S. Rte. 1, and Rte. 187; 20 miles southwest of Machias.

The birding is superb around Jonesport and Beals Island, a pair of fishing communities joined by a bridge over Moosabec Reach. A handful of stately homes ring Jonesport's Sawyer Square, where Sawyer Memorial Congregational Church's exquisite stained-glass windows are illuminated at night. But the towns are less geared to travelers than those on the Schoodic Peninsula. Lobster traps are still piled in the yards, and lobster-boat races near Moosabec Reach are the highlight of the community's annual Independence Day celebration. Right next to Beals Island, Great Wass Island, connected to it by a bridge, is home to a namesake preserve with rugged trails to the coast.

GETTING HERE AND AROUND

In Columbia Falls Route 187, a loop road, heads down to Jonesport, where a bridge leads to Beals Island. Route 187 returns to U.S. 1 in Jonesboro.

MACHIAS

20 miles northeast of Jonesport.

The Machias area—Machiasport, East Machias, and Machias, the Washington County seat—lays claim to being the site of the first naval battle of the Revolutionary War, which took place in what is now Machiasport. Despite being outnumbered and out-armed, a small group of Machias men under the leadership of Jeremiah O'Brien captured the armed British schooner *Margaretta*. That battle, fought on June 12, 1775, is now known as the "Lexington of the Sea." The town's other claim to fame is wild blueberries. On the third weekend in August the annual Machias Wild Blueberry Festival is a community celebration complete with parade, crafts fair, concerts, and plenty of blueberry dishes.

ESSENTIALS

Visitor Information Machias Bay Area Chamber of Commerce ✉ *85 Main St., Suite 2* ☎ *207/255–4402* 🌐 *www.machiaschamber.org.*

EXPLORING

Burnham Tavern Museum. It was in this gambrel-roofed tavern home that the men of Machias laid the plans that culminated in the capture of the *Margaretta* in 1775. After the Revolutionary War's first naval battle, wounded British sailors were brought here. Tour guides highlight exhibits and tell colorful stories of early settlers. Period furnishings and household items show what life was like in Colonial times. On the National Register of Historic Places, the dwelling is among the 21 in the country deemed most important to the Revolution. ✉ *14 Colonial Way* ☎ *207/255–6930* 🌐 *www.burnhamtavern.com* 🎟 *$5* 🕒 *Mid-June–Sept., weekdays 9:30–4.*

WHERE TO EAT

$$$ MODERN AMERICAN

🍴 **Riverside Inn & Restaurant.** A bright yellow exterior invites a stop at this delightful restaurant in a former sea captain's home perched on the bank of the Machias River, as are the restaurant's vegetable and herb gardens. Ask for a table in the sunroom, which has water views and opens to the other dining room. You can enjoy a drink on the deck. The chef-owner brings a special flair to traditional dishes, such as pork served with a pistachio crust. His signature dish is salmon stuffed with crabmeat and shrimp. In summer months the menu includes dressed-up dinner salads—try pairing one with standout appetizers like hake cakes and red-tuna wontons. Also an inn with Victorian touches, Riverside has two guest rooms in the main house and two suites in the coach house. [$] *Average main: $28* ✉ *608 Main St., East Machias* ☎ *207/255–4134, 888/255–4344* 🌐 *www.riversideinn-maine.com* 🕒 *Closed Jan. and Mon. Closed Tues. and Wed. in Feb.–May, Nov., and Dec. No lunch.*

DID YOU KNOW?

Atlantic puffin colonies were reintroduced to the Maine Coast by the Maine Audubon Society's Project Puffin. Get a closer look at these seabirds and their distinctive beaks on a puffin cruise from Cutler to Machias Seal Island.

LUBEC

28 miles northeast of Machias via U.S. 1 and Rte. 189.

Lubec is one of the first places in the United States to see the sunrise. A popular destination for outdoors enthusiasts, it offers plenty of opportunities for hiking and biking, and the birding is renowned. It's a good base for day trips to New Brunswick's Campobello Island, reached by a bridge—the only one to the island—from downtown Lubec. The main attraction there, Roosevelt Campobello International Park, operates a visitor center that also provides information about the region generally on the U.S. side of the border. It's in Whiting at the corner of U.S. 1 and Route 189, the road to Lubec. The village is perched at the end of a narrow strip of land at the end of Route 189, so you often can see water in three directions in this special off-the-beaten-path place.

GETTING HERE AND AROUND

In summer you can take a water taxi from here to Eastport—about a mile by boat, but 40 miles by the circuitous northerly land route. From U.S. 1 in Whiting, Route 189 leads to Lubec; it's about 13 miles to the village.

SPORTS AND THE OUTDOORS

West Quoddy Head Light. The easternmost point of land in the United States is marked by candy-striped West Quoddy Head Light. In 1806 President Thomas Jefferson signed an order authorizing construction of a lighthouse on this site. You can't climb the tower, but the former lightkeeper's house has a museum with a video showing the interior and displays on Lubec's maritime past. A gallery displays works by artists who live or summer in the area. A mystical 2-mile path along the cliffs at Quoddy Head State Park, one of five trails, yields magnificent views of Canada's cliff-clad Grand Manan Island. Whales can often be sighted offshore. The 540-acre park has a picnic area. ✉ *973 S. Lubec Rd., off Rte. 189* ☎ *207/733–0911* 🌐 *www.parksandlands.com* 🎟 *$3* 🕓 *Daily, 9–sunset.*

WHERE TO EAT AND STAY

$$ SEAFOOD 🍴 **Uncle Kippy's.** There isn't much of a view from the picture windows, but locals don't mind—they come here for the satisfying seafood. The dining room is large and has a bar. Entrées include seafood dinners and combo platters and some chicken and meat dishes. There are burgers, too, and the fresh-dough pizza is popular. You can order from the lunch or dinner menu. A take-out window and ice-cream bar are open May through September. [$] *Average main: $16* ✉ *170 Main St.* ☎ *207/733–2400* 🌐 *www.unclekippys.com.*

$ B&B/INN 🏨 **Peacock House.** Five generations of the Peacock family lived in this 1860 sea captain's home before it was converted into an inn. **Pros:** piano and fireplace in living room; lovely garden off deck; think-of-everything innkeepers direct guests to area's tucked-away spots. **Cons:** not on the water. [$] *Rooms from: $103* ✉ *27 Summer St.* ☎ *207/733–2403, 888/305–0036* 🌐 *www.peacockhouse.com* 🛏 *3 rooms, 4 suites* 🕓 *Closed Nov.–Apr.* 🍽 *Breakfast.*

CAMPOBELLO ISLAND, CANADA

28 miles east of Machias.

A popular excursion from Lubec, New Brunswick's Campobello Island has two fishing villages, Welshpool and Wilson's Beach. The only bridge is from Lubec, but in summer a car ferry shuttles passengers from Campobello Island to Deer Island, where you can continue on to the Canadian mainland.

GETTING HERE AND AROUND

After coming across the bridge from Lubec, Route 774 runs from one end of the island to the other, taking you through the two villages and to Roosevelt Campobello International Park.

EXPLORING

Roosevelt Campobello International Park. Neatly manicured Campobello Island has always had a special appeal for the wealthy and famous. It was here that President Franklin Roosevelt and his family spent summers. You can take a self-guided tour of the 34-room Roosevelt Cottage that was presented to Eleanor and Franklin as a wedding gift. The wicker-filled structure looks essentially as it did when the family was in residence. A visitor center has displays about the Roosevelts and Canadian-American relations. Eleanor Roosevelt Teas are held at 11 and 3 daily in the neighboring Hubbard Cottage. A joint project of the American and the Canadian governments, this park is crisscrossed with interesting hiking trails. Groomed dirt roads attract bikers. Eagle Hill Bog has a wooden walkway and signs identifying rare plants. ■ TIP→ **Note that the Islands are on Atlantic Time, which is an hour later than EST.** ⊠ *459 Rte. 774, Welshpool, New Brunswick, Canada* ☎ *506/752–2922, 877/851–6663* ⊕ *www.fdr.net* ⊠ *Free* ☉ *House and visitor center: Memorial Day weekend–Columbus Day, daily 10–6.*

WHERE TO EAT

$$
SEAFOOD
FAMILY

✕ **Family Fisheries.** Seafood lovers know that fried fish doesn't have to be greasy. That's why people keep heading across the international bridge to eat at this family establishment in Wilson's Beach. The freshest seafood is delivered to the restaurant, where you can bring your own wine ($2 corking fee). Order fried haddock, scallops, shrimp, or clams alone or as part of a platter. Eat in the large dining room or near the playground at picnic tables or in a screened room. Lobsters are cooked outside and also sold live or steamed to go. You can buy ice cream at the take-out window, and the restaurant serves breakfast in July and August. $ *Average main: C$15* ⊠ *1977 Rte. 774, Wilson's Beach, New Brunswick, Canada* ☎ *506/752–2470* ⊕ *www.family-fisheries.webs. com* ☉ *Closed late Oct.–early Apr.*

EASTPORT

39 miles northeast of Lubec via Rte. 189, U.S. 1, and Rte. 190; 109 miles north of Ellsworth via U.S. 1 and Rte. 190.

Connected by a granite causeway to the mainland at Pleasant Point Reservation, Eastport has wonderful views of the nearby islands, and you can sometimes spot whales from the waterfront because the harbor is so deep. Known for its diverse architecture, the island city was one of the nation's busiest seaports in the early 1800s. On the weekend after Labor Day the Eastport Pirate Festival brings folks out in pirate attire for a ship race, parade, fireworks, cutlass "battles" by reenactors, and other events, including a children's breakfast and schooner ride with pirates.

Get downtown early to secure a viewing spot for Maine's largest July 4th parade. On the weekend of the second Sunday in August, locals celebrate Sipayik Indian Days at the Pleasant Point Reservation. This festival of Passamaquoddy culture includes canoe races, dancing, drumming, children's games, fireworks, and traditional dancing.

GETTING HERE AND AROUND

From U.S. 1 Route 190 leads to the Island City. Continue on Washington Street to the water. You can also take a water taxi from here to Lubec—1 mile or so by boat but about 40 by land—in the summer.

ESSENTIALS

Visitor Information Eastport Area Chamber of Commerce ☎ *207/853–4644* 🌐 *www.eastport.net.*

WHERE TO EAT

$$ SEAFOOD FAMILY 🍴 **Chowder House.** Just north of downtown Eastport, this expansive waterfront eatery sits on the pier next to where the ferry docks. Built atop an old cannery foundation, it has original details such as wood beams and a stone wall. Eat in the downstairs pub, upstairs in the dining room, or on the large deck. The house specialties include a smoked fish appetizer and seafood pasta in a wine-and-cheese sauce. Lunch, served until 4, includes fried seafood plates, burgers, wraps, and sandwiches. [$] *Average main: $17* ✉ *167 Water St.* ☎ *207/853–4700* 🌐 *eastportchowderhouse.org* 🕓 *Closed mid-Oct.–mid-May.*

TRAVEL SMART
NEW ENGLAND

GETTING HERE AND AROUND

New England's largest and most cosmopolitan city, Boston, is the region's major transportation and cultural center. Secondary hubs include Hartford, Connecticut, and Portland, Maine. Your best bet for exploring is to travel by car—flying within the region is expensive and driving distances between most attractions are short. Inside most cities, public transportation is a viable—and often preferable—means for getting around. Passenger ferry service is available to outlying islands (some vessels accommodate vehicles).

See the Getting Here and Around section at the beginning of each chapter for more transportation information.

▌ AIR TRAVEL

Most travelers visiting New England head for a major gateway, such as Boston, Providence, Hartford/Springfield, Manchester, or even New York City or Albany, and then rent a car to explore the region. The New England states form a fairly compact region, with few important destinations more than six hours apart by car. It's costly and generally impractical to fly within New England, the exceptions being the island resort destinations of Martha's Vineyard and Nantucket in Massachusetts and Block Island in Rhode Island, which have regular service from Boston and a few other regional airports.

Boston's Logan Airport is one of the nation's most important domestic and international airports, with direct flights arriving from all over North America and internationally. New England's other major airports receive few international flights (mostly from Canada) but do offer a wide range of direct domestic flights to East Coast and Midwest destinations and, to a lesser extent, to the western United States. Some sample flying times to Boston are: from Chicago (2½ hours), London (6½ hours), and Los Angeles (6 hours).

Times from U.S. destinations are similar, if slightly shorter, to Albany and Hartford, assuming you can find direct flights.

AIRPORTS

The main gateway to New England is Boston's Logan International Airport (BOS). Bradley International Airport (BDL), in Windsor Locks, Connecticut, 12 miles north of Hartford, is convenient to Western Massachusetts and all of Connecticut. T. F. Green Airport (PVD), just outside Providence, Rhode Island, and Manchester Boston Regional Airport (MHT), in New Hampshire, are other major airports—and alternative gateways to Boston, which is a one-hour drive from each. Additional New England airports served by major carriers include Portland International Jetport (PWM) in Maine and Burlington International Airport (BTV) in Vermont. Other airports are in Albany, New York (ALB, near Western Massachusetts and Vermont); Westchester County, New York (HPN, near Southern Connecticut); Bangor, Maine (BGR); and Barnstable Municipal in Hyannis, Massachusetts (HYA). You can access Nantucket and Martha's Vineyard via ferries from Hyannis or fly directly to the islands' airports.

Airport Information Albany International Airport ✉ *737 Albany Shaker Rd., Albany, New York* ☎ *518/242–2200* ⊕ *www.albanyairport. com.* **Bangor International Airport** ✉ *287 Godfrey Blvd., Bangor, Maine* ☎ *207/992–4600* ⊕ *www.flybangor.com.* **Barnstable Municipal Airport** ✉ *480 Barnstable Rd., Hyannis, Massachusetts* ☎ *508/775–2020* ⊕ *www.town. barnstable.ma.us/airport.* **Bradley International Airport** ✉ *Schoephoester Rd., Windsor Locks, Connecticut* ☎ *860/292–2000* ⊕ *www. bradleyairport.com.* **Burlington International Airport** ✉ *1200 Airport Dr, South Burlington, Vermont* ☎ *802/863–1889* ⊕ *www. burlingtonintlairport.com.* **Logan International Airport** ✉ *1 Harborside Dr., Boston, Massachusetts* ☎ *800/235–6426* ⊕ *www.massport. com.* **Manchester Boston Regional Airport**

✉ *1 Airport Rd., Manchester, New Hampshire* ☎ *603/624-6539* ⊕ *www.flymanchester.com.* **Martha's Vineyard Airport** ✉ *71 Airport Rd., West Tisbury, Massachusetts* ☎ *508/693-7022* ⊕ *www.mvyairport.com.* **Nantucket Memorial Airport** ✉ *14 Airport Rd., Nantucket, Massachusetts* ☎ *508/325-5300* ⊕ *www.nantucketairport.com.* **Portland International Jetport** ✉ *1001 Westbrook St., Portland, Maine* ☎ *207/874-8877* ⊕ *www.portlandjetport.org.* **T.F. Green Airport** ✉ *2000 Post Rd., Warwick, Rhode Island* ☎ *401/737-8222, 888/268-7222* ⊕ *www.pvdairport.com.* **Westchester County Airport-White Plains** ✉ *240 Westchester Airport County Rd., White Plains, New York* ☎ *914/995-4850* ⊕ *airport.westchestergov.com.*

FLIGHTS

Numerous airlines fly to and from Boston; additionally, the discount carrier Southwest Airlines flies to Albany, Boston, Hartford/Springfield, Providence, and Manchester, New Hampshire. Smaller or discount airlines serving Boston include AirTran, Cape Air, and JetBlue. Cape Air also provides service from Cape Cod and the islands to Providence and New Bedford. You can fly to Burlington from New York City on JetBlue, and you can fly to Boston from Atlantic City, Myrtle Beach, and Fort Lauderdale on Spirit Airlines. New England Airlines serves Block Island, with regularly scheduled flights from Westerly, Rhode Island.

Airline Contacts AirTran Airways ☎ *800/247-8726* ⊕ *www.airtran.com.* **American Airlines** ☎ *800/433-7300* ⊕ *www.aa.com.* **Cape Air** ☎ *800/352-0714* ⊕ *www.capeair.com.* **Delta Airlines** ☎ *800/221-1212* ⊕ *www.delta.com.* **JetBlue** ☎ *800/538-2583* ⊕ *www.jetblue.com.* **New England Airlines** ☎ *800/243-2460* ⊕ *www.block-island.com/nea.* **Southwest Airlines** ☎ *800/435-9792* ⊕ *www.southwest.com.* **Spirit Airlines** ☎ *801/772-7117* ⊕ *www.spirit.com.* **United Airlines** ☎ *800/864-8331* ⊕ *www.united.com.* **US Airways** ☎ *800/428-4322* ⊕ *www.usairways.com.*

▌ BOAT TRAVEL

Principal ferry routes in New England connect New Bedford on the mainland and Cape Cod with Martha's Vineyard and Nantucket, Boston with Provincetown, southern Rhode Island with Block Island, and Connecticut with New York's Long Island and Block Island. Other routes provide access to many islands off the Maine Coast. Ferries cross Lake Champlain between Vermont and upstate New York. International service between Portland, Yarmouth, and Bar Harbor, Maine, and Nova Scotia, is also available. With the exception of the Lake Champlain ferries—which are first-come, first-served—car reservations are advisable.

▌ BUS TRAVEL

Regional bus service is relatively plentiful throughout New England. It can be a handy and affordable means of getting around, as buses travel many routes that trains do not.

Concord Coach runs buses between Boston and Concord, New Hampshire, Portland, Maine, and Bangor, Maine. C&J sends Wi-Fi–equipped buses up the New Hampshire coast to Newburyport, Massachusetts, Dover, New Hampshire, Durham, New Hampshire, and Portsmouth, New Hampshire, and also provides service to New York City. Concord and C&J both leave from Boston's South Station (which is connected to the Amtrak station) and Logan Airport.

Information C&J ☎ *800/258-7111* ⊕ *www.ridecj.com.* **Concord Coach** ☎ *800/639-3317* ⊕ *www.concordcoachlines.com.*

With fares starting at just $1 if you reserve early enough, BoltBus runs buses with Wi-Fi and electrical outlets between Boston, New York, Philadelphia, and Washington, D.C. Megabus also offers low fares, and its Wi-Fi–equipped buses serve New York City and many other points on the East Coast. BoltBus and Megabus use Boston's South Station.

Bus Information BoltBus ☎ *877/265-8287*
⊕ *www.boltbus.com.* **Megabus** ☎ *877/462-6342* ⊕ *us.megabus.com.*

▌ CAR TRAVEL

New England is best explored by car. Areas in the interior are largely without heavy traffic and congestion. Coastal New England is more congested (especially getting to and from Cape Cod during the summer) and parking can be hard to find or expensive in Boston, Providence, and the many smaller resort towns along the coast. Still, a car is typically the best way to get around even on the coast (though you may want to park it at your hotel in Boston or on Cape Cod and use it as little as possible). In the interior, especially Western Massachusetts, Vermont, New Hampshire, and Maine, public transportation options are limited and a car is almost necessary. Note that Interstate 90 (the Massachusetts Turnpike) is a toll road throughout Massachusetts. If you rent a car at Logan International Airport, allow plenty of time to return it—as much as 60 minutes to be on the safe side.

GASOLINE

Gas stations are easy to find along major highways and in most communities throughout the region. At this writing, the average price of a gallon of regular unleaded gas in New England is $3.57. However, prices vary from station to station within any city. The majority of stations are self-serve with pumps that accept credit cards, though you may find a holdout full-service station on occasion. Tipping is not expected at these.

PARKING

In Boston and other large cities, finding a spot on the street can be time-consuming. Your best bet is to park in a garage, but the rates are upward of $20 a day. In smaller cities, street parking is usually simpler, though parking garages are convenient and less expensive than their big-city counterparts. Pay attention to signs—some cities allow only residents to park on certain streets. In most small towns parking is not a problem, though some beach and lake parking areas are reserved for those with resident stickers.

ROAD CONDITIONS

Major state and U.S. routes are generally well maintained, with snowplows at the ready during the winter to salt and plow road surfaces soon after the flakes begin to fall. Traffic is heaviest around Boston, Hartford, and New Haven, especially during rush hour. Secondary state routes and rural roads can be a mixed bag; generally, Route 1 is well maintained, but with slower traffic that can get locally congested in even the smallest coastal towns.

Boston motorists are notorious for driving aggressively. Streets in the Boston area are confusing, so a GPS unit can be very helpful.

ROADSIDE EMERGENCIES

Throughout New England, call 911 for any travel emergency, such as an accident or a serious health concern. For breakdowns, dial a towing service.

RULES OF THE ROAD

On city streets the speed limit is 30 mph unless otherwise posted; on rural roads the speed limit ranges from 40 to 50 mph unless otherwise posted. Interstate speeds range from 50 to 65 mph, depending on how densely populated the area is. Throughout the region, you're permitted to make a right turn on red except where posted. Be alert for one-way streets in congested communities, such as Boston and Providence.

State law requires that drivers and all passengers wear seat belts at all times. Always strap children under age five or 40 pounds into approved child-safety seats.

You will encounter many traffic circles/rotaries if you drive in New England (especially in the Boston area). Remember that cars entering traffic circles must yield to cars that are already in the circle. Some rotaries have two lanes, which complicates things. If you're leaving the rotary at the next possible exit, enter from the right lane. If you're leaving the rotary at any exit after the first possible exit, enter from the left lane (which becomes the inner lane of the circle); you can also exit the circle directly from this lane—though check your right side so you don't side-swipe a driver who's incorrectly in the right lane.

CAR RENTAL

A car is the most practical way to get around New England. The major airports serving the region all have on-site car-rental agencies. If you're traveling to the area by bus or train, you might consider renting a car once you arrive. A few train or bus stations have one or two major car-rental agencies on-site.

Rates at the area's major airport, Boston's Logan Airport, begin at around $50 a day and $200 a week for an economy car with air-conditioning, automatic transmission, and unlimited mileage. The same car might go for around $70 a day and $300 a week at a smaller airport such as Portland International Jetport. These rates do not include state tax on car rentals, which varies depending on the airport but generally runs 12% to 15%. Generally, it costs less to rent a car outside of an airport, but factor into the value whether it is easy or difficult to get there with your luggage.

Most agencies won't rent to you if you're under the age of 21 and several major agencies will not rent to anyone under 25. When picking up a rental car, non-U.S. residents need a voucher for any prepaid reservation that was made in their home country, a passport, a driver's license, and a travel policy that covers each driver. Boston's Logan Airport is large, spread out, and usually congested, so if you will be returning a rental vehicle there, make sure to allow plenty of time to take care of it before heading for your flight.

Major Rental Agencies
Alamo ☎ 877/222–9075 ⊕ www.alamo.com. **Avis** ☎ 800/331–1212 ⊕ www.avis.com. **Budget** ☎ 800/527–0700 ⊕ www.budget.com. **Hertz** ☎ 800/654–3131 ⊕ www.hertz.

com. **National Car Rental** ☎ 877/222–9058 ⊕ www.nationalcar.com.

▌TRAIN TRAVEL

Amtrak offers frequent daily service along its Northeast Corridor route from Washington, D.C., Philadelphia, and New York to Boston. Amtrak's high-speed Acela trains link Boston and Washington, with stops at New York, Philadelphia, etc., along the way. The *Downeaster* connects Boston with Portland, Maine, with stops in coastal New Hampshire.

Other Amtrak services include the *Vermonter* between Washington, D.C., and St. Albans, Vermont, the *Ethan Allen Express* between New York and Rutland, Vermont, and the *Lake Shore Limited* between Boston and Chicago, with stops at Pittsfield, Springfield, Worcester, and Framingham, Massachusetts. These trains run on a daily basis. Allow 15 to 30 minutes to make train connections.

Several commuter services are handy for travelers. The Massachusetts Bay Transportation Authority (MBTA) connects Boston with outlying areas on the north and south shores of the state. Metro-North Railroad's New Haven Line offers service from New York City along the Connecticut coast up to New Haven. The line also reaches as far north as Danbury and Waterbury.

Information Amtrak ☎ 800/872–7245 ⊕ www.amtrak.com. **Massachusetts Bay Transportation Authority** (*MBTA*). ☎ 617/222–3200, 800/392–6100 ⊕ www.mbta.com. **Metro-North Railroad** ☎ 212/532–4900, 877/690–5114 ⊕ new.mta.info/mnr.

ESSENTIALS

▌ ACCOMMODATIONS

In New England you can bed down in a basic chain hotel or a luxurious grande dame, but unless you're staying in a city, this is really bed-and-breakfast land. Charming—and sometimes historic—inns, small hotels, and B&Bs dot the region and provide a glimpse of local life.

⇨ *Prices in the reviews are the lowest cost of a standard double room in high season.*

BED-AND-BREAKFASTS

Historic B&Bs and inns are found throughout New England. In many less touristy areas B&Bs offer an affordable alternative to chain properties. In most major towns, expect to pay about the same or more for a historic inn. Many of the region's finest restaurants are attached to country inns, so you often don't have to go far for the best meal in town. Quite a few inns and B&Bs serve substantial breakfasts.

Reservation Services Bed & Breakfast.com ☎ 512/322–2710, 800/462–2632 ⊕ www.bedandbreakfast.com. **Bed & Breakfast Inns Online** ☎ 800/215–7365 ⊕ www.bbonline.com. **BnB Finder.com** ☎ 888/469–6663 ⊕ www.bnbfinder.com.

HOUSE AND APARTMENT RENTALS

In New England you are most likely to find a house, apartment, or condo rental in areas in which ownership of second homes is common, such as beach resorts and ski country. Home-exchange directories sometimes list rentals as well as exchanges. Another good bet is to contact real-estate agents in the area in which you are interested.

Contacts Home Away ☎ 512/782–0805 ⊕ www.homeaway.com. **Interhome** ☎ 800/882–6864 ⊕ www.interhomeusa.com. **Villas International** ☎ 415/499–9490, 800/221–2260 ⊕ www.villasintl.com.

HOTELS

Major hotel and motel chains are amply represented in New England. The region is also liberally supplied with small, independent motels, which run the gamut from the tired to the tidy. Don't overlook these mom-and-pop operations; they frequently offer cheerful, convenient accommodations at lower rates than the chains.

Reservations are always a good idea, particularly in summer and in winter resort areas; in college towns in September and at graduation time in spring; and at areas renowned for autumn foliage.

Most hotels and motels will hold your reservation until 6 pm; call ahead if you plan to arrive late. All will hold a late reservation for you if you guarantee your reservation with a credit-card number.

Note that in Massachusetts, by state law, all hotels are no-smoking. All hotels listed have private baths unless otherwise noted.

Information New England Inns & Resorts Association ☎ 603/964–6689 ⊕ www.newenglandinnsandresorts.com.

▌ CHILDREN IN NEW ENGLAND

Throughout New England you'll have no problem finding comparatively inexpensive kid-friendly hotels and family-style restaurants—as well as some museums, beaches, parks, planetariums, and lighthouses. Keep in mind that B&Bs are not always suitable for kids—many flat-out refuse to accommodate children. Also, some of the quieter and more rural areas lack child-oriented attractions.

Favorite destinations for family vacations in New England include Boston, Cape Cod, the White Mountains, Mystic and southeastern Connecticut, and coastal Maine, but in general, the entire region has plenty to offer families.

LODGING

New England has many family-oriented resorts with lively children's programs. You'll also find farms that accept guests and can be lots of fun for children. Rental houses and apartments abound, particularly around ski areas. In the off-season, these can be economical as well as comfortable. Some country inns, especially those with a quiet, romantic atmosphere and those furnished with antiques, are less enthusiastic about little ones.

Most hotels in New England allow children under a certain age to stay in their parents' room at no extra charge, but others charge for them as extra adults; find out the cutoff age. Note that in Maine hotels and inns cannot put age restrictions on children unless they have five or fewer rooms.

Most lodgings that welcome infants and small children will provide a crib or cot, but remember to give advance notice so that one will be available for you. Many family resorts make special accommodations for small children during meals.

TRANSPORTATION

Each New England state has specific requirements regarding age and weight requirements for children in car seats. If you will need a car seat, make sure your rental-car agency provides them and reserve well in advance.

▮ COMMUNICATIONS

INTERNET

Most major chain hotels and many smaller motels throughout New England now offer wired or wireless Internet access (often both). Many have a desktop computer available for guest use. Access is often free, but be sure to ask about possible fees when you book. Many coffee shops offer Wi-Fi, as do most libraries. Cybercafes lists more than 4,000 Internet cafés worldwide.

Contacts Cybercafes ⊕ *www.cybercafes.com.*

▮ EATING OUT

Although certain ingredients and preparations are common to the region as a whole, New England's cuisine varies greatly from place to place. Urban centers like Boston, Providence, New Haven, and Portland and upscale resort areas such as the Berkshires, Martha's Vineyard, and Nantucket have stellar restaurants, many of them with culinary luminaries at the helm and a reputation for creative—and occasionally daring—menus.

Elsewhere, restaurant food tends more toward the simple, traditional, and conservative. Towns and cities have a great variety of international restaurants, especially excellent Italian, French, Japanese, Indian, and Thai eateries. There are also quite a few diners, which typically present patrons with page after page of inexpensive, short-order cooking and often stay open until the wee hours.

The proximity to the ocean accounts for a number of restaurants, often tiny shacks, serving very fresh seafood. The area's numerous boutique dairy, meat, and vegetable suppliers account for other choice ingredients. In fact, menus in the more upscale and tourism-driven communities often note which Vermont dairy or Berkshires produce farm a particular goat cheese or heirloom tomato came from.

For information on food-related health issues, see Health below.

MEALS AND MEALTIMES

For an early breakfast, pick places that cater to a working clientele. City, town, and roadside establishments specializing in breakfast for early workers often open their doors at 5 or 6 am. At country inns and B&Bs, breakfast is seldom served before 8 am; if you need to get an earlier start, ask ahead of time. Lunch generally runs from around 11 am to 2:30 pm; dinner is usually served from 6 to 9 pm (with early-bird specials sometimes beginning at 5). Only in the larger cities will you find dinner much later than 9 pm. Many restaurants in New England are closed

Monday and sometimes Sunday or Tuesday, although this is never true in resort areas in high season. However, resort-town eateries often shut down completely in the off-season.

Unless otherwise noted, the restaurants listed *in this guide* are open daily for lunch and dinner.

PAYING

Credit cards are accepted for meals throughout New England in all but the most modest establishments. *Prices in the reviews are the average cost of a main course at dinner or, if dinner is not served, at lunch.*

RESERVATIONS AND DRESS

It's a good idea to make a reservation if you can. We only mention them specifically when reservations are essential (there's no other way you'll ever get a table) or when they are not accepted. For popular restaurants, book as far ahead as you can (often 30 days) and reconfirm as soon as you arrive. (Large parties should always call ahead to check the reservations policy.) We mention dress only when men are required to wear a jacket or a jacket and tie.

WINE, BEER, AND SPIRITS

New England is no stranger to microbrews. The granddaddy of New England's independent breweries is the Boston Beer Company, maker of Samuel Adams. Following the Sam Adams lead in offering hearty English-style ales and special seasonal brews are breweries such as Vermont's Long Trail, Maine's Shipyard, and New Hampshire's Smuttynose Brewing Co. Green Mountain Cidery makes Woodchuck hard cider in Middlebury, Vermont.

New England is beginning to earn some respect as a wine-producing region. Varietals capable of withstanding the region's harsh winters have been the basis of promising enterprises such as Rhode Island's Sakonnet Vineyards, Chicama Vineyards on Martha's Vineyard, and Connecticut's Hopkins Vineyard (part

of the Connecticut Wine Trail). Even Vermont is getting into the act with the Snow Farm Vineyard in the Lake Champlain Islands and Boyden Valley Winery in Cambridge.

Although a patchwork of state and local regulations affect the hours and locations of places that sell alcoholic beverages (for example, Massachusetts bans "happy hours"), New England licensing laws are fairly liberal. State-owned or -franchised stores sell hard liquor in New Hampshire, Maine, and Vermont; many travelers have found that New Hampshire offers the region's lowest prices. Look for state-run liquor "supermarkets" on Interstate highways in the southern part of New Hampshire.

▌ HEALTH

Lyme disease, so named for its having been first reported in the town of Lyme, Connecticut, is a potentially debilitating disease carried by deer ticks. They thrive in dry, brush-covered areas, particularly in coastal areas. Always use insect repellent; the potential for outbreaks of Lyme disease makes it imperative that you protect yourself from ticks from early spring through summer. To prevent bites, wear light-color clothing and tuck pant legs into socks. Look for black ticks about the size of a pinhead around hairlines and the warmest parts of the body. If you have been bitten, consult a physician, especially if you see the telltale bull's-eye bite pattern. Flu-like symptoms often accompany a Lyme infection. Early treatment is imperative.

New England's two greatest insect pests are black flies and mosquitoes. The former are a phenomenon of late spring and early summer and are generally a problem only in the densely wooded areas of the far north. Mosquitoes, however, are a nuisance just about everywhere. The best protection against both pests is repellent containing DEET; if you're camping in the woods during black fly season, you'll also want to use fine mesh screening in eating and sleeping areas and even wear mesh headgear. A particular pest of coastal areas, especially salt marshes, is the greenhead fly. Their bite is nasty, they are hard to kill, and they are best repelled by a liberal application of Avon Skin So Soft or a similar product.

Coastal waters attract seafood lovers who enjoy harvesting their own clams, mussels, and even lobsters; permits are required and casual harvesting of lobsters is strictly forbidden. Amateur clammers should be aware that New England shellfish beds are periodically visited by red tides, during which microorganisms can render shellfish poisonous. To keep abreast of the situation, inquire when you apply for a license (usually at town halls or police stations) and pay attention to red tide postings as you travel.

▌ HOURS OF OPERATION

Hours in New England differ little from those in other parts of the United States. Within the region, shops and other businesses tend to keep slightly later hours in larger cities and along the coast, which is generally more populated than interior New England.

Most major museums and attractions are open daily or six days a week (with Monday being the most likely day of closing). Hours are often shorter on Saturday and especially Sunday, and some prominent museums stay open late one or two nights a week, usually Tuesday, Thursday, or Friday. New England also has quite a few smaller museums—historical societies, small art galleries, highly specialized collections—that open only a few days a week and sometimes only by appointment in winter or slow periods.

▌ MONEY

It costs a bit more to travel in most of New England than it does in the rest of the country, the most costly areas being Boston and the coastal resort towns. There are also a fair number of somewhat posh inns and restaurants in the Berkshires, northwestern Connecticut, and parts of Vermont and New Hampshire. ATMs are plentiful and larger denomination bills (as well as credit cards) are readily accepted in tourist destinations during the high season.

Prices throughout this guide are given for adults. Substantially reduced fees are almost always available for children, students, and senior citizens.

CREDIT CARDS

Major credit cards are readily accepted throughout New England, though in rural areas you may encounter difficulties or the acceptance of only MasterCard or Visa (also note that if you'll be making an excursion into Canada, many outlets there accept Visa but not MasterCard).

Reporting Lost Cards American Express ☎ 800/528–4800 ⊕ www.americanexpress. com. **Diners Club** ☎ 800/234-6377 ⊕ www. dinersclub.com. **Discover** ☎ 800/347–2683 ⊕ www.discover.com. **MasterCard** ☎ 800/627–8372 ⊕ www.mastercard.us. **Visa** ☎ 800/847–2911 ⊕ usa.visa.com.

▌ PACKING

The principal rule on weather in New England, is that there are no rules. A cold, foggy morning in spring can and often does become a bright, 60°F afternoon. A summer breeze can suddenly turn chilly and rain often appears with little warning. Thus, the best advice on how to dress is to layer your clothing so that you can peel off or add garments as needed for comfort. Showers are frequent, so pack a raincoat and umbrella. Even in summer you should bring long pants, a sweater or two, and a waterproof windbreaker, for evenings are often chilly and sea spray can make things cool.

Casual sportswear—walking shoes and jeans or khakis—will take you almost everywhere, but swimsuits and bare feet will not: shirts and shoes are required attire at even the most casual venues. Dress in restaurants is generally casual, except at some of the distinguished restaurants of Boston, Newport, and Maine Coast towns such as Kennebunkport, a few inns in the Berkshires, and in Litchfield and Fairfield counties in Connecticut. Upscale resorts, at the very least, will require men to wear collared shirts at dinner, and jeans are often frowned upon.

In summer, bring a hat and sunscreen. Remember also to pack insect repellent; to prevent Lyme disease you'll need to guard against ticks from early spring through summer (⇨ *Health*).

▌ SAFETY

Rural New England is one of the country's safest regions, so much so that residents often leave their doors unlocked. In the cities, particularly in Boston, observe the usual precautions. You should avoid out-of-the-way or poorly lighted areas at night; clutch handbags close to your body and don't let them out of your sight; and be on your guard in subways and buses, not only during the deserted wee hours but in crowded rush hours, when pickpockets are at work. Keep your valuables in hotel safes. Try to use ATMs in busy, well-lighted places such as bank lobbies.

If your vehicle breaks down in a rural area, pull as far off the road as possible, tie a handkerchief to your radio antenna (or use flares at night—check if your rental agency can provide them), and stay in your car with the doors locked until help arrives. Don't pick up hitchhikers. If you're planning to leave a car overnight to make use of off-road trails or camping facilities, make arrangements for a supervised parking area if at all possible. Cars left at trailhead parking lots are subject to theft and vandalism.

The universal telephone number for crime and other emergencies throughout New England is 911.

TIPPING GUIDELINES FOR NEW ENGLAND	
Bartender	$1 to $5 per round of drinks, depending on the number of drinks
Bellhop	$1 to $2 per bag, depending on the level of the hotel
Hotel Concierge	$5 or more, if he or she performs a service for you
Hotel Doorman	$1–$2 if he helps you get a cab
Hotel Maid	$1–$3 a day (either daily or at the end of your stay, in cash)
Hotel Room-Service Waiter	$1 to $2 per delivery, even if a service charge has been added
Porter at Airport or Train Station	$1 per bag
Skycap at Airport	$1 to $3 per bag checked
Taxi Driver	15%–20%, but round up the fare to the next dollar amount
Tour Guide	15% of the cost of the tour
Valet Parking Attendant	$1–$2, but only when you get your car
Waiter	15%–20%, with 20% being the norm at high-end restaurants; nothing additional if a service charge is added to the bill
Other Attendants	Restroom attendants in more expensive restaurants expect some small change or $1. Tip coat-check personnel at least $1–$2 per item checked unless there is a fee, then nothing.

TAXES

Sales taxes in New England are as follows: Connecticut 6.35%; Maine 5.5%; Massachusetts 6.25%; Rhode Island 7%; Vermont 6%. No sales tax is charged in New Hampshire. Some states and municipalities levy an additional tax (from 1% to 10%) on lodging or restaurant meals. Alcoholic beverages are sometimes taxed at a higher rate than that applied to meals.

TIME

New England operates on Eastern Standard Time and follows daylight saving time. When it is noon in Boston it is 9 am in Los Angeles, 11 am in Chicago, 5 pm in London, and 3 am the following day in Sydney. When taking a ferry to Nova Scotia, remember that the province operates on Atlantic Standard Time and, therefore, is an hour ahead.

TOURS

Insight Vacations offers a selection of fall foliage tours. Contiki Vacations, specialists in vacations for 18- to 35-year-olds, has a few tours available that pass through parts of New England as well as the rest of the Northeast.

Recommended Companies Contiki Vacations ☎ *866/266–8454* ⊕ *contiki.com*. **Insight Vacations** ☎ *888/680–1241* ⊕ *www. insightvacations.com/us*.

SPECIAL-INTEREST TOURS
BICYCLING AND HIKING
Contacts Bike New England ☎ *978/979–6598* ⊕ *www.bikenewengland.com*. **TrekAmerica** ☎ *800/873–5872* ⊕ *www.trekamerica.com*. **Urban Adventours** ☎ *617/670–0637* ⊕ *www. urbanadventours.com*.

CULINARY
Contacts Creative Culinary Tours ☎ *888/889–8681* ⊕ *www.creativeculinarytours.com*.

CULTURE
Contacts New England Vacation Tours ☎ *800/742–7669* ⊕ *www. newenglandvacationtours.com*. **Northeast Unlimited Tours** ☎ *800/759–6820* ⊕ *www. newenglandtours.com*. **Wolfe Adventures & Tours** ☎ *888/449–6533* ⊕ *www.wolfetours.com*.

SKIING
Contacts New England Action Sports ☎ *800/477–7669* ⊕ *www.skitrip.net*.

VISITOR INFORMATION

Each New England state provides a helpful free information kit, including a guidebook, map, and listings of attractions and events. All include listings and advertisements for lodging and dining establishments. Each state also has an official website with material on sights and lodgings; most of these sites have a calendar of events and other special features.

Contacts Greater Boston Convention & Visitors Bureau ☎ *617/536–4100* ⊕ *www. bostonusa.com*. **Connecticut Commission on Culture and Tourism** ☎ *888/288–4748* ⊕ *www.ctvisit.com*. **Maine Office of Tourism** ☎ *888/624–6345* ⊕ *www.visitmaine. com*. **Massachusetts Office of Travel and Tourism** ☎ *800/227–6277, 617/973–8500* ⊕ *www.massvacation.com*. **New Hampshire Division of Travel and Tourism Development** ☎ *603/271–2665* ⊕ *www.visitnh.gov*. **Rhode Island Tourism Division** ☎ *800/556–2484* ⊕ *www.visitrhodeisland.com*. **Vermont Department of Tourism and Marketing** ☎ *802/828–3237, 800/837–6668* ⊕ *www. vermontvacation.com*.

ONLINE RESOURCES
Check out the official home page of each New England state for information on state government as well as links to state agencies with information on doing business, working, studying, living, and traveling in these areas. GORP is a terrific general resource for just about every kind of recreational activity. You can narrow your search using the "Park Finder"

for a wide range of topics, ranging from backpacking to sailing to nature viewing. *Yankee,* New England's premier regional magazine, also publishes an informative travel website. Another great Web resource is Visit New England.

Online Info GORP ⊕ *www.gorp.com.* **Visit New England** ⊕ *www.visitnewengland.com.* **Yankee** ⊕ *www.yankeemagazine.com/travel.*

INDEX

PHOTO CREDITS

Front cover: SIME/eStock Photo [Description: Farmhouse, Vermont]. 1, Kindra Clineff. 2, (c) Stu99 I Dreamstime.com. 5, Kindra Clineff. Chapter 1: Experience New England: 8-9, Kindra Clineff. 10, Natalia Bratslavsky/iStockphoto. 11 (left), Denis Jr. Tangney/iStockphoto. 11 (right), William Britten / iStockphoto. 15 (left), Michael Dwyer /Alamy. 15 (right), Rhona Wise/Icon Sports Media, Inc. 16, Chris Coe / age fotostock. 17, Jerry and Marcy Monkman/EcoPhotography.com/Aurora Photos. 18 (left), Ken Canning/iStockphoto. 18 (top right), Kindra Clineff. 18 (bottom right), iStockphoto. 19 (left), Chee-Onn Leong/Shutterstock. 19 (right), Kindra Clineff. 20 (left), drewthehobbit/Shutterstock. 20 (top center), Kindra Clineff. 20 (top right), T. Markley/Shutterstock. 20 (bottom right), Kindra Clineff. 21 (left), Kindra Clineff. 21 (top right), Natalia Bratslavsky/iStockphoto. 21 (bottom right), muffi nman71xx/Flickr. 22, Dennis Curran/Vermont Dept. of Tourism & Marketing. 23 (left), Rod Kaye/ iStockphoto. 23 (right), Ken Canning/Flickr. 24, Eric Foltz/iStockphoto. 25, Wikimedia Commons. 27, Michael Czosnek/iStockphoto. 28, Denis Jr. Tangney/iStockphoto. 29 (left), Jeff Greenberg / age fotostock. 29 (right), Sheldon Kralstein/iStockphoto. 30, Jason Ganser/iStockphoto. 31 (left), Hnin Khine/ iStockphoto. 31 (right), kworth30/wikipedia.org. 32, Denis Jr. Tangney/iStockphoto. 33, Kindra Clineff. 34, Kindra Clineff. Chapter 2: Best Fall Foliage Drives & Road Trips: 35, (c) Aivoges I Dreamstime.com. 36-37, Ken Canning/iStockphoto. 39 (top left), Micha=Ç Krakowiak/iStockphoto. 39 (top center), Lisa Thornberg/iStockphoto. 39 (top right), Scott Cramer/iStockphoto. 39 (bottom left), Steffen Foerster Photography/Shutterstock. 39 (bottom center), iStockphoto. 39 (bottom right), Paul Aniszewski/Shutterstock. 40 (top), Denis Jr. Tangney/iStockphoto. 40 (bottom), Kevin Davidson/ iStockphoto. 41, Kindra Clineff. 42, Kindra Clineff. 43, (c) Donlan I Dreamstime.com. 44, Denis Jr. Tangney/iStockphoto. 45, Denis Jr. Tangney/iStockphoto. 46, Franz Marc Frei /age fotostock. 47, Calvin G. York /Hunt Hill Farm Trust. 48, Kindra Clineff. 49, Kindra Clineff. 50, Heeb Christian / age fotostock. 51, Sarah Kennedy/iStockphoto. 52, Mary Ann Alwan / Alamy. 53, iStockphoto. 54, Denis Jr. Tangney/iStockphoto. 55, The Wilhelm Reich Infant Trust. 56, Jason Orender/iStockphoto. Chapter 3: Boston: 67, Kindra Clineff. 68, Kindra Clineff. 69, ojbyrne/Flickr. 70, ChrisDag/Flickr. 71 (top), Kindra Clineff. 71 (bottom), Kindra Clineff. 72, David Eby/Shutterstock. 78-79, Kindra Clineff. 82, Kindra Clineff. 83 (top left), MCS@ fl ickr/Flickr. 83 (top center), A. H. C. / age fotostock. 83 (top right), cliff1066ô/Flickr. 83 (center left), Classic Vision / age fotostock. 83 (center right), Classic Vision / age fotostock. 83 (bottom), Kindra Clineff. 84, Kindra Clineff. 85 (top left), Kindra Clineff. 85 (top right), Freedom Trail Foundation. 85 (center left), Tony the Misfi t/Flickr. 85 (center right), Kindra Clineff. 85 (bottom left), Tim Grafft/MOTT . 85 (bottom center), Scott Orr/iStockphoto. 85 (bottom right), Kindra Clineff. 86 (top), Kindra Clineff. 86 (bottom), Jim Reynolds/Wikimedia Commons. 87 (top), revjim5000/Flickr. 87 (bottom), Kindra Clineff. 88, Kindra Clineff. 100, Kindra Clineff. 104, Kindra Clineff. 107, Allie_Caulfi ed/Flickr. 108, Isabella Stewart Gardner Museum, Boston. 112, Harvard Crimson. 145, Steve Dunwell / age fotostock. 150, Megapress / Alamy. 156, Public Domain. 158, Kindra Clineff. 167, Kindra Clineff. 172, Kindra Clineff. Chapter 4: Cape Cod, Martha's Vineyard, and Nantucket: 175, Kindra Clineff. 177, Denis Jr. Tangney/iStockphoto. 178, Denis Jr. Tangney/iStockphoto. 179 (top), Kenneth Wiedemann/iStockphoto. 179 (bottom), Kindra Clineff. 180, (c) Mwaits Dreamstime.com. 181 (top), (c) Jtunney I Dreamstime.com. 181 (bottom), (c) Ktphotog I Dreamstime.com. 182, Denis Jr. Tangney/iStockphoto. 189, Kindra Clineff. 192, Nantucket Historical Association. 193, Michael S. Nolan / age fotostock. 194, Kindra Clineff. 195 (top), Kindra Clineff. 195 (center), Penobscot Marine Museum. 195 (bottom left), Random House, Inc. 195 (bottom right), Kindra Clineff. 197, Jeff Greenberg / age fotostock. 201, Kindra Clineff. 204, Julie O'Neil/CCMNH. 215, Kindra Clineff. 221, Guido Caroti. 229, Denis Jr. Tangney/iStockphoto. 236, Kindra Clineff. 238, Kindra Clineff. Chapter 5: The Berkshires and Western Massachusetts: 241, Kindra Clineff. 242, Denis Jr. Tangney/iStockphoto. 243 (top left), Allan Pospisil/iStockphoto. 243 (top right), Denis Jr. Tangney/ iStockphoto. 243 (bottom), Denis Jr. Tangney/iStockphoto. 244, Kevin Kennefi ck. 249, Sterling and Francine Clark Art Institute, Williamstown, Massachusetts. 252-253, mkromer/Flickr. 257, Denis Jr. Tangney/iStockphoto. 263, wikipedia.org. 266, Denis Jr. Tangney/iStockphoto. 275, Kindra Clineff. 282, Kindra Clineff. Chapter 6: Connecticut: 285, Louis DiBacco /iStockphoto. 286, Rene, C Cartier/ iStockphoto. 287 (top), Jaco le Roux/iStockphoto. 287 (bottom), Denis Jr. Tangney/iStockphoto. 288, Kindra Clineff. 296, Alex Nason. 301, Kindra Clineff. 303, Kindra Clineff. 309, Denis Jr. Tangney/ iStockphoto. 315, Ken Wiedemann/iStockphoto. 319, Kindra Clineff. 321 (left), Karen Gentry/Shutterstock. 321 (right), Jochen Tack / age fotostock . 321 (bottom), Marc Dietrich/Shutterstock. 322 (top left), Johann Helgason/Flickr. 322 (top right), Kindra Clineff. 322 (bottom left), robcocquyt/Shutterstock. 322 (center right), Cre8tive Images/Shutterstock. 322 (bottom right), Matthew Gough/Shutterstock. 323 (top left), Guitar75/Shutterstock. 323 (top right), Artur Bogacki/Shutterstock. 323 (bottom left), Kindra Clineff. 323 (center right), libraryimages.net/Flickr. 323 (bottom right), iStockphoto. 324,

Kindra Clineff. 325 (left), Kindra Clineff. 325 (right), Kindra Clineff. 326, Kindra Clineff. 327 (top), Kindra Clineff. 327 (bottom), Lise Gagne/iStockphoto. 334, Kindra Clineff. 336, scaredy_kat/Flickr. 343, Kindra Clineff. Chapter 7: Rhode Island: 349, Kindra Clineff. 350 (top), Denis Jr. Tangney/iStockphoto. 350 (bottom), Steve Geer/iStockphoto. 351, Steve Geer/iStockphoto. 352, Denis Jr. Tangney/iStockphoto. 358, Kenneth C. Zirkel/iStockphoto. 363, Denis Jr. Tangney/iStockphoto. 374, iStockphoto. 383, Ken Wiedemann/iStockphoto. 398, (top left), The Preservation Society of Newport County. 398 (top right) & 399, The Preservation Society of Newport County. 398 (bottom left), Carolyn M Carpenter/Shutterstock. 398 (bottom right), The Preservation Society of Newport County. 400 (top), The Preservation Society of Newport County. 400 (bottom), Library of Congress Prints and Photographs Division. 401 (left), Kindra Clineff. 401 (top right), Library of Congress Prints and Photographs Division. 401 (right center top), wikipedia.org. 401 (right center bottom), Library of Congress Prints and Photographs Division. 401 (bottom right), Frymire Archive /Alamy. 402, The Preservation Society of Newport County. 403 (top left), Sergio Orsanigo. 403 (top right), The Preservation Society of Newport County. 403 (bottom), Travel Bug/Shutterstock. 411, SuperStock/age fotostock. 414, Kindra Clineff. 417, Denis Jr. Tangney/iStockphoto. 420, Kindra Clineff. 423, Kindra Clineff. 427, Kindra Clineff. Chapter 8: Vermont: 429, Kindra Clineff. 430 (top), Marcio Silva/iStockphoto. 430 (bottom), Denis Jr. Tangney/iStockphoto. 431, Denis Jr. Tangney/iStockphoto. 432, S. Greg Panosian/iStockphoto. 438, Kindra Clineff. 441, Kindra Clineff. 442, Kindra Clineff. 444, Kindra Clineff. 448, Hildene. 453, Lee Krohn Photography, Manchester, Vermont. 459, Kindra Clineff. 460, Kindra Clineff. 467, Simon Pearce. 469, Dale Halbur/iStockphoto. 474–75, S. Greg Panosian/iStockphoto. 481, Kindra Clineff. 483, Fraser Hall / age fotostock. 491, Dennis Curran/ age fotostock. 492, Skye Chalmers Photography, inc. 493 (left), Henryk T Kaiser / age fotostock. 493 (right), Hubert Schriebl. 494 (left), Marcio Silva/iStockphoto. 494 (right), Hubert Schriebl. 495, SMUGGLERS' NOTCH RESORT/Ski Vermont. 486, Okemo Mountain Resort. 505, Kindra Clineff. 508, Skye Chalmers/State of Vermont. 513, Kindra Clineff. 516, Alan Copson / age fotostock. 519, Jack Sumberg. Chapter 9: New Hampshire: 521, Denis Jr. Tangney/iStockphoto. 522 (top), Denis Jr. Tangney/iStockphoto. 522 (bottom), Ken Canning/iStockphoto. 524, Sebastien Cote/iStockphoto. 531, Kindra Clineff. 532, Kindra Clineff. 534, Denis Jr. Tangney/iStockphoto. 542-543, cyanocorax/Flickr. 544, NHDTTD/Dave Martsolf. 546, DAVID NOBLE PHOTOGRAPHY/ Alamy. 553, Kindra Clineff. 555, Roy Rainford / age fotostock. 563 (top), Jerry and Marcy Monkman/EcoPhotography.com / Alamy. 563 (bottom), Liz Van Steenburgh/Shutterstock. 564, Kindra Clineff. 565, Mike Kautz/AMC. 566 (left), nialat/Shutterstock. 566 (top right), RestonImages/Shutterstock. 566 (bottom right), nialat/Shutterstock. 567 (top left), jadimages/Shutterstock. 567 (right), rebvt/Shutterstock. 567 (bottom left), Ansgar Walk/wikipedia.org. 567 (bottom center), J. Carmichael/wikipedia.org. 569, Matty Symons/Shutterstock. 570, Danita Delimont / Alamy. 571, Frank Siteman / age fotostock. 578, Kindra Clineff. 584, First Light / Alamy. 588, Kenneth C. Zirkel/iStockphoto. 590, gailf548/Flickr. 596, Kindra Clineff. 599, Jet Lowe/Wikimedia Commons. 603, Currier Museum of Art/Jose Martinez. 609, Franz Marc Frei / age fotostock. 611, Andre Jenny / Alamy. Chapter 10: Inland Maine: 617, Jeff Martone/Flickr. 618, Kenneth C. Zirkel/iStockphoto. 619, Stephen G Page/iStockphoto. 620, BrendanReals/Shutterstock. 630, D A Horchner / age fotostock. 636–637, Kazela/Shutterstock. Chapter 11: Maine Coast: 645, SuperStock/age fotostock. 646 (top), Denis Jr. Tangney/iStockphoto. 646 (bottom), Paul Tessier/iStockphoto. 647, Andrea Pelletier/iStockphoto. 648, Aimin Tang/iStockphoto. 653, ARCO/L Weyers / age fotostock. 661, Perry B. Johnson / age fotostock. 669, Lucid Images / age fotostock. 674, SuperStock/age fotostock. 679, Jeff Greenberg / age fotostock. 680, Lee Coursey/Flickr. 695, Jeff Greenberg / Alamy. 696, Jim Kidd / Alamy. 698, Michael Czosnek/iStockphoto. 699, SuperStock / age fotostock. 700 (left), Maine State Museum. 700 (right), David Cannings-Bushell/iStockphoto. 701, Paul D. Lemke/iStockphoto. 702, Michael Rickard/Shutterstock. 703 (left), Robert Campbell. 703 (top right), Casey Jordan. 703 (bottom right), Dave Johnston. 704 (top), Kenneth Keifer/Shutterstock. 704 (center), Doug Lemke/Shutterstock. 704 (bottom), liz west/wikipedia.org. 707, Raymond Forbes / age fotostock. 712, David Mathies/iStockphoto. 717, Kindra Clineff. 721, Kindra Clineff. 733, Kindra Clineff. 740-741, Alan Majchrowicz/ age fotostock. 745, Kindra Clineff. 748-749, Lyle Fink/iStockphoto. Back cover (from left to right): Ron and Patty Thomas/iStockphoto; Chee-Onn Leong/Shutterstock; Denis Jr. Tangney/iStockphoto. Spine: (c) Babar760 | Dreamstime.com.

NOTES

NOTES

NOTES

NOTES